# Indonesia

Ryan Ver

Celeste

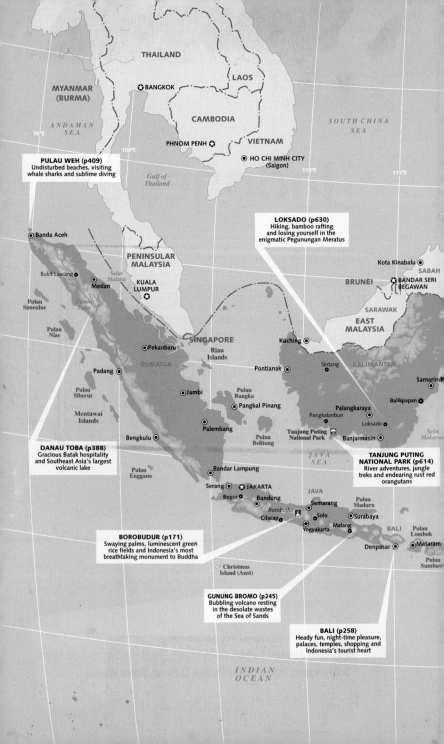

**PULAU WEH (p409)**
Undisturbed beaches, visiting whale sharks and sublime diving

**LOKSADO (p630)**
Hiking, bamboo rafting and losing yourself in the enigmatic Pegunungan Meratus

**DANAU TOBA (p388)**
Gracious Batak hospitality and Southeast Asia's largest volcanic lake

**TANJUNG PUTING NATIONAL PARK (p614)**
River adventures, jungle treks and endearing rust red orangutans

**BOROBUDUR (p171)**
Swaying palms, luminescent green rice fields and Indonesia's most breathtaking monument to Buddha

**GUNUNG BROMO (p245)**
Bubbling volcano resting in the desolate wastes of the Sea of Sands

**BALI (p258)**
Heady fun, night-time pleasure, palaces, temples, shopping and Indonesia's tourist heart

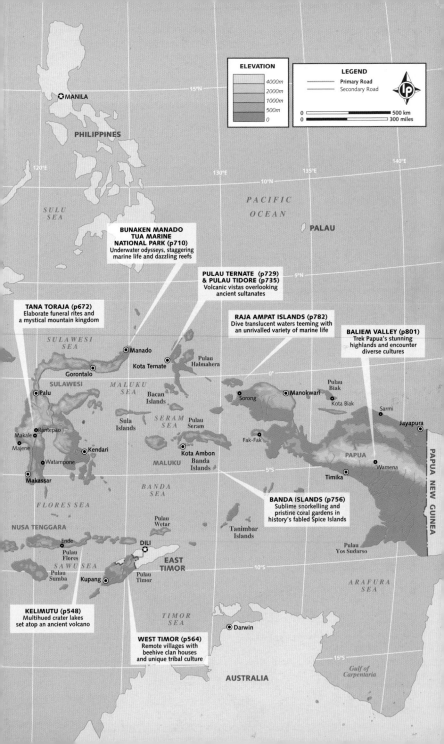

**ELEVATION**

4000m
2000m
1000m
500m
0

**LEGEND**

Primary Road
Secondary Road

0 — 500 km
0 — 300 miles

MANILA

PHILIPPINES

SULU
SEA

PACIFIC
OCEAN

PALAU

**BUNAKEN MANADO TUA MARINE NATIONAL PARK (p710)**
Underwater odysseys, staggering marine life and dazzling reefs

**PULAU TERNATE (p729) & PULAU TIDORE (p735)**
Volcanic vistas overlooking ancient sultanates

**TANA TORAJA (p672)**
Elaborate funeral rites and a mystical mountain kingdom

**RAJA AMPAT ISLANDS (p782)**
Dive translucent waters teeming with an unrivalled variety of marine life

**BALIEM VALLEY (p801)**
Trek Papua's stunning highlands and encounter diverse cultures

SULAWESI
SEA

Manado

Kota Ternate

Pulau
Halmahera

Gorontalo

SULAWESI

MALUKU
SEA

Bacan
Islands

Palu

Sorong

Manokwari

Pulau
Biak

Kota Biak

Sarmi

Jayapura

Sula
Islands

SERAM
SEA

Pulau
Seram

Makale
Rantepao

PAPUA

Majene

Kendari

Kota Ambon

Banda
Islands

Fak-Fak

Watampone

MALUKU

Wamena

Makassar

Timika

BANDA
SEA

5°S

PAPUA NEW GUINEA

FLORES SEA

**BANDA ISLANDS (p756)**
Sublime snorkelling and pristine coral gardens in history's fabled Spice Islands

NUSA TENGGARA

Pulau
Wetar

Tanimbar
Islands

Ende

Pulau
Flores

DILI

EAST
TIMOR

Pulau
Yos Sudarso

Pulau
Sumba

SAWU
SEA

Kupang

Pulau
Timor

ARAFURA
SEA

**KELIMUTU (p548)**
Multihued crater lakes set atop an ancient volcano

TIMOR
SEA

Darwin

**WEST TIMOR (p564)**
Remote villages with beehive clan houses and unique tribal culture

AUSTRALIA

Gulf of
Carpentaria

# On the Road

**RYAN VER BERKMOES Coordinating Author**
I'd been following coursing streams of water across Bali's impossibly green rice fields all day in search of new little places to stay. I was thinking just how serene it was when I saw this sign and thought 'Aha! I can just stay for good and start a new clean career.'

**MUHAMMAD COHEN** Jungle cruising doesn't get much better than on Sungai Ohong (p644), travelling between the longhouses at Tanjung Isuy and Mancong in a motor canoe.

**CELESTE BRASH** No don't worry, I didn't take a bite. Forest rat is sold raw to prepare yourself. The Tomohon market (p714) is a showcase of all sorts of local critters getting butchered. It was one of the goriest places I've ever been – not for the faint-hearted.

**MARK ELLIOTT** Skin-crisping sunshine turned to cascading rain as I juddered 'home' to Saumlaki (p769). But by the time I'd changed, and patted dry my passport, the clouds were swirling away, replaced by one of the most symphonic tropical sunsets I'd ever seen.

**TRENT HOLDEN** Here's me in Banda Aceh in front of a fishing boat swept several kilometres onto the roof of a villager's house. The monument (p406) stands as a stark reminder of the sheer ferocity of the 2004 Boxing Day tsunami that destroyed the region. The good news is that the city has been rebuilt as good as ever.

**JOHN NOBLE** No idea who this ugly but amiable character in a Balinese garden was. But I liked his mossy texture and daily fresh flowers. Note to the Lion Air passenger at Ambon who stole the book under my arm: I'll get you one day.

**ADAM SKOLNICK** After a four-hour delay, this Pelni cruiser finally pulled into Lewoleba's (p558) gritty harbour after 2am. At which time I, the boat's lone *bule* (foreigner), collapsed for a few hours sleep and woke up to shafts of sunlight in my eyes and these guys hovering over me, guarding my belongings. God bless the good people of way-out Indonesia.

**STEVE WATERS** The scenery's looking a lot better than I am after spending two hours on the back of a moped getting to the sublime Harau Valley (p437). The effort is worth it, because it's a truly magical place. Gibbons are howling away in the forest, and large blue butterflies dance in the grass by the roadside. But I really need a drink.

**IAIN STEWART** I'm outside Surabaya's 15th-century Mesjid Ampel (p222), one of Indonesia's holiest mosques and location of *wali songo* Sunan Ampel's tomb. To approach this monument you have to pass through the labyrinthine lanes of the city's Arab Quarter, past hundreds of stalls selling Islamic souvenirs to pilgrims – like the skull cap I'm wearing.

*For full author biographies see p875.*

# Indonesia Highlights

Indonesia is an infinitely varied mosaic of images: from no other place will travellers return with such a diverse and rarely overlapping collection of memories. Remote islands, exotic cultures, teeming cities, perfect beaches, captivating wildlife and extraordinary arts are just a few parts of the bigger work of art that is this huge and diverse nation.

MARK EL

## 1 BANDA ISLANDS

Overcoming all those transport obstacles makes reaching the brilliant Banda Islands (p756) a thrill in itself. There you'll find such colour in the reefs and clarity in the water that snorkelling feels like you've fallen into a tropical aquarium. Set amid soaring buttressed *kenari* trees, the crumbling fortresses whisper colonial secrets. And for breakfast you can spread your pancakes with jam made of nutmeg – once worth its weight in gold.

**Mark Elliott**

## GOING APE

Take a boat trip along Sungai Sekonyer for close encounters with orangutans, human beings' third-closest relatives. Tanjung Puting National Park (p614) is one of the best places left to see these critically endangered great apes up close in their natural habitat.

**Muhammad Cohen**

**3**

ANDREW BROWNBILL

PETER PTSCHELINZEW

## 2
## DIVING & EXPLORING KOMODO NATIONAL PARK

Drop into crystal-clear seas swirling with colourful clouds of fish, soar over pristine coral and commune with huge schools of sharks and manta rays, pods of dolphins and whales. Then stroll Komodo Island's (p528) pink beaches, trek through the marsh and climb up steep mountains in search of the infamous Komodo dragon. Simply spectacular.

**Adam Skolnick**

MARK ELLIOT

## 4
## MOROTAI'S OFFSHORE JEWELS

Pulau Dodola (p740) is one of those idyllic desert islands that film stars generally snap up. But this one is all yours to explore. Dodola's white sand caresses the feet and forms a beautiful natural causeway between the island's two palm-hung halves. Heading back to Daruba, don't miss Pulau Zum Zum (p740), where General MacArthur had a base and where locals are still trawling up rusty WWII weaponry.

**Mark Elliott**

## BATU KARAS

When Java's teeming cities just get too much, this tiny isolated surf spot (p160) is just the place to recharge and reconnect with the island. The waves here are superb, with relatively gentle surf ideal for beginners (as well as more challenging breaks).

**Iain Stewart**

**6**

IAIN STEW

TIM ROCK

**5**

## THE GILI LIFESTYLE

Just a two-hour speedboat ride from Bali are three luscious drops of white sand that deliver everything from serene solitude to barefoot luxury, fine dining and all-night dance parties. Add in the superb diving (the deep reef attracts sharks, turtles and rays throughout the year), and it's no wonder the Gilis (p492) have become Indonesia's hottest new destination.

**Adam Skolnick**

PETER PTSCHELINZ

**7**

## IDYLLIC ISLE

Pulau Derawan (p648) is the island you dreamt of when you packed for Indonesia: a simple, friendly fishing village fringed with white-sand beaches and surrounded by phenomenal marine life. Walk with sea turtle escorts to your simple room built on piles over clear Sangalaki Archipelago waters. Electricity runs from dusk to dawn only, and it seems time barely runs at all.

**Muhammad Cohen**

## DIVING BUNAKEN

With a bottle on your back or a snorkel in your mouth, you'll see some of the most stunning coral walls anywhere in the world around the drop-offs surrounding Pulau Bunaken (p710). Look for tiny neon-coloured nudibranches between the swaying sea anemones, check out treelike corals of every possible description and gasp for more air as a sea turtle swims past you to take a breath at the surface.

**Celeste Brash**

MARK WEBSTER

PAUL BEINSSEN

## 8 ART FOR THE AGES

Coming around a corner on Monkey Forest Rd in Ubud (p306) I was busy stepping around the mangy, greedy monkeys when I almost walked into the sweetest little parade I've seen. A children's procession was marching up the road at a pace almost too swift for their churning, shorts-clad legs. Banging drums, waving ceremonial umbrellas and even a Barong (mythical lion-dog creature) illustrate what for these kids is an early chapter in a lifetime of artistic expressions of their beliefs.

**Ryan Ver Berkmoes**

STEPHANE VICTOR

## 10 CLUBBING IN INDONESIA

Many parts of the archipelago may be culturally conservative, but the clubbing scene in Jakarta (p113) and Kuta (p277) is arguably the wildest in Southeast Asia. With home-grown superstar DJs, colossal venues and legions of young up-for-it clubbers, these are cities where the night goes on and on. And on.

**Iain Stewart**

GREG ELMS

## BASTIONG PORT

Pulau Ternate (p729) comes vibrantly to life in this marvellously chaotic harbour area: boats bobbing, market stalls peddling, speedboats weaving, children diving and unnamed family eateries roasting up superb-value fresh-fish dinners. And all with the spectacular backdrop of Tidore's perfect volcanic cone.

**Mark Elliott**

**12**

## 11 TANA TORAJA

From majestic rice-terraced valleys to the gory ceremonial butchering of water buffalo, Tana Toraja (p672) is an assault on the senses. Hike through bucolic villages, visit cave-burial sites that look like they came to life from the pages of *National Geographic* and take part in a palm-wine-swilling funeral ceremony highlighted by dancing and animal sacrifices; this region is simply unforgettable.

**Celeste Brash**

JOHN N

## 13 BALIEM HANGING BRIDGES

South of Wamena, Sungai Baliem (p807) becomes the fiercest, most raging torrent I've ever encountered. And you have to cross it on wobbly hanging footbridges. Locals do it without a thought. The secret: don't look at the water, but do look where you're putting your feet!

**John Noble**

## 14 DANAU SENTANI

The lake (p792) you fly over as you approach Papua's main airport is surrounded by ageless fishing and craft-making villages of stilt houses, aeons removed from the hustle and bustle of towns and airports. And the lake itself has a beauty that I can only call surreal.

**John Noble**

## 15 TREKKING IN THE BALIEM VALLEY

The friendliness of the mountain people was one of the many delights of trekking in Papua's Baliem Valley (p801). I met this group between Kilise and Tangma. I never found out where they had come from, or where they were going, but I was enchanted by their smiles.

**John Noble**

## 16 CANDI SUKUH

Perched halfway up a volcano, this remarkable temple (p205) enjoys a spectacular position overlooking the Solo plain. Many of the carvings here display signs of a fertility cult, and Sukuh has been dubbed the 'erotic' temple.

**Iain Stewart**

## 17 ANOTHER BEACH?

Peering over the edge of a cliff near Bingin (p290) I spotted yet another perfect little hidden white-sand cove, cooled by mist from the awesome surf breaks directly in front. Wait, was that the fifth one I'd seen down here near Ulu Watu, or the sixth?

**Ryan Ver Berkmoes**

# Contents

# Regional Map Contents

# Destination Indonesia

The numbers astound even as they boggle: 17,000 islands (or is it 20,000?), 8000 inhabited (or is it 11,000?), 300 languages spoken (or is it 400?); the list goes on.

The world's fourth most populace country – 240 million and counting – is a sultry kaleidoscope that runs along the equator for 5000km. It may well be the last great adventure on Earth. From the western tip of Sumatra to the eastern edge of Papua is a nation that defies homogenisation. A land of so many cultures, peoples, animals, customs, plants, features, artworks and foods that it is like 100 countries melded into one (or is it 200?).

And we're talking differences that aren't just about an accent or a preference for goat over pork, we are talking about people who are as radically different from each other as if they came from different continents. No man may be an island but here every island is a unique blend of the men, women and children who live upon it. Over time deep and rich cultures have evolved, from the mysteries of the spiritual Balinese to the utterly non-Western belief system of the Asmat people of Papua.

Venturing through the islands of Indonesia you'll see a land as diverse and unusual as those living upon it. Look at Sulawesi on a map, say what you think, and you'll save yourself the cost of an ink blot test at a shrink. Or view Sumatra from the air and be humbled by a legion of nearly 100 volcanoes marching off into the distance, several capable of blowing at any time.

Dramatic sights are the norm. There's the sublime: an orangutan lounging in a tree; the artful: a Balinese dancer executing precise moves that make a robot seem loose-limbed; the idyllic: a deserted stretch of blinding white sand on Sumbawa set off by azure water and virescent jungled hills; the astonishing: the mobs in a cool and glitzy Jakarta mall on a Sunday; the humbling: a woman bent double with a load of firewood on Sumatra; the solemn: the quiet magnificence of Borobudur.

As diverse as Indonesia is, perhaps what's so remarkable about the place is how often it is the same. Sure there may be those 300 spoken languages (or was it 400?) but virtually everybody can speak one language: Bahasa Indonesia, a tongue that helps unify this sprawling, chaotic collection of peoples with a past that's had more drama than a picnic on Krakatau in say, 1883. Destructive colonialism, revolution, mass slaughter, ethnic warfare, dictatorship and more have been part of daily life in Indonesia in just the past 100 years. That's one of the reasons why the national elections of 2009 are so remarkable: they were unremarkable.

More than a dozen parties waged high-energy campaigns. Rallies throughout the myriad islands were passionate and vibrant. Yet what happened in the end? President Susilo Bambang Yudhoyono's incumbent Democratic Party won. In the midst of global economic chaos (time for another Krakatau allusion), Indonesians chose to go with the status quo. This is a remarkable development for a nation where the looting of a single KFC by protestors with a, er, beef, is portrayed in the West as a complete breakdown of civil order.

But it wasn't that long ago, barely a decade, when there was blood in the streets from Lombok to the Malukus as religious and political factions settled scores and simply ran amok. Having a boring election is balm for a nation with such recent bad memories. And it is balm for anyone worried that the world's largest Muslim nation (numerous large religious minorities aside) could somehow come under the influence of radical groups dedicated to

**FAST FACTS**

Population: 240 million

Median age: 26.7 years

GDP per capita: US$2150

Number of islands: 17,000–20,000

Number of mobile phones in use: 30 million

Population density Java: 1000 per sq km

Population density Papua: under seven per sq km

Identified species of flowering plants: 28,000 and rising

Number of endangered mammals: 147

reversing the so far relatively successful Indonesian experiment in modest secularism. Although memories of bombings earlier in the decade in Bali and Jakarta had faded significantly, the 2009 Jakarta hotel bombings, which killed nine, reminded all that Indonesia will continue to have security challenges.

Yet look again at the boring election. The optimistically named Prosperous Justice Party (Partai Keadilan Sejahtera; PKS) which campaigned with a goal of bringing Islamic Shariah law to Indonesia received 8% of the vote after it and poll watchers had predicted a share of as much as 15%.

It was a heartening moment for those who believe Indonesia must continue to be a nation of all its people, no matter which of the 300 (or 400?) languages they prefer. Yet one election does not make anyone think there are not scores of challenges ahead. Just ask a yoga instructor on Bali. A quasi-governmental body, the Ulema Council, has issued a ban on the seemingly innocuous and uncontroversial practice of stress management on the grounds that the ancient Hindu elements of yoga are incompatible with the Muslim faith.

This only added to fears stoked by the passage in 2008 of a so-called anti-pornography law that potentially made many traditional forms of behaviour across the archipelago illegal – from wearing penis gourds on Papua, to the modest gyrations of traditional Javanese dancers (to say nothing of the brazenly topless on Bali's beaches). With recent memories of religious and ethnic violence still sharp in many places, anything that could stoke new divisions is anathema to many. Thus the general relief after the 'boring' 2009 elections.

In contrast, however, is the excitement expressed across Indonesia at the results of a different election, this one far way in the US. You'd have to find yourself a pretty remote rock in the Bandas to *maybe* find an Indonesian who couldn't tell you that President Barack Obama moved to Jakarta in 1967 with his mother and step-father and attended primary school there for four years (see p100). The president's memories in interviews may seem to focus on his love of *bakso* (meatball) soup but for locals he might as well have lived in the country his entire life. You simply cannot underestimate the pride felt over the ascent of 'one of theirs'. Certainly it means there will be a honeymoon in relations between the world's number three and number four most-populated countries. (On a side note: Obama's election coincided with a massive surge in popularity of American-style reality TV shows.)

Indonesia with its 17,000 islands (or was it 20,000?) is also, unfortunately, challenged by concerns that make political worries pale. Modern life in a place that hadn't changed in previous eons has come at a huge cost. Pollution, illegal land use, deforestation, rampant corruption (it places at 125 on Transparency International's corruption perceptions index; neighbours Malaysia and Singapore are at 47 and four respectively) and poverty (US$50 a month is big wages here) imperil the very fabric of the nation. Plus there's the ever-present possibility of natural disaster, as seen by the 2004 tsunami and the 2006 Yogya and 2009 Sumatra earthquakes.

Yet, visiting this ever-intriguing, ever-intoxicating land you'll see these problems, but more often you'll see the promise. And more often you'll live the promise of the last great adventure on Earth. Sitting in the open door of a train whizzing across Java, idling away time on deck on a ferry bound for Kalimantan, hanging on to the back of a scooter on Flores or simply trekking through wilderness you're sure no one has seen before, you'll enjoy endless exploration of the infinite diversity of Indonesia's 17,000 islands (or was it…).

# Getting Started

Indonesia is big, cheap, rough and effortless. It's everything to everyone, a choose-your-own-adventure travel destination. With little more than a passport, sunscreen and a day's notice, urban-fatigue victims arrive dazed at Denpasar to recover in comfortable Balinese resorts. With a bit of planning and preparation, explorers can put packs to their backs and lose themselves for two months – needing just time, energy and a keen sense of adventure as companions.

## WHEN TO GO

Straddling the equator, Indonesia tends to have a fairly even climate year-round. Rather than four seasons, Indonesia has two – wet and dry – and there are no extremes of winter and summer.

In most parts of Indonesia, the wet season falls between October and April (low season), and the dry season between May and September (high season). Rain tends to come in sudden tropical downpours, but it can also rain nonstop for days. In some parts of the country, such as Bali, the difference between the seasons is modest – the dry season just seems to be slightly hotter and slightly drier than the wet season. In other areas, such as Nusa Tenggara, the differences are very pronounced, with droughts in the dry season and floods in the wet.

See Climate Charts (p826) for more information.

Though travel in the wet season is not usually a major problem in most parts of Indonesia, mud-clogged back roads can be a deterrent (or landslides on Java). The December to February rains can make travel more difficult in Nusa Tenggara, Kalimantan and Papua. The rains shift in Sumatra, peaking from October to January in the north, and from January to February in the south. In contrast, parts of the Moluccas literally shine in January.

In most cases, experiencing an Indonesian festival is reason enough to head to a destination; but read the coverage in this book, as some events may make travel difficult. Check for local holidays (p832), when public transport can be clogged and some businesses close. Also, Indonesia's burgeoning middle class likes to travel and they seem to *all* hit the roads – and skies – when there is a major holiday.

It's also good to be aware of holidays elsewhere if visiting Bali. School holidays and Christmas bring hordes of fun-seekers from Australia, for example, booking up rooms by the thousands. Europeans travel in July and August to a swath of islands, but usually not in numbers to make for anything more than enjoyable sunset drinking companions.

## COSTS & MONEY

Costs vary depending on where you go, but Indonesia remains one of the best-value travel destinations in Asia. Hotels, food and transport are all inexpensive in US dollar terms.

Accommodation is usually the greatest expense of Indonesian travel, followed by special activities like tours, treks, dives and the like. But three square warung (simple eatery) meals can cost you as little as US$3 (about 10,000Rp or less per meal), but even if you dine in decent local restaurants, you still won't spend much more than US$10 per day (around 30,000Rp per meal) on food. Simply put, the more you live like a local, the less you will spend.

If you confine yourself to Sumatra, Java and Nusa Tenggara, a shoestring traveller can spend as little as US$20 per day. A midrange budget starts at about US$50 per day, which will get you an air-conditioned hotel room, an occasional tour and car hire. Midrange accommodation is more expensive in Balinese resorts, so budget for at least US$70 per day there. Top-end travellers will end up spending anything above US$100 a day, although there are few places on earth where that amount can get such good value. See p817 for details on the price categories used in this book.

Travellers' centres with lots of competition, such as Danau Toba, Yogyakarta and Bali, can be superb value for accommodation and food. The latter in particular can be amazing value. A superb grilled seafood meal with drinks in a lovely spot might cost as much as US$10. Sulawesi and Nusa Tenggara are good budget options.

Elsewhere, budget accommodation can be limited and prices are higher because competition is less fierce. Accommodation prices in Maluku and Papua can be twice as high as in tourist towns, and transport costs on Kalimantan are relatively high.

Transport expenses also increase once you get into the outer provinces. In Bali, Sumatra, Java and Nusa Tenggara there's very little need to take to the air, but in Papua you often have no choice but to fly. Flying is more expensive than other forms of transport, though still cheap in dollar terms as new budget airlines are offering stiff competition. Petrol prices are volatile – only recently have they begun to mirror world prices – bus fares remain cheap. See p847 for details on getting around.

## TRAVELLING RESPONSIBLY

The best way to responsibly visit Indonesia is to try to be as least-invasive as possible. Resources are often scarce and serving travellers can have a huge impact on local ecology through water use, refuse etc. Travelling green is of

### HOW MUCH?

Snorkel hire 20,000-50,000Rp

Bike hire 15,000-30,000Rp

Ikat (hand-dyed cloth) 500,000Rp plus

Cruise to see orangutans 150,000Rp

Economy passage on a ferry from Java to Kalimantan 165,000Rp

First-class passage, same boat: 500,000Rp

See also Lonely Planet Index, inside front cover

---

### DON'T LEAVE HOME WITHOUT...

- checking the visa situation (p839) – it's constantly changing and constantly frustrating
- an emergency stash of cash for remote or isolated areas (in Rupiah after you're in Indonesia)
- a hat, sunglasses and sunscreen – the Indonesian sun is relentless
- sturdy boots and sandals
- locks for your luggage – it's better to be safe than sorry (p828)
- an empty bag to haul your shopping home
- an effective set of earplugs for the mosque and traffic wake-up calls
- a snorkel and mask for areas outside of tourist centres
- a torch (flashlight)
- dental floss, tampons and shaving cream – they're harder to come by than your average toiletries
- waterproof jacket – it's the tropics, it rains...a lot
- antimalarial tablets if going rural and DEET repellent (see p859)
- sleeping bag if trekking
- extra memory card for the camera
- photos of loved ones – even pets – at home, they're amazing ice breakers
- a mental note to purchase a sarong once you're in Indonesia – it's a fashion statement, blanket, beach mat, top sheet, mattress cover, towel and shade from the pounding sun.

course easier than it sounds, especially in a country where environmental awareness is still nascent at best, but consider the following tips:

- Watch your use of water – demand often outstrips supply. Take up your hotel on its offer to save lots of water, by not washing your sheets and towels every day. Don't stay at a place with a pool, especially if the ocean is next door.
- Don't hit the bottle – those bottles are convenient but they add up. The zillions of such bottles tossed away each year are a major blight. Still, you're wise not to refill from the tap, so what do you do? Ask your hotel or eatery if you can refill from their huge containers of drinking water if they have them. Look for bottle refilling stations.
- Conserve power – sure you want to save your own energy on a sweltering afternoon, but using air-con strains an already overloaded system. Open the windows at night for often cooler breezes. Turn off the air-con (if you have it) when you go out.
- Don't drive yourself crazy – the traffic is already bad, why add another vehicle to it? Can you take a bus or bemo instead of a chartered or rental car? Would a hike or bicycle trip somewhere be more enjoyable than a road journey to an overvisited tourist spot? You can hire a bike for US$3 per day or less.
- Slow down – if you have the time, enjoy a ferry, don't fly. The train on Java is a democratic experience.
- Don't feed the animals – insist on tour guides not relying on feeding local wildlife such as orangutans to ensure sightings on treks.
- Eat local – warungs have food sourced locally and their food is usually the freshest.
- Trek responsibly – see p821
- Dive responsibly – see p820

For organisations that have more information on the local environment and may be able to use your help in protecting it, see p840. See also this book's GreenDex (p904) for attractions, tours and accommodation choices selected by the authors because they meet our criteria for sustainable tourism.

## TRAVEL LITERATURE

Wrapping your head around Indonesian culture can be a daunting task, as the country's history, economics, politics and culture have been widely interpreted and documented by a host of writers. Literature about Java and Bali is relatively common, but anything about the other islands can be hard to find. However we list favourite books at the start of each chapter. The following will all help you get in the mood before your trip:

Lyall Watson's *Gifts of Unknown Things* observes the symbiotic relationship of a community and its environment on an unnamed Indonesian island. The value of the natural world features highly in the book, and fans describe it as life affirming.

Tim Flannery's *Throwim Way Leg* is a must for Papuan inspiration. The author recounts his scientific expeditions to the province, where he discovered new species in Indiana Jones-style adventures. And it's all true!

The pages explode (!) in Simon Winchester's highly readable *Krakatoa – The Day the World Exploded,* which melds history, geology and politics, all centred on the 1883 eruption of Krakatau – the world's biggest bang.

*In Search of Moby Dick,* by Tim Severin, is an engagingly written search for the globe's last whale-hunters that includes an extended stay in the remote whaling village of Lamalera, Nusa Tenggara.

*Indonesia: People and Histories* by Jean Gelman Taylor is passionately written and throws new light on Indonesian history by telling it from both Indonesian and outsiders' perspectives, covering the lives of ordinary folk as well as rulers.

*The Year of Living Dangerously* by Christopher J Koch is the harrowing tale of a journalist in Sukarno's Indonesia of 1965. Many have seen the movie with a young Mel Gibson and Linda Hunt. The book is more harrowing.

# TOP 10

## ADVENTURES

Indonesia has as many adventures as islands but here are some great ones.

1 Sampling the deserted islands, volcanoes and jungle of untouristed Maluku (p724), the original Spice Islands.

2 Taking in the mummies, markets and culture of Papua's Baliem Valley (p801).

3 Snorkelling the remarkably clear and shallow dive spots of the Banda Islands (p756).

4 Braving the elements, sun bears and jungle in Kalimantan's Kayan Mentarang National Park (p594) or Apokayan Highlands (p650).

5 Surfing the legendary Desert Point (p487) in southwest Lombok.

6 Tramping through coffee plantations and waterfalls around Bali's Munduk (p354).

7 Marvelling at the 6km-wide crater lake and summit views of Lombok's Gunung Rinjani (p506).

8 Spotting orangutans, gibbons, macaques and kingfishers in Tanjung Puting National Park (p614).

9 Getting a bird's-eye view of Sumatra's smoking guns, Gunung Sinabung (p386) and Gunung Sibayak (p385).

10 Discovering pristine wilderness and beaches in Java's remote Ujung Kulon National Park (p133).

## FESTIVALS

Indonesians have myriad festivals, religious and otherwise; that are worth a journey.

1 Nyale Fishing Festival (February or March; p513) – hundreds flock to catch a glimpse of Lombok's first *nyale* (wormlike fish) at this huge fishing festival.

2 Pasola (February or March; p589) – ritual warfare marks Nusa Tenggara's harvest festival.

3 Waisak (May; p174) – Buddha's birth and enlightenment are celebrated by thousands of monks and pilgrims in Borobudur.

4 Festival Teluk Kendari (Kendari Bay Festival; April; p719) – partying and dragon-boat races in Sulawesi's Kendari.

5 Yogya Arts Festival (June to July; p183) – a month-long smorgasbord of shows and exhibitions in Java's cultural capital.

6 Bali Arts Festival (June to July; p296) – A celebration of Bali's sublime dance, music and crafts.

7 Tana Toraja funeral festival (July to September; p677) – Toraja people from all over Indonesia return to Sulawesi to celebrate these annual funeral rituals.

8 *Bidar* race (August; p831) – dozens of vivid *bidar* (canoes) race in Sumatra's Palembang.

9 Baliem Valley Festival (August; p811) – a rich celebration of the Baliem Valley's diverse indigenous cultures.

10 Ubud Writers & Readers Festival (October; p314) – an internationally acclaimed writers' festival.

If you think travel's rugged now, delve into Helen and Frank Schreider's *Drums of Tonkin,* which documents their 1963 journey from Sumatra to Timor in an amphibious jeep: landslides, gun-toting soldiers and sea voyages galore.

*The Invisible Palace* by Jose Manuel Tesoro tells the true story of a journalist's murder in Yogyakarta during the twilight of the Suharto regime. It details the intricate webs within Indonesian society linking Islam, traditional beliefs, family, government and thuggery.

## INTERNET RESOURCES

The following sites are all good for giving you a feel for current events in Indonesia; some go further and explore the ever-evolving culture of the country.

**Antara** (www.antara.co.id/en) This is the site for the official Indonesian news agency; it has a searchable database.

**Inside Indonesia** (www.insideindonesia.org) Excellent website with news and thoughtful features.

**Indonesia Traveling** (www.indonesiatraveling.com) Fantastic site with detailed information about Indonesia's parks, nature reserves and the critters you might encounter. Also has links to charter sailing boats and much more.

**Jakarta Globe** (www.thejakartaglobe.com) The top-notch new national English-language newspaper.

**Jakarta Post** (www.thejakartapost.com) Indonesia's original English-language daily; good cultural coverage.

**LonelyPlanet.com** (www.lonelyplanet.com) Share knowledge and experiences with other travellers about islands that have been Lonely Planet favourites from the start.

# Itineraries
## CLASSIC ROUTES

### BEACHES, BARS, BODIES & BLISS    Two to Three Weeks/Bali to the Gilis

Start in Bali, where you can acclimatise in the resorts, clubs and shops of **Kuta** (p269). Dose up on sun at the beach, then feast on fabulous food and sling back cocktails in **Seminyak's** (p279) trendy haunts.

Head north to immerse yourself in the 'other' Bali – the culture, temples and rich history of **Ubud** (p306). Visit the Unesco-nominated **Gunung Kawi** (p323), an ancient site worthy of Indiana Jones, and the nearby craft villages. Take a cooking course or learn batik, woodcarving or silversmithing. Once you've exhausted your yen for culture, escape to the misty mountains for treks to waterfalls amid coffee plantations in and around **Munduk** (p354).

Next on the agenda is Lombok; from Bali's beachy port town of **Padangbai** (p331) take a ferry to **Lembar** (p487), Lombok's launching pad. Potter through the rice fields and Hindu temples around **Mataram** (p486), then head to **Senggigi** (p488) for indulgent resorts, fine beaches and uninterrupted R&R.

From Senggigi take a ferry to the deservedly celebrated **Gili Islands** (p492), where seamless beaches, translucent water and vivid reefs beg for snorkel-clad swimmers. Or if you're on a short timeframe, just fast ferry to the Gilis direct from Padangbai.

Bali and Lombok are the heart of Indonesia's tourist industry. This well-trodden 160km-long path starts in Kuta, snakes north through Bali to Ubud and skips over to Lombok before ending in the Gili Islands.

*Bali Sea*

BALI
Gunung Kawai
Munduk
Ubud
Padangbai
Seminyak
Kuta

*Selat Lombok*

Gili Islands
Senggigi
LOMBOK
Mataram
Lembar

**Nusa Penida**

*INDIAN OCEAN*

## THE JAVA JAUNT

**Three Weeks to Two Months/Jakarta to Bromo-Tengger-Semeru National Park**

Start your journey in **Jakarta** (p96) and wrap your senses around the dizzying smells, sounds, sights and people of Indonesia's teeming capital. Linger long enough to binge on Bintang beer and shopping, then head to **Bogor** (p134) to lose yourself in the sublime Kebun Raya botanic gardens.

From Bogor set a course east through Java's centre, traversing tea plantations and dramatic scenery to pass through the famed rice centre of **Cianjur** (p142). Visit **Gede Pangrango National Park** (p142) and take a day to reach the summit of Gunung Gede for jaw-dropping views. Continue your journey for a stint in the urban jungle of **Bandung** (p143). Satiate yearnings for the modern world in this city's hotels and restaurants, then make a quick exit from the chaos.

It's time to hit the coast, ditch the boots for a while and camp out in some well-earned calm – and that's where **Pangandaran** (p155), Java's premier beach resort, comes in. The national park, wide shorelines and a coastal party buzz dominate the visual and social landscapes here, and the accommodation is kind to all budgets.

After you've worshipped the sun for a week or so, pack the bags and head to **Yogyakarta** (p176), Java's cultural capital. Dabble in batik, amble through the *kraton* (walled city palace) and part with your rupiah at the vibrant markets. A day trip to majestic **Borobudur** (p171) is a must. From Yogyakarta make your way to the laid-back city of **Solo** (p198), via the enigmatic temples of **Prambanan** (p194). Finish your Java expedition with a visit to the awesome **Bromo-Tengger-Semeru National Park** (p245), spending your last night on the lip of Tengger crater.

Positively churning with life, Java has the lion's share of Indonesia's population, and a wealth of culture and landscapes to match. This 800km route takes in its highlights, beginning in the teeming capital Jakarta and ending in the awe-inspiring peaks of Bromo-Tengger-Semeru National Park.

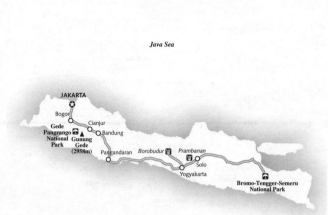

*Java Sea*

*INDIAN OCEAN*

## INDONESIA'S ISLAND CORE     One Month/Lombok To Bali the Long Way

Start on **Lombok** (p478), which has good air connections to the rest of Indonesia and Singapore. Head out to the **Gili Islands** (p492), three perfect droplets of white sand speckled with palm trees and surrounded by coral reefs teeming with marine life. Base yourself on **Gili Trawangan** (p498) where there's a great travellers' scene to hear tales from others and get inspired at fabled beach bars. Follow in the wake of generations of travellers on a boat from Lombok to **Flores** (p540), but choose carefully as standards vary. You'll see beautiful coastline along Sumbawa, stop for some snorkelling in **Pulau Satonda** (p522) and take a dragon-spotting hike on **Komodo** (p529). Take some time in the agreeable port town of **Labuanbajo** (p534) and head off-shore for some diving. From here you'll need to fly to Makassar on Sulawesi, this may require connecting *someplace*. In **Makassar** (p659), pause amid the pandemonium for excellent seafood and fun nightlife. But don't overdo it, as you want to be fully alive for the elaborate funeral ceremonies in **Tana Toraja** (p672), an eight-hour bus trip from Makassar. From here, another long bus ride (13 hours) takes you to the transport hub of **Poso** (p689), where you may wish to break your journey at the tidy lakeside town of **Tentena** (p687). A five-hour bus ride from Poso gets you to **Ampana** (p695) where you take a ferry to your reward: the amazing, beautiful and beguiling **Togean Islands** (p696). Spend your days island- and hammock-hopping between iconic beaches. Tearing yourself away, take a boat to **Gorontalo** (p697) and from there bus it to **Manado** (p704) where you can get a flight connection to **Bali** (p258) and spend the rest of your time chasing bliss.

**Beaches, underwater beauty, nasty lizards, transformative culture and more await you on a classic 4000km journey that begins in the mellow climes of Lombok, takes you through Komodo and a bit of Flores, and then on to Sulawesi for funeral ceremonies and yet more beaches before ending in Bali.**

# ROADS LESS TRAVELLED

This 3000km adventure concentrates on the underexplored east and the Moluccas. It takes in Papua's sublime Danau Sentani and the beguiling Baliem Valley before heading to the diving wonderland of the Raja Ampat Islands. Maluku's Pulau Ambon and Banda Islands provide a change of scene before the route heads south to West Timor and Flores.

## THE GREAT EAST
**One Month/Papua to Flores**

Papua is the launching pad for this route, which can be done in 30 days with judicious use of flights. Start at the transport hub of **Jayapura** (p789). But you'll only be there long enough to charter a boat to visit the magnificent **Danau Sentani** (p794), a 96.5-sq-km lake with 19 islands perfect for inland island-hopping.

Back on dry land, take to the air to get to the beautiful **Baliem Valley** (p801), rich in culture and trek-worthy mountain scenery. The valley is home to the Dani people, an ethnic group who have eschewed most modern things and live a traditional life. Next it's back to Jayapura for a flight to **Sorong** (p780), a base for trips out to the **Raja Ampat Islands** (p782) – a paradise for divers and snorkellers with Indonesia's most abundant and varied marine life. It's also good for birdwatchers and sublime tropical-island scenery. From Sorong you have your choice of transport: fly and this itinerary definitely can be done in a month, or take Pelni (a line of passenger ships), but make certain you have a 60-day visa, or Pelni it to Kota Ambon on Maluku's **Pulau Ambon** (p742). Dose up on urban comfort and culture, then take a ferry (often frustrating) or plane to the crystaline seas, multicoloured reefs and empty beaches of the **Banda Islands** (p756).

After indulging in sun and isolation, either fly to **Kupang** (p567) in West Timor or enjoy a Pelni march, connecting through Makassar. If heading to Kupang, visit villages in the surrounding areas, then jump over to **Rote** (p575) for relaxed coastal vibes. For a perfect ending, make your way to **Flores** (p532), a rugged volcanic island with fishing villages, thriving culture and dramatic terrain.

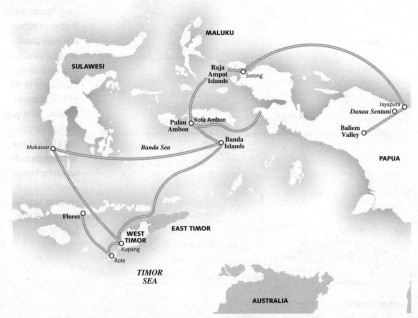

## POSTCARDS COME TO LIFE    Six to Eight Weeks/Kalimantan to Sulawesi

Unassuming **Pangkalan Bun** (p611) is the entry point to this excursion – it's the launching pad for trips into glorious **Tanjung Puting National Park** (p614), one of Indonesia's best orangutan haunts. Scan the canopy for their amber bodies from the top of a houseboat as it ambles down the beautiful Sungai Kumai, then fly back to reality in colourful **Banjarmasin** (p623). Dabble in Kalimantan's most beguiling city – brave a 5am call for the animated floating markets, then cruise the canals and meet the locals at dusk.

From Banjarmasin, travel overland to **Samarinda** (p637) and make an expedition along **Sungai Mahakam** (p642). Several days upstream will land you in the river's western reaches, which are peppered with semitraditional Dayak villages and preserved forests.

From Samarinda catch the weekly Pelni ferry to **Makassar** (p659) to marvel at colonial Dutch architecture and gorge on some of Indonesia's best seafood. Chart a course due north for vast and mesmerising **Tana Toraja** (p672), home to Sulawesi's most fascinating indigenous culture. Then spot spritely tarsiers and discover ancient megaliths at **Lore Lindu National Park** (p690).

Continue north and settle in central Sulawesi for hiking around Indonesia's third largest lake, **Danau Poso** (p689). From here escape the 'mainland' and plant yourself on the blissful **Togean Islands** (p696). Finally, head all the way north and escape life entirely by snorkelling or diving along unbelievably rich coral drop-offs – some of Asia's best – at chilled-out **Pulau Bunaken** (p710).

**Some of Indonesia's best-known but least-visited sights highlight this 2700-odd-km route that takes in the orangutans of magical Tanjung Puting National Park and the Dayak people of Kalimantan's interior, before skipping over to Sulawesi for Toraja funeral ceremonies, river rapids, mountain treks, beaches and underwater amazement.**

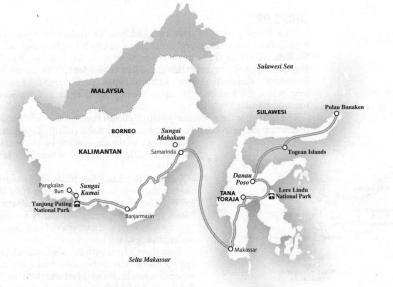

# TAILORED TRIPS

## BEGUILING BEASTIES

Indonesia's natural world is so vast and diverse that scientists seem to discover new species at the drop of a hat.

High on the list of must-sees are the enigmatic orangutans, best viewed at Sumatra's Bukit Lawang (p378) and Kalimantan's **Tanjung Puting National Park** (p614) and **Kutai National Park** (p641). This last conservation area is also populated by gibbons, macaques, proboscis monkeys, sun bears, clouded leopards and a whole host more. In east Kalimantan the wetlands around **Muara Pahu** (p644) are home to the pint-sized Irrawaddy dolphin.

Papua is the perennial flavour of the zoologist month: expeditions into the remote **Foja Mountains** (see p776) regularly uncover teeming communities of unknown frogs, birds, marsupials and more; the best way to reach them is by booking a tour (p779). You can catch a glimpse of Australianesque fauna in **Wasur National Park** (p814), or you can try spotting the rare bird of paradise in the islands around **Pulau Biak** (p796).

In Nusa Tenggara you'll encounter the gargantuan Komodo dragon, which dwells in the depths of **Komodo** (p528).

For butterflies bigger than your hand and exquisite birdlife, head to Sulawesi's **Lore Lindu National Park** (p690). The island is also home to **Tangkoko-Batuangas Dua Saudara Nature Reserve** (p716), which is both accessible and rich in birdlife and other fauna.

## SURF'S UP

With a dizzying array of coastlines and beaches, Indonesia is a surfing mecca. The most obvious and easiest place to catch a wave is Bali, where **Ulu Watu** (p291) on the west coast serves up three left-handers. Nearby, **Bingin** (p290) is the next best thing, and **Nusa Lembongan** (p301) has reached legendary status on the circuit. **Kuta** and **Legian** (p269) lured avid surfers long before the beaches were discovered by the crowds, and the waves remain a constant.

The hardy test their mettle at Lombok's **Desert Point** (p487) and then skip over to Sumbawa to catch the feisty tubes near **Maluk** (p518). Experienced surfers flock to the challenging breaks at **Lakey Peak** (p523). The surf capital of Sumba is **Baing** (p584).

Sumatra also has a few treats up its coastal sleeves, the most famous of which is **Pulau Nias** (p395). Also on Sumatra, the sublime **Mentawai Islands** (p425) are gaining popularity for their year-round swells, and a number of surf charters are beginning to sail here.

Then there's Java, with the world-class **G-Land** (p254) inside Alas Purwo National Park, and superlative reef breaks near **Pelabuhan Ratu** (p139). Beginners can find their balance on the friendly surf at **Batu Karas** (p160).

## UNDERWATER ODYSSEYS

With more than 17,000 islands under its archipelago belt, Indonesia boggles the minds of divers and snorkellers with a feast of underwater adventures.

Maluku's **Banda Islands** (p756) are encircled by dense coral gardens, cascading drop-offs and superb marine life. Best of all, they're so remote you may score this underwater vista all to yourself.

Oversized fish, sleepy sea fans and gaping canyons lounge beneath the ocean's surface near Sumatra's **Pulau Weh** (p409). The pick of the destinations here are the 20 dive sites around **Long Angen** (p412), the stomping ground for majestic manta rays, lion fish and morays.

Sulawesi's spectacular **Pulau Bunaken** (p710) simmers with more than 300 species of fish and coral types. Countless drop-offs, caves and valleys provide ample viewing for days of diving, and turtles, rays, sharks and dolphins are common visitors.

Off Papua, the **Raja Ampat Islands** (p782) have divers in raptures for their sheer numbers and variety of fish, and the huge reef systems with hundreds of hard and soft corals.

Off Kalimantan's northeast corner, **Pulau Derawan** (p648) is the best base for the Sangalaki Archipelago, as indicated by the turtles who nest here regularly and the schools of tuna who shimmy offshore.

In Nusa Tenggara, a diverse range of marine life simmers underwater in the **Gili Islands** (p497), and around **Komodo** and **Labuanbajo** (see p531).

## GUNUNG BAGGING

Indonesia's undulating landscapes encompass enough peaks and troughs to keep even marathon trekkers happy.

There's good walking to be found around Sumatra's **Gunung Sinabung** (p386) and **Gunung Sibayak** (p385), but serious explorers can brave the jungle beasties in the interior of **Gunung Leuser National Park** (p417).

Java's Unesco World Heritage–listed **Ujung Kulon National Park** (p133) is a remote outpost of untouched wilderness, and a three-day hike through the park reveals pristine forest and diverse wildlife. At the island's southeast tip, the **Ijen Plateau** (p250) is peppered with volcanic cones and offers a spectacular day trek to a sulphur lake.

The cascading rice fields around Sulawesi's **Tana Toraja** (p672) give way to excellent highland trekking, with soaring summits and cool-water swimming pools. Treks last anywhere from several hours to several days – highlights include the 2150m-high **Gunung Sesean** (p681). You can also mingle with the wildlife on treks in **Lore Lindu National Park** (p690).

Intrepid hikers should head to Papua's sublime **Baliem Valley** (p801). But for a real challenge, they should consider **Carstensz Pyramid** (Puncak Jaya; p776), at 5030m, it's the highest peak not just in Indonesia but in all Oceania. For this expedition you'll need experienced guides (p779).

Kalimantan's interior also provides excellent opportunities for hikers with time and experience, particularly around **Loksado** (p630) in Pegunungan Meratus (Meratus Mountains) and in the **Apokayan Highlands** (p650).

# History

Indonesia is a young country and even the idea of a single nation encompassing all of its territory is barely a century old. The word Indonesia itself was little known until the 1920s, when colonial subjects of the Dutch East Indies seized on it as the name for the independent nation they dreamed of. Their dream was realised in 1949 after a long, hard battle to throw off colonial rule. Since then independent Indonesia's growing pains have encompassed rebellions, religious strife, three decades of military dictatorship, much bloodshed, extremes of wealth and poverty, and expansionist adventures into neighbouring territories. Today, economic development has come a long way and Indonesia is maturing as a multi-party democracy, though not without its problem areas.

Before Indonesia, there was the Dutch East Indies – itself an idea that mutated repeatedly over three centuries as hundreds of disparate island states came one by one under the umbrella of a colonial administration. And before that, there were thousands of islands with connections of commerce and culture, some of which were sometimes grouped together under the same ruler, while others were often not even united within themselves.

The story of how Indonesia became is a colourful dance of migrants and invaders, rebels and religions, kingdoms and empires, choreographed by Indonesia's island nature and its location on millennia-old Asian trade routes. It's a story full of heroes and villains, victors and victims, but the strangest tale of all is just how these 17,000-plus islands with their 739 languages and diverse cultures ever came to be a nation at all.

> The name Indonesia was coined in the 1850s by a Scot, James Logan (editor of the Singapore-published *Journal of the Indian Archipelago and Eastern Asia*) as a shorter equivalent for the term Indian Archipelago.

## THE TRADING ARCHIPELAGO

Indonesians inhabit a diverse island world where a short sea voyage or journey inland can take a traveller into a whole new ecosystem providing a different set of useful commodities. Long ago forest dwellers were already collecting colourful bird feathers and tree resins and exchanging them for turtle shells or salt from people who lived by the sea. Some of these goods would find their way to nearby islands, from which they then reached more distant islands, and so on. By about 500 BC, routes sailed by Indonesian islanders began to overlap with those of sailors from mainland Asia. So it was that, 2000 years ago, bird-of-paradise feathers from Papua could be depicted on beautiful bronze drums cast by the Dong Son people of Vietnam, and some of the drums then ended up in Java, Sumatra and Bali.

Indonesia's main western islands – Sumatra, Kalimantan and Java – lie in the middle of the sea routes linking Arabia, India, China and Japan. Indonesia

> Simple iron tools, such as axes and plough tips, arrived from China around 200 BC, spurring Indonesians to find their own metal deposits and make their own knives, arrowheads, urns and jewellery.

## TIMELINE

| 60,000–40,000 BC | About 8000 BC | About 2000 BC |
|---|---|---|
| Indonesia's western islands are still connected to the Asian mainland. The first Homo sapiens arrive, probably ancestors of the Melanesians in today's population, who are now found mainly in Papua. | Sea levels rise after the end of the last glacial period, separating Sumatra, Borneo, Java and Bali from the Asian mainland, and the island of New Guinea from Australia. | Austronesian people originating from Taiwan, ancestors of most of today's Indonesians, start to arrive, probably by sea routes. They absorb or displace Melanesians. The earliest evidence of settlements dates from the 6th century BC. |

was destined to become a crossroads of Asia, and trade has been its lifeblood for at least 2000 years. It has brought with it nearly all the biggest changes the archipelago has seen through the centuries – new people, new ideas, new crops, new technologies, new religions, new wars, new rulers.

## INDIAN INFLUENCE & SRIWIJAYA

Contact between Indonesia and India goes back a long way. Pepper plants, originally from India, were spicing up western Indonesian food as early as 600 BC. Indonesian clothing got a lot smarter when boats from Indonesia reached India by the 2nd century BC and brought back cotton plants. In the early centuries AD, Hindu traders from southern India started to settle along the coast of mainland Southeast Asia. From there they found their way to early coastal trading settlements in Java, Sumatra and Kalimantan. The Indians brought jewellery, fine cloth, pottery, as well as Hindu and Buddhist culture.

From the 4th century AD, Chinese travellers too arrived in Indonesian ports, and in the 7th century Chinese reports started mentioning the port state of Sriwijaya. Buddhist Sriwijaya, in the Palembang-Jambi area of southeast Sumatra, may have been a grouping of ports or a single kingdom whose capital sometimes changed location. It was a powerful state, and its sailors were able to collect pepper, ivory, resins, feathers, turtle shells, mother of pearl and much more from Sumatra and ports around the Java Sea, and carry them to China, from which they brought back silk, ceramics and iron. An entrepôt for Indian, Indonesian, Arab, Southeast Asian and, eventually, Chinese traders, Sriwijaya remained important until the 14th century.

> Sriwijaya sailors travelled to Kalimantan riverside towns for gold, diamonds and beeswax, which they bought with rice, salt, iron tools and textiles.

> In 1292, Marco Polo visited Aceh and noted that local inhabitants had already converted to Islam.

## TRADERS FROM ARABIA

The first Muslim traders from Arabia appeared in Indonesian ports within a few decades of the death of the Prophet Mohammed in AD 632. Arabian ships bound for China, carrying spices and rare woods or Indian cloth, would call in at Sumatra or other Indonesian islands to add local products such as aromatic woods, resins and camphor to their cargoes. By the 13th century, Arabs had established settlements in major Indonesian ports. Sulaiman bin Abdullah bin al-Basir, ruler of the small north Sumatran port of Lamreh in the early 13th century, was the first Indonesian ruler known to have adopted Islam and taken the title Sultan.

## MAJAPAHIT

The first Indonesian sultanates came into being while the greatest of Indonesia's Hindu-Buddhist states, Majapahit, was flourishing in eastern Java. Like the earlier Sriwijaya, Majapahit's success was trade-based. Its powerful fleets exacted tribute from ports spread from Sumatra to Papua (disobedient states were 'wiped out completely' by the Majapahit navies,

> The Majapahit kingdom reached its zenith during the reign of King Hayam Wuruk (1350–89) who was ably assisted by his prime minister and brilliant military commander Gajah Mada. Their names mean, respectively, Rotting Chicken and Rutting Elephant.

| 500–1 BC | 5th Century AD | 7th–13th Centuries |
|---|---|---|
| Local trade routes mesh with mainland Asia's. Chinese iron tools, large Vietnamese bronze drums and Indian glass beads reach Indonesia. Local products such as tree resins, feathers, spices and shells reach India and China. | Under influence from India, some Indonesian trading ports have turned from animism to Hinduism or Buddhism. Indonesia's earliest known inscriptions, in the Indian learned language Sanskrit, are carved in west Java and near Kutai, Kalimantan. | Buddhist Sriwijaya in southeast Sumatra dominates in western Indonesia, with a trading network stretching at least as far as India and China. It may have been a collection of ports or a single state. |

**THE CHINESE IN INDONESIA**

As Indonesian trading states grew richer and more complex they came increasingly to rely on their growing numbers of Chinese settlers to oil the wheels of their economies. Indonesia's first recorded Chinese settlement was located at Pasai, Sumatra in the 11th century. By the 17th century, Chinese were filling a whole spectrum of roles as middlemen, artisans, labourers, tax-collectors, businessmen, financiers, farmers and keepers of shops, brothels and opium dens. Today ethnic-Chinese Indonesians own many of the country's biggest and most profitable businesses. For centuries they have also been the subject of jealousy and hatred, and the victims of repeated outbreaks of violence, including during the shocking 1998 Jakarta riots.

according to court poet Prapanca), and enabled its traders to dominate the lucrative commerce between Sumatran ports and China. Prapanca reported that traders in Majapahit ports came from Cambodia, Vietnam and Thailand. He also claimed, less credibly, that Majapahit ruled a hundred foreign countries. Majapahit was eventually conquered by one of the newly Islamic north Java ports, Demak, in 1478.

*Jean Gelman Taylor's Indonesia: People and Histories is a fascinating telling of Indonesian history, from both Indonesian and outsiders' perspectives, covering the lives of ordinary folk and rulers.*

## SPICES & THE PORTUGUESE

As Islam continued to spread around the archipelago, another new breed of trader arrived – Europeans. With advanced ship design and navigation technology, European sailors could now cross oceans in search of wealth. Portuguese ships crossed the Indian Ocean from southern Africa to India and then pushed on eastward. In 1511 they conquered Melaka, key to the vital Strait of Melaka between Sumatra and Malaya, and set up bases strung across Indonesia. They also established settlements in mainland ports from India to China and Japan.

The prize that drew the Portuguese to Indonesia was three little plant products long prized in Europe, China, the Islamic world and Indonesia itself: cloves, nutmeg and mace. All three, in high demand because they made food taste more interesting, were native to Maluku, the Spice Islands of eastern Indonesia. Cloves (the sun-dried flower buds of a type of myrtle tree) were produced on a few small islands off the west coast of Halmahera. Nutmeg and mace, both from the nut of the nutmeg tree, came from the Banda Islands. The sultans of the small Maluku islands of Ternate and Tidore controlled most of the already valuable trade in these spices.

*Nathaniel's Nutmeg by Giles Milton offers a fascinating account of the battle to control trade from the Spice Islands.*

Portuguese traders joined western Indonesians in buying spices in Maluku. They brought exotic new things to the islands such as clocks, firearms, sweet potatoes and Christianity. Clove and nutmeg cultivation was stepped up to meet their demand. After they fell out with the Ternate sultan Babullah and were expelled in 1575, they set up on nearby Pulau Ambon instead.

| 8th–9th Centuries | 1294–1478 | 13th–15th Centuries |
| --- | --- | --- |
| The Buddhist Sailendra and Hindu Sanjaya (or Mataram) kingdoms flourish on Java's central plains, creating the huge Borobudur and Prambanan temple complexes respectively. | The Hindu-Buddhist Majapahit kingdom, based in eastern Java, monopolises trade between Sumatra and China and exacts tribute from settlements across Indonesia. The splendid Majapahit court is imitated by many later Indonesian states. | Influenced by Arab merchants, two north Sumatran towns, Pasai and Lamreh, adopt Islam, followed later by Melaka on the Malay peninsula, the eastern island of Ternate and northern Java ports including Demak, which conquers Majapahit. |

The Portuguese also traded at Aceh (north Sumatra) and Banten (northwest Java), where the principal product was pepper, which had also been used for many centuries to liven up taste buds in Europe, China and elsewhere.

In the 17th century the Portuguese were pushed out of the Indonesian condiment business by a more determined, better armed and better financed rival. The newcomers didn't just want to buy spices, they wanted to drive other Europeans out of Asian trade altogether. They were the Dutch (p38).

# FROM ANIMISM TO ISLAM

The earliest Indonesians were animists – they believed animate and inanimate objects had their own life force or spirit, and that events could be influenced by offerings, rituals or forms of magic. Indonesia's scattered prehistoric sites, and animist societies that have survived into modern times, provide evidence that there was often a belief in an afterlife and supernatural controlling powers, and that the spirits of the dead were believed to influence events. Megaliths, found from Pulau Nias (p395) to Sumba (p577) and Sulawesi's Lore Lindu National Park (p690), are one manifestation of ancestor cults. Some megaliths may be 5000 years old, but in Sumba animist religion is still alive and well, and concrete versions of megalithic tombs are still being erected.

Banten's rise to importance began both when the Portuguese took Melaka, and Muslim traders started to sail down the west coast of Sumatra instead of through the Strait of Melaka.

## HINDUISM & BUDDHISM

It was contact with the comparatively wealthy cultures of India in the first few centuries AD that first led Indonesians to adopt new belief systems. Indian traders who settled in Indonesia continued to practice Hinduism, or its offshoot Buddhism. Some built their own temples and brought in priests, monks, teachers or scribes. Impressed local Indonesian rulers started to use the Indian titles Raja or Maharaja or add the royal suffix *varman* to their names. It was a short step for them to cement their ties with the Indian world by adopting the Indians' religion or philosophy too. The earliest records of Indianised local rulers are 5th-century stone inscriptions in Sanskrit, found in west Java and near Kutai (now Tenggarong), Kalimantan. These record decrees and tales of the glorious deeds of the kings Purnavarman and Mulavarman, respectively.

In the 1650s and 1660s Banten's Sultan Ageng Tirtajasa decreed that all men aged 16 or over must tend 500 pepper plants.

The major Indonesian states from then until the 15th century were all Hindu or Buddhist. Sriwijaya, based in southern Sumatra, was predominantly Buddhist. In central Java in the 8th and 9th centuries, the Buddhist Sailendra kingdom and the predominantly Hindu Sanjaya (or Mataram) kingdom constructed the great temple complexes of Borobudur (p171) and Prambanan (p194) respectively. They sought to recreate Indian civilisation in a Javanese landscape, and Indian gods such as Shiva and Vishnu were believed to inhabit the Javanese heavens, though this did not obliterate

*An Empire of the East* by Norman Lewis visits Indonesia's hot spots from the distant and more recent past in travelogue form.

| 1505 | 16th –17th Centuries | 1595 |
|---|---|---|
| Portuguese ships reach Indonesian waters. Interested in Indonesian spices, the Portuguese go on to establish trading settlements across the archipelago, joining Indians, Arabs, Chinese, Malays and islanders in the pan-Asian sea trade. | Islam continues to spread around Indonesian ports. The Islamic Mataram kingdom is founded (1581) in the lands of the old Hindu Sanjaya kingdom in central Java by a general from Demak's successor state Pajang. | Four small Dutch ships under Cornelis de Houtman reach the pepper port Banten in northwest Java, and sign a friendship treaty. Despite setbacks, the expedition returns home with enough spices to make a small profit. |

traditional beliefs in magical forces or nature spirits. In the 10th century, wealth and power on Java shifted to the east of the island, where a series of Hindu-Buddhist kingdoms dominated till the late 15th century. The greatest of these was Majapahit (1294–1478), based at Trowulan (p228). Javanese Indian culture also spread to Bali (which remains Hindu to this day) and parts of Sumatra.

## ISLAM

Majapahit was eventually undone by the next major religion to reach Indonesia – Islam. Muslim Arab traders had appeared in Indonesia as early as the 7th century. By the 13th century Arabs had established settlements in major Indonesian ports, and it was then that the first local rulers, at Lamreh and Pasai in north Sumatra, adopted Islam. Gradually over the next two centuries, then more rapidly, other Indonesian ports with Muslim communities switched to Islam. Their rulers would become persuaded by Islamic teachings and, keen to join a successful international network, would usually take the title Sultan to proclaim their conversion. Melaka on the Malay Peninsula, controlling the strategic Strait of Melaka, switched to Islam in 1436 and became a model for other Muslim states to emulate.

In Java, Sumatra and Sulawesi, some Muslim states spread Islam by military conquest. The conversion of several north Java ports in the late 15th century meant that Hindu-Buddhist Majapahit was hemmed in by hostile states and it was one of these, Demak, that conquered Majapahit in 1478.

Indonesian Islam has always had a 'folk religion' aspect in that legends of Islamic saints, holy men and feats of magic, and pilgrimages to sites associated with them, have played an important part in Muslim life. Tradition has it that Islam was brought to Java by nine *wali* (saints) who converted local populations through war or feats of magic.

The greatest of the Indonesian Muslim kingdoms, Mataram, was founded in 1581 in the area of Java where the Sailendra and Sanjaya kingdoms had flourished centuries earlier. Its second ruler, Senopati, was a descendant of Hindu princes and helped to incorporate some of the Hindu past, and older animist beliefs, into the new Muslim world.

> Islam was a focus for resistance to the Dutch in the Diponegoro War in Java (1825–30) and the Padri War (1810–37) and Aceh War (1873–1903) in Sumatra.

## CHRISTIANITY

The last major religion to reach Indonesia was Christianity. The Catholic Portuguese made some conversions among Islamic communities in Maluku and Sulawesi in the 16th century, but most reverted to Islam. The Protestant Dutch, who gradually took control over the whole archipelago between the 17th and 20th centuries, made little effort to spread Christianity. Missionaries active in the 19th and 20th centuries were steered to regions where Islam was weak or nonexistent, such as the Minahasa and Toraja areas of Sulawesi, the Batak area of Sumatra, and Dutch New Guinea (now Papua).

| 1602 | 1611–1700 | 1670–1755 |
|---|---|---|
| Holland merges competing merchant companies into the VOC (United East Indian Company). It aims to drive other European nations out of Asian trade, especially in spices, with a mixture of warfare and exclusive trading deals. | From its headquarters at Batavia (now Jakarta), the VOC expands its control through deals, alliances and battles with Indonesian sultans. A chain of Dutch-controlled ports leads to the Spice Islands and around Asia. | VOC involvement in Mataram's internal turmoils eventually brings it control of the kingdom. In 1755 it splits Mataram into two kingdoms, with capitals at Yogyakarta and Surakarta (Solo). The Dutch now effectively control all Java. |

# RAJAS & SULTANS

The Hindu, Buddhist and Muslim states of Indonesia were not charitable organisations dedicated to their subjects' welfare. The great majority were absolute monarchies or sultanates, whose rulers claimed to be at least partly divine. Their subjects were there to produce food or goods which they could pay as tribute to the ruler, or to do business from which they could pay taxes, or to fight in armies or navies, or to fill roles in the royal entourage from astrologer to poet to tax collector to concubine. Land was generally considered to belong to the ruler, who permitted the subjects to use it in exchange for taxes and tribute. Slaves were an integral part of the scene well into the 19th century.

Other states could pay tribute too and the largest kingdoms or sultanates, such as the Java-based Hindu-Buddhist Majapahit (1294–1478) and Muslim Mataram (1581–1755), built trading empires based on tribute from other peoples whom they kept in line through the threat of a military bashing. Majapahit lived on in the memory of later Indonesian states for the fine manners, ceremony and arts of its court, and because some of its princes and princesses had married into the ruling families of Muslim sultanates. Many later rulers would assert their credentials by reference to family connections with the Majapahit kingdom.

Shared religion was no bar to belligerence. Sultan Agung of Mataram had no qualms about conquering neighbouring Muslim states in the 1620s when he wanted to tighten control over the export routes for Mataram's rice, sugar and teak. Nor did past loyalty or even blood ties guarantee personal favour. In the first year of his reign, Agung's successor Amangkurat I massacred at least 6000 subjects, including his father's advisers and his own half-brothers and their families, to remove any possible challenges to his authority.

The coming of Europeans in the 16th and 17th centuries introduced new ways for Indonesian states and contenders to get one over on their rivals. They could use the Europeans as trading partners or mercenaries or allies, and if the Europeans became too powerful or demanding, they expected they could get rid of them. In Maluku, the Muslim sultanate of Ternate a small but wealthy clove-growing island, drove out the Portuguese, its former trading partners, in 1575. It later awarded the Dutch a monopoly on the sale of its spices and used the revenue to build up its war fleet and extract tribute from other statelets. Ternate eventually controlled 72 tax-paying tributaries around Maluku and Sulawesi.

Such agreements, and alliances and conquests, eventually gave the Dutch a hold over much Indonesian trade and territory. Their involvements in the endless internal feuds of the powerful Javanese Mataram kingdom won them such a stranglehold over the region that in 1749 the dying king Pakubuwono II willed them control over his kingdom. In 1755 the Dutch resolved yet another Mataram succession dispute by splitting it into two kingdoms, with

Ternate's sea power was built on its *kora-kora* war boats, powered by 200 rowers.

| 1795–1824 | 1800 | 1825–30 |
|---|---|---|
| In the Napoleonic Wars, Britain takes several Dutch possessions in the East Indies. An 1824 agreement divides the region into Dutch and British spheres of influence, similar to the territories of modern Indonesia and Malaysia. | The now overstretched, corrupt and bankrupt VOC is wound up. Its territories pass to the Netherlands crown, converting a trading empire into a colonial one, the Netherlands East Indies. | Prince Diponegoro, supported by many Muslims, the poor and some fellow Javanese aristocrats, rebels against Yogyakarta's King Hamengkubuwono V and his European and Chinese backers. 200,000 Javanese die, most from famine and disease. |

capitals at Surakarta (Solo) and Yogyakarta. Both royal families later split again, so that by the early 19th century there were four rival royal houses in this tiny part of central Java.

So long as local rulers and aristocrats cooperated, the Dutch were content to leave them in place, and these traditional rulers eventually became the top rank of the 'Native' branch of the colonial civil service, continuing to run their kingdoms under the supervision of a sprinkling of Dutch administrators.

The Dutch introduced coffee to Indonesia in 1696. United East India Company (VOC) officials got west Java nobles to instruct their farmers to grow coffee bushes, paying with cash and textiles for the harvested beans.

# DUTCH DOMINATION

When the Dutch first arrived at Banten in 1595 and set up the United East Indian Company (Vereenigde Oost-Indische Compagnie; VOC) to conduct all their business in the East Indies in 1602, they did not plan to end up running the whole of what came to be Indonesia. They just wanted to drive other European powers out of the lucrative spice trade in Indonesia. Their strategy was to sign exclusive trade agreements with local rulers where possible, and to impose their will by military force where necessary. Their powerful fleets and effective soldiers made them a potent ally for local strongmen, and in return the Dutch could extract valuable trading rights.

The British, keen to profit from the spice trade, kept control of the Maluku island of Run until 1667. Then they swapped it for a Dutch-controlled island, Manhattan.

## MOVING IN

In the beginning the Dutch concentrated primarily on the spice trade. In 1605 they drove the Portuguese out of Ambon. They then set up their own chain of settlements in Muslim ports along the route to the Spice Islands, with their headquarters at Jayakarta, a small vassal port of Banten in northwest Java. When Banten, with English help, tried to expel them in 1619, the Dutch beat off the attack, rebuilt the town and renamed it Batavia. Today it's called Jakarta.

By varied means the Dutch took control of Banda in 1621, Melaka in 1641, Tidore in 1657, Makassar in 1669, and then several Javanese ports. In Banda they exterminated or expelled almost the whole population in the 1620s and replaced them with slave-worked nutmeg plantations.

Makassar fleets visited the northern Australian coast for centuries, fishing for trepang and introducing Aborigines in the area to metal tools, pottery and tobacco, until they were banned around 1900. This legacy is acknowledged in Makassar's Museum Balla Lompoa.

The Javanese Mataram kingdom tried unsuccessfully to drive the Dutch out of Batavia in 1628 and again in 1629. In the 1640s, Mataram's King Amangkurat I, facing a host of internal challenges, decided it was wiser to make peace with the VOC. He went further and gave it the sole licence to carry Mataram goods.

While Chinese, Arabs and Indians continued to trade in Indonesia in the 17th and 18th centuries, the VOC ended up with all the best business. Asian traders carried rice, fruit and coconuts from one part of the archipelago to another; Dutch ships carried spices, timber, textiles and metals to other Asian ports and Europe.

| 1820s–1910 | 1830–70 | 1845–1900 |
| --- | --- | --- |
| Holland takes control of nearly all the archipelago through economic expansion, agreements with local aristocrats and warfare. Many aristocrats become representatives of the Dutch administration. Resource-rich Aceh wages guerrilla resistance. | The Cultivation System: two million Javanese peasants have to grow and pay tax in export crops (coffee, tea, tobacco, indigo, sugar). Holland is saved from bankruptcy, some peasants prosper, but others suffer hardship and famine. | The Liberal period: private (European) enterprise is encouraged, forced cultivation is wound down. Roads, ports, shipping services are improved; railways are built. Notoriously brutal rubber and tobacco plantations develop on Sumatra. |

## THE CULTIVATION SYSTEM

The VOC's trading successes brought it an ever larger and costlier web of commitments around the archipelago. By 1800 it controlled most of Java and parts of Maluku, Sulawesi, Sumatra and Timor. It was overstretched, and corrupt – and bankrupt. The Dutch crown took over the company's possessions but then lost them (first to France, then to Britain) during the Napoleonic Wars. Control was restored to the Dutch in 1816 following the Anglo-Dutch Treaty of 1814.

Progress in the Dutch colony was further delayed by the devastating Diponegoro War in Java (1825–30). After this, Holland desperately needed to make the East Indies profitable. Its answer was the new Cultivation (or Culture) System. Up to two million Javanese peasants were obliged to grow the export crops of coffee, tea, tobacco, indigo or sugar, and pay a proportion of their crop in tax, and sell the rest to the government at fixed prices. This saved Holland from bankruptcy, and while some villagers prospered, the cultivation system also resulted in famines, loss of rice-growing lands, poverty and corruption.

Indonesian farmers were forced to cultivate the indigo plant so that the Dutch could sell the extracted dye in Europe, where it fetched a high price.

## LIBERAL PERIOD

As the 19th century progressed, the Cultivation System was scaled back, and European private enterprise was encouraged to take over export agriculture. Privately owned rubber and tobacco plantations, both of which featured brutal working conditions, helped to extend Dutch control into eastern Sumatra. The colonial administration concentrated on creating a favourable investment climate by the construction of railways, improving roads and shipping services, and quashing unrest. They also waged military campaigns to subjugate the last non-compliant local statelets. The Banjarmasin sultanate in Kalimantan came under direct Dutch rule in 1863 after a four-year war; resource-rich Aceh in northern Sumatra was finally subdued in 1903 after 30 years of vicious warfare; southwest Sulawesi was occupied from 1900 to 1910; and Bali was brought to heel, after several attempts, in 1906. Some Balinese aristocrats killed their families and retainers and committed suicide rather than submit to the Dutch. In the late 19th century Holland, Britain and Germany all agreed to divide up the unexplored island of New Guinea.

During the 19th century, the Dutch set up plantations of the cinchona tree, the bark of which contains quinine: the most effective anti-malarial of the time.

## THE ETHICAL POLICY

The end of the 19th century saw the rise of a new Dutch awareness of the problems and needs of the Indonesian people. The result was the Ethical Policy, launched in 1901, which aimed to raise Indonesians' welfare and purchasing power through better irrigation, education, health and credit, and with a decentralised government. The Ethical Policy's immediate effects were mixed, and its benefits often accrued to Europeans rather than Indonesians.

| 1901 | 1912 | 1920 |
| --- | --- | --- |
| The Ethical Policy is introduced to raise Indonesian welfare through better irrigation, education, health and credit. Implementation is patchy: Europeans benefit most. But education and the growth of cities spawn a new Indonesian middle class. | Sarekat Islam (Islamic Union) emerges as a Javanese Muslim economic assistance group, with anti-Christian and anti-Chinese tendencies. Linking with other groups, it grows into a million-member anticolonial movement active throughout the colony. | The Indonesian Communist Party (PKI) is founded as a splinter from Sarekat Islam. A pro-independence party with support from urban workers, it is sidelined when uprisings in Java (1926) and Sumatra (1927) are suppressed by the Dutch. |

An increase in private land ownership increased the number of locals without land. Local revolts and strikes were fairly frequent. But the colony's trade continued to grow. By the 1930s the Dutch East Indies was providing most of the world's quinine and pepper, over one-third of its rubber and almost one-fifth of its tea, sugar, coffee and oil.

# BREAKING FREE

The longer-term effects of the Ethical Policy were truly revolutionary. Wider education spawned a new class of Indonesians aware of colonial injustices, international political developments and the value of their own cultures. These people were soon starting up diverse new political and religious groups and publications, some of which were expressly dedicated to ending Dutch colonial rule.

## THE FIRST NATIONALISTS

Today Indonesians look back to 1908 as the year their independence movement began. This was when Budi Utomo (Glorious Endeavour) was founded. Led by upper-class, Dutch-educated, Indonesian men, Budi Utomo wanted to revive monarchy and modernise Javanese culture for the 20th century. It was soon followed by more radical groups. Sarekat Islam (Islamic Union), which emerged in 1912, began as a Javanese Muslim economic mutual-help group, with a strong anti-Christian and anti-Chinese streak. Linking with other groups, it grew steadily into a million-member anticolonial movement trying to connect villagers throughout the colony with the educated elite.

In 1920 the Indonesian Communist Party (PKI), which had operated within Sarekat Islam, split off on its own. A pro-independence party with support from urban workers, it launched uprisings in Java (1926) and Sumatra (1927) but was neutralised when these were quashed by the Dutch, who imprisoned and exiled thousands of communists.

A key moment in the growth of nationalist consciousness came in 1928 when the All Indonesia Youth Congress proclaimed its historic Youth Pledge, establishing goals of one national identity (Indonesian), one country (Indonesia) and one language (the version of Malay called Bahasa Indonesia). Meanwhile the Indonesian National Party (PNI), which emerged in 1927 from the Bandung Study Group led by a young engineer, Sukarno, was rapidly becoming the most powerful Indonesian nationalist organisation – with the result that in 1930 the Dutch jailed its leaders.

Nationalist sentiment remained high through the 1930s, but even when Germany invaded the Netherlands in 1940, the Dutch colonial government was determined to hold fast.

Clove-impregnated *kretek* cigarettes, popular throughout Indonesia today, were first marketed by Nitisemito, a man from Kudus, Java, in 1906. His Bal Tiga (Three Balls) brand grew into one of the biggest Indonesian-owned businesses in the Dutch East Indies.

The 1860 novel *Max Havelaar* by Multatuli (Edward Douwes Dekker), revealing the nefarious effects of the Cultivation System, was one of the main reasons for the emergence of the Ethical Policy, through its profound effect on Dutch opinion.

The Australian National University's Asian Studies Virtual Library (http://coombs.anu.edu.au) is a great resource with heaps of links on Indonesian history and issues

| 1927 | 1942 | 1942–45 |
|---|---|---|
| The Indonesian National Party (PNI) emerges from the Bandung Study Group led by a young engineer, Sukarno. It grows quickly into the most powerful pro-independence organisation. In 1930 its leaders are jailed. | Japan invades Indonesia with little resistance. European military and civilians are sent to prison camps. Indonesians initially welcome the Japanese as liberators, but sentiment changes as the harshness of the occupation becomes apparent. | The Japanese collaborate with nationalist leaders such as Sukarno and Mohammed Hatta because of their anti-Dutch sentiments, and establish an Indonesian militia that later forms the backbone of the anti-Dutch resistance after WWII. |

## WWII

Everything changed when Japan invaded the Dutch East Indies in 1942 and swept aside Dutch and Allied resistance. Almost 200,000 Dutch and Chinese civilians and Allied military were put into prison camps, in some of which 30% of the inmates would die. Many Indonesians at first welcomed the Japanese as liberators, but feelings changed as they were subjected to slave labour and starvation. The 3½ year Japanese occupation did however strengthen the Indonesian nationalist movement, as the Japanese used anti-Dutch nationalists to help them run things and allowed them limited political activity. Sukarno was permitted to travel around giving nationalist speeches. The Japanese also set up Indonesian home-defence militias, whose training proved useful in the Indonesians' later military struggle against the Dutch.

As defeat for Japan loomed in May 1945, the Investigating Agency for Preparation of Independence met in Jakarta. This Japanese-established committee of Indonesian nationalists proposed a constitution, philosophy (Pancasila; see p46) and extents (the whole Dutch East Indies) for a future Indonesian republic.

Yogyakarta's Sultan Hamengkubuwono IX (1912–88) was one Indonesian aristocrat who sided with the national-ists against the Dutch. He later held a series of Indonesian cabinet posts, including as Suharto's vice-president in the 1970s.

## THE REVOLUTION

When Japan announced its surrender on 15 August 1945, a group of *pemuda* (radical young nationalists) kidnapped Sukarno and his colleague Mohammed Hatta and pressured them to declare immediate Indonesian independence, which they did at Sukarno's Jakarta home on 17 August (you can see the text of their proclamation on the 100,000Rp banknote). A government was formed, with Sukarno president and Hatta the vice-president.

British and Australian forces arrived to disarm the Japanese and hold the Indonesian nationalists until the Dutch could send their own forces. But Indonesians wanted independence. Some, like Sukarno and Hatta, favoured a negotiated path to freedom; others wanted to fight to get it as fast as possible. The early months of the revolution were a particularly chaotic period: with massacres of Chinese, Dutch and Eurasian civilians and Indonesian aristocrats; attempted communist revolutions in some areas; and clashes between Indonesian struggle groups and the British and Japanese. In the bloody Battle of Surabaya in November 1945, thousands died: not just from British bombing and in street fighting with the British, but also in nationalist atrocities against local civilians. In December the nationalists managed to pull diverse struggle groups together into a republican army.

By 1946, 55,000 Dutch troops had arrived. They soon re-captured major cities on Java and Sumatra. Ruthless tactics by Captain Raymond Westerling in southern Sulawesi saw at least 6000 Indonesians executed (40,000 by some accounts). The first of two big Dutch offensives – called 'police actions' – reduced republican territory to limited areas of Java and Sumatra in August 1947, with its capital at Yogyakarta.

Anyone interested in the WWII campaigns in Indonesia, and the sites and relics that can be found there today, should check out the fascinating Pacific Wrecks (www .pacificwrecks.com).

*Revolt In Paradise* by Scottish-American author K'tut Tantri is a gripping portrayal of her involve-ment in Indonesia's fight for independence. Timothy Lindsey's *The Romance of K'tut Tantri and Indonesia* offers great background to the original.

| Aug 1945 | Sep–Nov 1945 | 1946–49 |
|---|---|---|
| Japan surrenders on 15 August. Indonesian nationalist students kidnap Sukarno and Hatta and pressure them to declare imme-diate independence, which they do on 17 August. A government is formed, with Sukarno presi-dent and Hatta vice-president. | Allied troops disarm the Japanese and hold Indonesian nationalists. Sukarno wants in-dependence through diplomacy, but other nationalists want to fight. The Battle of Surabaya between British and nationalist forces leaves thousands dead. | With the arrival of Dutch troops to regain control, the nationalists organise struggle groups into a Republican Army. Despite Dutch offensives and rifts between Sukarno's government, Muslim movements and the Commu-nists, resistance continues. |

The first *becak* (tricycle rickshaws) appeared on the streets of Batavia (Jakarta) in 1936.

Differences among the Indonesian forces erupted viciously. In Madiun, Java, the republican army and Muslim militias fought pro-communist forces in August 1948, leaving 8000 dead. The second Dutch 'police action' in December 1948 won the Dutch more territory, and they captured Sukarno, Hatta and their prime minister Sutan Syahrir. But the independence forces kept up a guerrilla struggle, and international (especially US) opinion turned against the Dutch. Realising that its cause was unwinnable, the Netherlands finally transferred sovereignty over the Dutch East Indies (apart from Dutch New Guinea) to the Indonesian republic on 27 December 1949. At least 70,000, possibly as many as 200,000, Indonesians had lost their lives in the revolution, along with 700 Dutch and British troops and some thousands of Japanese troops and European, Chinese and Eurasian civilians.

# 'BUNG' KARNO

Independent Indonesia had a troubled infancy. Tensions between Muslims and communists persisted, with the secular nationalists like Sukarno and Hatta trying to hold everything together. The economy was in a sorry state after almost a decade of conflict, and a drop in commodity prices in the early 1950s made things worse.

At the entrance to a neighbourhood or village you may see an arch with the words 'Dirgahayu RI' painted across it. This translates as 'Long live the Republic of Indonesia' and the arch has been built to celebrate Independence Day, 17 August.

## EARLY DIVISIONS

There were some who wanted Indonesia to be an Islamic republic, and there were some who didn't want their home territories to be part of Indonesia at all. The western-Java-based Darul Islam (House of Islam) wanted a society under Islamic law. It linked up with similar organisations in Kalimantan, Aceh and south Sulawesi to wage guerrilla war against the republic, which lasted until 1962 in western Java. In Maluku, Ambonese former soldiers of the Dutch colonial army declared an independent South Moluccas Republic in 1950. They were defeated within a few months.

## GUIDED DEMOCRACY

Sukarno's anti-Western tendencies also saw him ban Hollywood movies and rock 'n roll music.

Coalition governments drawn from diverse parties and factions never lasted long, and when the much-postponed parliamentary elections were finally held in 1955, no party won more than a quarter of the vote. In 1956, after a visit to communist China, Sukarno began to expound his ideas on a more appropriate political system for Indonesia. He wanted to replace Western-style democracy, which he derided as rule by '50 per cent plus one', with something more in the Indonesian village tradition of achieving consensus through discussion. The outcome was 'Guided Democracy', effectively an uneasy coalition between the military, religious groups and communists, with increasing power concentrated in the hands of the president (ie himself). In

| 1949 | 1950–62 | 1955 |
|---|---|---|
| Faced with an unwinnable war and hostile international opinion, the Netherlands transfers sovereignty over the Dutch East Indies (apart from Netherlands New Guinea) to the Indonesian republic. | Armed movements challenge the republic. Darul Islam (House of Islam) wages guerrilla war in several islands, continuing until 1962 in western Java. Regionalist rebellions break out in Sumatra and Sulawesi (1958). | The PNI, regarded as Sukarno's party, tops the polls in much-postponed parliamentary elections, but no clear winner emerges. Short-lived coalition governments continue. The economy struggles following a drop in commodity prices. |

## NATION CREATION

The founders of independent Indonesia knew they had to forge some kind of national conscious if the post-colonial state was to hold together. The Dutch East Indies, though under one administration, had remained a rather disparate collection of kingdoms and sultanates. Indonesian nationalists in the early 20th century looked back to the mightiest kingdoms within the archipelago from past eras, such as Sriwijaya and Majapahit, as evidence of earlier powerful 'Indonesian' empires. Once independence was achieved, the nationalists created a set of national heroes, most of whom were awarded this status for their anti-Dutch activities. Indonesian street names and banknotes still perpetuate the memory, or myths, of many of these people:

**Diponegoro, Pangeran (1785–1855)** This Muslim prince from Yogyakarta rebelled against his own king and the Dutch in the Diponegoro War (or Java War) of 1825–30.

**Gajah Mada (d 1364)** Prime minister in the Javanese Majapahit kingdom who was also a brilliant military commander. He helped King Jayanegara defeat rebels but later arranged the king's murder because he took his wife!

**Imam Bonjol (1772-1864)** Leader of a central Sumatran fundamentalist Islamic rebellion in the Padri War (1810-37), he initially rose up against the local Minangkabau rulers and ended up fighting the Dutch who came to their aid.

**Monginsidi, Wolter (1925–49)** During the revolution, the Dutch captured and shot 24-year-old Monginsidi who had inspired the youth of Sulawesi to fight the colonialists.

**Pattimura (Thomas Matulessy; 1783–1817)** Matulessy led a short-lived anti-Dutch uprising in Maluku in 1817; for sparing the life of a six-year-old Dutch boy he gained the nickname Pattimura (Big-Hearted).

**Sisingamangaraja (1849–1907)** The last of a long line of Batak kings who had ruled since the 16th century, Sisingamangaraja became a leader of anti-Dutch resistance. Shot in error while trying to surrender, he still managed to gasp out 'Ay, Sisingamangaraja' as he expired.

**Subroto, Gatot (1907–62)** Fought for Indonesian independence in the 1940s and helped quell the communists in 1948. He became military governor of Surakarta and helped found Indonesia's national defence academy.

**Sudarso, Yos (1925–62)** Deputy chief of the Indonesian navy staff, Sudarso was one of those killed when his motor torpedo boat was sunk by the Dutch during the 'liberation' of Papua.

**Sudirman (1915–50)** A leader of the resistance against the Dutch, General Sudirman was chosen as the first commander-in-chief of the Indonesian army in 1949.

**Syahrir, Sutan (1909–66)** Syahrir was a nationalist leader in Java in the 1930s. During WWII he refused to cooperate with the Japanese. Prime minister from 1945 to 1947, he led Indonesia's attempt to negotiate independence from the Dutch.

**Thamrin, Mohammed (1894–1941)** A nationalist leader and politician in the 1920s and '30s, Thamrin died in jail after being arrested by the Dutch for his links to the Japanese.

**Yani, Ahmad (1922–65)** Hero of the military struggle against the Dutch, who became army chief of staff and was among those killed in the attempted coup of 1 October 1965.

1959 Sukarno also took on the job of prime minister for good measure. The elected legislature was dissolved in 1960, and of the political parties only the PKI continued to have any clout.

Sukarno's growing accumulation of power was one factor behind regional rebellions in Sumatra and Sulawesi in 1958, led by senior military and civilian

| 1957 | 1961–63 | 1963–66 |
| --- | --- | --- |
| Sukarno proclaims 'Guided Democracy', supposedly in the village tradition of achieving consensus through discussion. A military-Muslim-communist coalition replaces Western-style democracy. The army becomes the bedrock of national unity. | With the economy in the doldrums, Sukarno adopts an increasingly aggressive posture towards Netherlands New Guinea. Indonesia takes control there in 1963. Subsequent opposition from the local Papuan people is brutally put down. | Sukarno stages *konfrontasi* (confrontation) with the newly formed Malaysia. Fighting takes place along the Indonesia-Malaysia border in Borneo. The communist party (PKI) organises land seizures by hungry peasants in Java and other islands. |

One of Pramoedya Ananta Toer's earlier books, *Tales from Djakarta*, gives readers a backstreet view of the capital during the rocky early days of independence and the rise of military control.

The Asia-Africa Conference staged at Bandung in 1955 launched the Non-Aligned Movement, comprising countries that wanted to align with neither the USA nor the USSR. It also gave birth to the term Third World, originally meaning countries that belonged to neither Cold-War bloc.

figures. The rebels, who had backing from the CIA, were also opposed to the increasing influence of the communists, the corruption and inefficiency in central government, and the use of export earnings from the outer islands to import rice and consumer goods for Java. The rebellions were smashed within a few months and in response Sukarno forged a new alliance with Indonesia's army.

## MONUMENTS & CONFRONTATIONS

Unable to lift the economy from the doldrums, Sukarno built a series of ostentatious nationalist monuments as substitutes for real development – such as Jakarta's National Monument (Monas, also dubbed 'Sukarno's last erection'; p105) and Mesjid Istiqlal (p106). He diverted Indonesians' attention outward with a lot of bluster and aggression towards the supposedly threatening remnants of Western imperialism around Indonesia, Dutch New Guinea and Malaysia.

The New Guinea issue had already led Indonesia to seize all Dutch assets in the country and expel 50,000 Dutch people in 1957–58 after the UN rejected Indonesian claims to Dutch New Guinea. Bolstered by Soviet military backing, Indonesia finally took control of the territory in 1963 after a few military sorties and, more importantly, US pressure on the Netherlands to hand over. Subsequent opposition from the local Papuan population was brutally put down.

From 1963–66 Sukarno staged *konfrontasi* (confrontation) with the recently formed Federation of Malaysia, which he considered a British puppet. Intermittent fighting along the Indonesia–Malaysia border in Borneo never seriously threatened Malaysia's survival.

## COUP & ANTI-COMMUNIST PURGE

Meanwhile back in the heartland, the PKI was encouraging peasants to seize land without waiting for official redistribution, leading to violent clashes in eastern Java and Bali. By 1965 the PKI claimed three million members, controlled the biggest trade union organisation and the biggest peasant grouping, and had penetrated the government apparatus extensively. Sukarno saw it as a potential counterweight to the army, whose increasing power now had him worried, and decided to arm the PKI by creating a new militia. This led to heightened tensions with the regular armed forces, and rumours started to circulate of a planned communist coup.

In 1965, Indonesia's PKI was the largest communist party in the world outside the Soviet Union and China.

On 1 October 1965, military rebels shot dead six top generals in and near Jakarta. General Suharto, head of the army's Strategic Reserve, quickly mobilised forces against the rebels and by the next day it was clear the putsch had failed. Just who was behind it still remains a mystery (see opposite), but there's no mystery about its consequences. The armed forces under Suharto, and armed anti-communist civilians, took it as a cue to ruthlessly target both

| 1964–65 | 1965 | 1965–1966 |
| --- | --- | --- |
| Worried by the military's growing power, Sukarno decides to arm the communist party by creating a new militia, heightening tensions with the regular forces. Rumours of a planned communist coup circulate. | On October 1, military rebels shoot dead six top generals in and near Jakarta. General Suharto, head of the army's Strategic Reserve, mobilises forces against the rebels and by next day it is clear the coup has failed. | The armed forces, under Suharto, and armed anti-communist civilians take the attempted coup as a cue to slaughter communists and supposed communists. Around 500,000 are killed, chiefly in Java, Bali and Sumatra. |

---

### WHOSE COUP?

Some things about the 1965 attempted coup have never quite added up. Six of the country's top generals were killed by a group of officers who included members of Sukarno's palace guard and who said they were acting to save Sukarno's leadership – presumably from the threat of a plot. If that was really what they were doing, it was a very botched job.

These rebels appear to have made no effort to organise support elsewhere in the armed forces or the country. Both Sukarno and the communist leader DN Aidit visited the rebels at Halim air base near Jakarta but kept their distance from events – Sukarno leaving for the mountains in a helicopter and Aidit instructing his party to take no action and remain calm. If the officers expected the armed forces simply to fall into line under Sukarno's leadership, or the communists to rise up and take over, they miscalculated fatally.

The biggest question mark hangs over why they didn't also eliminate General Suharto, who was at least as senior as several of the generals they did kill. There is even a theory that Suharto himself might have been behind the attempted coup. Given his manipulatory talent and inscrutability, this can't be ruled out, though no evidence to confirm it has ever come to light.

---

communists and supposed communists. By March 1966, 500,000 or more people were killed, chiefly in Java, Bali and Sumatra. The anti-communist purge provided cover for settling all sorts of old scores.

## SUKARNO PUSHED ASIDE

Sukarno remained president but Suharto set about manoeuvring himself into supreme power. On 11 March 1966, Suharto's troops surrounded Sukarno's presidential palace, and Sukarno signed the 11 March Order, permitting Suharto to act on his own initiative to restore order. Sukarno loyalists in the forces and cabinet were soon arrested, and a new six-man inner cabinet including Suharto was established. After further anti-Sukarno purges and demonstrations, the People's Consultative Assembly (MPR) named Suharto acting president in March 1967. A year later, with Sukarno now under house arrest, the MPR appointed Suharto president.

Sukarno died of natural causes in 1970. An inspirational orator and charismatic leader, he is still held in great affection and esteem by many Indonesians, who often refer to him as Bung Karno – *bung* meaning 'buddy' or 'brother'. He was a flamboyant, complicated and highly intelligent character with a Javanese father and Balinese mother, and was fluent in several languages. His influences, apart from Islam, included Marxism, Javanese and Balinese mysticism, a mainly Dutch education and the theosophy movement. He had at least eight wives (up to four at once) at a time when polygamy was no longer very common in Indonesia. Throughout his political career he strove to unite Indonesians and, more than anyone else, he was the architect and creator of Indonesia.

Peter Weir's gripping *The Year of Living Dangerously* (1982), based on the eponymous novel by Australian Christopher Koch (1978), stars Mel Gibson as a young Australian reporter caught up in Indonesia's 1965 upheavals. Mel's best movie?

The film and novel title *The Year of Living Dangerously* is that of a major 1964 speech by Sukarno, which was drawn from Italian leader Mussolini's slogan 'Live Dangerously', which itself was originally penned by 19th-century German philosopher Friedrich Nietzsche!

| 1966–1968 | 1967 | 1971 |
|---|---|---|
| When Suharto's troops surround his palace, Sukarno signs the 11 March Order (1966), permitting Suharto to act independently. After anti-Sukarno demonstrations and purges of loyalists, the MPR names Suharto president (March 1968). | Suharto's 'New Order', supported by the West, holds Indonesia together under military dictatorship for the next 30 years. The economy develops, dissent is crushed and corruption rages. | The army party Golkar wins 236 of the 360 elective seats in the MPR, which now also includes 276 military and 207 Suharto appointees. A veneer of pseudo-democracy is maintained throughout the Suharto years. |

---

**PANCASILA – THE FIVE PRINCIPLES**

In government buildings and TV broadcasts, on highway markers and school uniforms you'll see the *garuda,* Indonesia's mythical bird and national symbol. On its breast are the five symbols of the philosophical doctrine of Indonesia's unitary state, Pancasila (which means Five Principles in Sanskrit and Pali, the sacred languages of Hinduism and Buddhism). Pancasila was first expounded by Sukarno in 1945 as a synthesis of Western democracy, Islam, Marxism and indigenous village traditions. Enshrined in that year's constitution, it was raised to the level of a mantra by Suharto's New Order regime. Suharto's successor BJ Habibie annulled the requirement that Pancasila must form the basic principle of all organisations, but it remains an important national creed. The five symbols:

**Star** Represents faith in God, through Islam, Christianity, Buddhism, Hinduism or any other religion.
**Chain** Represents humanitarianism within Indonesia and in relations with humankind as a whole.
**Banyan tree** Represents nationalism and unity between Indonesia's many ethnic groups.
**Buffalo** Symbolises representative government.
**Rice and cotton** Represents social justice.

---

Two great history books have the same name: *A History of Modern Indonesia.* MC Ricklefs offers a very readable account with extra focus on Java, while Adrian Vickers draws on the life of Pramoedya Ananta Toer to help tell the nation's story.

If he developed megalomaniac tendencies, they were perhaps in part a product of his high ambitions for the country. In some ways he acted like a Javanese puppet master on a grand scale – trying to keep the balance by playing off competing factions and movements against each other. In the end the puppets took over the show.

# 'PAK' HARTO

Once the dust had settled on the killing of communists and supposed communists, and a million or so political prisoners had been put behind bars, the 31 years of Suharto's rule were really one of the duller periods of Indonesian history. Such a tight lid was kept on opposition, protest and freedom of speech that there was almost no public debate. Under the New Order, as Suharto's regime was known, everybody just had to do what he and his generals told them to, if they weren't already dead or imprisoned.

## CAREER SOLDIER

Whereas Sukarno had led with charisma, Suharto's speeches seemed designed to stifle discussion rather than inspire. 'Enigmatic' was one of the kinder epithets used in his obituaries when he died in 2008. The normally restrained *Economist* magazine called him a 'kleptocrat' and 'a cold-war monster', behind whose 'pudgily smooth, benign-looking face lay ruthless cruelty'. Suharto wielded a supreme talent for manipulating events in his own interests and outwitting opponents of all kinds.

| 1975 | 1979–84 | 1989 |
| --- | --- | --- |
| Indonesia invades and annexes former Portuguese colony East Timor, where left-wing party Fretilin has won a power struggle. Fretilin wages guerrilla war for over 20 years. At least 125,000 die in fighting, famines and repression. | The government's transmigration program, started by Sukarno, reaches its peak with almost 2.5 million people moving to outer islands from overpopulated Java, Bali and Madura during these years. The program is finally ended in 2000. | The Free Aceh Movement (GAM), founded in 1976, reemerges as a guerrilla force, fighting for independence for the conservatively Islamic Sumatran region of Aceh. An estimated 15,000 people die in an insurgency lasting till 2005. |

Born in Java in 1921, he was always a soldier, from the day he joined the Dutch colonial army in his late teens. He rose quickly up the ranks of the Indonesian army in the 1950s, and was involved in putting down the South Moluccas and Darul Islam rebellions. He was transferred to a staff college after being implicated in opium and sugar smuggling in 1959, but in 1962 Sukarno appointed him to lead the military campaign against Dutch New Guinea. At the time of the attempted coup in 1965 he was the most senior army man not targeted by the rebels.

## THE NEW ORDER

The New Order did give Indonesia stability of a sort, and a longish period of pretty steady economic development. Whereas Indonesians had thought of Sukarno as Bung Karno, Suharto was never more than the more formal Pak (Father) Harto, but he liked to be thought of as Bapak Pembangunan – the Father of Development. Authoritarianism was considered the necessary price for economic progress.

Suharto and his generals believed Indonesia had to be kept together at all costs and this meant minimising political activity and squashing any potentially divisive movements – be they Islamic radicals, communists or the separatist rebels of Aceh, Papua (former Dutch New Guinea) and East Timor.

The armed forces considered themselves the indispensable protectors of Indonesian unity and it was during the Suharto years that their 'dual function' *(dwifungsi)* of supervising Indonesia's internal governance as well as defending the country became most deeply entrenched. Suppression of dissent was the norm, and censorship kept the populace ignorant of anything the regime wanted kept quiet.

In 1975 the industrial empire Pertamina, a personal fiefdom of General Ibnu Sutowo that controlled Indonesia's oil production and much more, crashed with debts greater than the national budget and was bailed out by the government.

## SUHARTO INC

Near absolute power allowed the forces and Suharto's family and business associates to get away with almost anything. The army was not just a security force, it ran hundreds of businesses, legal and illegal, supposedly to supplement its inadequate funding from government. Corruption went hand-in-hand with secrecy and most notorious was the Suharto family itself. Suharto's wife Ibu Tien (nicknamed Madam Tien Per Cent) controlled the state monopoly on the import and milling of wheat; his daughter Tutut won the 1987 contract to build the Jakarta toll road; his son Tommy gained a monopoly on the cloves used in Indonesia's ultra-popular *kretek* cigarettes in 1989.

In 1995 Indonesia was ranked the most corrupt of all the 41 countries assessed in the first-ever Corruption Index published by Transparency International (TI). In 2004 TI placed Suharto at the top of its all-time world corruption table, with an alleged embezzlement figure of between US$15 billion and US$35 billion from his 32 years in power.

Indonesia's most prominent and worthwhile English-language newspaper is the long-running daily *Jakarta Post* (www.thejakartapost.com). Coverage can be a little patchy, but it does give a reasonable picture of what's happening in the country.

| 1990s | 1997–1998 | 1998 |
|---|---|---|
| NGOs, many of them started by young middle-class Indonesians, emerge as a focus of dissent, campaigning on issues from peasant dispossessions to destructive logging and restrictions on Islamic organisations. | The Asian currency crisis savages Indonesia's economy, sparking riots. After troops kill four students at a Jakarta demonstration in May 1998, rioting and looting cause an estimated 1200 deaths. Suharto steps down on 21 May. | Vice-president BJ Habibie becomes president. He releases political prisoners and relaxes censorship, but the army kills at least 12 in a Jakarta student protest. Christian/Muslim violence erupts in Jakarta and elsewhere, especially Maluku. |

## DEMOCRATIC VENEER

Whereas Sukarno had rejected US aid in favour of support from the USSR and China, Suharto's anti-communism and Indonesia's mineral wealth won him support from Western nations. The US and Japan built the biggest stakes in the country's oil, mineral and other resources.

The New Order always maintained a superficial veneer of elections and democracy. 'Functional groups' (*golongan karya,* or *golkar* for short) such as civil servants, the military, and the employed and employers (who together formed one group), became the basis of social and political organisation. In the 1971 elections to the MPR, more than half the seats were allocated to the military and Suharto's personal appointees. Of the remaining elective seats, the Golkar political entity (not officially considered a party) won well over half. Golkar continued to dominate elections throughout the Suharto period amid widespread allegations of bribery, violence and threats by the regime. In 1973, other parties were compulsorily merged – the four Muslim parties into the Development Unity Party (PPP), and all the rest into the Indonesian Democratic Party (PDI). Political activity in the villages was banned altogether.

## EXTENDING INDONESIA

Suharto's regime saw to it that the former Dutch New Guinea stayed in Indonesia by staging a travesty of a confirmatory vote in 1969. Just over 1000 selected Papuan 'representatives' were pressured into voting unanimously for continued integration with Indonesia, in what was named the Act of Free Choice.

In 1975 the left-wing party Fretilin won a power struggle within the newly independent former Portuguese colony East Timor. The western part of Timor island, a former Dutch possession, was Indonesian. Horrified at the prospect of a left-wing government in a neighbouring state, Indonesia invaded and annexed East Timor. Fretilin kept up a guerrilla struggle and at least 125,000 Timorese died in fighting, famines and repression over the next 2½ decades.

## THE END OF THE NEW ORDER

When the Cold War ended, the West became less ready to turn a blind eye to both human rights abuses and the absence of democracy in Indonesia. In response to simmering discontent, the regime launched a period of freer political discussion known as 'Openness' in 1989. Openness closed abruptly in 1994 when the press became too rude about the regime.

The end of the New Order was finally precipitated by the Asian currency crisis of 1997, which savaged Indonesia's economy. Millions lost their jobs and rising prices sparked riots. Suharto faced unprecedented widespread calls for his resignation. Antigovernment rallies spread from universities

| **1999** | **Jun–Oct 1999** | **1999–2001** |
|---|---|---|
| Habibie agrees to a referendum in East Timor: resulting in a 78% vote for independence. Militias backed by Indonesian military conduct a murderous terror campaign before and after the vote. East Timor finally achieves independence in 2002. | Following Indonesia's first free election since 1955, Abdurrahman Wahid of the country's largest Islamic organisation, Nahdatul Ulama (Rise of the Scholars), becomes president as leader of a multi-party coalition. | Wahid tries to reform government, tackle corruption, reduce military power, bring Suharto to justice and address the grievances of Aceh and Papua. But his efforts are hamstrung by military, Suhartoist and Islamic opponents. |

to city streets, and when four students at Jakarta's Trisakti University were shot dead by troops in May 1998, the city erupted in rioting and looting. An estimated 1200 were killed. Hardest hit were the Chinese, whose businesses were looted and destroyed, with shocking tales of rape and murder emerging afterwards. Even Suharto's own ministers were now calling for his resignation, and he finally resigned on 21 May.

# THE ROAD TO DEMOCRACY

Suharto's fall ushered in a period known as *reformasi* (reform), three tumultuous years in which elective democracy, free expression and human rights all advanced, and attempts were made to deal with the grievances of East Timor, Aceh and Papua. It was an era with many positives and some disasters. *Reformasi* ground to a halt when Megawati Sukarnoputri, Sukarno's daughter, became president in 2002. Since 2004, President Susilo Bambang Yudhoyono (known as SBY), a retired general with moderately liberal leanings, has pursued a cautious, undramatic style of governing which has steered Indonesia free of serious troubles, produced some reforms and kept the economy afloat. SBY was re-elected for a second presidential term with an increased share of the vote in 2009. Though survivors from the Suharto era still dominate politics, the 2009 elections, peaceful and without major corruption scandals, showed that Indonesian democracy had put down roots.

In *Madness Descending,* British journalist Richard Lloyd Parry gives a first-hand account of the upheavals precipitated by the end of the Suharto regime in 1998.

## THE HABIBIE PRESIDENCY

Suharto's vice-president BJ Habibie stepped up as president when Suharto resigned. Habibie released political prisoners, relaxed censorship and promised elections, but he still tried to ban demonstrations and reaffirmed the political role of the unpopular army. When students marched on parliament in November 1998, demanding immediate elections, the army killed at least 12 and injured hundreds. Tensions between Christians and Muslims in some parts of Indonesia also erupted into violence – especially Maluku, where thousands died in incidents between early 1999 and 2002 (see p726).

*Inside Indonesia* (www .insideindonesia.org) provides excellent articles covering everything from political power plays to art-house films.

Habibie agreed to a UN-organised referendum in East Timor, where human rights abuses, reported by Amnesty International among others, had blackened Indonesia's name internationally. In the September 1999 vote, 78% of East Timorese chose independence. But the event was accompanied by a terror campaign by pro-Indonesia militia groups and Indonesian security forces, which according to Amnesty International killed an estimated 1300 people, and left much of East Timor's infrastructure ruined. Order was only restored by the arrival of a UN peacekeeping force. East Timor finally gained full independence in 2002.

| 2001 | 2001–04 | 2002 |
|---|---|---|
| Violence erupts in Kalimantan between indigenous Dayaks and Madurese migrants. Over a million people are displaced by conflicts in East Timor, Maluku, Kalimantan and elsewhere. The MPR dismisses Wahid for alleged corruption and incompetence. | Vice-president Megawati Sukarnoputri, Sukarno's daughter, leading the PDI-P (Indonesian Democratic Party – Struggle) and supported by many conservative elements, succeeds Wahid. | A bomb attack in Kuta, Bali, kills 202, mainly foreign tourists. The Islamic militant group Jemaah Islamiah is blamed. Several of its members are jailed in the following years, and three are executed in 2008. |

## UNHAPPY EXTREMITIES

Two regions at opposite ends of Indonesia have failed to fall in line with the notion of a unitary state, encompassing all the former Dutch East Indies, that has been espoused by all leaders of independent Indonesia.

The conservatively Islamic, resource-rich region of Aceh was only brought under Dutch rule by a 35-year war ending in 1908. After the Dutch departed, Aceh wasn't happy about Indonesian rule either. The Free Aceh Movement (Gerakan Aceh Merdeka; GAM), founded in 1976, gathered steam after 1989, waging a guerrilla struggle for Acehnese independence. The 1990s saw Aceh under something close to military rule, with the population suffering both atrocities by the Indonesian army and intimidation by GAM. Extended peace talks began in 2002, but when these collapsed in 2003, Aceh was placed under martial law and the Indonesian army launched its biggest assault since the 1975 invasion of East Timor.

Everything changed with the tsunami on 26 December 2004, which wrought its biggest devastation on Aceh, killing some 170,000 people and leaving about 500,000 homeless. The government was forced to allow foreign aid organisations into Aceh and to restart negotiations with GAM. A peace deal in August 2005 formally ended three decades of armed struggle which had cost an estimated 15,000 lives. GAM agreed to become an unarmed political movement and the government agreed to withdraw its troops from Aceh, give the province greater autonomy, allow Islamic law and let it keep a greater share of its oil and gas revenues. A former GAM commander, Irwandi Yusuf, was elected as provincial governor in direct elections in December 2006.

Whether this will prove a lasting solution for Aceh still remains to be seen. Much distrust lingers between the Indonesian authorities and ex-GAM members. Indonesian troops returned to Aceh (as reconstruction workers) and pro-Indonesian militias in the interior did not disband. Ex-GAM members have been accused of intimidation and extortion. Most observers agreed that the year 2009, when most of the post-tsunami aid programmes were due to end, was likely to be key to future prospects.

## THE WAHID & MEGAWATI PRESIDENCIES

Indonesia's first free parliamentary elections for 44 years took place in June 1999. No party received a clear mandate, but the MPR elected Muslim preacher Abdurrahman Wahid president as leader of a coalition. The eccentric Wahid, from the country's largest Islamic organisation, Nahdatul Ulama (Rise of the Scholars), was blind, had suffered two strokes and disliked formal dress and hierarchies. He embarked on an ambitious program to rein in the military, reform the legal and financial systems, promote religious tolerance, tackle corruption, bring Suharto to justice, and resolve the problems of Aceh and Papua. He even apologised to the victims of the 1965–66 massacres. Unsurprisingly, all this upset everybody who was anybody, and in July 2001 the MPR dismissed Wahid over alleged incompetence and corruption. Further ethnic violence erupted that year in Kalimantan, where indigenous Dayaks turned on migrants from the island of Madura.

*Abdurrahman Wahid, Indonesia's reformist president from 1999–2001, is universally known as Gus Dur – Gus being a Javanese familiar title and Dur a short form of Abdurrahman.*

| Mar 2004 | Oct 2004 | Dec 2004 |
|---|---|---|
| Anticorruption group Transparency International puts Suharto at the top of its all-time world corruption table, with an alleged embezzlement figure of between US$15 billion and US$35 billion from his 32 years in power. | In Indonesia's first direct presidential elections, Susilo Bambang Yudhoyono (SBY) of the new Democratic Party, a former general regarded as a liberal, wins a run-off vote against Megawati. | Over 200,000 Indonesians die in the 26 December tsunami that devastates large areas of Sumatra, especially Aceh. SBY restarts peace talks with the GAM rebels there, leading to a peace deal in 2005. |

Like Aceh, Papua wasn't brought into the Dutch East Indies until late in the colonial period and has always shown a strong distaste for Indonesian rule. Papuan people are culturally distinct from other Indonesians, being of dark-skinned Melanesian stock and having had very limited contact with the outside world until the 20th century. Today most of them are Christian. Resistance to Indonesian rule has continued ever since Sukarno's takeover in 1963, in the form of sporadic guerrilla attacks by the Organisasi Papua Merdeka (Free Papua Organisation; OPM), which is armed chiefly with bows, arrows and spears, and in non-violent forms such as demonstrations and raisings of the banned Papuan independence flag, the Morning Star. The Indonesian security forces have generally responded with disproportionate force to any type of resistance, including at times aerial attacks on villages.

Papua is a resource-rich region seen by many Indonesians as ripe for exploitation. It has about 1% of Indonesia's population on about 22% of Indonesia's land area. It has timber, fish, oil, and the world's biggest seams of gold and copper. Added to these reasons why Jakarta wouldn't want to let it go are the more than one million Indonesians who have migrated to Papua in the past 40 years, and now make up nearly half the region's population.

During the *reformasi* (reform) period following Suharto's fall in 1998, many Papuans hoped that independence might be on the cards. A congress of 2500 Papuans meeting in Jayapura in the year 2000 declared that Papua no longer recognised Indonesian rule, and consequently set out to seek a UN-sponsored referendum on Papuan independence. But the security forces soon had the movement's leaders either in jail or dead, and moved to quash popular independence protests.

Papua's economy and administration are dominated by non-Papuans, fuelling the indigenous people's grievances and making an Aceh-type autonomy solution impossible. Security-force abuses in Papua – torture, murder, rape – continue to be reported by human rights organisations. Pro-independence sentiment among Papuans remains high, and an end to Papua's troubles seems as far away as ever.

Vice-president Megawati of the Indonesian Democratic Party – Struggle (PDI-P) took over as president in Wahid's place. Supported by many conservative, old-guard elements, Megawati had none of her father's flair or vision and did little for reform in her three years in office. Corruption, human rights abuses and military abuse of power continued, and this, along with terrorist bombings in Bali and Jakarta, helped to discourage foreign support and investment.

Golkar's share of the vote fell from 70% to 20% in the first post-Suharto elections in 1999.

## SBY IN CHARGE

The year 2004 saw Indonesia's first-ever direct popular vote for president. Susilo Bambang Yudhoyono (SBY), leading the new Democratic Party (formed as his personal political vehicle), won in a run-off vote against Megawati. A popular and pragmatic politician, SBY quickly won favour by making sure foreign aid could get to tsunami-devastated Aceh and sealing a peace deal with Aceh's GAM rebels (see opposite).

| 2004–09 | 2006 | 2007 |
|---|---|---|
| SBY's presidency sees progress against B-list corruption. The army is edged away from politics and compelled to divest most of its business enterprises. But many human-rights abusers continue to be leniently treated. | Bantul, near Yogyakarta, Central Java, is hit by an earthquake on 27 May – 6000 die and 200,000 are left homeless across the region. | SBY orders a review of Indonesia's transport system after a series of air, ferry and rail disasters. The EU bans Indonesian airlines from Europe. Transport disasters continue. |

SBY's unspectacular but stable presidency saw the military forced to divest most of their business enterprises and edged away from politics (they lost their reserved seats in parliament in 2004). There was also progress against corruption. A former head of Indonesia's central bank, an MP, a governor of Aceh province and a mayor of Medan were all among those jailed thanks to the Corruption Eradication Commission, established in 2002. But no really big fish were netted – Suharto, for example, managed to cheat justice all the way to his death in 2008. The courts also continued to deal surprisingly leniently with many human rights abusers. No convictions of army leaders believed to have orchestrated the 1999 violence in East Timor have been upheld.

Fears of an upsurge in Islamic radicalism, especially after the Bali and Jakarta terrorist bombings of 2002 to 2005, proved largely unfounded. Despite isolated attacks on Indonesian Christians, the existence of hardline organisations such as the vigilante group Islam Defenders' Front (FPI), and the Jakarta hotel bombings of July 2009 that killed nine (which police believed was the work of an offshoot of Jemaah Islamiah, the organisation blamed for the 2002 Bali bombing), the great majority of Indonesian Muslims are moderate. Islamic parties receive a sizeable share of the vote in elections and can influence government policies, but they can only do so by remaining in the political mainstream.

Indonesians clearly appreciated the stability and non-confrontational style of SBY's presidency, and his successful handling of the economy, for they re-elected him for another five years, with over 60% of the vote, in 2009. The scale of his victory over Megawati Sukarnoputri and Jusuf Kalla of Golkar was such that only one round of voting was needed.

Interestingly neither religion nor ethnicity played a major part in determining how people voted, suggesting that many Indonesians valued democracy, peace and economic progress above sectarian or regional issues. Indonesia's two largest Islamic organisations, Nahdatul Ulama and Muhammadiyah, which together have over 50 million members, both publicly supported the candidacy of Jusuf Kalla, yet SBY won a majority of votes from members of both organisations.

The size of SBY's election victory gave him a great chance to take decisive action to spur economic progress and step up the pace of reform. He vowed to intensify the anticorruption campaign and efforts for good governance. With Indonesia handling the world recession better than other Southeast Asian countries – it was still expecting growth of 4% in 2009 while some neighbouring countries were slipping into recession – the country was also well placed to take advantage of the hoped-for upswing in the world economy.

---

Of 18 people tried by an Indonesian human-rights court for abuses in East Timor in 1999, only militia leader Eurico Guterres was convicted. His conviction for a massacre of 12 people was quashed by the Indonesian Supreme Court in 2008.

---

The word *sembako* refers to Indonesia's nine essential culinary ingredients: rice, sugar, eggs, meat, flour, corn, fuel, cooking oil and salt. When any of these become unavailable or more costly, repercussions can be felt right through to the presidency.

---

| **2009** | **Sept 17th 2009** | **Sept 30th 2009** |
| --- | --- | --- |
| SBY is re-elected president with over 60% of the vote. Indonesia is weathering the world recession relatively well and SBY promises to step up reform and the anticorruption campaign. | Terrorist leader Nordin M Top is killed in a shootout with police on the outskirts of Solo, Java. Top was alleged to be the mastermind in a string of major terrorist attacks in Indonesia from 2002 to 2009 resulting in the death of over 200 people. | Padang, the capital city of West Sumatra, is rocked by an earthquake that strikes 57km southwest of Pariaman. Measuring 7.6 in magnitude, the earthquake completely destroys many buildings, and kills many as 5000 people. |

# The Culture

## THE NATIONAL PSYCHE

Indonesia comprises a massively diverse range of societies and cultures; the differences between, say, the Sumbanese and Sundanese are as marked as those between the Swedes and Sicilians. Even so, a strong national Indonesian identity has emerged, originally through the struggle for independence and, following that, through education programs and the promotion of Bahasa Indonesia as the national language. This is despite the fact that Indonesia continues to be stretched by opposing forces: 'strict' Islam versus 'moderate' Islam, Islam versus Christianity versus Hinduism, outer islands versus Java, country versus city, modern versus traditional, rich versus poor, the 21st century versus the past.

These differences may challenge social cohesion and have at times been used as an excuse to incite conflict, but the nation still prevails. And, with notable exceptions like Papua, the bonds have grown stronger, with the notion of an Indonesian identity overlapping rather than supplanting the nation's many pre-existing regional cultures. The national slogan, *Bhinneka Tunggal Ika* (Unity in Diversity) – even though its words are old Javanese – has been adopted by Indonesians across widely varying ethnic and social standpoints. Perhaps this is why Indonesians are often keen to strike up a conversation with a traveller: everyone has their own story and perspective.

*The Jakarta – Indonesia – Urban Blog (http://tbelfield.wordpress.com) is a terrific collage of information, opinions and links on Indonesian arts, culture and society.*

A cultural element that bridges both the regional and the national is religion – the Pancasila principle of belief in a god holds firm (see boxed text, p46). Though Indonesia is predominantly Islamic, in many places Islam is interwoven with traditional customs, giving it unique qualities and characteristics. Some areas are Christian or animist and, to leaven the mix, Bali has its own unique brand of Hinduism. Religion plays a role in the everyday: mosques and *musholla* (prayer rooms) are in constant use, and the vibrant Hindu ceremonies of Bali are a daily occurrence, to the delight of many visitors.

Mobile phones, SUVs, ATMs, shopping malls, house- and techno-driven nightclubs and other facets of international modernity have found purchase in Indonesia. But while the main cities and tourist resorts can appear technologically rich, other areas remain untouched by the mod cons many city dwellers take for granted. And even where modernisation has taken hold, it's clear that Indonesians have a very traditionalist heart. As well as adherence to religious and ethnic traditions, social customs are maintained. Politeness to strangers is a deeply ingrained habit throughout most of the archipelago. Elders are still accorded great respect. When visiting someone's home, elders are always greeted first, and often customary permission to depart is also offered. This can occur whether in a high-rise in Medan or a hut in the Baliem Valley.

*Indonesia: An Introduction to Contemporary Traditions by Ian Chalmers covers everything from language to the struggle for democracy.*

## LIFESTYLE

Daily life for Indonesians has changed rapidly in the last decade or two. These days, many people live away from their home region and the role of women has extended well beyond domestic duties to include career and study (see p61). Nevertheless, the importance of the family remains high. This is evident during such festivals as Lebaran (the end of the Islamic fasting month), when highways become gridlocked with those returning home to loved ones. Even at weekends, many travel for hours to spend a day with their relatives. In many ways, the notions of family and regional identity have become more pronounced: as people move away from small-scale communities and enter the milieu of the cities, the sense of belonging becomes more valued.

Beyond family, the main social unit is the village. Half the population still lives in rural areas where labour in the fields, the home or the market is the basis of daily life. So, for younger Indonesians, is school – though not for as many as might be hoped. Nine out of 10 children complete the five years of primary schooling, but only six out of 10 get through secondary school. Kids from poorer families have to start supplementing the family income at an early age.

The village spirit isn't restricted to rural areas: the backstreets of Jakarta, for example, are home to tightknit neighbourhoods where kids run from house to house and everyone knows who owns which chicken. A sense of community may also evolve in a *kos* (apartment with shared facilities), where tenants, far from their families, come together for meals and companionship.

Villages can also act as something of a welfare system during tough times. They operate a grassroots system of mutual help called *gotong-royong*. But as more and more people move to large cities, this social safety net has thinned, which, in turn, has increased the prevalence of begging or crime.

For the many Indonesians who still live in their home regions, customs and traditions remain a part of the everyday: the Toraja of Sulawesi continue to build traditional houses due to their social importance (see boxed text, p676); the focus of a Sumbanese village remains the gravestones of their ancestors due to the influence they are believed to have in daily happenings (see p580). These aren't customs offered attention once a year – they are a part of life. And even where modernity has found purchase, age-old traditions can still underpin life: Bali, for example, still scrupulously observes its annual day of silence, Nyepi (Balinese Lunar New Year), when literally all activity stops and everyone stays at home (or in their hotels) so that evil spirits will think the island uninhabited and leave it alone.

Life for women in Indonesian society is, like so many other things, full of contradictions. While many are well educated and well employed, and women in cities can enjoy bars and clubbing just like men, traditional family roles are still strong (see p61). The pressures of conservative Islam (p59) make many women wary that recently gained freedoms may be eroded.

---

### SMALL TALK

One thing that takes many visitors by surprise in Indonesia is what may seem overinquisitiveness from complete strangers. *Dari mana?* (Where do you come from?) and *Mau kemana?* (Where are you going?) are questions you'll be asked by people you simply pass on the street. They may be quickly followed by *Tinggal dimana?* (Where are you staying?), *Jalan sendiri?* (Are you travelling alone?) or even *Sudah kawin?* (Are you married?). Visitors can find these questions intrusive or irritating, and in tourist hotspots they may just be a prelude to a sales pitch, but more often they are simply polite greetings and an expression of interest in a foreigner. A short answer or a Bahasa Indonesia greeting, with a smile, is a polite and adequate response. If you don't want to say exactly where you're going, just *Jalan-jalan* (Walking around) or *Makan angin* (literally 'Eating wind', ie 'Walking') is fine.

If you get into a slightly longer conversation, it's polite to ask some of the same questions in return. Indonesians like to be asked about their family and, if they are married, *Anak-anak ada?* (Do you have children?) is always a good question. When you've had enough chatter, you can answer the question 'Where are you going?' even if it hasn't been asked.

A smile goes a very long way in Indonesia. It's said Indonesians have a smile for every emotion, and keeping one on your face even in a difficult situation helps to avoid giving offence. Indonesians generally seek consensus rather than disagreement, so maintaining a sense of accord, however tenuous, is a good idea in all dealings. Anger or aggressive behaviour is considered poor form.

## TRAVELLER TACT

Understanding a few basic Indonesian courtesies and customs not only helps you avoid gaffes but also enriches your own travel experience. For a larger discussion of how you can minimise your impact while travelling, see p21.

### Dress & Etiquette

Skimpy beach attire, exposing large areas of skin in public, and open displays of affection are alien to most Indonesians. They may be tolerated in tourist resorts but elsewhere it's wise to adapt to local norms. Even shorts on men are considered bizarre by many people, although they don't usually attract open disapproval.

In places of worship it's essential to dress and behave respectfully. In mosques you must be well covered and women must don headscarves, but everyone must remove their shoes. In Bali you should tie a sash or *selandang* (traditional scarf) around your waist before entering temples – some have them for hire.

It's also customary to take off your shoes when entering many people's homes.

Never pass anything to someone with your left hand only. To show added respect, use both hands. Standing with hands on hips can be interpreted as aggressive, and sitting with the soles of your feet pointed towards someone is a sign of disrespect.

### Visiting Villages

Some villages receive busloads of visitors and are almost tourist theme parks, but in general wandering into a village is like entering someone's home, and a few rules of etiquette apply. It's polite to first introduce yourself to the *kepala desa* (village head) or another senior person.

Some villages that are used to visitors have a visitors' book, where you sign in and make a donation (10,000Rp is usually sufficient). In more remote villages, it's best to go with a guide, especially if language difficulty is likely. A guide can make the introductions, teach you protocol and explain points of interest.

For tips on visiting longhouses, see boxed text, p604.

Contradictions also run through the status of gays in Indonesian society. Plenty of Indonesians of both sexes are actively gay, and except in some very conservative areas such as Aceh, active repression is absent. But so is positive recognition of gay identity or gay rights. *Waria* (transgender or transvestite) performers and prostitutes have quite a high profile. Otherwise gay behaviour is, by and large, accepted without being particularly approved. Bali, with its big international scene, and some Javanese cities have the most open gay life.

## ECONOMY

Indonesia's economy is big. Its Gross Domestic Product (GDP), at US$511 billion in 2008, is almost half as big as India's and more than double that of its neighbour Malaysia. When you break that down per person, however, a more revealing picture emerges. Indonesia's GDP per person of US$2150 in 2008 was more than double India's – but Malaysia's was four times as big and Australia's 22 times as big.

Despite a big advance in the past four decades, Indonesia remains a poor country. The average school teacher earns the rupiah equivalent of just over US$100 a month; a typical shop worker gets about half that. The glitzy shopping malls that have sprung up in cities, and the obvious prosperity of an urban minority, belie the fact that about one in every two Indonesians still lives on less than US$2 per day. Some 100 million still live without electricity. And the overall national figures hide big differences between regions. People in oil-rich East Kalimantan have about 12 times as much to live on every month as people in undeveloped East Nusa Tenggara.

The Suharto dictatorship stamped out much originality and creativity, although some writers such as poet and playwright WS Rendra did have work published that spotlighted the negative side of Suharto's New Order. The major writer to emerge since Suharto's fall is Ayu Utami, who has been translated into English and explores different levels of Indonesian society and touchy issues such as sex, politics and religion in her books *Saman* and *Larung*.

*The annual Ubud Writers & Readers Festival (www .ubudwritersfestival.com) in Bali, held around October, showcases both local and international writers.*

## Painting

Galleries in the wealthier neighbourhoods of Jakarta are the epicentre of Indonesia's contemporary art scene, which has mushroomed in the past decade with a full panoply of installations, sculptures, performance art and more, and which can be either extremely original, eye-catching and thought-provoking, or the opposite. Jakarta and Yogyakarta both hold big biennale art events; at the time of writing the next ones were due in early 2011 and early 2010 respectively.

Traditionally, painting was an art for decorating palaces and places of worship, typically with religious or legendary subject matter. Foreign artists in Bali in the 1930s inspired a revolution in painting there: artists began to depict everyday scenes in new, more realistic, less crowded canvases. Others developed an attractive 'primitivist' style. Much Balinese art today is mass-produced tourist-market stuff, though there are also talented and original artists working there. Indonesia's most celebrated 20th-century painter was the Javanese expressionist Affandi (1907–90; see p181), who liked to paint by squeezing the paint straight out of the tube.

*A good place to check in on the contemporary art scene in Indonesia is Universes in Universe (www.universes-in-uni verse.de/english.htm).*

## Architecture

Indonesia is home to a vast and spectacular variety of architecture, from religious and royal buildings to traditional styles of home-building which can differ hugely from one part of the archipelago to another. Indian, Chinese, Arabic and European influences have all added their mark to locally developed styles.

The great 8th and 9th-century temples of Borobudur, Prambanan and the Dieng Plateau, in Central Java, all show the Indian influence that predominated in the Hindu-Buddhist period. Indian style, albeit with a distinctive local flavour, persists today in the Hindu temples of Bali, where the leaders of the Hindu-Buddhist Majapahit kingdom took refuge after being driven from Java in the 16th century.

For their own homes Indonesians developed a range of eye-catching structures whose grandeur depended on the family that built them. Timber construction, often with stilts, and elaborate thatched roofs of palm leaves or grass are common to many traditional housing forms around the archipelago. The use of stilts helps to reduce heat and humidity and avoid mud, floods and pests. Tana Toraja in Sulawesi, Pulau Nias off Sumatra, and the Batak and Minangkabau areas of Sumatra exhibit some of the most spectacular vernacular architecture, with high, curved roofs.

*Bali Style, by Barbara Walker and Rio Helmi, is a lavishly photographed look at Balinese design, architecture and interior decoration. In the same series is Java Style.*

Royal palaces around Indonesia are often developments of basic local housing styles, even if far more elaborate as in the case of Javanese *kraton* (walled palaces). Yogyakarta's *kraton* is effectively a city within a city inhabited by over 25,000 people.

The Dutch colonists initially built poorly ventilated houses in European style but eventually a hybrid Indo-European style emerged, using elements such as the Javanese *pendopo* (open-sided pavilion) and *joglo* (a high-pitched roof). International styles such as art deco started to arrive in the late 19th century as large numbers of factories, train stations, hotels, hospitals and other public buildings went up in the later colonial period. Bandung in Java has one of the world's largest collections of 1920s art deco buildings.

Early independent Indonesia had little money to spare for major building projects, though President Sukarno did find the funds for a few prestige projects such as Jakarta's huge and resplendent Mesjid Istiqlal (p106). The economic progress of the Suharto years saw Indonesia's cities spawn their quota of standard international high-rise office blocks and uninspired government buildings, though tourism helped to foster original, even spectacular hybrids of local and international styles in some hotels in Bali and elsewhere.

## BALINESE ARCHITECTURE

The basic feature of Balinese architecture is the *bale* (pronounced 'ba-lay'), a rectangular, open-sided pavilion with a steeply pitched roof of palm thatch. A family compound will have a number of *bale* for eating, sleeping and working. The focus of a community is the *bale banjar,* a large pavilion for meeting, debate, gamelan practise and so on. Buildings such as restaurants and the lobby areas of hotels are often modelled on the *bale* – they are airy, spacious and handsomely proportioned.

Like the other arts, architecture has traditionally served the religious life of Bali. Balinese houses, although attractive, have never been lavished with the architectural attention that is given to temples. Even Balinese palaces are modest compared with the more important temples. Temples are designed to fixed rules and formulas, with sculpture serving as an adjunct, a finishing touch to these design guidelines.

## MOSQUES IN INDONESIA

It's generally no problem for travellers to visit mosques, as long as appropriately modest clothing is worn – there is usually a place to leave shoes, and headscarves are often available for hire. Mosque interiors are normally empty except for five main features: the *mihrab* (a wall niche marking the direction of Mecca); the *mimbar* (a raised pulpit, often canopied, with a staircase); a stand to hold the Koran; a screen to provide privacy for important worshippers; and a water source for ablutions. There are no seats and if there is any ornamentation at all, it will be verses from the Koran.

### TOP 5 CLASSICAL MOSQUES

Indonesia's most revered mosques tend to be those built in the 15th and 16th centuries in Javanese towns that were among the first to convert to Islam. The 'classical' architectural style of these mosques includes tiered roofs clearly influenced by the Hindu culture that Islam had then only recently supplanted. They are curiously reminiscent of Hindu temples still seen on Bali today. During the Suharto era in the late 20th century, hundreds of standardised, prefabricated mosques were shipped and erected all around Indonesia in pale imitation of this classical Javanese style. Java's top five classical mosques:

- Mesjid Agung, Demak (p214)
- Mesjid Al-Manar, Kudus (p215)
- Mesjid Agung, Cirebon (p164)
- Mesjid Agung, Banten (p119)
- Mesjid Besar, Yogyakarta (p181)

The Yogyakarta mosque was built in the 18th century but is very much in the tradition of the other, earlier ones. Kudus also has a highly unusual brick minaret that may have been the watchtower of an earlier Hindu temple.

Kalimantan). Jackfruit is a common, cheap wood, though it tends to warp and split. Generally, local carvers use woods at hand: heavy ironwood and *meranti* (a hard wood) in Kalimantan, and *belalu* (a light wood) in Bali.

## Textiles

### IKAT

The Indonesian word 'ikat', meaning 'to tie' or 'to bind', signifies the intricately patterned cloth of threads that are painstakingly tie-dyed before being woven together. Ikat is produced in many regions, most notably in Nusa Tenggara.

Ikat garments come in an incredible diversity of colours and patterns: the spectacular ikat of Sumba and the elaborately patterned work of Flores (including *kapita*, used to wrap the dead) are the best known.

### MAKING IKAT

Traditionally, ikat is made of hand-spun cotton. The whole process of ikat production – from planting the cotton to folding the finished product – is performed by women. Once the cotton is harvested, it is spun with a spindle. The thread is strengthened by immersing it in baths of crushed cassava, rice or maize, then threaded onto a winder.

Traditional dyes are made from natural sources. The most complex processes result in a rusty colour known as *kombu* (produced from the bark and roots of the *kombu* tree). Blue dyes come from the indigo plant, and purple or brown can be produced by dyeing the cloth deep blue and then dyeing it again with *kombu*.

Any sections that are not coloured are bound together with dye-resistant fibre. Each colour requires a separate tying-and-dyeing process. The sequence of colouring takes into consideration the effect of each application of dye. This stage requires great skill, as the dyer has to work out – before the threads are woven – exactly which parts of the thread are to receive which colour in order to create the pattern of the final cloth. After the thread has been dyed, the cloth is woven on a simple hand loom.

### ORIGINS & MEANING OF IKAT

Ikat technique was most likely introduced 2000 years ago by Dongson migrants from southern China and Vietnam.

Ikat styles vary according to the village and the gender of the wearer, and some styles are reserved for special purposes. In parts of Nusa Tenggara, high-quality ikat is part of a bride's dowry. Until recently on Sumba, only members of the highest clans could make and wear ikat textiles. Certain motifs were traditionally reserved for noble families (as on Sumba and Rote) or members of a specific tribe or clan (as on Sabu or among the Atoni of West Timor). The function of ikat as an indicator of social status has since declined.

### MOTIFS & PATTERNS

Some experts believe that motifs found on Sumba, such as front views of people, animals and birds, stem from an artistic tradition even older than

In Tenganan (Bali), a cloth called *gringsing* is woven using a rare method of double ikat in which both warp and weft threads are predyed.

---

**IKAT SEASONS**

There are traditional times for the production of ikat. On Sumba the thread is spun between July and October, and the patterns bound between September and December. After the rains end in April, the dyeing is carried out. In August the weaving starts – more than a year after work on the thread began.

---

**CHOOSING IKAT**

Unless you are looking for inexpensive machine-made ikat, shopping is best left to the experts. Even trekking out to an 'ikat village' may be in vain: the photogenic woman sitting at a wooden loom may be only for show. But if you insist, here are some tips on recognising the traditional product:

- Thread – hand-spun cotton has a less perfect 'twist' to it than factory cloth.

- Weave – hand-woven cloth, whether made from hand-spun or factory thread, feels rougher and, when new, stiffer than machine-woven cloth. It will probably have minor imperfections in the weave.

- Dyes – until you've seen enough ikat to get a feel for whether colours are natural or chemical, you often have to rely on your instincts as to whether they are 'earthy' enough. Some cloths contain both natural and artificial dyes.

- Dyeing method – the patterns on cloths which have been individually tie-dyed using the traditional method are rarely perfectly defined, but they're unlikely to have the detached specks of colour that often appear on mass-dyed cloth.

- Age – no matter what anybody tells you, there are very few antique cloths around. There are several processes to make cloth look old.

---

Dongson, whose influence was geometric motifs like diamond and key shapes (which often go together), meanders and spirals.

One strong influence was *patola* cloth from Gujarat in India. In the 16th and 17th centuries these became highly prized in Indonesia, and one characteristic motif – a hexagon framing a four-pronged star – was copied by local ikat weavers. On the best *patola* and geometric ikat, repeated small patterns combine to form larger patterns, like a mandala. Over the past century, European styles have influenced the motifs used in ikat.

## Songket

*Songket* is silk cloth interwoven with gold or silver threads, although imitation silver or gold is often used in modern pieces. *Songket* is most commonly found in heavily Islamic regions, such as Aceh and among the coastal Malays, but Bali also has a strong *songket* tradition.

## Batik

The technique of applying wax or other dye-resistant substances (like rice paste) to cloth to produce a design is found in many parts of the world, but none is as famous as the batik of Java. Javanese batik dates from the 12th century, and opinion is divided as to whether batik is an indigenous craft or imported from India along with Hindu religious and cultural traditions.

The word 'batik' is an old Javanese word meaning 'to dot'. Javanese batik was a major weapon in the arsenal of social status competition in the royal courts. The ability to devote extensive resources to the painstaking creation of fine batik demonstrated wealth and power. Certain designs indicated courtly rank, and a courtier risked public humiliation, or worse, by daring to wear the wrong sarong.

The finest batik is *batik tulis* (hand-painted or literally 'written' batik). Designs are first traced out onto cloth, then patterns are drawn in hot wax with a *canting*, a pen-like instrument. The wax-covered areas resist colour change when immersed in a dye bath. The waxing and dyeing, with increasingly darker shades, continues until the final colours are achieved. Wax is added to protect previously dyed areas or scraped off to expose new areas to the dye. Finally, all the wax is scraped off and the cloth boiled to remove all traces of wax.

A great resource on Balinese culture and life is www.murnis.com. Click on Culture for explanations on everything from kids' names to what one wears to a ceremony and the weaving of the garments.

During the mid-19th century, as the demand far outstripped the supply, came the technical innovation of *batik cap,* in which the wax pattern is applied with a metal stamp. Most *batik cap* fabrics feature repeated geometric patterns, often with fine details finished by hand. *Batik cap* is regarded as true batik, not to be confused with screen-printed cloth which completely bypasses the waxing process and is often passed off as batik.

Batik was a dying art until the 1960s, when several innovative artists and designers, notably Harjonogoro of Surakarta and Iwan Tirta of Jakarta, revitalised the tradition by blending the staid court designs with vibrant motifs from Java's north coast, and using batik in fashion and interior design. The court cities of Yogyakarta and Solo remain major batik centres.

Batik painting, an odd blend of craft and art that all-too-often is neither, remains popular in Yogyakarta, where it was invented as a pastime for unemployed youth. Though most batik painting is tourist schlock, there are a handful of talented artists working in the medium.

## Ceramics

Indonesia's position on the trade routes saw the import of large amounts of ceramics from China, making it a fertile hunting ground for antique Chinese ceramics dating back to the Han dynasty. The best examples of truly indigenous ceramics are the terracottas from the Majapahit kingdom of East Java.

Indonesian pottery is usually unglazed and handworked, although the wheel is also used. Pieces are seldom painted. Potters around Mojokerto, close to the original Majapahit capital, still produce terracottas, but the best-known pottery centre in Java is just outside Yogyakarta at Kasongan, where intricate, large figurines and pots are produced.

In the Singkawang area of West Kalimantan, the descendants of Chinese potters produce a unique style of utilitarian pottery.

Lombok pottery has an earthy, primitive look, with subtle colouring. Balinese ceramics show a stronger Western influence and are more likely to be glazed.

## Basketwork & Beadwork

Some of the finest basketwork in Indonesia comes from Lombok. The spiral woven rattan work is very fine and large baskets are woven using this method; smaller receptacles topped with wooden carvings are also popular.

In Java, Tasikmalaya is a major cane-weaving centre, often adapting baskets and vessels to modern uses with the introduction of zips and plastic linings. The Minangkabau people, centred around Bukittinggi, also produce interesting palm-leaf bags and purses, while the *lontar* palm is used extensively in weaving on West Timor, Rote and other outer eastern islands. The Dayak of Kalimantan produce some superb woven baskets and string bags.

*Indonesian Primitive Art* by Irwin Hersey is an illustrated guide to the art of the outer islands.

Some of the most colourful and attractive beadwork is made by the Toraja of Sulawesi. Beadwork can be found all over Nusa Tenggara and in the Dayak region of Kalimantan. Small, highly prized cowrie shells are used like beads and are found on Dayak and Lombok works, though the best application of these shells is as intricate beading in Sumbanese tapestries.

## Kris

No ordinary knife, the wavy-bladed traditional dagger known as a kris is a mandatory possession of a Javanese gentleman; it's said to be endowed with supernatural powers and to be treated with the utmost respect. A kris owner ritually bathes and polishes his weapon, stores it in an auspicious location, and pays close attention to every rattle and scrape emanating from the blade and sheath in the dead of the night.

Some think the Javanese kris (from *iris,* meaning 'to cut') is derived from the bronze daggers produced by the Dongson around the 1st century AD. Bas-reliefs of a kris appear in the 14th-century Panataran temple complex

---

**TOPENG – MASKS**

Although carved masks exist throughout the archipelago, the most readily identifiable form of mask is the *topeng*, used in *wayang topeng*, the masked dance-dramas of Java and Bali. Dancers perform local tales or adaptations of Hindu epics such as the Mahabharata, with the masks used to represent different characters. Masks vary from the stylised but plain masks of Central and West Java to the heavily carved masks of East Java. Balinese masks are less stylised and more naturalistic than in Java – the Balinese save their love of colour and detail for the masks of the Barong dance, starring a mythical lion-dog creature who fights tirelessly against evil.

---

in East Java, and the carrying of the kris as a custom in Java was noted in 15th-century Chinese records. The kris remains an integral part of men's ceremonial dress.

Distinctive features, the number of curves in the blade and the damascene design on the blade are read to indicate good or bad fortune for its owner. The number of curves in the blade has symbolic meaning: five curves symbolise the five Pandava brothers of the Mahabharata epic; three represents fire, ardour and passion. Although the blade is the most important part of the kris, the hilt and scabbard are also beautifully decorated.

Although the kris is mostly associated with Java and Bali, larger and less ornate variations are found in Sumatra, Kalimantan and Sulawesi.

## Puppets

The most famous puppets of Indonesia are the carved leather *wayang kulit* puppets. These intricate lace figures are cut from buffalo hide with a sharp, chisel-like stylus, and then painted. They are produced in Bali and Java, particularly in Central Java. The leaf-shaped *kayon* representing the 'tree' or 'mountain of life' is also made of leather and is used to end scenes during a performance.

*Wayang golek* are three-dimensional wooden puppets found in Central and West Java. The *wayang klitik* puppets are the rarer flat wooden puppets of East Java.

## Metalwork

The bronze age in Indonesia began when metalwork was introduced by the Dongson culture, and it peaked with the Hindu-Buddhist empires of Java. Brassware was mostly of Indian and Islamic influence. Today, some of the best brass workmanship is that of the Minangkabau in Sumatra, but brassware is also produced in Java, South Kalimantan and Sulawesi.

The most important ironwork objects are knives and swords such as the Javanese kris and the *parang* of Kalimantan. *Parang* are sacred weapons used in everything from clearing jungle to – at one time – head-hunting. Scabbards for ceremonial *parang* are intricately decorated with beads, shells and feathers.

For an overall guide to Indonesian crafts, *Arts and Crafts of Indonesia* by Anne Richter is detailed and beautifully illustrated.

## Jewellery

The ubiquitous *toko mas* (gold shop) found in every Indonesian city is mostly an investment house selling gold jewellery by weight – design and workmanship take a back seat. However, gold and silverwork does have a long history in Indonesia. Some of the best gold jewellery comes from Aceh, where fine filigree work is produced, while chunky bracelets and earrings are produced in the Batak region.

Balinese jewellery is nearly always handworked and rarely involves casting techniques. Balinese work is innovative, employing both traditional designs

---

**GIFTS: LOW**

Looking to show close friends and relatives just how deep you plunged into Indonesian culture? Then give them a penis gourd.

Papua is the sweet spot for Indonesian penis gourds; in one stroke you can come up with a gift that will literally keep giving. Traditionally used by indigenous men in the province's highlands, they are attached to the testicles by a small loop of fibre. Sizes, shapes and colours vary across cultural groups but you can pick one up for around 5000Rp to 60,000Rp. A good place to check out the merchandise is **Wamena** (p805). Remember: bargain hard as competition is stiff.

If you'd rather not give something as intimate as a penis gourd, then perhaps you should do just the opposite and give the prized possession of head-hunters everywhere: a mandau from Kalimantan. Once the Dayak weapon of choice, this indigenous machete is still slung from the hips of most men in the Kalimantan interior. You can purchase traditional pieces for around 100,000Rp to 250,000Rp. A good place to shop is in the longhouse village of Tanjung Isuy (p643).

Obviously, you'll need to check a bag to get a *mandau* home, but you can probably simply wear your new gourd.

---

and those adapted from jewellery presented by Western buyers. The traditional centre for Balinese jewellery is Celuk.

Kota Gede in Yogyakarta is famous for its fine filigree work. Silverware from here tends to be more traditional, but new designs are also being adapted. As well as jewellery, Kota Gede produces a wide range of silver tableware.

## SPORT

Soccer and badminton are the national sporting obsessions. Indonesian badminton players – many of them ethnic Chinese – regularly win Olympic gold medals and the Thomas Cup (the world men's team championship), and you'll see courts set up almost anywhere there's space. Indonesian soccer teams are abysmally unsuccessful in international competitions, but that doesn't stop the game being hugely popular. The Indonesia Super League comprises 18 teams from Sumatra to Papua, all with their fanatical followers and most with confusingly similar names beginning with 'Persi...' (from Persatuan Sepakbola Indonesia, meaning 'Indonesian Football Club').

Volleyball is played in villages everywhere, and you may also see people playing *sepak takraw* (also known as *sepak raga*). Played with a rattan ball, it's a cross between volleyball and soccer and, except when serving, only the feet and head are used, resulting in amazing acrobatics.

*Pencak silat,* Indonesia's own form of martial arts, is most popular in Java and Sumatra. It takes different forms from place to place and is practised both as a form of self-defence and as artistic performance with musical accompaniment. It uses not only hands and feet but also some weapons, including sticks and swords.

Many regions, particularly those with a history of tribal warfare, stage traditional contests of various kinds to accompany weddings, harvest festivals and other ceremonial events. Mock battles are sometimes staged in Papua, *caci* whip fights are a speciality in Flores and men fight with sticks and shields in Lombok, but the most spectacular ceremonial fight is Sumba's *pasola* (see boxed text, p589), where every February and March horse riders in traditional dress hurl spears at each other.

The easiest place to find out which soccer club is from where is Wikipedia's Liga Indonesia page.

Jakartacasual (http://ja kartacasual.blogspot .com) is a great English-language source for Indonesian soccer news. You can check the schedule (*jadwal*) at www.antv sports.com or www .bli-online.com.

# Environment

## THE LAND

It makes sense that Indonesians call their country Tanah Air Kita (literally, 'Our Land and Water'), as it's the world's most expansive archipelago. Indonesia's land area of 1,920,000 sq km is speckled along the equator for 5000km, from Sabang off the northern tip of Sumatra, to a little beyond Merauke in Papua. The official count of islands has tended to change over the years, with different surveys producing varying results. However, it is likely there are over 18,000 bits of land rising above the high-tide mark, of which about 6000 are inhabited.

On most of the main islands, the landscape is dominated by volcanic cones, most long dormant, others very much active. Some of these volcanoes have erupted with such force that they have literally made history. The ash clouds from the cataclysmic 1815 eruption of Gunung Tambora in Sumbawa modified the global climate for a year, causing massive crop failures in Europe. The 1883 eruption of Krakatau between Java and Sumatra, which generated tsunamis that killed tens of thousands, was the first global media event, thanks to the newly completed global telegraph network.

Indonesia is home to no fewer than 129 active volcanoes, the most of any nation. See p131 for details.

The archipelago's ubiquitous volcanoes play a pivotal role in most Indonesian cultures. In Bali and Java, major places of worship grace the slopes of prominent volcanic cones, and eruptions are taken as demonstrations of divine disappointment or anger.

On most islands, all land below the lifeless craters of active volcanoes is – or was – covered in dense forest. The high rainfall and year-round humidity means that Indonesia has it all: from cloud and high alpine forests to the world's second largest expanse of tropical rainforest. However, most of this is disappearing at an alarming rate as timber, agricultural and mining companies continue to plunder the region's resources (see p76).

Indonesia also boasts extensive – and endangered – stands of mangrove (p76), particularly along the east coast of Sumatra, the Riau Islands, the southern coast of Kalimantan and Papua.

First published in 1869, *The Malay Archipelago* by Alfred Russel Wallace is a classic account of this famous naturalist's wanderings throughout the Indonesian islands.

Indonesia's diverse vegetation, mountainous terrain and widely scattered islands have been integral in shaping its history and astoundingly diverse culture. Looking at the big picture, this country has served as a crossroad between India, China and beyond – it was a convenient midway point where cultures crossed over, and merchants met and exchanged goods. However, difficult travel *within* Indonesia, due to seas, dense forests and rough volcanic terrain, contributed to the establishment of distinct cultural entities in the various regions.

### Equatorial Climate

The regular equatorial climate in most of the country means that the rhythm of life for many Indonesian farmers is based less on the annual fluctuations of the seasons than on the growth patterns of their crops. In areas with heavy rainfall and terraced rice-field cultivation, there is no set planting season or harvest season but a continuous flow of activity, where at any one time one hillside may demonstrate the whole cycle of rice cultivation, from ploughing to harvesting. Such intense agricultural activity has supported kingdoms and continues to feed the densely populated regions.

### WILDLIFE

From tiny tarsiers to massive stinking flowers, the range of natural attractions in Indonesia is phenomenal. In 2006, the discovery of several new species of wildlife in Papua's Foja mountain range highlighted the archipelago's astounding biodiversity. Unfortunately, discoveries are lagging far behind destruction of natural habitats, meaning that much of Indonesia's rich biological heritage will pass unrecorded into extinction.

## Animals

The Greater Sunda islands, comprising Sumatra, Java, Kalimantan and Bali, were once highland regions of a land mass, now called the Sunda Shelf, that extended from the Asian mainland. Some large Asian land animals still survive in this area, including tigers, rhinoceroses, leopards and sun bears. Despite frequent claims of sightings, the Javan tiger is probably extinct. The Sumatran tiger is fighting for survival, literally, as there have been several incidents of tigers killing loggers trespassing in protected habitats. Leopards (the black leopard, or panther, is more common in Southeast Asia) are rare but still live in Sumatra and in Java's Ujung Kulon National Park (p133). This park is also home to the rare, almost extinct, one-horned Javan rhinoceros. Rhinos have not fared well in Indonesia and the two-horned variety, found in Sumatra, is also on the endangered list.

Perhaps the most famous, and most endangered Indonesian animal is the orangutan (literally, 'man of the forest'). These long-haired red apes are found only in Sumatra and Kalimantan. For more on these fascinating creatures, see the boxed text, p379. Various species of the graceful gibbon also exist throughout the region, as do other primate species.

Sumatran elephants are another celebrity endangered species, being driven into overcrowded, underfunded refuges as their forest habitats are cleared for plantations and farming. Kalimantan also has a few wild elephants in the northeast at Sebuku Sembakung (p651), but they are very rare and the species is most probably introduced.

## Small Fry

Lying across the centre of Indonesia are the islands of Sulawesi, Nusa Tenggara and Maluku, all of which have long been isolated from the continental land mass, and make up part of the Wallecea transition zone between Asian and Australian species. Animals in this region have always been much smaller than those in the west. There's no rhinos or tigers here. Rather, look for intriguing species such as Sulawesi's *anoa* (dwarf buffalo), a wallowing animal that looks like a cross between a deer and a cow and stands only about 80cm high. Also in Sulawesi is the *babi rusa* (deer pig), with great curving tusks that come out the side of the mouth and through the top of the snout. The bulbous beaked hornbills are found across west Indonesia, but the *enggang Sulawesi* (Buton hornbill), with its brightly coloured beak and neck, is one of the most spectacular of the species. One hard-to-see animal is the tarsier, a tiny, nocturnal primate of North Sulawesi that looks, for all the world, like a mythical gremlin.

Maluku shows similarities with Sulawesi, but with fewer wildlife species. The *babi rusa* and smaller mammals are here, as are some primates, but it seems most of the migratory waves bypassed Maluku. However, it is noted for its butterflies – Pulau Seram has reported some enormous species – and bird life, particularly the *nuri raja* (Amboina king parrot), a large, magnificently coloured bird.

From Lombok eastwards, the fauna of Nusa Tenggara reflects the more arid conditions of these islands (see p656). Large Asian mammals are nonexistent, though there is fossil evidence that pygmy elephants once lived here. Asian bird species diminish further east and Australian birds are found on the eastern islands. Nusa Tenggara has one astonishing and famous animal, the

---

Two good illustrated books on Indonesian wildlife are *The Wildlife of Indonesia* by Kathy MacKinnon and *Wild Indonesia* by Tony and Jane Whitten.

The Birds of Java and Bali by Derek Holmes and Stephen Nash is one of the best bird-watching guides available. *The Birds of Sulawesi* by Derek Holmes and Karen Phillipps is also worthwhile.

Komodo dragon, the world's largest lizard, found only on Komodo (p530) and a few neighbouring islands.

Wildlife at the eastern end of the nation has a closer connection to that which scurries around Australia – as Papua and the Aru Islands were both once part of the Australian landmass and lie on the Sahul Shelf. Papua is the only part of Indonesia to have Australian marsupials such as tree kangaroos, bandicoots, echidnas and ring-tailed possums.

There are also Australian reptiles such as crocodiles and frilled-neck lizards. Then there's Papua's extraordinary birdlife: the area is home to over 600 species, the most famous being the cassowary and bird of paradise.

*A Photographic Guide to the Birds of Indonesia by Morten Strange is a good bird identification guide.*

## Plants

The clock is ticking for many of Indonesia's endemic plant species, but sufficient expanses of natural rainforest remain to experience some of the archipelago's floral and arboreal wonders. See p126 for details.

# NATIONAL PARKS & PROTECTED AREAS

Despite a constant nipping at the edges by illegal loggers and settlers, Indonesia still has large tracts of protected forest and national parks. The parks are managed by the Directorate General of Forest Protection and Nature Conservation (PHKA or KSDA). Many new national parks have been proclaimed in recent years. National parks receive greater international recognition and funding than nature, wildlife and marine reserves, of which there are also many in Indonesia. For more on the national parks, see p132.

*Keeping birds has been a part of Indonesian culture for centuries. It's common to see caged songbirds and they are sold in most markets.*

### TOP 10 NATIONAL PARKS & RESERVES

| Park | Location | Features | Activities | Best time to visit | Page |
|---|---|---|---|---|---|
| Gunung Leuser | Sumatra | biologically diverse conservation area, rivers, rainforest, mountains; tigers, rhinoceroses, elephants, orangutans, primates such as the white-breasted Thomas leaf monkey | orangutan viewing, wildlife spotting, bird watching; trekking, rafting | Dec–Mar | p417 |
| Tanjung Puting | Kalimantan | tropical rainforest, mangrove forest, wetlands; macaques, proboscis monkeys, diverse wildlife | orangutan viewing, bird watching | May–Sep | p614 |
| Kelimutu | Nusa Tenggara | coloured lakes | vulcanology, short walks | Apr–Sep | p548 |
| Gunung Rinjani | Nusa Tenggara | volcano | trekking, volcano climbing | Apr–Sep | p506 |
| Ujung Kulon | Java | lowland rainforest, scrub, grassy plains, swamps, sandy beaches; one-horned rhinoceroses, otters, squirrels, leaf monkeys, gibbons | jungle walks; wildlife spotting | Apr–Oct | p133 |
| Gunung Bromo | Java | volcanic landscape | crater climbing | Apr–Oct | p245 |
| Pulau Bunaken | Sulawesi | coral fringed islands | snorkelling, diving, island lazing | Jun–Jan | p710 |
| Kerinci Seblat | Sumatra | mountainous rainforest, one of Sumatra's highest peaks | trekking; wildlife spotting, bird watching | Dec–Mar | p442 |
| Komodo | Nusa Tenggara | Komodo dragon | snorkelling, diving; being chased by wildlife | Apr–Sep | p529 |
| Bali Barat | Bali | low hills, grasslands, coral fringed coasts | snorkelling, diving; wildlife spotting | year round | p347 |

---

**WE DARE YOU**

Everyday eating in Indonesia can be strange and there are some specialities that make for a real culture shock:

■ It's not a staple, but dog is eaten in North Sulawesi and the Batak region of Sumatra. They are, however, surreptitious about canine consumption and you'll never see the word *anjing* (dog) advertised. The Bataks call dog *B1* (pronounced beh *sah*-tuh), as dog in the local language is *biang*, which has one 'b'. They call *babi* (pig) *B2*. In North Sulawesi, Fido is known as *rw* (pronounced *err*-weh), in which 'r' stands for *rintek* (soft) and 'w' stands for *wu'uk* (fur).

■ The durian has a serious public image problem. This fruit's spiky skin looks like a Spanish Inquisition torture tool; opening it releases the fruit's odorous power. Many claim that durian is an acquired taste, but there is no record of anyone 'acquiring' a taste for this 'King of Fruits'. You develop either an abiding disgust, or an insatiable passion, from the first contact.

■ Balinese specialities are readily available in Denpasar and other towns. Look for *warung* advertising *siobak* (minced pig's head, stomach, tongue and skin cooked with spices). A pig's head (a real one) in the display case indicates *babi guling* (spit-roasted pork).

■ Avocado juice: take an avocado, blend with ice and condensed milk (or chocolate syrup) and serve. Indonesians don't consider this strange, as the avocado is just another sweet fruit.

---

*nasi liwet* (rice with coconut milk, unripe papaya, garlic and shallots, served with chicken or egg) and *serabi* (coconut-milk pancakes topped with chocolate, banana or jackfruit).

There's a lot of crossover between Central and East Javan cuisine. Fish is popular, especially *pecel lele* (deep-fried catfish served with rice and *pecel*). The best *pecel* (peanut sauce) comes from the town of Madiun.

Two very popular Madurese dishes are *soto Madura* (beef soup with lime, pepper, peanuts, chilli and ginger) and *sate Madura* (skewered meat with sweet soy sauce).

## Bali

Balinese specialities are increasingly easy to find, as tourist-oriented restaurants and cafes offer high-quality Balinese dishes, with several options of spiciness. Many restaurants offer the grandest Balinese dish, *babi guling* (spit-roast pig stuffed with chilli, turmeric, garlic and ginger) on a day's notice. Also popular is *bebek betutu* (duck stuffed with spices, wrapped in banana leaves and coconut husks, and cooked in embers). The local sate, *sate lilit*, is made with minced, spiced meat pressed onto skewers. Spicy, fleshy dishes like *lawar* (salad of chopped coconut, garlic and chilli with pork or chicken meat and blood) are generally only available outside tourist areas.

## Sumatra

In West Sumatra, beef is used in *rendang* (beef coconut curry). The region is the home of Padang cuisine (see p423), and the market in Bukittinggi is a great place to sample *nasi Kapau* (cuisine from the village of Kapau). It's similar to Padang food but uses more vegetables. There's also *ampiang dadiah* (buffalo yoghurt with palm-sugar syrup, coconut and rice) and *bubur kampiun* (mung-bean porridge with banana and rice yoghurt).

In North Sumatra, the Acehnese love their *kare* or *gulai* (curry). The Bataks have a taste for pig and, to a lesser extent, dog (see boxed text, above). Pork features in *babi panggang* (pork boiled in vinegar and pig blood, and then roasted).

Rice in the field is called *padi;* rice grain at the market is called *beras;* cooked rice on your plate is called *nasi*.

The culinary capital of South Sumatra is Palembang, famous for *pempek* (deep-fried fish and sago dumpling; also called *empek-empek*). South Sumatra is also home to *pindang* (spicy fish soup with soy and tamarind) and *ikan brengkes* (fish in a spicy, durian-based sauce). Palembang's sweetie is *srikaya* (green custard made from sticky rice, sugar, coconut milk and egg).

## Nusa Tenggara

In dry East Nusa Tenggara you'll eat less rice (although much is imported) and more sago, corn, cassava and taro. Fish remains popular and one local dish is Sumbawa's *sepat* (shredded fish in coconut and mango sauce).

The Sasak people of Lombok like spicy *ayam taliwang* (roasted chicken served with a peanut, tomato, chilli and lime dip) and *pelecing* sauce (made with chilli, shrimp paste and tomato). Also recommended is *sate pusut* (minced meat or fish sate, mixed with coconut, and grilled on sugar-cane skewers). Nonmeat dishes include *kelor* (soup with vegetables) and *timun urap* (cucumber with coconut, onion and garlic).

Lonely Planet's *World Food Indonesia*, by Patrick Witton, looks at the history and culture of Indonesian cuisine.

## Kalimantan

Dayak food varies, but you may sample *rembang,* a sour fruit that's made into *sayur asem rembang* (sour vegetable soup). In Banjarmasin, the Banjar make *pepes ikan* (spiced fish cooked in banana leaves with tamarind and lemon grass). Kandangan town is famous for *ketupat Kandangan* (fish and pressed rice with lime-infused coconut sauce). The regional soup, *soto Banjar,* is a chicken broth made creamy by mashing boiled eggs into the stock. Chicken also goes into *ayam masak habang,* cooked with large red chillies.

## Sulawesi

South Sulawesi locals love seafood, especially *ikan bakar* (grilled fish). Another local dish is *coto Makassar* (soup of beef innards, pepper, cumin and lemon grass). For sugar cravers, there's *es pallubutun* (coconut custard and banana in coconut milk and syrup).

The Toraja people have their own distinct cuisine (see p678) with a heavy emphasis on tastes of indigenous ingredients, many of them odd to Western palettes.

If a North Sulawesi dish has the name *rica-rica,* it's prepared with a paste of chilli, shallots, ginger and lime. Fish and chicken are two versions (also look out for dog). Things get very fishy with *bakasang* (flavouring paste made with fermented fish), sometimes used in *bubur tinotuan* (porridge made with corn, cassava, rice, pumpkin, fish paste and chilli).

*Cradle of Flavor* by James Oseland (the editor of *Saveur* magazine) is a beautiful tome covering the foods of Indonesia and its neighbours.

## Maluku

A typical Maluku meal is tuna and *dabu-dabu* (raw vegetables with a chilli and fish-paste sauce). Sometimes fish is made into *kohu-kohu* (fish salad with citrus fruit and chilli). Sago pith is used to make porridge, bread and *mutiara* (small, jelly-like 'beans' that are added to desserts and sweet drinks). Boiled cassava (*kasbi*) is a staple in peoples' homes as it's cheaper than rice. For more, see (p747).

## Papua

In the highlands of Papua the sweet potato is king. The Dani people grow around 60 varieties, some of which can only be eaten by the elders. Other plants, such as sago palms, are also cultivated. The locals eat the pith of the sago palm and also leave the plant to rot so they can collect and eat beetle grubs. On special occasions, chickens and pigs are cooked in earth ovens.

**FRUITY DELIGHTS**

It's worth making a trip to Indonesia just to sample the tropical fruits:

- *Belimbing* (star fruit) is cool and crisp; slice one to see how it gets its name.
- Durian is the spiky fruit people either love or hate (see boxed text, p80).
- *Jambu air* (water apple) is a pink bell-shaped fruit with crisp and refreshing flesh.
- *Manggis* (mangosteen) is a small purple fruit with white fleshy segments and fantastic flavour.
- *Nangka* (jackfruit) is an enormous, spiky fruit that can weigh over 20kg. Inside are segments of yellow, moist, sweet flesh with a slightly rubbery texture. The flesh can be eaten fresh or cooked in a curry.
- *Rambutan* is a bright-red fruit covered in soft spines; the name means 'hairy'. Break it open to reveal a delicious white fruit similar to lychee.
- *Salak* is recognisable by its brown 'snakeskin' covering. Peel it off to reveal segments that resemble something between an apple and a walnut.
- *Sirsak* (soursop or zurzak) is a warty, green-skinned fruit with a white, pulpy interior that has a slightly lemonish taste.

## DRINKS
### Tea
Indonesia's most popular brew is black tea with sugar. If you don't want sugar ask for *teh pahit* (bitter tea), and if you want milk buy yourself a cow. Various forms of ginger tea are popular, including *bandrek* (ginger tea with coconut and pepper) and *wedang jahe* (ginger tea with peanuts and agar cubes slurped from a bowl).

### Coffee
Indonesian coffee, especially from Sulawesi, is of exceptional quality, though most of the best stuff is exported. Warungs serve a chewy concoction called *kopi tubruk* (ground coffee with sugar and boiling water). Most urban cafes and restaurants offer quality coffee, and gourmet brands are available in most supermarkets.

### Ice & Fruit Drinks
Indonesia's *es* (ice drinks) are not only refreshing, they are visually stimulating, made with syrups, fruit and jellies. There are plenty of places serving *es jus* (iced fruit juice) or cordial-spiked *kelapa muda* (young coconut juice). But beware of ice outside of urban areas (ice in cities is made with filtered water).

### Alcoholic Drinks
Islam may be the predominant religion in Indonesia, but there's a range of alcohol available, including *tuak* (palm-sap wine), *arak* (rice or palm-sap wine) and Balinese *brem* (rice wine). Of the domestic breweries, iconic Bintang, a clean, slightly sweet lager, is the most preferred choice of beer for many. Note that bureaucratic snafu has made it hard to import alcoholic beverages into Indonesia. While not an issue in Maluku, it does mean that you will be hard-pressed to find Australian wine or British gin on Bali. You'll also need to be careful when buying *arak* as there have been cases where it has been adulterated with chemicals that have proved deadly in recent times.

## CELEBRATIONS

Whether a marriage, funeral or party with friends, food – and lots of it – is essential. Celebratory meals can include any combination of dishes, but for special occasions a *tumpeng* is the centrepiece: a pyramid of yellow rice, the tip of which is cut off and offered to the VIP. Meat is always served, often a speciality such as Sumatran *rendang* or Balinese *babi guling*. Once formalities are over (Indonesians love speeches) it's time for guests to dig in.

### Muslims

For Muslims, the largest celebrations are Ramadan (the fasting month, which ends with the Lebaran holiday; see p831) and Idul Adha. Each day of Ramadan, Muslims rise before sunrise to eat the only meal before sunset. It may sound like a bad time to be in Indonesia – you may have to plan meals and go without lunch – but when sunset comes, the locals' appreciation of a good meal is contagious. The first thing Indonesians eat after fasting is *kolak* (fruit in coconut milk) as a gentle way to reacquaint the body with food. Then, after prayers, the evening meal begins with aplomb. In some areas, such as in Bukittinggi, cooks set out food on the street. People gather to savour and enjoy their food as a community. Foreign guests are always made welcome.

After Ramadan, many travel to celebrate Lebaran with their families. During Lebaran, *ketupat* (rice steamed in packets of woven coconut fronds) are hung everywhere, like Christmas bells and holly.

Seventy days after Lebaran is Idul Adha, marked by the sight of goats tethered to posts on both city streets and rural pathways throughout the archipelago. Individuals or community groups buy these unfortunate animals to sacrifice in commemoration of Abraham's willingness to sacrifice his son at divine command. This is one of Indonesia's most anticipated festivals, as the sacrificial meat is distributed to the poor in each community.

### Balinese

The Balinese calendar is peppered with festivals including Kedaso (the 10th full-moon festival) and Penampahan (a purification festival). Such celebrations are always observed with a communal meal, sometimes eaten together from one massive banana leaf piled with dishes.

Festivals aside, every day in Bali you'll see food used to symbolise devotion: rice in woven banana-leaf pockets are placed in doorways, beside rice fields, at bus terminals – wherever a god or spirit may reside. Larger offerings studded with whole chickens and produce are made to mark special occasions such as *odalan* (anniversary of a temple). You'll see processions of women gracefully balancing offerings on their heads as they make their way to the temple. Bali's offerings are made by female-only collectives called *anyaman*, which also have a social aspect.

## WHERE TO EAT & DRINK

Outside of major cities and tourist areas, there are few choices for dining out in Indonesia. Warungs are simple, open-air eateries providing a small range of dishes. Often their success comes from cooking one dish better than anyone else. *Rumah makan* (eating house) or *restoran* refers to anything that is a step above a warung. Offerings may be as simple as those from a warung but usually include more choices of meat and vegetable dishes, and spicy accompaniments.

As Indonesia's middle class grows, the warung is also going upmarket. In urban areas, a restaurant by any other name advertises itself as a 'warung', and serves simple, local dishes. These 'flash' warung can be a good deal for travellers, as the full kitchens and proper water supplies raise hygiene levels – in most cases.

Indonesia's markets are wonderful examples of how food feeds both the soul and the stomach. There's no refrigeration, so freshness is dependent on quick turnover. You'll also find a huge range of sweet and savoury snacks. Supermarkets and convenience stores are also common in cities.

For information on business hours, see p823. For tips on healthy eating, see p859.

## Quick Eats

As many Indonesians can't afford fine service and surrounds, the most authentic food is found at street level. Even high rollers know this, so everyone dines at stalls or gets their noodle fix from roving vendors who carry their victuals in two bundles connected by a stick over their shoulders: a stove and wok on one side, and ready-to-fry ingredients on the other.

Then there's *kaki lima* (roving vendors) whose carts hold a work bench, stove and cabinet. '*Kaki lima*' means 'five legs': two for the wheels of the cart, one for the stand and two for the legs of the vendor. You'll find any and every type of dish, drink and snack sold from a *kaki lima*. Some have a permanent spot, others roam the streets, calling out what they are selling or making a signature sound, such as the 'tock' of a wooden *bakso* bell. In some places, sate sellers operate from a boat-shaped cart, with bells jingling to attract the hungry.

## VEGETARIANS & VEGANS

Vegetarians will be pleased to know that tempe and *tahu* (tofu) are in abundance, sold as chunky slabs of *tempe penyet* (deep-fried tempe), *tempe kering* (diced tempe stir-fried with sweet soy sauce) and *tahu isi* (deep-fried stuffed tofu). Finding fresh vegies requires more effort. Look for Chinese establishments; they can whip up *cap cai* (mixed vegetables). Vegetarian fried-rice or noodles can be found at many other eateries. A huge number of places, including Padang restaurants, offer *nasi campur* (rice with a choice of side dishes). Here you can avoid meat and go for things like tofu, tempeh, jackfruit dishes, egg dishes and leafy vegies. If meat is in a dish it's usually pretty obvious, but ask about hidden things like *terasi* (fish paste), often used in sambal. Vegans should be wary of condensed milk – often added to juices and pancakes. Vendors with blenders mix up some fine fresh fruit concoctions. And there's fantastic fruit available at the local market (see p82).

## EATING WITH KIDS

There's always the fear that a hidden chilli is going to make your child explode. But most Indonesian children dread chilli attacks, so a proprietor will often warn you if a dish is spicy. In any case, you can always ask '*Pedas tidak?*' ('Is it spicy?') or '*Makanan tidak pedas ada?*' ('Are there nonspicy dishes?').

Children may enjoy nasi goreng, *mie goreng* (fried noodles), *bakso* (meatball soup), *mie rebus* (noodle soup), *perkedel* (fritters), *pisang goreng* (banana fritters), sate, *bubur* (rice porridge), fruit and fruit drinks. Indonesia's sugar-rich iced drinks are useful secret weapons for when energy levels are low. All of these are available at street stalls and restaurants. Not available, however, are highchairs and kiddy menus. That's not to say children aren't welcome; in fact, they'll probably get more attention than they can handle.

If your little fella yearns for familiar tastes, supermarkets stock Western foods; and fast-food places are around. Be warned that heat can hit hard, so make sure children are getting enough fluids.

**INDONESIA'S TOP FIVE**

Our authors pick their favourite meals.

**Cak Asm** (p297) The *cumi cumi* (calamari) with *telor asin* sauce is a heavenly mixture of eggs and garlic. The resulting buttery, crispy goodness may be the best dish you have in Bali. And proof that you can eat superbly in a local joint and spend about US$1.          *Ryan Ver Berkmoes*

**Warung Opera** (p187) Run by a very extrovert Indonesian host called Donny, who was taught to cook by his mother (her portrait gazes at you approvingly while you dine...). Food is superb homestyle Indonesian – the humble nasi goreng takes on a different meaning here. Donny broke off half-way through our meal to sing hymns with his Catholic brethren in the back of the warung, the night air filled with vocal harmonies.          *Iain Stewart*

**Jenny's Restaurant** (p393) I asked Jenny what the most traditional Batak dish was. I was informed that at weddings and parties they always cooked *saksang* as the celebration dish. Myself and a few other travellers ordered some up and feasted on the rich and tasty stew with pig's blood dripping down our faces like we were Batak royalty-cum-vampires. You'll need to order a day in advance.          *Guyan Mitra*

**Lombok Lounge** (p514) It looks and feels like a standard issue backpacker haunt, but I ignored their scrolls of Western 'classics' (chicken cordon bleu anyone?) because the waitress assured me that their chilli crab was not to be missed. Good advice. Sweat poured, as I sucked out every last sliver with Zen-like intensity, destroying countless napkins and a few Bintang in the process.          *Adam Skolnick*

**Duta Café** (p791) This Jayapura warung only opens in the evenings and serves unbeatable *ikan bakar* (fish grilled over open coals) with five different sambals lined up on your table. Perfect with a long *es jeruk*.          *John Noble*

## HABITS & CUSTOMS

With a population of over 245 million, you'd expect a little variety in Indonesia's culinary customs. There will be no surprises if you are eating at a restaurant, apart from the lack of a menu. However if eating at someone's house, see the boxed text, p86 for suggestions on fitting in – or at least not offending, especially if someone invites you into their home for a meal.

## COOKING COURSES

If you want to carry on enjoying the tastes of Indonesia after you go home after your holiday, Bali has several cooking schools where you can learn everything from how to shop in the markets to the basics and on to advanced cooking techniques. Best of all though is that you get to eat what you make!

Two of the best:

**Bumbu Bali Cooking School** (p295) Long-time resident and cookbook author Heinz von Holzen runs a cooking school from his excellent South Bali restaurant.

**Casa Luna Cooking Courses** (p313). Part of Ubud empressario Janet De Neefe's empire, half-day courses cover cooking techniques, ingredients and the cultural background of the Balinese kitchen.

## EAT YOUR WORDS

Want to buy mangoes at a market or eat *rendang* at a restaurant? Don't be left speechless; check out the Language chapter on p865 for pronunciation guidelines.

MSG is widely used in Indonesia. In warungs, you can try asking the cook to hold off on the *ajinomoto*. If you get a look of blank incomprehension, well, hey, the headache only lasts for a couple of hours.

---

**TRAVELLER TACT – DINING**

In Indonesia hospitality is highly regarded. If you're invited to someone's home for a meal, you'll be treated warmly and social hiccups will be ignored. Nevertheless, here are some tips to make the experience more enjoyable for everyone:

■ When food or drink is presented, wait until your host invites you to eat.

■ Indonesians rarely eat at the table, preferring to sit on a mat or around the lounge room.

■ Don't be surprised if, when invited to a home, you're the only one eating. This is your host's way of showing you're special, and you should have choice pickings. But don't eat huge amounts, as these dishes will feed others later. Fill up on rice and take a spoonful from each dish served.

■ While chopsticks are available at Chinese-Indonesian eateries, and a fork and spoon in restaurants, most Indonesians prefer to eat with their hands. In a warung, it is acceptable to rinse your fingers with drinking water, letting the drops fall to the ground. Use only your right hand. If left-handed, ask for a spoon.

■ In Islamic areas, be sure not to eat and drink in public during Ramadan. Restaurants do stay open, though they usually cover the door so as not to cause offence.

■ Though antismoking regulations are becoming common, smoking remains acceptable anywhere, anytime.

■ Men and women dining together is the norm. An invitation to a meal from (or for) the opposite sex may be considered an 'expression of interest', as it is in most countries.

---

## Useful Phrases

Knowing these basic phrases will help make ordering a meal easier.

| | |
|---|---|
| **Where is a (cheap) restaurant?** | *Di mana ada rumah makan (murah)?* |
| **I want...** | *Saya mau...* |
| to eat | *makan* |
| to drink | *minum* |
| **Can you please bring me...?** | *Bisa minta...?* |
| a knife | *pisau* |
| a fork | *garpu* |
| a spoon | *sendok* |
| (some) water | *air minum (lagi)* |
| **I can't eat...** | *Saya tidak mau makan...* |
| eggs | *telur* |
| meat | *daging* |
| peanuts | *kacang tanah* |
| **Not too spicy, please.** | *Jangan terlalu pedas.* |
| **What's that?** | *Apa itu?* |
| **What are they eating?** | *Mereka makan apa?* |
| **That was delicious!** | *Ini enak sekali!* |

## Food Glossary

| | |
|---|---|
| *acar* | pickle; cucumber or other vegetables in a mixture of vinegar, salt, sugar and water |
| *air* | water |
| *arak* | spirits distilled from palm sap or rice |
| *ayam* | chicken; fried chicken is *ayam goreng* |

| | |
|---|---|
| *babi* | pork; since most Indonesians are Muslim, pork is generally only found in market stalls and restaurants run by the Chinese, and in areas where there are non-Muslim populations, such as Bali, Papua and Tana Toraja on Sulawesi |
| *bakar* | barbecued, roasted |
| *bakso/ba'so* | meatball soup |
| *bandrek* | ginger tea with coconut and pepper |
| *brem* | rice wine |
| *bubur* | rice porridge |
| *cassava* | known as tapioca in English; a long, thin, dark brown root which looks something like a shrivelled turnip |
| *colenak* | roasted cassava with coconut sauce |
| *daging kambing* | goat |
| *daging sapi* | beef |
| *es buah* | combination of crushed ice, condensed milk, shaved coconut, syrup, jelly and fruit |
| *gado gado* | very popular dish of steamed bean sprouts and various vegetables, served with a spicy peanut sauce |
| *gudeg* | jackfruit curry |
| *ikan* | fish |
| *jajanan* | snacks |
| *karedok* | salad of long beans, bean sprouts and cucumber with spicy sauce |
| *kelepon* | green rice-flour balls with a palm-sugar filling |
| *ketoprak* | noodles, bean sprouts and tofu with soy and peanut sauce |
| *ketupat tahu* | pressed rice, bean sprouts and tofu with soy and peanut sauce |
| *kopi* | coffee |
| *krupuk* | shrimp with cassava flour, or fish flakes with rice dough, cut into slices and fried to a crisp |
| *lombok* | chilli |
| *lontong* | rice steamed in a banana leaf |
| *martabak* | a pancake-like dish stuffed with meat, egg and vegetables |
| *mie goreng* | fried wheat-flour noodles, served with vegetables or meat |
| *nasi* | rice |
| *nasi campur* | steamed rice topped with a little bit of everything – some vegetables, some meat, a bit of fish, a *krupuk* or two; usually a tasty and filling meal |
| *nasi goreng* | fried rice |
| *nasi liwet* | rice with coconut milk, unripe papaya, garlic and shallots, served with chicken or egg |
| *nasi uduk* | rice cooked in coconut milk, served with meat, tofu and/or vegetables |
| *nasi putih* | white (*putih*) rice, usually steamed |
| *pecel* | peanut sauce |
| *pecel lele* | deep-fried catfish served with rice and *pecel* |
| *pempek (empek-empek)* | deep fried/grilled fish and sago balls (from Palembang) |
| *pisang goreng* | fried banana fritters |
| *roti* | bread; nearly always white and sweet |
| *sambal* | a hot, spicy chilli sauce served as an accompaniment with most meals |
| *sate* | small pieces of various types of meat grilled on a skewer and served with peanut sauce |
| *sayur* | vegetables |
| *serabi* | coconut-milk pancakes topped with chocolate, banana or jackfruit |
| *soto* | meat and vegetable broth; soup |
| *soto Bandung* | beef-and-vegetable soup with lemon grass |
| *soto Betawi* | beef soup |
| *soto Madura* | beef soup with lime, pepper, peanuts, chilli and ginger |
| *tahu* | tofu or soybean curd |
| *teh* | tea; tea without sugar is *teh pahit* |
| *telur* | egg |
| *tuak* | palm-sap wine |
| *udang* | prawns or shrimps |
| *ulen* | roasted sticky rice with peanut sauce |

# Java

The heart of the nation, Java is an island of megacities, mesmerising natural beauty, and complex, profound traditions in art, dance, spiritualism and learning.

Generally the cities are pretty uninspiring: pollution levels are high and they're plagued by environmental issues. That said, personal security is rarely an issue, and it's perfectly safe to explore most Javanese towns at night, snacking with locals on the street. And this is the one corner of Indonesia (Bali excepted) with vibrant nightlife and an exciting music scene, so the big cities are good places to catch a new indie band or local DJ.

Leaving the cities you'll find a Java of bewitching landscapes – iridescent rice paddies, villages of terracotta-tiled houses, bubbling streams and patches of dense jungle-clad hills. Verdant and fecund, this is one of the most fertile regions on earth, with three annual crops possible in some areas. And with over 40 volcanoes forming a spiky backbone, almost every journey in Java passes a succession of giant, often smoking cones.

Transport is better than in most parts of Indonesia. By road it can be slow going, though, unless you're on one of the new toll roads. The rail network is reliable and frequent, with trains ranging from dirt-cheap trundlers to fairly swift air-conditioned services.

Javanese people tend to be the best-educated and most worldly in the country, so it's an excellent place to really get to grips with Indonesia and learn what makes it tick. Switched-on young Javanese have set up several excellent new community tourism initiatives, which present an ideal opportunity for travellers to hook up with locals.

---

## HIGHLIGHTS

- Experiencing the magnificent temple of **Borobudur** (p171) at sunrise, when early-morning mist clings to the surrounding necklace of hills

- Gazing over the vast, ethereal caldera of **Bromo** (p245) and Semeru from the lofty lookout of Gunung Penanjakan

- Hiking mountain trails to the sublime crater lake of **Kawah Ijen** (p250) along with an army of strong-armed sulphur miners

- Time-travelling to Java's golden age in the cultural capital of **Yogyakarta** (p176)

- Getting off the beaten path and exploring Java's magnificent national parks: **Ujung Kulon** (p133), **Meru Betiri** (p253), **Alas Purwo** (p254) and **Baluran** (p256)

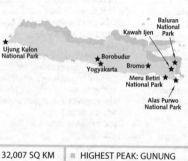

Ujung Kulon National Park ★
Borobudur ★
Yogyakarta ★
Bromo ★
Kawah Ijen ★
Baluran National Park ★
Meru Betiri National Park ★
Alas Purwo National Park ★

---

| ◼ POPULATION: 134 MILLION | ◼ LAND AREA: 132,007 SQ KM | ◼ HIGHEST PEAK: GUNUNG SEMERU (3676M) |

# HISTORY

Java has a history of epic proportions and a record of human habitation that extends back 1.7 million years to when 'Java Man' (see the boxed text, below) roamed the river banks of Sungai Bengawan Solo in Central Java. Waves of migrants followed, moving down through Southeast Asia.

## Early Javanese Kingdoms

Blessed with exceptional fertility from its mineral-rich volcanic soil, Java has long played host to intensive *sawah* (wet rice) agriculture, which required close cooperation between villages. Out of village alliances, small principalities emerged, including the Hindu Mataram kingdom, founded by the ruler Sanjaya, in the 8th century. Mataram's religion centred on the god Shiva, and produced some of Java's earliest Hindu temples on the Dieng Plateau (p169).

The Sailendra dynasty followed, overseeing Buddhism's heyday and the building of Borobudur (p171). But Hinduism and Buddhism continued to coexist and the massive Hindu Prambanan complex (p194) was constructed within a century of Borobudur.

Mataram eventually fell, perhaps at the hands of the Sumatra-based Sriwijaya kingdom. The Javanese revival began in AD 1019 under King Airlangga, a semi-legendary figure who formed the first royal link with Bali and divided his territory into two kingdoms, which he gave to his sons Janggala and Kediri.

Early in the 13th century the legendary commoner Ken Angrok briefly succeeded in uniting much of Central and East Java, defeating Kediri and bringing Janggala under his control. Javanese culture flourished brightly, and striking Shiva-Buddhist temples were built (see p238). However, much of West Java still remained under the influence of the Sriwijaya kingdom at this time.

The emergence of an expansionist new power, the much-celebrated Majapahit kingdom, pushed aside the Sriwijaya and Singosari kingdoms. Ruling from Trowulan (p228), it became the first Javanese commercial kingdom, with its own ports and shipping lanes, trading with China and most of Southeast Asia, and growing to claim sovereignty over the entire Indonesian archipelago. Today its influence endures as a representation of a Javanese golden age, its royal colours of scarlet

### JAVA MAN

Charles Darwin's *On the Origin of Species* (1859) spawned a new generation of naturalists in the 19th century, and his theories sparked acrimonious debate across the world. Ernst Haeckel's *The History of Natural Creation* (1874) expounded Darwin's theory of evolution and surmised that primitive humans had evolved from a common ape-man ancestor, the famous 'missing link'.

One student of the new theories, Dutch physician Eugene Dubois, went to Java in 1889 after hearing of the uncovering of a skull at Wajak, near Tulung Agung in East Java. Dubois worked at the dig, uncovering other fossils closely related to modern humans. In 1891 at Trinil in East Java's Ngawi district, Dubois unearthed an older skullcap, along with a femur and three teeth he later classified as originating from *Pithecanthropus erectus*, a low-browed, prominent-jawed early human ancestor, dating from the Middle Pleistocene epoch. His published findings of 'Java Man' caused such a storm in Europe that Dubois even reburied his discovery for 30 years.

Since Dubois' findings, many older examples of *Homo erectus* (the name subsequently given to *Pithecanthropus erectus*) have been uncovered in Java. The most important and most numerous findings have been at Sangiran, where in the 1930s Ralph von Koenigswald found fossils dating back to around one million BC; in 1936, at Perning near Mojokerto, the skull of a child was discovered and was purported to be even older. Most findings have been along Sungai Bengawan Solo in Central and East Java.

Geochronologists have now dated the bones of Java's oldest *Homo erectus* specimens at 1.7 million years, but also postulate that the youngest fossils may be less than 40,000 years old. This means that *Homo erectus* existed in Java at the same time as *Homo sapiens*, who arrived on the island some 60,000 years ago, and reignites the debate about whether humankind evolved in Africa and migrated from there, or whether humans evolved on several continents concurrently. Those interested in learning more should pick up a copy of Carl Swisher, Garniss Curtis and Roger Lewin's extremely readable book *Java Man*.

# JAVA

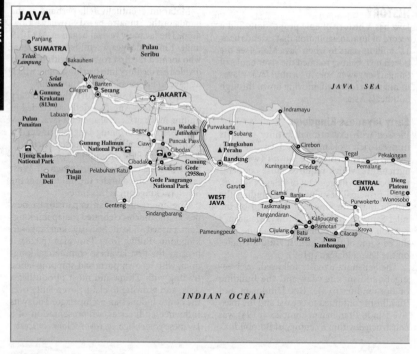

and white used on the Indonesian flag and its name invoked by nationalists.

## Islamic Kingdoms

Islamic influence grew in Java as the Majapahit kingdom faded, and by the 15th and 16th centuries Muslim kingdoms such as Demak (p214), Cirebon (p162) and Banten (p119) were on the ascent.

Demak's military incursions into East Java forced many Hindu-Buddhists eastwards to Bali, and in 1524 it took the port of Banten and then Sunda Kelapa (now Jakarta), before later overrunning Cirebon. But by the end of the 16th century the Muslim kingdom of Mataram (p180) had risen to control huge swaths of Central and East Java. Banten still remained independent, however, and grew to become a powerful maritime capital, holding sway over much of West Java. By the 17th century, Mataram and Banten were the only two powers in Java left to face the arrival of the Dutch.

## Dutch Period

The arrival of the Dutch and their eventual domination of Java is summarised in the History chapter (p38); a snapshot of Javanese resistance follows.

As the Dutch set up camp in Batavia (Jakarta), Banten remained a powerful force under Sultan Agung, but unfortunately civil war within the royal house led to Dutch intervention and its eventual collapse.

The Mataram kingdom was another matter. As the power of the Dutch grew, the empire began to disintegrate, and by the 18th century infighting was taking its toll. The first two Javanese Wars of Succession were resolved by the treaty of 1743 (restoring the ruler Pakubuwono II to his battered court), but the price of concessions to the colonial power was high.

Pakubuwono II established a new court at Solo (Surakarta; p198), but rivalry soon re-emerged, resulting in the third Javanese War of Succession in 1746. The Dutch rapidly lost patience and split the kingdom in three, creating the royal houses of Solo and Yogyakarta (p176), and the smaller domain of Mangkunegaran (p200) within Solo.

Resentment and resistance to Dutch influence continued to simmer, erupting in the

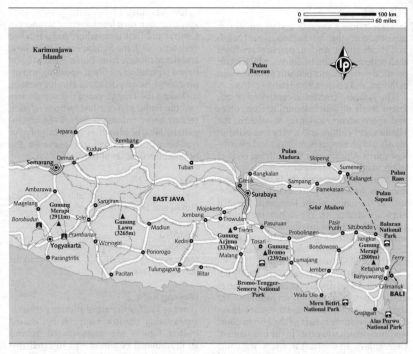

anti-Dutch Java War of 1825–30 as the rebel Prince Pangeran Diponegoro challenged but ultimately failed to defeat the colonists. Subsequently Javanese courts became little more than ritual establishments concentrating on traditional ceremonies and artistic patronage, overseen by a Dutch *residen* (governor), but with very limited political clout.

## Java Today

For Java's, and Indonesia's, struggle for independence from the Dutch and the subsequent growing pains, see the History chapter (p38).

Java still rules the roost when it comes to political and economic life in Indonesia. It has the bulk of the country's industry, is easily its most developed island, and has over the years received the lion's share of foreign investment.

The economic crisis of the late '90s hit hard, when huge numbers of urban workers lost their jobs and rioters targeted Chinese communities in cities including Solo (p198) and Jakarta (p99). But Java bounced back relatively quickly, and enjoyed a period of comparative stability and growing prosperity in the early 20th century. Glittering shopping malls and a new interisland expressway network are the most obvious signs of Java's steady (if unspectacular) modernisation.

Bali apart, Java is the most outward-looking island in Indonesia, and its literate, educated population is the most closely connected to the rest of the world. Extraneous influences matter here, and Java is both the most Westernised island in the country and also the corner of the nation most influenced by radical pan-Islamic ideology. Whilst most Javanese are moderate Muslims, there's an increasingly vocal conservative population (as well as tiny numbers of fanatics prepared to cause death and destruction in the name of *jihad*). The Bali bombers all came from Java, and Java-based terrorists targeted foreign investments in Jakarta in 2003 and 2004, as well as several international hotels in 2009.

But when it comes to the ballot box, the Javanese as a whole have consistently favoured secular rather then religious political parties: in the 2009 elections Islamist parties saw their share of the vote drop slightly.

JAVA

# CULTURE

Javanese culture is an exotic and incredibly rich mix of customs that date back to animist beliefs and Hindu times. Ancient practices are fused with endemic Muslim traditions, which retain mystical *sufi* elements beneath more obvious orthodox and conservative Islamic culture.

The Javanese cosmos is composed of different levels of belief stemming from older and more accommodating mysticism, the Hindu court culture and a very real belief in ghosts and numerous benevolent and malevolent spirits. Underneath the unifying code of Islam, magic power is concentrated in amulets and heirlooms (especially the Javanese dagger known as the kris), in parts of the human body, such as the nails and the hair, and in sacred musical instruments. The *dukun* (faith healer and herbal doctor or mystic) is still consulted when illness strikes. *Jamu* (traditional medicine) potions are widely taken to do everything from boost libido to cure asthma.

Refinement and politeness are highly regarded, and loud displays of emotion, coarseness, vulgarity and flamboyant behaviour are considered *kasar* (bad manners; coarse). *Halus* (refined) Javanese is part of the Hindu court tradition, which still exists in the heartland of Central Java. In contrast to Islam, the court tradition has a hierarchical world view, based on privilege and often guided by the gods or nature spirits.

Indirectness is a Javanese trait that stems from an unwillingness to make others feel uncomfortable. It is impolite to point out mistakes and sensitivities, or to directly criticise authority.

Java has three main ethnic groups, each speaking their own language: the Javanese of Central and East Java (where *halus* is taken very seriously); the Sundanese of West Java; and the Madurese from Pulau Madura (who have a reputation for blunt-speaking and informality). Small pockets of Hindus remain, including the Tenggerese of the Bromo area and the Badui of West Java, whose religion retains many animist beliefs. Even metropolitan Jakarta identifies its own polyglot tradition in the Betawi, the name for the original inhabitants of the city.

## Arts

Javanese culture is a cocktail of pre-Hindu, Hindu and Islamic influences.

### WAYANG

Javanese *wayang* (puppet) theatre has been a major way of preserving the Hindu- Buddhist heritage in Java.

#### Wayang Kulit

*Wayang kulit* is the art of theatre performances using shadow puppets. Perforated leather figures are manipulated behind an illuminated cotton screen to retell stories, which are usually based on Hindu epics the Ramayana and Mahabharata. Unsurprisingly, *wayang kulit* owes much to Indian tradition.

In a traditional performance, a whole night might be devoted to just one *lakon* (drama). Many *wayang kulit* figures and stories have a specific mystical function; certain stories are

---

**TOP FIVE READS**

Armchair travellers and those who like to read up on background knowledge before travelling should consider picking up one or more of the following.

■ *Jakarta Inside Out* by Daniel Ziv. A collection of humorous short stories tackling the vibrant underbelly of Indonesia's capital.

■ *Krakatoa* by Simon Winchester. An excellent, if a tad exhausting, historical account of the build-up to the largest bang ever recorded on planet earth.

■ *Java Man* by Garniss Curtis, Carl Swisher and Roger Lewin. One of the most thorough offerings on the continuing debate over the prehistoric skulls found in Central Java in 1936.

■ *The Religion of Java* by Clifford Geertz. A classic book on Javanese religion, culture and values. It's slightly dated (it was based on research done in the 1950s) but is nonetheless fascinating reading.

■ *Javanese Culture* by Koentjaraningrat. One of the most comprehensive studies of Javanese society, history, culture and beliefs. This excellent reference book covers everything from Javanese toilet training to kinship lines.

---

**JAVA AMBASSADORS**

Several excellent new community tourism initiatives have recently emerged in Java, all run by passionate and committed young Javanese eager to show travellers the best of their island. There's no better way to get to grips with the zeitgeist of the world's most populous island than sharing a day or two (and a laugh) with a local. Alongside sightseeing, other possibilities include school visits, volunteer work opportunities, cooking classes and visits to home industries like tofu kitchens.

In Cianjur (see the boxed text, p147) there's a great home stay program. Borobudur's Jaker community tourism network (p174) will enlighten you about life and customs in rural Java, while in nearby Yogyakarta Rumah Guides (p182) is a well-informed bunch of young local guides. And over in East Java you'll find the Malang Tourism Ambassadors (p235), the perfect hosts for that region.

---

performed to protect a crop, a village or even individuals.

By the 11th century, *wayang* performances with leather puppets flourished in Java, and by the end of the 18th century *wayang kulit* had developed most of the details we see today. The standardisation of the puppet designs is traditionally attributed to King Raden Patah of Demak, a 16th-century Islamic king.

The creation of a puppet is an art form in itself. First, an outline is cut using a knife, then the fine details are carved out using small chisels and a hammer. When the carving is finished, the movable arms are attached and the puppet is painted. Lines are drawn in and accentuated with black ink before the *cempurit*, the stick of horn used to hold the puppet upright, is attached.

The leaf-shaped *kayon* represents the 'tree' or 'mountain of life', and is used to end scenes or to symbolise wind, mountains, obstacles, clouds or the sea.

The characters in *wayang* are brought to life by a single *dalang* (puppeteer), who might manipulate dozens of figures during a performance. The *dalang* must be a linguist, capable of speaking both the language of the audience and the ancient Kawi language of the aristocratic protagonists of the play. He must also be able to reproduce the different voices of the characters, as well as be responsible for directing the accompanying gamelan orchestra (see right).

### Wayang Golek

Three-dimensional wooden puppets, *wayang golek* have movable heads and arms, and are manipulated in the same way as shadow puppets. They are most popular in West Java.

First used in north-coast towns as a vehicle to facilitate the spread of Islam, *wayang golek* is a popular, robust parody of the stylised, aristocratic *wayang kulit* play. In the early 19th century, a Sundanese prince of Sumedang had a set of wooden puppets made to correspond exactly to the *wayang kulit* puppets of the Javanese courts and was therefore able to perform the Hindu epics.

*Wayang golek* uses the same stories as the *wayang kulit*, but also has its own set, inspired by Islamic myths.

Sometimes a *wayang golek* puppet is used at the end of a *wayang kulit* play to symbolise the transition back from the world of two dimensions.

### Other Wayang

*Wayang klitik* or *kerucil* is popular in East Java and uses flat wooden puppets carved in low relief. This type of *wayang* is performed without a shadow screen. *Wayang orang* (also known as *wayang wong*) is a dance-drama in which real people dance the part of the *wayang* characters.

*Wayang topeng* is similar to *wayang orang*, only dancers don masks.

### GAMELAN

A gamelan is a traditional orchestra of some 60 to 80 musical instruments, consisting of a large percussion section – which includes bronze 'kettle drums', xylophones, and gongs – accompanied by spike fiddles and bamboo flutes.

The sound produced by a gamelan can range from harmonious to eerie (but always hypnotic), with the tempo and intensity of sound undulating on a regular basis. Expect to hear powerful waves of music one minute

JAVA

### SUNDANESE MUSIC & DANCE

Sundanese instrument makers are highly innovative and are capable of producing a sweet sound from just about anything. Of their better-known designs, the *kecapi* (a type of plucked lute) is the most idiosyncratic and is often accompanied by the *suling*, a soft-toned bamboo flute that fades in and out of the long, vibrating notes of the *kecapi*. The *angklung* is more ungainly in appearance and consists of a series of bamboo pieces of differing length and diameter, loosely suspended from a bamboo frame. When shaken, it produces an unlikely echoing sound.

Another traditional form is *gamelan degung*. This is played like Central Javanese gamelan, by a small ensemble, but with the addition of a set of small, suspended gongs (*degung*) and an accompanying *suling*. The music produced exists in the hinterland and has a sound somewhere between the soporific Central Javan and livelier Balinese styles of gamelan.

The best-known contemporary West Javan dance form, Jaipongan, is a whirlwind of fast drumming and erotic movement, interspersed with a good dose of *pencak silat* (Indonesian martial arts) and a flick of New York–style break dancing. Jaipongan is a recent mutation of a more traditional Sundanese form called Ketuktilu, in which a group of professional female dancers (sometimes prostitutes) dance for male spectators.

Other dance forms include Longser, Joker and Ogel. Longser and Joker involve the passing of a sash between two couples. Ogel is a slow and exhaustive form, featuring measured movements and a rehearsal regime that many young performers simply lack the time or patience for.

and a single instrument holding court the next.

More often than not gamelan music can be heard at *wayang* performances, but gamelan concerts are also quite common throughout Java.

## GETTING THERE & AWAY
### Air
Jakarta (p115) is Indonesia's busiest international arrival point and has numerous international connections on national and low-cost airlines to destinations throughout Asia and beyond. International flights to regional Javanese airports have increased greatly in recent years, offering useful alternative routes that allow you to bypass Jakarta completely. Surabaya (p226) has a few international flights, as do Solo (p203), Bandung (p149), Yogyakarta (p189) and Semarang (p212).

Domestic flights have dropped in price in recent years and are now a very convenient way to get around Indonesia. Book early during holiday season. You can get to anywhere in Indonesia from Jakarta, and all the main regional airports are offering an expanding network of connections through the archipelago.

### Sea
Jakarta is the main hub for Pelni passenger ships (see p115) that run all over Indonesia,

but no international connections exist. It's possible (but slow going) to get to/from Singapore by using the ferries that run between Pulau Bintan in the Riau archipelago (off the Sumatran coast) and Singapore. From Pulau Bintan there are Pelni boats to/from Jakarta.

#### BALI
Ferries run round the clock between Banyuwangi/Ketapang harbour in East Java (p256) and Gilimanuk in Bali. From Ketapang, numerous buses and trains travel to the rest of Java. An easier alternative is to take a through-bus from Denpasar to any major city in Java – these buses include the ferry journey.

#### SUMATRA
Ferries shuttle between the Javanese port of Merak (p121) and Bakauheni in southern Sumatra, 24 hours a day. From both ports, regular buses head for the main centres of their respective islands. Long-distance buses run from Jakarta (p116) to all the main cities in Sumatra. Work on a new bridge across Selat Sunda (Sunda Strait) linking Sumatra and Java is scheduled to begin in 2012 (and finish by 2025).

The long bus journeys in Sumatra can take their toll, and as most points of interest are in North Sumatra, most travellers prefer to fly there.

# GETTING AROUND

The traditional east–west route across Java is Jakarta–Bogor–Bandung–Pangandaran–Yogyakarta–Solo–Surabaya–Gunung Bromo and on to Bali. However, new flight connections mean that there are now many more potential points of entry (and exit), such as flying into Semarang and heading down to Yogyakarta from there.

## Air

Domestic flight routes in Java are expanding rapidly and can be very inexpensive. Surabaya–Jakarta is very popular and covered by AirAsia and five other airlines. Flight information is listed throughout the chapter and in the Transport chapter (p847).

## Boat

Ferries and boats sail to the island groups Pulau Seribu (p119) and Karimunjawa (p218). Krakatau (p123) can only be reached by boat.

## Bus

Buses are the main form of transport in Java. The normal practice is simply to front up at a bus terminal and catch the first one out; you shouldn't have to wait more than half an hour on the main intercity routes. Services range from hot economy-class buses to smart air-conditioned luxury coaches.

Tickets for buses are purchased on board, although tickets for *patas* (express) and luxury buses can be bought in advance at bus terminals, bus agents in the city centres, and sometimes hotels.

Small minibuses that cover shorter routes and back runs are commonly called *angkot* and shouldn't be confused with very useful door-to-door minibuses *(travel)*. The latter are air-con minibuses that travel all over Java and pick you up at your hotel and drop you off wherever you want to go in the destination city.

Many terminals (in Jakarta, Surabaya and Bandung, for instance) are located a long way from the centre of town. In these cities, the train is usually a better alternative.

## Car & Motorcycle

Driving in Java is not for the faint-hearted; most big cities are constantly *macet* (gridlocked) and main routes can be hellishly clogged. Accidents often result in large pay-offs or pricey lawsuits and a number of drivers are killed every year by angry crowds exacting mob justice following an accident.

Self-drive car hire is rarely available in Java. It's far more common (and a much better option) to hire a car and driver, which saves a lot of hassle. Rates start from as low as 275,000Rp per day, but the average price is nearer 500,000Rp (which includes petrol and the driver's meals and accommodation costs). Hiring a car and driver is an excellent way to explore the remote sights of East Java, or the temples around Solo.

Scooters are the favoured mode of transport for most Javanese, and hiring one yourself can be a good way to get to the island's quieter corners, like the coastal strip near Pangandaran. Rental prices start at around 40,000Rp per day, and should include a proper helmet. Java's roads are no place to try your hand at riding for the first time.

## Train

Java has a decent, if hardly speedy, rail service running right across the island. It connects with ferries to Bali (at Banyuwangi/Ketapang) and Sumatra (Merak). The service runs fairly efficiently and some classes are comfortable by developing-world standards. Punctuality is generally quite good.

A complete train timetable to Java, the InfoKA, is supposedly available from the larger train stations, but we've never seen one. A better option is to check timetables online at www.infoka.kereta-api.com, a clunky but useful website. Timetables are displayed on boards at stations and printed *jadwal* (timetables) are available at main stations (for that station).

If you can, select a train that begins in the city you are departing from, thus guaranteeing a seat; obtaining a seat on through-trains can sometimes prove difficult.

The railway's **Train Information Service** ( ☎ 0361-227 131; www.kereta-api.com) has more information (on the website, '*jadwal*' means schedule).

### CLASSES

Top of the range are the fairly fast 1st-class trains that operate to/from Jakarta. Usually indicated by an *Argo* prefix, they are well-maintained and comfortable, with reclining seats, air-conditioning, a complimentary meal and drink, video and plenty of legroom. The carriages used are ageing, however, so don't expect a luxury service. Tariffs are quite affordable; the Jakarta–Yogya trip costs about 230,000Rp.

Express trains, which offer business-class (*bisnis*) and executive-class (*eksekutif*) carriages, are one step down. *Bisnis* carriages can get very hot (there's no air-con), but the seats are quite comfortable and tickets are cheap. Executive class offers air-con and reclining seats and sometimes a video or snack. Rolling stock used in both these classes is quite old, however, and cleanliness standards could be better.

Java's most popular class with the masses is economy (*ekonomi*). Cheap, basic, slow, smoke-filled, excessively crowded, and a riot of livestock, hawkers, musicians and all manner of produce, these chicken trains move the country around and halt at *every* stop (except, quite often, a city's central one). Seats on these trains are hard (literally) to get and cannot be booked. Some, however, have been upgraded – designated 'economy plus' – and are limited express with padded seats that can be booked.

### RESERVATIONS

Purchasing tickets at ticket windows is usually straightforward. The bigger cities have helpful information desks; otherwise information is usually handed out with authority by the *kepala stasiun* (station master) or one of his cohorts.

Business- and executive-class trains can be booked weeks in advance at the appropriate ticket window. Some travel agencies and hotels can also buy tickets for you.

For basic economy-class trains, tickets go on sale an hour before departure – just roll up, buy a ticket and hope that you can get a seat. The better economy-class services can be booked up to a week in advance for a small extra fee.

It's usually possible to get a ticket in any class on the day of departure if you're travelling on a weekday, but seats should be booked ahead for weekend travel. Note that it's virtually impossible to get a seat during the main holiday periods, when enterprising *calo* (scalpers) buy large numbers of tickets and fob them off to desperate passengers at a hefty mark-up. Avoid planning a trip during the Idul Fitri public holiday, when the entire island is on the move and tickets are as rare as a snowfall in Jakarta.

# JAKARTA

☎ 021 / pop 8.9 million

Jakarta is a hard city to love. One of the world's greatest megalopolises, its grey, relentlessly urban sprawl spreads for tens of kilometres across a flood-prone plain with barely a park to break the concrete monotony.

And yet beneath the unappealing facade of high-rises, slums and gridlocked streets, this is a city of surprises and many faces. The 'Big Durian' is actually a far from threatening place, and its citizens are a remarkably good-natured, optimistic and positive bunch. Compared to many of the world's capitals, crime levels are very low (as is the cost of living, with four-star hotels starting at US$50 a night).

From the steamy, richly scented streets of Chinatown to the city's riotous, decadent nightlife, Jakarta is filled with unexpected corners. Here it's possible to rub shoulders with Indonesia's future leaders, artists, thinkers, movers and shakers in a bohemian cafe or a sleek lounge bar and go clubbing till dawn (and beyond).

Jakarta certainly isn't a primary tourist destination, but parts of the atmospheric old city (Kota) offer an interesting insight into the capital's long history, and there are a handful of good museums and dozens of swanky shopping malls. Though Jakarta's infamous traffic jams still choke the city, an ever-expanding modern busway network has speeded up travel considerably in recent years.

So if you really want to get under the skin of Indonesia, a visit to this mammoth city (the Greater Jakarta conurbation exceeds 20 million people) is essential.

## HISTORY

Jakarta's earliest history centres on the port of Sunda Kelapa, in the north of the modern city. When the Portuguese arrived in 1522, Sunda Kelapa was a bustling port of the Pajajaran dynasty, the last Hindu kingdom of West Java. By 1527 the Portuguese had gained a foothold in the city, but were driven out by Sunan Gunungjati, the Muslim saint and leader of Demak. He renamed the city Jayakarta, meaning 'victorious city', and it became a fiefdom of the Banten sultanate.

At the beginning of the 17th century the Dutch and English jostled for power in the city, and in late 1618 the Jayakartans, backed

## WAYANG CHARACTERS

The *wayang* characters are often based on figures from the Mahabharata and Ramayana. In the Mahabharata, the Kauravas are essentially the forces of greed and evil, while the Pandavas represent refinement and enlightenment.

At a *wayang* or dance performance the *halus* characters tend to be smaller and more elegant in proportion; their legs are slender, and their heads are tilted downwards, representing humility. The *kasar* characters are often muscular and hairy, with upturned heads.

Colour is also of great significance. Red often indicates aggressiveness, greed or anger. Black and blue indicate calm, spiritual awareness and maturity. Gold and yellow are reserved for the highest nobles, and white symbolises virtue.

### Mahabharata Characters

Bima is the second-eldest of the Pandavas. He is big, burly and aggressive. He is able to fly and is the most powerful warrior on the battlefield, but he also has infinite kindness and a firm adherence to principle.

The svelte figure of Arjuna is a fitting representative of the noble class, with good looks and a keen sense of virtue. He can be fickle, but he remains *halus*. Arjuna's charioteer is Krishna, an incarnation of the god Vishnu, who plays the dual role of spiritual adviser and ruthless, Machiavellian politician.

The dwarf clown Semar is an incarnation of a god. He is a great source of wisdom and advice to Arjuna – but his body is squat, with an enormous posterior, a bulging belly and a predisposition for explosive farting.

Gareng, Petruk and Bagong are Semar's three sons and are awkward, comic figures. Despite their ungainly appearances, they are the mouthpieces of truth and wisdom.

On the Kaurava side, Duryudana is the handsome, powerful leader, too easily influenced by the evil designs of his uncle, Sangkuni. Karna is actually a Pandava, brought up by the rival family but, adhering to the code of the warrior, he stands by his king and so dies tragically at the hands of Arjuna.

### Ramayana Characters

The characters of the Ramayana are a little more clear-cut. Like Arjuna, Rama is the ideal man and his wife Sita (or sometimes Shinta) is the ideal wife. Rawana's warrior brother, Kumbakarna, however, is more complex. He knows that Rawana is evil but is bound by the ethics of the Ksatria warrior to support his brother to the extremely grisly end.

by the British, besieged the Vereenigde Oost-Indische Compagnie (VOC) fortress. The Dutch managed to fend off the attackers until May 1619 when, under the command of Jan Pieterszoon Coen, reinforcements stormed the town and reduced it to ashes. A stronger shoreline fortress was built and the town was renamed 'Batavia' after a tribe that once occupied parts of the Netherlands in Roman times. It soon became the capital of the Dutch East Indies.

Within the walls of Batavia the prosperous Dutch built tall houses and pestilential canals in an attempt to create an Amsterdam in the tropics. By the early 18th century, the city's population had swelled, boosted by both Javanase and Chinese eager to take advantage of Batavia's commercial prospects.

By 1740 ethnic unrest in the Chinese quarters had grown to dangerous levels and on 9 October violence broke out on Batavia's streets; around 5000 Chinese were massacred. A year later Chinese inhabitants were moved to Glodok, outside the city walls. Other Batavians, discouraged by the severe epidemics between 1735 and 1780, also moved, and the city began to spread far south of the port.

Dutch colonial rule came to an end with the Japanese occupation in 1942 and the name 'Jakarta' was restored, but it wasn't until 1950 that Jakarta officially became the capital of the new republic.

Over the next four decades, the capital struggled under the weight of an ever-increasing population of poor migrants, but

JAVA

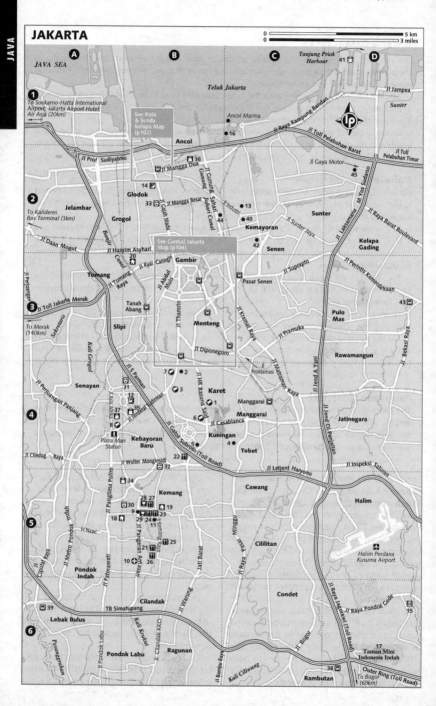

# JAKARTA

0 — 5 km
0 — 3 miles

**A** **B** **C** **D**

*JAVA SEA*

*Teluk Jakarta*

Tanjung Priok
Harbour

Jl Jampea

**1** To Soekarno-Hatta International
Airport; Jakarta Airport Hotel;
Air Asia (20km)

Ancol Marina

Sunter

Ancol

See Kota
& Sunda
Kelapa Map
(p102)

Jl Raya Kampung Bandan

Jl Toll Pelabuhan Barat

Jl Toll
Pelabuhan Timur

Jl Prof Sudiyatmo

Jl Gaya Motor

Jl Mangga Dua

Glodok

**2** To Kalideres
Bus Terminal (3km)

Jelambar

Grogol

Jl Mangga Besar

Jl Mangga Dua

Jl Gunung Sahari

Jl Industri

Sunter

Kemayoran

Jl Sunter Jaya

Kelapa
Gading

Jl Raya Barat Boulevard

Jl Perintis Kemerdekaan

Jl Daan Mogot

Jl Hasyim Ashyari

Jl Kyai

Canning

Gambir

Jl Abdul Muis

Pasar Senen

Jl Suprapto

Tomang

Jl Tomang
Raya

Jl Thamrin

Menteng

Jl Kramat Raya

Jl Pramuka

Pulo
Mas

Tanah
Abang

Slipi

Jl Diponegoro

Jl Matraman Raya

Rawamangun

**3** To Jl Toll Jakarta Merak

To Merak
(140km)

Proklamasi

Jl Jend A Yani

Senayan

Jl HR Rasuna Said

Karet

Manggarai

Manggarai

Jatinegara

Jl Jend DI Panjaitan

**4** Jl Perjuangan Panjang

Jl Gatot Subroto (Toll Road)

Jl Casablanca

Kuningan

Tebet

Kebayoran
Baru

Pizza Man
Statue

Jl Ciledug   Raya

Jl Wolter Monginsidi

Jl Letjen Haryono

Jl Inspeksi Saluran

Cawang

Halim

**5** Kemang

Jl Panglima Polim

Jl Metro Pondok Indah

Jl Pangeran Antasari

Jl Ciputat Raya

Cililitan

Halim Perdana
Kusuma Airport

Pondok
Indah

Cilandak

TB Simatupang

Condet

Jl Raya Pondok Gede

**6** Lebak Bulus

Pondok Labu

Ragunan

Rambutan

Taman Mini
Indonesia Indah

Outer Ring (Toll Road)
To Bogor
(60km)

by the 1990s Jakarta's economic situation had turned around. This all changed, however, with the economic collapse of 1997. The capital quickly became a political battleground and the epicentre of protests demanding Suharto's resignation.

After months of tension, the army fired live ammunition into a group of students on 12 May 1998; four were killed. Jakarta erupted in three days of rioting as thousands took to the streets and looted malls. The Chinese were hardest hit, with shocking tales of rape and murder emerging after the riots.

In recent years Jakarta has suffered on several fronts. Severe floods (which strike each rainy season) cause massive damage to homes and infrastructure. Terrorists have targeted Western interests. The July 2009 suicide bomb blasts that targeted the US-owned Ritz-Carlton and JW Marriott hotels followed previous attacks on the Australian embassy in 2004 and Marriott in 2003.

The city faces many challenges. Millions live in desperate poverty, many in flood-prone areas. Jakarta's public transport system has improved with the introduction of the busway, but it remains woefully inefficient compared with the metro networks now in place in many Chinese cities, Bangkok and Kuala Lumpur. There's much to be done before Jakarta becomes a modern metropolis.

## ORIENTATION

Jakarta sprawls around 30km from the docks to the suburbs of south Jakarta, covering 661 sq km. The city centre fans out from around Merdeka Sq (Lapangan Merdeka), which contains the central landmark of Sukarno's towering gold-tipped National Monument (Monas). Merdeka Sq is one of the city's central focal points, along with a number of other centres that are all separated by vast traffic jams and sweltering heat.

Just south of Monas is Jl Jaksa, the traditional backpacker centre, which is well placed for the historic north of the city and transport links, with busways and the main train station, Gambir, close by.

North of Monas is the old city of Kota, containing most of Jakarta's meagre tourist attractions, while nearby is the schooner harbour of Sunda Kelapa. The modern harbour, Tanjung Priok, is several kilometres along the coast to the east, past the Taman Impian Jaya Ancol recreation park.

The main thoroughfare in the central part of the city is Jl Thamrin, which stretches south of Monas and Merdeka Sq down to the Welcome Monument roundabout; it's lined with big hotels and shopping centres.

Continuing south, Jl Thamrin becomes Jl Jenderal Sudirman, home to more hotels, large banks and office blocks. Further south are the affluent suburban areas of Kebayoran Baru, Pondok Indah and Kemang, with their own

A block west of the square is **Kali Besar**, the great canal along Sungai Ciliwung. This was once a high-class residential area and on the west bank of the river are the last of the homes that date from the early 18th century. One of the most impressive is the red-tiled facade of **Toko Merah** (Red Shop; Map p102; Jl Kali Besar Barat), which was once the home of Governor General van Imhoff. There are plans to convert this house into a museum dedicated to the Dutch period. At the northern end of Kali Besar is the last remaining Dutch drawbridge, the **Chicken Market Bridge** (Map p102), which dates from the 17th century.

To reach Taman Fatahillah, take the busway Korridor I from Blok M or Jl Thamrin to Kota train station and walk. Trains from Gondangdia, near Jl Jaksa, also run here. A taxi will cost around 30,000Rp from Jl Thamrin.

### MUSEUM WAYANG

This **puppet museum** (Map p102; ☎ 692 9560; Taman Fatahillah; admission 2000Rp; ☒ 9am-1.30pm Tue-Fri & Sun, to 12.30pm Sat) has one of the best collections of *wayang* puppets in Java and its dusty cabinets are full of a multitude of characters. The collection includes puppets from not only Indonesia but also China, Vietnam, India, Cambodia and Europe, and masks used by dancers. There are free wayang performances here on Sunday at 10am.

Formerly the Museum of Old Batavia, the building itself dates from 1912. In the downstairs courtyard, you'll find memorials to Dutch governor generals who were once buried here, including Jan Pieterszoon Coen, founder of Batavia.

Be warned that we have received reports of a scam involving freelance guides at this museum, who pressure you into making exorbitant purchases after a tour of the exhibits.

### MUSEUM SEJARAH JAKARTA

The **Jakarta History Museum** (Map p102; Taman Fatahillah; admission 2000Rp; ☒ 9am-3pm Tue-Sun) is housed in the old town hall of Batavia, a stately Dutch-style structure that was once the epicentre of an empire. This bell-towered building, built in 1627, served the administration of the city and was also used by the city law courts.

Today it's a typically poorly presented municipal museum of peeling plasterwork and lots of heavy, carved ebony and teak furniture

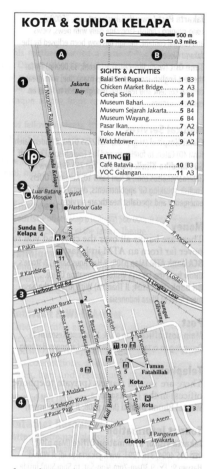

**KOTA & SUNDA KELAPA**

0 ———— 500 m
0 ———— 0.3 miles

| SIGHTS & ACTIVITIES | |
| --- | --- |
| Balai Seni Rupa............1 | B3 |
| Chicken Market Bridge....2 | A3 |
| Gereja Sion..................3 | B4 |
| Museum Bahari...............4 | A2 |
| Museum Sejarah Jakarta...5 | B4 |
| Museum Wayang..............6 | B3 |
| Pasar Ikan....................7 | A3 |
| Toko Merah...................8 | A4 |
| Watchtower...................9 | A2 |

| EATING | |
| --- | --- |
| Café Batavia.................10 | B3 |
| VOC Galangan................11 | A3 |

from the Dutch period (plus a disparate collection of exhibits collected from across the nation). But you will find the odd exquisite piece, such as the stunning black granite sculpture of Kali, a Hindu goddess associated with death and destruction.

In the back courtyard is a strange memorial stone to Pieter Erbervelt, put to death in 1722 for allegedly conspiring to massacre the Dutch inhabitants of Batavia, and the huge bronze **Cannon Si Jagur** that once graced Taman Fatahillah. This Portuguese cannon, brought to Batavia as a trophy of war after the fall of Melaka in 1641, tapers at one end into a large clenched fist, with the thumb protruding between the index and middle fingers. This suggestive fist is a sexual symbol in Indonesia, and childless women would offer flowers and sit astride the cannon in the hope of becoming mothers.

### BALAI SENI RUPA

Built between 1866 and 1870, the former Palace of Justice building is now a **Fine Arts Museum** (Map p102; Taman Fatahillah; admission 2000Rp; 9am-1.30pm Tue-Sun). It houses contemporary paintings with works by prominent artists, including Affandi, Raden Saleh and Ida Bagus Made. Part of the building is also a ceramics museum, with Chinese ceramics and Majapahit terracottas.

### GEREJA SION

Near the Kota train station, this **church** (Map p102; Jl Pangeran Jayakarta) dates from 1695 and is the oldest remaining church in Jakarta. Also known as Gereja Portugis (Portuguese Church), it was built just outside the old city walls for slaves captured from Portuguese trading ports. The exterior of the church is very plain, but inside there are copper chandeliers, a baroque pulpit and the original organ.

## Sunda Kelapa

A kilometre north of Taman Fatahillah, the old port of **Sunda Kelapa** (Map p102; admission 2000Rp) is full of magnificent Makassar schooners (*pinisi*). The dock scene here has barely changed for centuries, and porters unload cargo from these sailing ships by hand and trolley. Sadly, the port itself is rundown and its waters grotesquely polluted these days.

Ambitious plans exist to redevelop the entire Sunda Kelapa area and open new museums in the crumbling buildings, though these proposals have been stalled for years.

### MUSEUM BAHARI

Near the entrance to Sunda Kelapa, several old VOC warehouses (dating back to 1652) have been converted into the **Museum Bahari** (Map p102; ☎ 669 3406; www.museumbahari.org; admission 2000Rp; 9am-3pm Tue-Sun). This is a good place to learn about the city's maritime history, and though the wonderful old buildings (some renovated) are echoingly empty there are some good information panels (in English and Bahasa Indonesia). Under the heavy wooden beams of the vast old storage premises are various random exhibits: a sextant (used for astronomical navigation), various traditional boats from around Indonesia, the shell of a giant clam, plenty of pickled fish and a lighthouse lamp or two. The sentry posts outside are part of the old city wall.

Just before the entrance to the museum is a **watchtower** (Map p102; admission 5000Rp), built in 1839 to sight and direct traffic to the port. There are good views over the harbour, but opening hours are haphazard – ask for the caretaker if it is closed.

Further along the same street from the museum is the early-morning **Pasar Ikan** (fish market; Map p102). It's an intense, colourful scene of busy crowds around dawn, when the day's catch is sold. Later in the day household items and a growing collection of souvenirs are sold.

## Glodok

The neighbourhood of Glodok, the traditional enclave of the Chinese, is an archetypical downtown district full of bustling lanes, street markets, a shabby mall or two and some of the world's most decadent nightlife. It was also the site of the terrible riots of May and November 1998, which reduced huge swaths of the area to ash and rubble.

Most of the fun here is simply experiencing the (very) Chinese vibe of the place, eating some dumplings and browsing the myriad stalls and stores selling everything from traditional medicines to dodgy DVDs. Be sure to wander down the impossibly narrow **Petak Sembilan street market** (Map p98) off Jl Pancoran, lined with crooked houses with red-tiled roofs. It's a total assault on the senses, with skinned frogs and live bugs for sale next to an open sewer.

At the western end of the market is the large Chinese Buddhist temple compound of **Jin de Yuan** (Map p98; Dharma Bhakti Temple; www.jindeyuan.org; Jl Kemenangan III 13), which dates from 1755 and is one of the most important in the city. The main structure has an unusual roof crowned by two dragons eating pearls, while the interior is richly atmospheric: dense incense and candle smoke cloud the Buddha statues, ancient bells and drums, and there's some wonderful calligraphy.

## Central Jakarta

If a centre for this sprawling city had to be chosen, then Merdeka Sq (Lapangan Merdeka) would be it. This huge grassy expanse is home to Sukarno's monument to the nation, and is surrounded by a couple of museums and some fine colonial buildings.

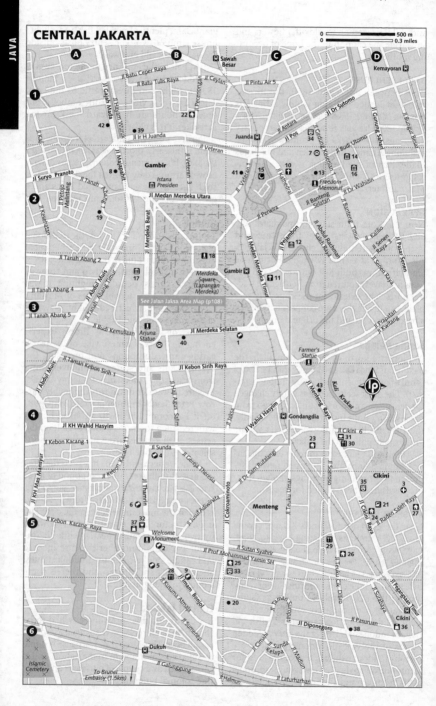

# CENTRAL JAKARTA

## MUSEUM NASIONAL

On the western side of Merdeka Sq, the **National Museum** (Map p104; ☎ 381 1551; www.museum nasional.org; adult/child 750/250Rp; ⏰ 8.30am-2.30pm Tue-Sat), built in 1862, is the best of its kind in Indonesia and is the one museum in the city that's an essential visit. A very impressive new wing was added on the north side of the neo-classical colonial structure in 2007. No photographs are allowed.

The museum has an enormous collection. Around the open courtyard is some magnificent statuary including a colossal 4.5m stone image of a Bhairawa king from Rambahan in Sumatra who is shown trampling on human skulls. The ethnology section is superb, with Dayak puppets and wooden statues from Nias bearing beards (a sign of wisdom) plus some fascinating textiles.

Over in the spacious new wing there are four floors with sections devoted to the origin of mankind in Indonesia, including a model of the Flores 'hobbit' (see the boxed text, p539). There's also a superb display of gold treasures from Candi Brahu in Central Java, including some glittering necklaces, armbands and a bowl depicting scenes from the Ramayana.

Outside the museum is a bronze elephant that was presented by the King of Thailand in 1871; thus the museum building is popularly known as the Gedung Gajah (Elephant House).

The **Indonesian Heritage Society** ( ☎ 572 5870; www.heritagejkt.org) organises free English tours of the museum at 10.30am every Tuesday and Thursday, every second Saturday and the last Sunday in the month. Tours in French, Japanese and Korean are also available; consult the website for details.

## MONAS

Ingloriously dubbed 'Sukarno's final erection', this 132m-high **National Monument** (Monumen Nasional, Monas; Map p104; ⏰ 8.30am-5pm, closed last Mon of every month), towering over Merdeka Sq, is both Jakarta's principal landmark and the most famous architectural extravagance of the former president. Begun in 1961, this typically masculine column was not completed until 1975, when it was officially opened by Suharto. The monument is constructed from Italian marble, and is topped with a sculpted flame, gilded with 35kg of gold leaf.

In the base of the monument, the **National History Museum** (adult/child 1500/500Rp) tells the story of Indonesia's independence struggle in 48 dioramas using *Thunderbirds*-like models. The numerous uprisings against the Dutch are overstated but interesting; Sukarno is barely mentioned and the events surrounding the 1965 coup are a whitewash.

Expect smog-tainted views from the top of the monument (adult/child 5000/2500Rp). Avoid Sunday and holidays, when the queues for the lift are long.

## TAMAN PRASASTI

To the northwest of the National Museum is **Taman Prasasti** (Park of Inscription; Map p104; Jl Tanah Abang; admission 2000Rp; ⏰ 9am-3pm Tue-Thu & Sun, to

2.30pm Fri, to 12.30pm Sat), which is actually the Kebon Jahe Cemetery; important figures from the colonial era are buried here.

### LAPANGAN BANTENG
Just east of Merdeka Sq, in front of the Hotel Borobudur Jakarta, **Lapangan Banteng** (Banteng Sq, formerly the Waterlooplein; Map p104) was laid out by the Dutch in the 19th century, and the area has some of Jakarta's best colonial architecture.

The **Catholic cathedral** (Map p104) has twin spires and was built in 1901 to replace an earlier church. Facing the cathedral is Jakarta's principal place of Muslim worship, the striking, modernist **Mesjid Istiqlal** (Map p104), which was completed in 1978 to a design by Catholic architect Frederich Silaban. The mosque has five levels, representing the five pillars of Islam; its dome is 45m across and its minaret tops 90m. During Ramadan over 200,000 worshippers can be accommodated here. Non-Muslim visitors are welcome. You have to sign in first and then you'll be shown around by an English-speaking guide (who will expect a tip).

To the east of Lapangan Banteng is the **Mahkamah Agung** (Supreme Court; Map p104), built in 1848, and next door is the **Ministry of Finance Building** (Map p104), formerly the Witte Huis (White House). This grand government complex was built by Daendels in 1809 as the administrative centre for the Dutch government.

To the southwest is **Gedung Pancasila** (Map p104; Jl Pejambon), which is an imposing neo-classical building built in 1830 as the Dutch army commander's residence. It later became the meeting hall of the Volksraad (People's Council), but is best known as the place where Sukarno made his famous Pancasila speech in 1945, laying the foundation for Indonesia's constitution. Just west along Jl Pejambon from Gedung Pancasila is the **Emanuel Church** (Map p104), another classic building dating from 1893.

## Southern Jakarta
In the southern reaches of the city reside a couple of attractions that require a day trip to fully enjoy.

### TAMAN MINI INDONESIA INDAH
In the city's southeast, near Kampung Rambutan, **Taman Mini Indonesia Indah** (Map p98; ☎ 545 4545; Jl Raya Pondok Gede; adult/child 6000/4000Rp; ⏰ 8am-5pm) is a 'whole country in one park'.

This 100-hectare park has full-scale traditional houses for each of Indonesia's provinces, with displays of regional handicrafts and clothing, and even a mini-scale Borobudur. Museums, theatres and an IMAX cinema are scattered throughout the grounds, which all command additional entrance fees. Free cultural performances are staged in selected regional houses (usually around 10am); Sunday is the big day for cultural events, but shows are also held during the week.

You can walk or drive your own car around Taman Mini. Free shuttle buses operate regularly, or you can take the monorail or cable car that go from one end of the park to the other. Taman Mini is about 18km from the city centre; allow about an hour to get there and at least three hours to look around. To get there, take a Koridor 7 bus to the Kampung Rambutan terminal and then a T15 metro-mini to the park entrance. A taxi from central Jakarta costs about 70,000Rp.

### MUSEUM PANCASILA SAKTI
Just north of Taman Mini, this **museum** (Map p98; ☎ 840 0423; Jl Raya Pondok Gede; 3000Rp; ⏰ 8am-4.30pm) is a bizarre homage to anti-communism. Inside you'll find dioramas depicting Communist crimes, photos of the 1960s show trials, and even bullet hole–ridden military uniforms. There's a large monument to the self-appointed 'saviours of the nation'.

## ACTIVITIES
### Fitness & Yoga
Jakarta has several public swimming pools. The best option in the centre (within walking distance of Jalan Jaksa) is the 50m **pool** (Map p104; Jl Cikini Raya; admission 20,000Rp; ⏰ 7am-8pm) behind the Hotel Formule 1 in Cikini. There's another 50m pool over in Senayan inside the **Bung Karno stadium complex** (Map p98; Jl Jenderal Sudirman; per swim 5000Rp; ⏰ 7am-9pm), which also has squash, tennis and badminton courts, plus rackets for hire.

**Bikram Yoga** (Map p98; ☎ 719 7379; Sabbero House, Jl Kemang Raya 10A; www.bikramyogajakarta.com; per session 100,000Rp) gets good reports for its hot yoga, Vinyasa, Asthanga and beginners' classes.

### Massage
Jakarta has massage establishments that range from ultra-luxe spas to dodgy set-ups that are

simply fronts for brothels. The hygienic and elegant massage and sauna facilities and professional masseurs at **Bersih Sehat** (Map p108; ☎ 390 0204; www.dayugroup.web.id; Jl Wahid Hasyim 106; 1hr massage from 110,000Rp; ☙ 10am-9pm) are highly recommended. For a real treat, the spa facilities at the Alila Jakarta hotel (p110) are excellent, where massages are available from US$30 per hour.

## JAKARTA FOR CHILDREN
### Taman Impian Jaya Ancol

Along the bay front, between Kota and Tanjung Priok, the people's **'Dreamland'** (Map p98; ☎ 6471 0497; www.ancol.com; basic admission incl entry to Pasar Seni 12,000Rp; ☙ 24hr) is built on land reclaimed in 1962. This 300-hectare, landscaped recreation park, providing non-stop entertainment, has hotels, theatres and a variety of sporting and leisure facilities including bowling. It's easily the city's best entertainment for kids in the city.

Taman Impian Jaya Ancol's prime attractions include **Pasar Seni** (Art Market), which has sidewalk cafes, a host of craft shops, cable-car rides, art exhibitions, and live music every Friday and Saturday night, and **Seaworld** ( ☎ 641 0080; www.seaworldindonesia.com; Mon-Fri 30,000Rp, Sat & Sun 40,000Rp; ☙ 9am-6pm), with its 'sharkquarium', dugongs and turtles. At the **Gelanggang Samudra** ( ☎ 640 6677; Mon-Fri 40,000Rp, Sat & Sun 50,000Rp; ☙ 11am-6pm Mon-Thu, 2-8pm Fri, 11am-8pm Sat & Sun) you can swim with dolphins.

Over in the **Gelanggang Renang** ( ☎ 640 6677; Mon-Fri 40,000Rp, Sat & Sun 50,000Rp; ☙ 11am-6pm Mon-Thu, 2-8pm Fri, 11am-8pm Sat & Sun) water-park complex there's a wave pool and slide pool plus two artificial beaches.

The biggest draw card in the larger Ancol recreation park is **Dunia Fantasi** (Fantasy Land; ☎ 6471 2000; Mon-Fri 60,000Rp, Sat & Sun 80,000Rp; ☙ 11am-6pm Mon-Thu, 2-8pm Fri, 11am-8pm Sat & Sun), a fun park that must have raised eyebrows at the Disney legal department. Spectacular rides here include the Halilintar twisted rollercoaster ride, the Niagra flume ride and a Ferris wheel. The park gets very crowded on weekends, but on weekdays it's fairly quiet. Take a bus or city train to Kota train station, then bus 64, 65, 125 or *angkot* 51. A taxi will cost around 45,000Rp from Jl Thamrin.

## TOURS

Numerous travel agencies offer daily tours of Jakarta. Bookings can be made through the tourist office and major hotels.

**Gray Line** ( ☎ 630 8105; www.grayline.com) Offers city tours (from US$35) and many other trips, including Pulau Seribu (p118; from US$140) and Bogor's botanical gardens (p135; US$85).

**Indonesian Heritage Society** Located at Museum Nasional. Offers city tours for 100,000Rp; see p105.

## FESTIVALS & EVENTS
### March

**Java Jazz Festival** Held in early March at the Jakarta Convention Center in Senayan and attracts some acclaimed international artists. Day passes cost around 350,000Rp.

### June/July

**Jakarta Anniversary** On 22 June, this marks the establishment of the city by Gunungjati back in 1527, and is celebrated with fireworks and the Jakarta Fair (fairground event held at the Jakarta Fairgrounds, Map p98, from late June until mid-July).

### August

**Independence Day** Indonesia's independence is celebrated on 17 August and the parades in Jakarta are the biggest in the country.

**Jalan Jaksa Street Fair** Features Betawi dance, theatre and music, as well as popular modern performances. Street stalls sell food and souvenirs, and art and photography exhibits are also staged. It is held for one week in August.

### December

**JiFFest** (Jakarta International Film Festival; www.jiffest .org) Indonesia's premier film festival takes place in early December.

## SLEEPING

Jakarta has some excellent deals in the mid-range and top-end hotel sectors, with promotional rates slashed as low as US$50 a night for luxury places; check websites or call the hotels direct for the best deals. Falling visitor numbers have seen standards slip badly in many of the traditional budget haunts; backpackers should consider forking out for a midrange hotel in this city.

### Jalan Jaksa Area

This is the travellers' ghetto in Jakarta, but today it's a shadow of its former gap-year glory and looking pretty rundown. The handful of remaining budget places are looking grungy, but the area does have some decent midrange options and plenty of restaurants and bars. Jaksa is conveniently located near

JAVA

hotel has comfortable, well-insulated rooms, a bar and a restaurant. Six-hour rates are available for US$78. Note that the room rate doesn't include the tax of 21%.

## Other Areas

**Alila Jakarta** (Map p104; ☎ 231 6008; www.alila.com/jakarta; Jl Pecenongan 7-17; r from US$80; 🅧 🖵 🛜 🕃) Of the two hotels in the Alila group, Alila Jakarta offers top-end facilities married with modern design, a gorgeous outdoor pool, spa and gym and mighty fine complimentary buffet breakfasts. Note that you must add 21% tax to the room rate. Rooms are nonsmoking.

**Kemang Icon** (Map p98; ☎ 719 7989; www.alilahotels.com/kemangicon; Jl Kemang Raya 1; r from US$150; 🅧 🖵 🛜 🕃) In terms of location, this place – the other Alila option – can't be beat as it's in the heart of south Jakarta's buzzing Kemang area. Here all the apartment-sized suites boast cutting-edge design, iPods, and state-of-the-art bathrooms, plus there's a rooftop lap pool and restaurant-lounge. Note that you must add 21% tax to the room rate. Nonsmoking.

**Dharmawangsa** (Map p98; ☎ 725 8181; www.the-dharmawangsa.com; r from US$195; 🅧 🖵 🛜 🕃) The most luxurious hotel in the city, the Dharmawangsa exudes style and class, with huge rooms and unmatched standards of service (each guest is assigned a private butler!). The leisure facilities (including two pools, spa, squash and tennis courts) and restaurants are also outstanding. Note that you must add 21% tax to the room rate. Nonsmoking.

## EATING

This is a terrific city for eating out. There are seriously stylish restaurants with international menus in the upmarket enclaves of southern Jakarta like Kemang and excellent inexpensive food courts in the dozens of malls spread throughout the city.

Tasty street grub is everywhere, but one excellent hot spot is Jl Pecenongan (Map p104), where there's everything from *sate babi* (pork sate) to fresh seafood. It's about 500m north of Monas.

And if you just can't face one more bowl of *nasi goreng*, don't fear, as there's a cosmopolitan choice of exotic cuisine – including Mexican, Vietnamese and Middle Eastern places.

## Jalan Jaksa Area

Jl Jaksa has a decent selection of backpacker-geared cafes and a few more authentic places. Breakfasts are often very good value.

**KL Village** (Map p108; ☎ 3192 5219; Jl Jaksa 21-23; mains from 15,000Rp; ⏰ 7am-11pm Sun-Wed, 24hr Thu-Sat; 🛜) Deservedly popular new Malaysian place with pavement tables under a covered terrace. Offers great curries (try the *kambing masala*), Western food, terrific juices and fruit shakes (but no beer).

**Memories** (Map p108; Jl Jaksa 17; mains 20,000Rp; ⏰ 24hr) Classic Jaksa haunt of fresh-in-town backpackers and seen-it-all expats. There's plenty of Chinese food, set breakfasts (from 19,000Rp), a book exchange and CNN on round the clock. It even has a few budget rooms upstairs.

**Blueberry Pancake House** (Map p108; ☎ 390 4701; Jl Wahid Hasyim 53; mains from 20,000Rp; 🛜) Below the Cipta hotel, this smart little restaurant is good for Indonesian food, pasta and snacks at moderate prices and offers a welcome air-conditioned retreat from Jaksa's steamy streets. The pancakes are only so-so, though.

**Sate Khas Senayan** (Map p108; ☎ 3192 6238; Jl Kebon Sirih Raya 31A; mains from 25,000Rp; ⏰ 11.30am-10pm) Excellent two-storey air-con restaurant at the northern end of Jl Jaksa, renowned for its superb sate, *rawon buntut* (oxtail stew) and other classic Indonesian dishes.

**Shanghai Blue 1920** (Map p108; ☎ 391 8690; Jl Kebon Sirih Raya 77-79; mains from 45,000Rp; ⏰ 12.30-11pm) A five-minute walk from the northern end of Jaksa, two fine restaurants occupy the same historic building. Downstairs, Shanghai Blue serves *masakan peranakan* (Chinese and traditional Indonesian cuisine) in a large room dripping with furniture and artefacts rescued from an old Batavia tea house.

**ourpick Samarra** (Map p108; ☎ 392 0384; Jl Kebon Sirih Raya 79; mains from 45,000Rp; ⏰ 12.30pm-1am) The upstairs option has an intimate opium-den atmosphere, with secluded tables, subtle lighting, oriental antiques and a great outdoor terrace (with DJs spinning lounge and house music on weekends). The food here encompasses flavours from the Middle East, Indonesian classics and some of the most creative salads in town.

Also worth a try:

**Pappa Kafe** (Map p108; Jl Jaksa 41; mains 20,000Rp) Offers travellers' fare at fair rates under fairy lights.

**Popeye's** (Map p108; cnr Jl Hali Agus Salim & Jl Kebon Sirih Raya; mains 20,000Rp) Flies the flag for junk-food fetishists, serving an assortment of deep-fried fish and chicken.

## Kota, Sunda Kelapa & Glodok

**Santong Kuo Tieh 68** (Map p98; ☎ 692 4716; Jl Pancoran; 10 dumplings 20,000Rp; ☺ 10am-9pm) For fried or steamed Chinese pork dumplings, look no further than this humble but highly popular little place; you'll see cooks preparing them out front. The *bakso ikan isi* (fish balls) are also good.

**VOC Galangan** (Map p102; ☎ 667 8501; Jl Kakap 1; snacks & meals from 12,500Rp; ☺ 9am-5pm) Occupying the premises of a beautifully restored warehouse that dates back to 1628, this is a fabulously atmospheric cafe – enjoy a drink or meal inside the beamed interior or on the terrace, which overlooks a grassy courtyard where there's a vintage car and horse-buggy carriage. Manager Derek Courbois runs a tight ship, and prices are very reasonable for dishes like *gado gado* (13,500Rp) given the setting.

**Café Batavia** (Map p102; ☎ 691 5531; Jl Pintu Besar Utara 14; mains 50,000Rp) An essential visit if you're in Kota, this historic restaurant sits pretty, overlooking Taman Fatahillah. Its teak floors and art deco furniture make a richly atmospheric setting, though the menu is overly grandiose and seems to be stuck in 1970s nostalgia. As it's often woefully empty you may opt to have a coffee or a cocktail instead.

## Cikini & Menteng

**Vietopia** (Map p104; ☎ 391 5893; Jl Cikini Raya 33; mains 25,000-50,000Rp; ☺ 11.30am-10.30pm; ☜) Authentic Vietnamese food, including steaming *pho* noodle broth, and plenty of delicious chicken, beef and seafood mains – green papaya with shrimp is gorgeous. All dishes are moderately priced and delicately spiced and the surroundings are very attractive, with Zen-influenced minimalist decor and bamboo plants.

**our pick** **Lara Djonggrang** (Map p104; ☎ 315 3252; Jl Teuku Cik Ditiro 4; mains 45,000-150,000Rp; ☺ 12.30-11pm) An attractive selection of dishes from around the archipelago, stunning decor that mixes traditional Indonesian flair with North African charm, atmospheric lighting and a great wine list make this one stunning place to eat.

**Lan Na Thai/Hazara/El Wajh** (Map p104; ☎ 315 0424; www.facebars.com; Jl Kusuma Atmaja 85; mains 70,000-120,000Rp; ☺ 11.30am-11pm) This four-in-one venue (Face Bar, see p112, is also located here) is great for North Indian food, including wonderful tandoori choices in Hazara, exquisite Thai cuisine in Lan Na Thai and delectable Moroccan dishes in El Wajh.

## Kemang Area

In addition to the following upmarket places Kemang has a couple of excellent food courts. The best of these is the huge **Kemang Food Festival** (Map p98; Jl Kemang Raya; meals from 12,000Rp; ☺ 11.30am-11pm), which has 50 or so stalls rustling up *roti canai* (Indian-style flaky flat bread), Japanese noodles, and Iranian, Arabic and Indonesian food. On weekend nights there's a real buzz here and the place is crammed. Over the road, the smaller **Kemang Food Square** (Map p98; Jl Kemang Raya; meals from 15,000Rp; ☺ 11.30am-11pm) also has stalls.

**WWWok** (Map p98; ☎ 719 3928; Jl Kemang Raya 9 J-K; mains 35,000-85,000Rp; ☜) Cafe-bar-restaurant with a really relaxed boho vibe that's popular with a freelance media crowd and students. There are plenty of sofas and space, pool tables and a menu of Chinese and Indonesian faves.

**Payon** (Map p98; ☎ 719 4826; Jl Kemang Raya 17; mains 40,000-110,000Rp; ☺ 11.30am-11pm) This feels like a secret garden, as you dine under a delightful open pagoda set well off the road and surrounded by greenery. Payon is a very civilized setting for authentic Javanese cuisine.

**Casa** (Map p98; ☎ 719 9289; www.casajakarta.com; Jl Kemang Raya 8B; mains 45,000-90,000Rp; ☜) Stylish, modern cafe-restaurant with large plate-glass windows overlooking the happening Kemang strip. There's always a buzz about this place, with quality lounge music and a straightforward menu of pizza, grilled meats, pasta and salads.

**Anatolia** (Map p98; ☎ 719 4658; Jl Kemang Raya 110A; mains 50,000-100,000Rp; ☺ 5.30-11pm) Authentic Turkish cuisine with an exceptional choice of mezze (including dozens of veggie dishes), succulent lamb and chicken kebabs and *pide* (Turkish-style pizza). Belly dancers strut their stuff here on Friday and Saturday night.

**Kinara** (Map p98; ☎ 719 2677; Jl Kemang Raya 78B; mains 55,000-125,000Rp; ☺ 11.30am-11pm) The mock medieval doors guarding Kinara lead to an opulent interior of grand arches that's an impressive setting for some of the finest Indian dishes in Jakarta – plump samosas, sublime chicken tikka and plenty of vegetarian choices.

**Toscana** (Map p98; ☎ 718 1217; Jl Kemang Raya 120; mains 85,000-195,000Rp; ☺ 5.30-11pm) Elegant Italian place renowned for its pizzas (baked in a wood-fired oven) and great fish dishes (try the John Dory with red-pepper puree). Also boasts a good selection of Tuscan wines.

**Blowfish** (Map p98; ☎ 5297 1234; www.blowfish-puro .com; City Plaza at Wisma Mulia, Jl Gatot Subroto 42; meals 120,000-300,000Rp; ☉ 6-11pm) Blowfish has a new location in Kuningan, situated 3km north of Kemang, but the quality of its Japanese cuisine (the sushi and sashimi here is sea spray–fresh) remains unchanged. Or if that doesn't tickle your tuna, you can head over to **Puro** (under the same management) for gourmet Italian food. Both of these places have contemporary decor, steep prices and gorgeous bar areas and are popular with Jakarta's beautiful crowd.

# DRINKING
## Bars

If you're expecting Jakarta, as the capital of the world's largest Muslim country, to be a pretty sober city with little in the way of drinking culture, think again. Bars are spread throughout the city, with down-to-earth (and down-at-heel) places grouped around Jalan Jaksa, swish lounge bars concentrated in Kemang and south Jakarta, and many more places in-between, including a strip of expat bars in Blok M (consult www.jakartablokm.com for more on these).

Note that most bars stay open till around 1am or 2am, sometimes later on weekends, and all establishments listed under Live Music (opposite) rank highly as drinking spots.

**Red Square** (Map p98; ☎ 5790 1281; Plaza Senayan Arcadia, Jl New Delhi 9) A hip, lively and fashionable vodka bar, Red Square has floor-to-ceiling stocks of Russia's favourite tipple. It even has a walk-in freezer for knocking back slammers. There's hip electronic music in the early evening and harder progressive house later on.

**Burgundy** (Map p104; ☎ 390 1234; Grand Hyatt Hotel, Jl Thamrin) One of Jakarta's most upmarket drinking haunts, with spectacularly expensive cocktails, avant-garde decor, a cigar humidor and more beautiful people than you can shake a daiquiri at.

**Cork & Screw** (Map p104; ☎ 3192 8996; Plaza Indonesia, Jl Kebon Kacang Raya) Seriously swanky bar-cum-restaurant with the city's best selection of wine – just choose your vintage from the hundreds of bottles on display. As wine is very heavily taxed in Indonesia, make sure your wallet is suitably stuffed.

**Eastern Promise** (Map p98; ☎ 7179 0151; Jl Kemang Raya 5; ☜ ) A classic British-style pub in the heart of Kemang, with a pool table, a welcoming atmosphere and filling Western and Indian grub. Service is prompt and friendly, the beer's cold and there's live music on weekends. It's a key expat hang-out.

**ourpick** **Melly's** (Map p108; Jl Wahid Hasyim 84; ☜ ) The best bet in the Jaksa area for a couple of drinks, this quirky little place attracts a good mix of locals and Westerners, has cheap snacks and beer (a large Bintang is 22,000Rp), and plenty of loungy sitting areas. It's open-sided (so it doesn't get too smoky) and there's a popular quiz here every Wednesday.

**Tabac** (Map p98; ☎ 390 1234; Jl Kemang Raya 25) Perhaps Jakarta's most unusual bar; the lobby to this place is actually a cigar store, and the bar is located behind a secret entrance (hint: push the door of the telephone kiosk). Inside it's like a private club, all wood panelling and comfortable seating. Pricey (a small Bintang is 40,000Rp) and draws a good mix of locals and expats.

The following restaurants also have great bars:

**Blowfish** (Map p98; ☎ 5297 1234; www.blowfish-puro .com; City Plaza at Wisma Mulia, Jl Gatot Subroto 42) A very happening and exclusive bar where DJs spin the latest club tunes till late.

**Café Batavia** (Map p102; ☎ 691 5531; Jl Pintu Besar Utara 14) *The* place for a cocktail or just a cool Bintang in north Jakarta.

**Face Bar** (Map p104; ☎ 315 0424; www.facebars.com; Jl Kusuma Atmaja 85) Part of the Lan Na Thai, Hazara and El Wajh venue (p111), this hip lounge bar has plenty of subdued reds and dark woods.

## Cafes

Cafe culture has taken off in Jakarta in the last few years and all the malls have a Starbucks or Starbucks-style coffee house selling extortionately priced cappuccinos and lattes. Yet every humble warung in town should be able to rustle up a cup of wonderfully strong Javanese coffee (ask for *kopi java* or *kopi hitam*) for between 2000Rp and 6000Rp.

**Bakoel Koffie** (Map p104; ☎ 3193 6608; Jl Cikini Raya 25; coffees from 10,000Rp; ☜ ) Occupying a fine old Dutch building, this is a really relaxed and atmospheric cafe, with vintage furniture, art on the walls and lots of little corners with Jakartan professionals tapping away on their laptops. Only the finest beans from Java, Sulawesi and Sumatra are used, and snacks and cakes are served.

---

**A CUP OF JAVA**

Java is so synonymous with coffee, one of the world's favourite drugs – sorry, *drinks* – that in some countries the term java has become a catch phrase for a cup of the hot, brown stuff.

Coffee was introduced to Indonesia by the Dutch, who initially founded plantations around Jakarta, Sukabumi and Bogor. Due to the country's excellent coffee-growing conditions, plantations began springing up across Java, and even in parts of Sulawesi and Sumatra. Early on, the prominent coffee was arabica; arabica coffees were traditionally named after the port they were exported from, hence the common worldwide terms of java and mocha (from Yemen) for coffee.

Commonly thought of as a bean, coffee is actually a fruit pit or berry. Around 2000 berries are needed to make one pound of coffee. The most expensive coffee in the world, fetching US$300 a pound, is *kopi luwak*, a fully flavoured coffee produced in Java (it is also exported from the Philippines, Vietnam and southern India). What makes *kopi luwak* – also known as civet coffee – so expensive is the process by which it gains its unusually rich flavour. The local palm civet, a catlike animal, gorges itself on coffee berries and passes the inner pit through its digestive tract unharmed. Along the way the pits are affected by the animal's stomach enzymes and come out the other end smelling of roses (or rich coffee in this case). The coffee has been appetisingly nicknamed 'cat poop' or 'monkey poo' coffee.

Today, Indonesia is the fourth-largest producer of coffee in the world after Brazil, Vietnam and Colombia. Robusta has replaced arabica as the leading coffee of choice, currently making up some 88% of the country's exports. For further reading on Indonesia's love affair with coffee pick up a copy of *A Cup of Java* by Gabriella Teggia and Mark Hanusz.

---

# ENTERTAINMENT

Jakarta is Indonesia's most broad-minded, sophisticated and decadent city, with the nightlife to match. The club scene can be nothing short of incendiary. Note that things can be a lot quieter during Ramadan.

The live music scene is also vibrant, with grunge, indie and reggae bands particularly popular with Jakarta's thousands of students.

Check the entertainment pages of *Time Out Jakarta* or *Jakarta Kini* for films, concerts and special events.

## Cultural Performances

Museum Wayang (p102) holds *wayang kulit* and *golek* performances on Sunday between 10am and 2pm.

**Taman Ismail Marzuki** (TIM; Map p104; ☎ 3193 7325; www.tamanismailmarzuki.com; Jl Cikini Raya 73) TIM is Jakarta's principal cultural centre, with a cinema, theatres (performances include Javanese dance, plays and gamelan concerts), two art galleries and several restaurants in the complex. The tourist office and listings magazines have program details.

**Gedung Kesenian Jakarta** (Map p104; ☎ 380 8282; Jl Gedung Kesenian 1) Hosts traditional dance and theatre, as well as European classical music and dance.

**Erasmus Huis** (Map p98; ☎ 524 1069; www.mfa.nl/erasmushuis; Jl HR Rasuna Said Kav S-3) This cultural centre holds regular cultural events and exhibitions.

## Live Music

**West Pacific** (Map p108; ☎ 391 2025; Jl Thamrin 12) Hosts indie/alternative bands and also has an extensive restaurant menu. It's below Jaya Pub.

**BB's** (Map p104; ☎ 3193 1890; Jl Cokroaminoto) Really popular with students, this scruffy multi-storeyed bar showcases emerging acoustic, blues and reggae bands. Drinks are quite reasonable, especially if you order beer by the pitcher. Friday night is the big night here; entrance is 30,000Rp.

**Jaya Pub** (Map p108; Jl Thamrin 12) This Jakarta institution has been around for more than 30 years and isn't showing signs of slowing down. Expect an older crowd and live bluesy rock performers.

**Nine Muses Club** (Map p98; ☎ 722 1188; www.ninemusesclub.com; Jl Wijaya I 25, Kebayoran Baru) Upmarket European-style bar-restaurant where the jazz artists, pianists and Latin bands draw an older crowd.

## Clubs

Jakarta is the clubbing mecca of Southeast Asia. The city has some great venues (from dark 'n'

JAVA

sleazy to polished and pricey), internationally renowned DJs, world-class sound systems and some of the planet's longest party sessions (some clubs open around the clock for the entire weekend!). Entrance is typically 50,000Rp to 80,000Rp but includes a free drink. Clubs open around 9pm, but they don't really get going until midnight; most close around 4am.

**Centro** (Map p98; ☎ 7278 0818; www.centrojakarta .net; Jl Dharmawangsa IX) A huge club that attracts international DJs on a regular basis.

**Embassy** (Map p98; ☎ 574 3704; www.embassytheclub .com; Taman Ria Senayan, Jl Gatot Subroto) One the most respected clubs in the city, its three levels include the main room for house and R&B, and the basement for techno and tribal sounds.

**Stadium** (Map p98; ☎ 626 3323; www.stadium jakarta.com; Jl Hayum Waruk 111 FF-JJ) The big daddy of Jakarta's scene, this club has the heritage (established in 1997), the reputation (DJs including Sasha and Dave Seaman have spun here), the capacity (around 4000), the sound system and the crowd. There are four levels, but the main room is where the prime dance-floor action is – a dark, cavernous space of pounding beats full of clubbers in sunglasses. This ain't no disco – alcohol is not the drug of choice, and Stadium has a distinctly underground vibe. Its weekend session is totally hardcore – beginning on Thursday evening and running until Monday morning.

**X2** (Map p98; ☎ 572 5560; www.x2club.net; Plaza Senayan, Jl Asia Afrika 8) Huge upmarket club with futuristic lighting, three dance zones (house and R&B/hip hop and trance/progressive sounds) plus a cocktail lounge. Entrance is a hefty 100,000Rp on weekend nights.

## SHOPPING

Shopping is one of Jakarta's biggest attractions. Clothes, shoes, bags and electrical goods (including DVDs) are very cheap, especially those that are locally made. Brand-name goods are available in profusion, but the genuine ones are rarely any cheaper than you could get them at home. Jakarta has handicrafts from almost everywhere in Indonesia, and while prices are higher than in the places of origin, it's a good opportunity to get an idea of prices if you have just arrived, or to make last-minute purchases if you are just leaving.

### Arts & Handicrafts

Jl Kebon Sirih Timur (Map p108), the street east of Jl Jaksa, has a number of shops that sell antiques and curios. The quality is high, but so are the prices. Jl Palatehan 1 is just to the north of the Blok M bus terminal (Map p98), and has some interesting antique and craft shops.

**Flea market** (Map p104; Jl Surabaya) Jakarta's famous flea market is in Menteng. It has woodcarvings, furniture, textiles, jewellery and many (often instant) antiques. Bargain like crazy – prices may be up to 10 times the value of the goods.

**Pasar Seni** (Map p98; Taman Impian Jaya Ancol) In north Jakarta, this is a good place to look for regional handicrafts and to see many of them being made.

**Pasaraya department store** (Map p98; Jl Iskandarsyah II/2) Opposite Blok M Mall, Pasaraya has two huge floors that seem to go on forever and are devoted to batik and handicrafts from throughout the archipelago.

### Shopping Centres

Jakarta has more shopping centres than you could spend a month of Sundays in, and the general rule in the capital is, the bigger, the better.

**Pasar Pagi Mangga Dua** (Map p98; Jl Mangga Dua) This is an enormous wholesale market with some of Jakarta's cheapest clothes, accessories and shoes, as well as a host of other goods. Quality can be a problem, though.

**Mangga Dua Mall** (Map p98; Jl Mangga Dua) Across the road from Pasar Pagi Mangga Dua, this is the place for computers, electronics, DVDs and CDs (and even Russian watches). The surrounding area has other malls, making it Southeast Asia's biggest shopping precinct.

**Blok M Mall** (Map p98; Kebayoran Baru) This mall by the large bus terminal has scores of small, reasonably priced shops offering clothes, shoes, CDs and DVDs.

**Plaza Indonesia** (Map p104; www.plazaindonesia.com; Jl Thamrin; 🛜) Exclusive Plaza Indonesia tops Jakarta's A list for shopping centres, with dozens of designer stores. There's a good, surprisingly inexpensive food court in the basement.

**Plaza Senayan** (Map p98; www.plaza-senayan.com; Jl Asia Afrika; 🛜) This huge plaza has a cinema, one of the city's best clubs (X2; see left) and stores including Marks & Spencer and Prada – though prices are very steep.

**FX Mall** (Map p98; Jl Jenderal Sudirman; 🛜) An upmarket mall in the Senayan district, the main attraction here is the 72m transparent cylindrical slide that shoots you down six stories in about 12 seconds – spend 100,000Rp and the ride is free.

## GETTING THERE & AWAY

Jakarta is the main international gateway to Indonesia; for details on arriving here from overseas, see the Transport chapter (p842). Jakarta is also a major centre for domestic travel, with extensive bus, train, air and boat connections.

### Air

All international and domestic flights operate from Sukarno-Hatta international airport (off Map p98). Consult www.jakartaairport online.com for airport information and schedules. The city's second airport, Halim, is no longer used for passenger flights. For information on departure tax and international airlines, see the boxed text, p843, and p842 respectively.

Domestic airline offices in Jakarta include the following.

**AirAsia** (off Map p98; ☎ 5050 5088; www.airasia.com; Sukarno-Hatta international airport)

**Batavia Air** (Map p104; ☎ 3899 9888; www.batavia-air .co.id; Jl Ir H Juanda 15)

**Garuda** (Map p104; ☎ 231 1801, 0804 180 7807; www.garuda-indonesia.com; Garuda Bldg, Jl Merdeka Selatan 13)

**Lion Air** (Map p104; ☎ 632 6039; www.lionair.co.id; Jl Gajah Mada 7)

**Mandala Air** (Map p108; ☎ 314 4838, 0804 123 4567; www.mandalaair.com; Jl Wahid Hasyim 84-88)

**Merpati** (Map p98; ☎ 654 8888, 0800-101 2345; www.merpati.co.id; Jl Angkasa Blok B/15 Kav 2-3, Kemayoran)

**Sriwijaya Airlines** (Map p98; ☎ 640 5566; www .sriwijayaair-online.com; Jl Gunung Sahari)

### Boat

See p848 for information on the Pelni shipping services that operate on regular weekly, two-week and four-week schedules to ports all over the archipelago. The **Pelni ticketing office** (Map p98; ☎ 421 2893; www.pelni.com; Jl Angkasa 18) is northeast of the city centre in Kemayoran. Tickets (plus commission) can also be bought from designated Pelni agents: **Menara Buana Surya** (Map p104; ☎ 314 2464; Jl Menteng Raya 29), in the Tedja Buana building, 500m east of Jl Jaksa; or **Kerta Jaya** (Map p104; ☎ 345 1518; Jl Veteran 1 27), opposite Mesjid Istiqlal.

Direct Pelni destinations from Jakarta include Padang, Tanjung Pandan (Pulau Belitung), Surabaya, Semarang, Belawan, Kijang (Pulau Bintan) and Batam. Some of the most useful services include the *Ganda Dewata*, which sails to/from Makassar and the *Kelud* to Batam (near Singapore). To Kalimantan, the *Leuser* goes via Tanjung Pandan to Pontianak.

Pelni ships all arrive at and depart from Pelabuhan Satu (dock No 1) at Tanjung Priok, 13km northeast of the city centre. Busway Koridor 10 (at the time of writing, slated to begin in mid-2009) should provide the fastest connection to the port, and Koridor 12 should provide an additional link some time in 2010. A taxi from Jl Jaksa costs around 70,000Rp. The **information centre** ( ☎ 436 7487) at the front of the dock No 1 arrival hall can be helpful, or try the nearby **Pelni Information Office** (Map p98; ☎ 430 1260; Jl Palmas 2), though you can't buy tickets here!

There are no longer any hydrofoils sailing between Jakarta and Batam.

### Bus

Jakarta's four major bus terminals – Kalideres, Kampung Rambutan, Pulo Gadung and Lebak Bulus – are all a long way from the city centre. Take the TransJakarta busway to these terminals as the journey can take hours otherwise. Trains are generally a better alternative for travelling to/from Jakarta.

Tickets (some including travel to the terminals) for the better buses can be bought from agencies (see p101).

#### KALIDERES

About 15km northwest of Merdeka Sq, this terminal (off Map p98) serves points to the west of Jakarta. Frequent buses run to Merak (28,000Rp, two hours) and Labuan (36,000Rp, 3½ hours). A few buses go through to Sumatra from Kalideres, but most Sumatra buses leave from Pulo Gadung bus terminal.

#### KAMPUNG RAMBUTAN

Buses that travel to areas south and southwest of Jakarta leave from this big bus terminal (Map p98), some 18km south of the centre. It mostly handles buses to West Java, including Bogor (normal/air-con 9000/12,000Rp, 45 minutes), Cianjur (26,000Rp, 2½ hours) and Bandung, via the toll road/Puncak Pass, (42,000Rp, three/four hours). Services also run to Pangandaran (from 65,000Rp, eight hours) and Pelabuan Ratu (31,000Rp, four hours) from here.

### PULO GADUNG

Twelve kilometres east of the city centre, Pulo Gadung (Map p98) has buses to Bandung, Central and East Java, Sumatra, Bali and even Nusa Tenggara. This wild bus terminal is the busiest in Indonesia. The terminal is divided into two sections: one for buses to the east and the other for Sumatra.

To points east, frequent buses go to virtually all cities in Central and East Java, and Bali. Destinations include Bandung, via the toll road (42,000Rp, three hours), Cirebon (from 48,000Rp, five hours) and Yogyakarta (from 90,000Rp, 12 hours).

Sumatra is a long haul from Jakarta by bus; most travellers fly these days. Services to Sumatra tend to leave between 10am and 3pm. Destinations include Bengkulu (from 210,000Rp), Palembang (from 180,000Rp) and even Padang (from 250,000Rp). Prices listed are for air-con deluxe buses with reclining seats and toilets.

### LEBAK BULUS

This terminal (Map p98) is 16km south of the city centre, and is another departure point for the long-distance deluxe buses to Yogyakarta, Surabaya and Bali. Most bus departures are scheduled for the late afternoon or evening.

## Car & Motorcycle

See opposite for details on car hire in Jakarta.

## Minibus

Door-to-door *travel* minibuses are not a good option in Jakarta because it can take hours to pick up or drop off passengers in the traffic jams. Some travel agencies book them, but you may have to go to a depot on the city outskirts.

**Media Taxis** (Map p108; ☎ 390 9010; Jl Johar 15) Has minibuses to Bandung (75,000Rp).

## Train

Jakarta's four main train stations are quite central, making trains the easiest way out of the city. The most convenient and important is Gambir station (Map p104), on the eastern side of Merdeka Sq, a 15-minute walk from Jl Jaksa. Gambir handles express trains to Bogor, Bandung, Yogyakarta, Solo, Semarang and Surabaya. Some Gambir trains also stop at Kota station (Map p102) in the north of the city. The Pasar Senen train station (Map p98) is to the east and mostly has economy-class trains. Tanah Abang (Map p98) train station has economy trains to the west.

For express trains, tickets can be bought in advance at the booking offices at the northern end of Gambir train station, while the ticket windows at the southern end are for tickets bought on the day of departure. Check timetables online at www.infoka.kereta-api.com, or consult the helpful staff at the station's **information office** ( ☎ 692 9194).

There's a (slightly pricey) taxi booking desk inside Gambir station; the fare to Jl Jaksa is 35,000Rp.

### BOGOR

Comfortable *Pakuan Express* trains (8500Rp, one hour) leave from Juanda (Map p98) and Gambir stations roughly every hour until 9pm. No-frills trains (4000Rp, 90 minutes) also run this route, about every 30 minutes, but can be horribly crowded during rush hours (watch your gear).

### BANDUNG

There are frequent trains to Bandung along a scenic hilly track, but be sure to book in advance (especially on weekends and public holidays).

Six efficient and comfortable *Parahyangan* services depart from Gambir train station daily for Bandung (business/executive 45,000/65,000Rp, 3¼hr) between 5.15am and 4.30pm. Seven more luxurious *Argo Gede* services (executive 75,000Rp, three hours) cover the same route between 6.10am and 7.30pm.

### CIREBON

Most trains that run along the north coast or to Yogyakarta go through Cirebon. Two of the best services from Gambir station are the *Cirebon Express* (business/executive 60,000/75,000Rp, three hours) with five daily departures, and the *Argo Jati* (business/executive 70,000/85,000Rp, three hours), which runs twice daily at 9am and 5.10pm.

### YOGYAKARTA & SOLO

The most luxurious trains are the *Argo Lawu* (220,000Rp, 8¼ hours), departing at 8pm, and the *Argo Dwipangga* (225,000Rp, 8¼ hours), departing at 8am. These trains go to Solo and stop at Yogyakarta, 45 minutes before Solo, but cost the same to either destination.

Cheaper services from the Pasar Senen train station to Yogyakarta are the *Fajar Yogyakarta* (business 110,000Rp, 8½ hours), departing at 6.20am, and the *Senja Utama Yogya* (110,000Rp, nine hours) at 7.20pm. The *Senja Solo* goes to Solo (110,000Rp, 10 hours) at 8.30pm and also stops in Yogyakarta.

### SURABAYA

Most trains between Jakarta and Surabaya take the shorter northern route via Semarang, though a few take the longer southern route via Yogyakarta. Trains from Gambir range from the *Gumerang* (business 140,000Rp, 13 hours) that departs at 6pm to the smart *Argo Bromo Anggrek* (special executive class from 260,000Rp, 9½ hours), which departs at 9.30am and 9.30pm.

# GETTING AROUND
## To/From the Airport

Jakarta's Sukarno-Hatta international airport is 35km west of the city centre. A toll road links the airport to the city and the journey takes about an hour (longer during rush hour).

**Damri** ( ☎ 460 3708, 550 1290) airport buses (20,000Rp, every 30 minutes) run between 5am and 7pm between the airport and Gambir train station (near Jl Jaksa) and several other points in the city including Blok M. From Gambir train station to Jl Jaksa, a taxi is a minimum of around 35,000Rp, or you could

walk (it's just under 1km). Damri buses also run regularly to Bandung (115,000Rp) and Bogor (55,000Rp).

Taxis from the airport to Jl Thamrin/Jl Jaksa cost about 140,000Rp including tolls. Book via the official taxi desks to be safe, rather than using the unlicensed drivers outside.

A new train line is being constructed between Manggarai station in central Jakarta and the airport; it's expected to be operational sometime in 2010.

## Bus

Jakarta has a very decent new TransJakarta busway system (see the boxed text, below), which has really speeded up city travel in recent years. Other buses are not very useful for visitors as they are much slower, hotter (no air-con) and crowded (pickpockets can be a problem). Nevertheless you may come across regular city buses, *patas* ('express') buses and orange Metro minibuses from time to time; fares cost between 2000Rp and 3000Rp.

The tourist office can provide a little information on buses around Jakarta, though at the time of research its city map did not plot the busway routes.

## Car

Jakarta has branches of the major car-rental operators, including **Avis** (Map p104; ☎ 314 2900; www.avis.co.id; Jl Diponegoro 25), and **Trac Astra** (Map p98; ☎ 650 6565; www.trac.astra.co.id; Jl Gaya Motor 1/10). Alternatively, enquire in travel agencies, as a vehicle with driver may be the most economical option.

---

### TRANSJAKARTA BUSWAY

Jakarta has a new network of clean, air-conditioned buses called TransJakarta that run on busways (designated lanes that are closed to all other traffic). Journey times have been slashed, and they now represent by far the quickest way to get around the city.

Most busways have been constructed in the centre of existing highways, and stations have been positioned at (roughly) 1km intervals. Access is via elevated walkways and each station has a shelter. Eight busway lines (called *koridor*) were up and running at the time of research, with a total of 15 planned, which should eventually form a network from Tanjung Priok south to Kampung Rambutan.

Tickets cost 3500Rp, payable before you board, which covers you to any destination in the network (regardless of how many *koridor* you use). Buses (running 5am to 10pm) are well maintained and not too crowded, as conductors (usually) ensure that maximum passenger numbers are not exceeded.

The busway system has been a great success, but as most middle- and upper-class Jakartans remain as addicted as ever to their cars, the city's famous traffic jams look set to continue for a good few years yet.

JAVA

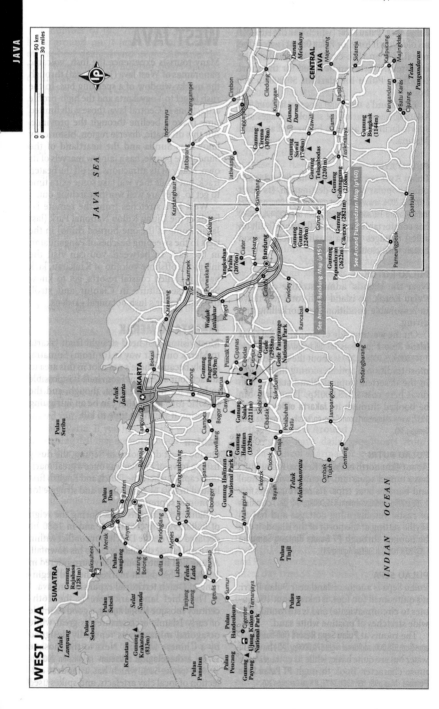

## WEST JAVA

by Banten's Debus followers. (The Debus tradition involves masochistic activities like self-piercing, which the faithful are said to be able to perform without drawing blood).

Directly across from the mosque is the large grass-covered site of the early ruler Hasanuddin's fortified palace, the **Surosowan**, which was wrecked in the bloody civil war during the reign of Sultan Agung (and again by the Dutch in 1832).

Other points of interest around the mosque include the massive ruins of **Fort Speelwijk** to the northwest; opposite the entrance to the fort is a **Chinese temple**, dating from the 18th century. Back along the road to Serang are the huge, crumbling walls and archways of the **Kaibon** palace, and nearby is the **tomb of Maulana Yusuf**, who died in 1580.

### GETTING THERE & AWAY
Take a bus from Jakarta's Kalideres bus terminal to Serang (15,000Rp, 1½ hours), 10km south of Banten, from where a minibus (3000Rp, 20 minutes) will drop you near the Mesjid Agung.

## Pulau Dua Bird Sanctuary
Off the north coast at Banten, Pulau Dua is one of Indonesia's major bird sanctuaries. The island has a large resident population – mainly herons, storks and cormorants – but the peak time is between March and July, when great numbers of migratory birds flock here for the breeding season.

It's a half-hour trip by chartered boat from the Karanghantu harbour in Banten, but you can walk across the fish ponds (via bridges) to the island. From Banten, take an *angkot* 5km east to Sawahluhur village. The trail to the island starts 100m or so before the village and then it's a hot 1km walk, weaving between the fish ponds – just keep heading for the trees on the horizon. There is a PHKA post with a derelict hut that has bare wooden beds and not much else. If you are planning to stay, bring food and water.

## MERAK
☎ 0254
Right on the northwestern tip of Java, 140km from Jakarta, Merak is an ugly port town, the terminus for ferries shuttling to and from Bakauheni on the southern end of Sumatra. In a decade or so a new Selat Sunda bridge should connect Java and Sumatra here, but for

now you'll be boarding a boat between these two great islands. If you're stuck in Merek **Hotel Anda** ( ☎ 571 041; Jl Raya Pulorida 4; r from 60,000Rp, with air-con from 110,000Rp; ❄ ) will do for a night; it's right opposite the ferry terminal.

### Getting There & Away
The bus terminal and train station are at the ferry dock.

#### BOAT
Ferries to Bakauheni in Sumatra depart every 30 minutes, 24 hours a day (see also p474). Ferries cost 15,000/18,000Rp in economy/business class and take around three hours. Much faster speedboats (42,000Rp, 45 minutes) also make this crossing, but these don't run in heavy seas. The through-buses to Bandarlampung are the easiest option.

#### BUS
There are frequent buses making the run between Merak and Jakarta (economy 20,000Rp, three hours; express 28,000Rp, two hours). Most terminate at Jakarta's Kalideres bus terminal, but buses also run to/from Pulo Gadung and Kampung Rambutan. Other buses run all over Java, including Bogor (40,000Rp) and Bandung (normal/air-con 42,000/55,000Rp).

Buses leave from the front of the Merak bus terminal for Serang (7000Rp) and Cilegon (5000Rp); for Labuan (12,000Rp), a change at Cilegon is required.

#### TRAIN
A business train to Jakarta (18,000Rp, 3¼ hours) departs at 12.30pm but is sometimes cancelled; a slower economy-class train (5500Rp, four hours) leaves at 2pm.

## WEST-COAST BEACHES
The west-coast beaches of Java have some good swimming spots, sparkling white sands and even a little surf. They're popular with weekending Jakartans, though few travellers make it out here.

Apart from the multiplying resorts, the area is sparsely populated. The main place of interest is Carita, for arranging tours to Krakatau, visible on the horizon from most of the resorts, and Ujung Kulon National Park. Strangely, this area is also notorious for motorcycle theft; if you bring your own vehicle, keep a close eye on it.

## Anyer & Around
☎ 0254

Anyer, some 14km to the southwest of Cilegon, is easily the most upmarket village along the this coastline. Here you'll find the west coast's semi-luxurious resorts and decent beaches. Anyer was once a big Dutch port before being totally destroyed by the tidal waves generated by the Krakatau eruption. The **Anyer lighthouse** dates from 1885.

Karang Bolong, 11km south of Anyer and 30km north of Labuan, also has a good beach. A huge stand of rock forms a natural archway from the land to the sea.

### SLEEPING & EATING
Most hotels here are pricey and not great value (and rates increase on weekends).

**Hotel Mambruk Anyer** ( ☎ 601 602; www.mambruk .co.id; r incl breakfast from 900,000Rp; ❄ ➋ ) The Mambruk Anyer occupies a huge coastal plot and has dozens of rooms, cottages and villas, though the beach is slimline. Facilities include tennis courts and two pools. It's the first place south of the Anyer lighthouse.

**our pick** **Griya Anyer Spa** ( ☎ 602 577; Jl Griya Anyer, km 127; www.dayugroup.web.id; villas 400,000Rp) This superb spa-restaurant-hotel has two lovely villas that can sleep four (book well ahead) and a fine Japanese restaurant serving sushi and bento sets (60,000Rp), teriyaki dishes and tempura in elegant surrounds. The spa is one of the most professional in West Java, with moderately priced massages (from 110,000Rp per hour) and spa treatments including aroma-therapy and body scrubs. It's located on the very northern edge of Anyer.

Seafood warungs are scattered along the coast from Anyer to Karang Bolong and provide the only cheap dining.

### GETTING THERE & AWAY
Most visitors to Anyer go by car from Jakarta – 2½ to three hours via the toll road (turn off at Cilegon). By bus from Jakarta, take a Merak bus and get off at Cilegon, from where infrequent buses and frequent minibuses run to Labuan via Anyer (6000Rp) and Karang Bolong.

## Carita
☎ 0253

Carita has a more rustic and laidback feel than Anyer and a certain scruffy charm. The beach is wide, and there's some good swimming and a few moderately priced accommodation options. Trips to Krakatau (opposite) and Ujung Kulon National Park (p133) are best organised here.

The hotel Sunset View is the best place for information. Heading north from Labuan port, the usual access point, Carita proper starts around 8km further on.

### SIGHTS & ACTIVITIES
About 2km from Carita over the rice paddies you can see the village of **Sindanglaut** (End of the Sea), which is where the giant tsunami of 1883 ended its destructive run. **Hutan Wisata Carita** is a forest reserve with walks through the hills and jungle. **Curug Gendang** waterfall is a three-hour return hike through the reserve.

Travel agencies including **Black Rhino** ( ☎ 802 818; blackrhinojava@yahoo.com), next to the Sunset View hotel, can arrange diving (as can Rakata Hotel); two-dive excursions start at 750,000Rp including equipment rental. The best diving is in Ujung Kulon National Park, but Krakatau and Pulau Sanghiang are also of interest.

### TOURS
Virtually everyone in town will try to peddle you a Krakatau tour. Check your tour boat first as waves can be rough, and make sure it has a radio on board. Black Rhino (above) and Rakata Hotel receive good reports; after bargaining, day trips to Krakatau start from around 1,800,000Rp. Trips to Ujung Kulon cost from US$280 per person for four days and three nights; overnight trips to Badui villages start at US$150.

### SLEEPING & EATING
**Sunset View** ( ☎ 801 075; r 85,000Rp, with air-con 150,000Rp; ❄ ) The cheapest option on this stretch, though the small, poky rooms could do with a really good scrub.

**Rakata Hotel** ( ☎ 801 171; r 90,000Rp, with air-con & TV 175,000Rp; ❄ ) Another inexpensive option, the Rakata offers reasonably priced rooms, though tariffs jump on weekends. The restaurant serves up good seafood and tours can be set up here.

**Carita Baka Baka** ( ☎ 801 126; r from 160,000Rp, family bungalows from 450,000Rp; ❄ ) It's looking a bit weary these days, and maintenance is not what it should be, but this midrange place has an idyllic spot right on the beach and is surrounded by palm trees. Rates double at weekends.

**Mutiara Carita** ( ☎ 801 069; www.mutiara-carita .com; r from 450,000Rp, cottages from 800,000Rp; 🖭 🖳 ) Stylish rooms and thatched cottages, some with beachfront aspects, in a large, leafy complex that has a tennis court, pool tables (and, unfortunately, karaoke). The kids' facilities and activities are excellent here.

**Krakatau Surf Carita** ( ☎ 803 848; villas from 635,000Rp; 🖭 🖳 ) This place has three classes of well-constructed, attractive detached bungalows (with either two or four bedrooms) right on the beach, with a view of the crashing surf. Prices rise by 30% on weekends. Add 21% tax to room rates.

**Valentine Restaurant** (meals from 30,000Rp) Carita has scores of inexpensive local places that specialise in fish and seafood, but for a smarter setting head to this elegant place, opposite the Krakatau Surf, which has a long menu of meat and fish dishes.

### GETTING THERE & AWAY
To get to Carita from Jakarta, take a bus to Labuan and then an *angkot* to Carita (5000Rp). To Anyer, an *angkot* costs 7000Rp.

## LABUAN
☎ 0253
The dreary little port of Labuan is merely a jumping-off point for Carita or for Ujung Kulon National Park (p133), but it is home to the helpful **Labuan PHKA office** ( ☎ 801 731), located 2km north of town towards Carita.

Frequent buses depart from Kalideres bus terminal in Jakarta for Labuan (36,000Rp, 3½ hours). Regular buses also operate between Labuan and Bogor (38,000Rp, four hours). *Angkots* for Carita (5000Rp, 30 minutes) leave from the market, 100m from the Labuan bus terminal.

## TANJUNG LESUNG
☎ 0253
Tanjung Lesung, 30km southwest of Labuan, is a quiet and unspoilt peninsula with beautiful beaches and traditional Sundanese villages. Accommodation is limited in this region, with no budget options.

**Tanjung Lesung Sailing Club** ( ☎ 0813 8515 1999; www.tanjunglesung.com/sailing.html; cottages weekdays/ weekends from 275,000/345,000Rp; 🛜 ) has attractive, good-value cottages with huge beds and mozzie nets in a great setting just off the resort's sandy bay. There's a bar and restaurant here and it's obviously a great place for

sailors (boats are available from 62,000Rp per hour). Sailing instruction is available from English-speaking staff. Add 21% tax to room rates.

**Tanjung Lesung Resort Hotel** ( ☎ 802 900, in Jakarta 021-6856 7118; www.tanjunglesung.com; cottages weekdays/weekends from US$68/150; 🖭 🖳 🖵 ) is a good choice, with three classes of cottages, sleeping between two and seven people, all of a high standard. There's a huge ocean-facing pool, lovely grounds, a spa and a restaurant. Add 21% tax to room rates.

From Labuan, *angkot* run to Citeureup (9000Rp, 45 minutes), the odd one continuing down towards Tanjung Lesung. However, you may have to hire an *ojek* for the final part of the journey.

## GUNUNG KRAKATAU
The legendary peak of Krakatau, the most famous of the world's famous volcanoes, is a name almost everyone knows – but few actually know of its location (take the film makers of *Krakatoa, East of Java*, for instance). Resting in relative peace some 50km from the West Java coast and 40km from Sumatra, the volcano is nowadays a shadow of its former self – a small group of disconnected islands centred on **Anak Krakatau** (Child of Krakatau), a volcanic mass that has been on the boil since 1928.

The highlight of any trip to Krakatau is rounding Pulau Rakata and first glimpsing the menacing peak of Krakatau's child.

### Information
**Labuan PHKA office** ( ☎ 801 731; ⏰ 8am-4pm Mon-Fri) has information on the volcano; otherwise consult your hotel reception for information on tours and Anak Krakatau's current activity status.

### Activities
Krakatau is only accessible by boat. It's often possible to land on the eastern side of Anak Krakatau, but this is very much dependent on volcanic activity. If conditions are favourable, organised tours usually take visitors about 150m up the side of Anak Krakatau. Walking to the edge of the caldera is never advisable – people have been killed by flying rocks. Always seek qualified advice before making any trip to the volcano.

After Krakatau, tours usually move on to hike and snorkel on neighbouring islands.

## DAY INTO NIGHT

Few volcanoes have as explosive a place in history as Krakatau, the island that blew itself apart in 1883. Turning day into night and hurling devastating tsunamis against the shores of Java and Sumatra, Krakatau quickly became vulcanology's A-list celebrity.

Few would have guessed that Krakatau would have snuffed itself out with such a devastating swan song. It had been dormant since 1680 and was regarded as little more than a familiar nautical landmark for maritime traffic passing through the narrow Selat Sunda.

But from May through to early August in 1883, passing ships reported moderate activity, and by 26 August Krakatau was raging.

At 10am on 27 August 1883, Krakatau erupted so explosively that on the island of Rodriguez, more than 4600km to the southwest, a police chief reported hearing the booming of 'heavy guns from eastward'.

With its cataclysmic eruptions, Krakatau sent up a column of ash 80km high and threw into the air nearly 20 cu kilometres of rock. Ash fell on Singapore 840km to the north and on ships as far as 6000km away; darkness covered Selat Sunda from 10am on 27 August until dawn the next day.

Far more destructive were the great ocean waves that were triggered by the collapse of Krakatau's cones into its empty belly. A tsunami more than 40m high swept over the nearby shores of Java and Sumatra, and the sea wave's passage was recorded far from Krakatau, reaching Aden (on the Arabian peninsula) in 12 hours over a distance 'travelled by a good steamer in 12 days'. Measurable wave effects were even said to have reached the English Channel. Coastal Java and Sumatra were devastated: 165 villages were destroyed and more than 36,000 people were killed.

The following day a telegram sent to Singapore from Batavia (160km east of Krakatau) reported odd details such as 'fish dizzy and caught with glee by natives', and for three years, ash clouds circled the earth, creating strange and spectacular sunsets.

The astonishing return of life to the devastated islands has been the subject of scientific study ever since. Not a single plant was found on Krakatau a few months after the event; 100 years later – although the only fauna are snakes, insects, rats, bats and birds – it seems almost as though the vegetation was never disturbed.

Krakatau may have blown itself to smithereens, but it is currently being replaced by Anak Krakatau, which has been on the ascendant ever since its first appearance nearly 80 years ago. It has a restless and uncertain temperament, sending out showers of glowing rocks and belching smoke and ashes.

## Getting There & Away

Most visitors to Krakatau come from Carita or the other beach resorts on the west coast of Java. However, Krakatau officially lies in Sumatra's Lampung province, and it is slightly quicker and cheaper to reach Krakatau from the small port of Kalianda (p000), 30km north of the ferry terminal at Bakauheni.

Tour operators out of Carita (see p122) will take down the names of interested travellers wanting to share a ride, but usually the numbers just aren't available and you will have to charter.

Prices vary depending on the quality of the boat, but always charter the best boat you can afford. During the rainy season (November to March) there are strong currents and rough seas, but even during the dry season strong southeast winds can whip up the swells and make a crossing inadvisable. Krakatau is a 90-minute ride from Carita in a fast boat when weather conditions are fine. It's a long one-day trip, but it's definitely worth the effort – *if* you can hire a safe boat.

Small fishing boats may be cheap, but so are the tales of travellers who spent the night, or longer, adrift in high swells. Reliable boats with radios and life jackets start at 1,800,000Rp for a small utility boat (maximum of six people) and go up to around 3,300,000Rp for faster boats (eight to 10 people). These can be organised through Carita agents or **Marina Lippo** ( ☎ 0253-801 525) in Carita.

**Wanawisata Alamhayati** ( ☎ 571 0392) also arranges expensive tours to Krakatau from Jakarta.

*(Continued on page 133)*

# Natural
# Indonesia

From volcanoes to orangutans, from dense jungle to coral reefs, Indonesia is a riot of action, colour and beauty. Travelling the islands is like a treasure hunt: the infinite diversity of nature across the archipelago will astound. It may have the world's fourth-largest populace, but Indonesia is also home to a fabulous variety of flora and fauna.

## ANIMALS

Indonesia's wildlife is as diverse as everything else about the archipelago. Great apes, tigers, elephants and monkeys – lots of monkeys – plus one mean lizard are just some of the more-notable critters you may encounter. And then there are the thousands of species that you've never seen on a nature special or in a zoo. Case in point: the one-horned Javan rhinoceros, one of the world's most critically endangered mammals, whose last refuge in Indonesia is the Ujung Kulon National Park (p133). Add in life underwater, and the biodiversity here is astonishing. See p74 for full details.

### Orangutans

Exemplifying a placid lifestyle that appeals to many a human slacker, Indonesia's orangutans are an iconic part of the nation's image. The world's largest arboreal mammal, they once swung through the forest canopy throughout all of Southeast Asia, but are now found only in Sumatra and Borneo. Researchers fear that the few that do remain will not survive the continued loss of habitat to logging and agriculture.

Deeply fascinating to view, orangutans have an important role in drawing people

## top five

### PLACES TO SEE ORANGUTANS

Although Sumatra is famous for orangutans, don't underestimate Kalimantan.

**Sumatra – Bukit Lawang** (p378) Home to over 5000 orangutans, Bukit Lawang is one of the world's top spots for viewing these great apes.

**Kalimantan – Betung Kerihun National Park** (p605) Hugging the border with Malaysia, here you can venture up wild rivers to find orangutans.

**Kalimantan – Danau Sentarum National Park** (p605) Spot crocodiles, monkeys and our ginger-haired relatives in the marshes of this national park.

**Kalimantan – Tanjung Puting National Park** (p614) Our favourite place to spot orangutans in their natural habitat. This gem offers the world's easiest adventure travel.

**Kalimantan – Kutai National Park** (p641) Offering the chance to see truly wild orangutans, here you'll find 200,000 hectares of diverse ecosystems. Treks encounter some of Indonesia's most unusual fauna.

Orangutan in Tanjung Puting National Park (p614)
ANDREW BROWNBILL

No prizes for guessing who the star attractions are at Komodo National Park (p528), Komodo
KARL LEHMANN

into the Indonesian wilds. Travellers exposed to the exotic beauty of these lands often return home ready to fight for its salvation. For more on orangutans, see p379 and p381.

At the other end of the scale, the Sangkulirang Mountains in East Kalimantan are home to easily the least disturbed orangutans on the planet: the 2000 here were only discovered in 2008. This is very remote country; Sangkulirang (Map p633) is the closest town, while Kutai National Park (p641) is to the south.

## Komodo Dragons

Tales of beasts with huge claws, menacing teeth and evil yellow forked tongues floated around the islands of Nusa Tenggara for centuries until only about 100 years ago, when the first Westerners brought one out of its namesake island home near Flores.

And as menacing as these 2.5m-long lizards look, their disposition is worse. Scores of humans have perished after being attacked, and the Komodos regularly stalk and eat small deer. One researcher compared the sound of a Komodo pounding across the ground in pursuit to that of a machine gun. Only in 2009 was one of the lizard's deadly secrets revealed: venom in its bite that sends the victim into shock and prevents blood from clotting. Yikes!

For more on Komodos, see p530.

Swim with turtles at Pulau Menjangan (p347), Bali
TIM ROCK

## Birds

Astrapias, sicklebills, riflebirds and manucodes are just some of the exotic and
beautifully feathered creatures you'll see
in the skies of Indonesia. On Papua alone,
there isn't just one type of bird called 'bird
of paradise', but 30 (see p788). For many
birdwatchers, the dream of a lifetime is to
witness a pair of these birds perform their
spectacular mating dance.

Birdwatching is popular in many of the
national parks; guides will always be ready
to point out birds, although they may not
know much more about them than you.
Periplus's illustrated guidebook *Birding In-
donesia* makes a good companion. On Kalimantan, Tangkoko-Batuangas Dua Saudara
Nature Reserve (p716) has regular birdwatching tours. On Bali, you can go on guided walks
looking for birds in and around Ubud (p313).

Papua easily wins the birdwatching crown, however. Its range of birds includes migrating species from Australia and as far as Siberia. See the boxed text, p788, for an idea of the
myriad bird-spotting opportunities.

## Life Underwater

Indonesia's incredible range of life on land is easily matched beneath the waves. The waters
around Komodo, Sulawesi, the east coast of Papua, and even some spots in Java and Bali
are home to a kaleidoscopic array of corals, reef dwellers and pelagics.

Huge sunfish, up to 2.5m in length and twice as high, are a much-treasured sight for
divers. These enigmatic fish can usually be found feeding on jellyfish and plankton in the
balmy waters around many of Indonesia's islands large and small. Manta rays are also found
in abundance. Even above the waves you're likely to see porpoises or other sea mammals.

For recommendations of the best dive sites, see p820.

---

### top five

**PLACES FOR
WATCHING WILDLIFE**

**Bali – Pulau Menjangan** (p347) Famous for a
dozen superb dive sites that can be reached on
a day trip from anywhere on the island.

**Nusa Tenggara – Komodo National Park**
(p529) The legendary Komodo dragon reigns
supreme.

**Papua – Danau Habbema** (p811) Cuscus, birds
of paradise and maybe tree kangaroos are
found near this isolated lake.

**Sulawesi – Lore Lindu National Park** (p690)
Tarsiers, birds of paradise, monkeys and more
are found in this protected area.

**Sumatra – Gunung Leuser National Park**
(p417) Famous for orangutans, but also home
to monkeys, elephants and tigers.

## PLANTS

Simply wandering a deserted back lane in Bali, a cathedral of bamboo arching over the road, will be enough to convince you of Indonesia's botanical magic.

Whether cultivated or wild, frangipani trees are alive with fragrant blooms, many ready to drop into your hand. Head off on a trek and be prepared for a profusion of orchids (2500 different species at last count), flowers, vines and magnificent brooding banyan trees. You can expect a riot of bougainvillea, lotus blossoms, hibiscus and a kaleidoscope of other blooms across the archipelago. Impossibly complex heliconias hang from vines in all their multifaceted crimson, orange and golden glory. In forested areas, teak, clove, rattan and a plethora of palms are among the trees providing welcome shade from the equatorial sun.

Amid all of the luxuriant flora are many edible plants. Passionfruit is common as are bananas. Look for coffee plantations, especially in the hills of Bali near Munduk (p354). On the Maluku – the original Spice Islands – you can still catch the scent of vanilla. Throughout Indonesia, markets abound with oodles of tropical fruits and citrus.

But it wouldn't be Indonesia without some real characters. Consider *Rafflesia arnoldii,* the world's largest flower, and the *Amorphophallus titanium,* the world's tallest flower. Both can be found on Sumatra and parts of Kalimantan and Java. In fact, the former may well be the world's stinkiest flower (p436).

See the world's largest (and stinkiest) flower, the *Rafflesia arnoldii,* in West Sumatra (p436)

KARL LEHMANN

Stand in awe beneath Indonesia's second-largest volcano, the classic Gunung Rinjani (p506), Lombok
JAMES

## GUNUNG API – FIRE MOUNTAINS

If you're keen to ascend spectacular peaks, watch the sun rise through the haze of steaming craters and peer into the earth's bubbling core, you've come to the right place. Indonesia is *the* destination for volcano enthusiasts. This is thanks to the fact that it lies on a significant segment of the Pacific 'Ring of Fire', where two large crustal plates (the Indian Ocean and western Pacific) are forced under the massive Eurasian plate, where they melt at approximately 100km beneath the surface. Some of the magma rises and erupts to form the string of volcanic islands across Indonesia. Its volcanoes do erupt, sometimes with shocking consequences (see Krakatau, p123). With tectonic activity comes devastating earthquakes and tsunamis, such as those of Boxing Day 2004, off Java in July 2006 and Sumatra in 2009.

# TOP VOLCANOES

## Java

- **Gunung Bromo** (p245) Journey to Bromo, a sacred and eerie peak surrounded by the desolate Sea of Sands.
- **Gunung Merapi** (p192) Tackle the lush, jungle-covered slopes of Merapi, an almost perfectly conical volcano dominating the cultural heartland of Java.
- **Gunung Krakatau** (p123) Take a boat trip to see the remnants, and new beginnings, of one of the world's A-list volcanoes.
- **Kawah Ijen** (p250) Spend the night at a peaceful coffee plantation before climbing this volcano to view its remarkable turquoise sulphur lake.

## Bali

- **Gunung Agung** (p330) Take one of the numerous routes up and down Bali's tallest and most sacred mountain; include seldom-visited temples in your journey.

## Sumatra

- **Gunung Sibayak** (p385) Enjoy an easy and rewarding day hike, just outside Berastagi – a few hours' bus ride from Medan.
- **Gunung Merapi** (p411) Climb Sumatra's most restless volcano in the middle of the night for a sunrise view from the top.
- **Gunung Kerinci** (p442) Brave this challenging ascent up into the heavens on Sumatra's highest peak.

## Nusa Tenggara

- **Gunung Rinjani** (p506) Join pilgrims at the summit of this sacred peak, which has a huge crater lake overlooked by the active cone of Gunung Baru.
- **Kelimutu** (p548) Wonder at the ethereal scenery atop this volcano, with its three differently coloured crater lakes and lunar landscape.
- **Wawo Muda** (p544) Climb the summit of this cone, which only emerged in 2001, and view several small lakes of a rusty red hue.

## Maluku

- **Gunung Api Gamalama** (p734) Catch the view from Ternate of lovely Tidore and its string of offshore volcanoes.
- **Gunung Api** (p761) Scramble up this volcano in the Banda Islands to experience the awesome sunrise views.

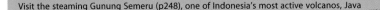

Visit the steaming Gunung Semeru (p248), one of Indonesia's most active volcanos, Java
JANE SWEENEY

Life is a beach at the Togean Islands (p696)
GREG ELMS

## top five
**BEAUTY SPOTS**

Jaw-dropping beauty can be found across Indonesia, often when you least expect it. Here's five of our favourites (culled from a long list):

**Gunung Bromo** (p245) It may not be Java's tallest volcano, but it's easily its most magnificent. From its summit you can see two other volcanoes (one in various stages of activity), all set in the vast caldera of yet another volcano.

**Pulau Weh** (p409) An idyllic tropical island off Sumatra that has superb diving in its azure waters.

**Togean Islands** (p696) An adventure to reach, but more than repay the effort with rings of perfect beaches, dense jade-green forests and a perfect low-key vibe.

**Banda Islands** (p756) On the verge of being descended upon by the tourist mobs, but like cookies in a jar to a kid, the Banda Islands remain tantalisingly out of reach. The 10 islands spiral and twist around each other, agleam with white, deserted sands.

**Danau Sentani** (p794) A lake near the coast of Papua that's dotted along the shore with timeless fishing villages built on stilts over the reflecting waters. At sunset (and sunrise) the water glows with every colour in the rainbow.

## NATIONAL PARKS

Most of Indonesia's national parks are very isolated, but the extra effort required to get to them is more than rewarded by the country's magnificent wilderness. Visitor facilities are minimal at best, but at many of the parks you'll find locals who are enthusiastic about *their* park and ready to guide you to its hidden gems. For further information, see p75.

Tents, sleeping bags and other gear are often available in most major towns. Many parks have an entrance gate, where you register and pay a minimal fee, and hire a guide. If there is no entrance gate, you should first visit the nearest Perlindungan Hutan dan Konservasi Alam (PHKA) office to check conditions and report your intended route. The Ministry of Forestry, which runs the parks, has a useful website: www.dephut.go.id.

*(Continued from page 124)*

# UJUNG KULON NATIONAL PARK

On the remote southwestern tip of Java, this Unesco World Heritage–listed **national park** (admission 59,500Rp) covers about 760 sq km of land, including large Pulau Panaitan. Because of its isolation and difficult access, Ujung Kulon has remained an outpost of prime rainforest and untouched wilderness in heavily developed Java; alongside some fine opportunities for hiking, it also has good beaches with intact coral reefs. Few people visit the park (which was Indonesia's first national park), but it is one of the most rewarding, if remote environments in all Java.

Ujung Kulon is best known as the last refuge in Indonesia of the one-horned Javan rhinoceros. There are only thought to be around 55 in Ujung Kulon (and perhaps a dozen or so in Vietnam), so it's one of the globe's most critically endangered mammals. That said, numbers are thought to be stable here, and breeding is occurring: in 2006 evidence of at least four baby rhinos was confirmed.

Javan rhinos are an extremely rare sight and you are far more likely to come across banteng (wild cattle), wild pigs, otters, squirrels, leaf monkeys and gibbons. Panthers also live in the forest and crocodiles in the river estuaries, but these are also rare. Green turtles nest in some of the bays and Ujung Kulon also has a wide variety of bird life. On Pulau Peucang, sambar deer, long-tailed macaques and big monitor lizards are common, and there is good snorkelling around coral reefs.

The main park area is on the peninsula, but it also includes the nearby island of Panaitan and the smaller offshore islands of Peucang and Handeuleum. Much of the peninsula is dense lowland rainforest and a mixture of scrub, grassy plains, swamps, pandanus palms and long stretches of sandy beach on the west and south coasts. Walking trails follow the coast around much of the peninsula and loop around Gunung Payung on the western tip.

## Information

The **Labuan PHKA office** ( ☎ 801 731; ◷ 8am-4pm Mon-Fri) is a useful source of information, but you pay your entry fee when you enter the park at the park office in Tamanjaya or on the islands. Try to pick up a copy of the excellent, but rarely available, *Visitor's Guidebook* to the *Trails of Ujung Kulon National Park* (25,000Rp) from the park office.

The best time to visit Ujung Kulon is in the dry season (April to October), when the sea is generally calm and the reserve less boggy. Be aware that malaria has been reported in Ujung Kulon.

Guides must be hired for hiking in the park and cost around 275,000Rp per day. Bring along lightweight food, such as packaged noodles, and drinking water if you are trekking; otherwise food can be organised by tour operators or the park wardens. Supplies are available in Tamanjaya, but in Sumur and Labuan there is more choice.

## Activities

Tamanjaya village, the entry point to the park, has accommodation and can arrange guides for the three-day hike across to the west coast and on to Pulau Peucang. This is the most rewarding way to explore the park and its diversity. It can be tackled by anyone of reasonable fitness but is not a stroll.

Conditions on the trail are basic – there are rough shelters, but some are almost derelict. If you have a tent, bring it. The trail heads to the south coast and the hut near Pantai Cibandawoh. The second day is a five-hour walk along the beach to the hut at Sungai Cibunar – rivers have to be waded through. On the third day, most hikers cross over the hills to the west coast at Cidaon, opposite Peucang. An alternative and longer trail with good coastal scenery goes from Cibunar via Sanghiang Sirah and the lighthouse at Tanjung Layar, the westernmost tip of mainland Java.

**Pulau Peucang** is the other main entry into the park but can only be reached by chartered boat. Good but expensive accommodation and a restaurant are run by a private tour company, **Wanawisata Alamhayati** ( ☎ 571 0392). Peucang also has beautiful white-sand beaches and coral reefs on the sheltered eastern coast. Hikers might be able to hitch a lift on a boat out of Peucang, but don't count on it.

There is also comfortable but simple accommodation at **Pulau Handeuleum**, which is ringed by mangroves and doesn't have Peucang's attractions. Boats or canoes can be hired for the short crossing to Cigenter, on the mainland opposite Pulau Handeuleum, and other trails can be explored on this side of the park.

JAVA

Large **Pulau Panaitan** is more expensive to reach but has some fine beaches and hiking. It is a day's walk between the PHKA posts at Legon Butun and Legon Haji, or you can walk to the top of Gunung Raksa, topped by a Hindu statue of Ganesh, from Citambuyung on the east coast. Panaitan is a legendary **surfing** spot (see the boxed text, p824), with breaks including the infamous One Palm Point, a left-hand barrel that spins over a sharp reef. The controversial surf camp located here is now closed and surf tours are once again heading to Panaitan.

## Tours

Most tours from Carita, as offered by travel agencies such as **Black Rhino** ( ☎ 802 818; blackrhinojava@yahoo.com) are four days/three nights with a transfer by car to Sumur, then a boat to Handeuleum (about seven to eight hours), where you camp. Then you trek to Jamang and camp overnight at the ranger's post. The next day you can explore around Tanjung Alang Alang and the nearby beaches, then return. The all-inclusive tours cost around US$265 per person for a minimum of four.

Boat hire from Labuan or Carita can also be arranged. A three-day return trip to Pulau Peucang costs around US$350 in a speedboat (2½ hours, maximum six people). The park office in Tamanjaya can arrange boat transfers to the islands for around 2,000,000Rp.

**Wanawisata Alamhayati** ( ☎ 571 0392) has allinclusive, two-day, three-night tours to Pulau Peucang for around US$300 per person, depending on accommodation, for a minimum of two people.

Surf packages are also available to Panaitan; Bali-based **Surf Panaitan** ( ☎ 0361-850 0254; www .surfpanaitan.com) charges from US$740 for a seven-day trip, including transfers from Jakarta airport.

## Sleeping & Eating

Advance bookings are recommended for Pulau Peucang and Handeuleum, particularly at weekends. Within the park you can camp or stay at the primitive huts for a small fee. Bring food for yourself and your guide.

**Pulau Umang** ( ☎ 0813 8034 5450; www.pulau-umang .com; weekday/weekend r 750,000/1,500,000Rp; ☒ ☒ ) It's not exactly a Robinson Crusoe experience, but this island has plenty going for it, with fine cottages, built in a kind of contemporarymeets-rustic style right on a white-sand beach,

and has two pools, spas and some snorkelling offshore. It's an idyllic spot, but beware the jet-skis and banana boats, and the restaurant and service standards could be better. Pulau Umang is just offshore from the village of Sumur.

Other options:

**Flora A & B bungalows** (d US$80; ☒ ) On Pulau Peucang and much more luxurious than its guest house; has hot water and fridges. Add 15% tax to all rates, including meals in the very good restaurant.

**Pulau Handeuleum guest house** (r 120,000Rp) In pleasant surroundings with a kitchen – bring your own food, as the island has no other dining options. Add 15% tax to room rates.

**Pulau Peucang guest house** (d 440,000Rp)
**Sunda Jaya homestay** (r per person 50,000Rp) In Tamanjaya; basic digs and meals.
**Wisma Wisata Alam** ( ☎ 0253-802 224; Jl Dermaga; r 50,000-65,000Rp) Also in Tamanjaya; homestay with simple rooms and good views of Krakatau.

## Getting There & Away

The cheapest way to get to the park is by minibus from Labuan to Sumur (32,000Rp, 3½ hours), and then an *ojek* to Tamanjaya (50,000Rp, one hour) along a badly rutted road.

Or you could charter a boat to get here. Given the long stretch of open sea, fork out for a decent one. Surf tours use their own transport.

## BOGOR

☎ 0251 / pop 830,000

'A romantic little village' is how Sir Stamford Raffles described Bogor when he made it his country home during the British interregnum. As an oasis of unpredictable European weather – it is credited with 322 thunderstorms a year – cool, quiet Bogor was long the chosen retreat of starch-collared colonials escaping the stifling and crowded capital.

Today, the long arm of Jakarta reaches almost the whole way to Bogor, and while a ribbon of green still just about survives between the two, the city is already choked with the overspill of the capital's perennial traffic problem.

But while Bogor's transformation into a distant Jakartan suburb continues apace, the real oasis remains untouched. Planted in the very centre of the city, with the traffic passing idly by, Bogor's botanical gardens are truly world class.

The gardens can be visited as a day trip from Jakarta, or since the capital is only an hour away, Bogor can be used as a cooler and more manageable base from which to visit the capital. From Bogor you can venture to the mountains that surround the city or continue on to Bandung or Pelabuhan Ratu.

Though Bogor stands at a height of only 290m, it's appreciably cooler than Jakarta. Visitors in the wet season should bear in mind the town's 'City of Rain' moniker.

## Information

Wartels can be found next to the post office and train station. There's free wi-fi at the Botani Square mall. Bogor has plenty of banks. Both those listed below have an ATM.

**BCA bank** (Jl Ir H Juanda 28)

**BII bank** (Jl Dewi Sartika)

**Internet** (Jl Merdeka; per hr 7000Rp)

**PHKA Headquarters** (Jl Ir H Juanda 15; ☻ 7am-2.30pm Mon-Thu, to 11am Fri) The official body for the administration of all of Indonesia's wildlife reserves and national parks; located next to the main garden gates.

**Post office** Just south of the western entrance to the gardens; also has internet access.

**Tourist office** ( ☎ 081 111 0347; agus_pribadi@hotmail .com; Jl Dewi Sartika 51; ☻ 8am-4pm) Outrageously, the city authorities fail to provide the committed staff at this very helpful office a landline phone. The team here can help out with most queries, provide a city map, and offer excellent, well-priced tours (p137).

## Sights
### KEBUN RAYA

At the heart of Bogor are the fabulous botanical gardens, known as the **Kebun Raya** (Great Garden; www.bogor.indo.net.id/kri; admission 9500Rp; ☻ 8am-5pm), the city's green lung of around 87 hectares. Governor General Raffles first developed a garden here, but the spacious grounds of the Istana Bogor (Presidential Palace) were expanded by Dutch botanist Professor Reinwardt, with assistance from London's Kew Gardens, and officially opened in 1817. It was from these gardens that various colonial cash crops, such as tea, cassava, tobacco and cinchona, were developed by Dutch botanists including Johannes Teysmann, during the infamous Cultivation Period in the 19th century. The park is still a major centre for botanical research in Indonesia. This was the one place in Indonesia George W Bush visited when he dropped by the country in 2006.

Allow yourself at least half a day to enjoy Kebun Raya, while keen gardeners could spend a week here and not be bored. It's tricky to pick out highlights in such a verdant wonderland – there are more than 15,000 species of trees and plants – but the gardens are said to contain 400 types of magnificent palms, including the footstool palm native to Indonesia, which tops 40m. There's a good stock of graceful pandan trees (look out for their unusual aerial roots) and some huge agave (used to make tequila) and cacti in the Mexican section. Drop by the Orchid House (admission an extra 2000Rp) and take in the lovely ponds, which have giant water lilies over a metre across, and look out for monitor lizards, exotic bird life and deer.

Near the main entrance of the gardens is a small **monument**, erected in memory of Olivia Raffles, who died in 1814 and was buried in Batavia. There is also a **cemetery** near the palace with Dutch headstones including the tomb of DJ de Eerens, a former governor general.

Crowds flock here on Sunday, but the gardens are quiet at most other times. The southern gate is the main entrance and home to Bogor's only touts; other gates are only open on Sunday and holidays. There's a great cafe-restaurant inside the gardens (see p138).

### ZOOLOGICAL MUSEUM

Near the entrance to the botanical gardens, this **museum** (admission 2000Rp; ☻ 8am-4pm Sat-Thu, to noon Fri) has a motley but interesting collection of zoological oddities, including the skeleton of a blue whale, giant stick insects, beetles as big as tennis balls and a pooch-sized Flores rat.

### ISTANA BOGOR

In the northwestern corner of the botanical gardens, the summer palace of the president was formerly the opulent official residence of the Dutch governors general from 1870 to 1942.

Today, herds of white-spotted deer roam the immaculate lawns and the building contains Sukarno's huge art collection, which largely focuses on the female figure. The palace is only open to groups (minimum 10) by prior arrangement, and children are not allowed inside. Contact the tourist office for more information.

### OTHER SIGHTS

The **Batutulis** is an inscribed stone dedicated to Sri Baduga Maharaja (1482–1521), a Pajaran

# BOGOR & KEBUN RAYA

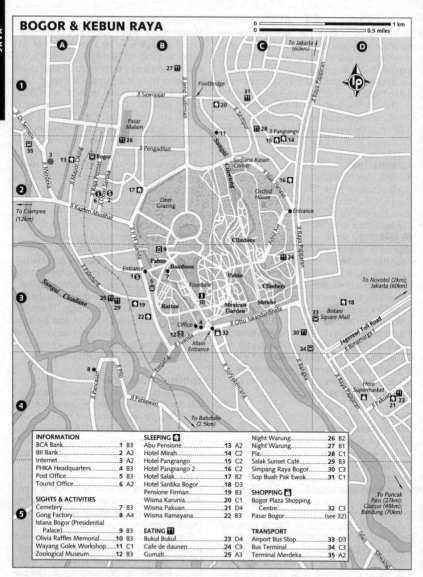

| INFORMATION | |
|---|---|
| BCA Bank | 1 B3 |
| BII Bank | 2 A2 |
| Internet | 3 A2 |
| PHKA Headquarters | 4 B3 |
| Post Office | 5 B3 |
| Tourist Office | 6 A2 |

| SIGHTS & ACTIVITIES | |
|---|---|
| Cemetery | 7 B3 |
| Gong Factory | 8 A4 |
| Istana Bogor (Presidential Palace) | 9 B3 |
| Olivia Raffles Memorial | 10 B3 |
| Wayang Golek Workshop | 11 C1 |
| Zoological Museum | 12 B3 |

| SLEEPING | |
|---|---|
| Abu Pensione | 13 A2 |
| Hotel Mirah | 14 C2 |
| Hotel Pangrango | 15 C2 |
| Hotel Pangrango 2 | 16 C2 |
| Hotel Salak | 17 B2 |
| Hotel Santika Bogor | 18 D3 |
| Pensione Firman | 19 B3 |
| Wisma Karunia | 20 C1 |
| Wisma Pakuan | 21 D4 |
| Wisma Ramayana | 22 B3 |

| EATING | |
|---|---|
| Bukul Bukul | 23 D4 |
| Cafe de daunen | 24 C3 |
| Gumati | 25 A3 |

| Night Warung | 26 B2 |
|---|---|
| Night Warung | 27 B1 |
| Pia | 28 C1 |
| Salak Sunset Café | 29 B3 |
| Simpang Raya Bogor | 30 C3 |
| Sop Buah Pak Ewok | 31 C1 |

| SHOPPING | |
|---|---|
| Bogor Plaza Shopping Centre | 32 C3 |
| Pasar Bogor | (see 32) |

| TRANSPORT | |
|---|---|
| Airport Bus Stop | 33 D3 |
| Bus Terminal | 34 C3 |
| Terminal Merdeka | 35 A2 |

king credited with great mystical power. The stone is housed in a small shrine visited by pilgrims – remove your shoes and pay a small donation before entering. Batutulis is 2.5km south of the botanical gardens, on Jl Batutulis. It's almost opposite the former home of Sukarno. His request to be buried here was ignored by Suharto, who wanted the

former president's grave as far away from the capital as possible.

One of the few remaining gongsmiths in West Java is located in Bogor. Visitors are welcome to drop by the **gong factory** ( ☎ 832 4132; Jl Pancasan 17), where gamelan instruments are smelted over a charcoal fire. As it takes two weeks to beat a copper gong into shape you may want to tip the workers here a note or two. A few pricey gongs and *wayang golek* puppets are on sale.

Pak Dase makes quality puppets at his **wayang golek workshop** (Lebak Kantin RT 02/VI), down by the river, just north of the botanical gardens. Take the footbridge to Wisma Karunia (see right) from Jl Jenderal Sudirman and ask for Pak Dase in the labyrinthine *kampung* (village).

## Tours

Tours of Bogor taking in a working-class *kampung*, and various cottage industries including a gong factory and tofu and *krupuk* (prawn cracker) kitchens can be arranged through the tourist office (see p135) for around 150,000/250,000Rp per half-day/day. Four-day, three-night eco-trips to Halimun National Park cost €200, while two-night trips to Garut and Pangandaran are €150. Some of the excellent English-speaking guides here include Nyoman and **Agus** (agus_pribadi@hotmail.com).

**Alwi** ( ☎ 0813 8434 3711; alwiadin@yahoo.com), who used to work in the office here, also organises excellent tours in the Bogor area. It's possible to visit local villages to teach children English in exchange for food and lodging.

## Sleeping
### BUDGET

Bogor has quite a few family-run budget places, though standards have slipped a little as the number of travellers passing through has declined. Most are on the west side of the gardens.

**Pensione Firman** ( ☎ 832 3246; Jl Paledang 48; r 60,000-140,000Rp) This venerable guest house has been serving travellers for decades and, though it's looking decidedly ramshackle these days, it's still a secure and friendly base – English-speaking owner Warda looks after her guests well, offers cheap meals and serves up free tea. Rooms here are very basic, though.

**Abu Pensione** ( ☎ 832 2893; Jl Mayor Oking 15; r with fan 90,000-150,000Rp, with air-con & hot water 220,000Rp; ❄ ) This is a good choice near the train station, with a selection of decent, clean rooms set at the rear of the property around a pleasant, quiet garden. There's a great little cafe, with cheap grub and views over a gurgling stream. Selfi, a guide based here, offers good (if a little pricey) city tours from 200,000Rp for a half-day trip.

**Wisma Pakuan** ( ☎ 831 9430; Jl Pakuan 12; r with balcony 150,000Rp, with air-con 200,000Rp; ❄ ) Pakuan occupies a large, modern family home a short stroll from the bus terminal. Rooms are very generously sized, in good condition and have hot-water bathrooms, but ask for one at the rear, as it's located on a busy street.

Also recommended:

**Wisma Karunia** ( ☎ 832 3411; Jl Sempur 33-35; r without private bathroom 60,000Rp, s/d with private bathroom 60,000/85,000Rp) A hike from the centre, but it offers a quiet base and it's run by friendly folk.

**Wisma Ramayana** ( ☎ 832 0364; Jl Ir H Juanda 54; r 80,000Rp) Worth considering as it's so close to the gardens, but some rooms are a tad damp.

### MIDRANGE & TOP END

Bogor is strangely lacking in good midrange options.

**Hotel Pangrango 2** ( ☎ 832 1482; Jl Raya Pajajaran 32; budget/standard r 215,000/545,000Rp; ❄ ⊠ ) Large concrete hotel offering spacious if dated standard rooms and a good restaurant, but traffic noise can be an issue here. Note that no alcohol is served.

**Hotel Mirah** ( ☎ 834 8040; www.mirahhotelbogor.com; Jl Pangrango 9A; r from 349,000Rp, ste 785,000Rp; ❄ 🛜 ⊠ ) A gaudily opulent hotel with a variety of rooms: the older doubles are bland, but rooms in the impressive newer wing are much better. All have free wi-fi and a large, flat-screen, multi-channel TV.

**Novotel** ( ☎ 827 1555; www.novotel-bogor.com; Bogor Raya; r from US$62; ❄ 🖥 🛜 ⊠ ) Arguably the best hotel in the city, set just east of the centre, the nonsmoking Novotel has its own 18-hole golf course. Standards are high here and rates are moderate given the comfort levels and facilities, which include a spa, a well-equipped gym, a tennis court and two restaurants.

**Hotel Salak** ( ☎ 837 3111; www.hotelsalak.co.id; Jl Ir H Juanda 8; r from 720,000Rp; ❄ 🖥 ⊠ ) Large colonial-style hotel within walking distance of the gardens with a plethora of cafes and restaurants and good business facilities. Rooms are spacious and comfortable enough, but would benefit from a make-over. Add 21% tax to room rates.

**Hotel Santika Bogor** ( ☎ 840 0707; www.santika.com/bogor; Jl Raya Pajajaran; r from 750,000Rp; ❄ 🖥 🛜 ⊠ ) Huge new nonsmoking hotel just behind the Botani Square mall that ticks all the right boxes in terms of minimalist design, though perhaps the effect is just a little soulless. Check the website for promotional deals.

Or try:

**Hotel Pangrango** ( ☎ 832 8284; Jl Pangrango 23; http://hotel-pangrango.co.id; r/deluxe r incl breakfast 325,000/550,000Rp; ❖ ⓐ ) The carpeted rooms are looking old-fashioned at this peculiar mock-Tudor setting, though they are spacious. This is a booze-free hotel.

## Eating & Drinking

Both the Bogor Trade Mall and the upmarket Botani Square shopping malls have good food courts including Western-style fast food, Indonesian favourites and cafes. Cheap warungs appear at night along Jl Dewi Sartika and Jl Jenderal Sudirman.

**Sop Buah Pak Ewok** ( ☎ 215 1369; Jl Bukittunggul 5; fruit punch 7000Rp) This is a great, very casual place popular with students for its inexpensive, delicious and refreshing bowls of fruit punch, which are tropical fruits of the season served up with ice. Other snacks including noodles and rice dishes are available.

**Pia** ( ☎ 832 9765; Jl Pangrango 10; pies from 11,000Rp) A stylish little eatery with low tables facing a narrow courtyard/car park, this place is renowned throughout West Java for its apple pie (though other fruit flavours including strawberry are available, and there are plenty of savoury options including chicken). It's also good for a bowl of soup, coffee or juice.

**Simpang Raya Bogor** ( ☎ 420 1577; Jl Raya Pajajaran; meals from 15,000Rp) A huge Pandang restaurant serving up Sumatra's finest and spiciest. Heaves with customers by early evening; stroll on in and find a seat wherever there's room.

**Bukul Bukul** ( ☎ 838 4905; Jl Pakuan 14; mains 16,000-22,000Rp; ❖ 11.30am-10pm) Sleek and stylish restaurant with a Zen-like garden that makes a great setting for a meal, Bukul Bukul is surprisingly affordable. It specialises in Indonesian and Sundanese cuisine. No alcohol is served, but there's a mocktail list, or you're welcome to BYO for no charge.

**Gumati** ( ☎ 832 4318; www.cafegumati.com; Jl Paledang 28; mains 15,000-59,000Rp; ❖ 10am-10pm) An imposing restaurant with wonderful vistas over Bogor's red-tiled rooftops to Gunung Salak from its two huge terraces – there's even a small pool here. You'll find an extensive menu, with tapas-style snacks and specials (try the *paket timbal komplit*, which gives you a selection of dishes); no booze though.

**Café de Daunen** ( ☎ 835 0023; meals 25,000-59,000Rp) Inside the botanical gardens, this is the nicest setting in town for a meal, with sweeping views down across a meadow to the water lily ponds. It's a little pricey, but the revamped menu has tasty food including fish and chips, pasta and good Indonesian dishes. For a refreshing drink try the *bandrek* (tea made with ginger and herbs).

**Salak Sunset Café** (Jl Paledang 38; mains 20,000Rp) For a beer, your best bet is this low-key place, geared to travellers, with cool Bintang and Western food such as pizzas and spaghetti.

## Getting There & Away

### BUS

Every 15 minutes or so, buses depart from Jakarta's Kampung Rambutan bus terminal (normal/air-con 9000/12,000Rp, 45 minutes).

Hourly air-conditioned Damri buses head direct to Jakarta's Sukarno-Hatta airport (55,000Rp) from 4am to 6pm from Jl Raya Pajajaran.

Buses depart frequently to Cianjur (14,000/20,000Rp, two hours) and Bandung (30,000/42,000Rp, 3½ hours), but at weekends these buses are not allowed to go via the scenic Puncak Pass and therefore travel via Sukabumi. Other bus destinations from Bogor include Pelabuhan Ratu (27,000Rp, three hours) and Labuan (38,000Rp, four hours).

Air-con, door-to-door *travel* minibuses go to Bandung for 60,000Rp. **Dimas Dewa** ( ☎ 653 671) has the best buses. Phone for a pick-up.

Damri air-con buses run approximately hourly (55,000Rp) to/from Jakarta's Sukarno-Hatta international airport from a bus stop on Jl Raya Pajajaran, across the road from the bus station.

### CAR

Bogor is a good place to hire a car and driver for a trip around the countryside; ask the tourist board to recommend someone – many speak English. Prices start at around 450,000Rp per day.

### TRAIN

Comfortable *Pakuan* express trains (8500Rp, one hour) leave Bogor for the capital roughly every hour. Economy trains (4500Rp, 1½ hours) run even more frequently but are usually packed.

## Getting Around

Green *angkot* minibuses (2000Rp) shuttle around town, particularly between the bus terminal and train station. Blue *angkot* run to outlying districts and terminate at Terminal Merdeka. *Angkot* 03 does an anticlockwise loop of the botanical gardens on its way to Jl Kapten Muslihat, near the train station. To the bus terminal from the train station take *angkot* 06.

Becak are banned from the main road encircling the gardens. Taxis are extremely rare in Bogor.

## AROUND BOGOR

### Batutulis (Purnawarman Stone)

Those in need of reminding that all great empires come to an end can head for Batutulis, where sits the large black boulder on which King Purnawarman inscribed his name and footprint around AD 450. His rather immodest inscription, in the Palawa script of South India, is uncannily reminiscent of Percy Shelley's *Ozymandias*, and reads: 'This is the footstep of King Purnawarman of Tarumanegara kingdom, the great conqueror of the world'.

The Ciampea boulder has been raised from its original place and embedded in the shallow water of Sungai Ciaruteun. The inscription on the stone is still remarkably clear after more than 1500 years.

Minibuses make the run to Batutulis from the village of Ciampea, about 12km northwest of Bogor.

### Gunung Halimun National Park

This national park is home to some primary rainforest, but the park has mixed usage and also includes plantations such as the Nirmala Tea Estate. The dominant feature of the park is the rich montane forest in the highland regions around **Gunung Halimun** (1929m), which is the highest peak.

Visitor facilities at the park are undeveloped and park administration is handled by the Gede Pangrango National Park (p142) at Cibodas, located some distance away. The most-visited attractions in the park are the waterfalls near Cikidang and those near the Nirmala estate, but the big drawcard is **white-water rafting. Pt Lintas Seram Nusantara** ( ☎ 021-835 5885; www .arusliar.co.id) in Jakarta organises white-water rafting on the Class II to IV (depending on

season) Sungai Citarak on the southeastern edge of the park. Prices start at 185,000Rp for an hour-long trip up to 425,000Rp for a full day excursion.

The usual access (you need your own transport) is through Cibadak on the Bogor–Pelabuhan Ratu road, from where you turn off to Cikadang and then on to the Nirmala Tea Estate. Rainfall in the park is between 4000mm and 6000mm per year, most of which falls from October to May, when a visit is more or less out of the question.

Speak to the staff at the tourist board in Bogor (p135) about setting up a trip to Halimun.

## SUKABUMI & SELABINTANA

☎ 0266

Sukabumi is a thriving provincial city of 300,000 people at the foot of Pangrango and Gede volcanoes. The main reason to visit is for bus connections to Bandung and Pelabuhan Ratu or to visit Selabintana, a small hill resort 7km north of town.

Selabintana is much less developed than the Puncak Pass resort area to the north of Gunung Gede. It is possible to walk up the hillside to **Sawer Waterfall** and on to **Gunung Gede**, but there is no PHKA post in Selabintana. Selabintana has a golf course, swimming pools and a good selection of midrange hotels.

The old-fashioned, slightly faded **Hotel Selabintana** ( ☎ 221 501; Jl Selabintana, km 7; r from 240,000Rp, VIP bungalows 435,000Rp; 🏊 ) is for sport junkies; it has a golf course, tennis and volleyball courts, two swimming pools and a bar-restaurant for afters. There are rooms or large bungalows with antique furniture. Minibuses from Sukabumi (take a 10 from the Yogyakarta department store) to Selabintana run straight up to the foot of Gunung Gede and terminate at the hotel. Add 21% tax to room prices.

## PELABUHAN RATU

☎ 0266

At the rear of a huge horseshoe-shaped bay, about 90km south of Bogor, Pelabuhan Ratu is a popular seaside retreat for Jakartans. The town itself is pretty humdrum – saved only by its long black-sand beach and the colourful outrigger fishing boats crowding the harbour. Most people come here for the fine surf beaches to the west.

Legend has it that Pelabuhan Ratu (which translates as 'Harbour of the Queen') actually witnessed the creation of Nyai Loro Kidul, the malevolent goddess who takes fishermen and swimmers off to her watery kingdom. Don't wear green on the beach or in the water (it's *her* colour), and in the Hotel Indonesia Samudra a room is set aside for meditating mystics wishing to contact the Queen of the South Seas.

## Information

The **tourist office** ( ☎ 433 544; Jl Kidang Kencana; ☯ 9am-4pm Mon-Fri) is within easy walking distance of the bus terminal – just head for the water. You'll find a wartel next door. The **BCA bank** (Jl Siliwangi) has an ATM and will change US dollars, and there are several other ATMs on the same street.

## Sights & Activities

The coastline here is pounded by crashing surf, and swimming can be treacherous, so take extreme care. Drownings do occur in spite of the warning signs. There are several excellent **surfing** spots in the region; for a really detailed guide consult the Pondok Kecana website (www.ombaktujuh.net).

Aside from its huge **fish market**, Pelabuhan Ratu won't hold your interest for long – it's best to head west once you've got your bearings. **Cimaja**, 8km west of Pelabuhan Ratu, has a pebble beach and some of the south coast's best waves at the **Ombak Tujuh** (Seven Waves) surf break. This is also the place to arrange diving, fishing or motorcycling trips. Surf lessons can be set up here for around 100,000Rp per day (excluding soft board rental); call **Iman** ( ☎ 0857 2305 8595) or **Mumu** ( ☎ 0812 890 1580).

**Pantai Karang Hawu**, 13km west of Pelabuhan Ratu, is a towering cliff with caves, rocks and pools created by a large lava flow. According to legend, it was from the rocks of Karang Hawu that Nyai Loro Kidul leapt into the mighty ocean to regain her lost beauty and never returned. Stairs lead up to a small *kramat* (shrine) at the top.

Further west, about 2km past Cisolok, are the **Cipanas hot springs**. Boiling water sprays into the river, and you can soak downstream where the hot and cold waters mingle. It is a very scenic area; you can walk a few kilometres upstream through the lush forest to a waterfall. Cipanas has changing sheds, warungs and crowds on the weekend.

**Goa Lalay** is a bat cave that's about 4km southeast of Pelabuhan Ratu. It's of limited interest except at sunset, when thousands of small bats flutter off into the night sky.

## Sleeping & Eating

Pelabuhan Ratu is very quiet in the week and fills up at weekends and during holidays.

### PELABUHAN RATU & CITEPUS

Pelabuhan Ratu (and Citepus 3km to the west) have an excess of uninspiring hotels and losmen that are poor value for money. Cimaja, 8km to the west, is far more attractive.

**Hotel Inna Samudra** ( ☎ 431 200; Citepus; s/d from 470,000/560,000Rp; ✹ ☻ ) It's said that Sukarno ordered the construction of this hotel, which was quite luxurious back in the 1960s and still remains a period piece, with most of the faded furnishings still in situ. It has its own beach, and all rooms face the ocean rollers. Room 308 is said to be the haunt of the Queen of the South Seas, and nonguests are free to take a look. Add 21% tax to room rates.

**Queen Restaurant** ( ☎ 431 229; Jl Kidang Kencana; mains 30,000-60,000Rp) On the western end of the harbourfront in Pelabuhan Ratu, this huge Chinese restaurant is the best in town, with a long menu of tempting seafood dishes.

### CIMAJA

This enjoyable, relaxed little place is by far the best base in the area. There's a good choice of accommodation and restaurants and excellent waves on tap offshore (plus a couple of surf shops). The village is split in two by Sungai Cimaja; most accommodation is on the east bank. The following places are listed in the order you approach them from Pelabuhan Ratu.

**Pondok Kencana** ( ☎ 431 465; www.ombaktujuh.net; dm 30,000Rp, r 100,000Rp, bungalows from 240,000Rp; ☻ ) An Australian-owned place with a choice of good-quality wooden bungalows in several price categories, plus a pub-restaurant with Western food such as lamb chops, ham steaks and BLT sandwiches (meals from 40,000Rp). Diving and fishing trips can be organised here. Add 15% tax to room rates.

**Green Room** ( ☎ 432 608; r with fan 50,000Rp) An excellent choice for a budget bed, this simple little place has plain but pleasant digs, and the shared bathrooms are kept very clean. The bar-restaurant has cold beer and Western food including sandwiches and spaghetti carbonara (meals from 25,000Rp).

**Rumah Makan Mirasa** ( ☎ 436 337; r 50,000-70,000Rp) Just past the Didesa, this humble little eatery serves up filling portions of Indonesian grub (meals 15,000Rp) and has simple fan-cooled rooms with no frills.

**Sunset Plaza** ( ☎ 431 125, 0815-7202 2360; r/ste 350,000/500,000Rp; ❄ ▯ ) Just west of Any's, this new hotel has a prime beachfront location. All the spacious, commodious rooms enjoy full-frontal ocean vistas while the suites have four-poster beds. The bar area is terrific, wrapping around two sides of the structure. A 25m hotel pool and a campground (over the road) are both planned. Meals cost from 30,000Rp.

**ourpick Cimaja Square** ( ☎ 644 0800; http://cimajasquare.com; Jl Raya Cisolok; bungalows US$40-60; ▯ ☞ ) This excellent new place offers gorgeous, comfortable wooden bungalows with kitchens, front decks and thatched roofs in a quintessentially Indonesian rice paddy setting. The roadside restaurant has a bistro feel, with tasty Indonesian and European food (meals from 28,000Rp) and stylish bamboo seating.

**Didesa** ( ☎ 433 288; www.didesa.co.id; Jl Raya Cisolok 23; r/ste 460,000/550,000Rp; ☕ ) A well-run, comfortable option with a large beachfront plot and plush bungalows on stilts. You'll also find a sun terrace, surf shop/repair service, a tower for checking wave conditions, and live reggae every Saturday night.

**Café Loma** (Jl Raya Cisolok, meals from 12,000Rp) A great little log cabin–style warung, with gingham tablecloths and cheap local grub like *cap cay*, plus cold beer.

**Any's Tavern** ( ☎ 431 184; www.anystavern.com; Jl Cisolok Raya, km 12; mains around 40,000Rp) What's this? A large, welcoming, stylish and efficient bar-cum-restaurant in the middle of nowhere – well, over Sungai Cimaja anyway. German-owned Any's promises ice-cold beer and has a lengthy cocktail list and a menu of filling fare like bratwurst and chorizo sandwiches. Motorcycling trips can be organised here.

### Getting There & Away

Pelabuhan Ratu is around four hours from Jakarta; regular buses (31,000Rp) run to/from the Kampung Rambutan terminal until 3pm. Buses run throughout the day from Bogor (27,000Rp, three hours) and hourly from Sukabumi (20,000Rp, 2¼ hours). Buses from Sukabumi continue on via Pelabuhan Ratu and Cimaja to Cisolok, and it's possible to continue right along the south coast by a variety of connections.

### Getting Around

*Angkot* run regularly between Pelabuhan Ratu and Cisolok (6000Rp). Motorbikes can be hired for around 60,000Rp per day from locals in Cimaja.

## PUNCAK PASS AREA

Snaking through sleepy tea plantations and terraced fields, the road over the 1500m-high Puncak Pass between Bogor and Cianjur rolls through some of West Java's most sensational scenery. But sadly the Puncak area has fallen victim to its own beauty: usually gridlocked, the highway is lined by an ugly sprawl of overpriced motels, factory-shopping outlets and vacation homes. Weekends are pandemonium (and buses are not even allowed to use the highway because of the congestion). That said, there are a couple of pleasant highland hotels.

Just east of Cisarua, about 12km from Bogor, is the turn-off to **Taman Safari Indonesia** ( ☎ 0251-250 000; www.tamansafari.com; adult/child under 6 years 70,000/60,000Rp, car 15,000Rp; ☽ 9am-5pm), a drive-through safari park with animals including zebras and red pandas, children's rides, animal shows, a pool and plenty of restaurants. A park bus does tours for those without a car.

In the foothills, 7km before the Puncak summit, are the lush, tea-carpeted hills of **Gunung Mas Estate** ( ☎ 0251-252 501; ☽ 9am-5pm Tue-Sun). You can tour the tea factory (7000Rp), which is a couple of kilometres from the highway, or combine it with a guided walk through the plantation itself (60,000Rp). The estate **guest house** (r basic/deluxe 185,000/245,000Rp, bungalows from 600,000Rp) is a quiet, relaxing mountain lodge; add 50,000Rp to all rates on weekends. On the Bandung side of the pass, the historic **Puncak Pass Hotel** ( ☎ 0263-512 503; www.puncakpassresort.com; r/bungalows from 500,000/950,000Rp; ☕ ) is from the Dutch era and has tastefully renovated bungalows that have a classy, polished charm and terrific alpine views.

### Cibodas

☎ 0263

Cibodas, the next village over the Puncak Pass, is famous for its stunning gardens, the **Kebun Raya Cibodas** ( ☎ 512 233; www.bebe.indo.net.id; per person/car 6000/15,500Rp; ☽ 8am-4pm), which are an extension of the Bogor botanical gardens. Spread over the steep lower slopes of Gunung Gede and Gunung Pangrango at an altitude of 1300m to 1440m, these lush gardens are one of the dampest places in Java. The Dutch tried to cultivate quinine here (its bark is used in malaria medication), though the East Javan climate proved more suitable.

You'll find an outstanding collection of ferns, palms, 65 species of eucalypt, Mexican mountain pines, and glasshouses bursting with cacti and succulents. A road loops around the gardens, passing via the Japanese garden with its cherry trees, and there are also paths leading through forests of bamboo to the impressive Cismun waterfall.

There are two guest houses (see below) and a couple of inexpensive cafes in the gardens. Visitors must pay 2000Rp to enter Cibodas village.

### SLEEPING & EATING

**ourpick** Cibodas Guest House ( ☎ 512 051; r from 125,000Rp) At this outstanding little Balinese-owned place, very attractive and well-priced rooms are perched on a shelf overlooking a valley. All come with balcony, sprung mattresses and private bathroom (and hot water on request). The restaurant here (meals 20,000Rp to 50,000Rp) is equally fine and makes the most of the views, serving good Western and Indonesian food, and Bintang. It's about 4km south of the entrance to the gardens.

**Freddy's Homestay** ( ☎ 515 473; r without mandi incl breakfast 150,000Rp) Located down a narrow alleyway 500m before the gardens, Freddy's is *the* base in the area for birders. Rooms here are very simple: they are clean but well overpriced. Nevertheless, this homestay does offer good information and bird books to browse, and guides can be hired. Meals are available too.

**Guest houses** ( ☎ reservations 512 233) Of the two guest houses in the gardens, Wisma Medinella (r from 275,000Rp) is the one to book; it's a lovely new (but rustic) stone-and-timber building with neat little rooms with pine furniture. Wisma Tamu (r from 300,000Rp) has far more basic accommodation, though the house does have character. Both are a 1km walk uphill from the gate. Book ahead and note that student groups often reserve the entire houses on weekends.

### GETTING THERE & AWAY

For travel information from Jakarta and Bogor, see opposite. The turn-off to Cibodas is on the Bogor–Bandung Hwy, a few kilometres west of Cipanas. The gardens are 5km off the main road. Yellow *angkot* run from the roadside in Cipanas up to the gardens (3000Rp, 15 minutes).

## Gede Pangrango National Park

The Cibodas gardens are right next to the main entrance to Gede Pangrango National Park, the highlight of which is the climb to the 2958m peak of the volcanically active Gunung Gede. From the top of Gede on a clear day you can see Jakarta, Cirebon and even Pelabuhan Ratu on the south coast – well, Raffles reported that he could.

Register for the climb and obtain your permit (6000Rp, 3000Rp for Cibeureum Falls only) from the PHKA office just outside the gardens' entrance. The office has an information centre and pamphlets on the park, which is noted for its alpine forest and bird life, including the rare Javan eagle. Guides to the summit can also be hired here for around 300,000Rp at the office, or for around 350,000Rp at Freddy's (left).

From Cibodas, the trail passes **Telaga Biru** (15 minutes), which is a blue-green lake. **Cibeureum Falls** (one hour away) lie just off the main trail. Most picnickers only go this far, though some continue on to the **hot springs**, 2½ hours from the gate. The trail continues to climb another 1½ hours to **Kandang Badak**, where a hut has been built on the saddle between the peaks of Gunung Gede and Gunung Pangrango (3019m). Take the trail to the right for a hard three-hour climb to Pangrango. Most hikers turn left for the easier, but still steep, 1½-hour climb to Gede, which has more spectacular views. The **Gede Crater** lies below the summit, and you can continue on to the **Suryakencana Meadow**.

The 10km hike right to the top of Gunung Gede takes at least 10 hours there and back, so you should start as early as possible and take warm clothes (night temperatures can drop to 5°C), food, water and a torch (flashlight). Most hikers leave by 2am to reach the summit in the early morning before the mists roll in. Register at the park office the day before. The main trails are easy to follow. The hike should only be undertaken in the dry season from May to October.

## Cianjur
☎ 0263 / pop 156,000
East of Cibobas it's 19km to Cianjur, a market town that's famed throughout Java for

the quality of its rice; indeed the town is enveloped by shimmering green paddy fields. Cianjur has a certain relaxed provincial charm, and a few sights of interest in the surrounding district, but most people are here to learn about Sundanese culture and mix with locals as part of the highly successful homestay program here.

You'll find several banks (with ATMs) on the main drag, Jl Cokroaminoto, and internet cafes are grouped together on Jl Siti Jenab.

### SIGHTS

Cianjur itself has few attractions, but it's possible to visit a huge **plastic recycling plant** to learn about waste management here. Plastic is sent here from all over West Java to be separated by hand, then washed, chopped and dried before being sent on to plastic manufacturers.

Around 18km northeast of town, **Jangari** is an intriguing 'floating village' on a large reservoir that has a substantial fish-farming community where fish are fattened for Jakartan dining tables. You can hire a boat here (around 75,000Rp) to get across the lake to a great restaurant (meals cost around 25,000Rp).

The lush hillsides and processing plants of the **Gedeh tea plantation** (admission free; 8am-4pm Mon-Sat), 15km northwest of town, are also well worth a visit.

Cianjur also makes a good base for trips to the Cibonas gardens, and down to the coast at Pelabuhan Ratu (p139).

### SLEEPING & EATING

Most travellers stay with local families in Cianjur (see the boxed text, p147). The region is famous for its sweet, spicy cuisine and there are several delicious dishes unique to the area. Be sure to try the local *lontong* (sticky rice with tofu in a delicious, sweet coconut sauce); there are several warung on Jl Dewisartika that specialise in this dish. Some of the best beef sate in Java, locally known as *marangi*, is served up right on the street – there's a great place at the corner of Dr Muwardi and Jl Cokroaminoto in the town centre.

After dark, **BCNY** (Jl A Rahamam Hakin 40; 5-11pm) is a cool hang-out – an open-air food court that has live music at weekends.

**Lendel Hotel** ( 263 268; Jl Dr Muwardi 165C; r with fan from 120,000Rp, with air-con 190,000-275,000Rp; ) Offers a choice of spacious rooms in good condition, with wardrobe and TV, that are grouped around fish ponds in a garden with palm trees. Bathrooms are all cold-water *mandi*, though.

**RM Batagor Ihsan** ( 280 737; Jl Juanda 55; meals from 8000Rp) This place gets the locals' vote as the best spot for *batagor* (crispy tofu), which is either eaten with *krin* (peanut sauce) or as part of a *kuah* soup with onion and garlic.

**Lotek LP** ( 264 554; Jl Aria Cikundang 76; meals 10,000Rp) A roadside warung that serves up the best *gado gado* in Cianjur, plus authentically sweet and sticky *sate marangi* (4000Rp per stick).

### GETTING THERE & AWAY

On weekdays buses leave Jakarta's Kampung Rambutan every 30 minutes to Cipanas (normal/air-con 17,000/23,000Rp, two hours) and Cianjur (21,000/26,000Rp, 2½ hours). At weekends (when traffic is terrible around Puncuk Pass) buses are routed via Sukabumi (add an extra hour to your journey time, and 5000Rp). Buses to/from Bandung (14,000/20,000Rp, 1¾ hours) run every half-hour.

There are buses to Bogor from Cianjur (14,000/20,000Rp, two hours) and the highway by Cipanas every 20 minutes; *angkot* ply the route on Sunday.

## BANDUNG

 022 / pop 2.4 million

After the bottle-green hills of Cibondas and the Puncak Pass, the sprawling bulk of Bandung hits you like a baseball bat across the back of the head. Once the 'Paris of Java', the city is now a throng of congested, polluted streets and endless suburbs, and any romantic notions of colonial glamour have long disappeared. This is one of Indonesia's megacities (the Bandung conurbation is home to over seven million people) and West Java's capital, and it likes everyone to know it.

But not everything has gone to pot. Among the shopping malls and business hotels you'll find a dynamic, major city that's on the move. It attracts workers, intellectuals and students from across the archipelago, and its industries, restaurants and cafes throb with life. Today, grandiose art deco buildings, heaving market stalls, *becak* and multiplexes jostle for space in the city.

Bandung was originally established in the late 19th century as a colonial garrison town,

JAVA

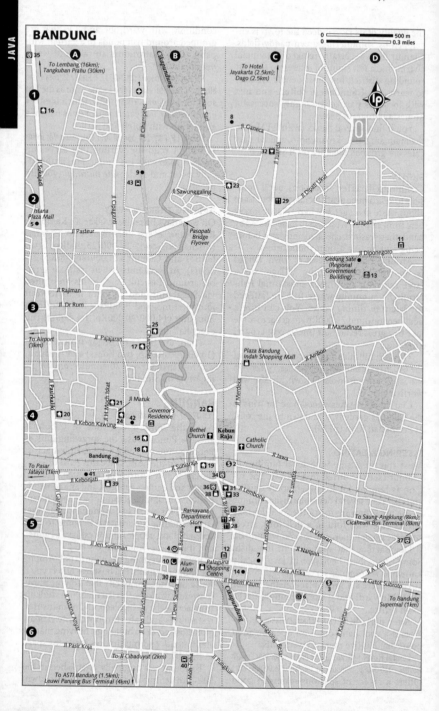

# BANDUNG

0 — 500 m
0 — 0.3 miles

To Lembang (16km);
Tangkuban Prahu (30km)

To Hotel
Jayakarta (2.5km);
Dago (2.5km)

Jl Cikapundung

Jl Champelas

Jl Tamun Sari

Jl Ganeca

Jl Juanda

Jl Sawunggaling

Jl Dipati Ukur

Pasopati
Bridge
Flyover

Jl Surapati

Jl Diponegoro

Istana
Plaza Mall

Jl Pasteur

Gedung Sate
(Regional
Government
Building)

Jl Rajiman

Jl Dr Rum

Jl Martadinata

To Airport
(3km)

Jl Pajajaran

Jl Champelas

Plaza Bandung
Indah Shopping Mall

Jl Ambon

Jl Pasirkaliki

Jl H Moch Iskat

Jl Matuk

Jl Merdeka

Governor's
Residence

Jl Kebon Kawung

Bethel
Church

Kebun
Raja

Catholic
Church

Bandung

Jl Jawa

To Pasar
Jatayu (1km)

Jl Kebonjati

Jl Suniaraja

Jl S Sumatra

Jl Lembong

To Saung Angklung (8km);
Cicaheum Bus Terminal (8km)

Jl ABC

Ramayana
Department
Store

Jl Lambiong

Jl Veteran

Jl Jen Sudirman

Jl Banceuy

Jl Naripan

Jl Cibadak

Alun-
Alun

Palaguna
Shopping
Centre

Jl Asia Afrika

Jl A Yani

To Bandung
Supermal (1km)

Jl Oto Iskandardinata

Jl Dewi Sartika

Jl Dalem Kaum

Jl Cikapundung

Jl Gatot Subroto

Jl Astana Anyar

Jl Lengkong Besar

Jl Karapitan

Jl Pasir Koja

To Jl Cibaduyut (2km)

Jl Moh Toha

Jl Pungkur

To ASTI Bandung (1.5km);
Leuwi Panjang Bus Terminal (4km)

but it rapidly acquired importance as a commercial and educational centre. Because of its pleasant climate – it stands at 750m above sea level – the Dutch even had plans to make it the capital prior to WWII. The city's most notable entry in the history books was as host of the Asia-Africa conference in 1955.

The main attraction of Bandung is its proximity to sights: high volcanic peaks, hot springs and enormous tea plantations are all easy day trips from the city.

## Orientation

Bandung spreads out over the northern foothills of a huge plateau surrounded by high mountain ridges. The main part of the city lies south of the train line, and is centred on Jl Asia Afrika and the *alun-alun* (main public square). Along Jl Asia Afrika are the tourist office, post office, banks and some fine art deco hotels. Jl Braga just north of here has a strip of bars and cafes.

In colonial times, the train tracks divided the riff-raff in the south from the Dutch city in the north, and the social divide still rings true. The genteel tree-lined streets and upmarket residential areas in the north harbour most of Bandung's cosmopolitan restaurants (and the key student area around Jeans St) and are bordered by the hills of Dago.

## Information
### BOOKSHOPS

**Periplus** ( ☎ 0888 135 7697; Istana Plaza Mall, Jl Pasir Kaliki; ⏰ 9am-7pm) Excellent selection of English books, maps and magazines including some Lonely Planet guidebooks.

### INTERNET ACCESS

Most of the upmarket shopping malls including the Bandung Supermal and Braga City Walk have free wi-fi.

**X-net** (Jl Lengkong Kecil 38) Access for 5000Rp per hour.

### MEDICAL SERVICES

**Adventist Hospital** ( ☎ 203 4386; Jl Cihampelas 161) A missionary hospital with English-speaking staff.

### MONEY

Banks with ATMs are scattered across Bandung.

**Bank Mandiri** (Jl Merdeka) Has an ATM and exchanges travellers cheques.

**Golden Megah moneychanger** (Jl Asia Afrika 142) Offers decent rates for cash dollars and euros.

### POST

**Main post office** (cnr Jl Banceuy & Jl Asia Afrika)

### TELEPHONE

Wartel aplenty can be found just south of the train station.

### TOURIST INFORMATION

**Bandung Tourist Information Centre** ( ☎ 420 6644; Jl Asia Afrika; ⏰ 9am-5pm Mon-Sat, to 2pm Sun) Managed by the very helpful Ajid Suriana, this office is located in the foyer of the central mosque. There's also a desk at the train station. Offers excellent free booklets, maps and information on cultural events.

## Sights

### CITY CENTRE

The **Museum Konperensi** (Conference Museum; Jl Asia Afrika; admission free; ☑ 9am-3pm Mon-Fri) inside the Gedung Merdeka (Freedom Building) is dedicated to the Asia-Africa conference of 1955. The scanty exhibits are pretty disappointing, but there are a few interesting photos of Sukarno, Nehru, Ho Chi Minh, Nasser and other developing world leaders of the 1950s.

For a bird's-eye view of central Bandung, climb the easterly tower of **Masjid Agung** (Jl Asia Afrika; admission 2000Rp; ☑ 9am-5pm Sat & Sun), next to the *alun-alun*.

There are some very fine Dutch art deco structures to admire on Jl Jenderal Sudirman and Jl Asia Afrika, two of the best being the **Grand Hotel Preanger** (p148) and the **Savoy Homann Hotel** (p148), both of which have imposing facades.

### NORTH OF THE CENTRE

About 3km north of the centre, the **Museum Geologi** (Geological Museum; Jl Diponegoro 57; admission free; ☑ 9am-3.30pm Mon-Thu, to 1.30pm Sat & Sun) is housed in the massive old headquarters of the Dutch Geological Service. It's a good place to get to grips with all matters geological and volcanic in Indonesia, though there's almost no information in English. Nevertheless it's worth an hour or so poking around the lava stones, crystals and bones that include a model of *Tyrannosaurus rex* and a mammoth. *Angkot* bound for 'Sadang Serang' leave the train station; get off at the Gedung Sate (Regional Government) complex, about 300m from the museum.

While you're in the neighbourhood, dip into the **Museum Prangko** (Stamp Museum; Jl Diponegoro; admission free; ☑ 9am-3pm Mon-Fri) in the northeastern corner of the Gedung Sate complex. As well as thousands of stamps from around the world, the museum has everything from postboxes to pushcarts used since colonial times.

### BANDUNG INSTITUTE OF TECHNOLOGY

Further north of Gedung Sate is the **Bandung Institute of Technology** (ITB; Jl Ganeca), set in spacious grounds and gardens with some bizarre hybrid Indo-European architecture.

Opened in 1920, ITB was the first university open to Indonesians. Sukarno studied here and formed the Bandung Study Club, which later grew into the pro-independence Partai Nasional Indonesia (PNI). The institute has maintained a reputation for political activism, and students here published the *White Book of the 1978 Students' Struggle*, which alleged corruption in high places. In 1998, in the lead-up to Suharto's downfall, up to 100,000 students rallied daily.

The ITB also has an excellent fine arts school, and its **art gallery** (admission free; ☑ on request) can be visited. Across from the main gate is a useful canteen in the *asrama mahasiswa* (student dorm complex), where many of the students congregate.

To reach the ITB, take a Lembang or Dago *angkot* from the train station and then walk down Jl Ganeca.

### DAGO

At the end of Jl Merdeka, Jl Juanda climbs up to Dago Hill to the north, overlooking the city. The famous, but now very faded, **Dago Thee Huis** (Dago Tea House; ☎ 250 5364; admission 1000Rp) offers city views through a tangle of power lines and a forest of radio towers. The complex has a cafe-restaurant, outdoor and indoor theatres and a small children's playground.

On the main road, 100m past the teahouse turn-off, a path leads down to **Curug Dago** (Dago Waterfall). From here you can walk along the river to **Taman Hutan Raya Ir H Juanda**, which is a pleasant forest park with another waterfall and walking paths. By road, the park entrance is 2km past the Dago bemo terminal.

**Gua Pakar** is in fact an ammunition store hacked out by the Japanese during the war. Further north is **Gua Belanda**, which is the same deal but built by the Dutch. A tunnel cuts right through the mountain to the start of the trail that leads all the way to **Maribaya** (p150) along Sungai Cikapundung.

### 'JEANS' STREET

Bandung's celebrated 'Jeans' Street, Jl Cihampelas is one of the main student areas of the city and lined with cafes, boutiques, stalls and clothes stores (look out for very kitsch giant plastercast statues of Rambo, Superman and the like that shops use as advertising symbols).

### ADU DOMBA

These noisy ram-butting fights, held most Sundays between 9am and 1pm, are wildly popular in Bandung. Animal lovers won't like it a bit but, like Spain's bullfights, they're a sight to behold, and at least the rams only walk away with a sore head. Consult the Tourist Information Centre (p145) for the latest program of events.

## Tours

Freelance English-speaking tour guide **Ahmadi** ( ☎ 0852 2106 3788; enoss_travellers@yahoo.com) runs good one-day tours (300,000Rp per person) of the sights to the north and south of the city, and can set up trips on to Garut and Pangandaran (around 800,000Rp). Hotel Guntur also offers similar trips.

## Sleeping

### BUDGET

Many of Bandung's very cheapest places close to the train station on Jl Kebonjati are looking very rundown these days and the area is very dark after nightfall. Backpackers should reckon on having to up their budgets in this prosperous city.

**Guest House Pos Cihampelas** ( ☎ 423 5213; Jl Cihampelas 12; r economy/standard from 50,000/90,000Rp; ❄ ) The best bet in the city for a cheap bed, this place has a plethora of different rooms – from humble but clean economy options with shared bathroom facilities to air-con doubles. English is spoken, and there's a lounge area and a very cheap in-house warung (meals from 10,000Rp).

**Hotel Patradissa** ( ☎ 420 6680; Jl H Moch Iskat 8; r 120,000-200,000R; ❄ ) This slightly quirky guest house may be old-fashioned in appearance, but it's secure, staff are friendly and helpful, and the location is quiet. There are plenty of rooms, all with a chintzy touch that granny would approve of, and some have air-con. Breakfast is included.

**Hotel Gunter** ( ☎ 420 3763; Jl Oto Iskandarinata 20; r with/without air-con 175,000/150,000Rp; ❄ ) Gunter vaguely resembles a motel, and has clean, spacious rooms complete with 1970s-style fur-

nishings. All have a porch area with chairs that face a central garden bursting with flowering shrubs and topiary. Tours can be organised here. Prices rise a little at weekends.

**Edelweiss** ( ☎ 203 2369; Jl Sukajadi 206; r with air-con & TV from 180,000Rp; ❄ ) A well-run, quiet and clean guest house with plain, orderly rooms that offer good value for money. It's a fair hike from the centre, but as there's a factory outlet in the compound (and plenty more close by) it's ideal for shopaholics. Staff are helpful, and breakfast is included.

Or try:
**Hotel Patradissa 2** ( ☎ 420 6657; Jl Wastukencana 7A; d from 135,000Rp; ❄ ) A newer option in the Patradissa empire; most rooms here have air-con.

### MIDRANGE

Bandung has plenty of midrange hotels, especially north of the train station and along Jl Gardujati, but most are old and faded.

**ourpick Hotel Serena** ( ☎ 420 4317; http://serena bandung.multiply.com; Jl Maruk 4-6; r incl breakfast from 238,000Rp; ❄ ) This classy little modern hotel offers outstanding value and a good degree of minimalist style. All rooms are smart, with comfortable beds and reading lights, and immaculately clean. The hot-water bathrooms have a sparkle. There's a restaurant too with tasty, well-priced local grub. Prices rise 10% at weekends.

**Hotel Kedaton** ( ☎ 421 9898; www.hotelkedaton.com; Jl Suniaraja 14; r from 490,000Rp; ❄ ▣ ) A large concrete hotel in a central location with an abundance of spacious rooms that are comfortable but slightly dated in terms of presentation. Worth considering for its excellent facilities though, as there's a good gym, a spa and an attractive pool area.

**Arion Swiss-Belhotel** ( ☎ 424 0000; www.swiss -belhotel.com; Jl Oto Iskandarinata 16; r from 655,000Rp; ❄ ▣ 📶 ▣ ) Modern nonsmoking hotel with roomy, immaculate accommodation and

---

**LIVE WITH THE LOCALS**

The **Cianjur homestay program** ( ☎ 081 7085 6691; www.cianjuradventure.com) is a superb initiative set up by author Yudi Sujana, who lived for years in New Zealand, that allows travellers to experience life in a non-touristy town in Java. Yudi and his team all speak fluent English, so it's a wonderful opportunity to get to understand Sundanese and Indonesian culture. School visits, sightseeing trips, hikes (and occasionally some volunteer-work opportunities) are offered at backpacking rates. Guests pay US$12 per person per day, which includes family accommodation and three meals; it's best to book a place a few days in advance. Airport pick-ups and drop-offs can also be arranged at very moderate rates, allowing you to bypass Jakarta completely.

JAVA

excellent facilities including multichannel TV and high-speed internet. The top floor has a pool, a spa and a fitness centre.

**Hotel Jayakarta** ( ☎ 250 5888; www.jayakartahotels resorts.com; Jl Juanda 381; r from 770,000Rp; ⊠ ) Up near the Dago Tea House, this is a well-regarded, nonsmoking four-star hotel. Offers sweeping views from its top-floor rooms and there's a great spa.

Or consider:

**Hotel Sawunggaling** ( ☎ 421 8254; Jl Sawunggaling 13; r from 280,000Rp; ⊠ ) Attractive hotel, out near ITB with some colonial style. It occupies a quiet corner and rooms are big and comfy.

**Hotel Mutiara** ( ☎ 420 0333; www.mutiarahotel.com; Jl Kebon Kawung 60; r incl breakfast from 488,000Rp; ⊠ ⊡ ⊠ ) A polished, motel-style place with a range of well-equipped and well-presented rooms. Also has a restaurant and bar.

**TOP END**

Like any big city, Bandung has a glut of luxury hotels, all with swimming pools. Most offer good discounts, so shop around.

**Savoy Homann Hotel** ( ☎ 423 2244; www.savoyhomann -hotel.com; Jl Asia Afrika 112; r/ste from 660,000/840,000Rp; ⊠ ⊡ ⊜ ⊠ ) Dating back to 1921, this wonderful-looking hotel has a superb sweeping facade, and the rooms and communal areas retain real art deco class, with period lighting and stylish detailing galore. Call for a free pick-up from the train station or airport.

**Novotel** ( ☎ 421 1001; www.novotel.com; Jl Cihampelas 23; r from 720,000Rp; ⊠ ⊡ ⊜ ⊠ ) By far the most contemporary hotel in the city, this seriously stylish new monument to luxury is no show pony and delivers on every level, with well-trained staff, free cable internet access and wi-fi, a great gym and spa, and an excellent restaurant. Nonsmoking.

Another option:

**Grand Hotel Preanger** ( ☎ 423 1631; www.preanger .aerowisata.com; Jl Asia Afrika 181; r from 785,000Rp; ste from 1,350,000Rp; ⊠ ⊠ ) Historic hotel that retains some art deco charm, but there's an ugly modern extension and the rooms are overpriced. Check out the terrific English pub, though.

## Eating

Jl Braga has a strip of cafes, restaurants and bakeries, but the city's really swanky, hip new places are concentrated in the north. For cheap food check out the night warungs on Jl Cikapundung Barat, across from the *alun-alun*.

**London Bakery** ( Jl Braga 37; cakes from 2000Rp) Stylish little cafe with coffee, cakes, snacks and light meals including pasta and sandwiches. You'll find a few magazines and copies of the *Jakarta Post* to read here, though traffic noise is intense.

**Bandung Supermal** ( Jl Gatot Subroto 289; meals 10,000-45,000Rp) In the east of the city, this upmarket shopping mall has a good food court, tons of fast-food joints, cafes and a Bread Talk bakery.

**Utami** ( ☎ 7078 7075; Jl Cihampelas 12; meals 12,000-20,000Rp) This is a very clean, attractive little eatery where a great deal of care is taken over the food – you'll find plenty of fresh greens, tasty *ayam goreng* and two feisty sambals to add a little extra spice to your plate.

**New Braga Café** ( ☎ 421 1567; Jl Braga 15; meals 12,000-21,000Rp; ⊗ 11.30am-9.30pm, closed Fri) An excellent, friendly Sundanese restaurant in an elegant building that dates back to colonial days. All the food is laid out on covered plates and bowls for you to choose from; *bakar ayam seuhah* (spicy roast chicken) is the house speciality, and there are plenty of vegetarian dishes.

**Warung Nasi Ampera** ( Jl Dewi Sartika 8; meals 14,000Rp; ⊗ 24hr) Just south of the *alun-alun*, this clean place is the best of several traditional Sundanese places on this road. Serves up delicious fresh tempeh (cake made from fermented soybeans) and curries around the clock.

**our pick Kiosk** (Braga City Walk, Jl Braga; meals 15,000-20,000Rp; ⊜ ) This great little mini-food court on the ground floor of the Braga City Walk is ideal for sampling some unusual snacks such as *pempek* (fish or egg fried with sago in a rich, dark sauce) from Sumatra and noodle dishes. Drinks include milky *teh tarik* (cardamom chai) and loads of yummy juices, from blueberry to *sirsak* (soursop).

**Prefere 72** ( ☎ 253 4338; Jl Juanda 72; meals from 25,000Rp; ⊗ 10am-midnight, to 2am Fri & Sat; ⊜ ) A library, cafe and restaurant rolled into one hip modernist building, this is one of the most happening places in fashionable north Bandung. You'll find pasta, snacks and rice and noodle dishes on the menu.

**Momiji** ( ☎ 420 3786; Jl Braga 64; mains 27,000-60,000Rp; ⊗ noon-10.30pm) Momiji is a traditional Japanese restaurant with a relaxed, civilised ambience. Prices are surprisingly moderate given the surroundings and quality of the sushi, noodle, teriyaki and teppanyaki dishes here.

## Drinking

After dark Jl Braga has a typical downtown vibe, with small bars, karaoke lounges and live-music venues. Up in north Bandung Jeans St is a popular hang-out for students (though there are few bars here), while rich kids gravitate to the hip places along Jl Juanda.

**Roempoet** (Jl Braga 80) Intimate bar with live bands (mainly playing covers) and a social vibe. Sizzling sate is also served up (mains 20,000Rp) here.

**North Sea Bar** (Jl Braga 82) The beer flows into the wee small hours at this pub-style expat and bar-girl hang-out. There's a popular pool table.

**R Café & Lounge** (Jl Juanda 97; 🛜) Happening, very metropolitan bar-cafe with a terrace facing busy Juanda, stylish seating, mocktails and cocktails. It's above a spa–fitness centre.

## Entertainment

### CULTURAL PERFORMANCES

Bandung is the place to see Sundanese performing arts; however, performance times are haphazard – check with the Tourist Information Centre for the latest schedules.

**Rumentang Siang** (☎ 423 3562; Jl Baranangsiang 1) Bandung's premier performing arts centre, where *wayang golek*, Jaipongan (West Javanese dance), *pencak silat* (the art of self-defence), Sandiwara (traditional Javanese theatre) and *ketoprak* (popular Javanese folk theatre) performances are held.

**ASTI-Bandung** (☎ 731 4982; Jl Buah Batu 212) In the southern part of the city, this is a school for traditional Sundanese arts – music, dancing and *pencak silat*.

**Saung Angklung** (☎ 727 1714; Jl Padasuka 118; performances 80,000Rp; 🕙 10.30am-5pm) *Angklung* (bamboo musical instrument) performances take place at Pak Ujo's Saung Angklung in the east of the city. You can also see the instruments being made here. Performances are held most afternoons at 3.30pm.

### LIVE MUSIC

Bar-cum-restaurant, Roempoet (above) has a relaxed, informal air and live bands most evenings.

**Classic Rock Café** (☎ 420 7982; Jl Lembong 1; www.classicrockcafe.co.id) For those about to rock – don your denim 'n' leather and head here. The whole place reeks of 1970s nostalgia, but try telling the regulars that the world has moved on. There's a live rock band nightly at 10pm and a modest (or no) entrance fee.

### CLUBS

Bandung has a vibrant clubbing scene and Indonesian and visiting DJs play to big crowds here. The unpretentious **New Braga Club** (☎ 423 2006; Jl Braga) is a good bet in the downtown district. Elsewhere in the city, **Mansion** (☎ 081 861 3743; Paris Van Java Mall, Jl Sukajadi 137-139) is a very popular dance club that draws a glam crowd; turntablists including the Martinez Brothers have spun their stuff here.

## Shopping

With a roster of glitzy malls and factory outlets, shopaholics come here from as far as Malaysia in search of labels and bargains. Jl Cibaduyut, in southwest Bandung, is to shoes what Jl Cihampelas is to jeans. Check out Jl Braga for antique and curio stores.

**Bandung Supermal** (www.bandungsupermal.com; Jl Gatot Subroto 289; 🛜) Has one of the largest Hero supermarkets in Indonesia, a bowling alley, cinemas, and more than 200 shops including Mango and Next.

**Braga City Walk** (Jl Braga; 🛜) Small upmarket shopping mall with plenty of boutiques, a food court, a cinema, a gym, a spa and a supermarket.

**Pak Ruhiyat** (No 78/17B) Down a small, unnamed alley behind Jl Pangarang 22, this small shop produces *wayang golek* puppets and masks.

**Saung Angklung** (☎ 727 1714; Jl Padasuka 118) Traditional Sundanese musical instruments can be bought at this bamboo workshop.

Markets to explore in Bandung:

**Pasar Baru** (Jl Kebonjati) Somewhat grotty central market, but good for fresh fruit.

**Pasar Jatayu** (Jl Arjuna) One kilometre west of the train station, this flea market is where a few collectables hide in piles of junk.

## Getting There & Away

### AIR

Bandung airport is served by **Merpati** (☎ 426 0253; www.merpati.co.id; Jl Kebon Kawung 16), flying to Batam and Surabaya; **Garuda** (☎ 420 9468; Grand Hotel Preanger, Jl Asia Afrika 181), which flies to Singapore; **AirAsia** (☎ 5050 5088; www.airasia.com), connecting Bandung with Kuala Lumpur and Singapore; and **Sriwijaya Air** (☎ 640 5566; www.sriwijayaair-online.com), with planes to Surabaya and on to Denpasar.

**JAVA**

### BUS

Five kilometres south of the city centre, **Leuwi Panjang bus terminal** (Jl Sukarno Hatta) has buses west to places such as Cianjur (normal/air-con 14,000/20,000Rp, 1¾ hours), Bogor (30,000/42,000Rp, 3¼ hours) and to Jakarta's Kampung Rambutan bus terminal (36,000Rp to 45,000Rp, three hours). Buses to Bogor are not allowed to take the scenic Puncak Pass route on weekends.

Buses to the east leave from the Cicaheum bus terminal on the eastern outskirts of the city. They include Cirebon (normal/air-con 26,000/38,000Rp, four hours), Garut (14,000Rp, two hours) and Pangandaran (52,000Rp, six hours).

**X-Trans** ( ☎ 204 2955; Jl Cihampelas 57) offers an hourly shuttle bus service to various drop-off points in central Jakarta (70,000Rp, 2½ hours), and also direct hourly buses to Jakarta airport (90,000Rp, three hours). **Sari Harum** ( ☎ 607 7065) has an air-con *travel* minibus to Pangandaran (80,000Rp, five hours) at 6am. Both **Kramatdjati** ( ☎ 423 9860; Jl Kebonjati 96) and **Pahala Kencana** ( ☎ 423 2911; Jl Kebonjati 90) run luxury buses to long-distance destinations, such as Yogyakarta (85,000Rp).

### TRAIN

Six comfortable *Parahyangan* (business/executive 45,000/65,000Rp, 3¼ hours) trains connect Bandung with Jakarta's Gambir station daily. Seven additional and more luxurious *Argo Gede* (executive 75,000Rp, three hours) trains also cover this route.

Several trains operate on the Bandung–Banjar–Yogyakarta line, most continuing on to Surabaya. The business-class *Mutiara Selatan* passes through Bandung at 5pm on its way to Yogyakarta (110,000Rp) and Surabaya (135,000Rp). The *Lodaya* leaves Bandung at 8am for Yogyakarta and Solo (business/executive 100,000/165,000Rp).

## Getting Around
### TO/FROM THE AIRPORT

Bandung's Husein Sastranegara airport is 4km northwest of town; it costs around 50,000Rp to get there by taxi from the centre.

### BUS, ANGKOT & TAXI

Bandung has a fairly good, if crowded, Damri city bus service that charges a fixed 2000Rp. Buses 9 and 11 run from west to east down Jl Asia Afrika to Cicaheum bus terminal.

*Angkot* run on set routes all over town between numerous stations. From Stasiun Hall (St Hall), on the southern side of the train station, *angkot* go to Dago, Ledeng and other stations. When returning, catch any *angkot* displaying 'St Hall'. Abdul Muis (Abd Muis), south of the *alun-alun* on Jl Dewi Sartika, and Cicaheum are the other main *angkot* terminals. *Angkot* cost from 2000Rp to 3000Rp.

For a taxi call the ever-reliable **Bluebird** ( ☎ 756 1234). Becak are now very rare in central Bandung.

## NORTH OF BANDUNG
### Lembang
☎ 022

The town of Lembang was once a noted hill resort but is now a busy little market town. Most visitors keep heading further up the hills, but if you're looking for a quick break from Bandung, 16km to the south, then it's a decent option.

The colonial-era **Grand Hotel Lembang** ( ☎ 278 6671; www.grandhotellembang.com; Jl Raya Lembang 272; weekday/weekend r from 360,000/422,000Rp; ☑ ) dates from 1921 and was once a fashionable base for the Dutch. It's a sprawling place with 191 recently renovated rooms and a smart, modern bistro, plus beautiful gardens and tennis courts.

### Maribaya Hot Springs

Maribaya, 5km east of Lembang, has a thermal spa, landscaped gardens and a thundering waterfall (admission 5000Rp). It's another tourist spot, crowded on Sunday, but worth visiting. You can extend your Tangkuban Prahu (below) trip by walking from the bottom end of the gardens down through a brilliant, deep and wooded river gorge all the way to Dago. There's a good track, and if you allow about two hours for the walk (6km), you can be at a Dago vantage point for sunset. From there it's only a short trip by *angkot* back to Bandung.

### Tangkuban Prahu

The 'overturned *perahu*' volcano crater is 30km north of Bandung. Years ago the centre of Tangkuban Prahu collapsed under the weight of built-up ash and, instead of the usual conical volcano shape, it has a flat, elongated summit with a huge caldera.

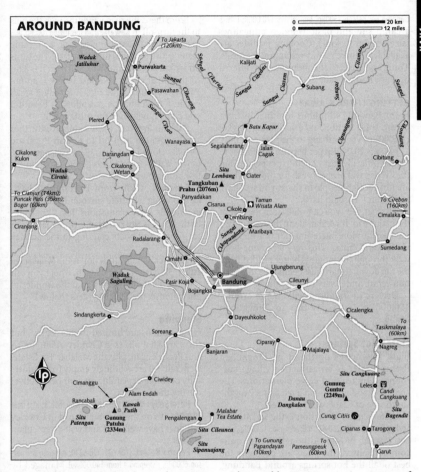

**AROUND BANDUNG**

At 2076m Tangkuban Prahu can be quite cool, and around noon the mist starts to roll in through the trees, so try to go early. The crater is easily accessible by car, so it's very much a tourist trap.

At the crater are an **information centre** ( 7am-5pm), warungs and a parade of pedlars hustling postcards, souvenirs and other junk. It's a tacky jumble that detracts from the scenery, but you can escape this bedlam of activity.

The huge **crater** is an impressive sight. Tangkuban Prahu still emits sulphur fumes – access to the volcano is occasionally denied when volcanic activity increases, but it's usually open. The last serious eruption occurred in 1969.

It's possible to circumnavigate most of the caldera in around two hours. **Kawah Ratu** is the huge 'Queen Crater' at the top. Walk around the rim of the main crater for about 20 minutes for views of the secondary crater, **Kawah Upas**. The trail leads further along a ridge between the two craters and returns to the car park, but it is steep and slippery in parts – exercise caution. A better and less-crowded walk is to **Kawah Domas**, a volcanic area of steaming and bubbling geysers that can be reached by a side trail to the top. You can also head off across country towards Ciater or Lembang; guides can be hired for around 50,000Rp per hour.

Just north of the town of Cikole, the outdoor centre **Taman Wisata Alam** ( 022-9115 0480;

camping per person 7500Rp, bungalows 170,000Rp) has a camp site and basic wooden bungalows (sleeping up to four). Cooking facilities are available, or there's a tiny restaurant for meals. Tours and treks to the mountain are offered by staff. Book ahead.

**GETTING THERE & AWAY**
From Bandung's minibus terminal in front of the train station, take a Subang *angkot* (10,000Rp) via Lembang to the park entrance.

Entry is 20,000Rp per person. Minibuses to the top officially cost 12,000Rp per person, but the drivers will probably ask for more; if there are not enough people to share, you will have to charter – bargain hard.

Alternatively, you can walk from the gate at the main road. It's 4.5km along the road or you can take the more interesting side trail that goes via Kawah Domas. This very steep one-hour walk through the jungle is better tackled from the top down. It starts just behind the information centre and is very easy to follow.

Drivers in Bandung will charge around 450,000Rp for a day-trip to Tangkuban Prahu.

## Ciater Hot Springs
Eight kilometres northeast of Tangkuban Prahu, Ciater is an attractive village surrounded by tea and clove plantations. The area has good walks, and a tea factory on the south side of Ciater can be visited.

Ciater's main attraction is the **Sari Ater Hot Spring Resort** ( ☎ 0260-471 700; admission 12,000Rp, pools extra 20,000Rp;  24hr). Although they're quite commercialised, the pools are probably the best of all the hot springs around Bandung. Rooms (from 250,000Rp) and rustic bungalows are available here.

Ciater has plenty of small *penginapan* (lodging houses) with rooms starting at around 40,000Rp.

You can walk to Ciater – about 12km across country – from Tangkuban Prahu, or flag down an *angkot* at the entrance point to Tangkuban Prahu.

## SOUTH OF BANDUNG
☎ 022
Less developed than the resorts to the north, the mountains south of Bandung have fewer facilities, but are quieter. The road south of Bandung leads to **Ciwidey**, a town where every second house has a strawberry patch.

From there, the road winds through the hills to the turn-off to **Kawah Putih** (per person 7000Rp, plus motorbike/car 1000/5000Rp;  7am-5pm), a volcanic crater with a beautiful turquoise lake. The turn-off is 6km before Rancabali, and then it is 8km to the small crater lake just below Gunung Patuha (2334m). Although it is only a small crater, Kawah Putih is exceptionally beautiful and eerily quiet when the mists roll in.

Back on the road, a few kilometres further south from the turn-off to Kawah Putih are two developed hot springs at **Cimanggu**; the newer **Walini** complex has big hot pools and a few bungalows.

**Rancabali**, 42km from Bandung, is basically one big tea estate surrounded by rolling green hills of tea plantations. Just 2km south of the town is **Situ Patengan**, a pretty lake with tea rooms and boats catering to the Sunday crowds.

The area's main attraction is the **Malabar Tea Estate**, 5km from Pengalengan, where you can tour the plantations and stay at the wonderful guest house, the Malabar Mess (below).

## Sleeping
Hotel options are limited in this region, but there are a few places in Ciwidey, Alam Endah and Pengalengan, plus the Malabar Tea Estate. Generally all are echoingly empty (or wonderfully peaceful, depending on your perspective) during the week.

**Hotel Selly** ( ☎ 592 8261; Jl Raya Rancabali, km 1; r from 70,000Rp) It's on the busy main road in Ciwidey but does have well-kept and well-swept, plain rooms.

**Patuha Resort** ( ☎ 022-720 8310; camping per person 6000Rp, r sleeping 4 from 140,000Rp) Managed by the Forestry Commission, this place in Alam Endah is geared to students on outdoor-pursuits trips. Its 12 wooden cabins are clean and comfortable and there's a canteen for inexpensive meals.

**Malabar Mess** ( ☎ 597 9401; weekday/weekend r from 176,000/231,000Rp) Located at an altitude of 1500m, this fine colonial guest house enjoys a delightfully temperate climate in tea plantations near the town of Pengalengan. Furnished with Dutch antiques, it's a great place to kick back for a few days. Book through the estate's Bandung office ( ☎ 022-203 8996).

## Getting There & Away
From Bandung's Leuwi Panjang terminal, frequent buses run to Ciwidey (10,000Rp,

1¼ hours). From Ciwidey *angkot* run to Situ Patengan (7000Rp). Kawah Putih is not serviced by regular public transport, but you'll find plenty of *ojek* (10,000Rp) in Alam Endah. Buses also run directly to Pengalengan (8000Rp), where *ojek* hang out at the bus terminal.

## BANDUNG TO PANGANDARAN

Heading southeast from Bandung, the road passes through rolling hills and stunning volcanic peaks skirting – at a safe distance – the particularly explosive **Gunung Papandayan** (2622m). This is the Bandung–Yogyakarta road as far as Banjar; the Bandung–Yogyakarta train line passes through Tasikmalaya and Banjar, but not Garut. After the choked streets of Jakarta and Bandung, these quieter back roads are a pleasure.

### Garut & Cipanas
☎ 0262

Sixty-three kilometres southeast of Bandung, Garut is a once-lovely spa town that's now become featureless sprawl and leatherware centre. But 6km north of here the lovely village of Cipanas makes a much more tranquil base for a day or two exploring some stunning volcanic scenery and soaking away any travelling tensions in a hot spring–fed bath or pool.

From Cipanas, the **Curug Citiis** waterfall is a three-hour walk away up the mountain; it's a four-hour hike further on to the peak of Gunung Guntur. Leave by 5am for good views.

The region is famed for its *dodol* – a confectionery of coconut milk, palm sugar and sticky rice. The 'Picnic' brand is the best quality, and it is possible to visit the **factory** (Jl Pasundan 102) in Garut.

#### SLEEPING
Cipanas has a good choice of places to stay; all are strung along Jl Raya Cipanas, the resort's single road. Most rooms are equipped with water piped in from the hot springs. Many of the flashier hotels have swimming pools heated by the springs; if you're staying at a cheaper option, it's possible to use the pools for a minimal fee (7000/3000Rp for adults/children). Prices quoted here are weekday rates; expect anything between a 15% and 40% increase on weekends.

**Hotel Tirta Merta** ( ☎ 231 112; r from 85,000Rp) Perhaps the best choice for a cheap base in Cipanas, this place has clean rooms, cheerful staff and plenty of decorative concrete tree stumps.

**Hotel Nurgraha** ( ☎ 234 829; r from 125,000Rp; ☒ ) Offers decent value, with well-presented if ageing rooms and bungalows with wooden floors and balconies. There are sunset views of the thermal pool, rice fields and coconut trees.

**Cipanas Indah** ( ☎ 233 736; r from 135,000Rp, VIP r 295,000Rp; ☒ ) Simple, clean rooms and attractive bungalows grouped around a pool. Prices rise substantially at weekends.

**Tirtagangga Hotel** ( ☎ 232 549; www.tirtagangga -hotel.com; r/ste from 325,000/815,000Rp; ☒ ) Large, low-rise hotel offering stylish and well-presented accommodation, a large pool surrounded by palm trees and a good-quality restaurant.

**Sumber Alam** ( ☎ 238 000; r 345,000-1,140,000Rp; ☒ ) This upmarket resort has fine thatched-and-timber bungalows built around a huge pool and pond. It's a popular family hang-out, particularly on weekends.

**Danau Dariza** ( ☎ 243 693; www.danaudariza.com; bungalows from US$66; ☒ ) If you're travelling with kids this large resort could be a good choice as it has a huge hot spring–fed water park complete with plunging water slides and pools. Accommodation is in quite tasteful mock-traditional wooden bungalows.

#### GETTING THERE & AWAY
Buses and *angkot* leave from the Guntur terminal in Garut, in the north of the town. Garut is easily reached by bus from Bandung (14,000Rp, two hours) and also from Tasikmalaya (16,000Rp, two hours). For Pangandaran, take another bus from Tasikmalaya.

Regular *angkot* run around town and to Cipanas (*angkot* 4, 2000Rp).

A car or minibus with driver can be rented in Cipanas – ask around the hotels. A trip to Papandayan will cost 350,000Rp to 500,000Rp, depending on the quality of the car and your bargaining skills.

### Around Garut
Near Leles, about 10km north of Garut, is **Candi Cangkuang**, which is one of the few remaining Hindu temples in West Java. Dating from the 8th century, some of its stones were found to have been carved into tombstones for a nearby Islamic cemetery. The restored temple lies on the edge of Situ Cangkuang,

a small lake. It has become something of a tourist trap, but it's a beautiful spot. From Garut take a green *angkot* to Leles (3000Rp) on the highway and then another *angkot* or horse-drawn *dilman* (two-wheeled buggy; 5000Rp per person) for the 3km to Candi Cangkuang. Rafts across the lake to the temple cost 25,000Rp.

Twenty-eight kilometres to the southwest of Garut, twin-peaked **Gunung Papandayan** is one of the most active volcanoes in West Java. Papandayan exploded in 1772, a catastrophe that killed more than 3000. It erupted again in 2002, and thousands were forced to flee when pyroclastic flows devastated the area. Papandayan is once again open to visitors, but check first with locals before setting out.

The bubbling yellow crater (Kawah Papandayan) just below the peak is an impressive sight and clearly visible from the Garut valley on clear mornings. To get there, take a Cikajang minibus and get off at the turn-off on the outskirts of Cisurupan (5000Rp), where you can catch a waiting *ojek* (25,000Rp one way, 13km).

From the car park area it is an easy half-hour walk to the crater, which is riddled with bubbling mud pools, steam vents and crumbling sulphur deposits. Take care – keep well to the right when ascending through the crater; it may pay to hire a guide (around 250,000Rp per day; from the PHKA office, as the car park area is generally full of cowboys) for closer inspection. For fine views, go very early in the morning before the clouds roll in. Gunung Papandayan's summit is a two-hour walk beyond the crater, and there are fields of Javan edelweiss near the top. PHKA staff can arrange a camping permit.

To the east of Garut town, **Gunung Telagabodas** (2201m) has a bubbling green sulphurous crater lake. To get to Telagabodas, take an *angkot* to Wanaraja (4000Rp) and an *ojek* (12,000Rp) to the parking area and then walk to the crater. Craters to the west of Garut that can be visited are **Kawah Darajat**, 26km away, and **Kawah Kamojang**, 23km away, the site of a geothermal plant that has defused the once spectacular geyser activity and replaced it with huge pipes.

Halfway between Garut and Tasikmalaya is **Kampung Naga**, a beautiful traditional Sundanese village of thatch-roofed timber houses nestled next to a river and surrounded by precipitous hillsides. Crowds of tourists pass through here during the dry season, but it's still a lovely spot. There are 360 steps up to the car park on the main highway. Freelance guides will offer to explain local customs, but they ask a hefty 50,000Rp for a tour.

## Tasikmalaya
☎ 0265

Sixty kilometres east of Garut, Tasikmalaya is an unremarkable town on the road to Pangandaran, though the surrounding area has a few points of interest. Tasik has plenty of hotels; the **Crown Mahkota Graha** ( ☎ 332 282; Jl Martadinata 45; r 245,000-445,000Rp; 🅿 🅿 ), with its restaurant and tidy rooms, is the best.

From Tasikmalaya, buses operate to Bandung (38,000Rp, four hours), Garut (20,000Rp, two hours) and Pangandaran (30,000Rp, three hours). The main bus terminal is 4km from the town centre on the eastern outskirts. Tasikmalaya is also on the main train line.

### Around Tasikmalaya

For cheap rattan crafts, for which the area is famous, visit the village of **Rajapolah** (12km north of Tasikmalaya on the road to Bandung), where many of the weavers work.

The hot spring **Cipanas Galunggung** is 20km northwest and lies at the foot of **Gunung Galunggung** (2168m), a volcano that exploded dramatically in 1982, killing 68 people. From the hot springs recreation park, a trail leads to a small waterfall and then on to Galunggung crater, 3km away. A steep road to the crater is an easier walk but less scenic. From Tasikmalaya's main bus terminal take an *angkot* to Bantar on the highway. From there, *ojek* will cover the final 14km along a rough road for around 25,000Rp.

**Situ Lengkong** is about 40km north of Tasikmalaya and 500m from the village of Panjalu. It's a serene lake that was formed when the Hindu ruler of Panjalu dammed the valley. There is a forested island in the middle and boats can be hired to take you around the lake. Panjalu village has a small **museum** containing the heirlooms of the kings of Panjalu. Situ Lengkong can be reached by bus from Tasikmalaya or from Kawali terminal, where *angkot* run the 20km to Ciamis.

On the highway to Banjar and Pangandaran, 16km southeast of Ciamis, **Karang Komulyan** is the excavated site of the ancient Galuh kingdom. It's often said that Galuh was both the first Hindu and the first Muslim kingdom in Java, but this Neolithic settlement dating from around the 5th century points to the pre-Hindu period. Only a few stone walls and foundations remain of the 'palace', store, prayer and bathing areas, but it is a beautiful walk through the jungle and bamboo groves down to the confluence of the swift Ciliwung and Citanduy rivers. A large car park and government-built cottages next to the park are attempts to make it a major tourist stop.

## Banjar

Banjar, 42km east of Tasikmalaya, is a large, bustling town and major junction on the Bandung–Yogyakarta road and rail route. From here a side road heads down to Pangandaran.

The bus terminal is 4km west of town on the highway. Many buses can be caught as they come through the centre of town near the train station. From Banjar buses go to Pangandaran (17,000Rp, two hours), Bandung, Purwokerto and Jakarta.

Banjar is not a good place to catch trains, since most are crowded through-trains. If you're heading east to Yogyakarta and Solo from Pangandaran, Sidareja station (p159) is more convenient, cheaper and quicker. For Bandung, the *Lodaya* passes through Banjar at 2.08pm and the *Argo Wilis* at 4.35pm.

## PANGANDARAN
☎ 0265

Situated on a narrow isthmus, with a broad sweep of sand on either side and a thickly forested national park on the nearby headland, Pangandaran is Java's premier beach resort. Walk away from the centre and the coastal scenery is reduced to its raw elements: a strip of dark sand, a vast, empty ocean and an enormous, gently curving horizon.

Most of the year Pangandaran is a quiet, tranquil place to enjoy walks along the sweeping sands or through the forest, but the town fills up on holidays (and weekends). The heavy swell that relentlessly pummels the impressive beach doesn't make for great swimming, though there are some more secluded spots along the coast. But as the surf is consistently good, it's a great place to get out on a board, or learn how to (surfing lessons can be easily arranged).

Pangandaran was hit hard by a tsunami in 2006 (a different one from the disaster that devastated Banda Aceh in Sumatra) that killed around 600 people and wiped out several hotels here. But the town is very much open for business again and there's little evidence of its impact today. Many hotels have been modernised and upgraded since the tsunami. Sadly, less attention has been devoted to the beach, which is littered with plastic and flotsam and in dire need of a clean-up.

### Orientation

Pangandaran extends for about 2km from the bus terminal to the national-park boundary in the south. The town is flanked by the west and east beaches, and bisected by the main street, Jl Kidang Pananjung. The west beach is a wide sweep of sand and the main resort strip. The east beach is a quieter, fishing beach, and not much sand remains since a retaining wall was built.

### Information

A 3500Rp admission charge is levied at the gates on entering Pangandaran. There's no tourist office in town.

**BNI ATM** (Jl Merdeka) There's a second branch on Jl Bulak Laut.

**BRI bank** (Jl Kidang Pananjung) Changes cash dollars and major brands of travellers cheques.

**Magic Mushroom Books** (Jl Pasanggrahan) Sells Western titles from a psychedelic shack and also changes money.

**Post office** (Jl Kidang Pananjung)

**Telkom** (Jl Kidang Pananjung)

**Tiara Internet** (Jl Kidang Pananjung; per hr 12,000Rp)

**YK** (Jl Pamugaran; per hr 15,000Rp) Helpful internet cafe with modern terminals and reasonable speed net connection.

### Sights & Activities

The **Taman Nasional Pangandaran** (Pangandaran National Park; admission 5500Rp; ☼ dawn-dusk), which takes up the entire southern end of Pangandaran, is a wild expanse of dense jungle. Within its boundaries live porcupines, *kijang* (barking deer), hornbills, scorpions and monkeys (including Javan gibbons). Small bays within the park enclose pretty tree-fringed beaches. Occasionally, the park is even used as a temporary home for elephants being transported around the archipelago. The park is divided into two sections: the recreation park and the jungle. Due to environmental degradation, the jungle is usually off limits.

hotel's trump card is its very attractive pool area (and not its aloof reception staff).

**Villa Angela** ( ☎ 639 641; Jl Pamugaran; r 100,000-150,000Rp; ⊠ ) Offering superb value, this new guest house has spacious rooms (all with TV and bathroom) in two attractive villa-style houses. It's run by a welcoming family and has a nice little garden. There's free tea/coffee and parking.

Other recommendations:

**Hotel Melati Nugraha** ( ☎ 639 225; Jl Pasanggrahan 3; r 45,000Rp) A row of very cheap, clean if bare rooms facing a grassy plot.

**Komodo** ( ☎ 630 753; Jl Bulak Laut 105; r 80,000-100,000Rp; ⊠ ) Friendly, family-owned place with spotless, if gaudy, large rooms.

### MIDRANGE & TOP END

Many of Pangandaran's midrange and top-end hotels have been upgraded since the tsunami. Weekday prices are given; expect to pay 15% to 30% more at some places on weekends.

**Adam's Homestay** ( ☎ 639 396; www.adamshomestay .com; Jl Pamugaran; r 160,000-440,000Rp; ⊠ 🔲 ) This a really relaxing, enjoyable place to stay, with a good, if slightly pricey, restaurant. Offers gorgeous, artistically presented rooms (many with balconies, beamed ceilings and outdoor bathrooms) spread around a verdant tropical garden that's just bursting with exotic plants and ponds.

**Pantai Sari** ( ☎ 639 175; Jl Bulak Laut 80; r incl breakfast 200,000-250,000Rp; ⊠ ) This renovated hotel has a very flash reception and though the rooms are more prosaic they're good value – spacious and very clean with flat-screen TVs, modern furniture and new beds.

**Hotel Century** ( ☎ 639 171; Jl Bulak Laut 86; r 250,000-300,000Rp; ⊠ ) Opening in late 2008, this modern hotel has smart rooms with a minimalist design, all with TV and air-con and some with sea views. Breakfast is included.

**Laut Biru** ( ☎ 639 360; www.lautbiru.com; Jl Jaga Lautan 17-18; r 400,000Rp; ⊠ 🛜 ⊠ ) A new modernist hotel at the southern end of the main beach that has huge rooms (each with twin beds, stylish dark-wood furniture and a balcony) that tick all the right contemporary boxes.

**Sunrise Beach Hotel** ( ☎ 639 220; Jl Kidang Pananjung 185; r 550,000-650,000Rp; ste from 800,000; ⊠ 🔲 ) Arguably Pangandaran's best hotel, this small resort has well-presented, spacious rooms (some with sea views), 24-hour room service and a restaurant and bar. Breakfast is included.

## Eating

Pangandaran is famous for its excellent seafood. For cheap Indonesian nosh, the town has many warungs.

**Warung Dapur** (Jl Bulak Laut 181; meals from 10,000Rp) Humble, inexpensive and friendly warung with bamboo walls and seats and a street terrace where you can watch the world go by. Try the *ayam bakar* (barbecued chicken) or *soto* (meat and vegetable broth).

**Batagor Bandung** ( ☎ 630 166; Jl Kidang Pananjung 116; snacks/meals 10,000/20,000Rp) Also known as the Green Garden Cafe, this excellent place has a relaxed boho vibe with artwork on display and tables set back off the street. *Batagor* (crispy tofu) is the delicious house speciality, but it also serves up other Indonesian dishes and great fresh juices.

**Relax Restaurant** ( ☎ 630 377; Jl Bulak Laut 74; mains 20,000Rp) Long-running Swiss-owned restaurant with a restrained, enjoyably formal air. The menu covers both Western and Indonesian fare, and service is prompt and efficient. Breakfast with the homemade bread is a treat.

**Sarimbit** (Jl Pantai Timor; meals around 25,000Rp) This simple local place is one of several fresh-fish restaurants facing east beach, and has tables facing the sea. Feast on red snapper or jumbo prawns cooked with a sauce of your choice.

**Chez Mama Cilacap** ( ☎ 630 098; Jl Kidang Pananjung 187; mains from 28,000Rp) This large restaurant has a good reputation and specialises in seafood, especially crab, fresh from the market.

**Pasar Ikan** (Fish Market; Jl Raya Timor; large fish 30,000-50,000Rp) Pangandaran's fish market occupies a little square that's situated just off the east beach. This is a great place for fresh fish and seafood – just choose what you want from the glistening iced displays, pay according to weight, and it's served up with a sauce (usually oyster or sweet-and-sour) within minutes.

## Drinking

**Bamboo Café** (Jl Pamugaran) Bamboo Café is fine for a cold Bintang, and though it has a great aspect over the ocean it's looking a bit shabby these days. The food's very average (mains from 15,000Rp).

**Mungil Steak House** (Jl Pamugaran) This log cabin bills itself as a 'steak house' for some bizarre reason, but it works much better as a bar (the food here – mains are 12,000Rp to 50,000Rp –

is greasy and takes hours to arrive). As well as beer it sell jugs of *arak*, and the sea views are top-drawer.

**De Coffee House** (Jl Pamugaran; coffee 2000-40,000Rp) Smart new cafe with stylish decor and a long long list of coffees (including Irish, hazelnut-flavoured and cappuccino), though most of the prices are absurd. Food including omelettes are also available.

## Getting There & Away

Pangandaran lies roughly halfway between Bandung and Yogyakarta. Most people get here by road as there's no train station close by, but it's perfectly possible to arrive by rail and bus. Speak to staff at the Mini Tiga Homestay for impartial transport advice and possible routes, and you can book tickets there too.

### BOAT

The once-popular backwater boat trip east of Pangandaran via Majingklak harbour to Cilacap is now effectively dead in the water due to dwindling numbers and better road and rail connections. It can still be done, but you'll have to charter your own *compreng* (wooden boat) to make the journey, which is very scenic, passing through rich swampland. Boatmen in Majingklak will do the three-hour trip for 300,000Rp after very hard bargaining. From Cilacap there are direct buses to Yogyakarta (48,000Rp, five hours).

### BUS

Local buses run from Pangandaran's main bus terminal to Tasikmalaya (30,000Rp, three hours), Ciamis (24,000Rp, 2½ hours), Banjar (17,000Rp, two hours) and Sidareja (10,000Rp, 1¼ hours). Buses also run along the west coast as far as Cijulang (8000Rp, 40 minutes).

Many *patas* buses to Jakarta and Bandung leave from the Sari Bakti Utama depot, just north of town, and Budiman bus company depot, about 2km west of Pangandaran along Jl Merdeka. Other services also leave from the main terminal. Buses leave for Bandung every one to two hours (52,000Rp, six hours) and for Jakarta's Kampung Rambutan terminal (65,000Rp to 80,000Rp, eight hours), mainly between 7pm and 9pm.

The most comfortable way to travel to Bandung is aboard a **Sari Harum** ( ☎ 639 276)

door-to-door *travel* minibus for 90,000Rp. **Perkasa Jaya minibuses** ( ☎ 639 607) pick up from hotels for the trip to Jakarta's Kampung Rambutan terminal (130,000Rp, eight hours).

### CAR

Travel agencies rent minibuses with drivers for about 700,000Rp per day including driver and petrol. The most popular trip is a three-day tour to Yogyakarta, usually via Wonosobo for the first night, Dieng for sunrise, then on to Borobudur. The final day is to Yogyakarta via Prambanan.

### TRAIN

The nearest stations are Banjar to the north and Sidareja on the east side. Both have regular local bus connections to Pangandaran. From Bandung to Banjar the most convenient trains are the *Argo Wilis* (executive class 175,000Rp, 3½ hours), which leaves at 7am, and the *Lodaya* (executive/business class 110,000/165,000Rp, 3½ hours), departing at 8am. You'll then have to hop on a local bus (17,000Rp, two hours), which leave every 20 minutes down to Pangandaran.

Train times and connections are not good or convenient from Yogyakarta to Sidareja. But if you're heading east to Yogya there's a very useful *bisnis* train (50,000Rp, 3½ hours) at 12.10pm from Sidareja direct to Yogya. You can't reserve seats on this train, but it's not usually crowded and it's possible to upgrade to an executive air-conditioned carriage once you're on board for an extra 50,000Rp. To make this connection either take a Budiman local bus from Pangandaran to Sidareja or hire a car to drop you off (150,000Rp). Travel agents and hotels including Mini Tiga Homestay can help with travel arrangements and tickets on this route via Sidareja, which is the quickest and most comfortable way to travel to Yogya.

## Getting Around

Pangandaran's brightly painted becak start at around 5000Rp and require heavy negotiation; see the warning about the local becak mafia, p157.

Bicycles can be rented for 20,000Rp per day, and motorcycles cost around 50,000Rp per day, excluding petrol; **Wawan Rental** ( ☎ 0852 2380 1257; Jl Pamugaran) rents out well-maintained bikes.

## AROUND PANGANDARAN

The scenic coastline around Pangandaran has some terrific surf beaches, forests, lagoons, fishing villages and a recreational park or two. It's a joy to explore by motorbike, or hotels and travel agencies can set up guided trips.

### West of Pangandaran

Heading west of town you travel along a pretty but busy coastal road lined with palm trees that runs through small villages and paddy fields. The once-popular backpacker hang-out of Cikembulan just west of Pangandaran was wiped out by the 2006 tsunami; for more on this, see the boxed text, opposite.

At the tiny village of **Ciokoto**, 6km along this road, there's a large *wayang golek* workshop, with high-quality puppets for sale (400,000Rp to 1,000,000Rp). Next up is **Karang Tirta**, a lagoon set back from the beach with *bagang* (fishing platforms). It's 16km from Pangandaran and 2km south of the highway. **Batu Hiu** (Shark Rock) is 23km from Pangandaran and 1km from the highway, and has a recreational park atop the cliffs with views along the coast.

Inland from Parigi, near Cigugur, **Gunung Tilu** hilltop has fine views and is included in some of the tour itineraries. **Sungai Citumang** is reached by a rough and hard-to-find inland road from Karang Benda, and has a small dam from where you can walk upstream to a beautiful gorge – 'Green Canyon II' in Pangandaran tour parlance.

### GREEN CANYON

The number one tour from Pangandaran is to Green Canyon (Cujang Taneuh); it's clearly signposted at several points along the highway. Many tour operators in Pangandaran run trips here for 150,000Rp and include 'countryside' excursions to make a full-day tour. To get there yourself, hire a boat from the Green Canyon river harbour on the highway, 1km

before the turn-off to Batu Karas. Boats cost 75,000Rp for a maximum of five people and operate daily from 7.30am to 4pm. They travel up the jungle-fringed, emerald-green river to a waterfall and a beautiful canyon where there's swimming (though the current is often strong here). Boatmen work on a return-trip schedule of just 45 minutes, which only gives you about 15 minutes to swim and explore the narrowest and most beautiful part of the canyon; if you want to stay longer you'll have to pay extra.

### Batu Karas

☎ 0265 / pop 3000

The idyllic fishing village and emerging surfing hot spot of Batu Karas, 32km west of Pangandaran, is one of the most enjoyable places to kick back in Java. It's a tiny one-lane settlement, separated by a wooded promontory, and has a low-key, very relaxed charm. There are two fine beaches, with sheltered sections that are usually calm enough for good swimming, but most visitors are here for the breaks, and there's a lot of surf talk. This is one of the best places in Java to learn to surf. The locally run surf co-op here charges 80,000Rp per person per day for lessons; board hire is extra (around 35,000Rp).

#### SLEEPING & EATING

**Teratai** (r 90,000-135,000Rp) Budget-friendly, family-owned place with large rooms and clean *mandis* scattered around a large grassy plot.

**Reef Hotel** (☎ 0813 2034 0193; r from 120,000Rp) Enjoys a great position right opposite one of the main surf breaks on the north side of the village, but the twin-bed rooms are overpriced and plain.

**Bonsai Bungalows** (☎ 709 3199; r 150,000Rp, bungalows 400,000Rp; ❄ ) This is a good choice, with well-constructed, very clean and tidy thatched accommodation either in neat little

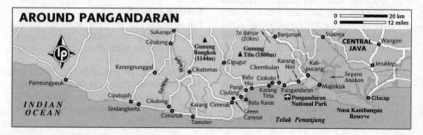

**AROUND PANGANDARAN**

## LOCAL VOICE: GECKO

In the previous edition of this guidebook, the sole 'our pick' in the Pangandaran area was Delta Gecko, a bohemian beach-side hang-out for travellers and creative Indonesians. But then the 2006 tsunami struck Java's southern coast.

Agus 'Gecko' Ramadhi, one of the founders of Delta Gecko, is an artist from Bandung but has been living in Pangandaran for years.

'I first came to Pangandaran in 1982. There was no electricity and only three losmen. I was studying art but hated studying and I was addicted to narcotics. I had two pet geckos – that's how I got my nickname, 'Gecko' – but they both died when my friend fed them tobacco. I painted 14 gecko designs in their memory, which were all bought by a Japanese guy.

We opened Delta Gecko in 1990, with a German partner and my ex-wife, Christina. I helped design and construct a lot of the bungalows, all from natural materials like bamboo and wood. We separated all our rubbish and composted. Gradually we created a mini-zoo. We had many animals – a porcupine, purple herons, wild pigs, three kinds of eagles as well as chickens, ducks geese and goats. We did tours the right way – going up the Green Canyon in canoes, not using motor boats, so people could see the birds and wildlife.

I built a 7m gecko from papier mâché and bamboo to celebrate 50 years of Indonesian independence. We carried it through the streets of Pangandaran – the children loved it. Our parties – every Wednesday – were famous. We had our own *pongdut* band and everyone would dance after dinner around a big beach bonfire. Sometimes we stayed up till sunrise. And no drugs! Just *arak* (palm wine) and beer.

On the day of the tsunami I remember it was my coffee time, four o'clock. We had no guests that day; the last one had checked out the day before. I was lying in my house at the back of Delta Gecko. There was no warning because the electricity was down. I heard a woman scream; the kitchen wall had fallen down. I ran. I ran like a madman. After about 100m the water hit me. It came up to my knees, but I got away.

Everything was gone except one bungalow. I lost my best friend, Iwan, and his little daughter Vanessa. He used to play music for the guests every night.

Afterwards it was so difficult. I had no money, no income. I would love to rebuild a kind of Delta Gecko but make it more an art space. I am lucky that I have a good friend who gives me room so I can paint and show my work.'

Agus's art can be seen at Batagor Bandung (p158).

---

fan-cooled wooden rooms with verandahs or huge air-con bungalows that can sleep six. The Tsunami bar here sells cold Bintang.

**Panireman Riverside** ( ☎ 0812 7255 8666; bungalows incl breakfast 250,000-400,000Rp) A new place in a lovely riverbank setting, 1km before the entrance to the village. The nine thatched bungalows, built in local style but with modern amenities including sprung mattresses, have front decks overlooking the river. Popular with students at weekends, it's usually very peaceful here during the week, and there's a restaurant. Very little English is spoken, however. Kayaks (20,000Rp per hour), dinghys (150,000Rp per hour) and jet-skis (60,000Rp for 15 minutes) are for hire.

**Java Cove** ( ☎ 708 2020; www.javacovebeachhotel .com; economy r 120,000Rp, luxury r 420,000-620,000Rp; ❋ ) Gorgeous Australian-owned beachfront hotel that offers beautiful, if a little pricey,

contemporary-chic rooms as well as no-frills economy options. There's a decked, surf-facing garden with a coffee and ice-cream bar, and Western treats like meat pies and pizzas are available. Add 15% tax to room rates.

Eating options:

**Sederhana** (mains 8000-18,000Rp) Catch a bite to eat while watching the waves here.

**Kang Ayi** ( ☎ 708 2025; mains 10,000-20,000Rp) Neighbours Sederhana.

**Popeye** (mains 10,000-20,000Rp) Opposite Bonsai Bungalows, this chalet-like place has good omelettes and Indo food.

## GETTING THERE & AWAY

You have to pay a toll of 3900Rp to enter the village. Batu Karas can be reached from Pangandaran by taking a bus to Cijulang (7000Rp) and then an *ojek* over the pretty bamboo bridge for 6000Rp.

## East of Pangandaran

The main Pangandaran–Banjar road runs east initially, passing a series of bays and beaches exposed to the full force of the Indian Ocean. The first of these, about 8km along the road, is **Karang Nini** (entrance fee 3500Rp), where there's a group of warung on a headland, picnic areas beneath pandan trees and some bare, unattractive **bungalows** (per night 220,000Rp). The eastern section of beach here is superb, with a sweeping expanse of sand and crashing surf. Walk for 15 minutes along this beach and you'll reach a beautiful river estuary, its banks lined with tropical forest and patrolled by gliding eagles. Karang Nini is about 3km south of the highway.

Pushing eastwards you get views over **Nusa Kambangan** (p167), the last port of call on this planet for the Bali bombers who were executed on this island prison in 2008. Around 7km from Karang Nini, there's a turn-off for the scruffy harbour of **Majingklak**, which sits on the western bank of Segara Anakan lagoon. There are no longer scheduled boats to Cilacap, but boatmen might be persuaded to take you there; expect to pay upwards of 300,000Rp for the three-hour trip. It's possible to charter a boat to explore the lagoon for 60,000Rp an hour after persistent bargaining.

## CIREBON

☎ 0231 / pop 230,000

Well off the tourist trail, on the sunburnt north coast, Cirebon is a cultural melting pot, blending the scattered remains of the ancient Islamic kingdom that once had its base here with a more contemporary cocktail of Javanese, Sundanese and Chinese culture.

Compared to many of Java's cities, Cirebon is refreshingly laid-back. And with venerable *kraton* (walled city palaces), a thriving batik industry and one of the north coast's biggest fishing fleets, it's a worthwhile stopover for seafood lovers and inquisitive travellers. Cirebon is famous for its batik; *tari topeng*, a type of masked dance; and *tarling*, music blending guitar, *suling* and voice.

Cirebon was one of the independent sultanates founded by Sunan Gunungjati of Demak in the early 16th century. Later the powerful kingdoms of Banten and Mataram fought over the town, which declared its allegiance to Sultan Agung of Mataram but was finally ceded to the Dutch in 1677. By a further treaty signed in 1705, Cirebon became a Dutch protectorate, jointly administered by three sultans whose courts at that time rivalled those of Central Java in opulence and splendour.

## Information

Banks and ATMs can be found all over town; a branch of BII Bank is located at the northern end of Jl Siliwangi.

**Elganet** (Ruko Grand Centre B/4; per hr 5500Rp) Internet access.

**Main post office** (Jl Yos Sudarso) Near the harbour.

**Telkom** (Jl Yos Sudarso) For international telephone calls and faxes.

**Tourist office** ( ☎ 486 856; Jl Dharsono 5; ✆ 7am-3pm Mon-Fri) Lies 5km out of town on the bypass road, near Gua Sunyaragi. Staff are helpful here, but printed information is lacking.

## Sights & Activities

### KRATON KESEPUHAN

At the southern end of Jl Lemah Wungkuk, **Kraton Kesepuhan** (admission 3000Rp, camera 2000Rp; ✆ 8am-4pm Mon-Thu & Sat, 8-11am & 1-4pm Fri, 8am-4pm Sun) is the oldest and best preserved of Cirebon's *kraton*. Built in 1527, its architectural style is a curious blend of Sundanese, Javanese, Islamic, Chinese and Dutch. Although this is the home of the sultan of Kesepuhan, part of the building is open to visitors. Inside is a pavilion with walls dotted with blue-and-white Delft tiles (many depicting biblical scenes), a marble floor and a ceiling hung with glittering French chandeliers.

The *kraton* museum has an interesting, if poorly displayed collection of *wayang* puppets, kris, cannons, furniture, Portuguese armour (weighing in at an impressive 45kg) and ancient royal clothes. The pièce de résistance is the Kereta Singa Barong, a 16th-century gilded chariot with the trunk of an elephant (Hindu), the body and head of a dragon (Chinese-Buddhist), golden wings (Egyptian-Islamic) and the paws of a tiger. It was traditionally pulled by four white buffaloes and the suspension apparently flapped the wings and waggled the creature's tongue. It is quite possibly the wildest carriage you'll ever see.

Entry to the *kraton* includes a guided tour (payment at your discretion), which finishes in the *kraton's* museum. Here there are spice boxes, French crystal and relics from Portugal and Holland. Look out for the Javanese-Hindu Kama Sutra woodcarving.

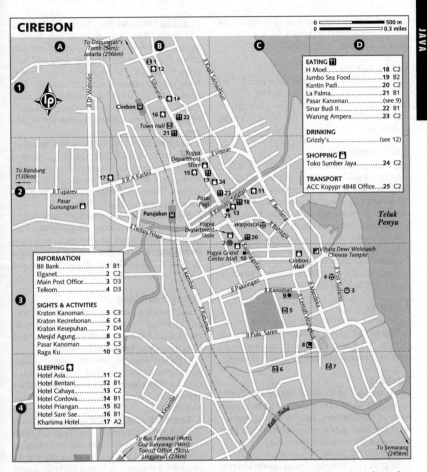

**CIREBON**

0   500 m
0   0.3 miles

To Gunungjati's
Tomb (5km);
Jakarta (256km)

To Bandung
(130km)

*Teluk
Penyu*

To Bus Terminal (4km);
Gua Sunyaragi (4km);
Tourist Office (5km);
Linggarjati (23km)

To Semarang
(245km)

| INFORMATION | | |
|---|---|---|
| BII Bank | **1** | B1 |
| Elganet | **2** | C2 |
| Main Post Office | **3** | D3 |
| Telkom | **4** | D3 |

| SIGHTS & ACTIVITIES | | |
|---|---|---|
| Kraton Kanoman | **5** | C3 |
| Kraton Kecirebonan | **6** | C4 |
| Kraton Kesepuhan | **7** | D4 |
| Mesjid Agung | **8** | C3 |
| Pasar Kanoman | **9** | C3 |
| Raga Ku | **10** | C3 |

| SLEEPING | | |
|---|---|---|
| Hotel Asia | **11** | C2 |
| Hotel Bentani | **12** | B1 |
| Hotel Cahaya | **13** | C2 |
| Hotel Cordova | **14** | B1 |
| Hotel Priangan | **15** | B2 |
| Hotel Sare Sae | **16** | B1 |
| Kharisma Hotel | **17** | A2 |

| EATING | | |
|---|---|---|
| H Moel | **18** | C2 |
| Jumbo Sea Food | **19** | B2 |
| Kantin Padi | **20** | C2 |
| La Palma | **21** | B1 |
| Pasar Kanoman | (see 9) | |
| Sinar Budi II | **22** | B1 |
| Warung Ampera | **23** | C2 |

| DRINKING | | |
|---|---|---|
| Grizzly's | (see 12) | |

| SHOPPING | | |
|---|---|---|
| Toko Sumber Jaya | **24** | C2 |

| TRANSPORT | | |
|---|---|---|
| ACC Kopypr 4848 Office | **25** | C2 |

## KRATON KANOMAN

A short walk from Kraton Kesepuhan, **Kraton Kanoman** (admission by donation; 8am-5pm) was constructed in 1588 but is now in poor shape. The Kanoman dynasty was founded by Sultan Badaruddin, who broke away from the main sultanate after a lineage dispute with the sixth sultan's heir. Outside the *kraton* is a red-brick, Balinese-style compound and a massive banyan tree. Further on past the white stone lions is the *kraton*, a smaller, neglected cousin of Kraton Kesepuhan.

The museum here has some intriguing carvings (one featuring a reptile king) amidst layers of dust. Again it's the sultan's chariot that steals the show, however. This version is in exactly the same style as the one over in

Kraton Kesepuhan, but here they claim that theirs is the original – rivalry for the sultanate still exists, it seems. The *pendopo* (large open-sided pavilion) and its inner altar were closed for renovation at the time of research.

The colourful **Pasar Kanoman**, just in front of the *kraton*, is at its most vibrant in the morning and is worth a visit in its own right.

## KRATON KECIREBONAN

Although it's classed as a *kraton*, this is really only a house occupied by members of the current royal family, descendants of Raja Kanomin, who broke away from the 10th Kesepuhan sultanate. Wander in, knock on the door and someone will be happy to show you around. Built in 1839, the house has fine colonial architecture and a small collection of swords, documents and other royal memorabilia. A donation is expected.

### MESJID AGUNG
On the western side of the field in front of Kraton Kesepuhan is Mesjid Agung. One of the oldest mosques in Java, it has a tiered roof and is similar in style to the Mesjid Agung in Banten.

### GUA SUNYARAGI
Approximately 4km southwest of town is this bizarre ruined 'cave' – a grotto of rocks, red brick and plaster, honeycombed with secret chambers, tiny doors and staircases that lead nowhere. It was originally a water palace for a sultan of Cirebon in the early 18th century and owes its present shape to a Chinese architect who had a go at it in 1852. It's often frequented by local students who, at the sight of a tourist, are more than happy to practise their English, even from 50m away.

## Activities
Sightseeing involves a lot of legwork. Head to **Raga Ku** ( ☎ 339 1099; Jl Karanggetas 6; massages from 45,000Rp; ☼ 9-9pm) for an excellent, very inexpensive massage; reflexology is also available.

## Sleeping
**Hotel Cordova** ( ☎ 204 677; Jl Siliwangi 87; r 40,000-154,000Rp; ☒ ▢ ☎) The renovated lobby is quite fancy at the Cordova, but the rooms haven't been touched: they're old-fashioned but kept clean enough; some have air-con.

**Hotel Asia** ( ☎ 204 905; Jl Kalibaru Selatan 11A; r 55,000-85,000Rp; ☒) It's looking a bit weary these days, but this fine old Dutch-Indonesian inn does have character. Rooms are basic, but fine for a night and there's a courtyard for your breakfast.

**Hotel Cahaya** ( ☎ 206 018; Jl Kalibaru Selatan 47; r 75,000-125,000Rp; ☒) This well-run place is popular with visiting salesmen and has plain, functional and clean rooms in a central location, the more expensive options have air-con and hot water. A free *nasi goreng* breakfast is included in the restaurant below.

**Hotel Priangan** ( ☎ 200 296; Jl Siliwangi 108; r 75,000-210,000Rp; ☒) Set back from the street, this slightly quirky place has ageing but decent rooms that face a narrow garden. Watch your head entering the bathroom – ceilings are very low!

**ourpick Hotel Sare Sae** ( ☎ 209 489; Jl Siliwangi 70; r 250,000-300,000Rp; ☒ ☎) The Sare Sae is a terrific newish hotel, with excellent comfort levels for the price, helpful staff and real style. Rooms, set to the rear of the property, have exposed beams, chunky wooden furniture and unusual bathrooms with zany *mandi*/showers. Enjoy your complimentary breakfast on the decked terrace above fish ponds.

**Kharisma Hotel** ( ☎ 207 668; kh-hotel@telkom.net; Jl RA Kartini 60; r from 376,000Rp; ☒ ▣) Kharisma is one of Cirebon's better midrange hotels; book one of the very spacious rooms in its new section. There's a restaurant and a couple of bars here for late-night drinks.

**Hotel Bentani** ( ☎ 203 246; www.bentani-hotel.com; Jl Siliwangi 69; r 500,000-622,000Rp; ☒ ▢ ☎ ▣) This garish-looking hotel has 88 spacious rooms with rattan furniture that are well-maintained and clean. The pool is small; there's a spa and a bar. Discounts are available.

## Eating & Drinking
Cheap warungs serving seafood and snacks can be found along Jl Kalibaru Selatan near Hotel Asia. For ultra-fresh exotic fruit, head directly to **Pasar Kanoman** (Jl Kanoman).

**La Palma** (Jl Siliwangi 86; cakes from 2000Rp; ☼ 7.30am-6pm) A period piece housed in an old Dutch villa, La Palma looks as if it hasn't changed for generations. Serves cakes, snacks and pastries. Nonsmoking.

**Kantin Padi** ( ☎ 208 836; Jl Karanggetas 51; meals 10,000-20,000Rp) Opposite the Yogya Grand Center Mall, this new place was just opening when we passed by. We recommend you do too, for the Indonesian food is super-fresh and no MSG is used – *nasi kunming* (yellow rice) is the house specialty.

**Warung Ampera** ( ☎ 201 205; Jl Siliwangi 247; meals from 12,000Rp) The hottest place in town, this new upmarket warung serves traditional Javanese food in modern surrounds. Choose from buffet-style displays – there are always plenty of delicious fish dishes. Ampera also has wonderful fresh juices.

**H Moel** ( ☎ 206 886; Jl Kalibaru Selatan 69; mains 12,000-65,000Rp) Huge place that has a city-wide reputation for its seafood; try the *ikan bakar* (from 25,000Rp). There's an open kitchen, so you can see the chefs at work.

**Sinar Budi II** ( ☎ 208 045; Jl Siliwangi 97; meals from 15,000Rp) For Padang food in Cirebon don't look any further.

**Jumbo Sea Food** ( ☎ 200 170; Jl Siliwangi 191; mains 27,000-50,000Rp) Another huge fish restaurant, the Jumbo is renowned for its hot plates and seafood grills.

For a drink:

**Grizzly's** (Jl Siliwangi 69) In the Hotel Bentani, this bar is about the only game in town, and has regular drinks specials.

## Shopping

**Toko Sumber Jaya** (Jl Siliwangi 211 & 229) The two branches of this store stock all sorts of *oleh-oleh* (souvenirs) from Cirebon including pottery and bamboo crafts.

## Getting There & Away

There are no longer any Pelni boats to or from Cirebon.

### BUS

The Cirebon bus terminal is 4km southwest of the centre of town.

Normal/air-con buses run between Cirebon and Jakarta (42,000/58,000Rp, four hours), Bandung (26,000/38,000Rp, four hours), Pekalongan (34,000/44,000Rp, four hours); and Semarang (50,000/66,000Rp, seven hours), as well as many of Java's main cities.

For *travel* from Cirebon, the **ACC Kopyor 4848 office** ( ☎ 204 343; Jl Karanggetas 9) operates minibuses to Bandung (60,000Rp, four hours) and Semarang (100,000Rp, seven hours).

### TRAIN

Cirebon is serviced by frequent trains that run on both the main northern Jakarta–Semarang–Surabaya train line and the southern Jakarta–Yogyakarta–Surabaya line. The better services leave from Cirebon's main train station, just off Jl Siliwangi. Crowded economy-class trains leave from the Parujakan train station further south.

For Jakarta's Gambir station, the *Cirebon Express* (business/executive class 60,000/75,000Rp, three hours) departs from Cirebon five times daily. To Yogyakarta, the business-class *Fajar Yogya* (110,000Rp, five hours) departs at 9.35am.

## Getting Around

Cirebon's city minibus *(angkutan kota)* services operate from behind the main bus terminal; a fixed 2000Rp fare is charged.

Cirebon has legions of pushy becak; you'll get harassed constantly. A ride from the train station to Pasar Pagi costs around 10,000Rp.

There are also taxis, but meters are seemingly reserved for family members and royalty.

## AROUND CIREBON

In the royal cemetery, 5km north of Cirebon, is the **tomb of Sunan Gunungjati**, who died in 1570. The most revered of Cirebon's kings, Gunungjati was also one of the nine *wali songo* (saintly men who spread Islam throughout Java), and his tomb is one of the holiest places in the country. The inner tombs are only open once a month on Kliwon Thursday of the Javanese calendar (the calendar is a combination of the normal seven-day week and the five-day Javanese market week), and at Idul Fitri and Maulud Nabi Muhammed (see p832). Pilgrims sit in contemplation and pray outside the doors on other days. Along from Sunan Gunungjati's tomb is the tomb of his first wife, who was Chinese – this tomb attracts Chinese worshippers.

**Linggarjati**, a small mountain resort 23km south of Cirebon, was assured of its place in the history books when, in 1946, representatives of the republican government and the returning Dutch occupying forces met to negotiate a British-sponsored cooperation agreement. Terms were thrashed out in a colonial hotel at the foot of **Gunung Cirema** (3078m), once a retreat from the heat for Cirebon's Dutch residents. Sukarno briefly attended, but the Linggarjati Agreement was soon swept aside as the war for independence escalated. The hotel is now **Gedung Naksa**, a museum recreating the events.

To reach Linggarjati, take a Kuningan bus from Cirebon to Cilimus (5000Rp) and then an *angkot* (3000Rp) or *andong* (horse-drawn passenger cart) to either resort.

# CENTRAL JAVA

Jakarta may be the nation's capital, but the Javan identity is at its strongest here, in the island's historic heartland. As the seat of Java's first major Indianised civilisation, as well as the great Islamic sultanates centred on the *kraton* of Yogyakarta and Solo, Central Java (Jawa Tengah) remains the province in which the island's cultural pulse beats loudest.

Even though Central Java has a reputation for a short fuse when dealing with religious and political sentiments, it's a relaxed, easy-going province for tourists. Yogyakarta, at the centre

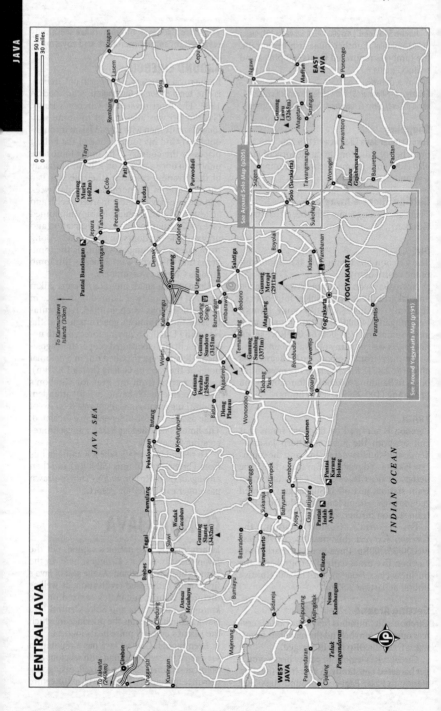

# CENTRAL JAVA

of its own quasi-independent 'special region' stretching from the south coast to Gunung Merapi, and Solo, just 65km to the northeast of Yogyakarta, are Java's most interesting cities. But even Semarang, the province's busy, maritime capital, has its fair share of charm and is, like its more bombastic tourist centres, an intriguing fusion of Java's past and future. Most, though, will find the intricate Borobudur and Prambanan temples the highlight of any trip to the centre of this stunning island.

## CILACAP

☎ 0282 / pop 210,000

Over the border from West Java, Cilacap is an unhurried city of wide boulevards and has the only natural harbour with deep-water berthing facilities on Java's south coast. Very few travellers pass through here now there are no regular boats plying the backwater trip to Pangandaran.

The **tourist office** ( ☎ 534 481; Jl A Yani 8; ⏰ 8am-3.30pm Mon-Fri, 7.30am-1pm Sat) is opposite the Hotel Wijayakusuma.

### Sights & Activities

Built between 1861 and 1879, **Benteng Pendem** (admission 2000Rp; ⏰ 8am-4pm) is an impressive Dutch fort complex at the entrance to the old harbour. It has intact barracks (bring a torch to explore properly, as they're rather dark) and massive ramparts, and is one of the best-preserved colonial garrisons in Java.

The fort overlooks a long stretch of dirty sand, **Pantai Teluk Penyu**. This popular local beach has souvenir stalls that sell an array of shells and trinkets.

For better beaches – complete with white sand – head to **Nusa Kambangan**, a long island south of the port. This island contains no fewer than four high-security prisons (and five inactive ones); former inmates have included the Bali bombers and Tommy Suharto. There are fine beaches to explore, but swimming can be treacherous. Keep a lookout for white-bellied fish eagles surfing the thermals. Ferries sail from Cilacap at 7am (30,000Rp) and return in the late afternoon.

### Sleeping & Eating

**Hotel Anggrek** ( ☎ 533 835; Jl Anggrek 16; r with shared mandi/air-con 45,000/75,000Rp; ☒ ) For a cheap bed, consider this place, which has spartan and reasonably clean rooms. It's about a five-minute walk to Jl Yani, the main drag.

**Hotel Mutiara Cilacap** ( ☎ 531 545; mutiaracilacap @intanhotels.com; Jl Gatot Subroto 136; r from 550,000Rp; ☒ ☐ ☒ ) This is the best hotel in town, with business-class facilities, comfortable, spacious rooms, and a decent restaurant plus a bar and cafe.

**Restaurant Perapatan/Sien Hieng** (Jl A Yani 62; mains around 30,000Rp) Long-running Chinese place that has the best rep in Cilacap. The seafood dishes excel here.

### Getting There & Away
#### BOAT
Only charter boats are now plying the backwaters from Cilacap to Majingklak. See p162 for more information on trips. The jetty is near the big Pertamina installations.

The Cilacap **bus terminal** (Jl Gatot Subroto) is 3km north of the city centre. Buses run between Cilacap and Pangandaran (32,000Rp, three hours), Yogyakarta (48,000Rp, five hours) and Purwokerto (14,000Rp, 1½ hours), where you'll need to change for Wonosobo.

For door-to-door minibuses to Yogyakarta (70,000Rp) call **Toko Djadi** ( ☎ 533 490; Jl A Yani 72); for Purwokerto (20,000Rp) use **Nusantara Express** ( ☎ 533 301; Jl Perwira).

Cilacap's central train station is just off Jl A Yani. Very few trains now operate from here, but the *Purwojaya* leaves for Jakarta (executive/business class 150,000/80,000Rp, five hours) at 6.30pm.

## PURWOKERTO

A surprisingly clean city with some architectural reminders of the Dutch colonial era, Purwokerto is a crossroads for travellers heading between Wonosobo and Pangandaran. There are hotels here, but you're better off staying at the mountain resort of Baturaden, 14km to the north.

The train station is close to the city centre and the bus terminal is about 2km south. Buses run to all major centres, including Wonosobo (28,000Rp, three hours), Banjar and Yogyakarta. Infrequent direct buses go to Baturaden (6000Rp), or catch an *angkot* from Pasar Wage (6000Rp) in town.

## WONOSOBO

☎ 0286 / pop 110,000

Wonosobo is the main gateway to the Dieng Plateau. At 900m above sea level in the central mountain range, it has a comfortable

Warna (Coloured Lake), Candi Bima (Bima Temple), Kawah Sikidang (Sikidang Crater), and then back to Candi Gatutkaca, the Arjuna Complex and the village. Many other lakes and craters around Dieng are scattered over a large area and are difficult to reach.

## Information

Entrance prices have risen recently for the temples and natural sights in Dieng. A cost-saving ticket used to exist that covered you for the main sights, but at research time this appeared to have been discontinued – expect to have to pay for each attraction separately.

The BRI bank, near Hotel Gunung Mas, changes US dollars.

## Sights

### TEMPLES

The five main temples that form the **Arjuna Complex** (20,000Rp) are clustered together on the central plain. They are Shiva temples, but like the other Dieng temples they have been named after the heroes of the *wayang* stories of the Mahabharata epic: Arjuna, Puntadewa, Srikandi, Sembadra and Semar. All have mouth-shaped doorways and strange bell-shaped windows and some locals leave offerings, burn incense and meditate here. Raised walkways link the temples (as most of this land is waterlogged), but you can see the remains of ancient underground tunnels, which once drained the marshy flatlands.

Just southwest of the Arjuna Complex are **Candi Gatutkaca**, two small **museums** (admission incl in Arjuna ticket price; 8am-3pm) and a modest cafe. The site museum contains statues and sculptures from the temples, including Shiva's carrier, Nandi the bull – with the body of a man and the head of a bull, it is a unique representation in Hindu iconography. There's also a headless image of Shiva himself, depicted in the lotus position, while a gargoyle sporting an erection is distinctly animist. The second museum, a new building directly behind the site museum, has lots of information about the geology of Dieng, the folklore associated with the plateau and more carved statues. All the display information here is in Bahasa Indonesia only.

Further south, **Candi Bima** is unique in Java, its *kudu* (sculpted heads) looking like spectators peering out of windows.

The restored **Candi Dwarawati** is on the northern outskirts of the village. Near the entrance to Dieng at the river, **Tuk Bima Lukar** is an ancient bathing spring. It was once a holy place and is said to be a fountain of youth.

### OTHER SIGHTS

The road south from Dieng Plateau Homestay passes a mushroom factory and a flower garden before the turn-off to beautiful **Telaga Warna** (7000Rp; 8am-4.30pm), which has turquoise hues from the bubbling sulphur deposits around its shores. A trail leads anticlockwise to the adjoining lake, **Telaga Pengilon**, and the holy **Gua Semar**, a renowned meditation cave. Return to the main road via the indistinct trail that leads around Telaga Pengilon and up the terraced hillside. The colours of the lakes are better viewed from up high.

From Telaga Warna it's about 1km along the main road to Candi Bima, and then another 1.2km to **Kawah Sikidang** (5000Rp), a volcanic crater with steaming vents and frantically bubbling mud ponds. Exercise extreme caution here – there are no guard rails to keep you from slipping off the sometimes muddy trails into the scalding-hot waters. **Kawah Sibentang** is a less spectacular crater nearby, and **Telaga Lumut** is another small lake.

South of the geothermal station, the paved road leads on to **Sembungan**, said to be the highest village in Java, at 2300m. Potato farming has made this large village relatively wealthy – it sends an inordinate number of pilgrims to Mecca.

**Gunung Sikunir**, 1km past Sembungan, and the shallow lake of **Telaga Cebong**, just beyond the village, are the main attractions in this area. Views from Sikunir are spectacular, stretching across Dieng and east as far as Merapi and Merbabu volcanoes on a clear day. To reach the hill in time for sunrise, start at 4am from Dieng village. It's a one-hour walk to Sembungan and another 30 minutes to the top of the hill. Dieng Plateau Homestay and Hotel & Restaurant Bu Jono both offer guides for 45,000Rp per person.

Other attractions to the west are more difficult to reach. **Telaga Merdada** is a large lake, with a mushroom factory next to it. **Kawah Sileri**, 2km off the main road and 6km from Dieng, is a smoking crater area with a hot lake. A cave, **Gua Jimat**, is a 1km walk through the fields from the main road.

Nine kilometres from Dieng village is the trail to **Kawah Candradimuka**; it's a pleasant 1.5km walk to this crater through the fields.

Another trail branches off to two lakes: **Telaga Nila** and (a longer, two-hour walk away) **Telaga Dringo**. Just a few hundred metres past the turn-off to Kawah Candradimuka is **Sumur Jalatunda**. This well is in fact a deep hole some 100m across with vertical walls plunging down to bright-green waters.

Another popular spot to see the sunrise and views of the valley is the **lookout point** on the Wonosobo road, 5km back towards Wonosobo.

## Sleeping & Eating

Dieng's dozen or more guest houses are notoriously poor value. Spartan conditions and draughty, semi-clean rooms are the norm. Beware that hot water is not always forthcoming. A new midrange hotel was nearing completion when we were in town. It's located right opposite the entrance road from Wonosobo (and painted a not-very-fetching dirty-pink colour).

**Dieng Plateau Homestay** ( ☎ 0813 2779 1565; Jl Raya, km 26; r 40,000Rp) Ubersparse place where the very basic rooms have concrete floors, a stick or two of furniture and rough blankets. That said, Titu, who works here, is a very amusing and hospitable guy who runs tours (sunrise trips are 50,000Rp) and will help you out in any way he can. The chilly, bare restaurant downstairs was closed for renovation when we visited but should soon reopen and serve typical travellers' fare.

**Hotel & Restaurant Bu Jono** ( ☎ 642 046, 0813 2845 5401; Jl Raya, km 26; r 50,000-75,000Rp) 'Hotel' is pushing it (considerably), but this simple place does have a certain quirky, if ramshackle charm. All rooms are small (one bed comes equipped with a Superman headboard!) and there are three shared hot-water *mandis*. The restaurant is actually a good place to eat, and even has tablecloths; try the high-altitude, energy-giving, carb-attack Swiss rosti. Staff are friendly here, supply good local information and offer tours.

**Hotel Gunung Mas** ( ☎ 334 2017; r 100,000, with hot water 150,000Rp) This is the most 'upmarket' hotel in town. Reception is not particularly friendly, and staff may enquire if couples are married (co-habiting is not on the agenda here, folks) and ask you to pay in advance. Still, at least the rooms are kept clean and in are good condition.

Food is not Dieng's strong suit; Hotel & Restaurant Bu Jono is your best bet and has

beer, but be prepared to wait for your nosebag. The cafe near the museums may or may not be open. While in town you must try the local herb, *purwaceng*, which is a kind of Dieng-style coca leaf that gives you a lift (if not a buzz). It's added to tea and coffee and for sale around town and at the entrance to the Arjuna Complex.

## Getting There & Away

Dieng is 26km from Wonosobo (8000Rp, one hour), which is the usual access point. Buses continue on to Batur (3000Rp from Dieng), where you can catch a further bus to Pekalongan (27,000Rp, three hours) via a steep and bumpy but paved road.

It's possible to reach Dieng from Yogyakarta in one day (including a stop at Borobudur) by public bus, provided you leave early enough to make the connection; the route is Yogyakarta–Borubudur–Magelang–Wonosobo–Dieng. Travel agents in Yogyakarta offer day trips that include Borobudur, but you'll spend most of your time on a bus and (unless you're very fortunate) generally end up seeing Dieng clouded in mist.

# BOROBUDUR
☎ 0293

Like Angkor Wat in Cambodia and Bagan in Myanmar, Java's Borobudur makes the rest of Southeast Asia's spectacular sites seem almost incidental. Looming out of a patchwork of bottle-green paddies and swaying palms, this colossal Buddhist monument has survived Gunung Merapi's ash flows, terrorist bombs and the 2006 earthquake to remain as enigmatic and beautiful as it must have been 1200 years ago.

However, in recent years the impact of mass tourism (on holidays up to 90,000 people ascend the temple) has put extreme pressure on Borobudur and conservationists are declaring that urgent measures are now necessary to ensure its survival.

It's well worth planning to spend a few days in the Borobudur region, which is a supremely beautiful landscape of impossibly green rice fields and traditional rice-growing *kampung*, all overlooked by soaring volcanic peaks.

This region is establishing itself as Indonesia's most important centre for Buddhism, and there are now three monasteries in the surrounding district. Visitors are welcome and you can even join the monks at prayer time for chanting; see p174.

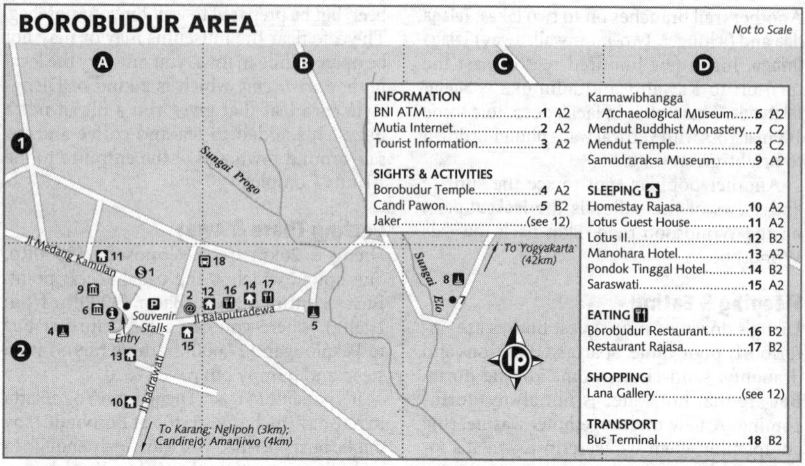
BOROBUDUR AREA
Not to Scale
A
B
C
D
1
2
Sungai Progo
Jl Medang Kamulan
Souvenir Stalls
Entry
Jl Balaputradewa
Jl Badrawati
Sungai Elo
To Yogyakarta (42km)
To Karang; Nglipoh (3km); Candirejo; Amanjiwo (4km)
INFORMATION
BNI ATM 1 A2
Mutia Internet 2 A2
Tourist Information 3 A2
SIGHTS & ACTIVITIES
Borobudur Temple 4 A2
Candi Pawon 5 B2
Jaker (see 12)
Karmawibhangga Archaeological Museum 6 A2
Mendut Buddhist Monastery 7 C2
Mendut Temple 8 C2
Samudraraksa Museum 9 A2
SLEEPING
Homestay Rajasa 10 A2
Lotus Guest House 11 A2
Lotus II 12 B2
Manohara Hotel 13 A2
Pondok Tinggal Hotel 14 B2
Saraswati 15 A2
EATING
Borobudur Restaurant 16 B2
Restaurant Rajasa 17 B2
SHOPPING
Lana Gallery (see 12)
TRANSPORT
Bus Terminal 18 B2

## History

Rulers of the Sailendra dynasty built Borobudur some time between AD 750 and AD 850. Little else is known about Borobudur's early history, but the Sailendras must have recruited a huge workforce, as some 60,000 cu metres of stone had to be hewn, transported and carved during its construction. The name Borobudur is possibly derived from the Sanskrit words 'Vihara Buddha Uhr', which mean 'Buddhist Monastery on the Hill'.

With the decline of Buddhism and the shift of power to East Java, Borobudur was abandoned soon after completion and for centuries lay forgotten, buried under layers of volcanic ash. It was only in 1815, when Sir Thomas Stamford Raffles governed Java, that the site was cleared and the sheer magnitude of the builders' imagination and technical skill was revealed. Early in the 20th century the Dutch began to tackle the restoration of Borobudur, but over the years the supporting hill had become waterlogged and the whole immense stone mass started to subside. A mammoth US$25-million Unesco-sponsored restoration project was undertaken between 1973 and 1983 to stabilise and restore the monument. This involved taking most of it apart stone by stone, adding new concrete foundations, inserting PVC and a lead drainage system, and then putting the whole shebang back together again.

On 21 January 1985, bombs planted by opponents of Suharto exploded on the upper layers of Borobudur. Many of the smaller stupas were damaged, but the temple has once again been fully restored, demonstrating the structure's resilience. In 1991 Borobudur gained the status of a World Heritage Site.

## Orientation & Information

The small, bustling village of Borobudur consists of around a dozen or so hotels and guest houses, scores of warungs and innumerable souvenir stalls The bus terminal is less than 10 minutes' walk from the monument.

For standard tourist information contact the **information office** (☎ 788 266; www.borobudurpark.com; admission to temple US$12; 6am-5.30pm) just beyond the temple's entrance. Official guides are available at the smart new entrance lobby; they charge 50,000Rp for a 90-minute tour (up to 20 people).

**BNI ATM** (Jl Medang Kamulan) Near the temple's entrance.

**Mutia Internet** (Jl Balaputradewa; per hr 3000Rp) Speeds are pedestrian.

## Sights

### BOROBUDUR TEMPLE

Borobudur is built from two million stone blocks in the form of a massive symmetrical stupa, literally wrapped around a small hill. It stands solidly on its 118m by 118m base. Six square terraces are topped by three circular ones, with four stairways leading up through finely carved gateways to the top. The paintwork is long gone, but it's thought that the grey stone of Borobudur was at one time washed with a colour to catch the sun.

Viewed from the air, the structure resembles a colossal three-dimensional tantric mandala (symbolic circular figure). It has been suggested, in fact, that the people of the Buddhist community that once supported Borobudur were early Vajrayana or Tantric Buddhists who used it as a walk-through mandala.

The monument was conceived as a Buddhist vision of the cosmos in stone, starting in the everyday world and spiralling up to nirvana, the Buddhist heaven. At the base of the monument is a series of reliefs representing a world dominated by passion and desire, where the good are rewarded by reincarnation as a higher form of life, while the evil are punished by a lowlier reincarnation. These carvings and their carnal scenes are covered by stone to hide them from view, but they are partly visible on the southern side.

Starting at the main eastern gateway, go clockwise (as one should around all Buddhist monuments) around the galleries of the stupa. Although Borobudur is impressive for its sheer bulk, the delicate sculptural work when viewed close up is exquisite. The pilgrim's walk is about 5km long and takes you along narrow corridors past nearly 1460 richly decorated narrative panels and 1212 decorative panels in which the sculptors have carved a virtual textbook of Buddhist doctrines as well as many aspects of Javanese life 1000 years ago – a continual procession of ships and elephants, musicians and dancing girls, warriors and kings.

On the third level there's a lengthy panel sequence about a dream of Queen Maya, which involved a vision of white elephants with six tusks. Monks and courtiers interpret this as a premonition that her son would become a Buddha, and the sequence continues until the birth of Prince Siddhartha and his journey to become a Buddha. Many other panels are related to Buddhist concepts of cause and effect or karma.

Some 432 serene-faced Buddha images stare out from open chambers above the galleries, while 72 more Buddha images sit only partly visible in latticed stupas on the top three terraces – one is considered the lucky Buddha. The top platform is circular, signifying never-ending nirvana.

Admission to the temple includes entrance to **Karmawibhangga archaeological museum**, which is just east of the monument and contains 4000 original stones and carvings from Borobudur,

an exhibition of tools and chemicals used in its restoration, and some interesting photographs, including some recording the damage caused by the 1985 bomb.

Close by, the new **Samudraraksa museum** is dedicated to the importance of the ocean and sea trade in Indonesia. There's an 18m wooden outrigger here, a replica of a boat depicted on one of Borobudur's panels. This boat was sailed to Madagascar and on to Ghana in West Africa in 2003, a voyage that retraced ancient Javanese trading links – the original spice trade – with the continent over a thousand years ago.

An audiovisual show at the Manohara Hotel costs 5000Rp, and there are a few other attractions at Borobudur, including a children's playground and a tacky magic museum.

Borobudur is Indonesia's single most popular tourist attraction; it can be crowded and noisy, especially on weekends. Hawkers both outside and inside the archaeological park can be very pushy but are sometimes put off if you tell them in Bahasa Indonesia that you are a resident of Yogyakarta (*saya tinggal di Yogyakarta*). The finest time to see Borobudur and capture something of the spirit of the temple is at dawn or sunset, but you won't have it to yourself. These are popular times for the bus loads of tour groups to visit Borobudur. The temple is usually at its quietest during Ramadan.

It is, however, possible to beat the crowds at sunrise; for 300,000Rp (150,000Rp if you're a guest at the hotel) Manohara Hotel lets visitors enter the temple's grounds at 4.30am. A passport is required for entry.

### MENDUT TEMPLE

This exquisite **temple** (admission 3300Rp; ☺ 8am-4pm), around 3.5km east of Borobudur, may look insignificant compared with its mighty neighbour, but it houses the most outstanding statue in its original setting of any temple in Java. The magnificent 3m-high figure of Buddha is flanked by Bodhisattvas: Lokesvara on the left and Vairapana on the right. The Buddha is also notable for his posture: instead of the usual lotus position, he sits Western-style with both feet on the ground.

The Mendut temple, also called Venu Vana Mandira (Temple in the Bamboo Grove), was discovered in 1836, and restoration attempts were made by the Dutch between 1897 and

1904. The gracefully carved relief panels on its outer walls are among the finest and largest examples of Hindu-Javanese art in the country.

The statues are particularly evocative at night, when spotlit against the evening sky, and the inner chamber appears charged with an almost supernatural energy. Guards here will sometimes allow visitors to enter Mendut after dark if accompanied with a local guide (speak to Jaker; see right).

Next to the temple is the **Mendut Buddhist Monastery**. You can join the monks here for prayers at around 6pm every day, and meditation courses are often held in December.

### CANDI PAWON

Around 1.5km east of Borobudur, this small solitary **temple** (admission 3300Rp; ⊙ 8am-4pm) is similar in design and decoration to the Mendut temple. It is not a stupa but resembles a Central Javanese temple, with its broad base, central body and pyramidal roof. Elaborately carved relief panels adorn its sides. Pot-bellied dwarfs pouring riches over the entrance to this temple suggest that it was dedicated to Kuvera, the Buddhist god of fortune.

### NEARBY VILLAGES

Away from the temples, the region around Borobudur is supremely beautiful – a verdant, incredibly fertile and classically Javanese landscape of villages and rice fields. Borubudur itself sits in a large bowl-shaped valley ringed by mountains and volcanoes that the locals call *mahagelan* – the giant bracelet.

Around 3km southwest of the monument, the small village of **Karang** is prime tofu-making terrain. There are several kitchens in the village, each producing around 50kg of *tahu* daily using traditional methods, cooking with coconut oil over a wood fire. The next settlement of **Nglipoh** is a ceramics centre, where locals say claypots have been made for over 1000 years; everyone in the village is involved in production in some way. Today mostly *ibu* (cooking vessels) are made, though glazed ashtrays and other pots are for sale too. The potters are very friendly and will let you try your hand on their wheels (just expect a giggle or two).

At **Candirejo**, 3km from Borobudur, locals have set up a **homestay program** ( ☎ 789 675; ind 3 meals 200,000Rp) that allows you to experience life in a Javanese village. Trekking, rafting

(125,000Rp) and tours (60,000Rp) of local home industries including palm sugar and *krupuk* kitchens are also offered.

## Tours

**Jaker** ( ☎ 0293-788 845; jackpriyana@yahoo.com.sg) is a group of guides and local activists based in the small settlement of Borobudur that surrounds the world's largest Buddhist monument. All Jaker members were born in the area (some in a *kampung* that no longer exists after the temple compound was expanded in the 1990s). If you want to explore the region around Borobudur, Jaker can provide expert local knowledge; many guides speak fluent English. Backpacking rates are charged for trips to **Selogriyo** (towering rice terraces and a small Hindu temple), **Tuksongo** (a centre of glass-noodle production), tofu and pottery villages, and to **Mahitan hill** for sunrise over the Borobudur monument.

## Festivals & Events

**Festival of Borobudur** Around June the Festival of Borobudur kicks off with a *Ramayana*-style dance, and goes on to feature folk-dancing competitions, handicrafts, white-water rafting and other activities.

**Waisak** The Buddha's birth, his enlightenment and his reaching of nirvana are all celebrated on the full-moon day of Waisak. A great procession of saffron-robed monks travels from Mendut to Pawon then Borobudur, where candles are lit and flowers strewn about as offerings, followed by praying and chanting. This holiest of Buddhist events attracts thousands of pilgrims, and usually falls in May.

## Sleeping

Presently little of the millions of dollars that the Borobudur monument generates trickles down to the people who live in its vicinity – many hotels are owned by Jakartan (or foreign) interests. Jaker (above) is campaigning to get discounts for visitors who stay in locally owned hotels.

**Pondok Tinggal Hotel** ( ☎ 788 145; Jl Balaputradewa 32; dm 15,000Rp; r with fan 70,000-90,000Rp; with air-con from 120,000Rp; ⊠ ) First impressions of this large hotel constructed of bamboo and timber are that it looks far too grand for budget travellers, but actually there's an excellent choice of inexpensive rooms around an attractive, peaceful garden, and even a couple of dorms. Don't expect much in the way of atmosphere, but there's a small *wayang* 'museum' and a decent restaurant too.

**Lotus Guest House** ( ☎ 788 281; Jl Medang Kamulan 2; r incl breakfast from 60,000-200,000Rp) North of the temple, Lotus is one of the original guest houses in Borobudur and it's still run by the same super-hospitable family. The 23 bare rooms scattered over a rambling building are very basic but kept clean, and there's plenty of space to read a book, free tea/coffee, and very cheap and tasty food.

**our pick** **Lotus II** ( ☎ 788 845; jackpriyana@yahoo .com.sg; Jl Balaputradewa 54; r incl breakfast 150,000Rp; 🌊 ) An outstanding guest house that's owned by one of the founders of Jaker (see opposite), so there's great local information and it's the ideal place to set up a tour. Most of the artistically styled rooms here are exceptionally large, with mosquito nets draped from high ceilings and lovely comfy beds, but also bathrooms (with tubs) bigger than most losmen rooms. There's also a wonderful rear balcony with views directly onto rice fields that's the ideal spot for an afternoon tea or beer.

**Homestay Rajasa** ( ☎ 788 276; ariswara_sutomo@ yahoo.com; Jl Badrawati 2; r with fan & cold water/air-con & hot water 160,000/275,000Rp; 🌊 ) A popular guest house that makes a very homey base, with rooms at the rear of a villa that face rice fields (through railings). Prices have ramped up in recent years, and though it remains a good place to stay the 14 rooms are quite plain for the tariffs asked. There's a pleasant, open-air restaurant and free afternoon tea/coffee.

**Manohara Hotel** ( ☎ 788 131; www.yogyes.com/ manohara; r incl breakfast from 575,000Rp; 🌊 ) Set within the grounds of Borubudur, this nonsmoking hotel enjoys an unrivalled location. Rooms are comfortable and very well kept, if slightly dated, with carpets, a small TV and a porch. There's a good restaurant-cafe facing the monument. Unlimited entry to Borobudur is included, so if there are two of you the savings are substantial.

**Saraswati** ( ☎ 788 843; www.saraswatiborobudur .com; Jl Balaputradewa 10; r from US$99, ste from US$157; 🌊 🖳 🛜 🍴 ) New, nonsmoking hotel a short walk from the monument with a grand, chintzy lobby and plush rooms set to the rear of the property with elegant furniture. The hotel's trump card is its delightful, shady pool area.

**Amanjiwo** ( ☎ 788 333; www.amanresorts.com/aman-jiwo; r US$700-2600; 🌊 🖳 🛜 🍴 ) Amanjiwo rivals Borobudur temple in architectural extravagance. Perched on a hillside 4km south of Borobudur, with panoramic views towards

the stupa, this monument to luxury has it all. Stupendously exclusive suites, many with their own pool, are some of the finest in Indonesia. The complex has two tennis courts, a 40m pool and a wonderful spa. David Beckham stayed here in 2007. Nonsmoking. Add 21% tax to room rates.

## Eating

Of the hotel restaurants, Lotus Guest House scores for cheap local food (try the *soto*) and has great juices, while Homestay Rajasa caters well to vegetarians. There are countless warungs outside the monument enclosure and around the bus terminal.

**Restaurant Rajasa** ( ☎ 789 690; Jl Balaputradewa; meals 20,000-30,000Rp) This is a lovely, intimate restaurant in a traditional Javanese house that has good Indonesian food: try a curry, or duck cooked in butter.

**Borobudur Restaurant** ( ☎ 788 109; Jl Balaputradewa; buffet 40,000Rp; ⏱ 11.30am-9pm) Large restaurant geared to tour groups with tables positioned near rice fields. Worth considering for its Javanese lunchtime buffet (40,000Rp).

## Shopping

There's an excess of touristy tat and cheapo souvenir stalls around the entrance to the monument.

**Lana Gallery** ( ☎ 0813 9207 7763; Jl Balaputradewa 56) For something completely different, check out the terrific contemporary art available here.

## Getting There & Away

Direct buses make the 42km trip from Yogyakarta's bus terminal to Borobudur (12,000Rp, 1½ hours) via Muntilan. These buses skirt the central city but can also be caught at Jombor, about 4km north of Yogyakarta on Jl Magelang, near the northern ring road. Bus 5 runs from Jombor to the city centre.

From Borobudur terminal buses go regularly to Magelang (5000Rp) until 4pm.

In Borobudur a becak should cost 5000Rp to 7000Rp to anywhere in the village. It's a fine walk to Mendut and Pawon; otherwise a bus or bemo is 2000Rp to hop from one temple to the next. Bicycles (20,000Rp) and motorbikes (50,000Rp) can be hired from hotels.

Tours of Borobudur (p182) are easily arranged in Yogyakarta with the Prawirotaman or Sosrowijayan agents.

## YOGYAKARTA

☎ 0274 / pop 700,000

If Jakarta is Java's financial and industrial powerhouse, Yogyakarta is its soul. Central to the island's artistic and intellectual heritage, Yogyakarta (pronounced 'Jogjakarta'), called Yogya for short, is where the Javanese language is at its purest, Java's arts at their brightest and its traditions at their most visible.

Fiercely independent and protective of its customs, Yogya is now the site of an uneasy truce between the old ways of life and the onslaught of modernity. Still headed by its sultan, whose *kraton* remains the hub of traditional life, contemporary Yogya is nevertheless as much a city of cybercafes, lounge bars and traffic jams as batik, gamelan and ritual. But while the process of modernisation homogenises many of Java's cities, Yogya continues to juggle past and present with relative ease, sustaining a slower, more conservative way of life in the quiet *kampung* that thrive only a stone's throw from the throbbing main streets.

Yogya's potency has long outweighed its size, and it remains Java's premier tourist city, with countless hotels, restaurants and attractions of its own. The city is also an ideal base for exploring nearby attractions, including Indonesia's most important archaeological sites, Borobudur and Prambanan.

### History

Yogyakarta owes its establishment to Prince Mangkubumi, who in 1755 returned to the former seat of Mataram and built the *kraton* of Yogyakarta. He took the title of sultan, adopted the name of Hamengkubuwono (The Universe on the Lap of the King) and created the most powerful Javanese state since the 17th century.

Yogya has always been a symbol of resistance to colonial rule; it was the heart of Diponegoro's Java War (1825–30) and became the capital of the republic from 1946 until independence in 1949.

When the Dutch occupied Yogya in 1948, the patriotic sultan locked himself in the *kraton* and let rebels use the palace as their headquarters. The Dutch did not dare move against the sultan for fear of arousing the anger of millions of Javanese who looked upon him almost as a god. As a result of the sultan's support of the rebels, Yogya was granted the status of a special region when independence finally came.

### Orientation

It's easy to find your way around Yogya. Jl Malioboro, named after the Duke of Marlborough, is the main road and runs straight down from the train station to the *kraton* at the far end. The road becomes Jl A Yani further south but is generally referred to as Jl Malioboro. The tourist office and many souvenir shops and stalls are along this street and most of the budget places to stay are west of it, in the Jl Sosrowijayan area near the railway line.

The old, walled *kraton* is the centre of old Yogya, where you will also find the Taman Sari (Water Castle), Pasar Ngasem (Bird Market) and numerous batik galleries. There's a second hotel and restaurant enclave south of the *kraton,* around Jl Prawirotaman.

### MAPS

The city's **tourist information office** (Map p177; ☎ 566 000; Jl Malioboro 16; ☑ 8am-7pm Mon-Thu, to 6pm Fri & Sat) produces a decent map of the city and also has a useful TransYogya busway map.

### Information

The website www.yogyes.com is a useful portal to the city.

#### BOOKSTORES

**Gramedia** (off Map p177; ☎ 433 1141; Ambarukmo Plaza, Jl Laksda Adisucipto) This branch, 5km west of the centre, stocks a few new English-language titles.

**Lucky Boomerang** (Map p184; ☎ 895 006; Gang 1 67) Has used guidebooks and fiction, Periplus maps and books, plus souvenirs.

#### INTERNET ACCESS

Internet cafes can be found all over town, although many of the cheaper cafes (3000Rp per hour) are located north of Jl Diponegoro.

**Internet Queen** (Map p184; Jl Pasar Kembang 17; per hr 7000Rp; ☑ 24hr) Pretty speedy place that also has scanning and fax facilities and offers cheap international calls.

**11 Net** (Map p185; Jl Parangtritis; per hr 5000Rp) Equipped with modern terminals; speeds are quite respectable.

#### MEDICAL SERVICES

**Ludira Husada Tama Hospital** (Map p177; ☎ 620 333; Jl Wiratama 4; ☑ 24hr)

#### MONEY

There are numerous banks (and a few money changers) in the tourist areas. ATMs are very widespread throughout the city.

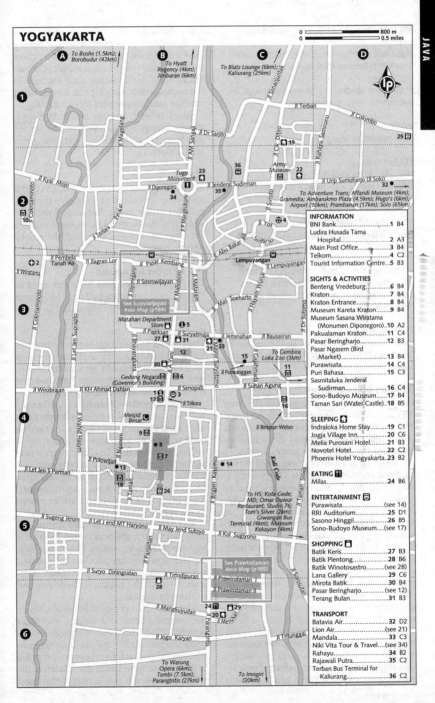

# YOGYAKARTA

0 — 800 m
0 — 0.5 miles

To Boshe (1.5km);
Borobudur (42km)

To Hyatt
Regency (4km);
Jimbaran (6km)

To Blatz Lounge (6km);
Kaliurang (25km)

Jl Terban

Jl Colombo

Jl Dr Sarjito

Jl Magelang

Jl AM Sangaji

Jl Cik Ditiro

Jl Simanjuntak

Jl Rahayu Samirono

25

Tugu
Monument

23

Jl Jenderal Sudirman

36

Army
Museum

22

Jl Urip Sumoharjo (Jl Solo)

32

Jl Kyai Mojo

Jl Diponegoro

34

35

Jl P Mangkubumi

To Adventure Trans; Affandi Museum (4km);
Gramedia; Ambarukmo Plaza (4.5km); Hugo's (6km);
Airport (10km); Prambanan (17km); Solo (65km)

Jl Cokroaminoto

10

Jl Tentara Pelajar

Jl Yos Sudarso

4

Jl Pembela
Tanah Air

2

Jl Wiratama

Jl Jlagran Lor

Pasar Kembang

Jl Malioboro

Jl Abu Bakar Ali

Lempuyangan

Jl Lempuyangan

Jl Cokroaminoto

Jl Poncowinatan

Jl Sosrowijayan

Jl Mataram

Jl Mas Soeharto

Jl Hayam Wuruk

Jl Dr Sutomo

See Sosrowijayan
Area Map (p184)

Jl Let Jen Suprapto

Matahari Department
Store

5

9

Jl Pajeksan

27

31

Jl Suryatmaja

Jl Jeminahan

Jl Bausasran

Jl Bhayangkara

12

21

33

To Gembira
Loka Zoo (3km)

15

Jl Cik Gembia

11

Jl Wirobrajan

30

6

Gedung Negara
(Governor's Building)

Jl Senopati

Jl Purwanggan

Jl Sultan Agung

16

Jl KH Ahmad Dahlan

3

Jl Trikora

1

17

Mesjid
Besar

Jl Bintaran Wetan

Jl Wahid Hasyim

9

8

7

Jl Ngasem

Jl Polowijan

13

14

Kali Code

Jl Let Jen S Parman

18

26

To HS; Kota Gede;
MD; Omar Duwur
Restaurant; Studio 76;
Tom's Silver (2km);
Giwangan Bus
Terminal (4km); Museum
Kekayon (4km)

Jl Sugeng Jeroni

Jl Let J end MT Haryono

Jl May Jend Sutoyo

Jl Kol Sugiyono

Jl Taman Siswo

Jl Prajatan

Jl Suryo Diningratan

Jl Tirtodipuran

Jl Prawirotaman I

See Prawirotaman
Area Map (p185)

Jl Prawirotaman II

28

Jl Mangkuyudan

24

20

29

Jl Menukan

Jl Jogo Karyan

Jl Parangtritis

Jl Tritunggal

Jl Sprosutan

To Warung
Opera (6km);
Tembi (7.5km);
Parangtritis (27km)

To Imogiri
(20km)

## INFORMATION
BNI Bank...................................1 B4
Ludira Husada Tama
  Hospital..................................2 A3
Main Post Office.......................3 B4
Telkom.....................................4 C2
Tourist Information Centre.....5 B3

## SIGHTS & ACTIVITIES
Benteng Vredeburg...............6 B4
Kraton......................................7 B4
Kraton Entrance......................8 B4
Museum Kareta Kraton.........9 B4
Museum Sasana Wiratama
  (Monumen Diponegoro)...10 A2
Pakualaman Kraton...............11 C4
Pasar Beringharjo.................12 B3
Pasar Ngasem (Bird
  Market).................................13 B4
Purawisata............................14 C4
Puri Bahasa...........................15 C3
Sasmitaluka Jenderal
  Sudirman.............................16 C4
Sono-Budoyo Museum........17 B4
Taman Sari (Water Castle)...18 B5

## SLEEPING
Indraloka Home Stay...........19 C1
Jogja Village Inn...................20 C6
Melia Purosani Hotel............21 B3
Novotel Hotel.......................22 C2
Phoenix Hotel Yogyakarta..23 B2

## EATING
Milas......................................24 B6

## ENTERTAINMENT
Purawisata........................(see 14)
RRI Auditorium....................25 D1
Sasono Hinggil.....................26 B5
Sono-Budoyo Museum....(see 17)

## SHOPPING
Batik Keris............................27 B3
Batik Plentong......................28 B6
Batik Winotosastro.........(see 28)
Lana Gallery..........................29 C6
Mirota Batik..........................30 B4
Pasar Beringharjo.............(see 12)
Terang Bulan........................31 B3

## TRANSPORT
Batavia Air............................32 D2
Lion Air.............................(see 21)
Mandala................................33 C3
Niki Vita Tour & Travel....(see 34)
Rahayu..................................34 B2
Rajawali Putra......................35 C2
Terban Bus Terminal for
  Kaliurang.............................36 C2

**BNI bank** (Map p177; Jl Trikora 1) Opposite the main post office.

**Mulia** (Map p184; Inna Garuda Hotel, Jl Malioboro 60) Along with Pt Barumun Abadi, this has the best exchange rates in Yogya.

**Pt Barumun Abadi** (Map p184; Inna Garuda Hotel, Jl Malioboro 60) Offers competitive rates.

### POST
**Main post office** (Map p177; Jl Senopati)

### TELEPHONE
Wartels are located all over town.

**Telkom** (Map p177; Jl Yos Sudarso) One kilometre east of Jl Malioboro.

### TOURIST INFORMATION
**Tourist Information Centre** (Map p177; ☎ 566 000; Jl Malioboro 16; ✆ 8am-7pm Mon-Thu, to 6pm Fri & Sat) A well-organised office with helpful staff, free maps and good transport information. Produces a number of publications (including a calendar of events). Also has counters at the airport and on the eastern side of the Tugu train station.

### TRAVEL AGENCIES
**Great Tours** (Map p184; ☎ 583 221; Jl Sosrowijayan 29) Good for sunrise tours, bus and minibus tickets and tours to places including Bromo and Ijen.

## Dangers & Annoyances
Hassle from smooth-talking batik salesmen is a constant issue for every traveller in town. The tourist board get hosts of complaints about these sharks, who may strike up conversations pretending to be guides. Inevitably you'll end up at a gallery where you'll get the hard sell and they'll rake in a big commission if you buy. A time-honoured scam is to pressure you to visit a 'special export' batik collection, a 'fine art student exhibition' or an 'official government store' – there are no official shops or galleries in the city.

Some of these dodgy batik salesmen hang around the *kraton* (right), where they tell you that the *kraton* is closed or there are no performances, but they might offer to show you to the 'sultan's batik workshop' (which is actually just a very expensive commission-paying showroom).

Be aware too that due to a schism in the ruling family there are actually two separate entrances, and ticket offices, at the *kraton*. One entrance (with a 5000Rp charge) only allows you to view a small area, which contains some dioramas and horse carriages; it may be signposted 'Pagelaran.' Official-looking guys with IDs will try to shepherd you in here before inviting you to look at some of the 'sultan's batik'. This is *not* the main entrance to the *kraton*, which has a big clock by its ticket window (and an entrance fee of 12,500Rp).

Becak drivers are very pushy in Yogya; those offering 'special rates' of 1000Rp for one hour are also trying to get you into a batik gallery.

## Sights
Most of Yogya's sights are in a small central area of the city centred on the *kraton* complex, and just to the north. But away from here and out in the eastern and southern suburbs are other attractions, including the quirky Affandi museum.

### THE KRATON & AROUND
The historic *kraton* area harbours most of Yogya's most important buildings and tourist attractions and is eminently walkable.

### Kraton
The cultural and political heart of this fascinating, independently minded city is the huge palace of the sultans of Yogya, or **kraton** (p177; ☎ 373 321; admission 12,500Rp, camera 1000Rp; guided tour by donation; ✆ 8am-2pm Sat-Thu, to 1pm Fri).

Be sure to read the warning under Dangers & Annoyances, left, about the two *kraton* ticket offices and entrances, and scams practised by batik sellers who hang around here.

Effectively a walled city, this unique compound is home to around 25,000 people, and has its own market, shops, batik and silver cottage industries, schools, and mosques. Around 1000 of its residents are employed by the sultan.

The *kraton* suffered damage during the 2006 earthquake and was closed for a time but is open again for visitors. Disappointingly, the treasures here are poorly displayed and not well labelled – don't expect much information to put the palace, its buildings and contents in context.

The innermost group of buildings, where the current sultan still resides, was built between 1755 and 1756, although extensions were made during the long reign of Hamengkubuwono I. European-style touches to the interior were added much later, in the 1920s. Structurally this is one of the finest

**YOGYA IN...**

**Two Days**

Start your day with a visit to the **kraton** (opposite) and a traditional performance of gamelan, *wayang* or dance, then spend the afternoon exploring the *kampung* surrounding the sultan's palace and nearby **Taman Sari** (below). End your afternoon with a wander through the city's squawking bird market, **Pasar Ngasem** (p180).

Your second day could start with a wander down Jl Malioboro scouting for batik bargains, and a meander through Yogya's main market, **Pasar Beringharjo** (p180). A becak ride to **Kota Gede** (p180) to seek out silver could be finished off with a trip to the Prawirotaman district and a meal at the hip and happening **Via Via** (p186) restaurant.

**Four Days**

After exploring the city of Yogya it's time to get out and see wonders within striking distance of the city. Rise early and catch the sunrise at the incomparable Buddhist temple of **Borobudur** (p171), before exploring the verdant countryside and fascinating villages around the monument, ideally with a community guide from Jaker (see p174).

On day four move on to **Prambanan** (p194), the Hindu masterpiece on the other side of the city; it's fun to make a whole day of it by cycling there via some of the minor outlying temples.

examples of Javanese palace architecture, providing a series of luxurious halls and spacious courtyards and pavilions. The sense of tradition holds strong in Yogya, and the palace is attended by very dignified elderly retainers who still wear traditional Javanese dress.

The centre of the *kraton* is the reception hall, the Bangsal Kencana (Golden Pavilion), with its marble floor, intricately decorated roof, Dutch-style stained glass windows and great columns of carved teak. A large part of the *kraton* is used as a museum and holds an extensive collection, including gifts from European monarchs, gilt copies of the sacred *pusaka* (heirlooms of the royal family) and gamelan instruments. One of the most interesting rooms contains the royal family tree, old photographs of grand mass weddings and portraits of the former sultans of Yogya.

A modern memorial building within the *kraton* is dedicated to the beloved Sultan Hamengkubuwono IX, with photographs and personal effects (including his desk, and, slightly bizarrely, some cutlery he used when in Holland).

Other points of interest within the *kraton* include the 'male' and 'female' entrances, indicated by giant-sized 'he' and 'she' dragons (although the dragons look very similar). Outside the *kraton*, in the centre of the northern square, there are two sacred *waringin* (banyan trees), where, in the days of feudal Java, white-robed petitioners would patiently sit hoping to catch the eye of the king. In the *alun-alun kidul* (southern square), two similar **banyan trees** are said to bring great fortune if you can walk between them without mishap blindfolded; on Friday and Saturday nights you can see the youth of Yogya attempting the feat to a chorus of laughter from friends.

There are **performances** (🕙 10am-noon) in the *kraton's* inner pavilion that are included in your 12,500Rp entrance ticket. There's gamelan on Monday, Tuesday and Thursday, *wayang golek* on Wednesday, Javanese singing and poems on Friday, *wayang kulit* on Saturday and classical dance on Sunday.

The *kraton's* entrance is on the northwestern side. It's closed on national holidays and for special *kraton* ceremonies.

**Taman Sari**

Just southwest of the *kraton* is this **complex** (Map p177; admission 7000Rp; 🕙 8am-3.30pm), which once served as a splendid pleasure park of palaces, pools and waterways for the sultan and his entourage. The Portuguese architect of this elaborate retreat, built between 1758 and 1765, was from Batavia – the story goes that the sultan had him executed in order to keep his hidden pleasure rooms secret.

The complex, which is also known by its old Dutch name *waterkasteel* (water castle), was damaged first by Diponegoro's Java War, and an earthquake in 1865 helped finish the job. While much of what you see today lies in ruins, the bathing pools have been restored. From the tower overlooking the pools, the sultan was able to dally with his wives and witness the goings-on below.

The entrance to the restored bathing pools is on Jl Taman. Batik touts will try to lure you to a batik gallery or pretend to be official guides – shake them off.

### Pasar Ngasem

At the edge of Taman Sari, Yogya's **bird market** (Map p177; Jl Polowijan; ⏱ 8am-5pm) is a colourful menagerie crowded with hundreds of budgerigars, orioles and singing turtle doves. Pigeons are the big business here (for training, not eating), but occasionally owls and raptors are also sold.

Snakes (including sometimes cobras and pythons), lizards, iguanas and other animals are also for sale, as are big trays of bird feed (swarming maggots and ants). From the back of Pasar Ngasem, an alleyway leads up to the broken walls of Taman Sari for fine views across Yogya.

### Museums Around the Kraton

Near the *kraton* entrance, **Museum Kareta Kraton** (Map p177; admission 7500Rp, camera 1000Rp; ⏱ 8am-2pm Sat-Thu, to noon Fri) has exhibits of the opulent chariots of the sultans, although the bug-eyed horse statues are almost more interesting than the main event.

Across the main square in front of the *kraton*, **Sono-Budoyo Museum** (Map p177; ☎ 376 775; admission 5000Rp; ⏱ 8am-1.30pm Tue-Thu, to 11.15am Fri, to noon Sat & Sun) is the pick of Yogya's museums, even if it is dusty and dimly lit. It has a first-class collection of Javanese art, including *wayang kulit* puppets, *topeng* (masks), kris and batik. It also has a courtyard packed with Hindu statuary and artefacts from further afield, including superb Balinese carvings. *Wayang kulit* performances are held here (p187).

Just north of here, on the opposite side of Jl A Yani, is the **Benteng Vredeburg** (Map p177; Jl A Yani 6; admission 3500Rp; ⏱ 8.30am-1.30pm Tue-Thu, to 11am Fri, to noon Sat & Sun), a Dutch-era fort that's been converted into a museum. It houses dioramas showing the history of the independence movement in Yogyakarta. The architecture is worth a look, but the dioramas are designed for Indonesian patriots.

The small **Pakualaman Kraton** (Map p177; Jl Sultan Agung; ⏱ 9.30am-1.30pm Tue, Thu & Sun), 1km east of

Benteng Vredeburg, houses a small museum, a *pendopo* that can hold a full gamelan orchestra, and a curious colonial house. Outside opening times you can explore the grounds. Close by is **Sasmitaluka Jenderal Sudirman** (Map p177; Jl Bintaran Wetan 3; admission by donation; ⏱ 8am-noon Tue-Sun), the memorial home of General Sudirman, who commanded revolutionary forces and died shortly after the siege of Yogya in 1948.

### Pasar Beringharjo

Yogya's **main market** (Map p177; Jl A Yani; ⏱ 8am-4.30pm), 800m north of the *kraton* on the southern continuation of Jl Malioboro, is a lively and fascinating place. The renovated front section has a wide range of batik – mostly inexpensive *batik cap* (stamped batik) – while the 2nd floor is dedicated to cheap clothes and shoes. Most interesting of all, though, is the old section towards the back. Crammed with warungs and stalls selling a huge variety of fruit and vegetables, this is still very much a traditional market. The range of *rempah rempah* (spices) on the 1st floor is quite something.

### Purawisata

In the evening you can head along to the **Purawisata** (Map p177; Jl Brigjen Katamso), an amusement park noted more for its dance performances, but there are also rides, fun-fair games and a *pasar seni* (art market) with a basic collection of souvenirs.

### EASTERN YOGYAKARTA

The east of the city has several more interesting sights, including the silver village of Kota Gede and a couple of museums.

### Kota Gede

Kota Gede (off Map p177) has been famed as the hub of Yogya's silver industry since the 1930s. But this quiet old town, which is now a suburb of Yogyakarta, was the first capital of the Mataram kingdom, founded by Panembahan Senopati in 1582. Senopati is buried in the small mossy graveyard of an old mosque located to the south of the town's central market. You can visit the **sacred tomb** (admission 1000Rp; ⏱ around 9am-noon Sun, Mon & Thu, around 1-3pm Fri), but be sure to wear conservative dress when visiting. On days when the tomb is closed there is not much to see here.

Jl Kemasan, the main street leading into town from the north, is lined with busy silver workshops. Most of the shops have similar stock, including hand-beaten bowls, boxes, fine filigree and modern jewellery (see p188).

Kota Gede is about 5km southeast of Jl Malioboro. Catch bus 3A or 3B, take a becak (about 18,000Rp), or cycle there; it's flat most of the way.

## Museums

One of Indonesia's most celebrated artists, Affandi lived and worked in a wonderfully quirky riverside house-cum-studio, about 6km east of the town centre. Today his former home is the **Affandi Museum** (off Map p177; ☎ 562 593; www.affandi.org; Jl Laksda Adisucipto 167; admission incl 1 soft drink 20,000Rp, camera 10,000Rp; ☻ 9am-4pm except holidays), which has an extensive collection of his paintings, including some astonishing self-portraits. Affandi's work is displayed in two large Gaudiesque buildings that he designed himself and also contain a few personal items, including a boy racer's dream: a lime-green-and-yellow customized 1967 Galant car with an oversized rear spoiler.

Paintings by his daughter Kartika and other artists are also exhibited. There's a great little cafe here, and Affandi's artistic touch even extends to the *mushullah* (prayer room), which occupies a converted horse carriage, painted in technicolour tones – it looks like a psychedelic gypsy cart. Catch bus 1A to reach this museum from Jl Malioboro.

A little further east, **Museum Kekayon** (off Map p177; ☎ 379 058; Jl Raya Jogja Wonosari 277; admission 3000Rp; ☻ 9am-4pm Tue-Sun) is dedicated to the history of Indonesian people and has a priceless antique *wayang* collection gathered from all over the nation.

## Zoo

Yogya's **Gembira Loka Zoo** (off Map p177; admission 8000Rp; ☻ 8am-6pm), about 5km east of Jl A Yani, has its fair share of cramped cages, but on the whole it is spacious and has some interesting exotica such as some Komodo dragons, which are successfully breeding.

## OTHER AREAS

In the northwest of the city, 1.5km west of the Tugu train station, **Museum Sasana Wiratama** (Monumen Diponegoro; Map p177; admission by donation; ☻ 8am-noon Tue-Sun) honours the Indonesian

hero Prince Diponegoro, who was leader of the bloody but futile rebellion of 1825–30 against the Dutch. A motley collection of the prince's belongings and other exhibits are kept in the small museum at his former Yogya residence.

Down in the deep south of the city, **Tembi** (off Map p177; ☎ 368 000; www.tembi.net; admission by donation; ☻ 9am-4pm) is a Javanese cultural centre in a lovely position surrounded by rice paddies. The fine old wooden houses here contain an outstanding collection of kris, a few *wayang* puppets, batik and basketry and some historic photographs of Yogya. There's a highly recommended restaurant and accommodation too. To get to Tembi, jump aboard any bus bound for Parangtritis beach from Jl Parangtritis and get off at kilometre 8.4 on the highway; Tembi is 400m east of here along a side road.

## Walking Tour

Yogya is a very manageable city and many of its blockbuster sights can be seen on foot. A good place to start a walking tour is **Tugu train station (1)**, from where **Jl Malioboro (2)**, Yogya's premier shopping street, is laid out in front of you. Head south along Jl Malioboro until it intersects with Jl Suryatmajan, from which point Malioboro becomes Jl A Yani. Only one block south of Jl Suryatmajan is the market **Pasar Beringharjo (3**; opposite), and only another block south again is the city's old Dutch fort, **Benteng Vredeburg (4**; opposite).

Continuing south once more, cross Jl Senopati onto Jl Trikora and the **alun-alun (5)** will appear. Swing right and past the **Sono-Budoyo Museum (6**; opposite) before heading south again, walking by the **Mesjid Besar** (Grand Mosque; **7**) and **Museum Kareta Kraton (8**; opposite). The entrance to the **Kraton (9**; p178) is only a few metres to the left.

From the *kraton*, head west until you hit Jl Ngasem, then turn left. Walk south and the city's **bird market (10**; opposite) will be impossible to miss. Take Jl Taman east from outside the bird market; it quickly turns south and passes the **Taman Sari (11**; p179). At the end of Jl Taman turn left and make a beeline for the city's southern **alun-alun (12)**. If you're with friends (or are simply feeling adventurous), have yourself blindfolded and try your luck walking between the square's two banyan trees; local folklore predicts good fortune for those who succeed.

JAVA

## WALKING TOUR

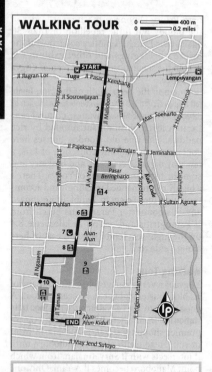

### WALK FACTS

**Start** Tugu train station
**Finish** *alun-alun kidul*
**Distance** 3km
**Duration** Two hours, excluding stops at attractions along the way

Finish off with a restorative cup of *ronde* (ginger tea) from one of the street vendors here, who also sell barbecued corn on the cob and *mie goreng* (fried noodles).

## Courses

Yogya has plenty of places offering a variety of courses, with everything from batik painting to Bahasa Indonesia classes on offer. The Tourist Information Centre (p178) also has a list of places offering courses.

**Losmen Lucy** (Map p184; ☎ 513 429) Cheap batik courses – a full day costs around 110,000Rp (after bargaining!).

**Puri Bahasa** (Map p177; ☎ 588 192; puriindo@indosat .net.id; Jl Purwanggan 15) A professional language school offering Bahasa Indonesia classes (US$7 per hour for

one-on-one tuition). Family homestays can be arranged, starting at 450,000Rp per week.

**Studio 76** (off Map p177; ☎ 714 7676; Jl Purbayan, Kota Gede) Runs good full-day silversmith courses (220,000Rp per person including lunch and 10g of silver to play around with).

**Via Via** (Map p185; ☎ 386 557; www.viaviacafe.com; Jl Prawirotaman I 30) Has excellent half-day cooking (85,000Rp), batik- and silver jewellery–making (both 80,000Rp) courses.

## Tours

**Rumah Guides** (Map p185; ☎ 386 432; www.inspirasi-indonesiaholidays.com; Rumah Eyang, Gang Sartono 823, Jl Parangtritis) is an excellent new community project run by young Yogya citizens eager to show you their city and the surrounding area. Tours of the city (150,000Rp per day) and to Borobudur, Dieng and beyond can be set up in their Prawirotaman area office. It's also possible to stay with local families as part of a homestay program (US$12 per day including all meals).

Tour agents on Jl Prawirotaman (Map p185) and in the Sosrowijayan area (Map p184) offer a host of tour options at similar prices. Typical day tours and per-person rates (excluding entrance fees):

**Borobudur** 70,000Rp.
**Dieng** 175,000Rp.
**Gedung Songo and Ambarawa** 175,000Rp.
**Prambanan** 80,000Rp.
**Prambanan and Parangtritis** 175,000Rp.
**Solo, Sukuh and Tawangmangu** 200,000Rp.
**Sunrise at Gunung Merapi** 200,000Rp.

Longer tours, such as to Gunung Bromo and on to Bali (from 330,000Rp for two days and one night) and Bromo/Ijen (600,000Rp for three days and two nights) are also offered. Tours are often dependent on getting enough people to fill a minibus (usually a minimum of four), and prices vary depending on whether air-con is provided. Note that tours may also stop at batik or silver galleries to earn extra commission for tour operators.

Operators also arrange cars with driver, with rates starting at 75,000Rp per hour or around 400,000Rp per day.

**Adventure Trans** (off Map p177; ☎ 0813 2806 1771; www.adventuretrans.net; Jl Raya Seturan 13) Adventure travel agent specialising in upmarket tours to Bali via Bromo and Ijen. Also offers trekking and rafting trips.

**Jogya Trans** ( ☎ 0816 426 0124; Gang 04/09, Madurejo, Prambanan) Professional agency that can provide cars and minibuses with drivers and also arrange bespoke tours.

**Kartika Trekking** (Map p184; ☎ 562 016; Jl Sosrowijayan 10) Agent specialising in trekking trips to Gunung Merapi. Recommended by locals and readers.

## Festivals & Events
**Gerebeg** The three Gerebeg festivals – held each year at the end of January and April and the beginning of November – are Java's most colourful and grand processions. In traditional court dress, palace guards and retainers, not to mention large floats of decorated mountains of rice, all make their way to the mosque, west of the *kraton*, to the sound of prayer and gamelan music.

**Arts Festival** Yogya hosts this annual festival from 7 June to 7 July. Offers a wide range of shows and exhibitions. Most events are held at the Benteng Vredeburg.

## Sleeping
Yogya has Java's best range of guest houses and hotels, many offering excellent value for money. During the high season – July, August and around Christmas and New Year – things can get crowded. Outside these times, you should have no problem finding a bed and discounts should be easy to come by.

### BUDGET
#### Sosrowijayan Area
Most of Yogya's cheap hotels are in the *gang* (alleys) of the Sosrowijayan area immediately south of the train line, which still has a real *kampung* atmosphere. Running between Jl Pasar Kembang and Jl Sosrowijayan, Gang Sosrowijayan I and II are lined with cheap accommodation. Standards in many places have slipped in recent years as backpacker numbers have declined, but there are still some good options.

**Tiffa Art Shop & Losmen** (Map p184; ☎ 512 841; tiffa artshop@yahoo.com; s/d 40,000/70,000Rp) An excellent little losmen owned by a hospitable family, with accommodation above an art shop. All the four rooms are smallish but have private *mandi* and there's a communal balcony where you can tuck into your free breakfast and tea/coffee. They also rent out motorbikes here, from 50,000Rp a day.

**Dewi Homestay** (Map p184; ☎ 516 014; dewi homestay@hotmail.com; r 50,000-75,000Rp) This converted house has some charm, with rooms with four-poster beds and massive mosquito nets, though there's not much natural light – perfect if you want a really deep sleep.

**Losmen Lucy** (Map p184; ☎ 513 429; s/d 70,000/80,000Rp) One of the best losmen in Yogya, this place tries much harder than most.

The 12 fan-cooled rooms here are kept really spick and span and the beds still have some spring; all have en-suite *mandi* with Asian toilets. The owner offers good batik-painting classes.

**our pick Losmen Setia Kawan** (Map p184; ☎ 512 452; www.bedhots.com; economy r 70,000-100,000Rp; r with air-con 125,000-200,000Rp; ✉ 💻) First choice in Sosrowijayan, this is a superb, very inviting and well-run place that occupies a fine old artistically decorated house. There are nice touches evident everywhere, with classic Vespa scooters in the lobby, a rooftop patio, a lounge area with TV/DVDs and a row of computers for internet access. Rooms are smallish but very attractive, though the swirling, hippy-dippy wall murals are a bit much to wake up to.

**Bladok Losmen & Restaurant** (Map p184; ☎ 560 452; Jl Sosrowijayan 76; r 80,000Rp, with balcony 120,000Rp, with air-con from 195,000Rp; ✉ 💻) A great lodge of real character and charm, Bladok caters to both budget and midrange travellers, and justifiably remains a perennial favourite. All the rooms have lovely chunky wooden beds and furniture, and crisp, fresh linen; rooms 11 and 12 have balconies. There's an excellent restaurant here too.

**Hotel Asia-Afrika** (Map p184; ☎ 566 219; Jl Pasar Kembang 21; r with fan 175,000Rp, with air-con from 210,000Rp; ✉ 💻) This hotel's rooms are not quite as glam as the swish marble lobby would indicate but are still good value. The decent-sized pool and sun loungers make it a tempting choice.

Also recommended:

**Jaya Losmen** (Map p184; ☎ 515 035; Gang II 79; s/d with shared mandi 35,000/40,000Rp) A pad to crash.

**Superman's Losmen** (Map p184; ☎ 515 007; r 45,000Rp) Simple losmen on Gang I with very basic rooms.

**Rejeki Homestay** (Map p184; ☎ 516 084; r 70,000Rp) Eleven neat, clean doubles and twins, with a stick or two of furniture, that all have fan and private *mandi*.

#### Prawirotaman Area
This area is definitely more upmarket than Sosrowijayan and has a few cheap places mixing it with lots of midrange choices. Plenty of hotels have a pool here – a huge bonus after a day spent sightseeing in the sun.

**Delta Homestay** (Map p185; ☎ 727 1047; www .dutagardenhotel.com; Jl Prawirotaman II 597A; s/d 75,000/85,000Rp, with mandi 105,000/115,000Rp, with air-con 140,000/150,000Rp; ✉ 💻) An outstanding little hotel with a selection of small but perfectly formed rooms, each with a little porch, grouped around a great pool. It's very peaceful here and breakfast is included; book ahead.

**Rumah Eyang** (Map p185; ☎ 823 2084; Gang Sartono 823, Jl Parangtritis; r incl breakfast from 80,000Rp, with air-con from 120,000Rp; ✸ 🖥 ) This converted suburban dwelling operates as a guest house for artists and makes a great place to mix with locals. Rooms are simple and moderately comfortable, but there's a great garden area with sculptures and a cafe. This is the HQ of Rumah Guides (see p182), so Yogya info is right on the money.

**Rose Guest House** (Map p185; ☎ 377 991; Jl Prawirotaman I 22; r with fan from 85,000Rp, with air-con from 120,000Rp; ✸ 🖥 ) This is a 1970s-style Indonesian hotel that hasn't been renovated, with plain, spacious tiled rooms. It's a little unloved but worth considering for its nice pool.

**Prambanan Guest House** (Map p185; ☎ 376 167; Jl Prawirotaman I 14; r with cold shower/air-con 90,000/160,000Rp; ✸ 🖥 ) A well-run place with an attractive garden and attentive staff, Prambanan is a very good option. Cheaper rooms are plain, but the

better doubles are comfortable and have bamboo trimmings and ikat-style textiles draped on good-quality beds.

**Hotel Winotosatro** (Map p185; ☎ 387 110; Jl Parangtritis 92A; r 140,000-160,000Rp, deluxe r 230,000Rp; ✸ 🖥 ) This large hotel in a peaceful location is divided into two sections with good-value, spacious rooms that all have air-con, TV and wooden furniture. The wonderful oval pool here must be 40m across.

**Harmony Inn** (off Map p185; ☎ 387 135; Gang Sartono, Jl Parangtritis; r 175,000Rp; ✸ 🖥 ) On the western side of Jl Parangtritis, this good-value place has spacious rooms with rattan furniture, TVs, and bathrooms with hot water and a tub. There's a great pool at the back with sun loungers and a cafe.

### MIDRANGE
#### Sosrowijayan Area
**Gloria Amanda** (Map p184; ☎ 565 286; www.gloriaa manda-hotel.com; Jl Sosrowijayan 195; r with fan 150,000Rp, with air-con from 270,000Rp; ✸ 🖥 ) Situated down a little lane, this modern place has 35 very neat if plain, smallish air-con rooms with good beds and TVs.

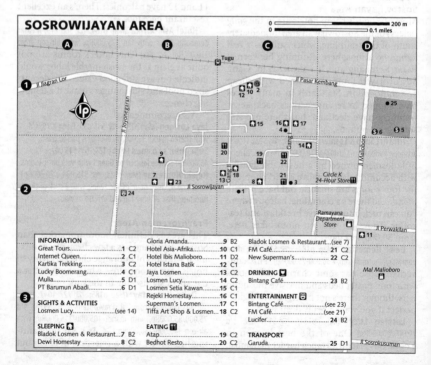

## SOSROWIJAYAN AREA

0 — 200 m
0 — 0.1 miles

| INFORMATION | |
|---|---|
| Great Tours | 1 C2 |
| Internet Queen | 2 C1 |
| Kartika Trekking | 3 C2 |
| Lucky Boomerang | 4 C1 |
| Mulia | 5 D1 |
| PT Barumun Abadi | 6 D1 |

| SIGHTS & ACTIVITIES | |
|---|---|
| Losmen Lucy | (see 14) |

| SLEEPING | |
|---|---|
| Bladok Losmen & Restaurant | 7 B2 |
| Dewi Homestay | 8 C2 |

| | |
|---|---|
| Gloria Amanda | 9 B2 |
| Hotel Asia-Afrika | 10 C1 |
| Hotel Ibis Malioboro | 11 D2 |
| Hotel Istana Batik | 12 C1 |
| Jaya Losmen | 13 C2 |
| Losmen Lucy | 14 C2 |
| Losmen Setia Kawan | 15 C1 |
| Rejeki Homestay | 16 C1 |
| Superman's Losmen | 17 C1 |
| Tiffa Art Shop & Losmen | 18 C2 |

| EATING | |
|---|---|
| Atap | 19 C2 |
| Bedhot Resto | 20 C2 |

| | |
|---|---|
| Bladok Losmen & Restaurant | (see 7) |
| FM Café | 21 C2 |
| New Superman's | 22 C2 |

| DRINKING | |
|---|---|
| Bintang Café | 23 B2 |

| ENTERTAINMENT | |
|---|---|
| Bintang Café | (see 23) |
| FM Café | (see 21) |
| Lucifer | 24 B2 |

| TRANSPORT | |
|---|---|
| Garuda | 25 D1 |

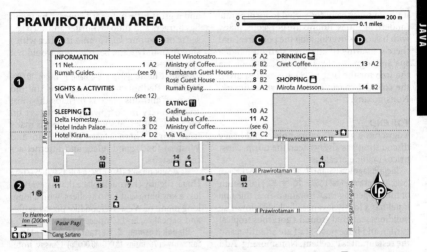

**PRAWIROTAMAN AREA**

0 — 200 m
0 — 0.1 miles

**INFORMATION**
11 Net....................................1 A2
Rumah Guides.....................(see 9)

**SIGHTS & ACTIVITIES**
Via Via..................................(see 12)

**SLEEPING**
Delta Homestay....................2 B2
Hotel Indah Palace................3 D2
Hotel Kirana.........................4 D2

Hotel Winotosatro................5 A2
Ministry of Coffee.................6 B2
Prambanan Guest House.......7 B2
Rose Guest House.................8 B2
Rumah Eyang.......................9 A2

**EATING**
Gading................................10 A2
Laba Laba Cafe....................11 A2
Ministry of Coffee...............(see 6)
Via Via...............................12 C2

**DRINKING**
Civet Coffee........................13 A2

**SHOPPING**
Mirota Moesson...................14 B2

---

**Hotel Istana Batik** (Map p184; ☎ 587 012; www.diana grouphotel.com; Jl Pasar Kembang 29; r 300,000-350,000Rp; ❄ 🛜 🍴 ) Istana Batik is what locals call *tradisional* – it has real Javanese character, with elaborately carved wooden furniture in its fine lobby and spacious rooms. Some fixtures and fittings are looking a little dated, but it's still a comfortable and convenient base.

### Prawirotaman Area

**Ministry of Coffee** (Map p185; ☎ 747 3828; www .ministryofcoffee.com; Jl Prawirotaman I 15A; s/d from 300,000/330,000Rp; ❄ 🛜 ) This cutting-edge cafe-library has not only delectable coffee but also a few comfortable, stylish rooms, all with air-con, safety boxes and free wi-fi and most with little balconies.

**Hotel Kirana** (Map p185; ☎ 376 000; kirana.hotel@ gmail.com; Jl Prawirotaman I 45; s/d incl breakfast from 370,000/390,000Rp; ❄ 🛜 ) A hip-looking new minimalist hotel, but rooms are not large, and though modern and well-presented, they're a bit pricey. You'll find a nice lounge and garden area at the rear. A discount is in order.

**Hotel Indah Palace** (Map p185; ☎ 383 738; www .hotelindahpalace.com; Jl Sisingamangaraja 74; s/d incl breakfast from 468,000Rp; ❄ 🛜 ) Modern midranger with plush, comfortable rooms set around a pool. The attractive restaurant, with its soaring wood-beamed roof, is good.

### Other Areas

**Indraloka Home Stay** (Map p177; ☎ 564 341; manung gal@yogya.wasantara.net.id; Jl Cik Ditiro 18; r incl breakfast, air-con & hot water from 225,000Rp; ❄ ) An intimate homestay with bags of charm, antique furniture, faded but classy old-world decor and a small garden out back. The cheaper rooms are quite poky, so shell out for the more expensive ones. It's north of Jl Sudirman.

**Tembi** (off Map p177; ☎ 368 000; www.tembi.net; Jl Parangtritis, km 8.4; bungalows 368,100-634,500Rp, family bungalows 918,000Rp; ❄ 🍴 ) On the road to the beach, this cultural centre (see p181) has seven commodious wooden bungalows, built in traditional Javanese style, with four-poster beds and wonderful open-air bathrooms. The location is semi-rural, with paddy fields all around, so it's best to have your own transport. Breakfast is included and there's a great restaurant too.

**Hotel Ibis Malioboro** (Map p184; ☎ 516 974; admin@ibisyogya.com; Jl Malioboro 52-58; r from 456,000Rp; ❄ 🖥 🍴 ) It's no beauty, but this nonsmoking central hotel is very convenient for shopping and offers homogenous but fully functional business-class comfort.

**Novotel Hotel** (Map p177; ☎ 580 930; admin@novo telyogya.com; Jl Jenderal Sudirman 89; r from 504,000Rp; ❄ 🖥 🛜 🍴 ) It may be a chain hotel, but it's a fine example of the genre, with sleek, contemporary decor, helpful English-speaking staff and excellent facilities including a good gym. Nonsmoking.

**our pick Phoenix Hotel Yogyakarta** (Map p177; ☎ 566 617; info@thephoenixyogya.com; Jl Jenderal Sudirman 9-11; r from 545,000Rp; ❄ 🖥 🛜 🍴 ) This historic hotel, part of the Accor chain, is easily the best in its class in Yogya. Dating back to 1918, it's been sensitively converted to incorporate modern facilities. Rooms are gorgeous, many with balconies overlooking the pool area, and there's an army of attentive staff on hand, a spa and a great cafe. Tariffs asked (book via the web for the best rates) are modest given the colonial charm of this Yogya landmark. Nonsmoking.

### TOP END

Yogya has a glut of luxury hotels, and heavy discounting has always been the norm. Most prices include breakfast.

**Jogja Village Inn** (Map p177; ☎ 373 031; www.jvidusun .co.id; Jl Menukan 5; r from US$75; ❄ 🛈 🅿) Just south of the happening Prawirotaman area, this fine hotel has a lovely Javanese feel, with low-rise buildings scattered around a gorgeous tropical garden and huge pool. Staff are attentive, and the restaurant is excellent. Nonsmoking. Add 21% tax to room rates.

**Melia Purosani Hotel** (Map p177; ☎ 589 521; www.solmelia.com; Jl Mayor Suryotomo 31; r from US$79; ❄ 🛈 🅿) This luxury colossus enjoys a very central location just east of Jl Malioboro. Its range of facilities includes a spa and a fitness centre, and it offers competitive deals via its website. Nonsmoking. Add 21% tax to room rates.

**Hyatt Regency** (off Map p177; ☎ 869 123; www.yogya karta.regency.hyatt.com; Jl Palagan Pelajar; r from US$115; ❄ 🛈 🅿) Sitting pretty in 24 hectares of landscaped grounds in the northern outskirts of the city, this luxury hotel has a golf course, tennis courts and a huge pool. Nonsmoking. Add 21% tax to room rates.

## Eating

### SOSROWIJAYAN AREA

For cheap and cheerful Indonesian and Western nosh, this area fits the bill (and your pocket) nicely. It's also the place to join locals for a bite to eat; after 10pm, the souvenir vendors along the northern end of Jl Malioboro pack up and a *lesahan* area (where diners sit on straw mats) comes alive. Here you can try Yogya's famous *ayam goreng* (deep-fried chicken soaked in coconut milk) and listen to young Indonesians strumming their guitars into the wee small hours.

A whole host of good warungs also lines Jl Pasar Kembang, beside the train line.

**Atap** (Map p184; ☎ 0856 4318 2004; Jl Sosrowijayan GT 1/113; dishes from 10,000Rp; ⏱ 5.30-10pm) Bohemian restaurant with tables made from car tyres

and a great little outdoor terrace. The menu has burgers and Indo favourites and a wicked sense of humour: *kopi osama* is coffee with a shot of brandy – the bearded one would not approve.

**Bedhot Resto** (Map p184; Gang II; mains 10,000-22,000Rp) Bedhot means 'creative' in old Javanese and this place is perhaps the most stylish eatery in Sosrowijayan, with art on the walls, batik tablecloths and menus made from bark. There's tasty Indonesian and Western food, good juices and internet access upstairs.

**New Superman's** (Map p184; meals 15,000-25,000Rp) Huge, slightly charmless place that's nevertheless a key hang-out for travellers, with a long, long menu of Western food like pizzas, jaffles and pancakes, and Chinese food.

**Bladok Losmen & Restaurant** (Map p184; Jl Sosrowijayan 76; mains 18,000-40,000Rp) Classy hotel restaurant with a wholesome and inviting air, and a mainly European menu.

**FM Café** (Map p184; Jl Sosrowijayan 14; mains around 20,000Rp) FM Café has a great courtyard setting and an eclectic menu ranging from *nasi goreng* to pizza. Happy hour is gloriously lengthy, lasting from 1pm to 8pm; bands perform here on Friday night.

### PRAWIROTAMAN AREA

**our pick Via Via** (Map p185; ☎ 386 557; www.viaviacafe .com; Jl Prawirotaman I 30; mains 14,000-28,000Rp; 🛈) A simply outstanding and very cosmopolitan venue, this cool cafe-restaurant gets virtually everything right. The menu is tempting, with very fresh, inventive Indonesian and Western food at fair prices, a few tapas, wine by the glass and healthy juices. The decor mixes exposed concrete and bamboo screens, and there's a great outdoor terrace.

**Ministry of Coffee** (Map p185; ☎ 747 3828; www.ministry ofcoffee.com; Jl Prawirotaman I 15A; meals 20,000Rp) A landmark modernist structure, with a library (with English-language books and magazines) upstairs and a cafe below. It's ideal for an espresso or latte, but the food (mainly snacks and cakes) is pretty average.

**Milas** (Map p177; ☎ 742 3399; Jl Prawirotaman IV 127; meals from 20,000Rp) This secret garden restaurant, located down a quiet side road, is a project centre for street youth. Offers tasty vegetarian cooking: healthy snacks, sandwiches, salads and organic coffee.

**Laba Laba Cafe** (Map p185; Jl Prawirotaman I 2; mains 20,000Rp) Laba Laba (which means 'spider') has a great rear garden that's an ideal setting for some filling European or Indonesian food.

**Gading** (Map p185; ☎ 659 6921; Jl Prawirotaman I 9; mains 20,000-48,000Rp) A civilised restaurant with pleasant seating and lighting and a menu of Indonesian and Western food – the thin-crust pizza here is great. There's live music on Wednesday, Friday and Sunday.

### OTHER AREAS

**Tembi** (off Map p177; ☎ 368 000; www.tembi.net; Jl Parangtritis, km 8.4; meals 8000-25,000Rp) Way down south, this lovely little restaurant specialises in traditional Javanese dishes. There are some startling things on the menu here, including squirrel and stir-fried sparrow, alongside more familiar options. It's part of the Tembi cultural centre (p181).

**Jimbaran** (off Map p177; ☎ 745 2882; Jl Damai; fish per ounce 8000Rp, lobster & prawns per ounce from 12,000Rp; ☉ noon-10pm) Overlooking rice fields (or kids' football pitch, depending on the season), this enjoyable place specialises in seafood. Everything is priced by the ounce; feast on crab, lobster, prawns and fresh fish. Jimbaran is about 6km north of Yogya, and about 2km north of the Hyatt.

**ourpick Warung Opera** (off Map p177; ☎ 718 1977; Jl Parangtritis, km 6.3; mains 10,000-30,000Rp; ☉ 5-10pm) Occupying a wonderful traditional Javanese house built from teak, this unusual and bohemian restaurant is an outstanding place to sample home-style Indonesian dishes. Donny, the flamboyant owner, also does fortune reading from coffee cups.

**Omar Duwur Restaurant** (off Map p177; ☎ 374 952; www.omahdhuwur.net; Jl Mondorakan 252; mains 32,000-125,000Rp; ☎ ) Out in Kota Gede, this is one of Yogya's best restaurants, with a lavish setting in a 150-year-old colonial mansion. Offers a wide selection of Western (try the rack of lamb) and Eastern dishes (the chicken masala is great).

## Drinking

There's not much drinking culture evident in Yogya, but if you want to sip a few beers both Sosrowijayan (along Jl Sosrowijayan) and Prawirotaman (along Jl Pangritis) have a bar or two.

**Bintang Café** (Map p184; Jl Sosrowijayan 54; mains 15,000Rp) This (un)imaginatively named place in the Sosrowijayan backpacking manor has live music and is one of the liveliest places around here. The food is bog-standard fare.

**Civet Coffee** (Map p185; Jl Prawirotaman I; snacks 16,000Rp; ☎ ) A stylish new cafe with a tempting choice of coffee, including gourmet blends like arabica Toraja, plus sandwiches and snacks. Wi-fi is free for 20 minutes and 6000Rp per hour afterwards.

## Entertainment

If you've ever wanted to see traditional Javanese performing arts, this is the place. Dance, *wayang* or gamelan is performed every morning at the *kraton* (p179), and provides a useful introduction to Javanese arts. Check with the tourist office for current listings and any special events.

Most famous of all performances is the spectacular Ramayana ballet (p197) held in the open air at Prambanan in the dry season.

### WAYANG KULIT

Leather-puppet performances can be seen at several places around Yogya every night of the week.

**Sasono Hinggil** (Map p177; South Main Sq) Most of the centres offer shortened versions for tourists, but here in the *alun-alun selatan* of the *kraton*, marathon all-night performances are held every second Saturday from 9pm to 5am (20,000Rp). Bring a pillow.

**Sono-Budoyo Museum** (Map p177; ☎ 376 775; admission 5000Rp) This museum holds popular two-hour performances nightly from 8pm to 10pm (20,000Rp). The first half-hour involves the reading of the story in Javanese, so most travellers skip this and arrive later.

### DANCE

Most performances are based on the Ramayana or at least billed as 'Ramayana ballet' because of the famed performances at Prambanan.

**Purawisata** (Map p177; ☎ 375 705; Jl Brigjen Katamso) This amusement park stages Ramayana performances daily at 8pm (tickets 120,000Rp). You can dine here and watch the show.

### OTHER PERFORMANCES

**RRI auditorium** (Map p177; cnr Jl Gejayan & Jl Colombo) Here you can see *ketoprak* performances from 8pm to midnight on the first Saturday of every month for 20,000Rp.

### LIVE MUSIC

**Blatz Lounge** (off Map p177; ☎ 748 8898; Jl Kaliurang, Km 6.3; ☎ ) Groovy cocktail bar that hosts smooth

upon reaching Bali. Purchase your ticket from a reliable agent and check up-to-date information with other travellers and on Lonely Planet's Thorn Tree internet forum.

### TRAIN

Centrally located, Yogya's **Tugu train station** (Map p184; ☎ 514 270) handles all business- and executive-class trains. Economy-class trains also depart from and arrive at Lempuyangan station (Map p177), 1km to the east.

The comfortable *Taksaka* (from 150,000Rp, eight hours) departs twice daily for Jakarta at 10am and 8pm. Or the best train is the executive *Argo Lawu* (from 220,000Rp, seven hours), which leaves at 8.53am.

Very regular trains run to Solo, including *Pramek* (7000Rp, one hour), which departs six times daily from Tugu.

For Surabaya, the best option is the executive *Argo Wilis* (from 150,000Rp, 5½ hours), which leaves at 2.22pm. Otherwise there are plenty of night trains, including the *Mutiara Selatan* (business class 110,000Rp, six hours), departing at 1.13am.

Heading for Bandung, trains include the *Lodaya* (business/executive class from 100,000/165,000Rp, 8½ hours), which passes through Yogya at 9.24pm.

From Lempuyangan train station, most of the economy-class services are overnight trains that run between Surabaya and Jakarta (40,000Rp, 11 hours) and Bandung (35,000Rp, 10 hours).

## Getting Around
### TO/FROM THE AIRPORT

Yogya's Adi Sucipto airport, 10km east of the centre, is very well connected to the city by public transport. Buses 3A and 1A (3000Rp) leave from the terminal for Jl Malioboro. *Pramek* trains (see above) stop at Maguwo station, which is right by the airport as well.

Taxis from the airport cost 50,000Rp to the city centre, and are slightly cheaper going to the airport on the meter.

### BECAK & ANDONG

Yogyakarta has an oversupply of becak; it is impossible to go anywhere in the main tourist areas without being greeted by choruses of 'becak'. Fares cost around 2000Rp per kilometre, but the minimum fare for tourists is usually around 4000Rp, and the

asking rate is a lot more. The trip from Jl Prawirotaman to Jl Malioboro costs at least 8000Rp. Avoid becak drivers who offer cheap hourly rates unless you want to do the rounds of all the batik galleries that offer commission. There are also horse-drawn *andong* around town, which cost about the same or less than becak.

### BICYCLE

Bikes cost as little as 15,000Rp a day from hotels, or try the shops at the southern end of Gang I in Sosrowijayan. Always lock your bike and look for bicycle *parkir*, who will look after your bike for some spare change.

### BUS

Yogya has a reliable new bus system called the TransJogja busway. These modern air-conditioned buses run from 6am to 10pm on six routes around the city to as far away as Prambanan. Tickets cost 3000Rp per journey, or 27,000Rp for a carnet of 10. TransJogja buses only stop at the designated bus shelters.

Bus 1A is a very useful service, running from Jl Malioboro as far as Jl Senopati, then northeast past the Affandi Museum, Ambarukmo Plaza and the airport to the ruins of Prambanan. Bus 3B connects Giwangan bus terminal with the airport and Prambanan before heading west to Jl Malioboro. TransJogja route maps are available at the Tourist Information Centre.

There are also older regular buses (2000Rp), which stop everywhere.

### CAR & MOTORCYCLE

Travel agencies on Jl Sosrowijayan and Jl Prawirotaman rent out cars with drivers for trips in and around town for 70,000Rp per hour, with or without petrol, depending on the travel agent. They have inflated price lists for more distant destinations, but you can usually get a car or small minibus with driver for around 700,000Rp per day.

Motorcycles can be hired for approximately 50,000Rp a day, sometimes less. An international driving permit is required by law, but they are not often checked.

### TAXI

Taxis have meters and are quite efficient, costing 5000Rp for the first kilometre, then 2500Rp for each subsequent kilometre.

# AROUND YOGYAKARTA
## Imogiri

A royal graveyard perched on a hilltop 20km south of Yogyakarta, Imogiri was first built by Sultan Agung in 1645 to serve as his own mausoleum. Since then almost all his successors and other prominent members of the royal family have been buried here. The cemetery contains three major courtyards – in the central courtyard are the tombs of Sultan Agung and succeeding Mataram kings; to the left are the tombs of the *susuhunan* (sultan or king) of Solo and to the right are those of the sultans of Yogyakarta. The tomb of Hamengkubuwono IX, the father of the present sultan, is one of the most visited graves.

Of major interest to pilgrims is the **tomb of Sultan Agung** (admission 1000Rp; 10am-1pm Sun & Mon, 1.30-4pm Fri). There is no objection to visitors joining the pilgrims at these specified times, although to enter the tombs you must don full Javanese court dress, which can be hired for a small fee.

It's an impressive site, reached by a daunting flight of 345 steps. From the top of the stairway, a walkway circles the whole complex and leads to the actual hill summit, with a superb view over Yogyakarta to Gunung Merapi.

*Angkots* and buses from Yogyakarta (4000Rp) stop at the car park, from where it is about 500m to the base of the hill and the start of the steps. Like most pilgrimage sites, there will be various demands for 'donations'. The only compulsory entry charge is payable when you sign the visitors' book, inside the main compound.

## Kasongan

Yogyakarta's prime pottery centre is Kasongan, where dozens of workshops produce pots and some superb figurines, giant dragons and peacocks. Kasongan pottery is generally sold painted or unpainted – very little glazing work is done. The village was very badly hit by the 2006 earthquake, but production has now resumed and visitors are very welcome (especially if they open their wallets).

Catch a Bantul-bound bus and get off on the main road at the entrance to the village, 6.5km south of Yogyakarta. It is then about a 1km walk to the centre of the village and most of the pottery workshops.

## Parangtritis
☎ 0274

Windswept and sandblasted, with crashing waves on one side and craggy, looming cliffs on the other, Parangtritis has all the makings of a lonely seaside town. Or at least it would do if it weren't for the thousands of local tourists who flock here every weekend. Weekends in Yogyakarta's favourite seaside escape are a whirlwind of overpriced hotels, jostling crowds and souvenir salespeople.

During the week, however, Parangtritis becomes that slightly forlorn resort. Prices fall, an eerie quiet descends and it becomes a half-decent place to spend the day. There are some great dunes to explore once you're away from the main stretch of beach, which is marred by litter.

It's best to respect local superstitions and not wear green if you visit Parangtritis.

### SIGHTS

The seas off Parangtritis are extremely dangerous, but you can swim safely in *pemandian* (freshwater pools) at the base of the hill near the village, where spring water spills out from

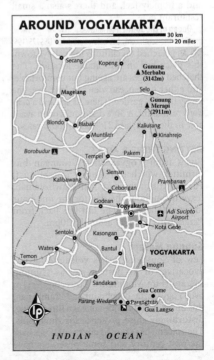

**AROUND YOGYAKARTA**

0 ———————— 30 km
0 ———————— 20 miles

Secang • Kopeng •  Gunung ▲ Merbabu (3142m)

Magelang •  Selo •  Gunung ▲ Merapi (2911m)

Blondo •  • Blabak  Kaliurang •  • Kinahrejo
• Muntilan

Borobudur 🏛  Tempel •  Pakem •

Kalibawang •  Sleman •  Prambanan 🏛
• Cebongan

Godean •  Yogyakarta ◉  Adi Sucipto ✈ Airport
•  Kota Gede
Sentolo •  Kasongan •

Wates •  Bantul •  **YOGYAKARTA**
Temon •

• Imogiri

Sandakan •  Gua Cerme •

Parang Wedang • • Parangtritis 🏛
• Gua Langse

*INDIAN   OCEAN*

the hilltop through high bamboo pipes. If you'd prefer hot springs, head for **Parang Wedang**, just beyond the nearby village of Parangkusumo.

Trails along the hills above the sea to the east of Parangtritis lead to a meditation cave, **Gua Cerme**. A couple of kilometres from the town and past the Queen of the South resort is **Gua Langse**, used by mystics as a meditation cave.

### FESTIVALS & EVENTS

Like so many places along the south coast, Parangtritis is a centre for the worship of Nyai Loro Kidul; during the annual festival of **Labuhan** staged to appease her, the sultans of Yogyakarta still send offerings to the sacred point at Parangkusumo.

### SLEEPING & EATING

The main drag to the beach is lined with basic hotels and warungs. Alternatively, some of the better options are on the main road, to the east of the bus terminal. During the week, some places have rooms with *mandis* for as little as 30,000Rp.

**Losmen Dinasti** ( ☎ 368 536; r from 40,000Rp) A basic place with simple, plain but clean rooms and a homely feel, and there's also a small restaurant here.

**Queen of the South** (Puri Ratu Kidul; ☎ 367 196; www.queen-of-the-south.com; bungalows/ste from US$125/195; ✖ ✿ ) Perched on clifftops high above town, this place has an unbeatable location. The thatched cottages are ageing but comfortable, and either have ocean views or look over the lovely tropical garden. There's a spa and a *pendopo* restaurant. A 50% discount is often available in the week; add 21% tax to room rates.

### GETTING THERE & AWAY

Buses from Yogyakarta's Giwangan bus terminal, which can also be caught on Jl Parangtritis at the end of Jl Prawirotaman, leave throughout the day for the one-hour journey (8000Rp). The last bus back from Parangtritis leaves at around 5.30pm.

## Gunung Merapi

Few of Southeast Asia's volcanoes are as evocative, or as destructive, as Gunung Merapi (Fire Mountain). Towering 2911m over Yogyakarta, Borobudur and Prambanan, this immense Fujiesque cone is a threatening, disturbingly close presence for thousands. The volcano has erupted dozens of times over the past century and some observers have theorised that it was even responsible for the mysterious evacuation of Borobudur and the collapse of the old Mataram kingdom during the 11th century.

Merapi is revered and feared in equal measure. Every year, offerings from Yogya's *kraton* are made to appease the mountain's foul temper, in conjunction with offerings to the Queen of the South Seas at Parangtritis.

But Merapi isn't so easy to appease. On 22 November 1994 it erupted, killing more than 60 people, and it has been on the boil ever since. In 2006 28,000 people were evacuated as lava and pyroclastic flows cascaded from its upper slopes.

Such is its threat, Merapi is one of only 16 'decade volcanoes' in the world, a definition bestowed by the United Nations–sponsored International Decade for Natural Disaster Reduction for particularly explosive peaks.

Eruptions, however, have not put a stop to people living on the mountain. With a population density of 690 people per sq km, Merapi supports hundreds of small communities.

The hill resort of Kaliurang, 25km north of Yogyakarta, is the main access point for views of Merapi and makes a wonderful break from the city. Yogyakarta travel agencies also sell night trips for views of the lava flows – there are several good viewpoints – but you can also do this yourself. Take a bus for Kaliurang (7000Rp, one hour) from the Giwangan terminal, get off at the Kaliurang Hill Resort, then catch one of the waiting *ojek* (8000Rp) to the viewpoint of Kalu Aden, from where there's a wonderful perspective of the lava action.

### CLIMBING GUNUNG MERAPI

Merapi is frequently declared off-limits to visitors. But if conditions permit, climbing the summit is possible in the dry season (April to September). There are three possible routes, but the most popular path is from the small village of Selo, on the northern side of the mountain. Even then *extreme caution* is advised.

During quiet periods, a 1am start from Selo is necessary to reach the summit for dawn (a four- to five-hour trip). After a 2km walk through the village to Pos Merapi, the abandoned vulcanology post, the steady but steep climb begins. It is a tough, demanding walk, but manageable by anyone with a reasonable level of fitness.

The last stages are through loose volcanic scree, but guides may stop short of the summit. Check with your guide whether it is possible to go to the top before setting off. Treks from Selo are not always well organised. Guides should warn against climbing if it looks dangerous. While they don't want to endanger lives, they may be prepared to take risks in order to be paid. Even during quieter periods, Merapi can suddenly throw out a stream of lava; in September 2002 an Indonesian student was killed when he got lost and fell into a ravine. There are two vents where lava can be seen, but it is not advisable to approach them.

Check the latest situation in Kaliurang, but at the time of writing the climb to the peak from Kaliurang had been strictly off limits since 1994 because of volcanic activity. **Christian Awuy** ( ☎ 081 7541 2572), owner of Vogels Hostel, has organised climbs for years and is an essential first reference point.

Alternatively, you can contact the **Merapi Volcano Observatory** ( ☎ 0274-514180, 0274-514192; Jl Cendana 15, Kaliurang), or Kartika Trekking (p183) in Yogyakarta.

## Kaliurang
☎ 0274
Kaliurang, 25km north of Yogyakarta, is the nearest hill resort to the city. At 900m, it has a cool, refreshing climate. During the rainy season, Kaliurang often sits in a thick blanket of cloud, but on clear days the views of Merapi are magical.

All visitors to Kaliurang must pay a 2500Rp entrance fee.

### SIGHTS & ACTIVITIES
One of Java's finest museums, **Ullen Sentalu** ( ☎ 895 161; www.ullensentalu.com; admission 45,000Rp, students 25,000Rp; ☻ 9am-3.30pm Tue-Sun) is a surprise find on the slopes of Merapi. This large complex has a principal structure that resembles a Bavarian baron's mansion, and extensive gardens and courtyards to explore. Ullen Sentalu is dedicated entirely to the richness of Javanese culture, and has an outstanding collection of fine art, including oil paintings and sculpture. Unusually, it focuses heavily on notable women of Java, particularly the wives of sultans, through pictures and stories. Batik also takes pride of place; here you can gauge the subtle differences between Yogya and Solo designs, alongside those from coastal towns

to the north. There's a great restaurant here, a high-quality contemporary art gallery, and a souvenir store loaded with top-grade batik. Admission includes a two-hour tour with a knowledgeable English-speaking guide, and copious cups of refreshing spice-flavoured tea.

There's also an excellent **forest park** (Hutan Wisata Kaliurang; admission 1000Rp; ☻ 8am-4pm) on the slopes of the mountain. Maps at the park entrance show areas you are allowed to explore. Heed them and don't venture further; in a sudden eruption lava can flow down the mountain at 300km/h. At the time of writing you could take the 15-minute walk to the Promojiwo viewpoint for views of Merapi and then on to the Tlogo Muncar waterfall, which is just a trickle in the dry season, and then back to the entrance.

Vogels Hostel arranges **mountain walks** to see the lava flows. The five-hour return trek starts at 3am and climbs 1400m up the mountain to see the glowing lava at its best (from 60,000Rp per person). Overnight camping trips (from 180,000Rp), village tours and birdwatching walks can also be arranged. A minimum of two people is required for all trips.

### SLEEPING & EATING
Kaliurang is a sprawling, slightly scruffy-around-the-edges resort with more than 100 places to sleep.

**Vogels Hostel** ( ☎ 895 208; Jl Astamulya 76; dm 15,000Rp, d with shared facilities 20,000-25,000Rp, bungalows with bath and hot water 100,000Rp) Vogels is a travellers' institution and has been serving up the same mixture of cheap accommodation, hearty food and excellent information for years. The owner, Christian Awuy, is a particular authority on Merapi and its many moods.

**Hotel Satriafi** ( ☎ 895 128; Jl Kesehatan 193; r with/without hot water & TV from 110,000/85,000Rp) Clean, quite basic rooms that are a step up from those at Vogels.

**Hotel Kano** ( ☎ 895 342; Jl Giri Kondang; r with TV & hot water 200,000-300,000Rp) In the heart of Kaliurang, this large art deco–style hotel has a selection of bright, comfortable rooms that are in decent shape, and a good cafe-restaurant.

**Restaurant Joyo** (Jl Astamulya 63; mains around 10,000Rp) Half-shop, half-restaurant Jojo has tasty Chinese and Indonesian food and some eclectic traditional artefacts for sale. It's over the road from Vogels.

## GETTING THERE & AWAY

*Angkot* from Yogyakarta's Terban station to Kaliurang cost 7000Rp; the last leaves at 4pm. A taxi from Malioboro will cost around 90,000Rp.

## Selo

On the northern slopes of Gunung Merapi, 50km west of Solo, Selo has a few basic home-stays where guides can be arranged for the Merapi climb. The views of the mountain from the village are superb.

From Selo it is a very steep, four-hour trek to the volcano's summit (see p192), and about 2½ hours for the descent. At the top the sulphurous fumes can be overpowering – take great care. It's not advisable to attempt this climb in the rainy season, or after heavy downpours at any time of year.

The host at popular **Pak Auto** (r per person 25,000Rp) has been guiding trips to the summit for years. Accommodation is very basic but clean. Elderly Pak Darto rarely ventures far these days, but both of his sons (Sutrisno and Yudi) work as guides and know the route. Prices are variable depending on how many people are in the group and the risk factor. Count on a minimum of 120,000Rp for one person, or upwards of 150,000Rp for two or more people.

**Hotel Agung Merapi** ( ☎ 0276-326 025; r from 75,000Rp) is in poor shape, but it represents a (small) step up in quality from Pak Auto; it also has a restaurant.

Selo is most easily reached from Solo: take a bus to Magelang, stopping at Selo (14,000Rp, two hours) on the way. However, the route from Yogyakarta is far more beautiful. Take a Magelang bus to Blabak (8000Rp, one hour) and an *angkot* or bus to Selo (6000Rp). Travel agents in Solo and Yogyakarta arrange Merapi climbing trips via Selo.

## PRAMBANAN

☎ 0274

On the road to Solo, 17km northeast of Yogyakarta, the temples of Prambanan are the best remaining examples of Java's period of Hindu cultural development. Not only do these temples form the largest Hindu temple complex in Java, but the wealth of sculptural detail on the great Shiva temple makes it easily the most outstanding example of Hindu art.

All the temples in the Prambanan area were built between the 8th and 10th cen-turies AD, when Java was ruled by the Buddhist Sailendras in the south and the Hindu Sanjayas of Old Mataram in the north. Possibly by the second half of the 9th century, these two dynasties were united by the marriage of Rakai Pikatan of Hindu Mataram and the Buddhist Sailendra princess Pramodhavardhani. This may explain why a number of temples, including those of the Prambanan temple complex and the smaller Plaosan group, reveal Shivaite and Buddhist elements in architecture and sculpture. These two elements are also found to some degree in India and Nepal.

Following this creative burst over a pe-riod of two centuries, the Prambanan Plain was abandoned when the Hindu-Javanese kings moved to East Java. In the middle of the 16th century there is said to have been a great earthquake that toppled many of the temples. In the centuries that fol-lowed, their destruction was accelerated by treasure hunters and locals searching for building materials. Most temples have now been restored to some extent, and, like Borobudur, Prambanan made the Unesco World Heritage list in 1991.

Prambanan suffered extensive damage in the 2006 earthquake. Though the temples sur-vived, hundreds of stone blocks collapsed to the ground or were cracked (479 in the Shiva temple alone). Parts of the complex are now fenced off and some temples are covered in scaffolding. It will take years to fully restore Prambanan. That said, Prambanan is certainly still well worth a visit, and you can get within a few metres of (if not enter) all the main monuments.

## Orientation & Information

The **Prambanan temples** ( ☎ 496 401; adult/student US$11/6; ☀ 6am-6pm, last admission 5.15pm) are usu-ally visited from Yogyakarta (17km away), but they can also be visited from Solo (50km away). The main temple complex lies on the Yogyakarta–Solo highway, opposite the slightly grimy suburb of Prambanan. From the main entrance on the southeastern side, it's about a 10-minute walk to the core of the site. Behind it, on the western side near the highway, is the outdoor theatre where the Ramayana ballet is performed.

To the north of the largest Shiva Mahadeva temple is the archaeological museum. Further north are smaller, partly renovated temples leading to Candi Sewu. A 'minitrain' (5000Rp) from the museum loops to Candi Sewu. All of these temples form the main Prambanan complex.

On the left after passing through the main gate there is a small information desk with info on the site and Ramayana performances. As at Borobudur, the admission price includes camera fees and admission to the museum. Guides charge 60,000Rp for a one-hour tour for one to 20 people. There is also an audiovisual show every 30 minutes (2000Rp).

Most of the other (seldom-visited) outlying temples are within a 5km radius of Prambanan village. You'll need at least half a day to see them on foot, or they can be explored by bicycle or motorcycle if you ride to Prambanan. A standard entry fee of 5000Rp applies to most of the outlying temples.

The best time to visit Prambanan is in the early morning or late in the day, when it's quiet, though you can never expect to get Prambanan to yourself – expect plenty of attention from visiting school groups and requests for photos.

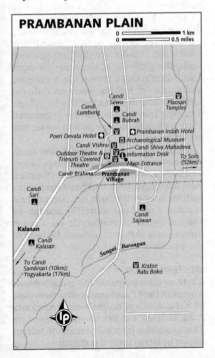

**PRAMBANAN PLAIN**

0 — 1 km
0 — 0.5 miles

Candi Sewu
Candi Lumbung
Plaosan Temples
Candi Bubrah
Poeri Devata Hotel
Archaeological Museum
Prambanan Indah Hotel
Candi Vishnu
Candi Shiva Mahadeva
Outdoor Theatre & Trimurti Covered Theatre
Information Desk
Main Entrance
To Solo (52km)
Candi Brahma
Prambanan Village
Candi Sari
Candi Sajiwan
Kalasan
Candi Kalasan
Sungai Barongan
To Candi Sambisari (10km); Yogyakarta (17km)
Kraton Ratu Boko

## Sights
### PRAMBANAN TEMPLES

The huge Prambanan complex was erected in the middle of the 9th century – around 50 years later than Borobudur – but little is known about its early history. It's thought that it was built by Rakai Pikatan to commemorate the return of a Hindu dynasty to sole power in Java.

Prambanan was in ruins for years, and while efforts were made in 1885 to clear the site, it was not until 1937 that reconstruction was first attempted. Of the original group, the outer compound contains the remains of 244 temples. Eight minor and eight main temples stand in the highest central courtyard.

### Candi Shiva Mahadeva

This temple, dedicated to Shiva, is not only the largest of the temples but also the finest. At the time of research it was not possible to get really close to the monument, but there's still plenty to admire from a distance.

The main spire soars 47m and the temple is lavishly carved. The 'medallions' that decorate its base have a characteristic Prambanan motif – small lions in niches flanked by *kalpatura* (trees of heaven) and a menagerie of stylised half-human and half-bird *kinnara* (heavenly beings). The vibrant scenes carved onto the inner wall of the gallery encircling the temple are from the Ramayana – they tell how Lord Rama's wife, Sita, is abducted and how Hanuman the monkey god and Sugriwa the white monkey general eventually find and release her.

The following descriptions apply to the temple's interior, which has not been accessible since the earthquake of 2006, but may reopen in the lifetime of this guidebook. The main chamber at the top of the eastern stairway has a four-armed statue of Shiva the Destroyer and is notable for the fact that this mightiest of Hindu gods stands on a huge lotus pedestal, a symbol of Buddhism. In the southern cell is the pot-bellied and bearded Agastya, an incarnation of Shiva as divine teacher; in the western cell is a superb image of the elephant-headed Ganesha, Shiva's son. In the northern cell, Durga, Shiva's consort, can be seen killing the demon buffalo. Some people believe that the Durga image is actually an image of the Slender Virgin, who, legend has it, was turned to stone by a man she refused to marry. She is still an object of pilgrimage and her name is often used for the temple group.

## Candi Vishnu

It's still possible to get up front and personal with this magnificent temple, which touches 33m, and sits just north of Candi Shiva Mahadeva. Its magnificent reliefs tell the story of Lord Krishna, a hero of the Mahabharata epic, and you can ascend its stone staircase to the inner chamber and see a four-armed image of Vishnu the Preserver.

## Candi Brahma

Candi Vishnu's twin temple, Candi Brahma, is south of Candi Shiva Mahadeva and carved with the final scenes of the Ramayana. It has a spectacular 'monster mouth' doorway. Again, you will probably not be able to gain access to its inner chamber, which contains a four-headed statue of Brahma, the god of creation.

## Candi Sewu

The 'Thousand Temples', dating from around AD 850, originally consisted of a large central Buddhist temple surrounded by four rings of 240 smaller 'guard' temples. Outside the compound stood four sanctuaries at the points of the compass, of which Candi Bubrah is the most southern one. The renovated main temple has finely carved niches around its inner gallery – these niches once held bronze statues.

## PLAOSAN TEMPLES

This northeastern group of temples is 3km from the Prambanan complex. It can be reached on foot by taking the road north from the main gate, going past Candi Sewu and then walking east (right) for about 1km.

Built around the same time as the Prambanan temple group by Rakai Pikatan, the Plaosan temples combine both Hindu and Buddhist religious symbols and carvings. Plaosan Lor (Plaosan North) comprises two restored, identical main temples, surrounded by some 126 small shrines and solid stupas, most of which are now just a jumble of stone.

Two giant *dwarapala* (temple guardian statues) stand at the front of each main temple. The main temples, notable for their unusual three-part design, are two-storey,

three-room structures, with an imitation storey above and a tiered roof of stupas rising to a single, larger one in the centre. Inside each room are impressive stone Bodhisattvas on either side of an empty lotus pedestal, and intricately carved *kala* (dragon) heads above the many windows. The bronze Buddhas that once sat on the lotus pedestals have been removed.

Plaosan Kidul (Plaosan South) has more stupas and the remnants of a temple, but little renovation work has been done.

## SOUTHERN GROUP
### Candi Sajiwan

Not far from the village of Sajiwan, about 1.5km southeast of Prambanan village, are the ruins of this Buddhist temple. Around the temple's base are carvings from the Jataka (episodes from the Buddha's various lives).

### Kraton Ratu Boko

Perched on top of a hill overlooking Prambanan, Kraton Ratu Boko (Palace of King Boko), a huge Hindu palace complex dating from the 9th century, is believed to have been the central court of the mighty Mataram kingdom. Little remains of the original complex. Renovations, while only partially successful, have included new stonework. You can see the large gateway, walls, the platform of the main *pendopo*, Candi Pembakaran (Royal Crematorium) and a series of bathing places on different levels leading down to the nearby village. The view from this site to the Prambanan Plain is magnificent, especially at sunset, and worth the walk.

To reach Ratu Boko, travel 1.5km south on the road from Prambanan village to just southwest of where the river crosses the road. Near the 'Yogya 18km' signpost a steep rocky path leads up to the main site. Altogether it is about a one-hour walk. The site can be reached by car or motorcycle via a much longer route that goes around the back of the mountain.

### WESTERN GROUP

There are three temples in this group between Yogyakarta and Prambanan, two of them close to Kalasan village on the main Yogyakarta road. Kalasan and Prambanan villages are 3km apart, so it is probably easiest to take an *angkot* or bus to cover this stretch.

## Candi Kalasan

Standing 50m off the main road near Kalasan village, this temple is one of the oldest Buddhist temples on the Prambanan Plain. A Sanskrit inscription of AD 778 refers to a temple dedicated to the female Bodhisattva, Tara, though the existing structure appears to have been built around the original one some years later. It has been partially restored during this century and has some fine detailed carvings on its southern side, where a huge, ornate *kala* head glowers over the doorway. At one time it was completely covered in coloured, shining stucco, and traces of the hard, stonelike 'diamond plaster' that provided a base for paintwork can still be seen. The inner chamber of Kalasan once sheltered a huge bronze image of Buddha or Tara.

## Candi Sari

About 200m north from Candi Kalasan, in the middle of coconut and banana groves, the Sari Temple has the three-part design of the larger Plaosan temple but is probably slightly older. Some experts believe that its 2nd floor may have served as a dormitory for the Buddhist priests who took care of Candi Kalasan. The sculptured reliefs around the exterior are similar to those of Kalasan but are in much better condition.

## Candi Sambisari

A country lane runs to this isolated temple, about 2.5km north of the main road. Sambisari is a Shiva temple and possibly the latest temple at Prambanan to be erected by the Mataram kingdom. It was discovered by a farmer in 1966. Excavated from under ancient layers of protective volcanic ash and dust, it lies almost 6m below the surface of the surrounding fields and is remarkable for its perfectly preserved state. The inner sanctum of the temple is dominated by a large lingam and yoni (stylised penis and vagina), typical of Shiva temples.

## Sleeping

There are a few options close to Prambanan, but very few people stay here, given its proximity to Yogyakarta.

**Prambanan Indah** ( ☎ 497 353; Jl Candi Sewu 8; r with fan/air-con 85,000/210,000Rp; ste 291,000Rp; ✴ ) The large hotel is close to the core of the site and some rooms have temple views.

**Poeri Devata Hotel** ( ☎ 496 435; garden/temple view cottages 500,000/600,000Rp; ✴ ⬛ ) Down a quiet lane at the northwestern corner of the temple complex, this midrange hotel has bungalows with outdoor bathrooms set in attractive gardens, and a restaurant.

## Entertainment

**Ramayana Ballet** ( ☎ 496 408; www.borobudurpark.com) Held at the outdoor theatre just west of the main temple complex, the famous Ramayana Ballet is Java's most spectacular dance-drama. The story of Rama and Shinta unfolds over four successive nights, twice or three times each month from May to October (the dry season), leading up to the full moon. With the magnificent floodlit Candi Shiva Mahadeva as a backdrop, nearly 200 dancers and gamelan musicians take part in a spectacle of monkey armies, giants on stilts, clashing battles and acrobatics.

Performances last from 7.30pm to 9.30pm. Tickets are sold in Yogyakarta through the tourist information office (p178) and travel agencies (p178) at the same price that you'll pay at the theatre box office, but they usually offer packages that include transport direct from your hotel for 30,000Rp to 50,000Rp extra. Tickets cost 50,000Rp for economy seats, 100,000Rp for 1st-class seats, 125,000Rp for special class and 200,000Rp for VIP seats (padded chairs up the front). All seats have a good view and are not too far from the stage, but the cheapest seats are stone benches that are situated side on to the stage.

Alternatively, the *Ramayana Ballet Full Story* is a good two-hour performance (condensing the epic into one night), and alternates with the four-part episodic performances. It features only 50 performers but is still a fine spectacle, held at the Trimurti Covered Theatre from November to April. Performances start at 7.30pm every Tuesday and Thursday.

## Getting There & Away

### BICYCLE & MOTORCYCLE

You can visit all the temples by bicycle from Yogya. The most pleasant route, though it's a longer ride, is to take Jl Senopati out past the zoo to the eastern ring road, where you turn left. Follow this right up to Jl Solo, turn right and then left at Jl Babarsari. Go past the Sahid Garden Hotel and follow the road anticlockwise around the school to the Selokan Mataram. This canal runs parallel to the Solo road, about 1.5km to the north, for around 6km to Kalasan, about 2km before Prambanan.

To view the western temples you really need to come back via the Solo road. The turn-off north to Candi Sambisari from the Solo road crosses the canal before leading another 1km to the temple. You can visit the temple, backtrack to the canal path and continue back to Yogyakarta.

If you are coming by motorcycle, you can combine the visit with a trip to Kaliurang. From Kaliurang, instead of going back to the main Yogyakarta–Solo road, take the 'Solo Alternatif' route signposted in the village of Pakem, about halfway between Yogyakarta and Kaliurang. From there the road passes through some beautiful countryside, before tipping you onto the main highway just before Prambanan's main entrance.

### BUS

From Yogyakarta, take TransYogya bus 1A (3000Rp, 40 minutes) from Jl Malioboro. From Solo, buses take 1½ hours and cost 13,000Rp.

## SOLO (SURAKARTA)

☎ 0271 / pop 560,000

Arguably the epicentre of Javanese identity and tradition, Solo is one of the least westernised cities in the island. An eternal rival to Yogyakarta, this conservative city often plays second fiddle to its more conspicuous neighbour. But with backstreet *kampung* and elegant *kraton*, traditional markets and gleaming malls, Solo has more than enough to warrant at least an overnight visit. And as there are some fascinating temples close by, it also makes a great base for forays into the lush hills of Central Java.

In many ways, Solo is also Java writ small, incorporating its vices and virtues and embodying much of its heritage. On the downside, the island's notoriously fickle temper tends to flare in Solo first – the city has been the backdrop for some of the worst riots in Java's recent history. On the upside, the city's long and distinguished past as a seat of the great Mataram empire means that it competes with Yogyakarta as the hub of Javanese culture.

Solo attracts many students and scholars to its academies of music and dance. The city is an excellent place to see traditional perform-

ing arts, and traditional crafts, especially batik, are also well represented, as Solo is a major textile centre.

## History

Surakarta's founding in 1745 has a mystical history. Following the sacking of the Mataram court at Kartosuro in 1742, the *susuhunan*, Pakubuwono II, decided to look for a more auspicious site. According to legend, 'voices' told the king to go to the village because 'it is the place decreed by Allah and it will become a great and prosperous city'.

Pakubuwono II died after only four years in the city, and his heir, Pakubuwono III, managed to lose half of his kingdom to the court of Yogyakarta. Pakubuwono X (1893–1938), however, had more luck. He revived the prestige of the court through the promotion of culture and gave no time to fighting rival royals.

Following WWII, the royal court fumbled opportunities to play a positive role in the revolution, and lost out badly to Yogyakarta, which became the seat of the independent government. The palaces of the city soon became mere symbols of ancient Javanese feudalism and aristocracy.

With the overthrow of Suharto, Solo erupted following the riots in Jakarta in May 1998. For two days rioters went on a rampage, systematically looting and burning every shopping centre and department store and targeting Chinese-owned businesses.

Today things have settled down again, and sleek new shopping malls have risen from the ashes of the old. But Solo retains a reputation amongst Javanese as a hotbed of radicalism, and its *madrassahs* (Islamic schools) have maintained links to extremist groups such as Jemaah Islamiah.

## Orientation

Jl Slamet Riyadi, the broad and busy avenue running east–west through the centre of Solo, is the main thoroughfare; most hotels and restaurants are on or just off it. For most of its length it's a one-way street (east–west) between 8pm and 6am.

Solo's Balapan train station is situated in the northern part of the city, about 2km from the city centre; the main bus terminal, Tirtonadi, is 1.5km north again. The Gilingan minibus terminal is near the bus terminal.

The oldest part of the city is centred on the Kraton Surakarta to the southeast.

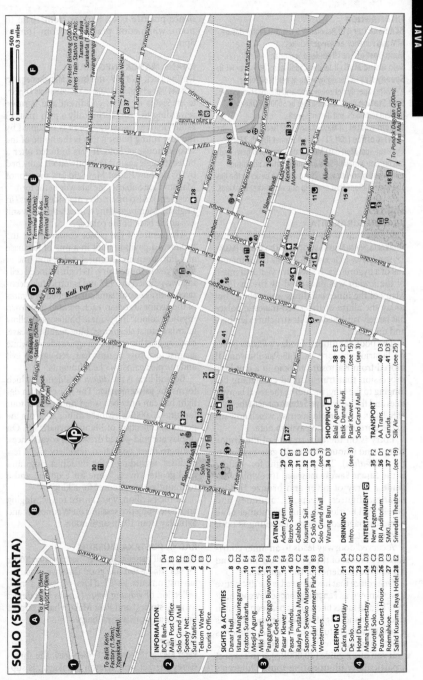

# SOLO (SURAKARTA)

## Information

**BCA bank** (cnr Jl Dr Rajiman & Jl Gatot Subroto) Has an ATM and currency-exchange facilities.

**Main post office** (Jl Jenderal Sudirman)

**Solo Grand Mall** (Jl Jenderal Sudirman; 🛜 ) Free wi-fi.

**Speedy Net** (Jl Ronggowarsito 4; per hr 6000Rp; 🕑 24hr) Speedy net connection and plenty of computers.

**Surf Station** (Jl Dr Surtono; per hr 5000Rp) Offers modern terminals and decent speeds.

**Telkom wartel** (Jl Mayor Kusmanto) Near the post office.

**Tourist office** ( ☎ 711 435; Jl Slamet Riyadi 275; 🕑 8am-4pm Mon-Sat) Most staff are helpful here, and can provide a map of Solo and information on cultural events and places to visit. There are also desks at the bus and train stations that can help out with ticket bookings.

## Sights

### KRATON SURAKARTA

Once the hub of an empire, today the **Kraton Surakarta** (Kraton Kasunanan; ☎ 656 432; admission 8000Rp; 🕑 9am-2pm Tue-Fri, to 3pm Sat & Sun) is a faded memorial of a bygone era. It's worth a visit, but much of the *kraton* was destroyed by fire in 1985. Many of the inner buildings were rebuilt, but today the allure of this once-majestic palace has largely vanished and its structures left bare and unloved.

The poor condition of today's *kraton* belies its illustrious history. In 1745 Pakubuwono II moved from Kartosuro to Solo in a day-long procession that transplanted everything belonging to the king, including the royal banyan trees and the sacred **Nyai Setomo cannon** (the twin of Si Jagur, p102, in old Jakarta), which now sits in the northern palace pavilion here.

Entry is on the eastern side of the *kraton* compound (though the main gateway fronts the *alun-alun*). The main sight for visitors is the **Sasono Sewoko museum**. Its exhibits include a array of silver and bronze Hindu-Javanese figures, weapons, antiques and other royal heirlooms, plus the mother of all horse carriage collections. Labelling is poor or nonexistent.

A carved doorway leads to an inner courtyard , but most of the *kraton* is off-limits and it's still the residence of the *susuhunan*.

One edifice that has survived is the distinctive tower known as **Panggung Songgo Buwono**, built in 1782 and looks like a cross between a Dutch clocktower and a lighthouse. Its upper storey is a meditation sanctum where the *susuhunan* is said to commune with Nyai Loro Kidul.

If you hire a guide (20,000Rp), don't expect a particularly illuminating tour. Children's dance practice is on Sunday from 10am to noon, while adult practice is from 1pm to 3pm.

### ISTANA MANGKUNEGARAN

Dating back to 1757, the **Istana Mangkunegaran** ( ☎ 644 946; admission 10,000Rp; 🕑 8.30am-4pm Mon-Sat, to 1pm Sun) is in better condition and is more rewarding to visit. Technically a *puri* (palace) rather than a *kraton* (a *kraton* is occupied by the first ruling house), this is the home of the second house of Solo. It was founded after a bitter struggle against Pakubuwono II launched by his nephew Raden Mas Said (an ancestor of Madam Tien Suharto, the late wife of the former president). Also offers decent guided tours (in English). Members of the aristocratic family still live at the back of the palace.

The centre of the palace compound is the *pendopo*, a pavilion built in a mix of Javanese and European architectural styles, and one of the largest in the country. Its high, rounded ceiling was painted in 1937 and is intricately decorated with a central flame surrounded by figures of the Javanese zodiac, each painted in its own mystical colour. In Javanese philosophy yellow guards against sleepiness, blue against disease, black against hunger, green against desire, white against lust, rose against fear, red against evil and purple against wicked thoughts.

Behind here is the *dalem* (residence), which forms the **palace museum**. The museum is a delight but can only be visited on a guided tour (around 20,000Rp). Most exhibits are from the personal collection of Mangkunegara VII. On display are gold-plated dresses for royal dances, a superb mask collection, jewellery and a few oddities, including huge Buddhist rings and gold genital covers – one for a queen, and a (diminutive) penis cover for a king.

At the pavilion, you can see music, singing and dance-practice sessions on Wednesday and Saturday from 10am until noon.

### RADYA PUSTAKA MUSEUM

This small **museum** (Jl Slamet Riyadi; admission 1000Rp; 🕑 9am-1pm Tue-Sun) has good displays of gamelan instruments, jewelled kris, puppets, a small collection of *wayang beber* (scrolls that depict *wayang* stories) and Raja Mala, a hairy puppet figurehead from a royal barge.

### MARKETS

**Pasar Klewer** (Jl Secoyudan; 🕑 8am-6pm), the three-storey market near Kraton Surakarta, is supposedly the largest batik and textile market in Indonesia. This is the place to buy batik.

**Pasar Triwindu** (Jl Diponegoro; 9am-4pm or 5pm Mon-Sat), Solo's flea market, was closed for renovation at the time of research but should reopen in 2010. Expect antiques and bric-a-brac galore.

**Pasar Gede** (Jl Urip Sumoharjo; 8am-6pm) is the city's largest general market, selling all manner of produce, particularly fruit and vegetables.

At the northwestern end of Jl Raden Mas Said, **Pasar Depok** ( 8am-5pm Mon-Sat) is Solo's squawking bird market.

### OTHER SIGHTS

**Danar Hadi** ( 722 042; www.houseofdanarhadi.com; Jl Slamet Riyadi 261; admission 15,000Rp; 9.30am-4pm) is a small museum big on batik, with a terrific collection of antique and royal textiles from Java, China and beyond. It occupies a stunning whitewashed colonial building. Entry includes a guided tour in English, which explains the history of the many pieces (10,000 in the collection), though no photos are allowed. There's a workshop where you can watch craftswomen at work creating new masterpieces. There's an upmarket storeroom and souvenir shop too.

On the western side of the *alun-alun*, **Mesjid Agung**, featuring classical Javanese architecture, is the largest and most sacred mosque in Solo.

Solo's **Sriwedari Amusement Park** (admission 3000Rp; 5-10pm Mon-Fri, 5-11pm Sat, 9am-10pm Sat) has fair rides and sideshow stalls. Nightly *wayang orang* performances (and other cultural shows) are held here.

### Courses

There's little demand these days, but contact the tourist office (p199) for a list of places offering batik courses. Warung Baru (p202) has batik courses for 85,000Rp, including T-shirt.

### Tours

Guesthouses and travel agents including **Miki Tours** ( 653 278; Jl Yos Sudarso 17) run tours to Candi Sukuh, Gunung Merapi and Gunung Lawu. Prices depend on numbers, but a day trip for two people with a car and guide starts at around 500,000Rp.

Bicycle tours (from 75,000Rp) to sites around the city are popular in Solo, taking in gamelan and batik-making, *arak* and rice-cracker processing. **Westerners** ( 633 106; Kemlayan Kidul 11) and Miki Tours offer such trips.

If you want to set up your own tour to places around Solo, see Getting Around, p204.

### Festivals & Events

These are two of the best of the many local festivals:

**Kirab Pusaka** (Heirloom Procession) Held on the first day of the Javanese month of Suro (between March and May) since 1633, these colourful processions start at Istana Mangkunegaran in the early evening and continue late into the night.

**Sekaten** Marks the birth of the Prophet Muhammed and is held in the Islamic month of Maurud (from May to July). Comprises two ceremonies with a week in between. Culminates with a fair erected in the *alun-alun* and the sharing out of a rice mountain.

### Sleeping
#### BUDGET

Solo has some good budget hotels. Almost all offer travel information, tours, bus bookings, bicycles for rent, breakfast, and free tea/coffee.

**Pondok Dagdan** ( 669 324; Jl Carangan Baluarti 42; r without mandi 35,000Rp) In the shadow of Kraton Surakarta, Dagdan has simple rooms around a leafy courtyard, and a welcoming owner. Is popular with students and English teachers.

**Mama Homestay** ( 652 248; Kauman Gang III; s/d incl breakfast 40,000/55,000Rp) If you're looking for a welcoming homestay and don't mind very basic digs, Mama's is worth considering. The three rooms here all have shared cold-water *mandi*.

**Paradiso Guest House** ( 652 960; Kemlayan Kidul 1; r with/without mandi from 55,000/40,000Rp) 'Paradise' may be pushing it a bit, but this is still a fine place to stay as you'll be lodging in a historic white residence of real character with ornate lighting and mirrors.

**Cakra Homestay** ( 634 743; Jl Cakra II 15; r with/without mandi 75,000/65,000Rp, with air-con 100,000Rp; ) An excellent choice for those interested in Javanese culture, which staff are keen to promote, and it also has a nice pool at the rear of the charming, traditional house. Cakra loses marks on the rooms, which are plain but functional. There's often a gamelan performance in the evening.

**Hotel Bintang** ( 648 737; Jl Ir Sutami 104; r from 99,000Rp; ) The location, 2km northeast of the centre, is a bit inconvenient, but the modern rooms here are in good condition, many with hot-water bathrooms, and there's a cafe.

#### MIDRANGE

Many of the hotels in this bracket are strung along or just off Jl Slamet Riyadi west of the city centre.

**Hotel Dana** (☎ 711 976; www.hoteldanasolo.com; Jl Slamet Riyadi 286; r/ste incl breakfast from 245,000/495,000Rp; ❄ ) In the heart of town, this once-grand colonial place still has some fine features, but most of the comfortable rooms are to the rear in motel-style blocks. There's a good garden cafe.

**De Solo** (☎ 714 887; de_solo@yahoo.co.id; Jl Dr Sutomo 8; r/ste incl breakfast from 300,000/750,000Rp; ❄ ) Solo's first boutique hotel has class and style, and makes a restful place to stay. Smallish 'semi-Zen' rooms lack real wow factor but are uncluttered and modern. Staff are very accommodating here and there's an attractive little garden cafe.

**our pick Roemahkoe** (☎ 714 024; www.roemah koe.info; Jl Dr Rajiman 501; r/ste incl breakfast from 430,000/490,000Rp; ❄ ☎ ) For a truly memorable place to stay, this incredibly classy art deco landmark won't disappoint. Roemahkoe has been sensitively renovated, and boasts a wood-panelled lobby with stained-glass windows. The 13 commodious rooms are very competitively priced and juxtapose modern facilities with period features superbly. Corridors and walls are positively dripping in (very) fine art and photographs, and the restaurant is wonderful. However, staff do not speak much English.

**Sahid Kusuma Raya Hotel** (☎ 646 356; haku suma@indo.net.id; Jl Sugiyopranoto 20; r from 480,000Rp; ❄ ▯ ☎ ▣ ) This hotel is centred on an elegant colonial structure, with modern buildings set around it. The pool is huge and staff are hospitable, though the restaurant is overpriced.

**Novotel Solo** (☎ 724 555; reservation@novotelsolo .com; Jl Slamet Riyadi 272; r from 523,000Rp; ❄ ▯ ☎ ▣ ) This luxury four-star hotel has a central location, well-trained staff and excellent facilities including a spa and fitness centre. Its bar is a popular late-night haunt. Nonsmoking.

**TOP END**

Solo isn't loaded with truly top-end hotels.

**Lor'in** (☎ 724 500; www.lor-in.com; Jl Adisucipto 47; r US$70-110, ste from US$200; ❄ ▯ ☎ ▣ ) This huge resort's trump card is its absolutely stunning tropical garden, complete with towering palms, dramatic statues and a vast pool. Rooms are comfortable and spacious and the gym is excellent. Special offers sometimes cut standard room prices as low as US$55. It's 5km northwest of the centre. Nonsmoking.

## Eating & Drinking

Solo has a superb street-food tradition and a great new traffic-free area called **Galabo** (Jl Slamet Riyadi; ☽ 5-11pm) where you can sample it. Galabo is a kind of open-air food court with around 90 stalls – tuck into local specialties like *nasi gudeg* (unripe jackfruit served with rice, chicken and spices), *nasi liwet* (rice cooked in coconut milk and eaten with a host of side dishes) or the beef noodle soup *timlo solo* here. It's very sociable, though you'll have to bring your own Bintang.

In daylight hours, or if it's raining, try the more conventional food court in the Solo Grand Mall on Jl Slamet Riyadi, which has Indo-Japanese food, steamboats and a juice bar.

**Warung Baru** (☎ 656 369; Jl Ahmad Dahlan 23; mains from 8500Rp) A long-time travellers' hang-out, the Baru bakes great bread, but the rest of the enormous menu can be pretty mediocre. Still, the friendly owners arrange tours and batik classes.

**Kusuma Sari** (☎ 656 406; Jl Yos Sudarso 81; mains around 8000Rp) Very inexpensive, no-frills place serving steaks, chicken dishes and ice cream.

**Adem Ayem** (☎ 716 992; Jl Slamet Riyadi 342; meals around 15,000Rp) An ever-popular *rumah makan* (eating house), this place has a large dining room with swirling fans and photos of ye olde Surakarta. Everyone is here for the chicken – either fried, or served up *gudeg*-style.

**Mas Mul** (Jl Veteran; meals around 60,000Rp; ☽ 3-11pm) A snake restaurant where you can select a live victim for sataying or frying, wash it down with serpent blood, and then take the skin home as a gruesome souvenir. If you're so inclined, of course.

**O Solo Mio** (☎ 727 264; Jl Slamet Riyadi 253; pizzas around 40,000Rp; ☽ 11.30am-10.30pm) Authentic Italian that's as close as you'll get to a taste of the homeland in Central Java; it has a wood-fired pizza oven and delicious pasta.

**Bizztro Saraswati** (☎ 717 100; Jl Yosodipuro 122; meals from 25,000Rp; ☽ 3pm-midnight; ☎ ) A stylish, up-market new European-owned place with an open-air lounge area, dining rooms and elegant furnishings. Serves good snacks, meals (try the NZ beef ribs), cold beer and superb coffee.

There are very few bars in Solo. The only place in the centre that might be worth a look is the flash **Intro** (☎ 742 669; Solo Grand Mall, Jl Slamet Riyadi), which has live music on weekends but is pretty dead during the week.

## Entertainment

### CULTURAL PERFORMANCES

Solo is an excellent place to see traditional Javanese performing arts; contact the tourist office for the latest schedules. Istana Mangkunegaran (p200) and Kraton Surakarta (p199) both have traditional Javanese dance practice.

At the back of Sriwedari Amusement Park, **Sriwedari Theatre** (admission 3000Rp; �) performances 8-10pm) has a long-running *wayang orang* troupe – it's well worth dropping by to experience this masked dance-drama; you can come and go as you please.

**RRI auditorium** ( ☎ 641 178; Jl Abdul Rahman Saleh 51) RRI holds an eclectic program of cultural performances, including *wayang orang* and *ketoprak*.

**SMKI** ( ☎ 632 225; Jl Kepatihan Wetan) The high school for the performing arts has dance practice from around 8am to noon Monday to Thursday and Saturday, and 8am to 11am Friday.

**Taman Budaya Surakarta** (TBS; ☎ 635 414; Jl Ir Sutami 57) This cultural centre hosts all-night *wayang kulit* performances; private dance lessons are also available.

### NIGHTCLUBS

This is not a big party town, but Solo has a few clubs. All alternate cheesy bands with DJs playing pounding dance music.

**New Legenda** (Jl Suryo Pranoto) Popular city-centre club playing *dangdut* (popular Indonesian music characterised by wailing vocals and a strong beat), techno and Indo chart hits.

## Shopping

Solo is one of Indonesia's main textile centres, producing not only its own unique, traditional batik but every kind of fabric for domestic use and export.

For everyday shopping, check out the markets (p200) or the **Solo Grand Mall** (Jl Slamet Riyadi).

### BATIK

The following are all large, well-established manufacturers with showrooms for their range of sophisticated work.

**Batik Keris factory** ( ☎ 714 400; ☉ 8am-5pm Mon-Sat) In Lawiyan, west of the city, this is one place to see the batik process up close. Its shop (Jl Yos Sudarso 62) has icy air-con, a cafe and two full floors of fixed-price batik bags, skirts and shirts.

**Batik Danar Hadi** (Jl Slamet Riyadi 261) Danar Hadi is an important Solonese manufacturer and has a good store at its museum-cum-showroom (p201).

**Pasar Klewer** (Jl Secoyudan) Has hundreds of stalls selling fabrics.

### CURIOS

Kris and other souvenirs can be purchased from street vendors found at the eastern side of the *alun-alun* near Kraton Surakarta. The gem sellers have a mind-boggling array of semi-precious stones. Jl Dr Rajiman (Secoyudan), which runs along the southern edge of the *alun-alun*, is the goldsmiths street.

**Balai Agung** (Jl Kyai Gede Sala) On the north side of the *alun-alun* you can see high-quality *wayang kulit* puppets being made (and put through their paces). Gamelan sets are also on sale too.

For information about Solo's flea market, **Pasar Triwindu** (Jl Diponegoro), see p200.

## Getting There & Away

### AIR

A new terminal is scheduled to open at Solo's Adi Sumarmo airport in late 2009, and should result in more frequent flight connections. Currently there are just two international flights.

**AirAsia** ( ☎ 5050 5088; www.airasia.com) connects Solo to Kuala Lumpur daily. On Tuesday, Thursday and Saturday, **Silk Air** ( ☎ 724 604/5; www.silkair.com; Novotel Hotel, Jl Slamet Riyadi 272) flies to/from Singapore.

Domestic services include very regular flights to Jakarta with **Garuda** ( ☎ 630 082; Hotel Cakra, Jl Slamet Riyadi 201) and **Sriwijaya Airlines** ( ☎ 723 777; www.sriwijayaair-online.com; airport).

### BUS

The Tirtonadi bus terminal is 3km from the centre of the city. Only economy buses leave from here to destinations such as Prambanan (13,000Rp, 1½ hours), Yogyakarta (from 13,000Rp, two hours) and Semarang (26,000Rp, 3¼ hours). Buses also travel to a number of destinations in East Java including Surabaya (52,000Rp, seven hours) and Malang (60,000Rp, eight hours).

Near the bus terminal, the Gilingan minibus terminal has express air-con minibuses to almost as many destinations as the larger buses.

*Travel* minibuses go to Yogyakarta (25,000Rp), Semarang (45,000Rp), Surabaya and Malang (80,000Rp) and Jakarta (170,000Rp). **Citra** ( ☎ 713 684), based at Gilingan, runs *travel* minibuses to most main cities; call for a pick-up. Homestays, cafes and travel agents also sell these tickets.

### TRAIN

Solo is located on the main Jakarta–Yogyakarta–Surabaya train line and most trains stop at **Balapan** ( ☎ 714 039), the main train station.

Seventeen daily trains connect Solo with Yogyakarta, so you won't have to wait long. The *Pramek* (business class 7000Rp, one hour) trains are reasonably comfortable but not air-conditioned.

Express trains to Jakarta include the 8am *Argo Lawu* (executive class 220,000Rp, eight hours), which is the most luxurious day train, and the *Senja Utama* (business class from 100,000Rp, 10½ hours), which leaves at 6pm.

The *Lodaya* (business/executive class 100,000/165,000Rp, nine hours) departs for Bandung at 8am and 8.30pm daily, while the *Sancaka* (business/executive class 55,000/80,000Rp, five hours) heads for Surabaya twice daily.

Jebres train station in the northeast of Solo has a few very slow economy-class services to Surabaya and Jakarta.

### Getting Around

A taxi to/from Adi Sumarmo airport, 10km northwest of the city centre, costs around 55,000Rp, or you can take a bus to Kartosuro and then another to the airport. For a taxi, metered **Kosti Solo taxis** ( ☎ 856 300) are reliable. Becak cost about 7000Rp from the train station or bus terminal into the centre. Public buses run up and down Riyadi and cost 2000Rp.

Many homestays and travellers' cafes can arrange bike hire for around 15,000Rp or a motorcycle for about 60,000Rp a day.

Solo can be an extremely inexpensive place to set up car hire. Avoid homestays and hotels and book direct with **AA Trans** ( ☎ 632 8121; Hotel Keprabon, Jl Ahmad Dahlan 8), and you'll pay 275,000Rp for a 12-hour hire period in a modern air-con car, with driver, excluding

petrol. Due to complicated Javanese business protocol this company is reluctant to offer pick-ups from your hotel (many of whom have their own car-hire deals); in that case, arrange to meet your driver at their office instead.

## AROUND SOLO
### Sangiran

Sangiran is a very important archaeological excavation site (so important it gained World Heritage status in 1996), where some of the best examples of fossilised skulls of prehistoric 'Java Man' *(Pithecanthropus erectus)* were unearthed by a Dutch professor in 1936 (see the boxed text, p89).

The town's main (if not only) attraction is its small **museum** (admission 10,000Rp; ⊙ 9am-4pm Tue-Sun), with a few skulls (one of *Homo erectus*), various pig and hippopotamus teeth, and fossil exhibits, including huge mammoth bones and tusks. Souvenir stalls outside sell bones, 'mammoth tusks' carved from stone and other dubious fossil junk. Guides will also offer to take you to the area where shells and other fossils have been found in the crumbling slopes of the hill.

Take a Purwodadi bus from Solo's main bus terminal to Kalijambe (3000Rp). Ask for Sangiran and you will be dropped at the turn-off, 15km from Solo. It is then 4km to the museum (around 10,000Rp by *ojek*).

### Gunung Lawu

Towering Gunung Lawu (3265m), lying on the border of Central and East Java, is one of the holiest mountains in Java. Mysterious Hindu temples dot its slopes and each year thousands of pilgrims seeking spiritual enlightenment climb its peak.

Although popular history has it that when Majapahit fell to Islam, the Hindu elite all fled east to Bali, Javanese lore relates that Brawijaya V, the last king of Majapahit, went west. Brawijaya's son, Raden Patah, was the leader of Demak and led the conquering forces of Islam against Majapahit, but rather than fight his own son, Brawijaya retreated to Gunung Lawu to seek spiritual enlightenment. There he achieved nirvana as Sunan Lawu, and today pilgrims come to the mountain to seek his spiritual guidance or to achieve magic powers.

The unique temples on the mountain – some of the last Hindu temples built in Java before

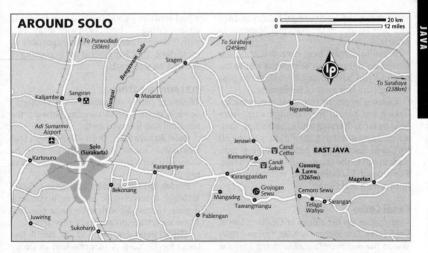

**AROUND SOLO**

the region converted to Islam – show the influence of the later *wayang* style of East Java, though they incorporate elements of fertility worship. The most famous temple is Candi Sukuh; Candi Cetho is another large complex that still attracts Hindu worshippers.

### CLIMBING GUNUNG LAWU

*Angkot* between Tawangmangu and Sarangan pass Cemoro Sewu (5000Rp), 5km from Sarangan on the East and Central Java border. This small village is the starting point for the 6.7km hike to the summit of Gunung Lawu. Thousands of pilgrims flock to the summit on 1 Suro, the start of the Javanese new year, but pilgrims and holidaying students make the night climb throughout the year, especially on Saturday night. Most start around 8pm, reaching the peak at around 2am for meditation.

For the best chance of witnessing a clear sunrise, start by midnight at the latest. It is a long, steady hike, but one of the easiest mountains in Java to tackle. The stone path is easy to follow – bring a torch (flashlight). Alternatively, guides can make a night climb easier and can lead you to the various pilgrimage sites along the way. Guides in Cemoro Sewu cost around 100,000Rp. Sign in at the PHKA post before starting the climb (admission to walk 2000Rp).

## Candi Sukuh

In a magnificent position on the slopes of Gunung Lawu, 900m above the Solo plain,

**Candi Sukuh** (admission 10,000Rp; ☉ 7am-4.30pm) is one of Java's most enigmatic and striking temples. It's not a large site, but it has a large, truncated pyramid of rough-hewn stone, and there are some fascinating reliefs and statues. It's clear that a fertility cult was practised here: several sniggeringly explicit carvings have led it to be dubbed the 'erotic' temple. It's a quiet, isolated place with a strange, potent atmosphere.

Built in the 15th century during the declining years of the Majapahit kingdom, Candi Sukuh seems to have nothing whatsoever to do with other Javanese Hindu and Buddhist temples. The origins of its builders and strange sculptural style (with crude, squat and distorted figures carved in the *wayang* style found in East Java) remain a mystery and it seems to mark a reappearance of the pre-Hindu animism that existed 1500 years before.

At the gateway before the temple are a large stone lingam and yoni. Flowers are still often scattered here, and locals believe these symbols were used to determine whether a wife had been faithful, or a wife-to-be was still a virgin. The woman had to wear a sarong and jump across the lingam – if the sarong fell off, her infidelity was proven. Other interesting cult objects include a monument depicting Bima, the Mahabharata warrior hero, with Narada, the messenger of the gods, both in a stylised womb. Another monument depicts Bima passing through the womb at his birth. In the top courtyard three enormous flat-backed turtles stand like sacrificial altars. A 2m lingam once topped the pyramid, but it was removed by Sir Stamford Raffles in 1815 and now resides in the National Museum in Jakarta.

If you're driving here note that there are almost no signposts to help direct you to the site and you have to pay a small fee to pass through the *kampung* of Kemuning.

Coming by public transport is very tricky. Take a bus bound for Tawangmangu from Solo as far as Karangpandan (6000Rp), then a Kemuning minibus (3000Rp) to the turn-off to Candi Sukuh; from here it's a steep 2km walk uphill to the site or a 10,000Rp *ojek* ride. For around 35,000Rp, *ojeks* will take you to both Sukuh and Cetho.

## Candi Cetho

Even higher up the slopes of Gunung Lawu, **Candi Cetho** (Ceto; admission 10,000Rp; ⏰ 7am-4.30pm) sits on the southern face of Gunung Lawu at around 1400m. Thought to date from around 1350, this *candi* closely resembles a Balinese temple in appearance, though it combines elements of Shivaism and fertility worship. It's a larger temple than Sukuh and is spread over terraces rising up the misty hillside. There's little carving here, but the stonework is well constructed and close-fitting. The entrance is marked by temple guardians and you'll find a striking platform with a turtle head and a large lingam on the upper terrace. Balinese Hindus visit Candi Cetho to make offerings on auspicious days.

Because of the effort required to reach Cetho, few visitors make it here – which is one of its attractions. The temple is 9km by road past the Sukuh turn-off. See above for transport details.

## Tawangmangu
☎ 0271

Tawangmangu, a large hill resort on the western side of Gunung Lawu, is a popular weekend retreat for Solonese. It's a pleasant enough, if sprawling, place to escape the city heat and do a hike or two in the hills.

### SIGHTS & ACTIVITIES

About 2km from town, **Grojogan Sewu** (admission 3500Rp; ⏰ 6am-6pm), a 100m-high waterfall, is a favourite playground for monkeys. It's reached by a long flight of steps down a hillside, but you probably won't want to have a dip in the very chilly and dirty swimming pool. From the bottom of the waterfall

a trail leads to a good track to Candi Sukuh, an interesting 2½-hour, 6km walk away. This path is steep in parts but is also negotiable by motorbike. *Ojek* hang out at the beginning of the trail on weekends.

### SLEEPING & EATING

There are plenty of losmen on Jl Grojogan Sewu, a quieter street running between the waterfall and Jl Raya Lawu.

**Hotel Wahayu Sari** ( ☎ 697 470; Jl Grojogan Sewu 6; r 80,000Rp) One of the best options near the waterfall, with simple but acceptably clean rooms.

**Pondok Sari** ( ☎ 697 088; Jl Utara Taman; r 120,000-180,000Rp) A motel-style place with spacious if plain rooms, all with little front porches. There's a restaurant and kids' play area.

**ourpick Hotel Bintang** ( ☎ 696 269; Jl Raya Lawu; r from 150,000Rp) A surprise find in sleepy Tawangmangu, this outstanding new modern hotel has three floors of sleek, contemporary rooms, all with card-entry door, dark wood furniture, LCD TV and stylish lighting. Expect the opening tariffs quoted here to rise as the hotel becomes established. There's a mini-mart, and a cafe is planned.

**ourpick Warung Grio** ( ☎ 700 7413; set meals 45,000Rp) For a really memorable, rural setting for a meal, this riverside warung, part of an outdoor activity centre, can't be beat. Absolutely delicious traditional Javanese dishes are cooked on log fires and you eat under wooden shelters overlooking a fast-flowing stream. The freshly cooked food takes time to prepare, so expect to wait a while. It's 2km west of Tawangmangu, on the road back to Solo.

For cheaper eats, the road near the waterfall is inundated with warungs.

### GETTING THERE & AWAY

Buses travel to Solo (12,000Rp) and less-frequent *angkot* go to Sarangan (7000Rp). Minibuses (2000Rp) loop through town from the bus terminal up the main road, across to the waterfall and back.

## Sarangan
☎ 0351

Just over the provincial border in East Java, 13km from Tawangmangu, Sarangan is a weekend resort set around the banks of a small lake. The journey here is beautiful, ascending steeply through the thick forest that clings to the shoulder of Gunung Lawu volcano before plunging down to the lakeshore.

Sarangan is crowded at weekends, when speedboats zip and pedalos potter around the lake, but very quiet at other times. At 1287m, the climate is fresh and it makes a good base for tackling Lawu.

Speedboats cost 40,000Rp per person for a quick whiz around the lake; pedalos are 30,000Rp per hour.

### SLEEPING
Prices rise on weekends.

**Hotel Merah** ( ☎ 888 182; Jl Raya Telaga; r 125,000-600,000Rp) Painted (appropriately) bright red, the Merah has rooms and apartments that lack character, but many do have direct lake vistas. The restaurant is ideal for a meal with a view.

**Villa Joglo** ( ☎ 888 509; Jl Raya Telaga; r/ste from 150,000/300,000Rp) This friendly place on the main drag to the lakeshore has rooms and apartment-style accommodation, some with two and three bedrooms. All are in tip-top condition. The owners are friendly but speak no English.

**Nirwana** ( ☎ 888 498; Jl Raya Telaga; ste 200,000-450,000Rp) New four-storey place with smart, bright and airy suites that all have a living area, a modern hot-water bathroom and from one to five bedrooms.

There are several places on the lakeshore, including **Nusa Indah** ( ☎ 888 333; meals from 12,000Rp), which also sells cold Bintang.

*Angkot* make the run to Tawangmangu (9000Rp), passing Cemoro Sewu for the climb to Gunung Lawu, but they only leave when full.

## Mangadeg

Near Karangpandan, a road branches south from the main Solo–Tawangmangu road about 5km to Mangadeg, the burial hill of Solo's royal Mangkunegoro family. Make a small donation and visit the graves or simply take in the superb views.

Just 500m away in the same sacred hills, the lavish **Astana Giribangun** is the Suharto family burial place, where the former president and military dictator was buried in 2008, alongside the grave of his wife. Tens of thousands lined the route of his funeral cortege from Solo airport to Astana Giribangun, and thousands more visit this traditional Javanese *pendopo*-style burial monument to pay their respects every year.

Just past Mangadeg is **Pablengan**, the former bathing pools of the Mangkunegoro, which has dilapidated, ancient pavilions fed by seven types of spring water.

## NORTH COAST
Central Java's north coast features little on the itineraries of most travellers, but this steamy strip of land is not without its charm.

For starters, the towns dotting the north coast are steeped in history. For many centuries the coast was the centre for trade with merchants from Arabia, India and China, who brought with them not only goods but also ideas and cultures. In the 15th and 16th centuries the area was a springboard for Islam into Java, and the tombs of the country's great saints all lie between Semarang and Surabaya (with the exception of Sunan Gunungjati in Cirebon).

The north coast's rich craft traditions are also impressive. Pekalongan is celebrated for its batik, while Jepara is a major centre for wooden furniture. If the sweet smell of *kretek* (clove cigarettes) is to your liking, then a trip to Kudus, the birthplace of the *kretek*, may appeal.

Central Java's capital, Semarang, is located here, and while it won't hold your interest for too long, it is a gateway to the splendid (and often forgotten) Karimunjawa Islands and the peaceful mountains between it and Yogyakarta.

## PEKALONGAN
☎ 0285 / pop 260,000
On the north coast between Semarang and Cirebon, Pekalongan (its name is said to be derived from the Chinese *a-pek-along-an*, meaning 'a place for catching fish') is known as Kota Batik (Batik City), and its batiks are some of the most sought after in Indonesia. It is less formal, more colourful and more innovative in design than the traditional styles of Yogyakarta and Solo.

Pekalongan is a steamy city that sees few tourists, but it does have a neglected, old-fashioned atmosphere and an ethnically diverse population.

### Information
**BII bank** (Jl Diponegoro 4)
**Main post office** (Kantor Pos dan Giro) Opposite the Balai Kota on the *alun-alun*.
**Telkom office** (Jl Merak 2) Next door to the main post office. International telephone calls can be made here.

plantation's organic tea and coffee in the historic Club House. Losari is located near Grabag, some 12km southwest of Ambarawa. From Ambarawa, it's best to take a taxi (40,000Rp) to the resort; note that 21% tax must be added to room rates.

Ambarawa can be reached by public bus from Semarang (7000Rp, one hour) and Yogyakarta (31,000Rp, three hours) via Magelang.

## BANDUNGAN
☎ 0298

Bandungan is a pleasant hill resort at 980m, but the main attraction is the nearby Gedung Songo temples. It's a good base for exploring the temples and train museum at Ambarawa, and for escaping the heat of the north coast. There are several hotels here, as it's something of a weekend resort for folk from Semarang.

In town, **Hotel Parahita** ( ☎ 711 017; r 60,000Rp), just down the back road to Semarang from the market, has basic rooms and a friendly owner who speaks no English.

**Hotel Rawa Pening Eltricia** ( ☎ 711 445; r from 140,000Rp, cottages from 250,000Rp; ☎ ) has great views from its hilltop perch and a terraced garden. Rooms are in good shape, and it has a lovely old colonial-style restaurant and a tennis court.

Buses make the run directly from Semarang to Bandungan (10,000Rp). If you are coming from the south, get off at Ambarawa and take an *angkot* to Bandungan (2000Rp).

## GEDUNG SONGO TEMPLES
These nine (Gedung Songo means 'nine buildings' in Javanese) small **Hindu temples** (admission 5000Rp; ☉ 7am-5pm) are scattered along the tops of the foothills around Gunung Ungaran. The temples are not huge, but the setting is magnificent. The 1000m perch gives one of the most spectacular views in Java – south across shimmering Danau Rawa Pening to Gunung Merbabu and, behind it, smouldering Gunung Merapi; and west to Gunung Sumbing and Gunung Sundoro.

Built in the 8th century AD and devoted to Shiva and Vishnu, five of the temples are in good condition after major restoration in the 1980s; however, most of the carvings were lost. A hill path goes past three temple groupings – the temples at the third grouping are the most impressive. Halfway up, the trail leads down to a ravine and hot sulphur

springs, and then up again to the final temple and its expansive views. The 3km loop can be walked in an hour, but allow longer to savour the atmosphere. Horses can also be hired.

Arrive early in the morning for the best views. A couple of small hotels with rooms for around 40,000Rp are just outside the gate. Camping inside the temple complex is also possible, for a small fee.

The temples are about 6km from Bandungan. Take a Sumawono bus (2000Rp) 3km to the turn-off to the temples. Buses also run from Semarang and Ambarawa (4000Rp). The final 3km uphill to Gedung Songo (3000Rp) can be tackled either by foot or *ojek* (10,000Rp).

## DEMAK
Demak was the springboard from which Islam made its leap into Java. As the capital of the island's first Islamic state, it was from here that the Hindu Majapahit kingdom was conquered and much of Java's interior was converted.

The town's economic heyday has now passed and even the sea has retreated several kilometres, leaving this former port landlocked. But the role this small town, 25km east of Semarang, once played has not been forgotten, and Demak's **Mesjid Agung** remains one of the archipelago's foremost Muslim pilgrimage sites.

Constructed in 1466, this is Java's oldest mosque. Legend tells how it was built from wood by the *wali songo* in a single night. Four main pillars in the central hall were originally made by four of the Muslim saints, and one pillar, erected by Sunan Kalijaga, is said to be made from scraps of timber magically fused together.

The history of the mosque is outlined in the small **museum** (admission by donation; ☉ 8am-5pm) to the side. Some of the original woodwork, including magnificent carved doors, is on display.

The tombs of Demak's rulers are next to the mosque; the tomb of Raden Trenggono (leader of Demak's greatest military campaigns), however, attracts the most pilgrims. During Grebeg Besar, when various heirlooms are ritually cleansed, thousands of pilgrims visit Demak (the date is different each year; check with Semarang's Central Java Tourist Office – see p209).

The mosque is on the main road in the centre of town, beside the *alun-alun*, and through-buses from either Semarang or Kudus (6000Rp) can drop you right outside.

## KUDUS

☎ 0291 / pop 90,000

Kudus takes its name from the Arabic word *al-Quds* – the Arabic name for Jerusalem. Founded by the Muslim saint Sunan Kudus, it's an important pilgrimage site. Like much of Java, Kudus retains links with its Hindu past and the slaughter of cows is still forbidden here.

The town itself is quite industrial today and holds little charm unless you're a hardened *kretek* smoker. This is where the first clove cigarettes were produced, and today Kudus is still a stronghold of *kretek* production.

### Information

The **BII bank** (Jl Dr Lukmonohadi) has an ATM, and there are several more inside the Taman Bojana food complex (p216). You'll find the **tourist office** ( ☎ 435 958; Komplek Kriday Wisata; 7am-2pm Mon-Thu, to 11am Fri, to 12.30pm Sat) in the

east of town (look out for the concrete animals). Though it doesn't have much information it can direct you to local home industries, including woodcarving workshops.

### Sights
#### OLD TOWN

West of the river, **Kauman**, the oldest part of town, has narrow streets and the feel of a *kasbah* in the Middle East, with traders selling religious souvenirs, dates, prayer beads and caps.

Here you'll find the **Mesjid Al-Manar** (also known as Al-Aqsa); constructed in 1549 by Sunan Kudus, it's famous for its red-brick *menara* (minaret). This minaret may have originally been the watchtower of the Hindu temple the mosque is said to be built on. Its curiously squat form and flared sides certainly have more in common with Balinese than with Islamic architecture; climb to its upper balcony to see a huge *bedug* (drum) that's still used to summon the faithful to prayer.

From the courtyards behind the mosque, a palm-lined path leads to the imposing **Tomb of Sunan Kudus**, shrouded with a curtain of lace. The narrow doorway, draped with heavy gold-embroidered curtains, leads through to an inner chamber and the grave. During Buka Luwur, held once a year on 10 Muharram of the Islamic calendar, the curtains around the tomb are changed and thousands of pilgrims flock to Kudus for the ceremony.

#### KRETEK

Kudus is a massive centre of *kretek* production – there are said to be 25 factories in the town. Djarum, which started in 1951, is the main employer and third-biggest *kretek* manufacturer in Indonesia. Tours of its modern **factory** ( ☎ 431 901; www.djarum.com; Jl A Yani 28) leave at 9am Monday to Friday and are free of charge. It's incredible to see the women rollers at work, a blur of hand and eye coordination. **Sukun**, outside the town, still produces *rokok klobot*, the original *kretek* rolled in corn leaves.

The **Kretek Museum** (donations accepted; Jl Museum Kretek Jati Kulon; 8am-2pm Sat-Thu) has exhibits of a number of interesting photographs and implements used in *kretek* production (almost all explanations are in Bahasa Indonesia). Next door, **Rumah Adat** is a traditional wooden Kudus house exhibiting the fabulous carving work the town is noted for.

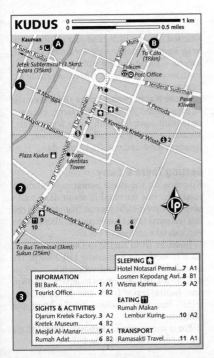

**KUDUS**

0 — 1 km
0 — 0.5 miles

| INFORMATION | |
|---|---|
| BII Bank | 1 A1 |
| Tourist Office | 2 B2 |

| SIGHTS & ACTIVITIES | |
|---|---|
| Djarum Kretek Factory | 3 A2 |
| Kretek Museum | 4 B2 |
| Mesjid Al-Manar | 5 A1 |
| Rumah Adat | 6 B2 |

| SLEEPING | |
|---|---|
| Hotel Notasari Permai | 7 A1 |
| Losmen Kepodang Asri | 8 B1 |
| Wisma Karima | 9 A2 |

| EATING | |
|---|---|
| Rumah Makan | |
| Lembur Kuring | 10 A2 |

| TRANSPORT | |
|---|---|
| Ramasakti Travel | 11 A1 |

Map labels:
Kauman
Jl Sunan Kudus
Jl Sunan Muria
Jetek Subterminal (3.5km); Jepara (35km)
To Colo (18km)
Telkom
Post Office
Jl Mangga
Jl Jenderal Sudirman
Pasar Kliwon
Jl Pemuda
Jl Dr Ramelan
Jl A Yani
Jl Mayor H Basuno
Jl Komplek Kriday Wisata
Plaza Kudus
Tugu Identitas Tower
Jl Dr Lukmonohadi
Jl Agil Kusumadya
Jl Museum Kretek Jati Kulon
To Bus Terminal (3km); Sukun (25km)

**KRETEK CIGARETTES**

If Java has a smell, it is the sweet, spicy scent of the clove-flavoured *kretek*. The *kretek* has only been around since the early 20th century, but today the addiction is nationwide and accounts for 90% of the cigarette market, while sales of *rokok putih* (cigarettes without cloves) are languishing. So high is the consumption of cloves used in the *kretek* industry that Indonesia, traditionally a supplier of cloves in world markets, has become a substantial net importer from other world centres.

The invention of the *kretek* is attributed to a Kudus man, Nitisemito, who claimed the cigarettes relieved his asthma. He mixed tobacco with crushed cloves rolled in *rokok klobot* (corn leaves) – this was the prototype for his Bal Tiga brand, which he began selling in 1906.

Kudus became the centre for the *kretek* industry and at one stage the town had more than 200 factories, though today fewer than 50 cottage industries and a few large factories remain. Rationalisation in the industry has seen *kretek* production dominated by big producers, such as Sampoerna in Surabaya, Gudang Garam in Kediri, and Djarum in Kudus. Nitisemito became a victim of the industry he started and died bankrupt in 1953.

Although filtered *kretek* are produced by modern machinery – Djarum churns out up to 140 million a day – nonfiltered *kretek* are still rolled by hand on simple wooden rolling machines. The best rollers can turn out about 4000 cigarettes in a day.

As to the claim that *kretek* are good for smoker's cough, cloves are a natural anaesthetic and so do have a numbing effect on the throat. Any other claims to aiding health stop there – the tar and nicotine levels in the raw, slowly cured tobaccos are so high that some countries have banned or restricted their import.

Filtered *kretek* now dominate the market. There are now 'mild' versions on offer, but for the *kretek* purist, the conical, crackling, nonfiltered *kretek* has no substitute – Sampoerna's Dji Sam Soe ('234') brand is regarded as the Rolls Royce of *kretek*. To see Sampoerna rollers in action visit the factory in Surabaya (p222).

## Sleeping & Eating

Few people stay in Kudus, but there are some inexpensive options.

You have to try *soto kudus* (a rich chicken soup), which the town is famous for. It's usually served up bright yellow (from turmeric) with lots of garlic, and the chicken is sometimes shredded. *Jenang kudus* is a sweet that's made of glutinous rice, brown sugar and coconut.

The best place for inexpensive food and local specialties is Taman Bojana, a food-stall complex on the main roundabout in the centre of town.

**Wisma Karima** ( ☎ 431 712; Jl Museum Kretek Jati Kulon 3; r with/without mandi 60,000/40,000Rp, with air-con 100,000Rp; ✴ ) A popular budget hotel with well-presented rooms and welcoming owners, although it suffers from traffic noise.

**Losmen Kepodang Asri** ( ☎ 433 795; Jl Kepodang 17; r 60,000Rp) An alternative budget choice, this simple place has spartan, clean rooms and no frills.

**Hotel Notasari Permai** ( ☎ 437 245; Jl Kepodang 12; r 100,000Rp, r with air-con, TV & minibar from 175,000Rp; ✴ ⬛ ) This good hotel has a quiet location

situated down a little lane just off the main drag and has clean, well-scrubbed if plain rooms – those on the upper floor benefit from more natural light. There's a restaurant here too.

**Rumah Makan Lembur Kuring** (Jl Agil Kusumadya 35; mains 12,000-30,000Rp) At this large, pleasant restaurant complete with water features and statues you can tuck into tasty Sundanese and Javanese food under a shady pagoda.

## Getting There & Away

Kudus is on the main Semarang–Surabaya road. The bus terminal is about 4km south of town. City minibuses run from behind the bus terminal to the town centre (2000Rp), or you can take an *ojek* or *becak*.

Buses go from Kudus to Demak (4000Rp, 30 minutes) and Semarang (10,000Rp, 1½ hours), while brown-and-yellow minibuses go to Colo for 6000Rp. Buses to Jepara (7000Rp, one hour) leave from the Jetak subterminal, 4km west of town (2000Rp by purple minibus).

For *travel* minibuses **Ramasakti Travel** ( ☎ 432 153; Jl A Yani 110) is recommended.

## AROUND KUDUS

The small hill resort of **Colo**, 700m up the slopes of Gunung Muria, is 18km north of Kudus. Colo is famed for its **Tomb of Sunan Muria** (Raden Umar Said), one of the nine *wali songo* buried here in 1469. Built in the 19th century, the mosque surrounding the tomb is high on a ridge overlooking the plains to the south. Pilgrims pray at the tomb, and during Buka Luwur, held in Colo on 16 Muharram of the Islamic calendar, up to 10,000 pilgrims line the road to the top.

A waterfall, **Air Terjun Monthel**, is 1.5km away or about a half-hour stroll from the village.

Local artist Mustaqim paints and sculpts out of his **Taqim Arts Studio** in the village of Kajar, 1km from Colo. Visits can be arranged through the tourist office in Kudus (p215) .

## JEPARA

☎ **0291** / pop **51,000**

Famed as the best woodcarving centre in Java, Jepara's booming furniture business has brought it all the trappings of prosperity. It's also as sleepy as an afternoon becak driver and more affluent than many of Java's small towns, making it a tranquil spot to take a break from the road.

If you are just here for the furniture, then the road into town passes more woodcarving workshops than you can shake a table leg at.

### Information

The town's **tourist office** (☎ 591 493; www.gojepara .com; Jl AR Hakim 51; ☽ 8am-4pm Mon-Thu, 7-11am Fri) in the western part has very helpful staff, and runs a particularly informative website.

### Sights

The **Museum RA Kartini** (admission 2000Rp; ☽ 8am-2pm), on the north side of the *alun-alun*, is named after one of Indonesia's most celebrated women (see the boxed text, p218). One room is devoted to Kartini and contains portraits of her (and her family) plus memorabilia including letters. Other rooms contain assorted archaeological findings, including a yoni and lingga, and local art and artefacts, including some fine woodcarvings and ceramics. There's also the 16m skeleton of whale that was washed up in Karimunjawa.

It is sometimes possible to visit Kartini's old rooms – if you contact the tourist office

first – which are now local government offices on the eastern side of the *alun-alun*.

Heading north from the museum, cross the river and veer left up the hill to the old Dutch **Benteng VOC**. Over the last 50 years the fort's stonework has been pillaged, but the site has good views across town to the Java Sea. The cemetery nearby has some Dutch graves.

The most popular seaside recreation park and beach is **Pantai Kartini**, 3km west of town – locals often call it Pemandian. From there you can rent a boat (around 75,000Rp return) to nearby **Pulau Panjang**, which has excellent white-sand beaches. Café SA (below) offers fishing trips to the island as well.

### Sleeping

**Pondok Wisma Kota Baru** (☎ 593 356; Pantai Kartini; r with/without air-con 90,000/60,000Rp; ▨ ) A modest homestay within view of the ocean. The humble but well-swept rooms all have shared *mandi*.

**Hotel Elim** (☎ 591 406; Jl Dr Soetomo 13-15; r 65,000Rp, r with hot water, air-con & TV from 145,000Rp; ▨ ) This small hotel is ageing a tad, but it's still worth considering as the 22 rooms are in decent condition. Manager Thomas is helpful and can assist with transport, and there's a pleasant outdoor restaurant.

**Kalingga Star** (☎ 591 054; Jl Dr Soetomo 16; r with air-con 125,000Rp, ste from 195,000Rp; ▨ ) A large hotel with a range of tiled rooms in different price categories; most are spacious but a bit soulless. It's a couple of doors down from Hotel Elim and has a restaurant.

**Palm Beach Jepara** (☎ 594 446; www.palm beachjepara.com; Jl Tirta Samudra 191; cottages from 800,000Rp; ▨ ▨ ▨ ) This resort has very spacious cottages right on the beach, tastefully furnished and each with a living room and kitchenette. The pool area is fringed by palms and the restaurant serves good Indonesian and Western cuisine. Discounts are available in mid-week.

### Eating

**Pondok Rasa** (Jl Pahlawan 2; mains 8000-20,000Rp) Just across the river from the *alun-alun*, Rasa has a pleasant garden setting and tasty Indonesian food served *lesahan* style.

**Café SA** (☎ 081 7955 2266; Pantai Kartini; fish meals from 25,000Rp) For super-fresh crab, jumbo prawns and steamed or fried fish, SA is a good choice. It's right on the beach.

**Yam-Yam** (☎ 598 755; Jl Pantai Karang Kebagusan, km 5; meals from 40,000Rp) This seriously good, new,

**AN INDO ICON**

Raden Ajeng Kartini, a writer, feminist and progressive thinker, was born in 1879, the daughter of the *bupati* (regent) of Jepara. She grew up in the *bupati*'s residence, on the eastern side of the *alun-alun*, excelled at school and learnt to speak fluent Dutch by the age of 12. It was in this residence that Kartini spent her *pingit* ('confinement' in Javanese), when girls from 12 to 16 are kept in virtual imprisonment and forbidden to venture outside the family home. She later used her education to campaign for women's rights and against colonialism, before dying at the age of 24 just after the birth of her first child. The date 21 April, known as 'Kartini Day' is a national holiday in Indonesia in recognition of her work.

modish place has a prime seafront plot and serves exquisite Thai and Indonesian food, plus some Western dishes.

## Shopping

Intricately carved *jati* (teak) and mahogany furniture and relief panels are on display at shops and factories all around Jepara. However, the main carpentry centre is the village of **Tahunan**, 4km south of Jepara on the road to Kudus, where it's wall-to-wall furniture.

Brightly coloured, Sumba-style *ikat* weavings using traditional motifs are woven in the village of **Torso**, situated 14km south of Jepara and 2km off the main road. Other original designs are also produced; unusually, men predominantly do the weaving here. Srikandi Ratu and Lestari Indah are two workshops that have fixed-price showrooms.

**Pecangaan**, 18km south of Jepara, produces rings, bracelets and other jewellery from *monel* (a stainless-steel alloy).

## Getting There & Around

Frequent buses make the trip from Jepara to Kudus (7000Rp, one hour) and Semarang (12,000Rp, 1¾ hours). A few buses also go to Surabaya, but Kudus has more connections.

Becak are cheap and the best way to get around. From the terminal, about 1km west of the town centre, 5000Rp will get you to anywhere in town.

## AROUND JEPARA
### Mantingan

The mosque and tomb of Ratu Kali Nyamat, the great warrior-queen, are in Mantingan village, 4km south of Jepara. Kali Nyamat twice laid siege to Portugal's Melaka stronghold in the latter part of the 16th century.

The mosque, dating to 1549, was restored some years ago and the tomb lies to the side of it. The mosque is noted for its Hindu-style embellishments and medallions.

Mantingan is easily reached from Jepara. *Angkudes* (minibuses) from the bus terminal can drop you outside the mosque for 2000Rp.

### Beaches

Jepara has some fine white-sand beaches. **Pantai Bandengan** (aka Tirta Samudra), 8km northeast of town, is one of the best beaches on the north coast. The main public section can be littered, but a short walk away the sand is clean, the water clear and the swimming safe. To get there from Jepara, take a brown-and-yellow bemo (2000Rp) from Jl Pattimura. On weekdays you may have to charter a whole bemo (around 30,000Rp).

## KARIMUNJAWA
☎ 0297 / pop 8000

The dazzling offshore archipelago of Karimunjawa, a marine national park, consists of 27 coral-fringed islands that lie about 90km north of Jepara. The white-sand beaches are sublime but rarely visited by travellers.

Relatively difficult to reach (particularly in the rainy season) and with only limited facilities, the archipelago is still little more than a pinprick on the tourist trail. Wealthy Indonesians and scuba divers count for most of the visitors here.

The archipelago is divided into zones to protect the rich ecosystem here. Zone One is completely out of bounds to all except national park rangers, with other areas set aside for sustainable tourism.

### Orientation

The main island, **Pulau Karimunjawa**, is home to most of the islanders and the majority of the archipelago's facilities. It is also the site of the islands' only real town, **Karimunjawa**, and, despite widespread mangroves, some reasonable beaches. A small airport is located on adjacent **Pulau Kemujan**.

### Information

The islands don't have a tourist office per se, but a small information booth at the harbour is usually open to greet boats. Semarang tourist office p209 can also help out with practicalities. Pulau Karimunjawa is home to both a wartel and a post office.

### Sights & Activities

If you can find one of the rangers, they may be able to organise a hike up Pulau Karimunjawa's 600m peak, **Gunung Gendero**, but the real attractions lie offshore. The uninhabited islands of **Menjangan Besar** and **Menjangan Kecil** both have sweeping white sands and good **snorkelling** and are within easy reach of Karimunjawa town.

Further out, **Pulau Menyawakan** is the site of Karimunjawa's only major resort. **Pulau Nyamuk**, **Pulau Parang**, **Pulau Bengkoang** and **Pulau Genting** are all home to small, traditional communities. The reefs around many of these islands offer good **diving** and snorkelling, which can be arranged through the Kura Kura Resort on Pulau Menyawakan.

As a marine park, many parts of Karimunjawa are off-limits. **Pulau Burung** and **Pulau Geleang** are home to nests of sea eagles and are strictly protected.

The islands can experience violent weather in January and February; during this time, flights and boat trips can be badly disrupted.

### Sleeping & Eating

The main village of Karimunjawa has a handful of homestays and one *wisma* (guest house); the tourist office in Semarang (p209) can help out with names and contact numbers.

**Prapatan** ( ☎ 312 227; Jl Dermaga Baru; r 70,000Rp) A cheerful homestay in Karimunjawa's main village; for an extra 40,000Rp the host will also provide three meals a day.

**Wisma Wisata** ( ☎ 312 118; r 75,000Rp) On the *alun-alun*, Wisata is a decent choice for a budget bed, with beer, clean rooms and a good spot near the harbour.

**Karimunjawa Inn** ( ☎ 312 253; www.karimunjawainn .com; r with fan/air-con 96,000/272,000Rp; ☒ ) Formerly the Melati, this hotel is near the main town on Pulau Karimunjawa. Offers a choice of accommodation, from fan-cooled rooms to air-con

bungalows; all are spotless if a little dated. It's surrounded by plenty of greenery and there's a open-air restaurant with great fish and squid dishes (meals from 15,000Rp) and sea views. Book ahead for weekend visits.

**Nirvana Laut** ( ☎ 024-659 2854; www.karimun-jawa .com; r from US$55; ☒ ) Right on a white-sand beach with good snorkelling, this small resort has four rooms (two with en suite) in a attractive house with a kitchen that's ideal for small groups. Additionally, the eight luxurious suites here have panoramic sea views and teak floors. There's a great decked restaurant area and plenty of fresh seafood available.

**Kura Kura Resort** ( ☎ Jepara 0291-595 932; www .kurakuraresort.com; minimum 2 nights from US$175; ☒ ☒ ) This five-star PADI scuba diving resort is situated on its own private island, with a bar, a restaurant and water sports facilities, and about 800m of fine, white sand. Prices are per person per night and include good-quality bungalow accommodation, flights (or speedboat connections) and meals. Hefty supplements are charged if boats or planes from the mainland aren't full (a minimum of three people is needed for planes to take off).

**Ibu Joice** (Jl Pattimura) Run by Joice, a friendly local who speaks English and sells food, snacks and beer; she will cook meals (if asked in advance) and can help with transport and island info.

**Ester's** (mains around 20,000Rp) On the *alun-alun*; serves up seafood and Indonesian staples.

### Getting There & Away

Kura Kura Resort operates the only planes flying into Karimunjawa. Most flights shuttle guests between the resort and Semarang or Yogyakarta, and last-minute deals can be as low as 350,000Rp and 500,000Rp respectively. Four-seater Cessnas can also be chartered.

The *Muria* sails to Karimunjawa (economy/ VIP 24,000/60,000Rp, seven hours) from Pantai Kartini in Jepara on Wednesday and Saturday at 8.30am, returning from Karimunjawa on Monday and Thursday at the same time.

From Semarang the *Kartini I* (business/ executive class 115,000/135,000Rp, 3½ hours) leaves at 9am Saturday and returns at 2pm Sunday from Karimunjawa. Tickets can be reserved via the tourist information office in Semarang or on ☎ 024-760 5660.

From Pulau Karimunjawa, it costs around 400,000Rp to charter a wooden boat for a

Transnet (cnr Jl Pemuda & Jl Basuki Rahmat; per hr 6000Rp; ⊗ 24hr)

## MEDICAL SERVICES
**Rumah Sakit Darmo** ( ☎ 567 6253; Jl Raya Darmo 90) Hospital with English- and Dutch-speaking doctors.

## MONEY
Jl Pemuda has plenty of banks with ATMs, as does Tunjungan Plaza.
**BNI Bank** (Jl Pemuda) Offers good rates and has an ATM.

## POST
**Main post office** (Jl Kebon Rojo) Inconveniently located 4km north of the city centre.

## TOURIST INFORMATION
**Tourist Information Centre** ( ☎ 534 0444; www .sparklingsurabaya.com; Jl Pemuda; ⊗ 9am-5pm Mon-Sat) Has helpful English-speaking staff and plenty of leaflets, and a good free colour map is offered.
**East Java Regional Tourist Office** ( ☎ 853 1822; Jl Wisata Menanggal; ⊗ 7am-2pm Mon-Fri) About 3km south of the centre; has a few brochures on the province.

## Sights
### OLD CITY
Even though much of Surabaya's historical cen-tre is literally falling to pieces, the old city eas-ily wins the 'Most Attractive Neighbourhood' prize. With crumbling Dutch architecture, a fascinating Arab quarter and strong Chinese influences, it's also by far the most atmospheric and idiosyncratic area of Surabaya to explore.

From the old city you can then head north to the **Kalimas harbour**, where brightly painted *pinisi* from Sulawesi and Kalimantan unload their wares.

### Jembatan Merah
A good place to start a wander around the old city is **Jembatan Merah**, the bridge that saw fierce fighting during Indonesia's battle for independence. Jl Jembatan Merah, running south of the bus terminal along the canal, is a grungy replica of Amsterdam, but worthy (although rundown) examples of **Dutch archi-tecture** can be seen here. Another impressive structure is the Indo-European-style **Gedung PTP XXII** government office building on Jl Merak Cendrawasih.

### House of Sampoerna
Just northwest of Jembatan Merah is the city's best-presented attraction, the **House of** **Sampoerna** ( ⊗ 353 9000; www.houseofsampoerna.com; Jl Taman Sampoerna; admission free; ⊗ 9am-9.30pm) which is the home of one of Indonesia's most famous *kretek* cigarette manufacturers. Whatever you think about the tobacco industry, this factory and museum makes a fascinating place to visit. The building itself is a wonderful 19th-century Dutch structure, originally an orphanage but later converted into a theatre (indeed Charlie Chaplin once dropped by). The former lobby now forms the museum and is something of a shrine to the Sampoerna empire, with exhibits on the use of cloves and the history of *kretek* in Indonesia alongside uniforms and drums of the Sampoerna marching band and other quirky company curios.

Upstairs there's a bird's-eye perspective of the factory's shop floor, where hundreds of women hand roll, trim and pack the Dji Sam Soe brand (banned from most countries as the tar content is so strong). The fastest roll-ers here churn out 4000 cigarettes a day, their fingers a blur of motion.

You'll be accompanied throughout your visit by a highly informative, English-speak-ing guide, and there's a superb cafe-restaurant here too.

### Chinatown
East of Jembatan Merah is Surabaya's **Chinatown**, with hundreds of small businesses and warehouses. Becak and hand-pulled carts are still the best way to transport goods in the crowded, narrow streets. **Pasar Pabean** (Jl Pabean) is a sprawling, darkly lit market, where you can buy everything from Madurese chickens to Chinese crockery.

Further east, near the canal, the stunningly atmospheric **Kong Co Kong Tik Cun Ong temple** (Jl Dukuh) is primarily Buddhist, but has a variety of Confucian and Taoist altars if you can see them through the plumes of incense smoke.

### Arab Quarter (Qubah)
A warren of narrow lanes, Surabaya's Arab Quarter has the atmosphere and appearance of a Middle Eastern *medina*, with stalls selling prayer beads, *peci* (black Muslim felt hats) and other religious paraphernalia, alongside perfumes, dates and a plastic camel or two. All alleys lead to the **Mesjid Ampel** (Jl Ampel Suci), the most sacred mosque in Surabaya; it was here that Sunan Ampel, one of the *wali songo* who brought Islam to Java, was buried in 1481. The mosque itself is a huge space, the vast

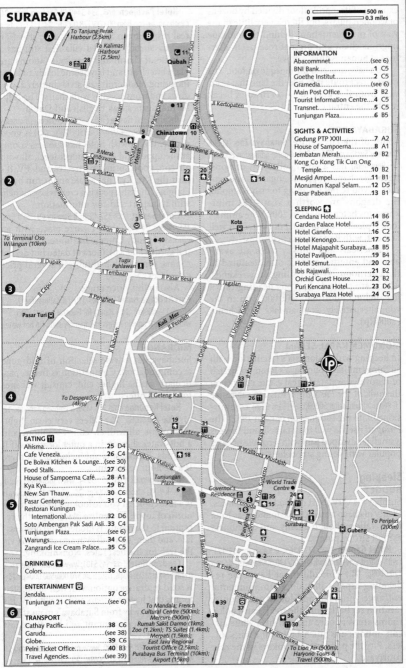

# SURABAYA

0 — 500 m
0 — 0.3 miles

expanse of its marble floor divided by dozens of wooden pillars, but there's very little in the way of ornamentation. Behind the mosque pilgrims chant and present rose-petal offerings at Sunan Ampel's grave.

You have to access the mosque on foot. The most direct route is to take the lane that leads west from Jl Ampel Suci – a crowd of becak marks the entrance.

### SURABAYA ZOO

South of the city centre, **Surabaya Zoo** (Kebun Binatang Surabaya, KBS; Jl Diponegoro; admission 8000Rp; ☙9am-4pm) has a good collection of lions, tigers, elephants, hippos, kangaroos and reptiles. If you're not planning to visit Komodo, the dragons are worth a visit – 32 mini-komodos hatched here in 2009. The animals look typically nonchalant, but the park is well laid out, with large, open enclosures.

Camel-cart and donkey rides are available and entertainment is often featured in the afternoon. Avoid visiting on weekends, which are packed. Any bus heading down Jl Panglima Sudirman will take you to the zoo; alternatively, you can take an M bemo (2000Rp).

### MONUMEN KAPAL SELAM

In keeping with Indonesia's fascination with all things military, Surabaya's foremost stretch of renovated waterside real estate centres on the hulk of the *Pasopati*, a Russian **submarine** (Jl Pemuda; admission 5000Rp; ☙9am-9pm) commissioned into the Indonesian navy in 1962. The *Pasopati* itself is well maintained, and there is a small landscaped **park** with a couple of cafes popular with young smoochers.

## Sleeping
### BUDGET

Surabaya is very short of good budget places. Plenty of cheap hotels can be found near Kota train station, though quality and cleanliness are not strong points.

**Hotel Ganefo** ( ☎ 371 1169; Jl Kapasan 169-171; r with shared/private mandi 80,000/120,000Rp, with air-con 120,000Rp; ✷ ) This old-timer has some redeeming aspects including a monumental entrance verandah and lobby and a quiet location set back from the road. Fan-cooled rooms are very bare and cell-like, while air-con options are much better, if a bit soulless. Pity the poor caged monkeys in the rear courtyard.

**Hotel Paviljoen** ( ☎ 534 3449; Jl Genteng Besar 94; r with fan/air-con from 90,000/128,000Rp; ✷ ) This is a real respite from Surabaya's manic streets, a slightly shabby colonial villa that still has a twinkle of charm and grandeur. Rooms are plain but clean, and have some lovely touches including Mediterranean-style shuttered windows and front porches with chairs. The helpful managers speak English and Dutch.

**Orchid Guest House** ( ☎ 355 0211; orchidguesthouseby @yahoo.com; Jl Bongkaran 49; d 150,000Rp; ✷ ) A good choice, this newish hotel has spotless rooms at the upper end of the budget level, all with air-con, good spring mattresses and TV. It's near the Kya Kya, has a cafe and is run by an obliging English-speaking crew who can help with transport and city information.

**Hotel Semut** ( ☎ 352 4578; Jl Samudra 9-15; d from 155,000Rp; ✷ ) Slightly bizarre place with an excess of gaudy Chinese furniture, a slim central garden and a plethora of dated but decent rooms, some with bathtubs, in several price categories.

Also in this price range:

**Puri Kencana Hotel** ( ☎ 503 3161; Jl Kalimantan 9; r from 115,000Rp; ✷ ) Handy for Gubeng train station, with simple if ageing rooms and friendly staff. No hot water.

### MIDRANGE

Surabaya has a wide selection of midrange accommodation. Competition is fierce, particularly at the higher end; consult websites for special offers.

**Hotel Kenongo** ( ☎ 534 1359; Jl Embong Kenongo 12; r 195,000-230,000Rp; ✷ ) Offers very clean, light, airy rooms, all with air-con, TV, phone and a hot-water shower; in a quiet location off Jl Pemuda. Breakfast is not included, but there is a 24-hour restaurant.

**Ibis Rajawali** ( ☎ 353 9994; www.ibishotel.com; Jl Rajawali 9-11; r from 360,000Rp; ✷ ▯ 🛜 ) Rajawali is a fine choice if you're looking to stay in the north of town. The entire place, from the reception to the rooms, is modern and business-like, and there's a small gym and spa. Book via the web for the best rates. Nonsmoking.

**Cendana Hotel** ( ☎ 545 5101; www.cendanahotel.com; Jl Kombes Pol M Doeryat 6; r/ste from 370,000/500,000Rp; ✷ ) A solid midrange option with well-appointed rooms that have minibars and satellite TV. It's located just away from Surabaya's main streets and has a cafe-restaurant and bar. Breakfast is included.

**Mercure** ( ☎ 562 3000; www.mercuresurabaya.com; Jl Raya Darmo 68-78; r from 502,000Rp; ✷ ▯ 🛜 ) Large centrally located hotel that's part of the Accor Group's empire in Surabaya. Its facilities are excellent, with a lovely tree-fringed pool area at the rear that's a peaceful retreat, plus a great cafe-restaurant where you can sample local *jamu*. Rooms are modern, stylish and spacious and have free internet access. Nonsmoking.

**Garden Palace Hotel** ( ☎ 534 4056; www.gardenhotel .co.id; Jl Yos Sudarso 11; s/d from 525,000Rp; 🅿 💻 🆒 ) This huge concrete monolith is not a palace, but it does have an ostentatious marble lobby complete with giant chandelier. The rooms are a little dated in design terms but generous in size. A complimentary airport shuttle is usually offered.

Also in the running:

**Surabaya Plaza Hotel** ( ☎ 531 6833; www.prime plazahotels.com; Jl Pemuda 31-37; r from US$70; 🅿 💻 🛜 🆒 ) One of Surabaya's ritzier establishments; well located in the thick of things. Rooms range from standard to plush suites. Nonsmoking.

## TOP END

Surabaya has a glut of luxury hotels and competition is cut-throat, with some excellent deals available. Most are geared to business travellers.

**TS Suites** ( ☎ 563 1222; www.tssuites.com; Surabaya Town Sq, Jl Hayam Wuruk 6; r from US$90; 🅿 💻 ) For a very different take on the luxury experience, these hip, spacious suites represent the height of Surabaya chic and have free fast internet and minibar (except booze!) and other niceties. Located above one of the city's most popular malls, so you won't have to walk far to access dozens of restaurants, cafes and a large cinema complex. Nonsmoking.

**our pick** **Hotel Majapahit Surabaya** ( ☎ 545 4333; www.hotel-majapahit.com; Jl Tunjungan 65; r from US$110; 🅿 💻 🛜 🆒 ) This superb colonial hotel built in 1910 is head and shoulders above the competition in terms of class and atmosphere. It's all very tasteful indeed, with colonnaded courtyards, fountains and verdant greenery and also very competitively priced – the rooms lack nothing in terms of facilities. Staff are extremely helpful and well trained, and the Sarkies Chinese restaurant is one of the best in the city. Nonsmoking.

## Eating

You won't be left hungry in Surabaya – the city has a huge array of eating options. Local dishes include *rawon*, a thick, black beef soup that tastes better than it sounds.

For cheap eats, **Pasar Genteng** (Jl Genteng Besar; mains 8000Rp; 🕑 9am-9pm) has good night warungs. Late-night munchies can also be had at the offshoot of Jl Pemuda, opposite the Plaza Surabaya, which buzzes with food-stall activity around the clock, or the strip of warungs with their backs to the river along Jl Kayun.

Sadly the once-throbbing Chinese night market **Kya Kya** (Jl Kembang Jepun; 🕑 6pm-11pm) in the old city is now far less popular, though there are still a few food stalls here.

For an air-conditioned setting, **Tunjungan Plaza** (Jl Tunjungan) has a colossal selection of squeaky-clean Asian (including a great sushi bar), Western restaurants and cafes; the food court is on the 5th floor.

**Zangrandi Ice Cream Palace** ( ☎ 534 5820; Jl Yos Sudarso 15; ice creams from 3000Rp) This ice-cream parlour has been famous since Dutch times, and is still going strong. Traffic noise is a real issue here, however.

**Soto Ambengan Pak Sadi Asli** ( ☎ 532 3998; Jl Ambengan 3A; mains 20,000Rp) This is the original location of a chain with several branches across Surabaya. Everyone is here for the delicious *soto ayam* (chicken soup), which is served up with herbs, turmeric, plenty of peanuts and an egg or two if you want.

**Ahisma** ( ☎ 535 0466; Jl Kusuma Bangsa 80; mains from 25,000Rp; 🕑 noon-10pm) A welcome surprise, this elegant upmarket vegetarian restaurant has well-presented salads, tofu meals, soups, and lots of rice and noodle dishes; no MSG is used. It's owned and run by a welcoming Indo-Chinese family and there's a small (veggie) deli here too for snacks and biscuits. Nonsmoking.

**our pick** **House of Sampoerna Café** ( ☎ 353 9000; Jl Taman Sampoerna; meals 20,000-82,000Rp; 🛜 ) The House of Sampoerna cigarette factory cafe, occupying a gorgeous colonial structure complete with stained-glass windows and classy seating, is the perfect spot for a meal. The menu is divided into east and west sections, with *rawon* and Singapore laksa from the former and fish and chips from the latter standing out. There are great desserts, a full bar, espresso coffee (and even a nonsmoking section!).

**Cafe Venezia** ( ☎ 534 3335; Jl Ambengan 16; mains from 40,000Rp; 🕑 11.30am-10pm) Venezia is a slightly faded old-school establishment in a venerable Dutch villa that offers Korean, Japanese and Indonesian dishes and 'proper' service.

JAVA

**New San Thauw** ( ☎ 503 5776; Jl Raya Gubeng 64; fish & crab per 100g from 9000Rp) San Thauw offers seafood that only comes fresher directly from the sea; choose your meal from the tank. Also serves some unusual dishes like cassava leaf soup.

**De Boliva Kitchen & Lounge** ( ☎ 596 3202; Jl Raya Gubeng 66; meals from 40,000Rp) A popular, if pricey, Western-style cafe with filling sandwiches (try the wholewheat BLT). Its desserts are famous, with crepes, sorbets and ice cream galore (including low-fat options).

**Restoran Kuningan International** ( ☎ 503 5103; Jl Kalimantan 14; mains 45,000-200,000Rp; ⏱ 5-10.30pm) For a splurge, this top-class restaurant, housed in a converted Dutch villa, is renowned for its seafood – try the lobster.

## Drinking

There are very few bars in Surabaya. Those located in upmarket hotels (which often double as clubs) are a few of the only options.

**Colors** ( ☎ 503 0562; www.colorspub.com; Jl Sumatra 81) Very popular with expats, this large pub-restaurant has live music and a DJ every night. The bartenders and some locals will treat you like a long-lost cousin, and there's good Western food too.

**Desperados** ( ☎ 566 1550; Shangri La Hotel, Jl Mayjend Sungkono 120) Popular hotel bar west of the centre with live music; try the margaritas. There's a cover charge of around 40,000Rp.

## Entertainment

### CULTURAL PERFORMANCES

**Jendala** ( ☎ 531 4073; Jl Sonokembang 4-6) This restaurant, in a beautiful colonial lodge, has a varied program of so-called 'culturetainment', ranging from theatre to dance to disco.

### CINEMA

Cinema complexes are found all around the city.

**Tunjungan 21** ( Tunjungan Plaza, Jl Tunjungan) One of the best in town, this large cinema complex shows recent Hollywood releases in English and has good sound quality.

## Getting There & Away

### AIR

Surabaya is Indonesia's third-busiest airport and has a few international connections and an expanding selection of domestic routes, including direct flights to Lombok and Kalimantan.

Airlines operating out of Surabaya include the following.

**AirAsia** ( ☎ 5050 5088; www.airasia.com) Flies to Johor Bahru and Kuala Lumpur.

**Batavia Air** ( ☎ 504 9666; www.batavia-air.co.id; airport) Operates flights to Ambon, Denpasar, Balikpapan, Banjarmasin, Jakarta, Kupang, Makassar, Mataram, Palangkaraya, Pontianak, Tarakan and Yogyakarta.

**Cathay Pacific** ( ☎ 0804 188 8888; www.cathaypacific .com; Hyatt Regency, Jl Basuki Rachmat 124-128) Flies daily to/from Hong Kong

**Garuda** ( ☎ 080 7142 7832, 24hr booking line 546 8505; www.garuda-indonesia.com; Hyatt Regency, Jl Basuki Rahmat 124-128) Connections to Singapore, Denpasar, Hong Kong, and several flights daily to Jakarta.

**Lion Air** ( ☎ 503 611; www.lionair.co.id; Jl Sulawesi 75) Flights to Ambon, Denpasar, Balikpapan, Banjarmasin, Batam, Jakarta, Makassar, Manado, Mataram, Ternate and Yogyakarta.

**Mandala** ( ☎ 561 0777; www.mandalaair.com; Jl Raya Diponegoro 91D) Flies to Denpasar, Balikpapan, Batam, Jakarta, Malang, Semarang and Solo.

**Merpati** ( ☎ 568 8111; www.merpati.co.id; Jl Darmo 109-111) Has plenty of connections including routes to Kuala Lumpur, Bandung, Denpasar, Jakarta, Kupang, Makassar, Manado, Mataram and Yogyakarta.

Travel agencies sell domestic tickets at a small discount and international tickets with a bigger cut. Agencies include the large, well-established **Haryono Tours & Travel** ( ☎ 503 4000; www .haryonotours.com; Jl Sulawesi 27-29; ⏱ 8am-5pm Mon-Fri, to 1pm Sat).

### BOAT

Surabaya is an important port and a major transport hub for ships to the other islands. Boats depart from Tanjung Perak harbour; bus P1 from outside Tunjungan Plaza heads here.

Several Pelni ships sail to Makassar in Sulawesi (economy/1st class from 182,00/558,000Rp), and Pontianak (209,000/664,000Rp) in Kalimantan. See the Transport chapter (p848) or head to the **Pelni ticket office** ( ☎ 352 1044; www.pelni.co.id; Jl Pahlawan 112) for more information.

Ferries no longer run to Madura now that the Suramadu Bridge has been completed.

### BUS

Surabaya's main bus terminal is called Purabaya; it's 10km south of the city centre. Crowded Damri buses run between the bus terminal and the Jl Tunjungan/Jl Pemuda intersection in the city centre. A metered taxi costs around 50,000Rp.

Note all buses heading south of Surabaya on the toll road get caught up in heavy traffic around the Gembol junction because of the snarl-up around the mud volcano (see the boxed text, p228); during rush hour this can add an hour to your journey. Buses from Purabaya head to Malang (10,000/15,000Rp, two to three hours), Probolinggo (14,000/22,000Rp, around three hours), Banyuwangi (36,000/51,000Rp, seven hours), Solo (52,000/70,000Rp, seven hours) and Yogyakarta (58,000/76,000Rp, 8½ hours). Buses also operate from Purabaya bus terminal to Madura.

Luxury buses from Purabaya also do the long hauls to Solo, Yogyakarta, Bandung and Denpasar. Most are night buses leaving in the late afternoon or evening. Bookings can be made at Purabaya bus terminal, or travel agencies in the city centre sell tickets with a mark-up. The most convenient bus agents are those on Jl Basuki Rahmat. Intercity buses are not allowed to enter the city, so you will have to go to Purabaya to catch your bus.

Buses along the north coast to Kudus (normal/ *patas* 54,000/74,000Rp, eight hours) and Semarang (60,000/82,000Rp, nine hours) depart from Terminal Oso Wilangun, 10km west of the city.

### MINIBUS

Door-to-door *travel* minibuses collect passengers from their hotels and homes, which saves a slog to the terminal, but they aren't always quicker because of the time spent driving between pick-ups.

Destinations and sample fares include Malang (35,000Rp), Solo (80,000Rp), Yogyakarta (85,000Rp) and Semarang (95,000Rp). Hotels can make bookings and arrange pick-up or you can try the agencies along Basuki Rahmat.

### TRAIN

From Jakarta, trains taking the fast northern route via Semarang arrive at the Pasar Turi train station southwest of Kota train station. Trains taking the southern route via Yogyakarta, and trains from Banyuwangi and Malang, arrive at Gubeng and most carry on through to Kota. **Gubeng train station** (☎ 503 3115) is much more central and sells tickets for all trains.

Most Jakarta-bound trains leave from **Pasar Turi** (☎ 534 5014), including the luxury *Argo Bromo Anggrek* (from 260,000Rp, 10½ hours), which leaves at 8am and 8pm, and the *Gumarang* (business class 140,000Rp, executive class from 240,000Rp, 12½ hours), departing at 5.30pm.

From Gubeng, the slower *Bima* (executive class 220,000Rp, 13 hours) departs at 4pm for Jakarta via Yogyakarta (executive class 140,000Rp, five hours), and the business-class *Mutiara Selatan* (120,000Rp, 13 hours) at 4.35pm for Bandung.

The *Sancaka* is a convenient day train for Yogyakarta, leaving Gubeng at 7am and 3pm for Solo (4½ hours) and Yogyakarta (5½ hours); it costs from 55,000/80,000Rp in business/executive class to either destination.

The reinstated business-class *Malang Ekspres* is the best option for Malang (11,000Rp, two hours), leaving Gubeng at 10am daily. There are also a few very slow economy trains; most continue on to Blitar.

Heading east, the *Mutiara Timur* goes to Banyuwangi (business/executive class from 60,000/80,000Rp, six hours) via Probolinggo at 9.15am and 10.35pm.

## Getting Around
### TO/FROM THE AIRPORT

Taxis from Juanda airport (17km) operate on a coupon system and cost around 85,000Rp to the city centre; from the city centre expect to pay a little more. Add on another 8000Rp for toll road fees.

There are also regular Damri buses (15,000Rp) from the airport to Purabaya bus terminal, and then on to the city centre.

### BUS

Surabaya has an extensive Damri city bus network, with normal buses (2000Rp) and *patas* buses (3000Rp per journey). Watch out for pickpockets, as buses can be very crowded.

One of the most useful services is the *patas* P1 bus, which runs from Purabaya bus terminal past the zoo and into the city along Jl Basuki Rahmat. It then turns down Jl Bubutan and continues on to Tanjung Perak harbour. In the reverse direction, catch it on Jl Tunjungan. The normal buses also cover the same route.

Surabaya also has plenty of bemos labelled A, B and so on, and all charge 2000Rp, depending on the length of the journey. Bemo M runs to the zoo.

Kalianget (35,000Rp) in the east of Madura island. The ferry departs Jangkar at 2pm (Monday to Wednesday, Friday and Saturday, six hours) and at 4pm on Thursday and Sunday, when it sails via Pulau Sapudi and takes 10 hours. Schedules change regularly, so it's a good idea to phone ahead. Buses run from Situbondo to Jangkar, or you can take a bus to Asembagus, then a becak or *andong* for the 4.5km trip to Jangkar. From Kalianget, the ferry departs at 8am daily. Minibus 'O' (2500Rp, 20 minutes) travels between Kalianget and Sumenep.

### GETTING AROUND

From Bangkalan, buses run along the main highway to Pamekasan (17,000Rp, 2½ hours) and Sumenep (25,000Rp, four hours). Minibuses also travel along the northern route to Arosbaya, Tanjungbumi, Pasongsongan and Ambunten.

To see something of the island, it's interesting to take a bus from Pamekasan inland through tobacco country to Waru, and then another on to Pasongsongan, from where you can head back to Sumenep via Ambunten and Slopeng.

Madura's roads are almost all paved and in excellent condition, with relatively little traffic. As the island is mostly flat, Madura is a good cycling destination, although it does get very hot.

## South Coast

The first port of call for most visitors is **Kamal**, a scruffy town of little importance to sightseers. Many head directly to **Bangkalan**, the next town north of Kamal, to watch the bull races. If you've time to kill before a race, **Museum Cakraningrat** ( 8am-2pm Mon-Sat) will entertain you for an hour or so with displays on Madurese history and culture and exhibits including a gamelan and traditional tools. For a day trip you could do worse than head to the beach at **Sambilangan**, 7km south of town, where there's a lonely 90m lighthouse that gazes out over the Madura strait.

**Sampang**, 61km from Bangkalan, also stages bull races and is the centre of the regency of the same name. **Camplong**, 9km further east, is a safe and popular, if grungy, swimming beach on the south coast. The Pertamina storage tanks nearby do nothing for its visual appeal, but it is a breezy oasis from the hot interior of Madura.

About another 15km further east is the important town of **Pamekasan**, the island's capital. Bull races are held in and around Pamekasan every Sunday from the end of July until early October; during October each year it throbs with the festivities of the **Kerapan Sapi Grand Final**. The **BCA bank** (Jl Jokotole;  9am-2pm Mon-Fri), just east of the *alun-alun*, changes money and has an ATM.

About 35km east of Pamekasan, before Bluto, is **Karduluk**, a woodcarving centre.

### SLEEPING

Bangkalan has a few places to stay, and the island's capital has a handful of hotels and several losmen.

**Losmen Gatra** (  0324-322 045; Jl Agus Salim 18, Pamekasan; r 40,000Rp) For a cheap bed head to this simple losmen.

**Hotel Ramayana** (  0324-324 575; Jl Niaga 55, Pamekasan; r from 50,000Rp, with air-con from 110,000Rp;  ) A step up in quality and comfort from the Gatra.

**Hotel Ningrat** (  031-309 5388; Jl Kahaji Muhammed Kholil 113, Bangkalan; r 60,000-125,000Rp, with air-con 210,000Rp;  ) Smallish clean rooms, and bigger air-con options decorated in traditional Madurese style, are on offer here.

**Hotel Camplong** (  0323-321 568; r 130,000Rp) In Camplong, this imaginatively named hotel is a reasonable place to bed down for the night.

## Sumenep
 0328 / pop 99,000
Compared with the rest of Madura, Sumenep, in the far east of the island, is a sleepy, refined town, with a Mediterranean air and quiet, lazy streets. The goats and belching pick-ups that clog the streets of the island's other main communities are a rarity here and by midafternoon the whole town seems to settle into a slow, collective siesta. With dozens of crumbling villas and a fine *kraton* and mosque, it is easily Madura's most interesting town.

### INFORMATION

Madura's only **tourist office** (  667 148; kurniadi@consultant.com; Jl Sutomo 5;  7am-3.30pm Tue-Sat) is run by the very enthusiastic and knowledgeable Adi Wijaya, who can answer most queries and help out with transport information relating to both Sumenep and the island. He also acts as guide.

Sumenep has several internet places, all charging around 4000Rp per hour; the fastest is on Jl KH Wahid Hasyim. The post office

### A BULL RACE AT PACE

In Madurese folklore, the tradition of *kerapan sapi* began long ago when plough teams raced each other across the arid fields. This pastime was encouraged by Panembahan Sumolo, an early king of Sumenep. Today, with stud-bull breeding big business on Madura, *kerapan sapi* are an incentive for the Madurese to produce good stock. Only bulls of a high standard can be entered for important races – the Madurese keep their young bulls in superb condition, dosing them with an assortment of medicinal herbs, honey, beer and raw eggs.

Traditional races are run in bull-racing stadiums all over Madura. Practice trials are held throughout the year, but the main season starts in late August and September, when contests are held at district and regency levels. The finest bulls fight it out for the big prize in October at the grand final in Pamekasan, the island's capital.

This is the biggest and most colourful festival and as many as 100 bulls, wearing richly decorated halters, ribbons and flowers, are paraded through town to a loud fanfare. For each race, two pairs of bulls, stripped of their finery, are matched, with their 'jockeys' perched behind on wooden sleds. Gamelan music is played to excite the bulls and then, after being fed a generous tot of *arak*, they're released and charge flat out down the track – just as often plunging straight into the crowd. The race is over in a flash – the best time recorded so far is nine seconds over 100m. After the elimination heats the victors get to spend the rest of the year as studs.

Pamekasan is the main centre for bull racing, but Bangkalan, Sampang, Sumenep and some of the surrounding villages also host races. The East Java Calendar of Events, available from tourist offices in Surabaya (p222), has a general schedule for the main races, but if you are on Madura over a weekend during the main season, you can be guaranteed that races or practices will be held somewhere on the island.

---

is on the road to Kalianget, and the Telkom office is further out past the Chinese temple. BCA and BNI banks are on Jl Trunojoyo; both have ATMs and change cash.

### SIGHTS

Occupied by the present *bupati* of Sumenep, the **kraton** and its **taman sari** (pleasure garden; admission included in carriage-house museum entry; ☉ 7am-5pm) were built in 1750 by Panembahan Sumolo, son of Queen Raden Ayu Tirtonegoro and her spouse, Bendoro Saud. The bathing pools once used by the royal women are still here, though they're no longer in use. Part of the *kraton* building is a small museum with an interesting collection of royal possessions, including Madurese furniture, stone sculptures and *binggel* (heavy silver anklets worn by Madurese women). The complex can only be visited on a guided tour arranged at the royal carriage-house museum.

Opposite the *kraton*, the **royal carriage-house museum** (admission 1000Rp; ☉ 7am-5pm) contains the throne of Queen Tirtonegoro and a Chinese-style bed, which is reputedly 300 years old. On the first Sunday of the month, **traditional dance or gamelan practice** (admission free; ☉ 10am-1pm) is held at the *kraton*.

Sumenep's 18th-century **Mesjid Jamik** is notable for its three-tiered Meru-style roof, Chinese porcelain tiles and ceramics. Sumenep also has a **Chinese temple.**

The tombs of the royal family are at the **Asta Tinggi cemetery**, which looks out over the town from a peaceful hilltop 2km northwest of the centre. The main royal tombs are decorated with carved and painted panels; two depict dragons said to represent the colonial invasion of Sumenep. The biggest mausoleum is that of Panembahan Notokusomo (1762–1811), but it is the grave of Tirtonegoro that attracts pilgrims from all over Madura and Java. One of the small pavilions in the outer courtyard still bears the mark of an assassin's sword from an unsuccessful attempt to murder Bendoro Saud.

Sumenep is a centre for champion bull breeding, and on most Saturday mornings practice **bull races** can be seen at the Giling stadium.

### FESTIVALS & EVENTS

The **Festival of Sumenep** is usually celebrated bi-annually on 31 October and marks the founding of the town, with a program of cultural performances.

JAVA

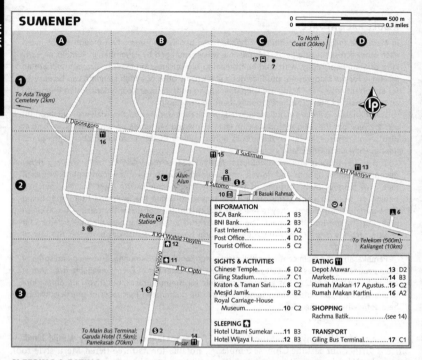

**SUMENEP**

| INFORMATION | |
|---|---|
| BCA Bank | **1** B3 |
| BNI Bank | **2** B3 |
| Fast Internet | **3** A2 |
| Post Office | **4** D2 |
| Tourist Office | **5** C2 |

| SIGHTS & ACTIVITIES | |
|---|---|
| Chinese Temple | **6** D2 |
| Giling Stadium | **7** C1 |
| Kraton & Taman Sari | **8** C2 |
| Mesjid Jamik | **9** B2 |
| Royal Carriage-House Museum | **10** C2 |

| SLEEPING | |
|---|---|
| Hotel Utami Sumekar | **11** B3 |
| Hotel Wijaya I | **12** B3 |

| EATING | |
|---|---|
| Depot Mawar | **13** D2 |
| Markets | **14** B3 |
| Rumah Makan 17 Agustus | **15** C2 |
| Rumah Makan Kartini | **16** A2 |

| SHOPPING | |
|---|---|
| Rachma Batik | (see 14) |

| TRANSPORT | |
|---|---|
| Giling Bus Terminal | **17** C1 |

## SLEEPING & EATING

**Hotel Wijaya I** ( ☎ 662 433; Jl Trunojoyo 45-47; r with/without air-con from 90,000/35,000Rp; ☒ ) Right in the centre of town, Wijaya I is one of the best of a bunch of bad budget places. Rooms are plain and reasonably clean and there's a restaurant and a wartel here.

**Garuda Hotel** ( ☎ 662 424; Jl KH Wahid Hasyim 3; r 50,000-175,000Rp, ste 225,000Rp; ☒ ) Set back from the road, and very handy for the bus terminal, this new hotel is the most comfortable place in town. It has a wide range of accommodation, from no-frills economy digs with fans to large rooms with air-con and en-suite bathrooms.

**Hotel Utami Sumekar** ( ☎ 672 221; Jl Trunojoyo 53; s/d 100,000/120,000Rp, ste from 145,000Rp; ☒ ) A large, slightly ramshackle hotel with a selection of ageing rooms in a quiet location.

You won't go hungry in Sumenep, as there are plenty of good, inexpensive eateries. Be sure to order the local speciality *sate kambing* (lamb sate), which is often served with raw shallots and rice cakes. Good places include **Depot Mawar** ( ☎ 662 178; Jl KH Mansyur 55; meals 10,000Rp), **Rumah Makan Kartini** ( ☎ 662 431; Jl Diponegoro 83; mains around 9000Rp) and **Rumah**

**Makan 17 Agustus** ( ☎ 662 255; Jl Sudirman 34; meals from 10,000Rp).

There are good day and night markets down a lane next to the BNI bank.

## SHOPPING

The main business in town is antiques, but the best stuff is carted off by the truckload to Bali and Jakarta. Every second house seems to have something for sale. Sumenep is a centre for batik on Madura.

In the market, Rachma Batik has good-quality gear and fair prices.

## GETTING THERE & AWAY

Sumenep's main bus terminal is on the southern side of town, a 6000Rp becak ride from the centre. Buses leave roughly hourly until 4pm for Surabaya's Purabaya bus terminal (normal/*patas* 28,000/38,000Rp, four hours), and there are also direct buses to Banyuwangi, Malang, Semarang, Jakarta and Denpasar. Bus agents along Jl Trunojoyo sell tickets.

The Giling bus terminal for *angkots* to the north is right near the stadium, 1.5km from the market, or around 7000Rp by becak.

From Giling minibuses go to Lombang, Slopeng, Ambunten and other north-coast destinations.

## Around Sumenep

From Sumenep, the road to **Kalianget**, 10km southeast, passes many fine villas with facades of heavy, white columns under overhanging red-tiled roofs. About halfway between the two towns are the ruins of a Dutch **fort** dating from 1785, which once had four bastions, though only a perimeter wall and a couple of gateways remain. Next to the fort is a Dutch cemetery.

The Kalianget region is a centre for **salt production** – you'll see great mounds of the white powder piled up for export if you pass by in the dry season. Daily boats sail from here for Jangkar in East Java (p229) and to other islands in the Sumenep district.

You can go **snorkelling** at Pulau Talango, just offshore.

## North Coast

Fishing villages and their brightly painted *perahu* (boats) dot the north coast. The coast is lined with sandy beaches, but few are particularly wonderful.

Near Arosbaya, 27km north of Kamal, the tombs of the Cakraningrat royalty are at **Air Mata** (Tears) cemetery, superbly situated on the edge of a small ravine. The ornately carved *gunungan* (*wayang* mountain motif) headstone on the grave of Ratu Ibu, consort of Cakraningrat I, is the most impressive and is on the highest terrace. The turn-off to Air Mata is just before Arosbaya. From the coast road it's a 4km walk inland.

The village of **Tanjungbumi** is situated on the northwest coast of Madura, about 60km from Kamal. Although primarily a fishing village, it is also a manufacturing centre for traditional Madurese batik and *perahu*.

**Pasongsongan** is a fishing village on the beach, where it may be possible to stay with villagers. Further east, **Ambunten** is the largest settlement on the north coast and has a bustling market. Just over the bridge, you can walk along the picturesque river, which is lined with *perahu*, and through the fishing village to the beach.

Just outside Ambunten to the east, **Slopeng** has a wide beach with sand dunes, coconut palms and usually calm water for swimming, but it is not always clean. Men fish the shallower water with large cantilevered hand nets, which are rarely seen elsewhere in Java.

Slopeng is also known for its *topeng* making. Its beach is best visited on a day trip from Sumenep, only 20km away.

The stunning white sands of **Pantai Lombang**, 30km northeast of Sumenep, form the best beach in Madura. There's no development here to spoil the idyllic scene. Locals harvest tree saplings for the bonsai market, and sell coconuts to visitors.

## MALANG

☎ 0341 / pop 760,000

With leafy, colonial-era boulevards and a breezy climate, Malang moves at a far more leisurely pace than the regional capital, Surabaya, sprawling over the hilltops with the airs and graces of an overgrown market town. It's a cultured city with several important universities and home to a large student population.

Established by the Dutch in the closing decades of the 18th century, Malang earned its first fortunes from coffee, which flourished on the surrounding hillsides. Today, the city's colonial grandeur is quickly disappearing behind the homogenous facades of more modern developments, but there's still much to admire for now.

And with a number of Hindu temples and sights outside the city, Malang makes an ideal base to explore this intriguing corner of East Java.

To get the most from the city and region, try to hook up with one of the city's Malang Tourism Ambassadors (p235).

## Orientation

City life revolves around the *alun-alun* and the busy streets flowing into Jl Agus Salim and Jl Pasar Besar near the central market. This is where you'll find the main shopping plazas, restaurants, cinemas and many of Malang's hotels. Banks are northwest of the *alun-alun* along Jl Basuki Rahmat. Many of Malang's best restaurants are in the west of the city. For more historical wanderings, start with the circular Jl Tugu.

## Information

Malang has plenty of banks with ATMs; most are congregated along Jl Basuki Rahmat, including BCA; or try Lippo Bank, opposite the *alun-alun*.

## AROUND MALANG
### Singosari Temples
The Singosari temples lie in a ring around Malang and are mostly funerary temples dedicated to the kings of the Singosari dynasty (AD 1222 to 1292), the precursors of the Majapahit kingdom.

### CANDI SINGOSARI
Situated right in the village of Singosari, 12km north of Malang, this **temple** (admission free; ☯ 7am-5pm) stands 500m off the main Malang–Surabaya road. One of the last monuments erected to the Singosari dynasty, the temple was built in 1304 in honour of King Kertanegara, the fifth and last Singosari king, who died in 1292 in a palace uprising. The main structure of the temple was completed, but for some reason the sculptors never finished their task. Only the top part has any ornamentation and the *kala* heads have been left strangely stark. Of the statues that once inhabited the temple's chambers, only the statue of Agastya, the Shivaite teacher who walked across the water to Java, remains. Statues of Durga and Ganesha once found in the temple are now both exhibited in the National Museum in Jakarta. Locals visit this temple to meditate as well as to leave offerings of flower petals.

About 200m beyond the temple are two enormous figures of *dwarapala* (guardians against evil spirits) wearing clusters of skulls and twisted serpents.

To reach Singosari, take a green *angkot* (4000Rp) from Malang's Arjosari bus terminal and get off at the Singosari market on the highway.

### CANDI SUMBERAWAN
This small, squat **Buddhist stupa** (admission free; ☯ 7am-5pm) lies in the foothills of Gunung Arjuna, about 5km northwest of Singosari. Originating from a later period than the Singosari temples, it was built to commemorate the visit of Hayam Wuruk, the great Majapahit king, who visited the area in 1359.

Take an *angkot* (2500Rp) from Singosari *pasar* on the highway to Desa Sumberawan, and then walk 500m down the road to the canal, turn right and follow the canal through picturesque rice paddies for 1km to the temple. This delightful walk is the highlight of the visit.

Young men use the canal for washing themselves, so don't be surprised to see a naked body or two en route to the stupa. In Javanese culture it's polite to avert your eyes, and the boys will duck down into the water in fits of giggles as you pass by.

Sumberawan village is a **shoemaking** centre where wooden soles are shaped by hand for export to Bali; prospective purchasers can drop by the Echarispen's family home at Jl Candirawan 17.

### CANDI JAGO
Along a small road near the market in Tumpang, 22km from Malang, **Candi Jago** (Jajaghu; admission 5000Rp; ☯ 7am-5pm) was built between 1268 and 1280 and is thought to be a memorial to the fourth Singosari king, Vishnuvardhana. The temple has some interesting decorative carving – in the three-dimensional, *wayang kulit* style typical of East Java – from the Jataka and the Mahabharata. This primarily Buddhist temple also has Javanese-Hindu statues, including a six-armed, death-dealing goddess and a lingam, the symbol of Shiva's male potency. There are two photocopied leaflets available at the entrance you can consult to learn about its history.

To reach Candi Jago take a white *angkot* from Malang's Arjosari bus terminal to Tumpang (4000Rp).

Tumpang is also home to the **Mangun Dhama Arts Centre** ( ☎ 0341-787 907; www.mangun-dharma .com), which has Javanese dance classes and performances, plus some gamelan, *wayang* and woodcarving courses. *Wayang kulit* and dance shows can be staged if pre-arranged, and books, dance DVDs, masks, puppets and batik are usually for sale.

If coming from Singosari, go to Blimbing where the road to Tumpang branches off the highway, and then catch a minibus. In Tumpang, the temple is only a short stroll from the main road.

### CANDI KIDAL
This graceful **temple** (admission 5000Rp; ☯ 24hr), a fine example of East Javanese architecture, is 7km south of Candi Jago. It's now 12m high but originally topped 17m. Built around 1260 as the burial shrine of King Anusapati (the second Singosari king, who died in 1248), it is tapering and slender, with pictures of the Garuda (mythical man-bird) on three sides,

# AROUND MALANG

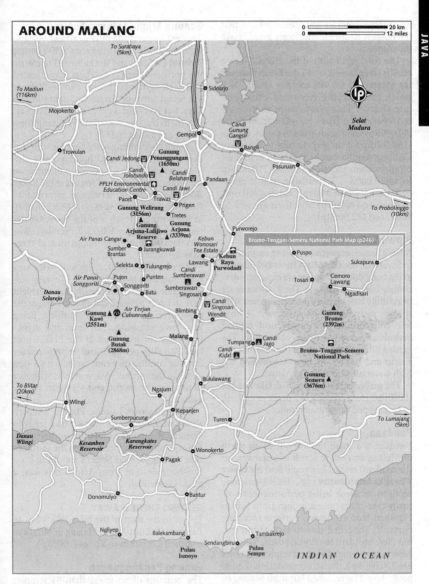

| 0 | 20 km |
| 0 | 12 miles |

To Surabaya (5km)

To Madiun (116km)

Mojokerto

Sidoarjo

Trowulan

Gempol

Candi Gunung Gangsir

Bangil

Selat Madura

Candi Jedong

Gunung Penanggungan (1650m)

Candi Jolotundo

Candi Belahan

Pandaan

Pasuruan

PPLH Environmental Education Centre

Candi Jawi

Pacet

Trawas

Prigen

Gunung Welirang (3156m)

Tretes

To Probolinggo (10km)

Ganung Arjuna-Lalijiwo Reserve

Gunung Arjuna (3339m)

Air Panas Cangar

Kebun Wonosari Tea Estate

Purworejo

Bromo-Tengger-Semeru National Park Map (p246)

Sumber Brantas

Jurangkuwali

Lawang

Kebun Raya Purwodadi

Puspo

Sukapura

Selekta

Tulungrejo

Candi Sumberawan

Tosari

Cemoro Lawang

Air Panas Songgoriti

Pujun

Punten

Songgoriti

Sumberawan

Ngadisari

Danau Selorejo

Batu

Singosari

Candi Singosari

Gunung Kawi (2551m)

Air Terjun Cubanrondo

Blimbing

Wendit

Gunung Bromo (2392m)

Gunung Butak (2868m)

Malang

Tumpang

Candi Jago

Bromo-Tengger-Semeru National Park

Candi Kidal

To Blitar (20km)

Ngajum

Bululawang

Gunung Semeru (3676m)

Wlingi

Kepanjen

Turen

To Lumajang (5km)

Sumberpucung

Danau Wlingi

Kesamben Reservoir

Karangkates Reservoir

Wonokerto

Pagak

Donomulyo

Bantur

Ngliyep

Balekambang

Tambakrejo

Sendangbiru

Pulau Ismoyo

Pulau Sempu

INDIAN OCEAN

bold, glowering *kala* heads and medallions of the *haruna* and Garuda symbols. Two *kala makara* (dragons) guard the steps – like those at the *kraton* steps in Yogyakarta, one is male and the other female.

Hourly brown *angkot* (3000Rp) run from Tumpang market to Candi Kidal; the last one returns at 4pm.

## Lawang

☎ 0341 / pop 200,000

Lawang, an ugly, sprawling city 18km north of Malang, is eminently forgettable, but the **Hotel Niagara** is a notable five-storey, pink art nouveau building. This once-grand hotel has seen better days, but it's fun to poke around its teak-panelled and antique-tiled interior if management will let you. Rumour has it that the hotel is haunted, and locals avoid it like the plague.

The road just south of the Hotel Niagara climbs steeply west up to the **Kebun Wonosari tea estate** ( ☎ 426 032; admission 6000Rp; 🔊 ), which has sweeping views and a temperature climate. This agrotourism venture offers everything from tea-plantation tours (40,000Rp) and a mini-train to tennis. Guides (160,000Rp for the day) to hike to the top of Gunung Arjuna can be arranged here. Best of all, accommodation (rooms 110,000Rp to 1,020,000Rp) is available in this glorious setting. From Malang, catch a *mikrolet* to Lawang (4000Rp) and then an *ojek* to Wonosari (12,000Rp).

## Purwodadi

A few kilometres north of Lawang on the road to Surabaya, the **Kebun Raya Purwodadi** (admission 4000Rp, tours 7500Rp; 🕑 7am-4pm) are expansive dry-climate botanical gardens. The 85 hectares are beautifully landscaped and contain over 3000 species, including 80 kinds of palm, a huge fern collection, a Mexican section, myriad orchids and many varieties of bamboo. The garden office to the south of the entrance has a map and leaflets. **Air Terjun Cobanbaung** is a high waterfall next to the gardens.

The gardens are easily reached; take any bus (5000Rp) from Malang to Surabaya and ask to be dropped off at the entrance.

## Pandaan

Pandaan is a small town about 45km north of Malang and 40km south of Surabaya, on the road to Tretes. Here you'll find the **Candra Wilwatika Amphitheatre** ( ☎ 0343-631 842), where modern Javanese ballet performances normally take place once a month from July to October. Unfortunately, performances are currently cancelled due to lack of interest, but there are plans to reinstate them. You can, however, overnight at the complex (doubles are 230,000Rp); the accommodation is quite basic. To get there, take a bus from Malang or Surabaya, and then a Tretes-bound minibus. The theatre is 1km from Pandaan, right on the main road to Tretes.

Also on the main road to Tretes, a few kilometres from Pandaan before Prigen, **Candi Jawi** (admission free; 🕑 7am-5pm) is an early 14th-century Hindu temple, built to honour King Kertanegara.

## Gunung Arjuna-Lalijiwo Reserve

This reserve includes the dormant volcano **Gunung Arjuna** (3339m), the semi-active **Gunung Welirang** (3156m) and the Lalijiwo Plateau on the northern slopes of Arjuna. Experienced and well-equipped hikers can walk from the resort town of Tretes to Selekta in two days, but you need a guide to go all the way. Alternatively, you can climb Welirang from Tretes or Lawang (p239).

A well-used hiking path, popular with students on weekends and holidays, and also with soul-searchers who come to meditate on the mountain, begins in Tretes near the Kakak Bodo Recreation Reserve. Get information from the **PHKA post** ( ☎ 081 2178 8956; Jl Wilis 523) in the northern reaches of the town. Guides can be hired here for 300,000Rp per day; allow two days to climb one mountain and three days for both.

It's a hard, five-hour, 17km walk to the very basic huts used by the Gunung Welirang sulphur collectors. Hikers usually stay overnight here in order to reach the summit before the clouds roll in around mid-morning. Bring your own camping gear, food and drinking water (or hire it all at the PHKA post for 120,000Rp per day), and be prepared for freezing conditions. From the huts it's a 4km climb to the summit. Allow at least six hours in total for the ascent, and 4½ hours for the descent.

The trail passes Lalijiwo Plateau, a superb alpine meadow, from where a trail leads to Gunung Arjuna, the more demanding peak. From Arjuna a trail leads down the southern side to Junggo, near Selekta and Batu. It's a five-hour descent from Arjuna this way; a guide is essential.

### GETTING THERE & AWAY

To get to the start of the hike, take a bus to Pandaan (8000Rp) from Malang or Surabaya and then a minibus to Tretes (7000Rp).

## Gunung Penanggungan

The remains of no fewer than 81 temples are scattered over the slopes of Gunung Penanggungan (1650m), a sacred Hindu mountain said to be the peak of Mt Mahameru, which according to legend, broke off and landed at its present site when Mt Mahameru was transported from India to Indonesia.

Historically this was a very important pilgrimage site for Hindus, and a few Javanese mystics, meditators and Hindus still visit the mountain today. Pilgrims make their way to the top of the mountain and stop to bathe in the holy springs adorned with Hindu statuary. The two main bathing places are **Candi Jolotundo** and **Candi Belahan**, the best examples of remaining Hindu art. Both are difficult to reach.

In a stunning setting on the evergreen western slopes of Penanggungan, **PPLH Environmental Education Centre** ( ☎ 0321-722 1045; dm 20,000Rp, bungalows 240,000Rp) is a supremely relaxing place. It mainly caters to groups, but its hiking packages (guides 90,000Rp) and herbal medicine and ecology courses are also open to individuals. There's a good organic restaurant and fine accommodation in pretty bungalows or more basic dorms. During the week you'll generally have the place to yourself, aside from the occasional school group passing through. To get there, take a Trawas-bound bemo (7000Rp) from Pandaan and an *ojek* (10,000Rp) from Trawas.

For somewhere more luxurious, head to the fine **Grand Trawas Hotel** ( ☎ 0343-880 015; www .grandtrawas.com; r/ste incl breakfast from 500,000/700,000Rp; 🖳 ) in Trawas, where all rooms have balconies overlooking Penanggungan. Nonsmoking.

## Batu

☎ 0341 / pop 79,000

Batu, 15km northwest of Malang, is a large hill resort on the lower reaches of Gunung Arjuna, surrounded by volcanic peaks.

Azahari Husin, a Malaysian bomb maker linked with Jemaah Islamiah and the Bali bombings, was cornered and killed here in 2005, but it's not a militant town (most people are happy holidaymakers from Malang and Surabaya).

There are several banks with ATMs near the *alun-alun*.

### SIGHTS

Without leaving the confines of Batu, the only sight is the **apple and strawberry orchard** surrounding the Kusuma Agrowisata hotel. **Tours** (incl electric truck ride 25,000Rp; 🕑 8am-4pm) are offered, and the price includes a piece of fruit or two and entry to the mini-zoo.

**Songgoriti**, 3km west of Batu, has well-known **hot springs** (admission 8000Rp; 🕑 7.30am-5pm) and a small, ancient Hindu temple in the grounds of the Hotel Air Panas Songgoriti. Nearby, Pasar Wisata is a tourist market sell-ing mostly apples, bonsai plants, and stone mortars and pestles. The waterfall **Air Terjun Cubanrondo** (admission 10,000Rp; 🕑 7.30am-5pm) is 5km southwest of Songgoriti.

**Selekta**, a small resort 5km further up the mountain from Batu and 1km off the main road, is home to the **Pemandian Selekta**, a large swimming pool with a superb setting in landscaped **gardens** (admission 12,500Rp; 🕑 7.30am-5pm).

Higher up the mountain, the small village of **Sumber Brantas**, far above Selekta, is at the source of Sungai Brantas. From here you can walk 2km to **Air Panas Cangar** (admission 5000Rp; 🕑 7.30am-5pm), a hot springs high in the mountains surrounded by forest and mist.

### SLEEPING

Accommodation is available in Batu, Songgoriti and all along the road to Selekta at Punten and at Tulungrejo, where the road to Selekta turns off. Songgoriti and Selekta are small, quiet resorts; Selekta has the best views. Batu has the best facilities but is more built-up.

Add around 25% to the prices listed here for weekend rates.

**Hotel Baru** ( ☎ 591 775; Jl Agus Salim 27; d 50,000-80,000Rp) A decent guest house with friendly staff and neat, simple tiled rooms with TV. No sheets (only blankets) are provided, and bathrooms are all cold water.

**Mutiara Baru** ( ☎ 511 259; Jl Panglima Sudirman 89; r 100,000-300,000Rp; 🖳 ) It's better than it looks from the street. Deluxe rooms are airy and light and face the garden and pool at the rear; economy rooms are perfunctory but clean.

**Hotel Kartika Wijaya** ( ☎ 592 600; www.kartika wjaya.com; Jl Panglima Sudirman 127; r incl breakfast from 450,000-675,000Rp; 🖳 🖳 ) A very grand colonial residence, Kartika Wijaya has a stately twin-towered facade and a lobby with a stained-glass map of Java. The grounds are huge – there's a vast lawn dotted with palms, tennis courts and a jogging track. Rooms are carpeted and generously sized, if a little plain.

**Kusuma Agrowisata** ( ☎ 593 333; www.kusumaagro wisatahotel.com; Jl Abdul Gani Atas; r from 560,000Rp; 🖳 🖳 ) A vast resort-cum-orchard with dinky little cottages and immaculate rooms in mani-cured grounds 3km south of Batu. There's a disco, and tours of the orchard and strawberry farm are included in the rate.

## EATING

Jl Panglima Sudirman is lined with restaurants and warungs.

**Pantara Café** (Jl Panglima Sudirman 123; mains around 15,000Rp) An atmospheric local eatery that serves East Javan dishes in bamboo surroundings.

**Waroeng Ba Be** ( ☎ 502 5300; www.waroengba -be.com; Jl Raya Beji 142; meals 15,000-30,000Rp; ) A stylish faux-traditional place with some tables overlooking rice fields and others under the large main *pendopo*-style structure. Excellent snacks (spring rolls, calamari), Chinese dishes, noodles, and even a dish or two from India and Mexico. There's live jazz or blues daily at 7pm. Ba Be is 3km east of the centre on the road to Malang.

### GETTING THERE & AWAY

From Malang's Landungsari bus terminal take a Kediri bus or one of the frequent pink *mikrolet* to Batu (3500Rp, 30 minutes). Batu's bus terminal is 2km from the centre of town – take another *mikrolet* (1500Rp) from here to Jl Panglima Sudirman.

From the bus terminal, orange *mikrolet* run to Selekta (3000Rp, 30 minutes) and Sumber Brantas (6000Rp, one hour). *Mikrolet* turn off to Sumber Brantas at Jurangkuwali village. For Air Panas Cangar, walk 2km straight ahead from Jurangkuwali.

An *ojek* to Selekta costs 12,000Rp.

## Gunung Kawi

On Gunung Kawi (2551m), west of Malang and 18km northwest of Kepanjen, is the tomb of the Muslim sage Kanjeng Penembahan Djoego, who died in 1871. Descended from Pakubuwono I, king of the Mataram empire, the sage is better known as Mbah Jugo.

From the parking area, a long path leads up the slope past tacky souvenir stalls and beggars. Before the tombs at the top, there's a mosque, a Buddhist temple and the house of Mbah Jugo, which draws Indonesians of all faiths and Chinese worshippers from across Asia. Legend has it that the saint will answer the prayers of fortune-seeking pilgrims. Apparently he did so for one Chinese couple, who went on to form one of Indonesia's biggest *kretek* companies.

Gunung Kawi can be reached by taking a bus to Kepanjen (7000Rp), 3km east of the turn-off, and then a minibus (7000Rp) for the final 19km.

## South-Coast Beaches

The coast south of Malang has some good beaches, but facilities are limited. **Sendangbiru** is a picturesque fishing village separated by a narrow channel from **Pulau Sempu**. This island nature reserve has a couple of lakes, **Telaga Lele** and **Telaga Sat**, both ringed by jungle. Boats can be hired (around 125,000Rp return) to get you to Sempu. Take your own provisions.

A few kilometres before Sendangbiru, a rough track to the left leads 3km to **Tambakrejo**, a small fishing village with a sweeping sandy bay, which despite the surf is generally safe for swimming.

**Balekambang** is best known for its picturesque Hindu temple on the small island of Pulau Ismoyo, connected by a footbridge to the beach. Balekambang is one of the most popular beaches and is crowded on weekends. Accommodation in the village is basic.

### GETTING THERE & AWAY

Minibuses from Malang's Gadang bus terminal travel the 69km to Sendangbiru (14,000Rp, two hours), past the turn-off to Tambakrejo; otherwise take a bus to Turen and then another to Sendangbiru. For Balekambang, buses run direct from Malang for 10,000Rp.

## BLITAR

☎ 0342 / pop 140,000

Blitar makes a good base for visiting Panataran temple and the spectacular active volcano of Gunung Kelud. It's also of interest as the site of former president Sukarno's home and memorial.

## Information

There are several banks in town including **BCA bank** (Jl Merdeka), with an ATM. **Telkom** (Jl A Yani 10) is the place to go for international telephone calls; it's on the eastern continuation of Jl Merdeka. **Warnet Mitra** (Jl Lawu 71; per hr 3000Rp) has internet access and is behind the main street. The post office is next to the train station.

## Sights

### MAKAM BUNG KARNO

At Sentul, 2km north of the town centre on the road to Panataran, former president Sukarno's grave is marked by an elaborate **monument** (admission by donation; 7am-5pm). Sukarno (or Bung Karno) is widely regarded as the father of the Indonesian nation, although he was only reinstated as a national hero in 1978.

Despite family requests that he be buried at his home in Bogor, Sukarno was buried in an unmarked grave next to his mother in Blitar. His father's grave was also moved from Jakarta to Blitar. It was only in 1978 that the lavish million-dollar monument was built and the grave site was opened to visitors. There's also a small museum here devoted to the man, which has hundreds of historic photographs of Sukarno with heads of state including John F Kennedy and Ho Chi Minh.

The monument has an undeniable poignancy, and thousands of Indonesian pilgrims come here each year to pay their respects. Sadly, as you leave, things descend abruptly into tacky consumerism as you're directed through a seemingly never-ending maze of souvenir stalls.

A becak from the Blitar town centre is around 8000Rp. Panataran-bound *angkudes* (yellow minibuses; 2000Rp) pass by; ask for the *makam* (grave). s

### OTHER SIGHTS

For a more personal look into the life of Sukarno, head for the **Museum Sukarno** (Jl Sultan Agung 59; admission by donation; ☺ 7am-5pm), located in the house where he lived as a boy. Photos, revolutionary posters and memorabilia (including a Bung Karno clock!) line the front sitting room, and you can see the great man's bedroom and check out his old Mercedes in the garage. The museum is about 1.5km from the centre of town.

Blitar's large **Pasar Legi**, next to the bus terminal, is also worth a gander.

### Sleeping & Eating

**Hotel Sri Rejeki** ( ☎ 801 718; Jl TGP 13; r with/without mandi from 50,000/35,000Rp, with air-con & breakfast from 80,000Rp; ✦ ) This place is a good deal, with a range of clean rooms, some with TV and Western toilets, but none with hot water. It's centrally located and staff are friendly.

**our pick** **Hotel Tugu Blitar** ( ☎ 801 766; www.tugu hotels.com; Jl Merdeka 173; r 100,000-300,000Rp, ste from 450,000Rp; ✦ ⊚ ) A historic hotel of real grandeur and Javanese character, with wonderfully spacious suites in the Dutch colonial section and good-value rooms in a separate block at the rear. Staff are delightful, and service is impeccable in the open-sided restaurant, which is decorated with fine art. Complimentary afternoon tea and Javanese snacks are served. A pool is planned. Nonsmoking; add 21% tax to room rates.

Blitar has some good restaurants on Jl Merdeka:

**RM Retno** ( ☎ 802 158; Jl Ir Sukarno 37A; meals 10,000Rp) Around 300m from Sukarno's grave, this is a great local place serving inexpensive East Javanese food. The lunch buffet is a knockout, with a huge choice of varied fare including fried catfish and lots of tempeh treats, while strong local coffee costs just 1000Rp.

**Ramayana** (Jl Merdeka 65; mains around 17,000Rp) Large Chinese establishment east of the *alun-alun*.

### Getting There & Away

Regular buses run from Blitar to Malang (12,000Rp, two hours) and Surabaya (31,000Rp, four hours), as well as Solo (42,000Rp, six hours). The bus terminal is 4km south of town along Jl Veteran (2000Rp by *angkot* from the centre). *Angkudes* run from the western end of Jl Merdeka to Panataran temple for 3000Rp, passing close to Makam Bung Karno; you'll have to walk the last 300m or so.

Blitar has a few useful train connections. Heading west, the *Matarmaja* leaves at 4.42pm from Blitar to Solo, Semarang, Cirebon and Jakarta (50,000Rp, 13 hours), and east at 5.54am for Malang. Or the *Gajayana* runs to Jakarta (from 270,000Rp, 11½hours) via Solo and Yogya at 5.56pm.

Hiring a car and driver makes a lot of sense to see the sights around town; the Hotel Tugu Blitar can organise this for 400,000Rp per day.

## PANATARAN

The **Hindu temples** (admission by donation; ☺ temple complex 7am-5pm) at Panataran are the largest intact Majapahit temples, and the finest examples of East Javanese architecture and sculpture. Construction began in 1197, during the Singosari dynasty, with building work continuing for another 250 years. Most of the important surviving structures date from the great years of the Majapahit kingdom during the 14th century.

Around the base of the first-level platform, the comic-strip carvings tell the story of a test between the fat, meat-eating Bubukshah and the thin, vegetarian Gagang Aking.

Further on is the small Dated Temple, so called because of the date '1291' (AD 1369) carved over the entrance. On the next level are colossal serpents snaking endlessly around the Naga Temple, which once housed valuable sacred objects.

At the rear stands the Mother Temple, whose lowest panels depict stories from the Ramayana. Behind is a small royal *mandi* with a frieze depicting lizards, bulls and dragons around its walls.

Three hundred metres beyond the turn-off to the temples, the **Museum Panataran** (admission by donation; 8am-2pm Tue-Thu, Sat & Sun, to 11am Fri) has an impressive collection of statuary from the complex, but labelling is poor.

Panataran is 16km from Blitar (4000Rp by bus), and 3km north of the village of Nglegok.

## GUNUNG KELUD

Around 30km directly north of Panataran, **Gunung Kelud** (1731m) is one of Java's most active, accessible and rewarding volcanoes to visit, with a plunging crater, steaming vents and a small crater lake. Kelud is in a near-permanent state of growl – an eruption in 1919 killed 5000 people and one in 2007 sent smoke 2.5km into the air and created a new cone within the caldera.

To get to the crater itself you have to walk through a 200m tunnel, built under the Japanese occupation. A path snakes up the side of the crater to a viewpoint of the whole scene.

Entrance to Gunung Kelud is controlled at a **gateway** (admission 15,000Rp; 6.30am-4pm Mon-Fri, 6am-5pm Sat-Sun) 10km before the summit because of the active nature of the beast.

There's no public transport to Kelud; the nearest village served by *angkot* from Blitar is Watus, from where you'll have to hire an *ojek* (around 25,000Rp) to the entrance gateway, and another (50,000Rp return) up to the car park close to the summit. If you can afford it, it's far easier to get there with your own wheels.

## PACITAN

☎ 0357

A long way from anywhere, the small south-coast town of Pacitan lies near the border with Central Java, on a horseshoe bay ringed by rocky cliffs. Pacitan's **Pantai Ria Teleng**, 4km from town, has golden sand and some surf. Swimming is possible when the seas are calm – the safest area is towards the fishing boats at the southwestern end of the bay, where there is also a swimming pool.

Pacitan has several banks with ATMs and a warnet on the main street. The helpful **Tourist Information Office** ( ☎ 885 326; Jl WR Suprapmanto;

7am-3pm Mon-Thu, to 11am Fri) is 2km from Hotel Pacitan.

The beach is the main reason to visit Pacitan, and home to **Happy Bay Beach Bungalows** ( ☎ 881 474; r 70,000Rp, private bungalows 85,000Rp), which has comfortable accommodation, and bicycles (15,000Rp) and motorbikes (50,000Rp) for hire. Otherwise, **Srikandi** ( ☎ 881 252; Jl A Yani 67; r with TV & fan/air-con 100,000/145,000Rp; ) is a good choice, overlooking rice paddies on the western edge of the town. It has a restaurant.

### Getting There & Away

Buses run here from Solo (26,000Rp, 4½ hours) and also from Ponorogo (12,000Rp, two hours) via a scenic road. From Ponorogo, direct buses go to Blitar (21,000Rp, three hours).

Pacitan's bus terminal is 500m from the centre of town on the road to Solo and the beach. Buses from Solo pass the turn-off to the beach and can drop you there.

## AROUND PACITAN

At Punung village, on the Solo road 30km northwest of Pacitan, is the turn-off to the limestone caves of **Goa Putri**, 2km away, and the much more impressive **Gua Gong**, 8km from the highway, the largest and most spectacular cave system in the area.

The more famous **Gua Tabuhan** (Musical Cave) is 4km north on the highway beyond Punung, and then another 4km from there. This huge limestone cavern is said to have been a refuge for the 19th-century guerrilla leader Prince Diponegoro. Guides will give an excellent 'orchestral' performance by striking rocks against stalactites, each in perfect pitch, and echoing pure gamelan melodies. The concert lasts about 10 minutes. You must hire a guide and lamp.

This is also agate country, and hawkers sell reasonably priced polished stones and rings.

## PROBOLINGGO

☎ 0335 / pop 180,000

Probolinggo has a rep as a producer of Java's finest mangoes, but for most travellers it's a bustling, featureless transit point on the route to Gunung Bromo. You won't want to hang around here long.

### Information

The main post office and most of the banks are on Jl Suroyo, which leads off the main street (Jl Panglima Sudirman) to the train station.

---

### PROBOLINGGO PROBLEMS

Of all the bus terminals in Java, Probolinggo's has the worst reputation. It's by no means dangerous, just not very honest. Travellers have reported problems with arranging onward tickets, particularly at night, when overcharging is the norm. Even what looks like a reputable ticket agent may charge double or even triple the standard price. The best thing to do is find the bus you need and pay the fare on board; at least you'll have a chance to compare prices with other passengers. Also, when travelling to Probolinggo, make it clear to the ticket collector you want to be dropped off at the Bayuangga bus terminal; we've received letters from travellers complaining of being left at random travel agents and charged exorbitant fares for bus tickets.

Thieves are common on the buses in East Java, especially on buses departing from Probolinggo.

---

## Sleeping & Eating

**Hotel Bromo Permai** ( ☎ 422 256; Jl Panglima Sudirman 327; r 65,000Rp, with air-con 90,000-180,000Rp; ✖ 💻 ) It's on a mega-busy street, but the plain, clean rooms are all situated well to the rear around a garden where noise is not an issue. There's a warnet and good travel info, and breakfast is included.

**Hotel Paramita** ( ☎ 421 535; Jl Siaman 7; r incl breakfast 75,000-225,000Rp; ✖ ) Just off the town's main drag, this place's bunkerlike entrance is very unappealing, but its accommodation is set to the side around a lovely peaceful garden. It's worth paying a little extra here for a better room.

**Sumber Hidup** ( ☎ 421 413; Jl Dr Mosh Saleh 2; mains 12,000-25,000Rp; ⏱ 11.30am-10pm) Serves filling Chinese food, including sweet-and-sour pork, and Indonesian dishes. Doubles as an ice-cream parlour.

**Restaurant Malang** (Jl Panglima Sudirman 104; mains from 15,000Rp) Has a big menu and cold beer.

## Getting There & Away

### BUS

Probolinggo's Bayuangga bus terminal is located about 5km from town on the road to Gunung Bromo. Yellow *angkot* run to/from the main street and the train station for 2000Rp. Buses to Banyuwangi are very frequent. Advance bookings for the long-distance executive buses will cost a little more – shop around.

From Probolinggo, buses travel to Bondowoso (15,000Rp 2½ hours) and Surabaya (economy/air-con 14,000/22,000Rp, around three hours) about every 30 minutes, though note that due to traffic chaos around Gembol (see the boxed text, p228), delays are guaranteed during rush hour and holiday periods. Other destinations covered are Malang (14,000/21,000Rp, 2½ hours), Banyuwangi (35,000/50,000Rp, five hours) via Situbondo, Yogyakarta (58,000/85,000Rp, nine hours), and Denpasar (78,000/115,000Rp, 11 hours).

### MINIBUS

Gunung Bromo minibuses leave from a stop just up from Probolinggo's Bayuangga bus terminal, heading for Cemoro Lawang (15,000Rp, two hours) via Ngadisari (12,000Rp, 1½ hours) until around 5pm. The late-afternoon buses charge more to Cemoro Lawang, when fewer passengers travel beyond Ngadisari. Make sure it goes all the way to Cemoro Lawang when you board.

### TRAIN

About 2km north of town, the train station is 6km from the bus terminal. Probolinggo is on the Surabaya–Banyuwangi line. Most services are economy class. The *Mutiara Timur* costs from 60,000/80,000Rp (business/executive) to Surabaya (departing at 1.31pm, two hours) or the same rate to Banyuwangi (departing at 11.10am, five hours). The slow economy-class *Sri Tanjung* goes west to Solo via Surabaya at 11.36am or east to Banyuwangi at 5.08pm.

### TAXI

Taxis and freelance car drivers meet trains, and wait for business at the bus station. A trip up to Cemoro Lawang costs around 180,000Rp after bargaining, more if it's late in the day.

## GUNUNG BROMO & BROMO-TENGGER-SEMERU NATIONAL PARK

☎ 0335

A lunaresque landscape of epic proportions and surreal beauty, Gunung Bromo is one of Indonesia's most breathtaking sights.

Compared with Java's other major peaks, Gunung Bromo (2392m) is a midget, but this volcano's beauty is in its setting, not its size. Rising from the guts of the ancient Tengger caldera, Bromo is one of three volcanoes to have emerged from a vast crater, stretching 10km across. Flanked by the peaks of Kursi (2581m) and Batok (2440m), the steaming cone of Bromo stands in a sea of ashen, volcanic sand, surrounded by the towering cliffs of the crater's edge. Nearby, Gunung Semeru (3676m), Java's highest peak and one of its most active volcanoes, throws its shadow – and occasionally its ash – over the whole scene.

The immense size of the crater, the supernatural beauty of the scenery and the dramatic highland light really are something very special indeed. Mercifully, Bromo has completely escaped the tacky commercialism that besmirches many Indonesian beauty spots. And though the local Tengger people may press you into accepting a horse ride across the crater bed, there's little in the way of serious hassle, and it's still very easy to connect spiritually with this sacred peak.

## Orientation & Information

Probolinggo is the usual access point, but Bromo can be approached from a number of routes, including Wonokitri from the northwest and Ngadas from the southwest. At any time of year it's cold on these mountains and night temperatures can drop to single figures.

Whichever approach you take, an entrance fee of 25,000Rp is payable. Information is available from the **PHKA post** ( ☎ 541 038; 🕒 8am-3pm Tue-Sun), opposite Hotel Bromo Permai in Cemoro Lawang, and at the **PHKA post** ( ☎ 0343-571 048; 🕒 8am-3pm Tue-Sun) on the southern outskirts of Wonokitri. Both extend their opening hours during busy periods. The park's official office is located in Malang (p234).

There's a BNI ATM close to the crater lip in Cemoro Lawang.

## Activities

Gunung Bromo is at its ethereal best at sunrise, when the colours are most impressive, and virtually all tours are planned to enable you to experience the mountain at this time. But visibility is usually good throughout the day in the dry season, even though the slopes

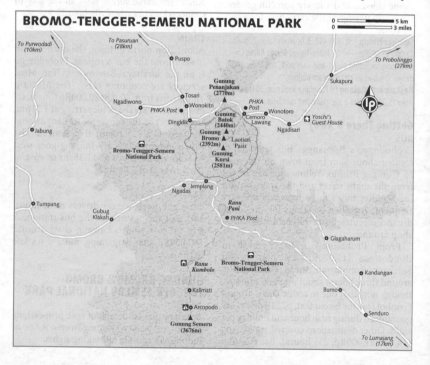

### BROMO-TENGGER-SEMERU NATIONAL PARK

---

### THE LEGENDS OF BROMO

Unsurprisingly, the eerie landscape of Bromo and its neighbouring volcanoes has spawned countless myths and legends. It is said that the Tengger crater was originally dug out with just half a coconut shell by an ogre smitten with love for a princess.

But Bromo is of particular religious significance to the Hindu Tengger people, who still populate the massif and first fled here to escape the wave of Islam that broke over the Majapahit kingdom in the 16th century. The Tengger believe that Bromo once fell within the realm of the childless King Joko Seger and Queen Roro Anteng, who asked the god of the volcano for assistance in producing an heir. The god obliged, giving them 25 children, but demanded that the youngest, a handsome boy named Dian Kusuma, be sacrificed to the flames in return. When the queen later refused to fulfil her promise, the young Dian bravely sacrificed himself to save the kingdom from retribution.

Today, the mountain is appeased during the annual Kasada festival (the park's PHKA offices can tell you when it occurs during the year), when local Tenggerese come to Bromo to throw offerings of vegetables, chickens and money into the crater of the volcano.

---

below Cemoro Lawang may be covered in mist. Later in the day you'll also avoid the dawn crowds, especially during busy holiday periods. In the wet season it's often bright and clear at dawn but quickly clouds over.

### PROBOLINGGO APPROACH

This is the easiest and most popular route. From Probolinggo, it's 28km to Sukapura, then another 7km to Ngadisari and then 3km to Cemoro Lawang. Minibuses ply the route all the way to Cemoro Lawang from Probolinggo.

Most people get up at around 4am and head up to the neighbouring peak of **Gunung Penanjakan** (2770m), which offers the best vistas (and photographs) of the entire Bromo landscape, with Gunung Semeru puffing away on the horizon. Hired 4WDs (around 275,000Rp for a sunrise tour) climb up to Penanjakan for dawn. Alternatively, it is two hours on foot. After sunrise, 4WDs head back down the steep lip of the crater and then over the Laotian Pasir (Sand Sea) to the base of Bromo.

If you want to just hike to Bromo from Cemoro Lawang, it's a 3km (40-minute) walk down the crater wall and across the eerie Laotian Pasir to the slopes of Bromo. White stone markers are easy to follow during the day but can be more elusive in the dark. Make sure you climb the right cone (!); Bromo has a stone staircase. Some hikers, disorientated in the dark, have attempted to climb neighbouring Batok.

After ascending the 253 steps you'll come face to face with the steaming, sulphurous guts of the volcano. From the lip there are sweeping views back across the Laotian Pasir to the lip of the crater and over to Batok and the Hindu temple (this only opens on auspicious days in the pilgrim calendar) at its base.

From Cemoro Lawang, trekkers can also take an interesting walk across the Laotian Pasir to Ngadas (8km), on the southern rim of the Tengger crater. You'll need to start early in order to get to Malang by evening.

### WONOKITRI APPROACH

Small tour groups come this way to do the trip to Gunung Penanjakan, which can be reached by sealed road, or by a 4WD, which can drive all the way to the base of Bromo. Wonokitri can be approached from Pasuruan on the main northern highway, or coming from Malang you can turn off at Purwodadi just after Lawang.

From Pasuruan take an *angkot* to Puspo (7000Rp) and then another to Tosari (5000Rp), 36km from Pasuruan. From the Purwodadi turn-off, catch an *angkot* to the market town of Nongkojajar (7000Rp) then an *ojek* to Tosari (20,000Rp to 25,000Rp). Note that the latter route is not a common tourist trail, so you may have to hunt for an *ojek* to take you the last leg.

From Tosari market another *ojek* will take you to Wonokitri (10,000Rp), from where 4WDs can be hired for the last stretch to Bromo (300,000Rp, less in the afternoon), including a side trip to Gunung Penanjakan. Cheaper *ojek* can also be hired (75,000Rp to Penanjakan).

From Wonokitri, it's 5km along a good road to Dingklik on the edge of the crater, from where superb views can be had. From Dingklik the road forks – down to Bromo or 4km up along the paved road to Gunung Penanjakan for even better views. From Penanjakan a walking trail leads to Cemoro Lawang. The 6km paved road from Dingklik down to the Laotian Pasir is very steep but spectacular. From the bottom it is then 3km across the sand to Bromo.

## NGADAS APPROACH

It is also possible to trek into the crater from Ngadas (at 2140m one of the highest in- habited villages in Java) to the southwest of Gunung Bromo, although it is more often done in the reverse direction as a trek out from Bromo or as an approach to climbing Gunung Semeru. This is definitely a trek for those willing and able to rough it a bit, but it is very rewarding.

Transport to the area is erratic and only available in the morning. From Malang take a *mikrolet* to Tumpang (p237), or from Surabaya take a bus to Blimbing, just north of Malang, then a *mikrolet* to Tumpang. From here take another *mikrolet* to Gubug Klakah (4000Rp), from where it's 12km to Ngadas (this track is only suitable for 4WD vehi- cles). From Ngadas it is 2km to Jemplang at the crater rim, and then three hours on foot (12km) across the floor of the Tengger crater to Gunung Bromo and on to Cemoro Lawang. From Jemplang, you can also head south for the Gunung Semeru climb.

## CLIMBING GUNUNG SEMERU

Part of the huge Tengger Massif, the classic cone of Gunung Semeru is the highest peak in Java, at 3676m. Also known as Mahameru (Great Mountain), it is looked on by Hindus as the most sacred mountain of all and the father of Gunung Agung on Bali.

Semeru is one of Java's most active peaks and has been in a near-constant state of erup- tion since 1818. In 1981, 250 people were killed during one of its worst eruptions, and it exploded as recently as March 2009. At the time of writing the mountain was open to climbers, but this situation could change at any time; check with the local tourist office, other travellers or the nearest *pos pengama- tan* (observation post) for Gunung Semeru's status.

It's a rough three-day trek to the summit, and you must be well equipped and prepared for camping overnight. Nights on the moun- tain are freezing and inexperienced climbers have died of exposure. The best time to make the climb is May to October.

Hikers usually come through Tumpang in the west, from where you can charter 4WDs to Ranu Pani (550,000Rp return), the start of the trek. If you want to do it economically under your own steam, take a minibus from Tumpang to Gubug Klakah, and then hike up the 12km to Ngadas, and then on to Jemplang. It is also possible to cross the Laotian Pasir from Gunung Bromo (12km) to Jemplang, from where you take the road that skirts around the crater rim before heading south to Ranu Pani (6km, 1½ hours on foot).

Ranu Pani is a lake with a small village nearby. Pak Tasrip runs a homestay cost- ing 90,000Rp per person (meals are served). He can help organise a climb of Gunung Semeru, and he also rents out sleeping bags, which are essential. Ranu Pani is the usual overnight rest spot, and the Ranu Pani **PHKA post** ( ☎ Tumpang office 0341-787 972) is towards the lake. Hikers *must* register with the PHKA, who will have the latest info about condi- tions. Guides (from 200,000Rp for one day; 95,000Rp for porters) are not essential but recommended.

The main trail begins behind the PHKA post. This newish trail is lined with scrubby growth but is an easier walk than the old trail, which is steeper. Both trails lead to Ranu Kumbolo crater lake (2400m), 13km or 3½ hours from Ranu Pani. From Ranu Kumbolo, which has a shelter, the trail climbs to Kalimati (three hours), at the foot of the mountain. From Kalimati it is a steep 1½-hour climb to Arcopodo, where there is a camp site for the second night on the mountain.

From Arcopodo, it is a short, steep climb to the start of the volcanic sands, and then a tough three-hour climb through loose scree to the peak. Semeru explodes every half-hour and these gases and belching lava make the mountain dangerous – stay well away from vents. On a clear day, there are breathtak- ing views of Java's north and south coasts, as well as vistas of Bali. To see the sunrise it is necessary to start at 2am for the summit. It is possible to make it back to Ranu Pani on the same day.

## Sleeping & Eating

### CEMORO LAWANG

On the lip of the Tengger crater overlooking Bromo, Cemoro Lawang is the most popular place to stay. There's not much choice and hotel prices are inflated, but it's an attractive, relaxed little place and the cool climate can come as quite a relief. Rates increase at weekends and during high season (by around 20%). For some reason the village is plagued by flies, though it's not dirty.

**Cemara Indah Hotel** ( ☎ 541 019; old block r with/ without mandi from 170,000/50,000Rp, with air-con, TV & hot water 350,000Rp; ⊠ ) Enjoys a great position on the edge of the crater, but the staff can be a bit tour-pushy and the so-so rooms are not great value.

**Hotel Bromo Permai I** ( ☎ 541 049; economy r 99,000Rp, cottages with hot shower from 240,000Rp) Ageing but reasonable cottages with porches and a huge log cabin–style restaurant with a slightly pricey menu.

**Cafe Lava Hostel** ( ☎ 541 020; r with shared bath from 100,000Rp, with breakfast & hot shower 200,000-350,000Rp) Tumbling down the side of the mountain, this is the best base in town for travellers, with a sociable vibe and English-speaking staff. Unfortunately, it's jacked up its rates steeply in the last few years. Economy rooms have been renovated and are clean and neat if bare, while the smarter rooms are attractive (all have little porches with valley views). The restaurant serves up filling, inexpensive Indonesian and Western grub and Bintang, and is the best place in town to get a group together for the 4WD ride up Penanjakan.

**Lava View Lodge** ( ☎ 541 009; www.globaladventure indonesia.com/lava view lodge.htm; r 350,000Rp, bungalows from 400,000Rp) This is a well-run hotel located 500m along a side road on the eastern side of the village. Annoyingly, management has ramped prices right up here – due to the lack of competition it's the only decent midranger in town – but it's still a decent place, even if rates are too steep. At least the views are superb, wooden rooms comfortable, staff are helpful and the large restaurant is good.

There are a couple of warungs near the PHKA office.

### NGADISARI & WONOTORO

**Yoschi's Guest House** ( ☎ 0335-541 018; yoschi_bromo@ telkom.net; r with/without shower 170,000/90,000Rp, cottages with hot water from 330,000Rp; ▢ ) A friendly, hospitable place with loads of character, this alpine chalet–style place has a good vibe, tasty food and friendly staff. Rooms are a little small but comfortable, and there's a peaceful garden. Tours and transport for the 4km to Bromo (50,000Rp person) are also offered.

**Java Banana** ( ☎ 0335-541 193; www.java-banana .com; r 650,000-2,000,000Rp) A gorgeous, supersleek new mountain lodge, about 3km from Cemoro Lawang in Wonotoro village. Largely built from wood, with accommodation that's of a very high standard – many rooms are not large but are superbly finished at least. There's a fine cafe-restaurant, and a sauna and spa is planned. Check out the stunning gallery here, which exhibits very fine photography.

### TOSARI & WONOKITRI

It's possible to stay with villagers in Wonokitri or at the **Surya Nata Homestay** (r from 100,000Rp). Wonokitri's PHKA office can help with this.

**Bromo Cottages** ( ☎ 0343-571 222; www.bromocottages .com; r from 600,000Rp, cottages from 750,000Rp) With a great aspect from its hillside location in Tosari, Bromo Cottages is a large resort with pleasant but dated rooms and cottages, plus a restaurant. Transport and tours to Bromo can be set up.

## Getting There & Away

Probolinggo (see p245) is the main gateway to Bromo. Hotels in Cemoro Lawang and Ngadisari can book long-distance bus tickets from Probolinggo to Yogyakarta (125,000Rp to 140,000Rp) and Denpasar (125,000Rp to 140,000Rp).

Travel agencies in Solo and Yogyakarta book minibuses to Bromo (from 110,000Rp; see p189 for more information about options from Yogya). These are not luxury minibuses, and sometimes they run a bigger bus to Probolinggo and change there. Tours to Bromo are easily organised in Malang, and you can also arrange 4WD hire in hotels and travel agents there.

## BONDOWOSO

☎ 0332 / pop 73,000

Bondowoso, 34km southwest of Situbondo, is one of the cleanest towns in Java – itself an attraction – and the home of some of the island's best *tape*, a tasty, sweet-and-sour snack made from boiled vegetable roots. It's merely a transit point for nearby attractions such as Ijen but does have banks with ATMs and internet facilities. Tours to Ijen can be organised here.

**Hotel Anugerah** ( ☎ 421 870; Jl Sutoyo 12; r 75,000Rp, with TV/air-con 100,000/150,000Rp; ✖ ) A friendly place run by a hospitable Christian family, this hotel has a wide selection of rooms. All have slightly odd colour schemes but are clean and most are spacious. Good home-cooked meals (around 12,000Rp) are available and trips to Ijen (500,000Rp return) are offered.

**Palm Hotel** ( ☎ 421 201; www.palm-hotel.net; Jl A Yani 32; r with fan & mandi/air-con from 80,000/200,000Rp; ✖ ⏰ ) Just south of the huge, grassy *alun-alun*, this is a fine hotel with immaculate, modern rooms, many with excellent facilities, a lovely pool and rooftop bar. The restaurant is one of the best in town and transport to Ijen can be arranged. A very complex discount scheme is used here – just make sure you get one!

*Tape* can be found on Jl PB Sudirman, where dozens of shops sell it by the basket (15,000Rp). The '321' brand is reportedly the best.

There are many (cramped) minibuses to Ijen (17,500Rp), all leaving before noon, for the 2½-hour trip. Other destinations from Bondowoso include Jember (6000Rp, 45 minutes), Probolinggo (15,000Rp, two hours) and Surabaya (normal/air-con 32,000/45,0000Rp, five hours).

## IJEN PLATEAU

The fabled Ijen Plateau is a vast volcanic region dominated by the three cones of Ijen (2368m), Merapi (2800m) and Raung (3332m). A beautiful and thickly forested alpine area, these thinly populated highlands harbour coffee plantations and a few isolated settlements – Gunung Ijen is Javanese for 'Lonely Mountain'. Access roads to the plateau are poor, and perhaps because of this visitor numbers are low.

Virtually everyone that does come is here for the hike up to the spectacular crater lake of Kawah Ijen. But with sweeping vistas and a temperate climate, the plateau could make a great base for a few days up in the clouds away from the crowds.

## Sights & Activities
### KAWAH IJEN HIKE

The magnificent turquoise sulphur lake of Kawah Ijen lies at 2148m above sea level and is surrounded by the volcano's sheer crater walls. Ijen's last major eruption was in 1936, though a minor ash explosion occurred in 1952. At the edge of the lake, sulphurous smoke billows out from the volcano's vent and the lake bubbles when activity increases.

Ijen is a major sulphur-gathering centre (see the boxed text, below) and you'll pass the collectors as you hike up the trail. Most now ask for a fee for photographs, though a cigarette will usually be accepted as payment.

The ideal time to make the Kawah Ijen hike is in the dry season between April and October, but though the path is steep, it's not too slippy so it's certainly worth a try in rainy season if you have a clear day. Make it for sunrise if you can.

The starting point for the trek to the crater is the **PHKA post** ( ⏰ 7am-5pm) at Pos Paltuding, which can be reached from Bondowoso or Banyuwangi. Sign in and pay your 15,000Rp entry fee here. The steep 3km path up to the observation post (where there's a tea house) takes just over an hour; keep an eye out for gibbons. From the post it's a further

---

**A HEAVY LOAD**

The Ijen volcano produces a lot of sulphur, and around 300 collectors (all men) work here, getting up at between 2am and 4am to hike up the crater to hack out the yellow stuff by hand. Their only protection against the cone's noxious fumes are cotton scarfs, which they tie around their noses. These DIY miners then spend the next six or so hours scurrying back down the volcano with loads of 60kg to 80kg on their backs.

It's incredibly tough work that pays very little (around 600Rp per kilo), and yet the physical exercise keeps the collectors incredibly fit – few report health problems despite breathing great lungfuls of sulphurous fumes virtually every day of their lives. A 72-year-old still climbs Ijen most days and locals say there's a centurion living in the village. Ijen sulphur is used for cosmetics and medicine, and is added to fertilizer and insecticides. Historically, sulphur was commonly called brimstone.

30-minute walk to the lip of the wind-blasted crater and its stunning views.

From the crater, a steep, gravelly path leads down to the sulphur deposits and the steaming lake. The walk down takes about 30 minutes; the path is slippery in parts and the sulphur fumes towards the bottom can be overwhelming. Take great care – a French tourist fell and died some years ago.

Back at the lip of the crater, turn left for the climb to the crater's highest point (2368m) and magnificent views, or keep walking anticlockwise for even more expansive vistas of the lake. On the other side of the lake, opposite the vent, the trail disappears into crumbling volcanic rock and deep ravines.

### COFFEE PLANTATIONS

Java's finest coffee, both arabica and robusta varieties, is produced in the Ijen Plateau area, as well as cacao, cloves and rubber. It's possible to visit various coffee plantations, including **Kebun Kalisat** (admission 50,000Rp) and **Kebun Balawan** (admission free); visits will usually include a wander through coffee groves and an impromptu tour of the plantation's factory. The latter plantation has thermal pools and a gushing thermal waterfall (2000Rp) set among lush jungle. Both plantations have accommodation.

## Sleeping & Eating

You'll find a couple of store-warungs at the PHKA post where you can get hot tea or a snack.

**Pos Paltuding** (dm 50,000Rp, r 120,000Rp, Pesanggrahan cottages 350,000Rp) The PHKA post at the start of the Kawah Ijen hike has a bare, chilly cottage with three comfortable rooms. There's no hot water and blankets are not provided, so bring a sleeping bag. The post also has an open-sided shelter for campers.

**Arabika** ( ☎ 0811 350 5881, 0828-330 1347; r incl breakfast from 125,000-245,000Rp) The Kebun Kalisat coffee plantation maintains this pleasant guest house, 1km from the main road. There are three choices of rooms, ranging from bare but serviceable to spacious and comfortable; all have hot water and a bathtub in which to enjoy it. Service is friendly, meals are served, and there's ping pong. It's at Sempol, 13km before Pos Paltuding on the Bondowoso side.

**Kartimore** ( ☎ 0813 3619 9110; r 175,000-300,000Rp; 🐾 ) These rooms are located in the Kebun

Balawan coffee plantation some 7km from Sempol. There are quite respectable, clean rooms in a long row, or for a real (if very faded) colonial experience sleep in the original Dutch lodge, which dates back to 1894. There's a spring-fed hot tub; the swimming pool is chilly. Meals are served and tours are available. An *ojek* from Sempol is about 20,000Rp.

**Jampit Villa** ( ☎ 031-352 4893, Jember 0331-486 861; ptpn12@rad.net.id; villa 1,000,000Rp; 🐾 ) Kebun Kalisat coffee plantation owns this luxurious villa, 14km south of Sempol at Jampit. The villa sleeps 20 and has a kitchen and a communal living room. Book through PT Perkubunan Nusantara XII ( ☎ 0331-486 861; Jl Gajah Mada 249) in Jember.

**Ijen Resort** ( ☎ 0333-773 3338; www.ijendiscovery .com; Dusun Randuagung, Licin; r from US$115, ste US$195; 🐾 ) In the remote eastern foothills of the Ijen Plateau, this top-end resort has magnificent views over rice terraces. Rooms are more than inviting, with stone floors, open-air bathrooms and vistas of the Ijen cones or Bali. There's fine cooking in the restaurant, while tours and transport can be fixed. The resort is about 25 minutes from Banyuwangi on the road up to Ijen. Add 21% tax to room rates.

Sempol village has a couple of warungs if you need a place to eat. Pos Paltuding has a small shop for provisions and a cafe serving little more than noodles.

## Getting There & Away

It is possible to travel nearly all the way to Kawah Ijen by public transport, but most visitors charter transport.

### FROM BONDOWOSO

From Wonosari, 8km from Bondowoso towards Situbondo, a badly potholed road runs via Sukosari and Sempol all the way to Pos Paltuding. It's in poor shape and slow going, but a 4WD was not necessary at the time of research. Sign in at the coffee-plantation checkpoints (around 4000Rp) on the way. Both the Palm Hotel and Hotel Anugerah in Bondowoso (p249) can arrange day tours.

Several minibuses run from Bondowoso to Sempol (17,500Rp, 2½ hours), but only until noon. You should be able to find someone in Sempol who will take you the 13km to Pos Paltuding on the back of their motorbike for around 35,000Rp one way. At Pos Paltuding,

coverage here. Staff can provide meals (around 12,000Rp), but it's safer to bring your own food – you can stock up in Sarongan, or the Sukamade estate in the nearby plantation has a shop selling basic supplies. If you have your own equipment, you can also camp on the beach (15,000Rp per tent).

**Wisma Sukamade** ( ☎ 0331-484 711; r from 120,000Rp) Approximately 5km north of the beach, Sukamade plantation has good-quality accommodation with electricity and all the creature comforts. It has a variety of rooms and meals are provided. However, it's not as convenient unless you have your own transport or are on a tour.

### Getting There & Away

It is a long, bumpy trip to Meru Betiri, even by 4WD vehicle.

The most direct way to Sukamade from Banyuwangi or Jember is to first take a bus to Jajag (14,000Rp, 1½ hours), then a minibus to Pesanggaran (8000Rp, one hour). From Pesanggaran take a taxi (the local name for a public truck) to Sukamade (25,000Rp, two hours). The taxi leaves Pesanggaran at noon on the dot (a rarity in Java); to make it on time, you'll need to leave Jember around 6.30am.

The taxi passes through Sarongan, a small town where you can stock up on supplies. *Ojeks* to Sukamade (around 60,000Rp) can be arranged here, but generally only in the dry season; during the wet the rivers are impassable. There are two river crossings: the deeper one further south and the shallower crossing further upstream. If the river is up but not flooded, you can wade across and get another *ojek* or walk the 4km to Mess Pantai. The taxi has no problem with swollen rivers unless there is severe flooding.

About 4km on from Sarongan you reach the Rajegwesi PHKA post at the entrance to the park; this is a good place to check on the condition of the river.

## ALAS PURWO NATIONAL PARK

This 434-sq-km national park occupies the whole of the remote Blambangan Peninsula on the southeastern tip of Java. Facilities are limited and it is not easy to reach, but Alas Purwo has fine beaches, good opportunities for wildlife spotting, and savannah, mangrove and lowland monsoon forests. Apart from day trippers and local beach parties on weekends, the park gets few visitors.

Alas Purwo means First Forest in Javanese – according to legend, this is where the earth first emerged from the ocean. Many soul-searchers and mystics flock here during the month of Suro, which marks the Javanese New Year. These pilgrims meditate in caves and pray to Nyai Loro Kidul. **Pura Giri Selokah**, a Hindu temple in the park, also attracts many pilgrims, especially during Pagerwesi, the Hindu new year.

The huge surf at Plengkung, on the isolated southeastern tip of the peninsula, forms one of the best left-handed waves in the world, breaking over a shallow reef in a perfect tube. Surfers have dubbed it **G-Land** (for Grajagan, another name for the area). It's best between April and September.

### Orientation & Information

Surfers come by charter boat from Grajagan at the western end of the bay, but the usual park entry is by road via the village of Pasar Anyar, which has a large national park office and interpretive centre. Call in here to check on accommodation; alternatively, check with the head office (opposite) in Banyuwangi.

The actual gateway to the park is at Rowobendo, 10km south along a bad road, where you need to pay your admission fee (20,000Rp). From Rowobendo the road runs past the temple before hitting the beach at Trianggulasi, 2km away. Trianggulasi has hut accommodation but nothing else.

### Sights & Activities

This limestone peninsula is relatively flat and the rolling hills reach a peak of only 322m. Alas Purwo has plenty of lowland coastal forest but few trails to explore it – vast expanses of the eastern park are untrammelled, even by park staff.

Using Trianggulasi as a base, there are some interesting short walks. The white-sand beach here is beautiful, but swimming is usually dangerous.

The **Sadengan** grazing ground has the largest herd of wild banteng in Java, and *kijang* (deer) and peacocks are seen here from the viewing tower. This beautiful meadow backed by forest is a 2km walk from Trianggulasi along a road and then a swampy trail.

Alas Purwo also has a small population of *ajag* (Asiatic wild dogs), jungle fowl, leaf monkeys, *muntjac* deer, sambar deer and leopards. The park guards can arrange interesting, although often fruitless, night leopard-spotting expeditions for around 100,000Rp.

Guards can also arrange a motorbike trip to the turtle hatchery at **Ngagelan**, or you can walk. It's 6km from Rowobendo along a rough road, or a 7km walk along the beach at low tide from Trianggulasi.

It is also possible to walk along the beach all the way to Plengkung via **Pancur**, 3km southeast of Trianggulasi, where there is a small waterfall that flows onto the beach, another PHKA post and a camping ground.

From Pancur a trail heads 2km inland through some good forest to **Gua Istana**, a small cave, and another 2km further on to **Gua Padepokan**.

From Pancur it is a further 11km walk (two hours) around Teluk Grajagan to the fine beach at **Plengkung** and one of Asia's premier surfing spots. The surf camps at Plengkung are by no means five-star but do provide unexpected luxury in the wilderness.

## Tours

The bigger and better surf camps, away from the beach at Plengkung, are for tours only. Everyone comes on a surfing package that includes all transfers, usually from Bali.

**Bobby's Camp** ( ☎ bookings in Bali 0361-755 588; www.grajagan.com; ✎ ▣ ☎ ) The biggest camp with three standards of bungalow in shady grounds with a restaurant and bar. There's beach volleyball, and boat and fishing trips can be arranged. It's run out of Kuta, Bali, and offers three-night packages from US$350.

**G-Land Joyo's Surf Camp** ( ☎ bookings in Bali 0361-763 166; www.g-land.com; ✎ ▣ ) Good-quality thatched wooden bungalows with fan or air-con and most of the facilities a surfer could want: cold beer, a large screen for sports, pool tables, internet access and table tennis. Surf guides and a doctor are based here. Packages start at US$300 for three nights. Joyo's is open November to March only.

## Sleeping & Eating

**Pesanggrahan** ( ☎ 0333-428 675; s/d 50,000/75,000Rp) Close to the beach at Trianggulasi, this PHKA establishment has elevated bungalows. The rooms are spartan, with only a bed. Water is from a well, and electricity is provided by a generator. Though primitive, this is a lovely, relaxing spot and many who come for a day or two end up staying longer.

Staff here *may* sell supplies and cook meals in the high season, but it's best to bring all food and drink with you. Trianggulasi has no warungs and is deserted if no guests stay,

but the Pesanggrahan has a kitchen with a kerosene stove and hurricane lamps.

The PHKA office at Pasar Anyar has a shop selling basic provisions for visitors, such as packet noodles, but it is better to stock up on food at the general stores in Dambuntung, where the bus drops you. There is also a camping ground and a PHKA post at Pancur.

## Getting There & Away

From Banyuwangi's southern Brawijaya bus terminal there are buses to Kalipahit (12,000Rp, 1½ hours) via Benculuk and Tegaldelimo until 4pm. Buses can drop you at the small village of Dambuntung, where you can stock up on food. Then take an *ojek* for around 40,000Rp to 60,000Rp first to the park office in Pasar Anyar, 3km from Dambuntung, to check on accommodation, and then on to the park. The 12km road from Pasar Anyar to Trianggulasi is badly potholed but is flat and negotiable by car.

It's possible to hire 4WDs (around 700,000Rp) in Banyuwangi for one-day trips to Plengkung.

## BANYUWANGI

☎ 0333 / pop 110,000

The end of the line, Java's land's end is a pleasant-enough town, but there's no reason to hang around here.

Confusingly, the ferry terminus for Bali, bus terminal and train station are all some 8km north of town in the port of Ketapang, though all transport uses 'Banyuwangi' as a destination.

## Information

**Alas Purwo National Park head office** ( ☎ 428 675; Jl A Yani 108; ☺ 7.30am-3.30pm Mon-Thu, to 11am Fri) Two kilometres south of the town centre.

**Baluran National Park head office** ( ☎ 424 119; Jl Agus Salim 132; ☺ 7am-3.30pm Mon-Thu, to 11am Fri) Four kilometres southwest of the centre.

**Banyuwangi Tourist Office** ( ☎ 424 172; Jl Ahmad Yani 78; ☺ 7am-4pm Mon-Thu, to 11am Fri) A helpful office. Mr Aekanu ( ☎ 081 5590 5197; aekanu@plasa.com), who works here, speaks Dutch and some English and organises tours.

## Sights

One of the few sights in Banyuwangi is the **Kongco Tan Hu Cin Jin Chinese temple** (Jl Ikam Gurani 54); built in 1784, it's well worth a peek.

Banyuwangi Tourist Office has a small **museum** devoted to culture from the area.

## Sleeping & Eating

**Hotel Baru** ( ☎ 421 369; Jl MT Haryono 82-84; r with fan/air-con 50,000/110,000Rp; ✷ ) A short walk south of the *alun-alun*, this is a clean little place with friendly staff, a choice of rooms and a cafe-restaurant.

**Hotel Ketapang Indah** ( ☎ 422 280; www.ketapangindah.com; Jl Gatot Subroto, Ketapang; r from 265,000Rp, seaview r 475,000Rp; ✷ ✷ ) A stylish, well-run hotel with attractive rooms and cottages, built in traditional Javanese design in the spacious grounds of a coconut plantation. There are fine views of Bali and a large restaurant; it's 2km south of the ferry terminal.

For cheap eats, there are warungs on the corner of Jl MT Haryono and Jl Wahid Haysim.

## Getting There & Away

### BOAT

Ferries from Ketapang depart roughly every 30 minutes around the clock for Gilimanuk in Bali. The ferry costs 7500Rp for passengers, 23,700Rp for a rider and motorcycle, and 126,400Rp for a car, including driver. Through-buses between Bali and Java include the fare in the bus ticket and are the easiest option.

Pelni ships no longer call at Banyuwangi.

### BUS

Banyuwangi has two bus terminals. The Sri Tanjung terminal is 3km north of the Bali ferry terminal at Ketapang, and 11km north of town. Buses from this terminal travel to northern destinations, such as Baluran (8000Rp, one hour), Probolinggo (normal/*patas* 35,000/50,000Rp, five hours) and Surabaya (36,000/51,000Rp, seven hours). Buses also go right through to Yogyakarta (*patas* 115,000Rp, 15 hours) and Denpasar (from 45,000Rp, five hours including the ferry trip).

Brawijaya terminal (also known as Karang Ente), 4km south of town, has most of the buses to the south. These include Kalipahit (12,000Rp, 1½ hours), Kalibaru (14,000Rp, two hours) and Jember (21,000Rp, three hours).

### TRAIN

The main Banyuwangi train station is just a few hundred metres north of the ferry terminal.

The express *Mutiara Timur* leaves at 9am and 10.20pm for Probolinggo (4½ hours) and Surabaya (business/executive 60,000/80,000Rp, 6½ hours). Economy-class trains include the *Sri Tanjung*, which leaves at 6am for Yogyakarta (41,000Rp, 17 hours).

# BALURAN NATIONAL PARK

Baluran National Park harbours an amazingly diverse range of ecosystems in a 250-sq-km chunk of northeastern Java. Extensive grasslands cover parts of the park, providing rich grazing for Javanese wild oxen (banteng), *kijang* and water buffalos and making it ideal terrain for Africa-style safari excursions in 4WDs. You should see a wide range of wildlife here.

Large sections of this prime savannah were taken over by acacia thorn scrub (which was introduced as a fire break), but park rangers are steadily clearing this prickly invader from Baluran and the grasslands are reclaiming lost ground.

All kinds of tours can be organised: safari trips, hiking up the Baluran crater, visiting local villages to learn about home industries, and snorkelling on offshore coral reefs.

## Orientation & Information

Wonorejo, on the main coast road between Surabaya and Banyuwangi, is the main service town for the park and has stores for food supplies. You'll find the **PHKA office** ( ☎ 0333-461 650; ⏱ 7am-5pm) on the highway, where guides can be arranged for around 200,000Rp per day. The park's head office (p255) is in Banyuwangi. Entrance costs 20,000Rp and an extra 6000Rp is charged for a car.

Baluran can be visited at any time of the year, but the dry season (June to November) is usually the best time because the animals congregate near the waterholes at Bekol and Bama.

## Sights & Activities

Baluran is rich in wildlife and supports important populations of around 500 Timor deer and 200 banteng, plus sambar deer, *muntjac* deer, two species of monkey, and wild boars. Visit in July and August and you may see male Timor deer rutting for breeding rights.

The park is home to leopards, but there have only been two recent sightings. Bird life is excellent, with green peafowl, red and green jungle fowl, hornbills, white-bellied woodpeckers and bee-eaters all quite easy to see.

On the hill above the guest houses at Bekol there is a viewing tower that provides a panoramic view over a 300-hectare clearing. Banteng and deer can be seen here, and wild dogs can sometimes be seen hunting, usually in the early morning. There are walking trails around Bekol.

Bama, on the coast, is a 3km walk or drive from Bekol. It has accommodation and a beach with coral offshore that offers fair **snorkelling**. It's a popular weekend retreat for local families, but it's peaceful at other times. Watch out for the cheeky long-tailed macaques here, who have been known to pinch food.

The nearby coastal forest has numerous waterholes and is a good place to see water monitor lizards and sometimes wild boars.

Rosa's Ecolodge offers several **tours** of Baluran: wildlife-watching trips in specially converted 4WDs (600,000Rp), snorkelling (600,000Rp), bicycling trips and hikes to the Baluran crater.

## Sleeping

Bookings can be made in advance through the Baluran National Park head office (p255) in Banyuwangi. Most visitors tend to day trip, so accommodation is often available, but it pays to book, especially in the peak June to August holiday period.

At Bekol, 12km into the park, **Pesanggrahan** (per person 25,000Rp) has six basic rooms; there's a *mandi* and kitchen here. Bekol also has two *wisma* (guesthouse); **Wisma Tamu** (beds per person 45,000Rp) has three simple rooms with attached *mandis*, while **Wisma Peneliti** (beds per person 60,000Rp) is a little more comfortable.

Bama beach, 3km east of Bekol, also has simple losmen. **Bama Guesthouse** (beds per person 35,000Rp) is a very basic option with cooking facilities (bring your own food). **Rumah Panggung** (cottages 200,000Rp) is bigger, newer and cosier but closer to the waterhole than the beach.

**Rosa's Ecolodge** ( ☎ 0338-453 005; www.rosasecolodge .com; Ds Sidomulyo RT 03/03, Sumberwaru; r incl breakfast 350,000Rp; 🐾 🖳 ) This guest house is run by Rene and Rosa, who are passionate and informative about the Baluran, and good hosts. The spacious rooms are immaculately kept, with tiled floors you could eat off, bathrooms with Western toilets, and front porches. Buffet-style meals of tasty Javanese food are served in the charming restaurant. This homestay is very much geared to guests booking its (quite pricey) Baluran tours, with profits channelled into community development and education, so priority is given to tour-bookers during busy times. It's on the northern edge of the park in the village of Sumberwaru.

The canteen at Bekol sells drinks and packet noodles, but meals are cooked only for groups of 10 or more.

## Getting There & Away

Surabaya to Banyuwangi buses taking the coast road via Probolinggo all pass right by the (almost hidden) park entrance. From Banyuwangi it's only a half-hour journey (5000Rp). Coming from the west, Baluran is four hours from Probolinggo.

PHKA rangers at the entrance can arrange an *ojek* (around 30,000Rp) to take you the next 12km to Bekol; the road is poor but usually passable in a Kijang 4WD or high-clearance car.

# Bali

**BALI**

Impossibly green rice terraces, pulse-pounding surf, enchanting Hindu temple ceremonies, mesmerising dance performances, ribbons of beaches, a truly charming people: there are as many images of Bali as there are flowers on the ubiquitous frangipani trees.

This small island – you can drive the entire coast in one day – looms large for any visit to Indonesia. No place is more visitor-friendly. Hotels range from surfer dives where the fun never stops to sybaritic retreats in the lush mountains. The shopping, from hackneyed baubles to designer duds will put 'extra bag' at the top of your list. You can dine on local foods bursting with flavours fresh from the markets or let a world-class chef take you on a culinary journey around the globe. From a cold Bintang at sunset to an epic night clubbing, your social whirl is limited only by your own fortitude. And when comes time to relax, you can get a cheap beach massage or lose yourself in an all-day spa.

And small obviously doesn't mean homogeneous. Manic Kuta segues into luxurious Seminyak. The artistic swirl of Ubud is a counterpoint to misty treks amid the volcanoes. Mellow beach towns like Amed, Lovina and Pemuteran are found right round the coast and just offshore is the laid-back idyll of Nusa Lembongan.

As you stumble upon the exquisite little religious offerings that seem to materialise everywhere as if by magic, you'll see that their tiny tapestry of colours and textures is a metaphor for Bali itself.

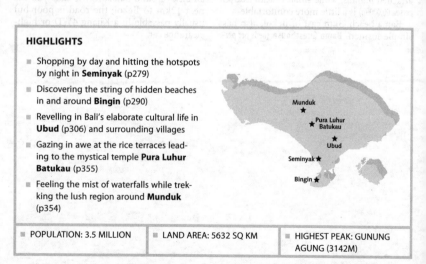

## HIGHLIGHTS

- Shopping by day and hitting the hotspots by night in **Seminyak** (p279)

- Discovering the string of hidden beaches in and around **Bingin** (p290)

- Revelling in Bali's elaborate cultural life in **Ubud** (p306) and surrounding villages

- Gazing in awe at the rice terraces leading to the mystical temple **Pura Luhur Batukau** (p355)

- Feeling the mist of waterfalls while trekking the lush region around **Munduk** (p354)

★ Munduk
★ Pura Luhur Batukau
★ Ubud
★ Seminyak
★ Bingin

| ■ POPULATION: 3.5 MILLION | ■ LAND AREA: 5632 SQ KM | ■ HIGHEST PEAK: GUNUNG AGUNG (3142M) |

# HISTORY

It's certain that Bali has been populated since early prehistoric times, but the oldest human artefacts found are 3000-year-old stone tools and earthenware vessels from Cekik. Not much is known of Bali during the period when Indian traders brought Hinduism to the Indonesian archipelago, but the earliest written records are stone inscriptions dating from around the 9th century. By that time, rice was being grown under the complex irrigation system known as *subak,* and there were precursors of the religious and cultural traditions that can be traced to the present day.

## Hindu Influence

Hindu Java began to spread its influence into Bali during the reign of King Airlangga, from 1019 to 1042. At the age of 16, Airlangga had fled into the forests of western Java when his uncle lost the throne. He gradually gained support, won back the kingdom once ruled by his uncle and went on to become one of Java's greatest kings. Airlangga's mother had moved to Bali and remarried shortly after his birth, so when he gained the throne there was an immediate link between Java and Bali. At this time, the courtly Javanese language known as Kawi came into use among the royalty of Bali, and the stunning rock-cut memorials seen at Gunung Kawi near Tampaksiring (p323) are a clear architectural link between Bali and 11th-century Java.

After Airlangga's death, Bali retained its semi-independent status until Kertanagara became king of the Singasari dynasty in Java two centuries later. Kertanagara conquered Bali in 1284, but his power lasted only eight years until he was murdered and his kingdom collapsed. With Java in turmoil, Bali regained its autonomy and the Pejeng dynasty, centred near modern-day Ubud, rose to great power. In 1343 Gajah Mada, the legendary chief minister of the Majapahit kingdom, defeated the Pejeng king Dalem Bedaulu and brought Bali back under Javanese influence.

Although Gajah Mada brought much of the Indonesian archipelago under Majapahit control, Bali was the furthest extent of its power. Here the 'capital' moved to Gelgel, near modern-day Semarapura (once known as Klungkung), around the late 14th century, and for the next two centuries this was the base for the 'king of Bali', the Dewa Agung. The Majapahit kingdom collapsed into disputing sultanates. However, the Gelgel dynasty in Bali, under Dalem Batur Enggong, extended its power eastwards to the neighbouring island of Lombok and even crossed the strait to Java.

As the Majapahit kingdom fell apart, many of its intelligentsia moved to Bali, including the priest Nirartha, who is credited with introducing many of the complexities of Balinese religion to the island. Artists, dancers, musicians and actors also fled to Bali at this time, and the island experienced an explosion of cultural activities. The final great exodus to Bali took place in 1478.

## European Contact

The first Europeans to set foot in Bali were Dutch seafarers in 1597. Setting a tradition that prevails to the present, they fell in love with the island, and when Cornelius Houtman – the ship's captain – prepared to set sail from Bali, some of his crew refused to leave with him. At that time, Balinese prosperity and artistic activity, at least among the royalty, were at a peak, and the king who befriended Houtman had 200 wives and a chariot pulled by two white buffaloes, not to mention a retinue of 50 dwarfs. When the Dutch returned to Indonesia in later years, they were interested in profit, not culture, and barely gave Bali a second glance.

## Dutch Conquest

In 1710 the capital of the Gelgel kingdom was shifted to nearby Klungkung (now called Semarapura), but local discontent was growing, lesser rulers were breaking away from Gelgel domination and the Dutch began to move in, using the old policy of divide and conquer. In 1846 the Dutch used Balinese salvage claims over shipwrecks as the pretext to land military forces in northern Bali. In 1894 the Dutch chose to support the Sasaks of Lombok in a rebellion against their Balinese raja. After some bloody battles, the Balinese were defeated in Lombok, and with northern Bali firmly under Dutch control, southern Bali was not likely to retain its independence for long. Once again, salvaging disputes gave the Dutch the excuse they needed to move in. A Chinese ship was wrecked off Sanur in 1904 and ransacked by the Balinese. The Dutch demanded that the raja of Badung (southern Bali) pay 3000 silver dollars in damages – this was refused. In 1906 Dutch warships appeared at Sanur; Dutch forces landed and, despite Balinese opposition, marched the 5km to the outskirts of Denpasar.

BALI

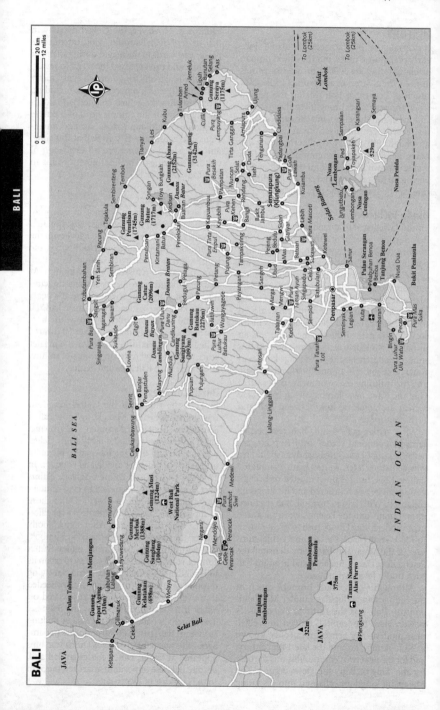

On 20 September 1906, the Dutch mounted a naval bombardment of Denpasar and then commenced their final assault. The three rajas of Badung realised that they were outnumbered and outgunned, and that defeat was inevitable. Surrender and exile, however, was the worst imaginable outcome, so they decided to take the honourable path of a suicidal *puputan* – a fight to the death.

The Dutch begged the Balinese to surrender rather than make their hopeless stand, but their pleas went unheard and wave after wave of the Balinese nobility marched forward to their deaths. In all, nearly 4000 Balinese died in the *puputan*. Later, the Dutch marched east towards Tabanan, taking the raja of Tabanan prisoner, but he committed suicide rather than face the disgrace of exile.

The kingdoms of Karangasem and Gianyar had already capitulated to the Dutch and were allowed to retain some powers, but other kingdoms were defeated and the rulers exiled. Finally, the raja of Klungkung (p327) followed the lead of Badung and once more the Dutch faced a *puputan*. With this last obstacle disposed of, all of Bali was now under Dutch control and became part of the Dutch East Indies. Dutch rule over Bali was short-lived, however, as Indonesia fell to the Japanese in WWII.

### Independence

On 17 August 1945, just after WWII ended, the Indonesian leader Sukarno proclaimed the nation's independence, but it took four years to convince the Dutch that they were not going to get their great colony back. In a virtual repeat of the *puputan* nearly half a century earlier, a Balinese resistance group was wiped out in the Battle of Marga on 20 November 1946; Bali's airport, Ngurah Rai, is named after its leader. It was not until 1949 that the Dutch finally recognised Indonesia's independence.

The huge volcanic eruption of Gunung Agung in 1963 killed thousands, devastated vast areas of the island and forced many Balinese to accept transmigration to other parts of Indonesia. Two years later, in the wake of the attempted communist coup, Bali became the scene of some of the bloodiest anticommunist killings in Indonesia. These were perhaps inflamed by some mystical desire to purge the land of evil, but also came about because the radical agenda of land

reform and abolition of the caste system was a threat to traditional Balinese values. The brutality of the killings was in shocking contrast to the stereotype of the 'gentle' Balinese.

### Modern Bali

The tourism boom, which started in the early 1970s, has brought many changes, and has helped pay for improvements in roads, telecommunications, education and health. Though tourism has had some marked adverse environmental and social effects, Bali's unique culture has proved to be remarkably resilient. Beginning in the 1990s there has been vocal public opposition to some controversial tourist developments, which indicates that Balinese people will play a more active role in the development of their island.

Bali, like most places, has also been affected by global politics. In October 2002, two simultaneous bomb explosions in Kuta – targeting an area frequented by tourists – injured or killed more than 500 people (p273). Tourism (meaning the economy) was devastated and was dealt another blow in 2005 when more bombs went off, albeit with less loss of life. Since then however, Bali has been on a roll. It elected the hero of the 2002 bombing investigations, Made Pastika, governor. A record two million visitors turned up in 2008 and development is everywhere. People are starting to ask: 'Can we be too popular?'

## CULTURE

Bali's culture strips the cliché from the word unique. The version of Hinduism practiced with great fervour is found no place else in the world and has inspired fervent artistic expressions that charms visitors.

The population in Bali is almost all Indonesian; 95% are of Balinese Hindu descent and could be described as ethnic Balinese. The remaining residents are mostly from other parts of the country, particularly Java.

Balinese have traditional caste divisions that resemble the Indian Hindu system, although there are no 'untouchables'. Nor is there separation of labour based on caste, except for the Brahmana priesthood. Over 90% of the population belong to the common Sudra caste, which now includes many wealthy Balinese. The main significance of caste is in religious roles and rituals, and its influence on Balinese language.

The traditional Balinese society is intensely communal; the organisation of villages, the cultivation of farmlands and even the creative arts are communal efforts. A person belongs to their family, clan, caste and to the village as a whole. The roles of the sexes are fairly well delineated, with certain tasks handled by women and others reserved for men. For instance, the running of the household is very much the woman's task, while caring for animals is mostly a male preserve.

Balinese society is held together by collective responsibility. If a woman enters a temple while menstruating, for instance, it is a kind of irreverence, an insult to the gods, and their displeasure falls not just on the transgressor but on the whole community. This collective responsibility produces considerable pressure on the individual to conform to *adat* – the traditional values and customs that form the core of society.

## Religion

You can't get away from religion in Bali – there are temples in every village, shrines in every field and offerings made at every corner.

The Balinese are nominally Hindus, but Balinese Hinduism is half-a-world away from that of India. When the Majapahits evacuated to Bali they took with them their religion and its rituals, as well as their art, literature, music and culture. The Balinese already had strong religious beliefs and an active cultural life, and the new influences were simply overlaid on existing practices – hence the peculiar Balinese interpretation of Hinduism.

The Balinese worship the same gods as the Hindus of India – the trinity of Brahma, Shiva and Vishnu – but they also have a supreme god, Sanghyang Widi. Unlike in India, the trinity is never seen – a vacant shrine or empty throne tells all. Nor is Sanghyang Widi often worshipped, though villagers may pray to him when they have settled new land and are about to build a new village. Other Hindu gods such as Ganesh, Shiva's elephant-headed son, may occasionally appear, but a great many purely Balinese gods, spirits and entities have far more relevance in everyday life.

The Balinese believe that spirits are everywhere, an indication that animism is the basis of much of their religion. Good spirits dwell in the mountains and bring prosperity to the people, while giants and demons lurk beneath the sea, and bad spirits haunt the woods and desolate beaches. The people live between these two opposites and their rituals strive to maintain this middle ground. Offerings are carefully put out every morning to pay homage to the good spirits and nonchalantly placed on the ground to placate the bad ones.

### TEMPLES

The word for temple is *pura*, which is a Sanskrit word meaning 'a space surrounded by a wall'. As in so much of Balinese religion, the temples, though nominally Hindu, owe much to the pre-Majapahit era. Their *kaja, kelod* or *kangin* (alignment towards the mountains, the sea or the sunrise) is in deference to spirits that are more animist than Hindu.

Almost every village has at least three temples. The most important is the *pura puseh* (temple of origin), which is dedicated to the village founders and is at the *kaja* end of the village. In the middle of the village is the *pura desa* for the spirits that protect the village community in its day-to-day life. At the *kelod* end of the village is the *pura dalem* (temple of the dead). The graveyard is also here and the temple will often include representations of Durga, the terrible incarnation of Shiva's wife.

Families worship their ancestors in family temples, clans in clan temples and the whole village in the *pura puseh*. Certain temples in Bali are of such importance that they are deemed to be owned by the whole island rather than by individual villages. These include Pura Besakih (p329) on the slopes of Gunung Agung, the most revered place in Bali, often called 'The Mother Temple'.

The simple shrines or thrones you see – for example, in rice fields or next to sacred old trees – are not real temples, as they are not walled. You'll find these shrines in all sorts of places, often overlooking intersections or dangerous curves in the road to protect road users.

For much of the year Balinese temples are deserted, but on holy days it's believed that the deities and ancestral spirits descend from heaven to visit their devotees, and the temples come alive with days of frenetic activity and nights of drama and dance. Temple festivals come at least once every Balinese year (210

### TOP FIVE TEMPLES

- Pura Luhur Ulu Watu (p291), on the Bukit Peninsula, one of Bali's nine directional temples, with a spectacular cliff-top location.

- Pura Tirta Empul (p323) at Tampaksaring, renowned for its beauty and nearby springs and bathing pools.

- Pura Luhur Batukau (p355) on the slopes of Gunung Batukau, with its cool, misty atmosphere.

- Pura Kehen (p326), state temple of the Bangli kingdom and miniature version of Pura Besakih.

- Pura Maduwe Karang (p358), near Kubutambahan, an elaborate seaside temple with some surprising carvings.

days). Because most villages have at least three temples, you're assured of at least five or six annual festivals in every village. The full-moon periods, around the end of September to the beginning of October, or early to mid-April, are often times of important festivals. Galungan-Kuningan is a 10-day festival when *lots* of activity takes place at family and community temples all over the island.

## Arts

The Balinese had no words for 'art' and 'artist' because, traditionally, art has never been regarded as something to be treasured for its own sake. Prior to the tourism boom, art was just part of everyday life, and what was produced went into temples, palaces or festivals. Although respected, the painter or carver was not considered a member of some special elite, the artist's work was not signed and there were no galleries or craft shops.

It's a different story today, with thousands of art outlets tucked into every possible crevice. Although much Balinese art is churned out quickly as cheap souvenirs, buried beneath the reproductions of reproductions there's still much beautiful work to be found.

Even the simplest activities are carried out with care, precision and artistic flair. Just glance at those little offering trays thrown down on the ground for the demons every morning – each one a throwaway work of art. Look at the temple offerings, the artistically stacked pyramids of fruit or other beautifully decorated foods. Look for *penjor*, long decorated bamboo poles at doorways during festivals, the woven decorative palm-leaf strips called *lamak*, stylised female figures known as *cili* and the intricately carved coconut-shell wall-hangings.

Most visitors to the island discover the greatest concentration of the arts in and around Ubud (p306).

### BALINESE PAINTING

The art form most influenced both by Western ideas and tourist demand is painting. Traditional painting was very limited in style and subject matter, and was used primarily for temple decoration. The arrival of Western artists following WWI introduced new subject matters and materials with which artists could work.

Traditional Balinese painting was strictly limited to three basic kinds: *langse, iders-iders*

BALI

**TOP FIVE BALI READS**

The stacks of books about Bali are like coconuts on trees, there are so many they could easily topple over and hit you on the head. However, here's five you'll enjoy before or during your stay.

*Eat, Pray, Love* by Elizabeth Gilbert is a publishing sensation. Fans of the lurid, self-absorbed prose flock to Ubud looking for their own prince.

Diana Darling's *The Painted Alphabet* is based on a Balinese epic poem with all the usual ingredients: good, evil, a quest, baby-swapping and various mystical events. It's a gentle and beguiling way to get your head into Balinese folklore.

*A House in Bali* by Colin McPhee is the timeless classic about a Canadian who experienced Balinese cultural and village life to the core in the 1930s.

*Gecko's Complaint* is a morality tale presented as an old Balinese children's fable. The recent Periplus edition is richly illustrated.

*Bali Blues* by Jeremy Allan is a highly readable tale of love set in the tumultuous year after the 2002 bombings. It contains many an insight into life on the island.

and calendars. *Langse* are the large, rectangular hangings used as decoration or curtains in palaces or temples. *Iders-iders* are scroll paintings that are hung along the eaves of temples. The calendars are usually astrological, showing the auspicious days of each month.

Most of the paintings were narratives with mythological themes, illustrating stories from Hindu epics and literature. Paintings were executed in the *wayang* style – the flat two-dimensional style that imitates the *wayang kulit* (shadow puppets), with the figures invariably shown in three-quarter view. The colours that artists could use were strictly limited to a set list of shades (red, blue, brown, yellow and light ochre for flesh).

In these narratives the same characters appeared in several different scenes, each depicting an episode from the story. The individual scenes were usually bordered by mountains, flames or ornamental walls. The deities, princes and heroes were identified by opulent clothing, jewellery, elaborate headdresses and by their graceful postures and gestures; and the devils and giants by their bulging eyes, canine teeth, bulbous noses and bulky bodies. As always, Ubud is the place to both ponder the best paintings in museums (p307) and to sift through the works of many in galleries.

## ARCHITECTURE

Architecture has an important role in Bali that transcends the mere visual and gets to the heart of matters spiritual. Much of the unique look of Bali's architecture has deep religious and cultural significance. For more, see p65.

## SCULPTURE

In small or less-important temples, sculpture may be limited or even nonexistent, while in other temples – particularly some of the exuberantly detailed temples of northern Bali – it may be almost overwhelming in its detail and intricacy. Throughout the island you will see elaborate carved stone decorations and accents. These are relatively easy to produce with the soft local stones.

## WOODCARVING

Especially around Ubud, woodcarvers produce highly stylised and elongated figures, leaving the wood in its natural state rather than painting it, as was the traditional practice. Others carve delightful animal figures, some totally realistic and others wonderful caricatures, while other artists carve whole tree trunks into ghostly, intertwined 'totem poles' or curiously exaggerated and distorted figures.

## DANCE

Many visitors are seduced by the haunting and melodic charms of a dance performance in Ubud (p320), a quintessential Bali experience.

Music, dance and drama are closely related in Bali. In fact, dance and drama are synonymous, though some 'dances' are more drama and less dance, and others more dance and less drama.

Balinese dance tends to be precise, shifting and jerky, like the accompanying gamelan music, which has abrupt shifts of tempo and dramatic changes between silence and crashing noise. There's virtually no physical contact in Balinese dancing – each dancer moves independently, but every movement of wrist, hand and finger is important. Even facial expressions are carefully choreographed to convey the character of the dance.

The dances are a blend of seriousness and slapstick. Basically, they are straightforward ripping yarns, where you cheer the goodies and boo the baddies. Some dances have a comic element, with clowns who counterbalance the staid, noble characters. The clowns often have to convey the story to the audience, since the noble characters may use the classical Javanese Kawi language, while the clowns (usually servants of the noble characters) converse in Balinese.

Dances are a regular part of almost every temple festival, and Bali has no shortage of these. There are also dances virtually every night at tourist centres, although the most authentic are found in and around Ubud.

### Kecak

One of the best-known dances of Bali is the Kecak. It is unusual because it does not have a gamelan accompaniment. Instead, the background is provided by a chanting 'choir' of men who provide the 'chak-a-chak-a-chak' noise that distinguishes the dance.

The Kecak tells the tale of the Ramayana, the quest of Prince Rama to rescue his wife Sita after she had been kidnapped by Rawana, the King of Lanka. Rama is accompanied to Lanka by Sugriwa, the king of the monkeys, with his monkey army. Throughout the Kecak dance, the circle of men, all bare-chested and wearing checked cloth around their waists, provide a nonstop accompaniment, rising to a crescendo as they play the monkey army and fight it out with Rawana and his cronies. The chanting is accompanied by the movements of the monkey army whose members sway back and forth, raise their hands in unison, flutter their fingers and lean left and right, all with an eerily exciting coordination.

### Barong & Rangda

The Barong Keket is half shaggy dog, half lion – and is played by two men in much the same way as a circus clown-horse. Its opponent is the *rangda* (witch).

The Barong represents good and protects the village from the *rangda*, but is also a mischievous creature. It flounces into the temple courtyard, snaps its jaws at the gamelan, dances around and enjoys the acclaim of its supporters – a group of men with kris. Then the *rangda* makes her appearance, with long tongue lolling, pendulous breasts wobbling, human entrails draped around her neck, fangs protruding from her mouth and sabre-like fingernails clawing the air.

The two duel with their magical powers, and the Barong's supporters draw their kris and rush in to attack the witch. The *rangda* puts them in a trance and the men try to stab themselves, but the Barong also has great magical powers and casts a spell that stops the kris from harming the men. This is the most dramatic part of the dance – as the gamelan rings crazily the men rush back and forth, waving their kris around, all but foaming at the mouth, sometimes even rolling on the ground in a desperate attempt to stab themselves. Finally, the *rangda* retires defeated – good has won again. Good must always triumph over evil in Bali, and no matter how many times the spectators have seen the performance or how well they know the outcome, the battle itself remains all-important.

### Legong

This is the most graceful of Balinese dances and, to connoisseurs of Balinese dancing, the one of most interest.

There are various forms of the Legong but the Legong Kraton (Legong of the Palace) is the one most often performed. A performance involves just three dancers – the two Legongs and their 'attendant' known as the Condong. The Legongs are identically dressed in tightly bound gold brocade. So tightly are they encased that it's something of a mystery how they manage to move with such agility and speed. Their faces are elaborately made up, their eyebrows plucked and repainted, and their hair decorated with frangipanis.

The dance relates how a king takes a maiden, Rangkesari, captive. When Rangkesari's brother comes to release her, he begs the king to let her free rather than go to war. The king refuses and on his way to the battle meets a bird bringing ill omens. He ignores the bird and continues on to meet Rangkesari's brother, who kills him. The dance, however, relates only the lead up to the battle and ends with the bird's appearance. When the king leaves the stage he is going to the battle that will end in his death.

BALI

The dance starts with an introduction by the Condong. She departs as the Legongs enter. The Legongs dance solo, in close identical formation, and even in a mirror-image formation when they dance a nose-to-nose love scene. They relate the king's sad departure from his queen, Rangkesari's request that he release her and the king's departure for battle. Finally, the Condong reappears with tiny golden wings as the bird of ill-fortune and the dance ends.

### GAMELAN

As in Sumatra and Java, Balinese music is based around the gamelan orchestra. The whole gamelan orchestra is known as a *gong* – an old fashioned *gong gede* or a more modern *gong kebyar*. There are even more ancient forms of the gamelan, such as the *gong selunding*, still occasionally played in Bali Aga villages like Tenganan.

Although the instruments used are much the same, Balinese gamelan is very different from the more gentle, reserved and formal form you'll hear in Java. Balinese gamelan often sounds like everyone is going for it full pelt. In Java gamelan music is rarely heard except at special performances, whereas in Bali you'll hear gamelan playing everywhere you go.

## GETTING THERE & AWAY

For important visa information, see p839.

### Air

The only airport in Bali, Ngurah Rai Airport (DPS) is just south of Kuta, however it is sometimes referred to internationally as Denpasar (which is 15km north) or on some internet flight booking sites as Bali.

The airport is modern; renovations planned for 2010 will greatly expand it. Services include, internet centres, upscale lounges, left-luggage, ATMs, exchange counters etc.

The **domestic terminal** ( ☎ 0361-751011) and **international terminal** ( ☎ 0361-751011) are a few hundred metres apart.

International airlines flying to and from Bali include:

**AirAsia** (AK; ☎ 0361-760116; www.airasia.com; ticket office outside international terminal) Serves Kota Kinabalu, Kuala Lumpur and Kuching in Malaysia, connects to London.

**Cathay Pacific Airways** (CX; ☎ 0361-766931; www.cathaypacific.com) Serves Hong Kong.

**China Airlines** (CI; ☎ 0361-754856; www.china-airlines.com) Serves Taipei.

**Eva Air** (BR; ☎ 0361-751011; www.evaair.com) Serves Taipei.

**Garuda Indonesia** (GA; Map pp298-9; ☎ 0361-227824; www.garuda-indonesia.com; Jl Sugianyar 5, Denpasar) Serves Australia and major cities in Asia direct.

**Japan Airlines** (JL; ☎ 0361-757077; www.jal.co.jp) Serves Tokyo.

**Jetstar/Qantas Airways** (QF; Map p286; ☎ 0361-288331; www.qantas.com.au; Grand Bali Beach Hotel, Sanur) Serves Australia.

**Korean Air** (KE; ☎ 0361-768377; www.koreanair.com) Serves Seoul.

**Lion Air** (JT; ☎ 0804-177 8899; www.lionair.co.id) Serves Singapore.

**Malaysia Airlines** (MH; ☎ 0361-764995; www.mas.com.my) Serves Kuala Lumpur.

**Pacific Blue** (DJ; ☎ +61 7 3295 2296; www.flypacificblue.com) Offshoot of Australia's Virgin Blue.

**Singapore Airlines** (SQ; Map p270; ☎ 0361-768388; www.singaporeair.com; GOI Bldg, Airport Parking Lot) Several Singapore flights daily.

**Thai Airways International** (TG; Map p286; ☎ 0361-288141; www.thaiair.com; Grand Bali Beach Hotel, Sanur) Serves Bangkok.

Domestic services in Bali seem to be in a constant state of flux. However competition is fierce and you can usually find flights to a range of destinations for under US$100. The best thing to do is to go to the airport and shop at the airline ticket offices. Often you'll come close to long-distance bus and ferry fares. Places served often from Bali include Jakarta, Surabaya, Lombok, Yogyakarta, Bima, Maumere, Bandung, Kupang and more.

**AirAsia** (AK; www.airasia.com) Fast-growing Malaysian-based budget carrier with a web of Indonesian domestic flights.

**Batavia Air** (7P; www.batavia-air.co.id) Serves numerous destinations; has the enigmatic slogan: 'Trust us to fly'.

**Garuda Indonesia** (GA; www.garuda-indonesia.com) The national carrier serves numerous cities.

**Lion Air** (JT; www.lionair.co.id) Fast-expanding budget carrier has a web of services across the archipelago; carried the most passengers in 2008.

---

### DEPARTURE TAX

The departure tax from Bali and Lombok is 30,000Rp domestic and 150,000Rp international. Have the exact amount for the officer.

**Mandala Airlines** (RI; www.mandalaair.com) Serves major routes.

**Merpati Airlines** (MZ; www.merpati.co.id) Serves many smaller Indonesian cities, in addition to the main ones.

## Bus
### JAVA

Many buses from numerous bus companies travel daily between the Ubung terminal in Denpasar and major cities in Java (via ferry); most travel overnight. Fares vary between operators, and depend on what sort of comfort you want – it's worth paying extra for a decent seat and air-con. For details, see p300.

## Sea
### JAVA

Ferries operate between Gilimanuk in western Bali and Ketapang (Java), see p346.

### LOMBOK

This island is accessible by regular public boat from Padangbai, see p331. Fast boats for tourists serve the Gili Islands (p492).

### OTHER INDONESIAN ISLANDS

The Pelni ship *Kelimutu* wanders the archipelago on a month-long route that links Bali (Benoa Harbour; p289) with Surabaya and then Bima, Makassar, Ambon, Banda, Tual and points further east. Prices are dependent on the route and the class of travel, and this can vary widely in price. Check for details locally but in general, fares, even in 1st class, are very low, eg Bali to Surabaya on Java is US$35.

You can inquire and book at the **Pelni offices** in Tuban (Map p270; ☎ 0361-763963, 021-7918 0606; www.pelni.co.id; Jl Raya Kuta 299; ☉ 8am-noon & 1-4pm Mon-Fri, 8am-1pm Sat) and at the harbour in Benoa (Map p270; ☎ 0361-721377; ☉ 8am-4pm Mon-Fri, 8am-12.30pm Sat).

## GETTING AROUND

Bali is a small island with good roads and regular, inexpensive public transport. Traffic is heavy throughout the south and east as far as Semarapura and west across to the port of Gilimanuk. Roads are more pleasant on the rest of the island. If you rent your own vehicle, it's generally not hard to find your way around – main roads have some signs and maps are readily available. Off the main routes, most roads are surfaced but often potholed and signage is not good.

It's worth noting that many pricier restaurants in places such as South Bali and Ubud will arrange free transport to/from the establishment. Just ask.

## To/From the Airport

From the official counters, just outside the airport terminals, there are supposedly fixed-price taxis. However, efforts may be made to charge you at the high end of each range and if you say you don't have a room booking, there will be heavy pressure to go to a commission-paying hotel. The costs are (depending on drop-off point):

| Destination | Cost |
| --- | --- |
| Denpasar | 70,000-90,000Rp |
| Jimbaran | 75,000-95,000Rp |
| Kuta Beach | 45,000-50,000Rp |
| Legian | 55,000-65,000Rp |
| Nusa Dua | 95,000-105,000Rp |
| Sanur | 95,000Rp |
| Seminyak | 70,000-80,000Rp |
| Ubud | 195,000-225,000Rp |

If you have a surfboard, you'll be charged at least 35,000Rp extra, depending on its size. Ignore any touts that aren't part of the official scheme. Many hotels will offer to pick you up at the airport, however there's no need to use this service if it costs more than the above rates.

The thrifty can walk from the international and domestic terminals across the airport car park to the right (northeast) and continue a couple of hundred metres through the vehicle exit to the airport road (ignoring any touts along the way), where you can hail a regular cab for about half the above amounts.

Any taxi will take you to the airport at a metered rate that should be much less than the taxis from the airport.

## Bemo

Most of Bali's public transport is provided by cramped minibuses, usually called bemo, but on some longer routes the vehicle may be a full-sized bus. Denpasar is the transport hub of Bali and has bus/bemo terminals for all the various destinations. Travel in southern Bali often requires travelling via one or more of the Denpasar terminals, which can make for an inconvenient and time-consuming trip.

The fare between main towns may be posted at the terminals, or you can ask around. You can also flag down a bemo pretty much anywhere along its route; you will likely be charged the *harga turis* (tourist price). Ask a local the correct fare before starting a journey, or watch what people pay and give the same when you get off. Local rides cost a minimum of 4000Rp.

Note that as seemingly everyone on Bali has bought a motorbike, the bemo/bus network has suffered. Service hours are short and frequencies may be few.

Beware of pickpockets on bemos – they often have an accomplice to distract you, or use a package to hide the activity.

## Bicycle

A famous temple carving (p358) shows the Dutch artist WOJ Nieuwenkamp pedalling through Bali in 1904. Bali's roads have improved greatly since then and more and more people are touring the island by *sepeda* (bicycle). Many visitors are using bikes around the towns and for day trips in Bali. Ask at your accommodation about where you can rent a good bike; hotels often have their own. Generally, prices range from 20,000Rp to 30,000Rp per day.

## Boat

Boats of various sizes serve Nusa Lembongan (p304) and Nusa Penida (p305) from Benoa Harbour, Sanur and Padangbai.

## Car & Motorcycle

A small Suzuki or Toyota 4WD is the typical rental vehicle in Bali. Typical costs are 150,000Rp to 180,000Rp per day, including insurance and unlimited kilometres but not including fuel. Hiring a car with driver will cost around 350,000Rp to 600,000Rp for an eight- to 10-hour day.

Motorcycles are a popular way to get around Bali, but can be dangerous. Most rental motorcycles are between 90cc and 125cc, with 100cc being the usual size. Rental charges vary with the bike, period of hire and demand. The longer the hire period the lower the rate; the bigger or newer the bike the higher the rate. Typically you can expect to pay from around 30,000 to 40,000Rp a day. This includes a flimsy helmet, which is compulsory and provides protection against sunburn but not much else.

You can arrange rentals from any place you are staying, or in tourist areas just by walking down the street. Offers will pour forth.

## Taxi

Metered taxis are common in South Bali. They are essential for getting around Kuta and Seminyak, where you can easily flag one down. Elsewhere, they're often a lot less hassle than haggling with bemo jockeys and charter drivers.

The usual rate for a taxi is 5000Rp flag fall and 4000Rp per kilometre, but the rate is higher in the evening. If you phone for a taxi, the minimum charge is 10,000Rp. Any driver who claims meter problems or who won't use it should be avoided.

By far the most reputable taxi agency is **Bali Taxi** ( ☎ 0361-701111; www.bluebirdgroup.com), which uses distinctive blue vehicles with the words 'Bluebird Group' over the windshield (watch out for fakes). Drivers speak reasonable English, won't offer you illicit opportunities and use the meter at all times. Many expats will use no other firm and the drivers are often fascinating conversationalists.

After Bali Taxi, standards decline rapidly. Some are acceptable, although you may have a hassle getting the driver to use the meter and fending off offers for shopping, massage etc.

## Tourist Shuttle Bus

Tourist shuttle buses travel between the main tourist centres in Bali and connect to destinations on Lombok. Shuttle buses are quicker, more comfortable and more convenient than public transport. But if you're with a group of three or more people (or sometimes even two), it may be cheaper to charter a vehicle.

**Perama** (www.peramatour.com) has a near monopoly on this service in Bali. At least one bus a day links the main Bali tourist centres with more frequent services to the airport. There are also services along the east coast between Lovina and Candidasa via Amed by demand.

Fares are reasonable (for example, Kuta to Lovina is 100,000Rp). Be sure to book your trip at least a day ahead in order to confirm schedules. It is important to understand where Perama buses stop as you may need to pay an extra 5000Rp to get to/from your hotel. Some routes involve changing buses.

# SOUTH BALI

For many people South Bali *is* Bali; for many others it is anything but. Chaotic Kuta and upscale Seminyak throb around the clock. In the south, the Bukit Peninsula is home to some of the island's largest resorts, while in the east Sanur follows the subdued beat of its reef-protected surf. The coasts feature a fine range of beaches.

## KUTA & LEGIAN
☎ 0361

The Kuta region is overwhelmingly Bali's largest and tackiest tourist beach resort. Most visitors come here sooner or later because it's close to the airport and has the greatest range of budget hotels, restaurants and tourist facilities. Some find the area overdeveloped and seedy, but if you have a taste for a busy beach scene, souvenir shopping and bawdy nightlife, you will probably have a great time. Go elsewhere on the island if you want an actual Balinese experience.

It is fashionable to disparage Kuta and its immediate neighbour to the north, Legian, for their rampant development, low-brow nightlife and crass commercialism, but the cosmopolitan mixture of beach-party hedonism and entrepreneurial energy can be fun. It's not pretty, but it's not dull either, and the amazing growth is evidence that a lot of people find something to like in Kuta.

Kuta has the most diversions and the best beach – but the worst traffic and most persistent hawkers.

Legian is a slightly quieter version of Kuta and seems to appeal mostly to sun-seekers who have outgrown Kuta. The hotels are slightly more genteel, as is everything else.

Tuban, a small area between Kuta and the airport to the south, is short on character but does boast several large hotels and a vast shopping centre.

### History

Mads Lange, a Danish copra trader and an adventurer of the 19th century, established a successful trading enterprise near modern Kuta, and had some success in mediating between local rajas and the Dutch, who were encroaching from the north. His business soured in the 1850s, and in 1856 he died suddenly, perhaps murdered. His grave, and a monument erected later, are near Kuta's night market.

The original Kuta Beach Hotel was started by a Californian couple in the 1930s, but closed with the Japanese occupation of Bali in 1942 during WWII. In the late 1960s, Kuta became a stop on the hippie trail between Australia and Europe, and an untouched 'secret' surf spot. Accommodation opened and by the early 1970s Kuta had a delightfully laid-back atmosphere. Enterprising Indonesians seized opportunities to profit from the tourist trade, often in partnership with foreigners who wanted a pretext for staying longer.

As Kuta expanded, Legian further north became the quiet alternative, but now you can't tell where one ends and the other begins. Immediately north again, Seminyak continues north from Legian. All this has taken its toll, and the area is a chaotic mixture of shops, bars, restaurants and hotels on a confusing maze of streets and alleys, often congested with heavy traffic, thick with fumes and painfully noisy.

### Orientation

The Kuta region is a disorienting place – it's flat, with few landmarks or signs, and the streets and alleys are crooked and often walled on one or both sides so it feels like a maze. The busy Jl Legian runs roughly parallel to the beach through Legian and Kuta. It's a two-way street in Legian, but in most of Kuta it's one way going south, except for an infuriating block near Jl Melasti where it's one way going north.

Between Jl Legian and the beach is a tangle of narrow side streets, with an amazing hodgepodge of tiny hotels, souvenir stalls, warungs (food stalls), bars, construction sites and even a few remaining coconut palms. A small lane or alley is known as a *gang*; most are unsigned and too small for cars, although this doesn't stop some drivers from trying. The best known are called Poppies Gang I and II – use these as landmarks. You'll find most of the bigger shops, restaurants and nightspots situated along Jl Legian and a few of the main streets that head towards the beach.

Many streets have more than one name. See the boxed text, p282, for more information on the confusing street names in the region.

⊗ 10am-9pm) at the Wisata Beach Inn offers a cream bath that has set the hearts of many spa-o-philes a-twitter with delight. Located off the main street, this lovely spa has very competitive prices.

## Kuta for Children

Except for the traffic, the Kuta area is a pretty good place for kids. With supervision – and sunscreen! – they can cavort on the beach for hours. Almost all the hotels and resorts above the surfer-dude category have pools.

**Amazone** (Map p270; Discovery Shopping Mall, Jl Kartika Plaza, Tuban; ⊗ 10am-10pm) Has hundreds of screeching arcade games on the top floor of the mall.

**Waterbom Park** (Map p270; ☎ 755676; www.water bom.com; Jl Kartika Plaza, Tuban; adult/child US$21/11; ⊗ 9am-6pm) Popular activities for kids at this park include waterslides and pools.

Further afield, see p313 for details on popular rafting trips in Bali's hills and p325 for info on the popular Bali Safari and Marine Park.

## Tours

A vast range of tours all around Bali, from half-day to three-day tours, can be booked through touts or hotels in Kuta. These tours are a quick and easy way to see a few sights if your time is limited and you don't want to rent or charter a vehicle. Prices range from US$25 to US$50.

## Sleeping

Kuta, Legian and Tuban have hundreds of places for you to stay. The top-end hotels are along the beachfront, midrange places are mostly on the bigger roads between Jl Legian and the beach, and the cheapest losmen (basic, often family-run, accommodation) are generally along the smaller lanes in between.

### BUDGET

The best budget accommodation is in a losmen with rooms facing a central garden. Look for a place that is far enough off the main roads to be quiet, but close enough so that getting to the beach, shops and restaurants isn't a problem. Luxuries like air-con and pools have become common, although the cheapest rooms are fan- and cold-water-only.

### Kuta

Many of the cheap places in Kuta are along the tiny alleys and lanes between Jl Legian and the beach in central Kuta. This is a good place to base yourself: it's quiet, but only a short walk from the beach, shops and nightlife. Jl Benesari is a great place to stay, close to the beach and quieter than the Poppies Gangs. Gang Sorga is another top pick, with scores of options.

**Puri Agung Homestay** (Map p272; ☎ 750054; off Poppies Gang I; s/d 30,000/50,000Rp) The budget winner in Kuta. Hungover surfers will appreciate the 12 dark, cold-water-only rooms at this attractive little place that features a tiny grotto-like garden. Nonvampires can find more light on the top floor.

**Komala Indah I** (Map p272; ☎ 753185; Jl Benesari; r 50,000-150,000Rp; ⊠) The rooms here are set around a pleasant garden; the cheapest of the 30 rooms have squat toilets, fans and twin beds only. It's part of the Komala empire that dates back to the early days of Kuta tourism.

**Kedin's II** (Map p272; ☎ 763554; Gang Sorga; s/d from 80,000/110,000Rp; ⊠ ⌨) One of the best budget choices. Here the 16 cold-water-only rooms (with showers) have hints of style and verandahs with fine views of the gardens and the good-sized pool.

**Gemini Star Hotel** (Map p272; ☎ 750558; aquariusho tel@yahoo.com; Poppies Gang II; r 90,000-185,000Rp; ⊠ ⌨) Only the monosyllabic mutterings of lounging surfers interrupt the peace at this small, quiet hotel on a narrow alley. Two two-storey blocks shelter the sunny and surprisingly large pool area. Cheap rooms have fans and hot water; more money adds air-con and fridges.

**Mimpi Bungalows** (Map p272; ☎ 751848; kumimpi @yahoo.com.sg; Gang Sorga; r 150,000-200,000Rp; ⊠ ⌨) The cheapest of the 10 bungalow-style rooms here are the best value. The private gardens boast orchids and shade, and the pool is a good size. The owner, Made Supatra, is a tireless promoter of Kuta.

### Legian

The streets are wider here and the pace is less frenetic than just south in Kuta. Budget places tend to be larger as well. Wander off the main roads for some quiet gems.

**Senen Beach Inn** (Map p272; ☎ 755470; Gang Camplung Mas 25; r 50,000-70,000Rp) In a quiet little *gang* near Jl Melasti, this 18-room, cold-water-only place is run by friendly young guys. Rooms have outdoor bathrooms and are set around a small garden. There are several other family-run cheapies hidden back here.

**Sri Beach Inn** (Map p272; ☎ 755897; Gang Legian Tewngah; r 60,000Rp) Follow a series of paths into the heart of old Legian. When you hear the rustle of palms overhead, you're close to this homestay with eight simple, clean rooms. The gardens get lovelier by the year; agree to a monthly rate and watch them grow.

## MIDRANGE

The bulk of accommodation in the Kuta area falls into the midrange category, especially in Legian. Quality varies widely, with some places offering quite a bit in terms of location, amenities and service. Leave the rest for hapless groups.

### Kuta

These places are handy to the beach.

**Suji Bungalow** (Map p272; ☎ 765804; www.suji bglw.com; off Poppies Gang I; r US$20-32; ✖ ☑ ☐ 🛜) You can have your choice of 47 bungalows and rooms in two-storey blocks set in a spacious, quiet garden around a pool (which has a slide into the kiddie area) at this cheery place. The verandahs and terraces are good for relaxing.

**Un's Hotel** (Map p272; ☎ 757409; www.unshotel .com; Jl Benesari; s/d US$26/36, with air-con US$38/45; ✖ ☑ ☐ 🛜) A hidden entrance sets the tone for the secluded feel of Un's. It's a two-storey place with bougainvillea spilling over the pool-facing balconies. The 30 spacious rooms in a facing pair of two-storey blocks (the southern one is quieter) feature antiques, comfy cane loungers and open-air bathrooms.

**Bali Bungalo** (Map p272; ☎ 755109; www.bali-bungalo .com; off Jl Pantai Kuta; r from 375,000Rp; ✖ ☑) Large rooms close to the beach yet away from irritations are a big part of the appeal of this older, 44-room hotel. It's well maintained and there are prancing statues of horses to inspire horseplay in the pool. Rooms are in two-storey buildings and have patios/porches.

**Poppies Cottages** (Map p272; ☎ 751059; www.poppies bali.com; Poppies Gang I; r US$75-100; ✖ ☑ ☐ 🛜) This Kuta institution has a lush, green garden setting for its 20 thatch-roofed cottages with outdoor sunken baths. Bed choices include kings and twins. The pool is surrounded by stone sculptures and water fountains in a garden that almost makes you forget you are in the heart of Kuta.

### Legian

Further north, many hotels have great locations on the beach. There's a crop of good-value places along Jl Lebak Bene.

**Three Brothers Inn** (Map p272; ☎ 751566; www .threebrothersbungalows.com; off Jl Padma Utara; r US$20-35, with air-con US$25-45; ✖ ☑) Twisting banyan trees shade scores of brick bungalows holding 83 rooms in the Brothers' sprawling and garden-like grounds. The fan rooms are the best option, but all rooms are spacious, some with alluring outdoor bathrooms (all have tubs). Top-end rooms have DVD players.

**Hotel Kumala Pantai** (Map p272; ☎ 755500; www.ku malapantai.com; Jl Werkudara; r US$50-70; ✖ ☑ ☐ 🛜) One of the better deals in Legian. The 108 rooms (20 in a new building) are large, with marble bathrooms that have a separate shower and tub. The three-storey blocks are set in nicely landscaped grounds across from popular Double Six beach.

**Sari Beach Inn** (Map p272; ☎ 751635; sbi@indo.net .id; off Jl Padma Utara; r US$50-90; ✖ ☑) Follow your ears down a long *gang* to the roar of the surf at this great-value beachside hotel that defines mellow. The 24 rooms have patios and the best have big soaking tubs. The grassy grounds boast many little statues and water features.

**Lokha Legian** (Map p272; ☎ 766 7601; www.thelokha legian.com; Jl Padma; r from US$90; ✖ ☑ ☐ 🛜) This modern and stylish place in Legian sets the midrange standard. The 49 rooms are not huge but neither are the prices. The closed-in, U-shaped block overlooks a large pool, and pals from Perth shout from one terrace to the next. The beach is a five-minute walk.

## TOP END

Beachfront hotels in Kuta actually front busy Jl Pantai Kuta while most of Legian's top hotels (and some more modest forms) front a fine swath of beach and a road closed to traffic – in effect, a long promenade.

### Legian

Most of the top-end places in Legian are directly opposite the beach on stretches of road closed to traffic. These tend to be relaxed places favoured by families.

**Bali Mandira Hotel** (Map p272; ☎ 751381; www .balimandira.com; Jl Pantai Kuta; r US$110-180, cottage from US$160; ✖ ☑ ☐ 🛜) Gardens filled with bird of paradise flowers set the tone at this 191-room full-service resort. Cottages have modern interiors, and the bathrooms are partly open-air. A dramatic pool at the peak of a stone ziggurat (which houses a spa) offers sweeping ocean views, as does the cafe. Wi-fi is best near reception.

BALI

**O-CE-N Bali** (Map p272; ☎ 737400; www.outrigger .com; Jl Arjuna 88X; r US$150-300; ✕ ⚘ ☐ ☎ ) Flashy but not trashy, this vowel-challenged resort looms over a very popular stretch of Double Six Beach. The 112 rooms scattered about the concrete complex range from hotel-simple to apartment-deluxe; none are far from the myriad of water features.

## Eating

There's a profusion of places to eat around Kuta and Legian. Cafes with their cheap menus of Indonesian standards, sandwiches and pizza are ubiquitous. Other forms of Asian fare can be found as well and there are numerous places serving fresh seafood. But don't expect a village experience; signs bearing come-ons like 'Bloody good tucker mate' abound.

If you're looking for the laid-back scene of a classic travellers cafe, wander the *gang* and look for the crowds. Often what's busy one night will be quiet the next. For quick snacks and 4am stubbies, Circle K convenience stores are everywhere and are open 24 hours.

### TUBAN

In most cases the best feature of the beach-front hotels for nonguests are the beachside cafes, which are good for a tropical snack or a sunset drink.

**Kafe Batan Waru** (Map p270; ☎ 766303; Jl Kartika Plaza; mains 25,000-50,000Rp) The Tuban branch of one of Ubud's best eateries (p318) is a slicked-up version of a warung (food stall), albeit with excellent and creative Asian and local fare. There's also good coffee, baked goods and magazines.

**B Couple Bar n' Grill** (Map p270; ☎ 761414; Jl Kartika Plaza; mains from 30,000Rp; ✕ 24hr) A vibrant mix of upscale local families and a swath of tourists (menus are even in Russian) tuck into Jimbaran-style grilled seafood in this slick operation. Pool tables and live music add to the din while flames flare in the open kitchens.

### KUTA
#### On the Beach

Busy Jl Pantai Kuta keeps beachside businesses to a minimum in Kuta. Beach vendors are pretty much limited to drinks.

**Kuta Food Court** (Map p272; Jl Pantai Kuta; meals from 7000Rp; ✕ 5pm-3am) A slick, modern version of a night market, this open-air collection of food stalls are as tidy as they come. Choose from a

vast array of local specialities plus seafood from Jimbaran. Dine for as little as 7000Rp with karaoke and cover bands thrown in for free (although some may say this is a cost).

### Central Kuta

**Kuta night market** (Map p272; Jl Blambangan; dishes 5000-15,000Rp; ✕ 6pm-midnight) This enclave of stalls and plastic chairs bustles with locals and tourism workers chowing down on hot-off-the-wok treats, grilled goods and other fresh foods.

**Made's Warung** (Map p272; ☎ 755297; Jl Pantai Kuta; dishes 15,000-90,000Rp) Made's was the original tourist warung in Kuta. Through the years, the Westernised Indonesian menu has been much copied. Classic dishes such as *nasi campur* (rice served with side dishes) are served with attitude and authority. Although not the hub it once was, Made's is still a pleasant spot.

**Poppies Restaurant** (Map p272; ☎ 751059; Poppies Gang I; dishes 30,000-100,000Rp; ☎ ) Right on its namesake *gang*, long-running Poppies is popular for its lush garden setting, which has a timeless romance. The menu combines upscale Western (avocado and shrimp) and Balinese (your own little grill of sate) tastes.

### Along Jalan Legian

The eating choices along Jl Legian seem endless, but avoid tables close to the busy street.

**Aroma's Café** (Map p272; ☎ 751003; Jl Legian; dishes 20,000-45,000Rp) A gentle garden setting encircled by water fountains is a perfect place to start the day over great juices, breakfasts and coffee. Other times the menu has good versions of Western and Indonesian classics.

**Kopi Pot** (Map p272; ☎ 752614; Jl Legian; dishes 25,000-60,000Rp; ☎ ) Shaded by trees, Kopi Pot is a favourite, popular for its coffees, milkshakes and desserts. The multilevel, open-air dining area sits back from noxious Jl Legian.

### On & Near Poppies Gang II

**Rainbow Cafe** (Map p272; ☎ 765730; Poppies Gang II; mains from 20,000Rp) Join generations of Kuta denizens quaffing the afternoon away. Deeply shaded, the vibe here is little changed in years. Many current customers are the offspring of backpackers who met at adjoining tables.

**Alleycats** (Map p272; ☎ 08 1747 65148; off Poppies Gang II; dishes 20,000-40,000Rp) Homesick Brits can tuck into a Sunday roast or a breakfast replete with beans at this shady cafe in a courtyard off the Poppies II madness.

BALI

**Balcony** (Map p272; ☎ 757409; Jl Benesari 16; dishes 20,000-80,000Rp) The Balcony has a breezy tropical design and sits above the din of Jl Benesari below. Get ready for the day with a long menu of eggs and pancakes. At night there's something for everyone, although the grilled steak and seafood skewers are a speciality.

### LEGIAN
Some of the beachside hotels have restaurants – often Italian – with nice views. Better still is the clutch of places at the end of Jl Double Six that afford views of sandy action by day, strolling fun-seekers by night and sunsets in between. Along the streets of Legian, the ho-hum mix with the superb, so take your time choosing.

**Warung Yogya** (Map p272; ☎ 750835; Jl Padma Utara; dishes 10,000-15,000Rp) A real find in the tourist heart of Legian, this basic warung is spotless and serves up hearty portions of Balinese classics. The *gado gado* comes with a huge bowl of peanut sauce.

**Warung Asia** (Map p272; ☎ 742 0202; off Jl Double Six & Jl Pura Bagus Taruna; dishes 10,000-30,000Rp; ☎) Look down a couple of little *gang* for this dollhouse of a cafe. Traditional Thai dishes are paired with an authentic Italian espresso machine; lose your afternoon over the many newspapers.

**Warung Murah** (Map p272; ☎ 732082; Jl Arjuna; meals from 20,000Rp) Lunch goes swimmingly at this authentic warung specialising in seafood. An array of grilled fish awaits; if you prefer fowl over fin, the *sate ayam* (chicken sate) is succulent *and* a bargain.

**ourpick Indo-National** (Map p272; ☎ 759883; Jl Padma 17; mains 20,000-90,000Rp) Kerry and Milton Turner's popular restaurant is a home-away-from-home for legions of fans. Grab a cold one with the crew up front at the bar with a sweeping view of Legian's action. Or head back to a pair of shady and romantic tables. Order the heaping grilled seafood platter and Bali's best garlic bread.

### Double Six Beach
These places are right on the popular beach, which is always thronging with locals and visitors alike. The following is good come sunset.

**Zanzibar** (Map p272; ☎ 733529; Jl Double Six; dishes 30,000-70,000Rp) A flash rehab has added a second level with views over the shady trees. The menu is a typical mix of Indo-pasta-

sandwiches and very good thin-crust pizza, but that's not your priority – get a large table with a group and enjoy the beachy views.

## Entertainment
Around 6pm every day, sunset on the beach is the big attraction, perhaps while enjoying a drink at a cafe with a sea view. Later on, even as the temperature diminishes, the action heats up, especially at the raging clubs of Kuta. Many spend their evening at one of the hipster joints in Seminyak (p283) before working their way south to oblivion.

Check out the free mag, *The Beat* (www.beatmag.com), for good club listings and other 'what's on' news.

### BALINESE DANCE & MUSIC
The Ubud area (p320) is really the place to go for authentic dance, and you'll see offers from tour operators in many hotels. But note that you won't get back to Kuta until after 10pm with most of these. Local performances are geared for tourists who treat culture like vitamins and are often perfunctory at best.

### BARS & CLUBS
Most bars are free to enter, and often have special drink promotions and 'happy hours' between about 5pm and 8pm. During the low season, when tourist numbers are down, you might have to visit quite a few venues to find one with any life. Ambience ranges from the laid-back vibe of the surfer dives to the high-concept nightclubs with their long drink menus and hordes of prowling servers.

You'll find many low-key boozers, amid their flashier brethren, along Jl Legian.

**Apache Reggae Bar** (Map p272; ☎ 761212; Jl Legian 146; ☽ 11pm-4am) One of the rowdier spots in Kuta, Apache jams in locals and visitors, many of whom are on the make. The music is loud, but that pounding you feel the next day is from the free-flowing *arak* (colourless, distilled palm wine) served in huge plastic jugs.

**Double Six Club** (Map p272; ☎ 081 2462 7733; www.doublesixclub.com; Jl Double Six; ☽ 11pm-6am) This legendary club (and namesake for the beach, road and more) continues reinventing itself. The swimming pool is still there and so is the bungee jump. Top international DJs play a mix of dance tunes in a sleek open-air pavilion. A cafe up front adds glitz to sunset drinks.

**Ocean Beach Club** (Map p272; ☎ 755423; www.esc bali.com; Jl Pantai Kuta; ☽ 11am-late) This flash place occupies a swath of prime real estate across from the beach. Lounge on vivid red pillows and watch the sunset, or plunge into the pool – before or after your stint at the pool bar.

**Sky Garden Lounge** (Map p272; ☎ 756362; www .escbali.com; Jl Legian 61; ☯ 24hr) Part of the ESC empire (which includes the Ocean Beach Club, p277), this multilevel palace of flash, flirts with height restrictions from its rooftop bar. Look for top DJs, a ground-level cafe and paparazzi-wannabes.

## Shopping

Many people spend – literally – a major part of their trip shopping. Kuta has a vast concentration of cheap places, as well as huge, flashy surf-gear emporiums on Kuta Sq and Jl Legian. As you head north along the latter into Legian, the quality of the shops improves and you start finding cute little boutiques, especially past Jl Melasti. Jl Double Six (Arjuna) is lined with wholesale fabric, clothing and craft stores, giving it a bazaar feel. Continue into Seminyak (see p283) for absolutely fabulous shopping.

Simple stalls with T-shirts, souvenirs and schlock – especially schlock – are everywhere (especially along the Poppies). The top-selling gift for those left at home are penis-shaped bottle openers in a range of colours and sizes. Bargain hard to avoid paying a stiff price.

### ARTS & CRAFTS

Shops in Kuta and Legian sell arts and crafts from almost every part of the island, from Mas woodcarvings to Kamasan paintings to Gianyar textiles. There are also many interesting pieces from other parts of Indonesia, some of questionable authenticity and value.

**Kiky Shop** (Map p272; ☎ 081 9161 24351; Jl Pantai Kuta 6) *The* place to live the cliché and buy a bongo drum. Finely crafted instruments from around Indonesia are on sale.

### BEACHWEAR & SURF SHOPS

A huge range of surf shops sells big-name surf gear – including Mambo, Rip Curl and Billabong – although goods may be only marginally cheaper than overseas. Local names include Surfer Girl and Quicksilver. Most have numerous locations in South Bali.

### CLOTHING

The local fashion industry has diversified from beach gear to sportswear and fashion clothing. From the intersection with Jl Padma,

go north on Jl Legian to Seminyak for the most interesting clothing shops.

**IO & CO** (Map p272; ☎ 754093; Jl Legian 361) Gauzy, silky and fashionable women's wear in a sleek multilevel air-con shop. This Bali label also sells housewares in vibrant patterns.

**Joger** (Map p270; Jl Raya Tuban; ☯ 11am-6pm) Look for the mobs of Indonesian tourists in front of this huge T-shirt shop east of Tuban. The sign out front says *'Pabrik kata-kata'*, which means 'factory of words'. The T-shirts are nationally iconic and bear sayings in Bahasa Indonesia that are wry, funny or simply arch.

### DEPARTMENT STORES & MALLS

**Carrefour** (Map p270; ☎ 847 7222; Jl Sunset; ☯ 9am-10pm) This vast outlet of the French discount chain combines lots of small shops (books, computers, bikinis etc) with one huge hypermarket. It's the place to stock up on staples and there's a large ready-to-eat section and a food court as well. The downside, however, is inescapable: it's a mall.

**Discovery Shopping Mall** (Map p270; ☎ 755522; www.discoveryshoppingmall.com; Jl Kartika Plaza; ☯ 9am-9pm) Maybe if they hadn't gone and ruined the shoreline… Anyway, this huge, hulking and popular enclosed Tuban mall is built on the water and is filled with stores of every kind, including the large Centro (☎ 769629) and trendy Sogo (☎ 769555) department stores.

**Matahari** (Map p272; ☎ 757588; Kuta Sq; ☯ 9.30am-10pm) This store has the basics – fairly staid clothing, a floor full of souvenirs, jewellery and a supermarket. You can find most things here, including some decent-quality luggage should you need extra bags to haul your wretched excess home.

## Getting There & Away

### BEMO

Dark-blue public bemo (minibuses) regularly travel between Kuta and the Tegal terminal in Denpasar – the fare should be 8000Rp. The route goes from a **bemo stop** onto Jl Raya Kuta near Jl Pantai Kuta, looping past the beach and then on Jl Melasti and back past Bemo Corner (Map p272) for the trip back to Denpasar.

### BUS
### Public Bus

For public buses to anywhere in Bali, you'll have to go to the appropriate terminal in Denpasar first; see above.

## Tourist Shuttle Bus

**Perama** (Map p272; ☎ 751551; www.peramatour.com; Jl Legian 39; ⏰ 7am-10pm) is the main shuttle-bus operation in town, and will sometimes pick you up from your hotel for free (confirm this with them when making arrangements). Perama usually has at least one bus a day to all of its destinations.

| Destination | Fare | Duration |
|---|---|---|
| Candidasa | 60,000Rp | 3½hr |
| Lovina | 125,000Rp | 4½hr |
| Padangbai | 60,000Rp | 3hr |
| Sanur | 25,000Rp | 30min |
| Ubud | 50,000Rp | 1½hr |

## Getting Around

See p267 for details on getting around. Besides the frequent taxis, you can rent a scooter – often with a surfboard rack – or a bike. Just ask at where you are staying. One of the nicest ways to get around the Kuta and Legian area is by foot, along the beach.

## SEMINYAK

Seminyak may be immediately north of Kuta and Legian, but in many respects it feels like it's almost on another island. It's flash, brash, phoney and filled with bony models and expats.

It's also home to dozens of restaurants and clubs – when a hot new place opens, it's usually in Seminyak. Along Jl Raya Seminyak and Jl Laksmana, and the odd side street, there are a wealth of creative shops and galleries, and world-class hotels line the beach. And what a beach it is, as deep and sandy as Kuta's but less crowded.

## Orientation

The southern border of Seminyak runs north of Jl Double Six (Jl Arjuna). Jl Raya Seminyak is the continuation of Jl Legian from Kuta and is lined with shops. Jl Abimanyu runs to the beach and passes many bars and restaurants.

Jl Laksmana also heads west towards the beach. From here, things get real tricky as the road wanders north through a part of Seminyak that some people call Petitenget, that's properly called Jl Pantai Kaya Aya, but is also known by its old name: Jl Oberoi. See the boxed text on p282, for more information on the confusing street names in the region.

## Information

Most hotels have broadband connections for guests, and many cafes offer free wi-fi for patrons as noted in the listings. ATMs can be found along all the main roads.

For medical services, see the Kuta & Legian section (p271).

**Periplus Bookshop** Seminyak Sq ( ☎ 736851; Jl Laksmana) Bali Deli ( ⏰ 734578; Jl Kunti) The island-wide chain of lavishly-fitted bookshops has enough design books to have you fitting out even your garage in Bali Style; also stocks best sellers, magazines and newspapers.

**Taiga Pharmacy** ( ☎ 732621; Jl Raya Seminyak 19; ⏰ 24hr) Across from Bintang Supermarket, it has a full range of prescription medications.

## Sights

North of the string of hotels on Jl Pantai Kaya Aya, **Pura Petitenget** is an important temple and a scene of many ceremonies. It is one of a string of sea temples that stretches from Pura Luhur Ulu Watu on the Bukit Peninsula north to Tanah Lot in western Bali. It honours the visit of a 16th-century priest.

## Activities

Because of the limited road access, the beaches in Seminyak tend to be less crowded than further south in Kuta. This also means that it's less patrolled and the water conditions are less monitored. The odds of encountering dangerous rip tides and other hazards are ever-present, especially as you head north.

### SPAS

Look for lavish spas in all of the top hotels in Seminyak.

**Jari Menari** ( ☎ 736740; Jl Raya Seminyak 47; ⏰ 10am-9pm) has won international acclaim. Its name means 'dancing fingers' and your body will be one happy dance floor. The all-male staff use massage techniques that emphasise rhythm. Fees start at 250,000Rp for 75 minutes.

The name says it all at **Chill** ( ☎ 734701; Jl Kunti; ⏰ 10am-10pm). This Zen place embraces reflexology, with treatments starting at 80,000Rp.

## Sleeping

Seminyak has a good range of places to stay, from world-class resorts like the Oberoi to more humble hotels hidden away on backstreets. This is also the start of villa-land, which runs north from here through the vanishing rice fields. For details on booking a private villa, see p819. The 2009 opening of

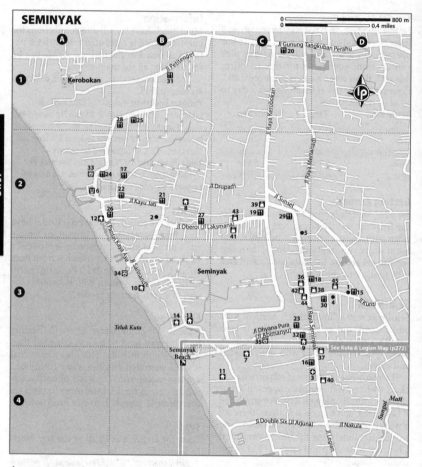

SEMINYAK

the new W Hotel on the beach north of the Legian was very flashy.

## BUDGET

**Ned's Hide-Away** ( ☎ 731270; nedshide@dps.centrim.net.id; Gang Bima 3; r from 100,000Rp) Named after Aussie icon Ned Kelly, this simple, 15-room, two-storey place is popular with those hoping to lie low between bouts of fun. Rooms have hot water and there's a character-filled bar. Look for the sign on Jl Raya Seminyak north of Bintang Supermarket.

## MIDRANGE

**Raja Gardens** ( ☎ 730494; jdw@eksadata.com; Jl Abimanyu; r 300,000-500,000Rp; ❷ ❷ ▢ ❝ ) Enjoy spacious, grassy grounds in this quiet inn almost on the

beach. Rooms are fairly barebones but there are open-air bathrooms and plenty of potted plants. The basic rate gets you cold water and a fan; more money buys hot water, air-con and a fridge.

**Green Room** ( ☎ 731412; www.thegreenroombali.com; Jl Abimanyu 63B; r 300,000-550,000Rp; ❷ ❝ ) A new-age cheapie, the Green Room evokes Robinson Crusoe from its hammocks to its banana-tree motif. Lounge around the small inkblot-shaped pool or chill in the open *bale* (Balinese open-sided pavilion with steeply pitched thatched roof) with its media centre. Among the 14 rooms in a two-storey block are ones with jungle themes.

**Sarinande Beach Inn** ( ☎ 730383; www.sarinandehotel.com; Jl Sarinande 15; s/d US$30/32; ❷ ❷ ▢ ❝ )

BALI

An excellent-value place. The 24 rooms are in two-storey blocks around a small pool; the decor is older but everything is well maintained. Amenities include fridges, satellite TV and a cafe. The beach is three minutes away by foot.

**ourpick Villa Kresna** ( ☎ 730317; www.villa-kresna.com; Jl Sarinande 19; r US$40-85, villas US$150-220; ❄ ⚅ 🖳 🛜 ) The beach is only 50m from this cute, idiosyncratic property tucked away on a small *gang*. The 10 art-filled units are mostly suites, which have a nice flow-through design with both public and private patios. A small, sinuous pool wanders through the property.

**Mutiara Bali** ( ☎ 708888; www.mutiarabali.com; Jl Karang Mas Sejahtera 88; r US$60-90, villas from US$250; ❄ ⚅ 🖳 🛜 ) Although hidden on a small road behind Jl Laksmana, the Mutiara is close to everything: fine dining – two minutes; the beach – five minutes, etc. There are 29 good-sized and nicely furnished rooms in two-storey blocks around a frangipani-draped pool area. Seventeen large private villas occupy one half of the compound.

### TOP END

**Samaya** ( ☎ 731149; www.thesamayabali.com; Jl Pantai Kaya Aya; villas from US$300; ❄ ⚅ 🖳 🛜 ) The beachfront Samaya is one of the best choices if you want to step from your room to the sand. The 24 villas in the beachside compound are attractive, roomy and have small pools. Another compound across the road trades location for even larger units. Food, from breakfast onwards, is creative and superb.

**Oberoi** ( ☎ 730361; www.oberoihotels.com; Jl Laksmana; r from US$220, villas from US$500; ❄ ⚅ 🖳 🛜 ) One of the world's top hotels, the beauti-

fully understated Oberoi has been a refined Balinese-style beachside retreat since 1971. All accommodation has private verandahs and as you move up through the food chain, additional features include private villas, ocean views and private, walled pools. From the cafe overlooking the almost-private sweep of beach, to the numerous luxuries, this is a place to spoil yourself.

## Eating

Jl Laksmana is the focus of Seminyak eating but there are interesting choices virtually everywhere. Note that where indicated, some restaurants morph into clubs as the night wears on. Conversely, some of the places listed under Entertainment (p283) also do decent food.

### JL ABIMANYU

**Jef Burgers** ( ☎ 081 7473 4311; Jl Dhyana Pura 24; dishes from 13,000Rp; ⏰ 24hr) Munchies central: Jef cooks up burgers around the clock (customised if you like), from a small grill out front.

**Zula Vegetarian Paradise** ( ☎ 732723; Jl Dhyana Pura 5; dishes 15,000-40,000Rp; ⏰ 8am-4pm) It's all vegetarian at this newly enlarged cafe, where you can get tofu cheese, a tofu spring roll and tofu cheesecake. Or go wild with a brown-rice surprise.

### JALAN RAYA SEMINYAK

**Warung Ibu Made** (Jl Raya Seminyak; meals 10,000Rp; ⏰ 7am-7pm) The woks roar almost dawn to dusk amid the constant hubbub on this busy corner of Jl Raya Seminyak. It's one of a few simple stalls. The meals from this warung couldn't be fresher and put to shame some of the Western fakery just down the road.

**BALI**

---

**PICK A NAME, ANY NAME**

Some streets in Kuta, Legian and Seminyak have more than one name. Many streets are unofficially named after a well-known temple and/or business place, or according to the direction they head. In recent years there has been an attempt to impose official – and usually more Balinese – names on the streets. But the old, unofficial names are still common.

| Old (unofficial) | New (official) |
| --- | --- |
| Jl Dhyana Pura/Jl Gado Gado | Jl Abimanyu |
| Jl Double Six | Jl Arjuna |
| Jl Kartika Plaza | Jl Dewi Sartika |
| Jl Oberoi | Jl Laksmana |
| Jl Padma | Jl Yudistra |
| Jl Pantai Kuta | Jl Pantai Banjar Pande Mas |
| Jl Pura Bagus Taruna/Rum Jungle Rd | Jl Werkudara |
| Jl Raya Seminyak | Northern stretch: Jl Raya Basangkasa |
| Jl Satria | Jl Kediri |
| Jl Segara | Jl Jenggala |
| Poppies Gang II | Jl Batu Bolong |

---

**Café Moka** ( ☎ 731424; Jl Raya Seminyak; meals 18,000-40,000Rp; 🖳 ) Enjoy French-style baked goods at this popular bakery and cafe. Many escape the heat and linger here for hours. The bulletin board spills over with notices.

**Warung Italia** ( ☎ 737437; Jl Kunti 2; meals from 20,000Rp; ⏱ 8am-7pm) The climax in any classic warung happens at lunch, when happy diners walk down the displays and have their plates filled with a wide selection of treats. No matter what they choose, the price is the same (and it's low). Here, warung-style meets Italian as diners select from a range of pastas, salads and more.

**JL KAYU JATI & JL LAKSMANA**

Saddled by some with the unimaginative name 'Eat Street', this restaurant row has scores of choices. Stroll the strip and see what sparks a craving. Prices are uniformly popular.

**Ibu Mangku** ( ☎ 780 1824; Jl Kayu Jati; meals 15,000Rp) Look for the cabs in front of this bamboo place that serves superb minced-chicken sate redolent with lemongrass and other spices.

**Grocer & Grind** ( ☎ 081 735 4104; Jl Kayu Jati 3X; mains 20,000-60,000Rp; 🖳 ) Keep your vistas limited and you might think you're at just another sleek Sydney cafe, but look around and you're unmistakably in Bali, albeit one of the trendiest bits. Classic sandwiches, salads and big breakfasts issue forth from the open kitchen. Eat in the open-air or choose air-con tables in the deli area.

**Corner Store** ( ☎ 730276; Jl Laksmana 10A; dishes 30,000-60,000Rp; ⏱ 7am-5pm) Seminyak's fashionistas gather here most mornings (aka

Tuck Shop to the expats) to dish the gossip and breakfast on upscale, healthy fare like organic muesli. Tell everyone you're a 'cushion designer' and look bored under the beautiful frangipani tree.

**Ultimo** ( ☎ 738720; Jl Laksmana 104; mains 30,000-100,000Rp) *Uno:* find a table overlooking the street action or out the back in one of the gardens. *Due:* choose from the surprisingly authentic Italian menu. *Tre:* marvel at the efficient service from the army of servers. *Quattro:* smile at the reasonable bill.

**ourpick Sate Bali** ( ☎ 736734; Jl Oberoi 22; mains from 40,000Rp; ⏱ 11am-10pm) Some very fine traditional Balinese dishes are served at this small cafe run by chef Nyoman Sudiyasa. The multicourse *rijsttafel* (200,000Rp) is a symphony of tastes including the addictive *babi kecap* (pork in a soy sauce) and *tum bebek* (minced duck in banana leaf).

**NORTHERN SEMINYAK**

Some of Bali's most interesting restaurants are found amid the curving roads and villas here.

**Warung Sulawesi** (Jl Petitenget; meal 15,000Rp ⏱ 11am-4pm) Set back from the road in a family compound, enjoy fabulously fresh Balinese and Indonesian food served in classic warung style (you choose white or yellow rice, then pick from a captivating array of dishes). The long beans, yum!

**Waroeng Bonita** ( ☎ 731918; www.bonitabali.com; Jl Petitenget 2000x; dishes 30,000-70,000Rp) Balinese dishes such as *ikan rica-rica* (fresh fish stir-fried in a spicy green chilli sauce) and the classic, spicy beef rendang are the specialities here. Nab a table under the trees, unless it's Baliwood night when the staff are dragooned into performing with drag queens in an unmissable and flamboyant spectacle.

**Sarong** ( ☎ 737809; www.sarongbali.com; Jl Petitenget 19X; mains US$5-10; ☽ noon-10pm) The food is almost as magical as the setting at this top-end, high-concept restaurant. Largely open to the evening breezes, the dining room has plush furniture and gleaming place settings that twinkle in the candlelight. Opt for tables out back where you can let the stars do the twinkling. The food spans the globe – small plates are popular for an evening spent enjoying the commodious bar.

**Living Room** ( ☎ 735735; www.livingroombali.com; Jl Petitenget; mains 80,000-100,000Rp; ☽ noon-late) At night, hundreds of candles twinkle on and about the scores of outdoor tables at this fusion of Balinese thatching with colonial posh. The fusion menu combines French classics with Asian flair – think Saigon before things went pear-shaped. The famous soundtrack? Fusion of course (house, jazz and trance).

**Blossom** ( ☎ 735552; www.balisentosa.com; Sentosa Private Villas & Spa, Jl Pura Telaga Waja; meals from US$30) Arguably Bali's finest restaurant, Blossom is certainly one of the most captivating. Occupying much of the ground level of the ultraposh Sentosa Villas, the restaurant has widely spaced tables in an elegant open-air space overlooking smoothly flowing water features. The menu changes often but is always global in outlook and creative in execution.

### SELF-CATERING

**Bali Deli** ( ☎ 738686; Jl Kunti 117X; 🖳 📶 ) The lavish deli counter at this upscale market is loaded with imported cheese, meats and baked goods. This is the place to start a special meal. The breezy cafe also has a good, fresh menu.

**Bintang Supermarket** ( ☎ 730552; Jl Raya Seminyak 17) Always busy, this large supermarket is the stock-up favourite among expats.

## Entertainment

Like your vision at 2am, the division between restaurant, bar and club blurs in Seminyak. For instance, Living Room (above) and Sarong (above) have large and inviting bars that fill with people who never take a crack at a menu. Meanwhile, Ku De Ta (right) and

Hu'u (below) serve good food to the partying masses. Although Seminyak lacks any real hardcore clubs where you can greet the dawn (or vice versa), stalwarts head south to Kuta in the wee hours.

### JL ABIMANYU

Numerous bars line Jl Abimanyu (aka Jl Dhyana Pura), although noise-sensitive locals complain if things get too raucous.

**Q-Bar** ( ☎ 762361; Jl Abimanyu; ☽ 8pm-3am) This bright and always-popular bar caters to gay clubbers. The music of choice is house. There are good views of the action – inside and out – from the upper floor.

### JL LAKSMANA

**Hu'u** ( ☎ 736443; www.huubali.com; Jl Pantai Kaya Aya; ☽ 4pm-late) There's a menu someplace, but really, this spot is all about air-kissing, seeing and making the scene, an enchanting outdoor garden and pavilion. Action peaks around midnight before the club exodus begins.

**Ku De Ta** ( ☎ 736969; www.kudeta.net; Jl Laksmana; ☽ 7am-1am) Hardly an article gets written about Bali that doesn't mention this beachside lounge, heaving with Bali's beautiful and their attendant scenesters. Perfect your 'bored' look over drinks, although the gorgeous sunsets shine through many a sneer.

## Shopping

Seminyak shops could occupy days of your trip. Designer boutiques (Bali has a thriving fashion industry), funky stores, slick galleries, wholesale emporiums and family-run workshops are just some of the choices.

The action picks up in the south from Kuta and Legian (p278) and heads north along Jl Legian and Jl Raya Seminyak. The retail strip branches off into the prime real estate of Jl Laksmana while continuing north on Jl Raya Kerobokan.

**Ashitaba** ( ☎ 737054; Jl Raya Seminyak 6) Tenganan, the Aga village of East Bali (p334), produces the intricate and beautiful rattan items sold here. Containers, bowls, purses and more (from US$5) display the very fine weaving.

**Bananas Batik** ( ☎ 730938; www.bananasbatik.com; Jl Raya Seminyak) Flouncy clothes for women that you don't have to travel to the source for – the exquisite duds are made near Candidasa.

**Biasa** ( ☎ 730308; www.biasabali.com; Jl Raya Seminyak 36) This is Bali-based designer Susanna Perini's premier store. Her line of tropical wear for men and women combines cottons, silks and embroidery.

**Blue Glue** ( ☎ 844 5956; Jl Raya Seminyak) Has a collection of Bali-made bathing suits from teensy to trendy.

**Divine Diva** ( ☎ 731903; Jl Oberoi 1A) Bali-made breezy styles for fuller female figures. A friend calls it: 'the essence of agelessness'.

**ET Club** ( ☎ 730902; Jl Raya Seminyak 14A) Out-of-this-world prices on designer knock-offs and bohemian bags, belts, shoes and clothes.

**Lily Jean** ( ☎ 734864; Jl Oberoi 102X) Saucy knickers underpin sexy women's clothing that both dares and flirts; most are Bali-made.

**Luna Collection** ( ☎ 081 139 8909; Jl Raya Seminyak) Handmade sterling silver jewellery in a range of designs. The local craftsmen are quite creative and the mother-of-pearl works are museum quality.

**Morena** ( ☎ 745 3531; Jl Oberoi 69) Puerto Rican-born Wilma sells her line of sexy, flouncy, comfy and colourful women's clothes here.

**Sabbatha** ( ☎ 731756; Jl Raya Seminyak 97) Megabling! The glitter, glam and gold here are almost blinding and that's just what customers want. On one of the nicest stretches of shops.

**Uma and Leopold** ( ☎ 733670; www.umaandleopold.com; Jl Kunti 8x) Luxe clothes and little frilly things to put on before slipping off…

## Getting There & Around

Most transport information is the same as for Kuta (p278). Metered taxis are easily hailed. A taxi to the heart of Kuta will be about 15,000Rp. You can beat the traffic, save the ozone and have a good stroll by walking south down the beach. Legian is about 15 minutes away.

# NORTH OF SEMINYAK
☎ 0361

Growth is marching north and west along the coast, much of it anchored by the endless swath of beach. Kerobokan is morphing into Seminyak; cloistered villas here lure the well-heeled who whisk past –in air-con comfort – stooped rice farmers.

Small roads lead off the main clogged artery that runs to Pura Tanah Lot. Use these to reach beaches at Berewa, Canggu and Echo Beach (Batu Mejan). These are uncrowded and wild, with pounding surf, perilous swimming and sweeping views to the south.

Getting to most of the places below is only convenient with your own transport or by

taxi. Think 25,000Rp or more from Kuta, 15,000Rp from Seminyak.

## Kerobokan

The next area north of Seminyak is seamlessly blending with the south.

Situated at the corner of Jl Raya Kerobokan and Jl Gunung Tangkuban Perahu, there's a scrumptious little **fruit market** (Map p280) where you can do your lab work in Bali fruits and veg 101.

**Warung Gossip** (Map p270; ☎ 081 7970 3209; Jl Pengubengan Kauh; meals from 20,000Rp; ☺ noon-4pm) is always popular thanks to its Westernised versions of Balinese warung staples.

## Berewa

The greyish beach, secluded among rice fields and villas, is about 2km up the sand from Seminyak and about 10km by roundabout lanes. There are a couple of surfer cafes by the pounding surf. The grey, volcanic sand here slopes steeply into the foaming waters.

One person described **Desa Seni** (Map p270; ☎ 844 6392; www.desaseni.com; Jl Kayu Putih 13; r US$150-300; ✖ ⊠ ⌨ �𝅘 ) as like a 'hippie Four Seasons', and that's not far off. Classic wooden homes have been brought to the site from across Indonesia and turned into luxurious quarters. Guests enjoy a menu of organic and healthy cuisine while pondering which yoga class, spa session or cultural event to sign up for.

## Canggu

A popular surf spot, Canggu draws a lot of locals and expat residents at weekends. Access to the paved parking area costs 2000Rp and there are cafes and warung for those who work up an appetite in the water or watching others in the water.

To get to Canggu, go west at Kerobokan or south at Kayutulang. Taxis from Kuta will cost 40,000Rp or more.

## Echo Beach

Just 500m northwest of Canggu Beach is Echo Beach, or Batu Mejan. It has reached critical mass in popularity and has become its own scene. Shops are moving in and the burgeoning number of cafes includes **Mandira Cafe** (Map p270; Jl Pura Batu Mejan; dishes 8000-15,000Rp), which has a timeless menu of jaffles, banana pancakes, club sandwiches and smoothies.

Slicker yet, the **Beach House** (Map p270; ☎ 738471; Jl Pura Batu Mejan; dishes 30,000-80,000Rp; ⏿ ) faces the waves and draws stylish loungers. It has a variety of couches and picnic tables where you can enjoy the menu of breakfasts, salads, grilled fare and more.

## SANUR
☎ 0361

Sanur is a genteel alternative to Kuta. The white-sand beach is sheltered by a reef. The resulting low-key surf contributes to Sanur's nickname 'Snore', although this is also attributable to the area's status as a haven for expat retirees. Some parents prefer the beach at Sanur because its calmness makes it a good place for small children to play.

Sanur was one of the places favoured by Westerners during their prewar discovery of Bali. Artists Miguel Covarrubias, Adrien Jean Le Mayeur and Walter Spies, anthropologist Jane Belo and choreographer Katharane Mershon all spent time here.

## Orientation

Sanur stretches for about 5km along an east-facing coastline, with the lush and green land-scaped grounds of resorts fronting right onto the sandy beach. The appalling Grand Bali Beach Hotel, located at the northern end of the strip, fronts the best stretch of beach. West of the beachfront hotels is the noisy main drag, Jl Danau Tamblingan, with hotels, oodles of tourist shops, restaurants and cafes.

Jl Ngurah Rai, commonly called Bypass Rd, skirts the western side of the resort area, and is the main link to Kuta and the airport.

## Information

There are numerous ATMs and banks along Jl Danau Tamblingan. Most hotels have some form of internet access as do many cafes and bars

**Guardian Pharmacy** ( ☎ 284343; Jl Danau Tamblingan 134) The chain pharmacy has a doctor on call.

**Periplus** ( ☎ 282790; Hardy's Supermarket, Jl Danau Tamblingan 136) Good selection of glossy books, best-sellers and periodicals.

**Police station** ( ☎ 288597; Jl Ngurah Rai)

## Sights

Sanur's **beachfront walk** was the first in Bali and from day one has been delighting locals and visitors alike. Over 4km long, it follows the sand south as it curves to the west. Lots of cafes with tables in the sand will give you plenty of reason to pause. Offshore you'll see gnarled fishermen in woven bamboo hats standing in the shallows rod-fishing for a living.

### MUSEUM LE MAYEUR

The Belgian artist Adrien Jean Le Mayeur de Merpes (1880–1958) arrived in Bali in 1932. Three years later, he met and married the beautiful Legong dancer Ni Polok when she was just 15. They lived in this compound, which houses the museum, when Sanur was still a quiet fishing village. The main house must have been delightful – a peaceful and elegant home filled with art and antiques right by the tranquil beach. After the artist's death, Ni Polok lived in the house until she died in 1985.

Despite security (some Le Mayeur paintings have sold for US$150,000) and conservation problems, almost 90 Le Mayeur paintings are displayed inside the **museum** ( ☎ 286201; adult/child 2000/1000Rp; ⏰ 7.30am-3.30pm) in a naturalistic Balinese interior of woven fibres. Some of Le Mayeur's early works are Impressionist paintings from his travels in Africa, India, the Mediterranean and the South Pacific. The works from the 1950s are in much better condition, displaying the vibrant colours that later became popular with young Balinese artists. Look for the haunting black-and-white photos of Ni Polok.

### STONE PILLAR

The pillar, down a narrow lane across from a Circle K and to the left as you face Pura Belangjong, is Bali's oldest dated artefact and has ancient inscriptions recounting military victories of more than a thousand years ago. These inscriptions are in Sanskrit and are evidence of Hindu influence 300 years before the arrival of the Majapahit court.

## Activities
### DIVING & SNORKELLING

The diving near Sanur is not great, but the reef has a good variety of fish and offers quite good snorkelling. Sanur is the best departure point for dive trips to Nusa Lembongan. Among several good options, **Crystal Divers** ( ☎ 286737; www.crystal-divers.com; Jl Danau Tamblingan 168; intro dives from US$25) is a slick diving operation and has its own hotel, the Crystal Santai Hotel.

### SPAS

Most of the large beachside hotels have spas. **Jamu Traditional Spa** ( ☎ 286595; www.jamutraditional spa.com; Jl Danau Tamblingan 41; massage from US$45) has a beautifully carved teak-and-stone entry that sets the mood.

## WATER SPORTS
Various water sports are offered at kiosks along the beach: close to Museum Le Mayeur; near Sanur Beach Market; and at **Surya Water Sports** ( ☎ 287956; www.suryadive.com; Jl Duyung 10),

which is the largest. You can go parasailing (US$20 per go), snorkelling by boat (US$30, two hours), windsurfing (US$30, one hour), or enjoy a two-tank dive at the nearby reef (US$50).

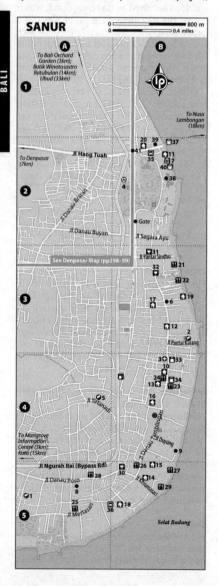

## Sleeping

Usually the best places to stay are right on the beach; however, beware of properties that have been coasting for decades. Modest budgets will find comfort on the nonbeach side of Jl Danau Tamblingan.

### BUDGET

**Keke Homestay** ( ☎ 287282; Jl Danau Tamblingan 96; r 60,000-135,000Rp; 🞫 ) Set 150m down a *gang* from the noisy road, Keke welcomes backpackers into its genial family. The seven quiet, clean rooms vary from fan-only to air-con cool.

**Watering Hole I** ( ☎ 288289; www.wateringhole sanurbali.com; Jl Hang Tuah 37; r 60,000-150,000Rp; 🞫 🖳 ) In the northern part of Sanur, the Hole is a busy, friendly place close to the Nusa Lembongan boats. It has 20 pleasant, clean rooms; the cheapest have fans and cold water.

**Jati Homestay** ( ☎ 281730; www.hoteljatiandhome stay.com; Jl Danau Tamblingan 168; r 200,000Rp; 🞫 ) Jati means 'genuine' and you will feel right at home at this attractive inn. The 15 bungalow-style rooms are situated in pretty grounds; some of the units have small kitchens.

**Hotel Bali Rita** ( ☎ 282630; balirita@hotmail.com; Jl Danau Tamblingan 174; r 250,000Rp; 🞫 ) Lovely Rita is tailor-made for those who want a traditional-style bungalow room in a nice garden. The 12 rooms here are large, with big fridges and tubs in open-air bathrooms. The beach is 10 minutes east.

### MIDRANGE

**Flashbacks** ( ☎ 281682; www.flashbacks-chb.com; Jl Danau Tamblingan 106; s/d 145,000/165,000Rp, bungalows 335,000/360,000Rp; 🞫 🞫 ) This welcoming place has nine rooms that vary greatly in size. The better ones are bungalows or suites while more modest rooms share bathrooms and have cold water. The lovely design takes a lot of cues from traditional Balinese style. Porch Café (p288) is out the front.

**Hotel Segara Agung** ( ☎ 288446; www.segaraagung .com; Jl Duyung 43; r US$25-50; 🞫 🞫 🖳 ) Down a quiet, sandy lane lined with villas, the hotel is only a three-minute walk from the beach. The 16 rooms are clean though spartan; the cheapest are fan and cold-water-only.

**Hotel Palm Garden** (Taman Palem; ☎ 287041; www .palmgarden-bali.com; Jl Kesumasari 3; r from 275,000Rp; 🞫 🞫 ) Everything is low-key here, from the 17 large rooms (with satellite TVs and fridges) to the relaxed service and pretty

---

**GETTING HIGH OVER SANUR**

Travelling South Bali you can't help but notice scores of kites overhead much of the year. These creations are often huge (10m or more in length, with tails stretching another 100m) and fly at altitudes that worry pilots. Many have noisemakers that make eerie humming and buzzing noises. Like much in Bali there are spiritual roots: the kites are meant to figuratively whisper into the ears of the gods suggestions that abundant harvests might be nice. But for many Balinese, kite flying is simply a really fun hobby.

Each July, hundreds of Balinese and international teams descend upon Sanur for the **Bali Kite Festival**. They compete for an array of honours in such categories as original design and flight endurance.

---

grounds. It's one minute to the beach; there is a nice medium-sized pool with a small waterfall.

**Diwangkara Beach Hotel** ( ☎ 288577; www .holidayvillahotelbali.com; Jl Hang Tuah 54; r US$65, villas US$90-180; 🞫 🞫 🖳 📶 ) Facing the beach near the end of Jl Hang Tuah, this 38-unit hotel has traditional Balinese architecture and richly decorated rooms. Pool villas have their own plunge pool right off a wooden terrace.

### TOP END

**Puri Santrian** ( ☎ 288009; www.santrian.com; Jl Mertasari; r from US$110, bungalows from US$150; 🞫 🞫 🖳 ) Lush gardens, three large pools with fountains, a tennis court and beach frontage, as well as 184 comfortable, well-equipped rooms make this a popular choice. Many rooms are in older-style bungalows, others in two- and three-storey blocks.

ourpick **Tandjung Sari** ( ☎ 288441; www.tandjung sari.com; Jl Danau Tamblingan 29; bungalows US$170-270; 🞫 🞫 🖳 📶 ) The mature trees along the shaded driveway set the gracious tone at this Sanur veteran, which was one of the first Balinese boutique hotels. The 26 traditional-style bungalows are superbly decorated with crafts and antiques.

## Eating

Dine on the beach in a traditional open-air pavilion or in a genial bar – the choice is yours in Sanur. Although there are plenty of uninspired

tubs. Although it's close to the beach and has a large pool and manicured gardens, it does not have a top-end level of service, so make sure you get a deal.

**Jimbaran Puri Bali** (Map p270; ☎ 701605; www .jimbaranpuribali.com; Jl Yoga Perkanti; cottages US$150-400; ✖ ☒ ☐ ) This beachside resort is set in nice grounds complete with a mazelike pool that looks onto open ocean. The 41 cottages have private gardens, large terraces and stylish room design with sunken tubs.

### EATING

Jimbaran's seafood warung are the destination of tourists across the south. The open-sided affairs are right on the beach and perfect for enjoying sea breezes and sunsets.

The usual deal is to select your seafood fresh from iced displays or tanks, and to pay according to weight. Expect to pay around 40,000Rp per 100g for live lobster, 15,000Rp to 25,000Rp for prawns, and 9000Rp for fish, squid and clams. Prices are open to negotiation and the accuracy of the scales is a joke among locals. Agree to a price before ordering. Some places simplify things with fixed menu prices.

The best kitchens marinate the fish in garlic and lime, then douse it with chilli and oil while grilling over coconut husks.

The longest row of warung is at the **northern seafood warung** (Map p270), south of the fish market. This is the area you will be taken to by a taxi if you don't specify otherwise.

The **middle seafood warung** (Map p270) are in a compact group just south of Jl Pantai Jimbaran and Jl Pemelisan Agung. These seafood warung are the simplest affairs, with old-fashioned thatched roofs and wide-open sides.

The **southern seafood warung** (Map p270) are just north of the Four Seasons Jimbaran Bay. There's a parking area off Jl Bukit Permai and the places are right in a row. The beach here is well groomed with nice trees. Call for transport.

### GETTING THERE & AWAY

Public bemo from Tegal terminal in Denpasar go via Kuta to Jimbaran (12,000Rp), and continue to Nusa Dua. They don't run after about 4pm, but plenty of taxis wait around the beachfront warung in the evening to take diners home (about 35,000Rp to Kuta). Some of the seafood warung provide free transport if you call first.

## Balangan Beach

First of a string of small beaches backed by cliffs that run along the west coast of the Bukit Peninsula south to Ulu Watu, Balangan Beach is a real find. A long and low area at the base of the cliffs is covered with palm trees and is fronted by a ribbon of near-white sand. At the north end there is a small temple, **Pura Dalem Balangan** (Map p292); at the south end, a few surfer shacks cluster, renting out loungers and serving drinks.

Back on the bluff above the water are what are likely to be the first of many places to stay; both have cafes. The beach a is brief walk away.

**Balangan Sea View Bungalows** (Map p292; ☎ 780 0499; robbyandrosita@hotmail.com; r from 250,000Rp; ☒ ) is a cluster of six thatched bungalows and five rooms surrounding a small pool in an attractive compound.

At **Flower Bud Bungalows** (Map p292; ☎ 857 2062; www.flowerbudbalangan.com; r 250,000-450,000Rp), the raised thatched bungalows are well spaced around simple gardens. There's a certain Crusoe-esque motif, and fans and sprightly pillows are among the 'luxuries'. It is directly across from Balangan Sea View Bungalows.

Balangan Beach is 6km off the main Ulu Watu road via Cenggiling. Look for a sign at a crossroads on the main Ulu Watu road that reads 'Balangan'. Follow more signs; the road is often tortuous.

Taxis from the Kuta area cost at least 40,000Rp per hour for the round trip and waiting time.

## Pecatu Indah

This 400-hectare **resort complex** (Map p292; www.balipecatu.com) rises between central Bukit Peninsula and the coast. The land is arid but that hasn't stopped the developers from building a huge hotel, condos, houses and, worst of all, a water-sucking 18-hole golf course. The once popular and mellow beach known as Dreamland has been all but erased by a hulking development.

## Bingin

A fast-evolving scene, Bingin comprises several funky places to stay scattered across cliffs and one strip of white sand down below. A 1km dirt road turns off the paved road (look for the thicket of accommodation signs), which in turn branches off the main Ulu Watu road at the small village of Pecatu.

An elderly resident collects 3000Rp at a T-junction, which is near parking for the trail down to the **beach**. The surf here is often savage but the sands are calm and the roaring breakers mesmerising. The scenery here is simply superb, with virescent cliffs dropping down to a row of houses and the foaming edge of the azure sea.

### SLEEPING
Several places to stay enjoy the views while more modest places are set back. All have at least simple cafes, although for nightlife – like the rest of this coast – you'll be heading north to Kuta

**Bingin Garden** (Map p292; ☎ 081 6472 2002; tommy barrell76@yahoo.com; r from 150,000Rp) Four basic and new bungalows are set around tidy grounds back from the cliffs and 300m north of the toll gate. Each unit sleeps two and has cold water and a fan.

**Mu** (Map p292; ☎ 847 0976; www.mu-bali.com; r €55-185; ✻ ⚑ 🖳 ⚡) Turn left after the toll gate for the most stylish option in Bingin. Seven very individual bungalows with round, pointed thatched roofs are scattered about a compound dominated by a cliffside infinity pool. All have open-air living spaces; some have air-con bedrooms and hot tubs with a view.

## Impossibles Beach
Another of the isolated white-sand beaches and legendary surf spots that dot the coast, look for signs for Impossibles on the Ulu Watu road and then follow a 1km dirt track. In the right conditions, surfers enjoy long left-hand tubes.

## Padang Padang Beach
Small in size but not in perfection, this little cove is near the main Ulu Watu road where a stream flows into the sea. Parking is easy and it is a short walk. Experienced surfers into tubes flock here.

**Thomas Homestay** (Map p292; ☎ 081 23775 6030; r 100,000Rp) has stunning views up and down this spectacular coast. The seven simple rooms lie at the end of a very rough 400m track off the main road. You can easily walk down to the beach along a path through the palms.

## Ulu Watu & Around
Ulu Watu has become the generic name for the southwestern tip of the Bukit Peninsula. It includes the much-revered temple and

the fabled surf breaks at Padang Padang, Suluban and Ulu Watu. Surfers are most common in these parts, although a spate of villa-building is changing that. (In fact, authorities are waging war against new construction within about 2km of the temple.)

### SIGHTS & ACTIVITIES
**Pura Luhur Ulu Watu** (Map p292; admission incl sarong & sash rental 3000Rp, parking 1000Rp; ✻ 8am-7pm) is one of several important temples to the spirits of the sea along the south coast of Bali.

The temple is perched precipitously on the southwestern tip of the peninsula, atop sheer cliffs that drop straight into the pounding surf. You enter through an unusual arched gateway flanked by statues of Ganesha. At sunset, walk around the cliff top to the left (south) of the temple. Watch out for monkeys, who – when not reproducing – like to snatch sunglasses and anything else within reach. The views far out to sea are mesmerizing.

An enchanting **Kecak dance** (tickets 40,000Rp; ✻ 6-7pm) is held in the temple grounds at sunset. Although obviously set up for tourists, the gorgeous setting makes it one of the more delightful performances on the island.

**Ulu Watu**, or Ulu's, is a legendary surf spot – the stuff of dreams and nightmares. There are seven different breaks here, all reached through a cave where you go in the water (below). It's about 1km south of the fabled breaks at Padang Padang.

### SLEEPING
If you're not picky you can count on being able to find accommodation of some sort near the surf break of your choice. Expect to pay

---

**BEATING ULU WATU**

Observe where other surfers paddle out and follow them. If you are in doubt, ask someone. It is better having some knowledge than none at all. When the swell is bigger you will be swept to your right from the cave. Don't panic, it is an easy matter to paddle around the white water from down along the cliff. Coming back in you have to aim for the cave. When the swell is bigger, come from the southern side of the cave as the current runs to the north. If you miss the cave, paddle out again and repeat the procedure.

BALI

**BALI**

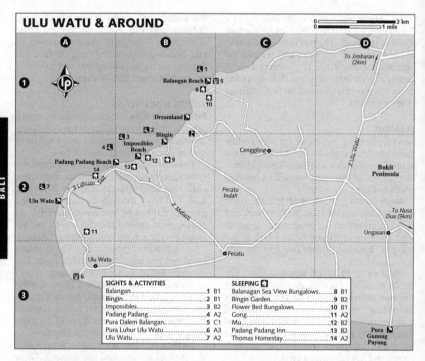

## ULU WATU & AROUND

at least 80,000Rp for a room with cold water, a fan and a shared bathroom. Many surfers choose to stay in Kuta and make the commute of less than an hour.

**Padang Padang Inn** (Map p292; ☎ 081 2391 3617; Jl Melasti 432; r from 80,000Rp) A better-than-average budget place, Padang Padang has 24 tidy rooms with private cold-water-only bathrooms and a little cafe. It can arrange all manner of surfing services like lessons, trips etc.

**Gong** (Map p292; ☎ 769976; thegongacc@yahoo.com; Jl Pantai Suluban; r from US$12) Few stay away long from the Gong. Eight tidy rooms with good ventilation and hot water face a small compound and have distant ocean views. There's also a cafe.

### Getting There & Away

The best way to see the region is with your own vehicle or by chartering a taxi.

Drivers' note: coming from the east to Pantai Suluban you will first encounter a gated parking area (5000Rp), which is about a 400m walk from the water. Continuing over a bridge, there is an older parking area (3000Rp) that is a hilly 200m from the water. Watch out for 'gate-keepers' looking for bonuses.

Public bemo to Ulu Watu are infrequent and stop running by midafternoon. Some from Kuta serve Jimbaran and Ulu Watu – it's best to catch one west of Tuban (on Jl Raya Kuta, outside the Supernova shopping centre) or in Jimbaran (on Jl Ulu Watu).

## Nusa Dua

Nusa Dua translates literally as 'Two Islands' – the islands are actually small raised headlands, each with a little temple. Nusa Dua is better known as Bali's gated beach-resort enclave – a gilded ghetto of enormous hotels. Here you will find no independent developments, no hawkers, no warung, no traffic, no pollution and no noise. The drawback is the isolation from any sense of Balinese community life; in many ways, you could be at any international tropical beach resort the world over.

As a planned resort, Nusa Dua is very spread out. You enter the enclave through one of the big gateways, and inside there are expansive lawns, manicured gardens and sweeping driveways leading to the lobbies of large hotels.

## BALI'S SOUTHERNMOST BEACH

At the crossroads on the Ulu Watu road, where the road to Balangan leads east, the road running west connects to Nusa Dua (opposite) and passes by a few isolated beaches on the way. One of the best is at **Pura Gunung Payung** (Map p292), a seaside temple about 3km south of the village of Ungasan. New concrete steps lead down the 400m cliff to a sweet swath of sand on the pounding ocean. Bring a picnic and a good book.

### SIGHTS & ACTIVITIES

The **Pasifika Museum** ( ☎ 774559; Bali Collection, Block P, Nusa Dua; admission 50,000Rp; ☼ 10am-6pm) has Asian and Balinese art by Arie Smit, Adrien Jean Le Mayeur and Theo Meier among others.

One of the nicest features of Nusa Dua is the 5km-long **beach promenade** that stretches the length of the resort and continues north along much of the beach in Tanjung Benoa. The walk is paved for most of its length.

The reef-protected beach at Nusa Dua is shallow at low tide, and the wave action is pretty limp. Worth a day trip from anywhere in South Bali, however, **Geger Beach** has a few mellow cafes and umbrella and lounger rentals. Expats in the know come here on weekends; on weekdays it's very quiet. It's reached by a small road outside of the Nusa Dua gates and south of the St Regis Bali Resort.

### SLEEPING

The Nusa Dua hotels are similar in several ways: they are all big (some are just plain huge) and they have long beachfronts. Each has several restaurants and bars, as well as various pools and other resort amenities. Some of these huge places are a bit long in the tooth, but if you're looking for an anonymous top-end resort experience, the following will do.

**Westin Resort** ( ☎ 771906; www.westin.com/bali; r from US$250; ✻ ☙ ☐ ☎ ) Attached to a large convention centre, the Westin has an air-conditioned lobby (a rarity) and vast public spaces. Guests in the 355 rooms enjoy the best pools in Nusa. There are waterfalls and more in this aquatic playground. The Kids Club has extensive activities and facilities. The landmark 2007 meetings on climate change were held here.

**St Regis Bali Resort** ( ☎ 847 8111; www.starwood hotels.com; ste from US$500; ✻ ☙ ☐ ☎ ) The newest Nusa Dua resort leaves most of the others in the sand. Every conceivable luxury from the electronics to the furnishings to the marble is provided. Pools abound and units are huge. Golf course and the beach adjoin.

### EATING

Restaurants can be found by the dozen in the huge resorts. Prices are high even by top-end Bali standards. For people not staying at the hotels, the best reason to venture in is if you want a bounteous Sunday brunch at one of the international chains.

**Warung Dobiel** (Jl Srikandi; meals from 15,000Rp; ☼ 8am-3pm) It's all about pork at this beloved open-front warung. Pork sate, pork soup, and green beans with shredded pork are among the favourites. The sautéed jackfruit will make you a convert; the green sambal is redolent with spices. Seating is on stools at long tables.

**Nusa Dua Beach Grill** ( ☎ 743 4779; Jl Pura Geger; mains 30,000-60,000Rp) A hidden gem, this warm-hued cafe is just south of Geger Beach on foot, but a circuitous 1.5km by car. The drink menu is long, the seafood fresh and the atmosphere redolent with assignations.

### SHOPPING

**Bali Collection** ( ☎ 771662) This shopping centre has had numerous name changes. The latest incarnation is mostly empty; a few souls try to make merry on their Bali holiday at the deserted Starbucks.

### GETTING THERE & AWAY

The fixed taxi fare from the airport is 85,000Rp; a metered taxi *to* the airport will be less. Taxis to/from Seminyak average 70,000Rp.

## Getting Around

Find out what shuttle-bus services your hotel provides before you start hailing taxis. A free **shuttle bus** ( ☎ 771662; ☼ 9am-10pm) connects all Nusa Dua and Tanjung Benoa resort hotels with the Bali Collection shopping centre about every hour. Better: use the delightful beach promenade.

## Tanjung Benoa

The peninsula of Tanjung Benoa extends about 4km north from Nusa Dua to the fishing village of Benoa. It is not a gated community

BALI

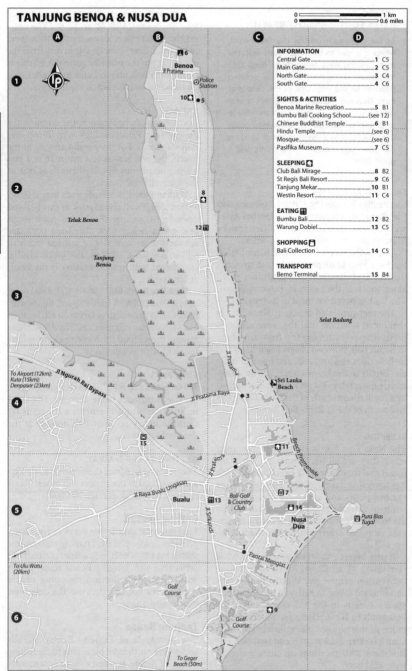

# TANJUNG BENOA & NUSA DUA

0 ——————— 1 km
0 ——————— 0.6 miles

**INFORMATION**
Central Gate...............................**1** C5
Main Gate..................................**2** C5
North Gate.................................**3** C4
South Gate.................................**4** C6

**SIGHTS & ACTIVITIES**
Benoa Marine Recreation............**5** B1
Bumbu Bali Cooking School......(see 12)
Chinese Buddhist Temple...........**6** B1
Hindu Temple.............................(see 6)
Mosque.....................................(see 6)
Pasifika Museum........................**7** C5

**SLEEPING** 🏠
Club Bali Mirage........................**8** B2
St Regis Bali Resort....................**9** C6
Tanjung Mekar..........................**10** B1
Westin Resort...........................**11** C4

**EATING** 🍴
Bumbu Bali...............................**12** B2
Warung Dobiel..........................**13** C5

**SHOPPING** 🛍
Bali Collection...........................**14** C5

**TRANSPORT**
Bemo Terminal..........................**15** B4

Benoa
Jl Pratama
Police Station

Teluk Benoa

Tanjung Benoa

Selat Badung

To Airport (12km);
Kuta (15km);
Denpasar (23km)

Jl Ngurah Rai Bypass

Jl Pratama

Jl Pratama Raya

Sri Lanka Beach

Beach Promenade

Jl Raya Bvalu Ungasan

Bualu

Jl Pratama

Jl Srikandi

Bali Golf & Country Club

Nusa Dua

Pura Bias Tugal

To Ulu Watu (20km)

Pantai Mengiat

Golf Course

Golf Course

To Geger Beach (50m)

by any means and resorts bump up against modest local homes.

Like beaches at Sanur and Nusa Dua, those here are protected from waves by an off-shore reef.

Modest restaurants and hotels are spread out along Jl Pratama, which runs the length of the peninsula. It may be one of the most perilous streets in South Bali for a stroll. There are few sidewalks and in many places nowhere to walk but on the narrow road.

### SIGHTS

Benoa is one of Bali's multidenominational corners, with an interesting **Chinese Buddhist temple**, a **mosque** and a **Hindu temple** within 100m of each other. It's an interesting little fishing town that makes for a good stroll.

### ACTIVITIES

Quite a few water-sports centres along Jl Pratama offer daytime diving, cruises, windsurfing, water-skiing etc. Check equipment and credentials before you sign up. Most have a thatched-roof bar and restaurant attached to their premises. Each morning convoys of buses arrive from all over South Bali bringing day trippers to enjoy the calm waters and various activities.

Among the established water-sports operators is **Benoa Marine Recreation** (BMR; ☎ 771757; www.bmrbali.com; Jl Pratama 99).

Water sports include the very popular parasailing (per round US$25) and jet skiing (per 15 minutes US$25). You'll need at least two people for banana-boat rides (per 15 minutes US$30), or glass-bottomed boat trips (60-minute tour US$25).

### COURSES

**Bumbu Bali Cooking School** (Map p294; ☎ 774502; www.balifoods.com; Jl Pratama; classes US$75; ☒ 6am-3pm Mon, Wed & Fri) Long-time resident and cookbook author Heinz von Holzen runs a renowned cooking school. The day starts with a visit to the markets of Jimbaran.

### SLEEPING

Accommodation here is a mixed bag. Several lesser resorts along the beach charge top-end prices. Some are time-share properties renting out rooms, while others are used almost exclusively by people on package tours.

**Tanjung Mekar** (☎ 081 2363 1374; Jl Pratama; r 120,000-150,000Rp; ☒) Set in a little garden back

from the street, this small family-run guesthouse has four simple, pleasant rooms, some with air-con.

**Club Bali Mirage** (☎ 772147; www.clubbalimirage .com; Jl Pratama 72; r from US$70; ☒ ☒) This compact, J-shaped resort has a good-sized free-form swimming pool. Palms shade the grounds and the beach is right out the front. Rooms feature bold colours, the better to jolt you out of your jet lag – or hangover. All 98 rooms have balconies or terraces. All-inclusive rates are available.

### EATING

Each hotel has several restaurants. There are also several tourist restaurants in or near Benoa.

**Bumbu Bali** (☎ 774502; www.balifoods.com; Jl Pratama; dishes 45,000-90,000Rp; ☒ noon-9pm) One of the finest restaurants on the island, Bumbu Bali serves the best Balinese food you'll have during your visit. Long-time resident and cookbook author Heinz von Holzen, his wife Puji and an enthusiastic staff serve exquisitely flavoured dishes beautifully. Many diners opt for one of several set menus (210,000Rp). There is a nearby lodge as well.

Von Holzen also runs a renowned **cooking school** (classes US$75; ☒ 6am-3pm Mon, Wed & Fri). The day starts with a visit to the markets of Jimbaran (p289).

### GETTING THERE & AROUND

Taxis from the airport cost 100,000Rp. Take a bemo to Bualu, then take one of the infrequent green bemo that shuttle up and down Jl Pratama (3000Rp) – after about 3pm bemo become really scarce on both routes. A metered taxi will be much easier and quicker. Or stroll the beach promenade.

# DENPASAR

☎ 0361 / pop 600,000

Sprawling, hectic and ever-growing, Bali's capital has been the focus of a lot of the island's growth and wealth over the last five decades. It can seem a daunting and chaotic place but spend a little time on its tree-lined streets in the relatively affluent government and business district of Renon and you'll discover a more genteel side.

Denpasar might not be a tropical paradise, but it's as much a part of 'the real Bali' as the rice paddies and cliff-top temples. This is the

## UBUNG

Well north of the town, on the road to Gilimanuk, Ubung is the terminal for northern and western Bali and most long-distance bus services. In the complex, there is a **tourist office** ( ☎ 427172) that provides help with fares and schedules. Arriving here by taxi guarantees a reception by baggage and ticket touts.

| Destination | Fare |
| --- | --- |
| Gilimanuk (for the ferry to Java) | 25,000Rp |
| Kediri (for Tanah Lot) | 7000Rp |
| Mengwi | 7000Rp |
| Munduk | 22,000Rp |
| Negara | 20,000Rp |
| Pancasari (for Danau Bratan) | 18,000Rp |
| Singaraja (via Pupuan or Bedugul) | 30,000Rp |
| Tabanan | 7000Rp |

## BATUBULAN

Located an inconvenient 6km northeast of Denpasar on a road to Ubud, this terminal is for destinations in eastern and central Bali.

| Destination | Fare |
| --- | --- |
| Amlapura | 20,000Rp |
| Bangli | 12,000Rp |
| Gianyar | 10,000Rp |
| Kintamani (via Tampaksiring) | 18,000Rp |
| Padangbai (for the Lombok ferry) | 18,000Rp |
| Sanur | 6000Rp |
| Semarapura | 18,000Rp |
| Singaraja (via Kintamani) | 30,000Rp |
| Singaraja (via Semarapura & Amlapura) | 30,000Rp |
| Ubud | 8000Rp |

## TEGAL

On the western side of town on Jl Iman Bonjol, Tegal is the terminal for Kuta and the Bukit Peninsula.

| Destination | Fare |
| --- | --- |
| Airport | 10,000Rp |
| Jimbaran | 12,000Rp |
| Kuta | 8000Rp |
| Legian | 8000Rp |
| Nusa Dua | 12,000Rp |
| Ulu Watu | 15,000Rp |

## GUNUNG AGUNG

This terminal, at the northwestern corner of town (look for orange bemo), is on Jl Gunung Agung, and has bemo to Kerobokan and Canggu (7000Rp).

## KERENENG

East of the town centre, Kereneng has bemo to Sanur (7000Rp).

## SANGLAH

On Jl Diponegoro, near the general hospital in the south of the city, Sanglah has bemo to Suwung and Benoa Harbour (7000Rp).

## WANGAYA

Near the centre of town, this small terminal is the departure point for bemo services to northern Denpasar and the outlying Ubung bus terminal (6000Rp).

## Bus

The usual route to Java is a bus (get one with air-con) from Denpasar's Ubung terminal to Surabaya (120,000Rp, 10 hours), which includes the short ferry trip across the Bali Strait. Other buses go as far as Yogyakarta (210,000Rp, 16 hours) and Jakarta (305,000Rp, 24 hours), usually travelling overnight.

Book directly at offices in the Ubung terminal, 3km north of the city centre. To Surabaya or even Jakarta, you may get on a bus within an hour of arriving at Ubung, but at busy times you should buy your ticket at least one day ahead.

## GETTING AROUND
### Bemo

Bemo take various circuitous routes from and between Denpasar's many bus/bemo terminals. They line up for various destinations at each terminal, or you can try and hail them from anywhere along the main roads – look for the destination sign above the driver's window. The Tegal–Nusa Dua bemo (dark blue in colour) is handy for Renon; and the Kereneng–Ubung bemo (turquoise) travels along Jl Gajah Mada, past the museum.

### Taxi

As in South Bali, taxis prowl the streets of Denpasar looking for fares. As always, the blue cabs of **Bali Taxi** ( ☎ 701111) are the most reliable choice.

# NUSA LEMBONGAN & ISLANDS

Look towards the open ocean southeast of Bali and the hazy bulk of Nusa Penida dominates the view. But for many visitors the real focus is Nusa Lembongan, which lurks in the shadow of its vastly larger neighbour. Here there's great surfing, quiet white beaches and the kind of funky vibe travellers cherish. It's a popular destination and justly so – it's an easy way to escape the hubbub of South Bali.

Nusa Penida is seldom visited, which means that its dramatic vistas and unchanged village life are yours to explore. Tiny Nusa Ceningan huddles between the larger islands. It is an interesting quick jaunt from Lembongan.

It's been a poor region for many years. Income from tourists is padded with seaweed cultivation. You'll see plots of cultivation in the waters off Jungutbatu and smell the stuff drying on land. Extracts are used as food additives in products like ice cream.

## NUSA LEMBONGAN
☎ 0366

It's the Bali many imagine but never find: simple rooms on the beach, cheap beers with incredible sunsets, days spent surfing and diving, and nights spent riffling through a favourite book or hanging with new friends.

Nusa Lembongan grows in popularity each year, but even as rooms for travellers proliferate, it remains a very mellow place. The 7000 hard-working locals welcome the extra money brought by visitors and time is marked by the crow of a rooster and the fall of a coconut.

### Orientation
Most surfers, divers and budget travellers stay at Jungutbatu Beach in the island's northwest, while more upmarket accommodation is farther south towards Mushroom Bay, where many of the day-trip cruise boats stop.

About 4km southwest along the sealed road from Jungutbatu is Lembongan village, the island's other town. Leaving Jungutbatu, when heading towards Lembongan village, you climb up a steep knoll that offers a wonderful view back over the beach.

### Information
It's vital that you bring sufficient cash for your stay, as there's no ATM. **Bank BPD** ( 8am-3pm Mon-Thu, 8am-1pm Fri) can exchange travellers cheques and cash but the rates are bad.

If the name **Money Changer** ( 8am-9pm) provokes images of the usurious being chased from the temple, you'd be right. Cash advances here on credit cards incur an 8% service charge.

**Pondok Baruna** ( ☎ 081 2390 0686) has public internet terminals. Wi-fi is being installed at many places.

## Sights
### JUNGUTBATU
The **beach** here, a lovely arc of white sand with clear blue water, has superb views across to Gunung Agung in Bali. The village itself is pleasant, with quiet lanes, no cars and a couple of temples, including **Pura Segara** and its enormous banyan tree.

### MUSHROOM BAY
This gorgeous little bay, unofficially named for the mushroom corals offshore, has a perfect crescent of white-sand beach. During the day, the tranquillity may be disturbed by banana-boat rides or parasailing. In the morning and the evening, it's delightful.

The most pleasant way to get here from Jungutbatu is to walk along the trail that starts from the southern end of the main beach and follows the coastline for a kilometre or so past a couple of little beaches.

### DREAM BEACH
Down a little track, on the south side of the island, this 150m crescent of white sand has pounding surf and a warung for sunset beers.

## Activities
Most places will rent bicycles for 30,000Rp per day, surfboards for 50,000Rp, and motorbikes for 30,000Rp per hour.

### SURFING
Surfing here is best in the dry season (April to September), when the winds come from the southeast. It's definitely not for beginners, and can be dangerous even for experts. There are three main breaks on the reef, all aptly named. From north to south are **Shipwreck**, **Lacerations** and **Playground**. Depending on where you're staying, you can paddle directly out to whichever of the three is closest; for others it's better to hire a boat. Prices are negotiable – from 20,000Rp for a one-way trip, and around 100,000Rp waiting time.

### DIVING
**World Diving** ( ☎ 081 2390 0686; www.world-diving.com), based at Pondok Baruna (p303) on Jungutbatu Beach, is well regarded. It offers a complete range of courses, including five-day PADI open-water courses for US$375, and dive trips from US$27 to US$40 per dive to sites around all three islands. See the boxed text, p303 for details on the area's dive sites.

want to avail yourself of the boat-greeting luggage carriers for the walk here along the hillside trail. It's a 15-minute up-and-down scenic walk from the boat-landing area.

**Tamarind Beach** ( ☎ 081 2398 4234; www.balitamarind.com; r 150,000-250,000Rp) Trance music plays in the simple common area at this wild tropical setting right on the beach. The six rooms are simple, with cold-water tubs for getting clean and cooling off. Ring ahead for a pick-up by outrigger from the boat-landing area on Jungutbatu Beach.

**Morin Lembongan** ( ☎ 081 2385 8396; wayman40 @hotmail.com; r US$30-45; 🖳 ) More lushly planted than many of the hillside places, Morin has four woodsy rooms with views over the water from their verandahs. It's cold-water and fan-only; be sure to bargain.

### MUSHROOM BAY

It's your own treasure island. This shallow bay has a nice beach and plenty of over-hanging trees. It offers the nicest lodging on Lembongan. Get here from Jungutbatu by road (10,000Rp) or boat (25,000Rp).

**Mushroom Beach Bungalows** ( ☎ 24515; www .mushroom-lembongan.com; r US$45-80; 🗷 🖳 ) Perched on a tiny knoll at the east end of Mushroom Bay, this family-run place has 11 rooms, some fan-only. There are good-sized bathtubs and a popular cliffside cafe for viewing sunsets.

**Nusa Lembongan Resort** ( ☎ 725864; www.nusa -lembongan.com; villas from US$185; 🗷 🖳 ) Twelve well-appointed and stylish villas overlooking the picture-perfect bay are the draw here. Flowering shrubs and trees highlight the lavish gardens. The resort has a creative terrace restaurant (meals US$10 to US$25) with views over the bay.

### Getting There & Away

Getting to or from Nusa Lembongan offers numerous choices. In descending order of speed are the fast boats like Scoot, the Perama boat and the public boats. Boats anchor off-shore, so be prepared to get your feet wet. And travel light – wheeled bags are comically inappropriate in the water and on the beach and dirt tracks. Porters will shoulder your steamer trunk for 10,000Rp.

#### SANUR

Public boats to Nusa Lembongan leave from the northern end of Sanur beach at 7.45am (45,000Rp, 1¾ to two hours). This is the

boat used for supplies, so you may have to share space with a melon. A faster public boat (150,000Rp, one hour) makes the run in under an hour: 3pm from Lembongan, 4pm from Sanur.

The Perama tourist boat leaves Sanur at 10.15am (100,000Rp, 1¾ hours). The Lembongan office is near the Mandara Beach Bungalows.

The speed champ is **Scoot** ( ☎ 0361-780 2255; one way/return US$18/30), a fast service (30 to 40 minutes) that flies over and through the waves. There are at least two returns daily; check schedules when you book.

For details on the Sanur end of the services, see p289.

#### BENOA HARBOUR

The day-tripping cruise boats to Nusa Lembongan from Benoa Harbour (p302) will usually take passengers only for about US$30 round-trip. Call to confirm. Alternatively, if you go on the full day trip and then decide you want to stay, you can return on a boat another day.

### Getting Around

The island is fairly small and you can easily walk most places. There are no cars. One-way rides on motorbikes or trucks cost 5000Rp.

## NUSA CENINGAN

There is a narrow suspension bridge crossing the lagoon between Nusa Lembongan and Nusa Ceningan, which makes it quite easy to explore the network of tracks on foot or by bicycle – not that there is much to see. The lagoon is filled with frames for seaweed farming and there's also a fishing village and several small agricultural plots. The island is quite hilly, and if you're up for it, you'll get glimpses of great scenery as you wander or cycle around the rough tracks.

This is one of the places you can visit with JED, the Village Ecotourism Network (see boxed text, p330).

## NUSA PENIDA
☎ 0366

The arid island of Nusa Penida is a limestone plateau with white-sand beaches on its north coast, and views over the water to the volcanoes in Bali. The beaches are not good for swimming as most of the shallows are filled with bamboo frames used for seaweed farming. The south coast has limestone cliffs dropping straight down to the sea and a row of offshore islets – it's rugged and spectacular scenery. The interior is hilly, with sparse-looking crops and old-fashioned villages. Nusa Penida can make for an adventurous daytrip from Nusa Lembongan.

Nusa Penida was once used as a place of banishment for criminals and other undesirables from the kingdom of Klungkung, and still has a somewhat sinister reputation. It's also thought to be home to demons.

Services are limited to small shops in the main towns. Bring cash and anything else you'll need.

## Sampalan

Sampalan, the main town on thinly populated Penida, is quiet and pleasant, with a market, schools and shops strung out along the curving coast road. The market area, where the bemos congregate, is in the middle of town.

**Made's Homestay** ( ☎ 0828 368 6709; r 100,000Rp) has four small, clean rooms in a pleasant garden. Breakfast is included. A small side road between the market and the harbour leads here.

## Toyapakeh

If you come by boat from Lembongan, you'll probably be dropped at the beach at Toyapakeh, a pretty town with lots of shady trees. The beach has clean white sand, clear blue water, a neat line of boats, and Gunung Agung as a backdrop. Step up from the beach and you're at the road head, where bemos can take you to Ped or Sampalan (5000Rp).

Offshore, the big grey thing that looks like a tuna-processing plant is the **Quicksilver pontoon** ( ☎ 0361-7425161; www.quicksilver-bali.com). Day trips (adult/child US$85/42.50) from Benoa Harbour include a buffet lunch, snorkelling, banana-boat rides and an excursion ashore to an extremely unattractive 'tourist village' of souvenir sellers.

## Around the Island

A trip around the island, following the north and east coasts, and crossing the hilly interior, can be completed in a few hours by motorcycle. The following description goes clockwise from Sampalan.

The coastal road from Sampalan curves and dips past bays with rows of fishing boats and offshore seaweed gardens. After about 6km, just before the village of Karangsari, steps go up on the right side of the road to the narrow entrance of **Goa Karangsari** caves. There are usually people who can provide a lantern and guide you through the cave for a small negotiable fee of around 20,000Rp each. The limestone cave is over 15m tall in some sections. It extends more than 200m through the hill and emerges on the other side to overlook a verdant valley.

Continue south past a naval station and several **temples** to Suana. Here the main road swings inland and climbs up into the hills, while a very rough side track goes southeast, past more interesting temples to **Semaya**, a fishing village with a sheltered beach and one of Bali's best dive sites offshore.

About 9km southwest of Suana, **Tanglad** is an old-fashioned village and a centre for traditional weaving. Rough roads south and east lead to isolated parts of the coast.

A scenic ridge-top road goes northwest from Tanglad. At Batukandik, a rough road and 1.5km track leads to a spectacular **waterfall** *(air terjun)* that crashes onto a small beach. Get a guide (20,000Rp) in Tanglad.

Back on the main road, continue to Batumadeg, past **Bukit Mundi** (the highest point on the island at 529m), through Klumpu to Sakti, which has traditional stone buildings. Return to the north coast at Toyapakeh.

The important temple of **Pura Dalem Penetaran Ped** is near the beach at Ped, a few kilometres east of Toyapakeh. It houses a shrine for the demon Jero Gede Macaling. The temple structure is sprawling and you will see many people making offerings for safe sea voyages from Nusa Penida. From there, the road follows the lush coast back to Sampalan.

## Getting There & Away

The strait between Nusa Penida and southern Bali is deep and subject to heavy swells – if there is a strong tide, boats often have to wait. Boats to and from Kusamba are not recommended.

### PADANGBAI

On the beach just east of the car park in Padangbai, you'll find the twin-engine fibre-glass boats that run across the strait to Buyuk, 1km west of Sampalan on Nusa Penida (30,000Rp, 45 minutes, four daily). The boats run between 7am and noon. A large and new car ferry has been built for the route but its operation is spotty, owing to insufficient government funding.

**BALI**

## NUSA LEMBONGAN
Boats runs between Toyapakeh and Jungutbatu (30,000Rp, one hour) between 5.30am and 6am. Enjoy the mangrove views on the way. Otherwise, charter a boat for 250,000Rp.

### Getting Around
To see the island you should charter your own bemo or private vehicle with driver for about 60,000Rp to 100,000Rp.

# UBUD

☎ 0361

Perched on the gentle slopes leading up towards the central mountains, Ubud is the other half of Bali's tourism duopoly. Unlike South Bali, however, Ubud's focus remains on the remarkable Balinese culture in its myriad forms.

It's not surprising that many people come to Ubud for a day or two and end up staying longer, drawn in by the rich culture and many activities. Besides the very popular dance-and-music shows, there are numerous courses on offer that allow you to become fully immersed in Balinese culture.

Ubud is home to good restaurants, cafes and streets of shops, many selling goods from the region's artisans. There's somewhere to stay for every budget, and no matter what the price you can enjoy lodgings that reflect the local Zeitgeist: artful, creative and serene.

Around Ubud are temples, ancient sites and whole villages producing handicrafts (albeit mostly for visitors). Although the growth of Ubud has engulfed several neighbouring villages, leading to an urban sprawl, parts of the surrounding countryside remain unspoiled, with lush rice paddies and towering coconut trees. You'd be remiss if you didn't walk one or more of the dozens of paths during your stay.

## ORIENTATION
The once small village of Ubud has expanded to encompass its neighbours – Campuan, Penestanan, Padangtegal, Peliatan and Pengosekan are all part of what we see as Ubud today. The centre of town is the junction of Monkey Forest Rd and Jl Raya Ubud, where the bustling market and bemo stops are found, as well as Ubud Palace and the main temple, Pura Desa Ubud. Monkey Forest Rd (officially Jl Wanara Wana, but always known

by its unofficial name) runs south to Sacred Monkey Forest Sanctuary and is lined with shops, hotels and restaurants.

Jl Raya Ubud ('Ubud Main Rd' – often Jl Raya for short) is the main east–west road. West of Ubud, the road drops steeply down to the ravine at Campuan, where an old suspension bridge, next to the new one, hangs over Sungai Wos (Wos River). West of Campuan, the pretty village of Penestanan is famous for its painters and bead-work. East and south of Ubud proper, the 'villages' of Peliatan, Nyuhkuning and Pengosekan are known variously for painting, woodcarving and traditional dance. The area north of Ubud is less densely settled, with picturesque paddies interspersed with small villages, many of which specialise in a local craft.

## INFORMATION
Along the main roads, you'll find most services you need.

### Bookshops
Ubud is the best place in Bali for book shopping. Shops typically carry newspapers such as the *International Herald Tribune*.

**Cinta Bookshop** (Map p310; ☎ 973295; Jl Dewi Sita) Nice assortment of used novels and vintage books about Bali.

**Ganesha Bookshop** (Map pp308-9; ☎ 970320; www .ganeshabooksbali.com; Jl Raya Ubud) Bali's best bookshop has an amazing amount of stock jammed into a small space. Excellent selection of titles on Indonesian studies, travel, arts, music and fiction (including used titles). Good recommendations and mail-order service.

**Neka Art Museum** (Map pp308-9; ☎ 975074; www .museumneka.com; Jl Raya Sanggingan; ☺ 9am-5pm) Good range of art books.

**Periplus** Monkey Forest Rd (Map p310; ☎ 975178); Jl Raya Campuan (Map pp308-9; ☎ 976149; Bintang Centre) The branch on Monkey Forest Rd is typically glossy; the Campuan branch is a large store with a small cafe.

### Emergency
**Police station** (Map pp308-9; ☎ 975316; Jl Raya Andong; ☺ 24hr) Located east, at Andong.

### Internet Access
The following two neighbouring places are a cut above average with fast broadband connections and large screens. Many of Ubud's cafes offer wi-fi as noted in the listings.

**@Highway** (Map pp308-9; ☎ 972107; Jl Raya Ubud; per min 500Rp; ☺ 24hr; ⚡ ) Full-service and very fast.

## Libraries

**Pondok Pecak Library & Learning Centre** (Map p310; ☎ 976194; Monkey Forest Rd; ◷ 9am-5pm Mon-Sat, 1-5pm Sun) On the far side of the football field, this relaxed place has a children's book section. Charges membership fees for library use. Small cafe and a pleasant reading area. See p313 for information on cultural courses.

## Medical Services

See p271 for additional medical resources for travellers.

**Mua Pharmacy** (Map p310; ☎ 974674; Monkey Forest Rd; ◷ 8am-9pm)

**Ubud Clinic** (Map pp308-9; ☎ 974911; www.ubud clinic.com; Jl Raya Campuan 36; ◷ 24hr) Best medical centre in Ubud. Charges start at 200,000Rp for a clinical consultation.

## Money

Ubud has numerous banks, ATMs and money-changers along Jl Raya Ubud and Monkey Forest Rd.

## Post

**Main post office** (Map pp308-9; Jl Jembawan; ◷ 8am-5pm) Has a sort-it-yourself poste restante system – address poste restante mail to Kantor Pos, Ubud 80571, Bali, Indonesia.

## Tourist Information

**Ubud Tourist Information** (Yaysan Bina Wisata; Map p310; ☎ 973285; Jl Raya Ubud; ◷ 8am-8pm) The one really useful tourist office in Bali. It has a good range of information and a noticeboard listing current happenings and activities. The staff can answer most regional questions and have up-to-date information on ceremonies and traditional dances held in the area; dance tickets are sold here.

# SIGHTS
## Palaces & Temples

**Ubud Palace** and **Puri Saren Agung** (Map p310; cnr Jl Raya Ubud & Jl Suweta) share space in the heart of Ubud. The compound has many ornate corners and was mostly built after the 1917 earthquake. The local royal family still lives here and you can wander around most of the large compound exploring the many traditional and not excessively ornate buildings.

Just north, **Pura Marajan Agung** (Map p310; Jl Suweta), has one of the finest gates you'll find and is the private temple for Ubud's royal family. **Pura Desa Ubud** (Map p310; Jl Raya Ubud) is the main temple for the Ubud community. Just a bit west is the very picturesque **Pura Taman**

**Saraswati** (Ubud Water Palace; Map p310; Jl Raya Ubud). Waters from the temple at the rear of the site feed the pond at the front, which is a riotous tangle of pink lotus blossoms. There are carvings that honour Dewi Saraswati, the goddess of wisdom and the arts, who has clearly given her blessing to Ubud.

## Art Museums
### MUSEUM PURI LUKISAN

This **Palace of Fine Arts** (Map p310; ☎ 975136; www.mpl-ubud.com; off Jl Raya Ubud; admission 20,000Rp; ◷ 9am-5pm) displays excellent examples of all schools of Balinese art. The modern Balinese art movement started in Ubud, where artists first used modern materials, were influenced by foreign styles and began to depict scenes of everyday Balinese life.

The pavilion straight ahead as you enter has a collection of early works from Ubud and the surrounding villages. The pavilion on the left has some colourful examples of the 'Young Artist' style of painting and a good selection of 'modern traditional' works. The pavilion on the right is used for temporary exhibitions, which change every month or so. Paintings are well displayed and labelled in English, and some of the artwork is often for sale.

You enter the museum by crossing a river gully beside the road and wander from building to building through a beautiful garden with pools, statues and fountains.

### NEKA ART MUSEUM

Quite distinct from Neka Gallery, the **Neka Art Museum** (Map pp308-9; ☎ 975074; www.museumneka .com; Jl Raya Sanggingan; adult/child 40,000Rp/free; ◷ 9am-5pm) is the creation of Suteja Neka, a private collector and dealer in Balinese art. It has an excellent and diverse collection and is the best place to learn about the development of painting in Bali.

The **Balinese Painting Hall** provides an overview of local painting, showing influences from classic *wayang kulit* puppetry through to abstract expressionism. The **Arie Smit Pavilion** features Smit's works and examples of the 'Young Artist' school, which he inspired. The **Lempad Pavilion** houses Bali's largest collection of works by I Gusti Nyoman Lempad.

The **Contemporary Indonesian Art Hall** has paintings by artists from other parts of Indonesia, many of whom have worked in Bali. Abdul Aziz, Affandi, Dullah and Anton

Kustia Wijaya, among others, are represented. The upper floor is devoted to the work of foreign artists, such as Louise Koke, Miguel Covarrubias, Rudolph Bonnet, Donald Friend, Han Snel and Antonio Blanco. It often hosts temporary exhibitions.

Bemos travelling between Ubud and Kintamani stop outside the museum.

### AGUNG RAI MUSEUM OF ART (ARMA)

Founded by Agung Rai as a museum, gallery and cultural centre, the impressive **ARMA** (Map pp308-9; ☎ 976659; www.armamuseum.com; Jl Raya Pengosekan; admission 25,000Rp; ⊗ 9am-6pm) is the only place in Bali to see works by the influential German artist Walter Spies. It also has works by 19th-century Javanese artist Raden Saleh. It exhibits classical Kamasan paintings, Batuan-style work from the 1930s and 1940s, and works by Lempad, Affandi, Sadali, Hofker, Bonnet and Le Mayeur. The collection is well labelled in English. Look for the enigmatic *Portrait of a Javanese Nobleman and his Wife* by Raden Saleh.

It's interesting to visit ARMA when local children practise **Balinese dancing** (⊗ 3-5pm Mon-Fri, 10.30am-noon Sun) and during **gamelan practice** (hours vary). See p320 for details on regular Legong and Kecak dance performances. See p313 for details on the numerous cultural courses offered here.

You can enter the museum grounds from the southern end of Jl Raya Pengosekan (there's parking near Kafe ARMA) or around the corner on Jl Pengosekan at the Kafe ARMA.

### MUSEUM RUDANA

This large, imposing **museum** (Map pp308-9; ☎ 975779; admission 20,000Rp; ⊗ 8am-5pm) is run by local politician and art lover Nyoman Rudana. The three floors contain interesting traditional paintings, including a calendar dated to the 1840s, some Lempad drawings and more modern pieces.

### BLANCO RENAISSANCE MUSEUM

The picture of Antonio Blanco mugging with Michael Jackson says it all. His namesake **Blanco Renaissance Museum** (Map pp308-9; ☎ 975502; Jl Raya Campuan; admission 50,000Rp; ⊗ 9am-5pm) captures the artist's theatrical spirit. Blanco came to Bali from Spain via the Philippines. He specialised in erotic art, illustrated poetry and playing the role of an eccentric artist à la Dali.

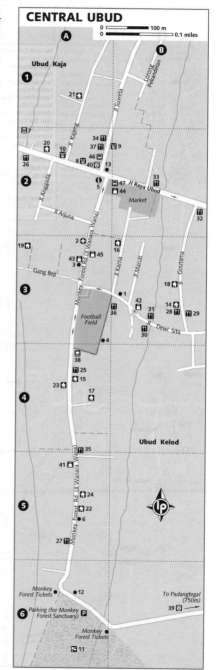

He died in Bali in 1999, and his flamboyant home is now this museum.

## Galleries

Ubud is dotted with galleries – every street and lane seems to have a place exhibiting artwork for sale. They vary enormously in the choice and quality of items on display.

### NEKA GALLERY

Operated by Suteja Neka, the **Neka Gallery** (Map pp308-9; ☎ 975034; Jl Raya Ubud; ⏰ 9am-5pm) is a separate entity from the Neka Art Museum. It has an extensive selection from all the schools of Balinese art, as well as works by European residents such as the renowned Arie Smit.

### SENIWATI GALLERY OF ART BY WOMEN

This **gallery** (Map pp308-9; ⏰ 975485; www.seniwati gallery.com; Jl Sriwedari 2B; ⏰ 9am-5pm Tue-Sun) exhibits works by more than 70 Balinese, Indonesian and resident foreign women artists. The information on many of the artists makes for fascinating reading.

### ADI'S STUDIO

'Look at this!' cry the signs around town plugging this interesting **gallery** (Map pp308-9; ☎ 977104; Jl Bisma 102; ⏰ 10am-5pm), and you should. Many of the better local artists display their works here, including Wayan Pasti, whose carvings give new meaning to 'pork'. It hosts occasional special events like live music.

### KETUT RUDI GALLERY

These sprawling **galleries** (☎ 974122; Pengosekan) showcase the works of more than 50 Ubud artists with techniques as varied as primitive and new realism. The gallery's namesake is on display as well; he favours an entertaining style that's best described as 'comical realism'.

## Artists' Homes

The home of Walter Spies is now part of **Hotel Tjampuhan** (p317). Dutch-born artist Han Snel lived in Ubud from the 1950s until his death in 1999, and his family runs **Siti Bungalows** on Jl Kajeng, where his work is exhibited in a gallery.

Music scholar Colin McPhee is well known thanks to his perennial favourite *A House in Bali*. Although the actual 1930s house is long gone, you can visit the riverside site (which shows up in photographs in the book) at **Sayan Terrace Resort** (p317).

## Sacred Monkey Forest Sanctuary

This cool and dense swath of jungle, officially called **Mandala Wisata Wanara Wana** (Map p310; ☎ 971304; www.monkeyforestubud.com; Monkey Forest Rd; adult/child 15,000/7500Rp; ⏰ 8am-6pm), houses three holy temples. The sanctuary is inhabited by a band of grey-haired and greedy long-tailed Balinese macaques who are nothing like the innocent-looking doe-eyed monkeys on the brochures.

The interesting **Pura Dalem Agung** (Temple of the Dead) is in the forest and has a real

### WALKS AROUND UBUD

There are lots of awe-inspiring walks to surrounding villages or through the rice paddies.

It's good to start walks at daybreak, before it gets too hot. In the walks below, distances are approximate and are measured with the Ubud Palace as the start and end point.

#### Monkey Forest & Penestanan

This 8km walk (Map pp308–9) features a good range of rice paddies and rural Ubud scenery.

Take your time strolling through the **Sacred Monkey Forest Sanctuary** (p311). Continue south on the lane to the village of **Nyuhkuning**, and turn west along the south end of the football field, then turn south down the narrow road. At the southern end of the village, turn right and follow the paved road across the bridge over Sungai Wos to Dangin Lebak. Take the track to the right just after the large Bale Banjar Dangin Lebak (Dangin Lebak Community Hall). From here follow paths due north through the rice paddies, and veer left, westwards through the rice paddies to a paved road to reach **Katik Lantang**, where you join a paved road that continues north to **Penestanan**, where many artists live. Follow the paved road through the village, veering east, and go down through a deep cutting and back to Ubud.

#### Campuan Ridge

This 8.5km walk (Map pp308–9) passes over the lush river valley of Sungai Wos, offering views of Gunung Agung and glimpses of small village communities and rice fields.

The walk leaves Jl Raya Campuan at the Warwick Ibah Luxury Villas. Enter the hotel driveway and take the path to the left, where a walkway crosses the river to Pura Gunung Lebah. From there follow the concrete path north, climbing up onto the ridge between the two rivers.

Continuing north along the Campuan ridge, the road improves as it passes through rice paddies and the small village of **Bangkiang Sidem**. On the outskirts of the village, an unsigned road heads west, which winds down to Sungai Cerik (the west branch of Sungai Wos), then climbs steeply up to **Payogan**. From here you can walk south to the main road and on to the centre of Ubud.

#### Penestanan & Sayan

The wonders of Sungai Ayung are the focus of this 6.5km walk (Map pp308–9), where you will jaunt below the luxury hotels built to take advantage of this lush, tropical river valley.

Just west of the Campuan bridge, a steep uphill road, Jl Raya Penestanan, bends away to the left and winds across the forested gully of Sungai Blangsuh to the artists' village of Penestanan. West of Penestanan, take a small road north that curves around to **Sayan** and the Sayan Terrace Resort (p317). The best place to get down to the riverside is just north of Sayan Terrace – follow the narrow tracks down.

Head north along the eastern side of Sungai Ayung, traversing steep slopes and rice paddies. After about 1.5km you'll reach the finishing point for many of the white-water rafting trips – a good but steep trail goes from there up to the main road at **Kedewatan**, where you can walk back to Ubud.

Indiana Jones feel to it. Look for the Rangda figures devouring children at the entrance to the inner temple.

You can enter through one of the three gates: the main one at the southern end of Monkey Forest Rd; 100m further east, near the car park; or from the southern side, on the lane from Nyuhkuning. Across from the main entrance, the forest's **office** (Map p310) accepts donations for a scheme to offset the carbon you created getting to Bali. Get a tree planted for 150,000Rp.

## ACTIVITIES
### Massage, Spas & Salons

Ubud brims with salons and spas where you can pamper yourself. In fact, visiting a spa is at the top of many a visitor's itinerary. Most higher-end hotels have (often lavish) spas. Peruse the range of holistic services on offer on the bulletin board outside Bali Buddha (p319) and you'll decide that simple yoga is for pikers.

**Eve Spa** (Map p310; ☎ 747 0910; Monkey Forest Rd; 1hr massage 75,000Rp; ☼ 9am-9pm) will cleanse you of toxins from eating an apple or other dubious substances. The menu is straightforward and affordable, and you can go on something of a spa orgy: an all-day festival of treatments is 325,000Rp.

**Ubud Sari Health Resort** (Map pp308-9; ☎ 974393; Jl Kajeng; 1hr massage US$30; ⏰ 8am-8pm) is a spa and hotel in one. It is a serious place with extensive treatments bearing names such as 'total tissue cleansing' (treatments use organic and other natural materials). Besides a long list of one-day spa and salon services, there are packages that include stays at the hotel (see p316).

**Wayan Nuriasih** (Map pp308-9; ☎ 742 6189; bali healer@hotmail.com; Jl Jembawan 5; ⏰ 9am-5pm), one of the stars of *Eat, Pray, Love* (p264), can work wonders with medicinal plants – many are for sale out front – as well as massage and other treatments. The 'vitamin lunch' is the antidote for a Bintang dinner.

**Yoga Barn** (Map pp308-9; ☎ 070992; www.balispirit .com; off Jl Pengosekan; classes from 90,000Rp; ⏰ 7am-8pm) sits in its own lotus position amid trees back near a river valley. The name exactly describes what you'll find – although this barn never needs shovelling. A huge range of classes in yoga and life-affirming offshoots are held through the week.

## Rafting

The nearby Sungai Ayung is the most popular river in Bali for white-water rafting. **Bali Adventure Tours** ( ☎ 721480; www.baliadventuretours .com) offers trips down Sungai Ayung from US$50 to US$90, and can combine rafting with a big choice of other outdoor activities.

Another operator offering rafting and other adventurous outings is **Sobek** ( ☎ 287059; www .balisobek.com).

## COURSES

Ubud is a very pleasant place to spend a few weeks developing your artistic skills, or learning about Balinese culture. Most places ask that you register in advance.

**Augung Rai Museum of Art** (ARMA; Map pp308-9; ☎ 976659; www.armamuseum.com; Jl Raya Pengosekan; classes US$25-50; ⏰ 9am-6pm) A cultural powerhouse offering classes in painting, woodcarving and batik. Other courses include Balinese history, Hinduism and architecture.

**Casa Luna Cooking Courses** (Map pp308-9; ☎ 973283; www.casalunabali.com; Honeymoon Guesthouse, Jl Bisma) Janet de Neefe and her team run regular cooking courses at Honeymoon Guesthouse. Half-day courses (250,000Rp) cover

ingredients, cooking techniques and the cultural background of the Balinese kitchen. Sunday tours cover sea-salt and palm-sugar production (300,000Rp).

**Kite Workshop** ( ☎ 081 3387 64495) Kites are a colourful part of Balinese culture. Programs are flexible and geared to families; classes are held in a village near Ubud and include materials and packing for getting the creations home.

**Nirvana Batik Course** (Map p310; ☎ 975415; www .nirvanaku.com; Nirvana Pension & Gallery, Jl Goutama 10; ⏰ classes 10am-3pm Mon-Sat) Nyoman Suradnya teaches highly regarded batik courses. Classes cost US$40 to US$150 depending on duration (one to five days).

**Nyoman Warsa** (Map p310; ☎ 974807; Pondok Bamboo Music Shop, Monkey Forest Rd) Offers courses in basic Balinese instruments. Simple mastery can take six months or more. Those with less time can try a flute lesson (per hour 50,000Rp).

**Pondok Pecak Library & Learning Centre** (Map p310; ☎ 976194; Monkey Forest Rd, on the far side of the football field; ⏰ 9am-5pm Mon-Sat, 1-5pm Sun) Painting and mask-carving classes. Sessions cost from 75,000Rp for one hour. Good resource centre for other courses offered locally.

**Santra Putra** (Map pp308-9; ☎ 977810; Penestan; classes per hr 100,000Rp) Intensive painting and drawing classes are run by abstract artist I Wayan Karja, whose studio is on site. Accommodation is also available; see p315.

**Threads of Life Indonesian Textile Arts Center** (Map pp308-9; ☎ 972187; www.threadsoflife.com; Jl Kajeng 24) Textile-appreciation courses in the gallery and educational studio last from one day to eight days. Some classes involve extensive travel around Bali and should be considered graduate level.

## TOURS

Day tours around Ubud are popular, especially ones that involve activities or themed programs.

**Bali Bird Walks** (Map pp308-9; ☎ 975009; www .balibirdwalk.com; Jl Raya Campuan; walks US$33; ⏰ Tue & Fri-Sun 9am-12.30pm) For the keen birdwatcher, this tour started by Victor Mason is still going strong. A gentle morning's walk (from the former Beggar's Bush Bar) will give you the opportunity to see maybe 30 of the 100 or so local species.

**Banyan Tree Cycling** ( ☎ 805 1620, 081 3387 98516; www.banyantree.wikispaces.com; tours from 360,000Rp) Has day-long tours of remote villages in the hills above Ubud. It's locally owned, and the tours emphasise interaction with villagers.

**Herb Walks** ( ☎ 975051; walks US$18; ⏰ 8.30am Mon-Thu) Four-hour walks through lush Bali landscape; medicinal and cooking herbs and plants are identified and explained in their natural environment. Includes herbal drinks. A great deal.

BALI

**Ubud Tourist Information** (Yaysan Bina Wisata; Map p310; ☎ 973285; Jl Raya Ubud; tours 125,000-200,000Rp; ☻ 8am-8pm) Runs interesting and affordable half- and full-day trips to a huge range of places, including Ulu Watu, Mengwi, Alas Kedaton and Tanah Lot, or Goa Gajah, Pejeng, Gunung Kawi and Kintamani.

## FESTIVALS & EVENTS

The Ubud area is one of the best places in Bali to see the many religious and cultural events that are celebrated on the island each year.

The **Ubud Writers & Readers Festival** (www .ubudwritersfestival.com) brings together scores of writers and readers from around the world in a celebration of writing – especially writing that touches on Bali. It is usually held in October.

## SLEEPING

Ubud has hundreds of places to stay. Choices range from simple little losmen to luxurious retreats that are among the best in the world. Generally, Ubud accommodation offers good value for money at any price level. A simple, clean room within a family home compound is the least-expensive option. The midrange hotels generally offer swimming pools and other amenities, while the top-end hotels are often perched on the edges of the deep river valleys, with superb views and service. (Although some very cheap places also boast amazing views that urge you to curl up with a book and contemplate.)

Addresses in Ubud can be imprecise – but signage at the end of a road will often list the names of all the places to stay. Away from the main roads there are no streetlights and it can be very difficult to find your way after dark. If walking, you will definitely want a torch (flashlight).

### Budget

Inexpensive family lodgings are very small, often with just two, three or four rooms. They tend to operate in clusters, so you can easily look at a few before making your choice.

#### CENTRAL UBUD

This was the first area developed for tourists in Ubud and there are many good-value homestays.

#### Monkey Forest Rd

**Frog Pond Inn** (Map p310; Monkey Forest Rd; r 80,000-120,000Rp) It's quiet, ultrabasic, friendly and

has eight rooms with open-air bathrooms and cold water. Enjoy the breakfast that has charmed generations of backpackers across Asia: banana pancakes.

**Mandia Bungalows** (Map p310; ☎ 970965; Monkey Forest Rd; r 100,000-130,000Rp) It's heliconia heaven in the lush gardens. The four bungalow-style rooms are shaded by coconut palms and cooled by ceiling fans. Porches have comfy loungers.

**Warsa's Garden Bungalows** (Map p310; ☎ 971548; Monkey Forest Rd; r 150,000-200,000Rp; ☒ ☒ ) A good-sized pool with fountains enlivens this comfy but simple place that's located in the heart of Monkey Forest action. The 10 rooms are reached through a traditional family-compound entrance. Some have tubs; some are fan-only.

#### East of Monkey Forest Rd

Small streets east of Monkey Forest Rd, including Jl Karna and Jl Maruti, have numerous, family-style homestays, which are secluded but close to the market and Jl Raya Ubud.

**Gandra House** (Map p310; ☎ 976529; Jl Karna; r from 100,000Rp) Modern bathrooms and spacious gardens are the highlights of this cold-water-only 10-room homestay. It's one of several family-run places on this street, so compare.

#### Jl Goutama

This charming street has several cheap, quiet and accessible places to stay.

**Agung Cottages** (Map p310; ☎ 975414; Jl Goutama; r 150,000-250,000Rp, villas 300,000Rp; ☒ ) Follow a short path to reach this slightly rural-feeling family compound. The six huge, spotless rooms (some fan-only) are set in gardens tended by a lovely family. It's well off the already quiet road.

**Nirvana Pension & Gallery** (Map p310; ☎ 975415; www.nirvanaku.com; Jl Goutama 10; s/d 200,000/250,000Rp) There are *alang alang* (woven thatch) roofs, a plethora of paintings, ornate doorways and six rooms with modern bathrooms in a secluded locale next to large family temple. Batik courses are also held here (p313).

#### North of Jl Raya Ubud

Both Jl Kajeng and Jl Suweta, leading north from Jl Raya, offer an excellent choice of budget lodgings, some quite close to the centre of town.

**Shanti Home Stay** (Map p310; ☎ 975421; Jl Kajeng 5; r 60,000-120,000Rp) This is a classic Ubud home-stay: you join four generations of the family – plus numerous cute pooches – in a compound with six rooms in bungalow-style units. Rooms are clean and some have hot water. The porches are spacious.

### NORTH OF THE CENTRE

Things get quiet as you head up the gentle slope from Jl Raya Ubud; note that some places are a kilometre or more to the north.

**Homestay Rumah Roda** (Map pp308-9; ☎ 975487; rumahroda@indo.net.id; Jl Kajeng 24; r 70,000-90,000Rp) Next door to the Threads of Life gallery on peaceful Jl Kajeng, Rumah Roda is a typically mellow homestay. The inn is dedicated to sound ecological principles and you can refill your water bottles here.

### EAST OF THE CENTRE

You can get to the heart of Ubud in less than 15 minutes by foot from this low-key part of town.

### Jl Hanoman

East of central Ubud, but still conveniently located, this area has several budget lodgings along Jl Hanoman.

**Artini Cottages 1** (Map pp308-9; ☎ 975348; www .artinicottage.com; Jl Hanoman; bungalows 150,000Rp) The Artini family runs a small empire of good-value guesthouses on Jl Hanoman. This, the original, is in an ornate family compound with many flowers. The three bungalows have hot water and large bathtubs.

**Nick's Homestay** (Map pp308-9; ☎ 975526; www .nickshotels-ubud.com; Jl Hanoman 57; US$15) Nick has a minor empire of three Ubud budget hotels. This, his simplest, is the best. Beds in the six bungalow-style rooms are made from bamboo logs. Watch family life from the copious porches.

### Tebesaya

A little further east, this quiet village comprises little more than its main street, Jl Sukma, which runs between two streams.

**Biangs** (Map pp308-9; ☎ 976520; Jl Sukma 28; r 50,000-100,000Rp) In a little garden, Biangs – meaning 'mama' – has six well-maintained rooms, all with hot water. The best rooms have views of a small valley. Should you need a Japanese novel, the book exchange is loaded.

### WEST OF THE CENTRE
### Jl Bisma

Paved with cement blocks inscribed by residents and donors, Jl Bisma runs into a plateau of rice fields.

**Pondok Indah** (Map pp308-9; ☎ 966323; off Jl Bisma; s/d 150,000/200,000Rp) Follow the swift-flowing waterways for 150m along a path hopping with frogs to this peaceful place where the top-floor terraces look over the fields. All five rooms have hot water.

**Bali Moon** (Map pp308-9; ☎ 978293; off Jl Bisma; r from 170,000Rp) Watch the moon rise over Gunung Batukau from this simple inn set with a few others down narrow paths between the rice fields. The four rooms are simple but have ambitions of style with open-air bathrooms with tubs. One 2nd floor room is the view-lovers' choice.

### Campuan & Penestanan

West of Ubud, but still within walking distance, simple rooms and bungalows in the rice fields are pitched at those seeking low-priced, longer-term lodgings. Most will offer discounted monthly rates (US$200 is average), and some larger bungalows are quite economical if you can share with a group of people.

Note that these places are a steep climb up a set of concrete stairs off Jl Raya Campuan. (You can avoid this by approaching from the west.)

**Santra Putra** (Map pp308-9; ☎ 977810; karjabali@ yahoo.com; off Jl Raya Campuan; r US$12-15) Run by internationally exhibited abstract artist I Wayan Karja (whose studio/gallery is also on site), this place has five big, open, airy rooms with hot water. Enjoy paddy-field views from all vantage points. Painting and drawing classes are offered by the artist; see p313.

**Kori Agung Bungalows** (Map pp308-9; ☎ 975166; off Jl Raya Campuan; r from 150,000Rp) On the terrace with other basic inns above Campuan. Rooms are basic but the location is ideal for those looking for leafy views and solitude. The only noise at night is water coursing through the rice fields.

## Midrange
### CENTRAL UBUD
### Jl Raya Ubud

Don't settle for a room with road noise along Ubud's main drag.

**Puri Saraswati Bungalows** (Map p310; ☎ 975164; www.purisaraswati.com; Jl Raya Ubud; r US$60-90; 🖁 🖳 )

BALI

Very central and pleasant with lovely gardens that open onto the Ubud Water Palace. The 18 rooms are well back from Jl Raya Ubud, so it's quiet. Some rooms are fan-only; interiors are simply furnished but have richly carved details.

### Monkey Forest Rd

**Ubud Inn** (Map p310; ☎ 975071; www.ubudinn.com; Monkey Forest Rd; r US$25-80; 🗶 🖵 ) Lush loses its meaning in Ubud, but this place takes it to a new level. The 30 rooms span several budgets: basic are fan-only; the rest are large, nicely furnished and have fridges. The L-shaped pool has a children's area.

**our pick** **Oka Wati Hotel** (Map p310; ☎ 973386; www .okawatihotel.com; off Monkey Forest Rd; r US$30-60; 🖵 ) Oka Wati (the owner) is a lovely lady who grew up near the Ubud Palace. The 19 rooms have large verandahs where the delightful staff will deliver your choice of breakfast. The decor features vintage details like four-poster beds; some rooms view a small rice field.

### NORTH OF THE CENTRE

**Ketut's Place** (Map pp308-9; ☎ 975304; www.ketuts place.com; Jl Suweta 40; r US$21-46; 🗶 🖵 ) The nine rooms here range from basic with fans to deluxe versions with air-con and bathtub. All have artful accents and enjoy a dramatic pool shimmering down the hillside and river-valley views. On some nights, an impressive Balinese feast is served by Ketut, a local luminary.

**Ubud Sari Health Resort** (Map pp308-9; ☎ 974393; www.ubudsari.com; Jl Kajeng; r US$35-60; 🗶 🖵 ) Like your colon after a week of treatments here, this 10-room health resort has been spiffed up. See p312 for details on the spa. The plants in the gardens are labelled for their medicinal qualities and the cafe serves organic, vegetarian fare. Guests can use the health facilities, including the sauna and whirlpool.

### EAST OF THE CENTRE

**Matahari Cottages** (Map pp308-9; ☎ 975459; www .matahariubud.com; Jl Jembawan; r US$35-60; 🗶 ) This delightful place has six flamboyant, themed rooms, including the 'Batavia Princess' and the 'Indian Pasha'. The library is a vision out of a 1920s fantasy. It also boasts a self-proclaimed 'jungle Jacuzzi' and a multicourse breakfast and high tea elaborately served on silver (free for guests). And in a nod to the modern day, the hotel fully recycles.

### SOUTH OF THE CENTRE

**Artini 3 Cottages** (Map pp308-9; ☎ 974147; www.artini ubudhotel.com; Jl Raya Pengosekan; r US$35-45; 🗶 🖵 ) The top choice of the Artini empire, the 16 rooms here are in attractive stone buildings arrayed around a spectacular pool area down by a stream. Get a room facing east for the best views through the palms. Room decor is comfortable but standard.

**Swasti Cottages** (Map pp308-9; ☎ 974079; www .baliswasti.com; Jl Nyuh Bulan; standard fan/air-con r 350,000/450,000Rp, Gladak 550,000Rp; 🗶 🖵 🛜 ) This popular French-run, 6-room property is a great hideaway. Guests come to stay in a sprawling garden setting, with a dedicated yoga/tai chi pavilion, a pool, and three classes of simple yet stylish rooms. Meals are accented by home-grown produce.

**Alam Indah** (Map pp308-9; ☎ 974629; www.alamindah bali.com; Jl Nyuh Bulan; r US$50-95; 🗶 🖵 ) Just south of the Monkey Forest in Nyuhkuning, this isolated and spacious resort has 10 rooms that are beautifully finished in natural materials to traditional designs. The Wos Valley views are entrancing, especially from the multilevel pool area. The walk in at night follows a driveway lined with tea candles.

### WEST OF THE CENTRE
### Jl Bisma

Close to town, this area retains rural charm while moving upmarket.

**Uma Sari Cottage** (Map pp308-9; ☎ 981538; www .umasari.com; Jl Bisma; r $30-40; 🗶 🖵 🖥 ) While ducks patrol the rice in the surrounding fields looking for bugs, you can waggle your tail in the jade-green pool. Most of the eight large rooms are fan-only; go for the upper floor, as the verandahs have the best views of the ducks in action. All have tubs.

**Sama's Cottages** (Map pp308-9; ☎ 973481; wayan _sarjana@yahoo.com; Jl Bisma; s/d US$33/39; 🖵 ) This lovely little hideaway is terraced down a hill. The bungalow-like rooms have lashings of Balinese style layered on absolute simplicity. The oval pool feels like a jungle oasis. Ask for low-season discounts.

**Honeymoon Guesthouse** (Map pp308-9; ☎ 973282; www.casalunabali.com; Jl Bisma; r 350,000-600,000Rp; 🗶 🖵 🖥 ) The 19 rooms here have terraces and tubs; some have air-con. There's a play area for kids. Avoid the dark rooms; some rooms have air-con and those near reception have wi-fi. See p313 for details about the cooking classes held here.

## Campuan & Penestanan

Just west of the Campuan bridge, steep Jl Raya Penestanan branches off to the left, and climbs up and around to Penestanan.

**Pager Bungalows** (Map pp308-9; ☎ 975433; Jl Raya Campuan; r 150,000-300,000Rp, villas 500,000Rp) Run by painter Nyoman Pageh and his family, this cute homestay hugs a verdant hillside location that feels like you're lost in the bottom of the spinach bowl on a salad bar. Two large bungalows face the compound; five more rooms are comfortable and have views.

**Hotel Tjampuhan** (Map pp308-9; ☎ 975368; www .pitamaharesorts-bali.com; Jl Raya Campuan; r US$65-120; 🐱 🏊) This venerable place overlooks the confluence of Sungai Wos and Campuan. The influential German artist Walter Spies lived here in the 1930s. Bungalow-style units spill down the hill and enjoy mesmerising valley views.

## Sayan & Ayung Valley

**Sayan Terrace Resort** (Map pp308-9; ☎ 974384; www.sayanterraceresort.com; Jl Raya Sayan; r US$80-160; 🐱 🏊 🖥 🛜) Gaze into the Sayan Valley from this venerable hotel and you'll understand why this was the site of Colin McPhee's namesake in *A House in Bali*; see p311 for details. Here the 11 rooms are simply decorated but are large and have *that* view.

## Top End

At this price range you have your choice of prime properties in the area. The big decision: close to town or not. Look for views, expansive pools, rooms with architectural features such as marble and/or outdoor bathrooms and a full range of amenities. Excellent service is a given.

### CENTRAL UBUD

**Ubud Village Hotel** (Map p310; ☎ 975571; www.theubud village.com; Monkey Forest Rd; r US$70-160; 🐱 🏊 🖥) Mainstream comfort is the order of the day at this centrally located 28-room hotel. Rooms have elegant traditional Balinese decor with plenty of teak and ikat, and the pool area is large. The owners have a luxe villa resort with the same name in Pengosekan.

### NORTH OF THE CENTRE

**Waka di Ume** (Map pp308-9; ☎ 973178; www.waka diumeubud.com; Jl Suweta; r US$150, villas from US$300; 🐱 🏊 🖥 🛜) Located a gentle 1.5km uphill from the centre, this elegant compound enjoys engrossing virescent views across rice fields. New and old styles mix in the large units; go for a villa with a view. Service is superb yet relaxed. Listening to gamelan practice echoing across the fields at night is quite magical.

### SOUTH OF THE CENTRE

**ARMA Resort** (Map pp308-9; ☎ 976659; www.arma resort.com; Jl Raya Pengosekan; r US$80-180, villas from US$375; 🐱 🖥 🏊) Get full Balinese cultural immersion at the hotel enclave of the ARMA compound (see p310 for details about the excellent museum and p313 for details on the range of courses offered). The expansive property has a large library and elegant gardens. Villas come with private pools.

### WEST OF THE CENTRE

Properties generally go from posh to posher as you near the fabled Ayung Valley.

### Campuan

**Warwick Ibah Luxury Villas & Spa** (Map pp308-9; ☎ 974466; www.warwickibah.com; off Jl Raya Campuan; ste US$200-530; 🐱 🏊 🖥 🛜) Overlooking the rushing waters of the Wos Valley, the Ibah offers refined luxury in 15 spacious, stylish individual suites and villas, which combine ancient and modern details. The swimming pool is set into the hillside amid gardens and lavish stone carvings.

### Sayan & Ayung Valley

Two kilometres west of Ubud, the fast-flowing Sungai Ayung has carved out a deep valley, its sides sculpted into terraced paddy fields or draped in thick rainforest. Overlooking this verdant valley are some of Bali's best hotels.

**Bambu Indah** (Map pp308-9; ☎ 975124; www .bambuindah.com; Baung; house US$200-500; 🏊 🖥 🛜) Famed expat entrepreneur John Hardy sold his namesake jewellery company in 2007 and became a hotelier. On a ridge near Sayan and his beloved Sungai Ayung, he's assembled a compound of four 100-year-old royal Javanese houses. Several outbuildings create a timeless village with underpinnings of luxury. The entire compound is run to a very 'green' standard.

**Amandari** (Map pp308-9; ☎ 975333; www.aman resorts.com; Kedewatan; ste from US$700; 🐱 🏊 🖥 🛜) In Kedewatan village, the storied Amandari does everything with charm and grace – sort of like a classical Balinese dancer. Superb views over the jungle and down to the river –

BALI

the 30m green-tiled swimming pool seems to drop right over the edge – are just some of the inducements.

## EATING

Ubud's restaurants offer the most diverse and interesting food on the island. It's a good place to try authentic Balinese dishes, as well as a range of other Asian and international cuisine.

A good **organic farmers market** is held each week, at Pizza Bagus (opposite) every Saturday from 8am to 1pm. **Bintang Supermarket** (Map pp308–9; Bintang Centre, Jl Raya Campuan) is well located and has a large range of food and other essentials.

### Central Ubud

#### JL RAYA UBUD

There are busy and tasty choices on Ubud's main street.

**Nomad** (Map p310; ☎ 977169; Jl Raya Ubud; dishes 15,000-60,000Rp) Offers a daily barbecue, often with a gamelan player providing the soundtrack. Balinese food is served in tapas-sized portions. Assume the position – lotus that is – at low Japanese-style tables.

**Casa Luna** (Map p310; ☎ 977409; Jl Raya Ubud; dishes 15,000-60,000Rp) Renaissance woman Janet de Neefe of cooking school (p313) and writers festival (p314) fame runs this ever-popular Indonesian-focused restaurant, which has recently been entirely rebuilt and looks better than ever.

**Rendezvousdoux** (Map p310; ☎ 747 0163; Jl Raya Ubud 14; dishes 20,000-35,000Rp; 🍴) How to define it? A fusion of French-accented forms: cafe, library and bookshop, Rendezvousdoux is the most creative spot on the street. Bonuses include global music (at times live) and historic films about Ubud on loop.

#### MONKEY FOREST RD

**Bumbu Bali** (Map p310; ☎ 976698; Monkey Forest Rd; dishes 15,000-50,000Rp) A good place for Balinese food in the heart of Ubud. The menu features dishes such as *lawar* (green bean salad), *ayam pelalah* (spicy shredded chicken salad) and *sambal goreng udang* (prawns in a tangy coconut-milk sauce).

**our pick Three Monkeys** (Map p310; ☎ 974830; Monkey Forest Rd; mains 20,000-50,000Rp) Mellow music and artworks set a cultured mood. The tables overlooking the rice field out the back make it magic. By day there are sandwiches, salads

and gelato. At night there's a fusion menu of Asian classics, including addictive Vietnamese summer prawn rolls.

**Coffee & Silver** (Map p310; ☎ 975354; Monkey Forest Rd; dishes 20,000-70,000Rp; 🕙 10am-midnight; 🛜) Tapas and more substantial items make up the menu at this comfortable cafe with seating inside and out. Vintage photos of Ubud line the walls. Many linger over the good coffee and other drinks for hours.

#### EAST OF MONKEY FOREST RD

**Juice Ja Café** (Map p310; ☎ 971056; Jl Dewi Sita; snacks from 15,000Rp; 🛜) Glass of spirulina? Dash of wheatgrass with your papaya juice? Organic fruits and vegetables go into the food at this funky bakery-cafe. Little brochures explain the provenance of items like the organic cashew nuts.

**Tutmak Café** (Map p310; ☎ 975754; Jl Dewi Sita; dishes 15,000-35,000Rp; 🛜) The breezy multilevel location here, facing both Jl Dewi Sita and the football field, is a popular place for a refreshing drink or a meal. Local comers on the make huddle around their laptops plotting their next move.

**Kafe Batan Waru** (Map p310; ☎ 977528; Jl Dewi Sita; dishes 20,000-70,000Rp) This ever-popular cafe has an expanded outdoor terrace. It serves consistently excellent Indonesian food, which is presented with a dash of colour and flair. The *mie goreng* noodles are made fresh daily – a noteworthy detail given the number of places that substitute pot noodles. Western dishes include sandwiches and salads.

#### JL GOUTAMA

Choose from several simple and funky eateries on this nearly traffic-free lane.

**Dewa Warung** (Map p310; Jl Goutama; dishes 5000-20,000Rp) When it rains, the tin roof sounds like a tap-dance convention and the bare light bulbs sway in the breeze. A little garden surrounds tables a few steps above the road where diners tuck into plates of sizzling fresh Indo fare.

**Devilicious** (Map p310; ☎ 745972; Jl Goutama; mains from 20,000Rp) Jl Goutama is a delightful street for a stroll and this cafe is one of the reasons why. Just wandering the narrow lane is like stepping back 30 years in Ubud, and creative little places like this place seem to appear like mushrooms after the rain. Look for theme nights like Cajun Fridays and Italian Tuesdays.

**NORTH OF JL RAYA UBUD**

**Warung Ibu Oka** (Map p310; Jl Suweta; dishes 15,000-20,000Rp; 11am-3pm) Join the lunchtime lines opposite Ubud Palace waiting for one thing: the eponymous Balinese-style roast suckling pig. Locals and expats in the know travel far for meat they say is the most tender and tasty on the island. Order a *spesial* to get the best cut.

**Terazo** (Map p310; 978941; Jl Suweta; dishes 30,000-80,000Rp) A popular restaurant serving creative Balinese fusion cuisine. The wine list is decent and features French, Italian and Australian choices. The spare interior is accented by evocative vintage travel posters and furnished with plush cane chairs. The beautiful framed tonic-ad reproduction tells you what you need to know about the bar.

## North of the Centre

**Roda Restaurant** (Map pp308-9; 975487; Jl Kajeng 24; dishes 7000-18,000Rp) Above Threads of Life (p313), Roda (which also rents rooms; p315), serves astonishingly cheap Balinese dishes with a wonderful overlay of local culture. The extended Roda family lives here and prepares dishes from recipes which have been handed down for generations.

## East of the Centre

**Warung Igelanca** (Map pp308-9; 974153; Jl Raya Ubud; dishes 8000-15,000Rp) Little bigger than a macaroni, this streetside diner is a temple for noodle lovers. Get 'em in dishes that range from Jakarta chicken noodle soup to North Sumatra fried rice noodles.

**Bali Buddha** (Map pp308-9; 976324; Jl Jembawan 1; dishes 15,000-40,000Rp) A local institution, Bali Buddha has a veggie cafe with a long list of healthy foods upstairs and a health-food store and bakery downstairs (the blueberry muffins, 6000Rp, are mighty fine). Raw foodists, vegans and just those in search of tasty food and drink will find much to like here. The bulletin board out the front is a community resource.

**JL HANOMAN**

**Masakan Padang** (Map pp308-9; Jl Hanoman; dishes 6000-15,000Rp; noon-1am) The bright-orange exterior at this Padang-style eatery – where you choose from the plates on display – hints at the fresh and spicy food within.

**Kafe** (Map pp308-9; 970992; www.balispirit.com; Jl Hanoman 44; dishes 15,000-40,000Rp; ) Part of Bali Spirit, a host group for several NGOs, Kafe has an organic menu great for veggie grazing or just having a coffee, juice or house-made natural soda.

## South of Ubud

Many highly regarded restaurants are found along the curves of Jl Raya Pengosekan. It's always worth seeing what's new.

**Pizza Bagus** (Map pp308-9; 978520; www.pizza bagus.com; Jl Raya Pengosekan; dishes 18,000-40,000Rp; ) Ubud's best pizza bakes up with a crispy thin crust here. Besides the long list of pizza options, there's pasta and sandwiches – all mostly organic. Tables are in and out, there's a play area and delivery.

## West of Ubud

The restaurants and cafes west of the centre are dotted among rice fields, lanes and roads.

**JL BISMA**

**Café des Artistes** (Map pp308-9; 972706; Jl Bisma 9X; dishes 22,000-90,000Rp; 10am-midnight) In a quiet perch up off Jl Raya Ubud, the popular Café des Artistes serves elaborate Belgian-accented food, superb steaks and daily specials. Local art is on display and the bar is refreshingly cultured. Enjoy the enveloping wicker seating inside or in front in a small garden. Book.

**SANGGINGAN**

**our pick** **Nasi Ayam Kedewatan** (Map pp308-9; 742 7168; Jl Raya Kedewatan; mains under 10,000Rp; 9am-6pm) Few locals making the trek up the hill pass this open-air place without stopping. The star is *sate lilit* (minced chicken sate), which here reaches heights that belie the common name. Chicken is minced, combined with a array of spices including lemongrass, then moulded onto bamboo skewers and grilled.

**Naughty Nuri's** (Map pp308-9; 977547; Jl Raya Sanggingan; dishes 15,000-60,000Rp) This legendary expat hang-out packs punters in for grilled steaks, tender ribs and burgers. Thursday-night grilled-tuna specials are wildly popular and something of a scene. This is a raw-boned joint where the stiff martinis make up for occasional lapses in the kitchen (which is mostly a barbecue out the front).

**Mozaic** (Map pp308-9; 975768; www.mozaic-bali .com; Jl Raya Sanggingan; meals 150,000-300,000Rp; 6-10pm Tue-Sun) Chef Chris Salans oversees this

## Car & Motorcycle

With numerous nearby attractions, many of which are difficult to reach by bemo, renting a vehicle is sensible. Ask at your accommodation.

# AROUND UBUD

☎ 0361

The region east and north of Ubud has many of the most ancient monuments and relics in Bali. Some of them predate the Majapahit era and raise as yet unanswered questions about Bali's history. Others are more recent, and in other instances, newer structures have been built on and around the ancient remains. They're interesting to history and archaeology buffs, but not that spectacular to look at – with the exception of Bali's own bit of Angkor at Gunung Kawi. Perhaps the best approach is to plan a whole day walking or cycling around the area, stopping at the places that interest you, but not treating any one as a destination in itself.

The area is thick with excursion possibilities. Besides the Elephant Cave, there's the Crazy Buffalo Temple. Heading north you find Bali's most important ancient site at Tampaksiring and a nearly forgotten shrine nearby, Pura Mengening, that rewards the adventurous.

## BEDULU

Bedulu was once the capital of a great kingdom. The legendary Dalem Bedaulu ruled the Pejeng dynasty from here, and was the last Balinese king to withstand the onslaught of the powerful Majapahits from Java. He was eventually defeated by Gajah Mada in 1343. The capital shifted several times after this, to Gelgel and then later to Semarapura (Klungkung).

### Sights

#### GOA GAJAH

About 1km east of Teges is **Goa Gajah** (Elephant Cave; Map pp308-9; adult/child 6000/3000Rp, parking 2000Rp; ☺ 8am-6pm). The origins of the cave are uncertain – one tale relates that it was created by the fingernail of the legendary giant Kebo Iwa. It probably dates at least to the 11th century, and it was certainly in existence at the time of the Majapahit takeover of Bali. In modern times the cave was rediscovered by Dutch archaeologists in 1923; the fountains and bathing pool were not unearthed until 1954.

The small cave is carved into a rock face and you enter through the cavernous mouth of a demon. The gigantic fingertips pressed beside the face of the demon push back a riotous jungle of surrounding stone carvings. Inside the T-shaped cave you can see fragmentary remains of lingam, the phallic symbols of the Hindu god Shiva, and their female counterpart the yoni, plus a statue of the elephant-headed god Ganesh. In the courtyard in front of the cave are two square bathing pools with water gushing into them from waterspouts held by six female figures. To the left of the cave entrance, in a small pavilion, is a statue of Hariti, surrounded by children. In Buddhist lore, Hariti was an evil woman who devoured children, but under the influence of Buddhism she reformed completely to become a protector of children and a symbol of fertility.

Try to get here before 10am, when the big tourist buses begin lumbering in like, well, modern elephants.

#### YEH PULU

A man having his hand munched by a boar is one of the scenes on the 25m-long **carved cliff face** (Map pp308-9; adult/child 6000/3000Rp) known as Yeh Pulu, believed to be a hermitage from the late 14th century. Apart from the figure of Ganesha, the elephant-headed son of Shiva, most of the scenes deal with everyday life, although the position and movement of the figures suggests that it could be read from left to right as a story. One theory is that they are events from the life of Krishna, the Hindu god.

Even if your interest in carved Hindu art is minor, this site is quite lovely and rarely will you have much company. From the entrance, it's a 300m lush, tropical walk to Yeh Pulu.

#### PURA SAMUAN TIGA

The majestic **Pura Samuan Tiga** (Temple of the Meeting of the Three; Map pp308-9) is about 200m east of the Bedulu junction. The name is possibly a reference to the Hindu trinity, or it may refer to meetings held here in the early 11th century. The imposing main gate was designed and built by I Gusti Nyoman Lempad, one of Bali's renowned artists and a native of Bedulu.

#### MUSEUM PURBAKALA

This archaeological **museum** (Map pp308-9; ☎ 942354; Jl Raya Tampaksiring; admission by donation;

8am-3pm Mon-Thu, 8am-12.30pm Fri) has a reasonable collection of artefacts from all over Bali, and most displays are in English. The exhibits in several small buildings include some of Bali's first pottery from near Gilimanuk, and sarcophagi dating from as early as 300 BC – some originating from Bangli are carved in the shape of a turtle, which has important cosmic associations in Balinese mythology. The museum is about 500m north of the Bedulu junction.

### Getting There & Away

About 3km east of Teges, the road from Ubud reaches a junction where you can turn south to Gianyar or north to Pejeng, Tampaksiring and Penelokan. Any Ubud to Gianyar bemo will drop you off at the Bedulu junction, from where you can walk. The road from Ubud is reasonably flat, so coming by bicycle is a good option.

## PEJENG

Further up the road to Tampaksiring is Pejeng and its famous temples. Like Bedulu, Pejeng was once an important seat of power, the capital of the Pejeng kingdom, which fell to the Majapahit invaders in 1343.

### Pura Kebo Edan

Also called the **Crazy Buffalo Temple** (Map pp308-9; 7am-6pm), this is not an imposing structure but is famous for its 3m-high statue, known as the Giant of Pejeng and thought to be about 700 years old. The temple is a place where prayer and offerings are thought to cure sick animals. It's on the western side of the road.

### Pura Pusering Jagat

This large **temple** (Navel of the World Temple; Map pp308-9) is said to be the centre of the old Pejeng kingdom. Dating from 1329, it is visited by young couples who pray at the stone lingam and yoni. Further back is a large stone urn with elaborate but worn carvings of gods and demons searching for the elixir of life in a depiction of the Mahabharata tale 'Churning the Sea of Milk'. The temple is on a small track running west of the main road.

### Pura Penataran Sasih

This **temple** (Map pp308-9; Jl Raya Tampaksiring) was once the state temple of the Pejeng kingdom. In the inner courtyard, high up in a pavilion and difficult to see in any detail, is the huge bronze drum known as the **Moon of Pejeng**. The hourglass-shaped drum is more than 2m long, the largest single-piece cast drum in the world. Estimates of its age vary from 1000 to 2000 years, and it is not certain whether it was made locally.

## TAMPAKSIRING

Tampaksiring is a small village about 18km northeast of Ubud with a large and important temple and the most impressive ancient site in Bali, Gunung Kawi. It sits in the Pakerisan Valley, and the entire area has been nominated for Unesco recognition.

### Sights

#### GUNUNG KAWI

On the northern outskirts of town, a sign points east off the main road to Gunung Kawi and its **ancient monuments** (adult/child 6000/3000Rp, parking 2000Rp; 7am-5pm). From the end of the access road, a steep, stone stairway leads down to the river, at one point making a cutting through an embankment of solid rock. There, in the bottom of this lush green river valley, is one of Bali's oldest and largest ancient monuments.

Gunung Kawi consists of 10 rock-cut *candi* (shrines) – memorials cut out of the rock face in imitation of actual statues. They stand in awe-inspiring 8m-high sheltered niches cut into the sheer cliff face. A solitary *candi* stands about a kilometre further down the valley to the south; this is reached by a trek through the rice paddies on the western side of the rushing river. Be prepared for long climbs up and down.

The five monuments on the eastern bank are probably dedicated to King Udayana, Queen Mahendradatta, their son Airlangga and his brothers Anak Wungsu and Marakata. While Airlangga ruled eastern Java, Anak Wungsu ruled Bali. The four monuments on the western side are, by this theory, to Anak Wungsu's chief concubines. Another theory is that the whole complex is dedicated to Anak Wungsu, his wives, concubines and, in the case of remote 10th *candi*, to a royal minister.

#### TIRTA EMPUL

A well-signposted fork in the road north of Tampaksiring leads to the popular holy springs at **Tirta Empul** (adult/child 6000/3000Rp, parking 2000Rp; 8am-6pm), discovered in AD 962 and believed to have magical powers. The springs bubble up into a large, crystal-clear pool within the temple and gush out through waterspouts into a bathing pool – they're the main source of Sungai Pakerisan, the river that rushes by Gunung Kawi only 1km or so away. Next to the springs, **Pura Tirta Empul** is one of Bali's most important temples.

Come in the early morning or late afternoon to avoid the tourist buses. You can also use the clean, segregated and free public baths here.

The exit route from the temple is through a lengthy warren of souvenir stalls – grit your teeth and follow the painted arrows on the ground to find your way out.

### Getting There & Away

Tampaksiring is an easy day trip from Ubud, or a stopover between Ubud and Danau Batur. If travelling by bemo, get a connection in Bedulu. Tirta Empul and Gunung Kawi are easy to find along the Penelokan to Ubud road, and are only about 1.5km apart.

## NORTH OF UBUD

Abused and abandoned logging elephants from Sumatra have been given refuge in Bali at the **Elephant Safari Park** ( ☎ 721480; www.bali adventuretours.com; adult/child US$16/8; ☒ 8am-5pm). Located in the cool, wet highlands of **Taro** (14km north of Ubud), the park is home to almost 30 elephants. Besides a full complement of exhibits about elephants, most people will probably want to *ride* an elephant (adult/child including admission US$53/36). The park has received praise for its conservation efforts; however, be careful you don't end up at one of the rogue parks, designed to divert the unwary to unsanctioned displays of elephants.

## SOUTH OF UBUD

The road between South Bali and Ubud is lined with places making and selling handicrafts. Many visitors shop along the route as they head to Ubud, sometimes by the busload, but much of the craftwork is actually done in small workshops and family compounds on quiet back roads.

For serious shopping and real flexibility in exploring these villages, it's worth renting or chartering your own transport, so you can explore the back roads and carry your purchases without any hassles. Note that your driver may receive a commission from any place you spend your money – this can add 20% to 30% or more to the cost of purchases. Also, a

driver may try to steer you to workshops or artisans that he favours, rather than those of most interest to you.

The following places are presented in the order you'll encounter them on the way to Ubud from the south.

### Batubulan

Stonecarving is the main craft of Batubulan, which means 'moon stone', and the temples around Batubulan are noted for their fine **sculptures**. You'll see hundreds of statues beside the road, and you're welcome to watch the workers, many of them young boys, chipping away at big blocks of soft volcanic stone.

The temples around Batubulan are, naturally, noted for their fine stonework. Just 200m to the east of the busy main road, **Pura Puseh Batubulan** is worth a visit for its moat filled with lotus flowers. Statues draw on ancient Hindu and Buddhist iconography and Balinese mythology; however, they are not old – many are copied from books on archaeology.

Batubulan is the major bemo terminal for eastern and central Bali – see p297 for details.

### Bali Bird Park & Rimba Reptil Park

Just north of Tegaltamu, the **bird park** ( ☎ 299352; www.bali-bird-park.com; adult/child US$14/7; ☒ 9am-5.30pm) boasts more than a thousand birds from over 250 different species, including rare *cendrawasih* (birds of paradise) from Irian Jaya and the all-but-vanished Bali starlings. Many are housed in special walk-through aviaries.

Next door, **Rimba Reptil Park** ( ☎ 299344; adult/child US$10/5; ☒ 9am-5pm) has about 20 species of creatures from Indonesia and Africa, as well as turtles, crocodiles, a python and a solitary Komodo dragon.

Both places are popular with kids. You can buy a combination ticket to both parks (adult/child US$20/10). Allow at least two hours for the bird park alone.

Many tours stop at the parks, or you can take a Batubulan–Ubud bemo, get off at the junction at Tegaltamu, and follow the signs north for about 600m.

### Singapadu

The centre of Singapadu is dominated by a huge **banyan tree**. The surrounding village has a traditional appearance, with walled family compounds and shady trees. You can visit the **Nyoman Suaka Home** (requested donation 10,000Rp; 9am-5pm), which is 50m off the main road, just south of the big tree. Pass through the old carved entrance to the walled family compound and you'll discover a classic Balinese home.

## Sukawati

Sukawati is a centre for the manufacture of wind chimes, temple umbrellas and masks. It has a busy **craft market** in an obvious, two-storey building on the main road – bemos stop right outside. Every type of quality craftwork and touristy trinket is on sale, at cheap prices for those who bargain hard. Across the road is the colourful morning produce market, with the old royal palace behind; it's worth a stop.

*Wayang kulit* (shadow puppets) and *topeng* (masks) are also made in the backstreets of Sukawati and in **Puaya**, about 1km northwest of the main road.

## Batuan

Batuan is a noted **painting centre** with scores of art galleries. Just west of the centre, the twin temples of **Pura Puseh** and **Pura Dasar** (admission to both 10,000Rp) are accessible studies in classic Balinese temple architecture. The carvings are elaborate and visitors are given the use of vermilion sarongs, which look good in photos.

## Mas

Mas means 'gold', but **woodcarving**, particularly mask carving, is the craft practised here. The road through Mas is lined with craft shops for the tour-bus loads, but there are plenty of smaller carving operations in the back lanes. Historically, carving was limited to temple decorations, dance masks and musical instruments, but in the 1930s carvers began to depict people and animals in a naturalistic way. Today it's hard to resist the oodles of winsome creatures produced here.

# EAST BALI

The eastern side of Bali is dominated by the mighty Gunung Agung, the 'navel of the world' and Bali's 'mother mountain'. The slopes of this and the other peaks at this end of the island hold some of the most verdant rice fields and tropical vistas you can imagine. It's a good place to have your own transport,

as you can simply 'get lost' wandering side roads and revel in the exquisite scenery.

The coast is dotted with beaches, many rough, rugged and untrammelled. Add in some ancient cultural sites and the popular areas of Sideman, Candidasa and Amed and you have an area that will lure you from the South Bali-Ubud juggernaut.

## COAST ROAD TO KUSAMBA
☎ 0361

Bali's coast road running from just north of Sanur east to a junction past Kusamba has been a hit since it opened in 2006.

The shoreline the new road follows is striking, with black-sand beaches and pounding waves. The entire coast has great religious significance and there are many temples. At the many small coastal-village beaches, cremation formalities reach their conclusion when the ashes are consigned to the sea. See the boxed text, p327 for details on sandy delights.

Kids love **Bali Safari & Marine Park** ( ☎ 950000; Prof Dr Ida Bagus Mantra Bypass; admission from US$25; 9am-5pm) and their parents are happy they love *someplace*. This big-ticket animal theme park is filled with critters whose species never set foot in Bali until their cage door opened. Displays are large and naturalistic. A huge menu of extra-cost options includes camel and elephant rides. The park is north of Lebih Beach.

## GIANYAR
☎ 0361

Gianyar is the capital of Gianyar district (which includes Ubud). It has some small **textile factories** on the west side of town, including **Tenun Ikat Setia Cili** ( ☎ 943409; Jl Astina Utara; 9am-5pm), where you can see ikat being woven and buy fabric and clothes. It's a place that most tourists will pass through, rather than spend time in.

Many people come to Gianyar to eat. *Babi guling* (spit-roast pig stuffed with chilli, turmeric, garlic and ginger) is a delicious local speciality. The descriptively named **Gianyar Babi Guleng** (Jl Jata; meals 5000-8000Rp; 7am-4pm) is favoured by locals among many competitors. It's in a tiny side street at the west end of the centre behind the bemo parking area.

Nearby are numerous stands selling fresh food, including delectable *piseng goreng* (fried banana). Also worth sampling for *babi guling* and other local treats are the food stalls in the

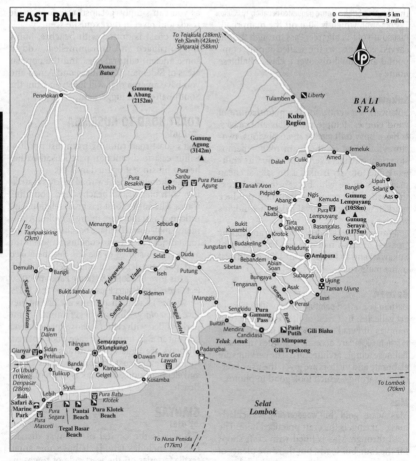

## EAST BALI

0 — 5 km
0 — 3 miles

To Tejakula (28km);
Yeh Sanih (42km);
Singaraja (58km)

Danau
Batur

Penelokan

Gunung
Abang
(2152m)

Tulamben    Liberty

BALI
SEA

Kubu
Region

Gunung
Agung
(3142m)

Jemeluk

Dalah    Culik    Amed    Bunutan

Pura
Besakih    Lebih    Pura
Sanbu    Pura Pasar
Agung    Tanah Aron
Pidpid

Lipah
Bangli    Selang
Kemuda    Aas
Ngis    Gunung
Lempuyang
(1058m)

Abang    Pura
Desi    Lempuyang    Gunung
Ababi    Seraya
(1175m)

Menanga    Sebudi    Bukit
Kusambi    Tirta
Gangga    Basangalas

To
Tampaksiring
(2km)    Muncan    Krotok    Tauka    Seraya

Rendang    Selat    Duda    Jungutan    Budakeling    Peladung    Amlapura

Demulih    Bangli    Iseh    Putung    Bebandem    Abian
Soan    Subagan

Bukit Jambal    Tabola    Sidemen    Sibetan    Bungaya    Asak    Ujung
Taman Ujung

Tenganan    Perasi

Manggis    Jasri

Pura
Dalem    Sengkidu    Pura
Gamang
Pass

Gianyar    Sidan    Tihingan    Semarapura
(Klungkung)    Buitan    Pasir
Putih    Gili Biaha

Peteluan    Banda    Dawan    Mendira    Gili Mimpang
Candidasa    Gili Tepekong

To Ubud
(10km);
Denpasar
(28km)    Tulikup    Kamasan    Pura Goa
Lawah    Padangbai    Teluk Amuk

Lebih    Siyut    Kusamba
Bali
Safari &
Marine
Park    Pura Batu
Klotek

Pura
Segara    Pantai
Beach    Pura Klotek
Beach    To Lombok
(70km)

Pura
Masceti    Tegal Basar
Beach

Selat
Lombok

To Nusa Penida
(17km)

---

food market ( 11am-2pm) and the busy **night market** ( 6-11pm). All of these places line both sides of the main section of Jl Ngurah Rai.

Regular bemo travel is between the main terminal in Gianyar and Batubulan terminal (10,000Rp). Gianyar is the junction for Ubud and Tampaksiring. The bemo terminal is on the west side of town, about 500 metres from the centre.

## BANGLI
☎ 0366

Halfway up the slope to Penelokan, Bangli – once the capital of a kingdom – has an interesting temple and cultural centre, though if there's no ceremony or festival happening, it's pretty quiet.

## Sights
### PURA KEHEN
The state temple of the Bangli kingdom, **Pura Kehen** (adult/child 6000/3000Rp;  9am-5pm) is one of the finest temples in east Bali; it's a little like a miniature version of Pura Besakih.

The temple is terraced up the hillside, with a great flight of steps leading to the beautifully decorated entrance. The first courtyard has a huge banyan tree with a *kulkul* (alarm drum) entwined in its branches. The inner courtyard has a *meru* (multiroofed shrine) with 11 roofs, and thrones for the Hindu trinity of Brahma, Shiva and Vishnu. The carvings are particularly intricate.

Tickets are sold at a gate about 100m to the west, but there may not be anyone there. Some sleepy souvenir stalls are in the car park, a few metres to the east of the temple gate.

### PURA DALEM PENUNGGEKAN

Just south of the centre, the exterior wall of this fascinating 'temple of the dead' features vivid relief carvings of wrong-doers getting their just desserts in the afterlife. One panel addresses the lurid fate of adulterers (men may find the viewing uncomfortable). Other panels portray sinners as monkeys, while another is a good representation of evil-doers begging to be spared the fires of hell.

## Eating

A *pasar malam* (night market), on the street beside the bemo terminal, has some excellent warung, and you'll also find some in the market area during the day.

## Getting There & Away

Bangli is located on the main road between Denpasar's Batubulan terminal (12,000Rp) and Gunung Batur, via Penelokan.

## SEMARAPURA (KLUNGKUNG)

☎ 0366

Semarapura was once the centre of Bali's most important kingdom, and a great artistic and cultural focal point. But on 28 April 1908 it was the site of a terrible *puputan,* one of the battles when Balinese – armed only with

hand-weapons – fought to an honourable death rather than surrender to the bullet-spraying Dutch. Today the remains of the palace make for a fascinating stop on your eastern explorations.

The town is still commonly called Klungkung, but has been officially renamed Semarapura; the latter appears on most signs and maps. There are ATMs in the centre and a large market with warung.

## Sights

### SEMARA PURA COMPLEX

When the Dewa Agung dynasty moved here in 1710, a new palace, the **Semara Pura** (adult/child 12,000/6000Rp, parking 1000Rp; ☼ 7am-6pm), was established. Most of the original palace and grounds were destroyed during Dutch attacks in 1908, and the **Pemedal Agung**, the gateway on the southern side of the square, is all that remains of the palace itself – the carved wooden doors are beautiful.

### Kertha Gosa

The 'Hall of Justice' was effectively the supreme court of the Klungkung kingdom, where disputes and cases that could not be settled at the village level were brought. This open-sided pavilion is a superb example of Klungkung architecture, and its ceiling is covered with fine paintings in the Klungkung style. The paintings, done on asbestos sheeting,

**BALI**

---

### COAST ROAD BEACHES

The coast road from Sanur heads east past long stretches of shore that until recently were reached only by long and narrow lanes from roads well inland. Development has yet to catch on here – excepting villas – so take advantage of the easy access to enjoy the beaches and the many important temples near the sand.

Don't expect white sand or even tan sand – the grains here are volcanic shades of grey. Swimming in the often pounding surf is dangerous. You'll need your own transport to reach these beaches. Except where noted, services are few, so bring your own drinking water and towels.

From west to east, recommended beaches include the following:

- **Saba Beach** has a small temple, covered shelters, a shady parking area and a short, junglelike drive from the coast road; it's about 12km east of Sanur.
- **Pura Masceti Beach**, 15km east of Sanur, has a few drink vendors. **Pura Masceti** is one of Bali's nine directional temples. It is right on the beach and is both architecturally significant and enlivened with gaudy statuary.
- **Lebih** has sand composed of mica that sparkles with a billion points of light. There are a couple of cafes. The large Sungai Pakerisan, which starts near Tampaksiring, reaches the sea near here. The impressive **Pura Segara** looks across the strait to Nusa Penida.
- **Pura Klotek Beach** has very fine black sand. The quiet at **Pura Batu Klotek** belies its great significance. Sacred statues are brought here from Pura Besakih (p329) for ritual cleansing.

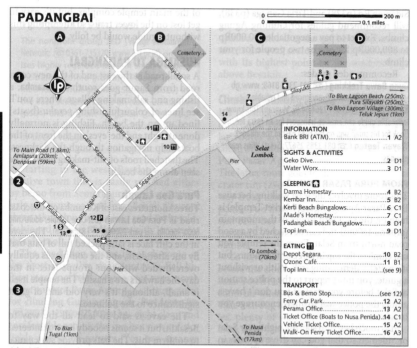

## PADANGBAI

To Main Road (1.8km);
Amlapura (20km);
Denpasar (59km)

To Bias
Tugal (1km)

Selat
Lombok

Pier

Pier

To Blue Lagoon Beach (250m);
Pura Silayukti (250m);
To Bloo Lagoon Village (300m);
Teluk Jepun (1km)

To Lombok
(70km)

To Nusa
Penida
(17km)

| INFORMATION | |
| --- | --- |
| Bank BRI (ATM).................................1 | A2 |
| **SIGHTS & ACTIVITIES** | |
| Geko Dive.........................................2 | D1 |
| Water Worx.......................................3 | D1 |
| **SLEEPING** | |
| Darma Homestay................................4 | B2 |
| Kembar Inn.......................................5 | B2 |
| Kerti Beach Bungalows.......................6 | C1 |
| Made's Homestay...............................7 | C1 |
| Padangbai Beach Bungalows...............8 | D1 |
| Topi Inn............................................9 | D1 |
| **EATING** | |
| Depot Segara...................................10 | B2 |
| Ozone Café......................................11 | B1 |
| Topi Inn........................................(see 9) | |
| **TRANSPORT** | |
| Bus & Bemo Stop...........................(see 12) | |
| Ferry Car Park.................................12 | A2 |
| Perama Office..................................13 | A2 |
| Ticket Office (Boats to Nusa Penida)...14 | C1 |
| Vehicle Ticket Office.........................15 | A2 |
| Walk-On Ferry Ticket Office...............16 | A3 |

## Sights

With its protected bay, Padangbai has a good beach. Others are nearby; walk southwest from the ferry terminal and follow the trail up the hill to idyllic **Bias Tugal**, also called Pantai Kecil (Little Beach), on the exposed coast outside the bay. Be careful in the water; it is subject to strong currents. There are a couple of daytime warung here.

On a headland at the northeast corner of the bay, a path uphill leads to three temples. On the other side is the small, light-sand **Blue Lagoon Beach**.

## Activities

### DIVING

There's some pretty good diving on the coral reefs around Padangbai, but the water can be a little cold and visibility is not always ideal. The most popular local dives are Blue Lagoon and Teluk Jepun (Jepun Bay), both in Teluk Amuk, the bay just east of Padangbai. There are a good variety of soft and hard corals and varied marine life, including sharks, turtles and wrasse, and a 40m wall at the Blue Lagoon.

Several good local outfits offer diving trips in the area, including to Gili Tepekong and Gili Biaha, and on to Tulamben and Nusa Penida. All dive prices are competitive, costing US$40 to US$90 for two boat dives, depending on the site. Dive courses are available.

Recommended operators, among the growing throng:

**Geko Dive** ( ☎ 41516; www.gekodive.com; Jl Silayukti) Has a nice cafe across from the beach.

**Water Worx** ( ☎ 41220; www.waterworxbali.com; Jl Silayukti) Another good dive operator; has a diving pool.

### SNORKELLING

One of the best and most accessible walk-in snorkel sites is off Blue Lagoon Beach. Note that it is subject to strong currents when the tide is out. Other sites such as Teluk Jepun can be reached by local boat (or check with the dive operators to see if they have any room on their dive boats). Snorkel sets cost about 30,000Rp per day.

Local *jukung* (boats) offer snorkelling trips (bring your own snorkelling gear) around Padangbai (50,000Rp per person per hour) and as far away as Nusa Lembongan (350,000Rp) for two passengers.

## Sleeping

Accommodation in Padangbai – like the town itself – is pretty laid-back. Prices are fairly cheap and it's pleasant enough here that there's no need to hurry through to or from Lombok if you want to hang out on the beach and in cafes with other travellers.

### VILLAGE

In the village, there are several tiny places in the alleys, some with a choice of small, cheap downstairs rooms or bigger, brighter upstairs rooms.

**Darma Homestay** ( ☎ 41394; Gang Segara III; r 60,000-150,000Rp; ✗ ) A classic Balinese family homestay. The more expensive of the 12 rooms have hot showers and air-con; go for the private room on the top floor.

**Kembar Inn** ( ☎ 41364; kembarinn@hotmail.com; r 100,000-250,000Rp; ✗ ) There are six rooms at this inn linked by a steep and narrow staircase. The best awaits at the top and has a private terrace with views.

### JALAN SILAYUKTI

On this little strip at the east end of the village, places are close together and right across from the sand.

**Made's Homestay** ( ☎ 41441; Jl Silayukti; s/d 50,000/60,000Rp; 🖳 ) Four basic, clean and simple rooms and internet access are the draws here.

**Topi Inn** ( ☎ 41424; www.topiinn.com; Jl Silayukti; r 50,000-60,000Rp; 🖳 🛜 ) Sitting at the end of the strip in a serene location, Topi has five pleasant rooms, some of which share bathrooms. The enthusiastic owners offer courses in topics as diverse as cooking and gamelan, among other diversions. The cafe is excellent.

**Kerti Beach Bungalows** ( ☎ 41391; Jl Silayukti; r 70,000-250,000Rp; ✗ 🖳 ) Go for the 19 rooms in pretty bungalows built in a long narrow strip rather than the rice barns. As you move up the rate ladder here, you gain hot water and air-con.

**Padangbai Beach Bungalows** ( ☎ 41417; Jl Silayukti; r 100,000-400,000Rp; ✗ 🛋 ) The bungalows are attractive, with open-air bathrooms, and set in a classic Balinese garden setting that now boasts a large pool across from the beach. The top rooms have air-con.

### BLUE LAGOON BEACH

**ourpick** **Bloo Lagoon Village** ( ☎ 41211; www.bloo lagoon.com; r US$75-200; ✗ 🛋 🖳 ) Perched above Blue Lagoon Beach, up hill from town, the 23 cottages and villas here are all designed in traditional thatched style and the compound is dedicated to sustainable practices. Units come with one, two or three bedrooms and are well thought out and stylish.

## Eating & Drinking

Beach fare and backpackers' staples are on offer in Padangbai – lots of fresh seafood, Indonesian classics, pizza and, yes, banana pancakes. You can easily laze away a few hours soaking up the scene at the places along Jl Segara and Jl Silayukti, which have harbour views during the day and cool breezes in the evening.

**Depot Segara** ( ☎ 41443; Jl Segara; dishes 10,000-30,000Rp) Fresh seafood such as barracuda, marlin and snapper are prepared in a variety of ways at this popular cafe. Enjoy harbour views from the slightly elevated terrace.

**Ozone Café** ( ☎ 41501; dishes 15,000-35,000Rp) This popular travellers' gathering spot has more character than every other place in East Bali combined. Slogans cover the walls; there is pizza and live music, sometimes by patrons.

**Topi Inn** ( ☎ 41424; Jl Silayukti; mains 18,000-40,000Rp) Juices, shakes and good coffees served up throughout the day. Breakfasts are big, and whatever is landed by the fishing boats outside the front door during the day is grilled by night.

## Getting There & Away

### BEMO

Padangbai is 2km south of the main Semarapura–Amlapura Rd. Bemo leave from the car park in front of the port; orange bemo go east through Candidasa to Amlapura (8000Rp); blue or white bemo go to Semarapura (8000Rp).

### BOAT

### Lombok

Public ferries travel nonstop between Padangbai and Lembar on Lombok. There are also fast boats for travellers to the Gili Islands and Lombok. For details on these services, see p481.

### Nusa Penida

For details on the fibreglass boats and car ferry that make the run to Nusa Penida, see p305.

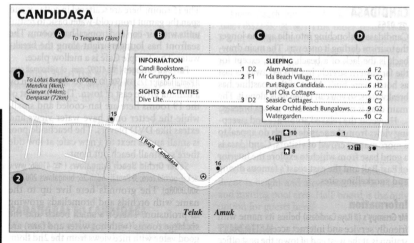

**CANDIDASA**

| | |
|---|---|
| **INFORMATION** | |
| Candi Bookstore..............................1 D2 | |
| Mr Grumpy's..................................2 F1 | |
| | |
| **SIGHTS & ACTIVITIES** | |
| Dive Lite.........................................3 D2 | |

| | |
|---|---|
| **SLEEPING** | |
| Alam Asmara...................................4 F2 | |
| Ida Beach Village............................5 G2 | |
| Puri Bagus Candidasa.....................6 H2 | |
| Puri Oka Cottages...........................7 G2 | |
| Seaside Cottages.............................8 C2 | |
| Sekar Orchid Beach Bungalows.......9 G2 | |
| Watergarden..................................10 C2 | |

To Tenganan (3km)

To Lotus Bungalows (100m);
Mendira (4km);
Gianyar (44km);
Denpasar (72km)

Jl Raya Candidasa

Teluk Amuk

## Eating & Drinking

There's a good range of eating options in Candidasa. Most restaurants are dotted along Jl Raya Candidasa and the traffic noise can be particularly unpleasant, although it improves after dark. Many of these places are also good for a drink.

**Legend Rock Café** (Jl Raya Candidasa; dishes 15,000-30,000Rp) A bar that also serves Western and Indonesian meals, this has live music many nights each week. It's a well-mannered place; as wild as things get in Candidasa.

**Temple Café** ( ☎ 41629; Seaside Cottages, Jl Raya Candidasa; dishes 15,000-35,000Rp) Global citizens can get a taste of home at this cafe attached to the Seaside Cottages. It has a few menu items from the owner's native Oz, such as Vegemite. The popular bar has a long drink list.

**Legong** ( ☎ 41052; Jl Raya Candidasa; mains 15,000-55,000Rp) This is the kind of family-run joint that you fall for thanks to homey touches such as vaguely incomprehensible banners that read: 'Don't leave before you come'.

**Watergarden Café** ( ☎ 41540; Jl Raya Candidasa; dishes 15,000-60,000Rp) Overlooking a carp pond, this stylish cafe maintains a peaceful atmosphere amid the zooming trucks thanks to an artfully placed wall. The food is a fusion of French and Asian touches.

**Vincent's** ( ☎ 41368; Jl Raya Candidasa; dishes 25,000-80,000Rp) Candi's best is a deep and open place with several distinct rooms and a lovely rear garden with rattan lounge furniture. The bar is an oasis of jazz. The menu combines excellent Balinese, fresh seafood and European dishes.

## Getting There & Away

Candidasa is on the main road between Amlapura and South Bali, but there's no terminal, so hail bemo (buses probably won't stop). You'll need to change in either Padangbai or Semarapura.

You can charter a ride to Amed in the far east for about 120,000Rp, and Kuta and the airport for 250,000Rp. Ask at your accommodation about vehicle and bicycle rental.

**Perama** ( ☎ 41114; Jl Raya Candidasa; ⏱ 7am-7pm) is at the western end of the strip.

| Destination | Fare | Duration |
|---|---|---|
| Kuta | 60,000Rp | 3½hr |
| Lovina | 150,000Rp | 5¼hr |
| Padangbai | 25,000Rp | 30min |
| Sanur | 60,000Rp | 2¾hr |
| Ubud | 50,000Rp | 1¾hr |

## CANDIDASA TO AMLAPURA

No longer anyone's secret, **Pasir Putih** is an idyllic white-sand beach whose name indeed means 'white sand'.

A row of thatched beach **warung** and **cafes** have appeared. You can get *nasi goreng* or grilled fish for little money. Bintang is of course on ice and loungers await bikini-clad bottoms. The beach itself is truly lovely: a long crescent of white sand backed by coconut trees. At one end cliffs provide shade. The surf is often mellow; bring snorkelling gear to explore the waters.

Look for crude signs along the coast road with either 'Virgin Beach Club', 'Jl Pasir Putih' or 'White Beach' near the village of Perasi. Turn off the main road (about 5km east of

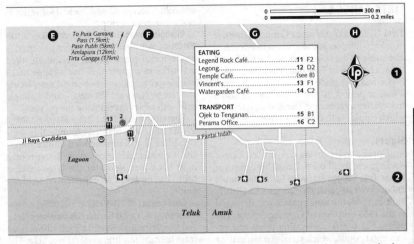

EATING
Legend Rock Café................11 F2
Legong.............................12 D2
Temple Café.....................(see 8)
Vincent's..........................13 F1
Watergarden Café.............14 C2

TRANSPORT
Ojek to Tenganan..............15 B1
Perama Office...................16 C2

Candidasa) and follow a pretty paved track for about 1.5km to a temple where locals will collect a fee (5000Rp). You can park here and walk the gentle hill down or drive a further 600m directly to the beach on a perilous road that barely qualifies as such.

## AMLAPURA
☎ 0363
Amlapura is the capital of Karangasem district, and the main town and transport junction in eastern Bali. The smallest of Bali's district capitals, it's a multicultural place with Chinese shophouses, several mosques and confusing one-way streets (which are the tidiest in Bali). It's worth a stop to see the royal palaces but a lack of options means you'll want to spend the night elsewhere, such as Tirta Gangga.

### Information
The **tourist office** (☎ 21196; www.karangasemtourism .com; Jl Diponegoro; ⏲ 7am-3pm Mon-Thu, 7am-noon Fri) offers the booklet *Agung Info*, which is filled with useful detail. Also check the website.
**Bank BRI** (Jl Gajah Mada) will change money. It has an international ATM as does **Hardy's Supermarket** (☎ 22363; Jl Diponegoro). The latter has good warung. There is a **pharmacy** (Apotik; Jl Ngurah Rai 47) and a small hospital across the street.

### Sights
Amlapura's three palaces, on Jl Teuk Umar, are stolid reminders of Karangasem's period as a kingdom at its most important when sup-

ported by Dutch colonial power in the late 19th and early 20th centuries.

Outside the **Puri Agung Karangasem** (Jl Teuku Umar; admission 10,000Rp; ⏲ 8am-5pm), there is an impressive three-tiered entry gate and beautiful sculpted panels. After you pass through the entry courtyard, a left turn takes you to the main building, known as the Maskerdam (Amsterdam), because it was the Karangasem kingdom's acquiescence to Dutch rule that allowed it to hang on long after the demise of the other Balinese kingdoms. Inside you can see several rooms, including the royal bedroom and a living room with furniture that was a gift from the Dutch royal family.

Across the street, **Puri Gede** (Jl Teuku Umar; donation requested; ⏲ 8am-6pm) is still used by the royal family and is surrounded by long walls. The palace grounds feature many brick buildings dating from the Dutch colonial period. Look for stone carvings and woodcarvings from the 19th century. The Rangki, the main palace building, has been returned to its glory and is surrounded by fish ponds. Catch the stern portrait of the late king AA Gede Putu.

The other royal palace building, **Puri Kertasura**, is not open to visitors.

### Getting There & Away
Amlapura is a major transport hub. Buses and bemo regularly ply the main road to Denpasar's Batubulan terminal (20,000Rp; roughly three hours) via Candidasa, Padangbai and Gianyar. Plenty of buses also go around the north coast to Singaraja (about 16,000Rp) via Tirta Gangga, Amed and Tulamben.

## TIRTA GANGGA
☎ 0363

Tirta Gangga (Water of the Ganges) is the site of a holy temple, some great water features and some of the best views of rice fields and the sea beyond in East Bali. High on a ridge, it is a relaxing place to stop for an hour or a longer period, which will allow for some treks in the surrounding terraced countryside, which ripples with coursing water.

### Sights

Amlapura's water-loving raja, the last king of Karangasem, built the palace of his dreams at **Taman Tirta Gangga** (adult/child 5000/3000Rp, parking 2000Rp; ☉ site 24hr, ticket office 6am-6pm). Originally built in 1948, the water palace was damaged in the 1963 eruption of Gunung Agung. The palace has several swimming pools and ornamental ponds, which serve as a fascinating reminder of the old days of the Balinese rajas. 'Pool A' (adult/child 6000/4000Rp) is the cleanest and is in the top part of the complex. It's a good place for a break and a stroll.

### Activities

**Hiking** in the surrounding hills is recommended. The rice terraces around Tirta Gangga are some of the most beautiful in Bali. Back roads and walking paths take you to many picturesque traditional villages. Or you can ascend the side of Gunung Agung. Guides are a good idea. Ask at any of the accommodation we've listed, especially Homestay Rijasa where the owner I Ketut Sarjana is an experienced guide. Another local guide who comes with good marks is **Komang Gede Sutama** (☎ 081 3387 70893).

Among the possible treks is a six-hour loop to Tenganan village, plus shorter ones across the local hills, which include visits to remote temples and all the stunning vistas you can handle. Rates average about 50,000Rp per hour for one or two people.

### Sleeping & Eating

Most places to stay have cafes with mains under 20,000Rp and there's another cluster by the sedate shops near the entrance. A small valley of rice terraces runs up the hill behind the parking area. It is a majestic vision of emerald steps receding into the distance.

With the exception of Tirta Ayu Hotel and Tirta Gangga Villas, most of the places to stay are cold-water-only and basic. Hot water is not a universal option.

**Dhangin Taman** (Friendly Hotel; ☎ 22059; r 50,000-100,000Rp) Adjacent to the water palace, this characterful place features elaborate tiled artworks in a garden. It has a range of 14 cold-water rooms – the cheapest ones facing the rice paddies are the best – and a simple cafe with tables overlooking the palace.

**Homestay Rijasa** (☎ 21873; r 80,000-150,000Rp) With elaborately planted grounds, this well-run place is a recommended choice opposite the water-palace entrance. Better rooms have hot water, good for the large soaking tubs. The owner is an experienced trekking guide.

**Good Karma** (☎ 22445; r 100,000-120,000Rp) A classic homestay, Good Karma has four very clean and simple bungalows and a good vibe derived from the surrounding pastoral rice field. The good cafe is close to the parking lot.

**Puri Sawah Bungalows** (☎ 21847; r 150,000-200,000Rp) Just up the road from the palace, Puri Sawah has four comfortable and spacious rooms and family bungalows that sleep six (with hot water). Besides Indo classics, the restaurant has some interesting sandwiches like 'avocado delight'.

**Tirta Ayu Hotel** (☎ 22503; www.hoteltirtagangga.com; villas US$50-100; ⚘) Right in the palace compound, this has four pleasant villas that are clean and have basic, modern decor in the limited palette of creams and coffees that's ubiquitous right now. Flop about like a fish in the hotel's private pool or use the vast palace facilities. The restaurant is a tad upscale (mains from 50,000Rp) and serves creative takes on local classics.

**Tirta Gangga Villas** (☎ 21383; www.tirtagangga-villas.com; villas US$120-400; ⚘) Built on the same terrace as the Tirta Ayu Hotel, the villas are parts of the old royal palace. Thoroughly updated – they have that classic Bali style motif – the villas look out over the water palace from large shady porches. Private cooks are available and you can arrange to rent the entire complex and preside over your own court.

**Genta Bali** (☎ 22436; dishes 10,000-20,000Rp) Across the road from the parking area, you can find a fine yoghurt drink here, as well as pasta and Indonesian food. It has an impressive list of puddings, including ones with banana, jackfruit and taro. Try out the black-rice wine.

## Getting There & Away

Bemos and minibuses making the east-coast haul between Amlapura and Singaraja stop at Tirta Gangga, right outside the water palace or any hotel further north. The fare to Amlapura should be 5000Rp.

## AMED & THE FAR EAST COAST
☎ 0363

Stretching from Amed to Bali's far eastern tip, this once-remote stretch of semi-arid coast draws visitors to a succession of small, scalloped, black-sand beaches, a relaxed atmosphere and excellent diving and snorkelling.

The coast here is often called simply 'Amed' but this is a misnomer, as the coast is a series of seaside *dusun* (small villages) that start with the actual Amed in the north and then run southeast to Aas. If you're looking to get away from crowds, this is the place to come and try some yoga. Everything is spread out, so you never feel like you're in the middle of anything much except maybe one of the small fishing villages.

Traditionally this area has been quite poor, with thin soils, low rainfall and very limited infrastructure. Villages rely on fishing, and colourful *jukung* (traditional boats) line up on every available piece of beach. Inland, the steep hillsides are generally too dry for rice – corn, peanuts and vegetables are the main crops.

## Orientation & Information

As noted, this entire 10km stretch of coast is often called 'Amed' by both tourists and marketing-minded locals. Jemeluk has cafes and a few shops; Lipah has warung, shops and a few services. Both have places with dial-up internet access. The closest ATM is in Amlapura.

Besides the main road via Tirta Gangga, you can also approach the Amed area from the south via a scenic curving and narrow road from Ujung.

## Activities
### DIVING & SNORKELLING

Snorkelling is excellent at several places along the coast. **Jemeluk** is a protected area where you can admire live coral and plentiful fish within 100m of the beach. There's a wreck of a Japanese fishing boat near **Aas**, offshore from Eka Purnama bungalows, and coral gardens

and colourful marine life at **Selang**. Almost every hotel rents snorkelling equipment for about 30,000Rp per day.

Scuba diving is good and the *Liberty* wreck at Tulamben (p341) is only a 20-minute drive away. There are two good operators with similar prices (eg local dives from about US$50, open-water dive course about US$350):

**Eco-dive** ( ☎ 23482; www.ecodivebali.com; Jemeluk) Full-service shop with simple accommodation for clients. Has led the way on environmental issues.

**Euro Dive** ( ☎ 23469; www.eurodivebali.com; Lipah) Has a new facility and offers packages with hotels.

### TREKKING

Quite a few trails go inland from the coast, up the slopes of Gunung Seraya (1175m) and to some little-visited villages. The countryside is sparsely vegetated and most trails are well defined, so you won't need a guide for shorter walks. Allow a good three hours to get to the top of Seraya, starting from the rocky ridge just east of Jemeluk Bay.

## Sleeping

The entire area is very spread out, so take this into consideration when choosing accommodation. You will also need to choose between staying in the little beachside villages or on the sunny and dry headlands connecting the inlets. The former puts you right on the sand and offers a small amount of community life while the latter gives you broad, sweeping vistas and isolation.

Accommodation can be found in every price category; almost every place has a restaurant or cafe. Places with noteworthy dining are indicated in the listings.

### EAST OF AMED VILLAGE

**Hotel Uyah Amed** ( ☎ 23462; hoteluyah@naturebali.com; r €27-40; ❇ 🔊 ) This cute place features four-poster beds set in stylish, conical interiors bathed in light. From all eight rooms (two with air-con) you can see the saltworks on the beach. The hotel makes the most of this by offering fascinating and free salt-making demonstrations

### JEMELUK

**Sama Sama Bungalows** ( ☎ 081 3373 82945; r 70,000-150,000Rp) There are two simple cold-water rooms in bungalows here (and a good seafood cafe) across from the beach. The family that runs things is often busy making kites.

**Galang Kangin Bungalows** ( ☎ 23480; bali_amed_gk @yahoo.co.jp; r 100,000Rp-300,000Rp; 🖳 ) Set on the hill side of the road amid a nice garden, the four rooms here mix and match fans, cold water, hot water and air-con. The beach is situated right over the foot path, as is the cafe.

**Aiona Garden of Health** ( ☎ 081 3381 61730; www .aionabali.com; bungalows €18-30) This eccentric place has enough signs outside that it qualifies as a genuine roadside attraction. The simple bungalows are shaded by mango trees and the natural food served seems to have fallen right out of the trees. Stays are a two-night minimum and you can partake of organic potions and lotions, classes in yoga, meditation, tarot reading etc.

### BUNUTAN

These places are on a sun-drenched, arid stretch of highland.

**Wawa-Wewe II** ( ☎ 23521; wawawewevillas@yahoo .com; r 200,000-250,000Rp; 🖳 💷 ) From the headlands, this nice and peaceful place has 10 bungalow-style rooms on lush grounds that shamble down to the water's edge. The natural-stone infinity pool is shaped like a Buddha and is near the water, as are two rooms with ocean views.

**Waeni's Sunset View Bungalows** ( ☎ 23515; made sani@hotmail.com; r 250,000-350,000Rp; 🖳 ) Waeni's is a hillside place with unusual rustic stone cottages that have gorgeous views of the mountains behind and the bay below. The eight rooms have a flash of creative style plus hot water. The cafe is a good place for a sunset drink.

### LIPAH

This village is just large enough for you to go wandering.

**Le Jardin** ( ☎ 081 3532 15753; limamarie@yahoo.fr; r €12-25; 🖳 ) Four rooms (some fan-only) are housed in shady thatched bungalows at this French-accented B&B. Open baths have garden decor and you can avail yourself of yoga, meditation etc. The beach on the cove is just steps away.

**Bayu Cottages** ( ☎ 23495; www.bayucottages.com; r €25-50; 🖳 💷 ) Bayu has six large, comfortable rooms with balconies overlooking the coast from the hillside above the road. There is a small swimming pool and many amenities including open-air marble bathrooms and satellite TV.

### SELANG

**Blue Moon Villas** ( ☎ 081 7473 8100; www.bluemoon villa.com; r from US$55, villas US$120-185; 🖳 💷 ) On a knoll across the road from the cliffs, Blue Moon is a small and upmarket place, complete with a little pool. The five rooms set in three villas have open-air stone bathrooms. The cafe takes usual fare and gives it a dash of panache.

### AAS

The butt end of the Amed coast is sparsely developed.

**ourpick Meditasi** (fax 22166; r 200,000-250,000Rp) There's nothing like chilled-out Aas for a respite from the pressures of life. Meditation and yoga help you relax, and the four rooms are close to good swimming and snorkelling. Open-air baths allow you to count the colours of the bougainvillea and frangipani that grow in profusion.

## Eating & Drinking

As already noted, most places to stay have cafes. Ones that are worth seeking out are listed here.

**Café Garam** ( ☎ 23462; Hotel Uyah Amed, east of Amed; dishes 14,000-40,000Rp) There's a relaxed feel here with pool tables and Balinese food plus the lyrical and haunting melodies of live Genjek music at 8pm on Wednesday and Saturday.

**Sails** ( ☎ 22006; Lehan; mains 30,000-60,000Rp) A high-concept restaurant with high standards for food, Sails is one big terrace with 180-degree views from its cliffside perch. Settle back in the chic blonde furniture and enjoy fusion hits like lamb medallions, spare ribs and grilled fillets of fresh fish with Balinese accents.

**Wawa-Wewe I** ( ☎ 23506; Lipah) Spend the evening here and you won't know your wawas from your wewes. This is the coast's most raucous bar – which by local standards means that sometimes it gets sorta loud. A vast CD collection is augmented by local bands on many nights. You can also eat here (mains from 15,000Rp).

## Getting There & Around

Most people drive here via the main highway from Amlapura to Culik. Public-transport options are limited. Minibuses and bemo from Singaraja and Amlapura pass through Culik, the turn-off for Amed. Infrequent public bemo go from Culik to Amed (3.5km), and some continue to Seraya until 1pm. A public bemo should cost around 8000Rp from Culik to Lipah.

You can also charter transport from Culik for a negotiable 45,000Rp (by *ojek* is less than half). Be careful to specify which hotel you wish to go to – if you agree on a price to 'Amed', you may be taken only to Amed village, far short of your destination.

Perama offers charter tourist-bus services from Candidasa (see p336); the cost is 125,000Rp each for a minimum of two people. This is similar to the cost of hiring a car and driver.

Many hotels rent bicycles for about 35,000Rp per day.

## KUBU REGION

Driving along the main road you will pass through vast old lava flows from Gunung Agung down to the sea. The landscape is strewn with lava, boulders and is nothing like the lush rice paddies elsewhere.

## TULAMBEN
☎ 0363

The big attraction here sunk over 60 years ago. The WWII wreck of the US cargo ship *Liberty* is among the best and most popular dive sites in Bali and this has given rise to an entire town based on scuba diving. Other great dive sites are nearby and even snorkellers can easily swim out and enjoy the wreck and the coral.

But if you don't plan to explore the briny waves, don't expect to hang out on the beach either. The shore is made up of rather beautiful, large washed stones, the kind that cost a fortune at a DIY store.

Tulamben is a quiet place, and is essentially built around the wreck – the hotels, all with cafes and many with dive shops, are spread along a 3km stretch either side of the main road.

### Activities
#### DIVING & SNORKELLING
The wreck of the *Liberty* is about 50m directly offshore from Puri Madha Bungalows (there's also a shady car park here; 2000Rp). Swim straight out and you'll see the stern rearing up from the depths, heavily encrusted with coral, and swarming with dozens of species of colourful fish – and with scuba divers

most of the day. Many divers commute to Tulamben from Candidasa or Lovina, and in busy times it can get quite crowded between 11am and 4pm, with up to 50 divers around the wreck at a time. Stay the night in Tulamben or – better – in nearby Amed and get an early start.

Most hotels have their own diving centre, and some will give a discount on accommodation if you dive with their centre. If you are an inexperienced diver, see p819 for tips on choosing a dive operation.

Among the many dive operators, **Tauch Terminal** ( ☎ 774504, 22911; www.tauch-terminal.com) is one of the longest-established operators in Bali. A four-day PADI open-water certificate course costs about €350. Expect to pay about €30/50 for one/two dives at Tulamben, and a little more for a night dive or dives around Amed.

Snorkelling gear is rented everywhere for 30,000Rp.

### Sleeping & Eating
At high tide, none of the places situated on the water have much rocky beach at all, but the waves are dramatic. Look for signs along the main road for the following places; most have their own dive operations. Every place to stay has at least a cafe.

**Ocean Sun** ( ☎ 22912; www.ocean-sun.com; r 60,000-70,000Rp) The budget choice of Tulamben, Ocean Sun has four bungalow-style rooms in a small garden on the hill side of the road. Units are clean and basic.

**Puri Madha Bungalows** ( ☎ 22921; r 70,000-300,000Rp; ﹡ ) Refurbished bungalow-style units are directly opposite the wreck on shore. Of the 12 rooms, the best have air-con and hot water. The spacious grounds feel like a public park.

**Tulamben Wreck Divers Resort** ( ☎ 23400; www .tulambenwreckdivers.com; r 200,000-400,000Rp; ﹡ ﹡ ﹡ ) There are seven rooms at this comfy two-storey complex on the hill side of the road. At the top end of the rate card, rooms have DVD players, air-con and fridges. All have hot water.

**Tauch Terminal Resort** ( ☎ 774504, 22911; www .tauch-terminal.com; r US$50-100; ﹡ ﹡ ) Down a side road at the shore, this sprawling hotel has 27 rooms in several categories. Many of the rooms are newly rebuilt and all are comfortable in a modern, motel-style way. Expect all amenities like satellite TV and fridges.

### Getting There & Away

Plenty of buses and bemos travel between Amlapura and Singaraja and will stop anywhere along the Tulamben road, but they're infrequent after 2pm. Expect to pay 8000Rp to either town.

Perama offers charter tourist-bus services from Candidasa; the cost is 125,000Rp each for a minimum of two people. This is similar to the cost of hiring a car and driver.

If you are driving to Lovina for the night, be sure to leave by about 3pm, so you will still have a little light when you get there. There's a petrol station just south of town.

## TULAMBEN TO YEH SANIH

North of Tulamben, the road continues to skirt the slopes of Gunung Agung, with frequent evidence of lava flows from the 1963 eruption. Further around, the outer crater of Gunung Batur slopes steeply down to the sea. The rainfall is low and you can generally count on sunny weather. The scenery is very stark in the dry season and it's thinly populated. The route has regular public transport, but it's easier to make stops and detours with your own vehicle.

At Les, a road goes inland to lovely **Air Terjun Yeh Mampeh**, said to be one of Bali's highest waterfalls. Look for a large sign located on the main road and then turn inland for 2km. Walk the last 2.5km or so on an obvious path by the stream. A 2000Rp donation is requested; there's no need to hire a guide.

The next main town is **Tejakula**, famous for its stream-fed public bathing area, said to have been built for washing horses, and often called the horse bath. The renovated bathing areas (separate for men and women) are behind walls topped by rows of elaborately decorated arches, and are regarded as a sacred area. The baths are 100m inland on a narrow road with lots of small shops – it's a quaint village, with some finely carved *kulkul* towers.

A remote retreat, **Alam Anda** ( ☎ 0361-750444; www.alamanda.de; r €40-160; ☒ ☒ ) is striking thanks to the efforts of the German architect-owner. The 30 units come in various sizes, from losmen rooms to cottages with views. All are well equipped and have artful thatch and bamboo motifs. A reef just offshore keeps the dive shop busy. The resort is near Sambirenteng.

# WEST BALI

Some of Bali's most sacred sites are in the west, from the ever-thronged Pura Tanah Lot to the Unesco-nominated Pura Taman Ayun. In between you can cruise along beside coursing streams on rural roads with bamboo arching overhead and fruit piling up below.

But the real star of the underachieving west is Taman Nasional Bali Barat (West Bali National Park), the only protected place of its kind on the island. Few who dive or snorkel the rich and pristine waters around Pulau Menjangan forget the experience. Others go for the challenge and trek through the savannah flats, mangroves and hillside jungles. Amid it all you'll find isolated resorts and hideaway inns in places like Balian Beach or Mengwi.

## TANAH LOT

☎ 0361

One of the most popular day trips from South Bali, **Pura Tanah Lot** (adult/child 10,000/5000Rp, car park 5000Rp) is the most visited and photographed temple in Bali. It's an obligatory stop, especially at sunset, and it is very commercialised. It has all the authenticity of a stage set – even the tower of rock that the temple sits upon is an artful reconstruction (the entire structure was crumbling). Over one-third of the rock you see is artificial.

For the Balinese, Pura Tanah Lot is one of the most important and venerated sea temples. Like Pura Luhur Ulu Watu (p291), at the tip of the southern Bukit Peninsula, it is closely associated with the Majapahit priest, Nirartha.

Tanah Lot, however, is a well-organised tourist trap. To reach the temple, a walkway runs through a sort of sideshow alley with dozens of souvenir shops down to the sea. To ease the task of making purchases, there is an ATM.

To visit the temple you should pick the correct time – everybody shows up for sunset and the mobs obliterate any spiritual feel the place has. If you visit before noon, crowds are few and the vendors are all but asleep.

### Getting There & Away

Coming from South Bali with your own transport, take the coastal road west from

Kerobokan, north of Seminyak, and follow the signs or the traffic. From other parts of Bali, turn off the Denpasar–Gilimanuk Rd near Kediri and follow the signs. During the pre- and post-sunset rush, traffic is awful.

By bemo, go from Denpasar's Ubung terminal to Tanah Lot (7000Rp) via Kediri, noting that bemo stop running by nightfall.

## PURA TAMAN AYUN

The huge state temple of **Pura Taman Ayun** (adult/child 5000/2500Rp; 8am-6pm), surrounded by a wide, elegant moat, was the main temple of the Mengwi kingdom, which survived until 1891, when it was conquered by the neighbouring kingdoms of Tabanan and Badung. The large, spacious temple was built in 1634 and then extensively renovated in 1937. It's a lovely place to wander around and its size means you can get away from speed-obsessed group-tour mobs ('Back on the bus!'). In the first courtyard you'll find a large, open, grassy expanse and in the inner courtyard there is a multitude of *meru* (multiroofed shrines).

Owing to its heritage, the temple has been nominated for Unesco recognition.

### Getting There & Away

Any bemo running between Denpasar (Ubung terminal) and Bedugul or Singaraja can drop you off at the roundabout in Mengwi, where signs indicate the road (250m) to the temple. Pura Taman Ayun is a stop-off on many organised tourist tours.

## MARGA

Northwest of the village, **Margarana memorial** (admission 5000Rp; 9am-5pm) commemorates the battle of Marga. On 20 November 1946, a force of 96 independence fighters was surrounded by a much larger and better-armed Dutch force fighting to regain Bali as a colony after the departure of the Japanese. The outcome was similar to the *puputan* of 40 years before. There was, however, one important difference: this time the Dutch suffered heavy casualties too, and this may have helped weaken their resolve to hang on to this rebellious colony.

Even with your own transport it's easy to get lost finding Marga and the memorial, so, as always, ask directions. You can easily combine this with a tour of the amazing Jatiluwih rice terraces (p355).

## TABANAN
☎ 0361

Tabanan is the capital of the district of the same name. Like many such towns in Bali, it's a large, well-organised place. It is also a renowned centre for dancing and gamelan playing, although public performances are essentially nil. Mario, the renowned dancer of the prewar period, hailed from Tabanan. His greatest achievement was to perfect the Kebyar dance, and he is also featured in Miguel Covarrubias' classic book, *Island of Bali*.

Playing a critical role in rural Balinese life, the *subak* is a village association that deals with water, water rights and irrigation (some of Bali's finest rice fields are in the surrounding region). The **Mandala Mathika Subak** (☎ 810315; Jl Raya Kediri; admission 5000Rp; 7am-4.30pm) is quite a large complex devoted to Tabanan's *subak* organisations. Within this is the **Subak Museum** with displays about the irrigation and cultivation of rice and the intricate social systems that govern it. The staff here are very sweet and will show you around; the exhibits themselves could use a little love.

All bemo and buses between Denpasar (Ubung terminal) and Gilimanuk stop at the terminal at the western end of Tabanan (7000Rp). The bemo terminal in the town centre only has transport to nearby villages.

## SOUTH OF TABANAN

There are not a lot of tourist attractions in the southern part of Tabanan district, but it's easy to access with your own transport. You can reach the main villages by local bemo from Tabanan, especially in the mornings. **Kediri** has Pasar Hewan, one of Bali's busiest cattle markets, and is the terminal for bemos to Pura Tanah Lot. About 10km south of Tabanan is **Pejaten**, a centre for the production of traditional pottery, including elaborate ornamental roof tiles. Porcelain clay objects, which are made purely for decorative use, can be seen in a few workshops in the village.

A little west of Tabanan, a road goes 8km south via Gubug to the secluded coast at **Yeh Gangga**. Here you can stay at **Bali Wisata Bungalows** (☎ 0361-7443561; www.baliwisatabungalows.com; Yeh Gangga; bungalows 200,000-400,000Rp; ), which has excellent views in a superb setting on 15km of rock and black-sand beach. The cheapest of the 12 rooms have cold water; the best have dramatic oceanfront vistas. It's family-run, and there's nothing fancy here.

BALI

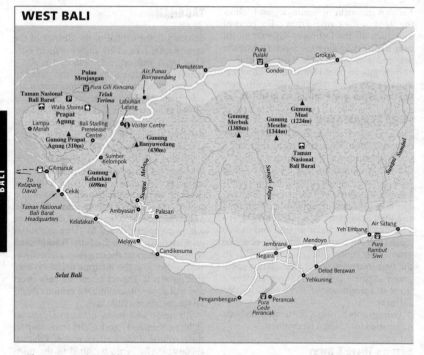

**WEST BALI**

The next road west from Tabanan turns down to the coast via **Kerambitan**, a village noted for its beautiful old buildings (including two 17th-century palaces); a tradition of *wayang*-style painting; and its own styles of music and dance, especially Tektekan, a ceremonial procession.

South of Kerambitan, you will pass through **Penarukan**, known for its stone- and woodcarvers, and also its dancers. Continue to the coast, where you'll find the beach at **Kelating** wide, black and usually deserted.

About 4km from southern Kerambitan is **Tibubiyu**. For a gorgeous drive through huge bamboo, fruit trees, rice paddies and more, take the scenic road northwest from Kerambitan to the main road.

## NORTH OF TABANAN

The area north of Tabanan is good to travel around with your own transport. There are some strictly B-level attractions; the real appeal here is just driving the back roads with trees canopying the road for a full-on tropical experience. Here you will see some of the finest rice terraces in Bali.

About 9km north of Tabanan the road reaches a fork. The left road goes to Pura Luhur Batukau via the hot springs at **Penatahan**. A few kilometres north of the hot springs, take a right turn at **Wangayagede** village and follow the road as it winds and soars through some beautiful countryside. At **Jatiluwih** (p355) you will be rewarded with vistas that exhaust your ability to describe green.

## BALIAN BEACH & LALANG-LINGGAH
☎ 0361

Located some 10km west of the junction with the road to the north at Antosari (p354) is Lalang-Linggah. Here a road (toll 2000Rp) leads 800m to the surf breaks near the mouth of Sungai Balian and the ever-more-popular scene at Balian Beach.

A rolling area of dunes and knolls overlooks the pounding surf here, which predictably is popular with surfers. A sort of critical mass of villas and beach accommodation has appeared here, and you can wander about between a few cafes and join other travellers for a beer and sunset.

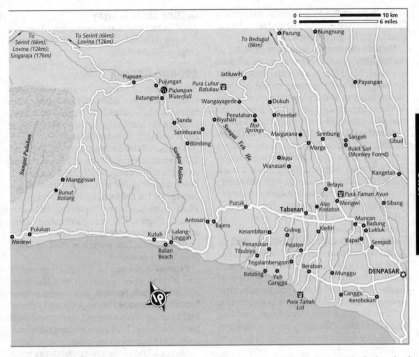

## Sleeping & Eating

All of the places listed below are close together. The way things are going, there will be more choices by the time you arrive.

**Made's Homestay** ( ☎ 081 2396 3335; r 100,000Rp) Three basic bungalow-style units back from the beach are surrounded by banana trees. The rooms are basic, clean, large enough to hold numerous surfboards and have cold-water showers.

**Balian Segara Homestay** ( ☎ 081 9164 56147; r 150,000-200,000Rp) Right down by the grey-sand beach, the three simple, clean cottages are set in a row, although views are a little obscured by dunes. The top unit has hot water. Try to overlook the marketing materials, which show the perils of Photoshop: huge waves break right over the homestay.

**Gajah Mina** ( ☎ 081 2381 1630; www.gajahminaresort.com; bungalows US$85-145; ✗ ⬚ ) Designed by the French architect-owner, this eight-unit boutique hotel is close to the ocean. The private, walled bungalows march out to a dramatic outcrop of stone surrounded by surf. The grounds are vast and there are little trails for wandering and pavilions for relaxing. The restaurant overlooks its own little bowl of rice terraces.

## JEMBRANA COAST

About 34km west of Tabanan you cross into Bali's most sparsely populated district, Jembrana. The main road follows the south coast most of the way to Negara. There's some beautiful scenery but little tourist development along the way, with the exception of the surf action at Medewi.

## Medewi

☎ 0365

Along the main road, a large sign points down the paved road (200m) to the surfing mecca of Pantai Medewi. The beach is a stretch of huge, smooth grey rocks interspersed among round black pebbles. It's a placid place where cattle graze by the beach. Medewi is noted not for its beach but for its *long* left-hand wave – there is little else here.

### SLEEPING & EATING

You'll find accommodation along the main lane to the surf break and down other lanes about 2km east. For a casual meal, some of the finest fare is freshly stir-fried and served up at a cart right by the beach/rocks.

**Mai Malu Restaurant & Guesthouse** ( ☎ 43897; s/d 70,000/90,000Rp) Near the highway on the Medewi side road, Mai Malu is a popular (and almost the only) hang-out, serving crowd-pleasing pizzas, burgers and Indonesian meals in its modern, breezy upstairs eating area. Eight cold-water rooms have the basics plus fans.

**Homestay CSB** ( ☎ 081 3386 67288; Pulukan; r 70,000-150,000Rp; ✼ ) Some 2km east of the Medewi surf break at Pulukan, look for signs along the main road. Venture 300m down a track and you'll find a great family with the beginnings of an empire. The best of the 10 simply furnished rooms have air-con, hot water and balconies with views that put anything in South Bali to shame.

**Medewi Beach Cottages** ( ☎ 40029; r US$45-75; ✼ ⟲ ) A large pool anchors 27 modern, comfortable rooms (with satellite TV) scattered about nice gardens right down by the surf break. The one off-note: security measures obstruct what should be a good view. Across the lane there's a lively two-storey building ostensibly called 'the party wing' with seven second-rate cold-water rooms (US$10) aimed at surfers.

## NEGARA
☎ 0365

Set amid the broad and fertile flatlands between the mountains and ocean, Negara is a prosperous little town, and a useful pit stop. Although it's a district capital, there's not much to see. Services include a **clinic** (Jl Arjuna). Several banks on the main commercial road (south of the Tabanan-Gilimanuk road), Jl Ngurah Rai, change money and have international ATMs.

### Eating

Numerous choices for meals line Jl Ngurah Rai. There are assorted warung in the market area at the traffic circle with Jl Pahlawan.

**Warung Lesehan** (Jl Ngurah Rai; mains from 4000Rp) A simple open-air place across from Hardy's has excellent fried fish and chicken redolent with local spices.

**Hardy's Supermarket** ( ☎ 40709; Jl Ngurah Rai; ✼ ) Hardy's has a popular albeit cacophonous indoor food court serving fresh, cheap chow. Dishes are generally under 4000Rp. This large supermarket has the best selection of goods in western Bali.

### Getting There & Away

Most bemo and minibuses from Denpasar (Ubung terminal) to Gilimanuk drop you in Negara (20,000Rp).

## AROUND NEGARA

At the southern fringe of Negara, **Loloan Timur** is largely a Bugis community (originally from Sulawesi) that retains 300-year-old traditions. Look for the distinctive houses on stilts, some decorated with wooden fretwork.

To reach **Delod Berawan**, turn off the main Gilimanuk–Denpasar Rd at Mendoyo and go south to the coast, which has a black-sand beach and irregular surf. This part of Bali is famous for the **bull races**, known as *mekepung*, which culminate in the Bupati Cup in Negara in early August. The racing animals are actually the normally docile water buffalo, which charge down a 2km stretch of road or beach pulling tiny chariots.

**Perancak** is the site of Nirartha's arrival in Bali in 1546, commemorated by a limestone temple, **Pura Gede Perancak**. Bull races are run at **Taman Wisata Perancak** ( ☎ 0365-42173), and Balinese buffets are sometimes staged for organised tours from South Bali. If you're travelling independently, give the park a ring before you go there.

Once capital of the region, **Jembrana** is the centre of the *gamelan jegog*, a gamelan using huge bamboo instruments that produce a very low-pitched, resonant sound. Performances often feature a number of gamelan groups engaging in musical contest. To see and hear them in action, time your arrival with a local festival, or ask in Negara where you might find a group practising.

## GILIMANUK
☎ 0365

Gilimanuk is the terminus for ferries that shuttle back and forth across the narrow strait to Java.

Most travellers to or from Java can get an onward ferry or bus straight away, and won't need to stop in Gilimanuk. The museum is the only attraction – the town is really a place one passes through quickly. Services are few; there are no ATMs.

This part of Bali has been occupied for thousands of years. The **Museum Situs Purbakala Gilimanuk** ( ☎ 61328; donation 5000Rp; ✼ 8am-4pm Mon-Fri) is centred on a family of skeletons thought to be 4000 years old, which were found locally in 2004. It's 500m east from the ferry port.

From fan-cooled singles to air-con suites you have your choice of basic accommodation at the 21-room **Hotel Lestari** ( ☎ 61504; r 65,000-325,000Rp; 🕸 ), which feels strangely suburban. It has a cafe.

## Getting There & Away

Frequent buses hurtle along the main road between Gilimanuk's huge bus depot and Denpasar's Ubung terminal (25,000Rp, two to three hours), or along the north-coast road to Singaraja (22,000Rp).

If you have wheels, watch out for the numerous police checkpoints around the terminal where commas are counted and the number of dots on i's checked on vehicle documents. Freelance 'fines' are common.

### FERRY

To get to and from Ketapang on Java (30 minutes; p608), car ferries (adult/child 6000/4500Rp, car and driver 95,000Rp, motorbike 31,000Rp) run around the clock.

## TAMAN NASIONAL BALI BARAT
☎ 0365

Call it nature's symphony. Most visitors to Bali's only national park, Taman Nasional Bali Barat (West Bali National Park), are struck by the mellifluous sounds from myriad birds. It's a place where you can hike through forests, enjoy the island's best diving at Pulau Menjangan and explore coastal mangroves.

The park covers 19,000 hectares of the western tip of Bali. An additional 55,000 hectares is protected in the national park extension, as well as almost 7000 hectares of coral reef and coastal waters. Together this represents a significant commitment to conservation on an island as densely populated as Bali, although the many firewood vendors lining the road are indicative of the challenges facing preservationists.

The **park headquarters** ( ☎ 61060; 🕙 7am-5pm) at Cekik displays a topographic model of the park area, and has a little information about plants and wildlife. The **Labuhan Lalang visitors centre** ( 🕙 7.30am-5pm) is in a hut located on the northern coast, where boats leave for Pulau Menjangan (p348).

The main roads to Gilimanuk go through the national park, but you don't have to pay an entrance fee just to drive through. If you want to stop and visit any of the sites within the park, you must buy a ticket (20,000Rp).

## Sights & Activities

By land, by boat or by water, the park awaits exploration. Most of the natural vegetation in the park is not tropical rainforest, which requires rain year-round, but coastal savannah, with deciduous trees that become bare in the dry season. The southern slopes receive more regular rainfall, and hence have more tropical vegetation, while the coastal lowlands have extensive mangroves.

### DIVING PULAU MENJANGAN

Bali's best-known dive area, Pulau Menjangan has a dozen superb dive sites. The diving is excellent – iconic tropical fish, soft corals, great visibility (usually), caves and a spectacular drop-off. One of the few complaints we've ever heard came from a reader who said that while snorkelling she kept getting water in her mouth because she was 'smiling so much'.

Of the dozen of so named sites here, most are close to shore and suitable for snorkellers or diving novices. Some decent snorkelling spots are not far from the jetty – ask the boatman where to go. Venture a bit out, however, and the depths turn inky black as the shallows drop off in dramatic cliffs, a magnet for experienced divers looking for wall dives. The Anker Wreck, a mysterious sunken ship, challenges even experts.

This uninhabited island boasts what is thought to be Bali's oldest temple, **Pura Gili Kencana**, dating from the 14th century. You can walk around the island in about an hour and most people who take to the waters here take a break on the unblemished beaches.

The closest and most convenient dive operators are found at Pemuteran (p363). Snorkellers can arrange for a boat (400,000Rp, four-hour trip) from the tiny dock at Labuhan Lalang (p348) just across the turquoise water from Menjangan. Warung here rent snorkelling gear (50,000Rp for four hours).

### BOAT TRIPS

The best way to explore the mangroves of Teluk Gilimanuk or the west side of Prapat Agung is by chartering a boat (maximum of five people) for about 250,000Rp per boat per hour, including guide and entrance fees. You can arrange this at either of the park offices. This is the ideal way to see bird life, including kingfishers, Javanese herons and plenty of others.

**BALI**

BALI

### TREKKING

All trekkers must be accompanied by an authorised guide. It's best to arrive the day before you want to trek, and make inquiries at the park offices in Cekik or Labuhan Lalang.

The set rates for guides in the park depend on the size of the group and the length of the trek – with one or two people it's 250,000Rp for one or two hours, 350,000Rp for three or four hours, and 600,000Rp for five to seven hours; all the prices are very negotiable. Early morning, say 6am, is the best time to start – it's cooler and you're more likely to see some wildlife. The following are two of the more popular treks.

From a trail west of Labuhan Lalang, hike around the mangroves at **Teluk Terima**. Then partially follow Sungai Terima into the hills and walk back down to the road along the steps at Makam Jayaprana. You might see grey macaques, deer and black monkeys (allow two to three hours).

From Sumber Kelompok, go up **Gunung Kelatakan** (698m), then down to the main road near Kelatakan village (six to seven hours). You may be able to get permission from park headquarters to stay overnight in the forest – if you don't have a tent, your guide can make a shelter from branches and leaves, which will be an adventure in itself. Clear streams abound in the dense woods.

### Sleeping

Park visitors will want to spend the night as close to the park as possible in order to get an early start. Gilimanuk (p346) is closest and has basic choices. Much nicer are the resorts in Labuhan Lalang (right). The best all-round choice is in Pemuteran (p363), 12km further east.

There is free and rough camping at the park headquarters in Cekik. A gratuity to the staff is greatly appreciated; you'll need your own gear.

### Getting There & Away

The national park is too far for a comfortable day trip from Ubud or South Bali, though many dive operators do it. Better to stay at one of the places suggested under Sleeping (above).

If you don't have transport, any Gilimanuk-bound bus or bemo from North or West Bali can drop you at park headquarters at Cekik (those from North Bali can also drop you at Labuhan Lalang).

## LABUHAN LALANG

To catch a boat to Pulau Menjangan (p347), head to the jetty at this small harbour in the national park. There's also a small park **visitors centre** ( ⏱ 7.30am-5pm) in a hut on the northern coast, and there are warung and a pleasant beach 200m to the east. The resorts and dive shops of Pemuteran (p363) are 11km northeast.

**Waka Shorea** ( ☎ 0362-94666; www.wakaexperience .com; r US$165, villas US$230; ❄ ⛱ ) is located in splendid isolation inside the park, a 10-minute boat ride from the hotel's reception area 100m east of Labuhan Lalang. The 16 naturalistic units are hidden in the forest, with decks above the trees and a dreamy pool.

# CENTRAL MOUNTAINS

Most of Bali's mountains are volcanoes; some are dormant, but some are definitely active. The mountains divide the gentle sweep of fertile land to the south from the narrow, more arid strip to the north. Northwest of Gunung Agung is the stark and spectacular caldera that contains the volcanic cone of Gunung Batur (1717m), the waters of Danau Batur and numerous smaller craters. In central Bali, around Bedugul, is another complex of volcanic craters and lakes, with much lusher vegetation.

It's all a big change from the coastal areas. Temperatures fall and you may need something more than shorts! There are two main routes through the mountains to the north coast (via Gunung Batur and via Bedugul), which allow you to make a circuit. There are treks to be had, clear lake waters to enjoy, plus a few other natural and sacred sites of note, especially the mysterious temple, Pura Luhur Batukau and nearby Unesco-nominated ancient rice terraces in and around Jatiluwih plus the stupendous hiking around the old colonial village of Munduk.

## GUNUNG BATUR
☎ 0366

Most day-visitors come on organised tours and stop at the crater rim at Penelokan for views and lunch; most overnight visitors stay in the villages around the lake. The views both from above and from lake level are truly wonderful – if you hit the area on a clear day.

## Orientation & Information

There are two main roads in the Gunung Batur area. The outer caldera-rim road links Penulisan and Penelokan, and from Penelokan you drop down onto the inner-rim road. The latter is rough in parts, especially the western side of the circuit, but drivable for all vehicles.

If you arrive by private vehicle, you will be stopped at ticket offices at Penelokan or Kubupenelokan; to save any hassle, you should stop and buy a ticket. Entry is 6000/3000Rp per adult/child. Bicycles are free (and should be, given the climb needed to get here). This ticket is for the whole Gunung Batur area; you shouldn't be charged again.

## Dangers & Annoyances

Gunung Batur has developed a well-deserved reputation as a money-grubbing place where visitors (mainly around Penelokan) are hassled by touts and wannabe mountain guides (mainly around the lake area). Of course the guides themselves can be a problem, see p350. Don't leave valuables in your car, especially at any car park at the start of a volcano trail. Don't even leave a helmet with a motorcycle.

## Trekking

The setting for Gunung Batur is otherworldly: it's like a giant dish, with the bottom half covered with water and a set of volcanic cones growing in the middle. Visit the area

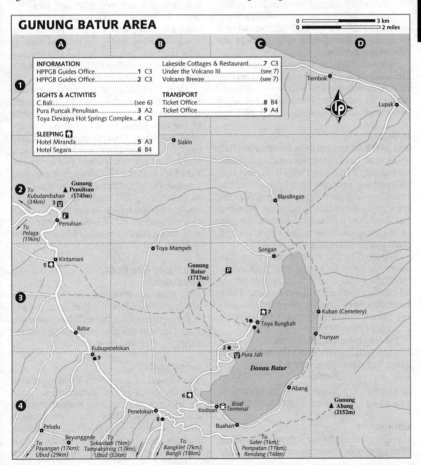

**GUNUNG BATUR AREA**

0 — 3 km
0 — 2 miles

**INFORMATION**
HPPGB Guides Office.....................**1** C3
HPPGB Guides Office.....................**2** C3

**SIGHTS & ACTIVITIES**
C.Bali.........................................(see 6)
Pura Puncak Penulisan...................**3** A2
Toya Devasya Hot Springs Complex...**4** C3

**SLEEPING**
Hotel Miranda...............................**5** A3
Hotel Segara.................................**6** B4

Lakeside Cottages & Restaurant........**7** C3
Under the Volcano III.....................(see 7)
Volcano Breeze.............................(see 7)

**TRANSPORT**
Ticket Office.................................**8** B4
Ticket Office.................................**9** A4

on a clear day and you'll understand what all the fuss is about. Soaring up in the centre of the huge outer crater is the cone of Gunung Batur (1717m), formed by a 1917 eruption. A cluster of smaller cones lies beside, created variously by eruptions in 1926, 1963, 1974 and 1994.

But is it worthwhile to go through the hassle and the expense of making the climb? You'll get some amazing pictures and come close to volcanic action not easily seen anywhere. But the flip side is that it's costly, you have to deal with various characters and at some point you may just say, 'I could have enjoyed all this from the carpark viewpoint in Penelokan.'

Even reputable and highly competent adventure tour operators from elsewhere in Bali cannot take their customers up Gunung Batur without paying the HPPGB (see below) and using one of their guides, so these tours are relatively expensive.

Pretty much all the accommodation in the area can help you put a trek together. They can recommend hassle-free alternatives to Batur such as the outer rim of the crater, or to other mountains such as Gunung Agung (p330).

### HPPGB

The **HPPGB** (Mt Batur Tour Guides Association; ☎ 52362; ☯ 3am–noon) has a monopoly on guided climbs up Gunung Batur. The HPPGB requires that all trekking agencies that operate on the mountain hire at least one of its guides for trips up the mountain. In addition, the cartel has developed a reputation for intimidation in requiring climbers to use its guides and during negotiations for its services.

Reported tactics have ranged from dire warnings given to people who inquired at its offices to physical threats against people attempting to climb without a guide. There have also been reports of guides stationing themselves outside hotels to intercept climbers.

Pinning these guys down on rates can be like trying to keep pace with the pea in a shell game, but expect to pay the following:

| Trek | Duration | Cost |
| --- | --- | --- |
| Batur Sunrise | 4–8am | 300,000–400,000Rp |
| Gunung Batur | 4–10am | 300,000–400,000Rp |

### EQUIPMENT

If you're climbing before sunrise, take a torch (flashlight) or be absolutely sure that your guide provides you with one. You'll need good strong footwear, a hat, a jumper and drinking water.

### ROUTES

Most travellers use one of two trails that start near Toya Bungkah.

The shorter one is straight up (three to four hours return), while a longer trek (five to six hours return) links the summit climb with the other craters.

The route from Toya Bungkah is pretty straightforward. Climbers have reported that they have easily made this journey without a HPPGB guide, although it shouldn't be tried while dark. The major obstacle is actually avoiding any hassle from the guides themselves. There are a few separate paths at first, but they all rejoin sooner or later and after about 30 minutes you'll be on a ridge with quite a well-defined track. It gets pretty steep towards the top and it can be hard walking over the loose volcanic sand – climbing up three steps and sliding back two. Allow about two hours to get to the top.

There is another route from the northeast, where a track enables you to use private transport to within about 45 minutes' walk of the top. From Toya Bungkah, take the road northeast towards Songan and take the left fork after about 3.5km at Serongga, just before Songan. Follow this inner-rim road for another 1.7km to a well-signposted track on the left, which climbs another 1km or so to a car park. From here, the walking track is easy to follow to the top. If you do this without an HPPGB guide, you can be sure that guides on motorbikes will appear to hassle you.

## The Outer-Rim Road
### PENELOKAN

On a clear day, Penelokan has superb views across to Gunung Batur and down to the lake at the bottom of the crater. It has numerous huge places catering to busloads of tourists. Enjoy the view and leave.

### KINTAMANI

The villages of Batur and Kintamani now virtually run together. Kintamani is famed for its large and colourful **market**, which is held every three days. The town is like a string bean: long, with pods of development. Activity starts early and by 11am the town is all packed up. If you don't want to go on a trek, the sunrise view from the road here is pretty good.

**Hotel Miranda** ( ☎ 52022; Jl Raya Kintamani, Kintamani; s/d 40,000/70,000Rp) is the only accommodation here. The six rooms are clean and very basic with squat toilets. It has good food and a welcome open fire at night. The informative owner, Made Senter, is an excellent trekking guide.

### PENULISAN

At a bend in the road, at the junction to Singaraja, several steep flights of steps lead to Bali's highest temple, **Pura Puncak Penulisan** at 1745m. The views from the temple are superb: facing north you can see over the rice terraces clear to the Singaraja coast.

## The Inner-Rim Road

The farming villages down on the lakeside grow onions and other aromatic crops. It's a crisp setting with often superb lake and mountain views.

### KEDISAN

A hairpin-bend road winds its way down from Penelokan to Kedisan on the shore of the lake. **C.Bali** ( ☎ 081 3532 00251; www.c-bali.com; Hotel Segara, Kedisan) is a ground-breaking tour company (operated by an Australian-Dutch couple) that offers bike tours around the craters and canoe tours on the lake. Prices start at US$40 and include pick-up across South Bali.

**Hotel Segara** ( ☎ 51136; hotelsegara@plasa.com; Kedisan; r 80,000-200,000Rp;) has bungalows set around a courtyard. The cheapest rooms have cold water; the best have hot water and bathtubs – perfect for soaking away the hypothermia.

### TOYA BUNGKAH

The main tourist centre is Toya Bungkah, which is scruffy but has a cute charm and a serene lakeside setting.

Beside the lake, **Toya Devasya** ( ☎ 51204; adult/child US$10/5; ☯ 8am-8pm) is built around a hot spring. The huge hot pool is 38°C while the comparatively brisk lake-fed pool is 20°C.

Unless noted, hotels only have cold water, which can be a boon for waking up for a sunset climb. Most have restaurants, some of which serve *ikan mujair*, a delicious small lake fish, which is barbecued to a crisp with onion, garlic and bamboo shoots.

---

**WHEN TO TREK**

The volcanically active area west of the main peak can be deadly, with explosions of steam and hot lava, unstable ground and sulphurous gases. To find out about current conditions, ask at your accommodation or in Toya Bungkah. Alternatively look at the website of the **Directorate of Volcanology and Geographical Hazard Mitigation** (www.vsi.esdm.go.id).

The active areas are sometimes closed to visitors for safety reasons – if this is the case, don't try it alone, and don't pay extra for an extended main crater trek that you won't be able to complete.

---

**Under the Volcano III** ( ☎ 081 3386 0081; r 70,000Rp) With a lovely, quiet lakeside location opposite vegetable plots, this inn has eight clean and pretty rooms; go for Room 1 right on the water. There are two other nearby inns in the Volcano empire, all run by the same lovely family.

**Lakeside Cottages & Restaurant** ( ☎ 51249; www .lakesidebali.com; r US$10-35; ☯ ) The lakeside pool at this option, at the end of the lane on the water's edge, makes it a top pick. Of the 11 rooms, the best have hot water and satellite TV. The restaurant serves home-style Japanese dishes.

**Volcano Breeze** ( ☎ 51824; dishes 15,000-25,000Rp) This sociable travellers cafe with local art on the walls serves fresh lake fish in many forms.

## Getting There & Around

From Batubulan terminal in Denpasar, bemos make regular trips to Kintamani (18,000Rp). You can also get a bus on the busy Denpasar (Batabulan)–Singaraja route, which makes stops in both Penelokan and Kintamani (about 18,000Rp). Alternatively, you can just hire a car or use a driver. From South Bali you can expect to pay at least 450,000Rp.

Orange bemo regularly shuttle back and forth around the crater rim, between Penelokan and Kintamani (8000Rp for tourists). Public bemo from Penelokan down to the lakeside villages go mostly in the morning (tourist price is about 6000Rp to Toya Bungkah). Later in the day, you may have to charter transport (40,000Rp or more).

# DANAU BRATAN

☎ 0368

Approaching from the south, you gradually leave the rice terraces behind and ascend into the cool, often misty mountain country around Danau Bratan. The name Bedugul is sometimes used to refer to the whole lakeside area, but strictly speaking, Bedugul is just the first place you reach at the top of the hill when coming up from South Bali. Candikuning is the main village in the area, and has an important and picturesque temple. Marvellous Munduk anchors a region with fine trekking to waterfalls and cloud-cloaked forests.

The choice of accommodation near the lake is limited as much of the area is geared towards domestic, not foreign, tourists. Many new inns aimed at international visitors are opening around Munduk.

Wherever you go, you are likely to see the tasty local strawberries on offer. Note that it is often misty and can get chilly up here.

## Candikuning

Dotting the western side of the lake, Candikuning is a haven for plant lovers. Its **market** (parking 1000Rp) is touristy but among the eager vendors of tat, you'll find locals shopping for fruit, veg, herbs, spices and potted plants. You'll find good cafes hidden in the corners. Privately run toilets in the southwest corner (5000Rp) are the cleanest for miles.

### SIGHTS

The **Bali Botanical Gardens** (Kebun Raya Eka Karya Bali; ☎ 21273; admission walking/driving 7000/12,000Rp, car parking 6000Rp; ☼ 7am-6pm) is a showplace. Established in 1959 as a branch of the national botanical gardens at Bogor, near Jakarta, it covers more than 154 hectares on the lower slopes of Gunung Pohen. The garden boasts an extensive collection of trees and flowers. The gorgeous orchid area is often locked to foil flower filchers; ask that it be unlocked.

Within the park, you can cavort like a bird or a squirrel at the **Bali Treetop Adventure Park** (www.balitreetop.com; adult/child US$20/13). Winches, ropes, nets and more let you explore the forest well above the ground.

Coming northwest from Bedugul, at a junction conspicuously marked with a large, phallic corn-cob sculpture, a small side road goes 600m west to the garden. It gets crowded on Sundays with local families.

The very important Hindu-Buddhist **Pura Ulun Danu Bratan** (adult/child 10,000/5000Rp, parking 2000Rp; ☼ tickets 7am-5pm, site 24hr) was founded in the 17th century. It is dedicated to Dewi Danu, the goddess of the waters, and is actually built on small islands, which means it is completely surrounded by the lake. Pilgrimages and ceremonies are held here to ensure that there is a supply of water for farmers all over Bali.

The tableau includes classical Hindu thatch-roofed *meru* reflected in the water and silhouetted against the often-cloudy mountain backdrop – a true Bali photo-cliché.

### ACTIVITIES

At the temple gardens, you can hire a four- passenger speedboat with a driver (150,000Rp per 30 minutes), a five-person rowboat with rower (100,000Rp per 30 minutes), or a two-person pedal boat (35,000Rp per 30 minutes).

For an almost surreal experience, take a quiet paddle across the lake and see Pura Ulun Danu Bratan at sunrise – arrange it with a boatman the night before.

### SLEEPING

The Bedugul and Candikuning area can make a good place for a break in exploring the highlands.

**Pondok Wisata Dahlia Indah** ( ☎ 21233; r 80,000-125,000Rp) In the village along a lane near the road to the botanical gardens, this is a decent budget option with 17 comfortable, clean rooms with hot-water showers set in a garden of mountain flowers.

**Enjung Beji Resort** ( ☎ 21490; cottages 250,000-500,000Rp) Just north of the temple and overlooking Danau Bratan is this peaceful, pleasant option. The 23 cottages are modern and clean. The nicest have outdoor showers and sunken baths.

### EATING

From simple market snacks to meals featuring the region's fresh strawberries, you'll have much to choose from. At the entrance to Pura Ulun Danu Bratan are several Padang warung, and there's a cafe with a view on the grounds.

**Roti Bedugal** ( ☎ 21838; snacks 5000Rp; ☼ 8am-6pm) Just north of the market, this tiny bakery produces fine versions of its namesake as well as croissants and other treats all day.

**Strawberry Stop** ( ☎ 21060; dishes 7000-20,000Rp; ☼ 8am-7pm) Here, north of the temple, locally grown strawberries star in milkshakes, juices,

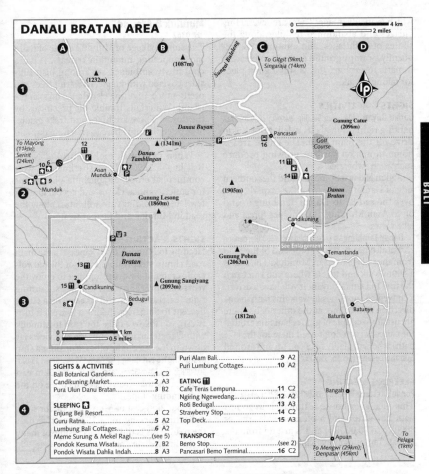

### DANAU BRATAN AREA

**SIGHTS & ACTIVITIES**
Bali Botanical Gardens.........................1 C2
Candikuning Market.............................2 A3
Pura Ulun Danu Bratan........................3 B2

**SLEEPING**
Enjung Beji Resort................................4 C2
Guru Ratna.........................................5 A2
Lumbung Bali Cottages.........................6 A2
Meme Surung & Mekel Ragi.............(see 5)
Pondok Kesuma Wisata........................7 B2
Pondok Wisata Dahlia Indah................8 A3

Puri Alam Bali......................................9 A2
Puri Lumbung Cottages.......................10 A2

**EATING**
Cafe Teras Lempuna...........................11 C2
Ngiring Ngewedang............................12 A2
Roti Bedugal.....................................13 A3
Strawberry Stop.................................14 C2
Top Deck..........................................15 A3

**TRANSPORT**
Bemo Stop....................................(see 2)
Pancasari Bemo Terminal....................16 C2

pancakes and more. Bananas are used when berries are out of season, which might drive you to drink the self-proclaimed 'dry' – ha! – strawberry wine (100,000Rp).

**Cafe Teras Lempuna** ( ☎ 0362-29312; dishes 15,000-40,000Rp; ✷ ) Also north of the temple, this indoor/outdoor cafe is stylish and modern. The menu ranges from burgers to Japanese and the coffees, teas and juices refresh no matter the temperature.

**Top Deck** ( ☎ 081 138 8697, 0361-877 9633; mains 20,000-50,000Rp; ✷ 9am-5pm) Hovering above Crackers, and with the same Australian owners, this airy cafe with an open kitchen looks over the market and has a full menu of creative Indo fare. At lunch there's a buffet option.

**GETTING THERE & AWAY**
Danau Bratan is beside the main north–south road, so it's easy to reach from South Bali or Lovina.

Although the main terminal is in Pancasari, most minibuses and bemo will stop along the road in Bedugul and Candikuning. There are frequent connections from Denpasar's Ubung terminal (18,000Rp) and Singaraja's Sukasada terminal (18,000Rp). For Gunung Batur, you have to connect through Singaraja or hire transport.

## Danau Buyan & Danau Tamblingan
Also northwest of Danau Bratan are two more lakes, Danau Buyan and Danau Tamblingan – neither has been heavily developed for tourism,

which is an advantage. There are several tiny villages and abandoned temples along the shores of both lakes, and although the frequently swampy ground makes it unpleasant in parts to explore, this is still a good place for taking a walk.

### SIGHTS & ACTIVITIES

**Danau Buyan** (admission 5000Rp, parking 2000Rp) has parking right on the lake, a delightful 1.5km drive off the main road. The entire area is home to market gardens growing produce such as strawberries.

A 4km **hiking trail** goes around the southern side of Danau Buyan from the carpark, then over the saddle to Danau Tamblingan and on to Asan Munduk. It combines forest and lake views.

**Danau Tamblingan** (adult/child 6000/3000Rp, parking 2000Rp) also has parking at the end of the road from the village of Asan Munduk. The lake is a 400m walk and this is where you can catch the trail to Danau Buyan. If you have a driver, a convenient option is to walk this path in one direction and be met at the other end. There are usually a couple of guides hanging around the car park (you don't need them for the lake path) who will gladly take you up and around **Gunung Lesong** (per 6hr 350,000Rp).

### SLEEPING & EATING

**Pondok Kesuma Wisata** ( ☎ 081 7472 8826; r 200,000Rp) This nice guesthouse features clean rooms with hot water and a pleasant cafe (dishes 8000Rp to 20,000Rp) and is just up from the Danau Tamblingan parking lot.

## Munduk & Around
☎ 0362

The simple village of Munduk is one of Bali's most appealing mountain retreats. It has a cool misty ambience set among lush hillsides covered with jungle, rice, fruit trees and pretty much anything else that grows on the island. Waterfalls tumble off precipices by the dozen. There are hikes and treks galore. Many people come here to trek for a day and stay a week.

When the Dutch took control of North Bali in the 1890s, they experimented with commercial crops, establishing plantations for coffee, vanilla, cloves and cocoa. Quite a few Dutch buildings are still intact along the road in Munduk and further west.

### SIGHTS & ACTIVITIES

Heading to Munduk from Pancasari, the main road climbs steeply up the rim of the old volcanic crater. It's worth stopping to enjoy the **views** back over the valley and lakes. Turning right (east) at the top will take you on a scenic descent to Singaraja. Taking a sharp left turn (west), you follow a ridge-top road to Munduk with Danau Buyan on one side and views far down to the sea on the other. Consider a stop at **Ngiring Ngewedang** ( ☎ 0828 365 146; dishes 15,000-40,000Rp; ☼ 10am-5pm), a coffeehouse 5km east of Munduk that grows its own coffee on the surrounding slopes.

About 2km east of Munduk look for signs indicating parking for a 15m **waterfall** near the road. This is the most accessible of many in the immediate area.

---

### SCENIC ROUTES BETWEEN THE COASTS

The two most popular routes between the southern and northern coasts are the roads via Kintamani and Bedugul, but there are two other routes over the mountains. Both branch north from the Denpasar to Gilimanuk road, one from Pulukan and the other from Antosari, and meet at Pupuan. At Mayong, you can turn east to Munduk or continue down to Seririt, west of Lovina on the north coast.

The Pulukan–Pupuan road climbs steeply up from the coast providing fine views back down to West Bali and the sea. The route also runs through spice-growing country – you'll see (and smell) spices laid out on mats by the road to dry. After about 10km and just before Manggissari, the narrow and winding road actually runs right through **Bunut Bolong** – an enormous tree that forms a complete tunnel. Further on, the road spirals down to Pupuan through some of Bali's most beautiful rice terraces.

The road from Antosari initially travels through rice fields, then climbs into the spice-growing country and finally descends through the coffee plantations to Pupuan. If you continue another 12km or so towards the north coast you reach Mayong, where you can turn east to Munduk and on to Danau Tamblingan and Danau Buyan.

Almost everything in the Munduk area is at an elevation of at least 1000m. Numerous trails are suitable for **treks** of two hours or much longer to coffee plantations, rice paddies, waterfalls, villages, or around both Danau Tamblingan and Danau Buyan. You will be able to arrange a guide through your lodgings.

### SLEEPING & EATING

Like mushrooms after the rain (they grow up here), accommodation is proliferating around Munduk. Enjoy simple old Dutch houses in the village or more naturalistic places in the countryside. Most have cafes, usually serving good local fare. There's a couple of cute warung along the road down to Seririt and North Bali.

**Guru Ratna** ( ☎ 92182; r 100,000-200,000Rp) The cheapest place in the village, this has five comfortable cold-water rooms in a colonial Dutch house. The best rooms have some style and nice porches. Ponder the distant ocean from the cafe.

**Meme Surung & Mekel Ragi** ( ☎ 92811; r US$20-24) These atmospheric old Dutch houses adjoin each other in the village and have two rooms. There are seven more rooms – all with hot showers – next door to the pair. Meme Surung has views.

**Puri Alam Bali** ( ☎ 081 2465 9815; www.purialambali .com; r 200,000-250,000Rp) Perched on a precipice at the east end of the village, Puri Alam Bali's eight rooms (all hot-water) have better views the higher you go. The rooftop cafe surveys the local scene from on high. Think of the long concrete stairs down from the road as trekking practice.

**Lumbung Bali Cottages** ( ☎ 92818; www.lumbung -bali.com; r US$45-125) About 800m east of Munduk, this country inn has nine traditional cottages overlooking the lush local terrain. The open-air bathrooms (with tubs) are as refreshing as the porches are relaxing. A short trail leads to a small waterfall.

**our pick Puri Lumbung Cottages** ( ☎ 92810; www .purilumbung.com; cottage US$68-160; 🖳 🛜 ) Founded by Nyoman Bagiarta to develop sustainable tourism, this lovely hotel has 14 bright two-storey cottages set among rice fields. Enjoy intoxicating views down to the coast from the upstairs balconies. Dozens of trekking options and courses, including dance and cooking, are offered. The hotel's restaurant, Warung Kopi Bali, is excellent. The hotel is on the right-hand side of the road, 700m before Munduk from Bedugul.

### GETTING THERE & AWAY

Bemos leave Ubung terminal in Denpasar for Munduk frequently (22,000Rp). Morning bemo from Candikuning also stop in Munduk (13,000Rp). If you're driving to or from the north coast, a decent road west of Munduk goes through a number of picturesque villages to Mayong (where you can head south to West Bali). The road then goes down to the sea at Seririt in North Bali.

## GUNUNG BATUKAU AREA

Often overlooked (probably a good thing given what the vendor hordes have done to Gunung Agung), Gunung Batukau is Bali's second-highest mountain (2276m), the third of Bali's three major mountains and the holy peak of the island's western end. Enjoy a magical visit to one of the island's holiest and most underrated temples, Pura Luhur Batukau, or just revel in the ancient rice-terrace greenery around Jatiluwih.

### Orientation

There are two main approaches to the Gunung Batukau area. The easiest is to go via Tabanan (see p343) and take the Pura Luhur Batukau road north 9km to a fork in the road. Take the one on the left (towards the temple) and go a further 5km to a junction near a school in Wangayagede village. Here you can continue straight to the temple or turn right (east) for the rice fields of Jatiluwih.

### Pura Luhur Batukau

On the slopes of Gunung Batukau, **Pura Luhur Batukau** (donation 10,000Rp) was the state temple when Tabanan was an independent kingdom. It has a seven-roofed *meru* dedicated to Maha Dewa, the mountain's guardian spirit.

The main pagoda-like structures have little doors shielding small ceremonial items. This is certainly the most spiritual major temple you can easily visit in Bali. There's a general lack of touts and other characters – including hordes of tourists. Facing the temple take a short walk around to the left to see a small white-water stream. The air vibrates with the coursing of water.

### Jatiluwih Rice Fields

At **Jatiluwih**, which means 'Truly Marvellous', you will be rewarded with vistas of centuries-old rice terraces that exhaust your ability to describe green. The locals will also be rewarded with your 'green', as there's a road toll for visitors (per person 10,000Rp, plus 5000Rp per car).

The terraces have been nominated for Unesco status. You'll understand why just viewing the panorama from the narrow, twisting 18km road, but get out for a **rice-field walk**. Follow the water as it runs through channels and bamboo pipes from one plot to the next.

Along the drive you'll pass a couple of warung with simple food served at tables overlooking the terraces.

### Getting There & Away
The only realistic way to explore the Gunung Batukau area is with your own transport.

# NORTH BALI

Although one-sixth of the island's population lives in North Bali, the vast region, centred on Singaraja and the Buleleng regency, is overlooked by many visitors who stay trapped in the South Bali-Ubud axis. And that's ironic

because the north was once the gateway to Bali, with Dutch steamers bringing the island's first visitors to the port in Singaraja.

Today, tourism in the north is focused on Lovina, the mellow beach town with cheap hotels and even cheaper sunset beer specials. To the west, Pemuteran charms all who discover the crescent of appealing resorts around a cute little bay. Diving is big here and all along the north coast.

Getting to North Bali for once lives up to the cliché: it's half the fun. Routes follow the thinly populated coastlines east and west, or, you can go up and over the central mountains by any number of routes, marvelling at crater lakes and maybe stopping for a misty trek on the way.

## YEH SANIH
☎ 0362
About 15km east of Singaraja, Yeh Sanih (also called Air Sanih) is a hassle-free seaside spot with a few guesthouses on a black-sand beachfront (albeit with a retaining wall). It's named for its fresh-water springs, **Air Sanih** (adult/child 3000/1000Rp; ☼ 8am-6pm), which are channelled

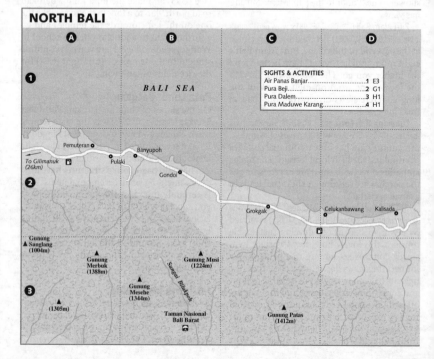

### NORTH BALI

**SIGHTS & ACTIVITIES**
| | |
|---|---|
| Air Panas Banjar | 1 E3 |
| Pura Beji | 2 G1 |
| Pura Dalem | 3 H1 |
| Pura Maduwe Karang | 4 H1 |

BALI SEA

Pemuteran
To Gilimanuk (26km)
Pulaki
Banyupoh
Gondoi
Grokgak
Celukanbawang      Kalisada

Gunung Sanglang (1004m)
Gunung Merbuk (1388m)
Gunung Mesehe (1344m)
Gunung Musi (1224m)
Sungai Blihdyoh
Taman Nasional Bali Barat
(1305m)
Gunung Patas (1412m)

into large swimming pools before flowing into the sea. The pools are particularly picturesque at sunset, when throngs of locals bathe under blooming frangipani trees.

**Pura Ponjok Batu** has a commanding location between the sea and the road, some 7km east of Yeh Sanih. It has some very fine limestone carvings in the central temple area.

A surprise in the area is **Art Zoo** (☻8am-6pm), 5.7km east of Yeh Sanih on the Singaraja road. The irrepressible American artist Symon owns this gallery and studio. It bursts with his own creativity that's at times vibrant, exotic and erotic.

### Sleeping & Eating

our pick **Cilik's Beach Garden** (☎ 26561; www.ciliks beachgarden.com; s/d €40/60, villas €60-160; 🖳 ) These custom-built villas, 3km east of Yeh Sanih, are large and have extensive private gardens. Other accommodation is in stylish *lumbung* (rice barns with round roofs) set in a delightful garden facing the ocean. There's a real emphasis on local culture; the owners have even more remote villas further south on the coast.

### Getting There & Away

Yeh Sanih is on the main road along the north coast. Frequent bemo (small minibuses) and buses from Singaraja stop outside the springs (8000Rp).

If heading to Amed or Tulamben, make certain you're on your way south from here by 4pm in order to arrive while there's still some light.

## SINGARAJA

☎ 0362

With a population of more than 100,000 people, Singaraja (which means 'Lion King' and somehow hasn't caused Disney to demand licensing fees) is Bali's second-largest city. With its tree-lined streets, surviving Dutch colonial buildings and charmingly moribund waterfront area north of Jl Erlangga, it's worth exploring for a few hours. Most people stay in nearby Lovina, however.

Singaraja was the centre of Dutch power in Bali and remained the administrative centre for the Lesser Sunda Islands (Bali through to Timor) until 1953. Today, Singaraja is a major educational and cultural centre.

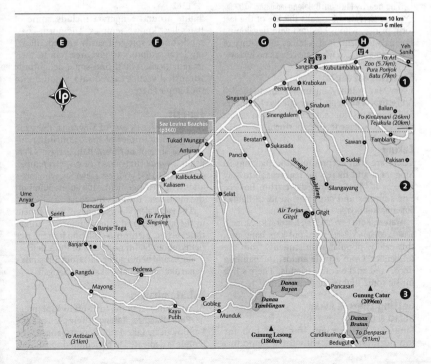

## Information

There are numerous banks and ATMs. Facilities include the following:

**Diparda** ( ☎ 25141; cnr Jl Veteran & Jl Gajah Mada; ☉ 7.30am-3.30pm Mon-Fri) The regional tourist office loves visitors. Ask about dance and other cultural events.

**RSUP Hospital** ( ☎ 22046; Jl Ngurah Rai; ☉ 24hr) Singaraja's hospital is the largest in northern Bali.

## Sights

### OLD HARBOUR & WATERFRONT

The conspicuous **Yudha Mandala Tama monument** commemorates a freedom fighter killed by gunfire from a Dutch warship early in the struggle for independence. Close by, there's the colourful Chinese temple **Ling Gwan Kiong**. There are a few old canals here as well and you can still get a little feel of the old colonial port.

### GEDONG KIRTYA LIBRARY & MUSEUM

This small historical **library** ( ☎ 22645; admission 10,000Rp; ☉ 8am-4pm Mon-Thu, 8am-1pm Fri) was established in 1928 by Dutch colonialists and named after the Sanskrit word 'to try'. It has a collection of *lontar* books as well as some even older written works.

The nearby **Museum Buleleng** (admission 10,000Rp; ☉ 9am-3.30pm Mon-Fri) recalls the life of the last local prince, who is credited with developing Lovina's tourism. It also traces the history of the region back to when there was no history.

## Festivals & Events

Every May or June, Singaraja is host to the **Bali Art Festival of Buleleng**. Over one week dancers and musicians from some of the region's most renowned village troupes perform.

## Eating

There are slim accommodation pickings in Singaraja, and there's no real reason to stay here as it's just a short drive from Lovina. For supplies and sundries, head to **Hardy's Supermarket** (Jl Pramuka; ☉ 6am-10pm).

**Warung Kota** ( ☎ 700 9737; Jl Ngurah Rai 22; meals 5000-15,000Rp; ☉ 24hr) The kool kats hang-out, this cafe is popular with students from the university. Grab a table amidst the bamboo decor and make some friends. There's live music some nights, movies others.

## Getting There & Away

### BEMO & BUS

Singaraja is the main transport hub for the northern coast, with three bemo/bus terminals. From the **Sukasada terminal**, 3km south of town, minibuses go to Denpasar (Ubung terminal, 30,000Rp) via Bedugul/Pancasari (15,000Rp) sporadically through the day.

The **Banyuasri terminal**, on the western side of town, has buses heading to Gilimanuk (22,000Rp, two hours) and Java, and plenty of blue bemo to Lovina (7000Rp).

The **Penarukan terminal**, 2km east of town, has bemo to Yeh Sanih (8000Rp) and Amlapura (18,000Rp, three hours) via the coastal road; and also minibuses to Denpasar (Batubulan terminal, 30,000Rp, three hours) via Kintamani.

### To Java

From Singaraja, several companies have overnight services to Surabaya (150,000Rp, 13 hours), which include the ferry trip across the Bali Strait. Other buses go as far as Yogyakarta (210,000Rp, 16 hours) and Jakarta (300,000Rp, 24 hours), usually travelling overnight – book at Banyuasri terminal a day before.

# AROUND SINGARAJA

☎ 0362

Sights around Singaraja include some of Bali's best-known temples. The north-coast sandstone is soft and easily carved, allowing local sculptors to give free rein to their imaginations. You'll find some delightfully whimsical scenes carved into a number of the temples here.

## Sangsit

A few kilometres east of Singaraja, there are two good examples of the colourful architectural style of northern Bali. Sangsit's **Pura Beji** is a *subak* (irrigated rice system) temple, dedicated to the goddess Dewi Sri, who looks after irrigated rice fields. It's about 500m off the main road towards the coast.

The **Pura Dalem** shows scenes of punishment in the afterlife, and other humorous, sometimes erotic, pictures. You'll find it in the rice fields, about 500m northeast of Pura Beji.

Buses and bemo going east from Singaraja's Penarukan terminal will stop at Sangsit.

## Kubutambahan

About 1km east of the turn-off to Kintamani is **Pura Maduwe Karang** (Temple of the Landowner). Like Pura Beji at Sangsit, the temple is dedicated to agricultural spirits, but this one looks after unirrigated land. This is one of the best temples in northern Bali, and is particularly noted for its sculpted panels, including the famous bicycle panel depicting a gentleman riding a bicycle with flower petals for wheels. Kubutambahan is on the Singaraja to Amlapura road, and there are regular bemos and buses.

## Gitgit

Situated about 11km south of Singaraja are the pretty – and pretty touristy – waterfalls of **Air Terjun Gitgit** (adult/child 6000/3000Rp) The well-signposted path (800m) from the main road in the village is lined with souvenir stalls and warung. The 40m falls are a good place for a picnic when it's not too busy, but litter can be an issue. There is another small waterfall, sometimes called **Gitgit Multitier Waterfall** (donation 5000Rp) situated about 2km further up the hill from the main falls and about 600m off the main road.

Buses and minibuses travel between the main Sukasada terminal in Singaraja and Denpasar (Ubung terminal), via Bedugul, and stop at Gitgit.

## LOVINA
☎ 0362

Relaxed is how people most often describe Lovina and they are correct. This low-key, low-rise beach resort is the polar opposite of Kuta. Days are slow and so are the nights.

Almost merging into Singaraja to the west, the town is really a string of coastal villages – Pemaron, Tukad Mungga, Anturan, Kalibukbuk, Kaliasem and Temukus – that have taken on this collective name.

Lovina is a convenient base for trips around the north coast or the central mountains. The beaches are made up of washed-out grey and black volcanic sand, and they are mostly clean near the hotel areas, but generally unspectacular. Reefs protect the shore, so the water is usually calm and clear.

### Orientation & Information

The Lovina tourist area stretches over 8km, but the main focus is Kalibukbuk, 10.5km west of Singaraja.

If you're planning a reading holiday in Lovina, come prepared. Other than some used-book stalls, there's no good source for new books or newspapers. The **main post office** is 1km west of central Kalibukbuk.

There is a **Bank BCA ATM** at the corner of Jl Bina Ria and Jl Raya Lovina, plus many more in Singaraja.

For internet access:

**Bits and Bytes** ( ☎ 081 755 2511; Jl Raya Lovina; per hr 25,000Rp;  8am-8pm) Fast connections plus wi-fi and laptop connections.

**Spice Cyber** ( ☎ 41305; Jl Bina Ria; per min 300Rp;  8am-midnight;  ) Wi-fi and printing.

### Sights & Activities
#### BEACHES

A sweet paved beach path runs along the sand in Kalibukbuk and extends in a circuitous path along the seashore. Enjoy the postcard view to the east of the mountainous North Bali coast.

Otherwise, the best beach areas include the main beach east of the **Dolphin Monument** as well as the curving stretch a bit west. The cluster of cheap hotels in Anturan are well-placed for fun on the sand.

#### DOLPHIN WATCHING

Sunrise boat trips to see dolphins are Lovina's much-hyped tourist attraction. Some days, no dolphins are sighted, but most of the time at least a few surface.

Expect constant hassle from your hotel and touts selling dolphin trips. The price is fixed at 50,000Rp per person by the boat-owners' cartel. Trips start at a nonholiday-like 6am and last about two hours. Note that the ocean can get pretty crowded with loud, roaring powerboats and there's great debate about what all this means to the dolphins.

#### DIVING

Scuba diving on the local reef is better at lower depths and night diving is popular. Many people stay here and dive Pulau Menjangan (p347), a two-hour drive west.

For a two-dive trip, including transport and all equipment, expect to pay about US$40 for a Lovina reef or night dive; and around US$60 to Tulamben or Pulau Menjangan.

**Spice Dive** ( ☎ 41509; www.balispicedive.com) offers PADI open-water certificate courses for about US$350. It's based at the west end of the beach path.

#### SNORKELLING

Generally, the water is clear and some parts of the reef are quite good for snorkelling. The best place is to the west, a few-hundred

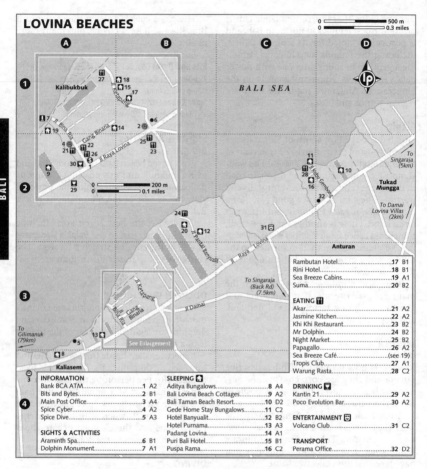

## LOVINA BEACHES

| INFORMATION | | | SLEEPING | | |
|---|---|---|---|---|---|
| Bank BCA ATM | 1 | A2 | Aditya Bungalows | 8 | A4 |
| Bits and Bytes | 2 | B1 | Bali Lovina Beach Cottages | 9 | A2 |
| Main Post Office | 3 | A4 | Bali Taman Beach Resort | 10 | D2 |
| Spice Cyber | 4 | A2 | Gede Home Stay Bungalows | 11 | C2 |
| Spice Dive | 5 | A3 | Hotel Banyualit | 12 | B2 |
| | | | Hotel Purnama | 13 | A3 |
| SIGHTS & ACTIVITIES | | | Padang Lovina | 14 | A1 |
| Araminth Spa | 6 | B1 | Puri Bali Hotel | 15 | B1 |
| Dolphin Monument | 7 | A1 | Puspa Rama | 16 | C2 |

| | | | |
|---|---|---|---|
| Rambutan Hotel | 17 | B1 |
| Rini Hotel | 18 | B1 |
| Sea Breeze Cabins | 19 | A1 |
| Suma | 20 | B2 |
| | | |
| **EATING** | | |
| Akar | 21 | A2 |
| Jasmine Kitchen | 22 | A2 |
| Khi Khi Restaurant | 23 | B2 |
| Mr Dolphin | 24 | B2 |
| Night Market | 25 | B2 |
| Papagallo | 26 | A2 |
| Sea Breeze Café | (see 19) | |
| Tropis Club | 27 | A1 |
| Warung Rasta | 28 | C2 |
| | | |
| **DRINKING** | | |
| Kantin 21 | 29 | A2 |
| Poco Evolution Bar | 30 | A2 |
| | | |
| **ENTERTAINMENT** | | |
| Volcano Club | 31 | C2 |
| | | |
| **TRANSPORT** | | |
| Perama Office | 32 | D2 |

metres offshore from Billibo Beach Cottages. Snorkelling gear costs about 30,000Rp per day.

### MASSAGE & SPAS

**Araminth Spa** ( ☎ 081 2384 4655; Jl Ketapang; massage from 105,000Rp; ☺ 10am-7pm) offers Balinese, Ayurveda and foot massage in a simple but soothing setting. It promotes 'vagina steaming', which involves dry, herbal smoke (75,000Rp).

## Sleeping

Hotels are spread out along the many side roads running off Jl Raya Lovina to the beach. There are decent places to stay in every price range.

### BUDGET
### Anturan

A few tiny side tracks and one proper sealed road, Jl Kubu Gembong, lead to this lively little fishing village, busy with swimming locals and moored fishing boats. It's a real travellers' hang-out though it's a long way from Lovina's evening delights.

**Puspa Rama** ( ☎ 42070; Jl Kubu Gembong; s/d incl breakfast 60,000/70,000Rp) One of several budget places on this street, Puspa Rama has grounds a few cuts above the others. The six rooms have hot water. Fruit trees abound – why not pick your own breakfast?

**Gede Home Stay Bungalows** ( ☎ 41526; Jl Kubu Gembong; r 70,000-120,000Rp; ☒ ) Don't forget to shake the sand off your feet as you enter this beachside nine-room homestay. Cheap rooms have cold water while better ones have hot water and air-con.

### Anturan to Kalibukbuk

Jl Pantai Banyualit has many hotels, although the beachfront area is not very inspiring.

**Suma** ( ☎ 41566; www.sumahotel.com; Jl Pantai Banyualit; r 150,000-400,000Rp; 🛏 🛒 🖳 ) In a mannered stone building, Suma has views of the sea from its upstairs rooms; the best have air-con and hot water. The pool is large and naturalistic; there's also a pleasant cafe. A much-renovated temple is nearby.

### Kalibukbuk

The 'centre' of Lovina is the village of Kalibukbuk. Jl Ketapang is marginally quieter and more pleasant than Jl Bina Ria. There are small *gang* off both.

**Padang Lovina** ( ☎ 41302; Gang Binaria; r 80,000-250,000Rp; 🛏 ) Down a narrow lane in the very heart of Kalibukbuk. There's no pretension at all around the 12 comfortable bungalow-style rooms set around spacious grounds teeming with flowers. The best rooms have air-con and tubs.

**Rini Hotel** ( ☎ 41386; rinihotel@telkom.net; Jl Ketapang; r 120,000-250,000Rp; 🛏 🖳 ) This tidy 30-room place has a large saltwater pool. Cheaper rooms have fans and cold water but the more expensive ones are huge, with air-con and hot water. In fact, should you come across a keg, you could have a party.

**Puri Bali Hotel** ( ☎ 41485; www.puribalilovina.com; Jl Ketapang; r 130,000-250,000Rp; 🛏 🖳 ) The pool area is set deep in a lush garden – you may hang out here all day. The better of the 30 rooms, with hot water and air-con, are simple but comfortable. The cheapest, with fans and cold water, are simply simple.

**Sea Breeze Cabins** ( ☎ 41138; r US$20, bungalows US$30-40; 🛏 🖳 ) One of the best choices in the heart of Kalibukbuk and right off Jl Bina Ria, the Sea Breeze has three appealing bungalows right on the pool and beach, some with sensational views from their verandahs. The two economy rooms have fans and hot water.

### West of Kalibukbuk

**Hotel Purnama** ( ☎ 41043; Jl Raya Lovina; s/d 40,000/50,000Rp) One of the best deals on this stretch, Purnama has seven clean cold-water rooms. The beach is a two-minute walk away.

However, the name is a misnomer: this is a family compound, and a friendly one at that.

### MIDRANGE

### Anturan

**Bali Taman Beach Resort** ( ☎ 41126; www.balitaman lovina.com; Jl Raya Lovina; r US$40-75; 🛏 🛒 🖳 ) Facing the busy road, but extending down to the beach, the Bali Taman has 30 rooms that vary widely – although all have pretty simple interiors. The best ones are bungalows with ocean views. The large pool faces the ocean and is surrounded by leafy gardens.

### Anturan to Kalibukbuk

**Hotel Banyualit** ( ☎ 41789; www.banyualit.com; Jl Pantai Banyualit; r 250,000-700,000Rp; 🛏 🖳 ) About 100m back from the beach, the Banyualit has a lush garden, statues and a large pool. The 22 rooms (all with air-con) offer great choice; best are the villas with whirlpools, fridges and large, shady patios. There's also a small spa.

### Kalibukbuk

**Rambutan Hotel** ☎ 41388; www.rambutan.org; Jl Ketepang; r US$12-65, villas from US$110; 🛏 🖳 ) The hotel, on one hectare of lush gardens, features two pools, a playground and games for all ages. The 31 rooms and villas are tasteful with lashings of Balinese style. The very cheapest have fans and cold water.

**Bali Lovina Beach Cottages** ( ☎ 41285; www .balilovinahotel.com; Jl Raya Lovina; r US$40-60; 🛏 🖳 ) The 30 rooms here are in mixed two-storey and bungalow-style units. Several surround the large pool (complete with dolphin statue) or face the beach. Room styles are basic but clean.

### West of Kalibukbuk

**Aditya Bungalows** ( ☎ 41059; www.adityalovina.com; Jl Raya Lovina; r 300,000-600,000Rp; 🛏 🖳 ) There are 64 rooms at this big place on a sandy beach. The best ones have views of the ocean and all have a good range of amenities and attractive bathrooms. Swim in the large pool or in the ocean? Sit on your patio while you're deciding.

## Eating

Just about every hotel has a cafe or restaurant. Close to the centre of Lovina you can find several places that go beyond the usual travellers' fare. Beachside places are good just for drinks if you're planning to do some hopping.

A small **night market** (Jl Raya Lovina; 5-11pm) is a good choice for fresh and cheap local food.

### ANTURAN
**Warung Rasta** (mains 15,000-30,000Rp) Right on a strip of beach lined with fishing boats. The menu not surprisingly leans towards simply grilled fresh seafood; given the name, the endless loop of music shouldn't surprise either. It's run by dudes who have clearly realised that lounging around here all day beats fishing.

### ANTURAN TO KALIBUKBUK
**Mr Dolphin** ( 081 3384 87612; Jl Pantai Banyualit; dishes 15,000-40,000Rp) Right on the beach, this cheery hang-out for dolphin-tour skippers serves a killer grilled seafood platter. There's live acoustic music most nights.

### KALIBUKBUK
**Khi Khi Restaurant** ( 41548; dishes 8000-100,000Rp) Well off Jl Raya Lovina and behind the night market, this barn of a place specialises in Chinese food and grilled seafood, including lobster. It's always popular in a rub-elbows-with-your-neighbour kind of way.

**Akar** ( 081 7972 4717; Jl Bina Ria; snacks from 18,000Rp) The many shades of green at this cute-as-a-baby-frog cafe aren't just for show. They reflect the earth-friendly ethics of the owners. Refill your water containers here and then enjoy organic smoothies and other refreshing treats. A tiny back porch overlooks the river.

**Sea Breeze Café** ( 41138; dishes 12,000-45,000Rp) Right by the beach off Jl Bina Ria, this cafe has a range of Indonesian and Western dishes and excellent breakfasts. It's a good spot for sunset drinks and ocean views.

**Tropis Club** ( 42090; Jl Ketepang; dishes 15,000-35,000Rp) The long menu at this beachside place includes wood-fired pizza. Choose a table under the soaring roof or out along the beach walkway. Sunset specials include cheap Bintang.

**Pappagallo** ( 41163; Jl Bina Ria; dishes 15,000-35,000Rp) This big, ambitious open-air restaurant brings some much-needed energy to the snoozy Kalibukbuk scene. There's all the beach standards plus good pizzas from a wood-burning oven. Opt for the wicker chairs on the breezy second level.

**Jasmine Kitchen** ( 41565; Gang Binaria; dishes 15,000-35,000Rp) As good as ever, the Thai fare at this elegant two-level restaurant is excellent.

The menu is long and authentic and the staff gracious. While soft jazz plays (and trays of peppers dry near the entrance), try the home-made ice cream for dessert.

## Drinking & Entertainment
Lovina's modest social scene centres on Kalibukbuk.

**Kantin 21** ( 081 2460 7791; Jl Raya Lovina; 11am-1am) Funky open-air place where you can watch traffic by day and groove to acoustic guitar or garage-band rock by night. There's a long drinks list, fresh juices and a few local snacks.

**Poco Evolution Bar** ( 41535; Jl Bina Ria; dishes 12,000-25,000Rp; 11am-1am) Movies are shown at various times, and cover bands perform at this popular bar-cafe. Classic travellers' fare is served at tables open to street life in front and the river in back.

**Volcano Club** (Jl Raya Lovina; 9pm-late Wed-Sat) There's nothing fancy about this big tropical disco in Anturan, where local and visiting partiers mix it up to local DJs until all hours.

## Getting There & Away
### BUS & BEMO
To reach Lovina from South Bali by public transport, you'll need to change in Singaraja. Regular blue bemo go from Singaraja's Banyuasri terminal to Kalibukbuk (about 7000Rp) – you can flag them down anywhere on the main road.

If you're coming by long-distance bus from the west you can ask to be dropped off anywhere along the main road.

### TOURIST SHUTTLE BUS
Perama buses stop at its office, in front of **Hotel Perama** ( 41161) on Jl Raya Lovina in Anturan. Passengers are then ferried to other points on the Lovina strip (10,000Rp).

| Destination | Fare | Duration |
| --- | --- | --- |
| Candidasa | 150,000Rp | 5½hr |
| Kuta | 125,000Rp | 4hr |
| Padangbai | 150,000Rp | 4¾hr |
| Sanur | 125,000Rp | 3¾hr |
| Ubud | 125,000Rp | 2¾hr |

## Getting Around
The Lovina strip is *very* spread out, but you can easily travel back and forth on bemo (3000Rp). Bikes are easily rented around town for about 30,000Rp per day.

## WEST OF LOVINA

The main road west of Lovina passes temples, farms and towns while it follows the thinly developed coast. You'll notice a lot of vineyards, where the grapes work overtime producing the sugar that's used in Bali's very sweet local vintages.

### Air Terjun Singsing

About 5km west of Lovina, a sign points to **Air Terjun Singsing** (Daybreak Waterfall). About 1km from the main road, there is a warung on the left and a car park on the right. Walk past the warung and along the path for about 200m to the lower falls. The waterfall is not huge, but the pool underneath is ideal for swimming. The water isn't crystal clear, but it's cooler than the sea and very refreshing.

The area is thick with tropical forest and makes a nice day trip from Lovina. The falls are more spectacular in the wet season (October to March), and may be just a trickle at other times.

### Air Panas Banjar
☎ 0362

These **hot springs** (adult/child 6000/3000Rp, parking 2000Rp; ⏲ 8am-6pm) are beautifully landscaped with lush tropical plants. You can relax here for a few hours and have lunch at the restaurant, or even stay the night.

Eight fierce-faced carved stone *naga* pour water from a natural hot spring into the first bath, which then overflows (via the mouths of five more *naga*), into a second, larger pool. In a third pool, 38°C water pours from 3m-high spouts to give you a pummelling massage.

From the bemo stop on the main road to the hot springs you can take an *ojek*; going back is a 2.4km downhill stroll.

## PEMUTERAN
☎ 0362

This oasis in the far northwest corner of Bali has a number of artful resorts set on a little bay that's alive with local life such as kids playing soccer until dark.

This is the place to come for a real beach getaway. Most people dive or snorkel the underwater wonders at nearby Menjangan (p347) while here.

Pemuteran is home to the nonprofit Reef Seen Turtle Project, run by the Australian-owned **Reef Seen Aquatics** ( ☎ 93001; www.reefseen .com). Turtle eggs and small turtles purchased

from locals are looked after here until they're ready for ocean release. More than 7000 turtles have been released since 1994 and for a small fee, you can release one yourself. It's just off the main road east of Pondok Sari.

Reef Seen also offers diving, boat cruises and horse riding. A PADI introductory dive costs US$60 and dives at Pemuteran/ Pulau Menjangan are US$60/70 for two dives. Sunset and sunrise cruises and glass-bottomed boat trips (per person 200,000Rp) are offered. Horse-riding treks pass through the local villages and beaches (from 300,000Rp for two hours).

**Easy Divers** ( ☎ 94736; www.easy-divers.eu) comes well recommended and the founder, Dusan Repic, has befriended many a diver new to Bali. Prices are similar to Reef Seen. It is on the main road near the Taman Sari and Pondok Sari hotels.

Pemuteran's hotels all have their own dive operations.

### Sleeping & Eating

Pemuteran has many mellow midrange and top-end choices, all located on the bay, which has nice sand and is good for swimming. There are small warung along the main drag, otherwise all the hotels have good, mostly modestly priced, restaurants.

Some of the hotels are accessed directly off the main road, others are off of a small road the follows the west side of the bay.

**Jubawa Home Stay** ( ☎ 94745; r 180,000-270,000Rp; 🍴 ) Not far from the Matahari on the south (hill) side of the road, this clean hotel is a good budget choice. The best of the 12 rooms have hot water and air-con. The cafe serves Balinese and Thai food and there is a popular bar.

**Reef Seen** ( ☎ 93001; www.reefseen.com; r 450,000Rp; 🍴 ) Five solid Balinese-style brick bungalows have air-con and open-air bathrooms with showers. This is a well-regarded dive centre (left).

**Pondok Sari** ( ☎ 92337; www.pondoksari.com; r US$50-160; 🍴 🛏 ) There are 30 rooms here set in densely planted gardens that assure privacy. The pool is down by the beach; the cafe has sweet water views through the trees. Traditional Balinese details abound; the bathrooms are open-air and are a calling card for the stone-carvers. Deluxe units have elaborate stone tubs among other details. The resort is just off the main road.

BALI

**Taman Sari Bali Cottage** ( ☎ 93264; www.balitaman sari.com; bungalows US$50-200; ❄ ☎ ▣ ) Thirty-one rooms are set in gorgeous bungalows (some quite grand) that feature intricate carvings and traditional artwork inside and out. The open-air bathrooms inspire extended ablutions. Most rooms are under US$100 – those over are quite grand. It's located on a long stretch of quiet beach on the bay. It's part of a reef restoration project.

**Taman Selini Beach Bungalows** ( ☎ 94746; www .tamanselini.com; r US$90-200; ❄ ☎ ) The 11 bungalows recall an older, refined Bali, from the quaint thatched roofs down to the antique carved doors and detailed stonework. Rooms, which open onto a small garden area, have four-poster beds and large outdoor bathrooms. The outdoor day-beds can be addictive. It's immediately east of Pondok Sari, on the beach and right off the main road.

## Getting There & Away

Pemuteran is served by any of the buses and bemo on the Gilimanuk–Lovina run. Labuhan Lalang (p348) and Taman Nasional Bali Barat are 12km west. It's a three- to four-hour drive from South Bali, either over the hills or around the west coast.

# Sumatra

Few isles tempt the imagination with the lure of adventure quite like the fierce land of Sumatra. The planet's sixth-largest island is vibrating with life – too often to the detriment of its disaster-hardened inhabitants, who live in the shadow of Sumatran Mother Nature: a mixed blessing of vast extremes.

Eruptions, earthquakes, floods and tsunamis are regular headline grabbers, and are steep costs of living in one of the world's richest ecosystems. Steaming volcanoes brew and bluster while standing guard over lakes that sleepily lap the edges of craters. The resulting soil makes for an ocean of green topography that dominates every vista, filling the land with a feast of flora and fauna. Orangutan-filled jungles host not only our red-haired cousins, but all sorts of monkeys that swing in the tree tops. A lucky few may spot tigers or even the timid Sumatran rhino.

Then there are the beaches. The tempestuous, tectonic coastline creates a constant unravelling of clear barrels of surf onto deserted beaches across Sumatra, making the area one of the great isolated surf meccas of the world.

Consistent with Indonesia's social make-up, the massive island is a spicy broth of mixed cultures, from the devout Muslims in Aceh to the hedonistic Batak Christians and the matrilineal Minangkabau of Padang. All get along (most of the time) and are unified by a fear, respect and love of the wild and wondrous land of Sumatra.

**SUMATRA**

## HIGHLIGHTS

- Lounging away a few days on the cool shores of **Danau Toba** (p388) and sharing a few drinks with the fun-loving Batak folk

- Ogling our orangutan cousins in the wild jungles of **Bukit Lawang** (p378)

- Hiking up beyond the clouds to the steaming peaks of the volcanoes around the hill town of **Berastagi** (p384)

- Swimming with sharks and turtles in the coral garden off **Pulau Weh** (p409), an underwater paradise

- Cruising around the lush paddy fields in the verdant countryside around **Bukittinggi** (p431), where the matrilineal Minangkabau built soaring-roofed houses and the women told the men what to do

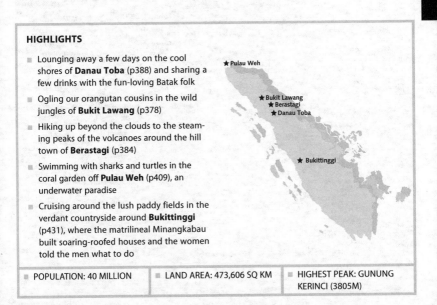

★ Pulau Weh

★ Bukit Lawang
★ Berastagi
★ Danau Toba

★ Bukittinggi

| ▓ POPULATION: 40 MILLION | ▓ LAND AREA: 473,606 SQ KM | ▓ HIGHEST PEAK: GUNUNG KERINCI (3805M) |

# SUMATRA

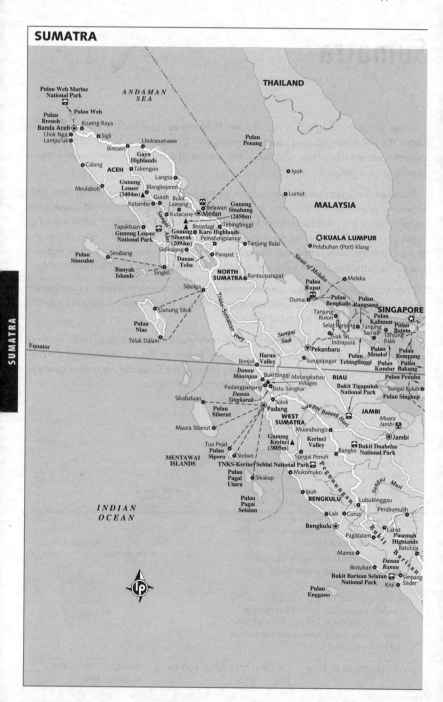

SUMATRA

THAILAND

*ANDAMAN SEA*

Pulau Weh Marine National Park
Pulau Weh
Pulau Breueh
Krueng Raya
Banda Aceh
Lhok Nga
Lampu'uk
Sigli
Lhokseumawe
Bireuen
Pulau Penang
Calang
Gayo Highlands
Takengon
ACEH
Langsa
Ipoh
Meulaboh
Gunung Leuser (3404m)
Blangkejeren
Gurah
Ketambe
Kutacane
Bukit Lawang
Belawan
Gunung Sinabung (2450m)
Medan
Berastagi
Tebingtinggi
Lumut
MALAYSIA
Tapaktuan
Gunung Leuser National Park
Gunung Sibayak (2094m)
Karo Highlands
Pematangsiantar
Tanjung Balai
KUALA LUMPUR
Pelabuhan (Port) Klang
Pulau Simeulue
Sinabang
Sidikalang
Danau Toba
Parapat
Banyak Islands
Singkil
NORTH SUMATRA
Rantauparapat
Sibolga
Pulau Rupat
Melaka
Gunung Sitoli
Trans-Sumatran Hwy
Dumai
Pulau Bengkalis
Pulau Rangsang
SINGAPORE
Tanjung Buton
Pulau Kalimun
Pulau Batam
Equator
Pulau Nias
Teluk Dalam
Selat Panjang
Tanjung Samak
Tanjung Balai
Sungai Siak
Siak Sri Indrapura
Pekanbaru
Pulau Mendol
Pulau Rempang
Harau Valley
Sungaipagar
Pulau Tebingtinggi
Pulau Kundur
Pulau Bakung
Pulau Penuba
Bonjol
Danau Maninjau
Bukittinggi
Minangkabau Villages
RIAU
Bukit Tigapuluh National Park
Sungai Buluh
Pulau Singkep
Padangpanjang
Danau Singkarak
Batu Sangkar
Sikabaluan
Solok
Sungai Batang Hari
JAMBI
Pulau Siberut
Padang
WEST SUMATRA
Muara Jambi
Muara Siberut
Muarabungo
Jambi
Tua Pejat
Pulau Sipora
Gunung Kerinci (3805m)
Kerinci Valley
Bukit Duabelas National Park
Bangko
MENTAWAI ISLANDS
Sioban
TNKS-Kerinci Seblat National Park
Sungai Penuh
Pulau Pagai Utara
Sikakap
Mukomuko
*INDIAN OCEAN*
Ipuh
BENGKULU
Lubuklinggau
Perabumulih
Pulau Pagai Selatan
Lais
Curup
Bengkulu
Pagaralam
Lahat
Pasemah Highlands
Baturaja
Manna
Bintuhan
Danau Ranau
Simpang Sinder
Bukit Barisan Selatan National Park
Krui
Pulau Enggano

Strait of Melaka

*Sungai Alas*

*Sungai Siak*

*Sungai Musi*

Pegunungan Bukit Barisan

IP

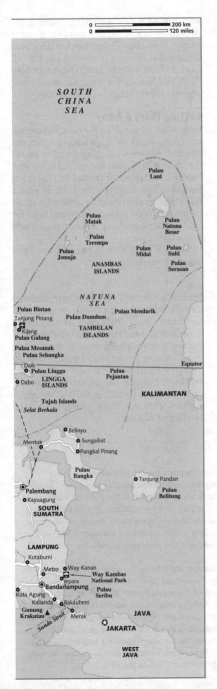

**SUMATRA**

## History

Pre-Islamic history is often more myth than fact, but archaeological evidence suggests that Sumatra was the gateway for migrating tribes from mainland Southeast Asia. Stone tools and shells unearthed north of Medan indicate that hunter-gatherers were living along the Strait of Melaka (Selat Malaka) 13,000 years ago. Two megalithic cultures appeared around 2000 years ago, one in the mountains of western Sumatra and the other on Pulau Nias.

The Strait of Melaka, an important trade route between China and India, exposed the east coast of Sumatra to the region's superpowers and cultural influences, such as Islam. The kingdom of Sriwijaya emerged as a local player at the end of the 7th century, with its capital presumably based near the modern city of Palembang. After Sriwijaya's influence waned, Aceh, at the northern tip of Sumatra, assumed control of trade through the strait. Aceh is presumably where Muslim sea traders first introduced Islam to Indonesia from Gujarat (western India). In the spirit of diplomacy and trade, the animist Acehnese adopted the faith of their visitors and continue to practise a more devout form of Islam than that found in neighbouring provinces. Aceh's control of the shipping route increased after its main rival, Melaka, fell to the Portuguese in 1511. The era of Aceh's sultanate prevailed until the beginning of the 17th century, when Dutch traders claimed a piece of the spice trade.

The most influential port of the day, Samudra (Ocean), near Lhokseumawe, eventually became the name that the traders used to refer to the entire island, alternatively known as Lesser Java. It was Marco Polo who corrupted the name to 'Sumatra' in his 1292 report on the area. In more poetic times, the island was known as Swarnadwipa (Island of Gold).

Throughout the colonial era, Sumatra saw many foreign powers stake a claim in its resources: the Dutch based themselves in the West Sumatran port of Padang, the British ruled in Bencoolen (now Bengkulu), American traders monopolised pepper exports from Aceh, and the Chinese exploited tin reserves on the islands of Bangka and Belitung, east of Palembang. Oil and coffee were other prized Sumatran exports.

In the early 19th century, the Dutch attempted to assert military control over all of Sumatra, a move met with resistance by its disparate tribes. In 1863, after three military expeditions, the Dutch finally established authority over Pulau Nias. Treaties and alliances brought other areas of Sumatra under Dutch rule, including Bengkulu, which the British willingly traded for Melaka.

A peace may have been brokered, but the Dutch were never welcomed in Sumatra. The island contributed several key figures to the independence struggle, including future vice president, Mohammed Hatta and the first prime minister, Sutan Syahrir. Yet despite this Sumatra was as dissatisfied with Jakarta's rule as it was with that of the Dutch. From 1958–61, rebel groups based in Bukittinggi and the mountains of South Sumatra resisted centralisation, leading to clashes with the Indonesian military. Fiercely independent Aceh, though, proved to be Jakarta's most troublesome region. Aceh's separatist movement started in the late 1970s and continued until 2006 (see p403), with brief spells of quiet counterbalanced with repression by the Indonesian military.

No human conflict could compare to the destruction of the 2004 Boxing Day tsunami, in which a 9.0-plus-magnitude earthquake off the northwestern coast of Sumatra triggered a regionwide tsunami. In Aceh province, the land mass closest to the epicentre, waves almost 15m high rose up like the mythical *naga* (sea serpent) and swallowed coastal development and dwellers. The Indonesian death count was estimated at more than 170,000 people, mainly in Aceh. An 8.7-magnitude aftershock that followed several months later

was centred near the island of Nias; it destroyed the capital city and killed hundreds of people. Most of the destruction has since been cleared and the area is moving on, but aid workers have become familiar faces in both Aceh and Nias and will remain in the most severely affected regions for some time.

## Getting There & Away

Once upon a time along the backpacker trail, travellers sailed the high seas to reach the island of Sumatra, touching down in one of the international ports: Batam, Belawan (near Medan), Pekanbaru or Dumai. But the era of budget airlines has made the friendly skies a faster and more affordable option for international arrivals. As fuel prices and fares for land and sea travel soar, airfares consistently take a nose dive.

Keep in mind that Sumatra is one hour behind Singapore time.

### AIR

Medan is Sumatra's primary international airport, with frequent flights to mainland Southeast Asian cities such as Singapore, Kuala Lumpur and Penang. In West Sumatra, Padang receives flights from Singapore and Kuala Lumpur several times a week. In eastern Sumatra, Palembang is linked to Singapore and Kuala Lumpur. The primary international carriers include Garuda Indonesia, Malaysian Airlines, Lion Air, Tiger Airways, Air Asia, Firefly and Silk Air.

---

**SUMATRA AU NATUREL**

Sumatra's natural endowments are superlative: it stretches nearly 2000km, from Banda Aceh in the north to Bakauheni in the south, is nearly bisected by the equator and covers an area of 473,606 sq km, almost the size of France. The island's backbone is the Bukit Barisan range, which runs most of the length of the west coast, merging with the highlands around Danau Toba and central Aceh. Forming the most dramatic peaks is an almost martial formation of almost 100 volcanoes, 15 of which are still active; the tallest is Gunung Kerinci, measuring 3805m. The string of islands off the west coast, including Nias and the Mentawai Islands, are geologically older than the rest of Sumatra.

The coastal lowlands on the east coast are swampy and drained by wide muddy rivers, such as Batang Hari, Siak and Musi, which empty into the shallow Strait of Melaka.

In its remaining forests, Sumatra boasts some of Indonesia's most interesting biodiversity. Flowers and primates top the naturalist's list. The *Rafflesia arnoldii*, the world's largest flower, and the *Amorphophallus titanium* (also known as the Titan Arum), the world's tallest flower, can be found in pockets of the Bukit Barisan jungle. The island is also home to endangered species such as the two-horned Sumatran rhino, the honey bear, the Sumatran elephant and the Sumatran tiger. But scientists from all over the world come to northern Sumatra's Gunung Leuser National Park, where more than 5000 orangutans are believed to still live in the wild.

**VISA ON ARRIVAL**

Regulations for visiting Indonesia are in flux. At the time of research, most nationalities could obtain a visa on arrival at the following international entry points, but check with an Indonesian consulate for the current situation.

- Pulau Batam: airport and the ports of Nongsa, Sekupang, Waterfront City (Teluk Senimba) and Batam Centre (p454).

- Pulau Bintan: ports of Tanjung Pinang, Bandar Bentan Telani Lagoi and Bandar Sri Udana Lobam in Tanjung Uban (p458).

- Medan: Polonia airport and Belawan port (p376).

- Pekanbaru: airport and port (p450).

- Padang: airport and Teluk Bayur port (p424).

- Dumai: Yos Sudarso port (p451).

- Sibolga: port (p394).

- Palembang: airport (p466).

You can also hop on a plane from Jakarta to every major Sumatran city aboard Garuda, Merpati, Jatayu, Mandala or Sriwijaya. Flights from Sumatra to other parts of Indonesia typically connect through Jakarta. One notable exception is Merpati's flight between Medan and Pontianak (Kalimantan).

All Sumatran airports charge a departure tax of 75,000Rp to 150,000Rp for international flights.

**BOAT**

Many travellers still heed the call of the sea and enter Sumatra by ferry from Malaysia. There are two primary port options: Melaka (Malaysia) to Dumai (Indonesia) or Penang (Malaysia) to Belawan (Indonesia). If you don't have a lot of time to explore Sumatra, Belawan is your best option, as it is a short bus ride from Medan (see p377), which sits at the centre of most tourist attractions. Dumai is on Sumatra's east coast and is a five-hour bus ride to Bukittinggi; see p451 for more information.

From Singapore, ferries make the quick hop to Pulau Batam and Bintan, the primary islands in the Riau archipelago. Mainly Singaporean weekenders heading to beaches and resorts in the Riau islands use these water routes.

From Batam, boats serve the following mainland Sumatran ports: Dumai, Palembang and Pekanbaru. Only a few backpackers depart Batam for Sumatra because all of these ports but Dumai are a long way from postcard-worthy spots. See Pulau Batam (p454) or Pulau Bintan (p459) for more information on boat transfer between Singapore and beyond.

Ferries swim across the narrow Sunda Strait, linking the southeastern tip of Sumatra at Bakauheni to Java's westernmost point of Merak. The sea crossing is a brief dip in a daylong voyage that requires several hours' worth of bus transport from both ports to Jakarta on the Java side and to Bandarlampung on the Sumatran side. See p472 for more details.

Pelni-operated boats still paddle between Indonesia's islands, carrying freight and families.

Check with local ticket agents for schedules and prices as both are subject to change.

## Getting Around

Most travellers travel by bus around Northern Sumatra and then hop on a plane to Java, largely avoiding Sumatra's highway system. Most of the island is mountainous jungle and the poorly maintained roads form a twisted pile of spaghetti on the undulating landscape. Don't count on getting anywhere very quickly on Sumatra.

Sumatra's airports are incongruously modern and numerous, providing a quick and cheap means of arrival or escape.

**AIR**

An hour on a plane is an attractive alternative to what may seem like an eternity on a bone-shaking bus. For long-distance travel, airfares are competitive with bus and ferry fares. Medan to Banda Aceh and Medan to Gunung Sitoli are two popular air hops.

Domestic carriers include Merpati, Mandala, Lion Air and Sriwijaya. Nusantara Buana Air (NBA) and Susi Air fly to minor destinations that the bigger airlines don't bother with.

All Sumatran airports charge an airport departure tax (between 20,000Rp and 40,000Rp) that is not included in your ticket. Ticket agents are located in the smallest of towns and typically charge 10% commission.

As cheap and convenient taking domestic flights may be, it's also important to take into account the environmental impact of air travel (see the boxed text, p844 for more information)

## BOAT

Most boat travel within Sumatra connects the main island with the many satellite islands lining the coast.

The most commonly used routes link Banda Aceh with Pulau Weh, Sibolga with Pulau Nias, and Padang with Pulau Siberut (in the Mentawai Islands chain). In the less-visited areas of southeastern Sumatra, Jambi, Palembang and Pekanbaru are important towns for river transport. The Riau islands of Batam and Bintan are also linked to southeastern port towns by ferry.

Most long-distance ferries have several classes, ranging from filthy and crowded to filthy and less crowded. An upgrade in class might be a necessary luxury.

## BUS

Bus is the most common mode of transport around Sumatra, and in many cases it's the only option for intercity travel. But it is far from efficient or comfortable. The primary thoroughfare is the Trans-Sumatran Hwy, which is little more than a jungle-bound track for petrol-eating beasts. Locals prefer the more affectionate term: 'chicken roads'. The pavement inexplicably disappears, oncoming vehicles must yield to one another, and the potholes are as big as moon craters. It is not uncommon during the rainy season for bridges to wash out and for mudslides to block the road.

Most trips take extra long because of road conditions. At this laborious pace you have plenty of time to soak up the views: cascades of deep, lush greens; terraced rice fields; mottled rushing rivers; and isolated villages gathered around the communal well.

Buses range from economy sardine cans to modern air-con coaches. At the top of the class structure are super-executive buses with reclining seats, deep-freeze air-con, toilets, and an all-night serenade of Scorpions albums. Many passengers come prepared with winter hats, gloves and earplugs.

Bus terminals in Sumatra can vary, from modern and organised to run-down and abandoned. In some towns, you can go straight to the bus terminal to buy tickets and board buses, while other towns rely on bus company offices located outside the terminals. Ticket prices vary greatly depending on the quality of the bus and the perceived gullibility of the traveller. It pays to shop around and to ask at your guest house about reliable companies; do be aware that some accommodation act as booking agents and charge a commission for their services.

## LOCAL TRANSPORT

The usual Indonesian forms of transport – bemo or *opelet* (small minibus), becak (bicycle-rickshaw) and *bendi* (two-person horse-drawn cart) – are available in Sumatran towns and cities. The base rate for a bemo or *opelet* is 1500Rp to 4000Rp; the minimum fare is 7000Rp for becak and 10,000Rp for *bendi*.

Establish a price for a becak ride before climbing aboard. For an *opelet,* you pay after you disembark.

## MINIBUS

For midrange and shorter journeys, many locals and travellers prefer to use minibus services, which can be more convenient than hustling out to the bus terminal. Some minibuses are in superb shape and provide door-to-door service, while others are a little rickety and shovel in more people than a clown car. Typically, tourists will end up paying more than the locals; negotiating a front seat ensures a little breathing room as the driver won't crowd his steering range.

## TRAIN

The only useful train service in Sumatra runs from Bandarlampung (p472) to Palembang, and then on to Lubuklinggau. There are also passenger trains from Medan to Pematangsiantar, Tanjung Balai and Rantauparapat – though these are rarely used by tourists.

# NORTH SUMATRA

For most visitors travelling through Indonesia on a race-against-time visa, this is the sole slice of Sumatra they'll taste. And with good reason: ogle the orangutans in Bukit Lawang, veer over the volcanoes of Berastagi and laze away on the shores of Danau Toba. All in, a well-trodden and worthy circuit that centres on Medan, the gateway metropolis of the north.

## SUMATRA IS BURNING

Every year smoke and haze from fires used to clear farmland and plantations choke the skies over the island and its neighbours, sometimes downing planes and closing schools as far away as Kuala Lumpur. Malaysia complains bitterly about its inconsiderate neighbour and promises are made by Indonesian officials that next year won't be as bad – until next year comes. As for Sumatra, fires are part of the family. In the evening, backyard burn piles are most communities' solution to a lack of municipal garbage collection. Minifires follow people throughout the day as most Sumatrans, men and women, are chain smokers. These clove-smoking dragons are so comfortable with a cigarette that it often looks like an extra digit. Cigarettes are so much more than a habit or a hobby: they are a social lubricant, the accepted payment for a medicine man and an offering to the deceased. Perhaps it is the influence of the smoking volcanoes that encourages the Sumatrans to light up.

North Sumatra stretches from the Indian Ocean to the Strait of Melaka and from sea to shining sea it is anything but homogeneous. The rolling landscape varies from sweaty plains to cool highlands, while the houses of worship switch between the metal-domed mosques to the arrow-straight steeples of Christian churches. The coastal Malays, relatives of peoples from mainland Southeast Asia, live along the Strait of Melaka and are the largest ethnic group. In the highlands around Danau Toba are the delightful Batak, a group which is further subdivided into five classes. If you can name them all then you've either married into the clan or are destined to. Then there are the Pesisirs (central Tapanuli) along the Indian Ocean coastline and the megalithic culture of Pulau Nias (p395).

North Sumatra has a population of almost 12 million and is an economically robust province, producing more than 30% of Indonesia's exports. Oil, palm oil, tea and rubber are produced in large quantities, and fine tobacco is grown in the rich soil around Medan.

## MEDAN

☎ 061 / pop 2 million

Sumatra's major metropolis, and Indonesia's third-largest city, is somewhat mythical in travellers' circles, regularly popping up in 'What's the worst place you've ever visited?' conversations in global backpacker bars. As ever, with these things, perspective plays a huge part in the Medan experience. For most tourists, just off the boat from squeaky-clean, multicultural Malaysia, the pollution, poverty and persistent cat calls of 'Hello mister!' could be an unnerving jolt of dirt-under-your-fingernails Asia. However, if you've worked your way north through Sumatra, and are

a little more immune to the culture shock, it's easier to see past the grime and discover an amenity-filled, leafy and modern town with more than a hint of crumbling Dutch-colonial charm.

First impressions are often misleading. Just when you had Medan dismissed as a chaotic nightmare, you'll pass by one of the city's grand marble mosques, fading art-deco buildings or smiling locals and it's just enough to make you realise its a city worth hanging around for.

### History

Medan has had several major incarnations. The plains were once used as a battlefield between the kingdoms of Aceh and Deli (the word *medan* translates as 'field' or 'battlefield') from the end of the 16th century to the early 17th century.

But more importantly, Medan was a planters' trading post, a civilised district of tidy lanes and open-air cafes for society-deprived plantation owners. An enterprising Dutch planter named Nienhuys introduced tobacco to the area in 1865, which ushered in prosperity, imported Chinese labourers and investment in infrastructure. In 1886 the Dutch made Medan the capital of North Sumatra and by the end of Dutch rule the population had grown to about 80,000.

Once the Dutch were kicked out following WWII, Medan tossed off its starched uniform and grew as it pleased. A wealthy merchant class, comprised mainly of ethnic Chinese, dominates the cosmopolitan side of town, while a handful of ethnic tribes from all over Sumatra make do in the run-down remainder. Animosity towards the Chinese erupted into violent rioting on Medan's streets on

SUMATRA

SUMATRA

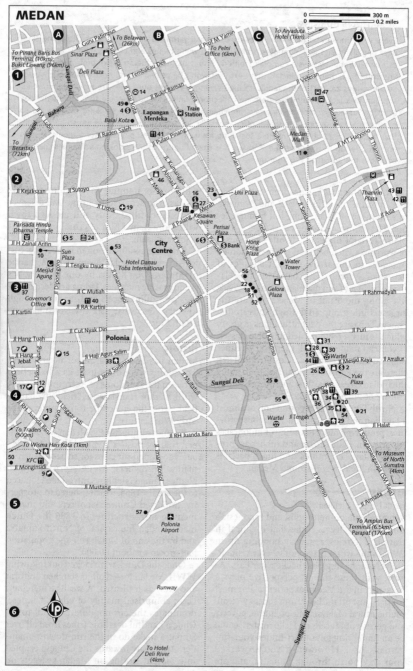

**MEDAN**

0        300 m
0        0.2 miles

To Pinang Baris Bus
Terminal (10km);
Bukit Lawang (96km)

To Belawan
(26km)

To Aryaduta
Hotel (1km)

Sinar Plaza

To Pelni
Office (6km)

Deli Plaza

Jl Guru Patimpus

Jl Putri Hijau

Jl Prof M Yamin

Jl Veteran

47

48

Jl Tembakau Deli

Jl Balai Kota

14

Jl Bukit Barisan

Jl MT Haryono

Jl Thamrin

Jl Bintang

49

4

Balai Kota

Lapangan
Merdeka

Train
Station

Medan
Mall

11

To Berastagi
(72km)

Jl Raden Saleh

41

Jl Pulau Pinang

Jl Sipongi

Jl Sutomo

Thamrin
Plaza

43

42

Jl Kejaksaan

Jl Sutoyo

Jl Mesjid

Jl Ahmad Yani

46

16

23

Uni Plaza

Jl Irian Barat

Jl Asia

Jl Listrik

19

45

27

Merah

Kesawan
Square

Jl Cirebon

Jl Senatugu

Jl Palang

Perisai
Plaza

Parisada Hindu
Dharma Temple

Jl H Zainal Arifin

5

24

City
Centre

6

Jl Pemuda

Bank

Hong
Kong
Plaza

Jl Pandu

10

Sun
Plaza

53

Hotel Danau
Toba International

Water
Tower

Mesjid
Agung

Jl Tengku Daud

Jl Imam Bonjol

56

37

Jl C Mutiah

22

18

51

Gelora
Plaza

Jl Rahmadyah

3

40

Jl RA Kartini

52

Jl Kartini

Jl Katamso

Jl Suprapto

Jl Puri

Jl Hang Tuah

Jl Cut Nyak Din

Polonia

31

Jl Amaliun

7

15

Jl Haji Agus Salim

28

30

Jl Hang
Jebat

33

Wartel

Mesjid Raya

Jl Rivai

Jl Jend Sudirman

44

2

17

12

Sungai Deli

26

Yuki
Plaza

Jl Utama

25

38

39

13

55

34

Jl Linggar Jati

35

20

54

Jl RH Juanda Baru

36

21

To Traders
(500m)

29

Jl Halat

To Wisma Hari Kota (1km)

8

Jl Tengah

Wartel

To Museum
of North
Sumatra
(4km)

50

32

KFC

9

Jl Monginsidi

Jl Mustang

Jl Imam Bonjol

57

Polonia
Airport

To Amplas Bus
Terminal (6.5km);
Parapat (176km)

Runway

Jl Armada

To Hotel
Deli River
(4km)

several occasions during the 1990s, and to this day there is still a noted division in the community.

## Orientation

The sprawling city of Medan radiates out from the confluence of the Sungai Deli and Sungai Babura. Most backpackers head to the neighbourhood surrounding Mesjid Raya on Jl Sisingamangaraja (SM Raja) for accommodation. North of this area is the city centre, organised around Jl Pandu and Jl Pemuda. The historic district occupies Jl Ahmad Yani around Lapangan Merdeka (Freedom Sq). The manicured part of town is Polonia, west of Sungai Deli following the spine of Jl Imam Bonjol. Little India is sandwiched between Jl H Zainal Arifin, Jl Imam Bonjol and Jl Cik Ditiro.

## Information
### BOOKSHOPS

Apart from Bukit Lawang and Danau Toba, Sumatra has little English reading material on offer, and Medan's slim pickings is a bumper crop compared to other stops on the road.

**Gramedia bookshop** Medan Mall ( ☎ 415 4422; Jl MT Haryono); Sun Plaza ( ☎ 4501354; Jl H Zainul Arifin) Good for maps, nonfiction and the occasional paperback.

### INTERNET ACCESS

Medan has speedy warnets (internet stalls) across the city, and internet access is also avail-

able at most of the large shopping plazas. Prices range from 3000Rp to 5000Rp per hour.

**Café Zelsy** (Jl SM Raja; ⏱ 9am-10pm)

**Dedeq Net** (Jl RH Juanda Baru; ⏱ 9.30am-midnight)

### MEDICAL SERVICES

For an ambulance, dial ☎ 118.

**Rumah Sakit Gleneagles** ( ☎ 456 6368; Jl Listrik 6) The best hospital in the city, with a 24-hour walk-in clinic and pharmacy, as well as English-speaking doctors and specialists.

### MONEY

Medan has branches of just about every bank operating in Indonesia. Most bank headquarters sit along the junction of Jl Diponegoro and Jl H Zainal Arifin.

**Bank Indonesia** (Jl Balai Kota)

**BCA bank** (Bank Central Asia; Jl H Zainal Arifin)

**BNI bank** (Bank Negara Indonesia; Jl Pemuda)

Try the following complexes for ATMs:

**ATM** (Yuki Plaza, Jl SM Raja)

**ATM** (Hotel Garuda Plaza, Jl SM Raja)

Shop around, as exchange rates can differ significantly from bank to bank. Medan typically offers the best rates on the island.

Outside of banking hours (see p823), there are moneychangers on the corner of Jl Sipiso-Piso and Jl SM Raja, as well as at travel agencies on Jl Katamso.

SUMATRA

## POST

**DHL** ( ☎ 453 2225; Jl SM Raja; ⓨ closed Sun) Next door to Hotel Sumatera.

**Main post office** (Jl Bukit Barisan; ⓨ 8am-6pm) Located in an old Dutch building on the main square; internet, fax and photocopying also available.

## TELEPHONE

International calls can be made at several wartel (private telephone offices) or international hotels around town; however, the line is often poor.

## TOURIST INFORMATION

There is a basic tourist-information office immediately to the right as you exit at the international airport terminal.

**North Sumatra Tourist Office** ( ☎ 452 8436; Jl Ahmad Yani 107; ⓨ 8am-4pm Mon-Fri) Provides excellent information, brochures and maps. Also displays traditional North Sumatran costumes.

## TRAVEL AGENCIES

Jl Katamso is packed with travel agencies that handle air tickets and ferry tickets.

**Perdana Express** ( ☎ 456 6222; Jl Katamso 35G) Sells Pelni and Penang ferry tickets.

**Sukma Tour & Ferry** ( ☎ 732 0421; Jl SM Raja 106) Sells Penang ferry tickets.

**Tobali Tour & Travel** ( ☎ 732 4472; Jl SM Raja 79C) For tourist buses to Danau Toba (80,000Rp, four hours).

**Trophy Tour** ( ☎ 415 5777; pttrophy@indosat.net.id; Jl Katamso 33D) Ticket agent for most of the airlines (1st floor), and tour operator (2nd floor).

## Dangers & Annoyances

Medan can seem like an untamed town at times, but while normal big-city common sense is required, the locals are generally as friendly as village folk.

## Sights

### ISTANA MAIMOON

Having recently received a much-needed lick of paint, the **Maimoon Palace** (Jl Katamso; admission by donation; ⓨ 9am-5pm) stands as grand as ever. Built by the sultan of Deli in 1888, the 30-room palace features Malay, Mogul and Italian influences. Only the main room is open to the public; it features the lavish inauguration throne. The back wing of the palace is occupied by members of the sultan's family. The current sultan, Aria Mahmud Lamanjiji, was only eight years old when he was installed as the 14th Sultan of Deli in 2005, replacing

his father, who died in a plane crash. He is the youngest sultan in Deli history. He currently resides in Sulawesi, and his role is purely ceremonial.

### MESJID RAYA

The impressive **Grand Mosque** (cnr Jl Mesjid Raya & SM Raja; admission by donation; ⓨ 9am-5pm, except prayer times) was commissioned by the sultan in 1906. The Moroccan-style building has towering ceilings, ornate carvings, Italian marble and stained glass from China.

### MUSEUMS

The **Museum of North Sumatra** ( ☎ 771 6792; Jl HM Joni 51; admission 750Rp; ⓨ 8.30am-12.30 & 1.30-4pm Tue-Sun) has a well-presented collection ranging from early North Sumatran civilisations to Hindu, Buddhist and Islamic periods to colonial and military history. Highlights include fine stone carvings from Nias and extravagantly carved wooden coffins.

**Bukit Barisan Military Museum** (Jl H Zainal Arifin 8; admission by donation; ⓨ 9am-3pm Mon-Fri) has a small collection of weapons, photos and memorabilia from WWII, the War of Independence and the Sumatran rebellion of 1958.

### COLONIAL MEDAN

Ghosts of Medan's colonial mercantile past are still visible along Jl Ahmad Yani from Jl Palang Merah north to Lapangan Merdeka. Some are still stately relics, while others have been gutted and turned into parking garages, demonstrating the enduring friendship between Indonesia and its former coloniser.

**Tjong A Fie Mansion** (www.tjongafieinstitute. com; Jl Ahmad Yani 105; admission incl guide 35,000Rp; ⓨ 10am-5pm), the former residence of a famous Chinese merchant, mixes Victorian and Chinese styles. It is intentionally similar to Tjong A Fie's cousin's (Cheong Fatt Tze) home in Penang. At the time of research the mansion was opened to the public for the first time since it was built in 1860. The exquisite hand-painted ceilings, Tjong's huge bedroom, interesting art pieces, an upstairs ballroom (which now exhibits work by local artists) and Taoist temples make the pricey admission worthwhile. If you're a fan of 1950s pulp fiction, you'll love his son's collection in the Chinese guestroom.

Across the street is Tip Top Restaurant (see p376), a historic spot for sipping colonial nostalgia. Further north is Lapangan Merdeka, a former parade ground surrounded by handsome colonial buildings, such as the Bank Indonesia, Balai Kota (Town Hall) and the post office.

For more information about Medan's colonial architecture, check out *Tours Through Historic Medan and its Surroundings,* by Dirk A Buiskool, a long-time Medan resident. The author also operates **Tri Jaya Tour & Travel** ( ☎ 703 2967; www.trijaya-travel.com; tours 65,000Rp), which offers historic city tours.

## Sleeping

The majority of accommodation is on or near Jl SM Raja. Most budget options have cold water only.

### BUDGET

**Ronna's Guesthouse I** ( ☎ 732 4556; ronnasaloon@yahoo .com; Jl Tengah 33; r with/without bathroom 40,000/20,000Rp) Friendly bright-yellow guest house with simple but perfectly fine rooms that make a great choice for those on a tight budget.

**Zakia Hotel** ( ☎ 732 2413; Jl Sipiso-Piso 12; s/d without bathroom 30,000/45,000Rp, r with bathroom 60,000-80,000Rp, r with air-con 120,000-130,000Rp; ☒ ) An old backpackers in the '90s, Zakia isn't a bad budget option but is in dire need of a refurb; none of its Western toilets have seats.

**our pick Ponduk Wisata Angel** (Hotel Angel; ☎ 732 0702; Jl SM Raja 70; s with fan & with/without bathroom 70,000/50,000Rp, s/d with air-con 130,000/150,000Rp; ☒ ) The best backpacker option in town. Angel's clean rooms are a swirl of vivid blues and yellows, a colour scheme that almost succeeds in offsetting the noisy traffic. It has a sociable street-front cafe (see p376).

**Hotel Raya** ( ☎ 7366601; hotel-raya@gmail.com; s Jl RH Juanda Baru 200; r with/without air-con 85,000/65,000Rp; ☒ ) A bit of an improvement on most of the other SM Raja cheapies, with large rooms looking out to the busy road.

**Wisma Hari Kota** ( ☎ 453 3113; Jl Lobak 14; r 77,000-100,000Rp, r with aircon 127,000-150,000Rp; ☒ ) Only 10 minutes from the airport, this family-run guest house has a friendly vibe and comfortable rooms with street-facing balconies. Breakfast is included (except for the cheaper rooms).

**JJ's Guesthouse** ( ☎ 457 8411; www.guesthousemedan .com; Jl Suryo 18; s/d incl breakfast 100,000/180,000Rp; ☒ ) In an old Dutch villa, JJ's has tidy boarding-house-style rooms run by a mannerly Dutch-speaking Indonesian woman. Opposite KFC; its lack of signage makes it tricky to find. The gates are locked, so you'll need to ring the doorbell tucked inside the left-hand side of the gate.

### MIDRANGE

Hotel tax and breakfast are included in the quoted rates.

**Hotel Sumatera** ( ☎ 732 1551; Jl SM Raja 35; r without bathroom 135,000, with air-con 230,000-285,000Rp; ☒ ▯ ) One of the comfiest sleeps out of the glut of hotels around SM Raja. You'll find that once you add another zero to the price tag the rooms in Medan start to look a lot better.

**Ibunda Hotel** ( ☎ 734 5555; Jl SM Raja 31; s 170,000Rp, d 220,000-300,000Rp; ☒ ) A cheery spot, with minty green walls and new tiled baths.

### TOP END

Medan's best hotels all have the standard top-end facilities you'd expect, such as fitness centres, swimming pools and 24-hour room service. You'll also find many of the international chain hotels in town. All rates include tax and breakfast.

**Polonia Hotel** ( ☎ 414 2222; www.hotelpolonia.com; Jl Jend Sudirman 14; r 350,000-680,000Rp, ste 1,200,000Rp; ☒ ▣ ▯ ⬚ ) Excellent-value top-end choice located in the aristocratic section of Medan, close to the airport.

**Garuda Plaza Hotel** ( ☎ 736 1111; www.garuda plaza.com; Jl SM Raja 18; r 490,000-1,200,000Rp, ste from 2,500,000Rp; ☒ ▣ ▯ ⬚ ) Almost hip, Garuda Plaza is Medan's homage to Jakarta, with modern, corporate accents. Discounts of up to 40% are available.

**Hotel Deli River** ( ☎ 703 2964; Jl Raya Namorambe 129; r 700,000Rp; ☒ ▣ ▯ ⬚ ) Outside the city chaos, this family-run hotel is shaded by fruit trees and overlooks the Deli River. The hotel provides free transfers from the airport.

**Aryaduta Hotel** ( ☎ 457 2999; www.aryaduta .com; Jl Kapten Maulana Lubis 8; r 700,000-1,580,000Rp; ☒ ▣ ▯ ⬚ ) One of Medan's newest luxury hotels is international class, with all the frills you'd expect for the price and sprawling high-rise views across the city. Don't be put off by the above-mall location.

## Eating

Medan has the most varied selection of cuisines in Sumatra, from basic Malay-style *mie* (noodle) and nasi (rice) joints, to top-class hotel restaurants.

Lots of simple warungs (food stalls) occupy the front courtyards of the houses in the little lanes around Mesjid Raya; the menu is on display with a few pre-made curries, coffee, tea and sometimes juices.

The main fruit market, **Pasar Ramai** (Ramani Market; Jl Thamrin), next to Thamrin Plaza, is a profusion of colours and smells, and has an impressive selection of local and imported tropical fruit.

**Majestik Bakery & Cafe** (Jl SM Raja 71; pastries 2000Rp) Keep the munchies at bay during a long bus ride with sweets from this super-sized bakery.

**Taman Rekreasi Seri Deli** (Jl SM Raja; dishes from 8000Rp; ☾ evening only) For basic Malay food, this venue, opposite the Mesjid Raya, is a slightly upmarket approach to stall dining. But the *kerupuk* (cracker) sellers, blind beggars and spoon players might find you more of an oddity than vice versa.

**Sehat Vegetarian** (Jl Thamrin; dishes from 10,000Rp; ☾ 6am-9pm; ✷) The place to go when you can't face another gado gado, this Chinese restaurant has a fascinating choice of unidentifiable vegetarian dishes.

**our pick Merdeka Walk** (Lapangan Merdeka, Jl Balai Kota; dishes 10,000-15,000Rp; ☾ 5-11pm; ☎) Inspired by Singapore's alfresco dining, this collection of outdoor cafes occupies Lapangan Merdeka with both fast food and proper restaurants. You can burn off the calories on a series of bizarre public-exercise equipment at the adjoining sports ground.

**Bollywood Food Centre** (☎ 453 6494; Jl Muara Takus 7; dishes from 12,000Rp) Lip-smacking Indian-style curries are a family affair at this blindingly bright restaurant in Little India (Kampung Keling). It also serves cold Bintang. Malay-Indian roti shops are located nearby.

**Ponduk Wisata Angel** (Jl SM Raja 70; mains 15,000-20,000Rp) With a laidback backpacker vibe, this cafe could almost pass for a beachside shack if it weren't for the insanely busy traffic along SM Raja. It does tasty Indonesian dishes and decent Western food. Sells cold beer.

**Corner Café Raya** (cnr Jl SM Raja & Sipiso-Piso 1; dishes 15,000-40,000Rp; ☾ 24hr) A Western-themed cafe serving breakfast fry-ups and burgers as well as Indonesian dishes.

**Tip Top Restaurant** (Jl Ahmad Yani 92; dishes 15,000-50,000Rp; ✷ ☎) Only the prices have changed at this old colonial relic, great for a drink of bygone imperialism. It offers tasty Indonesian, Chinese and Western dishes, including a good steak menu. The desserts are delicious.

**Medan Club** (Jl Kartini 36; dishes 30,000-80,000Rp) Wealthy and well-dressed expats sip cocktails and dine from the broad international menu, which includes Mexican, French and American dishes.

**Traders** (Jl Kapten Pattimura 423; mains 60,000-230,000Rp, Japanese menu 35,000-120,000Rp; ☾ noon-midnight; ✷) The very plush Traders is the perfect spot to blow your dining budget on sushi, snail chowder, lobster dishes or Australian Angus steaks. If you can somehow fit more food in, try the Avocado Mousse cake.

## Drinking

**Corner Café Raya** (cnr Jl SM Raja & Sipiso-Piso 1; ☾ 24hr) Cold beer and Western sports served to a heady mix of seedy sex-pats and fresh-faced backpackers, which makes its location directly opposite the Mesjid Raya mosque a little puzzling.

**Traders** (Jl Kapten Pattimura 423; ☾ noon-midnight) The front bar-restaurant has sport on the TV and is busiest on weekends, especially on two-for-one Friday night and all-you-can-drink beer on Sunday (90,000Rp). Out the back is a swanky blue neon–lit bar with pool tables and live music.

**Medan Club** (Jl Kartini 36) A local institution, the Medan Club is still the place for many well-to-do locals to socialise on weekends.

## Shopping

Medan has a number of interesting arts-and-crafts shops, particularly along Jl Ahmad Yani. **Toko Asli** (No 62), **Toko Rufino** (No 56) and **Toko Bali Arts** (No 68) all have selections of antique weaving, Dutch pottery and carvings.

Clothes, shoes, jewellery, electrical goods and cosmetics can be found at any of Medan's numerous multilevel shopping centres. Most also have well-stocked supermarkets.

## Getting There & Away

Medan is Sumatra's main international arrival and departure point.

### AIR

Medan's Polonia Airport is 2km south of the city centre. Remember that there is an airport tax for departing flights (see the boxed text on p847).

There are daily international flights from Medan to Singapore, Kuala Lumpur and Penang. Domestic flights connect Medan to Jakarta, Banda Aceh, Pekanbaru, Padang, Batam, Pontianak and Gunung Sitoli.

The following airlines have offices in Medan and serve the destinations as listed:

**Air Asia** ( ☎ 733 1988; www.airasia.com; Jl SM Raja 18) Inside Garuda Plaza Hotel; has flights to Jakarta, Kuala Lumpur.

**Garuda** ( ☎ 455 6777; Jl Monginsidi 340); Jl Balai Kota 2 ( ☎ 453 7844; Inna Dharma Deli, Jl Balai Kota 2) Jakarta, Banda Aceh.

**Kartika Air** ( ☎ 452 2433; Jl Katamso 37) Batam, Jambi, Palembang.

**Lion Air** ( ☎ 457 1122; Jl Katamso 41) Jakarta, Banda Aceh, Batam, Palembang, Penang.

**Malaysian Airlines** ( ☎ 451 9333; www.malaysiaair lines.com; Hotel Danau Toba International, Jl Imam Bonjol 17) Kuala Lumpur, Penang.

**Merpati** ( ☎ 736 6888; www.merpati.co.id/EN; SM Raja 92A) Pulau Simeulue, Sibolga, Gunung Sitoli.

**NBA** (Nusantara Buana Air; ☎ 453 4680; Jl Katamso) Singkil, Kutacane.

**Silk Air** ( ☎ 453 7744; www.silkair.com; Polonia Hotel, Jl Sudirman 14) Singapore.

**Sriwijaya Air** ( ☎ 455 2111; www.sriwijayaair-online .com, in Bahasa Indonesia; Jl Katamso 29) Jakarta, Banda Aceh, Batam, Pekanbaru.

**Susi Air** ( ☎ 785 2169; www.susiair.com; domestic airport) Pulau Simeulue, Meulaboh, Silangit.

## BOAT

High-speed ferries (one way/return 140/210 Malaysian ringgit; five hours; noon Tuesday, Thursday and Saturday) depart from the port of Belawan, 26km from Medan, to the Malaysian city of Penang.

A complimentary bus transfer to Belawan from Medan is available. There is a 35,000Rp surcharge for harbour tax. Tickets can be bought from agents on Jl Katamso or Jl SM Raja (see p374). Arriving in Belawan from Penang, the bus transfer to Medan is *not* included in the price. You can take the green *opelet* 81 between Belawan and Medan (8000Rp).

Pelni ships sail to Jakarta and Batam. The **Pelni office** ( ☎ 6622526; Jl Krakatau 17A) is 8km north of the city centre, but it is much easier to buy tickets and check schedules from the agencies on Jl Katamso.

## BUS

There are two major bus terminals in Medan: Amplas, serving southern destinations, and Pinang Baris, serving northern destinations. For long-distance travel, most people deal directly with the bus ticketing offices located outside of the terminals.

Amplas bus terminal is 6.5km south of the city centre along Jl SM Raja. Almost any *opelet* heading south on Jl SM Raja will get you to Amplas (3000Rp). Bus ticket offices line the street nearby at Km 6 and include the following:

**ALS** ( ☎ 786 6685) Serves Bukittinggi (economy 115,000Rp, air-con with/without toilet 150,000/135,000Rp, 22 hours)

**Kurnia** ( ☎ 786 4177) Runs buses with air-con and toilets to Parapat (22,000Rp, four hours), Jambi (250,000Rp, 30 hours) and Palembang (280,000Rp, 40 hours).

**Pelangi** ( ☎ 787 8822) Runs buses to Pekanbaru (air-con/super-executive 140,000/190,000Rp, 12 to 14 hours), Banda Aceh (air-con/executive 120,000/200,000Rp, 12 hours), Jambi (air-con/executive 265,000/370,000Rp, 28 to 30 hours) and Palembang (air-con/executive 290,000/370,000Rp, 40 hours).

There are frequent public buses to Parapat (economy/air-con 12,000/22,000Rp, four hours, 6am to 6pm), the jumping-off point to Danau Toba. Minibuses (80,000Rp, four hours, frequently up until 6pm) also leave from **Tobali Tour & Travel** ( ☎ 732 4472; Jl SM Raja 79C).

**Pinang Baris bus terminal** (Jl Gatot Subroto), 10km west of the city centre, serves northern destinations. Get there by taxi (40,000Rp) or by *opelet* 24, 37 or 64 (5000Rp).

There are frequent public buses to both Bukit Lawang (15,000Rp, three hours) and Berastagi (15,000Rp, 2½ hours) every half-hour between 5.30am and 6pm.

Although there are buses to Banda Aceh from Pinang Baris, it's easier to get to Banda Aceh from the Pelangi ticket agent near Amplas.

A minibus departs at 8pm daily for Singkil (80,000Rp, 10 hours), the departure point for boats to the Banyak Islands. Buses depart from **Singkil Raya** ( ☎ 081 26560739; Jl Bintan), past the caged-bird warehouses. Here you'll also find buses to Ketambe (100,000Rp, eight hours). Take *opelet* 53 from Jl SM Raja to Medan Mall.

## TRAIN

Rail services are very limited, with just two trains a day to Tanjung Balai (economy only, 10,000Rp). There are four trains daily to Rantauparapat (business/executive 40,000/60,000Rp).

## Getting Around

### TO/FROM THE AIRPORT

It is cheaper and less of a hassle to sail past the throng of taxi drivers to the becak queue at the airport gate (becak aren't allowed inside the airport). It should cost 10,000Rp to reach the hotel district on Jl SM Raja. If you like to haggle, a taxi ride should cost around 30,000Rp.

### PUBLIC TRANSPORT

Medan's got more *opelet* than you can shake a spoon player at. They cost 3000Rp for most in-town destinations. Here are a few helpful routes: white Mr X from Jl SM Raja to Kesawan Sq, Lapangan Merdeka and the train station; and yellow 64 from Maimoon Palace to Sun Plaza.

For becak, expect to pay about 8000Rp for most destinations. But they'll ask you to pay more than double that.

## BUKIT LAWANG

☎ 061 / pop 30,000

Lost in the depths of the Sumatran jungle is this sweet little tourist town built around the popularity of its orangutan-viewing centre. But Bukit Lawang has much more to offer beyond our red-haired cousins. It's very easy to while away a few days lounging in the many riverside hammocks, listening to the mating calls over the gushing river and watching the jungle life swing and sing around you. The surrounding jungle is one of the most biodiverse regions in the world, and is home to eight species of primate plus tiger, rhino, elephant, pangolin, leopard and cobras (though most of the larger mammals are very rarely seen).

Tourists, almost exclusively, come here to check out the orangutans. The conservation program has been operating on the eastern edge of the Gunung Leuser National Park since the 1970s. The national park is one of the orangutan's last remaining strongholds, with more than 5000 thought to be living in the wild here.

Since the village is only 96km northwest of Medan, Bukit Lawang is also one of the easiest places from which to make the leap into the jungle, a diverse and rugged forest crisscrossed by clear, fast-flowing rivers. Many tourists slip-slide through the mud and undergrowth on multiday treks and hobble back to the village to recuperate.

Bukit Lawang was extensively damaged by a flash flood in November 2003, which killed 239 people and destroyed much of the riverfront development. The essentials of the town and tourist infrastructure have been rebuilt but the community is still grieving for lost relatives and livelihoods.

## Orientation & Information

The nearby village of Gotong Royong, 2km southeast of Sungai Bohorok, has effectively become the new town centre. About a kilometre north of the bus stop, the stretch of riverside accommodation begins.

There are no banks, but you'll find money-changers along the strip. There is no post office here, but you can buy stamps from the shops and use a local post box. There is a market on Friday and on Sunday in Bohorok town, 15km away, where you will also find the nearest police station and medical clinic.

**Leuser Netwave** (per hr 25,000Rp; ⏰ 10am-10pm), at the top of a hill, has pricey and often unreliable internet connection. A few other internet cafes were opening up at the time of research.

**Bukit Lawang Guide Association** ( ⏰ 7am-2pm) Located across the street from the visitor centre, this place distributes a rate sheet for hikes.

**Bukit Lawang Visitors Centre** ( ⏰ 8am-3pm) Displays of flora and fauna found in Gunung Leuser National Park, plus a book of medicinal plants and their uses. Past visitors often record reviews of guides in the sign-in book.

**PHKA permit office** (park entrance; ⏰ 8am-10am & 3-4pm) Timed with the orangutan feedings, the rangers open up this office to collect permit fees; don't bother arranging permits in town. If you're taking another entrance to the park, guides can arrange permits for you.

## Dangers & Annoyances

Not so much a danger as an annoyance: there are 140 guides and rarely more than a dozen tourists in town, which means that the guide harangue starts on the bus before you've even left Medan. A friendly stranger hops aboard and makes a beeline to the nearest available seat. They are full of Bukit Lawang titbits and just so happen to be going in the same direction, or, imagine that, they're a guide. They'll then escort you to a guest house, sit you down and sign you up for a trek. The trick is to be polite and feel no obligation to book anything unless you want to.

**RED-HEADED COUSINS**

Orangutans, the world's largest arboreal mammals, once swung through the forest canopy throughout all of Southeast Asia, but are now found only in Sumatra and Borneo. Researchers fear that the few that do remain will not survive the continued loss of habitat to logging and agriculture.

While orangutans are extremely intelligent animals, their way of life isn't compatible with a shrinking forest. Orangutans are mostly vegetarians; they get big and strong (some males weigh up to 90kg) from a diet that would make a Californian hippie proud: fruit, shoots, leaves, nuts and tree bark, which they grind up with their powerful jaws and teeth. They also occasionally eat insects, eggs and small mammals.

All of the forest is their pantry, requiring them to migrate through a large territory following the fruit season. But they aren't social creatures; they prefer a solitary existence foraging during the day and building a new nest every night high up in the trees away from predators.

Orangutans have a long life span, often living up to 30- to 40-years old in the wild. They breed slowly and have few young. Females reach sexual maturity at about the age of 10 and remain fertile until about the age of 30, on average having only one baby every six years. Only the females raise the young, which stay with their mothers until reaching sexual maturity.

The 'orang hutan' (a Malay word for 'person of the forest') has an extremely expressive face, which has often suggested a very close kinship with the hairless ape (humans). But of all the great apes, the orangutans are considered to be the most distantly related to humans.

## Sights

### ORANGUTAN FEEDING CENTRE

Bukit Lawang's famous orangutan centre was set up in 1973 to help primates readjust to the wild after captivity or displacement through land clearing. Much of the original duties of the centre have been moved to more remote locations, but twice-daily feedings are still provided to semidependent orangutans. These events are open to the public (no guide required) and provide one of the closest views of the forest ape outside the confines of a zoo.

During the centre's decades-long operation, it has introduced 200 orangutans into the jungle and many of them have successfully mated with the wild population. Many of the animals have been kept as caged pets; the centre teaches them how to forage for food in the wild, build nests, climb trees and other essentials for survival after release. The orangutans are also treated for diseases that they contracted during contact with humans. The most recent release of an orangutan into the wild was in 2005.

Once the apes are on their own in the wild, the centre still provides supplementary feedings in case of awkward transitions or demanding circumstances. The feedings provided by the centre consist of milk and bananas and are considered a fairly bland diet compared with the diversity of food found in the forest. The semi-wild apes who appear at the centre's 'welfare' platform are typically nursing or pregnant females in need of an extra source of nutrition.

There are two feeding times a day: 8.30am to 9.30am and 3pm to 4pm. These are the only times visitors are allowed to enter the national park without a guide.

The feeding platform is located on the west bank of Sungai Bohorok within the park boundaries, about a 20-minute walk up from the village. The river crossing to the park office is made by dugout canoe. Permits are required to enter the park (20,000Rp) and are available from the **office** (☉ 8am-10am & 3-4pm) at the foot of the trail to the platform. If you have a camera/video camera you'll have to pay an additional 50,000/150,000Rp at the office, with no refunds if orangutans don't come to the feeding platform – during peak fruit season they often don't.

Since 1996 the centre has been closed to new arrivals, as the park is considered to be saturated with orangutans. A replacement quarantine centre, just outside Medan, opened in 2002 to carry on the rehabilitation efforts, but it is not open to the public. Originally funded by World Wildlife Fund and Frankfurt Zoological Society, the centre now falls under the management of the Indonesian government, which does not provide adequate financial resources. Park rangers are not paid in a timely fashion and permit money is sent directly to Jakarta. Despite these problems, the rangers are dedicated to their jobs and often supplement their incomes and their hands-on experience by working with foreign researchers.

Outside Gunung Leuser National Park, orangutans can be found in the Tanjung Puting and Kutai National Parks; in the Gunung Palung, Bukit Raja, Sebangau, Danau Sentarum and Betung Kerihun national parks in Kalimantan; as well as in neighbouring Sarawak and Sabah in Malaysia.

For more information about Sumatran orangutans try the **Sumatran Orangutan Society** (SOS; www.orangutans-sos.org) and the **Sumatran Orangutan Conservation Programme** (www.sumatranorangutan. com).

## Activities
### TREKKING

Treks into the Gunung Leuser National Park require a guide and can last anywhere from three hours to two days. Most people opt for two days so that they can spend the night in the jungle, which increases their likelihood of seeing orangutans and other critters in the wild. It is best to hike in a small group and to set off as early as possible.

Choosing a guide can be a tricky task as there are so many and the choice can be intimidating. Despite the pressure, take your time in choosing a guide. Talk to returning trekkers and decide how much jungle time you really need.

If you just want a few souvenir pictures and stories, find a guide you like. People who trekked with guides from the village have mainly positive feedback, with the greatest kudos going to the nightly meals and campfire socials. Common complaints range from guides who don't know enough about the flora and fauna, the bunching together of treks, and the feeding of orangutans.

Guide rates are fixed by the Sumatra Guide Association. For a minimum of three people it's €15 for a three-hour trek; €25 for a day trek; and €60/50 with/without rafting for a two-day trek including overnight camping in the jungle. Add €25 per extra day in the jungle. 'Rafting' back to town, which actually involves rubber tubes tied together, is a popular option that allows you to trek deeper into the jungle and makes for a fun and relaxing way to finish your trek. Prices include a visit to the feeding centre, basic meals, guide fees, camping equipment and the park permit. Camping involves a tarpaulin sheet thrown over bamboo poles, with everyone sleeping in the same tent.

A word of warning: trekking in the jungle is no stroll in the park. You'll encounter steep slippery ascents and precipitous drops amid intense humidity, so a good level of fitness is

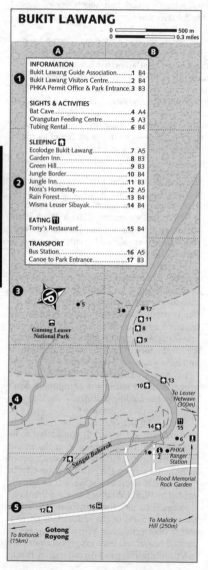

**BUKIT LAWANG**

0 ————— 500 m
0 ————— 0.3 miles

**INFORMATION**
Bukit Lawang Guide Association.........**1** B4
Bukit Lawang Visitors Centre.............**2** B4
PHKA Permit Office & Park Entrance.**3** B3

**SIGHTS & ACTIVITIES**
Bat Cave.........................................**4** A4
Orangutan Feeding Centre..............**5** A3
Tubing Rental.................................**6** B4

**SLEEPING**
Ecolodge Bukit Lawang....................**7** A5
Garden Inn.....................................**8** B3
Green Hill.......................................**9** B3
Jungle Border..................................**10** B4
Jungle Inn......................................**11** B3
Nora's Homestay.............................**12** A5
Rain Forest.....................................**13** B4
Wisma Leuser Sibayak.....................**14** B4

**EATING**
Tony's Restaurant...........................**15** B4

**TRANSPORT**
Bus Station.....................................**16** A5
Canoe to Park Entrance..................**17** B3

## SAVE THE ORANGUTANS

A tragic paradox of Bukit Lawang is that the tourist presence, which keeps the viewing and rehabilitation centre running, is killing the orangutan population. It's a vicious circle, because the tourists are needed to maintain Bukit Lawang as a profitable and protected region. However, orangutans are extremely susceptible to human disease, and the semi-wild orangutans that come into contact with humans every day are passing on diseases across the orangutan population. Just a mild cold can potentially kill an orangutan. Without the orangutans, there is no jungle, as their seed-filled faeces are needed to maintain and spread the plant life. There are no reliable figures available, but a great number of orangutans – young, old, wild and semiwild – are dying from some form of human illness, in particular influenza. Infant mortality is estimated to be as high as 75%.

Respected conservation scientist and owner of Green Hill lodge, Andrea Molyneaux, recommends these tourist guidelines for protecting the orangutan population in Bukit Lawang.

- The recommended maximum number of people per trekking group is seven: this controls the risk of human impacts and optimises your viewing experience.

- At the feeding platform you are allowed to stay for a maximum of 30 minutes. If you meet orangutans when trekking stay with them for no longer than 10 minutes.

- Visitors who are sick (eg cough, diarrhoea) should not go trekking or to the feeding platform. Please report any sickness to your guide or a ranger and your visit can be rescheduled. Rangers and guides can refuse a visit to anyone showing obvious signs of illness.

- Healthy visitors should not be closer than 10m to orangutans.

Observe the following etiquette when you are close to orangutans:

- Do not call the orangutans.

- Do not feed or give them drinks.

- Do not smoke, eat, drink, cough, sneeze or spit.

- Always stay in a close group and never lose contact with your guide.

- When possible you should sit when watching the orangutans.

- Show respect by being as silent as possible and using good body language (no shouting, no sudden movements, no making monkey sounds etc).

- Do not use flash photography. It will not be effective anyway.

- Do not approach or try to touch them and NEVER come between a mother and her baby.

When you are in the rainforest, abide by these guidelines:

- It is forbidden to enter the rainforest without a guide.

- Do not pressure your guide to get closer to animals, shake trees or give them food so you can take photographs.

- If you feel your guide has behaved inappropriately inform the guide office.

- Do not leave any litter in the forest, eg tissues, water bottles, cigarette butts, food scraps. It must be carried outside of the forest then disposed of. This includes fruit skins (such as banana, orange, rambutan), which may carry your germs.

- If you must defecate you should dig a hole at least 2ft deep. You can borrow a parang/machete from your guide. All faecal material and tissue must be buried.

- Do not disturb or collect anything from the forest such as flowers, insects, seeds etc.

Some of these may seem extreme but so is the situation, and due attention to these rules by tourists is vital if we are to maintain the orangutans' existence in and around Bukit Lawang.

SUMATRA

## THE NOTORIOUS MINA

The most well-known inhabitant of Bukit Lawang's jungle is a fiery female orangutan named Mina, who's earned a reputation among locals as the most feared, yet most loved, of the orangutans. She's known for her aggression towards humans – it seems every guide has a tale of a violent encounter with Mina at some point or another. At last count she'd attacked some 64 guides! Yet from the guides you'll hear nothing but love for this bad girl of the jungle, as nearly all run-ins result from tourists not heeding to guides' advice, and getting too close. Once held captive as a pet, the 29-year-old Mina is one of the first orangutans released into the wild here, and her aggression is largely a result of her expectation of being fed by humans. She is the perfect case study as to why tourists should ensure that they take the proper precautions by never feeding or coming too close to these magnificent apes.

essential. The trails can be well-worn paths or barely visible breaks in the underbrush. Pack at least two bottles of water per day. If you don't have trekking shoes, and have small feet, in town you may be able to buy a pair of cheap but reliable shoes with studded soles, the same as most guides wear.

### SHORT WALKS

There are a number of short walks around Bukit Lawang that don't require guides or permits.

The **canal** that runs alongside the river is an easy stroll through the village. In the evening everything gets washed in the rushing waters: frolicking kids, soiled bums, dirty laundry. Activities usually considered private are social in the communal waters.

The most interesting is a 20-minute walk, signposted from the Ecolodge Bukit Lawang, to a **bat cave**. This 2km walk passes through rubber plantations and patches of forest, and by a children's foster home. A lot of the trees are durian, so take care in late June and July, when the spiked fruits crash to the ground (there are signs warning people not to linger). You'll need a torch (flashlight) to explore the cave.

### TUBING

A shed along the river en route to the orangutan centre rents inflated truck inner tubes (10,000Rp per day), which can be used to ride the Sungai Bohorok rapids. On weekends, the river near the bridge resembles a water theme park, with Indonesian tourists having the time of their lives. Don't underestimate the river, though; currents are extremely strong and when the water is high, tubing is officially off limits, though few will tell you this. Tube at your own risk.

## Sleeping

The further upriver you go, the more likely you are to ogle the swinging monkeys and apes from your porch hammock. You won't find hot water or air-con at any of the guest houses. The following are listed in geographic order from south to north.

**Nora's Homestay** ( ☎ 081 36207 0656; r 40,000-50,000Rp) Nora's little cluster of bamboo huts between the rice fields and the main road is an old backpacker favourite with a reputation for being Sumatra's friendliest guest house. Many readers swear by it, despite the prettier-located guest houses upriver. Nora is very helpful with local information, though these days she's mostly found at Rain Forest (see below).

**Ecolodge Bukit Lawang** ( ☎ 081 2607 9983; http://ecolodge.yelweb.org; r incl breakfast s 130,000-275,000Rp, d 155,000-300,000Rp) Popular with package tourists, the village's most upmarket lodging has a range of hotel-style rooms. There are many commendable attempts at ecofriendly business: an organic garden provides produce for the restaurant, a medicinal-plant garden preserves the pharmaceutical aspects of the jungle, and there's recycling. Children under 10 stay free.

**Wisma Leuser Sibayak** ( ☎ 0813 6101 0736; r 50,000-60,000Rp) A basic cheapie that's worth a stay if you've arrived at night and don't fancy trekking up through the jungle path in the dark. Its rickety bridge across the river is rather frightening, though.

**Rain Forest** ( ☎ 081 362070656; d 30,000-40,000Rp) Nora (or 'Mama', as she calls herself) has recently opened this new spot on the river. The big house has rooms as close as you'll find on the water at bargain prices. Nora also has cooking classes for 100,000Rp, including meal.

**Green Hill** ( ☎ 081 26364 3775; www.greenhill-bukit lawang.com; dm 30,000Rp, r with/without bathroom incl breakfast 150,000Rp/60,000Rp) For a few more rupiah you get a lot more than what's offered by most of the competition. Run by English conservation scientist Andrea Molyneaux and her Sumatran husband, Green Hill has two lovely stilt-high rooms ideal for couples, where the en suite bamboo-shoot showers afford stunning jungle views while you wash. Also has dorms and cheaper rooms available.

**Garden Inn** ( ☎ 0812 6355 6285; fadill36@gmail.com; r 50,000-150,000Rp) A popular backpacker choice. The lovely high rooms look over the river and the jungle, plus there's a sweet little cafe for swapping monkey-spotting tales.

**Jungle Inn** ( ☎ 0813 6550 5005; superdjoe@yahoo.com; d 50,000-450,000Rp). The last guest house along the strip near the park entrance, Jungle Inn is an old favourite of many a reader. One room overlooks a waterfall, while another incorporates the hill's rock face, and the bathroom sprouts a shower from living ferns. Its only downsides are the sometimes unreliable information provided by staff and overcharging for treks.

At the time of research, a new ecolodge called **Jungle Border** was about to open across the river from Rain Forest guest house, with five bungalows at the edge of the jungle, organic food and a yoga centre planned.

## Eating

All the guest houses along the river en route to the park entrance serve Western food, barbecued fish, nasi goreng (fried rice), fruit salads and a laidback ambience. Here is also where the guides camp out for new arrivals.

**Tony's Restaurant** (mains 25,000Rp, pizzas 40,000-63,000Rp) Located further up the river, Tony's fires up tasty pizzas in a riverfront shack.

## Getting There & Away

There are direct buses to Medan's Pinang Baris bus terminal every half-hour between 5.30am and 5pm (10,000Rp, four hours). Minivans (15,000Rp, three hours) also leave for Medan throughout the day.

## TANGKAHAN

This is the place for a truly wild and off-the-map adventure. Having ticked off seeing the orangutans in Bukit Lawang, in-the-know ecotourists are now trickling north to experience the jungle aboard elephants in this undiscovered retreat.

Towards the end of the 1990s a few foreign ecologists and conscientious locals decided to take a stand against the palm-oil loggers that working in this wild part of northern Sumatra. Armed with a few rifles and machetes, and using elephants to patrol the jungle against loggers and poachers, the locals have gradually lobbied the government into declaring the region a protected area. Fast forward a decade and the once-doomed region is still home to all manner of apes, monkeys, lizards and, of course, elephants. Not so much a village as a bus stop, a park entrance and a handful of basic riverside bungalows on the wild banks of the Kualsa Buluh River, Tangkahan has a tiny community of amiable loggers-turned-guides selling an experience as close as you'll get to Tarzan living on this untamed isle.

## Sights & Activities

For many, the elephants are the main draw here: you can give them their morning bath (20,000Rp) or be taken on an elephant-back trek (one hour, 250,000Rp). But it's also a wonderful place to relax in the wild, exploring the jungle and taking isolated morning dips in the river. At the time of research there were also plans to offer four-day elephant treks from Tangkahan into Bukit Lawang.

Grade III white-water rafting is also a popular activity (450,000Rp).

## Sleeping

There are only four places to stay in the area, with little to separate each one. **Green Lodge** (r 100,000Rp), situated by the elephant-washing area, has simple wood cabins. On the other side of the river (listed in the order you'll find them once you've crossed the river), **Mega Inn**, **Bamboo Lodge** and **Jungle Lodge** all have fairly basic en suite bungalows with river views from 80,000Rp. All of the guest houses serve simple meals.

## Getting There & Away

There are three direct buses that depart daily to Medan's Pinang Baris terminal (20,000Rp, four hours). To get to Tangkahan from Bukit Lawang, take one of the many buses to Binjai (10,000Rp, 2½ hours), from where it is possible to change for a bus to Tangkahan (15,000Rp, 2½ hours). Alternatively, any of the local guides will take you direct from Bukit Lawang on a moped (150,000Rp, three hours) – be warned that the road is treacherous. Most Medan-based travel agents can arrange 4WD transport (600,000Rp, 2½ hours).

# BERASTAGI

☎ 0628 / pop 600,000

Escaping from the infernal heat of sea-level Medan, the colonial Dutch traders climbed high into the lush, cool, volcanic hills, took one look at the stunningly verdant, undulating landscape and decided to build a rural retreat where Berastagi (also called Brastagi) now stands.

Today weekending Medan folk and backpackers alike sigh a crisp, clear breath of relief when they arrive in this quaint agricultural escape situated high among Sumatra's steaming volcanoes. Though the town itself is not overly pretty, a concrete jungle set amid beautiful surrounds, as an agricultural trade centre its markets are always humming with activity, and modern-day snake-oil hawkers fill the sidewalks with 'big city' amusements for isolated country folk. On Sunday, the largely Christian community takes the babies and bibles out for worship.

Beyond the town are the green fields of the Karo Highlands, dominated by two volcanoes: Gunung Sinabung to the west and the smoking Gunung Sibayak to the north. Though you won't find lava in either Sibayak or Sinabung, each still has the feel of everything you hoped to experience from an active volcano, with steamy gases gushing from the fumaroles like a mad scientist's laboratory. These volcanoes are a day hike apiece, making them two of Sumatra's most accessible volcanoes, and the primary reason why tourists get off the bus here.

Berastagi is at an altitude of 1300m, and the climate is deliciously cool, sometimes even cold.

## Orientation

Berastagi is essentially a one-street town spread along Jl Veteran. The colourful Tugu Perjuangan (Combat Memorial), commemorating the Bataks' struggle against the Dutch in the 1800s, marks the centre of town. The hill to the northwest is Bukit Gundaling, a popular picnic spot.

## Information

**BNI bank** (Jl Veteran) With ATMs.
**BRI bank** (Jl Veteran) With ATMs.
**Sibayak Trans Tour &Travel** ( ☎ 91122; dicksonpelawi@yahoo.com; Jl Veteran 119) Books plane tickets and has information about local and onward travel.
**Post office** (Jl Veteran) Near the memorial at the northern end of the street.

**Telkom wartel** (Jl Veteran) Near the memorial at the northern end of the street is a 24-hour Telkom wartel, which has a Home Country Direct phone and internet.
**Tourist Information Centre** ( ☎ 91084; Jl Gundaling 1; ☺ 8am-5pm Mon-Sat) Has maps and can arrange guides.
**D'Z@S Net** (Jl Perwira; ☺ 7am-midnight) Decent-speed internet.

## Sights & Activities

Berastagi is underutilised as an escape from Indonesia's intensity. Most people spend a couple of days hiking here and then trek south to Danau Toba. But there is a lot of unhindered wandering you can do on foot and motorbike. .

### TRADITIONAL VILLAGES

There are some fine examples of traditional Karo Batak architecture in the villages around Berastagi. Most of the houses are no more than 60 years old – or possibly 100, but certainly not 400, as claimed by some guides.

#### Kampung Peceren

On the northern outskirts of Berastagi, this village has a cluster of traditional houses, which are still occupied. Any *opelet* heading north can drop you there (2000Rp). There's a 2000Rp entry fee to the village.

#### Lingga

The best-known and most visited of these villages is **Lingga** (admission 2000Rp), a few kilometres northwest of Kabanjahe. There is about a dozen traditional houses with characteristic horned roofs. Some, such as the *rumah rajah* (king's house), are occupied and in good condition; others, including the *sapo ganjang* (the house for young unmarried men), have almost collapsed.

There are regular *opelet* to Lingga from Kabanjahe (8000Rp).

#### Dokan

The charming little village of Dokan is approximately 16km south of Kabanjahe. Traditional houses are still in the majority and most are in good condition. Entry is by donation. You can get here by the occasional direct *opelet* from Kabanjahe (5000Rp).

### AIR TERJUN SIPISO-PISO

These narrow but impressive **falls** cascade 120m down to the north end of Danau Toba,

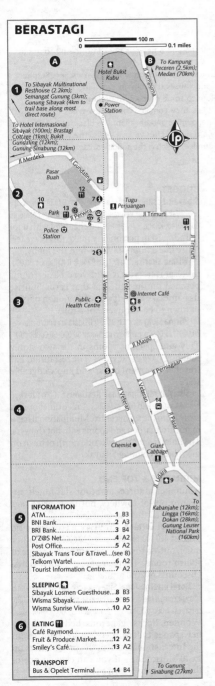

24km from Kabanjahe and about 300m from the main road. It is fairly easy to get here by yourself; take a bus from Kabanjahe to Merek (10,000Rp) and then walk or hitch a ride on a motorbike.

## TREKKING TO VOLCANOES

Trails on both volcanoes are neither clearly marked nor well maintained, and it is easy to get lost or lose your footing. During the wet season, paths can be extremely slippery or even washed out. The weather is variable and views from either mountain are far from guaranteed. Be prepared for abrupt weather changes (fog, cold temperatures and rain can sneak up during a clear day). Bring supplies such as food, drink, rain gear and a torch, in case you get caught out after dark.

### Gunung Sibayak

At 2094m, Gunung Sibayak is probably the most accessible of Indonesia's volcanoes. A guide is only essential if taking the route through the jungle, though if you're trekking alone it may be a good idea. Rates for guides are 150,000Rp for the easy way along the road, and 200,000Rp to 250,000Rp through the jungle. The hike can be done in five hours return, and you should set out as early as possible.

There are three ways to tackle the climb, depending on your energy level. The easiest way is to take the track that starts to the northwest of town, a 10-minute walk past the Sibayak Multinational Resthouse. Take the left-hand path beside the hut where you pay the entrance fee (1500Rp). From here it's 7km (about three hours) to the top and fairly easy to follow, mostly along a road. Finding the path down is a little tricky. When you reach the crater, turn 90 degrees to the right (anticlockwise), climb up to the rim and start looking for the stone steps down the other side of the mountain. If you can't find the steps, you can also go back the way you came.

On the descent you can stop off at the various **hot springs** (admission 3000-5000Rp) in Semangat Gunung, on the road back to Berastagi. You'll be disappointed if you're expecting natural springs; instead you'll find a complex of small concrete pools. As soon as you soak your aching muscles in its delightfully warm waters, you won't mind one bit. If you want privacy away from excitable children, it's a good idea to look at a few places scattered along the road, most of which are empty.

SUMATRA

---

**IN THE KNOW ON VOLCANOES**

There's nothing like an exhausting hike up a volcano and a nervous peek into the pit to ignite an interest in earth science.

Inside both Sibayak and Sinabung are fumaroles, vents through which gases escape. Sulphur is the most pungent of the steaming vapours and causes difficulty in breathing if you get too close. Sulphur also lends its brilliant yellow colour to some of the surrounding rocks.

Volcanic rocks are classified by how much silica they contain. The easiest types to identify within a volcanic crater are the subsets of rhyolite: pumice and obsidian. The black, glassy obsidian is formed when lava cools quickly, typically a result of effusive lava flows. The white porous material that gives way when you walk on it is pumice, which is the solidified version of a frothy, gas-filled lava eruption.

---

Alternatively, you can catch a local bus (5000Rp) to Semangat Gunung at the base of the volcano, from where it's a two-hour climb to the summit. There are steps part of the way, but this track is narrower and in poorer condition than the one from Berastagi.

The longest option is to trek through the jungle from Air Terjun Panorama; this waterfall is on the Medan road, about 5km north of Berastagi. Allow at least five hours for this walk.

Before setting out, pick up a map from Wisma Sibayak (see right) in Berastagi and peruse the guest book for comments and warnings about the hike.

### Gunung Sinabung

This peak, at 2450m, is considerably higher than Sibayak, with even more stunning views from the top. Be warned, though, that the clouds love mingling with the summit and can often obscure the vista.

Most guest houses recommend taking a guide (200,000Rp to 300,000Rp), as hikers have gotten lost and died. The path up the mountain from Danau Kawar is fairly well trodden by locals, but relying on a guide takes the guesswork out of timing your return to town or reading changing weather conditions. The climb takes six to eight hours depending on your skill and the descent route.

To reach the trailhead, take an *opelet* to Danau Kawar (7000Rp, 1½ hours). Entry fee is 2500Rp. There is a scenic camp site surrounding Danau Kawar for those travelling with gear.

### Sleeping

Jl Veteran sees extremely heavy traffic and many rooms in the centre of town are very noisy. Most provide detailed maps of Berastagi and the Karo Highlands.

**BUDGET**

**Sibayak Losmen Guesthouse** ( ☎ 91122; dicksonpelawi@yahoo.com; Jl Veteran 119; r with/without bathroom 60,000/40,000Rp; 🖳 🛜 ) Nice cheapies with a lot of Indonesian personality make this place feel more like a homestay. Wi-fi in the lobby.

**Wisma Sunrise View** ( ☎ 92404; Jl Kaliaga; r 50,000-60,000Rp) Here you'll find very basic rooms perched on the little hill that earns Sunrise its namesake view. It's just far enough outside of town to be a convenient stroll.

**Wisma Sibayak** ( ☎ 91104; Jl Udara 1; r with bathroom 80,000-125,000Rp, r without bathroom 50,000-60,000Rp; 🖳 ) Tidy and spacious rooms in the two-storey building have great views. The restaurant has traveller comment books and knowledgeable staff.

**Sibayak Multinational Resthouse** ( ☎ 91031; Jl Pendidikan 93; r 100,000-120,000Rp) A nice quiet option away from the town centre. Multinational has a manicured garden and rooms with hot showers. The hotel is a short *opelet* ride north of town on the road to Gunung Sibayak.

**MIDRANGE & TOP END**

A number of three- and four-star hotels appeal to out-of-towners, but their price tags don't match their standards.

**Brastagi Cottage** ( ☎ 91345; Jl Gundaling; d incl breakfast 450,000-550,000Rp, tr 730,000Rp) Another quiet, out-of-town possibility with a range of stylish rooms. There are great garden views. Discounts of 20% available.

**Hotel Internasional Sibayak** ( ☎ 20152; www.hotelsibayak.com; Jl Merdeka; d incl breakfast 750,000-900,000Rp, cottages 1,000,000Rp, ste 2,000,000-3,000,000Rp; 🖳 ) Wooden floors, generous beds, read-the-newspaper toilets: there's a lot right about the International, except the price. Offers up to 40% discount – if you can eke out one of these, then you'll earn a shiny frugal star.

## Eating & Drinking

The rich volcanic soils of the surrounding countryside supply much of North Sumatra's produce, which passes through Berastagi's colourful **produce and fruit markets**. Passionfruit is a local speciality, as is *marquisa Bandung,* a large, sweet, yellow-skinned fruit. The *marquisa asam manis,* a purple-skinned fruit, makes delicious drinks.

Most of the budget hotels have restaurants, but head into town for more diversity. Along Jl Veteran there's a variety of evening food stalls, as well as simple restaurants specialising in *tionghoa* (Chinese food). Because this is a Christian community, you'll see a lot of *babi* (pork) on the menu. Another local favourite is *pisang goreng* (fried banana).

**Café Raymond** (Jl Trimurti 49; mains 8000-20,000Rp ⊗ 7am-midnight) Berastagi's local bohemians hang out at Café Raymond, which serves fruit juices, beer and Western food.

**Smiley's Café** (Jl Perwira 1; ⊗ 8am-8pm; mains 10,000-23,000Rp) A rickety little cafe serving cheesy lasagne, local dishes and useful tourist advice.

## Getting There & Away

The **bus terminal** (Jl Veteran) is conveniently located near the centre of town. You can also catch buses to Medan (8000Rp, 2½ hours) anywhere along the main street; buses run to and from Padang Bulan in Medan between 6am and 8pm.

To reach Danau Toba without backtracking through Medan, catch an *opelet* to Kabanjahe (3500Rp, 15 minutes) and change to a bus for Pematangsiantar (15,000Rp, three hours), then connect with a Parapat-bound bus (15,000Rp, 1½ hours). It's a little bit of a pain but it gets you there eventually.

Berastagi is the southern approach for visits to Gunung Leuser National Park. To reach the park, catch a bus to Kutacane (50,000Rp, five hours).

## Getting Around

*Opelet* to the surrounding villages leave from the bus terminal. They run every few minutes between Berastagi and Kabanjahe (3500Rp), the major population and transport centre of the highlands. Local *opelet* are most easily waved down from the clock tower in town.

## PARAPAT
☎ 0625

The mainland departure point for Danau Toba, Parapat has everything a transiting tourist needs: transport, lodging and supplies.

The commercial sector of the town is clumped along the Trans-Sumatran Hwy (Jl SM Raja). Branching southwest towards the pier, Jl Pulau Samosir passes most of Parapat's hotels. After 1km, a right fork (Jl Haranggaol) leads to the pier, another kilometre southwest. The bus terminal is 2km east of town, but most buses pick up and drop off passengers at ticket agents along the highway or at the pier.

## Information

There is a string of moneychangers and a wartel along Jl Haranggaol.

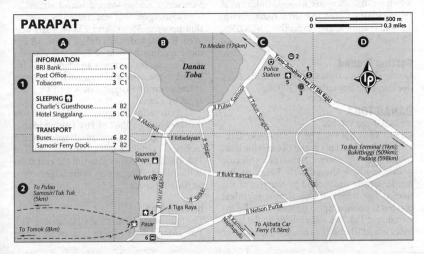

**BRI bank** (Jl SM Raja) Has an ATM.
**Tobacom** (Jl SM Raja 84; per hr 3500Rp; ⏱ 8am-10pm) Internet cafe.
**Post office** (Jl SM Raja)

## Sleeping & Eating

You'll have to crash for the night if your bus gets in after the last boat to Samosir. Here are a few options:

**Charlie's Guesthouse** (☎ 41277; Jl Tiga Raya 7; r 50,000Rp) Beside the ferry dock, Charlie's is cheap and close. It's run by a local Toba music legend.

**Hotel Singgalang** (☎ 41260; Jl SM Raja 52; r without bathroom 80,000Rp) A big Chinese-run place with basic rooms and a downstairs restaurant.

The highway strip (Jl SM Raja) is well equipped to feed the passing traveller, with every variety of Indonesian cuisine.

## Getting There & Away
### BOAT

For details of ferries to Samosir, see p394.

### BUS

The **bus terminal** (Jl SM Raja) is about 2km east of town on the way to Bukittinggi, but is not frequently used (so say the travel agents). Prices are highly negotiable, so shop around at the different ticket agents.

Buses to Medan (22,000Rp, five hours) are frequent, although services taper off in the afternoon. There are also minibuses (70,000Rp) that deliver passengers to Jl SM Raya in Medan. Other destinations include Sibolga (70,000Rp, six hours), Bukittinggi (economy/superexecutive 160,000/200,000Rp, 15 hours) and Padang (executive 220,000Rp, 17 hours).

## Getting Around

*Opelet* shuttle constantly between the ferry dock and the bus terminal (2000Rp).

## DANAU TOBA
☎ 0625 / pop 517, 000

Danau Toba has been part of traveller folklore for decades. This grand ocean-blue lake, found high up among Sumatra's volcanic peaks, is where the amiable Batak people reside, largely untouched by the rest of the world. The secret of this almost mythical place was opened up to travellers by the intrepid, and Tuk Tuk – the village on the lake's inner island – became as much a highlight for

Southeast Asian shoe-stringers as Haad Rin and Kuta. It was almost overrun with tourism: wild full-moon parties would kick off, and travellers in beach-bum mode would get 'stuck' on the island for months on end. Yet the world seems to have forgotten about Toba all over again, and the lazy, low-key lakeside days have returned to the Batak people, who warmly open their arms to the trickle of travellers that come.

Expect a chorus of '*horas*' ('welcome') to greet you at every turn, as the locals quietly strum away the afternoon on their guitars while passing around a flagon of jungle juice – the locals are proud, debaucherous Christians who love a drink.

For European and American missionaries this was once the 'heart of darkness', and the first evangelists met their makers by the tips of spears. Good timing brought survival and fame to a German missionary named Nommenson, whose arrival preceded a bumper crop, which encouraged the Bataks' King Sidabutar to incorporate the Christian faith with the community's animist beliefs.

The resulting blend of traditional culture and imported religion, observable in the Batak countryside, is the reality behind those exotic tales of mannered missionaries and cannibalistic natives.

## Orientation

Danau Toba is the largest lake in Southeast Asia, covering a massive 1707 sq km. In the middle of this huge expanse is Pulau Samosir, a wedge-shaped island almost as big as Singapore that was created by an eruption between 30,000 and 75,000 years ago. Well, Bahasa Indonesia calls it an island, but those visiting the west of Toba will discover that Samosir isn't actually an island at all. It's linked to the mainland by a narrow isthmus at the town of Pangururan – and then cut again by a canal.

Directly facing Parapat is another peninsula occupied by the village of Tuk Tuk, which has Samosir's greatest concentration of tourist facilities. Tomok, a few kilometres south of Tuk Tuk, is the main village on the east coast of the island. Pangururan is the largest town on the west coast.

## Information

The following facilities are all located in Tuk Tuk (Map p391). There is a small police

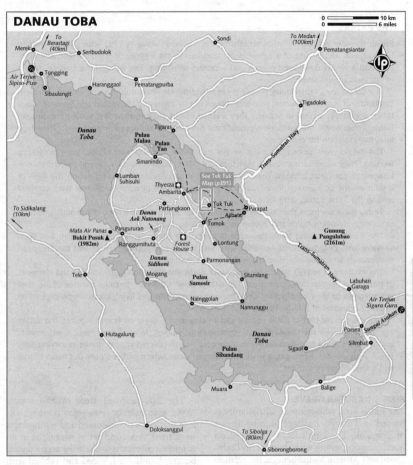

**DANAU TOBA**

SUMATRA

station at the top of the road leading to the Carolina Cottages (p392).

### BOOKSHOPS
Better load up on reading material in Toba, because the rest of Sumatra is a desert for the printed word. **Penny's Bookstore** and **Gokhan Library** have used and rental books, plus DVD hire for rainy days.

### INTERNET ACCESS
Internet access (10,000Rp per hour) is available at many of the guest houses.

### MEDICAL SERVICES
**Health centre** ( ☎ 451075) Small 24-hour place close to the turn-off to Carolina Cottages,

at the southern end of the peninsula. It's equipped to cope with cuts, bruises and other minor problems.

### MONEY
Be sure to change your money before you get to Samosir. Exchange rates at the island's hotels and moneychangers are pretty awful.

### POST
Samosir's only **post office** is in Ambarita, but several shops in Tuk Tuk sell stamps and have postboxes.

## Sights
The following sights and activities are located around Danau Toba (see map above).

## THE BATAKS

British traveller William Marsden astonished the 'civilised' world in 1783 when he returned to London with an account of a cannibalistic kingdom in the interior of Sumatra that, nevertheless, had a highly developed culture and a system of writing. The Bataks have been a subject of fascination ever since.

The Bataks are a Proto-Malay people descended from Neolithic mountain tribes from northern Thailand and Myanmar (Burma) who were driven out by migrating Mongolian and Siamese tribes. When the Bataks arrived in Sumatra they trekked inland, making their first settlements around Danau Toba, where the surrounding mountains provided a natural protective barrier. They lived in virtual isolation for centuries.

The Bataks were among the most warlike peoples in Sumatra, and villages were constantly feuding. They were so mistrustful that they did not build or maintain natural paths between villages, or construct bridges. The practice of ritual cannibalism, involving eating the flesh of a slain enemy or a person found guilty of a serious breach of *adat* (traditional law), survived among the Toba Bataks until 1816.

Today there are more than six million Bataks, divided into six main linguistic groups, and their lands extend 200km north and 300km south of Danau Toba.

The Bataks have long been squeezed between the Islamic strongholds of Aceh and West Sumatra and, despite several Acehnese attempts to conquer and convert, it was the European missionaries who finally quelled the waters with Christianity.

The majority of today's Bataks are Protestant Christians, although many still practise elements of traditional animist belief and ritual. The Bataks believe the banyan to be the tree of life; they tell a legend of their omnipotent god Ompung, who created all living creatures by dislodging decayed branches of a huge banyan into the sea.

Music is a great part of Batak culture and a Batak man is never far from his guitar. The Bataks are also famous for their powerful and emotive hymn singing. Most of their musical instruments are similar to those found elsewhere in Indonesia – cloth-covered copper gongs in varying sizes struck with wooden hammers; a small two-stringed violin, which makes a pure but harsh sound; and a kind of reedy clarinet.

### KING SIDABUTAR GRAVE

The Batak king who adopted Christianity is buried in Tomok, a village 5km southeast of Tuk Tuk. The king's image is carved on his tombstone, along with those of his bodyguard and Anteng Melila Senega, the woman the king is said to have loved for many years without fulfilment. The tomb is also decorated with carvings of *singa*, mythical creatures with grotesque three-horned heads and bulging eyes. Next door in death is the missionary who converted the tribe, the career equivalent of boy-band stardom. Next in the row is an older Batak royal tomb, which is used as a multilingual fertility shrine for childless couples, according to souvenir vendors.

The tombs are 500m up a narrow lane lined with souvenir stalls.

### STONE CHAIRS

More traditional Batak artistry and legend is on view in Ambarita, 5km north of Tanjung Tuk Tuk.

The 300-year-old **stone chairs** (admission 2000Rp; guides 20,000Rp; 🕑 8am-6pm) is where village matters were discussed and wrongdoers were tried. A second set of megaliths in an adjoining courtyard is where the accused were bound, blindfolded, sliced and rubbed with chilli and garlic before being beheaded.

Guides love to play up the story and ask for volunteers to demonstrate the process. It is customary to pay a small fee for the tale, or risk meeting a savoury death (just kidding).

### MUSEUM HUTA BOLON SIMANINDO

At the northern tip of the island, in Simanindo, there's a fine old traditional house that has been restored and now functions as a **museum** (admission 30,000Rp; 🕑 10am-5pm). It was formerly the home of Rajah Simalungun, a Batak king, and his 14 wives. Originally, the roof was decorated with 10 buffalo horns, which represented the 10 generations of the dynasty.

The museum has a small, interesting collection of brass cooking utensils, weapons,

Dutch and Chinese crockery, sculptures and Batak carvings.

Displays of traditional **Batak dancing** are performed at 10.30am from Monday to Saturday if enough tourists show up.

The village of Simanindo is 15km from Tuk Tuk and is accessible with a hired motorbike.

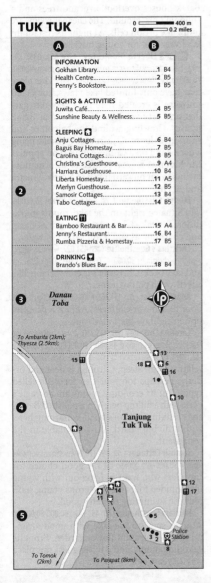

**TUK TUK**

0 ___ 400 m
0 ___ 0.2 miles

**INFORMATION**
Gokhan Library.........................1 B4
Health Centre..........................2 B5
Penny's Bookstore...................3 B5

**SIGHTS & ACTIVITIES**
Juwita Café...............................4 B5
Sunshine Beauty & Wellness......5 B5

**SLEEPING**
Anju Cottages...........................6 B4
Bagus Bay Homestay................7 B5
Carolina Cottages.....................8 B5
Christina's Guesthouse.............9 A4
Harriara Guesthouse...............10 B4
Liberta Homestay...................11 A5
Merlyn Guesthouse.................12 B5
Samosir Cottages....................13 B4
Tabo Cottages........................14 B5

**EATING**
Bamboo Restaurant & Bar.......15 A4
Jenny's Restaurant.................16 B4
Rumba Pizzeria & Homestay....17 B5

**DRINKING**
Brando's Blues Bar..................18 B4

*Danau Toba*

To Ambarita (2km);
Thyesza (2.5km);

*Tanjung Tuk Tuk*

Police Station

To Tomok (2km)
To Parapat (8km)

## SIMANINDO TO PANGURURAN

The road that follows the northern rind of Samosir between Simanindo and the town of Pangururan is a scenic ride through the Bataks' embrace of life and death. In the midst of the fertile rice fields are large multistorey **graves** decorated with the distinctive Batak-style house and a simple white cross. Reminiscent of Thai spirit houses, Batak graves reflect the animist attitudes of sheltering the dead. Cigarettes and cakes are offered to the deceased as memorials or as petitions for favours. Typical Christian holidays, such as Christmas, dictate special attention to the graves.

## Activities

In Tuk Tuk, **Sunshine Beauty & Wellness** (☎ 451 108; ☺ 8am-8pm) will turn beasts into beauties with facials, after-sun treatment and traditional massages (60,000Rp to 80,000Rp).

### CYCLING & MOTORCYCLING

Pulau Samosir's sleepy roads make the island perfect for exploring by motorbike or bicycle. Zipping through the scenic countryside enclosed by lush volcanic mountains and the stunning lake is the highlight of many who visit here. The rice paddies and friendly villages are cultivated around sober Protestant-style churches and tombs merging traditional Batak architecture and Christian crosses.

### SWIMMING

Danau Toba reaches a depth of 450m in places and is refreshingly cool. The best swimming on the south coast is said to be at Carolina Cottages, while many cottages on the north coast maintain weed-free swimming.

Across the isthmus, just before Pangururan, there are some *mata air panas* (hot springs) that the locals are extremely proud of. Most foreigners look around at the litter and decide that the waters are too hot.

### TREKKING

If you don't fully succumb to Samosir's anaesthetising atmosphere, there are a couple of interesting **treks** across the island. The trails aren't well marked and can be difficult to find, but ask at any of the guest houses for a map. In the wet season (December to March) the steep inclines are very muddy and slippery and can be quite dangerous.

SUMATRA

The central highlands of Samosir are about 700m above the lake and on a clear day afford stunning views of mist-cloaked mountains. The top of the escarpment forms a large plateau and at its heart is a small lake, Danau Sidihoni. Samosir's vast tracts of jungle have long since vanished and the only forest you will pass through on either walk is pine, and even this is only in small areas. However, there are many interesting cinnamon, clove and coffee plantations and some beautiful waterfalls.

Most people opt for the short trek from Ambarita to Pangunuran. It can be done in a day if you're fit and in a hurry, though it's best to stay overnight in one of the villages. The path starts opposite the bank in Ambarita. Keep walking straight at the escarpment and take the path to the right of the graveyard. The three-hour climb to the top is hard and steep. The path then leads to Partungkaon village (also called Dolok); here you can stay at **Jenny's Guest House** (r 5000Rp) or **John's Losmen** (☎ 0813 7678 7733; r 5000Rp). From Partungkaon, it's about five hours' walk to Panguraran via Danau Sidihoni.

The road between Tomok and **Forest House 1**, an interior guest house, is now paved and many visitors steer motorbikes up the escarpment to Danau Sidihoni.

Bring along wet-weather gear and some snacks. There are no warung along the way but you should be able to buy cups of coffee or even arrange accommodation at villages en route.

## Courses

The clouds that come steaming in off the surrounding mountains often bring cloudy and rainy days to Toba. A good way to pass a day indoors is by turning your hand to Indonesian and Batak cooking. **Juwita Café** (☎ 451 217) has four-hour cooking classes for 250,000Rp, held in an outdoor kitchen with magnificent views of the lake.

## Festivals & Events

The week-long **Danau Toba Festival** is held every year in mid-June. Canoe races are a highlight of the festival, but there are also Batak cultural performances.

## Sleeping

The best sleeping options are along the north and south coasts, where little guest houses are tucked in between village chores: washing the laundry on the rocks and collecting the news from neighbours.

All of the places listed here are located in Tuk Tuk (Map p391).

**Bagus Bay Homestay** (☎ 451 287; www.bagus-bay.page.tl; r with bathroom 75,000-150,000Rp; r without bathroom 20,000-30,000Rp; 💻) Rooms in traditional Batak houses overlook avocado trees and a children's playground. The cheaper rooms are more like prison cells. At night its restaurant is a lively spot for young travellers.

**our pick Liberta Homestay** (☎ 451 035; liberta_homestay@yahoo.com.co.id; r with bathroom 40,000-70,000Rp, r without bathroom 25,000Rp; 💻) This place may have only limited lake views, but a chill universe is created here by a lazy-day garden and arty versions of traditional Batak houses. Crawling around the balconies and shortened doors of the rooms feels like being a deck hand on a Chinese junk. The popular Mr Moon is a great source of information, including for onward travel to North Sumatra and Aceh.

**Merlyn Guesthouse** (☎ 451057; r 30,000-35,000Rp; 💻) Situated right on the lake; rooms in traditional Batak-style houses here are as cheap and charming as you'll find. Has hot water.

**Christina's Guesthouse** (☎ 451 027; www.xs4all.nl/~wiltheo/christina; r 30,000-45,000Rp, f 80,000Rp) Cheap and laid-back, Christina's is comfortable like a well-worn pair of jeans.

**Anju Cottages** (☎ 451265; r 40,000-50,000Rp) Next door to Samosir Cottages, Anju is a peaceful option right on the waterfront.

**Carolina Cottages** (☎ 415 210; www.carolinacottagelaketoba.blogspot.com; d 48,000-110,000Rp, f 250,000Rp; 💻 🛜) Considered Tuk Tuk's swankiest (a relative term) sleep, Carolina is neat and orderly, perhaps too much so for dishevelled types. But its economy rooms are an eagle's eyrie with a hilltop perch in a polished Batak-style building. There's good swimming here, with a diving board. Wi-fi available in the restaurant.

**Samosir Cottages** (☎ 451 170; www.samosircottages.com; r 50,000-375,000Rp; 💻) A good choice for travellers who want to hang out with young like-minded folk and boisterous young staff, plus the swimming is pretty good.

**Harriara Guesthouse** (☎ 451 183; r 60,000-80,000Rp) A great spot on the lake with good swimming and a pleasant flower garden. From its sparkling rooms, you'd never guess this place was 22 years old.

**PUPPET MASTERS**

A purely Batak tradition is the *sigalegale* puppet dance, once performed at funerals but now more often a part of wedding ceremonies. The life-sized puppet, carved from the wood of a banyan tree, is dressed in the traditional costume of red turban, loose shirt and blue sarong. The *sigalegale* stand up on long, wooden boxes where the operator makes them dance to gamelan (percussion orchestra) music accompanied by flute and drums.

One story of the origin of the *sigalegale* puppet concerns a widow who lived on Samosir. Bereft and lonely after the death of her husband, she made a wooden image of him and whenever she felt lonely hired a *dalang* (puppeteer-storyteller) to make the puppet dance and a *dukun* (mystic) to communicate with the soul of her husband.

Whatever its origins, the *sigalegale* soon became part of Batak culture and were used at funeral ceremonies to revive the souls of the dead and to communicate with them. Personal possessions of the deceased were used to decorate the puppet, and the *dukun* would invite the deceased's soul to enter the wooden puppet as it danced on top of the grave.

**Thyesza** ( ☎ 700 0443; www.flowerofsamosir.com; r 60,000Rp, r with hot water & breakfast 150,000Rp) Located out of town just past Ambarita, Thyesza is a great choice for those wanting some added peace and quiet away from Tuk Tuk's backpacker scene. Rooms are immaculate, and there's an option to stay in a Batak house. Offers free transport from Tuk Tuk on arrival.

**Tabo Cottages** ( ☎ 451 318; www.tabocottages.com; r incl breakfast 60,000-285,000Rp; ste 350,000-650,000Rp; 🖳 🛜 ) The professionals' choice, Tabo Cottages has a resort feel with modern rooms set in a beautiful garden. Lots of expats from Jakarta and Aceh bring the family here for a weekend getaway. Has a popular vegetarian restaurant and German bakery, and wi-fi in the lobby.

## Eating

The guest houses tend to mix eating and entertainment in the evening. Most restaurants serve the Batak speciality of barbecued carp (most from fish farms), sometimes accompanied by traditional dance performances.

The following restaurants are all located in Tuk Tuk (Map p391).

**our pick** **Jenny's Restaurant** (mains 20,000-45,000Rp) One of the busiest places on the island and with good reason. The smoky grilled fish fresh from the lake is simply the best in town. The fruit pancake is also highly recommended.

**Bamboo Restaurant & Bar** (mains 20,000-50,000Rp) With incredible lake views, Bamboo is a stylish place to watch the sun slink away, with cosy cushion seating, a down-tempo mood and a reliable menu. Does good cocktails, too.

**Rumba Pizzeria & Homestay** (mains 20,000-70,000Rp) On Saturday Rumba's will stay open late to show English Premiership football, served with delicious pizza where you pick your own ingredients. Also has magic mushrooms (legal in Danau Toba) on its menu.

## Drinking

**Brando's Blues Bar** ( ☎ 451084) There is a handful of foreigner-oriented bars, such as this one in between the local jungle-juice cafes. Happy hour is until 10pm.

## Entertainment

On most nights, music and spirits fill the night air with the kind of camaraderie that only grows in small villages. The Toba Bataks are extremely musical and passionate choruses erupt from invisible corners.

Today the parties are all local – celebrating a wedding, a new addition on a house or the return of a Toba expat. Invitations are gladly given and should be cordially accepted.

Bagus Bay and Samosir Cottages (see opposite) both have traditional Batak music and dance performances on Wednesday and Saturday evenings at 8.15pm.

## Shopping

Samosir's souvenir shops carry a huge range of cheap and tacky cotton T-shirts. For something slightly more original, local Gayo embroidery is made into a range of bags, cushion covers and place mats.

Around Tuk Tuk there are numerous woodcarvers selling a variety of figures, masks, boxes and *porhalaan* (traditional Batak calendars), as well as some traditional musical instruments.

## Getting There & Away
### BOAT
Ferries between Parapat and Tuk Tuk (7000Rp) operate about every hour from 8.30am to 6pm. Ferries stop at Bagus Bay (35 minutes); other stops are by request. The first and last ferries from Tuk Tuk leave at about 7am and 4pm, respectively; check exact times with your hotel. When leaving for Parapat, stand on your hotel jetty and wave a ferry down.

Five ferries a day shuttle vehicles and people between Ajibata, just south of Parapat, and Tomok. There are five departures per day between 7am and 9pm. The passenger fare is 4000Rp. Cars cost 75,000Rp, and places can be booked in advance at the **Ajibata office** ( ☎ 41194) or the **Tomok office** ( ☎ 451185).

### BUS
See Parapat (p388), the mainland transit point, for information on bus travel to/from Danau Toba.

On Samosir, to get to Berastagi you'll have to catch a bus from Tomok to Pangururan (12,000Rp, 45 minutes), from where you take another bus to Berastagi (27,000Rp, three hours). This bus goes via Sidikalang, which is also a transfer point to Kutacane and Tapaktuan (on the west coast).

## Getting Around
Local buses serve the whole of Samosir except Tuk Tuk, which is an inconvenience for those wanting to explore the island, although the peaceful, well-maintained roads are perfect for travelling by motorbike or bicycle. You can rent motorcycles in Tuk Tuk for 75,000Rp a day, which includes petrol and a helmet. Bicycle hire costs from 25,000Rp per day.

Minibuses run between Tomok and Ambarita (3000Rp), continuing to Simanindo (6000Rp) and Pangururan (12,000Rp). The road through the neck of the peninsula is a good spot to flag down these minibuses. Services dry up after 5pm.

## SIBOLGA
☎ 0631 / pop 90,000
The departure point for boats to Nias, Sibolga is a west-coast port town renowned for its touts. As tourist numbers decline, the hassles have diminished to a fish boil of touts when you step off the bus or boat.

Most boats like to get in and out of Sibolga as soon as possible, so it's best to arrive as early in the day as possible to ensure a place on a boat departing that day.

## Information
**BNI bank** (Jl Katamso) It is advisable to change money here or to use the ATM, as options on Nias are limited.
**Post office** (Jl Tobing; ⏲ 8am-6pm) Internet access available (per hr 5000Rp).
**Telkom wartel** (Jl A Yani 35) International phone calls can be made from here.

## Dangers & Annoyances
Dragging around surf gear can invite inflated prices: either be willing to bargain hard or accept a degree of extra 'service'.

A more serious scam involves being detained on suspicion of carrying drugs. Some travellers have reported being searched and intimidated by groups of uniformed officials demanding exorbitant bribes before releasing travellers.

Don't leave your bags unattended or with a 'helpful' guide.

## Sights
**Pantai Pandan** is a popular white-sand beach at the village of Pandan, 11km north of Sibolga. A few hundred metres further on is **Pantai Kalangan** (admission 2000Rp). Both beaches get very crowded at weekends, but are good places to pass the time while you're waiting to catch a boat from Sibolga. *Opelet* run to the beaches all day (3000Rp).

## Sleeping & Eating
If you get stuck overnight in Sibolga, try the following:
**Hotel Pasar Baru** ( ☎ 22167; cnr Jl Imam Bonjol & Raja Junjungan; d with fan 100,000Rp; d with air-con 180,000-250,000Rp; ✷ ) A decent enough place to sleep in a pinch.
**Hotel Wisata Indah** ( ☎ 23688; Jl Katamso 51; r incl breakfast from 350,000Rp; ✷ ▣ ) The only upmarket hotel in town, Wisata Indah has a pool, comfortable rooms and sea views. Nonguests can use the pool and showers for a day-use fee.

There are plenty of Padang restaurants and coffee shops directly across the street from the harbour.

## Getting There & Away
### BOAT
Ferries to Nias leave from the harbour at the end of Jl Horas. There are two port options for

Nias: the capital city of Gunung Sitoli, which is at the north of the island and a three-hour bus ride from the surf break; or Teluk Dalam, which is in the south and a 15-minute ride away.

Boats to Teluk Dalam are the obvious choice but they don't run every day. **PT Simeulue** ( ☎ 21497; Jl Sultan Bustani) runs a ferry to Teluk Dalam (11 hours).

If you arrive in Sibolga between Monday and Saturday, catch a Gunung Sitoli–bound boat (economy/air-con/cabin 69,000/103,000/155,000Rp, eight to 10 hours), which departs at 8pm every day but Sunday. **ASDP** ( ☎ 21752), in front of the harbour, runs a modern passenger- and car-ferry. The air-con class is the best value: seats recline, the room is fairly cool and generally quiet.

Ferries generally leave one to two hours late. If you arrive in Sibolga and are told you have just missed the boat it is often worth going to the harbour yourself to verify this.

Theoretically you don't have to pay extra to carry surfboards on either service but this is not always the case.

### BUS
Sibolga is a bit of a backwater as far as bus services are concerned, and the route is windy and inordinately slow. The bus terminal is on Jl SM Raja, 2km from the harbour. You can ask the bus driver to drop you off at the harbour. A becak between the two should be 5000Rp.

There are frequent departures for Bukittinggi (90,000Rp, 12 hours), Padang (125,000Rp, 14 hours), Medan (85,000Rp, 11 hours) and Parapat (60,000Rp, six hours).

There are also minivan services that shuttle folks between Sibolga and Medan (95,000Rp) – prices are highly negotiable.

# PULAU NIAS

The Indian Ocean roars onto Indonesia, arriving in one of the world's most spectacular surf breaks here on lonely Nias: a sizeable but solitary rock off the northern Sumatran coast. Surfers have been coming here for decades for the wave on superb Sorake Bay, which has deservedly kept this far-flung island on the international surfing circuit. The ancient megalithic monuments and traditional architecture will satisfy the hunger of any culture vulture.

At any one time, no more than a gaggle of surfers can be found paddling offshore, where, famously, you can while away the wait for your set ogling the sea turtles that dance and spin under the crystal-clear water below.

The locals have a reputation for being somewhat unfriendly. Apparently, the surfers back in the '70s weren't that respectful and there's been a surfer/local divide ever since. Grossly exaggerated tales of rip-offs and macho tussles don't help the reputation of either side, especially when the reality is that most folk get along just fine. But, as always, there are exceptions.

The tragic 2004 tsunami and the following aftershock, four months later, resulted in the deaths of over 600 people and the flattening of the capital city. The recovery program here hasn't been anywhere near as rapid as in Aceh; the local frustration is evident and sometimes gets taken out on tourists. Patience and understanding are absolute requirements for all on Nias.

### History
Local legend tells it that Niassans are the descendants of six gods who came to earth and settled in the central highlands. Anthropologists link them to just about everyone: the Bataks of Sumatra, the Naga of Assam in India, the aborigines of Taiwan and various Dayak groups in Kalimantan.

Nias history is the stuff of campfire tales in which locals practised headhunting and human sacrifice long after the rest of the world started fainting at the sight of blood.

Traditionally, Niassan villages were presided over by a village chief, who headed a council of elders. Beneath the aristocratic upper caste were the common people, and below them the slaves, who were often traded. Until the first years of the 19th century, Nias' only connection with the outside world was through the slave trade.

Sometimes villages would band together to form federations, which often fought each other. Prior to the Dutch conquest and the arrival of missionaries, intervillage warfare was fast and furious, spurred on by the desire for revenge, slaves or human heads. Heads were needed for stately burials, wedding dowries and the construction of new villages.

When the people weren't warring, they were farming, a tradition that continues

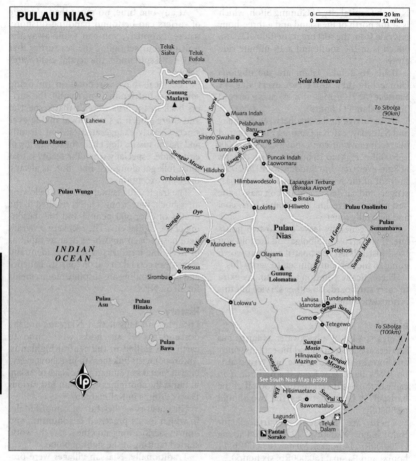

## PULAU NIAS

today. They cultivated yams, rice, maize and taro, despite the thick jungle, and raised pigs as a source of food and a symbol of wealth and prestige; the more pigs you had, the higher your status in the village. Gold and copper work, as well as woodcarving, were important industries.

The indigenous religion was thought to have been a combination of animism and ancestor worship, with some Hindu influences. Today the dominant religions on Nias are Christianity and Islam, overlaid with traditional beliefs.

The island did not come under full Dutch control until 1914. Today's population of about 639,000 is spread through more than 650 villages, most inaccessible by road.

## Orientation & Information

For a place known to the outside world, Nias is surprisingly underdeveloped and the earthquake undid any minor steps forward. Don't expect rapid transport across the island, internet connection or reliable mobile-phone coverage.

Gunung Sitoli, the island's biggest town, and Binaka, the only airport, are both in the north. The famous surf break is in the south at Pantai Sorake, accessible via the port town of Teluk Dalam. Some might refer to the surfing area as Teluk Lagundri, which is the bay that the waves barrel into.

Gunung Sitoli has two working ATMs, and there is one moneychanger in Teluk Dalam.

## Dangers & Annoyances

Chloroquine-resistant malaria has been reported on Nias, so be sure to take appropriate precautions.

## Getting There & Away

### AIR

**Merpati** ( ☎ 061-736 6888; www.merpati.co.id/en) has daily flights from Medan to Binaka airport, 17km south of Gunung Sitoli. Surfboards cost an extra 30,000Rp.

### BOAT

There are boats every night except Sunday from Gunung Sitoli to Sibolga. In theory, all services leave at 8pm, but in practice they seldom set sail before 10pm. Ticket prices are 69,000/103,000/155,000Rp for economy/air-con/cabin. **ASDP** (fax 0639-21554; Jl Yos Sudarso) has an office at the harbour in Gunung Sitoli.

Boats to Sibolga also leave from Teluk Dalam every Monday, Wednesday and Friday. Boat tickets to Sibolga can be bought at **PT Simeulue** ( ☎ 081 216 7033; Jl Saunigaho). Tickets cost 80,000/100,000Rp for economy/cabin class. **Pelni** ( ☎ 0639-21846; Jl Chengkeh) has as an irregular monthly boat to and from Padang.

## Getting Around

Getting around Nias can be slow. In Gunung Sitoli, the bus terminal is 1.5km south of the centre of town; an *opelet* from the pier costs 2000Rp.

From Gunung Sitoli, there are minibuses to the southern market town of Teluk Dalam (60,000Rp, three hours), which has transport to Lagundri, 13km away. You can also arrange transport directly to Sorake (75,000Rp). You will probably be charged extra to take a surfboard but always whittle down the initial quote as low as a smile can get. Services dry up in the afternoon, so aim to leave before noon.

To get to Sorake or Lagundri from Teluk Dalam, catch a local bus from the town centre (5000Rp). Losmen will also hunt the town looking for new arrivals and usually charge 10,000Rp for motorbike transfer.

## GUNUNG SITOLI
☎ 0639

Gunung Sitoli, on the northeastern coast of Nias, is the island's main town. It was badly damaged by the 28 March 2005 earthquake and reconstruction only really got underway in the last couple of years, at a pace that's agonisingly slow for the locals.

## Orientation & Information

The port is about 2km north of the centre of town, and the bus terminal is about 1.5km south, beyond the bridge. Businesses are clustered around the parade ground in the centre of town.

**Bank Sumut** (Jl Hatta) MasterCard-accessible ATM.
**BRI bank** ( ☎ 21946; Jl Imam Bonjol; ☯ 8am-4pm Mon-Fri) ATM available.
**Post office** (cnr Jl Gomo & Hatta) Opposite the parade ground.
**Public hospital** ( ☎ 21271; Jl Cipto M Kusomo) For dealing with minor emergencies.

## Sights

**Museum Pusaka Nias** ( ☎ 21920; Jl Yos Sudarso 134A; admission 2000Rp; ☯ 8am-noon & 1-5pm Tue-Sat, 2-5pm Sun) has a good collection of woodcarvings, stone sculptures and ceremonial objects. The garden has an interesting display of local plants and herbs and some models of traditional Niassan architecture.

If you're curious about viewing more examples of Nias' cultural heritage, see p400.

## Sleeping & Eating

Accommodation options in Gunung Sitoli have not been rebuilt since the earthquake. If you need to stay on the north coast to catch a departing flight, try these options outside the town centre.

**Wisma Soliga** ( ☎ 21815; d with fan/air-con from 50,000/100,000Rp; ☒ ) Located 4km south of town, this is a friendly, well-managed place with clean and spacious rooms.

**Miga Beach Bungalows** ( ☎ 21460; d incl breakfast 200,000-300,000Rp; ☒ ) About 1.5km out of town, Miga sits right on a small beach with comfortable rooms.

**Harmony Cottages** ( ☎ 22157; r incl breakfast 450,000Rp; ☒ ) Near Miga, a lovely jungle-clad, family-run place with simple but clean rooms.

To get to these hotels, catch an *angkot* from the bus terminal (2000Rp). A becak will cost about 15,000Rp. These hotels are 14km from the airport and can arrange transport for 30,000Rp per person.

There are lots of small **restaurants** along the main streets in Gunung Sitoli. **Bintang Terang** (Jl Sirao 10; mains 10,000Rp) has good seafood fried noodles.

**SUMATRA**

SUMATRA

---

**EARTH SHAKER**

Hardly at the centre of international events, remote Sumatra isn't exactly renowned for its influence on the rest of the world. That is, until you tally up all the times that violent natural disasters on the island have literally shaken the planet.

Take for instance the 1883 eruption of Krakatau, 40km off the southern Sumatra coast. This volcanic explosion was equivalent to that from 200 megatonnes of TNT, more powerful than the A-bomb dropped on Hiroshima. So much ash was hurled into the atmosphere that the sky was darkened for days and global temperatures were reduced by an average of 1.2 degrees Celsius for several years.

It is said that the blast that created Danau Toba some 100,000 years ago – before scientists were around to measure such rumblings – would have made Krakatau look like an after-dinner belch.

Then there was the 2004 Boxing Day earthquake, the world's second-largest recorded earthquake (magnitude 9.3). The resulting tsunami hit more than a dozen countries around the Indian Ocean, leaving more than 300,000 people dead or missing and millions displaced. The force of the event is said to have caused the earth to wobble on its axis and shifted surrounding landmasses southwest by up to 36m.

Few landmasses can claim to have literally moved the planet in the same way as Sumatra.

---

## TELUK DALAM
☎ 0631

This squat little port town is as loud and chaotic as much larger cities. You'll need to pass through Teluk Dalam for transit connections to the beach or to pick up provisions.

The **post office** (Jl Ahmad Yani) and **Telkom wartel** (Jl Ahmad Yani) are both near the harbour. There are lots of Indonesian banks, but none exchanges foreign currency. A **moneychanger** is situated across the street from the BRI bank.

## PANTAI SORAKE & TELUK LAGUNDRI
☎ 0630

A fish-hook piece of land creates the perfect horseshoe bay of Lagundri and the surf break at Sorake, which is said to be the best right-hander in the world. The main surfing season is June to October, and in July and August waves can be more than 4m high. Folks refer to this area interchangeably as Sorake or Lagundri.

The Boxing Day tsunami destroyed many of the family-run guest houses and restaurants on the beach. The businesses that could afford to rebuild are all located on Pantai Sorake, which is considered to be more protected from future disasters.

### Dangers & Annoyances
Times are tough here – not that hardship is an annoyance, but it creates disparity between a tourist's expectations for a holiday and the

locals' economic concerns. Many generous people who have a relationship with Nias have sponsored the rebuilding of local houses and bungalows destroyed by the tsunami, ostensibly in exchange for free accommodation, but more importantly as true grassroots giving. By circumventing aid organisations, many people can see tangible results from their disaster donations. The downside is that some locals view every new arrival here as a possible donor and the sales pitch can come from your losmen or from a stranger you meet on the beach, blurring the line between charity and con game. Unless you have a relationship with a family, it is not advisable to expect that your donation will be spent as promised. Be wary about donating to people you do not know, as the money may not be spent as promised.

Renting surf gear on the island is still a source of unexpected headaches. Be sure you pay a fair price; if it is too cheap, you'll probably pay for it at the end with inflated damage costs.

### Activities
#### SURFING
Surfing is to Nias what honeymooning is to the Maldives. It's the island's tourism raison d'être. Sorake's famous right consistently unrolls between June and October. Access to the wave is a quick paddle from the Keyhole, a break in the coral reef that lies between the beach and the bay.

The March 2005 earthquake lifted the Sorake reef up by about 1m, a shift that some say has improved the wave.

Folks also claim that the off-season waves are good for beginners, a term frequently misinterpreted by nonsurfers. If you've never surfed before, you're better off learning on a break with a sandy beach in a less-remote place.

Most surfers arrive with their own gear, but you can rent equipment from **Key Hole Surf Camp**, in front of the Keyhole.

There are also other breaks within the bay under certain conditions and a few rides elsewhere on the island.

### SWIMMING

A wide sandy beach starts just north of JJ Losmen (p400) and rounds the horseshoe bay all the way to the southeastern tip. A rind of dead coral separates Pantai Sorake from the water and swimming areas.

## Sleeping & Eating

The western part of the bay, known as Pantai Sorake, is the primary location for lodging since the tsunami destroyed much of the infrastructure elsewhere on the bay. Most surfers stay on the northern end so that they can watch the waves. Accommodation is in basic beach bungalows run by local families and usually costs between 25,000Rp and 80,000Rp.

It is expected that you eat your meals, especially dinner, at your losmen, and enquiries of where you've eaten can range from curiosity to accusation. In general, the more expensive the lodging, the less likely your hosts will care where you spend your money. Food is quite expensive on the island, with dinner prices averaging between 35,000Rp to 50,000Rp for a plate of fish or chicken.

The following guest houses run south to north:

**Morris Losmen** and **Eddy's Losmen** are next door to one another, a few minutes' walk from the waves. **Lisa's**, **Lili's** and **Peeruba Losmen** are clumped together on a sunny patch of sand just on the edge of the action.

**Key Hole Surf Camp** (from 90,000Rp), right in the thick of things, charges a little more, giving you the freedom to eat where you please. Next in line is **Toho Surf**, which has nice beachfront

SUMATRA

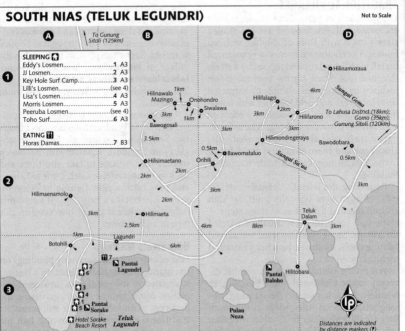

**SOUTH NIAS (TELUK LEGUNDRI)**                              Not to Scale

SLEEPING 🏠
Eddy's Losmen........................1 A3
JJ Losmen.............................2 A3
Key Hole Surf Camp...................3 A3
Lilli's Losmen........................(see 4)
Lisa's Losmen.........................4 A3
Morris Losmen.........................5 A3
Peeruba Losmen.......................(see 4)
Toho Surf.............................6 A3

EATING 🍴
Horas Damas...........................7 B3

---

**OFFSHORE SURFING**

Popular surfing destinations off Nias include the islands of Asu, Bawa and Hinako. More exposed than Nias itself, the islands see bigger and more-consistent waves. With a left-hander at Asu and a strong right-hander at Bawa, good surf is almost guaranteed regardless of wind direction.

The risk of malaria is high on these islands, particularly Bawa, which has a large swamp in its interior. Visitors should take proper precautions.

Sirombu on Nias' west coast is the jumping-off point for the islands. Ask around to see if any public buses will be heading there; otherwise you can charter transport for about 500,000Rp.

From Sirombu there are cargo boats (80,000Rp). You can also charter boats (500,000Rp, maximum of 10 people) from local fishermen at Teluk Dalam and save yourself the hassle of getting to Sirombu.

Bawa has several simple losmen (70,000Rp per night), including one run by an Indonesian named German. Bring your own food.

Surfers on Nias are saying that the earthquake adversely affected the waves on Asu. Now the ride is good only if the swell is high. Tours can be organised through **Sumatran Surfariis** (www.sumatransurfariis.com).

Pulau Tello, further south towards the Mentawai Islands, is another destination that can be reached by charter boat.

---

balconies. **JJ Losmen**, the last in the row, has freshly varnished wooden rooms.

The only development on this side of the bay is **Horas Damas**, an open-air restaurant with a view of the deep blue.

## TRADITIONAL VILLAGES

For hundreds of years, Nias residents built elaborate villages around cobble-stoned streets lined with rows of shiplike wooden houses. The traditional homes were balanced on tall wooden pylons and topped by a steep, thatched roof. Some say the boat motif was inspired by Dutch spice ships. Constructed from local teak and held together with hand-hewn wooden pegs, the houses are adorned with symbolic wooden carvings. The technology of traditional architecture proved quite absorbent and these structures fared better in the 2005 earthquake than modern concrete buildings.

Reflecting the island's defensive strategies, villages were typically built on high ground reached by dozens of stone steps. A stone wall for protection usually encircled the village. Stone was also used for carved bathing pools, staircases, benches, chairs and memorials.

Within the island there is geographic diversity in the traditional house building. In northern Nias, homes are freestanding, oblong structures on stilts, while in the south they are built shoulder to shoulder on either side of a long, paved courtyard. Emphasising the roof as the primary feature, southern Niassan houses are constructed using pylons and cross-beams slotted together without the use of bindings or nails.

### Gomo & Around

The villages around Gomo, in the central highlands, contain some of the island's best examples of stone carvings and *menhirs* (single standing stones), some thought to be 3000 years old. Such examples can be found in the village of **Tundrumbaho**, 5km from Gomo, **Lahusa Idanotae**, halfway between Gomo and Tundrumbaho, and at **Tetegewo**, 7km south of Gomo.

Unfortunately, Gomo is virtually inaccessible. Getting to Tundrumbaho involves a tough two-hour uphill slog through the steamy jungle. From Lagundri, negotiate with the losmen owners for someone to take you there and back by motorcycle, or catch a bus to Lahusa and then hitch a ride. Getting to Tetegewo is possible, but it's a long trip – it's probably only worthwhile if you're interested in this type of architecture.

### Hilinawalo Mazingo

One of only five such surviving buildings on the island, the **Omo Hada** (Chieftain's House) is situated in the prestigious 'upstream' direction of the remote village, garnering the first rays of morning light. It still serves its traditional purpose as a meeting hall for seven neighbouring villages and is currently undergoing restoration work by a local conservation group, North Sumatra Heritage, with funding from World Monuments Fund and corporate sponsors. In order to repair damages from age and climate, villagers have been trained in traditional carpentry skills, in turn preserving crafts that were nearing extinction.

The area is known as Eri Mazino and is 18km from Lagundri between Teluk Dalam and Lahusa district. You can take a public bus to Simpang Oge and then hire an *ojek* (motorcycle that takes passengers) from there or arrange transport directly from Lagundri. The last 8km of the trip is arduous due to poor road conditions.

### Bawomataluo

This is the most famous, and the most accessible, of the southern villages. It is also the setting for *lompat batu* (stone jumping), featured on Indonesia's 1000Rp note.

Bawomataluo (Sun Hill) is perched on a hill about 400m above sea level. The final approach is up 88 steep stone steps. Houses are arranged along two main stone-paved avenues that meet opposite the impressive **chief's house**, which is thought to be both the oldest and largest on Nias. Outside are stone tables where dead bodies were once left to decay.

Although Bawomataluo is worth exploring, tourism is in full swing here, with lots of eager knick-knack sellers.

There are also cultural displays of **war dances**, traditionally performed by young, single males, and **stone jumping**. The latter was once a form of war training; the jumpers had to leap over a 1.8m-high stone wall traditionally topped with pointed sticks. These days the sticks are left off – and the motivation is financial.

From Bawomataluo, you can see the rooftops of nearby **Orihili**. A stone staircase and a trail lead downhill to the village.

Bawomataluo is 15km from Teluk Dalam and is accessible by public bus (5000Rp).

### Hilisimaetano

There are more than 100 **traditional houses** in this large village, 16km northwest of Teluk Dalam. **Stone jumping** and **traditional dancing** are performed here during special events. Hilisimaetano can be reached by public transport from Teluk Dalam (5000Rp).

### Botohili & Hilimaeta

**Botohili** is a small village on the hillside above the peninsula of Pantai Lagundri. It has two rows of **traditional houses**, with a number of new houses breaking up the skyline. The remains of the original entrance, **stone chairs** and paving can still be seen.

**Hilimaeta** is similar to Botohili and is also within easy walking distance of Lagundri. The *lompat batu* pylon can still be seen here and there are a number of **stone monuments**, including a 2m-high stone penis. A long pathway of stone steps leads uphill to the village.

# ACEH

Over the years, this far-flung corner of the Indonesian archipelago has grabbed headlines for all the wrong reasons. Earthquakes, tsunamis, civil war and sharia law are the main associations people have with Sumatra's most northern state. The reconstruction from the Boxing Day tsunami that put this place on television screens around the world is near completion. However, the social wounds incurred by the natural disaster and previous civil war will take much longer to heal. Post-tsunami Aceh is still tender, guns have been laid down (for now), a degree of autonomy has been granted and there is now an air of new beginnings across the province.

For the visitor, politics and disasters are somewhat of a smokescreen. Intrepid travellers to the region are unearthing one of the few remaining undiscovered gems of Southeast

---

**TRAVELLING TO ACEH**

No special permit or permission is required to visit Aceh province. At one time foreign visitors were limited but since the 2004 tsunami these restrictions have been eased at the entry points to Aceh. Confusion does arise if you enquire with Indonesian embassies or outside of the island of Sumatra, as the Indonesian government has not yet disseminated an official decision on the matter. At the time of research a visa on arrival (VOA) at Banda Aceh airport was still not possible, though it was said to be very likely in the near future.

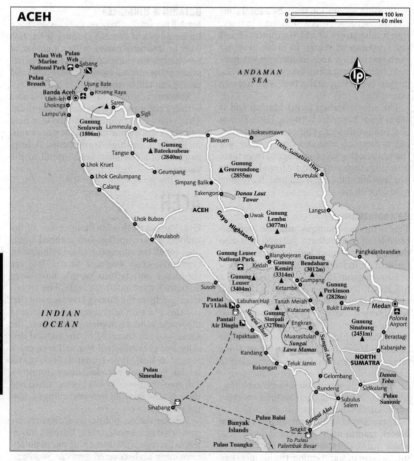

Asia. Rich, animal-filled jungle, misty coffee plantations and endless swaths of empty beach lick the coastline, not to mention the rainbow of pristine coral beneath the sea. The tourist infrastructure isn't great, with bungalows and guest houses making it up as they go along, for the most part. Western comforts aren't exactly the norm. But this is *the* 'I was there before it was discovered' destination of the moment, and a few sacrificed luxuries are the pay-off.

Through all of the disagreements and turmoil from recent events here, the locals have largely ignored the goldmine of tourism on which the state stands, and very little is being done to encourage tourists to come…leaving it ripe and ready for unbridled discovery.

## History

In the days of sailing ships, Aceh competed with Melaka on the Malay Peninsula for control of the important spice-trade route. Aceh was also Islam's entry to the archipelago. The capital, Banda Aceh, was an important centre of Islamic learning and a gateway for Muslims making the pilgrimage to Mecca.

The influx of traders and immigrants and the province's strategic position contributed to Aceh's wealth and importance. The main exports were pepper and gold; others included ivory, tin, tortoiseshell, camphor, aloe wood, sandalwood and spices. Though Aceh's power began to decline towards the end of the 17th century, the province remained independent of the Dutch until war was declared in 1871. It was 35 years before the fighting stopped and the last of the sultans, Tuanku Muhamat Dawot, surrendered.

In 1951 the Indonesian government incorporated Aceh's territory into the province of North Sumatra. The prominent Islamic Party was angered at being lumped together with the Christian Bataks, and proclaimed Aceh an independent Islamic Republic in September 1953. Prolonged conflict ensued, and in 1959 the government was forced to give Aceh 'special district' status, granting a high degree of autonomy in religious, cultural and educational matters. Despite this special status the government strengthened its grip on Aceh's huge natural-gas reserves.

In December 1976 Gerakan Aceh Merdeka (GAM; Free Aceh Movement) was formed and began fighting for independence. Fighting was limited in the early years of the struggle, but by 1989 GAM had gathered strength and launched a renewed attack on the Indonesian government.

---

### SHARIA LAW

Aceh considers itself the home and origin of Islam in Southeast Asia, with Islamic roots dating as far back as the 13th century. It prides itself on being the most strictly Islamic state in Indonesia. Since it was granted 'special autonomy' in 2002, Aceh has the power to apply sharia law to Islamic people, which contrasts with the traditionally moderate and secular attitude of the rest of Indonesia. A bill was passed on 14 September 2009, making sharia law official in Aceh. The most controversial amendment was the introduction of capital punishment for committing adultery, as well as a law prohibiting homosexuality. It's important to be informed and understand as much as possible about the local custom and laws that are exclusive to this unique state.

The main laws include:

- Muslims (male and female) must wear clothing in line with Islamic teaching
- the consumption, production and sale of alcohol is prohibited
- gambling is prohibited
- *khalwat* (proximity, where intimate contact is possible, between a male and female who have no marriage or kin relationship) is prohibited
- wealthy Muslims must pay *Zakat* (alms for the poor) to the Islamic treasury
- unmarried couples committing adultery can be sentenced to 100 lashings
- married people committing adultery can be sentenced to death by stoning
- homosexuality is prohibited.

So what does this mean for you? As far as Westerners are concerned the law is somewhat unclear, and it is generally up to the interpretation of the sharia police. Initially, Westerners and non-Muslims had been excused from observing most of the laws, but since 2006 the laws have become more applicable to everyone, especially if a Westerner is obstructing a Muslim from observing a law. For example, there have been instances of Western men being arrested for socialising with Muslim women (on a positive note, this means that this is one of the few parts of Southeast Asia where sleazy expats are nonexistent). Generally, Westerners are left to get on with it and tourist and aid-worker hang-outs tend to serve beer without recriminations, but technically it's still illegal and comes with the punishment of 40 lashes.

Under Acehnese law, punishments vary from a small fine to four-year sentences or even the death penalty, depending on the crime. Public (sometimes televised) canings attended by thousands of onlookers have drawn criticism from across the nation and within Aceh itself, as people fear that law makers are veering towards a more extreme state. Many of the objections from within Aceh come from women, some of whom claim that the manner in which the laws and punishments are enacted by the sharia police is sexist and unjust. However, international accusations that Aceh is a 'mini-Taliban' state are also gross exaggerations of the truth. Basically as long as visitors to the region act in a respectful fashion, you'll have no problems whatsoever.

By 1990 the area had been designated a 'special combat zone' and eight years of near-military rule followed. Amnesty International has reported years of human rights abuses perpetrated during this time. In the following years the army launched further attacks, while GAM intimidated whole villages into giving support to the rebel forces. Deaths, tortures, disappearances and arbitrary arrests occurred on a daily basis, with each side blaming the other. The ordinary people of Aceh were the real losers: tens of thousands of them were displaced and living in fear of both sides.

At the turn of the millennium, several steps towards peace were made: a brief ceasefire was declared in 2000, and in 2002 Jakarta granted a 'special autonomy' law allowing the province to keep up to 70% of oil and gas revenues and, controversially, implement sharia law. Peace talks were also initiated for the first time since the conflict began, and progressed for a year and a half before crumbling. For two years afterwards, all of the progress toward normality was quickly reversed. Martial law was declared in 2003, paving the way for a full-scale military assault on the separatists – the biggest military operation in Indonesia since the 1975 invasion of East Timor.

The 2004 tsunami provided the necessary counterpoint to open up the sealed province to relief organisations and to renew peace talks between Jakarta and the rebels. On 15 August 2005, a peace accord was signed in Helsinki and many of the important steps of the agreement have been met: GAM rebels successfully surrendered their weapons and the Indonesian troops have withdrawn from the province. Although optimism for a stable Aceh is tangible, some fear that the biggest obstacle to a lasting peace is steering the former GAM rebels into lives as productive citizens rather than low-level criminals. It remains very much a 'watch this space' region.



## BANDA ACEH

**☎ 0651 / pop 210,000**

Indonesian cities are rarely coupled with pleasant descriptions, but Banda Aceh breaks the mould. The sleepy provincial capital is an extremely pleasant spot to spend a few days. The village-like atmosphere and dusty, unobtrusive streets make for laid-back, easily explored town filled with cheery faces. The proud folk rarely betray the tragedy that they must have experienced during the Boxing Day tsunami; looking at the reconstructed city today it's impossible to reconcile it with the distraught images of 2004. In Banda Aceh alone, 61,000 people were killed and development outside of the city centre was reduced to a wasteland in a matter of a few hours. Today you'd hardly guess that anything had happened.

For a few years the city was awash with aid workers, who not only helped rebuild the pretty town you'll find today but also kick-started the economy to catering to nongovernmental organisations (NGOs). Prices soared as foreign expense accounts paid for taxis, steak dinners and overpriced hotel rooms. There is certainly a lull in the city now that the NGOs have gone, which, positively, means the city's infrastructure is well recovered, but sadly the NGO-inflated miniboom is over. However, now that Aceh has greater control over its resources, in particular oil, the town is relatively affluent and the streets, the homes and especially the mosques are well maintained and looked after.

Banda Aceh is a fiercely religious city and the ornate mosques are at the centre of daily life. In this devoutly Muslim city, religion and respect are everything. The hassles are few and the people are easygoing and extremely hospitable to visitors (Muhammad was a traveller, after all).

### Orientation

Banda Aceh is split in two by Sungai Krueng Aceh. In the southern part of the city is its best-known landmark, the Mesjid Raya Baiturrahman. Behind the mosque is the huge Pasar Aceh Central (central market), and adjoining the market is the main *opelet* terminal.

The residential neighbourhood in the southeast corner is referred to as Geuceu Komplek, and is home to some of the Banda Aceh's politicians and wealthy inhabitants.

North of the river is the city centre, where much of the rebuilding was concentrated and new homes now stand. The commercial spine is Jl Panglima Polem.

### Information

#### INTERNET ACCESS & POST

**Country Steakhouse** (off Jl Sri Ratu Safiatuddin; 🕑 noon-10pm) This restaurant has free wi-fi access for laptops.

**Jambo Internet** (Jl Panglima Polem 2; 🕑 24hr)

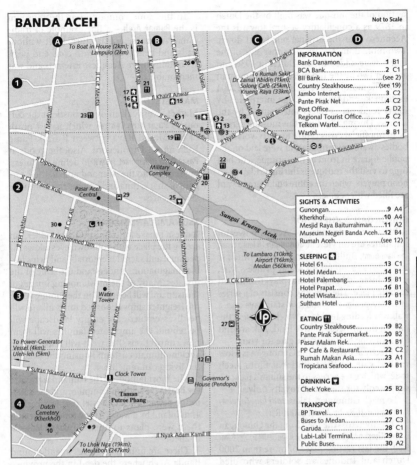

## BANDA ACEH

Not to Scale

**SUMATRA**

**Pante Pirak Net** (Jl Dhimurthala 19; ☉ 9am-10pm)
Next door to PP Cafe & Restaurant.
**Post office** (☎ 29487; Jl Bendahara 33; ☉ 8am-
4pm Mon-Fri) A short walk from the centre; also has
internet.

### MEDICAL SERVICES
**Rumah Sakit Dr Zainal Abidin** ( ☎ 26090, 22606; Jl
Nyak Arief ) One of the best hospitals in town.

### MONEY
There are lots of ATMs around town, mainly
on Jl Panglima Polem and on Jl Sri Ratu
Safiatuddin.
**BCA bank** (Jl Panglima Polem)
**BII bank** (Jl Panglima Polem)
**Bank Danamon** (Jl Sri Ratu Safiatuddin)

### TELEPHONE
**Telkom wartel** (Jl Daud Beureeh) Home Country Direct
phone.
**Wartel** (Jl Panglima Polem 11)

### TOURIST INFORMATION
**Regional tourist office** (Dinas Parawisata; ☎ 23692;
Jl Chik Kuta Karang 3) On the 1st level of a government
building; the staff are exceptionally friendly and have free
copies of an excellent guidebook to the province.

## Sights & Activities
### MESJID RAYA BAITURRAHMAN
With its brilliant white walls and liquorice-black
domes, the **Mesjid Raya Baiturrahman** (admission by
donation, headscarf required for women; ☉ 7-11am & 1.30-4pm)
is a dazzling sight on a sunny day. The first

section of the mosque was built by the Dutch in 1879 as a conciliatory gesture towards the Acehnese after the original one burnt down. Two more domes – one on either side of the first – were added by the Dutch in 1936 and another two by the Indonesian government in 1957. The mosque survived intact after the 2004 earthquake and tsunami, a sign interpreted by many residents as direct intervention by the Divine. During this time the mosque served as an unofficial crisis centre for survivors, and bodies awaiting identification were laid on the public square in front of the mosque. The best time to visit the mosque is during Friday afternoon prayers, when the entire building and yard are filled with people.

### GUNONGAN & KHERKHOF

All that remains today of Aceh's powerful sultanates are on view at **Gunongan** (Jl Teuku Umar; ☻ 8am-6pm). Built by Sultan Iskandar Muda (r 1607–36) as a gift for his Malay princess wife, it was intended as a private playground and bathing place. The building consists of a series of frosty peaks with narrow stairways and a walkway leading to ridges, which represent the hills of the princess' native land. Ask around for someone to unlock the gate for you.

Directly across from the Gunongan is a low vaulted gate, in the traditional Pintu Aceh style, which gave access to the sultan's palace – supposedly for the use of royalty only.

To reach Gunongan, take a *labi labi (opelet)* bound for Jl Kota Alam (3000Rp).

Directly across the road from the Gunongan is the **Kherkhof** (Dutch Cemetery; Jl Teuku Umar; ☻ 8am-6pm), the last resting place of more than 2000 Dutch and Indonesian soldiers who died fighting the Acehnese. The entrance is about 250m from the clock tower on the road to Uleh-leh. Tablets set into the walls by the entrance gate are inscribed with the names of the dead soldiers. The cemetery suffered some flooding from the tsunami.

To reach the Kherkhof take *labi labi* 9 or 10.

### MUSEUM NEGERI BANDA ACEH

The **Museum Negeri Banda Aceh** ( ☎ 23144; Jl Alauddin Mahmudsyah 12; admission 1000Rp; ☻ 8.00am-noon & 2-4pm Tue-Sun) has displays of Acehnese weaponry, household furnishings, ceremonial costumes, everyday clothing, gold jewellery, calligraphy and some magnificently carved *recong* (Acehnese daggers) and swords. It also has a display of a baby two-headed buffalo.

In the same compound as the museum is the **Rumah Aceh** – a fine example of traditional Acehnese architecture, built without nails and held together with cord and pegs. It contains more Acehnese artefacts and war memorabilia.

### MARKETS

Market lovers will enjoy the bustle at the colourful **Pasar Aceh Central**, which is just north of the Mesjid Raya between Jl Chik Pante Kulu and Jl Diponegoro. Also, the goods at **Pasar Ikan** (fish market; Jl SM Raja) define freshness: boats ease into the river and unload their cargoes of shark, tuna and prawns right onto the vendor carts.

### TSUNAMI LANDMARKS

It doesn't make for sunny postcard fodder, but seeing the place with your own eyes allows for personal and sacred memorials, and helps feeble imaginations understand the scale of the disaster. Many of the most moving images of the tsunami will be erased in the coming years: the freighter ships deposited miles inland will be disassembled, the empty landscape will be rebuilt, the amputated families will form new connections. But what will remain is an ancient human custom: housing the dead so the living can remember.

The most famous of the tsunami sights are the **boat in the house** in Lampulo, and the 2500-tonne **power-generator vessel** that was carried 4km inland by a wave. At the time of research there were plans to open a **Tsunami Museum** in 2010.

There are four mass graves in and around Banda Aceh where the dead in the province were buried. The largest site is **Lambaro**, located on the road to the airport, where 46,000 unidentified bodies were buried. Other grave sites include **Meuraxa**, **Lhok Nga** and **Darusalam**, where another 54,000 bodies were interred. Families who wish to mourn the loss of unlocated relatives choose one of the mass graves based on possible geographic proximity; they have no other evidence of where to lay their prayers.

### VOLUNTEERING OPPORTUNITIES

More than 1000 schools in Aceh were destroyed or damaged by the tsunami. Libraries were ruined, sports equipment swept out to sea, computer equipment lost. And then there's the human toll: some estimates claim

**TSUNAMI RELIEF**

The December 26 2004 tsunami killed more than 170,000 people in Aceh and destroyed infrastructure along 800km of coastline.

The tsunami was an unprecedented disaster and in Aceh alone even a decades-long separatist movement couldn't achieve the level of destruction that the ocean accomplished in a few hours. According to figures from the UN Development Program (UNDP), Aceh was in a state of emergency from January to May 2005. During that time, basic shelter and nutrition were provided, families reunited, dead bodies were recovered and buried, 70,000 cu metres of debris was removed and used in reconstruction efforts, and possible epidemics of water-borne diseases were averted.

Since then, rebuilding of homes and infrastructure has been slow, but according to the BRR (Aceh-Nias Rehabilitation and Reconstruction Agency) the majority of reconstruction has been completed. After four years of overseeing the massive task of rebuilding the earthquake- and tsunami-ravaged Aceh province, BRR officially closed down in April 2009.

BRR's chairman, Kuntoro Mangkusubroto, said during the agency's final press conference here that through cooperation with regional governments, donor countries, UN agencies and NGOs, and a US$3.25 billion budget, BBR had managed to rebuild Aceh as planned.

'The target was achieved. All numbers in the blueprint were achieved', he said. 'In the first blueprint, we were supposed to build 90,000 houses. But as of today, 140,304 housing units have already been constructed'.

In April 2009 the BRR stated that some 400 tsunami victim families were still living in temporary shelters. According to BRR many contractors had run away with the construction funds, forcing the reconstruction and rehousing to take much longer than initially anticipated.

During its four-year mandate, BRR built 13 airports and airstrips, 23 seaports, 1115 medical facilities, 1759 schools, 3696km of road, 363 bridges and 996 government buildings. It also assisted 195,726 small- and medium-sized enterprises, trained 155,182 workers and 39,663 teachers, and rehabilitated 1012.4 sq km of farmland.

There is an air of bitterness at the pace and standard of the disaster relief. Many of the locals claim that the homes have been built poorly and are only partly finished, many without electricity or running water.

The reality is that, while slow, the reconstruction is impressive. Most visitors to Aceh will probably take away that what's been done is quite remarkable, despite what some may say, and as Joachim Von Amsberg – the country director for the World Bank, which helped fund and supervise reconstruction efforts – stated in 2009, 'It's easy to make a big story out of the failures, but this actually is a success story. Aceh and Nias have been built back, and in some cases have been built back better'.

that 2500 teachers were killed and a third of the tsunami deaths were children. Rebuilding lives in Aceh also means rebuilding educational facilities.

**Forum Bangum Aceh** (FBA; ☎ 45204; www.forum bangunaceh.org) is the leading local NGO formed by Aceh residents to work directly and effectively with affected communities. The group has two ongoing projects: microeconomic packages to get businesses up and running, and educational outreach. To volunteer here you'll need to get an application form from the website, and positions are subject to availability. Because FBA is a small organisation, it is more responsive to short-term volunteers than the larger NGOs. Whatever your area of expertise, FBA will find a place for you.

## Sleeping

The influx of international aid workers jacked up the prices but not the standards of the few hotels left in town since the tsunami; there's very little for budget travellers.

**Hotel Palembang** ( ☎ 22044; Jl Khairil Anwar 49; r with fan 70,000-100,000Rp, with air-con 120,000Rp; 🎇 ) A basic place with dark, uninspiring rooms.

**Hotel Prapat** ( ☎ 22159; Jl Ahmad Yani 19; d with fan/air-con 100,000/200,000Rp; 🎇 ) One of the more affordable spots. From the outside Prapat has the feel of a cheap, run-down motel, but rooms are good value with Western toilet and clean sheets.

**Hotel Wisata** ( ☎ 21834; Jl Ahmad Yani 19-20; r 125,000-450,000Rp; 🖳 ) With a streamlined art-deco facade, Wisata has decent clean rooms with tiled floors and ultrasoft beds. Some rooms have ornate Victorian-style plaster ceilings.

**SUMATRA**

---

**LOCAL VOICE: RAHMADHANI SULAIMAN (DANNY), TSUNAMI SURVIVOR**

Rahmadhani Sulaiman (aka Danny) is Aceh's tourism promotion director, and a survivor of the 2004 Boxing Day tsunami.

**What were you doing on the day the tsunami hit Aceh?** My family and I were enjoying the sunshine together on a beautiful Sunday morning. We couldn't expect this to happen. At around 8am people start running, screaming 'Water come! Water come!'. We started running even though we couldn't see water. Many locals rushed to the higher elevation of the hills. From here we could see the water and that something was very wrong with the sea, though we didn't realise it was a tsunami. After a while people slowly came down from the mountains, and it's then we saw bodies and debris everywhere. I will never forget people screaming, crying and running without clear direction. It was a dreadful situation. Rumours were that entire islands were wiped out. There was no power, and no real information. Everything was so quiet except for crying. Life suddenly became so empty and frustrating. I and neighbours were encouraged to locate the injured people, and dead bodies to take them to safe places to be buried later. It was so frightening for me, but they are my people.

**What happened in the ensuing days?** Sanitation became very bad. Everyone was haunted with the image of the devastating tsunami. We could only try to survive and depend on each other. We had a little remaining food, but when finished – there was no more. People were searching for food, and there was high competition – lots of demand and little supply. After day three of tsunami, I tried to seek my family in Banda Aceh, so I borrowed my friend's motorcycle. I saw thousands of dead bodies in the city. On the left, in the centre, and the right. Everywhere was horrible. My wife and young sons were with me. They were not prepared for the sight of so many dead bodies. Not to mention the smell. Things that were supposed to be in the sea were in the street! We couldn't believe it to see ships in the roofs of houses and in hotel car parks. Finally, after a long time, we found our family member stranded in a safe place. It was such an emotional, important meeting.

Life wasn't so healthy, so we tried to escape the house because things were getting unbearable, so we moved to a friend's house in Lambaro (15km from Banda Aceh), though there it was the same situation.

**How about the clean up?** Due to this tragedy, maybe the worst natural disaster ever, Aceh received unprecedented attention from the international community. Today Aceh has made significant progress. People's lives are improving and they're better off than they were before economically and socio-culturally. People of Aceh are very thankful for everyone's kind help and to people who kindly donated money in order to build Aceh back better.

---

**Hotel Medan** ( ☎ 21501; fax 23514; Jl Ahmad Yani 15; r 175,000, r incl breakfast 200,000-350,000Rp; 🍴 💻 🛜 ) The business-style rooms are spotless and comfortable, with cable TV; wi-fi is available in the lobby. Reception has a photograph from the tsunami of a huge boat marooned in the hotel's carpark.

**Hotel 61** ( ☎ 638866; reservation@hotel61.web.id; Jl Panglima Polem 28; r incl breakfast 280,000-500,000Rp; 🍴 🛜 ) Here you'll find modern rooms that are much closer to international standards than others in town. Includes free transport from airport.

**Sulthan Hotel** ( ☎ 22469; Jl Sultan 1; r incl breakfast 200,000-834,000Rp, ste 1,246,000; 🍴 🛜 ) When the NGOs hit town, this was one of the only functional hotels. With its large modern rooms, it's been packed out ever since.

## Eating

The square at the junction of Jl Ahmad Yani and Jl Khairil Anwar is usually the setting for the **Pasar Malam Rek**, Banda Aceh's lively night food market. Many night food stalls are found on JL SM Raja.

**Pante Pirak supermarket** (Jl Pante Pirak; ⏰ until 10pm) Good for stocking up on supplies or just watching the buying habits of Banda Aceh's middle class.

**Rumah Makan Asia** (Jl Cut Meutia 37/39; mains 10,000Rp) Aceh's version of *masakan Padang* (Padang dish) has an array of zesty seafood dishes that waiters plonk on to your table, such as *ikan panggang* (baked fish).

**PP Cafe & Restaurant** (Jl H Dhimurthala 31; mains 12,000Rp; 🍴 🛜 ) Popular with local teenagers, PP's is a great place to escape the heat for a cold drink, a good selection of Indonesian food and some European dishes.

**Country Steakhouse** ( ☎ 24213; off Jl Sri Ratu Safiatuddin 45B; mains 15,000-100,000Rp; ☺ noon-10pm; ⊠ ☎ ) Well hidden down an alley, this wood-panelled restaurant was set up to cater for the international aid workers; now it's often empty. Serves New Zealand steaks, snapper and chips and other Western dishes. Also has beer and Australian red wine, and a TV showing BBC.

**Tropicana Seafood** (Jl SM Raja; mains from 20,000Rp; ⊠ ) Chinese restaurant serving delicious seafood dishes and cold Bintang. Vegetarians beware: even the 'mixed vegetables' contains chicken and prawns.

## Drinking

Because of sharia law, alcohol is not available as openly here as elsewhere in Indonesia, but Chinese restaurants, the Sulthan Hotel and Country Steak House serve beer. As long as it's kept quiet, most of the locals don't mind.

If you'd like to see what life is like without the fermented juice, follow the locals to the brewed replacement. Friendly locals sip strong Acehnese coffee and smoke at **Chek Yoke** (Jl Chik Pante Kulu), a coffee shop on the southern banks of the river, which serves delicious pastries.

Aceh's most famous coffee house is nicknamed **Solong Café** (Jasa Ayah Cafeteria; Sedia Bubuk Aceh, Ulee Kareng). One-pound bags of finely ground, locally grown coffee are for sale and make a delicious post-Indo gift. You'll need to take a taxi.

## Getting There & Away
### AIR
There are several flights a day from Banda Aceh to Medan and Jakarta on Garuda, Sriwijaya and Lion Air. Air Asia flies daily to Kuala Lumpur, and Firefly to Penang in Malaysia. **NBA** ( ☎ 333 777) is the best airline serving the region, with flights to Takengon, Kutacane, Singkil, Simeulue and Meulaboh.

**BP Travel** ( ☎ 32325; Jl Panglima Polem 75) is a helpful air-ticket agent. **Garuda** (Garuda Indonesia; ☎ 32523; Jl Daud Beureeh 9) also has an office in Banda Aceh.

### BOAT
After the tsunami, the port moved to Uleh-leh, 10km northwest of Banda Aceh's city centre. The road to the port goes straight through the tsunami's path – once a two car–garage suburb, now an eerie, empty landscape. See Pulau Weh for boat schedules and fare information (p410).

### BUS
South of the city centre you'll find the new **Terminal Bus Bathoh** (Jl Mohammed Hasan), which has numerous buses to Medan. Economy buses (100,000Rp, 14 hours) depart at 4pm, while air-con buses leave all day (120,000Rp, 11½ hours). The other option are the non-stop buses (200,000Rp, 10 hours) departing at 8.30pm and 9pm. Other bus services are likely to depart from here in the future.

The west-coast road from Banda Aceh to Meulaboh was destroyed by the 2004 tsunami, but has since been rebuilt (for the most part). Public buses depart from the land-bus terminal behind the mosque on Jl Mohammad Jam.

## Getting Around
Airport taxis charge a set rate of 70,000Rp for the 16km ride into town. A taxi from the airport to Uleh-leh port will cost 100,000Rp.

*Labi labi* are the main form of transport around town and cost 1500Rp. The **labi-labi terminal** (Jl Diponegoro) is that special breed of Indonesian mayhem.

For Uleh-leh (5000Rp, 30 minutes), take the blue *labi labi* signed 'Uleh-leh'. You can also reach Lhok Nga and Lampu'uk (10,000Rp).

From the bus station, a becak into town will cost around 15,000Rp. A becak around town should cost between 5000Rp and 10,000Rp, depending on your destination. From the centre of town to Geuceu Komplek, a becak should cost about 10,000Rp.

## PULAU WEH
☎ 0652 / pop 25,000

A tiny tropical rock off the tip of Sumatra, Weh is a little slice of peaceful living that rewards travellers who've journeyed up through the turbulent greater mainland below. After you've hiked around the mainland's jungles, volcanoes and lakes, it's time to jump into the languid waters of the Indian Ocean. Snorkellers and divers bubble through the great walls of swaying sea fans, deep canyons and rock pinnacles, while marvelling at the prehistorically gargantuan fish. This is one of the finest underwater hikes you'll find. Both figuratively and geographically, Pulau Weh is the cherry on top for many visitors to Sumatra.

Don't come expecting lazy days on sprawling beaches with swaying palms, though; the stretches of sand are generally short, rocky strips met by the ocean's emerald-green coral garden. Most visitors spend their days underwater, ogling the dazzling kaleidoscope of marine life. Along the newly paved island road are little villages with underwear-only kids playing in the yard, lazy cows tied up to a green patch of grass and scrappy goats looking for garden victims.

Pulau Weh is shaped roughly like a horseshoe. On the northeastern leg is the port town of Sabang, where most of Weh's population lives. The primary tourist beaches are Gapang and Iboih, which are about 20km away heading towards the northwestern leg. Some may try to argue that one beach is better than the other, but both have their charms.

Note that malaria has been reported on the island, so take the proper precautions.

It's always a little rainy on Weh, which has two monsoon seasons. But that shouldn't matter, as you'll be underwater most of the time anyway. Plus the rain keeps the island lush green and the water full of plankton, which draws in underwater giants such as manta rays and whale sharks.

The tsunami did give Weh a minor licking, but the island fared better than the mainland did. Many of the coastal businesses that were battered have since been rebuilt, and the villagers banded together to repair roads and replant trees.

A word of warning: such is Pulau Weh's allure, many a traveller's itinerary has been blown out by weeks or even months by what is regarded by many as the best diving in Southeast Asia.

### ACTIVITIES
People don't come to Weh for the nightlife or the bikinis. They come for the diving and snorkelling, which is considered some of the best in the Indian Ocean. On an average day, you're likely to spot morays, lionfish and stingrays. During plankton blooms, whale sharks come to graze. Unlike at other dive sites, the coral fields take a back seat to the sea life and landscapes. There are close to 20 dive sites around the island, most in and around Iboih and Gapang.

There are several dive operators on the island; the two main ones are listed here. Both offer PADI diving courses. At Iboih, **Rubiah**

**Tirta Divers** ( ☎ 332 4555; www.rubiahdivers.com; 1/2/3 dives all inclusive €25/45/60) is the oldest dive operation on the island.

At Gapang, **Lumba Lumba Diving Centre** ( ☎ 332 4133; 081 1682 787; www.lumbalumba.com; 1/2/5 dives all inclusive €25/45/100) is the centre of activity, with the comings and goings of wet-suited creatures. Ton and Marjan Egbers maintain a helpful website with detailed descriptions of dives and other need-to-know information. The centre's shop has internet access (500Rp per minute).

Snorkelling gear can be hired almost anywhere for around 20,000Rp per day.

### GETTING THERE & AWAY
Sabang is the port town on Pulau Weh. Fast ferries to Sabang leave the mainland from Uleh-leh, situated 5km northwest of Banda Aceh, at 9.30am and 3.30pm (economy/business/VIP 60,000/75,000/85,000Rp; 45 minutes to one hour). On Friday, the afternoon ferry departs at 4.30pm. Slow ferries (economy/air-con 11,500/36,500Rp, two hours) leave at 2pm on Monday, Tuesday, Thursday and Friday. On Wednesday, Saturday and Sunday there are two ferries, departing at 11am and 4pm, respectively. In the opposite direction, the slow ferry leaves at 8am daily, with an afternoon ferry on Wednesday, Saturday and Sunday at 2pm. The fast ferry leaves at 8.00am and 4pm daily. You should get to the port at least 45 minutes before departure to get a ticket. Ferry service is weather pending.

### GETTING AROUND
From the port, there are regular minibuses to Sabang (20,000Rp, 15 minutes), and Gapang and Iboih (50,000Rp, 40 minutes).You can catch a minibus from Jl Perdagangan in Sabang to Gapang and Iboih (30,000Rp).

## Sabang
The island's main township is an interesting mix of traditional fishing village and old colonial villas. During Dutch rule, Sabang was a major coal and water depot for steamships, but with the arrival of diesel power after WWII it went into decline.

During the 1970s it was a duty-free port, but this status was eliminated in 1986 and Sabang once again became a sleepy fishing town. Today the only industry – other than fishing – is rattan furniture.

Most people pass through Sabang fairly quickly en route to the tourist beaches, but return to town for provisions.

You'll find internet at **2 Net Communication** (per hr 6000Rp). The **post office** (Jl Perdagangan 66) is next door to the **telephone office** (☼ 24hr), which has a Home Country Direct phone.

**BRI bank** (Jl Perdagangan) changes travellers cheques and US dollars at terrible rates. It also has an unreliable ATM that's usually out of order; it's highly recommended that you change money at Banda Aceh. Alternatively, try your negotiating skills with the Chinese moneychangers scattered about town.

Sabang is surrounded by beautiful beaches. Just 10 minutes' walk away is **Pantai Paradiso**, a white-sand beach shaded by coconut palms. A little further on is **Pantai Kasih** (Lover's Beach), and about 30 minutes from town is **Pantai Sumur Tiga**, a popular picnic spot.

Other attractions around Sabang include **Danau Anak Laut**, a serene freshwater lake that supplies the island's water, and **Gunung Merapi**, a semi-active volcano, which holds boiling water in its caldera and occasionally puffs smoke.

### SLEEPING & EATING

Few people choose to stay in town unless they get stuck.

**Pom Losmen** ( ☎ 21148; Jl Teuku Umar 3; r with fan & shared bathroom 50,000-70,000Rp, r with air-con 175,000Rp; ✖ ) A local boarding house.

**Hotel Holiday** ( ☎ 21131; Jl Perdagangan 1; r without bathroom 75,000-100,000Rp, r with bathroom 175,000Rp, r with air-con 200,000-425,000Rp; ✖ ) A marked step up, Hotel Holiday is a Chinese-run hotel with solid, if not fashion-plate, rooms.

**our pick** **Freddies** ( ☎ 081 3602 5501; www.santai -sabang.com; Santai Sumur Tiga; r weekday 210,000-225,000Rp, weekend 250,000-275,000Rp) This delightful option overlooks a pretty stretch of white-sand beach with a coral reef, perfect for those content with snorkelling and some R&R. The list of alcohol is impressive and all food is cooked by Freddie, the South African owner. Located in Santai Sumur Tiga, 5km east of Sabang.

**Casa Nemo** ( ☎ 0812 692 2598; www.casanemo.com; Santai Sumur Tiga; weekday/weekend r 225,000/275,000Rp). Italian-owned, this is another excellent Santai Sumur Tiga option, with bungalows perched over a luxurious beach.

There are plenty of restaurants along the main street, Jl Perdagangan, serving cheap Padang food. There's also a fruit market near the BRI bank.

## Gapang

Occupying a sandy cove, Gapang is a lazy stretch of beach lined with shack restaurants and simple guest houses. The locals are friendly and the atmosphere is low-key and quiet, with dive chat dominating the evenings.

### SLEEPING & EATING

Gapang has the greatest variety of accommodation on the island, from pseudo-resorts to cheapie huts. A problem for budget-minded backpackers is that the old boom years under the NGOs forced the prices disproportionately high, meaning relative value for money is something you'll struggle to find on Weh.

**Ramadilla** (r 50,000-100,000Rp) The last guest house along the beach, Ramadilla features cabins that climb up the hill, plus a longhouse or two with a chieftain's view of the sea.

**Dang Dang Na** (r 100,000Rp) Formerly Ohana; here basic wooden bungalows on concrete stilts with ocean views and *mandis* (common Indonesian form of bath, consisting of a large water tank from which water is ladled over the body) are planted on the hillside.

**Lumba Lumba** ( ☎ 332 4133; www.lumbalumba .com/staying.html; r with/without bathroom €12/8, cottage €20-25; 🖳 🛜 ) Dutch-owned Lumba Lumba features some spanking-new wood-decked cottages with tiled rooms and Western toilets. Accommodation is for the exclusive use of those diving with this outfit, so it's often hard to find a room. The blue line marked high on the front entrance indicates the water level reached during the tsunami.

Two government-owned resorts, **Flamboyan** ( ☎ 081 360272270; d 250,000-400,000Rp; ✖ ) and **Leguna Resort** ( ☎ 22799; d 250,000Rp; ✖ ), are mostly avoided by Western tourists on account of their dire need of maintenance and the fact that they're often spookily empty. There was talk of both closing; whether this is permanent or for a much-needed refurbishment, you'll have to enquire on arrival.

Beachside cafes serving Western food absorb the evening breezes and postdive appetites. For lunch, head out to the main road, where a small warung does delicious *nasi bungus* (rice and curry served for takeaway in a banana leaf). Mama Donut is a local institution, walking the sand selling delicious vegetable samosas, doughnuts and fried bananas.

SUMATRA

## Iboih

More spread out than Gapang, Iboih (*ee*-boh) follows a rocky headland with a string of simple bungalows along a woodsy footpath. A small path leads through a stone gateway past the village well, and up and over a small hill to the bungalow strip.

Opposite Iboih, 100m offshore, is **Pulau Rubiah**, a densely forested island surrounded by spectacular coral reefs known as the **Sea Garden**. It is a favourite snorkelling and diving spot. The coral has been destroyed in places but there is still plenty to see, including turtles, manta ray, lionfish, tigerfish and occasional sharks.

If you are a strong swimmer it is possible to make your own way there. Beware of strong currents, especially at the southern tip of the island.

Adjacent to the Sea Garden is the **Iboih Forest nature reserve**. It has some good walks, and coastal caves that can be explored by boat.

### SLEEPING & EATING

Simple palm-thatched bungalows, many built on stilts and overhanging crystal-clear water, make up the majority of the accommodation here – the cheapest you'll find in Pulau Weh.

Most places are very similar, but it's best to do a wander before you declare a winner. If you are staying for several days, you can negotiate 50,000Rp a night for a basic bathroom and a fanless shack. The following bungalows are listed in geographic order as you'll approach them: of the more comfortable huts, **OONG's Bungalows** ( ☎ 0813 6070 0150; r without bathroom 50,000Rp) has the best value for money with its two waterfront shacks, while **Iboih Inn** ( ☎ 081 2699 1659; r 200,000Rp) has the most 'luxurious' shacks – but they are outrageously overpriced. **Yulia's** ( ☎ 0813 7727 9989; r without bathroom 70,000-80,000Rp) has the best rooms of the basic bunch and excellent front-door snorkelling.

Just off the main road are a few shops selling sundries, Indonesian lunches and coffee in front of a small beach. If you speak Bahasa Indonesia, this is where you can scoop up the village gossip.

Located next door to Rubiah Tirta Divers is **Sirkui Beach Café** with pricey internet, and **Mama's**, serving tasty meals and a view of the small beach that's popular with sunbathers. **Norma's**, the restaurant portion of OONG's

Bungalows, does a nightly seafood dinner around a communal table and serves beer amid scuba chat. Further down, **Yulia's** has shakes and light fare. Prices at these places tend to be around 25,000Rp for mains. There was also large overwater restaurant in construction at the time of research.

## Long Angen

This secluded beach on the western side of the island is ideally located for spectacular sunsets. The beach itself only exists for six months of the year – the sand is swept away by the sea from November to May.

## ACEH'S WEST COAST

Rounding the northwestern tip of Sumatra's finger of land is a string of little villages and endless beaches backed by densely forested hills, home to some interesting wildlife including tigers and bears. This is the perfect recipe for paradise, but several factors have conspired to keep the sands free of beach blankets: the unstable safety situation during the military occupation of Aceh, and the Boxing Day tsunami. Most of the houses along the coast are identical in design, having been rebuilt after villages were destroyed in 2004. For the moment the attractive, but still visibly scarred, west coast attracts only the more intrepid travellers and surfers in search of waves. Once the road from Banda Aceh to Calang is completed, no doubt it will open up more to tourists again.

### Lhoknga & Lampu'uk

☎ 0656 / pop Lhoknga 200, Lampu'uk 1000

Before the tsunami this area was a favourite spot of intrepid surfers and weekending locals from Banda Aceh. These coastal weekend spots, only 17km from Banda Aceh, were levelled by the tsunami. In Lampu'uk the wave travelled some 7km inland, killing four in five people. The reconstruction work is pretty much complete here and the disjointed families that have returned are trying to continue with their lives.

There's still very little in the way of accommodation here, although some of the bungalows along the beach in Lampu'uk are rented out by surfers. Also in Lampu'uk, **Joel's Restaurant** ( ☎ 0813 7528 7765; ⊗ 4pm-10pm Mon-Fri, 10am-10pm Sat & Sun), of the legendary Joel's Bungalows fame before the tsunami, had beach bungalows in construction at the

---

**THE LAST OF THE LAMNOS**

One tragic story resulting from the 2004 Boxing Day tsunami was the plight inflicted upon the Lamno people – a mixed blood Portuguese-Acehnese ethnic group living along Aceh's northwest coast. The Lamno people are famous among the Acehnese for their European appearance, and are affectionately referred to as the 'blue eyes of Aceh'. The Portuguese explorers first arrived in the region during the 16th century in search of spices; the Lamno people are their descendants. The Lamno villages were hard hit by the tsunami, destroying six villages and killed three in four people. Included in this figure were the remaining blue-eyes – all except a fisherman and his wife, who are said to be the last of the Lamnos. In actuality, there is no doubt that Lamno people still live in Banda Aceh and other parts of Aceh, but whether this recessive blue-eye gene will continue through generations seems unlikely.

---

time of research. It's a good spot for wood-fire pizza, beer and a spot of surf chat; it also rents surfboards. It's situated in the village, away from the beach.

Lhoknga has decent waves too, although it's beach is not as nice, particularly with the huge concrete factory and the nearby port.

Take *labi labi* 04 (20,000Rp, 20 minutes) from the *opelet* terminal in Banda Aceh for both Lhoknga and Lampu'uk.

## Calang & Meulaboh
☎ 0654/5

This coastal swath of Banda Aceh felt the ferocity of the tsunami more then anywhere else. The west-coast road from Banda Aceh to Meulaboh was destroyed by the tsunami. USAID contracted Halliburton to rebuild parts of the road – while not complete from Banda Aceh to Calang, the road is working again and being used. You'll need to make several river crossings with a rickety wooden car barge, complete with attached outboard motor.

Everything in the town of **Calang** was destroyed; the population was halved and infrastructure was wiped out and relocated 20km north of the original town. There's very little to see or do here. If you get stuck you can stay at **Khana Hotel** ( ☎ 0654-221 0127; r 110,000-275,000Rp).

Further south, **Meulaboh**, 240km from Banda Aceh, was the closest town to the earthquake's epicentre and is often referred to in the press as 'ground zero'. The town was completely destroyed and close to a third of the 120,000 population was killed. Reconstruction is underway, but sorting such epic destruction will take time. **Meuligou Hotel** ( ☎ 0655-700 7171; Jl Iskandar Muda 35; 275,000-495,000Rp; ✦ ) is one of the few places that survived the tsunami. You'll

find a few *very* basic losmen; if you're on a tight budget it's worth asking to see if anything new has opened up. **Speed Net** (Jl Iskandar Muda; per hr 4000Rp) has internet.

Bus services to Calang or Meulaboh are running again. The airport is operational and **Susi Air** (www.susiair.com) runs twice-weekly flights to Medan, while NBA flies to Medan and Banda Aceh.

Note that malaria can be a problem, so take precautions. Before going for a swim, be aware that some of the west-coast beaches have very strong currents.

## Pulau Simeulue
☎ 0650 / pop 70,000

The isolated island of Simeulue, about 150km west of Tapaktuan, is a rocky volcanic outcrop blanketed in rainforest and fringed with clove and coconut plantations. Few visitors make it this far – though the surfing is said to be excellent along the west coast.

You'll find simple **losmen** (r 40,000Rp) in Sinabang and Sibigo, or if you have a tent you can camp on the beach. The most comfortable sleeping option is the surf camp **Baneng Beach Retreat** ( ☎ 0813 6241 7692; www.simeulue.com; packages Nov-Apr US$115, May-Oct US$140) on the west coast. Packages include meals and transfers. Reef uplift from the earthquake has flattened out some of the famous surf breaks, but new spots are being discovered.

**Susi Air** ( ☎ 061-785 2169; www.susiair.com) has twice-daily flights from Medan, while **Merpati** ( ☎ 061-736 6888; www.merpati.co.id/EN) has three flights a week from Medan. NBA has flights to Banda Aceh. Enquire with a local travel agent for ticketing and schedules.

Ferries run from the mainland ports of Singkil and Labuhan Haji to Pulau Simeuleu's port town of Sinabang.

## Tapaktuan

☎ 0656 / pop 15,000

The sleepy seaside town of Tapaktuan, 200km south of Meulaboh, is the main town in South Aceh. It's very laid-back by Sumatran standards and, although it has few specific sights, it can be a pleasant place to hang out for a couple of days. Although its location would suggest otherwise, Tapaktuan was not noticeably affected by the tsunami. Many displaced people from other parts of Aceh have sought refuge here with relatives or friends.

Most places of importance are on the main street, Jl Merdeka, which runs along the coast. The town can be used as a base to explore the lowland **Kluet region** of Gunung Leuser National Park, about 45km south. Kluet's unspoilt swamp forests support the densest population of **primates** in Southeast Asia and are also good sites for **bird-watching**. It may be possible to hire guides through the national park office in Kandang, 38km south of Tapaktuan.

**Pantai Tu'i Lhok** and **Pantai Air Dingin**, about 18km north of Tapaktuan, are the best of several good beaches in the area. Opposite both beaches are waterfalls with natural plunge pools where you can cool off.

**Gua Kelam** (Dark Cave), 3km north of Tapaktuan, is a spectacular series of caves and tunnels that can be explored, but you'd be wise to take a guide. You can usually find a guide at the coffee shop by the river.

Most of the places to stay are located along Jl Merdeka. **Losmen Bukit Barisan** ( ☎ 21145; r 50,000Rp), an old Dutch house, is a friendly place with basic rooms and a certain shabby charm; and **Hotel Panorama** ( ☎ 21004; Jl Merdeka 33; d 55,000-135,000Rp; 🏊 ) is a large, modern hotel with a range of reasonable rooms. Otherwise try the comfortable **Metro Hotel** ( ☎ 0813 6053 8088; Jl Ben Mahmud 17; r incl breakfast 250,000Rp), a friendly guest house with some rooms looking out over the waves rolling into shore.

Jl Merdeka is also a good place to find a bite to eat. Seafood is a speciality and there are several **restaurants** selling delicious grilled fish for about 10,000Rp. After dark, the **night market** by the main pier, opposite Hotel Panorama, kicks into action. It's a lively place for a quick meal.

Bank BRI has a 24-hour ATM.

### GETTING THERE & AWAY

The west road is now working and in semidecent order. There's a daily bus from Banda Aceh (economy/air-con 100,000/170,000Rp, 10 hours); Medan (120,000Rp, 10 hours) via Berastagi and Sidikalang. From Sidikalang it's possible to get a direct bus to Pangururan (50,000Rp, two hours) on the west coast of Danau Toba.

NBA has two flights per week to Medan, and one per week (on Friday) to Banda Aceh.

## Singkil

☎ 0658 / pop 20,000

Singkil is a remote port at the mouth of Sungai Alas. It's a sleepy town with welcoming locals, although it merits a mention only as the departure point for boats to the Banyak Islands and Pulau Simeulue.

Catching a boat will mean spending a night in Singkil, with **Hotel Dina Amalia** ( ☎ 0856 6404 4354; elviandi_rs@yahoo.com; Jl Bahari; r 130,000-200,000Rp; 🏊 ) the best option. You can also find basic **losmen** (r 30,000Rp). Internet is at **Icang Promo** (Jl Bahari; per hr 5000Rp).

NBA has two flights to Medan and one flight to Banda Aceh per week. **Bombay Tours & Travel** ( ☎ 0813 7721 9667; Jl Mesjid 102) can organise flights to Medan as well as charter speedboats.

There are daily minibuses from Medan to Singkil (80,000Rp, nine hours) and from Banda Aceh (250,000Rp, 16 hours). If you're travelling from Berastagi, Danau Toba or Tapaktuan, you will need to change buses at Sidikalang and Subulus Salem.

For transport to Pulau Banyak, see opposite. There's also one overnight ferry per week to Sinabang, Pulau Simeulue (28,000Rp to 68,000Rp, Wednesday 6.30pm), arriving early the next morning.

## PULAU BANYAK

pop 5000

If you've ever dreamt about having a tropical island entirely to yourself, complete with palm trees, powdery white beaches and gin-clear waters, then Pulau Banyak is a great place to fulfil your Robinson Crusoe fantasy. A cluster of 99, mostly uninhabited islands, the Banyak (Many) Islands are situated about 30km west of Singkil. They are very remote and see few casual visitors. As well as beaches to laze on, Pulau Banyak has some great reef breaks for surfing, kayaking and snorkelling.

The 2004 Boxing Day earthquake and tsunami, followed by the 2005 Nias quake, destroyed many coastal dwellings and contaminated fresh-water wells. The main town on the island of Pulau Balai was permanently see-sawed by the quake, causing the west coast to rise by about 70cm and the east coast to drop below sea level. Its once-beautiful beaches were permanently washed away, hence most visitors only hang around to arrange transport to one of the other islands.

Your first port of call on Balai should be to **Yayasan Pulau Banyak** (YPB; ☎ 0813 6282 8449; luk manul.kim@gmail.com; Jl Makmur, Balai), an NGO that aims to develop ecotourism as an alternative livelihood for local communities. YPB can provide information on places to stay and transport, as well as guides and tents. It was set up to promote sea turtle conservation in the region, and continues to do excellent work. If you're keen to see turtles lay their eggs on the beach at Pulau Bangkaru, you'll need to obtain a permit first from YPB. It's also possible to do volunteer work, with duties including nightly beach patrols collecting data on the nesting turtle population. Enquire on their website at www.acehturtleconservation.org.

Tourists arriving on Balai will need to bring a copy of their passport and register at the police office.

Haloban on Pulau Tuangku is the other main village on the islands, which many visitors prefer over Balai; though it's not renowned for its beaches, it's more relaxed.

Malaria has been reported on the islands, so take suitable precautions.

## Sleeping & Eating

Sleeping options on Pulau Banyak are limited and basic, with only a few islands having bungalows. Camping is another option, and will allow you to stay exclusively on one of the many uninhabited idyllic islands. Tents can be arranged through Yayasan Pulau Banyak (see above).

If staying at one of the bungalows, or if you have a guide, you can arrange food on the islands; otherwise you'll have to bring provisions with you (or catch your own dinner!). It's a good idea to stock up on food and drinking water in Singkil. Sunglasses are essential, such is the intense glare from the sun.

If you get stuck at Balai, the best accommodation is at **Losmen Putri** ( ☎ 0813 9737 6499; r

with shared bathroom 20,000-85,000Rp, r with air-con 85,000-150,000Rp; 🅿 ). At Haloban you can stay at the losmen **Sederhana Aleng Moon** ( ☎ 0813 9745 8156; r 40,000Rp).

On **Pulau Palambak Basar**, you'll find basic bungalows at **Pap** ( ☎ 0812 6332 2839; r 50,000Rp) which has mosquito nets, and also the **Point** ( ☎ 0852 7744 2298; r 75,000Rp). Both look onto perfect white beaches and turquoise water. **Pulau Tailana** also has basic bungalows (50,000Rp), and there's a good chance that you'll have the entire island to yourself.

On **Ujung Lolok**, surfers can try **Banyak Island Lodge** ( ☎ 0813 6126 3491; www.banyakislandlodge.com; 9/12 nights package all-inclusive with flights AU$3190/3490), which also organises fishing trips.

## Getting There & Around

There is one ferry a week (Tuesday 8.30am) between the mainland port of Singkil and Balai (16,000Rp, four hours). It returns from Balai to Singkil on Wednesday at 8.30am.

Local boats depart Singkil (30,000Rp, 4½ hours) at around 8am to 9am on Monday, Thursday and Saturday. They return from Balai on Sunday, Wednesday and Friday. A boat leaves twice a week to Haloban (50,000Rp). Try calling **Mr Dasir** ( ☎ 0852 6111 0411) for further info.

By far the most convenient way to reach the islands is to charter a speedboat from Singkil (one way/return around 800,000/ 1,400,000Rp, two hours), although it is very expensive.

To travel between islands it's best to ask around at the port on Balai or enquire at YPB for local boats to islands (around 50,000Rp per two hours).

## GAYO HIGHLANDS

As long as the peace lasts, the interior of Aceh is ripe for off-the-path picking. This is coffee country, cool and mountainous with spectacular vistas and the odd view of wild jungle critters. The road from Takengon to Blangkejeran, the main towns of the Gayo Highlands, is astoundingly picturesque and can be used as an alternative route to or from Berastagi.

The Gayo people, who number about 250,000, lived an isolated existence until the advent of modern roads and transport. Like the neighbouring Acehnese, the Gayo are strict Muslims and were renowned for their fierce resistance to Dutch rule.

## Takengon

☎ 0643 / elev 1120m

Takengon is the largest town in the highlands, and while it is not particularly attractive it retains a relaxed charm, with a spectacular setting and a refreshing climate. The town is built on the shores of Danau Laut Tawar, a 26km-long stretch of water, surrounded by steep hills rising to volcanic peaks. Gunung Geureundong, to the north, rises 2855m.

### ORIENTATION & INFORMATION

All of the action is in the centre of town on Jl Lebe Kadir. You'll find the post office, a Telkom wartel, the police station and Mesjid Raya here. You can change money at **BRI bank** (Jl Yos Sudarso), which has an ATM. **HRC.Net** (Jl Sengeda; per hr 5000Rp) has internet, including wi-fi hotspots in its surrounds, access to which you can purchase by the hour.

### SIGHTS & ACTIVITIES

Takengon's main attractions are all natural. Admire the views, cruise around the lake in a *perahu* (dugout canoe) or explore caves, waterfalls and hot springs.

The best cave is **Loyang Koro** (Buffalo Caves; admission 3000Rp), 6km from town, which has some interesting stalagmites. Don't forget to bring a torch (flashlight).

At Simpang Balik, about 15km north of Takengon, the sulphurous **hot spring** (Wih Pesame; entry by donation) is set in a large concrete pool and is said to cure skin diseases.

In the week following Independence Day (17 August), Takengon hosts a regional **horse-racing carnival**, held at the track to the west of town. It's a highly spirited affair, with 12-year-old jockeys from all over the highlands riding bareback in the hope of glory.

### SLEEPING & EATING

**Hotel Buntu Kubu** (Jl Malem Dewa; r 65,000-140,000Rp) This hotel has a varied history: a former Dutch official residence, museum and Indonesian military post. Today it's a pretty horrible, run-down guest house, though it's the only cheap place in town.

**Hotel Mahara** ( ☎ 21728; Jl Sengeda 568; r incl breakfast 185,000-295,000Rp) New sparkling rooms with homely fittings arranged around an indoor Indonesian-style pond with bonsai trees.

**ourpick Hotel Renggali** ( ☎ 21144; Jl Bintang; d incl breakfast 250,000-550,000Rp) A wonderful location perched above the lake, Renggali's rooms are large and comfortable and open directly onto the calm lake and pleasant gardens – so it's surprising that it's often spookily empty. Situated 2km out of town.

**Rakan Singkile** (Jl Labe Kader 2; meals 10,000-25,000Rp) Tasty Chinese, Indonesian and Western dishes, as well as beer (17,000Rp).

**Pondok Laguna** (Jl Lintang, mains 12,000-30,000Rp) Best restaurant in town, with a good selection of vegetarian and seafood dishes. The back section is one giant adventure playground.

Delicious fresh Gayo coffee is available pretty much everywhere. A local speciality is *kopi telor kocok* – a raw egg and sugar creamed together in a glass and topped up with coffee.

### SHOPPING

Takengon is the place to buy traditional-style Gayo-Alas tapestry, which is made into clothes, belts, purses and cushion covers. At the market, it's sometimes possible to buy highly decorated engraved pottery called *keunire*, which is used in wedding ceremonies.

### GETTING THERE & AWAY

There's one bus a day to Medan at 7.30pm (air-con, 110,000Rp, 10 hours). There are also buses to Banda Aceh (85,000Rp, eight hours). Heading south, there are regular buses to Blangkejeran (80,000Rp, seven hours) and Ketambe (110,000Rp, nine hours). You would connect through these towns to reach Berastagi.

NBA flies has two flights a week to both Medan and Banda Aceh.

### GETTING AROUND

*Labi labi* leave from the southern end of Jl Baleatu. Fares around town cost 2000Rp. *Perahu* for lake cruising can be hired at the pier at the end of Jl Laut Tawar.

## Blangkejeran

Blangkejeran is the main town of the remote southern highlands. The area is recognised as the Gayo heartland and it's possible to hire guides to take you out to some of the smaller **villages**. Accommodation is available in several small guest houses. There are regular buses north to Banda Aceh via Takengon and south to Ketambe and Kutacane.

# GUNUNG LEUSER NATIONAL PARK

☎ 0629

The Aceh section of Gunung Leuser National Park has slipped under the tourist radar for years, seeing only a trickle of visitors as the masses head to the more hyped Bukit Lawang. Its jungle is basically the same minus the well-worn paths and tourists clambering about trying to spot semiwild orangutans. Here is the place for the *real* jungle experience. In the past it's been largely off limits due to the conflict, but now that there's peace in the region it's likely to receive the recognition it deserves.

The World Heritage-listed Gunung Leuser National Park is one of the world's most important and biologically diverse conservation areas. It is often described as a complete ecosystem laboratory because of the range of forest and species types.

Within the park's boundaries live some of the planet's most endangered and exotic species: tigers, rhinoceros, elephants and orangutans. Although your chances of seeing these celebrity animals are remote, you've got a reasonable chance of seeing orangutans, and you can be sure of encountering plenty of primates. The most common is the white-breasted Thomas' leaf monkey, which sports a brilliant, crested punk hairdo. Other resident species include leopards, bears and cobras.

Habitats range from the swamp forests of the west coast to the dense lowland rainforests of the interior. Much of the area around Ketambe is virgin forest. Above 1500m, the permanent mist has created moss forests rich in epiphytes and orchids. Rare flora includes two members of the rafflesia family, *Rafflesia acehensis* and *Rafflesia zippelnii*, which are found along Sungai Alas.

More than 300 bird species have been recorded in the park, including the bizarre rhinoceros hornbill, the helmeted hornbill and woodpeckers.

The park faces a great number of challenges. Poachers have virtually wiped out the crocodile population and have severely reduced the number of tigers and rhinoceros. According to the Indonesian Forum for the Environment, a fifth of the park has been adversely affected by illegal logging and road construction. A highly controversial road project called Ladia Galaska runs through the park, linking the eastern and western coasts of the province. Furthermore, during the conflict

in Aceh, the jungle was a stronghold of GAM militants, and the national park saw fighting between GAM and Indonesian troops.

This park receives a lot of rain throughout the year, but rain showers tend to lessen in frequency and duration from December to March.

## Ketambe (Gurah)

### ORIENTATION & INFORMATION

Ketambe (also called Gurah), in the heart of the Alas Valley, is one of the main access points to Gunung Leuser National Park. Directly across the river is Ketambe Research Station, a world-renowned conservation research station, which is off limits to tourists (see the boxed text, p418). Kutacane, 43km from Ketambe, is the closest town of any note and is the place to go for transport, ATMs and internet. For the latter, go to **Yom@** (Jl Iskandar 71; per hr 4000Rp; ⏰ 24hr).

Permits to the park (20,000Rp per day) can be arranged at guest houses in Ketambe. In theory you will need three photocopies of your passport but this is rarely required. Guides can be hired from any guest house in Gurah. If you want to see a certain plant or animal, ask around for the guides with that speciality.

Guide prices (one day 250,0000Rp, two days and one night 350,000Rp, three days and two nights 700,000Rp) are fixed by the Sumatran Guide Association. Non-English-speaking guides cost less. It's important that you support local guides if possible, rather than organising through Medan.

### TREKKING

For serious trekkers and jungle enthusiasts Ketambe offers a much more authentic experience than the trekking near Bukit Lawang. Be prepared for extreme terrain, hordes of leeches and swarms of stinging insects. Bring plenty of water. Here are a few options; guides can also tailor a trip to specific requests:

**Gurah Recreation Forest** The *hutan wisata* (recreation forest) at Gurah is a park within the national park. The forest's 92 sq km has walking tracks and viewing towers. The most popular walk involves a two-hour (5km) hike from Ketambe to hot springs by Sungai Alas. There's also a 6km walk to a waterfall.

**Bukit Lawang** Starting one hour south of Kutacane, this five-day trek through tough terrain passes over 20 river crossings. You have a good chance of seeing orangutans and gibbons, and the trek passes through areas that elephants are known to inhabit. You can arrange to have your luggage delivered to Bukit Lawang separately.

**KETAMBE RESEARCH STATION**

The Ketambe Research Station has been conducting extensive studies of the flora and fauna of Gunung Leuser National Park for almost 30 years.

In the early 1970s, Ketambe was home to Sumatra's orangutan rehabilitation program, but the project was relocated to Bukit Lawang to allow researchers to study the Ketambe region without the disruption of tourists. Nowadays the station's primary concern is hard-core conservation, research and species cataloguing. Both the centre and the surrounding forest are off limits to almost everyone but the Indonesian and international researchers.

The 450-hectare protected area consists mainly of primary lowland tropical forest and is home to a large number of primates, as well as Sumatran tigers, rhinoceros, sun bears, hornbills and snakes. Despite its protected status, a third of the area has been lost to illegal logging since 1999.

**Gunung Kemiri** At 3314m, this is the second-highest peak in Gunung Leuser National Park. The return trek takes five to six days, starting from the village of Gumpang, north of Ketambe. It takes in some of the park's richest primate habitat, with orangutans, macaques, siamangs and gibbons.

**Gunung Simpali** The trek to Gunung Simpali (3270m) is a one-week round trip starting from the village of Engkran and following the valley of Sungai Lawe Mamas. Rhinos live in this area. The Lawe Mamas is a wild, raging river that joins the Alas about 15km north of Kutacane.

**Gunung Leuser** The park's highest peak is, of course, Gunung Leuser (3404m). Only the fit should attempt the 14-day return trek to the summit. The walk starts from the village of Angusan, northwest of Blangkejeran.

### SLEEPING & EATING

Accommodation is scattered along the only road through Ketambe; guest houses are listed in geographical order as you arrive into town. Each has its own small restaurant.

**Pak Mus Guesthouse** ( ☎ 0813 8020 4305; r 50,000Rp) Charming family-run bungalows set beneath a forest backdrop. Thomas' leaf monkeys are often sighted feeding on the fruit trees.

**Pondok Wisata Ketambe** ( ☎ 24652; www.ketambe-indonesia.com; r 50,000-70,000Rp) Well-established guest house with knowledgeable staff.

**Wisma Sadar Wisata** ( ☎ 0852 7615 5741; r 50,000Rp) Here you'll find a range of good-value bungalows from basic older models to newer, more comfortable rooms overlooking the river. The friendly lady owner is great for a laugh.

**our pick Friendship Guesthouse** ( ☎ 0852 9688 3624; www.ketambe.com; r 50,000) This new spot has a beautiful location 150m upriver, with charming wooden bungalows and Western toilets. Staff are very friendly, and there are plenty of characters lurking about (Jhon Kanedi, aka JFK, is a classic!).

**Wisma Cinta Alam** ( ☎ 0852 7086 4580; r 30,000-60,000Rp) Another decent option along the river, whose owner is an experienced guide. A good choice for those keen on rafting.

The government-owned Gurah Bungalows is simply best avoided.

If you arrive in Kutacane too late to reach Gurah, you might have to spend the night at **Hotel Maroon** ( ☎ 21078; Jl Besar; r from 60,000-150,000Rp; 🛜 ); one of the better sleeping options in town, it's located in a quiet street parallel to the main road.

### GETTING THERE & AROUND

NBA flies from Kutacane to Medan and to Banda Aceh twice weekly.

Long-distance buses leave from the terminal in Kutacane for Medan's Pinang Baris terminal (50,000Rp, seven hours), Banda Aceh (190,000Rp, 20 hours) via Takengon (130,000Rp, eight hours) and Berastagi (50,000Rp, five hours). Along the way there are fine views of Gunung Sinabung and the Alas Valley.

From Kutacane there are countless *labi labi* to Ketambe (10,000Rp, one hour).

There are buses heading north to Blangkejeran (80,000Rp, three hours) and beyond.

## Kedah

Located 15km west of Blangkejeran, the small village of Kedah has seen very few visitors since the conflict in Aceh, making it ripe for off-the-beaten-track travel. At the northern edge of Gunung Leuser National Park, Kedah is a magnificent starting point for treks into the jungle, which is home to orangutans, gibbons and other exotic wildlife, birds and plants.

**Rainforest Lodge** ( ☎ 0859 6077 6934; www.gunung-leuser-trek.net; r without bathroom 80,000Rp) is run by the popular Mr Jali, with simple but pleasant bungalows in beautiful jungle surrounds. The lack of electricity adds greatly to its charm.

To get here catch a bus to Blangkejeran, from where you can take a motorbike taxi (40,000Rp, 20 minutes) to Kedah.

# WEST SUMATRA

From the air, Sumatra Barat looks as though a giant has plunged their hands into the equator, thrown it high into the air, and let it rain back down to earth. Fertile uplands ring jungle-clad volcanoes, waterfalls cascade into deep ravines and nature takes a breath in deep silent lakes. Rainforest still clings to the steepest slopes, while rice, tapioca, cinnamon and coffee bring in the wealth.

This is the heartland of the matriarchal Minangkabau, an intelligent, culturally rich and politically savvy people who have successfully exported their culture, language, cuisine and beliefs throughout Indonesia. Their unique buffalo-horned architecture dominates the cities and villages.

Hot, bustling Padang on the Indian Ocean is the gateway and provincial capital, though most tourists head straight for scenic Bukittinggi in the highlands. Surfers and trekkers flock to the perfect breaks and tribal culture of the Mentawai Islands, while nature

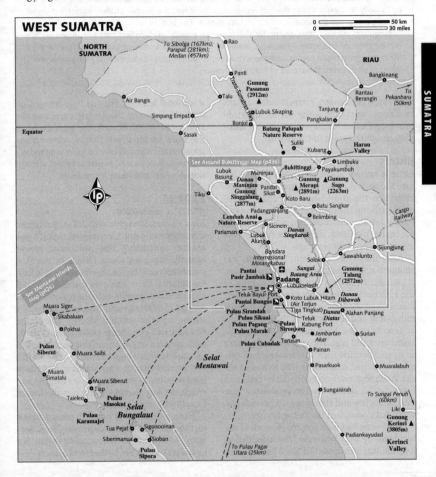

**WEST SUMATRA**

## THE MINANGKABAU

Legend has it that the Minangkabau are descended from the wandering Macedonian tyrant Alexander the Great. According to the story, the ancestors of the Minangkabau arrived in Sumatra under the leadership of King Maharjo Dirajo, the youngest son of Alexander.

Anthropologists, however, suggest that the Minangkabau arrived in West Sumatra from the Malay Peninsula some time between 1000 and 2000 BC, probably by following Sungai Batang Hari upstream from the Strait of Melaka to the highlands of the Bukit Barisan mountains.

Even if they don't have Alexander's bloodline, the Minangkabau reflect his wanderlust and love of battle, albeit in the milder form of buffalo fighting. Their success in buffalo fighting is believed to have bestowed the people with their tribal name, and the horns of the beast are the focus of their architecture and traditional costumes.

The legend of how the Minangkabau named themselves begins with an imminent attack by a Javanese king. Rather than pit two armies against each other, the Minangkabau proposed a fight between two bulls. When the time came, the West Sumatrans dispatched a tiny calf to fight the enormous Javanese bull, but the half-starved beast was outfitted with sharp metal spears to its horns. Believing the Javanese bull to be its mother, the calf rushed to suckle and ripped the bull's belly to shreds. When the bull finally dropped dead, the people of West Sumatra shouted *'Minangkabau, minangkabau!'*, which literally means 'The buffalo wins, the buffalo wins!'

Linguistic sticklers, though, prefer the far more prosaic explanation that Minangkabau is a combination of two words: *minanga,* meaning 'a river', and *kerbau,* meaning 'buffalo'. A third theory suggests that it comes from the archaic expression *pinang kabhu,* meaning 'original home' – Minangkabau being the cradle of Malay civilisation.

---

lovers explore Sumatra's largest national park in Kerinci, just across the border in Jambi province. Danau Maninjau remains the stunning, forgotten jewel in the crown.

## History

Little is known about the area's history before the arrival of Islam in the 14th century. However, the abundance of megalithic remains around the towns of Batu Sangkar and Payakumbuh, near Bukittinggi, suggest that the central highlands supported a sizable community some 2000 years ago.

After the arrival of Islam, the region was split into small Muslim states ruled by sultans. It remained this way until the beginning of the 19th century, when war erupted between followers of the Islamic fundamentalist Padri movement and supporters of the local chiefs, adherents to the Minangkabau *adat* (traditional laws and regulations). The Padris were so named because their leaders were haji, pilgrims who had made their way to Mecca via the Acehnese port of Pedir. They returned from the haj determined to establish a true Islamic society and stamp out the pre-Islamic ways that dominated the ruling houses.

The Padris had won control of much of the highlands by 1821 when the Dutch decided to join the fray in support of the Minangkabau

traditional leaders. The fighting dragged on until 1837, when the Dutch overcame the equator town of Bonjol, the stronghold of the Padri leader Imam Bonjol, whose name adorns street signs all over Indonesia. In today's Minangkabau society, a curious fusion of traditional beliefs and Islam is practised.

## PADANG

☎ 0751 / pop 960,000

Most visitors don't give Sumatra's third-largest city a second glance, convinced that it's just another simmering urbo-Indonesian sprawl of traffic, smog and chaos. Caught between the mountains and the sea, this once-humble fishing village is reinventing itself, aided by cheap airfares and its proximity to the region's power centres of Malaysia and Singapore. There's a strong sense of cultural identity among the youthful, well-educated population, and Padang is the modern face of Minangkabau culture and the cuisine Padang gave to the world. Sure, it's not without its problems, which include daily blackouts, but as you eat sate, sip a Bintang and watch the sun dive blood red into the Indian Ocean, who really cares?

Note: at the time of going to press, a major earthquake hit Padang, destroying large sections of town and the surrounding region. See boxed text, p422, for further information.

## Orientation & Information

While Padang's tentacles spread in all directions, the central area is reasonably compact. Most of the action is centred around the *pasar* (market) on Jl M Yamin, and the area immediately south bounded by Jl Iman Bonjol, the river and the sea. Jl Bundo Kandung contains top-end hotels, while cheaper digs can be found along Jl Hayam Wuruk and Jl Diponegoro/Veteran. The old colonial area on the river is home to Chinatown.

The main *opelet* terminal is across from the *pasar* and the airport is 20km north. Taxis are found outside any of the top-end hotels, and behind the museum on Jl Gereja. Boats to Siberut leave from one of two ports (for more information see Getting There & Away, p424).

### INTERNET ACCESS & POST
**Caroline Street Internet** (Jl Pondok 5F; per hr 6000Rp; 9am-9pm)
**Cyber West** (Jl Nipa Berok 10; per hr 5000Rp 9am-late)
**Post office** (Jl Azizchan 7; per hr 6000Rp)

### MEDICAL SERVICES
**Rumah Sakit Yos Sudarso** ( 33230; Jl Situjuh 1)
**Selasih Hospital** ( 51405; Jl Khatib Sulaiman 72)

### MONEY
There are ATMs all over town, and all major Indonesian banks are represented. The **Dipo International Hotel** (Jl Diponegoro 13) has a 24-hour moneychanger.
**BCA bank** (Jl Agus Salim 10)
**BII bank** (Bank Internasional Indonesia; Jl Sudirman 14)

**PADANG**

0 ———————— 500 m
0 ———————— 0.3 miles

**INFORMATION**
| | |
|---|---|
| Bank Mandiri | 1 C2 |
| BCA Bank | 2 C2 |
| Bevys Sumatra | 3 B3 |
| BII Bank | 4 C1 |
| BNI Bank | 5 B3 |
| BRI Bank | 6 C2 |
| Caroline Street Internet | 7 B3 |
| Cyber West | 8 B4 |
| Dipo International Hotel | 9 B3 |
| Ina Tours | (see 9) |
| Padang Tourism | 10 A4 |
| Post Office | 11 C3 |
| Rumah Sakit Yos Sudarso | 12 C1 |
| Sumatran Surfariis | (see 3) |

**SIGHTS & ACTIVITIES**
| | |
|---|---|
| Adityawarman Museum | 13 B3 |
| Taman Budaya Cultural Centre | 14 B3 |

**SLEEPING**
| | |
|---|---|
| Ambacang | 15 B3 |
| Bumiminang Hotel | 16 B3 |
| Hotel Inna Muara | 17 B3 |
| Hotel Nuansa | 18 A3 |
| Hotel Tiga Tiga | 19 B1 |
| Immanuel Hotel | 20 B4 |
| Spice Homestay | 21 B3 |
| Sriwijaya Hotel | 22 B1 |
| Wisma Mayang Sari | 23 C1 |

**EATING**
| | |
|---|---|
| Fellas | 24 B4 |
| France Modern Bakery | 25 B4 |
| Ikan Bakar ('Pak Agus') | 26 B4 |
| Mirama Café | 27 B3 |
| Nelayan Restaurant | 28 A3 |
| Pagi Sore | 29 B3 |
| Sari Raso | 30 B3 |
| Simpang Raya | 31 B3 |
| Taman Ria Pantai Padang | 32 A4 |

**SHOPPING**
| | |
|---|---|
| Pasar Raya | 33 B2 |
| Plaza Andalas | 34 B3 |
| Plaza Matahari | 35 B2 |

**TRANSPORT**
| | |
|---|---|
| Air Asia | 36 B3 |
| Boats to Pulau Siberut | 37 B4 |
| Garuda | 38 C2 |
| Mandala Air | 39 B1 |
| Opelet Terminal | 40 B3 |
| Sriwijaya Air | 41 C3 |
| Taxi Stand | 42 B3 |

To Pangeran Beach Hotel (3km); Vans For Bukittinggi & Kerinci (5km)

To Batavia Air (3km); Selasih Hospital (3km); Telkom Wartel (3km); Airport (20km); Bukittinggi (89km)

To Teluk Bayur (8km); Pantai Bungus (20km)

To Aie Pacah Bus Terminal (12km)

To Teluk Bayur (7.5km); Pantai Bungus (19.5km)

INDIAN OCEAN

Pantai Padang

Taman Siti Nurbaya

Gunung Padang (400m)

SUMATRA

---

**PADANG EARTHQUAKE 2009**

At 5.16pm on 30 September 2009, the city of Padang was devastated by a 7.6 magnitude earthquake that struck 57km southwest of Pariaman. At the time of going to print it was estimated that as many as 5000 people had been killed. Several places reviewed in this section were destroyed, including hotels, restaurants and hospitals. Some of these places will rise again, others won't. It's strongly advised to check the situation before you arrive.

Some remote villages in the Kerinci region were wiped out completely from landslides, while Mentawai, Bungus, Bukittinggi and Danau Maninjau escaped relatively unscathed.

---

**BNI bank** (Jl Bundo Kandung)
**BRI bank** (Jl Sudirman)

**TELEPHONE**
Mobile phones have killed the wartel scene. It's easier to purchase a pre-paid SIM and borrow a handset from your hotel.
**Telkom wartel** (cnr Jl Ahmad Dahlan & Khatib Sulaiman; ☽ 24hr) Huge Minangkabau-style building located north of the city centre.

**TOURIST INFORMATION**
**Tourism Padang** (Dinas Kebudayaan Dan Pariwisata; ☎ 34186; www.tourism.padang.go.id; Jl Samudera 1; ☽ 8am-2.30pm Mon-Fri, to 1pm Sat) Keep repeating 'tourist information' and eventually someone will give you an informative booklet. The website has a handy list of events.

## Sights & Activities

Padang's **colonial quarter** around Jl Batang Arau is laden with old Dutch and Chinese warehouses backing onto a river brimming with fishing boats. The beach along Jl Samudera is the best place to watch the sunset.

**Adityawarman Museum** (Jl Diponegoro; admission 1500Rp; ☽ 8am-4pm Tue-Sun), built in the Minangkabau tradition, has pleasant grounds, though non-Bahasa speakers may find the dusty collections detailing everyday Minangkabau life rather dry. The entrance is on Jl Gereja.

**Taman Budaya Cultural Centre** (☎ 22752; www.tamanbudaya-sumbar.org; Jl Diponegoro 31) stages sporadic dance performances, poetry readings, plays and art exhibitions. The events schedule is posted outside the building and on the website.

## Tours

Padang is the launching point for tours of the Mentawai Islands, famous for their hunter-gatherer culture, endemic flora and fauna, and world-class surfing. See p425 for more information.

## Festivals & Events

Don't miss the colourful dragon-boat festival held annually at the beginning of August to commemorate the city's founding.

The highlight of the West Sumatran cultural calendar is **Pesta Budaya Tabuik** (derived from the Islamic festival of Tabut), held at the seaside town of Pariaman, 36km north of Padang. It takes place at the beginning of the month of Muharam (based on the Islamic lunar calendar, usually January or February) to honour the martyrdom of Muhammed's grandchildren, Hassan and Hussein, at the battle of Kerbala.

Central to the festival is the *bouraq*, a winged horse-like creature with the head of a woman, which is believed to have descended to earth to collect the souls of dead heroes and take them to heaven.

## Sleeping

Hotels don't age well in Sumatra. Prepare to pay for comfort and location; always ask for a 'discount' and whether breakfast, tax and service charges are included.

### BUDGET & MIDRANGE

**Hotel Tiga Tiga** (☎ 22173; Jl Veteran 33; r incl breakfast 55,000-125,000Rp plus 10% tax; 🕸 ) North of the centre, this old travellers' dosser has cheap, simple rooms only five minutes' walk from the sea. Grab any white *opelet* heading up Jl Permuda.

**Immanuel Hotel** (☎ 28560; Jl Hayam Wuruk 43; r incl breakfast 100,000-250,000Rp; 🕸 ) Another travellers' standby, centrally located with simple rooms, helpful cheery staff and a welcome garden.

**our pick Spice Homestay** (☎ 841388; spicehomey@yahoo.com; Jl Dobi 34; r incl breakfast 110,000-330,000Rp plus 10% tax; 🕸 🖳 ) Fabulous tiny Balinese-style losmen in the centre, with beautiful rooms, a cosy lounge and great food.

**Wisma Mayang Sari** (☎ 23555; Jl Sudirman 19; r 130,000-330,000Rp plus 15% tax; 🕸 ) If only it were in the centre. Nice clean airy rooms with a leafy courtyard, stuck on a busy road to the north.

**Sriwijaya Hotel** ( ☎ 21942; thesriwijayahotel.com; Jl Veteran 26; r incl breakfast 250,000-325,000Rp; ⊠ ) If the Tiga's too grungy, then try this newbie across the road. Beautiful modern rooms look onto a quiet courtyard, and the ocean is (almost) close enough to smell.

**Hotel Nuansa** ( ☎ 26000; Jl Samudera 12; r incl breakfast 220,000-320,000Rp plus 10% tax; ⊠ ) Fantastic location opposite the main beach, though only the flashest rooms have a view.

### TOP END

Depending on the season, these hotels may offer big discounts, which bring the cheaper rooms back into the realms of mere mortals (check that tax and service are still included).

**Hotel Inna Muara** ( ☎ 35600; www.innamuara.com; Jl Gereja 34; r incl breakfast 625,000-850,000Rp; ⊠ 💻 ) The faux Minangkabau is a little tired, but with a discount the economy rooms aren't bad value.

**Ambacang Hotel** ( ☎ 39888; www.theambacanghotel.com; Jl Bundo Kandung 14-16; r incl breakfast from 650,000-1,500,000Rp plus 21% tax; ⊠ 💻 ) Sumptuous rooms, a day spa and the best nightclub in town.

**Bumiminang Hotel** ( ☎ 37555; www.bumiminang.com; Jl Bundo Kandung 20-28; r incl breakfast from 816,000-6,900,000Rp plus 21% tax; ⊠ 💻 🛁 ) The most expensive pad in town has a business centre and other trappings of the rich and powerful.

## Eating & Drinking

Start with the cuisine that conquered a nation, from these excellent proponents: **Pagi Sore** (Jl Pondok 143; dishes 8000Rp), **Sari Raso** ( ☎ 33498; Jl Karya 3; dishes 10,000Rp) and **Simpang Raya** (Jl Bundo Kandung; dishes 8000Rp).

**Taman Ria Pantai Padang** (Jl Samudera; mains 6000-8000Rp; ☾ dinner) Serves standard dishes with excellent sea views.

**Mirama Cafe** ( ☎ 23237; miramacaferst@hotmail.com; Jl Gereje 38; mains 21,000Rp) Offers pricey, blandeddown versions of Indonesian standards in a nice outdoor setting.

**Nelayan Restaurant** (Jl Samudera; mains 25,000Rp) Does great seafood the Chinese way.

**our pick** **Ikan Bakar 'Pak Agus'** ( ☎ 823 1799; Jl H O S Cokroaminoto 91; set meals from 25,000Rp) Pak Agus flames his dead sea creatures to perfection.

---

### MEET BREAKFAST, LUNCH & DINNER: PADANG CUISINE

Eating in a foreign land just got a whole lot easier thanks to Padang cuisine. Forget about pointing at a pot or snooping at your neighbour's meal. With Padang cuisine, you sit down and the whole kit and caboodle gets laid out in front of you. You decide which ones look tasty and push the others aside. You pay for what you eat – nibbling, sniffing and fondling included.

The drawback is that you never really know what you're eating, since there's no menu. If the dish contains liquid, it is usually a coconut-milk curry, a major component of Padang cuisine. The meaty dishes are most likely beef or buffalo, occasionally offal or (less likely) even dog. Some of the fun of Padang-ing is identifying the mystery meat. Because most dishes are cooked slowly and thoroughly, the difference between chicken and certain types of fish isn't so obvious.

The most famous Padang dish is *rendang,* in which chunks of beef or buffalo are simmered slowly in coconut milk until the sauce is reduced to a rich paste and the meat becomes dark and dried. Other popular dishes include *telor balado* (egg dusted with red chilli), *ikan panggang* (fish baked in coconut and chilli) and *gulai merah kambing* (red mutton curry).

Most couples pick one or two meat dishes and a vegetable, usually *kangkong* (water spinach), and load up with a plate or two of rice. Carbs are manna in Padang cuisine. Vegetarians should ask for tempeh or *tahu* (tofu), which comes doctored up in a spicy sambal. The orphan dishes are collected and returned to the display window, protected from curious flies by a lacy curtain.

Before digging into the meal – and we mean this literally, as your right hand is your utensil – wash up in the provided bowl of water. Food and sauces should be spooned onto your plate of rice, then mixed together with the fingers. The rice will be easier to handle if it is a little wet. Use your fingers to scoop up the food, and your thumb to push it into your mouth. It is messy even for people raised on it.

Padang cuisine has an earthy spiciness that might need a little sweet tea or water as a chaser. There is usually a tumbler of lukewarm water (a sign that it has been boiled for sterilisation) on the table.

After you've slurped and sucked your plate clean, wash up, let out a burp (or don't be surprised if your neighbour does) and fire up a cigarette.

The seafood is delivered fresh every afternoon. A set meal contains a whole barbecued fish, sides, rice and a drink.

Jl Sumadera and Jl Batang Arau are full of cheap warungs that spring to life at night, while discerning foodies head for Jl Pondok and Jl H O S Cokroaminoto. Juice wagons loiter near the end of Jl Hayam Wuruk. Grab a snack from the carts at the *opelet* station opposite the market. If pastries are your thing, try **France Modern Bakery** (Jl Batang Arau; mains 2000Rp) or any of the **Tokyo Bakery** franchises.

**Fellas** (Jl Hayam Wuruk 47; 🛜) is a Western-style wi-fi cafe by day; the evenings see it fill with trendy young locals sucking on hookahs and tourists getting liquored.

## Shopping

**Pasar Raya** (Jl Pasar Raya) – literally 'big market' – is the centre of Padang's shopping universe; most traveller necessities can be found here. Across the street, **Plaza Matahari** specialises in women's clothes, while the nearby **Plaza Andalas** (Jl M Yamin) is the place to hunt out a new cell phone. All three have a food court on their top floor.

## Getting There & Away

### AIR

Padang's airport, **Bandara Internasional Minangkabau** (BIM; off Jl Adinegoro) is located 20km north of town. The following airlines operate international and domestic flights. There is a 100,000Rp departure tax on international flights.

**Air Asia** ( ☎ 021 5050 5088; Hotel Huangtuah, Jl Pemuda 1) Flies twice daily to Kuala Lumpur, Malaysia.

**Batavia Air** ( ☎ 41502; www.batavia-air.co.id; Jl Khatib Sulaiman 63C) Flies three times daily to Jakarta.

**Fireflyz** (www.fireflyz.com.my) Has a daily propeller flight to Kuala Lumpur domestic airport (Subang), Malaysia.

**Garuda** ( ☎ 30737; www.garuda-indonesia.com; Jl Sudirman 2) Operates three flights daily to Jakarta.

**Lion Air** ( ☎ 786 4781; www.lionair.co.id; BIM) Flies to Jakarta four times daily.

**Mandala Air** ( ☎ 39737; www.mandalaair.com; Jl Veteran 20C) Flies daily to Jakarta, Medan and Batam.

**SMAC** ( ☎ 0813 6358 8828; BIM) Flies three times a week to Pulau Sipora in the Mentawai Islands.

**Sriwijaya Air** ( ☎ 811 777; www.sriwijayaair-online .com; Jl Proklamasi 39, Terandam) Daily flights to Jakarta and Medan.

**Tiger Airways** (www.tigerairways.com) Flights to Singapore on Tuesday, Thursday and Saturday.

### BOAT

Padang has three commonly used ports. Depending on the tide, boats to Siberut and other Mentawai islands will leave from either the river mouth (Sungai Muara) on Sungai Batang Arau, just south of Padang's city centre, or from Teluk Kabung port at Bungus, 20km (45 minutes) away. Check the boat's departure point with your travel agent on sailing day.

Teluk Bayur is the commercial freight port 8km from town and receives a monthly **Pelni** ( ☎ 61624; www.pelni.co.id) ship, MV *Lawit*, to/from Nias (economy/1st class 109,000/353,000Rp, 20 hours).

### BUS

The days of heading 12km out of town to the Bengkuang terminal at Aie Pacah are over. Most locals prefer to take minivans directly from Padang and, depending on your destination, these vans will even pick you up from your hotel.

Vans depart frequently for Bukittinggi (16,000Rp, two hours), from the city's northern fringes. **Tranex** ( ☎ 705 8577) has a depot 2km north of the Pangeran Beach Hotel, opposite the Indah Theatre. Catch any white *opelet* (2000Rp) heading north on Jl Permuda and ask for 'Tranex'. If coming from the airport and heading straight to Bukittinggi, take any bus from the terminal and alight at the motorway overpass (2km), where there's a pickup area.

Vans for Kerinci go to Sungai Penuh (70,000Rp, six hours) and leave from the same depot as Tranex.

Vans to other destinations including Parapat (for Danau Toba, 350,000Rp, 17 hours), Bengkulu (155,000Rp, 16 hours) and Sibolga (for Nias, 150,000Rp, 12 hours) will pick up from your hotel.

For Medan and Jakarta, it's cheaper and faster to fly.

## Getting Around

Airport taxis start from 100,000Rp. White **Damri** ( ☎ 780 6335) buses (18,000Rp) are a cheaper alternative and loop through Padang. Tell the conductor your street and they'll drop you at the right stop. Heading to the airport, they pass by Bumiminang Hotel and Jl Pemuda/Veteran. From Bukittinggi alight at the motorway overpass and take an *ojek* to the terminal.

There are numerous *opelet* around town, operating out of the Pasar Raya terminal off Jl M Yamin. The standard fare is 2000Rp. Motorcycle rental is from 80,000Rp per day.

## AROUND PADANG
### Beaches

If Padang's traffic is frying your brains, or you're waiting for a boat, kick back on one of the nearby beaches. **Pantai Bungus**, 23km south of Padang, is conveniently close to the ferry port of Teluk Kabung, but still sufficiently relaxed to unkink the most frazzled. There's a host of nearby islands to explore, plus the odd gem in the hinterland.

**Losmen Carlos** ( ☎ 751 153; Pantai Bungus; r 100,000-150,000Rp) has great beachside rooms and a laid-back vibe. It runs tours (200,000Rp) to Pulau Pagang and Pulau Sironjong, and can organise Siberut guides and trips to the hinterland.

**Tin Tin Homestay** ( ☎ 0812 6683 6668; losmen-tintin .tripod.com; r 50,000Rp) is a small, quiet family-run losmen with basic, netted rooms, situated 400m south of Losmen Carlos. Also offers island tours.

**Pulau Pagang** is beautiful small island, 90 minutes offshore, with white sandy beaches and a handful of basic bungalows. It's possible to rent a boat from Bungus and stay the night. Ask at your losmen, or among the local fishermen.

**Pulau Sikuai** and **Pulau Cubadak** both have expensive resorts. **Cubadak Paradiso Village** ( ☎ 081 2660 3766; www.cubadak-paradisovillage.com) is the better of the two; it also has a **dive school** ( ☎ 081 2663 7609).

Further south is **Pulau Marak**, which has a simiang (black gibbon) rehabilitation centre and miles of undisturbed coastline. While not officially open to the public, it's worth asking around.

Back on the mainland, and close to Teluk Kabung, the spectacular three-storey waterfall **Air Terjun Tiga Tingkat** (Three Tier Waterfall) is found in the village of Koto Lubuk Hitam.

**Jembatan Akar** (Bridge of Roots; Pulut-Pulut) is a living bridge over the Bayang River made from the entwined roots of weeping fig trees. Follow the highway south through Tarusan towards Painan, and turn left after Pasar Baru onto the Muara Air road, heading for Kampong Pulut-Pulut. The narrow road follows a scenic valley for another 23km. There's a small warung at the bridge. Transport can be arranged in Painan.

To reach Pantai Bungus, take a blue *opelet* labelled 'Kabung Bungus' (8000Rp, 60 minutes) or a taxi (100,000Rp).

**Pasir Jambak** is the best of several beaches north of Padang. **Uncle Jack's** ( ☎ 787 4719; r per person with meals 90,000Rp) has basic huts among the palms just behind the beach. Jack can organise snorkelling trips to nearby Pulau Sawo. He'll also do airport transfers for 50,000Rp.

*Opelet* 423 will get you to the turnoff for 5000Rp, but you'll have to take an *ojek* (7000Rp) the rest of the way.

## MENTAWAI ISLANDS

Though not a great distance from the mainland, Mentawai Islands and its people were kept isolated until the 19th century by strong winds, unpredictable currents and razor-sharp corals.

It's thought that the archipelago separated from Sumatra some 500,000 years ago, resulting in such unique flora and fauna that sees Mentawai ranked alongside Madagascar in terms of endemic primate population. Of particular interest is *Siamang kerdil*, a rare species of black and yellow monkey, named *simpai Mentawai* by the locals.

The largest island, Siberut, is home to the majority of the Mentawai population and is the most studied and protected island in the archipelago. About 60% of Siberut is still covered with tropical rainforest, which shelters a rich biological community that has earned it a designation as a Unesco biosphere reserve. The western half of the island is protected as the Siberut National Park (TNS).

Pulau Sipora is home to Tua Pejat, the seat of regional government and a surfer drop-off point. The archipelago's airport is located at Rokot. With only 10% original rainforest remaining, it's also the most developed of the Mentawai islands.

Further south are the Pulau Pagai islands – Utara (North) and Selatan (South), which rarely see independent travellers.

Change has come quickly to Mentawai. Tourism, logging, *transmigrasi* (a government-sponsored scheme enabling settlers to move from overcrowded regions to sparsely populated ones) and other government-backed attempts to mainstream the culture have separated the people from the jungle and whittled the jungle into profit. It isn't what it used to be, but it is a long way from being like everywhere else. And that keeps trekkers happily braving mud and

SUMATRA

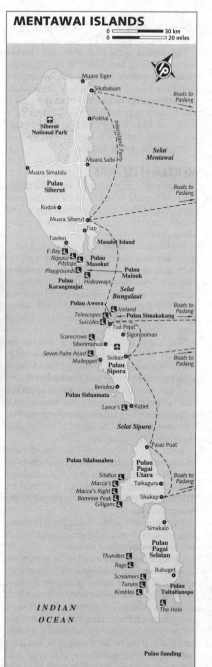

**MENTAWAI ISLANDS**

bugs to visit the remaining traditional communities. Surfers comprise the other Mentawai-bound pilgrims, many of whom rank Mentawai as the ride of their life. Slowly but surely resorts are grabbing a beachhead and starting a crab-like march against the forest, though with rising sea levels, nothing is guaranteed.

## Information

The islands are very undeveloped. Bring all necessities and plenty of cash.

**Siberut National Park** (TNS; Sejeterah; ☎ 0759-21109; ⏱ 8am-noon & 2-5pm Mon-Fri, 8am-noon Sat) The park office, a 10-minute *ojek* ride from the ferry jetty, is only useful if you speak Bahasa.

## Activities

### TREKKING

The river scene from *Apocalypse Now* flashes into your mind as you head upstream in a longboat and watch the people and villages growing wilder by the minute. Soon you're out of the canoe and following some shaman-eyed tribesman with crazy tattoos and a loincloth through the mud for the next few hours, passing waterfalls, balancing on slippery tree branches and swimming across rivers, to his humble abode on poles in the middle of nowhere.

There's been fervent discussion about the authenticity of these trips, and what actually constitutes a traditional lifestyle. The mud is real, and so are the tattoos – decide for yourself.

In the past, mainland tour agencies had a stranglehold on the tourist dollar, but times have changed. It is infinitely more flexible, rewarding and sustainable to turn up at Muara Siberut independently and tailor a trek to remote communities, than it is to be locked into a 10-day mainland-organised tour with a horde of strangers following a well-trodden route. Ask around at the jetty cafes in Maileppet and Muara Siberut. Prices start around 100,000Rp per day, but don't include transport, food, accommodation or tips. Clarify exactly what is and isn't included.

If you prefer a mainland-organised trek, prices in Bukittinggi start at around US$225/250 for six/10 days and normally include a guide, accommodation, food and transport. However, always check for any additional costs. Guides also hang around some of the losmen in Bungus, waiting for a boat home, and most hotels in Padang also offer tours.

For more on hiring guides, see p822.

## Trekking Essentials

Dress for mud wrestling. Most of your gear will get trashed, so bring as little as possible; electronic items have a particularly high attrition rate. Bear in mind you may need to swim the odd river.

Double bag everything in plastic bags and try to keep one set of clothes dry for evening use. Don't walk in beach sandals – one foot into deep bog and you'll never see them again. However, if you dislike having pig excrement between your toes, you might find them useful around the communities in the evenings.

Travel light. Large packs are a hindrance and anything tied to the outside is a goner. Forget rain gear, just accept that you're going to get wet. Bring a mosquito net if trekking independently; tour group accommodation should supply them (though check!). Water purification (tablets or Steripen) is recommended, as is a head torch.

Chloroquine-resistant malaria still exists on Siberut, so take appropriate precautions, though **Surf Aid** (www.surfaidinternational.org) has been actively working to limit its spread. DDT-strength insect repellent is advisable. Sanitation is poor, with the local river serving all purposes, so bring as much bottled water as you can.

May is generally the driest month, while October and November are the wettest – but it can rain any time. The seas between Siberut and the mainland can get very rough in June and July, when it can be too dangerous to sail.

You can buy most supplies in Muara Siberut, but they are much cheaper in Padang. You'll also need items for barter and gifts. You will be pestered for cigarettes, but day-to-day items might be more appropriate. Check with your guide what is sustainable.

### FIXERS – THE FINE ART OF FIXING A SURFING SAFARI

Surfers have latched onto what journalists and movie directors have known for years – if you need to get things done in a foreign country with the least amount of hassle, you need to find a local 'fixer'. Sure, you could just take an all-inclusive surf package with a tour company, but these cost a lot of money (something surfers are traditionally reluctant to part with), and besides, they lack a little, well, adventure.

A good fixer is worth their weight in gold. They will meet you at the airport and arrange portage of all your boards and gear, take you somewhere to freshen up, show you where you can procure various supplies (food, drinking water, beer – there's none where you're headed), then get the whole lot to the port and safely stowed on the ferry. They will have already arranged your arrival day to coincide with the ferry schedule, and secured you a cabin. On your return, they'll meet the ferry and get you and all your gear back to the airport.

You then need a second fixer out in the islands, who will meet your ferry, tee up a longboat, ship your gear, and drop you at a cheap losmen or basic hut somewhere close to your favourite break. They'll even arrange a cook if you want one. Of course, all this costs money, and rest assured, your fixer is taking a cut from everybody, but with careful planning and bargaining it's still going to be a whole lot cheaper than two weeks in a resort.

How do you find a fixer? Without any recommendations, your first trip will always be a learning curve and will involve equal quantities of patience, luck, and trial and error. Experienced surfers come back year after year and use the same fixers, boat drivers and hut owners. All business is conducted by mobile phone, and good fixers will also have email addresses. Ask around your hotel – chances are that desk clerk actually came from village A and his best mate now works in resort B and knows a boat driver who can hook you up with this guy who owns a shack on island C. Watch closely what other groups are doing, maybe you can share a taxi to the port, or bum a lift in a speedboat – all the time filling your mobile phone with contact numbers.

Who are these fixers? A lot are or were students, looking for some extra cash and a chance to practise their English/French/Portuguese. Some have worked in hotels and resorts and are well connected, as are others who are native to the islands.

There's nothing stopping you doing all this organising yourself, and the first time you probably will, but it's time and energy you'd most likely rather leave for the waves.

**THE MENTAWAIANS**

The untouched, the unbaptised and the unphotographed have long drawn Westerners to distant corners of the globe. And the Mentawaians have seen every sort of self-anointed discoverer: the colonial entrepreneurs hoping to harness the land for profit, missionaries trading medicine for souls, and modern-day tourists eager to experience life before the machine.

Very little is known about the origins of the Mentawaians, but it is assumed that they emigrated from Sumatra to Nias and made their way to Siberut from there.

In 1864 the Mentawai archipelago was nominally made a Dutch colony, but it was not until 1901, during the Russo-Japanese War, that the Dutch placed a garrison on the islands to prevent another foreign power using them as a naval base. In subsequent years it was the missionaries who had the most influence on the Mentawai people, creating fundamental changes in their culture.

At the time of contact with missionaries, the Mentawaians had their own language, *adat* (traditional laws and regulations) and religion, and were skilled boat builders. They lived a hunter-gatherer existence.

Traditional clothing was a loincloth made from the bark of the breadfruit tree for men and a bark skirt for women. Mentawaians wore bands of red-coloured rattan, beads and imported brass rings. They filed their teeth into points and decorated their bodies with tattoos.

After independence, the Indonesian government banned many of the Mentawaians' customs, such as tattoos, sharpened teeth and long hair. Although the ban has not been enforced, many villagers have adopted modern fashions.

Traditional villages are built along riverbanks and consist of one or more *uma* (communal house) surrounded by *lalep* (single-storey family houses). Several families live in the same building. Bachelors and widows have their own quarters, known as *rusuk,* identical to the family longhouse except they have no altar. Traditionally, the houses stand on wooden piles and are windowless.

Although essentially patriarchal, society is organised on egalitarian principles. There are no inherited titles or positions and no subordinate roles. It is the *uma,* not the village itself, which is pivotal to society. It is here that discussions affecting the community take place. Everyone is present at meetings, but the prominent men make most of the major decisions, including choosing a *rimata* (the person who leads religious affairs and is the community's spokesperson to the outside world), building an *uma,* clearing a forest or laying out a banana plantation.

## SURFING

Surfing is big business in Mentawai as the islands have consistent surf year-round at hundreds of legendary breaks. The season peaks between April and October.

In the past, charter boats were the primary means of reaching the top spots, but now land-based resorts have gained a toehold, and many fly in clients on all-inclusive packages.

With patience, attitude and a handful of contacts, however, it's possible to put together your own independent surfing safari for a fraction of the cost of a package tour (see the boxed text, p427). Losmen are blossoming throughout Mentawai, and chartering a longboat is relatively easy. Check some of the more popular surfing blogs, or Lonely Planet's own Thorntree forum, for the latest hotspots:

**GlobalSurfers** (www.globalsurfers.com)
**WannaSurf** (www.wannasurf.com)
**Lonely Planet Thorn Tree forum** (www.lonelyplanet.com/thorntree)

## Tours & Charters

The following companies can arrange trekking tours and surf charters.

**Bevys Sumatra** (Map p421; ☎ 34878; bevyssumatra@yahoo.com; Jl Pondok 121, Padang) A Padang-based agent who issues ferry tickets to Mentawai and organises trekking, surf and dive tours.

**Ina Tours** (Map p421; ☎ 31669; Dipo International Hotel, Jl Diponegoro 13, Padang) Located inside Dipo Hotel in Padang, this agent organises Mentawai cultural tours.

**Sumatran Surfariis** (Map p421; ☎ 34878; www.sumatransurfariis.com; Jl Pondok 121) Affiliated with Bevys, Sumatran Surfariis operates a variety of surf-boat charters; packages start from US$1600 for a 10-day tour.

On such occasions, the people of the *uma* carry out a religious festival known as *punen*. This usually involves ritual sacrifices of both pigs and chickens and, depending on the importance of the occasion, the festival can last for months, sometimes years. All kinds of everyday jobs and activities become taboo; work in the fields is stopped and strangers are denied access to the *uma*, its isolation being marked by a cordon of palm leaves and flowers.

The native Sibulungan religion is a form of animism, involving the worship of nature spirits and a belief in the existence of ghosts, as well as the soul. The chief nature spirits are those of the sky, the sea, the jungle and the earth. The sky spirits are considered the most influential. There are also two river spirits: *Ina Oinan* (Mother of Rivers) is beneficent, while *Kameinan* (Father's Sister) is regarded as evil. In addition, all inanimate objects have a *kina* (spirit), which gives them life.

The worship of the soul is of utmost importance, being vital to good health and longevity. The soul is believed to depart the body at various times during life before its ultimate escape at death. Sickness, for example, is the result of the temporary absence of the soul; dreams also signify that the soul is 'on vacation'.

When the soul leaves the body at death it is transformed into a *sanitu* (ghost). Mentawaians try to avoid these ghosts, whom they suspect of malevolently attempting to rob the living of their souls. To protect themselves, they place fetish sticks at every entrance to the village. This tactic is considered foolproof, provided no one has committed a ritual sin or broken a taboo.

German missionary August Lett was the first to attempt to convert the local people, but he was not entirely successful: eight years after his arrival Lett was murdered by the locals. Somehow the mission managed to survive and 11 baptisms had been recorded by 1916. There are now more than 80 Protestant churches throughout the islands.

More than 50 years after the Protestants, Catholic missionaries moved in to vie for converts. They opened a mission – a combined church, school and clinic – in south Siberut. Free medicines and clothes were given to any islander who became a Catholic, and by 1969 there were almost 3000 converts.

Islam began to make inroads when government officials were regularly appointed from Padang during the Dutch era, and then to complicate religious matters further, the Baha'í faith was introduced in 1955. Today more than half the population claims to be Protestant, 16% Catholic and 13% Muslim, while the rest have no official religion.

## Sleeping

Along with transport, accommodation will be your primary expense in Mentawai. Trekking guides will organise family homestays. Most of the private surf resorts don't accept short-term stays (less than seven days). However, there are alternatives.

If you're stuck in Muara Siberut without a guide, there is very basic accommodation at the **Sirruhuudin Hotel** (r 25,000Rp) on the waterfront (next to the pink Telkom shop), as well as the odd homestay (ask around the *pasar*).

There are basic losmen around most of the Mentawai ports, and simple beach huts (with/without cook from 175,000/75,000Rp) have sprung up around **E-Bay** and **Playgrounds**, to the south of Siberut. Bring all your supplies, drinking water and mosquito nets. To get there, either bum a lift off another group, or charter your a longboat from Muara Siberut (see p431).

You don't have to be a surfer to enjoy the pristine beach protected by a lagoon at **Masalot Island**, an hour from Muara Siberut. Boatmen from Siberut can arrange a local homestay.

**Katiet**, at the bottom of **Pulau Sipora** and home of the classic **Lance's** breaks, also has a few losmen. Catch a ferry from Bungus to **Sioban**, then try to find a speedboat (seat/whole boat 50,000/400,000Rp) heading south. Saturday (market day) is your best bet.

If you want wi-fi, three meals a day and hot showers, then bite the resort bullet. Transport from the mainland is normally included.

**Wavepark Resort** (Pulau Mainuk; ☎ 081 2663 5551; www.wavepark.com; minimum 7-night package, per day US$245) The first land-based resort on Mentawai, Wavepark has a front-row view of Hideaways. Rates include flights to and from the mainland.

**Macaroni's Resort** (Pulau Pagai Utara; ☎ 081374429357 www.macaronisresort.com; minimum 8-day package surfer/nonsurfer US$1525/1245; ☜) Bamboo villas built over the water; it's a quick speedboat transfer to Macca's and Macca's Right.

**Aloita Resort & Spa** (Pulau Simakakang; ☎ 34878; www.aloitaresort.com; minimum 3-night package, per day surfer/nonsurfer US$220/165) Eight bungalows occupy a private beach within shuttle's reach of Telescopes and Iceland. Also offers scuba diving and certification. Book through Bevys.

**Kandui Resort** (Pulau Karangmajat; ☎ US 1714 478 2487; www.mentawaiislands.com; minimum 10-night package from US$2350; ☜) Self-contained, wi-fi-enabled thatched bungalows with access to 4 Bobs and A-Frames. Price does not include transport.

**Pitstop Hill Resort** (Pulau Masokut, aka Nyang Nyang; www.pitstophill.com; per day from A$150) Sleeps six in a central house near the break of the same name. Close to E-Bay.

**Awera Island Surf Camp** (Pulau Awera; www.awerais land.com; per day from US$105;) This small low-key resort near Iceland sleeps six in twin-bunk dorms. Transport to the island not included.

## Getting There & Away

**Subang Merauke Airways** (SMA, previously SMAC; ☎ 0813 6358 8828) flies to Pulau Sipora (Rotok) on Tuesday, Thursday and Saturday (without/with surfboard 800,000/1,600,000Rp).

As there is no longer a speedboat, all ferries to Mentawai charge the same price (deck/cabin 105,000/125,000Rp) and usually take 10 hours. Unless you enjoy being squashed into a corner on a hard floor and continually trampled under the glare of the passage lights, pay extra for a cabin. All boats run overnight, and usually return the following evening (unless continuing). The ferry schedules are changing constantly so always check what's available on arrival in Padang. See below for the ferry schedule.

Tickets can be bought from **Bevys Sumatra** (Map p421; ☎ 34878; Jl Pondok 121). Remember to check which Padang port to leave from (see p424)

## Getting Around

Boats to Siberut arrive at the jetty in Maileppet. It's a 10-minute *ojek* ride (15,000Rp) to the

### FERRY SCHEDULE TO/FROM MENTAWAI ISLANDS

| Day | Boat | From | To |
|---|---|---|---|
| Mon | Ambu-Ambu | Tua Pejat | Padang |
|  | Beriloga | Sikakap | Padang |
|  | Simasin | Sikabaluan | Siberut–Tua Pejat–Padang |
|  | Sumber Rezeky | Padang | Siberut |
| Tue | Ambu-Ambu | Padang | Sikakap |
|  | Beriloga | Padang | Sikabaluan–Siberut |
|  | Sumber Rezeky | Siberut | Padang |
| Wed | Ambu-Ambu | Sikakap | Padang |
|  | Beriloga | Siberut | Padang |
|  | Sumber Rezeky | Padang | Tua Pejat |
| Thu | Ambu-Ambu | Padang | Tua Pejat# |
|  | Ambu-Ambu | Padang | Siberut* |
|  | Beriloga | Padang | Sikabaluan–Tua Pejat |
|  | Simasin | Padang | Sikabaluan–Siberut |
|  | Sumber Rezeky | Tua Pejat | Padang |
| Fri | Ambu-Ambu | Siberut* | Padang |
|  | Ambu-Ambu | Tua Pejat# | Padang |
|  | Beriloga | Sikabaluan | Padang |
|  | Simasin | Siberut | Padang |
|  | Sumber Rezeky | Padang | Sioban–Tua Pejat |
| Sat | Sumber Rezeky | Tua Pejat | Sioban–Padang |
| Sun | Ambu-Ambu | Padang | Tua Pejat |
|  | Beriloga | Padang | Sikakap |
|  | Simasin | Padang | Tua Pejat–Siberut–Sikabaluan |

\# - weeks 1 & 4
\* - weeks 2 & 3

SUMATRA

| FERRY SCHEDULE AROUND MENTAWAI ISLANDS | | |
|---|---|---|
| **Day** | **From** | **To** |
| Mon | Tua Pejat | Sioban–Pasar Puat–Sikakap |
| Tue | Sikakap | Pasar Puat–Sioban–Tua Pejat |
| Wed | Tua Pejat | Maulimuk–Siberut–Sikabaluan |
| Thu | Sikabaluan | Siberut–Maulimuk–Tua Pejat |
| Fri | Tua Pejat | Sioban–Pasar Puat–Sikakap |
| Sat | Sikakap | Pasar Puat–Sioban–Tua Pejat |

main village of **Muara Siberut**, where longboats can be hired. Sample charter fees (up to five passengers) include the following:
**Muara Siberut to E-Bay** 600,000Rp (1½ hours)
**E-Bay to Playgrounds** 300,000Rp (30 minutes)
**Playgrounds to Tua Paget** 1,200,000Rp (2½ hours)
**Sioban to Katiet** 400,000Rp (two hours)

In theory it's possible to island hop from Siberut all the way to Tua Pejat on Sipora via E-Bay and Playgrounds, but in reality it would work out cheaper (because you would have to keep the same boat or risk getting stranded) to return to Muara Siberut and take the inter-island ferry. See above for the ferry schedule.

Every Monday the *KM Sibulat* departs from Tua Pejat and winds its way through the islands. Tickets are 35,000Rp for one stop and the boat leaves at 9am each day.

# BUKITTINGGI
☎ 0752 / pop 95,000
Early on a bright, clear morning, the market town of Bukittinggi sits high above the valley mists as three sentinels – fire-breathing Merapi, benign Singgalang and distant Sago – all look on impassively. Sun-ripened crops grow fat in the rich volcanic soil, as frogs call in the paddies, *bendis* haul goods to the *pasar*, and the muezzin's call sits lightly on the town. Modern life seems far removed.

Until 9am. Then the traffic starts up, and soon there's a mile-long jam around the bus terminal and the air turns the colour of diesel. The mosques counter the traffic by cranking their amps to eleven, while hotel staff try to pass off cold bread and jam as breakfast.

Such is the incongruity of modern Bukittinggi, blessed by nature, choked by mortals. Lush. Fertile. Busy. And at 930m above sea level, deliciously temperate all year round.

The town (alternatively named Tri Arga, referring to the triumvirate of peaks) has had a chequered history, playing host at various times to Islamic reformists, Dutch colonials, Japanese invaders and Sumatran separatists.

Bukittinggi was once a mainstay of the banana-pancake trail, but regional instability, shorter visas, and the rise of low-cost air-carriers have seen the traveller tide reduced to a low ebb. However, locals are optimistic that the worst is over, and that numbers may again be on the increase.

## Orientation
The town centre is compact and most items of interest are easily reached on foot. By day, the *pasar* and clock-tower end is bustling. In the evenings the focus shifts to the bottom of Jl Ahmad Yani, where warungs open and travellers sip their drinks after a hard day's touring.

The Aur Kuning bus terminal is 2km south of the town centre.

## Information
### INTERNET ACCESS & POST
Internet cafes abound on Jl Ahmad Yani.
**Orange99.net** (Jl Ahmad Yani; per hr 4000Rp; ☒ 10am-late) Two locations.
**Harau Internet** (Jl Ahmad Yani; per hr 4000Rp)
**Turret Cafe** ( ☎ 625 956; Jl Ahmad Yani 140-142; internet access per hr 6000Rp)
**Post office** (Jl Sudirman; internet access per hr 6000Rp) South of town, near the bus terminal.

### MEDICAL SERVICES
**Rumah Sakit Sayang Bari** (Jl Dr Rivai)

### MONEY
Banks and ATMs are scattered along Jl Ahmad Yani.
**Lippo bank** (Jl Ahmad Yani)
**BNI Bank** (Jl Lenggogeni)
**BRI bank** (Jl Ahmed Yani)
**BRI bank** (Jl Istana)

### TELEPHONE
There are still a few wartel around town.
**Wartel** (Jl Yos Sudarso, next to Hotel Sari)
**Wartel** (Jl Ahmad Yani, near Aladdin Antiques)
**Wartel** (Jl Ahmad Yani, near Apache Cafe)
**Wartel** (Jl Sudirman, past the Tourist Office)

# BUKITTINGGI

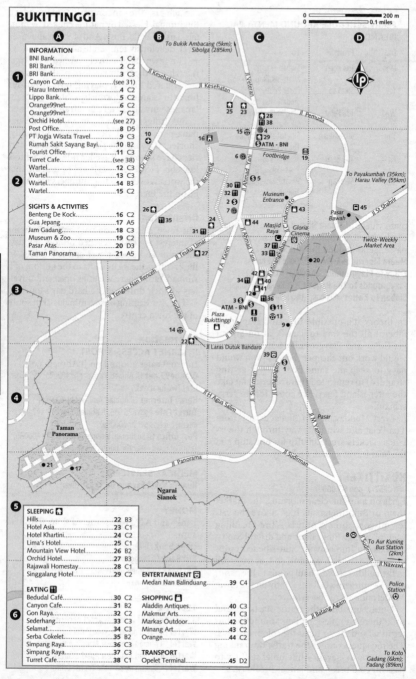

| A | B | C | D |

**INFORMATION**
| | |
|---|---|
| BNI Bank | **1** C4 |
| BRI Bank | **2** C2 |
| BRI Bank | **3** C3 |
| Canyon Cafe | (see 31) |
| Harau Internet | **4** C2 |
| Lippo Bank | **5** C2 |
| Orange99net | **6** C2 |
| Orange99net | **7** C2 |
| Orchid Hotel | (see 27) |
| Post Office | **8** D5 |
| PT Jogja Wisata Travel | **9** C3 |
| Rumah Sakit Sayang Bayi | **10** B2 |
| Tourist Office | **11** C3 |
| Turret Cafe | (see 38) |
| Wartel | **12** C3 |
| Wartel | **13** C3 |
| Wartel | **14** B3 |
| Wartel | **15** C2 |

**SIGHTS & ACTIVITIES**
| | |
|---|---|
| Benteng De Kock | **16** C2 |
| Gua Jepang | **17** A5 |
| Jam Gadang | **18** C3 |
| Museum & Zoo | **19** C2 |
| Pasar Atas | **20** D3 |
| Taman Panorama | **21** A5 |

**SLEEPING**
| | |
|---|---|
| Hills | **22** B3 |
| Hotel Asia | **23** C1 |
| Hotel Khartini | **24** C2 |
| Lima's Hotel | **25** C1 |
| Mountain View Hotel | **26** B2 |
| Orchid Hotel | **27** B3 |
| Rajawali Homestay | **28** C1 |
| Singgalang Hotel | **29** C2 |

**EATING**
| | |
|---|---|
| Bedudal Café | **30** C2 |
| Canyon Cafe | **31** B2 |
| Gon Raya | **32** C2 |
| Sederhang | **33** C3 |
| Selamat | **34** C3 |
| Serba Cokelet | **35** B2 |
| Simpang Raya | **36** C3 |
| Simpang Raya | **37** C3 |
| Turret Cafe | **38** C1 |

**ENTERTAINMENT**
| | |
|---|---|
| Medan Nan Balinduang | **39** C4 |

**SHOPPING**
| | |
|---|---|
| Aladdin Antiques | **40** C3 |
| Makmur Arts | **41** C3 |
| Markas Outdoor | **42** C3 |
| Minang Art | **43** C2 |
| Orange | **44** C2 |

**TRANSPORT**
| | |
|---|---|
| Opelet Terminal | **45** D2 |

SUMATRA

## TOURIST INFORMATION
**Tourist Office** (Jl Sudirman; ⏲ 7.45am-3pm) Opposite the clock tower; it's got maps, tours and tickets to cultural events.

## TRAVEL AGENCIES
Bukittinggi has plenty of travel agencies, most of them along Jl Ahmad Yani.

**PT Jogja Wisata Travel** ( ☎ 32634; Jl Perintis Kemerdekaan 17) At the bottom of the steps at the clock-tower side of the market. Staff can arrange airport transfers (40,000Rp) and flights.

Some traveller hotels and cafes also act as booking agents. The **Orchid Hotel** ( ☎ 32634; roni_orchid@hotmail.com; Jl Teuku Umar 11) and **Canyon Cafe** ( ☎ 21652; www.seruling-travel.com; Jl Teuku Umar 8) have previously proved reliable.

## Sights
**Pasar Atas** (located east of Jl Minangkabau) is a large, colourful market crammed with stalls selling fruit and vegetables, secondhand clothing and crafts. It's open daily, but the serious action is on Wednesday and Saturday, when the stalls overflow down the hill and villagers from the surrounding area come to haggle and have a look around.

**Benteng de Kock** (Benteng Fort; admission 5000Rp) was built by the Dutch during the Padri Wars, but apart from the moat and a few rusting cannons, there's not much to see, other than fine views over the town from its hilltop position.

A footbridge crosses over Jl Ahmad Yani to Taman Bundo Kandung, site of the **museum** and **zoo**. The museum, constructed in 1934 in Minangkabau style, is the oldest in the province; admission is 2000Rp. The zoo (included in the Benteng Fort admission) is just depressing.

**Taman Panorama** (Panorama Park; Jl Panorama; admission 5000Rp), on the southern edge of town, overlooks the deep Ngarai Sianok (Sianok Canyon), where fruit bats swoop at sunset. *Friendly* guides will approach visitors – settle on a price before continuing (around 20,000Rp) to avoid misunderstandings later – to lead you through **Gua Jepang** (Japanese Caves), wartime defensive tunnels built by Japanese slave labour. **Jam Gadang** (Big Clock Tower; btwn Jl Istana & Sudirman) is the town's focal point, where locals and tourists alike slurp ice creams and take snapshots under the leafy shade while vacant *bendis* look on. It was built in the 1920s

to house the clock, a gift from the Dutch queen; independence saw the retrofit of a Minangkabau roof.

## Tours
Local tours fall into two categories, culture or nature, and can range from a half-day meander through neighbouring villages to a three-day jungle trek to Danau Maninjau, or an overnight assault on Gunung Merapi.

Half-/full-day tours start at around 100,000Rp/175,000Rp, and multiday trekking is roughly 200,000Rp per day. Some tours have a minimum quota, though the **Orchid Hotel** runs solo tours by motorbike.

Guides hang out in all the cafes. Be clear about what you want and what is and isn't included. If going solo, make sure somebody knows who you're going with.

There's a healthy climbing scene here and a day on the cliffs is around US$35, but if you can find some locals and avoid the entrepreneurs, it'll work out cheaper.

## Sleeping
Bukittinggi's mosques have been strategically located to saturate the entire town with the predawn call to prayer.

Most hotels include a simple breakfast. Hotel tax is only applied to top-end options and can be negotiated. On holidays, rooms fill quickly with Indonesian visitors. In Bukittinggi's temperate climate, hot water is more desirable than air-con.

### BUDGET
**Rajawali Homestay** ( ☎ 26113; Jl Ahmad Yani 152; r 50,000Rp) The rooms are basic but cosy in this tiny homestay right in the centre. The irrepressible Ulrich is a fount of local knowledge and has detailed maps and advice on the area's attractions.

**Orchid Hotel** ( ☎ 32634; roni_orchid@hotmail.com; Jl Teuku Umar 11; r cold/hot water 75,000/100,000Rp) Roni runs this popular backpacker inn that features clean rooms and a friendly atmosphere, and he's able to tailor a tour to almost anywhere.

**Singgalang Hotel** ( ☎ 21576; Jl Ahmad Yani 130; r 120,000-150,000Rp) This basic cheapie is close to the action.

**Mountain View Hotel** ( ☎ 21621; Jl Yos Sodarso 31; r 150,000Rp) In a stunning location with a huge garden and plenty of room for vehicles. The simple rooms are great value.

SUMATRA

**MIXING BUSINESS WITH FRIENDSHIP**

In Indonesia, the line between business and socialising isn't as distinct as it is in the West. We expect printed prices and obvious sales tactics. Without a price tag, we assume that it is free or done out of friendship. On the other side of the cultural divide Sumatrans prefer business to resemble friendship: a little chit-chat, a steady sales pitch, and a sort of telepathic understanding that payment is expected. They'd rather be helpful instead of entrepreneurial, but necessity dictates an income. The sluggish state of the Sumatran economy means that unemployment is high, with an overload of young resourceful men supporting themselves by guiding too few tourists.

Once you realise that nothing is gratis, ask about prices. Don't assume that the quoted price is all-inclusive. You are expected to buy lunch and drinking water for your guide. If transport isn't included in the initial price, you should pay for this as well. A tip at the end is also welcome. Most are smokers and a pack costs about 10,000Rp. If all this seems steep, keep in mind that the guides have a couple of crumpled rupiah to their name and not a lot of other opportunities.

### MIDRANGE & TOP END

**Hotel Asia** ( ☎ 625277; Jl Kesehatan 38; r incl breakfast 100,000-250,000Rp; ❄ ) Centrally located, the Asia offers spotless rooms for a bargain price. The airy common balconies evoke a Himalayan vibe.

**Hotel Khartini** ( ☎ 22885; Jl Teuku Umar 6; r incl breakfast 150,000-250,000Rp) Clean, light-filled rooms, but it's very close to the mosque.

**Lima's Hotel** ( ☎ 22641; www.limashotelbukittinggi .com; Jl Kesehatan 34; r incl breakfast 250,000-400,000Rp plus 10% tax) Great views down the valley from the side of the hill. The economy rooms are spotless and well appointed.

**Hills** ( ☎ 35000; www.thehillshotel.com; Jl Laras Dutuk Bandaro; r 800,000-4,000,000Rp plus 21% tax; ❄ ▣ ☎ ) Commanding the heights like a Moorish citadel, and with more bling than a Paris catwalk, the most expensive place in town is usually full of VIPs and their security squads. At least grab a drink and watch the proceedings (or use the wi-fi).

### Eating

Bukittinggi has always been the one place in Sumatra where weary road bums can give their poor chilli-nuked organs a chance to recover, with lashings of lovingly bland western *makan* (food). OK, so sometimes the reality doesn't quite fit the dream, but hey, what did you expect?

**Canyon Cafe** ( ☎ 21652; Jl Teuku Umar 8; mains from 15,000Rp) Still playing Credence and waiting for the tide to change, but the food's always good.

**Turret Cafe** ( ☎ 625 956; Jl Ahmad Yani 140-142; mains from 20,000Rp; ▣ ) Good food, relaxed outdoor lounges, internet (per hour 6000Rp) and the best guacamole in town.

**Bedudal Café** (Jl Ahmad Yani; mains from 20,000Rp) All the old favourites in a cosy, intimate atmosphere, located on the main drag.

If you're pizza'd out, there are plenty of *nasi Padang* options. Try tiny **Sederhang** (Jl Minangkabau 63) and its mouth-watering choices; **Selamat** (upper Jl Ahmad Yani), located towards the clocktower; **Gon Raya** (Jl Ahmad Yani), in the middle of town; or either **Simpang Raya** (Jl Minangkabau) location. Dishes start at 8000Rp.

Need a chocolate muffin fix? Try the sublime offerings at **Serba Cokelet** (Jl Yos Sudarso 6A; ☺ 8am-4pm).

Jl Ahmad Yani comes alive at night with food stalls doing excellent sate and nasi/*mie goreng*. Locals rave about the sweet *lon tong* (a soupy concoction of coconut milk, rice, egg and whatever else is handy) served in a no-name tent opposite the Singgalang Hotel.

### Entertainment

**Medan Nan Balinduang** (Jl Lenggogeni; tickets 40,000Rp; ☎ 8.30pm) presents Minangkabau dance performances. Check with the tourist office for the latest schedule.

West Sumatrans love a good **bullfight**, known locally as *adu kerbau*. Unlike Spanish bullfighting, there is no (intended) bloodshed and the water-buffalo bulls are normally unharmed. Two animals of similar size and weight lock horns in a trial of strength. Whichever doesn't retreat, wins. Unfortunately, West Sumatrans also love a good punt, and betting reached such a frenzy that the provincial government banned bullfighting indefinitely.

However, where there's a will, there's a horse and Bukittinggi holds an annual race at Bukik Ambacang in early March. Horses are ridden bareback and jockeys wear regional costumes, vying to win kudos for their village, and something else for the onlookers' wallets. Solok and Sawahlunto also hold annual races.

## Shopping

Bukittinggi is a great place to shop for both the mundane and the bizarre: leather sandals, woven bags, false teeth, silver, karabiners, skate wear, batik shirts, antiques and curios. Box collectors can look out for a couple of Minangkabau versions. Brass *salapah panjang* (long boxes) are used for storing lime and tobacco, and silver *salapah padusi* for betel nut and lime.

Souvenir shops line Jl Minangkabau,while upper Jl Ahmad Yani is full of trendy clothes and antiques. Try **Minang Art** (☎ 35662; Jl Cindurmato 98A), **Aladdin Antiques** (☎ 33593; Jl Ahmad Yani 14) or **Makmur Arts** (☎ 22208; Jl Ahmad Yani 10).

For outdoor gear, check out **Orange** and **Markas Outdoors**, both on upper Jl Ahmad Yani.

Beautiful red and gold Minangkabau embroidery can be found in the *pasar*. Pillowcases, slippers and ceremonial wedding sashes all make easy-to-carry souvenirs.

## Getting There & Away

The chaos of the Aur Kuning bus terminal 2km south is easily reached by *opelet* (2000Rp). Ask for 'terminal'. Heading to town ask for 'Kampung China'.

Minivans run regularly to Padang (16,000Rp, two hours) and Solok (16,000Rp, two hours). Decrepit buses make the Danau Maninjau run (13,000Rp, 1½ hours), while a taxi starts at 160,000Rp.

Trans-Sumatran buses also stop here, though only zombies make it to Jakarta (from 250,000Rp, 35 hours); it's quicker and cheaper to fly from Padang. Ditto for Medan (from 200,000Rp, 20 hours), though you could jump off at Parapat (from 170,000Rp, 16 hours) for Lake Toba. You'll cross the equator en route, near Bonjol.

Minivans head west to Pekanbaru (100,000Rp, five hours), and there's a night bus direct to Dumai (110,000Rp, 10 hours) that connects with the Melaka ferry (250,000Rp, two hours). There is a handy bus to Sibolga (90,000, 12 hours) for Nias, and a few buses to Bengkulu (150,000Rp, 18

hours), Jambi (200,000Rp, 15 hours), Sungai Penuh for Kerinci (85,000Rp, 10 hours) and Palembang (140,000Rp, 20 hours), but most services leave from Padang.

## Getting Around

*Opelet* cost 2000Rp. *Bendi* start from 10,000Rp. An *ojek* from the bus terminal to the hotels costs 7,000Rp and a taxi costs 20,000Rp. Transfers direct to Padang airport can be arranged from any travel agent for 40,000Rp.

# AROUND BUKITTINGGI

While Bukittinggi is an interesting market town, visitors come to explore the Minangkabau countryside, hike up an active volcano or hunt for the fabled rafflesia.

## Handicraft Villages

Silversmiths occupy the old Dutch houses of **Koto Gadang**, 5km from Bukittinggi (*opelet* 2000Rp). Alternatively, it's an hour's walk from Taman Panorama.

**Pandai Sikat** (Clever Craftsmen) is famous for *songket* (silver- or gold-threaded cloth) weaving and woodcarving. The village is 13km from Bukittinggi. Take an *opelet* (5000Rp) from Aur Kuning.

## Minangkabau Sights

The rich volcanic soil of the hilly countryside around Bukittinggi oozes fertility. Stop by the roadside and you can spot cinnamon, betel nut, avocado, coffee, mango and papaya trees. Rice, tapioca and potatoes grow in terraces, while bamboo waterwheels feed irrigation ditches and drive wooden grinding mills.

Hopefully, you'll see a wedding parade. The bride and groom, dressed in full traditional regalia, are accompanied by musicians, family members and half the village. The Minangkabau tribal flags (red, black and yellow) typically mark the site of the festivities.

**Rumah Gadang Pagaruyung** (King's Palace) was a scaled-down replica of the former home of the rulers of the ancient Minangkabau kingdom of Payaruyung. Unfortunately, a fire razed it to the ground in 2007 and the reconstruction is still incomplete. Most tours now divert to **Istano Silinduang Bulan** (Silinduang Bulan; donation 2000Rp), the nearby Queen's Palace. This building is still used for important clan meetings, and a small donation is expected. Both palaces are located in the village of Silinduang Bulan,

5km north of Batu Sangkar, the heartland of the red Tanah Datar clan of Minangkabau.

Batu Sangkar is pleasant enough and can be reached via public bus (15,000Rp), where an *ojek* (3,000Rp) or minivan (2,000Rp) can take you the rest of the way to Silinduang Bulan.

Another popular tour stop is **Belimbing**, one of the largest surviving collections of traditional architecture in the highlands. Many of the homes are 300 years old and in various states of decay. Most owners have built modern homes nearby and use the relics for ceremonial purposes.

Ethno-musicologists make the pilgrimage to the town of **Padangpanjang**, 19km south of Bukittinggi, to see the **Conservatorium of Traditional Music** (STSI or ASKI; ☎ 0752-82077; Jl Bundo Kanduang 35; ❧ 8am-3pm Mon-Thu, to noon Fri). Minangkabau dance and music are preserved and performed here. Regular buses run between Bukittinggi, Padang and Padangpanjang (10,000Rp).

Train lovers head to Padangpanjang for Sunday's Museum Train trip to the old coal-mining town of **Sawahlunto**. Scenically stunning, this newly restored service runs alongside **Danau Singkarak**. The trip takes three hours (one way 60,000Rp, departs 7.30am) and there's two hours in Sawahlunto, where you can ride a steam train, visit the rail museum or head down a coal mine, before the return journey.

## Nature Reserves

West Sumatra is famous for its many orchid species and for the massive *Rafflesia arnoldii*, and *Amorphophallus titanium,* the largest flowers on the planet. The blossom of the parasitic rafflesia measures nearly a metre across and can weigh up to 11kg, while the inflorescence of *Amorphophallus* can extend to over 3m in circumference. Both flowers reek like road kill. The rafflesia typically blooms between August and November, whereas the Titan Arum flowers infrequently. The best place to find ripe blossoms is **Batang Palupuh Nature Reserve**, 16km north of Bukittinggi. Local buses to Palupuh, where guides can be hired, cost 5000Rp.

On the highway between Padang and Bukittinggi is the **Lembah Anai Nature Reserve**, which is renowned for its waterfalls, wild

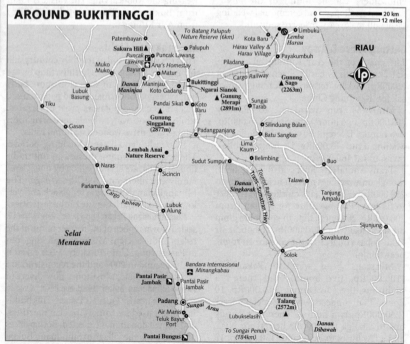

**AROUND BUKITTINGGI**

## WOMEN RULE

Though Muslim, Minangkabau society is still matrilineal. According to Minangkabau *adat* (traditional laws and regulations), property and wealth are passed down through the female line. Every Minangkabau belongs to his or her mother's clan. At the basic level of the clan is the *sapariouk*, those matri-related kin who eat together. These include the mother, the grandchildren and the son-in-law. The name comes from the word *periouk* (rice pot). The eldest living female is the matriarch. The most important male member of the household is the mother's eldest brother, who replaces the father in being responsible for the children's education, upbringing and marriage prospects. But consensus is at the core of the Minangkabau ruling philosophy and the division of power between the sexes is regarded as complementary – like the skin and the nail act together to form the fingertip, according to a local expression.

orchids and giant rafflesia. Any Bukittinggi–Padang bus can drop you nearby.

### Gunung Merapi

Looming large over Bukittinggi to the east is the smouldering summit of Gunung Merapi (2891m). Occasionally deemed too dangerous to climb, Merapi is Sumatra's most active volcano.

If Merapi's benign, then visitors typically hike overnight to view sunrise from the summit. The climb begins at the village of Koto Baru and it's normally a 12-hour round trip. You'll need good walking boots, warm clothing, a torch, food and drink.

It's unwise to attempt the climb alone, and people are advised to take a guide or join a group. Travel agencies in Bukittinggi do guided trips to Merapi for US$25 per person (minimum three people).

### Gunung Singgalang

Singgalang (2877m) is a more adventurous undertaking than Merapi, is rarely climbed by tourists. There are campsites by the beautiful crater lake, Telago Dewi.

### Harau Valley

Heading east from Bukittinggi takes you through the tapioca-growing area of **Piladang**, famous for *keropok* (tapioca crackers), and the sprawling agricultural centre of **Payakumbuh**. Of Minangkabau's three clans, this is the territory of the 50 Kota (50 villages) yellow branch. Paddies and daydreaming buffalos flank the narrow road that leads to the tiny village of Harau. Venture another 3km and spectacular 100m cliffs rise up to enclose the claustrophobic Harau Valley, 15km northeast of Payakumbuh and 55km from Bukittinggi.

Most tourists just pass through on a tour to **Lemba Harau** (admission 1000Rp), a set of waterfalls that either trickles or plummets, depending on the weather. However, Harau Valley is also the best-developed rock-climbing area in Sumatra, and those climbers who make the pilgrimage will be rewarded with long clean lines on plenty of sheer faces. The local climbers are very knowledgeable and worth seeking out. Check out climbing blogs such as **Climbing** (www.climbing.com) and **Rockclimbing.com** (www.rockclimbing.com) for more information.

Right under the cliffs in the narrowest part of the valley is **Echo Homestay** ( ☎ 775 0306; Tarantang Lb Limpato; r with shared bathroom 60,000Rp, r incl breakfast 350,000-450,000Rp), a stunningly beautiful place teeming with butterflies and surrounded by forests full of gibbons. Slum it in the basic thatched bungalows or pamper yourself in the Minangkabau-style cottages.

To get there take a local bus from Bukittinggi to Payakumbuh (10,000Rp), then a minivan to Harau village (5000Rp), and finally an *ojek* the rest of the way (5000Rp). Alternatively, take an *ojek* all the way from Payakumbah (15,000Rp). Harau can also be reached on a half-day tour from Bukittinggi for 100,000Rp.

## DANAU MANINJAU
☎ 0752

The first glimpse of this perfectly formed volcanic lake sucks your breath away as the dilapidated bus lurches over the caldera lip and hurtles towards the first of the 44 (yep, they're numbered) hairpin bends down to the lakeshore. Monkeys watch your progress from the crash barriers as the lush rainforest of the heights retreats from the ever-expanding farms and paddies of the lowlands.

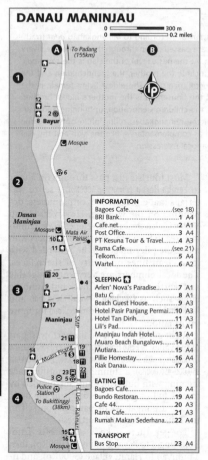

## DANAU MANINJAU

When the traveller tide receded from Bukittinggi, Danau Maninjau was left high and dry. The locals looked to more sustainable sources of income and aquaculture to fill the void. Fish farms now dot the lake foreshore.

Life travels slowly in Maninjau, making it the ideal place to kick back and do nothing. On the other hand, the rainforests and waterfalls of the caldera are just waiting to be explored.

Hopefully, the tide may again be turning as travellers begin to trickle back to one of Sumatra's most stunning destinations.

## Orientation & Information

Ground zero is the intersection where the Bukittinggi highway meets the lake road in the middle of Maninjau village. Turn left or right

and drive 60km and you'll end up back here. The lake is 17km long, 8km wide and 460m above sea level. Most places of interest spread out north along the road to Bayur (3.5km) and beyond. Tell the conductor where you're staying and you'll be dropped off at the right spot. The town is pretty much asleep by 9pm.

### INTERNET ACCESS

Internet in the area is slow and expensive.
**Bagoes Cafe** (per hr 10,000Rp; ☺ 10am-9pm)
**Rama Cafe** (per hr 10,000Rp; ☺ 9am-10pm)
**Cafe.net** (Bayur; per hr 10,000Rp)

### MONEY

There are no ATMs. The **BRI bank** in Maninjau should change foreign currency, otherwise try one of the larger hotels or the travel agent, but rates are much better in Bukittinggi.

### POST & TELEPHONE

The post office and Telkom wartel are next to each other at the intersection. There is another wartel on the road to Bayur.

### TRAVEL AGENCIES

**PT Kesuna Tour & Travel** ( ☎ 61422; kesumatravel@ yahoo.com; Jl Panunuran Air Hangat) Arranges air tickets and minibus charters to Padang (300,000Rp) and Bukittinggi (170,000Rp), and will also change money.

## Sights & Activities

Swimming and canoeing in the lake (warmed by subterranean springs) are still the main drawcards but there are plenty of other options.

The caldera is a hiker's dream, covered in rainforest, hiding waterfalls and traditional villages. Hike to the rim from Bayur, or cheat by catching the bus up the hill to Matur, then walking back down via the lookout at **Puncak Lawang**. Half-way to Bayur is **Ana's Homestay**, deep within the jungle.

If this all sounds a bit athletic, try unwinding in a hot spring. Failing all else, grab a moped and zoom off to Sinar Pagi, the point on Ujung Tanjung poking out from the far shore.

## Festivals & Events

**Rakik Rakik** is celebrated on the night before Idul Fitri (the end of Ramadan) by building a platform to hold a replica Minangkabau house and mosque. The offering is then floated out onto the lake on canoes, accompanied by fireworks and revelry.

## Sleeping

Aquaculture has transformed the Maninjau foreshore. Losmen that once overlooked pristine beaches now have views of fishponds and jetties. There are still beautiful spots, but you need to decide whether comfort, scenery, cost or access is your main priority.

Outside of Maninjau village, most losmen are reached by walking along rice-paddy paths, so look for the sign by the roadside. Truck tubes, canoes, bicycles and mopeds can normally be hired.

Distances listed here are from the intersection.

### MANINJAU

The majority of the town options front onto aquaculture.

**Riak Danau** ( ☎ 081 2679 08153; s/d 30,000/50,000Rp) The cheapest single in town, 500m north of the intersection.

**Pillie Homestay** ( ☎ 61048, 081 3633 73361; r 50,000Rp) Simple and cheap rooms 200m south of the intersection, with a lovely family and nice verandah.

**Beach Guest House** ( ☎ 61082; r 50,000; 🖳 ) Cheap rooms on a sunny beach, 600m north of town; they also rent bicycles and mopeds.

**Muaro Beach Bungalows** ( ☎ 61189; neni967@yayoo .com; Jl Muaro Pisang 53; r 50,000Rp) Down a maze of footpaths (about 300m northwest) on a nice stretch of private beach somehow free of fish ponds, these clean bungalows are the best value of the village group.

**Mutiara** ( ☎ 61049; ricojayamozart@yahoo.com; r with fan/air-con 100,000/150,000Rp) Next door to Pillie Homestay, the rooms here are clean and cool with great views from the deck.

**Maninjau Indah Hotel** ( ☎ 61018; Jl Telaga Biru 1; r 175,000-300,000Rp; 🌡 🖳 ) One of the best views in town, but the rooms in this large hotel are overpriced.

### GASANG

Between Maninjau and Bayur, there is a sprinkling of hotels, cheap losmen and restaurants.

**Hotel Tan Dirih** ( ☎ 61474; KM1 Desa Air Angek; r 150,000Rp) Good value rooms, but the deck looks at fishponds; 950m north of the crossroads in Maninjau.

**Hotel Pasir Panjang Permai** ( ☎ 61111; Desa Gasang; r 200,000-300,000Rp) Excellent rooms, with a great view from the breezy restaurant. It's 1.2km north of the crossroads.

### BAYUR

The following are all beyond Bayur village.

**Lili's Pad** (r 70,000Rp) Nice beach but these bungalows (3.8km north of Maninjau) need some work.

**Batu C** (r 40,000Rp) Next door to Lili's Pad, Batu C has cheap, sunny huts – but you can't escape the fishponds.

**'Arlen' Nova's Paradise** ( ☎ 081 5352 04714; novaf@ hotmail.com; Sungai-Rangeh; r 150,000Rp) Walk through rice paddies (5.5km north of Maninjau) to these beautiful bungalows on a private beach, with nary a fishpond in sight. It's easily the nicest place on the lake.

## Eating

Most of the guest houses serve standards such as nasi/mie goreng, some Western favourites and freshly caught fish. The bigger hotels also have restaurants. A few places in Maninjau village are also worth checking out.

**Bagoes Cafe** ( ☎ 61418; mains 12,000-25,000Rp; 🖳 ) Traveller-friendly place with all the usual faves and a few local dishes. It also runs movie nights. Internet access is 10,000Rp per hour.

**Rama Cafe** (ramacafe@ymail.com; mains 20,000-30,000Rp; 🖳 ) Share a *martabak* (20,000Rp) before hooking into a plate of *ikan panggang* (baked fish; 30,000Rp) while lazing on cush-

---

### WHO LET THE DOGS OUT

Unlike other parts of Southeast Asia, Sumatra is not overrun with packs of stray dogs. In Islam, dogs are regarded as impure and contact with the animal is prohibited. Then what is all that barking, you might ask? Minangkabau culture makes an exception to some of the Islamic precepts, especially when it comes to protecting crops. The farmer's great nemesis is the wild boar, which roots up vegetable patches during overnight feasts. To combat the intruder, farmers keep very vocal hunting dogs, usually tied up on leashes or kept in pens. All that caged energy is then unleashed on boar-hunting days, assigned to various villages throughout the year. In other hunting traditions, the prey is usually retrieved for the owner, but because pigs are also haram (forbidden) in Islamic law, the dogs get the spoils instead of the scraps.

ions amongst kites and drums. Look out for the excellent map. Internet access is 10,000Rp per hour.

**Cafe 44** ( ☎ 61238; mains 12,000Rp) Down by the lakeshore, this place has a good selection of local food – if you can find the cook. There are also a few cheap rooms (30,000Rp).

**Rumah Makan Sederhana** and **Bundo Restoran** (dishes from 8000Rp) both serve a good selection of Padang food.

## Getting There & Around

Buses run hourly between Maninjau and Bukittinggi (13,000Rp, 1½ hours). Taxis from Bukittinggi start from 160,000Rp. There is also an economy bus to/from Dumai (50,000Rp).

Several places rent out mountain bikes (per day 15,000Rp), motorcycles (per day 80,000Rp) and canoes (per day 15,000Rp).

Minivans (2000Rp) travel the lake road during daylight hours. Alternatively, an *ojek* from the intersection to Bayur will cost around 7000Rp.

# KERINCI VALLEY
☎ 0748 / pop 300,000

Kerinci is a stunning mountain valley tucked away high in the Bukit Barisan on Jambi's western border. Many of the cool, lush forests are protected as the Kerinci Seblat National Park. To the south is picturesque Danau Kerinci and a patchwork of rich farmland. Tea and cinnamon account for much of the valley's wealth, with the former ringing the higher villages and the latter forming a buffer between farmland and rainforest.

Minangkabau and native Kerincinese make up most of the population, with a sprinkling of Batak and Javanese who are drawn by the rich soil. Kerinci is in Jambi province but appears in this section because of its geographic proximity to Padang.

## Getting There & Away

Sungai Penuh doesn't have a bus terminal, but the bus companies all have offices near the market.

The shortest approach to Sungai Penuh is from Padang (70,000Rp, seven hours). If you're staying in Kersik Tua, let the driver know, as all minibuses pass through the town en route. **PO Cahaya Kerinci** ( ☎ 21421; Jl Diponegoro), **PO CW Safa Marwa** ( ☎ 22376; Jl Yos Sudarso 20) and **PO AYU Transport** ( ☎ 22074; Jl Cokroaminoto), all in

Sungai Penuh, run Padang-bound services. If you're leaving Kersik Tua for Padang or Bukittinggi, let the bus company know and they'll pick up from your losmen.

Other destinations include Dumai (200,000Rp, 18 hours), Bukittinggi (85,000Rp, 10 hours, nightly), Bangko (50,000Rp, five hours) and Bengkulu (100,000Rp, 16 hours, daily).

## Getting Around

Most places in the valley are accessible using the white minivans that leave from near the market. Sample destinations and fares are Danau Kerinci (8000Rp), Kersik Tua (7000Rp, one hour) and Pelompek (7000Rp, 80 minutes). Watch your pronounciation – Semurup and Semerap are in opposite directions.

## Sungai Penuh

Sungai Penuh (Full River) is the regional administrative centre and transport hub for the valley. Bang in the middle is a large, walled sports field and most necessities will be in one of the streets that radiate off here. There is a lively market and fast, reliable internet, but not much else to recommend a protracted stay. Most people get in and get out, heading for the more scenic climes of Kersik Tua.

### INFORMATION

**BNI ATM** (Jl Matadinata) Just off the main square near Hotel Jaya Wisata; accepts MasterCard and Visa.

**BNI Bank** (Jl Ahmad Yani) Will exchange cash and travellers cheques; opposite Hotel Matahari.

**TNKS** (Taman Nasional Kerinci Seblat; ☎ 323701; Jl Basuki Rahmat 11) The park (p442) HQ sells permits but ring first to check it's open. If closed, you can get permits from losmen in Kersik Tua.

**Post office** (Jl Sudirman 1)

**Telkom wartel** (internet per hr 5000Rp) Fast internet and IDD in the big building on the southern side of the sports field near Hotel Aroma.

### SIGHTS
#### Mesjid Agung Pondok Tinggi

Head west up Jl Sudirman (past the post office) and turn left, where you'll find this old wooden **mosque** (admission by donation 10,000Rp) with its pagoda-style roof. Built in 1874 without a single nail, the interior contains elaborately carved beams and old, Dutch tiles. Ask the caretaker for permission, and dress demurely.

## SLEEPING & EATING

Accommodation options in Sungai Penuh are fairly dire. Unless you're planning adventures in the not-so-exciting southern end of the park, try and head to Kersik Tua (p442).

**Hotel Matahari** ( ☎ 21061; Jl Ahmad Yani 25; d 55,000-175,000Rp) Sungai Penuh's first hotel is showing some wear and tear.

**Hotel Yani** ( ☎ 21409; Jl Muradi 1; d 60,000-185,000Rp) Next door to Minang Soto (see right), it's as good as it looks.

**Aroma Hotel** ( ☎ 21142; hotel.aroma@yahoo.com; Jl Imam Bonjol 14; d 80,000-210,000Rp) Conveniently located at the top corner of the square, the Aroma's budget rooms are better value than its expensive ones.

**Hotel Jaya Wisata** ( ☎ 21221; Jl Martadinata 7; r incl breakfast & fan/air-con 100,000/495,000Rp; 🗶 ) The flashest address in town fills up quickly.

Kerinci is known for the local speciality of *dendeng batokok*, charcoal-grilled strips of pounded beef. Street stalls pop up in the evening along Jl Teuku Umar, a block from the square. The fruit and produce market is at the southern end of Jl Diponegoro.

**Minang Soto** (Jl Muradi; dishes from 8000Rp) Busy Padang-style eatery, but watch you get what you ordered. The *tahu* arrives with *ayam*. Eat the *tahu*, pay for the *ayam* (chicken).

## Kersik Tua

Darjeeling it's not, but at 1500m, surrounded by tea plantations and dominated by the massive cone of Gunung Kerinci (3805m), Kersik Tua makes a pleasant base for exploring the wilder northern end of Kerinci Seblat.

The town sprawls along one side of the main road, with tea plantations and the mountain on the other. The national park turn-off is indicated by a *harimau* (Sumatran tiger) statue.

Trekking gear, supplies, guides and transport can all be arranged here. There's a market on Saturday and a BNI ATM. The village is 52km north of Sungai Penuh on the road to

**SUMATRA**

### ORANG PENDEK: LITTLE BIG FOOT

Every culture that has lived among trees tells stories about elusive creatures that straddle myth and reality. Tales about leprechauns, fairies and even Sasquatch have existed for so long that it is impossible to determine which came first: the spotting or the story. The Indonesian version of these myth makers is the *orang pendek*, which has been occasionally spotted but more frequently talked about in the Kerinci forests for generations.

Villagers who claim to have seen *orang pendek* describe the creature as being about 1m tall, more ape-like than human, but walking upright on the ground. The creature's reclusive habits made it a celebrity in local mythology. Common folk stories say that the *orang pendek* has feet that face backwards so that it can't be tracked through the forest or that it belongs to the supernatural not the world of flesh and blood. Others say that the first-hand accounts were only spottings of sun bears.

Scientists have joined the conversation by tramping through the forest hoping to document the existence of *orang pendek*. British researchers succeeded in making a plaster cast of an animal footprint that fits the *orang pendek* description and doesn't match any other known primate. Hair samples with no other documented matches have also led researchers to believe that there is merit to the local lore. Two members of Fauna & Flora International, a British-based research team, even reported separate sightings, but were unable to collect conclusive evidence. Researchers sponsored by the National Geographic Society have resumed the search by placing motion-sensitive cameras in strategic spots in the jungle. So little is known about this region and so many areas are so remote that researchers are hopeful that the *orang pendek* will eventually wander into the frame.

If nothing else, the *orang pendek* helps illuminate aspects of Sumatrans' linguistic and cultural relationship with the jungle. Bahasa Indonesia makes little distinction between man and ape, for example 'orang-utan' (forest man) or 'orang rimba' ('people of the forest', the preferred term for the Kubu tribe) may reflect a perceived blood tie between forest dwellers. This imprecision is often used for comic effect. A common joke is that the *orang pendek* (meaning 'short man') does indeed exist, followed by the punch line that the shortest person in the room is the missing link.

Padang and can be reached via any Padang–Kerinci bus.

There are several basic homestays. **Subandi Homestay** ( ☎ 357009, 081 2741 14273; subandi.home stay@gmail.com; just south of the tiger statue; r 90,000Rp) is the best base camp in the village. Subandi is a trove of local knowledge and can organise mountain, jungle and wildlife treks of varying difficulty and duration. His rooms are basic but clean, and his wife is an excellent cook catering for all tastes.

Other homestays include **Home Stay Paiman** ( ☎ 357030; r 65,000Rp), 200m south of Subandi (near the ATM), and **Home Stay B Darmin** ( ☎ 357070; r 65,000Rp), 300m north of the statue.

## Kerinci Seblat National Park (TNKS)

This is the largest national park in Sumatra, covering a 350km swath of the Bukit Barisan range and protecting 15,000 sq km of prime equatorial rainforest spread over four provinces, with almost 40% of the park falling within Jambi's boundaries.

Most of the protected area is dense rainforest; its inaccessibility the very reason it's one of the last strongholds of endangered species such as *harimau* and *badak* (Sumatran rhinoceros).

Because of the great elevation range within the park, Kerinci has a unique diversity of flora and fauna. Edelweiss and other high-altitude flowers grow in the forest. Lower altitudes bring pitcher plants, orchids, *Rafflesia* and the giant *Amorphophallus* (see p436).

As with many of Sumatra's protected areas, encroachment by farmers, illegal logging and poaching are all serious issues for Kerinci. According to park estimates, a total of 23,000 hectares (230 sq km) of forests were destroyed between 2002 and 2004.

TNKS sees few visitors and tourist infrastructure is nonexistent. Trekking opportunities typically focus on the northern region of the park, while the southern region is the traditional zone where local people are allowed to cultivate the land. Permits and guides are required to enter the park; both can be arranged at the TNKS office in Sungai Penuh (see p440) or through your losmen. There is a park office at the entrance to Danau Gunung Tujuh, but it's rarely staffed.

Permits cost 20,000Rp and guide rates are highly negotiable, ranging from 75,000Rp to 200,000Rp per day. Be sure to clarify exactly what the rate entails, as camping gear, food and transport may be considered additional costs.

Kerinci's climate is temperate, and downright cold as you gain altitude. Bring warm clothes and rain gear.

### GUNUNG KERINCI

Dominating the northern end of the park is the 3805m Gunung Kerinci, one of Sumatra's most active volcanoes (it last erupted in 2009) and Indonesia's highest non-Papuan peak. On clear days the summit offers fantastic views of Danau Gunung Tujuh (see below) and the surrounding valleys and mountains.

Summit treks usually start from the national park entrance, 5km from Kersik Tua, and tackle the mountain in two stages (see boxed text, opposite). The highest campsite, at 3400m, is normally reached after six hours. The following morning, allow an hour in the predawn to reach the summit by sunrise.

Botanists and twitchers from around the world come for the rare flora and fauna such as Javanese edelweiss, Schneider's pitta and the Crested Wood Partridge. *Nepthenes* (pitcher plants), squirrels, geckos and long-tailed macaques can be found in the lower forest.

The path is very steep and eroded, and above the treeline the scree is extremely slippery. A guide is mandatory and you'll need full camping gear and warm clothes, including a windproof jacket and head torch (all of which can be hired in Kersik Tua). Nights are freezing. Do not attempt the climb in wet weather.

Expect to pay around 700,000Rp for a fully guided trip with food, permits, transport and all gear thrown in. Fully self-sufficient parties needing a guide only will pay around 400,000Rp.

### DANAU GUNUNG TUJUH

At 1996m, the beautiful caldera of Danau Gunung Tujuh (Seven Mountain Lake) is the highest in Southeast Asia and makes for a pleasant day walk or multiday trek.

It takes 3½ hours to climb to the lake from the park entrance, which is 2km from the village of Pelompek. It's possible to camp near the lake. Subandi Homestay in Kersik Tua (see above) can organise two- or three-day treks including a canoe crossing.

## CLIMBING GUNUNG KERINCI *Steve Waters*

The *ojek* bumps it's way along the rough track for 5km through tea plantations until the road becomes impassable. Time to hoof it. My guide, Kemun, is shouldering most of the load including the tent and all the food, leaving myself with a light pack of warm clothes and rented sleeping bag.

The forest doesn't begin until the park entrance, and even there it's looking like it's on borrowed time, as farms keep pushing the boundaries. It's cooler under the canopy and the first thing I notice is bird song. Within 10 minutes we arrive at a small clearing, named Base Camp I.

Kemun is adept at pointing out wildlife and we spot various geckos, squirrels and quite a few birds. On glimpsing a long-blonde primate tail I ask Kemun 'what sort', thinking it's possibly a long-tailed macaque. He replies 'monkey'. Alas, neither of us have the language skills for further clarification.

The track is unmarked, though well defined, and not too steep in the early sections, and Base Camp II is reached after an hour. We take a break. Kemun supplies the snacks – pineapple cream biscuits. We push onto Shelter I, which takes 90 minutes of hard slog over tree roots to 2500m, where we take another break and eat some sticky-rice snacks Kemun has procured from the market.

The track steepens further and is greatly eroded, making for strenuous moves balancing on tree roots, and for a while I think I'm in southwest Tasmania in Australia. Alien shrieks from the shrubbery help me refocus and soon we arrive at Shelter II, at 3000m. There are no structures at these shelters, other than a few rusting poles or a slab of cement, and lots of litter. Slower groups normally spend the night at Shelter II.

Kemun produces a plastic container holding a Padang-style lunch of rice, noodles, potatoes, fried egg, chilli sardine and *rendang*. Fuelled up, we push onto Shelter III (3400m) where we'll spend the night. Just above the treeline, this campsite has sensational views of the whole valley, including Danau Gunung Tujuh.

Kemun sets up camp and gets a brew going while I snap away. The wind is fierce and we both start piling on the layers. By 4pm I'm wearing everything I've got, including a bike jacket, rented gloves and beanie. By 5pm we're both inside the tent, emerging briefly to check the sunset, as Kerinci's pyramid of shadow marches across the valley. Dinner is another plastic container containing an identical meal.

Kemun's brought insulating mats, but it's a cold, sleepless night in a crowded tent on hard ground with a thin sleeping bag. The muezzin's call from the valley comes as welcome relief, and we get a pre-dawn brew going.

Above Shelter III there is no real path, just the odd concrete pole to mark the way. The scree is extremely slippery and it pays to keep your hands free (hence the gloves). The sky is lightening behind Gunung Tujuh but it's still bitterly cold. The knife-edge rim of the caldera is reached in only an hour and we trade places in front of the camera as we soak in the view and try not to gag on the sulphurous fumes.

The descent back to Shelter III takes as long as the ascent due to the treacherous scree, but once we're packed and on the path proper we make good time and all too soon we are at the bottom and out of the forest. Here were are greeted by our transport, and are back in Kersik Tua in time for lunch.

Pelompek is 8km beyond Kersik Tua (bus 4000Rp) and 60km from Sungai Penuh (7000Rp). Hire an *ojek* (5000Rp) from Pelompek for the final trip to the park entrance. You'll need a park permit, and if TNKS (see left) is closed, ask next door at the tiny **Losmen Pak Edes** (r 50,000Rp) which also has two very basic rooms and can arrange guides.

### LADEH PANJANG

This region of rainforest, sulphur lakes and hot springs located on Gunung Kerinci's western flank is seldom visited, and is home to *harimau*, *badak*, tapir and *beruang* (bear). A five-day, 120km trek traverses the range and exits onto the highway north of Kerinci.

**DANAU KERINCI**

Danau Kerinci, 20km south of Sungai Penuh, is a small lake nestled beneath Gunung Raya (2535m). There is a popular recreational park and an annual festival, held in July, which displays traditional Kerinci dance and music. **Stone carvings** in the villages around the lake suggest that the area supported a sizable population in megalithic times. **Batu Gong** (Gong Stone), in the village of Muak, 25km from Sungai Penuh, is thought to have been carved 2000 years ago.

To reach the lake, catch a public bus from Sungai Penuh to Sanggaran Agung (8000Rp). The last return bus leaves around 4pm.

**AIR TERJUN**

Impressive waterfalls dot the whole valley. The easiest to find are the **Letter 'W' Waterfalls** (3000Rp) in 'Letter W' village 4km north of Pelompek. Look for the sign 'Air Terjun Telun Berasap' then walk 300m to a deep, fern-lined ravine where a thunderous torrent of water crashes onto rocks below.

Other falls include **Air Terjun 13 Tingkat** near Sungai Medang, and **Air Terjun Pauh Sago** near Batang Merangin on the Bangko Rd.

**GUA (CAVES)**

Locals believe that caves act as mediums for communicating with the supernatural, and that entry into these sacred spaces requires a modest ritual. Hiring a guide helps in the exploration of both the physical and esoteric landscapes.

The most extensive network of caves is situated outside the village of **Sengering**, including the celebrated **Gua Tiangko**. Obsidian-flake tools found in the cave indicate that it was occupied some 9000 years ago. The caves also contain some impressive natural formations.

Sengering is 9km from Sungai Manau, on the Bangko road. Buses leave Sungai Penuh for Bangko in the mornings.

There are cave paintings in **Gua Kasah**, 5km southeast from Kersik Tua, and two cave systems **Gua Kelelawar** and **Gua Belang** at Ting Kemulun near Sanggaran Agung.

**AIR PANAS (HOT SPRINGS)**

If you fancy a dip in some hot springs, make your way to either **Dusan Buru Air Panas** near Semurup (11km north of Sungai Penuh) or **Sungai Medang Air Panas** across the valley.

# BENGKULU

Cut off from its neighbours by the Bukit Barisan range, Bengkulu remains Sumatra's most isolated province – and nothing much seems to have changed here for years.

Few tourists make it this far, but those who do are rewarded with the simple pleasures of ordinary Indonesian life and an opportunity to learn Bahasa Indonesia without the support of bilingualism.

## History

Little is known of Bengkulu before it came under the influence of the Majapahits from Java at the end of the 13th century. Until then it appears to have existed in almost total isolation, divided between a number of small kingdoms such as Sungai Lebong in the Curup area. It even developed its own cuneiform script, *ka-ga-nga*.

In 1685, after having been kicked out of Banten in Java, the British moved into Bengkulu (Bencoolen, as they called it) in search of pepper. The venture was not exactly a roaring success. Isolation, boredom and constant rain sapped the British will, and malaria ravaged their numbers.

The colony was still not a likely prospect in 1818 when Sir Stamford Raffles arrived as its British-appointed ruler. In the short time he was there, Raffles made the pepper market profitable and planted cash crops of coffee, nutmeg and sugar cane. In 1824 Bengkulu was traded for the Dutch outpost of Melaka as a guarantee not to interfere with British interests in Singapore.

From 1938 to 1941 Bengkulu was a home-in-domestic-exile for Indonesia's first president, Sukarno.

## BENGKULU

☎ 0736 / pop 380,000

A quiet provincial capital, Bengkulu does not really have much for tourists to do except chat to the locals, most of whom don't speak English. Alternatively you could pass through as a UFO – unidentified foreign object.

## Orientation

Although Bengkulu is by the sea, most of the town is set back from the waterfront, touching only near the fort, Benteng Marlborough. The coast is unexpectedly

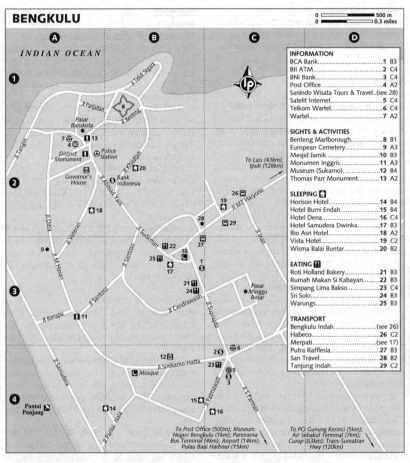

# BENGKULU

quiet and rural, just a kilometre or so from the town centre.

The city is divided up into the Kampung (the area around Benteng Marlborough), Simpang Lima (the intersection of Jl Suprapto, Parman, Fatmawati and Soekarno-Hatta) and Minggu (the area around Pasar Minggu). The commercial spine of Jl Suprapto and the nearby Pasar Minggu Besar are in the modern town centre, which is connected to the old-town area around the fort by the long and straight Jl Ahmad Yani/Jl Sudirman.

## Information
### INTERNET ACCESS
**Satelit Internet** (Jl S Parman 9; per hr 8000Rp; 10am-10pm)

### MONEY
There are plenty of ATMs around town.
**BCA Bank** (Jl Suprapto 150) The best place to exchange money.
**BII Bank** (Jl Suprapto) ATM.
**BNI Bank** (Jl S Parman) Travellers cheques and US dollars can be changed here.

### POST
**Main post office** (Jl S Parman) South of town centre; also has poste restante.
**Post office** (Jl RA Hadi 3) More convenient, opposite the Thomas Parr monument.

### TELEPHONE
**Telkom wartel** (cnr Jl Suprapto & Soekarno-Hatta; 7am-10pm) International calls can be made here.

### TRAVEL AGENCIES
**Sanindo Wisata Tours & Travel** ( ☎ 27522; Jl Mt Haryono 73) Sanindo Wisata can arrange historical city tours, as well as tours to the Curup tea plantations and offshore islands.

## Sights
Set on a hill overlooking the Indian Ocean, **Benteng Marlborough** (admission 2000Rp; ☉ 8am-7pm), a former British fort, was restored and opened to the public in 1984 after a long period of use by the Indonesian army. It became the seat of British power in Bengkulu after 1719, when it replaced nearby Fort York, of which nothing but the foundations remain. Despite its sturdy defences the fort was attacked and overrun twice – once by a local rebellion just after its completion in 1719, and then by the French in 1760. The old British gravestones at the entrance make poignant reading. There are a few interesting old engravings and copies of official correspondence from the time of British rule, and you can also see where the Dutch incarcerated Sukarno during his internal exile.

Bengkulu has a number of other reminders of its British history. The **Thomas Parr monument** (Jl Ahmad Yani), in front of the Pasar Barukota, was erected in memory of a British governor beheaded by locals in 1807. The **Monumen Inggris** (Jl M Hasan), near the beach, is dedicated to Captain Robert Hamilton, who died in 1793 'in command of the troops'.

Former president Sukarno was exiled to Bengkulu by the Dutch from 1938 until 1941. The small villa in which he lived is maintained as a **museum** (Jl Soekarno-Hatta; admission 2000Rp; ☉ 8am-4.30pm Mon-Thu, 8am-noon Sat & Sun). Exhibits include a few faded photos, a wardrobe and even his trusty bicycle. During his stay, Sukarno, who was an architect, designed the **Mesjid Jamik** (Bung Karno Mosque; cnr Jl Sudirman & Suprapto).

**Museum Negeri Bengkulu** ( ☎ 32099; Jl Pembangunan; admission by donation; ☉ 8am-4.30pm Tue-Thu, 8am-noon Sat & Sun) has a poorly labelled collection of standard Sumatran fare. Bring your own light if you want to see anything. The graves in the **European cemetery** (Jl Ditra) behind the small church are testament to the colonialists' vulnerability to malaria.

Bengkulu's main beach, **Pantai Panjang**, although not the best in Indonesia, is clean, generally deserted and a good place for a walk. Strong surf and currents make it unsafe for swimming.

## Sleeping
### BUDGET
**Vista Hotel** ( ☎ 20820; Jl MT Haryono 67; r incl snack with fan/air-con 40,000/170,000Rp; ✖ ) Located near the bus agents, Vista is excellent value. You might have forgotten what clean means in Sumatra, but Vista can remind you, with a good range of clean rooms.

**Wisma Balai Buntar** ( ☎ 21254; Jl Khadijah 122; r with fan/air-con 75,000/100,000Rp) In an old Dutch villa, this is Bengkulu's version of backpacker land. The enormous rooms are a little faded, but the neighbourhood is worth a wander.

**Hotel Samudera Dwinka** ( ☎ 21604; Jl Sudirman 246; r incl breakfast with fan/air-con 110,000/450,000Rp; ✖ ) Located in the centre of town, Hotel Samudera has rooms that are inexpensive without being depressing.

**Hotel Bumi Endah** ( ☎ 21665; fax 073 634 6442; Jl Fatmawati 29; r incl breakfast 198,000-374,000Rp; ✖ ) A friendly rambling hotel with quiet rooms and airy common spaces in a residential neighbourhood.

### MIDRANGE & TOP END
**Hotel Dena** ( ☎ 21066; Jl Fatmawati 28; r incl breakfast 195,000-250,000Rp; ✖ ) A popular option with clean, comfortable rooms – all with hot water.

**Rio Asri Hotel** ( ☎ 345 000; Jl Veteran 63; r incl breakfast 454,000-816,000Rp; ✖ ▣ ) For such a staid town, Rio Asri is a daring '80s-inspired design experiment. The rooms are equally as smart and some have high-top views over the garden city.

**Horison Hotel** ( ☎ 21722, 081 173 9304; dewita_grage@yahoo.com; Jl Pantai Nala 142; r incl breakfast 465,000-1,400,000Rp; ✖ ▣ ☞ ) The fanciest hotel in town, with well-dressed rooms and a swimming pool overlooking the beach.

## Eating
In the evening, several warungs cause a traffic jam along Jl Sudirman, serving freshly grilled seafood. Be sure to try the local favourites, *tempoyak* (durian and fish) and *martabak* (stuffed savoury pancake).

**Roti Holland Bakery** (Jl Suprapto 124; pastries 2000Rp; ☉ 8am-5pm) Chocolate doughnuts are wrapped thoughtfully in a cardboard box for those with self-control. The rest of us can tear into the pastries at the cafe tables.

**Sri Solo** (Jl Suprapto 118; mains 8000Rp; ☉ 10am-10pm) The equivalent of an ice-cream parlour, Sri Solo serves plates of *ayam baker* (grilled chicken) and tasty fruit juices to local families after church, gangs of school kids and courting couples.

**Rumah Makan Si Kabayan** (Jl Sudirman 51; mains from 35,000Rp; ⊗ 6-10pm) This is where Bengkulu entertains guests, with fitting VIP prices.

**Simpang Lima Bakso** (Jl Soekarno-Hatta; mains from 10,000Rp) Bengkulu is *bakso* (meatball-and-noodle soup) crazy and this simple warung does a thriving business beside the city's crazy five-way intersection.

### Getting There & Away
#### AIR
Merpati and Sriwijaya operate daily flights to Jakarta. The **Merpati office** ( ☎ 27111; Jl Sudirman 246) is in the Hotel Samudera Dwinka. Other tickets can be purchased through Sanindo Wisata Tours and Travel (see left).

#### BUS
Bengkulu has two bus terminals: the Air Sebakul terminal, 12km east of town, serves long-distance destinations, while Panorama terminal, 7km east, is used by local buses. However it is much easier to go to the bus company offices on Jl MT Haryono, as almost all long-distance destinations can be reached from here.

To get to Air Sebakul take a yellow *opelet* (2000Rp) to Panorama and then a white one (2000Rp) to Air Sebakul.

**Putra Rafflesia** ( ☎ 20313; Jl MT Haryono 12) services Palembang (economy 90,000Rp, 15 hours). **Bengkulu Indah** ( ☎ 22640; Jl MT Haryono) services a wide range of destinations. **San Travel** ( ☎ 21811; Jl MT Haryono 73) goes to Bukittinggi (economy/air-con 110,000/135,000Rp, 17 hours) and Padang (economy/air-con executive 110,000/150,000Rp) on Friday only.

**PO Gunung Kerinci** (Jl Bali 36) runs buses up the coast to Sungai Penuh in the Kerinci Valley (95,000Rp, 18 hours). **Tanjung Indah** (Jl MT Haryono 108) runs minivans to Palembang (160,000Rp) and other destinations.

**Habeco** (Jl MT Haryono), at the northern edge of town, has daily buses along the coast road to regional destinations, such as Lais (10,000Rp, two hours), Ipuh (40,000Rp, five hours) and Mukomuko (60,000Rp, eight hours).

### Getting Around
Airport taxis charge a standard 60,000Rp to town. The airport is 200m from the main road south, from where there are regular *opelet*

to town (2000Rp). Tell the driver where you want to stay or simply ask for the *benteng* (fort). *Opelet* and *ojek* also greet buses when they arrive at Jl MT Haryono/Jl Bali. *Opelet* fares to almost anywhere in town are 2000Rp; *ojek* are 5000Rp.

There are no fixed routes for *opelet;* tell the driver your destination or general area and you might get a nod of approval.

## NORTHERN BENGKULU
The coast road (Jl Manusurai Pantai), running north from Bengkulu to Padang, offers a number of possibilities for travellers.

The road is sealed all the way and the journey takes a mere 16 hours, a real quickie when measured by the Sumatran distance stick. However in the wet season the coast road is prone to wash-outs and landslides, so the going can be much slower.

The journey can be done in a number of short hops, stopping off at a town along the way for the hell of it; each town has at least one losmen. The first town north of Bengkulu is **Lais**. There are reputed to be elephants further north near **Ipuh**, around the mouth of Sungai Ipuh. **Mukomuko**, 200km north of Bengkulu, is the largest community on this stretch of road and was the northern outpost of the British colony of Bencoolen.

**Curup** is a small market town in the foothills of the Bukit Barisan, halfway between Bengkulu and Lubuklinggau. There are several surviving traditional homes and the town itself is in a valley watered by the upper reaches of Sungai Musi, which eventually flows through Palembang. Curup is a good base for visits to the surrounding mountains, including volcanic **Gunung Kaba**, 19km east of town, which has two large smouldering craters surrounded by dense rainforest.

There's nowhere to change money in Curup, so come prepared. Curup has a mediocre losmen and hotel to choose from.

### Getting There & Away
Padang–Bengkulu buses can stop off at the northern coastal towns. Curup can be reached by frequent connections to/from Bengkulu and Lubuklinggau.

## PULAU ENGGANO
This remote island, 100km off the coast of southern Bengkulu, is so isolated that until the early 20th century some Sumatrans believed

that it was inhabited entirely by women, who miraculously gave birth to children sired by the wind.

The island is featured on a map of Asia drawn in 1593. Enggano is Portuguese for 'deceit' or 'disappointment', which suggests that the Portuguese were the first Europeans to discover it. It wasn't until three years later that Dutch navigators first recorded it.

Enggano's original inhabitants are believed to have fled the Sumatran mainland when the Malays migrated there. Today the islanders live by cultivating rice, coffee, pepper, cloves and copra. Wild pigs, cattle and buffalo are abundant.

The island has an area of 680 sq km and there are no tourist facilities. **Malakoni** is the main harbour. The island is relatively flat (the highest point is Bua Bua, at 250m) and has a swampy coastline interspersed with some good **beaches** and **snorkelling**. Few tourists make it this far, so it's a good spot for budding linguists to practise their Bahasa Indonesia.

It is best to report to the *kepala desa* (village chief) and seek advice for lodging.

## Getting There & Around

In theory there are three boats a week from Bengkulu to Malakoni, but no one in Bengkulu was able to vouch for this service. Alternatively, go to the small port of Bintuhan, about 225km south of Bengkulu, and ask at the harbour.

The villages on the island are connected by tracks originally made by the Japanese and not very well maintained since. The only way to get around is to walk.

# RIAU

The landscape and character of Riau province is decidedly distinct from the northern and western rind of Sumatra. Rather than mountains and volcanoes, Riau's character was carved by rivers and narrow ocean passages. Trading towns sprang up along the important navigation route of the Strait of Melaka, across which Riau claims cultural cousins.

For the port towns, such as Pekanbaru, and the Riau islands, proximity to Singapore and Kuala Lumpur has ensured greater access to the outside world than those towns of the interior Sumatran jungle. The discovery of oil and gas reserves has also built an educated and middle-class population within an otherwise impoverished island.

The interior of the province more closely resembles Sumatra as a whole: sparse population, dense jungle, surviving pockets of nomadic peoples (including the Sakai, Kubu and Jambisal) and endangered species, such as the Sumatran rhinoceros and tiger.

A strain of chloroquine-resistant malaria has been reported on the Riau archipelago.

## History

Riau's position at the southern entrance to the Strait of Melaka, the gateway for trade between India and China, was strategically significant.

From the 16th century, the Riau Islands were ruled by a variety of Malay kingdoms, which had to fight off constant attacks by pirates and the Portuguese, Dutch and English. The Dutch eventually won control over the Strait of Melaka, and mainland Riau (then known as Siak) became their colony when the Sultan of Johor surrendered in 1745. However Dutch interest lay in ridding the seas of pirates, so they could get on with the serious business of trade, and they made little effort to develop the province.

Oil was discovered around Pekanbaru by US engineers before WWII, but it was the Japanese who drilled the first well at Rumbai, 10km north of the city. The country around Pekanbaru is criss-crossed by pipelines that connect the oil wells to refineries at Dumai, as ocean-going tankers cannot enter the heavily silted Sungai Siak.

## PEKANBARU
☎ 0761 / pop 750,000

Before the Americans struck oil, Pekanbaru was little more than a sleepy river port on Sungai Siak. Today it is Indonesia's oil capital, with all the hustle and bustle of modern cities. Pekanbaru's primary purpose for tourists is as a transit point between ferries from Singapore, but the increased affordability of air travel has curtailed the sea passage. Now only Western oil executives on business trips find themselves in Pekanbaru.

If you do decide to wander through, you'll spend most of your time accepting inexplicable gestures of kindness, from cafe conversations to instant friendships.

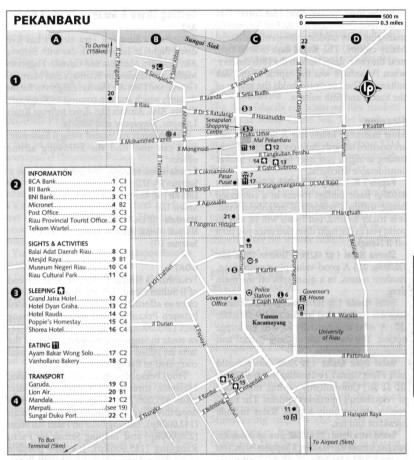

**PEKANBARU**

0 — 500 m
0 — 0.3 miles

**INFORMATION**
| | |
|---|---|
| BCA Bank | 1 C3 |
| BII Bank | 2 C1 |
| BNI Bank | 3 C1 |
| Micronet | 4 B2 |
| Post Office | 5 C3 |
| Riau Provincial Tourist Office | 6 C3 |
| Telkom Wartel | 7 C2 |

**SIGHTS & ACTIVITIES**
| | |
|---|---|
| Balai Adat Daerah Riau | 8 C3 |
| Mesjid Raya | 9 B1 |
| Museum Negeri Riau | 10 C4 |
| Riau Cultural Park | 11 C4 |

**SLEEPING**
| | |
|---|---|
| Grand Jatra Hotel | 12 C2 |
| Hotel Dyan Graha | 13 C2 |
| Hotel Rauda | 14 C2 |
| Poppie's Homestay | 15 C4 |
| Shorea Hotel | 16 C4 |

**EATING**
| | |
|---|---|
| Ayam Bakar Wong Solo | 17 C2 |
| Vanhollano Bakery | 18 C2 |

**TRANSPORT**
| | |
|---|---|
| Garuda | 19 C3 |
| Lion Air | 20 B1 |
| Mandala | 21 C2 |
| Merpati | (see 19) |
| Sungai Duku Port | 22 C1 |

SUMATRA

## Orientation

The main street of Pekanbaru is Jl Sudirman. Almost everything of importance to travellers – banks, hotels and offices – can be found here or close by. Speedboats leave from the Sungai Duku port. The bus terminal is 5km west of town.

## Information

Most of the city's banks and ATMs are spread along Jl Sudirman. There are plenty of travel agencies around town that can book plane and bus tickets as well as tours of the local area.
**BCA Bank** (Jl Sudirman 448)
**BII Bank** (Jl Nangka 4) Changes US and Singapore dollars (cash and travellers cheques).
**BNI Bank** (Jl Sudirman)

**Micronet** (Jl Mohammed Yamin 11; per hr 10,000Rp; ☺ 9am-10pm) Internet cafe and travel agency.
**Post office** (Jl Sudirman) Between Jl Hangtuah and Jl Kartini.
**Riau Provincial Tourist Office** ( ☎ 31562; Jl Gajah Mada 200; ☺ 8am-4pm Mon-Thu, 8-11am Fri)
**Telkom wartel** (Jl Sudirman; ☺ 8am-9pm) About 1km north of the post office.

## Sights

If you've got time to burn, you could check out the rather standard displays at **Museum Negeri Riau** (Jl Sudirman; admission 10,000Rp; ☺ 8am-2pm Mon-Thu & Sat, 8am-noon Fri). The neighbouring **Riau Cultural Park** (Jl Sudirman; ☺ 8am-2pm Mon-Thu & Sat, 8am-noon Fri) hosts occasional performances. Ask at the tourist office for details.

SUMATRA

# PULAU BATAM & PULAU BINTAN

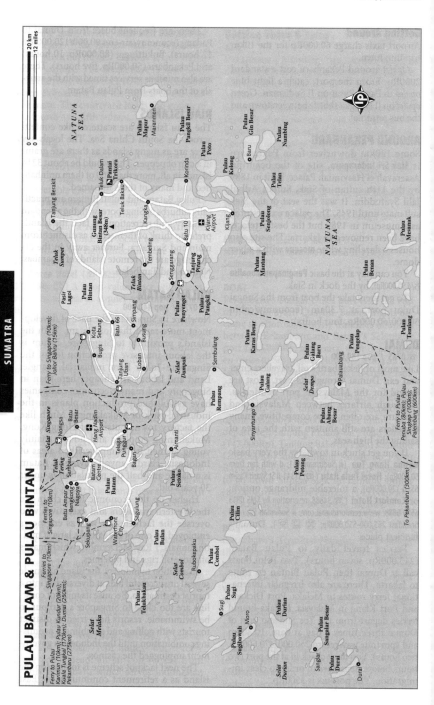

0                20 km
0            12 miles

Ferry to Pulau
Karimun (10km); Pulau Kundur (20km);
Kuala Tungkal (170km); Dumai (250km);
Pekanbaru (275km)

Ferries to
Singapore (10km)

Ferries to
Singapore (10km)

Ferry to Singapore (10km);
Johor Bahru (15km)

Selat Singapore

Selat
Meleka

NATUNA SEA

Tanjung Berakit

Pulau
Mapur

Marannen

Pantai
Trikora

Pulau
Pangkil Besar

Pulau
Gin Besar

Pulau
Numbing

Teluk Dalam

Baru

Pulau
Polo

Pulau
Kelong

Gunung
Bintan Besar
(348m)

Teluk Bakau

Kangka

Pulau
Telan

Teluk
Sumpat

Batu 10

Kijang
Airport

Kijang

Pulau
Senjoong

Pulau
Mesanak

Pulau
Bintan

Tembeling

Pasir
Lagoi

Teluk
Bintan

Simpang

Senggarang

Tanjung
Pinang

NATUNA SEA

Pulau
Mantang

Pulau
Benan

Kota
Sebung

Batu 66

Busung

Pulau
Penyenget

Pulau
Pangkil

Pulau
Temiang

Tanjung
Uban

Bugis

Loban

Selat
Dampuk

Pulau
Karas Besar

Sembulang

Pulau
Pengelip

Nongsa

Batu
Besar

Hang Nadim
Airport

Telaga
Punggur

Ainanti

Pulau
Rempang

Pulau
Galang

Pulau
Galang
Baru

Selat
Dempo

Palaubang

Ferry to Pulau
Penuba (80km); Pulau
Singkep (100km);
Palembang (600km)

Batu Ampar

Bengkong

Nagoya

Batam
Centre

Bagan

Pulau
Setoko

Sinyantungo

Pulau
Abang
Besar

Teluk
Tering

Sambau

Pulau
Batam

Saguling

Waterfront
City

Pulau
Petong

To Pekanbaru (300km)

Sekupang

Rubokepaku

Pulau
Cilim

Pulau
Bulan

Selat
Combol

Rubokepaku

Pulau
Combol

Pulau
Telukhakau

Pulau
Sugi

Sugi

Pulau
Durian

Pulau
Sugibawah

Moro

Pulau
Sangalar Besar

Selat
Durian

Sangalar

Pulau
Durai

Durai

Asians, Singaporeans and Jakarta-based Chinese. New housing complexes are going up faster than new factories.

Besides using Batam as a transit point for boats from Singapore to Sumatra, it is unlikely that a tourist would purposely come to Batam. The majority of foreigners here arrive on corporate assignments and find that the island has cultivated a bit of a boys' club ambience. The main town of Nagoya has plenty of girlie bars to make the buttoned-down execs feel like studs.

### ORIENTATION & INFORMATION

Most travellers to Batam arrive at the northern port of Sekupang by boat from Singapore. Sekupang has an international and domestic terminal next door to each other and all the short-term necessities that new arrivals need: immigration desk and money changers. There are no ATMs at Sekupang, so arrive with cash to avoid a taxi to Nagoya.

The main town on the island is Nagoya, with hotels, banks and other necessities. To the south is the island's administrative centre, Batam Centre, which also has port facilities.

Waterfront City and Nongsa are the surviving resort areas that attract Batam expats on weekends and package tourists from elsewhere in Asia.

On Batam, Singapore dollars are as easy to spend as the Indonesian rupiah.

## Nagoya

This is the original boom town, showing a lot more skin than you'll find in the rest of Sumatra. The heart of town is the Nagoya Entertainment District, where bars and massage parlours indulge male camaraderie with lap dances and take-home prizes. Although it ain't pretty, Nagoya is ultimately functional, with Western-geared food and entertainment sneaking in just under Singapore prices.

The city is divided up like Singapore into main avenues and tributary blocks and exhibits a certain Chinese industriousness similar to the city-state. Most of the hotels in Nagoya have travel agencies.

### INFORMATION

**Awal Brothers Hospital** ( ☎ 431 777; Jl Baloi) Western-trained doctors and international facilities, 7km south of Nagoya.

**Barelang Internet** (Komplek Batam Plaza 4; per hr 10,000Rp)

**Bank Danamon** (Jl Imam Bonjol) Across from Goodway Hotel.

**Batam Tourist Promotion Board** ( ☎ 322 871; next door to Sekupang domestic terminal) Can help with local information and hotel bookings but keeps erratic hours.

**Post office** (Jl Imam Bonjol)

### SLEEPING

**Hotel Grand Palace** ( ☎ 432 529; Komplek Nagoya Business Centre, Block 1; d from 100,000-170,000Rp; ❄ ) The best value around for those on a budget. The tiled-floor rooms come with air-con, hot water, cable TV and clean, sleepable beds.

**Hotel Bahari** ( ☎ 421 911; Komplek Nagoya Square, Block D; r incl breakfast from 140,000-330,000Rp; ❄ ) Bahari I and II occupy the block, with comfy concrete boxes and hot and cold showers. Breakfast included.

**Goodway Hotel** ( ☎ 426 888; www.goodwayhotel.com; Jl Imam Bonjol; r incl breakfast 590,000-750,000Rp; ❄ ⬛ ) Displaced gentleman are lucky to have this classic hotel in this far-flung corner of the world. The decor is subdued and the best rooms have balconies.

**Planet Holiday** ( ☎ 433 555; www.planetholidayho tel.com; Jl Raja Ali Haji; r incl breakfast 600,000-725,000Rp; ❄ ⬛ ⬛ ) Service is crisp, the rooms are modern and as the tallest building in town there are views over squatty Batam.

### EATING & DRINKING

Nagoya has a tasty mix of Indonesian and Chinese restaurants, and warungs.

**Grill Bar** ( ☎ 701 3670; Goodway Hotel, Jl Imam Bonjol; mains from 50,000Rp; ⏰ 10am-11pm) Chase away the nasi goreng blues with a meal of New Zealand Angus steaks at this cherished expat restaurant.

**Kedai Kopi Indah** (mains from 20,000Rp) A popular in-town stop for Chinese-style seafood dishes, such as pepper crab and fish claypot. Located behind Panorama Hotel.

**Golden Prawn** (Bengkong; mains from 50,000Rp) This famous *kelong* (open-air seafood restaurant) is considered one of the best on the island. Everything is charged by the kilo.

For local food, head to the **night market** (Jl Raja Ali Haji) or the big and raucous **Pujasera Nagoya** (food centre, opposite Hotel Sahid Rashinta).

**Goodway Wine Bar** ( ☎ 426 888; Goodway Hotel, Jl Imam Bonjol) Through the wild-west saloon doors is a comfortable tap room for unwinding expats. Kenneth, the publican, once peddled his 'very British' demeanour in Hollywood, a role he plays out here today.

SUMATRA

SUMATRA

## Waterfront City

Near the shipyards, Waterfront City's resorts are a strange occurrence: beachside resorts without beach activities. Instead they focus on resort diversions: swimming, spa-ing, golfing and organised activities. These resorts are heavily marketed to East Asians, mainly Koreans. Weekday discounts through travel agents might override the obvious drawbacks.

**Harris Resort** ( ☎ 381 888; d 599,000Rp; ✖ ▣ ▣ ) This fun-in-the-sun resort is targeted to families and folks of all ages.

**Holiday Inn Resort** ( ☎ 381 333; r incl breakfast S$181-194; ✖ ▣ ⬚ ▣ ) Mainly a corporate hotel, Holiday Inn has classically decorated suites with balconies overlooking the pool. The internationally recognised spa is a fave for Singaporeans who don't want to trek all the way to Bali.

## Nongsa

Batam's prettiest, but still unswimmable, beach occupies the less-developed Nongsa peninsula. Casino resorts had provided the biggest draw for nearby Singaporeans, but ever since the Indonesian government outlawed gambling, the area has quietened down.

**Turi Beach Resort** ( ☎ 761 086; d from S$125; ✖ ▣ ▣ ) Of the surviving resorts, Turi is the best and provides a close but delicious escape for Batam-bound visitors. The thatched-roof huts designed in the Balinese style have all the mid-life comforts and a linen-suit ambience.

Golf courses in Nongsa offer attractive promotional packages (from S$70 to S$100) during the week; Singapore-based travel agents typically have the best rates. Nongsa's two courses are **Tering Bay** ( ☎ 778 761; 818 Jl Hang Lekiu, Km 4), which was designed by Greg Norman, and **Palm Spring Golf Resort** ( ☎ 761 222; Jl Hang Leiku).

Nongsa's favourite *kelong* is the **Rezeki Kelong** (Batu Besar; mains from 50,000Rp).

## Getting There & Away

### AIR

Hang Nadim airport is on the eastern side of the Pulau Batam. Garuda, Merpati, Mandala, Bouraq and Air Asia operate to/from Jakarta. Merpati destinations also include Medan, Padang, Palembang, Jambi and Pekanbaru, as well as Pontianak in Kalimantan. Jatayu also flies to Medan.

### BOAT

Batam has five ports and services between Singapore, the Sumatran mainland and other Riau Islands.

#### To Pulau Bintan

The ferry dock at Telaga Punggur, 30km southeast of Nagoya, is the main port for speedboats to Bintan. The departure tax is 3500Rp.

Boats to Bintan's Tanjung Pinang (one way/return 45,000/85,000Rp, every 20 minutes from 7.30am to 5.50pm) take one hour. There are also boats to Bintan's Lagoi resort area (one way/return 110,000/190,000Rp, three daily).

#### To Elsewhere in Indonesia

The main reason travellers come to Batam is due to its links with the Sumatran mainland. Dumai Express and Surya Gemilang Jaya are the best of the domestic carriers.

Boats leave from Batam's Sekupang terminal to Pekanbaru (210,000Rp, six hours, two morning departures). In order to make the connection without spending the night on Batam, you'll need to catch the first ferry from Singapore at 7.30am and assume that the Indonesian boats are running late as usual.

There are also two morning boats from Sekupang to Dumai (220,000Rp, six hours), one morning boat to Kuala Tungkal (230,000Rp) on the Jambi coast, and three boats weekly to Palembang (305,000Rp, eight hours).

Other destinations from Sekupang port include Karimun (70,000Rp, one hour, hourly from 8am to 4pm) and Pulau Kundur (85,000Rp, two hours, hourly from 8am to 2.30pm).

Pelni ships pass through Batam to and from Belawan (the port for Medan) and Jakarta. The tickets can be bought at the domestic ferry terminal or at travel agencies in Nagoya.

#### Singapore

Frequent services shuttle between Singapore and Batam, taking between 25 minutes and 45 minutes depending on the pier. Tickets for all ferries to Singapore cost S$30/54 one way/return. There is a S$7 harbour-departure tax upon leaving Batam and an hour time difference between Indonesia and Singapore. Penguin has the biggest and fastest ferries (taking 25 minutes).

---

**ISLAND IN THE SUN**

Imagine an island made up of a handful of salt-white beaches, emerald waters and nobody but you and your personally selected guests. Robinson Crusoe goes luxury on **Pulau Pangkil** (www .pangkil.com; island hire for up to 10 guests from S$2600; 🔊 ) an exclusive private island available for hire. Guests have a choice of romantic 'Driftwood Palaces' to sleep in, which are scattered up and down the island's main two beaches. Butlers, maids, a swimming pool and all sorts of beach activities are on hand to ensure that island survival is as easy as possible. The tiny speck is around a 30-minute boat hop from Tanjung Pinang and regularly houses up to 30 guests, normally Western expats from Singapore, who take over the island as a single group and get up to all kinds of debauchery. The rule goes what happens on Pangkil stays on Pangkil.

---

Sekupang is most widely used by tourists because the terminal that receives boats from Singapore's Harbourfront Centre is next door to the domestic terminal for transfer to the Sumatran mainland. The boats to Singapore run approximately every hour from 6am to 6.45pm, and from Singapore to Batam from 7.30am to 8pm. Batam Centre and Waterfront City have services only to/from Singapore's Harbourfront Centre. The last boat to leave the island departs from Batam Centre at 9.30pm. Waterfront City's schedule is fairly limited, with only four departures per day. Ferries to Nongsa shuttle back and forth to Singapore's Tanah Merah, with eight departures per day between 8am and 8pm.

At Sekupang port don't buy a ticket from the many touts, and refuse any offers of 'assistance' to see you through immigration.

### Getting Around

Taxis are the primary way to get around Pulau Batam. Sample fares are as follows: from Sekupang to Nagoya (10,000Rp, 45 minutes) and Batam Centre to Nagoya (6,000Rp, 30 minutes). From the airport, it will cost 100,000Rp to Sekupang, 80,000Rp to Nagoya and 75,000Rp to Batam Centre.

Blue-and-white bemo shuttle between Nongsa and Nagoya (15,000Rp). There's also a public bus from Telaga Punggur to Nagoya (10,000Rp). A taxi on the same route is 75,000Rp.

## PULAU BINTAN
☎ 0771 / pop 200,000

Just across the water from Batam, Pulau Bintan has been receiving a billing as the next big luxury destination. Bintan is trying to market itself as the high-end playground for the new money from East Asia. Certainly, the

folk at Indonesia's marketing department are boasting Bintan to be the next Bali, which is more than optimistic but some of the beaches do justify the comparison.

There's little reason or means for a budget traveller to stop off here, but those with deeper pockets will find high-end resorts on the north side of the island, complete with delicious shores and all the trimmings.

### Tanjung Pinang

The main port town on the island is a bustling mercantile centre with more ethnic diversity than most Sumatran towns. There is lots of provincial-style shopping and nibbling on Chinese and Indonesian specialities. Located nearby are several traditional-style villages and temple attractions that tickle the culture-bone of the many weekending Singaporeans.

#### ORIENTATION & INFORMATION

The port, hotels, and other necessities are all within walking distance. There are plenty of ATMs around town and bank branches, mainly on Jl Teuku Umar.

**Bank Mandiri** (Jl Teuku Umar)

**BCA Bank** (Jl Ketapang)

**Bintan Internet Centre** (Jl Pos; per hr 10,000Rp; 🕓 9am-10pm)

**BNI Bank** (Jl Teuku Umar)

**Extreme Internet** (Jl Mawar 9A; per hr 10,000Rp; 🕓 10am-10pm) On the 2nd floor of a wartel office.

**Pinang Jaya Tour & Travel** ( ☎ 21267; Jl Bintan 44) Air tickets.

**Post office** (Jl Merdeka) Near the harbour, on Tanjung Pinang's main street.

**Tourist information centre** ( ☎ 31822; Jl Merdeka 5; 🕓 8am-5pm) Behind the police station; the helpful English-speaking staff organise city tours.

**Wartel** (Jl Bintan)

**Wartel** (Jl Merdeka)

SUMATRA

**TANJUNG PINANG**

0 _____ 200 m
0 _____ 0.1 miles

**A** **B** **C** NATUNA SEA **D**

| INFORMATION | |
| --- | --- |
| Bank Mandiri.....................1 | C3 |
| BCA Bank..........................2 | C2 |
| Bintan Internet Centre........3 | B2 |
| BNI Bank...........................4 | C3 |
| Extreme Internet.................5 | D3 |
| Pinang Jaya Tour & Travel....6 | C3 |
| Post Office........................7 | B3 |
| Tourist Information Centre....8 | B3 |
| Wartel..............................9 | C3 |
| Wartel.........................(see 7) | |

| SLEEPING | |
| --- | --- |
| Bong's Homestay..............10 | C3 |
| Hotel Laguna....................11 | C3 |
| Hotel Melia.......................12 | C3 |
| Hotel Surya......................13 | C3 |

| EATING | |
| --- | --- |
| Food Court.......................14 | D3 |
| Pasar Buah.......................15 | C2 |

| TRANSPORT | |
| --- | --- |
| Boat to Sungai Ular..............(see 19) | |
| Boats to Pulau Penyengat.....16 | B3 |
| Ferry & Speedboat Ticket Agents.17 | C3 |
| Ferry & Speedboat Ticket Agents.18 | B3 |
| Ferry to Senggarang............19 | C1 |
| Pelni...............................20 | C2 |

To Senggarang (5km);
Sungai Ular (15km)

Pejantan II

Jl Plantar II

Jl Pasar

Jl Gambir Baru

Jl Pasar Ikan

Lorong Merdeka

Chinese Temple

Jl Kelapang

Jl Temiang

Jl Mawar

Jl Teratai

Jl Terata

Jl Po

Bintan Indah Mall

Jl Merdeka

Lorong Bintan

Jl Teuku Umar

Jl Bakar Batu

Jl Gereja

Bestari Mall & Supermarket

Volleyball Stadium

To Bus Terminal (7km);
Pantai Trikora (45km);
Tanjung Uban (115km)

Main Pier

Boats to Batam (40km);
Singapore (60km);
Jakarta (900km)

To Pulau Penyengat (2km)

Police Station

Jl SM Amin

Jl Bintan

Lorong Bintan II

Jl Mesjid

Jl Yusuf Khahar

Mosque

Jl Tabib

**SIGHTS & ACTIVITIES**

You can stroll around Tanjung Pinang in a leisurely hour. The older part of town is found around the narrow piers near Jl Plantar II. The harbour hosts a constant stream of vessels, from tiny sampans to large freighters.

The following sites can be visited independently or through tour programs arranged with the tourist office.

**Pulau Penyenget**

Only a short hop across the harbour from Tanjung Pinang, tiny **Penyenget** was once the capital of the Riau rajahs. The island is believed to have been given to Rajah Riau-Lingga VI in 1805 by his brother-in-law, Sultan Mahmud, as a wedding present. Another historical footnote is that the Penyenget-based sultanate cooperated with Sir Stamford Raffles to hand over Singapore in exchange for British military protection in 1819.

The island is littered with interesting relics and can be walked in a couple of hours. The coastline is dotted with traditional Malay

stilted houses, while the ruins of the **old palace** of Rajah Ali and the **tombs** and **graveyards** of Rajah Jaafar and Rajah Ali are clearly signposted inland. The most impressive site is the sulphur-coloured **mosque**, with its many domes and minarets. Dress appropriately or you won't be allowed in.

There are frequent boats to Pulau Penyenget from Bintan's main pier (4000Rp, from 7am to 5pm). There's a 2000Rp entry charge at weekends.

**Senggarang**

A fascinating village sits just across the harbour from Tanjung Pinang. The star attraction is an old **Chinese temple**, now suspended in the roots of a huge banyan that has grown up through it.

The temple is to the left of the pier, where boats from Tanjung Pinang dock. Half a kilometre along the waterfront, **Vihara Darma Sasana**, a complex of three temples, all said to be more than a century old, occupy a large courtyard facing the sea.

Boats to Senggarang (15,000Rp) leave from Pejantan II wharf.

## Sungai Ular

Snake River swims through mangrove forests to **Jodoh temple**, the oldest Chinese temple in Riau Islands. The temple is decorated with gory murals depicting the trials and tortures of hell. You can charter a sampan (80,000Rp for five people) from Tanjung Pinang harbour.

### SLEEPING & EATING

All of Tanjung Pinang's accommodation is within walking distance of the harbour.

**Bong's Homestay** (Lorong Bintan II 20; d 30,000Rp) This alleyway home has been running since 1972 and has very basic rooms. The family speaks excellent English – specialist subjects include English Football and '70s rock.

**Hotel Surya** ( ☎ 318 387; Jl Bintan 49; s/d incl breakfast 55,000/90,000Rp; ✹ ) Quality varies at this multi-storey hotel. Fan rooms are basic concrete boxes, while some rooms have sunny windows and new paint.

**Hotel Laguna** ( ☎ 311 555; Jl Bintan 51; d incl breakfast 302,500-387,200Rp; ✹ 🛜 ) Tanjung Pinang's corporate stay, with big beds and walk-in shower.

**Hotel Melia** ( ☎ 21898; Jl Pos 25; d incl breakfast 262,500-525,000Rp; ✹ 🛜 ) Bright and airy rooms and enormous suites with views over the harbour.

In front of the volleyball stadium on Jl Teuku Umar, an open-air **food court** (mains 8000Rp) whips up tasty snacks.

If you're looking for Padang food, there are several places on Jl Plantar II serving good fish or jackfruit curries.

The colourful *pasar buah* (fruit market) is at the northern end of Jl Merdeka. In the evening there are several food stalls scattered around town serving *mie bangka*, a Hakka-style dumpling soup.

### GETTING THERE & AWAY

See p458 for transport options to/from Tangjung Pinang.

### GETTING AROUND

It is fairly easy to get around central Tangjung Pinang by catching one of the many *opelet* (3000Rp). The *opelet* don't have fixed routes, so tell the driver your destination and see if he agrees.

The bus terminal is inconveniently located 7km out of Tanjung Pinang, along the road to Pantai Trikora. But there aren't many services that leave from here.

To get to the outlying beaches is expensive. A taxi from Tanjung Pinang to Pantai Trikora is a long ride and will cost 250,000Rp. You can also fish around for share taxis, but most drivers won't want to cut a deal with a 'rich' foreigner. If you head out to the main highway, you can catch Barakit-bound public buses that pass through Trikora (20,000Rp).

Another not-so-affordable option is to rent a car, which gives you flexibility in exploring the beaches around the island. **Rico Rental** ( ☎ 315931; Jl Yos Sudarso 1) rents Kijang (4WD vehicles) for 250,000Rp per day (not including petrol). Renting a car in Tanjung Pinang is cheaper than relying on the resorts in Lagoi.

## Pantai Trikora & Around

Bintan's east coast is lined with rustic beaches and simple wooden bungalows. The main beach is **Pantai Trikora**, which is pretty enough at high tide but turns into miles of mud flats at low tide. The beaches to the north around Malangrupai have more consistent surf and turf. Regardless though, the area is relatively deserted: just you, the ocean and a few napping dogs. A group of small islands off Pantai Trikora are well worth visiting and there is good **snorkelling** outside the monsoon season (November to March).

### SLEEPING & EATING

Accommodation at Trikora is outside the village of Teluk Bakau. Hotels listed here can organise snorkelling trips to offshore islands (150,000Rp).

**Shady Shack** ( ☎ 081 3645 15223; www.lobo.kinemotion.de; d with breakfast S$25) A handful of weather-beaten shacks face directly to the sea. This is just a step above camping and is a good excuse not to shower or brush your teeth. Quad rooms also available (S$40).

**Gurindam Resort** ( ☎ 26234; Telok Bakau, Km 35; weekday/weekend d with breakfast 180,000/220,000Rp) Designed like an Islamic fishing village with stilt-frame bungalows built over the water, this is a dream come true for down-to-earth family getaways. There's fishing in the attached fish ponds, a thatched-roof restaurant big enough for energetic tots, and a small swimming beach.

## Lagoi

Bintan's resort area stretches along the northern coastline of the island along Pasir Lagoi, with acres of wilderness buffering the hotels from commoners to the south. Security is in full effect, with checkpoints at access roads and at hotel entrances. The beaches are sandy and swimmable, the resorts have polished four- and five-star service and there are water-sports activities and entertainment for all ages.

There are three golf courses in Lagoi designed by champion golfers: **Bintan Lagoon Resort Golf Club** ( ☎ 0770 691 388; www.bintanlagoon. com; green fees weekday/weekend S$65/70), **Laguna Bintan Golf Club** ( ☎ 0770 693 188; golf-bintan@banyantree.com; green fees weekday/weekend S$122/165) and top-rated **Ria Bintan Golf Club** ( ☎ 0770 692 839; www.riabintan. com; green fees weekday/weekend S$150/210). Packages include ferry from Singapore (weekday S$99 to S$169, weekends S$130 to S$229).

### SLEEPING

There are three resort compounds comprising several hotel clusters, private beaches and golf courses. Check with travel agents about weekday discounts, which can be as generous as 50%. See www.bintan-resorts.com for property details.

Of the three, we found the hotels within Laguna Bintan (Angsana Resort and Banyan Tree) and Nirwana Gardens (Nirwana Resort) compounds to be accommodating and well maintained.

**Angsana Resort & Spa Bintan** ( ☎ 0770 693 111; www.angsana.com; package incl breakfast weekday US$220-520, weekend US$281-607; 🅿 🛜 🌊 ) The more dressed-down companion to sophisticated Banyan Tree, Angsana is best suited to young professionals. The breezy common spaces are decorated in zesty citrus colours, with private rooms sporting a contemporary colonial style. The superior rooms are nice but the suites are super.

**Banyan Tree Bintan** ( ☎ 0770 693 100; www.banyantree.com; package incl breakfast weekday/weekend US$305/320; 🅿 🛜 🌊 ) More private and privileged than Angsana, Banyan Tree has famed spa facilities and a high-powered retreat deep in the jungle. The hotel shares the 900m-long beach with Angsana.

**Nirwana Resort Hotel** ( ☎ 0770 692 505; www.nirwanagardens.com; package incl breakfast weekday US$180-360, weekend US$228-440; 🅿 🛜 🌊 ) More targeted to local families, Nirwana is comfortable and unfussy, with sweet staff but not the best beach. The lagoon-style pool has a large baby pool area, but the grounds are little thirsty. The suites have sea views and huge bathrooms.

### GETTING AROUND

For Lagoi-bound visitors, most resorts organise shuttle service between the harbour at Kota Sebong and the hotels as part of the package price or for an additional S$6.

## Getting There & Away
### AIR

Kijang airport is currently used for cargo rather than passenger flights.

### BOAT

Bintan has three ports and services to Palau Batam, Singapore and other islands in the Riau archipelago.

Tanjung Pinang is the busiest harbour and the best option for folks planning to stay in Tanjung Pinang or Pantai Trikora. If you're bound for the resort area of Lagoi, the port at Kota Sebung is more convenient. Tanjung Uban is the third option.

### To Batam

Regular speedboats depart from the main pier in Tanjung Pinang for Telaga Punggur on Batam (45,000Rp, 45 minutes) from 7.45am to 4.45pm daily. There are also boats that go from Lagoi to Batam's Telaga Punggur (one way/return 100,000/170,000Rp).

### To Elsewhere in Indonesia

There are boats to Pekanbaru (280,000Rp, daily) and Dumai (220,000Rp, daily). Tickets for all of these destinations can be bought from agents on Jl Merdeka in Tanjung Pinang, just outside of the harbour entrance.

Daily ferries travel to other islands in the Riau chain, such as Pulau Karimum's Tanjung Balai (80,000Rp, 2½ hours), Pulau Lingga's Daik (70,000Rp, three hours), Sungai Buluh on Singkep (60,000Rp, three hours) and Penuba (80,000Rp, three hours). The Anugra Makmur company runs boats every 10 days to the remote Natuna Islands.

Pelni sails to Jakarta weekly from the southern port of Kijang. Travel agencies in Tanjung Pinang can supply tickets and schedules.

### To Malaysia

There are boats to Johor Bahru in Malaysia (150,000Rp, five departures daily) from Tanjung Pinang. Tickets can be bought from agents on Jl Merdeka in Tanjung Pinang, just outside of the harbour entrance.

**To Singapore**

Boats from Tanjung Pinang go to Singapore's Tanah Merah (one way S$24) between 7am and 6.30pm. There are more frequent services on the weekend.

**Bintan Resort Ferries** (www.brf.com.sg) is the only company that handles transport between Lagoi and Singapore; ticket prices vary based on day of week but start at S$26.

## OTHER RIAU ISLANDS

Few travellers reach the remote outer islands of Riau. Getting there is half the problem. Head to the better-serviced islands first, and you can usually organise to island-hop from there.

### Pulau Singkep

Singkep is the third-largest island in the archipelago. Huge tin mines once provided most of the island's jobs, but since their closure much of the population has moved elsewhere and the island has reverted to being a sleepy backwater.

The main town, **Dabo**, is shaded by lush trees and gardens and clustered around a central park. A large **mosque** dominates the skyline. The fish and vegetable **markets** near the harbour are interesting, and Jl Pasar Lamar is a good browsing and shopping area. **Batu Bedaun**, 4km from town, is a lovely white-sand beach fringed with palms.

There is accommodation available at the simple **Wisma Gapura Singkep** ( ☎ 0776 21136; Jl Perusalaan 41; d 50,000-240,000Rp).

You can eat at the **markets** behind Wisma Sri Indah or try any of the warungs on Jl Pasar Lama and Jl Merdeka. Food stalls and warungs pop up all over the place at night.

There's one boat a day to Tanjung Pinang on Pulau Bintan (57,000Rp, three hours) and daily ferries to Daik on Pulau Lingga. Boats dock at Singkep's northern port of Sungai Buluh, from where there are buses to Dabo. Several shops in Dabo act as ticket agencies.

### Pulau Penuba

Penuba is a small island wedged between Singkep and Lingga. It's an idyllic place to do little but swim, walk and read. There are some great beaches near the north-coast village of **Tanjung Dua** and others near the main settlement, **Penuba**, on the southeastern coast.

Penuba is a sleepy village centred around the **Attaqwa Mosque**. Accommodation is available at the house next door – ask around for the caretaker – and you can eat at several warungs along Jl Merdeka, the main street.

A daily boat travels to Penuba from Tanjung Pinang (80,000Rp, three hours) on Bintan, or you can charter a boat from Singkep for the half-hour trip.

### Pulau Lingga

Not much remains of the glory that was once the royal island of Lingga except a few neglected ruins. Today there are few creature comforts and little in the way of modern development. The island resembles a crown and rises sharply from the shore to form the three jungle-clad peaks of **Gunung Daik**. The central peak reaches 1163m and is the highest point in the archipelago. Locals maintain that it has never been climbed.

Daik, the main village and arrival point, is hidden 1km up a muddy river. The town itself is pretty much a single street, with some cargo wharves and about a dozen Chinese shops. It has a certain tropical, seedy charm and a very laid-back atmosphere.

The main site of historical interest is the modest ruin of the **palace** of Rajah Suleiman, the last rajah of Riau-Lingga. Next to the palace are the foundation stones of a building said to have housed the rajah's extensive harem. The palace was made of wood and little survives today, though the surrounding jungle hides overgrown bathing pools and squat toilets. The ruins are a two-hour walk from Daik and you'll need very clear directions or a guide to get you through the maze of overgrown forest paths.

On the outskirts of Daik the **Mesjid Sultan Lingga** houses the tomb of Rajah Mahmud I, who ruled in the early 19th century. A half-hour walk from town is the **Makam Bukit Cenckeh** (Cenckeh Hill Cemetery) on a hill overlooking the river. The crumbling graves of Rajah Abdul Rakhman (r 1812–31) and Rajah Muhammed (r 1832–41) are here. The remains of an old fort are nearby.

There is one basic **hotel** (d around 60,000Rp) in Daik, near the ferry dock on the main street. There are a few small **warungs** on the main street.

There are daily boats for the two-hour trip from Daik to Dabo on Singkep (50,000Rp), and there's also a daily service to Tanjung Pinang (80,000Rp, three hours) on Pulau Bintan.

## Natuna Islands

These islands are right off the beaten track and difficult to reach.

The population of **Pulau Natuna Besar** is fairly small, although there's an extensive *transmigrasi* program along Sungai Ulu, with settlers from Java growing cash crops such as peanuts and green peas.

The islands are noted for fine basket-weave **cloth** and various kinds of **traditional dance**. One particularly idiosyncratic local dance is a kind of *Thousand & One Arabian Nights* saga, incorporating episodes from Riau-Lingga history.

Ask in Tanjung Pinang on Pulau Bintan about infrequent boat services to Natuna.

# JAMBI

For such a centrally located province, Jambi is not easy to reach and sees few foreign visitors. The province occupies a 53,435-sq-km slice of central Sumatra, stretching from the highest peaks of the Bukit Barisan range in the west to the coastal swamps facing the Strait of Melaka in the east.

The eastern lowlands are mainly rubber and palm-oil plantations. Timber is also big business, as is oil; Jambi's main field is southeast of the capital (Jambi) on the South Sumatran border.

In the western portion of the province is the Kerinci Seblat National Park, home to Sumatra's highest peak, Gunung Kerinci (3805m), Sumatran tigers (Jambi's faunal mascot) and rhinos. The park is covered in the West Sumatra section (see p442) as Padang has more convenient transit links than Jambi.

Most of the province is sparsely populated; many are migrants from Java and Bali. In the province's fast disappearing forests, the Orang Rimba are an endangered hunter-gatherer tribe.

## History

The province of Jambi was the heartland of the ancient kingdom of Malayu, which first rose to prominence in the 7th century. Much of Malayu's history is closely and confusingly entwined with that of its main regional rival, the Palembang-based kingdom of Sriwijaya. The little that is known about Malayu has mostly been gleaned from the precise records maintained by the Chinese court of the time.

It is assumed that the temple ruins at Muara Jambi mark the site of Malayu's former capital, the ancient city of Jambi – known to the Chinese as Chan Pi. The Malayu sent their first delegation to China in 644 and the Chinese scholar I Tsing spent a month in Malayu in 672. When he returned 20 years later he found that Malayu had been conquered by Sriwijaya. The Sriwijayans appear to have remained in control until the sudden collapse of their empire at the beginning of the 11th century.

Following Sriwijaya's demise, Malayu re-emerged as an independent kingdom and stayed that way until it became a dependency of Java's Majapahit empire, which ruled from 1278 until 1520. It then came under the sway of the Minangkabau people of West Sumatra.

In 1616 the Dutch East India Company opened an office in Jambi and quickly formed a successful alliance with Sultan Muhammed Nakhruddin to protect its ships and cargoes from pirates. It also negotiated a trade monopoly with Nakhruddin and his successors. The major export was pepper, which was grown in great abundance. In 1901 the Dutch East India Company moved its headquarters to Palembang and effectively gave up its grip on Jambi.

## JAMBI

☎ 0741 / pop 490,000

The capital of Jambi province is the city of the same name, a busy river port about 155km from the mouth of Sungai Batang Hari. Jambi is not known as a tourist destination, but those who have wandered the markets and watched the city in action have found that somewhere can be more fun than nowhere.

## Orientation

Jambi sprawls over a wide area, a combination of the old Pasar Jambi district spreading south from the port, and the new suburbs of Kota Baru and Telanaipura to the west. Most of the banks, hotels and restaurants are in Pasar Jambi near the junction of Jl Gatot Subroto and Jl Raden Mattaher, while government buildings are out at Kota Baru.

## Information

There are plenty of ATMs around town. Jl Dr Sutomo is the primary bank street.

**Culture & Tourism Office** ( ☎ 445 056; Jl H Agus Salim, Kota Baru) The English-speaking staff are keen to promote the province and can organise city tours.

## ORANG RIMBA

Jambi's nomadic hunter-gatherers are known by many names: outsiders refer to the diverse tribes collectively as Kubu, an unflattering term, while they refer to themselves as Orang Rimba (People of the Forest) or Anak Dalam (Children of the Forest). Descended from the first wave of Malays to migrate to Sumatra, they once lived in highly mobile groups throughout Jambi's lowland forests.

As fixed communities began to dominate the province, the Orang Rimba retained their nomadic lifestyle and animistic beliefs, regarding their neighbours' adoption of Islam and agriculture as disrespectful towards the forest. Traditionally the Orang Rimba avoided contact with the outsiders, preferring to barter and trade by leaving goods on the fringes of the forest or relying on trusted intermediaries.

In the 1960s, the Indonesian government's social affairs and religion departments campaigned to assimilate the Orang Rimba into permanent camps and convert them to a monotheistic religion. Meanwhile the jungles were being transformed into palm-oil and rubber plantations during large-scale *transmigrasi* from Java and Bali.

Some Orang Rimba assimilated and are now economically marginalised within the plantations, while others live off government funds and then return to the forests. About 2500 Orang Rimba retain their traditional lifestyles within the shrinking forest. The groups were given special settlement rights within Bukit Duabelas and Bukit Tigapuluh National Parks, but the protected forests are as vulnerable to illegal logging and poaching as other Sumatran parks.

In the opinions of the NGO groups that work with the Orang Rimba, it isn't a question of *if* the tribes will lose their jungle traditions but *when*. In the spirit of practical idealism, the organisation **WARSI** (www.warsi.or.id) established its alternative educational outreach. Rather than forcing educational institutions on the Orang Rimba, teachers join those that will accept an outsider and teach the children how to read, write and count – the equivalent of knowing how to hunt and forage in the settled communities.

**Main Telkom wartel** (Jl Dr Sumantri) In Telanaipura.

**Post office** (Jl Sultan Thaha 9) Near the port.

**Thamrin Internet** (Jl Gatot Subroto 6; per hr 5000Rp; ☻ 10am-10pm) Internet access near Gloria Bookshop.

**Wartel** (Jl Raden Mattaher; ☻ 8am-9pm) More convenient than the main Telekom wartel; you can make international phone calls here.

## Sights & Activities

Jambi is the starting point for excursions to the archaeological site of Muara Jambi (see p462).

**Museum Negeri Propinsi Jambi** (cnr Jl Urip Sumoharjo & Prof Dr Sri Sudewi, Telanaipura; admission 2000Rp; ☻ 8.30am-3pm Mon-Fri), one of the city's few attractions, is out in Telanaipura. It has a selection of costumes and handicrafts, as well as a small historical display. Take an *ojek* (3000Rp to 4000Rp).

Nearby the museum is a **batik centre** that produces and sells traditional Jambi textiles featuring striking floral motifs. The centre also has a range of handicrafts from all over the province, including *songket* weaving and finely woven split-rattan baskets. The centre provides employment for local women.

## Sleeping

Accommodation in Jambi isn't much of a bargain, so you should opt for convenience instead. The most social spot to base yourself is near the market, behind the Novotel, where you'll find a cluster of midrange and top-end hotels.

**Lukman Language Exchange** (l_tanjung@yahoo .com) Delightful Jambi resident Lukman can provide lodging in his home in exchange for a few appearances by an English native speaker at his weekly tutoring sessions.

**Hotel Da'lia** ( ☎ 755 2309; Jl Camar 100; d with shared bathroom 70,000Rp, d with air-con 150,000Rp; ✴ ) Basic and clean, this is the best you'll get in the budget range.

**Hotel Abadi** ( ☎ 25600; Jl Gatot Subroto 92; d 410,000, d incl breakfast 550,000Rp; ✴ ▣ ▣ ☞ ) Otherwise average top-end rooms at Hotel Abadi are decorated with Jambi batik bedspreads for a local flair. Junior suites feature a tranquil balcony.

**Novotel** ( ☎ 27208; novotel@e-jambi.net; Jl Gatot Subroto 44; d 465,000-1,010,000Rp; ▣ ) Currently the most expensive hotel in town but far from being worth it.

## Eating

**Saimen Perancis** (Jl Raden Mattaher; pastries 2000Rp) An excellent bakery that also serves meals.

**Simpang Raya** (Jl Raden Mattaher 22; dishes 7000Rp) An old friend in the *nasi Padang* game.

**Munri Food Centre** (Jl Sultan Agung; mains 10,000Rp) More night-time eats set the night ablaze at this alfresco dining area.

**Ancol** (near Sungai Batang Hari) Just down from the Trade Centre, this is an evening destination for promenading and river breezes. Stalls sell local favourites, such as *nanas goreng* (fried pineapples) and *jagung bakar* (roasted corn slathered with coconut milk and chillis).

**Pasar Makanan** (Jl Sultan Iskandar Muda) Lots of regional Palembang specialities, which Jambi also claims as its own, get top billing at this busy market.

## Getting There & Away

### AIR

The Sultan Thaka Airport is 6km east of the centre. Batavia Air and Mandala fly to Jakarta daily. Merpati flies to Batam. Most tickets are available through travel agents, but **Mandala** (☎ 24341; Jl Gatot Subroto 42) also has an office.

### BOAT

**Ratu Intan Permata** (☎ 60234; Simpang Kawat, Jl M Yamin) operates connecting services from Jambi to the coastal town of Kuala Tungkal (50,000Rp, two hours), from where there are speedboats to Batam (210,000Rp, five hours).

### BUS

The highways to the south and north are in poor condition, making bus travel an arduous task. Bus-ticketing offices occupy two areas of town: **Simpang Rimbo**, 8km west of town, and **Simpang Kawat**, 3.5km southwest of town on Jl M Yamin.

There are frequent economy buses to Palembang (60,000Rp, seven hours).

**Ratu Intan Permata** (☎ 20784; Simpang Kawat, Jl M Yamin) has comfortable door-to-door minibus services to Pekanbaru (190,000Rp, eight hours), Bengkulu (180,000Rp, 10 hours), Palembang (110,000Rp, six hours) and Padang (180,000Rp, 13 hours).

**Safa Marwa** (☎ 65756; Jl Pattimura 77) runs a similar service to Sungai Penuh in the Kerinci Valley (70,000Rp, 10 hours).

Buses from Jambi depart from the companies' offices.

## Getting Around

Airport taxis charge a standard 60,000Rp for the 8km run into town. Local transport comprises the usual assortment of *ojek* and *opelet*. Rawasari *opelet* terminal, off Jl Raden Mattaher in the centre of town, is where all *opelet* start and finish their journeys. The standard fare is 2000Rp.

## MUARA JAMBI

The large temple complex at Muara Jambi, 26km downstream from Jambi, is the most important Hindu-Buddhist site in Sumatra. It is assumed that the temples mark the location of the ancient city of Jambi, capital of the kingdom of Malayu 1000 years ago. Most of the temples, known as *candi*, date from the 9th to the 13th centuries, when Jambi's power was at its peak. However the best of the artefacts have been taken to Jakarta.

For centuries the site lay abandoned and overgrown in the jungle on the banks of the Batang Hari. It was 'rediscovered' in 1920 by a British army expedition sent to explore the region.

### Sights

It's easy to spend all day at **Muara Jambi** (admission by donation; ☉ 8am-4pm). The forested site covers 12 sq km along the north bank of the Batang Hari. The entrance is through an ornate archway in the village of Muara Jambi and most places of interest are within a few minutes' walk of here.

Eight temples have been identified so far, each at the centre of its own low-walled compound. Some are accompanied by *perwara candi* (smaller side temples) and three have been restored to something close to their original form. The site is dotted with numerous *menapo* (smaller brick mounds), thought to be the ruins of other buildings – possibly dwellings for priests and other high officials.

The restored temple **Candi Gumpung**, straight ahead of the donation office, has a fiendish *makara* (demon head) guarding its steps. Excavation work here has yielded some important finds, including a *peripih* (stone box) containing sheets of gold inscribed with old Javanese characters, dating the temple back to the 9th century. A statue of Prajnyaparamita found here is now the star attraction at the small **site museum** nearby.

**Candi Tinggi**, 200m southeast of Candi Gumpung, is the finest of the temples uncovered so far. It dates from the 9th century but is built around another, older temple. A path leads east from Candi Tinggi to **Candi Astano**, 1.5km away, passing **Candi Kembar Batu** and lots of *menapo* along the way.

The temples on the western side of the site are yet to be restored. They remain pretty much as they were found – minus the jungle, which was cleared in the 1980s. The western sites are signposted from Candi Gumpung. First stop, after 900m, is **Candi Gedong Satu**, followed 150m further on by **Candi Gedong Dua**. They are independent temples despite what their names may suggest. The path continues west for another 1.5km to **Candi Kedaton**, the largest of the temples, then a further 900m northwest to **Candi Koto Mahligai**.

The dwellings of the ordinary Malayu people have long since disappeared. According to Chinese records, they lived along the river in stilted houses or in raft huts moored to the bank.

### Getting There & Away
There is no public transport to the park. You can charter a speedboat (300,000Rp) from Jambi's river pier to the site. You can also hire an *ojek* (35,000Rp).

# SOUTH SUMATRA

Like Riau and Jambi provinces, the eastern portion of South Sumatra shares a common Malay ancestry and influence from its proximity to the shipping lane of the Strait of Melaka. Rivers define the character of the eastern lowlands, while the western high peaks of the Bukit Barisan form the province's rugged underbelly. The provincial capital of Palembang was once the central seat of the Buddhist Sriwijaya empire, whose control once reached all the way up the Malay Peninsula.

Despite the province's illustrious past, there aren't very many surviving attractions, except for the hospitality that occurs in places where bilingual Indonesians don't get a lot of opportunity to practise their English.

## PALEMBANG
☎ 0711 / pop 1.67 million
Sumatra's second-largest city, Palembang is a manic concrete sprawl with little to offer anyone but the true urban enthusiast.

The town prospers as a major port and on the core industries of oil refining, fertiliser production and cement manufacturing, which all scent the air with a distinctive odour you might first mistake as your own funk.

Chances are you're passing north or south if you're here. While the city ain't much to look at, be sure to stick around for at least a meal – the spicy fare is subject of much debate (positive and negative) in Sumatra, and it's worth establishing your own opinion for gaining kudos on cuisine chat around the rest of the island.

### History
A thousand years ago Palembang was the centre of the highly developed Sriwijaya civilisation. The Chinese scholar I Tsing spent six months in Palembang in 672 and reported that 1000 monks, scholars and pilgrims were studying and translating Sanskrit there. At its peak in the 11th century, Sriwijaya ruled a huge slab of Southeast Asia, covering most of Sumatra, the Malay Peninsula, southern Thailand and Cambodia. Sriwijayan influence collapsed after the kingdom was conquered by the south Indian king Ravendra Choladewa in 1025. For the next 200 years, the void was partly filled by Sriwijaya's main regional rival, the Jambi-based kingdom of Malayu.

Few relics from this period remain – no sculptures, monuments or architecture of note – nor is there much of interest from the early 18th century, when Palembang was an Islamic kingdom. Most of the buildings of the latter era were destroyed in battles with the Dutch.

The city's name comes from two words: *pa* (place) and *limbang* (to pan for gold). The prosperity of the Sriwijayan city is said to have been based on gold found in local rivers.

### Orientation
Palembang sits astride Sungai Musi, the two halves of the city linked by the giant Jembatan Ampera (Ampera Bridge). The river is flanked by a hodgepodge of wooden houses on stilts. The southern side, Seberang Ulu, is where the majority of people live. Seberang Ilir, on the north bank, is the city's better half, where you'll find most of the government offices, shops, hotels and the wealthy residential districts. The main street, Jl Sudirman, runs north–south to the bridge. The bus terminal and train station are both on the southern side.

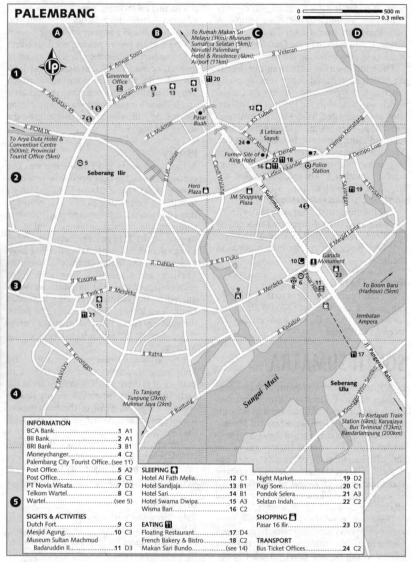

# PALEMBANG

## Information

Palembang has branches of all the major banks and there are ATMs all over the city. Outside banking hours, the bigger hotels are a better bet than money changers.

**BCA Bank** (Jl Kapitan Rivai)
**BII Bank** (Jl Kapitan Rivai)
**BRI Bank** (Jl Kapitan Rivai)

**Money changer** (Jl Kol Atmo)
**Palembang city tourist office** ( ☎ 358 450; Museum Sultan Machmud Badaruddin II, Jl Pasar Hilir 3) A useful office at the Museum Sultan Machmud Badaruddin II, off Jl Sudirman; the staff can arrange trips down the Sungai Musi and handicraft tours.

**Post office** (Jl Merdeka) Close to the river, next to the Garuda monument. Internet facilities available.

**Provincial tourist office** ( ☎ 357 348; Jl Demang Lebar Daun) A useful office outside of the centre of town.

**PT Novia Wisata** ( ☎ 512 584; Jl Jend A Yani 3) Agents here can book city and river tours and trips to Bangka and Danau Ranau, plus onward flights.

**Telkom wartel** (Jl Merdeka; ⏲ 8am-9pm) Next to the post office; international phone calls can be made here.

**Wartel** (Jl Kapitan Rivai)

## Sights

**Museum Sumatera Selatan** ( ☎ 422 382; Jl Sriwijaya 1, Km 5.5; admission 1000Rp; ⏲ 8am-4pm Sun-Thu, 8-11am Fri) is well worth a visit. It houses finds from Sriwijayan times, as well as megalithic carvings from the Pasemah Highlands, including the famous *batu gajah* (elephant stone). There is a magnificent *rumah limas* (traditional house) behind the museum. The museum is about 5km from the town centre off the road to the airport.

**Museum Sultan Machmud Badaruddin II** (Jl Pasar Hilir III; admission 1000Rp; ⏲ 8am-4pm Mon-Thu & Sat, 8-11am & 1.30-4pm Fri) has a few dust-covered exhibits.

Other Palembang attractions include the imposing **Mesjid Agung** (Jl Sudirman), built by Sultan Machmud Badaruddin at the beginning of the 19th century.

The remains of a late 18th–century **Dutch fort**, occupied today by the Indonesian army, can be seen to the north of Jl Merdeka. Only sections of the fort's outside walls still stand.

## Festivals & Events

Palembang's annual tourist event is the **bidar race** held on Sungai Musi in the middle of town every 17 August (Independence Day) and on 16 June (the city's birthday). A *bidar* (canoe) is about 25m long, 1m wide and is powered by up to 60 rowers.

## Sleeping

The midrange hotels in Palembang are typical Indonesian breeds: personality-less multistorey boxes with prices that make a backpacker wince. The upmarket business options are slowly but surely maturing to match international standards.

**Wisma Bari** ( ☎ 315 666; Jl Letnan Sayuti 55; d incl breakfast 137,000-176,000Rp; ✕ ) Well positioned in a quiet lane, the postmodern rooms are modest but tolerable.

**Hotel Al Fath Melia** ( ☎ 370 488; Jl KS Tuban 19; d incl breakfast 175,000-295,000Rp; ✕ ) The best you'll get for under $25. Set on a quiet street, a grand old staircase winds round to the lobby, giving an airy feel to the place. The staff were a delight when we called round.

**Hotel Sari** (Jl Sudirman 1301; d 200,000-240,000Rp; ✕ ) On a noisy junction, the ugly exterior hides half-decent rooms.

**Hotel Sandjaja** ( ☎ 362 222; info@sandjaja.com; Jl Kaptain Rivai 6193; d incl breakfast from 355,000Rp; ✕ 🖙 🖭 ) This smart, upmarket hotel has rooms that match what you would get back home for the same price, plus a few more fingerprints. But when measured on the Sumatran scale, this is top-grade.

**Hotel Swarna Dwipa** ( ☎ 313 322; Jl Tasik II; s/d incl breakfast 445,000/1,208,000Rp; ✕ 🖙 🖭 ) Located in a leafy area, this mini resort is filled with Indonesian bigwigs, but the rooms don't quite deliver.

**Novotel Palembang Hotel & Residence** ( ☎ 369 777; info@novotelpalembang.com; Jl R Sukamto 8A; d with breakfast 650,000-720,000Rp; ✕ 🖳 🖙 🖭 ) Outside of the town centre, the Novotel is a stone-fortress resort with the town's best rooms oriented around a central pool.

**Arya Duta Hotel & Convention Centre** ( ☎ 383 838; reservation.palembang@aryaduta.com; Jl POM IX; d with breakfast from 850,000Rp; ✕ 🖳 🖭 🖙 ) The very modern Arya Duta is decorated in the reigning trend of global minimalist. Business travellers stay here, self-contained style, for conferences.

## Eating

Palembang fare takes a while to get used to. The area's southern Indian influences are found in the spicy vegetable and fish dishes that are favoured. But it's the heavy use of the funky durian that sends many Westerners running.

The best-known dishes are *ikan brengkes* (fish served with a spicy durian-based sauce) and *pindang*, a spicy, clear fish soup. Another Palembang speciality is *pempek*, also known as *empek-empek*, a mixture of sago, fish and seasoning that is formed into balls and deep fried or grilled. Served with a spicy sauce, *pempek* is widely available from street stalls and warungs; you typically pay for what you eat.

Palembang food is normally served with a range of accompaniments. The main one is *tempoyak*, a combination of fermented durian, *terasi* (shrimp paste), lime juice and chilli that is mixed up with the fingers and added to the rice. *Sambal buah* (fruit sambals), made with pineapple or sliced green mangoes, are also popular.

SUMATRA

**Pondok Selera** (Jl Rambutan; mains from 5000Rp) Near the Songket Village, this open-air lunch spot pulls in the government workers for Palembang style *ayam baker* (grilled chicken) served with fresh vegetables and sambal.

**Selatan Indah** (Jl Letkol Iskandar 434; dishes from 6000Rp) A recommended joint for trying Palembang food where the English menu removes the lottery factor found in other places.

**Floating Restaurant** (Seberang Ulu; mains 5000-20,000Rp; ☾ noon-10pm) Directly across the Sungai Musi from the museum is Palembang's favourite date restaurant, serving local specialities.

**Rumah Makan Sri Melayu** ( ☎ 420 468; Jl Demang Lebar Daun; mains 25,000-35,000Rp) For the full immersion of Palembang food and culture, visit this showpiece restaurant with polished wooden seating around a stylish pond.

**French Bakery & Bistro** (Jl Kol Atmo; dishes 8000Rp) Near the bus ticket agents, this bakery and cafe offers all sorts of carb-loaded dishes and fancy coffee drinks.

The main **night market** (Jl Sayangan), to the east of Jl Sudirman, has dozens of noodle and sate stalls. Missing Padang food already? Load up at our old pals **Pagi Sore** (Jl Sudirman) and **Makan Sari Bundo** (Jl Kaptain Rivai).

## Shopping

**Tanjung Tunpung**, 2km from the town centre, is the handicraft village where Palembang's local *songket* industry is based. Ground-floor showrooms display sarongs used in marriage ceremonies and traditional costumes, as well as more functional scarves and textiles. Above the storefront are the workshops where it takes the young weavers a month to weave one sarong and chest wrap, as well as keep up with the daily soap operas.

**Makmur Jaya** ( ☎ 355 3720; Jl Ki Gede Ing Suro 12) Beyond tourist-market selections of fine silk and batiks.

**Pasar 16 Ilir** (Jl Mesjid Lama; ☾ 6am-6pm) Near the river, just off Jl Pangeran Ratu, this market sells batik and other textiles from Sumatra and Java, as well as house wares.

## Getting There & Away

### AIR

Sultan Badaruddin II airport is 12km north of town. There are flights by Silk Air to Singapore three times a week (US$90 to US$110). Garuda flies daily from Palembang to Yogyakarta (800,000Rp) and Surabaya (655,000Rp).

Garuda, Wings Air, Lion Air, Batavia Air and Sriwijaya all fly to Jakarta.

Merpati flies to Batam daily and then onto Medan four times a week. Garuda, Wings, Lion, Merpati, Jatayu and Batavia also have flights to Medan. Batavia Air serves Jambi daily. Air Asia flies daily to and from Kuala Lumpur, Malaysia.

**PT Novia Wisata** ( ☎ 512 584; Jl Jend A Yani 3) can handle all of these ticketing arrangements.

### BOAT

There are several services each day from Palembang's Boom Baru harbour to Mentok on Pulau Bangka (140,000Rp to 220,000Rp depending on class, four hours).

There are direct ferry services to Batam (business/VIP 285,000/345,000Rp, 10 hours). Boats depart from Boom Baru on Tuesday, Thursday and Saturday at 7.30am.

### BUS

The **Karyajaya Bus Terminal** (cnr Jl Sriwijaya Raya) is 12km from the town centre.

Most of the bigger companies have ticket offices on Jl Kol Atmo, just near the former Hotel King. These agents are convenient for buying advance tickets and checking departure times, but it is recommended to catch the bus at the terminal instead of dealing with the extra transfer fee and extra wait time from the agents' offices.

Sample destinations and fares include Bukittinggi (air-con 165,000Rp, 18 hours), Medan (260,000Rp, 36 hours) and Jakarta (air-con 190,000Rp, 20 hours).

There are several companies on Jl Veteran that offer door-to-door minibus services to Jambi (100,000Rp, six hours) and Bengkulu (140,000Rp, 15 hours).

### TRAIN

Kertapati train station is 8km from the city centre on the south side of the river. There are two daily train departures to Bandarlampung. The morning train has economy class only (45,000Rp); the evening train has executive (95,000Rp) and business (65,000Rp) classes. The trip takes nine to 10 hours.

There are also two trains that go northwest to Lubuklinggau (economy/business 15,000/70,000Rp) with a stop at Lahat (for the Pasemah Highlands). It's four hours to Lahat and seven to Lubuklinggau, but the fares are the same.

## Getting Around

*Opelet* around town cost a standard 2500Rp. They leave from around the huge roundabout at the junction of Jl Sudirman and Jl Merdeka.

Any *opelet* marked 'Karyajaya' (4000Rp) will get you to the bus terminal. Any *opelet* marked 'Kertapati' (4000Rp) will get you to the train station.

Taxis to the airport cost 60,000Rp to 80,000Rp. A taxi from the station to the town centre should cost around 40,000Rp.

## DANAU RANAU

Remote Danau Ranau, nestled in the middle of the southwestern Bukit Barisan range, is one of the least accessible and least developed of Sumatra's mountain lakes. It's an extremely peaceful spot and an excellent place to just relax or, if you're feeling energetic, go hiking in the surrounding mountains. It's possible to climb Gunung Seminung (1881m), the extinct volcano that dominates the region. Temperatures at Ranau seldom rise above a comfortable 25°C.

The main transport hub of the area is Simpang Sender, about 10km northwest of the lake. At the northern tip is Banding Agung, the main settlement. There is no bank, so change money before you get there.

There are several small hotels in Banding Agung, including **Losmen Batu Mega** (Jl Sugiwaras 269; d 80,000Rp) and **Hotel Seminung Permai** (Jl Akmal 89; d 90,000Rp). Jl Akmal is the main street leading down to the lake.

The village of Pusri also has accommodation, including **Danau Ranau Cottages** and **Wisma Pusri** (d 60,000-100,000Rp).

South of Simpang Sender on the western shore is **Wisma Danau Ranau** (d 150,000-200,000Rp), an upmarket place popular with tour groups.

Padang food is about all you'll find in the restaurants.

## Getting There & Away

Most routes to Danau Ranau go through the Trans-Sumatran Hwy town of Baturaja. There are two buses a day to Baturaja from the main bus terminal in Palembang (20,000Rp, four hours). The Palembang–Bandarlampung train line stops at Baturaja, which is about 3½ hours south of Palembang.

There are regular buses for the remaining 120km from Baturaja to Simpang Sender (15,000Rp, three hours), where you can pick up an *opelet* for the final 18km to Banding Agung (4000Rp). It's a good idea to arrive in Baturaja as early as possible to give yourself plenty of time to get a bus out again. If you do get stuck, there are dozens of uninspiring budget losmen to choose from.

## KRUI
☎ 0728

If southern Sumatra ever makes an impression on the tourist trail, Krui will be the beach bums' hang-out. Sweeping slithers of white sand lick the coast north and south of Krui, which to-date has only been discovered by intrepid surfers.

You can stay at **DWI Hotel** ( ☎ 51069; Jl Merdeka 172; d with fan 65,000Rp, d with air-con & breakfast 195,000Rp; 🛏 ) in the town centre. **Hotel Mutiara Alam** ( ☎ 51000; 3km south of Krui; d 80,000Rp) is an out-of-town possibility right on the beach.

Backpackers might not pay much attention to Krui but surfers come for the unhindered swells that roar in off the ocean. Right in front of the Karang Nyimbor surf break is the scenic and homely **Family Losmen** ( ☎ 081 3804 31486; 30min south of Krui; d 165,000Rp).

There are daily buses to Krui from Bandar Lampung (50,000Rp, six hours) and Bengkulu (75,000Rp, eight hours). *Opelet* depart regularly for Liwa (20,000Rp, one hour) and from there to Simpang Sender (for Danau Ranau).

## PASEMAH HIGHLANDS

The highlands, tucked away in the Bukit Barisan west of Lahat, are famous for the mysterious megalithic monuments that dot the landscape. The stones have been dated back about 3000 years, but little else is known about them or the civilisation that carved them. While the museums of Palembang and Jakarta now house the pick of the stones, there are still plenty left in situ.

The main town of the highlands is Pagaralam, 68km (two hours by bus) southwest of the Trans-Sumatran Hwy town of Lahat.

The best source of information about the highlands is the Hotel Mirasa in Pagaralam. There's nowhere to change money, so bring enough rupiah to see you through.

## Sights & Activities

The Pasemah carvings are considered to be the best examples of prehistoric stone sculpture in Indonesia and fall into two distinct styles. The early style dates from almost 3000 years ago and features fairly crude figures squatting with hands on knees or arms folded over chests. The best examples of this type are at a site called **Tinggi Hari**, 20km from Lahat, west of the small river town of Pulau Pinang.

The later style, incorporating expressive facial features, dates from about 2000 years ago and is far more elaborate. Examples include carvings of men riding, battling with snakes and struggling with elephants. There are also a couple of tigers – one guarding a representation of a human head between its paws. The natural curve of the rocks was used to create a three-dimensional effect, though all the sculptures are in bas-relief.

Sculptures of this style are found throughout the villages around Pagaralam, although some take a bit of seeking out. **Tegurwangi**, about 8km from Pagaralam on the road to Tanjung Sakti, is the home of the famous **Batu Beribu**, a cluster of four squat statues that sit under a small shelter by a stream. The site guardian will wander over and lead you to some nearby dolmen-style stone tombs. You can still make out a painting of three women and a dragon in one of them.

The village of **Berlubai**, 3km from Pagaralam, has its own **Batu Gajah** (Elephant Stone) sitting out among the rice paddies, as well as tombs and statues. There is a remarkable collection of stone carvings among the paddies near **Tanjung Aru**. Look out for the one of a man fighting a giant serpent.

### GUNUNG DEMPO

This dormant volcano is the highest (3159m) of the peaks surrounding the Pasemah Highlands and dominates the town of Pagaralam. Allow two full days to complete the climb. A guide is strongly recommended as trails can be difficult to find. The lower slopes are used as a tea-growing area, and there are *opelet* from Pagaralam to the tea factory.

## Sleeping

The best place to stay in the highlands is Pagaralam.

**Hotel Mirasa** ( ☎ 073 062 1484; Jl Mayor Ruslan; d with/without breakfast 175,000/65,000Rp) There is a range of rooms to choose from and the owner can organise transport to the sites or guides to climb Gunung Dempo. The hotel is on the edge of town, about 2km from the bus terminal.

**Hotel Telaga** ( ☎ 073 062 1081; Jl Serma Wanar; d from 40,000-100,000Rp) A basic place with simple but clean rooms and very little else.

If you get stuck in Lahat, there is **Hotel Permata** ( ☎ 073 132 1642; Jl Mayor Ruslan III 31; r fan/air-con 60,000/100,000Rp; 🐱 ), conveniently close to both the bus terminal and the train station.

## Getting There & Around

Every bus travelling along the Trans-Sumatran Hwy calls in at Lahat, nine hours northwest of Bandarlampung and 12 hours southeast of Padang. There are regular buses to Lahat from Palembang (55,000Rp, five hours), and the town is a stop on the train line from Palembang to Lubuklinggau. There are frequent small buses between Lahat and Pagaralam (20,000Rp, two hours).

There are *opelet* to the villages near Pagaralam from the town centre's *stasiun taksi* (taxi station). All local services cost 2000Rp.

## PULAU BANGKA
☎ 0717 / pop 790,000

Bangka is a large, sparsely populated island 25km off Sumatra's east coast. Bangka has several white-sand beaches and a peaceful way of life, but little in the way of alluring accommodation. Resort hotels were originally designed for wealthy visitors from Singapore and Malaysia, but they, like everyone else, have been spooked by security in Indonesia.

The island's name is derived from the word *wangka* (tin), which was discovered near Mentok in 1710. Tin is still mined on the island, although operations have been greatly scaled down in recent years.

There are only small pockets of natural forest left on Bangka with a large part of the land cleared for rubber, palm-oil and pepper plantations.

### Pangkal Pinang

Bangka's main town is Pangkal Pinang, a bustling business and transport centre with a population of about 140,000 people.

Most places of importance to travellers are close to the intersection of the main streets, Jl Sudirman and Jl Mesjid Jamik. The bus terminal and markets are nearby on Jl N Pegadaian.

#### SLEEPING

There are quite a few cheap losmen around the centre of town.

**Penginapan Srikandi** ( ☎ 421 884; Jl Mesjid Jamik 42; r with shared bath 70,000-80,000Rp) Simple and clean, and, best of all, cheap.

**Bukit Shofa Hotel** ( ☎ 421 062; Jl Mesjid Jamik 43; d 100,000-150,000Rp; ✷ ) A large, modern place with a choice of decent rooms.

**Sabrina Hotel** ( ☎ 422 424; Jl Diponegoro 73; d incl breakfast 175,000-400,000Rp; ✷ ) A midrange place with comfortable rooms on a quiet side street off Jl Sudirman.

### EATING
There are lots of small restaurants in Pangkal Pinang, including plenty of places along Jl Sudirman and in the markets near the main junction.

**Restaurant Asui Seafood** (Jl Kampung Bintang; seafood from 20,000Rp) Behind the BCA bank, this is the place to go for seafood. *Gebung*, known locally as 'chicken fish' because of the firmness of its flesh, is worth trying.

## Mentok
Mentok, on the northwestern tip of the island, is the port for boats to/from Palembang. Most people hop on a bus directly from the port to Pangkal Pinang.

In Mentok, there is little of interest other than a **memorial** to 22 Australian nurses shot dead by the Japanese during WWII.

If you get stuck, try **Tin Palace Hotel** (Jl Major Syafrie Rahman 1; s/d 70,000/90,000Rp; ✷ ).

## Beaches
The best beaches are on the northeastern coast around the town of Sungailiat, the island's administrative centre.

**Pantai Parai Tenggiri** is one of the most popular and is monopolised by the **Parai Beach Hotel** ( ☎ 94888; Jl Pantai Matras; d incl breakfast weekday/weekend 484,000/574,750Rp; ✷ ). The deserted **Pantai Matras**, 5km further on, is even better.

### Getting There & Away
Merpati flies three times a week to Jakarta (350,000Rp).

There are several services each day from Palembang's Boom Baru jetty to Mentok on Bangka (100,000Rp to 200,000Rp depending on class, four hours).

Pelni ships stop in at Mentok travelling to Bintan. The **Pelni office** ( ☎ 22743) is outside the port gates in Mentok.

### Getting Around
There is regular public transport between Bangka's main towns, but most *opelet* stop running in the mid-afternoon. After that taxis are the only option.

Airport taxis charge 50,000Rp for the 7km run into Pangkal Pinang.

There are public buses from Mentok to Pangkal Pinang (15,000Rp, three hours) and Sungailiat (20,000Rp, 3½ hours).

# LAMPUNG

At the very tip of this bow-shaped landmass is Sumatra's southernmost province, which was not given provincial status by Jakarta until 1964. Although the Lampungese have had a long history as a distinct culture, the most recent tug of Jakarta's gravitational force is altering Lampung's independent streak. Big-city TV news and fashions have crept across the Sunda Strait, as did Javanese settlers under the *transmigrasi* policies, designed to off-load excess population and turn a profit in the wilds of Sumatra.

Outside the provincial capital of Bandarlampung, the province's robust coffee plantations dominate the economy and the unclaimed forests, closely followed by timber and pepper. There are also large areas of rubber and palm-oil plantation.

Today many Jakarta weekenders hop over to tour the Krakatau volcano (p474) or visit the elephants of Way Kambas National Park (p472). The rugged western seaboard is ostensibly protected as the Bukit Barisan Selatan National Park.

## History
Long before Jakarta became the helm of this island chain, there's evidence that Lampung was part of the Palembang-based Sriwijayan empire until the 11th century, when the Jambi-based Malayu kingdom became the dominant regional power.

Megalithic remains at Pugungraharjo, on the plains to the east of Bandarlampung, are thought to date back more than 1000 years and point to a combination of Hindu and Buddhist influences. The site is believed to have been occupied until the 16th century.

Lampung has long been famous for its prized pepper crop, attracting the West Javanese sultanate of Banten to the area at the beginning of the 16th century and the Dutch East India Company in the late 17th century.

SUMATRA

The Dutch finally took control of Lampung in 1856 and launched the first of the *transmigrasi* schemes that sought to ease the chronic overcrowding in Java and Bali. Most migrants came to farm the fertile plains of eastern Lampung and today the area is something of a cultural melting pot.

# BANDARLAMPUNG
☎ 0721 / pop 850,000

Once a major backpacker thoroughfare connecting Java and Sumatra, you'll immediately notice the jump in 'Hello Misters' and toothy smiles as the locals welcome Western faces like a long lost relative – which, of course, passing travellers are in these parts.

Perched on the hills overlooking Teluk Lampung, Bandarlampung is the region's largest city and its administrative capital. The fourth-largest city in Sumatra, it is the product of an amalgamation of the old towns of Telukbetung (coastal) and Tanjungkarang (inland).

Krakatau and Way Kambis are the main spots to check out in the area when passing through.

## Orientation

Bandarlampung is something of an administrative creation and the now massive, sprawling city has no real heart. Most places of relevance to travellers are in Tanjungkarang, including the train station and the bulk of the hotels. The Rajabasa bus terminal is 10km north of the town centre; the airport is 24km away.

## Information

All the major banks have branches in Bandarlampung, and there are ATMs all over town.

**Arie Tour & Travel** ( ☎ 474 675; Jl Monginsidi 143) A helpful travel agent located outside the city centre.

**BCA Bank** (Jl Raden Intan 98) Offers the best exchange rates; a second branch is located on Jl Kartini.

**BII Bank** (Jl Kartini)

**BNI Bank** (Jl Kartini)

**Lippo Bank** (Jl Kartini)

**Post office** Main office (Jl KH Dahlan); central branch (Jl Kotaraja)

**Provincial tourist office** ( ☎ 266 184; Jl Sudirman 29) A helpful centre centrally located.

**Rumah Sakit Bumi Waras** (Jl W Monginsidi) Hospital.

**Squid Net** (Jl Raden Intan 88a; per hr 5000Rp; ⏰ 10am-8pm) Internet access.

**Telkom wartel** (Jl Majapahit; ⏰ 24hr) International and home-country-direct calls can be made here.

## Sights

The **Krakatau monument** (Jl Verteran, Telukbetung) is a lasting memorial to the force of the 1883 eruption and resulting tidal wave. Almost half of the 36,000 victims died in the 40m-high tidal wave that funnelled up Teluk Lampung and devastated Telukbetung. The huge steel maritime buoy that comprises the monument was washed out of Teluk Lampung and deposited on this hillside.

**Lampung Provincial Museum** (Jl Teuku Umar; ⏰ 9am-4.30pm Tue-Sun), 5km north of central Tanjungkarang, houses a dusty collection of bits and pieces – everything from Neolithic relics to stuffed animals. To reach the museum, catch a grey *opelet* (2500Rp).

## Sleeping

Bandarlampung has a nice selection of midrange hotels that line Jl Raden Intan, within walking distance or a short *ojek* ride from the train station.

**Kurnia Perdana Hotel** ( ☎ 262 030; Jl Raden Intan 114; d incl breakfast 150,000-250,000Rp; ✷ 🖥 ) Clean, comfortable rooms with TV, but no charm.

**Hotel Arinas** ( ☎ 266 778; Jl Raden Intan 35; d incl breakfast from 215,000-500,000Rp; ✷ ) Central with clean, comfortable, modern rooms, all with TV and hot water.

**Hotel Purnama** ( ☎ 261 448; Jl Raden Intan 77; d incl breakfast 230,000-630,000Rp; ✷ 🖥 ) The best option in this price range. It is well managed and maintained, with big comfortable rooms.

**Marco Polo Hotel** ( ☎ 262 511; Jl Dr Susilo 4; d incl breakfast 386,000-735,000Rp; ✷ 🖥 💺 ) Character is a permanent guest at this atmospheric old gent. Rooms are spacious and many have views of Teluk Lampung.

**Indra Puri Hotel** ( ☎ 258 258; Jl W Monginsidi 70; d incl breakfast 390,000-1,120,000Rp; 🖥 ) Perched high on a hill, the Indra Puri has beautiful rooms with excellent views of the bay.

**Sheraton Lampung** ( ☎ 486 666; Jl W Monginsidi 175; d incl breakfast 810,000-935,000Rp; ✷ 🖥 💺 ) An impressive place; the Sheraton is the most stylish hotel in town and offers a range of sporting activities onsite.

## Eating

The **market stalls** around the Bambu Kuning Plaza offer a wide range of snacks.

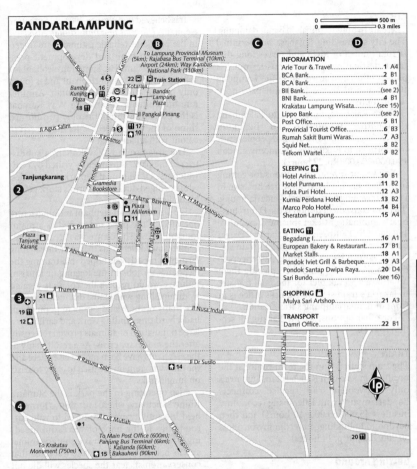

## BANDARLAMPUNG

| INFORMATION | |
|---|---|
| Arie Tour & Travel | 1 A4 |
| BCA Bank | 2 B1 |
| BCA Bank | 3 B1 |
| BII Bank | (see 2) |
| BNI Bank | 4 B1 |
| Krakatau Lampung Wisata | (see 15) |
| Lippo Bank | (see 2) |
| Post Office | 5 B2 |
| Provincial Tourist Office | 6 A3 |
| Rumah Sakit Bumi Waras | 7 A3 |
| Squid Net | 8 B2 |
| Telkom Wartel | 9 B2 |

| SLEEPING | |
|---|---|
| Hotel Arinas | 10 B1 |
| Hotel Purnama | 11 B2 |
| Indra Puri Hotel | 12 A3 |
| Kurnia Perdana Hotel | 13 B2 |
| Marco Polo Hotel | 14 B4 |
| Sheraton Lampung | 15 A4 |

| EATING | |
|---|---|
| Begadang I | 16 A1 |
| European Bakery & Restaurant | 17 B1 |
| Market Stalls | 18 A1 |
| Pondok Iviet Grill & Barbeque | 19 A3 |
| Pondok Santap Dwipa Raya | 20 D4 |
| Sari Bundo | (see 16) |

| SHOPPING | |
|---|---|
| Mulya Sari Artshop | 21 A3 |

| TRANSPORT | |
|---|---|
| Damri Office | 22 B1 |

SUMATRA

**Pondok Santap Dwipa Raya** (Jl Gatot Subroto; dishes from 15,000Rp) An upmarket Palembang-style place. It serves a delicious *sayur asam* (sour vegetable soup).

**Pondok Iviet Grill & Barbeque** (Jl W Monginsidi 64; steaks from 15,000Rp) A meat lover's paradise, with lots of steaks and grills to choose from.

**European Bakery & Restaurant** (Jl Raden Intan 35; pastries 2500Rp) For those in need of a sugar fix.

**Begadang I** (one of four in town) and **Sari Bundo** (dishes 6000Rp) are a couple of popular Padang restaurants near the markets on Jl Imam Bonjol.

## Shopping

Lampung produces weavings known as **ship cloths** (most feature ships), which use rich reds and blues to create primitive-looking geometric designs. Another type is *kain tapis*, a ceremonial cloth elaborately embroidered with gold thread.

**Mulya Sari Artshop** (Jl Thamrin 85) A good collection of both ship cloths and *kain tapis* can be found here.

## Getting There & Away

### AIR

The airport is 24km north of the city. There are flights every day to Jakarta through Merpati, Sriwijaya and Riau Air. Riau also flies to Palembang twice a week. Do note that Merpati flies to Halim Perdanakusuma Airport not Soekarno-Hatta airport. Arie Tour & Travel (see opposite) is a helpful travel agent.

## BUS

There are two bus terminals in Bandarlampung. The city's sprawling Rajabasa bus terminal is 10km north of town and serves long-distance destinations. Panjang bus terminal is 6km southeast of town along the Lampung Bay road and serves local and provincial destinations.

From Rajabasa, buses run to Palembang (90,000Rp, 10 hours) and Bengkulu (120,000Rp, 16 hours), but most people heading north go to Bukittinggi (economy/air-con 190,000/300,000Rp, 22 hours).

You've got several bus options for getting to the Bakauheni pier, from which boats go to Java. If travelling from central Bandarlampung, the most convenient option is the Damri bus–boat combination ticket (business/executive 110,000/130,000Rp, eight to 10 hours). Damri buses leave from Bandarlampung's train station at 9am and 9pm, shuttling passengers to the Bakahueni pier, and then picking them up at Java's Merak pier for the final transfer to Jakarta's train station. Damri's office is in front of Bandarlampung's train station.

For other options, see the Bakauheni section (p474).

## TRAIN

The train station is in the town centre at the northern mouth of Jl Raden Intan. Sumatra's only convenient rail service connects Bandarlampung with Palembang (economy/business 45,000/65,000, 10 hours) and then beyond to Lubuklinggau (economy/business 50,000/70,000Rp, 14 hours).

### Getting Around

For the airport, taxis charge 80,000Rp to 100,000Rp for the ride to/from town.

All *opelet* pass through the basement of the Bandar Lampung Plaza on Jl Raden Intan and the standard fare around town is 2000Rp.

To reach the Rajabasa bus terminal, take a green *opelet* (2500Rp). To reach the Panjang bus terminal, take a green *opelet* to Sukaraja and then transfer to a red *opelet* (2500Rp).

## WAY KAMBAS NATIONAL PARK

This national park is one of the oldest reserves in Indonesia. It occupies 1300 sq km of coastal lowland forest around Sungai Way Kambas on the east coast of Lampung. What little remains of the heavily logged forests is home to endangered species of elephants, rhinos and tigers.

It is believed that close to 200 wild Sumatran elephants (*Elephas maximus sumatrensis*) live in the park, but reliable estimates are uncertain and poaching and development pressures are constant. The Sumatran elephant is a subspecies of the Asian elephant and is found only in Sumatra and Kalimantan. Another rare but endemic creature in Way Kambas is the Sumatran rhino, the only two-horned rhino of the Asian species. Its hide is red in colour with a hairy coat.

The area around Way Kanan, a subdistrict of the park, is frequently visited by birdwatchers. Of the most remarkable species, white-winged duck and Storm's stork get the binoculars fogged up.

For some time an elephant training centre operated in the park and served as a major tourism draw. The centre was created to rehabilitate wild elephants that were threatening farmer's crops. It was hoped that training the elephants for jobs in the logging or tourism industry would resolve the conflicts created by diminishing wild lands. But the elephants, like many of the island's human population, had a hard time finding work and caring for a large population of animals proved too costly after the monetary crisis. As a result many of the elephants have been moved elsewhere and the ones who remain are used to carry tourists on jungle treks.

Also operating in the park is the Sumatra Rhino Sanctuary, where four rhinos formerly held in captivity are introduced to wild surroundings in the hope of successful breeding. The Sumatran rhino is a solitary animal and its habitat in the wild is so fractured that conservationists fear the species will die out without intervention. Breeding centres for rhinos are a controversial component of species-protection campaigns as they are expensive to maintain and have reported few successful births. For more information, visit the website of the **International Rhino Foundation** (www.rhinos-irf.org), one of the lead organisations involved with the centre and antipoaching patrols in the park.

For the average visitor not engaged in wildlife conservation, a visit to the park is a nice break from the concrete confines of Jakarta, but it's not a true wild safari. Most visitors are led through the forest on elephants or by canoes on the Sungai Way Kanan and surrounding waterways. The most commonly spotted animals on the tour include primates and birds. Herds of elephants are seen here from time to time but sightings of the Sumatran tiger are extremely rare.

A day trip to Way Kambas costs around US$50 per person for a minimum of two people and can be arranged through tour operators in Jakarta. Bandarlampung-based tour agents include Arie Tour & Travel (p470) and **Krakatau Lampung Wisata** ( ☎ 263 625, 486 666; Sheraton Lampung).

You could visit the park independently, but transport is limited and expensive. To strike out on your own, hire an *ojek* from Rajabasalama to Way Kanan, where you can hire a guide (50,000Rp to 100,000Rp) and arrange transport.

### Sleeping & Eating

Tourist facilities within the park are limited. About 13km from the entrance to the park is Way Kanan, where there is a collection of simple **guest houses** (100,000Rp) on the banks of Sungai Way Kanan. **Food stalls** nearby cater for day trippers and close after dark, so you'll need to bring food if you're staying the night.

### Getting There & Away

The entrance to Way Kambas is 110km from Bandarlampung.

There are buses from Bandarlampung's Rajabasa bus terminal to Jepara (25,000Rp, 2½ hours). They pass the entrance to Way Kambas, an arched gateway guarded by a stone elephant, in the village of Rajabasalama, 10km north of Jepara. Alternatively, you can catch a bus to Metro (10,000Rp, one hour) and then another to Rajabasalama (15,000Rp, 1½ hours).

From the park entrance, you can also hire a motorcycle to take you into the park and to pick you up.

## KALIANDA
☎ 0727

Kalianda is a quiet little town overlooking Teluk Lampung 30km north of the Bakauheni ferry terminal. The main reason for passing through is to visit Krakatau, but the town can also be used as an alternative base to Bandarlampung. Nearby are pretty white-sand beaches and simple fishing villages. Jakarta weekend refugees fed up with Bali have begun small migrations to Kalianda.

### Sights & Activities

Overlooking the town is **Gunung Rajabasa** (1281m), an easily scaleable volcano. Afterwards you can soak in the **hot springs** at Wartawan Beach, just beyond Canti. Beaches around Canti have relaxing sea breezes. An *opelet* to the beach costs 6000Rp.

Situated off the coast, **Pulau Sebuku** and **Pulau Sebesi** have snorkelling and swimming. Cargo boats leave from Canti to these islands, or you can charter a tour from the local fisherfolk.

To reach Krakatau, stop in at Hotel Beringin and ask about organised tours, or head down to the Canti harbour on weekends to pair up with local groups chartering boats.

### Sleeping & Eating

**Hotel Beringin** ( ☎ 322 008; Jl Kesuma Bangsa 75; d incl breakfast 55,000-75,000Rp) Close to the centre of town, this is an old Dutch villa with high ceilings and languid fans. The hotel has lots of information about local attractions and can arrange trips to nearby attractions.

**Kalianda Hotel** ( ☎ 322 392; d with fan/air-con 69,000/198,000Rp; ✖ ) On the way into town from the highway, this is a more upmarket choice.

**Laguna Helau** ( ☎ 081 172 7638; Jl Sinar Laut 81, Ketang; cottages from 250,000-700,000Rp) Just outside town, this ocean-side resort has cottages inspired by stilt-frame fishing villages nestled between a private beach and palm-fringed lagoon. Larger bungalows have four bedrooms and kitchen facilities.

The **food stalls** that appear in Kalianda's town centre at night are the best places to eat.

### Getting There & Around

There are regular buses between Kalianda and Bandarlampung's Rajabasa bus terminal (20,000Rp, 1½ hours). Most buses don't run right into Kalianda, but drop you on the highway at the turn-off to town. From there, simply cross the road and wait for an *opelet* into town (3000Rp). There are a few direct buses from the Bakauheni ferry terminal to Kalianda (20,000Rp), but it's usually quicker to catch any north-bound bus and get off at the junction for town.

There are regular *opelet* from Kalianda to Canti (5000Rp) and along the road that rings Gunung Rajabasa via Gayam and Pasuruan.

**SUMATRA**

There are also cargo boats from Canti to nearby Sebuku and Sebesi (15,000Rp). Canti can be reached by public bus.

## GUNUNG KRAKATAU

Krakatau may have come closer to destroying the planet than any other volcano in recent history, when it erupted in 1883. Tens of thousands were killed either by the resulting tidal wave or by the pyroclastic flows that crossed 40km of ocean to incinerate Sumatran coastal villages. Afterwards all that was left was a smouldering caldera where a cluster of uninhabited islands had once been. Perhaps peace had come, thought local villagers. But Krakatau, like all scrappy villains, re-awoke in 1927 and resulting eruptions built a new volcanic cone since christened Anak Krakatau (Child of Krakatau).

Tours to the island launch from West Java (see p123) or from Kalianda (p473) on the Sumatran coast. Organised tours typically cost US$90 per person. Hotel Beringin (p473) in Kalianda can also organise tours for 650,000Rp.

You can also join up with weekenders chartering boats from Canti, a fishing village outside of Kalianda, or from Pulau Sebesi. Charters usually cost 500,000Rp to 1,000,000Rp for 15 people.

## BAKAUHENI

Bakauheni is the major ferry terminal between Java and southern Sumatra.

There are frequent ferries between Bakauheni and Merak, Java's westernmost port. A fast ferry runs between the two ports every 30 minutes from 7am to 5pm and costs 42,000Rp; the crossing takes 45 minutes. A slow ferry runs every 30 minutes, 24 hours a day and costs economy/business 15,000/18,000Rp; the crossing takes three hours.

The journey between the two islands sounds like a snap until you factor in land transport between the ferry terminals and the major towns on either side. Bakauheni is 90km from Bandarlampung, a bus journey of about two hours. Buses to the port leave from the Bandarlampung town centre (see p472) or from the Panjang bus terminal (20,000Rp). A taxi to Bakauheni from Bandarlampung should cost 30,000Rp. In Java, the bus transfer from the port of Merak to Jakarta is another two-hour journey; see p115 for more information.

## BUKIT BARISAN SELATAN NATIONAL PARK

At the southern tip of Sumatra, this national park comprises one of the island's last stands of lowland forests. For this reason the World Wildlife Fund has ranked it as one of the planet's most biologically outstanding habitats and is working to conserve the park's remaining Sumatran rhinos and tigers. The park is also famous for many endemic bird species that prefer foothill climates, and several species of sea turtle that nest along the park's coastal zone.

Of the 365,000 hectares originally designated as protected, only 324,000 hectares remain untampered. The usual suspects are responsible: illegal logging and plantation conversion, and poachers are also at work.

Tourist infrastructure in the park is limited and most people visit on organised tours. The easiest access point into the park is through the town of Kota Agung, 80km west of Bandarlampung.

**Kantor Taman Nasional Bukit Barisan Selatan** ( ☎ 072 221 095; Jl Raya Terbaya, Kota Agung; 🕑 8am-4.30pm Mon-Thu, 8am-noon Fri) sells permits into the park (5000Rp) and can arrange guides and trekking information.

Less-accessible access points are Sukaraja, 20km west of Kota Agung, and Liwa, the northernmost entry way.

Kota Agung has several basic hotels and there is a camping ground near Sukaraja.

There are frequent buses from Bandarlampung to Kota Agung (10,000Rp).

# Nusa Tenggara

If you've ever dreamt of powder-white sand, azure bays, frothing hot springs and hidden traditional villages, then Nusa Tenggara is your wonderland. Here's an arc of islands that is lush and jungle-green in the north, more arid savannah in the south and in-between has some of the world's best diving, limitless surf breaks, and technicolor volcanic lakes. It's a land of pink-sand beaches, schooling sharks and rays, and the world's largest lizard: the swaggering, spellbinding Komodo dragon.

You'll also find a cultural diversity that is unmatched in Indonesia. East of Hindu Bali are the largely Islamic islands of Lombok and Sumbawa, followed by predominantly Catholic Flores, while Timor and the remote Alor and Solor Archipelagos have Protestant majorities. Throughout, animist rituals and tribal traditions thrive alongside the minarets, temples and chapels. Though Bahasa Indonesia is a unifying tongue, each main island has at least one native language, which is often subdivided into dialects. Eavesdrop on one of the weekly markets in the countryside and you'll hear several.

The easily accessed and ultimately seductive Gili Islands see the bulk of the tourism here, along with the rest of Lombok and its towering Gunung Rinjani (3726m). But those with a hunger for adventure head further east to Flores, charter boats to Komodo and back, then keep moving south and east where the *bule* (foreigner) crowds and creature comforts are thin on the ground and the travelling can be challenging and incredibly rewarding. In fact, you may fantasise about your next trip here before the first one is over.

## HIGHLIGHTS

- Gazing at the lunarlike landscape atop **Gunung Kelimutu** (p548), with its three astonishing crater lakes, each a different colour
- Trekking up the lush slopes of **Gunung Rinjani** (see boxed text, p508), the sacred volcano that dominates northern Lombok
- Coming face-to-face with the mother of all lizards in **Komodo** or **Rinca** (see boxed text, p530)
- Exploring the remote villages of **West Timor** (p564), characterised by their beehive-shaped clan houses, and experiencing the island's unique tribal culture, markets and textiles
- Snorkelling or diving in coral reefs teeming with marine life around the **Gili Islands** (see boxed text, p497) and **Komodo National Park** (see boxed text, p531)

Komodo & Rinca Islands
Gili Islands
Gunung Rinjani
Komodo National Park
Gunung Kelimutu
West Timor

| POPULATION: 8.3 MILLION | LAND AREA: 68,053 SQ KM | HIGHEST PEAK: GUNUNG RINJANI (3726M) |
|---|---|---|

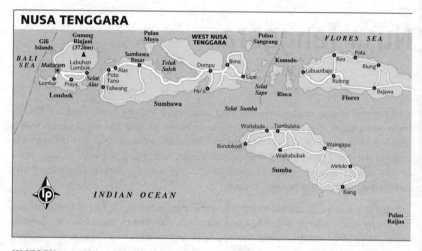

## HISTORY
Before the 15th century, the only external contact these islands had were sporadic visits from Chinese and Arab traders in search of sandalwood, spices and tortoiseshell. In 1512 the Portuguese landed in (and named) Flores, then Timor and Solor and brought Christianity to all three islands.

The Dutch muscled into the region in the 17th century, taking control of Kupang in 1653 and later shunting the Portuguese off to East Timor. But, with few resources to tempt them, they devoted little attention to Nusa Tenggara, only really establishing firm control over the area in the 20th century by forming alliances with tribal rajas. Crowns were stolen and redistributed, which has had a lasting effect on local politics. To this day, locals bicker over who the real Timor royals are.

Little changed after WWII, with the vast majority of people continuing to make a living from fishing or subsistence farming. Periodic droughts have been devastating: famine killed an estimated 50,000 in Lombok in 1966, provoking the government to implement a *transmigrasi* program that moved thousands of families from the island to other parts of the nation.

Today there remains very little industry in the region, apart from a colossal mine in Sumbawa; various international NGOs are also helping to develop tourism and seaweed farming in Flores and Alor. Many Nusa Tenggarans move to Java, Bali or Malaysia to find work. Tourism is expanding, however.

Dubai investors are deeply entrenched in South Lombok, and smaller-scale tourism development is underway in West Flores. Throw in Bali's continued growth and an increase in flights from Denpasar and Kupang, and the hope among local people is that this influx will help develop the region's poor infrastructure and eventually trickle down to them.

## WILDLIFE
The big brawny action hero is the Komodo dragon (see boxed text, p530), the world's largest lizard, which is easily spotted on the islands of Komodo and Rinca. Small numbers also exist in western Flores.

The coral reefs of Nusa Tenggara are some of the richest in the world, and there's an incredible array of marine life, from tiny reef dwellers such as nudibranchs, sea snails and pipefish to pelagic giants: manta and devil rays, gray and hammerhead sharks, pilot and blue whales, orcas and dolphins.

## CLIMATE
On the islands east of Bali, seasonal differences are more pronounced. The driest months are August and September, and the wettest months are between November and February. However, the duration of the seasons varies from island to island. The seasons in Lombok are more like those in Bali, with a dry season from April to September and a wet season from October to March. Much the same applies to both Sumbawa and Flores. The duration of the dry season increases the

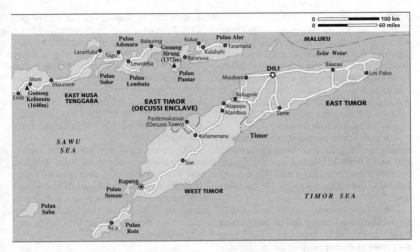

closer you get to Australia – the rusty land-scapes of Sumba and Timor contrast strongly with lush Flores.

## GETTING THERE & AROUND

Overland travel is arduous in mountain-ous Nusa Tenggara, particularly in Flores. Lombok, Sumbawa and Timor have fairly decent surfaced main roads and some comfortable bus services. Get off the highways and things slow down considerably, however. Ferry services are frequent and consistent in the dry season, but in the wet season, when the seas get rough, your ship may be cancelled for days, weeks even. Fortunately, several airlines now cover the main interisland routes, as few travellers who have endured the punishing long haul across Nusa Tenggara by surface transport are up for a repeat.

### Air

Most visitors use Bali as the international gateway to Nusa Tenggara. At research time, the only international flights to Nusa Tenggara were landing in Mataram, with twice-weekly connections to Singapore on Silk Air. Kupang is an international airport and rumours were swirling that the Darwin–Kupang hop, once jointly operated by Air North and Merpati, would resume in 2009.

Several airlines operate within Nusa Tenggara, but the most prolific are Merpati and Transnusa. ITA has new planes and operates the Denpasar–Mataram and Denpasar–Labuanbajo flights. Other airlines, including Adam, Lion, Batavia and Wings Air, concentrate on the main routes to/from Mataram and Kupang.

Merpati has shaped up in recent years, and ranks behind ITA as the second-best airline in the region. The choice is not always yours, however. Merpati and Transnusa monopolise few of the more remote hops. Air travel in Nusa Tenggara is not an exact science. Delays happen, and sometimes routes are cancelled for months and then resume abruptly. It's wise to book early, and reservations are essential in the peak August tourist season. If a flight is 'full', it is still worth going to the airport before departure, as there are often 'no-shows', making last-minute seats available.

Nusa Tenggara is not well connected to other parts of Indonesia, and you'll have to travel via Bali to get to Sulawesi, Maluku and Papua.

### Bicycle

Bicycles dominate the carless Gili Islands, but they are not a popular form of transport anywhere else in Nusa Tenggara. Long-distance cycling is an option on Lombok (though the roads are narrow and traffic can be quite heavy) and across the undulating terrain of Sumba and western Sumbawa. Cycling on volcanic Flores or mountainous Timor requires Tour de France levels of endurance, commitment (maybe even blood doping), though some riders do travel across both islands using buses to get their bikes up the steepest inclines and freewheeling downhill.

NUSA TENGGARA

## Boat

Pelni's *Awu, Kelimutu, Sirimau, Siguntang, Willis* and *Tilongkabila* ferries all service Nusa Tenggara. Schedules are provided under individual town entries in this chapter. Pelni's more basic Perintis cargo ships cover many routes and are an option if you get stuck. Ask at the office of the *syahbandar* (harbour master) or at the shipping offices. Cabins are almost always available for rent.

Fast and slow ferries also connect many of the islands. There are daily crossings between Bali and Lombok, Lombok and Sumbawa, Sumbawa and Flores, Larantuka (Flores) and Lembata, and between Kupang (Timor) and Rote.

Other ferry connections include weekly services between Kupang and Larantuka, and Ende (Flores) and Waingapu (Sumba). There are plenty of other possibilities; see the relevant sections of individual town entries for more details.

A popular way of travelling between Lombok and Flores or vice versa is on a boat tour, stopping at Komodo and other islands along the way. See the boxed text on p540 for more information.

## Bus

Aside from the main cross-island routes covered by air-con express coaches, travelling by bus is uncomfortable in Nusa Tenggara. Here's what you can expect: an oven-hot bus with legroom for a four-year-old, no shocks, errant betel-nut spittle, and an aromatic infusion of dried fish. Buses never leave on time. Sometimes they crawl around town for hours on endless loops looking for passengers – a maddening local practice called *keliling*. Don't underestimate journey times – a trip of only 100km may take up to four hours.

Most buses leave in the morning between 6am and 8am, so be prepared for early starts. There are also night buses between Mataram and Bima. Long-distance buses meet ferries for those travelling to or from Bali and Java.

Buying bus tickets for the right price can be a hassle as foreigners routinely get overcharged. Touts linger around hotels and bus terminals, willing to 'assist', but the true price is only available through the actual bus company office.

## Car & Motorcycle

Self-drive cars can be found at reasonable rates in Senggigi and Mataram on Lombok.

Remember to inspect the car thoroughly first, as insurance is often extremely basic, and you'll usually have to pay for any damage. Consider hiring a car with a driver from 350,000Rp a day including petrol. Elsewhere in Nusa Tenggara it's much more difficult and expensive to rent a car. Hotels are good contact points. Expect to pay from 450,000Rp to 700,000Rp a day, including driver and petrol. Bemo can be chartered for shorter trips.

If you are an experienced rider, motorcycling is a great way to see Nusa Tenggara, and you can transport your bike on ferries between most of the islands. If you want a real motorcycle, it's best to bring your own machine from Bali or Lombok. Short-term motorbike hires are possible virtually anywhere (from 50,000Rp to 75,000Rp a day).

# LOMBOK

Its proximity to Bali is one reason Lombok is the most popular destination in Nusa Tenggara, but its white-sand beaches, epic surf and spectacular diving also have something to do with it. Oh, and you'll probably notice mighty Gunung Rinjani (3726m), Indonesia's second-highest volcano. Rivers and waterfalls gush down its fissured slopes and feed the island's crops (which are chiefly rice, cashews, coffee and tobacco), while its summit – complete with hot springs and a dazzling crater lake – lures international trekkers as well as local Balinese Hindu and indigenous Sasak Muslim pilgrims hungry for divine blessings.

You won't want to miss the fabled Gili Islands – three exquisite droplets of white sand, sprinkled with coconut palms and surrounded by coral reefs teeming with marine life – where you'll nest in mod beach huts and feast on everything from humble *nasi campur* (rice with a choice of side dishes) to a fresh daily selection of grilled seafood to melt-in-your-mouth sashimi. You can happily burn daylight hours diving, snorkelling or chilling by the sea, and if you're nocturnal, you'll love Gili Trawangan's bar scene.

Lombok's dramatic south coast is a labyrinth of turquoise bays, white sand, world-class surf breaks, undulating tobacco fields and massive headlands. Given its drop-dead good looks, it's no surprise that it also happens to be the vortex of Lombok's onrushing US$600 million metamorphosis.

Thankfully, that transformation will take some time. So get Zen, forget about the future and enjoy Lombok's sweet, spacious and wild present.

## History

In the early 17th century Balinese warriors overthrew Lombok's Sasak royalty in the west, while the Makassarese invaded from the east. By 1750 the whole island was dominated by Bali's Hindu monarchy. In western Lombok, relations between the Balinese and the Sasaks were relatively harmonious, but in eastern Lombok peasant rebellions were common.

The Dutch intervened in the late 19th century and, after an initial defeat that cost 100 lives, they took control of Cakranegara. Here the last raja families were made martyrs during a grizzly *perang poepoetan* ritual. Men, women and children in white robes threw themselves upon perplexed Dutch soldiers, who shot to kill. Afterwards, the Dutch galvanized the support of the surviving Balinese and the Sasak aristocracy and soon controlled more than 500,000 people with 250 troops.

Even after Indonesian independence, Lombok continued to be dominated by its Balinese and Sasak elite. In 1958 Lombok was declared part of the new province of Nusa Tenggara Barat (West Nusa Tenggara) and Mataram became its administrative capital. Following the attempted coup in Jakarta in 1965, Lombok experienced mass killings of communists and ethnic Chinese.

Under former president Suharto's 'New Order', there was stability and some growth, but crop failures led to famine in 1966 and to severe food shortages in 1973. Many moved away from Lombok under the government-sponsored *transmigrasi* program.

Tourism took off in the 1980s but was mostly developed by outside investors and speculators. Indonesia descended into economic crisis and political turmoil in the late '90s, and on 17 January 2000, serious riots engulfed Mataram. Christians and Chinese were the primary victims, but the agitators were from outside Lombok. Ultimately all Lombok suffered, and the faint pulse of tourism was muted further by the Bali bombs of 2002 and 2005.

Then something miraculous happened. Lombok took off. Bali's recent resurgence in tourism has spilled over, big time. The Gili Islands, once a backpacking and diving stronghold, are setting new tourism records every year, with an influx of moneyed Indonesian tourists, villa developers and families eager to play on the carless isles. Luxury development has also swept through the mainland, in the north and south where Dubai suits envision the next Nusa Dua. There's even an expanded international airport in the works at Praya. Only time will tell if this bubble will expand exponentially or pop during the global recession.

## Culture

Lombok has a population of just over three million. Almost 90% of the people are Sasak, about 10% are Balinese, and there are small numbers of Chinese, Javanese, Bugis and Arabs.

Originally hill people, the Sasaks are now spread all over Lombok and are generally much poorer than the Balinese minority. Virtually all Sasaks are Muslims, but many retain much less orthodox Wektu Telu beliefs and ancient animist rituals. *Adat* (indigenous and animist traditions) is still fundamental to their way of life, particularly customs relating to birth, circumcision, courtship and marriage.

Sasaks show a fascination with heroic trials of strength, physical prowess and one-on-one contests. *Peresehan,* sometimes misleadingly called 'Sasak boxing', is a fight between two men using long rattan staves and small rectangular shields made of cowhide.

Most of Lombok's Chinese population lives in Ampenan or Cakranegara. The Chinese first came to Lombok with the Dutch as a cheap labour force, but after independence most stayed on and started businesses.

Lombok's Balinese are concentrated in the west. Before the arrival of Islam in the 15th century, Balinese Hindu culture dominated Lombok. Their temples still stand, and today the Balinese remain a powerful minority.

Lombok has an indigenous music style. The Tandak Gerok dance, theatre and singing to music played on bamboo flutes and on a two-stringed bowed lute called *rebab*. It's usually performed after harvesting or other hard physical labour, but it is also staged at traditional ceremonies. The Genggong

# LOMBOK

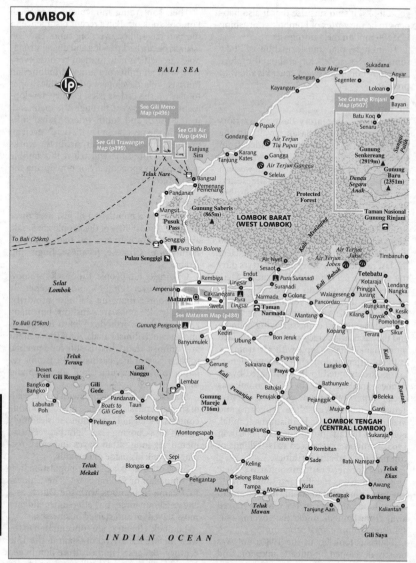

involves seven musicians using a simple collection of instruments, including a bamboo flute and a *rebab*.

A number of traditional dances are performed during seasonal ceremonies and rites of passage. The popular Cupak Gerantang, which originated in Java, tells the story of Panji, a romantic hero. A version of the Panji story, the Kayak Sando, featuring masked dancers, is found only in central and eastern Lombok. The Gandrung is about love and courtship, usually performed by the young men and women of Narmada, Lenek and Praya. Men and young boys in central and eastern Lombok love to perform the Oncer war dance.

0      20 km
0      12 miles

Kali Putih

Obel Obel

Gili
Lawang

Blantung

Gili
Sulat

Sajang

Protected
Forest

Sembalun
Lawang

Sugian

Gunung
Pengasingan

Sembalun
Bumbung

Sambelia

Gunung
Rinjani
(3726m)

Mayung
Putih

Gunung Nangi
(2330m)

Labuhan
Pandan

**LOMBOK TIMUR
(EAST LOMBOK)**

Gili
Pentangan

Pesugulan

Sapit

Labuhan
Lombok

To Sumbawa
(25km)

Swela

Pengadangan

Aikmel

Pringgasela

Lenek

Suralaga

Pringgabaya

Pulau
Belang

Anjani

Masbagik Timur

Masbagik

Selong

Pancor

Sakra

Labuhan Haji

Keruak

Jerowaru

Tanjung Luar

*Selat
Alas*

**Gili Maringki**

Ekas

Tanjung
Ringgit

Sekaroh

Maluk

Serewi

**Gili Melayu**

## Getting There & Away

### AIR

Lombok's Selaparang Airport has a decent terminal with a few shops to keep you occupied when your flight is inevitably delayed (unless you're on the first flight out). Domestic departure tax is now 30,000Rp and international departure tax is 150,000Rp. There has been wind blowing about a new international airport to be built near Praya for a number of years now, and with the impending South Lombok development those rumours may finally be coming true. At the time of writing authorities had publicised an opening date of 2010, but construction schedules said otherwise. **Jatatur** (Map p484; ☎ 0370-632 888; Mataram Mall, Mataram) is the best travel agent in Lombok. They book flights throughout Indonesia and take major credit cards.

**Batavia Air** ( ☎ 0370-648 998, 021-3899 9888; www .bataviaair.co.id) Flies daily to Surabaya and on to Jakarta.

**Garuda Indonesia** (Map p484; ☎ 0804 180 7807; www.garuda-indonesia.com; Hotel Lombok Raya, Mataram) Flies twice daily to Jakarta and once to Denpasar.

**IAT** ( ☎ 0370-639 589) Twice daily to Denpasar.

**Lion Air** (Map p484; ☎ 0370-629 333; www.lionair .co.id; Hotel Sahid Legi, Mataram) Flies direct to Jakarta.

**Merpati Airlines** (Map p484; ☎ 0370-621 111; www .merpati.co.id; Jl Pejanggik 69, Mataram) Flies to Denpasar three times daily.

**Silk Air** (Map p484; ☎ 0370-628 254; www.silkair.com; Hotel Lombok Raya, Mataram) Serves Singapore with three direct flights weekly (Monday, Thursday, Saturday).

**Transnusa/Trigana Airlines** ( ☎ 0370-616 2433; www.trigana-air.com) Three Denpasar flights a day.

**Wings Air** (Map p484; ☎ 0370-629 333; www.lionair .co.id; Hotel Sahid Legi, Mataram) Flies to Surabaya three times daily.

### BOAT

Lombok has 24-hour ferry connections with Sumbawa and Bali. Gili-bound fast and slow boats launch from Benoa, Serangan and Padangbai harbours in Bali, and Pelni ships steam in regularly from elsewhere in Indonesia.

Ferries travel between Padangbai (Bali) and Lembar (Lombok) every 90 minutes around the clock. Fares are 32,000Rp for foot passengers, 75,000Rp for motorcycles (with two passengers) and 479,000Rp for cars (up to four passengers). The trip takes four hours.

Much of the Gili Islands' recent tourist boom is due in large part to the speedboats that carry passengers directly from Bali. **Gili Cat** ( ☎ 0361-271 680; www.gilicat.com) leaves from Padangbai (660,000Rp, 2½ hours, 9am daily). **Blue Water Express** ( ☎ 0361-310 4558; www.bwsbali .com) leaves from Benoa Harbour (690,000Rp, 2½ hours). The new **Eka Jaya** ( ☎ 0361-752 277; www.baliekajaya.com) had just launched their Padangbai service (660,000Rp, 2½ hours) at research time.

NUSA TENGGARA

There's also a **Perama** (www.peramatour.com) shuttle bus and boat service (300,000Rp) from Padangbai, stopping at Senggigi (six hours) where for an additional 90,000Rp passengers can shift to smaller boats bound for the Gili Islands (one to 1½ hours).

Ferries also travel between Labuhan Lombok and Poto Tano on Sumbawa every 45 minutes (passenger 15,500Rp, motorcycle 75,000Rp, car 322,000Rp). They run 24 hours a day and the trip takes 1½ hours.

Pelni ships link Lembar with other parts of Indonesia. The *Awu* heads to Waingapu, Ende, Larantuka, Kupang and Kalabahi; the *Kelimutu* goes to Surabaya, Bima, Makassar, Ambon and Papua; and the *Tilongkabila* goes to Bima, Labuanbajo and Sulawesi. Buy tickets at the **Pelni office** (Map p484; ☎ 0370-637 212; Jl Industri 1; ☺ 8am-noon & 1-3.30pm Mon-Thu & Sat, 8-11am Fri) in Mataram.

### PUBLIC BUS

Mandalika terminal in Mataram is the departure point for major cities in Sumbawa, Bali and Java, via interisland ferries. For long-distance services, book tickets a day or two ahead at the terminal, or from a travel agency along Jl Pejanggik/Jl Selaparang in Mataram. If you get to the terminal before 8am, there may indeed be a spare seat on a bus going in your direction, but don't count on it, especially during holidays.

Among the destinations are Bima (economy/luxury 100,000/150,000Rp, 12 hours), Denpasar (luxury 135,000Rp, seven hours), Sumbawa Besar (economy/luxury 75,000/90,000Rp, six hours), Jakarta (luxury 375,000Rp, 38 hours), Surabaya (luxury 179,000Rp, 20 hours) and Yogyakarta (luxury 272,000Rp, 30 hours).

### TOURIST SHUTTLE BUS/BOAT

The Bali-based company **Perama** (www.perama tour.com) has tourist shuttle bus/boat services between the main tourist centres in Lombok (Senggigi, Gili Islands and Kuta) and most tourist centres in Bali (Ubud, Sanur and the Kuta region). Tickets can be booked directly or at any travel agency in Lombok or Bali.

## Getting Around

There is a good road across the middle of the island, between Mataram and Labuhan Lombok. Though narrow, the Mataram–Praya–Kuta and Mataram–Sengiggi–Anyar routes are also decent sealed roads. Public transport is generally restricted to the main routes; away from these, you need to hire a car or motorbike, or charter a bemo, *cidomo* (horse-drawn cart) or *ojek* (motorcycle taxi). During the wet season, remote roads are often flooded or washed away, particularly around the foothills of Gunung Rinjani.

### BUS & BEMO

The main terminal, Mandalika, is at Bertais, 6km southeast of central Mataram; other regional terminals are in Praya, Anyar and Pancor (near Selong). You may have to go via one or more of these terminals to get from one part of Lombok to another. A list of fixed fares should be displayed at the terminals. Public transport becomes scarce in the late afternoon and normally ceases after dark.

Chartering a bemo can be convenient and reasonably cheap – about 250,000Rp per bemo per day (including petrol), depending on distance and road conditions, although some bemos are restricted to specific routes or regions.

### CAR & MOTORCYCLE

Senggigi is the best place to organise car or motorcycle rental. Arrangements can be made in Mataram and other places, but rates are much higher. Hotels and travel agencies offer the most competitive rates; 'official' car-rental companies often have a wider range of vehicles but tend to be more expensive.

SUVs are best for Lombok's roads. Suzuki Jimmys cost from 150,000Rp per day, and Toyota Kijangs cost about 225,000Rp, excluding petrol. Discounts are offered for longer periods. Hiring a car with a driver is a very sensible and popular option as you won't be liable for any damage – expect to pay between 350,000Rp and 525,000Rp per day, depending on the season.

Motorbikes can be rented in Mataram and Senggigi for around 35,000Rp per day. Motorcycles run for 65,000Rp per day in Senggigi.

Indonesian law dictates that you should carry an International Driving Licence if you plan on operating a motor vehicle. Your rental agency won't request it, but police may ask for one at checkpoints, and will issue a fine (to be paid immediately) if you don't have it.

Check your insurance arrangements carefully. Some agencies do not offer any coverage at all, and others offer only basic coverage. Even insured Balinese vehicles are often not covered at all in Lombok. It is best to proceed to Lombok and arrange a rental in Senggigi.

# MATARAM
☎ 0370 / pop 330,000

Lombok's capital, a conglomeration of several separate towns – Ampenan (the port), Mataram (administrative centre), Cakranegara or Cakra (business centre), and Bertais-Sweta (transport hub), is a quintessential Indonesian city. Its chaotic, traffic-choked streets sprawl more than 10km from east to west. But it's also attractive, with broad tree-lined avenues and friendly, exuberant locals. Since sights are slim and the beaches are so close, few visitors choose to stay here – which is exactly why you should.

## Orientation
The four towns are spread along one main road – it starts as Jl Pabean in Ampenan, becomes Jl Yos Sudarso, then changes to Jl Langko, Jl Pejanggik and travels from Sweta to Bertais as Jl Selaparang. It's one-way throughout, running west to east. A parallel one-way road, Jl Tumpang Sari–Jl Panca Usaha–Jl Pancawarga–Jl Caturwarga–Jl Pendidikan, brings traffic back to the coast.

## Information
### EMERGENCY
**Police station** ( ☎ 631 225; Jl Langko) In an emergency, dial ☎ 110.
**Rumah Sakit Umum Mataram** ( ☎ 622 254; Jl Pejanggik 6) The best hospital on Lombok has English-speaking doctors.

### IMMIGRATION
**Kantor Imigrasi** ( ☎ 632 520; Jl Udayana 2; ☻ 8am-4pm Mon-Fri)

### INTERNET ACCESS & TELEPHONE
There are wartel on Jl Pejanggik and at the airport.
**Elian Internet** (Mataram Mall, Jl Panca Usaha; www.elianmedia.net; per hr 5000Rp; ☻ 24 hr)
**Telkom** ( ☎ 633 333; Jl Pendidikan 23; ☻ 24hr) Offers phone and fax services.

### MONEY
You'll find plenty of banks with ATMs scattered along Cakra's main drag, particularly on Jl Penanggik; most of them change cash and travellers cheques.

### POST
**Main post office** (Jl Sriwijaya 37; ☻ 8am-5pm Mon-Thu, 8-11am Fri, 8am-1pm Sat) Inconveniently located, but has internet and poste restante services.
**Sub-post office** (Jl Langko; ☻ 8am-4.30pm Mon-Thu, 8-11am Fri, 8am-1pm Sat) Near the Nitour Hotel.

### TOURIST INFORMATION
**West Lombok tourist office** ( ☎ 621 658; Jl Suprato 20; ☻ 7.30am-2pm Mon-Thu, 7.30-11am Fri, 8am-1pm Sat) Just a slim selection of maps and leaflets.
**West Nusa Tenggara tourist office** ( ☎ 634 800; Jl Singosari 2; ☻ 8am-2pm Mon-Thu, 8-11am Fri, 8am-12.30pm Sat) Friendly staff offers limited information.

## Sights
### MUSEUM NEGERI NUSA TENGGARA BARAT
This dusty **museum** ( ☎ 632 519; Jl Panji Tilar Negara 6; admission 20,000Rp; ☻ 8am-2pm Tue-Thu, Sat & Sun, 8-11am Fri) has exhibits on the geology, history and culture of Lombok and Sumbawa. There's an interesting collection of prehistoric pottery, massive bronze kettledrums and a captivating assortment of kris (traditional daggers) and *songket* (silver- or gold-threaded cloth). For an extra 40,000Rp, check out gold swords and jewellery that once belonged to Sumbawan sultans and Javanese kings.

### MAYURA WATER PALACE
Built in 1744, this **palace** (Jl Selaparang; admission by donation; ☻ 7am-7.30pm) includes the former king's family temple, a pilgrimage site for Lombok's Hindus on 24 December. In 1894 it was the site of bloody battles between the Dutch and Balinese. Unfortunately, it has become a neglected public park with a polluted artificial lake.

### PURA MERU
Opposite the water palace, **Pura Meru** (Jl Selaparang; admission by donation; ☻ 8am-5pm) is the largest and second most important Hindu temple on Lombok. Built in 1720 by Balinese prince Anak Agung Made Karang, it's dedicated to the Hindu trinity of Brahma, Vishnu and Shiva.

Wooden drums call believers to ceremonies (the June full moon is the most important, but the grounds are also packed on Christmas Eve) in the outer courtyard. The inner court has 33 small shrines and three thatched, teak-wood *meru* (multitiered shrines). The central *meru*, with 11 tiers, is Shiva's house; the *meru* to the north, with nine tiers, is Vishnu's; and the

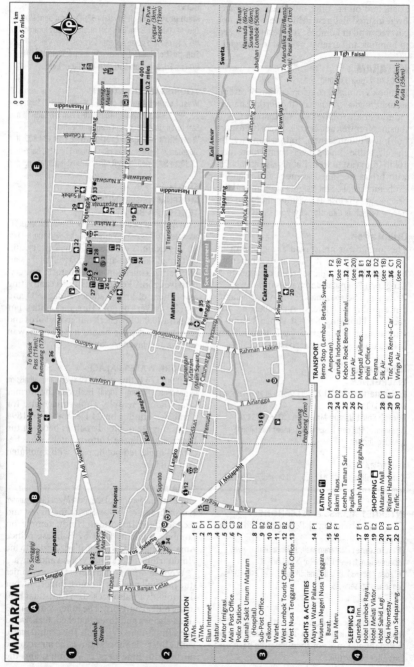

# MATARAM

NUSA TENGGARA

**INFORMATION**
| | |
|---|---|
| ATMs.....................................................1 | E1 |
| ATMs.....................................................2 | D1 |
| Eilan Internet.......................................3 | D1 |
| Jatatur.................................................4 | D1 |
| Kantor Imigrasi....................................5 | C2 |
| Main Post Office.................................6 | C3 |
| Police Station......................................7 | B2 |
| Rumah Sakit Umum Mataram | |
| (Hospital)..........................................8 | D2 |
| Sub-Post Office...................................9 | B2 |
| Telkom..............................................10 | B2 |
| Wartel...............................................11 | D1 |
| West Lombok Tourist Office...........12 | B2 |
| West Nusa Tenggara Tourist Office..13 | C3 |

**SIGHTS & ACTIVITIES**
| | |
|---|---|
| Mayura Water Palace.......................14 | F1 |
| Museum Negeri Nusa Tenggara | |
| Barat.............................................15 | B2 |
| Pura Meru.........................................16 | F1 |

**SLEEPING**
| | |
|---|---|
| Ganesha Inn.....................................17 | E1 |
| Hotel Lombok Raya..........................18 | D1 |
| Hotel Melati Viktor..........................19 | E2 |
| Hotel Sahid Legi..............................20 | D3 |
| Oka Homestay..................................21 | D1 |
| Zaitun Selaparang............................22 | D1 |

**EATING**
| | |
|---|---|
| Aroma...............................................23 | D1 |
| Bakmi Raos.......................................24 | D2 |
| Lesehan Taman Sari.........................25 | D1 |
| Papillion..........................................26 | D1 |
| Rumah Makan Dirgahayu..................27 | D1 |

**SHOPPING**
| | |
|---|---|
| Mataram Mall...................................28 | D1 |
| Rinjani Handwoven............................29 | E1 |
| Traffic...............................................30 | D1 |

**TRANSPORT**
| | |
|---|---|
| Bemo Stop (Lembar, Bertais, Sweta, | |
| Ampenan)........................................31 | F2 |
| Garuda Indonesia..........................(see 18) | |
| Kebon Roek Bemo Terminal..............32 | A1 |
| Lion Air.........................................(see 20) | |
| Merpati Airlines................................33 | E1 |
| Pelni Office.......................................34 | B2 |
| Perama..............................................35 | D2 |
| Silk Air..........................................(see 18) | |
| Trac Astra Rent-a-Car......................36 | C1 |
| Wings Air.......................................(see 20) | |

seven-tiered *meru* to the south is Brahma's. The *meru* also represent the three sacred mountains, Rinjani, Agung and Bromo, and the mythical Mount Meru.

The caretaker will lend you a sash and sarong if you need one.

## Activities
Lombok's back roads are ideal for bicycle touring. Two interesting routes are Mataram to Banyumulek and back via Gunung Pengsong, and along the coastal road from Mataram to Pemenang via Senggigi. If you feel energetic, return via the gorgeous yet steep road through Pusuk Pass.

## Sleeping
Most folks nest among Cakranegara's quiet streets off Jl Pejanggik/Jl Selaparang, east of Mataram Mall.

### BUDGET
**Ganesha Inn** ( ☎ 624 878; Jl Subak 1; s/d 30,000/40,000Rp) Stylish exterior, nice location, but some of the rooms are yellow at the edges.

**Oka Homestay** ( ☎ 622 406; Jl Repatmaya 5; d from 40,000Rp) Balinese-owned, this garden compound patrolled by three friendly poodles, is a great deal. Rooms are fan-cooled and quite clean.

**Hotel Melati Viktor** ( ☎ 633 830; Jl Abimanyu 1; d from 80,000Rp; 🕸 ) The high ceilings, clean rooms and Balinese-style courtyard, complete with Hindu statues, make this one of the best value places in town.

### MIDRANGE
**Zaitun Selaparang** ( ☎ 632 235; www.zaitun.hotels.com; Jl Pejanggik 41; standard/superior/deluxe 225,000/235,000/400,000Rp) In the thick of Cakra's commercial district, this minimall atrium hotel isn't fabulous, but it has new, recently remodelled rooms.

**Hotel Sahid Legi** ( ☎ 636 282; sahid@mataram.was antara.net.id; Jl Sriwijaya 81; r/deluxe 365,000/580,000Rp; 🕸 🌊 ) Once Mataram's grand dame of business hotels, thanks to the blend of modern and Indonesian design influences, three restaurants, international TV and a circular pool. But the halls are dark and even the deluxe rooms can be musty.

**our pick** **Hotel Lombok Raya** ( ☎ 632 305; lora @mataram.wasantara.net.id; Jl Panca Usaha 11; s/d from 390,000/525,000Rp, plus 21% tax; 🕸 🌊 ) This well-located hotel has spacious, comfortable rooms with balconies and all the mod cons including a terrific spa.

## Eating
You'll find Western fast-food outlets in Mataram Mall.

**Rumah Makan Dirgahayu** ( ☎ 637 559; Jl Cilinaya 19; rice dishes from 7000Rp, seafood from 25,000Rp) A popular Makassar-style place opposite the mall, with gurgling fountains and twirling ceiling fans.

**our pick** **Bakmi Raos** (Jl Panca Usaha); dishes 9000-20,000Rp) An authentic yet modern Indonesian noodle-and-soup joint behind the mall that attracts a steady stream of Mataram's hip, young and beautiful.

**Aroma** (Jl Pejanggik; meals from 15,000Rp) Popular among Mataram's Chinese Indonesian families, this modern, spotless Chinese seafood restaurant serves an outstanding fried gourami (35,000Rp) accompanied by a fiery sweet chilli sauce.

**Papillon** ( ☎ 632 308; Jl Cilinaya 1; dishes 19,000-45,000Rp) An upstart restaurant off the mall, with lamp-lit tables, red vinyl booths and an international menu.

**Lesehan Taman Sari** ( ☎ 629 909; Mataram Mall; meals 25,000Rp) Attached to the mall, this place wins with ambiance and multicourse, traditional Sasak meals served on banana leaves and enjoyed in *berugas* (raised thatched huts without walls).

## Shopping
For handicrafts try the outlets on Jl Raya Senggigi, which heads north from Ampenan.

**Mataram Mall** (Jl Selaparang; ⏰ 7am-7pm) A multistorey shopping mall with a supermarket, electronics and clothes stores as well as food stalls.

**Traffic** ( ☎ 0819 1792 8974; Jl Pejanggik; ⏰ 9am-9.30pm) Get your hipster, skate-punk fashion here.

**Rinjani Handwoven** ( ☎ 633 169; Jl Pejanggik 44) This is where you can see weavers in action and buy their work.

**Pasar Bertais** ( ⏰ 7am-5pm) A great place to get localised after you've overdosed on the *bule* circuit. There are no tourists at this market near the Mandalika bus terminal, but they have got everything else: fruit and veggies, fish (fresh and dried), baskets full of colourful, aromatic spices and grains, freshly butchered beef, palm sugar, pungent bricks of shrimp paste and cheaper handicrafts than you will find anywhere else in West Lombok.

## Getting There & Away

### BUS & BEMO

The sprawling, dusty Mandalika bus station in Bertais is the main bus and bemo terminal for the entire island and also for long-distance buses via ferry to Sumbawa, Bali and Java.

The terminal is fairly chaotic, so be sure to keep a level head to avoid the 'help' of the commission-happy touts. Long-distance buses leave from behind the main terminal building, while bemos and smaller buses leave from one of two car parks on either side.

Kebon Roek terminal in Ampenan has the bemo to Bertais (2000Rp) and services to Senggigi (4000Rp).

### TOURIST SHUTTLE BUS

Perama ( ☎ 635 928; www.peramatour.com; Jl Pejanggik 66) operates shuttle buses to popular destinations in Lombok (including Bangsal, Senggigi and Kuta) and Bali.

## Getting Around

### TO/FROM AIRPORT

Lombok's Selaparang Airport is on the north side of the city, 5km from Cakra. A taxi desk sells prepaid tickets: 30,000Rp to anywhere in Mataram, 85,000Rp to Senggigi, 125,000Rp to Bangsal and Lembar, 250,000Rp to Kuta, 400,000Rp to Senaru. Alternatively, walk out of the airport to Jl Adi Sucipto and take Bemo 7 to Ampenan.

### BEMO

Mataram is *very* spread out. Yellow bemos shuttle between Kebon Roek terminal in Ampenan and Mandalika terminal in Bertais (10km away) along the two main thoroughfares. Bemo terminals are good places to organise a charter trip. Outside the Cakranegara market (corner of Jl Hasanuddin and Jl Selaparang) there is a handy bemo stop for services to Bertais, Ampenan, Sweta and Lembar. The standard fare is 2000Rp, regardless of the distance.

### CAR & MOTORCYCLE

Most hotels can arrange chauffeured car hire (400,000Rp to 525,000Rp per day), but you'll find a better deal in Senggigi. Self-drivers should try Trac Astra Rent-a-Car ( ☎ 626 363; Jl Adi Sucipto 5, Rembiga Mataram; per day with driver/self-drive 525,000/360,000Rp).

## AROUND MATARAM

The gorgeous villages, rice fields and temples east of Mataram are reminiscent of some of Bali's best landscapes. You can easily visit all of the following places in half a day with your own transport.

## Pura Lingsar

This large **temple compound** (admission by donation; ☽ 7am-6pm) is the holiest in Lombok. Built in 1714 by King Anak Agung Ngurah, and nestled beautifully in the lush rice fields, it's multidenominational, with a temple for Balinese Hindus (Pura Gaduh) and one for followers of Lombok's mystical take on Islam, the Wektu Telu religion.

Pura Gaduh has four shrines: one orientated to Gunung Rinjani (seat of the gods on Lombok), one to Gunung Agung (seat of the gods in Bali) and a double shrine representing the union between the two islands.

The Wektu Telu temple is noted for its enclosed pond devoted to Lord Vishnu, and the holy eels, which can be enticed from their lair with hard-boiled eggs (available at stalls outside). It's considered good luck to feed them. You will be expected to rent a sash and/or sarong (or bring your own) to enter the temple.

A huge ritual battle, **Perang Topat**, is held here every year in November or December (the exact date depends on the lunar month). After a costumed parade, Hindus and Wektu pelt each other with *ketupat* (sticky rice in coconut leaves).

Pura Lingsar is 9km northeast of Mandalika. Take a bemo from the terminal to Narmada, and another to Lingsar. Ask to be dropped off near the entrance to the temple complex.

## Pura Suranadi

Set amid gorgeous countryside, holy **Pura Suranadi** (admission by donation; ☽ 7.30am-6pm) is worth a visit for its lovely gardens, which have a bubbling, icy natural spring and restored baths with ornate Balinese carvings (plus the obligatory holy eels).

Just opposite Pura Suranadi market, an entrance leads to **Hutan Wisata Suranadi** (admission 1000Rp; ☽ 8am-5pm), a quiet forest sanctuary good for short hikes and birdwatching.

The temple is 6km northwest of Narmada and served by frequent public bemos. Failing that, charter one.

## Sesaot & Around

Some 4km northeast of Pura Suranadi is Sesaot, a charming market town with an ice-cold, holy river that snakes from Gunung Rinjani into the forest. There are some gorgeous picnic spots and swimming holes here. Regular transport connects Narmada with Sesaot, and bites are available at the warungs along the main street.

Further east, **Air Nyet** is another pretty village with more options for swimming and picnics. Ask for directions to the unsigned turn-off in the middle of Sesaot. The bridge and road to Air Nyet are rough, but it's a lovely stroll (about 3km) from Sesaot.

## Gunung Pengsong

This hilltop **temple** (admission by donation; ☉ 7am-6pm), 9km south of Mataram, has spectacular views across undulating rice fields towards distant volcanoes and the sea. Japanese soldiers hid here towards the end of WWII, and cannon remnants can be found, as well as plenty of playful monkeys.

Once a year, in March or April, a buffalo is taken up the steep slope and sacrificed to give thanks for a good harvest. The **Desa Bersih festival** also occurs here at harvest time – houses and gardens are cleaned, fences whitewashed and roads and paths repaired. Once part of a ritual to rid the village of evil spirits, it's now held in honour of the rice goddess, Dewi Sri.

It's a 15-minute walk up to the temple top from the entrance. You'll need your own wheels to get here.

## Banyumulek

This is one of the two main **pottery centres** on Lombok, specialising in pots with a woven fibre covering, traditional urns and water flasks. It's close to the city – head south of Sweta on the main road to Lembar. After 6km veer right to Banyumulek.

# LEMBAR & THE SOUTHWESTERN PENINSULA

## Lembar
☎ 0370

Lembar is West Lombok's main port for ferries, tankers and Pelni liners. It's also a haven for would-be hustlers (touts even try and open your car door as they peddle bus tickets for Bali's tourist centres), but the setting – think azure inlets sheltered by jungled peninsulas – makes up for it. That doesn't mean you'll want

to crash here, and since bus connections to Mataram and Senggigi are abundant, you won't have to. If you do manage to get stuck, or need a bite, the clean, hospitable **Losmen Tidar** ( ☎ 681 444; Jl Raya Pelabuhan; r from 50,000Rp, cottages from 100,000Rp, all incl breakfast) 1km north of the ferry port, is an excellent deal. They serve up some mean Javanese food.

Plenty of bemos shuttle between Lembar and the Mandalika terminal in Bertais (3500Rp), or you can catch one at the market stop in Cakra (15,000Rp). See p481 for details on the ferries and boats between Bali and Lembar. Taxis cost 60,000Rp to Mataram and 100,000Rp to Senggigi.

## Southwestern Peninsula
☎ 0370

The jagged coastline west of Sekotong is blessed with deserted white-sand beaches, turquoise coves and tranquil offshore islands, which is why it has long been hyped as Lombok's next big tourist destination. And while vacation villas are beginning to sprout, it remains laid-back and pristine with few services for visitors. The narrow, paved road hugs the coast until Selegang, where a dirt track continues west past Bangko Bangko to Tanjung Desert (Desert Point), one of Asia's legendary 'lefts'. Waves are finicky, and the break can go from flat glass to cranking overhead barrels in an hour.

A few of the palm-dappled offshore islands with silky beaches and fine snorkelling are inhabited. Gili Nanggu and Gili Gede both have accommodation. Gede is also home to Bugis craftsman who build gorgeous wooden schooners.

### SLEEPING & EATING

Rooms and restaurants are slim on the ground, and some close in the rainy season. The **Sundancer Beach Resort** (www.sundancer.com) in Pelangan has been promising to bring upmarket, four-star sophistication to the peninsula for years now. Yet this massive compound of high-end modern apartments connected by pebbled footpaths is still not finished. At the time of writing they were due to open in 2010.

### Mainland

The following places are listed in the order you'll find them as you head southwest from Sekotong.

**Dolphins Lodge** ( ☎ 0819 1607 6770; Jl Raya Taun, Taun; r 500,000Rp) Breezy two-storey thatched wooden cabanas have queen beds, satellite TV, DVD players and fine terraces overlooking the sea. For 200,000Rp they'll shuttle you to Gili Nanggu.

**Bola Bola Paradis** ( ☎ 078 616 2156; www.bolabolaparadis.com; Jl Raya Palangan Sekotong; r 300,000-400,000Rp; 🞲) Just west of Pelangan, this nice midranger has superclean sweet octagonal bungalows, comfortable air-con rooms with tiled floors and private patios, and a funky restaurant/lounge (mains 25,000Rp to 75,000Rp) on grassy palm-shaded grounds that bleed into the sand.

**Nirvana Roemah Air** ( ☎ 660 8060; www.floatingvilla.com; Jl Raya Medang, Sekotong Barat; villas incl airport transfers US$100-125; 🞲) Enjoy secluded, floating luxury in the mangroves, 2km west of Sekotong. Book via the internet for substantial low season discounts.

**Hotel Aman Gati** ( ☎ 0817 5720 6699; Jl Raya Medang, Sekotong Barat; bungalows 250,000Rp; 🞲) Things get increasingly isolated on this end of Lombok, which makes these basic yet cosy bungalows – the last of their kind before the surf break – an oasis for wave hunters. Food is so-so at best, but views are lovely, and their boat shuttles surfers to the waves and back (300,000Rp, 30 minutes).

### Islands

**Secret Island Resort** ( ☎ 0818 0376 2001; www.secretislandresort.com; r 200,000Rp, bungalows 250,000Rp, 2-bed villas 1,000,000Rp; 🞲) Southwest Lombok's best island accommodation comes with fine sea or mountain views. The restaurant grills up dynamite seafood, and kayak, hiking, snorkelling and dive trips can be arranged. Call ahead for airport pick-up and/or free boat transfer from Pantai Tembowong.

**Gili Nanggu Cottages** ( ☎ 623 783; www.gilinanggu.com; cottages s/d 240,000/250,000Rp, bungalows 350,000Rp; 🞲) Nobody regrets crossing the Lembar channel to these rustic two-storey *lumbung* (rice barn) cottages just off the beach. Meals are 16,000Rp to 38,000Rp.

### GETTING THERE & AWAY

Bemos buzz between Lembar and Pelangan (1¾ hours, every 30 minutes) via Sekotong (25 minutes). West of Pelangan transport is less regular, but the route is still served by infrequent bemos until Selegang.

To reach Gili Nanggu, a return charter on a *prahu* (outrigger fishing boat) from Taun costs 250,000Rp. Public boats connect Tembowong with Gili Gede and Gili Rengit (both 8000Rp one-way), leaving from Putri Doyong losmen, 2km north of Pelangan. Alternatively, you can charter boats for 60,000Rp one-way or arrange a day trip around the islands for 250,000Rp.

## SENGGIGI

☎ 0370

Lombok's original tourist town rambles along a series of sweeping bays and wide beaches dappled in coconut palms. Blood-red views of Bali's Gunung Agung are revealed at sunset when locals congregate on the cliffs and watch yet another day turn to night. As darkness descends, the bright lanterns of the local fishing fleet glint like fallen stars against the black sea.

There are sweet, inexpensive guest houses, a few luxury hotels and dozens of restaurants and bars. Senggigi has everything, save a steady flow of tourists. However, with Lombok's growing popularity, that appears to be changing. And even if it is a relative ghost town when you roll through, the sheer beauty of the place is still worth staying a night or two.

### Orientation

The Senggigi area spans 10km of coastal road. Most shops, facilities and hotels are on the main road, Jl Raya Senggigi, which starts about 6km north of Ampenan. Mangsit, 5km north of the main strip, has some top-end properties. Street numbers are not used in Senggigi.

### Information
#### EMERGENCY

**Police station** ( ☎ 110) Next to the Pasar Seni.
**Senggigi Medical Clinic** ( ☎ 693 856; 🕗 8am-7pm) Based at the Senggigi Beach Hotel.
**Tourist Police** ( ☎ 632 733)

#### INTERNET ACCESS & TELEPHONE

Internet cafes on the main strip also double as wartel.
**Millennium Internet** ( ☎ 693 860; Jl Raya Senggigi; per min 500Rp; 🕗 24hr)

#### MONEY

Bank Central Asia (BCA) and Bank Negara Indonesia (BNI) on Jl Raya Senggigi both have ATMs and will exchange cash and travellers cheques.

#### POST

**Post office** (Jl Raya Senggigi; 🕗 8am-6pm)

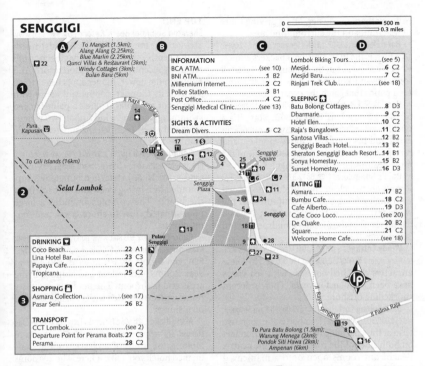

**SENGGIGI**

## Sights

It's not the grandest, but **Pura Batu Bolong** (admission by donation; 7am-7pm) is Lombok's sweetest Hindu temple. Join an ever-welcoming Balinese community as they leave offerings at the 14 altars and pagodas that tumble down a rocky volcanic outcropping into the foaming sea about 2km south of central Senggigi. The rock underneath the temple has a natural hole, hence the name (*batu bolong* literally means 'rock with hole'). The temple, orientated towards Gunung Agung, is a perfect sunset spot.

## Activities

### SNORKELLING & DIVING

There's reasonable snorkelling off the point in Senggigi, in the sheltered bay around the headland, and in front of Windy Cottages, a few kilometres north of the town. You can rent snorkelling gear (25,000Rp per day) along the beach near Senggigi Beach Hotel.

Diving trips from Senggigi normally visit the Gili Islands, so consider basing yourself there. The following are professional dive centres:

**Blue Marlin** ( 0812 376 6496; www.bluemarlindive.com; Holiday Resort Lombok; Alang Alang; Senggigi Beach Hotel)

**Dream Divers** ( 692 047; www.dreamdivers.com; Jl Raya Senggigi)

### BIKING & HIKING

**Lombok Biking Tours** ( 660 5792; Jl Raya Senggigi; day excursions per person from 200,000Rp) offers guided rides through the rural Sekotong region and the countryside around Lingsar and Suranadi.

Drop by the well-informed **Rinjani Trek Club** ( 693 202; rtc.senggigi@gmail.com; Jl Raya Senggigi) if you're interested in climbing the sacred volcano.

## Sleeping

Senggigi has no shortage of excellent accommodation spread up and down the coastal road. Outside peak times discounts of up to 50% are common.

### BUDGET

**Sonya Homestay** ( 0813 3989 9878; Jl Raya Senggigi; d from 50,000Rp) A shady family-run enclave of six rooms with nice patios and bright pink beds. Nathan, the owner, offers driving tours of Mataram and the surrounding area.

**Hotel Elen** ( ☎ 693 077; Jl Raya Senggigi; d from 55,000Rp; ⊠ ) Elen is the long-time backpackers choice. Rooms are basic, but those facing the waterfall fountain and koi pond come with spacious tiled patios that catch the ocean breeze.

**Pondok Siti Hawa** ( ☎ 693 414; Jl Raya Senggigi; s/d 60,000/100,000Rp) This isn't a homestay, it's a novelty act, starring an eccentric European expat and his family, a captive monkey, and ramshackle bamboo cottages set on one of the most beautiful beaches in Senggigi.

**Raja's Bungalows** ( ☎ 0812 377 0138; d 85,000Rp) Rooms are big, clean and tastefully decorated with high ceilings, gecko sculptures on the walls and outdoor bathrooms. But it's well within range of the mosque's loudspeaker and 300m from the sand.

**Windy Cottages** ( ☎ 693 191; Mangsit; cottages with cold/hot water 110,000/150,000Rp, r 140,000Rp; ⊠ ) These attractive thatched cottages with sea views have been popular for years. There's decent snorkelling offshore.

**Batu Bolong Cottages** ( ☎ 693 065; Jl Raya Senggigi; s/d 150,000/300,000Rp; ⊠ ) Bamboo is the operative term at this charming bungalow-style hotel set on both sides of the road south of the centre. Beachfront rooms open onto a manicured lawn that fades into white sand.

**Bulan Baru** ( ☎ 693 786; Mangsit; r 180,000Rp; ⊠ ⛭ ) Set in a lovely garden and a short walk from a fine sandy beach, this welcoming hotel has spacious, well-furnished rooms, all with mini-bar, air-con and hot-water bathrooms. No children allowed.

### MIDRANGE

**our pick** **Sunset Homestay** ( ☎ 692 020; www.sunsethouse-lombok.com; r 275,000/400,000Rp; ⊠ ) The six tastefully simple bungalows on a quiet stretch of shore come with all the mod cons and homey touches.

**Dharmarie** ( ☎ 693 050; www.dharmarie.com; r 300,000Rp; ⊠ ) These comfortable sea-view cottages with French doors and indoor/outdoor bathrooms are a great value. Breakfast is included.

**Santosa Villas** ( ☎ 693 090; www.santosavillas.com; standard/superior/deluxe/villa 560,000/650,000/1,500,000/3,000,000Rp; ⊠ ⛭ ) The recently renovated and rebranded Santosa resort has accommodation ranging from midrange to luxury villas on a nice beach and smack in the centre of the Senggigi strip.

### TOP END

**Sheraton Senggigi Beach Resort** ( ☎ 693 333; www.sheraton.com; r from 775,000Rp; ⊠ ⛭ ) Just north of the centre, the Sheraton has been, until relatively recently, Senggigi's top resort. And although the newer, hipper spots have stolen some of its thunder, rooms still come with terraces or balconies. There's a palm-fringed swimming pool and a kids' pool, two restaurants and a well-regarded spa and health club. Families love it.

**Senggigi Beach Hotel** ( ☎ 693 210; www.senggigibeach.aerowisata.com; r US$70, beach bungalows US$80, plus 21% tax; ⊠ ⛭ ) Detached bungalows surrounded by a lush garden and set back from the beach. The complex includes a large pool situated close to shore, a spa and tennis courts.

**Qunci Villas** ( ☎ 693 800; www.quncivillas.com; Mangsit; r with garden/ocean view US$70/95, plus 21% tax; ⊠ ⛭ ) Senggigi's most stylish hotel is also a great deal. Rooms have indoor and outdoor living areas and bathroom. The pool bar and tasty restaurant are outfitted with cool block-wood furnishings.

**Alang Alang** ( ☎ 693 518; www.alang-alang-villas.com; Mangsit; s/d bungalows US$95/100; ⊠ ⛭ ) If you're looking for more of a classic Indonesian-themed hotel, you'll like it here. The 20 rooms come with teak furnishings and are set in a lush, blooming garden. The small pool overlooks a thin sliver of beach where fishermen cast into the waves.

## Eating

Central Senggigi has far more restaurants than necessary, varying from local warungs to contemporary fine dining. Most offer free transport for evening diners – phone for a ride.For authentic Indonesian street food, head to the hillside warung on the route north to Mangsit where sate sizzles, pots of noodles bubble and corn cobs roast at dusk.

**Asmara** ( ☎ 693 619; www.asmara-group.com; mains 18,000-75,000Rp; ⊠ ) An ideal family choice, this place spans the culinary globe from tuna carpaccio to Wiener schnitzel to Lombok's own *sate pusut* (minced-meat or fish sate). It also has a playground and kids menu.

**De Quake** ( ☎ 693 694; mains from 23,000Rp; ⌚ 10am-10pm) Like The Square, this new spot blends pan-Asian cuisine with ambitious high design. It's right on the beach behind the art market.

**Cafe Coco Loco** ( ☎ 693 396; mains from 23,000Rp) Munch tempura, curries and fresh fish Lombok-style at this popular new cafe in the art market.

**Welcome Home Cafe** ( ☎ 693 833; Jl Raya Senggigi; mains 30,000Rp) Recalls that Jimmy Buffet feeling, with a fantastic knotted-wood bar, bamboo furniture, coral floors and fresh fish at reasonable prices.

**Cafe Alberto** ( ☎ 693 039; mains from 30,000Rp; 11am-11pm) Eat beachfront at this popular pizzeria on the sand.

**The Square** ( ☎ 693 688; Senggigi Square; mains 35,000Rp; 11am-11pm) Uber-hip design, with lounge seating, a blue-lit, open dining room and verandah sea views. Try the wok-tossed calamari with baby bok choy.

**Bumbu Cafe** (Jl Raya Senggigi; mains 35,000Rp) Popular choice for tasty pan-Asian fare. The owner says 'We always full!' – it's no coincidence.

**our pick** **Warung Manega** (Jl Raya Senggigi; meals 75,000-250,000Rp; 11am-11pm) If you fled Bali before experiencing the spectacular Jimbaran fish grills, you can make up for it at this sister restaurant to one of Jimbaran's finest. Choose from a fresh daily catch of barracuda, squid, snapper, grouper, lobster, tuna and prawns – all of which are grilled over smouldering coconut husks and served on candlelit tables in the sand.

## Drinking & Entertainment

Senggigi's nocturnal activity is mellow midweek with a mild spike on weekends. It revolves around a handful of bars with live music, a disco or two, and a rather conspicuous karaoke bar.

**our pick** **Coco Beach** ( ☎ 0817 578 0055; Pantai 2 Kerandangan, Jl Raya Senggigi; noon-10pm) Rent comfortable beachside bamboo *beruga* for sunset drinks where the coconut groves meet the sand north of Senggigi. Sip from a bar that serves traditional *jamu* tonics, fresh organic juices and tropical cocktails. Very popular with the moneyed Mataram set.

**Lina Hotel Bar** (beer small/large 10,000/13,000Rp) Lina's seafront deck is another great spot for a sundowner. Happy hour starts at 4pm and ends an hour after dusk.

**Papaya Cafe** ( ☎ 693 136; Jl Raya Senggigi) The decor is slick, with exposed stonewalls, rattan furniture and evocative Asmat art from Papua. There's a nice selection of liquor, and they have a tight house band that rocks.

**Tropicana** ( ☎ 693 432; www.tropicanalombok.com; admission 25,000Rp) Your cliché, cheeseball disco with DJs spinning Western pop, rock and a few Indo hits plus live bands. Be warned, you may be asked to participate in 'Mr & Miss Tropicana' contests.

## Shopping

Senggigi's shops are generally not well patronised. The **Pasar Seni** (Art Market; Jl Raya Senggigi) has some cheap handicraft stalls, but most of the wares here aren't worth your time. The **Asmara Collection** ( ☎ 693 619; Jl Raya Senggigi; 8am-11pm), on the other hand, is sensational. Here you will find authentic, handwoven Lombok textiles, intense tribal masks, carved hair combs and a lovely collection of jewellery.

## Getting There & Away

### BOAT

**Perama** ( ☎ 693 007; Jl Raya Senggigi) operates a daily boat service from Padangbai, Bali to Senggigi (p481; 300,000Rp, six hours), and from Senggigi to the Gili Islands (70,000Rp to 100,000Rp, one to 1½ hours), which enables you to avoid Bangsal. Gili dive schools (p493) also operate speedboat shuttles (from 120,000Rp per person) most days – contact them in advance.

### BUS

Regular bemos travel between Senggigi and Ampenan's Kebon Roek terminal (4000Rp, 40 minutes). Wave them down on the main drag. Headed to the Gilis? Organise a group and charter a bemo to Bangsal harbour (60,000Rp).

Perama has a few tourist shuttle bus/boat services daily between Senggigi and Kuta (Bali), Denpasar airport (150,000Rp), Ubud (150,000Rp) and other Lombok destinations, including Kuta (185,000Rp).

## Getting Around

If you stay within walking distance of the main drag, you won't need wheels. Motorbikes are readily available for hire in Senggigi and are the easiest way to get around. They rent for 35,000Rp per day plus petrol. Motorcycles go for 60,000Rp. Ask about rental at your hotel, or call Dino at **CCT Lombok** ( ☎ 668 1864, 0819 1715 9365). He also rents Kijangs (self-drive 300,000Rp, with driver 375,000Rp per day).

**NUSA TENGGARA**

# GILI ISLANDS

☎ 0370

For decades, travellers have made the hop from Bali for a dip in the turquoise-tinted, bathtub-warm waters of the tiny, irresistible Gili Islands, and stayed longer than they anticipated. Perhaps it's the deep-water coral reefs teeming with sharks, rays and reasonably friendly turtles? Maybe it's the serenity that comes with no motorised traffic? Or it could be the beachfront bungalows, long stretches of white sand and the friendly locals. Each of these pearls, located just off the northwestern tip of Lombok, has its own unique character, but they have one thing in common. They are all hard to leave.

Gili Air is the closest to the mainland, with plenty of stylish bungalows dotted among the palms. Mellow Gili Meno, the middle island, is the smallest, quietest, and makes for a wonderful chilled-out retreat.

Gili Trawangan, the furthest out, has been tagged as the 'party island'. And with three weekly parties and a groovy collection of beach bars, you can get loose here. But Trawangan is growing up, with stylish accommodation (including a number of inland vacation villas), a fun expat community and outstanding dining.

Bring ample rupiah with you to the islands – enough for a few extra days, at least. Though each island has shops and hotels that will change money and arrange cash advances from credit and debit cards, rates are low and commissions are high. It's also not uncommon for the ATM on Gili Trawangan to malfunction.

## Dangers & Annoyances

There are no police on the Gilis. Report theft to the island *kepala desa* (village head) immediately. They will stop all boats heading out and search passengers before they can leave the island. If you need help locating them or need someone to help you translate, the dive schools are a good point of contact. If you are on Gili Trawangan, notify Satgas, the community organisation that runs island affairs.

---

**GILI ISLANDS CURRENTS: WARNING**

The currents between the Gili Islands are very strong. Do not attempt to swim between the islands. People do get sucked out to sea.

---

Satgas uses its community contacts to resolve problems or track down stolen property with a minimum of fuss.

Incidents are very rare, but some foreign women have experienced sexual harassment and even assault while on the Gilis – it's best to walk home in pairs to the dark corners of the islands.

Jellyfish are common when strong winds blow from the mainland. Big ones leave a painful rash.

## Getting There & Away

The relatively new fast boats from Bali have fed the recent tourist boom. Seats sell out during July and August so be sure to book ahead. See p481 for price and contact details for these boat services.

There's also a cheaper direct service from Bali. Perama buses and their slow boat head to the Gilis via Padangbai (see p334) and Senggigi. Or you can fly to Mataram and make arrangements from there.

Coming from other parts of Lombok you can travel via Senggigi; via the public boats that leave from Bangsal (the cheapest route), you can charter your own boat from Bangsal (195,000Rp) or book passage on a private speedboat. Blue Marlin and Manta Dive (p500) on Gili Trawangan can arrange transfers (600,000Rp for up to three people). Speedboats use the Teluk Nare harbour south of Bangsal.

Coming by public transport, catch a bus or bemo to Pemenang, from where it's 1km by *cidomo* (3000Rp) to Bangsal Harbour. Bangsal is beyond annoying (see boxed text, opposite). The touts raise blood pressure for a living, and you should sooner ignore than trust them. Boat tickets are sold at the Koperasi harbour office on the beach. Public boats run roughly from 8am to 5pm, but don't leave until full (about 18 people). One-way fares at the time of research were 8000Rp to Gili Air, 9000Rp to Gili Meno and 10,000Rp to Gili Trawangan. Special charters can also be organised in Bangsal.

Boats pull up on the beach when they get to the Gilis. You'll have to wade ashore with your luggage.

## Getting Around

### BOAT

There's a twice-daily island-hopping boat service that loops between all three islands (20,000Rp to 23,000Rp). The morning boat leaves Air at 8.30am, stopping on Meno at

**BANGSAL GAUNTLET**

If you arrive to the principal Gili Islands port by bus, bemo or taxi, you will be dropped off at the Bangsal terminal – nearly a kilometre from the harbour, from which point irrepressible touts will hustle you non-stop. Do not buy a ticket from them. There is but one official Bangsal Harbour ticket office; it is on the beach left of the dirt road, and arranges all local boat transport – shuttle, public and chartered – to the Gilis. Buy a ticket elsewhere and you're getting played. You could also avoid Bangsal altogether by booking a speedboat transfer from Senggigi via one of the dive schools, taking one of the new speedboat services direct from Bali (the best choice), or by travelling with Perama from Bali or Mataram, Kuta, Lombok or Senggigi.

8.45am, Trawangan at 9.30am, Meno again at 9.45am and returning to Air at 9.45am. The afternoon boat leaves Air at 3pm, Meno at 3.15pm, Trawangan at 3.30pm, Meno at 4.15pm and gets back to Air at 4.30pm. Check the latest timetable at the islands' dock. You can also charter your own island-hopping boat (170,000Rp to 195,000Rp).

### CIDOMO

The Gilis are flat and easy enough to get around by foot or bicycle (p494). A torch (flashlight) is useful at night. You can buy one at local shops for around 25,000Rp. Hiring a *cidomo* for a clip-clop around an island is a great way to explore; a short trip costs between 20,000Rp and 35,000Rp. You'll pay 50,000Rp or more for a two-hour jaunt.

## Gili Air
### pop 1800

Closest to Lombok, Gili Air falls between Trawangan's sophistication and less-is-more Meno. It's a rural island, and like the other two was settled by Sasak and Bugis farmers who planted the lovely coconut groves that dominate the flat interior and cloak some of the better bungalows. On clear mornings you'll have stunning views of both Gunung Rinjani and Bali's Gunung Agung. The white-sand beaches are thin yet beautiful, lapped by turquoise water and sprinkled with laid-back beach bars and cafes. Traditionally, families have made Gili Air their offshore Lombok base, but Gili Trawangan has been gobbling up that market, so these days it's mostly couples lazing in the sun. Although it feels delightfully empty at times, Air is still the most populous of the Gili Islands.

### ORIENTATION

The main harbour is located at the southern end of the island, near the jetty; the **Koperasi** (☀ 8am-5.30pm) harbour office has a hut here with public boat prices marked clearly outside. Almost all accommodation and restaurants are on the east and south coasts, which have the best swimming beaches. A network of sand and dirt tracks criss-cross the island, but can get quite confusing. Keep it simple and stick to the coastal path around the island – it's a gorgeous 90-minute walk.

### INFORMATION

There's a small **Perama** (☎ 637 816) office next to the Gili Indah Hotel. **Gecko Cafe** (per min 500Rp; ☀ 8am-9pm) has the best web connection on the island. **Ozzy's Shop** (☎ 622 179; ☀ 8am-8pm), about halfway up the east coast, has a wartel and will change money, as will Hotel Gili Air, but exchange rates are poor. Blue Marlin charges 7% for cash advances on credit cards. There's a **medical clinic** (☀ 8am-6pm) in the village.

### ACTIVITIES
#### Snorkelling & Diving

There's great **snorkelling** all along the east-coast reef with more than its share of colourful fish. Gear can be hired from Ozzy's Shop and a number of beach bars for 20,000Rp a day. Check with dive centres about currents, as they can be extremely strong.

**Scuba diving** is excellent throughout the Gilis (see boxed text, p497). Gili Air has three established dive schools, **Blue Marlin Dive Centre** (☎ 634 387, 0812 377 0288; www.bluemarlindive.com), **Dream Divers** (☎ 634 547; www.dreamdivers.com), and **Manta Dive** (☎ 0813 5305 0462, 0813 3778 9047; www.manta-dive.com), which just opened its Gili Air branch on the east coast; plus one radical upstart, **7 Seas Dive Center** (☎ 0813 3877 7144; www.diveindonesia.com), which was breaking ground at research time, offering scooter diving, tech- and free-diving instruction, and has ambitious plans to cater scuba diving to the disabled.

NUSA TENGGARA

## Surfing

Directly off the southern tip of the island there's a long, peeling right-hand break that can get big. The dive schools will help you find a board.

## Cycling

Ozzy's Shop has bikes for hire for 25,000Rp a day. Pedalling on Gili Air can be fun. You'll have to walk it when you inevitably land in deep sand, and you're sure to roll into villagers' back yards if you explore the inland trails, but isn't that kind of accidental mingling the reason why you're here?

## SLEEPING

Most places are spread up and down the east coast. Prices quoted are high-season rates – expect substantial discounts in low season. The price categories below reflect those found on both the Gilis and Bali. See p817 for details.

### Budget

**Gili Air Santay** ( ☎ 0818 0375 8695, 0819 1599 3782; www .giliair-santay.com; d 80,000-180,000Rp) Set back from the beach in a quiet coconut grove, these spacious bamboo-and-timber huts are a good budget choice. The shoreside restaurant serves authentic Thai food (see opposite).

**Gusung Indah** ( ☎ 0812 378 9054; bungalows 100,000-150,000Rp) Nice bungalows, most with a sea view, served with a touch of attitude by the man in charge.

**Abdi Fantastik** ( ☎ 636 421; r 150,000Rp) Family-owned bungalows strung with hammocks, steps from the sea.

**Mawar Bungalows** ( ☎ 0813 6225 3995; bungalows 130,000-220,000Rp) Basic, thatched bungalows set 30m from the sea in the coconut grove. The new ones have Western-style toilets. All have hammocks and come with breakfast in a stylish dining area. They serve family dinners for guests and staff every night (50,000Rp per person).

**Resota Bungalows** ( ☎ 0818 0571 5769; bungalows 250,000Rp) Nestled in the coconut palms near the harbour, is this charming bungalow property. They feel new, and come with a stocked minibar and inviting hammocks.

**Sunrise Hotel** ( ☎ 642 370; bungalows 250,000-350,000Rp) Charming, if a bit aged. These two-storey thatched bungalows have outdoor living rooms and are set back from the beach.

**Sandy Cottages** ( ☎ 0812 378 9832; bungalows 250,000-400,000Rp; ) New stone and low-slung thatched bungalows. They offer great low-season deals.

GILI AIR

0 — 500 m
0 — 0.3 miles

BALI SEA

Takat Malang    Takat Sira

To Gili Meno (1.5km)

Boat Landing

Jetty

To Bangsal (3.5km)

## Midrange

**Corner Bungalows** (☎ 0819 1722 9543; bungalows 350,000Rp) Owned by a welcoming local family, these new (at the time of research) bamboo bungalows all have hammocks slung over a varnished deck.

**Manta Dive** (☎ 0813 5305 0462, 0813 3778 9047; www .manta-dive.com; bungalows US$50-65; 🖳 🖳 ) Manta are the innovators of the Zen mod-hut motif that has been replicated throughout the Gilis. These were brand new at research time with arched roofs, minimalist interiors, decks and outdoor baths.

**our pick** **Sejuk Cottages** (☎ 636 461, 0813 3953 5387; bungalows 450,000-650,000Rp; 🖳 🖳 ) Your experience will begin with an ice-blended latte – their welcome drink – which you'll slurp on the deck of your low-slung *lumbung* cottage or in the rooftop living room of your split-level bungalow. They all have outdoor baths, superb lighting and homey touches like hand-painted wardrobes. And they open onto a flower garden which fades into a coconut grove that sways to the sand.

**Villa Karang** (☎ 0813 3990 4440; bungalows from 500,000Rp; 🖳 ) This ambitious harbour resort is a mishmash of newer concrete and tile rooms and older thatched wood bungalows. For the money, it's not the best value. But it has a lovely pool area and it does book up.

## EATING

Gili Air dining isn't fancy, and service tends to be (painfully) slow, but you'll be seated cross-legged on cushions atop beachfront *berugas*, so no bitching! Most cafes serve simple Indonesian and Western dishes, and they almost all have wood-fired pizza ovens…for some unexplained reason.

**Tami's** (dishes 10,000-40,000Rp) A funky Sasak-themed cafe decorated with masks, bamboo furniture, dining platforms and shaggy new *berugas*. Try the *urap-urap* (cooked vegetables with grated, spiced coconut) and *ayam taliwang* (roasted chicken served with a peanut, tomato, chilli and lime dip). It also has a nightly fish grill.

**Ali Baba** (dishes 10,000-50,000Rp) A creative beachside *warung* infused with wacky coconut and seashell sculpture on a lovely rocky beach. It has the usual Indonesian, seafood and Western fare.

**Santay** (dishes 12,000-30,000Rp) The only Thai kitchen on Gili Air. Meals are served with gorgeous Rinjani views, if the Gods allow.

**Hikmah's** (baguettes 35,000-40,000Rp) Set on the island's southeast corner, it serves homemade baguettes. Choices include chicken-asparagus, smoked salmon and cream cheese, and brie with green pepper. It also rents snorkel gear for 20,000Rp per day.

**Harmony Cafe** (dishes 15,000-100,000Rp; ☽ 4-9pm) This is the island's classiest dinner spot. It's set on a bamboo pier, with pink tablecloths, ample pillows to lean into and exquisite sunset views. Come for a sundowner at happy hour (cocktails 25,000Rp) or for a full grilled fish dinner (50,000Rp to 100,000Rp).

**Wiwin Cafe** (dishes 25,000-45,000Rp) Its wood-fired pizzas smell divine and it has the most extensive veggie menu on the island.

Or try one of the following:

**Munchies** (dishes 7500-26,000Rp; ☽ noon-11pm) Serves good curries, fish and overflowing sandwiches.

**Gusung Indah** (☎ 0812 378 9054; dishes 15,000-40,000Rp) Sit under a beachfront *beruga* and feast on *opor ayam* (braised chicken in coconut milk), sandwiches or pasta.

## DRINKING

On full and dark moons the island can rock, but usually Gili Air is as mellow as Meno.

**our pick** **Zipp Bar** (☎ 0819 1593 5205; ☽ 7am-late) This beautiful teak bar, set on a sandy beach perfect for swimming, is the island's main hub of activity. It has an excellent booze selection, outstanding fresh-fruit cocktails and decent pub grub. It throws a beach party every full moon.

**Chill Out Bar** (☽ 11-2am) Popular with both visitors and locals, it has a good selection of spirits and cocktails.

**Blue Bar** (☽ 8.30am-late) You'll find comfy beach *berugas* and a great vibe here.

**Legend Pub** (☽ 10am-11.30pm Thu-Tue, happy hour 5-7pm, dark-moon party 10pm-2am) Your standard-issue island reggae bar. It throws monthly dark-moon parties.

## Gili Meno
### pop 300

Gili Meno is the smallest of the three islands and the perfect setting for your Robinson Crusoe fantasy. The beaches here are the best in the archipelago, and with a population of just 300 it's quiet day and night. Most of the accommodation is strung out along the east coast, near the widest and most picturesque beach. Inland you'll find scattered homesteads, coconut plantations and salt flats.

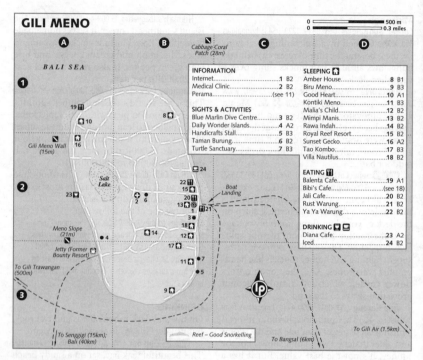

## GILI MENO

0 ——————————— 500 m
0 ——————————— 0.3 miles

| INFORMATION | | |
| --- | --- | --- |
| Internet.................................1 | B2 |
| Medical Clinic.......................2 | B2 |
| Perama...............................(see 11) |

| SIGHTS & ACTIVITIES | | |
| --- | --- | --- |
| Blue Marlin Dive Centre..........3 | B2 |
| Daily Wonder Islands...............4 | A2 |
| Handicrafts Stall.....................5 | B3 |
| Taman Burung.......................6 | B2 |
| Turtle Sanctuary....................7 | B3 |

| SLEEPING | | |
| --- | --- | --- |
| Amber House.......................8 | B1 |
| Biru Meno............................9 | B3 |
| Good Heart.........................10 | A1 |
| Kontiki Meno.......................11 | B3 |
| Malia's Child.......................12 | B2 |
| Mimpi Manis.......................13 | B2 |
| Rawa Indah.........................14 | B2 |
| Royal Reef Resort................15 | B2 |
| Sunset Gecko......................16 | A2 |
| Tao Kombo.........................17 | B3 |
| Villa Nautilus......................18 | B2 |

| EATING | | |
| --- | --- | --- |
| Balenta Cafe.......................19 | A1 |
| Bibi's Cafe.......................(see 18) |
| Jali Cafe.............................20 | B2 |
| Rust Warung.......................21 | B2 |
| Ya Ya Warung.....................22 | B2 |

| DRINKING | | |
| --- | --- | --- |
| Diana Cafe.........................23 | A2 |
| Iced..................................24 | B2 |

BALI SEA

Cabbage Coral Patch (28m)

Gili Meno Wall (15m)

Salt Lake

Meno Slope (21m)

Jetty (Former Bounty Resort)

Boat Landing

To Gili Trawangan (500m)

To Senggigi (15km); Bali (40km)

To Bangsal (6km)

To Gili Air (1.5km)

Reef – Good Snorkelling

## INFORMATION

There are a couple of minimarkets and a wartel near the boat landing; this is also where you can get access to **internet** (per min 600Rp). Money can be exchanged at poor rates at the Gazebo Meno and Kontiki Meno bungalows. **Perama** ( ☎ 632 824) is based at Kontiki Meno bungalows. A resident nurse attends the medical clinic near the bird park. Doctors are on call in Mataram.

## SIGHTS & ACTIVITIES

Gili Meno's 2500-sq-metre **Taman Burung** (bird park; ☎ 642 321; admission 50,000Rp; ☼ 9am-5pm) is home to 300 exotic birds from Asia and Australia, three demure kangaroos and a Komodo dragon. Birds are liberated from their cages three hours a day, to fly around an expansive atrium covered in netting.

Meno's **turtle sanctuary** (www.gilimenoturtles.com) is a complex of kiddie pools and bathtubs on the beach, bubbling with filters and teeming with baby turtles. The cute critters are nurtured until they're strong enough to be released into the wild with a minimum of predatory risk. The sanctuary releases about 250 turtles a year.

A late afternoon stroll around tiny Meno is a must. It can be completed in an hour and is best done with a few stops for sundowners along the way. Look for the ramshackle **handicrafts stall** just south of Kontiki. Blink and you'll miss it.

## Snorkelling & Diving

There's good snorkelling off the northeast coast near Amber House, on the west coast near Good Heart and also around the former jetty of the (abandoned) Bounty resort. Gear is available for 20,000Rp per day from several places on the eastern strip. For more on snorkelling and diving, see boxed text, opposite. **Daily Wonder Islands** ( ☎ 0818 0361 2402; per person 235,000Rp; ☼ tours depart at 9am & 2pm) offers half-day (four hours) snorkelling tours. Price includes hotel pick-up.

**Blue Marlin Dive Centre** ( ☎ 639 979, 0819 1719 3285; www.bluemarlindive.com) offers fun dives and courses from Discover Scuba to Divemaster.

## SLEEPING

Price categories below reflect those found on both the Gilis and Bali. See p817 for details.

NUSA TENGGARA

## Budget

**Tao Kombo** ( ☎ 0812 372 2174; tao_kombo@yahoo.com; bungalows 100,000-300,000Rp) About 200m inland, you'll find Meno's most unique bungalow property. There are open huts with bamboo screens instead of walls, and nicer, enclosed cottages with vaulted ceilings, thatched roofs and stone floors.

**Rawa Indah** ( ☎ 0819 1793 8813; bungalows 150,000Rp) Basic, bamboo, thatched, palm-shaded and dangling with seashell wind chimes.

**Good Heart** ( ☎ 0813 3955 6976; bungalows 200,000Rp) Excellent, friendly Balinese-owned place with a row of twin-deck *lumbung*-like bungalows sporting open-air fresh-water bathrooms.

**Mimpi Manis** ( ☎ 642 324; r 200,000Rp) Basic bamboo bungalows set back from the beach.

**Kontiki Meno** ( ☎ 632 824; cottages with fan/air-con 200,000/300,000Rp; 🌊 ) The beach is gorgeous, the seaside wooden platforms demand sunbathing, but the cold-water, cinderblock cottages are just okay.

---

### UNDERWATER GILIS

The Gili Islands are a superb dive destination. Marine life is plentiful and varied. Turtles, black-and white-tip reef sharks are common, and the microlife (small stuff) is excellent with seahorses, pipefish and lots of crustaceans. Around full moon, large schools of bumphead parrotfish appear to feast on coral spawns, while at other times of the year manta rays soar.

Though an El Niño–inspired bleaching damaged soft corals above 18m, the reefs are now in recovery. In front of every dive shop an electric current runs to a **Biorock reef**, which over time will evolve into a natural coral reef. This is a project of the Gili Eco Trust, a partnership that was formed between dive operators and the local community, which aims to improve the condition of the reefs and protect them in perpetuity. All divers help fund the trust by paying a one-off fee of 30,000Rp with their first dive – part of those funds go to locals who are actually paid not to fish.

The Gilis also have their share of virgin coral. **Hidden Reef**, a recently discovered site, pops with colourful life above 20m, and there's also an abundance of deep coral shelves and walls at around 30m, where the coral is, and always has been, pristine.

Safety standards are high in the Gilis despite the modest dive costs – there are no dodgy dive schools, and instructors and training are professional. Rates are fixed (no matter who you dive with) at US$35 a dive, with discounts for packages of five dives or more. A PADI Open Water course costs US$350, the Advanced course is US$275, and Divemaster starts at US$650.

Surrounded by coral reefs and with easy beach access, the Gilis offer superb snorkelling too. Masks, snorkels and fins can be hired for as little as 20,000Rp per day. On Trawangan, turtles appear on the reef right off the beach. You'll likely drift with the current, so be prepared to walk back. Around Gili Meno, the pier by the (closed) Bounty resort has prolific marine life, while over on Air, the walls off the east coast are good.

Some of the best dive sites:

**Deep Halik** This canyon-like site is ideally suited to drift diving. Black- and white-tip sharks are often seen at 28m to 30m.

**Deep Turbo** At around 30m, this site is perfect for Nitrox diving. It has impressive sea fans and leopard sharks hidden in the crevasses.

**Hans Reef** Off the northeast coast of Gili Air, and great for microlife including frogfish, ghostfish, seahorses and pipefish.

**Hidden Reef** (12-25m) Nestled between Meno and Air, and not yet flagged on most dive maps, this site has vibrant, pristine soft corals.

**Japanese Wreck** For experienced divers only (it lies at 45m), this Japanese WWII patrol boat suits Nitrox divers. You'll see prolific soft coral and lots of nudibranchs. Look out for lionfish and frogfish.

**Shark Point** (15-30m) Reef sharks and turtles are encountered regularly, along with schools of bumphead parrotfish and mantas. At shallow depths there can be a strong surge.

**Simon's Reef** (16-30m) The reef here is in excellent condition; you can see schools of trevally, and occasionally barracuda and leopard sharks.

**Sunset (Manta Point)** The sloping reef has good coral growth below 18m, including some impressive table coral. Large pelagics are frequently encountered and strong currents are rarely an issue.

NUSA TENGGARA

**Amber House** ( ☎ 0813 3756 9728; 250,000Rp) Attractive, circular bungalows with outdoor showers on the island's sleepy north end.

### Midrange

**Royal Reef Resort** ( ☎ 642 340; bungalows 300,000Rp) The name recalls an old-school yacht club. But it's just six large but basic, thatched bamboo bungalows opposite the marina. Um, that's a good thing.

**ourpick Sunset Gecko** ( ☎ 0813 5356 6774; www .thesunsetgecko.com; bungalows 350,000Rp; ⚡ ) These attractive thatched, two-storey A-frame bungalows have outdoor and indoor bedrooms, wood shutters and the best views on Meno.

**Malia's Child** ( ☎ 622 007; www.gilimeno-mallias .com; bungalows US$35) Some of the best bungalows on this end of Meno. They're thatched, bamboo and lined up along the deep white sand. If you want one, you'd better book ahead. They'll negotiate a lower daily rate for long stays.

**Biru Meno** ( ☎ 0813 365 7322; bungalows 450,000Rp) The staff are friendly, the bungalows are tastefully crafted from mostly native materials like bamboo and coral, and their beach is stunning. But without hot water, it's a touch overpriced.

**Villa Nautilus** ( ☎ 642 143; www.villanautilus.com; r €66; ⚡ ) Five deluxe detached villas, finished in contemporary style with natural wood, marble and limestone. Plenty of natural light floods the lounge, which opens onto a terrace.

### EATING & DRINKING

The beachfront restaurants near the boat landing all offer a soothing symbiosis of fine views with slow service.

**ourpick Rust Warung** ( ☎ 642 324; mains 8000-75,000Rp; ⚡ 7-10am, 11am-3.30pm, 6pm-late) This restaurant has beachfront *berugas* and a terrific assortment of fresh daily catch. Fish is perfectly grilled, glazed with garlic or sweet and sour sauce and served with grilled corn, cabbage salad and baked potato. If only its bar's soundtrack wouldn't bounce from Bollywood classics to techno club anthems to death metal.

**Jali Cafe** ( ☎ 639 800; dishes 10,000-20,000Rp) Friendly owners serve up tasty Indonesian, Sasak and curry dishes. At night they grill fresh fish and strum guitars by the fire. Everyone is welcome.

**Ya Ya Warung** (dishes 10,000-20,000Rp) It looks like a stiff breeze might blow over this lean-to

beach warung, and that's part of the charm. It serves all your Indo faves and a huge selection of pasta dishes.

**Balenta Cafe** (mains from 20,000Rp, fish at market price) Next to the Good Heart, this fantastic cafe has a full menu of Sasak and international food and a great seafood barbecue.

**Diana Cafe** ( ☎ 0818 057 7622; drinks 12,000-25,000Rp) The stilted *berugas* have cushions, coffee tables and ideal sunset views. It also has great snorkelling nearby and rents gear on the cheap (12,500Rp).

**Iced** (coffee 10,000-12,000Rp, scoops 6000Rp, sundaes 15,000-28,000Rp; ⚡ 8am-sunset) A half-dozen tables tastefully scattered on the white sand and shaded by parasols make this the perfect setting for iced coffee and...*ice cream!*

## Gili Trawangan
### pop 1500

Social but not trashy, relaxed but not boring, all-natural yet sprinkled with a collection of restaurants and bars that would satisfy any devout cosmopolitan, Gili Trawangan is the road-weary rambler's lucid fantasy.

The largest and most popular of the carless Gilis, Gili Trawangan first blipped on the tourism radar during the '90s, when Bali rose to global prominence and backpackers descended in search of white sand, warm water, rich reefs and a good party. Expectations were exceeded across the board. But thanks to an overt, entrenched weed and 'shrooms' trade, and three all-night ravelike events a week, it was that party label which stuck.

Gili Trawangan is a lot more than that now. Part of this latent maturity is due to a recent drug bust sparked by undercover cops who posed as humble DVD hawkers. But it also has something to do with the Bali fast boats, which shepherd over a diversified clientele of young families and moneyed weekenders from Singapore and Jakarta. Then there's the, ahem, 'maturing' expat community.

Yes, the once carefree dive entrepreneurs have families now. And they're building swanky villas, upscale dive schools and shabby chic cafes. Trawangan's Indonesian community has benefited from the surge in tourism here, as well. Some of the best new bars and bungalows are locally owned.

Agoraphobics needn't worry. Even with the new construction boom, the lightly developed northwest coast remains pristine – where the

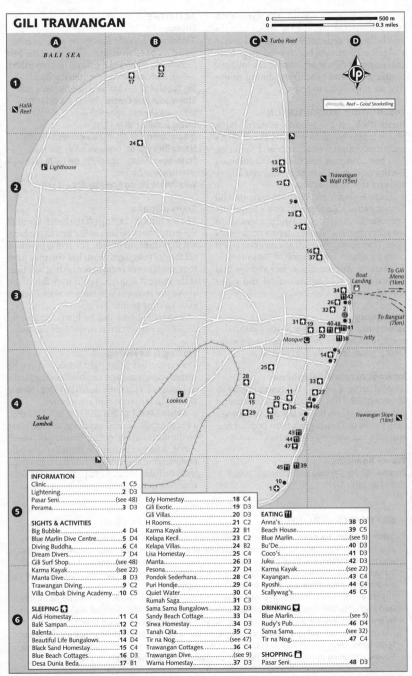

# GILI TRAWANGAN

0 ——————————— 500 m
0 ——————————— 0.3 miles

*BALI SEA*

*Halik Reef*

*Lighthouse*

*Turbo Reef*

*Reef – Good Snorkelling*

*Trawangan Wall (15m)*

*Boat Landing*

To Gili Meno (1km)

To Bangsal (7km)

*Mosque*

*Jetty*

*Lookout*

*Selat Lombok*

*Trawangan Slope (18m)*

**NUSA TENGGARA**

crowds are (much!) thinner, the water is the turquoise shade you dream about and the snorkelling is superb. Nest here and you're still just a 20-minute beach stroll away from that scrum of dive shops, sushi bars, lounges, reggae joints and beachfront dining rooms that are impossible to resist.

### ORIENTATION & INFORMATION

Boats dock on the island's eastern shore, which is also home to most of Trawangan's accommodation, restaurants and facilities. The best stretch of beach is on the stunning northwest corner. Stay here, and you'll have a longer trek to the action.

There is finally an ATM machine on Gili Trawangan at Villa Ombak but it's frequently out of service. Several stores will change cash or travellers cheques, but the rates are notoriously poor. Dive shops give cash advances on credit cards for a hefty commission of 7% to 10%.

There is no post office, but stamps and postcards are sold in the wartel and *pasar seni* (art market).

### Emergency

**Satgas** Contact this community organisation which controls security on the island via your hotel or dive school.
**Clinic** ( 9am-5pm) At the Villa Ombak Hotel.

### Internet Access & Telephone

Also offering a wartel, **Lightening** (internet access per min 500Rp) has a satellite-fed broadband connection. If you have a laptop, Scallywag's (p503), one of Trawangan's most popular restaurants, has wireless connection.

### Travel Agencies

**Perama** ( ☎ 638 514; www.peramatour.com) Located north of the jetty.

### ACTIVITIES
### Diving

Trawangan is made for divers, with six established scuba schools, including one of the best tech-diving schools in the world (see boxed text, p497), and one newcomer (Diving Buddha).
**Big Bubble** ( ☎ 625 020; www.bigbubblediving.com)
**Blue Marlin Dive Centre** ( ☎ 632 424, 0813 3993 0190; www.bluemarlindive.com)
**Diving Buddha** ( ☎ 644 179)
**Dream Divers** ( ☎ 634 496; www.dreamdivers.com)
**Manta Dive** ( ☎ 643 649; www.manta-dive.com)
**Trawangan Diving** ( ☎ 649 220, 0813 3770 2332; www.trawangandive.com)
**Villa Ombak Diving Academy** ( ☎ 638 531)

### Snorkelling

There's fun snorkelling off the beach north of the jetty. The coral isn't in the best shape here, but there are tons of fish. The reef is healthier off the northwestern coast, but you may have to scramble over coral to access it at low tide. If the current is quick, you'll have fun flying above the reef, but will have to walk back to your starting point.

Snorkelling gear can be hired for around 25,000Rp per day from shops near the jetty.

### Surfing & Kayaking

Trawangan has a fast right break that can be surfed year-round and can swell overhead. It's just south of Villa Ombak. **Gili Surf Shop** ( ☎ 0812 372 7615) in the *pasar seni* rents boards.

**Karma Kayak** ( ☎ 0818 0559 3710; tours 300,000Rp), a hotel, tapas bar and kayaking school, is set on the northern end of Gili Trawangan, where Astrid, a former champion stunt kayaker (she took silver at the 1991 world championship) leads half-day kayaking trips around the Gilis when currents allow.

---

### GILI T'S TECHNICALITIES

Simon Liddiard, founder and owner of Blue Marlin and the first Westerner with a Gili address, also happens to be one of the world's best tech-dive instructors. The Gilis' vibrant coral walls, which descend to more than 1000m beneath the surface, are his classrooms, and his curriculum includes Nitrox, Tri-Mix, Extended Range and Rebreather courses. Rebreathers recycle your air, are almost totally silent and allow for much longer dives.

Liddiard once held the world record for deepest dive with a Rebreather (170m), and his affable lead instructor Will Goodman, the perfect blend of London punk and dive god, owns the current record for the longest dive ever (30 hours). So you know you'll be in good hands.

Just remember, going deep (more than 45m) has a certain psychedelic effect on the brain. Technicolor coral throbs and sways, and you will be forgiven if you commune with a glowing, fluorescent green nudibranch and become convinced it holds the secrets of the universe.

## Walking & Cycling

Trawangan is fun to explore on foot or by bike. You can walk around the whole island in a couple of hours – if you finish at the hill on the southwestern corner (which has the remains of an old Japanese WWII gun placement), you'll have terrific sunset views of Bali's Gunung Agung.

Bikes are the preferred mode of transport and are easily hired from 25,000Rp per day. Your hotel can arrange rental or you can approach the bike shops on the main drag directly.

## SLEEPING

There are now more than 100 places to stay in Gili Trawangan. They range from simple village huts to mod Zen beach bungalows with outdoor baths to sprawling air-conditioned villas with private pools. The cheapest digs are in the village – where the mosque is everyone's alarm clock. You'll pay more for a beachside address. We like the island's rugged north coast.

All budget and most midrange places have brackish tap water. Pure water is available in some bungalows. High-season rates quoted here can drop up to 50% off-peak. Breakfast is included unless stated otherwise.

Price categories below reflect those found on both the Gilis and Bali. See p817 for details.

## Budget
**Sirwa Homestay** (s/d 40,000/45,000Rp) Spacious rooms – some have two double beds – with prices to suit those on a strict budget.

**Aldi Homestay** ( ☎ 0813 3954 1102; s/d 60,000/100,000Rp) Another village bargain. Some rooms are nicer than others, so check around. Look for the ripped-off logo of the German supermarket chain Aldi, which is also the name of the owner's son.

**Lisa Homestay** ( ☎ 0813 3952 3364; r 75,000Rp) Very friendly little place with airy and light tiled rooms that overlook a garden.

**Sandy Beach Cottage** ( ☎ 625 020; d from 100,000Rp) A shady hideaway, close to the action.

**Edy Homestay** (d from 120,000Rp) One of the best of the village cheapies. Rooms are very clean and come with ceiling fans.

**Warna Homestay** ( ☎ 623 859; d from 150,000Rp) Arguably the best value on the island, Warna has five sweet, tropical flower garden bungalows mere steps from the sea.

**Puri Hondje** (r 150,000Rp; ) Tucked away down a quiet village lane, these very stylish rooms overlook a small koi pond surrounded by bougainvillea and palms.

**Balenta** ( ☎ 0818 0520 3464; d from 180,000Rp) Next to the upmarket Good Heart, it's one of Gili Trawangan's better values. It's opposite a great stretch of beach and the rooms are large and immaculate.

**Pondok Sederhana** ( ☎ 0813 3860 9964; r 200,000Rp) At the foot of the hill, and run by a house-proud, friendly Balinese lady, the spotless rooms here face a neat little garden. Low-season discounts to 80,000Rp are available.

**Trawangan Cottages** ( ☎ 639 282; s/d 200,000/250,000Rp) These clean, freshly painted tiled rooms have built-in wood desks and a nice garden. Bathrooms could be cleaner. Long-stay discounts are available in off-peak season.

**Quiet Water** ( ☎ 0819 1753 1652; d from 250,000Rp) A plush yet affordable village choice with queen beds, soft linens, air-con, hot water and in-room DVD players.

## Midrange
**Black Sand Homestay** ( ☎ 0812 372 0353; r from 300,000Rp) One- and two-storey wooden bungalows are nestled in a sweet garden with views of the hill. Two-storey jobs come with TV and an outdoor bath. Management is hospitable, and prices drop in the low season.

**Tir na Nog** ( ☎ 639 463; tirnanog@mataram.wasantara .net.id; r from 300,000Rp; ) At the rear of the bar, these huge rooms with air-con have been thoughtfully designed and decorated; most have spacious private terraces and swanky modern bathrooms.

**Rumah Saga** ( ☎ 648 604, 0818 0571 4315; www.rumah saga.com; cottages 350,000-500,000Rp; ) Clean, modern cottages with TV, air-con and hot water are set around a lovely garden area with a nice pool. The large bungalows sleep up to three people.

**NUSA TENGGARA**

**Pesona** ( ☎ 660 7233; www.pesonaresort.com; r 400,000-600,000Rp; 🔀 ) You'll enjoy these new concrete and tile bungalows with inviting hammocks-laced porchside. The rooms, which are named for flowers, all have TVs, DVDs and safety boxes, and the shell-embedded terrazzo bathrooms are four-star quality.

**Sama Sama Bungalows** ( ☎ 0812 376 3650; r with air-con 400,000, deluxe lumbung 650,000Rp; 🔀 ) Combining natural materials with mod cons, these stylish rooms set back from the beach make a comfortable base.

**Beautiful Life Bungalows** ( ☎ 0818 0376 4102; bungalows 450,000Rp; 🔀 ) If you don't enjoy life in one of these new, clean, tiled garden bungalows, each with TV/DVD, air-con, and a front porch made for island slackers like you, it's your own fault.

**Tanah Qita** ( ☎ 639 159; bungalows 500,000Rp) Perhaps Trawangan's best new addition, these thatched, teak *lumbung*-style bungalows have high ceilings, outdoor bathrooms and style and grace to spare. The staff are marvellous. If they invite you to share a home-cooked Sasak meal, say 'yes, please'.

**Balé Sampan** ( ☎ 0813 3988 2153, 0813 3774 8469; www.balesampanbungalows.com; bungalows with garden/sea view 500,000/800,000Rp; 🔀 🍴 ) The name means 'boat house'. But there are no broken outboards, fishing nets and oily concrete floors here. Just fine modern-edge beach bungalows served with Yogja stone baths, a freshwater pool, plush duvet covers and a proper English breakfast.

**Manta** ( ☎ 643 649, 0812 376 4780; www.manta-dive .com; bungalows 550,000Rp; 🔀 🍴 ) This laid-back English-run dive centre introduced the mod-bungalow motif to the Gilis, and its own remain some of the most stylish. It's a fun place to be after the afternoon dive when beers flow.

**our pick Karma Kayak** ( ☎ 0818 0559 3710; bungalows 550,000Rp) A beautiful bungalow property on the tranquil north end, co-owned by a former champion kayaker. Owners and staff are lovely, the well-lit bungalows are spotless and the beach is absolutely gorgeous, especially at sunset. When we visited, a turtle nest hatched in the dunes less than 50m from the front gate. Spectacular!

**Blue Beach Cottages** ( ☎ 623 538; bungalows from 550,000Rp; 🔀 ) Native thatch meets mod-minimalist at this locally owned collection of sea-view cottages on the north end of the strip. There are outdoor bathrooms, queen beds, wide decks and glass doors. Large long-term and low-season discounts are available if you negotiate.

**Trawangan Dive** ( ☎ 649 220, 0813 3770 2332; www .trawangadive.com; bungalows US$60-80; 🔀 🍴 ) The swankiest dive school on the island – think luxe locker rooms with stone floors and a climate-controlled rebreather room – has just opened 12 stylish new rooms decked out in Indian limestone. They have fresh-water showers and a sunken pool bar.

**Kelapa Kecil** ( ☎ 0812 376 6496; bungalows US$70-90; 🔀 🍴 ) These sleek, minimalist mod bungalows have little luxuries like security boxes, limestone baths, a plunge pool, and are steps away from the sea.

**H Rooms** ( ☎ 639 248; villas from 800,000Rp) Directly behind Horizontal Lounge, these seriously chic minivillas offer space and style in abundance, each with a large sun terrace and private jacuzzi, living area with hi-fi and plasma TV, master bedroom and luxe open-air bathroom.

## Top End

**Desa Dunia Beda** ( ☎ 641 575; www.desaduniabeda.com; bungalows US$110-140 plus 21% tax; 🍴 ) Beautifully isolated on the north end are some astonishing rebuilt Javanese Joglo bungalows. Each is decked out with colonial-era antiques, including a four-poster bed, writing desk and sofa, and you'll dig the back-to-nature open-air bathrooms. The pool is small, but you have your own beach, so why quibble. This is a proper eco-retreat, so there's no air-con and no fresh water.

**Gili Exotic** ( ☎ 692 113, 0818 360 019; www.giliexotic .com; villas 1,500,000Rp; 🔀 🍴 📶 ) Sasak-owned and adjacent to the Gili Villas are these luxe wood, one-bedroom villas with classic Indo style and modern accents like satellite TV and wireless web access.

**Kelapa Villas** ( ☎ 632 424, 0812 375 6003; www.kelapa villas.com; villas US$150-550 plus 21% tax; 🔀 🍴 ) The villa complex that started the Trawangan luxe development boom. It has 14 villas, all privately owned, varying in size from one- to five-bedroom, less than half a click from the deserted western shore. The largest (which sleep up to eight people) are tropical palaces with granite kitchen counter tops, terrazzo baths and massive open-air rooms that spill onto a private pool deck, tropical flower garden and manicured lawn, which rolls toward the swaying palms. Bring a big group, and that gaudy price tag won't hurt too much.

NUSA TENGGARA

**Gili Villas** ( ☎ 0812 376 4780; www.gilivillasindonesia
.com; villas US$250; ⚏ ▣ ) Hidden in the village,
just inland from the art market is the latest
villa development on Trawangan. These are
ultramodern two-bedroom villas with Yogja
stone floors, indoor-outdoor kitchen, living
room and dining room, attentive staff and a
sweet pool deck. They're well located in the
middle of the action.

## EATING
It's easy to munch your way around the
world – from Indonesia to Japan to Spain and
Australia – in tiny Trawangan. In the evenings
several places display and grill fresh seafood.

**Anna's** (dishes from 8000Rp; ☽ 24hr) Opposite the
harbour is another tasty, local warung serving
*nasi campur* for 10,000Rp. It's the cheapest
meal in town, and it's damn good.

**Blue Marlin** (mains 9000-35,000Rp) Perhaps the
best fish grill on the island. Choose your
catch and enjoy it with a limitless buffet
of salads and sides. It's always cooked to
perfection.

**Bu'De** ( ☎ 0812 3637 9516; meals from 15,000Rp;
☽ 9am-7pm) Shoestringers and dive masters
now have a new place to inhale terrific local
food on the cheap. Choose from an array of
fresh, spicy food on display. The *nasi campur*
is special and usually comes with fried or curried chicken. Service is friendly and the bright
dining room is spotless.

**Beach House** ( ☎ 642 352; dishes 17,000-60,000Rp)
This once great restaurant isn't cheap, but
with plush, sand floor, seaside digs, a terrific fresh fish and salad bar selection and a
solid jazz and rock soundtrack, people keep
coming. The food has slipped a touch, but
the barmen are exceptional and it's still a
fun scene.

**Ryoshi** ( ☎ 639 463; dishes 17,000-48,000Rp) Another
delectable Bali import. The melt-in-your-
mouth tuna carpaccio should not be missed.

**Kayangan** (dishes from 20,000Rp) Across from
Ryoshi is a cheap and cheerful expat fave,
known for its tasty curries, sates and *gado
gado* (dish with mixed vegetables and peanut
sauce).

**Coco's** (espresso drinks from 15,000Rp, sandwiches
25,000Rp; ☽ 8am-6pm) If only there was a cafe
like this in every town, with mouth-watering
bacon and egg baguettes for breakfast and
roast turkey or meatball sandwiches at lunch.
The brownies, cakes, smoothies and shakes
are incredible too.

**Karma Kayak** ( ☎ 0818 0559 3710; tapas from 35,000Rp)
Tasty Spanish tapas (including house-cured
olives, exquisite garlic prawns and delicious
meatballs) are served on the beach, in *berugas*
or on tables and lounges made from driftwood. It's a popular spot at sunset.

**Juku** (grilled fish from 35,000Rp) Among local expats, Juku has long been known as the most
affordable and one of the best fish grills on the
island. Exceptional dishes like grilled barracuda with ginger glaze made its reputation.

**our pick Scallywag's** ( ☎ 631 945; meals from 45,000;
📶 ) Its open, shabby chic decor, and plush
patio seating help make this new hot spot a
major draw at all hours. But style only counts
if the food works, and it does. They have tender steaks, spicy chorizo, a daily selection of
fresh fish and Aussie pies, an organic ethos,
wireless internet, a full bar, terrific salads
(the chilli prawn salad is off the charts) and
exceptional deserts (including some truly
kick-ass ice cream). They do not always have
timely service, but you won't mind waiting
here.

## DRINKING & ENTERTAINMENT
Trawangan's rotating parties are no secret.
They fire up around 11pm and go on until
4am as imported DJs from Bali and beyond
mix techno, trance and house music (except
during Ramadan when the action is completely curtailed out of respect for local culture). At research time the party schedule
shifted between Blue Marlin (Monday), Tir
na Nog (Wednesday) and Rudy's (Friday).
But with this many cool beach bars, every
night is a good time.

**Blue Marlin** ( ☽ 8am-midnight Tue-Sun, 8am-3am Mon)
Of all the party bars, this upper-level venue
has the largest dance floor and the meanest
sound system – which pumps out trance and
tribal sounds on Monday.

**Tir na Nog** ( ☽ 7am-2am Wed-Mon, 7am-4am Tue)
Known simply and affectionately as 'The
Irish', it has a barnlike, sports-bar interior
with big screens, private thatched DVD
lounges that guests can use for free (their film
selection is huge), and a brilliant outdoor bar
with a live DJ that draws the biggest crowds in
town. Jameson comes cheap, and they have a
Wii video game system indoors (although it's
typically dominated by local dive professionals hell bent on bowling that elusive, perfect
300). Wednesday is their blow-out night, but
it's always fun here.

**Rudy's Pub** ( ☼ 8am-4am Fri, 8am-11pm Sat-Tue) Rudy's has as much to do with Gili T's party-hard reputation as all other bars combined. Mostly due to their weekly debaucherous Friday-night throwdowns and a preponderance of drinks and dishes involving a certain fungus. Drug bust? What drug bust?

**Sama Sama** ( ☼ 8am-late) Locally owned and easily the best reggae bar in Indonesia (and probably Southeast Asia). They have a top-end sound system, a killer live band at least six nights a week, and great barmen who mix tasty mojitos.

# NORTH & CENTRAL LOMBOK
☎ 0370

Lush and fertile, Lombok's scenic interior is stitched together with rice terraces, undulating tobacco fields, too many varieties of fruit and nut orchards to count, swatches of monkey forest, and it's capped by sacred Gunung Rinjani, which haemorrhages springs, rivers and waterfalls. Entwined in all this big nature are traditional Sasak settlements. Public transport is not frequent or consistent enough to rely on, but with wheels you can explore the black-sand fishing beaches, inland villages, and waterfalls, and if you're here in August you can attend the annual Sasak stick-fighting tournament.

## Bangsal to Bayan

The port of Bangsal is a hassle (see boxed text, p493), and public transport north from here is infrequent. Several minibuses go from Mandalika terminal in Bertais (Mataram) to Bayan, but you'll have to get connections in Pemenang and/or Anyar, which can be difficult to navigate. Simplify things and get your own wheels.

### SIRA

This peninsula has an insanely gorgeous white-sand **beach**, some snorkelling offshore where the reef is under recovery, and Lombok's two finest hotels. The rooms, villas and pavilions at **Oberoi Lombok** ( ☎ 638 444; www .oberoihotels.com; r from US$240, villas from US$350, plus 21% tax; ❄ ▯ ❀ ) ooze luxury, with sunken marble bathtubs, worn teak floors, antique entertainment armoire, oriental rugs and time-stopping verandahs, with sea and sunset views. The new **Tugu Hotel Lombok** ( ☎ 62011; www.tuguhotels.com; r from US$175 plus 21% tax; ❄ ▯ ❀ ) is likewise stunning. Owned by

one of Java's greatest antique collectors, the hotel lobby is set in a rebuilt 500-year-old home. Throughout the property you'll find fascinating wood paintings, masks, statues, doors, wardrobes and palatial beds. Deluxe rooms open onto private plunge pools and then the beach. The mosaic bathrooms (with deep tubs and rain showers) are fantastic. And the gallery, where some of the pieces are for sale, is museum quality.

Next door, the **Lombok Golf Kosaido Country Club** ( ☎ 640 137; per round incl caddy & cart US$80) is an attractive seaside 18-hole, 72-par course. Hole 9 faces glorious Teluk Sira, while holes 10 to 18 have exceptional Rinjani views. Guests who stay at Manta Dive or Gili Villas pay discounted member rates.

### GONDANG & AROUND

Just northeast of Gondang village, a 6km trail heads inland to **Air Terjun Tiu Pupas**, a 30m waterfall that's only worth seeing in the wet season. Trails continue from here to other wet-season waterfalls including **Air Terjun Gangga**, the most beautiful of all. A local guide will turn up at the trailhead to lead you there.

### BAYAN

Wektu Telu, Lombok's animist-tinted form of Islam, was born in humble thatched mosques nestled in these Rinjani foothills. The best example is **Masjid Kuno Bayan Beleq**, next to the village of Beleq. Its low-slung roof, dirt floors and bamboo walls reportedly date from 1634, making this mosque the oldest on Lombok. It's built on a square platform of river stones with a pagoda-like upper section. Inside is a huge old drum, which served as the call to prayer before PA systems. Ah, the good old days. With the exception of an annual pilgrimage, the mosque is usually dormant. Some of the outlying buildings are tombs, including one for the mosque's founding haji. You will be asked to sign a visitors' book and make a donation.

## Senaru & Batu Koq

These picturesque villages merge into one along a ridge with sweeping Rinjani and sea views. They are also way stations for would-be climbers. But even without a peak-bagging itch, the beautiful walking trails and spectacular waterfalls are worth spending a day or so.

## INFORMATION & ORIENTATION

The two villages are spread out along a single steep road which heads south to Rinjani. Batu Koq is about 3km south from Bayan, Senaru is a further 3km uphill.

**Rinjani Trek Centre** (RTC; ☎ 0868 1210 4132; www .info2lombok.com), at the southern end of the village, has good information on Rinjani and the surrounding area.

## SIGHTS & ACTIVITIES

Do not miss **Air Terjun Sindang Gila** (2000Rp), a spectacular set of falls 20 minutes' walk from Senaru. You'll stroll through forest and alongside an irrigation canal that follows the contour of the hill. Locals love to picnic by Sindang Gila. The hearty and foolish make for the creek, edge close, and then get pounded by the hard foaming cascade that explodes over black volcanic stone 40m above. If you crave a shot of life, join them.

Another 50 minutes uphill is **Air Terjun Tiu Kelep**, another waterfall with a swimming hole. The track is steep and tough at times. Guides are compulsory (25,000Rp).

Six kilometres south of Bayan is the traditional village of **Dusun Senaru**, where locals will invite you to chew betel nut (or tobacco) and show you around.

Community tourism activities can be arranged in most guest houses. They include a rice terrace and waterfall walk (50,000Rp), which takes in Sindang Gila, and the Senaru Panorama Walk (75,000Rp), led by female guides who blend stunning views with insight into local traditions.

## SLEEPING & EATING

These places are dotted along the road from Bayan to Senaru.

**Bukit Senaru Cottages** (r 75,000Rp) Shortly before Dusun Senaru, there are four decent semi-detached bungalows nestled in a sweet flower garden.

**Pondok Indah & Restaurant** ( ☎ 0817 578 8018; s/d 75,000/100,000Rp; 🖳 ) Simple rooms with great views of the valley and the sea beyond. It's owned and operated by the 'Rinjani Master'. There's ample parking, a good restaurant (dishes 7000Rp to 18,000Rp) and free internet.

**our pick** **Pondok Senaru & Restaurant** ( ☎ 622 868, 0868 1210 4141; r 200,000-350,000Rp) Perfectly perched on a cliff near the trail to the waterfalls. It offers easterly views of the rice-terraced valley from its recommended restaurant (dishes 13,000Rp to 21,000Rp) and spacious, spotless rooms that are the most comfortable digs in town.

Also worth considering is **Rinjani Homestay** ( ☎ 0817 575 0889; r 60,000Rp). A little further uphill, it has basic bamboo and tile bungalows with twin beds, and amazing views.

Head to **Emy Cafe** (dishes 5000-12,500Rp) or **Warung Galang Ijo** (dishes 13,000-18,500Rp), midway between Batu Koq and Senaru, for simple Sasak cuisine and cold drinks.

## GETTING THERE & AWAY

From Mandalika terminal in Mataram catch a bus to Anyar (20,000Rp, 2½ hours). Bemos leave Anyar for Senaru (7000Rp) every 20 minutes until 4.30pm. If you're coming from eastern Lombok, get off at the junction near Bayan, and hop a bemo to Senaru.

## The Sembalun Valley

☎ 0376

High on Gunung Rinjani's arid eastern slope is the beautiful Sembalun Valley, surrounded by farmland and golden foothills that turn green in the wet season. When high clouds part, Rinjani goes full-frontal from all angles. The valley has two main settlements, Sembalun Lawang and Sembalun Bumbung. Bumbung is wealthier but has no tourist facilities. Lawang is the best launch pad for Rinjani summit attempts, but it's no tourist magnet. Most trekkers base themselves in Senaru, which is reason enough to consider nesting here, among the relatively shy, sun-baked local Sasaks and Hindu Javanese who work the garlic fields. It's always interesting being the only foreigner(s) in town.

## INFORMATION & ACTIVITIES

The national-park rangers who staff the **Rinjani Information Centre** (RIC; ⏲ 6am-6pm) speak decent English and are well informed. They can hook you up with guides for day treks such as the four-hour **village walk** (per person 150,000Rp, minimum 2 people) and the strenuous slog to the **crater rim** (guide & park entrance fee 250,000Rp). The **wildflower walk** (per person incl guide, porters, meals & camping gear 550,000Rp) is a challenging two-day trek through blooming savannah. If you have your own gear and wish to hire guides and porters at day rates, the rangers will get you sorted for a summit attempt. Guides cost 100,000Rp per day and porters cost 80,000Rp per day.

The RIC has also helped local women to revive traditional weaving in Sembalun Lawang. Follow the signs from the village centre to their workshops.

### SLEEPING & EATING

The local hotel market is a bit bleak, but the RIC and their network of guides can help you find a homestay (75,000Rp). Wherever you stay, you will wash in frigid Rinjani water.

**Pondok Sembalun** ( ☎ 0852 3956 1340; r 75,000Rp) Stay in thatched, brick and bamboo bungalows set in a lovely garden. The restaurant serves basic Indo and Western fare, but that massive cell-tower is an eyesore.

**Lembah Rinjani** ( ☎ 0818 0365 2511; r 150,000Rp) The better of the two hotels in town. It has queen-size beds, spotless bathrooms and breathtaking mountain and sunrise views.

**Warung Madiya** (Jl Pariswata-Sembalun; meals from 10,000Rp) The rangers' choice for local food. It's across the street from the police station.

### GETTING THERE & AWAY

From Mandalika bus terminal in Mataram take a bus to Aikmel (12,000Rp) and change there for Sembalun Lawang (12,000Rp). Hourly trucks connect Lawang and Bumbung.

There's no public transport between Sembalun Lawang and Senaru; you'll have to charter an *ojek*, or a bemo for around 100,000Rp. Roads to Sembalun are sometimes closed in the wet season due to landslides.

## SAPIT

☎ 0376

On the southeastern slopes of Gunung Rinjani, Sapit is a tiny, very relaxed village with views across the sea to Sumbawa. *Open* (tall red-brick tobacco-drying buildings) loom above the lush landscape, and thick blocks of the local crop can be found in the market.

### Sights

Between Swela and Sapit, a side road leads to **Taman Lemor** (admission 3000Rp; ☒ 8am-4pm), a park with a spring-fed swimming pool and some monkeys. Further towards Pringgabaya, **Makam Selaparang** is the burial place of ancient Selaparang kings.

### Sleeping & Eating

**Hati Suci Homestay** ( ☎ 0818 545 655; www.hatisuci.tk; s 40,000-45,000Rp, d 75,000-85,000Rp) The budget bungalows come with en suite bathrooms set in

a blooming garden. The accommodation and restaurant (dishes 8000Rp to 18,000Rp) both offer stunning views over the sea to Sumbawa. Breakfast is included and hikes to Rinjani can be organised here.

### Getting There & Away

From Mataram or Central Lombok, head to Pringgabaya, which has frequent bemo connections to Sapit. Occasional bemos also go to Sapit from the Sembalun Valley.

## GUNUNG RINJANI

Rising over the northern half of Lombok, the mighty Gunung Rinjani (3726m), Indonesia's second-highest volcano, has spiritual gravitas. Balinese Hindus and Sasak Muslims consider it sacred and make pilgrimages to its peak and lake to leave offerings for the Gods. To the Balinese, who come once a year, Rinjani is one of three sacred mountains, along with Bali's Agung and Java's Bromo. Sasaks descend throughout the year around the full moon. International tourists also make the gruelling three-day trek. But we're generally after a more earthly satisfaction.

The mountain also has climatic significance. Its peak attracts a steady swirl of clouds which shower the valley and feed a tapestry of rice paddies, tobacco fields, cashew and mango trees, banana and coconut palms.

Inside the immense caldera, 600m below the rim, is a stunning, 6km-wide cobalt-blue lake, Danau Segara Anak (Child of the Sea). The Balinese toss their jewellery into the lake in a ceremony called *pekelan*, before they slog toward the sacred summit. The mountain's newest cone, Gunung Baru (or Gunung Barujari), which only emerged a couple of hundred years ago, rises from the lake's shores in all its ominous glory. It remains highly active and erupted as recently as October 2004. Natural hot springs bubble up within the crater. Locals suffering from skin diseases trek here with medicinal herbs to bathe and scrub.

Treks to the rim, lake and peak are challenging, and guides are mandatory. Climbing Rinjani during the wet season (November to March), when there's a real risk of landslides, is not at all advisable – the national-park office often completely forbids access to Rinjani for the first three months of each year. Between June and August there's minimal rain and few clouds, but come prepared with layers because it gets extremely cold at the summit.

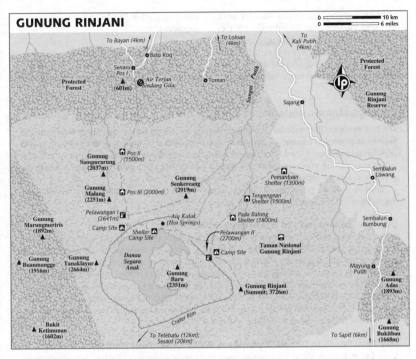

## GUNUNG RINJANI

Senaru has the best services for trekkers, and many treks begin there. This adds about 1000 vertical metres to the itinerary, so wise guides drive their guests to Sembalun Lawang on the eastern slope, and begin hiking from there.

### Organised Treks

The best and least expensive way to organise a trip is to head to either the Rinjani Trek Centre (p505) in Senaru or the Rinjani Information Centre (p505) in Sembalun Lawang. The centres use a rotation system so that all local guides get a slice of the trekking purse. And though guides are always eager for a gig, they are laid-back and easy to work with.

Whether you book through your losmen, or directly at the RTC or RIC, the same trek packages are offered, but in Senaru the prices often vary depending on demand and level of luxury. The most popular is the three-day, two-night trek from Senaru to Sembalun Lawang via the summit. It includes food, equipment, guide, porters, park fee and transport back to Senaru. This costs about 1,750,000Rp per person. An overnight trek to the crater rim from Senaru costs 1,000,000Rp for one person, 900,000Rp per head for two people and 750,000Rp per head for three.

Two Senaru outfitters stand out. **John's Adventures** ( ☎ 0817 578 8018; www.lombok-rinjani trek.com; per person 1,750,000Rp) has been leading Rinjani climbs since 1982. He has toilet tents, offers four meals a day, provides thick sleeping mats and starts hiking from Sembalun. **Galang Jo Expedition** ( ☎ 0819 1740 4198; for 2 people 2,300,000Rp) has competitive prices and a network of experienced guides.

In Sembalun Lawang the prices are uniform. Summit attempts cost 2,300,000Rp for two people; the per-person price falls for larger groups. All-day hikes to the crater rim (6am to 6pm) cost 1,500,000Rp per person.

### Guides & Porters

Hiking independently is prohibited, but if you abhor all-inclusive trekking packages, you can hire guides (100,000Rp per day) and porters (80,000Rp) at day rates. You'll have to bring your own camping gear and supplies. Make sure you take a radio

(10,000Rp per day) as well. Contract your guides and porters directly from the centres in Senaru and Sembalun Lawang. Guides are knowledgeable and informative, but won't carry anything for you, so take at least one porter. You'll need to arrange transport, and

bring ample food and water for you and your support team.

## Entrance Fee & Equipment

The entrance fee for the Gunung Rinjani National Park has ballooned to 150,000Rp –

### CLIMBING GUNUNG RINJANI

The best route on the mountain is the five-day trek (described below) that starts at Senaru and finishes at Sembalun Lawang. A strenuous dash from Senaru to the crater rim and back is also popular among short-timers. This trek is outlined on the Gunung Rinjani map (Map p507). A better map can be purchased from the Rinjani Trek Centre (RTC; p505) in Senaru – it is large, glossy and easy to understand.

Rinjani's trails are often closed during the wet season, particularly after heavy rainfall when the trail around the lake is vulnerable to land- and rockslides.

#### Day One: Senaru Pos I to Pos III (Five to Six Hours)

At the southern end of the village is the Rinjani Trek Centre (Pos I, 601m), where you register and pay the park fee. Just beyond the post, the trail forks – continue on the right fork. The trail climbs steadily through scrubby farmland to the signed entrance of Gunung Rinjani National Park. The wide trail climbs for another 2½ hours until you reach Pos II (1500m), where there's a shelter. Water can be found 100m down the slope from the trail, but it should be treated or boiled.

Another 1½ hours' steady ascent brings you to Pos III (2000m), where there are two shelters in disrepair. Water is 100m off the trail to the right, but sometimes evaporates in the dry season. Pos III is the place to camp at the end of the first day.

#### Day Two: Pos III to Danau Segara Anak & Aiq Kalak (Four Hours)

From Pos III, it takes about 1½ hours to reach the rim, Pelawangan I (2641m). Set off very early for the stunning sunrise. It's possible to camp at Pelawangan I, but level sites are limited, there's no water and it can be blustery.

It takes about two hours to descend to Danau Segara Anak and around to Aiq Kalak (hot springs). The first hour is a very steep descent and involves boulder-hopping. From the bottom of the crater wall it's an easy 30-minute walk across undulating terrain around the lake's edge. There are several places to camp, but most prefer to rest and recuperate near the hot springs. There are some caves nearby which are interesting but are not adequate shelter. The nicest campsites are at the lake's edge. Fresh water can be gathered from a spring near Aiq Kalak. The climb back up the rim is taxing – allow at least three hours and start early to make it back to Senaru in one day. Allow five hours from the rim down to Senaru. Or instead of retracing your steps, complete the Rinjani trek by continuing to Sembalun Lawang, where you can arrange transport back to Senaru (see p506).

#### Day Three: Aiq Kalak to Pelawangan II (Three to Four Hours)

The trail starts beside the last shelter at the hot springs and heads away from the lake for about 100m before veering right. It then traverses the northern slope of the crater, for an easy one-hour walk along the grassy slopes before you hit a steep, unforgiving rise; from the lake it takes about three hours to reach the crater rim (2639m). At the rim, a sign points the way back to Danau Segara Anak. Water can be found down the slope near the sign. The trail forks here – go straight on to Lawang or continue along the rim to the campsite of Pelawangan II (2700m). It's only about 10 minutes more to the campsite, which is on a bare ridge.

#### Day Four: Pelawangan II to Rinjani Summit (Five to Six Hours Return)

Gunung Rinjani stretches in an arc above the campsite at Pelawangan II and looks deceptively close. Start the climb at 3am in order to reach the summit in time for the sunrise and before the clouds roll in.

register and pay at the RTC in Senaru or the RIC in Sembalun Lawang before you begin climbing.

Sleeping bags and tents can be hired at either RTC or RIC. You'll also need solid footwear, layers of warm clothing, wet-weather gear, cooking equipment and a torch (flashlight), but these can also be hired from the RTC. Expect to pay about 75,000Rp a head per day for all your equipment.

Poaching firewood at high altitude is an environmental no-no, so take a stove. Also

---

It takes about 45 minutes to clamber up a steep, slippery and indistinct trail to the ridge that leads to Rinjani. Once on the ridge, it's a relatively easy walk uphill. That peak you see ahead isn't the finish line. After an hour, the real summit of Rinjani looms above you.

The trail gets steeper and steeper, and with just 350m to go before the summit, your footing deteriorates into loose scree – it's easiest to scramble on all fours. This section can take about an hour. The views from the top are magnificent on a clear day. In total it takes three hours or more to reach the summit, and two to get back down.

### Day Five: Pelawangan II to Sembalun Lawang (Five to Six Hours)

After bagging the peak, it's possible to reach Lawang the same day. After a two-hour descent, it's a long and hot three-hour walk back to the village. Head off early and make sure you've brought along plenty of water. From the campsite, head back along the ridge-crest trail. A couple of hundred metres past the turn-off to Danau Segara Anak there is a signposted right turn leading down a subsidiary ridge to Pada Balong and Sembalun Lawang. Once on the trail, it's easy to follow and takes around two hours to reach the bottom.

At the bottom of the ridge (where you'll find Pada Balong shelter; 1800m) the trail levels out and crosses undulating grassland all the way to Sembalun Lawang. After about an hour you will hit the Tengengean shelter (1500m); it's then another 30 minutes to Pemantuan shelter (1300m). Early in the season, long grass obscures the trail until about 30 minutes beyond Pemantuan. The trail crosses many bridges; at the final bridge, just before it climbs uphill to a lone tree, the trail seems to fork; take the right fork and climb the rise. From here, the trail follows the flank of Rinjani before swinging around to Lawang at the end. As always, a guide is essential.

### Variations

- Compress the last two days into one (racking up a hefty 10 to 11 hours on the trail). On the plus side, it's downhill all the way after the hard climb to the summit.

- Retrace your steps to Senaru after climbing to the summit, making a five-day circuit that includes another night at the hot springs.

- Another popular route is a three-day trek from Senaru to the hot springs and back. The first night is spent at Pos III and the second at the hot springs. The return to Senaru on the final day takes eight to nine hours.

- For (almost) instant gratification (if you travel light and climb fast), you can reach the crater rim from Senaru in about six hours. You'll gain an altitude of approximately 2040m in 10km. Armed with a torch (flashlight), some moonlight and a guide, set off at midnight to arrive for sunrise. The return takes about five hours.

- If you reach Pelawangan I early in the day, consider taking a side trip east along the crater rim for about 3km to Gunung Senkereang (2919m). This point overlooks the gap in the rim where the stream that comes from the hot springs flows down towards the sea. It's not an easy walk, however, and the track is narrow and very exposed in places – if you decide to do it, allow two hours.

- Start trekking from Sembalun Lawang, from where it takes six or seven hours to get to Pelawangan II. This is a shorter walk to the rim than from Senaru, with only a three-hour trek up the ridge.

pack up your rubbish, including toilet tissues. As the saying goes, 'take only pictures, leave only footprints'.

Excess baggage can be left at most losmen in Senaru or the RTC for 5000Rp per day.

## Food & Supplies

Trek organisers at RTC and RIC arrange food supplies. If you bring your own, buy most of your supplies in the Mataram markets, where it's cheaper and there's more choice. Bring a lighter, and drink more water than seems reasonable. Dehydration can spur altitude sickness.

## Getting There & Away

For transport options from Sembalun Lawang to Senaru, see p506. If you've purchased a trekking package, transport back to your point of origin is included.

## TETEBATU
☎ 0376

Laced with spring-fed streams and canals, sprinkled with traditional villages and blessed with rich soil, Tetebatu is a Sasak breadbasket. The surrounding countryside is quilted with tobacco and rice fields, fruit orchards and cow pastures that fade into remnant monkey forest where you'll find some fabulous waterfalls. At 400m it's also high enough on Rinjani's lower slopes to mute that hot, sticky coastal mercury. Dark nights come saturated in sound courtesy of a frog orchestra accompanied by countless gurgling brooks. Even insomniacs snore here.

Though small, the town is actually quite spread out, with facilities on roads north and east (nicknamed 'waterfall road') of the *ojek* stop in the centre of the village. There's a **wartel** (✆ 9am-9pm) next to Salabuse Cafe, but internet has yet to arrive.

## Sights & Activities

A shady 4km track leads from the main road, just north of the mosque, into **Taman Wisata Tetebatu** (Monkey Forest) with black monkeys and two waterfalls. Both waterfalls are accessible by private transport or a spectacular two-hour walk (one way) through rice fields from Tetebatu. If walking, hire a guide (80,000Rp to 100,000Rp), easily found through your hotel. The best ones describe the vegetation and village life, and make the experience even richer.

Locals still believe that water from **Air Terjun Jukut** (admission 20,000Rp) will increase hair growth. So if baldness frightens you, wade over and let the frigid cascade rain down on your man-scalp. It's a 2km walk from the car park at the end of the road.

Northwest of Tetebatu, **Air Terjun Joben** (admission 20,000Rp) is more of a public pool.

## Sleeping & Eating

**Pondok Tetebatu** ( ☎ 632 572; s/d 60,000/80,000Rp) North of the intersection, these detached, ranch-style rooms set around a flower garden are basic and could be cleaner, but the staff are fantastic, the restaurant, which specialises in Sasak cooking, is a good bet, and they offer guided walks through the villages and to the falls (50,000/80,000Rp village walk/falls walk).

**our pick** **Cendrawasih Cottages** ( ☎ 0818 0372 6709; r 90,000Rp) Sweet little *lumbung*-style cottages nestled in the rice fields. You'll sit on floor cushions in their stunning stilted restaurant, which has Sasak, Indonesian or Western grub (7000Rp to 22,000Rp) and 360-degree paddy views. It's about 500m east of the intersection.

**Wisma Soedjono** ( ☎ 21309; d 150,000-200,000Rp; ⚟ ) About 2km north of the intersection, these basic, functional rooms (with thin walls) and lovely two-storey, chalet-style cottages (with both balconies and verandahs) are scattered around the grounds of a rambling family farm.

**Green Orry** ( ☎ 632 233; cottages incl breakfast 175,000Rp) Twenty of the newest and cleanest rooms in town. It's a large, family-run place, and when the town blacks out (a frequent occurrence), they still have juice.

**Bale Bale** ( ☎ 0828 375 8688; dishes 10,000-22,000Rp) Tastefully candlelit, this streetside cafe has outstanding local food, such as fiery *pelecing kangkung* (spinach in tomato sauce) and Lombok-style *gado gado*. The friendly owner pours free shots of rice wine when the electricity falters.

## Getting There & Around

Public transport to this end of Lombok is infrequent and unpredictable. Buses do go from Mandalika terminal in Mataram to Pomotong (10,000Rp), on the main east–west highway. On market days (Monday and Wednesday) catch a bemo from here to Kotaraja (2000Rp), and an *ojek* (3000Rp) or *cidomo* (4000Rp) to Tetebatu.

Private cars (with drivers) can be arranged at Pondok Tetebatu (opposite) to all of Lombok's main destinations (250,000Rp to 500,000Rp for up to four passengers).

Pondok Tetebatu also rents bicycles and motorbikes for 15,000Rp and 50,000Rp per day, respectively.

## SOUTH OF TETEBATU

The nearest market town to Tetebatu is **Kotaraja**, the transport hub of the area. It's known for its skilled blacksmiths, and in August you can take in the annual **Sasak Stick Fighting** festivities. Fights are fierce, but end gracefully at the first sight of blood. There's a market on Monday and Wednesday mornings.

**Loyok** is noted for its fine basketry and **Rungkang** is known for its pottery, made from local black clay. You'll find home workshops in both villages.

**Masbagik** is a large town on Lombok's east–west highway with a huge cattle market on Monday afternoon, an imposing new mosque with elegant minarets, and the region's only reliable ATM. Look for the BCA sign opposite the mosque. **Masbagik Timur**, 1km east, is a centre for black-clay pottery and ceramic production.

## SOUTH LOMBOK

☎ 0370

Beaches just don't come any better. The water is warm, striped turquoise and curls into barrels. The sand is silky and snow-white, framed by massive headlands. And village life is still vibrant. You'll see seaweed and tobacco harvests, duck into tribal homes and listen to Sasak drum corps. Southern Lombok is noticeably drier and more sparsely populated, with limited roads and public transport, for now. But with long-anticipated hotel development on the immediate horizon, authentic tropical tranquillity may be on its way out. Especially in Kuta – which is the antithesis of Bali's version and the south coast's best base. Come soon.

## Praya

pop 37,000

Praya sprawls, with tree-lined streets and a few Dutch colonial relics. There's nothing of much interest right now, however, except a couple of ATMs on Jl Jend Sudirman, but soon Lombok's new international airport (at the time of writing due to open in 2010) will be

here, boosting the local economy – especially in the surrounding crafts villages. Until then, the bemo terminal, on the northwest side of town, is the transport hub for the region.

### Around Praya

Sukarara's main street is the domain of textile shops, where you can watch weavers work their looms. **Dharma Setya** ( ☎ 660 5204; ◷ 8am–5pm) has an incredible array of hand-woven Sasak textiles, including ikat and *songket*.

To reach Sukarara from Praya, take a bemo to Puyung along the main road. From there, hire a *cidomo* or walk the 2km to Sukarara.

### Penujak

Penujak is well known for its traditional *gerabah* pottery, made from chocolate-coloured terracotta, hand-burnished, and topped with braided bamboo. The pots are gorgeous, dirt-cheap and for sale in humble home studios. The best of the bunch belongs to **Wadiah** ( ☎ 0819 3316 0391), a local potter who is all smiles and has a terrific inventory. Find her opposite the cemetery.

Penujak is on the main road from Praya to the south coast; any bemo to Sengkol or Kuta will drop you off.

### Rembitan & Sade

The area from Sengkol down to Kuta is a centre for traditional Sasak culture where you can tour working Sasak villages, meet the villagers, check out their decorative rice barns *(lumbung)* and sip coffee in their homes, crafted from bamboo, mud, cow and buffalo dung and called *bale tani*.

Rembitan, aka Sasak Village, is on a hill just west of the main road. Forget the theme-park moniker, it boasts an authentic cluster of thatched houses and *lumbung*. Teens from the village offer short but interesting walking tours where they'll fill you in on village life. **Masjid Kuno**, an ancient thatched-roof mosque, crowns the nearby hill. It's a pilgrimage destination for Lombok's Muslims, as one of the founding fathers of Indonesian Islam is buried here.

A little further south is Sade, another traditional, picturesque village that has been extensively renovated. Many Sade villagers actually work and live part-time in Kuta. Donations are 'requested' by guides at both villages – 30,000Rp is enough, but you may have to pay extra for photos.

**NUSA TENGGARA**

## Kuta

Imagine a crescent bay – turquoise in the shallows and deep-blue further out. It licks a wide white-sand beach, backed by swaying trees and framed by domelike headlands. It's deserted – save a few fishermen, seaweed farmers and their children. Now imagine a coastline of nearly a dozen just like it, all backed by a dry, rugged range of coastal hills patched with lush tobacco fields, and you'll have a vague idea of Kuta's majesty.

For years it's been an under-the-radar surf paradise, thanks to the world-class beach and reef breaks within 30 minutes' drive, and the international packs of surfers who congregate here in August. But it's not all about the waves. The local, fun-loving Sasaks saturate Kuta with their charm, and the motley assortment of barefoot bars and cafes serve some terrific meals and good conversation. Unfortunately, this incarnation of Kuta is on the clock.

There have been whispers linking resort developers to Kuta's pristine coastline for nearly a decade. Now a Dubai development firm is involved, $600 million has been put on the table, and road construction to what folks on the ground claim will be a new Ritz Carlton began in January 2009 (see boxed text, below). Will this project involve a few well-placed, exclusive resorts or will it become another Nusa Dua? Nobody but the suits knows for sure, and they haven't been completely forthcoming. What is clear is that if you want to catch the last throes of Kuta natural, you'd better book now.

### INFORMATION & ORIENTATION

Several places change money, including the Kuta Indah Hotel (about 400m west of the junction) and Segare Anak Cottages (some 800m east of the junction), which is also a postal agency.

There's a wartel in town, and **Ketapang Cafe** (☺ 8am-11pm) has slow but functional internet access. The **market** fires up on Sunday and Wednesday.

Virtually everything in Kuta is on a single road that parallels the beach, and intersects the road from Praya.

### ACTIVITIES

#### Surfing

Plenty of good 'lefts' and 'rights' break on the reefs in Teluk Kuta, and more on the reefs east of Tanjung Aan. If you're after a reef break, local boatmen will buzz you out for around 70,000Rp. About 7km east of Kuta is the fishing village of **Gerupak**, where there are five reef breaks, including those way out by the mouth of the bay that demand a boat. The current charter rate is a negotiable 200,000Rp per day. West of Kuta, **Mawi** is absolutely gorgeous and offers consistent world-class surf. Expect company in the high season. Local surfers are privy to another handful of hidden breaks. If you happen to befriend one, you'll likely dodge the crowds and surf in relative peace.

Drop by the friendly, professional **Kimen Surf** (☎ 655 064; www.kuta-lombok.net), just west

---

### THE KUTA SITUATION

Emaar Property, a Dubai development concern, is poised to transform Kuta's pristine coast. The team planned their US$600 million takeover from Astari (see p514). We spoke to Gaz, one of the restaurant's owners, watched unnoticed as they unfurled blueprints and eyed a plot of land that stretches from the west end of Teluk Kuta to the east end of Tanjung Aan. Construction of a widened road to the site of their first new five-star hotel (possibly a Ritz Carlton) began at Tanjung Aan in January 2009. All the small businesses on Kuta's main road are in danger of being bulldozed when it too doubles in size.

Kuta's sea change was just a matter of time. Tommy Suharto, the former dictator's ne'er-do-well son, stockpiled coastal property for years, under an Indonesian law that allows government ministers to force owners to sell their land at will. But every time he began to build, locals torched the construction site, so he sold out to Dubai. Whether the Dubai developers bring economic opportunity, ecological and cultural awareness, or all of the above, remains to be seen.

Nobody in Kuta knows exactly what is about to happen; in Indonesia developers are not required to divulge information to the public. The public voice is still not very strong and there is a lack of consistent development standards. But the Emaar Property spokesman in Jakarta did tell us that 'this project involves multiple luxury hotels and golf courses and will be rolled out over the next 10 to 15 years.' Sounds like Nusa Dua to us.

of the junction, for swell forecasts, tips and information. Boards can be rented here (50,000Rp per day), repairs undertaken, lessons are offered (360,000Rp, four hours) and so are guided day trips. **Gloro** ( ☎ 0818 0576 5690) rents boards (35,000Rp per day) and offers lessons (200,000Rp, four hours).

### Diving

**Dive Zone** ( ☎ 660 3205; www.divezone-lombok.com) has two locations, one in town and the other at the Novotel Lombok Resort. They dive in Teluk Kuta (US$80 for two tanks) and at **Magnet** (US$120 for two tanks), a site famous for schooling hammerheads.

### SLEEPING

All accommodation is on or within walking distance of the beach, except for Mimpi Manis. Breakfast is included.

### Budget

**our pick** **Seger Reef Homestay** ( ☎ 655 528; r 80,000-100,000Rp) Ignore the ramshackle courtyard because these bright, spotless, family-owned bungalows across the street from the beach are the sweetest deal in town.

**Mimpi Manis** ( ☎ 0818 369 950; www.mimpimanis .com; s/d 80,000/130,000Rp; ✦ ) An inviting English-Balinese-owned guest house with two spotless rooms in a two-storey house, all with en suite shower and TV/DVD player. There's home-cooked food, plenty of good books to browse and DVDs to borrow. It's 2km inland from the beach, but the owners offer a free drop-off service and arrange bike and motorbike rental.

**Rinjani Bungalows** ( ☎ 654 849; s/d with fan 80,000/95,000Rp, with air-con 200,000/250,000Rp; ✦ ) This well-run place, situated 1km east of the junction, offers very clean bamboo bungalows with ikat bedspreads. The spacious, newer concrete bungalows have two double beds, hot water, hardwood furniture and cable TV.

**G'Day Inn** ( ☎ 655 342; s/d 90,000/100,000Rp) This friendly, family-run place offers clean rooms (some with hot water), as well as a cafe.

**Melon Homestay** ( ☎ 0817 367 892; r 100,000Rp, apt 150,000Rp) This place has two sweet apartments with a lounge and self-catering facilities, one with sea views from its balcony. There are a couple of smaller modern rooms with verandah and bathroom. It's about 400m east of the junction.

**Bungalow Anda** ( ☎ 655 049; r with fan/air-con 120,000/150,000Rp; ✦ ) Tiled bungalows are relatively charmless, but management is friendly, it's on the beach road and it tends to have vacancies during the August rush.

**Sekar Kuning** ( ☎ 654 856; r 150,000; ✦ ) A charming beach-road inn. Top-floor rooms have ocean views.

**Matahari Inn** ( ☎ 655 000; www.matahariinn.com; r 175,000-550,000Rp; ✦ ✦ ) Sure, it's OD'd on knick-knacks, but the lush tropical gardens and Balinese polish make it one of Kuta's better options.

**Surfers Inn** ( ☎ 655 582; www.lombok-surfersinn.com; r 180,000-400,000Rp; ✦ ✦ ) A very smart, stylish and orderly place with five classes of modern rooms, each with huge windows and large beds, and some with sofas. Book ahead as it's very popular.

### Top End

**Novotel Lombok** ( ☎ 653 333; www.novotel-lombok .com; r without/with terrace US$105/120, villa US$195, plus 21% tax; ✦ ✦ ) This appealing, Sasak-themed four-star resort spills onto a superb beach 3km east of the junction. Rooms have high sloping roofs and modern interiors. There are two pools, a wonderful spa, good restaurants, a swanky bar and a plethora of activities on offer including catamaran sailing, fishing and scuba diving. European families love it.

### EATING & DRINKING

There are some exceptional dishes hidden within Kuta's largely bland dining scene.

**Family Cafe** ( ☎ 653 748; mains 12,000-30,000Rp) You won't need that thick menu, just order the *sate pusut* (minced fish, chicken or beef mixed with fresh coconut, chilli and spices, moulded and grilled on lemongrass stalks) and *kangkung pelecing* (sautéed water spinach and bean sprouts, topped with tomato sauce and shredded coconut).

**Ketapang Cafe** ( ☎ 0878 6541 5209; meals 12,000-50,000Rp) There are three charming dining pagodas shaded by grass umbrellas, but you should belly up to the fine bamboo bar. The Indonesian fare is tasty and pizzas get rave reviews by the expat locals.

**Astari** (dishes 18,000-25,000Rp; ☟ 8.30am-6pm Tue-Sun) Perched on a mountaintop 2km west of town on the road to Mawan, this breezy, Moroccan-themed vegetarian lounge-restaurant has spectacular vistas of pristine bays and rocky peninsulas that take turns spilling further out to sea. And its delicious, health-conscious menu lives up to the setting. The blackboard always has a daily dish and drink of the day, but the mainstays are the focaccia sandwiches, salads and superb shakes (the coconut shake will make your beverage hall of fame immediately). You will not eat and run.

**our pick** **Lombok Lounge** ( ☎ 655 542) Yes, it has inexpensive Indonesian food and scrolls of pedestrian Western dishes. But you won't need to search the menu because you're here for the scintillating, finger-licking, meaty chilli crab (50,000Rp), a Chinese Indonesian classic. It's more than just the best meal in town, it's a full body experience. Wash it down with icy Bintang.

**Cafe Chili** (Novotel Lombok; breakfast buffet US$10; ☟ 8-10.30am) Breakfast lovers, rejoice! The Novotel opens its bottomless array of Western breakfast delights to all comers. Grab a table seaside and munch deeply.

**Shore Beach Bar** ( ☟ 10am-late, live band on Sat night) Owned by Kimen, Kuta's original surf entrepreneur, the open dance-hall interior has been recently renovated, the sound system is fantastic, there's breezy patio seating, cushy red booths and an expansive bar. If you're in town on a Saturday night, you'll probably wind up here.

### GETTING THERE & AWAY

Kuta is a hassle to reach by public transport. From Mandalika terminal in Mataram you'll have to go to Praya (5000Rp), then Sengkol

(3000Rp) and finally to Kuta (2000Rp). You'll usually have to change buses twice. Most opt for the shuttle-bus option offered by **Perama** ( ☎ 654 846) – from Mataram (125,000Rp, two hours), Senggigi (150,000Rp, 2½ hours) and the Gilis (225,000Rp, 3½ hours), or hire private transport.

### GETTING AROUND

*Ojeks* congregate around the main junction as you enter Kuta. Bemos go east of Kuta to Awang and Tanjung Aan (5000Rp), and west to Selong Blanak (10,000Rp). Most guest houses rent motorbikes for 40,000Rp to 50,000Rp per day.

## Around Kuta

Decent roads traverse the coast to the east and west, passing a seemingly endless series of beautiful bays punctuated by headlands.

The beach within walking distance of town, **Pantai Segar** is about 2km east around the first headland. The enormous rock of **Batu Kotak**, 2km further on, divides two glorious white-sand beaches. Continuing east, **Tanjung Aan** is an idyllic turquoise, horseshoe bay with five powder-white sand beaches. It's also the best swimming beach on this end of Kuta. Regrettably, it won't look like this for much longer (see boxed text, p512). The road continues another 2km to **Gerupak**, the fishing village with a market on Tuesday, a restaurant on the beach and five exceptional surf breaks. Alternatively, turn northeast just before Tanjung Aan and go to **Awang**, a busy fishing village with a sideline in seaweed harvesting. You could take a boat from Awang across the bay to Ekas (a charter costs around 120,000Rp) or to some of the other not-so-secret surf spots in this bay.

West of Kuta is yet another series of awesome beaches that all have sick surf when conditions are right. The road is potholed and very steep in places, detours inland and skirts tobacco, sweet potato and rice fields in between turn-offs to the sand.

The first left after Astari leads to **Mawan** (parking costs 3000/5000Rp for a motorbike/car), a sweet cove with a majestic old shade tree, a wide stretch of white sand that extends into the deep sea, and views of offshore islands. It's a terrific swimming beach when the undertow isn't too treacherous.

The very next left – although it's quite a bit further down the road – leads through a gate (admission 5000Rp) down a horribly rutted track to **Mawi** (parking 5000Rp), 16km from Kuta. Although the white-sand beach is relatively thin, it's still a stunning scene, with several additional beaches scattered around the bay. Surfers descend for the legendary barrels that roll in liberally. Sadly, thefts have been reported here.

After Mawi head back to the main road and when it forks, make a left into **Selong Blanak** village. Park and cross the rickety pedestrian bridge to a wide sugar-white beach with water streaked a thousand colours of blue, ideal for swimming.

From **Pengantap** the road climbs across a headland then descends to another superb bay; follow this around for about 1km, then look out for the turn-off west to **Blongas**, which is a very steep, rough and winding road with breathtaking scenery.

## EAST LOMBOK
☎ 0376

All that most travellers see of the east coast is Labuhan Lombok, the port for ferries to Sumbawa. But the real highlight is the remote southeastern peninsula. If you've ever wondered what Bali's Bukit looked like before all the villages, villas and surf rats, here's your chance.

### Labuhan Lombok
Labuhan Lombok (or Labuhan Kayangan) is the Sumbawa-bound ferry port. The town centre, 3km west of the ferry terminal, is a scruffy place with great views of Gunung Rinjani.

Try to avoid staying overnight as there's only one decent place, **Losmen Lima Tiga** Jl Raya Kayangan; r 55,000Rp). About 2.5km inland from the port on the main road, it's a family-run place with small rooms and shared bathrooms with western toilets and *mandis*. Warungs are scattered around the ferry terminal.

### GETTING THERE & AWAY
#### Bus & Bemo
Frequent buses and bemos travel between Labuhan Lombok and Mandalika terminal in Mataram (11,000Rp, two hours). Buses and bemos that don't go directly to Labuhan Lombok will drop you off at the port entrance, where you should catch another bemo to the ferry terminal. It's a long walk.

#### Ferry
See p517 for details on ferry connections between Lombok and Sumbawa, and p486 for bus connections between Mataram and Sumbawa.

### North Of Labuhan Lombok
Leaving Labuhan Lombok, look out for the giant mahogany trees about 4km north of the harbour. From Labuhan Pandan, or from further north at Sugian, you can charter a boat to the uninhabited **Gili Sulat** and **Gili Pentangan**. Both islands have lovely white beaches and good coral for snorkelling, but no facilities.

### South Of Labuhan Lombok
The capital of the East Lombok administrative district, **Selong**, has some dusty Dutch colonial buildings. The transport junction for the region is just west of Selong at **Pancor** where you can catch bemos to most points south.

**Tanjung Luar** is one of Lombok's main fishing ports and has lots of quaint Bugis-style houses on stilts. From there, the road swings west to **Keruak**, where wooden boats are built, and continues to **Sukaraja**, a traditional Sasak village. Just west of Keruak a road leads south to **Jerowaru** and the spectacular southeastern peninsula.

A sealed road branches west past Jerowaru to **Ekas**, where you'll find a huge bay framed by stunning sheer cliffs on both sides. There are two sensational surf breaks (inside and outside) at Ekas and boat charters to Awang across the bay. Or, you could just find **Heaven on the Planet** (☎ 0812 370 5393; www.heavenontheplanet .co.nz; per person all-inclusive for 5 days or less/6 days or more US$120/100; 🏊). Chalets are scattered among the cliffs (there is one beach chalet), where you'll have mind-blowing bird's-eye views of the sea and swell lines. It's especially magical at sunset, when the rippled bay flashes hot pink then melts into a deep purple, before the light fades and stars carpet a black-dome sky. Although Heaven does offer fun dives (US$37) on a wall

**NUSA TENGGARA**

lit by colourful soft corals, it is primarily a surf resort. From here you can paddle out to the inside break at Ekas or take the boat to the outside break. Heaven's groovy Kiwi owners recently opened a second resort, **Ocean Heaven**, right on Pantai Ekas. Both have tasty food, a full bar, friendly staff, and guests receive massages every second day. Room rates and contact details are the same at both resorts.

The roads here are confusing and pretty terrible, but if you reserve a room in Heaven, their angels provide free transfer. If you're already in Kuta, just charter a boat from Awang (see p514).

# SUMBAWA

Beautifully contorted and sprawling into the sea, Sumbawa is all volcanic ridges, terraced rice fields, jungled peninsulas and sheltered bays. The southwest coast is where Sumbawa is at her most spectacular, with a layered series of headlands and wide, silky white beaches that see incredible surf. The southeast is no slouch. It's also a bit more accessible, which explains why Lakey Peak has become Sumbawa's premier year-round surf magnet. Massive, climbable Gunung Tambora (2850m), a mountain that exploded so large it forever influenced the climate and topography of the island, looms in the north.

Though well connected to Bali and Lombok, Sumbawa is a very different sort of place. It's far less developed, much poorer and extremely conservative. Transport connections off the cross-island road are infrequent and uncomfortable, and most overland travellers don't even get off the bus in Sumbawa as they float and roll from Lombok to Flores. For now, it's the domain of surfers, miners and mullahs. But if you charter transport or rent a motorcycle, and take some time, you'll find more than a little bit of beauty.

## History

Before the 17th century Sumbawa had been subject to Javanese Hindu influence creeping east from Bali and Lombok, but it was the expansionist Makassarese states of Sulawesi who gained control of the island by force and, by 1625, Sumbawa's rulers had converted to Islam.

Soon West Sumbawa held sway over much of Lombok and this brought it into conflict with the Balinese during the 18th century. The wars had barely ceased when Gunung Tambora exploded in April 1815, killing tens of thousands. One of the most cataclysmic eruptions of modern times, it reduced a 4200m peak to approximately 2850m and devastated agricultural land. The following year was known as 'the year without a summer'. The sun was muted worldwide thanks to the tremendous amount of Tamboran ash in the atmosphere.

From the middle of the 19th century, immigrants repopulated Sumbawa, and the island's coastal regions now have small numbers of Javanese, Makassarese, Bugis, Sasaks and other ethnic groups.

In 1908 the Dutch intervened to prevent the prospect of a war between the three states that made up West Sumbawa. The sultans kept a fair degree of their power under the Dutch, but after Indonesian independence their titles were abolished; now their descendants hold official power only when they are functionaries of the national government. The only traces of the old sultanates are the palaces in Sumbawa Besar and Bima.

## Culture

Sumbawa is split between two distinct peoples. Those who speak Sumbawanese probably reached the west of the island from Lombok. Bimanese speakers dominate the Tambora Peninsula and the east. The shorter, darker-skinned and more outgoing Bimanese are more closely related to the people of Flores, while the western, more reserved Sumbawans are closer to the Sasaks of Lombok. Both languages have considerable variation in dialect.

Sumbawa is an overwhelmingly Islamic island, but in remote parts *adat* thrives under the veneer of Islam.

During festivals you may come across traditional Sumbawan fighting, a sort of bare-fisted boxing called *berempah*. Dynamic horse and water-buffalo races are held before the rice is planted.

## Dangers & Annoyances

Most Sumbawans are friendly and hospitable, but you may encounter some tension. Weeks before our arrival in 2009, there was significant civil unrest between the Dou Donggo people, who have long resented Bimanese control, and Bima police. Two died in the standoff.

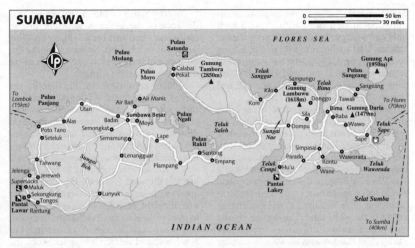

## Getting Around

Sumbawa's main highway is in great condition and runs from Taliwang (near the west coast) through Sumbawa Besar, Dompu and Bima to Sape (on the east coast). Fleets of long-distance buses, most of them air-conditioned and quite comfy, link all the towns on this road as far as Bima.

Car hire is possible through hotels in Sumbawa Besar or Bima, but prices are higher than in Bali or Lombok at about 450,000Rp per day, excluding petrol but including a driver. Plan on paying for your driver's meals and lodging as well. Motorcycles are a far cheaper option at 75,000Rp a day.

## WEST SUMBAWA

☎ 0372

West Sumbawa is drop-dead gorgeous. Beaches are wide, empty, sugar-white, framed with domelike headlands and backed by rolling jungled hills. Bays are just as spectacular, enormous and dynamic. They can be tranquil one hour and fold into overhead barrels the next. Sumbawa Besar is a humble Muslim town with a friendly population and a damn fine morning market. Pulau Moyo, a jungled jewel off the northern shore, has special diving and snorkelling, but it's difficult to access unless, of course, you're rolling with your black Amex at the ready.

## Poto Tano

Poto Tano, the main port for ferries to/from Lombok, is a ramshackle harbour, fringed by stilt-fishing villages with tremendous views of Gunung Rinjani. Pretty place, but there's no need to sleep here.

Ferries run every 45 minutes, 24 hours a day, between Labuhan Lombok and Poto Tano (15,500Rp, 1½ hours). You can also bring your hired car (322,000Rp) or motorcycle (75,000Rp). Through buses from Mataram to Sumbawa Besar or Bima include the ferry fare.

Buses meet the ferry and go to Taliwang (15,000Rp, one hour) and Sumbawa Besar (12,000Rp, two hours).

## Taliwang

It may be the regional capital and transport hub, but Taliwang is just a small, conservative village, 30km south of Poto Tano.

There's a BRI Bank with ATM on the main road, a few internet cafes and plenty of Padang-food warungs. The best eats are found at **Rumah Makan Totang Raja** ( ☎ 81387; Jl Jendral Sudirman 51; dishes 10,000-35,000Rp). Try their *ayam bakar pelecing*, aka *ayam taliwang*.

Buses go from Taliwang to Poto Tano (15,000Rp) almost hourly. Six buses a day head for Mataram (65,000Rp, six hours, last bus at 1.30pm) and around 30 a day go to Sumbawa Besar (25,000Rp, three hours). For Maluk there are two daily buses (10,000Rp, two hours) and regular bemos.

## Around Taliwang

**Lebok Taliwang**, Sumbawa's largest lake, is just off the highway south of Poto Tano. Look for the wetlands dotted with water lilies. **Poto**

**Batu**, 6km from Taliwang, is a favourite swimming spot among locals, with a cave, a blow hole and a decent beach. The muddy flats of **Labuhan-balat** are home to a Bugis stilt-fishing community on a spectacular bay – the first of several you'll see as you head south. It's 7km from Taliwang; take a truck or bemo here, and beware the motorbike buffalo rustlers.

From Taliwang, bemos and trucks run 11km south to Jereweh, from where it is 6km to the remarkable beach and enormous horseshoe bay at **Jelenga**, a humble country village with rice fields, goat farms and a tremendous 'left' break known as Scar Reef. **Sunset View** ( ☎ 0813 3716 7726; tr 200,000Rp) is the chilled-out, rustic surf lodge of your dreams with huge rooms, a ping-pong table, satellite TV, and garden that creeps to the white sand. The kitchen churns out burgers, seafood and curries. **Jelenga Mulia** ( ☎ 0813 5369 1920; bungalows 150,000Rp) is another solid option. The cute, simple beach huts are clean and have private outdoor baths.

## Maluk, Rantung & Sekongkang

As you keep moving south along the west coast, the beaches and bays work hard to outdo one another. Your first stop is the working-class commercial district of **Maluk**, 30km south of Taliwang. Yes, the town is ugly, but the beach is superb. The sand is a blend of white and gold, and the bay is buffered by two headlands: a massive rock to the north, and a long, slender peninsula to the south. Protected by an offshore reef, there's good swimming in the shallows, and when the swell hits, the reef sculpts barrels.

A massive open-pit copper and gold mine about 30km inland of Maluk has driven a wave of development and attracted international and domestic staff from the US, Australia and Java to the area. The Newmont mine employs about 10,000 workers, and had a huge impact on Maluk when it first opened, but most of the expat restaurant and bar traffic has now shifted to **Townside**, a private company enclave complete with health club, golf courses and the best hospital in Sumbawa. You need a personal invite to breach the gates, but you can arrange one with a week's notice. Some spill-over still trickles into Maluk, along with a pinch of the mining proceeds, which reach over 12 billion Rp in an average year. There's a **BNI bank** with ATM on Jl Raya Maluk, adjacent to the Trophy Hotel. Just south, **K-Link** (per hr 5000Rp) offers broadband access on Jl Raya Maluk.

Directly south of Maluk, within walking distance of the beach is **Supersuck**, one of Indonesia's best surf breaks. Many an aging surfer has proclaimed this wave to be the finest barrel of their lives. It only pumps in the dry season (May to October).

Fifteen kilometres further south, the spread-out settlement of **Sekongkang** includes three superb beaches with another handful of tremendous breaks. Pantai Rantung, 2km downhill from Sekongkang Atas, spills onto a secluded and majestic bay framed by 100m-high headlands. The water is crystal-clear and waves roll in year-round at **Yo Yo's**, a right break at the north end of the bay. **Hook**, which breaks at the edge of the northern bluff, is also a terrific right. **Supershit**, which breaks straight in front of the Rantung Beach Hotel, is a good, consistent beginner's break year-round, but gets heavy and delivers a long left when the swell comes in. The next bay down is where you'll find **Tropical**, another phenomenal beach (named for the resort) and home to great left and right breaks that beginners can enjoy all year. North of Rantung is Pantai **Lawar**, a tree-shaded stretch of white sand on a turquoise lagoon sheltered by volcanic bluffs draped in jungle. When the surf is flat, come here to swim, snorkel or spearfish.

### SLEEPING & EATING

The following hotels are listed in geographical order.

**Maluk Resort** ( ☎ 635 424; Jl Pasir Putih, Maluk; standard/deluxe 200,000/250,000Rp; ✖ ) One block west of the main road and steps from the sand is this pleasant, palm-studded three-star resort. Rooms are spotless with queen beds, wood furnishings, air-con and ceiling fans.

**Super Suck Hotel** ( ☎ 0812 3637 3122; jwscafe@yahoo.com; Maluk; dm 50,000Rp, standard with Western-style shared bath 200,000Rp, deluxe 400,000Rp; ✖ ☎ ) Accessible from Pantai Maluk or via the half-paved strip that meets the Maluk–Sekongkang road. Deluxe rooms are large and come with HBO and Cinemax, hot water and queen beds. The smaller, shared rooms also have cable TV and are quite clean. The American owner serves tasty Western breakfasts, burgers and seafood. He'll even arrange transport to the lodge from Mataram or Poto Tano if you email him in advance. Book ahead during the surf season.

**Rantung Beach Hotel** ( ☎ 0878 6393 5758; Rantung; s/d 50,000/80,000Rp; ✖ ) The region's cheapest option attracts budget surfers to their somewhat ramshackle rooms (which come with fans and mosquito nets). The young, hip Sasak-born management are full of surf tips and good vibrations.

**Rantung Restaurant & Cottages** ( ☎ 0812 375 4456; Rantung; cottages 650,000Rp; dishes 30,000-70,000Rp) Next door, the expat and Javanese mining crowd has enjoyed more than a few sundowners at this fantastic beach location. The food won't win any awards, but the new stylish cottages are the best beachfront option in the region. There are high ceilings, queen beds, nice wooden wardrobes, hot water, and they open onto leafy private decks with sea views.

**Depot Balikpapan** (Pantai Wisata Maluk, Maluk; meals 20,000-50,000Rp) Its fish-grill aroma stands out among the other stalls in Maluk's thatched beach dining complex, in a very good way. Fish plates come with a snarling, spicy *sambal* (chilli sauce).

**Lesehan Bu Diah** (0818 0525 4022, Jl Raya Maluk, Maluk; meals 10,000-80,000Rp; ☼ 11am-10pm) Sit cross-legged on the floor of wooden pagodas and dine on fresh seafood and Chinese Indo faves overlooking an artificial pond in a leafy garden. Located on Maluk's far south end, it gets a nice local dinner crowd.

### GETTING THERE & AWAY

Bemos travel between Taliwang and Maluk (10,000Rp, 2 hours) almost hourly from 7am to 6pm. Three buses leave Terminal Maluk, north of town across from the entrance to the Newmont mine (look for the big gates and massive parking area), for Sumbawa Besar (30,000Rp, four hours) at 7am, noon and 7pm daily.

## SUMBAWA BESAR

☎ 0371 / pop 56,000

Sumbawa Besar, often shortened to 'Sumbawa', is the principal market town of the island's western hemisphere. It's leafy, devoutly Muslim, and runs on the bushels of beans, rice and corn cultivated on the outskirts. It's also quite friendly and easy to navigate on foot, by *ojek* or horse cart (called *benhur*). There's not a lot to see here aside from the old palace (assuming it does eventually get rebuilt), a lazy mocha river that meanders through town and a lively morning market. Trips out to Pulau Moyo and to nearby villages are worthwhile but take time and money, which is why most travellers simply consider this town a respite on the trans-Sumbawa highway.

### Orientation

Sumbawa Besar is mostly doable on foot. Traffic runs in a high-speed Jl Hasanuddin–Jl Diponegoro loop. The best sleeping and eating options are clustered along Jl Hasanuddin.

### Information

**Bank Mega** (Jl Diponegoro 55; ☼ 8am-2.30pm Mon-Fri, 8am-noon Sat) ATM and cash advances available.

**BNI** (Jl Kartini 10; ☼ 8am-2.30pm Mon-Fri, 8am-noon Sat) Currency exchange and an ATM. There's also an ATM on Jl Kebayan, next to the supermarket.

**Klinik Lawang Gali** ( ☎ 270 5993; Jl Sudirman 18-20; per hr 11,000Rp) Brand-new hospital with ambulance services.

**Main post office** (Jl Garuda)

**Perlindungan Hutan dan Konservasi Alam** (PHKA; ☎ 23941; ☼ 8am-3pm Mon-Fri) The office of the national-park service has information about Pulau Moyo and can occasionally offer transport to the island for just 10,000Rp per person. It's about 4km southwest of town in the village of Nijang; take a bemo from the roundabout on Jl Garuda.

**Sejoli.Net** (Jl Hasanuddin 50; per hr 5000Rp; ☼ 8am-1am) Surf well for cheap.

**Sub-post office** (Jl Yos Sudarso) Closer to the town centre.

**Telkom** (Jl Yos Sudarso; ☼ 24hr) Still the cheapest place to make international calls.

**Tourist office** ( ☎ 23714; Jl Bungur 1; ☼ 7am-2pm Mon-Thu, to 11am Fri, to 1pm Sat) Just off Jl Garuda, 100m south of the main post office on the edge of town. Expect nothing more than a few brochures.

### Sights

Originally built over 200 years ago, the remains of the **Dalam Loka** (Sultan's Palace), a once-imposing structure that covers an entire city block, had deteriorated until near dereliction by the 1980s. A shoddy subsequent renovation included an ill-fitted tin roof hammered to the few remaining original pillars and carved beams, which is why Japanese archaeologists, with blessings from the Indonesian government, had dismantled it to the frame and were in the midst of a complete restoration at research time.

The descendants of the sultans now live in the **Balai Kuning** (Yellow House; ☎ 21101; Jl Dr Wahidin; tours for up to 10 people 100,000Rp), a handsome whitewashed mansion with a peaked shingled roof that was gifted to the royals by the Dutch on 11 February 1932. There are numerous artefacts from the days of the sultanate here. Call the day before to arrange a tour; otherwise admire it from **Sultan's Park** across the street.

NUSA TENGGARA

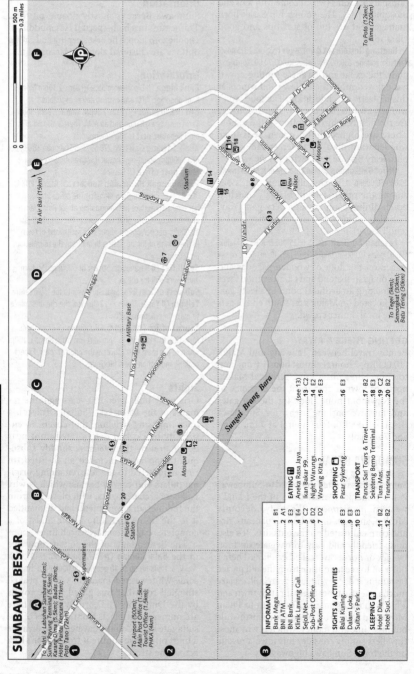

# SUMBAWA BESAR

0    500 m
0    0.3 miles

| INFORMATION | |
|---|---|
| Bank Mega | 1 B1 |
| BNI ATM | 2 A1 |
| BNI Bank | 3 E3 |
| Klinik Lawang Gali | 4 E4 |
| Sejoli.Net | 5 C2 |
| Sub-Post Office | 6 D2 |
| Telkom | 7 D2 |

| SIGHTS & ACTIVITIES | |
|---|---|
| Balai Kuning | 8 E3 |
| Dalam Loka | 9 E3 |
| Sultan's Park | 10 E3 |

| SLEEPING | |
|---|---|
| Hotel Dian | 11 B2 |
| Hotel Suci | 12 B2 |

| EATING | |
|---|---|
| Aneka Rasa Jaya | (see 13) |
| Ikan Bakar 99 | 13 C2 |
| Night Warungs | 14 E2 |
| Warung Kita 2 | 15 E3 |

| SHOPPING | |
|---|---|
| Pasar Syketeng | 16 E3 |

| TRANSPORT | |
|---|---|
| Panca Sari Tours & Travel | 17 B2 |
| Seketeng Bemo Terminal | 18 E3 |
| Tiara Mas | 19 C2 |
| Transnusa | 20 B2 |

Since you are waking up in Sumbawa, rise early and hit the steamy, exotic **Pasar Syketeng**. Beginning at 7am, its dank alleyways come alive as young and old descend to barter and haggle for every conceivable item from bras to live chickens. The fish market is interesting and the spicy aroma of chilli and turmeric compete with recently slaughtered beef for your olfactory attention. Locals are always happy to laugh and chat if you produce even a modicum of Bahasa Indonesia.

## Sleeping

Hotels congregate on Jl Hasanuddin. The nearby mosque provides free wake-up calls.

**Hotel Dian** ( ☎ 21708, 22297; Jl Hasanuddin 69; s/d with fan 45,000/60,000Rp, with air-con 90,000/135,000Rp; ✷ ) There's a wide variety of rooms here, and the best have air-con and spring beds. The worst feel like concrete cells. Still, it's reasonably clean and hospitable.

**our pick** **Hotel Suci** ( ☎ 21589; Jl Hasanuddin 57; d with fan 60,000Rp, with air-con 150,000Rp; ✷ ) Right next to the mosque is the top of the local lodging heap. Economy rooms aren't great, but the air-con rooms in the new building are large and airy, with high ceilings, and are reasonably clean. Service here is top-notch. It isn't fancy, but it feels good.

**Hotel Pantai Kencana** ( ☎ 270 8855; Jl Raya Tano Km 11; bungalows standard/deluxe 300,000/350,000Rp; ✷ ✷ ) A bit out of town, the grounds have seen better days. Still, the wooden bungalows are decent and on the beach. Deluxe bungalows come outfitted with air-con, TV and minibar, but it's the standard variety that enjoys the breeze and sea views.

## Eating

**Warung Kita 2** ( ☎ 23065; Jl Setiabudi 13; dishes 9000-17,000Rp) A bright, delicious pick 'n' mix diner with trays of broiled chicken, tasty fried shrimp, and curried green beans.

**Aneka Rasa Jaya** ( ☎ 21291, 23670; Jl Hasanuddin 16; dishes 12,000-55,000Rp) Clean and popular, this Chinese seafood house plates tender fish fillets, shrimp, squid, crab and scallops in oyster, Szechuan, and sweet and sour sauce. The *soto kepiting* (crab soup) is particularly popular.

**Ikan Bakar 99** ( ☎ 21102; Jl Hasanuddin 15; dishes 15,000-45,000Rp) Yes, the environs are not so savoury, but they do have tasty fresh seafood, and lots of it. Choose shrimp, squid, crab or fish and pair it with spicy Padang, oyster or butter sauce. Get it fried or grilled.

For cheap eats, make your way to the night warungs in front of the stadium, where you'll find sate sizzling.

## Getting There & Away

### AIR

At research time **Transnusa** ( ☎ 21565, 21370; Jl Hasanuddin 110) was Sumbawa Besar's only active carrier, with daily flights to Denpasar via Mataram. Flights depart at 8am Monday to Thursday and at 2.30pm Friday to Sunday. Departure tax is 10,000Rp.

### BUS

Sumbawa Besar's main long-distance bus station is **Terminal Sumur Payung**, 5.5km northwest of town on the highway, where seven bus lines run air-con coaches to Bima (90,000Rp, seven hours via Dompu) departing between 2pm and 3pm. Routes also include Poto Tano (25,000Rp, three hours, hourly 8am to midnight), Mataram (65,000Rp to 70,000Rp including ferry, six hours, departures at 8am, 10am and 9pm) and Denpasar (225,000Rp including ferries, around 12 hours, two daily). You can book tickets at **Tiara Mas** ( ☎ 21241; Jl Yos Sudarso). **Panca Sari Tours & Travel** ( ☎ 21513; Jl Diponegoro 49) books faster minibuses to Mataram (110,000Rp, departures 5.30am and 10.30pm).

## Getting Around

There are no taxis awaiting your arrival, but it's easy to walk into town from the airport, just 500m from the hotel cluster. Turn to your right as you exit the terminal and cross the bridge. Alternatively, take a yellow bemo (2000Rp) or an *ojek* (3000Rp).

The streets here, apart from the bemo speedway along Jl Hasanuddin, are relatively stress-free. Bemo and *benhur* cost 2000Rp for trips anywhere around town. The local **Seketeng bemo terminal** (Jl Setiabudi) is in front of the *pasar* (market).

A Kijang is 450,000Rp with a driver. Sumbawa's longest-tenured tour guide, **Gitasyata 'Iyat'** ( ☎ 0852 5366 4574), is knowledgeable, warm and easy to work with. He speaks terrific English. Motorcycles are best arranged in Lombok and ferried over to Poto Tano.

## AROUND SUMBAWA BESAR

All these attractions are tricky to reach by public transport. Ask at Hotel Suci (left) about hiring a local guide and transport charters.

## Pulau Moyo

A gently arcing crescent of jungled volcanic rock, Moyo – all 36,000 hectares of it – floats atop the gorgeous azure seas north of Sumbawa Besar. The same size as Singapore, it has almost no commercial development and is peopled by just five small villages. The majority of the island, and the rich reefs offshore, form a nature reserve laced with hiking and biking trails, dripping with waterfalls and offering some of the best diving west of Komodo. Loggerhead and green turtles hatch on the beaches, long-tail macaques patrol the canopy, and wild pigs, barking deer and a diverse bird population including megapodes all call Moyo home.

Unfortunately, accommodation is limited to just one expensive (like 'if you have to ask, you can't afford it' expensive) resort, but it is possible to visit Moyo on a day trip.

For transport contact the PHKA office (p519) in Sumbawa Besar; they may be able to shuttle you over for 10,000Rp per person. Otherwise, head to Air Bari, which is on the coast north of Sumbawa Besar. Public bemos (7000Rp, one hour) run to Air Bari three or four times daily, starting at around 7am. They leave from the turn-off to Air Bari, at the far end of Jl Sudirman.

From Air Bari, speedboats cost 100,000Rp per person (fishing boats and outriggers about half that) to the south coast of the island (3km away). The boats will take you to snorkelling spots Air Manis, and Tanjung Pasir (the better of the two). Good reefs with a plunging wall can be found all around the island if you are prepared to charter a boat for a bit longer. Just northeast of Pulau Moyo is small **Pulau Satonda**, which also has good beaches and tremendous snorkelling. It's three hours by boat from Air Bari.

With the recent demise of Sumbawa's Laguna Biru Resort, there are only two ways to dive at Pulau Moyo. You can join a Bali- or Lombok-based, Komodo-bound live-aboard or check in to the luscious Amanwana, the swankiest dive camp on the planet. There are worse fates.

The seas around Moyo get turbulent from December to March. If boat operators are hesitant to launch, they probably have good reason.

### SLEEPING

**Amanwana Resort** ( ☎ 22233; www.amanresorts.com; all-inclusive jungle tents s/d US$825, ocean tents US$925, plus 21%

tax; ❅ ) On Moyo's western side, Amanwana is the ultimate island hideaway. This is where the rich and famous go 'camping', albeit in lavish permanent tents with antique wood furnishings, king-sized beds, two sofas and, of course, air-con. But nature still rules here. The resort is built around diving, hiking and mountain biking, they sponsor turtle hatcheries, deer breeding and reef-protection projects. There's a full-service spa and a dive school where courses and dive trips are private. Guests arrive by private seaplane from Bali (US$400 return) or are shuttled over from mainland Sumbawa on an Aman cruiser.

## Other Sights & Activities

Some of the best ikat and *songket* sarongs are made by members of a women's weaving *klompok* (collective) in the conservative mountain village of **Poto**, 12km east of Sumbawa Besar and 2km from the small town of Moyo. Traditional designs include the *prahu* (outrigger boat) and ancestor head motif. You'll hear the clack of their looms from the street and are welcome to duck into their humble huts. The most intricate pieces take up to 45 days to produce. **Haj Masturi** ( ☎ 0852 3954 3485) is one of Poto's leading weavers. Call her when you get to town and she can show you around.

The hills south of Sumbawa Besar are home to a number of **traditional villages** and offer **hiking** possibilities. One of the more interesting villages is **Tepal**, where horses can be hired to venture higher into the forest, but you will need to charter a 4WD vehicle from Sumbawa Besar to get there.

Near **Batu Tering** are megalithic sarcophagi, carved with low-relief crocodile and human figures, believed to be the 2000-year-old **tombs** of ancient chiefs. Footprints in the stones are said to be those of the gods. Batu Tering is about 30km by bemo from Sumbawa Besar, via Semamung. Hire a guide in the village to visit the sarcophagi, which are 4km away.

**Air Beling** is a pretty waterfall in the southern mountains. Take the road south through Semamung to Brangrea, from where it is 6km along a rough road with many forks. It's usually inaccessible without a 4WD vehicle, and impossible to find without a guide.

If you have your own wheels and are doing the trans-Sumbawa disco, stop for lunch at **Warung Santong** (Pantai Santong; meals 25,000Rp; ❅ 24hr), a tasty fish shack teetering on the rocky shore at the island's midway point. Dine on fresh catch, grilled or fried, in the 'dining room', or on one of three stilted pagodas at the water's edge.

# EAST SUMBAWA
☎ 0373

Twisted into a shape all its own, and linguistically and culturally distinct from the west, the eastern half of Sumbawa sees the most visitors thanks to accessible year-round surf near Hu'u village. Adventurous souls may also want to tackle majestic Gunung Tambora, a mountain that changed the world. And there are a handful of traditional villages in the hills above chaotic Bima, the haywired commercial heart of East Sumbawa.

## Gunung Tambora

Looming over central Sumbawa is the 2850m volcano, Gunung Tambora. Its peak was obliterated during the epic eruption in April 1815 (see p516), which buried residents alive and forever altered the region's geography. Tambora, not deforestation, is the reason that the oldest trees on Moyo are under 200 years old. In 2004, University of Rhode Island and Indonesian vulcanologists unearthed bronze bowls and ceramic pots from a Pompeii-like village, which indicate that the region once had strong trading links with Vietnam and Cambodia.

But you're here to bag the peak. From the summit you'll have spectacular views of the 6km-wide caldera, which contains a two-coloured lake, and endless ocean vistas that stretch as far as Gunung Rinjani (Lombok). The base for ascents is the village of Pancasila near the town of Calabai on the western slope, which is five hours by a very crowded bus from Dompu (35,000Rp), two hours by wooden boat (250,000Rp plus petrol), or an hour by speedboat from Sumbawa Besar (500,000Rp plus petrol). From Calabai take a *benhur* (15,000Rp) or *ojek* (25,000Rp) to Pancasila, where guides and porters (100,000Rp each per day) can be easily arranged. Due to trail conditions, it can only be climbed in the dry season (June to October).

## Dompu

Nestled in a sweet coconut-studded valley with lush granite hills rising on both sides, Dompu, the seat of one of Sumbawa's former independent states, is Sumbawa's third-biggest town. There's a colourful market snaking through its back streets, but otherwise it's just an attractive pit stop for the road-weary.

Money can be changed at the **BNI bank** (Jl Nusantara; ⏱ 7.30am-3pm Mon-Fri, 8.30am-noon Sat), which has an ATM.

The best hotel is the hospitable **Wisma Samada** ( ☎ 21417; Jl Gajah Mada 18; standard d 55,000Rp, VIP with air-con d 110,000Rp; ✻ ), which has plenty of spacious rooms with attractive wooden beds and desks and private bathrooms. The gleaming **Rumah Makan Rinjani** ( ☎ 21445; Jl Sudirman; mains 5000-17,500Rp) serves up a delicious *nasi campur*. It also has a few rooms for rent.

### GETTING THERE & AWAY

Daily buses run from Ginte main bus terminal, 2km from the centre, to Bima (15,000Rp, two hours), Sape (15,000Rp, four hours) and Sumbawa Besar (35,000Rp, five hours). If availability allows, you can hop an air-con bus through to Mataram (110,000Rp). Several travel in convoy from Bima, passing by the terminal at 9pm.

Two buses leave the Lepardi local bus terminal on the southern side of town for Hu'u (15,000Rp, 1½ hours) at 7am and 2pm daily. From there you can charter an *ojek* (10,000Rp) to Pantai Lakey. At all other times you'll have to charter a car (300,000Rp).

## Hu'u & Pantai Lakey

Pantai Lakey, a gentle crescent of golden sand 3km south of Hu'u, is where Sumbawa's tourist pulse beats year-round, thanks to seven world-class surf breaks that curl and crash in one massive bay. **Lakey Peak** and **Lakey Pipe** are the best-known waves and are within paddle distance of the various hotels and bungalow properties. You can also paddle out to **Mangas**. You'll need to rent a motorbike or hire an *ojek* to get to **Cobblestone**, the one-time house break of local turned international surf star Oney Anwar (see boxed text, p524), and **Nangadoro**. **Periscope** is 150m from the sand and at the far north end of the bay near **Maci Point**, another good spot. Most surfers share the cost of a boat (500,000Rp, maximum five people) to get there and back. Waves can be very good (and very big) year-round, but the most consistent swell arrives between June and August. From August to October the wind blows in, which turns Pantai Lakey into Indonesia's best kite-surfing destination – regarded as one of the 10 best in the world.

---

**SURF DREAMS**

When he was just five years old, Oney Anwar found a broken nose-end of a surfboard and paddled to the outside reef at his native Lakey Peak. Fearless, he lined up with seasoned local and international surfers who laughed at the grom's ballsy antics.

No one is laughing now.

Sponsored by Rip Curl at 12 and national junior champion at 13, Anwar (now 16) is living on Australia's Gold Coast where he attends high school. Before and after class he is being groomed by some of the world's best fitness trainers and surf coaches to compete on the world tour like his idols, Mick Fanning and Kelly Slater. Not bad for a kid who grew up in a three-room hut, just steps from the Cobblestone break near Pantai Lakey.

'It's a special area if you're a surfer,' he says. 'We get good waves all year and people come from all over – Hawaii, Australia – to surf, which helped us locals learn new tricks and get better.'

Anwar's aerial displays and his innate ability to get barrels have earned him 11 junior titles in three years. But he has bigger dreams. 'I want to become the first Indonesian world champ, so I can support my country.'

---

Inexperienced surfers should take good care. Waves break over a shallow reef. At research time an experienced, sponsored surfer from California fractured vertebrae at Lakey Peak. The airlift didn't arrive for three days. Thankfully, he's expected to make a full recovery.

Hu'u is a small, poor, but very friendly fishing village, 3km north of Lakey. It's suffused with the scent of drying fish and blessed with breathtaking pink sunsets. When the swell gets really big, there's a beach break here as well.

### INFORMATION

Most hotels will change US and Australian dollars at poor rates; bring ample rupiah. There's a wartel at Balumba and an expensive but decent internet cafe at **Aman Gati** (per minute 1000Rp; ⏱ 7am-10pm).

### SLEEPING & EATING

There are plenty of decent-value digs strung along Pantai Lakey. Most places have their own restaurants. Prices fluctuate depending on the season. Options are listed in the order you reach them from Dompu.

**Mona Lisa Bungalows** (r with fan 50,000-75,000Rp, with air-con 100,000-150,000Rp; ✶) A popular, long-running choice with 22 rooms, from economy options with shared *mandi* to comfortable bungalows in a verdant garden. Safety deposit boxes are available, and there's a good restaurant.

**Balumba** (☎ 21682, 623 430; d with fan/air-con 100,000/150,000Rp; ✶) The cheaper rooms with private bathrooms, set around a garden, are not a bad value, while the air-con bungalows are only slightly better and are garishly pink. There's a small convenience store where you can buy beer, play ping-pong and use the wartel.

**Any Lestari** (☎ 21684; r with fan 75,000Rp, bungalow with air-con 150,000Rp; ✶) Fan rooms are quite large, but pretty basic. Air-con rooms in shingled bungalows have newer, tiled floors, and ownership isn't shy about filling every inch with mattresses so four surf rats can share the price of one air-con room.

**our pick Hotel Aman Gati** (☎ 623 031; www .lakeypeakamangati.com; Jl Raya Hu'u; s/d with fan 165,000/235,000Rp, s/d/tr with air-con 275,000/355,000/435,000Rp; ✶ 🖵 🏊) A Balinese-run, three-star spot with wood furnishings, high ceilings, crown mouldings, (almost) hot water, DVD players and international cable TV opposite Lakey Peak. The fan bungalows are the oldest, cheapest, and yet closest to the beach. All rooms are set around a lovely garden and beachfront pool. The meals (which include the typical Indo-Western tourist fare and veggie choices) are generous and quite good, and the beer is icy, which explains why folks who sleep elsewhere tend to eat (and drink) here.

**Alamanda Bungalows** (☎ 623 519; Jl Raya Hu'u; s/d 50,000/75,000Rp) Small concrete bungalows set on a patch of grass with high ceilings, ceiling fans and reasonably clean bathrooms with Western toilets.

### GETTING THERE & AWAY

From Dompu's main bus terminal take a bemo (2000Rp) or *benhur* to the Lepardi local terminal on the southern outskirts.

There are two (slow) buses daily as far as Hu'u (15,000Rp, 1½ hours), where you can hire an *ojek* (10,000Rp) to Pantai Lakey.

Try doing this with a surfboard and you'll see why so many people take a taxi from Bima airport (around 400,000Rp). Leaving Hu'u, there's one early morning bus, but any of the hotels can arrange a taxi (300,000Rp to Dongu, 400,000Rp to Bima).

## Donggo

From Sila, on the Dompu–Bima road, infrequent buses run to the traditional village of Donggo, the domain of the Dou Donggo (mountain people) who speak an antiquated form of the Bima language and may have descended from Sumbawa's original inhabitants. Numbering about 20,000, they've layered Islam and Christianity over their traditional beliefs in the last few decades, and they're slowly being absorbed into Bimanese culture, but not without a fight. Just a few weeks before research the latest episode of civil unrest took place between Dou Donggo youth and Bima police. By the time the intermittent monthlong battle was over, two people were dead. The most traditional village is **Mbawa**, where up until a decade ago people still wore distinctive black clothes. You'll find a few *uma leme* (traditional stilted houses with nearby rice barns) here, though most of the homes have replaced the thatched roof with corrugated tin. From Bima, it's 4km along a smooth road, and then 20km on an occasionally rough one up the mountain, where you'll have incredible views of terraced rice fields tumbling to the sea.

## BIMA & RABA
☎ 0374 / pop 71,000

Let's be frank. Bima will never be your favourite Indonesian getaway. Chalk it up to the traffic-choked streets, architecture that manages to be charmless and crumbling, and some fairly aggressive locals who are unlike those in the rest of Sumbawa. Still, if you keep your cool, you may find charm in the chaotic intensity of it all. Or you may want to flee to Raba, the much more orderly but dull administrative centre a few kilometres east. Together the twin towns form East Sumbawa's largest metropolitan centre.

Beneath its, um, exuberant veneer, Bima is a conservative Islamic place with one mediocre sight – the former sultan's palace. The

*pasar malam* (night market) in the Old Palace compound is also worth a wander.

Almost all the tourists who pass through are in transit between the waves at Lakey Peak and Bali, or plan on taking the ferry to Labuanbajo in Flores, the launch pad to Rinca and Komodo. Rest assured, the ferry between Sumbawa and Flores no longer stops at Komodo, no matter what some hustlers may claim.

## Information

### INTERNET ACCESS & TELEPHONE
**Internet & Game Center** (Jl Sumbawa; per hr 3000Rp)
**Telkom** (Jl Soekarno Hatta; ☇ 24hr) Adjacent to the tourist office.

### MONEY
**BNI bank** (Jl Sultan Hasanuddin; ☇ 8am-2pm Mon-Fri) Has an ATM and changes foreign currency.

### POST
**Main post office** (Jl Sultan Hasanuddin) Located a little way out.

### TOURIST INFORMATION
**Dinas Pariwisata** ( ☎ 44331; Jl Soekarno Hatta; ☇ 7am-3pm Mon-Fri, 7am-noon Sat) Friendly English speakers staff the tourist office in Raba's Kantor Bupati, 2km from Bima.

### TRAVEL AGENCIES
**Doro Parewa Makmur** ( ☎ 42926; Jl Sumbawa 16) Organises trips to Komodo and Rinca from Sape.
**PT Kristal Kencana Wisata** ( ☎ 43440, 44221; Jl Sumbawa 19) Merpati's official agent in Bima.
**Travel Lancar Jaya** ( ☎ 43737; Jl Sultan Hasanuddin 11) Also books Komodo-bound boats.

## Sights

The Sultan's Palace, former home of Bima's rulers, is now **Museum Asi Mbojo** (Jl Sultan Ibrahim; tourist admission 5000Rp; ☇ 8am-5pm Mon-Sat), a grabbag of dusty curios, including a royal crown, battle flags and weapons. Built in 1927, the palace had fallen into complete disrepair by the late 1950s but has since been restored and freshly painted. Look for the royal bedchamber.

The new palace, **Masjid Bima**, also looks pretty damn royal, with a gushing fountain and five towers. The patchy **sports field** opposite the palaces is the destination for soccer and volleyball games at dusk.

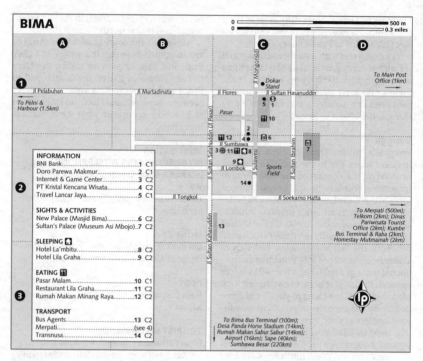

**BIMA**

## Activities

**Horse racing** is held four times a year, in May, July, August and December at the Desa Panda horse stadium, 14km from town on the airport road. There's a large grandstand, a gaggle of warungs and plenty of cheering as horses thunder around a dusty track. Racing – and gambling – peaks on 17 August as independence fever kicks in.

## Sleeping

**Hotel Lila Graha** ( ☎ 42740; fax 44705; Jl Lombok 6; d with fan 100,000-125,000Rp, with air-con 150,000-300,000Rp, plus 10% tax; ✗ ) One of two four-storey, blocklong hotels, each with a wide range of rooms. The economy rooms are poky, while some of those in the new wing have two beds, phones and hot water.

**Hotel La'mbitu** ( ☎ 42222; fax 42304; Jl Sumbawa 4; standard/superior/jr ste 110,000/170,000/250,000Rp; ✗ ) Virtually next door, and Bima's best choice. This is the newer, cleaner version with spotless tile floors, fresh paint and wood furnishings throughout. The top-floor rooms have direct access to a common terrace overlooking Bima's green hills.

**Homestay Mutmainah** ( ☎ 646 826, 42351; Jl Gajah Meda, Raba; d 350,000Rp; ✗ ☒ ) Set in a converted house in laid-back Raba. There are four-post beds, wardrobes, bathtubs, TV, air-con, hot water and rice-field views.

## Eating

**our pick Rumah Makan Sabur Sabur** ( ☎ 646 236; Jl Salahudin, Bandara; meals 9000Rp; ✆ 7am-6pm) These long wooden tables are always crowded with locals who come to munch *bandeng goreng* (a flash-fried freshwater fish). Like herring, you can eat it whole, bones and all. It's best combined with their fiery crushed-tomato *sambal*, torn leaves of lemon basil and a bit of rice. Wow!

**Rumah Makan Minang Raya** (Jl Sumbawa; mains 13,000-17,000Rp) A tasty Padang food haunt with fried and broiled shrimp, and stewed and curried chicken.

**Restaurant Lila Graha** (Jl Sumbawa; mains 15,000-25,000Rp) Attached to the hotel of the same name, this clean and friendly joint serves up Chinese and Indonesian reliables, with a few Western dishes thrown in.

Or dine cheap at the **pasar malam**, which sets up along the walking streets within the

Old Palace compound. There's fish and chicken sate grilling, *mie goreng* (fried noodles) and *nasi goreng* (fried rice) sizzling, *bakso* (meatball soup) and *gado gado* aplenty. As always, look for fresh ingredients and be discerning.

## Getting There & Away

### AIR

You can fly to Bima with **Merpati** ( ☎ 43440; Jl Sumbawa 19), which has daily flights to and from Denpasar (720,000Rp) where there are daily connections to Mataram, Ende and Kupang. **Transnusa** ( ☎ 647 251, Jl Sulawesi 26) also has daily flights to and from Denpasar (865,000Rp) via Mataram (489,000Rp).

Departure tax from Bima is 20,000Rp.

### BOAT

*Willis* travels monthly from Bima to Maumere, Larantuka, Papua, and back to Benoa in Bali. *Kelimutu* connects Bima with Larantuka, Benoa and Papua monthly. *Tilongkabila* sails to Labuanbajo and Sulawesi, and returns via Lembar and Benoa every two weeks. Travel agencies in town can organise tickets, since the **Pelni office** ( ☎ 42625; Jl Kesatria 2) is at Bima port.

### BUS

The Bima bus terminal is a 10-minute walk south along Jl Sultan Kaharuddin from the centre of town, though you can buy a ticket in advance from bus company offices on Jl Sultan Kaharuddin.

The majority of buses heading west to Lombok, via Sumbawa Besar, leave in a convoy (7pm to 7.30pm), but there is one daytime service departing at 9.30am. Fares to Mataram range from 100,000Rp for normal services (without air-con) to 150,000Rp for the luxury, air-con buses that take about 11 hours. Tiara Mas has the best buses. Many continue to Denpasar, arriving at 11am the next morning.

Local buses stop anywhere and everywhere. They run between 6am and 5pm. Destinations from Bima include Dompu (15,000Rp, two hours) and Sumbawa Besar (90,000Rp, seven hours).

Buses east to Sape go from Kumbe bus terminal in Raba, a 20-minute (2000Rp) bemo ride east of Bima. Pick up a yellow bemo on Jl Sultan Kaharuddin or Jl Soekarno Hatta. Buses leave Kumbe terminal for Sape (9000Rp, two hours) from about 6am until 5pm. If you leave at 6am sharp, you'll make it to Sape for the 9am ferry to Flores. Or sleep a little later and charter a car (200,000Rp, 1½ hours).

## Getting Around

The airport sits amid salt flats 17km from the centre. You can walk out to the main road and catch a passing bus. Alternatively, taxis meet arrivals, charging 80,000Rp to Bima or 400,000Rp to Hu'u.

A bemo around town costs 2000Rp per person; *benhur* are 5000Rp.

As there are no official rental agencies, try hiring a motorbike through your hotel or one of the travel agencies; expect to pay around 75,000Rp per day.

## AROUND BIMA

On the main highway between Bima and Sape, the Wawo area is noted for its traditional houses, *uma lengge*. The 'traditional' village of **Maria**, just off the highway, has examples of indigenous architecture, but the materials are modern. **Sambori**, located off a rugged road, has the real-deal grass roofs and some impressive three-storey houses. A chartered 4WD, compulsory for the trip, from either Sape or Bima will cost 500,000Rp.

The stunning Wera region extends northeast of Bima and includes some impressive scenery of rice terraces, gorges and views of the active **Gunung Api** (1950m). Bugis schooners are built in the village of **Sangeang**, 10km north of Tawali. Public transport is limited here, so renting a motorbike in Bima is the best way to explore.

## SAPE

☎ 0374

It's got a tumbledown port-town vibe, perfumed with the conspicuous scent of drying cuttlefish, but what it lacks in style it makes up for in soul. The outskirts are quilted in rice fields backed by jungled hills, and the streets are busy with *benhur* and bustling with early morning commerce. There's decent food and doable lodging here too, so if you are catching a ferry, consider this an alternative to the Bima madness.

There's a **PHKA Komodo Information Office** ( ☼ 8am-2pm Mon-Sat) 500m inland from the port with a few brochures and maps.

Sape's best lodging option is **Losmen Mutiara** (☎ 71337; Jl Pelabuhan Sape; economy/standard/deluxe r 35,000/80,000/100,000Rp; 🗱), right next to the port gates. Rooms are reasonably clean. The smiling ladies of **Rumah Makan Citra Minang** (Jl Pelabuhan Sape; meals 20,000Rp) bring Padang's finest and spiciest dishes to life. The cracked concrete floor and water-stained walls betray the quality and flavour of the food. **Arema Sape** (☎ 71015; Jl Pelabuhan Sape; dishes 8000-20,000Rp) is the cleaner, brighter option. The squid dishes look good. If you come for breakfast, order the pancake.

### Getting There & Around

**BOAT**

Regular breakdowns and heavy storms disrupt ferry services – always double-check the latest schedules in Bima and Sape. Or you can call **Cabang Sape** (☎ 71075; Jl Yos Sudarso, Pelabuhan Penye Berangan Sape). It operates the daily ferry to Labuanbajo (60,200Rp per person, 125,000Rp per motorcycle, eight to nine hours). Ferries are non-stop and leave at 9am daily. Tickets can be purchased at the pier about one hour before departure. Expect Indo heavy metal at high decibels if you're sitting outside, and assorted B-grade Hollywood flicks and kung fu movies indoors. Do not expect comfort.

It is possible to charter a boat to Komodo, but it's a much better idea to get to Labuanbajo and sort out a boat there, as many of the Sape-based vessels are not seaworthy and the seas around Komodo are notoriously treacherous. Travellers have even had to swim to shore after being shipwrecked.

There is also a ferry service connecting Sape with Waikelo (50,000Rp, eight hours) in West Sumba. It leaves Sape at around 10pm twice a week on Monday and Friday and returns from Waikelo on Tuesday and Saturday at 5pm.

**BUS**

Express buses with service to Lombok and Bali meet arriving ferries.

Buses leave every half hour for Raba (9000Rp, two hours) until around 5pm. From Raba take a bemo to Bima (2000Rp, 20 minutes), where you can catch local buses to Sumbawa destinations. Taxi drivers will no doubt claim buses have stopped running and you must charter their vehicle to Bima – ignore them.

# KOMODO & RINCA ISLANDS

Nestled between Sumbawa and Flores, the islands of Komodo and Rinca, their jagged hills carpeted with savannah and fringed with mangroves, are home to a few hundred fishermen and the legendary Komodo dragon (see boxed text, p530). The world's largest lizard, known locally as *ora*, it can reach over 3m in length and weigh up to 100kg. It hunts alone and feeds on animals as large as deer and buffalo, both of which are found here. The males also try to eat the females' eggs, inevitably sparking a vicious battle of the sexes.

These isolated islands are surrounded by some of the most tempestuous waters in Indonesia. The convergence of warm and cold water currents breeds nutritious thermal climes, rip tides and whirlpools that attract large schools of pelagics, from dolphins and sharks to manta rays and blue whales. The coral here is pristine. Add it all up and you have some of the best diving in the world, which is why liveaboards based in Bali and Lombok ply these waters between April and September when the crossing is smooth and the diving at its finest.

Rinca receives just as many visitors as Komodo because it's closest to Labuanbajo, Flores – the main departure point for trips to the Komodo National Park. Dragons are easy to spot, as they tend to hang around the camp kitchen. Komodo looks and feels wilder, the offshore dive sites are magnificent, but the dragons don't hang about the camps too often, so you have to hike to find them. A steady stream of visitors make their way here these days, but to understand how far off the beaten track it used to be, read *Zoo Quest for a Dragon* by naturalist and broadcaster David Attenborough, who filmed the dragons in 1956.

There are numerous hiking trails, but it's not permitted to explore without a guide, a forked staff his primary weapon, as dragons have very occasionally attacked (and killed) humans. Two villagers have died in the last 20 years, and three days before our visit a ranger was attacked on Rinca in his office while doing paperwork. He survived, but his bloodstains remained for all to see. Dragons are a docile bunch for the most part, but they could snap your leg as fast as they'll cut a goat's throat. Respect the beasts.

# KOMODO & RINCA ISLANDS

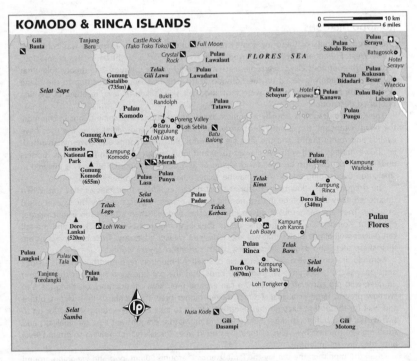

| 0 | 10 km |
| 0 | 6 miles |

## Visiting Komodo National Park

This **national park** (www.komodonationalpark.org), a Unesco World Heritage site, encompasses Komodo, Rinca, several neighbouring islands, and their incredibly rich marine ecosystem.

A three-day visitor permit includes your park entrance fee (40,000Rp adult or child) and the conservation fee (US$20 adult/US$10 child), collected on arrival by rangers.

A short, guided dragon-spotting trek is included with your entrance fee. For a longer, hour-long trek on Rinca you'll pay an additional 50,000Rp. On Komodo, where the hiking is superb, you can pay from 50,000Rp to 250,000Rp for guided treks that range from flat 3km strolls to steep 10km hikes up and over peaks and into deep valleys. Arrange your trek upon registration in Komodo. All guides speak some English and are very knowledgeable about the islands' flora and fauna. A camera permit is another 25,000Rp.

Komodo is one of the driest corners of Nusa Tenggara, and heavy rains are not common. However, the seas are calmest between April and September.

## KOMODO

Spectacular Komodo, its steep hillsides jade in the short wet season, frazzled by the sun and winds to a deep rusty red for most of the year, is the largest island in the national park. A succession of eastern peninsulas spread out like so many fingers, fringed in pink sand, thanks to the abundance of red coral reefs offshore. The recently renovated camp of **Loh Liang** and the PHKA office, where you can organise treks, is also on the east coast of the island.

The fishing village of **Kampung Komodo** is an hour-long walk south of Loh Liang. It's a friendly stilted Bugis village that's full of goats, chickens and children. The inhabitants are said to be descendants of convicts exiled to the island in the 19th century by one of the sultans in Sumbawa.

## Activities
### DRAGON SPOTTING

You're likely to see dragons if you do the standard stroll to Banu Nggulung, a dry riverbed about a half-hour walk from Loh Liang. The organised feeding of goats to dragons is a thing of the past, and dragons are now only

## KOMODO DRAGONS

There were rumours of these awesome creatures long before their existence was confirmed in the West. Fishers and pearl divers working in the area had brought back tales of ferocious lizards with enormous claws, fearsome teeth and forked yellow tongues. One theory holds that the Chinese dragon is based on the Komodo lizard. The first Dutch expedition to the island was in 1910; two of the dragons were shot and their skins taken to Java, resulting in the first published description.

The Komodo dragon is actually a monitor lizard. All monitors have some things in common: the head is tapered, the ear openings are visible, the neck is long and slender, the eyes have eyelids and round pupils, and the jaws are powerful. But the dragons also have massive bodies, powerful legs (each with five-clawed toes) and long, thick tails (which function as rudders underwater, but can also be used for grasping or as a potent weapon). The body is covered in small, non-overlapping scales; some may be spiny, others raised and bony.

The dragons' legs allow them to sprint short distances, lifting their tails as they run. When threatened, they'll take refuge in their normal resting places – holes, trees (for the smaller ones) or water. They are dangerous if driven into a corner and will then attack even a much larger opponent. Komodo dragons often rise up on their hind legs just before attacking, and the tail can deliver well-aimed blows that will knock down a weaker adversary. Their best weapons are their sharp teeth and dagger-sharp claws, which can inflict severe wounds.

Komodo dragons have a very keen sense of smell. All monitors feed on other animals – small ones on insects, larger ones on frogs and birds, and the *ora* (the local name for the dragon) on deer, wild pig and water buffalo. *Ora* can expand their jaws considerably, enabling them to swallow prey as large as a goat. To tackle even bigger prey, they ambush their victim, bite it and wait for the potent bacteria their mouths contain to take effect – waiting around for up to two weeks for a buffalo to die – before tucking in. Mature dragons are also cannibalistic, and small *ora* live the first five years of their lives up in trees for safety, not moving to ground level until they are 1m in length.

Of all the monitors, the *ora* lay the largest eggs – around 90mm long and weighing around 200g. The female lays 15 to 30 eggs at a time and often buries them in the wall of a dry river. She then protects her cache for three months from predators – including male dragons. The incubation period is nine months.

Komodo dragons are *not* relics of the dinosaur age; they're remarkably versatile, hardy modern lizards, if not exactly sensitive and New Age. Why they exist only on and around Komodo is a mystery, as is why males outnumber females by a ratio of 3.4 to one. Around 1300 *ora* live on Komodo, perhaps 1100 on Rinca and a small number (around 50) on the west coast of Flores. Today the *ora* are a protected species.

fed here when the PHKA wants to do a head count. Banu Nggulung still occasionally attracts dragons, but you're more likely to find them on your way here and back.

When you do come across a scaly beast, it's wise to keep a safe distance and move slowly and calmly. A telephoto lens is handy but not essential. It is also possible to spot dragons foraging for food and fresh water on some of the other walks, but it's never guaranteed.

### HIKING

Most visitors stay one night at Komodo and only do the short hike to **Banu Nggulung** – bad decision. The longer you hike, the more spectacular the scenery (think massive sea views, lonely beaches and bays, deep valleys that recall the Land of the Lost).

Walks from Loh Liang include the climb to the 538m-high **Gunung Ara** (200,000Rp, 9km, five hours return). The chances of seeing a dragon are slim, but there are expansive views from the top. **Poreng Valley** (150,000Rp, 5.5km, four to five hours return) is another potential dragon haunt, and has a more out-in-the-wild feeling than Banu Nggulung. The trail continues over **Bukit Randolph**, a memorial to the 79-year-old Randolph Von Reding who disappeared on Komodo in 1974, to **Loh Sebita** (150,000Rp, 9km, four hours). This is the best hike. It's challenging, the views are spectacular, you'll likely see a dragon or two, and you can organise your boat to pick you up in Loh Sebita, so you don't have to retrace your steps. There's also plenty of other wildlife, such as buffaloes, deer, wild boar and Komodo's rich bird life, including the fabled megapodes.

## SNORKELLING & DIVING

Almost everybody who visits the park hires a boat in Labuanbajo (see right). Boats always offer snorkelling (gear included) as part of the itinerary. Most folks snorkel around the small island of **Pulau Lasa** near Kampung Komodo, and just off the pink sands of **Pantai Merah** (Red Beach), which is just an hour's walk from Loh Liang.

Of course, diving is the thing here. Given the conditions – up and down currents, and chilly temperatures – and the effort involved in diving these amazing sites, it is not recommended for the inexperienced diver. But if you have 50 or more dives, stay calm and mind

your dive guide, you will have a tremendous experience. See boxed text, below for a full rundown.

## Getting There & Away

Ferries travelling between Sape and Labuanbajo haven't been stopping at Komodo for several years now, so the only way here is by some sort of charter. One way to arrive is on a boat tour between Lombok and Flores – these stop at Komodo for a night or two. See the boxed text, p540, for the pros and cons of such trips.

Labuanbajo is the best jumping-off point for Komodo and Rinca. It *is* possible to charter boats from Sape (see p528) in Sumbawa to Komodo, but be extremely cautious, as many boats here are barely seaworthy.

Two-day Komodo trips for up to six people cost a standard 1,500,000Rp from Labuanbajo. Price includes landings on Rinca and Komodo, meals and snorkelling gear.

---

### DIVING & SNORKELLING AROUND KOMODO & LABUANBAJO

Komodo National Park has some of the most exhilarating scuba diving in Indonesia. It's a region swept by strong currents and cold upswellings, created by the convergence of the warmer Flores Sea and the cooler Selat Sumba (Sumba Strait) – conditions that create rich plankton soup and an astonishing diversity of marine life. Mantas and whales are drawn here to feed on the plankton during their migration from the Indian Ocean to the South China Sea, while dolphins are also common in the waters between Komodo and Flores.

Among the several dozen dive sites mapped in the park are **Batu Bolong**, a split pinnacle with absolutely pristine coral and, compared to elsewhere in the park, light current; **Crystal Bommie** (aka Crystal Rock), with electric soft corals, turtles and schooling pelagics. We saw 19 reef and grey sharks in one dive. The currents are strong here and at **Castle Rock** (aka Tako Toko Toko), a tremendous sunrise dive site where, with a little luck, you'll dive with dolphins. Then there's **The Cauldron**, aka Manta Soupa a shallow drift dive over white sand where massive manta rays school and clean themselves on the rocks. If you've never seen mantas before, dive here. It's guaranteed.

When it comes to Komodo outfitters, there are several choices. You could sign up for day trips with the Labuanbajo dive shops (see p535). This is the cheapest way to go (800,000Rp for two dives). They operate year-round, but it's a long haul (up to three hours) to and from the sites, you can't customise your itinerary, and if you're diving multiple days this doesn't make much sense. If you are based out of Labuanbajo, the best bet is to arrange a private live-aboard through one of the dive shops. **CN Dive** ( ☎ 41159, 0813 3928 5913) offers live-aboards with unlimited diving and all meals from US$120 per day (two people minimum). They run trips off-season, when crowds are thin and you'll have the dive sites to yourself. They also have a fat, 40m luxury yacht (think mosaic showers, a plasma big-screen TV, air-con and two sun decks) available for live-aboard charters from US$250 per day (minimum two people). An absolute steal if it's available.

Several multiday live-aboard cruises also depart from Bali, Gili Trawangan and nearby Labuanbajo during the peak April to September season, when the seas are at their calmest. **Ikan Baru** ( ☎ 0813 534 4511; www.goodwilldiving.com; 7-day cruise from US$1350), a luxe Bugis schooner operated by Gili T's Trawangan Dive and led by world record holder Will Goodman, offers one of the best live-aboard experiences in Komodo.

## RINCA

Rinca is slightly smaller than Komodo and every bit as alluring. It's also close to Labuanbajo and easily done in a day trip. Boats arrive at the sheltered dock of Loh Kima. It's a five-minute walk through the mangroves, where you run across long-tail macaques and wild water buffalo grazing in the tidal marsh, to the PHKA camp at **Loh Buaya**, which has a ticket office and information centre, ramshackle wooden bungalows and a cafe. Keep the entrance ticket if you're heading to Komodo.

Two types of guided walks are offered. An hour's loop trail is included with your admission, or you could pay an extra 50,000Rp for a two-hour hike. As temperatures will inevitably be furnace-hot, most people opt for an hour of exploring the area close to the camp.

There are no set dragon-feeding places on Rinca, but there are often a half-dozen massive beasts near the camp kitchen at Loh Buaya. Finding dragons in the bush is not so easy, but the guides know spots where Komodo dragons sun themselves, and they'll show you dragon nests (the females dig huge burrows to lay their eggs, which they then guard for three months). Wildlife is much more abundant than on Komodo; in addition to the monkeys and buffalo you may find Timor deer, horses or even wild boar. Bird life includes spangled drongos, fish eagles, megapodes and orange-footed scrub fowl.

### Sleeping & Eating

Komodo's **PHKA camp** (per person per night 300,000Rp) accommodation just went through a renovation, but what once was a series of basic wood cabins is now an overpriced version of a basic Indo hotel, complete with musty interior. Rinca's large stilted cabins, on the other hand, are riddled with mould and falling apart. New bungalow construction was underway at research time. Most folks opt to sleep on the decks of their chartered boats – a lot more palatable, if a bit cramped.

Both camps have restaurants with a limited menu of *nasi/mie goreng*, fish and other simple meals.

### Getting There & Away

Chartering a boat to Rinca costs about 750,000Rp return from Labuanbajo. Boats usually leave at about 8am for the two-hour journey to the island and then return via snorkelling spots. You can book through your hotel, an agency or freelance agents in Labuanbajo, or speak directly to the captains at the harbour, which will allow you to size up the boat and check that the vessel has a radio and life jackets.

# FLORES

Flores is the kind of gorgeous that grabs hold of you tightly. There are empty white-sand beaches and bay islands, exceptional diving and snorkelling near Labuanbajo, and terrific muck diving near Maumere. An infinite sky-

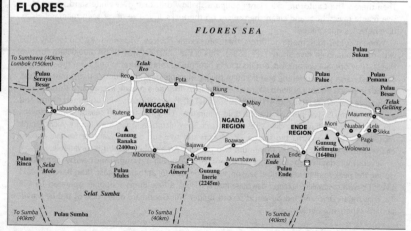

**FLORES**

*FLORES SEA*

line of perfectly shaped volcanoes craft knife-edge ridges, and spectacular river canyons are carpeted by a vast tapestry of hip-high, luminescent rice fields that undulate in the wind next to swaying palms. The serpentine, potholed 'trans-Flores highway' is long and slow, but never boring. It skirts waterfalls, conquers mountains, brushes by traditional villages in Bajawa, leads to the incredible multicoloured volcanic lakes of Kelimutu, and connects the east and west coasts. The Portuguese named it 'Flowers' when they colonised Flores in the 16th century. The name stuck (so did Catholicism) because of its sheer, wild beauty.

## History

A startling recent find near Ruteng indicates that a unique species of dwarf hominid lived in Flores until around 12,000 years ago (see boxed text, p539), although evidence has not yet been universally accepted by scientists.

Anthropologists and historians do agree that the island's diverse cultures developed from a common ancestry. Long before Europeans arrived in the 16th century, much of coastal Flores was firmly in the hands of the Makassarese and Bugis from southern Sulawesi. They brought gold, elephant tusks (used as currency), linen and copperware, and left with rubber, sea products, sandalwood, cinnamon, cotton and fabric. Bugis and Makassarese slave raids on the coasts of Flores were a common problem, forcing indigenous people to retreat inland. Eastern Flores was

controlled by Ternate in Maluku during the 15th and 16th centuries.

In 1512, Portuguese navigator Antonio de Abreu spotted Flores. Drawn by the lucrative sandalwood trade, the Portuguese built fortresses on Pulau Solor and at Ende, and named their landing site on the island's easternmost cape, Cabo das Flores. Christianity was a successful import, and today a church is the centrepiece of almost every village.

In the 17th century, the Dutch muscled the Portuguese out of most of Flores. By 1850 they had purchased Portugal's remaining enclaves in the area, including Larantuka, and were constantly confronted with rebellions and inter-tribal wars. Unrest continued until a major military campaign in 1907 subdued central and western Flores. Missionaries moved into the isolated western hills in the 1920s.

Today, western Flores is in the midst of a tourism boom. More visitors than ever are venturing to Labuanbajo to explore the Komodo and Rinca islands. A new luxury tower hotel just opened on the outskirts of Labuanbajo and a 100-room Jayakarta hotel is currently under construction. There's even talk of an expanded airport to accommodate direct flights from Singapore in the near future.

## Culture

The island's 1.8 million people are divided into five main linguistic and cultural groups. From west to east, these are the Manggarai (main town Ruteng), the Ngada (Bajawa), the

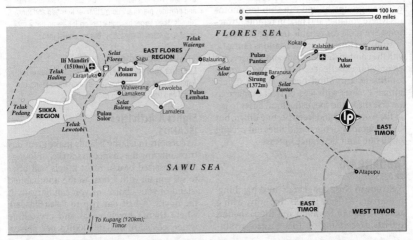

FLORES SEA

100 km
60 miles

Teluk Waienga

EAST FLORES REGION

Kokar • Kalabahi • Taramana

Selat Flores • Sagu • Balauring

Pulau Pantar

Pulau Alor

Ili Mandiri (1510m) • Larantuka • Pulau Adonara

Selat Alor

Gunung Sirung (1372m) • Baranusa

Selat Pantar

Teluk Hading

Waiwerang • Lewoleba

Lamakera

Pulau Lembata

SIKKA REGION

Selat Boleng

Pulau Solor

Lamalera

Teluk Pedang

Teluk Lewotobi

EAST TIMOR

SAWU SEA

• Atapupu

EAST TIMOR

WEST TIMOR

To Kupang (120km); Timor

closely related Ende and Lio peoples (Ende), the Sikkanese (Maumere) and the Lamaholot (Larantuka). In remote areas, some older people don't speak a word of Bahasa Indonesia, and their parents grew up in purely animist societies.

Physically, the people at the western end of the island are more Malay, while the other inhabitants of Flores are more Melanesian.

Around 85% of the people are Catholic, but in rural areas Christianity is welded onto *adat*. Animist rituals are still used for births, marriages and deaths and to mark important points in the agricultural calendar. Even educated, English-speaking Florinese participate in the odd chicken, pig or buffalo sacrifice to the ancestors when rice is planted.

Muslims congregate in fishing villages and coastal towns such as Ende (where they make up half the population).

## Getting Around

The 'trans-Flores highway' twists and tumbles nearly 700km from Labuanbajo to Larantuka, at the eastern end of the island. It's sealed, but often rutted and narrow. Buses are invariably small, cramped and overcrowded, but the stunning scenery certainly helps compensate. It is best to break up a trans-island journey to avoid the bus passengers' version of road rage.

For those with more money than time, car rental is available in Labuanbajo or Maumere. The trans-island rate is 500,000Rp to 550,000Rp per day, including driver and petrol. This is becoming a very popular option for small groups, as you can stop for photo-ops where you like, and take in remote attractions. See p538 for reliable transport fixers.

Motorcycling across the island is fantastic with the combination of roads and scenery, but it's only for experienced bikers, due to tough conditions and blind bends. A few super-human cyclists with legs of steel manage to traverse the island too, using local buses to get up the worst hills and freewheeling down, but the topography of the island rules out cycling for all but Tour de France outcasts.

## LABUANBAJO
☎ 0385

Welcome to Nusa Tenggara's 'next big thing' in tourism. At least it feels that way, with a steady stream of Komodo and Rinca–bound tourists descending on this gorgeous ram-shackle harbour, freckled with bay islands, blessed with surrealist sunsets and surrounded by rugged green hills. Dive and snorkelling boats leave day and night for world-class reefs in the nearby national park, there are sweet beach bungalows on empty islands closer to shore, and there's an ever-expanding collection of hotels and restaurants with a view.

### Information
#### INTERNET ACCESS & TELEPHONE
The Telkom office, 1km west of town, offers the best rates. The wartel near the waterfront seem to pluck high prices from the ether.
**Apik** (Jl Yos Sudarso; per hr 10,000Rp) The strongest connection in town.

#### MONEY
There are two banks with ATMs in Labuanbajo. They change travellers' cheques and dollars. Local moneychangers offer similar rates.
**BNI** (Jl Yos Sudarso; ☉ 8am-4.30pm Mon-Fri) ATM accepts Visa/Plus cards.
**BRI** (Jl Yos Sudarso; ☉ 8am-3.30pm Mon-Fri) Master-Card/Cirrus ATM only.

#### POST
**Post office** (Jl Yos Sudarso; ☉ 7am-2pm Mon-Sat)

#### TOURIST INFORMATION
**Dinas Pariwisata** ( ☎ 41170; ☉ 7am-2pm Mon-Thu & Sat, to 11am Fri) About 1km out of town on the road to the airport.
**PHKA information booth** ( ☎ 41005; tnkomodo@ indosat.net.id; Jl Yos Sudarso; ☉ 8am-2.30pm Mon-Thu, to 11am Fri) PHKA administers the Komodo National Park and provides practical information for Komodo and Rinca islands. Their larger headquarters on Jl Kasimo has a cool dragon skeleton in the lobby, but no tourist info.

#### TRAVEL AGENCIES
**Lantana Tours & Travel** ( ☎ 41289; Jl Soekarno Hatta) A helpful tour operator that can arrange trans-Flores car rental and trips to Komodo National Park.

### Sights & Activities
#### ISLANDS
Excursions to nearby islands make great day trips, offering the chance to snorkel or lounge on a deserted beach. Most hotels will offer to set you up with a boat to the uninhabited island of your choice, or you can bargain at the docks. A half-day trip to **Pulau Bidadari**, where there's lovely coral and crystalline water, costs around 100,000Rp per person

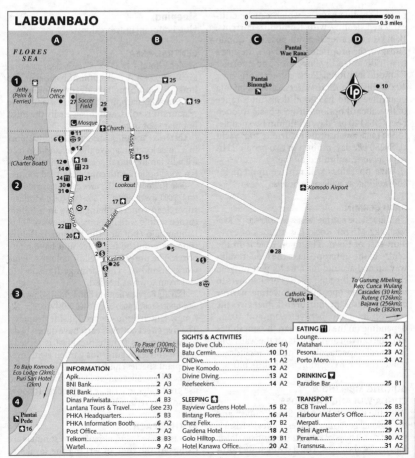

## LABUANBAJO

**SIGHTS & ACTIVITIES**
| | | |
|---|---|---|
| Bajo Dive Club | (see 14) | |
| Batu Cermin | **10** | D1 |
| CNDive | **11** | A2 |
| Dive Komodo | **12** | A2 |
| Divine Diving | **13** | A2 |
| Reefseekers | **14** | A2 |

**SLEEPING** 🏠
| | | |
|---|---|---|
| Bayview Gardens Hotel | **15** | B2 |
| Bintang Flores | **16** | A4 |
| Chez Felix | **17** | B2 |
| Gardena Hotel | **18** | A2 |
| Golo Hilltop | **19** | B1 |
| Hotel Kanawa Office | **20** | A2 |

**INFORMATION**
| | | |
|---|---|---|
| Apik | **1** | A3 |
| BNI Bank | **2** | A3 |
| BRI Bank | **3** | A3 |
| Dinas Pariwisata | **4** | B3 |
| Lantana Tours & Travel | (see 23) | |
| PHKA Headquarters | **5** | B3 |
| PHKA Information Booth | **6** | A2 |
| Post Office | **7** | A2 |
| Telkom | **8** | B3 |
| Wartel | **9** | A2 |

**EATING** 🍴
| | | |
|---|---|---|
| Lounge | **21** | A2 |
| Matahari | **22** | A2 |
| Pesona | **23** | A2 |
| Porto Moro | **24** | A2 |

**DRINKING** 🍸
| | | |
|---|---|---|
| Paradise Bar | **25** | B1 |

**TRANSPORT**
| | | |
|---|---|---|
| BCB Travel | **26** | B3 |
| Harbour Master's Office | **27** | A1 |
| Merpati | **28** | C3 |
| Pelni Agent | **29** | A1 |
| Perama | **30** | A2 |
| Transnusa | **31** | A2 |

with four or more passengers. You can snooze on **Pantai Waecicu** and snorkel around the tiny offshore islet of **Kukusan Kecil**. **Pulau Serayu** and **Pulau Kanawa** are both gorgeous and have basic beach-hut accommodation with free transport. Boats leave from the shoreline at the northern end of the main street.

### DIVING & SNORKELLING

With dive sites around the islands near Labuanbajo and the proximity of Komodo National Park, there are some excellent scuba opportunities here; see the boxed text on p531 for a full rundown.

Local dive operators share uniform prices. At research time the price was 800,000Rp for two dives around Rinca, plus a 200,000Rp

surcharge to stop and see the dragons. Custom dive safaris to the best northern Komodo sites are also available. Itineraries hover around 1,500,000Rp per person with a two- to four-person minimum depending on the dive shop. Dive offices are strung along or just off the seafront road:

**Bajo Dive Club** ( ☎ 41503; www.komododiver.com)
**CNDive** ( ☎ 41159, 0813 3928 5913)
**Dive Komodo** ( ☎ 41862; www.divekomodo.com)
**Divine Diving** ( ☎ 41948; www.divediving.info; Jl Soekarno Pelabuhan 1)
**Reefseekers** ( ☎ 41443; www.reefseekers.net)

It's best to chat with all the dive schools first, and survey their equipment and boats before you make a decision. We've heard reports of broken dive gauges, which can be critical when dealing with Komodo's currents. Bring a computer if at all possible. Condo Subagyo, the proprietor of CNDive, the area's first Indonesian dive operator and a former Komodo National Park ranger with over 10,000 dives in these waters, offers a 'manta guarantee', and has good deals on a range of live-aboard options, from a basic wooden boat (US$120 per day, minimum two people) to **Sila Lona**, an absurdly luxurious 40m yacht (US$250 per day, minimum two people). His trips include unlimited diving.

Dive operators will rent equipment for snorkelling, as will some hotels.

### BATU CERMIN

This **limestone outcrop** (admission 10,000Rp; ⊙ 8am-5pm), aka Mirror Rock, has a series of caves 4km east of town. The main cave is in the centre of the outcrop – take the ladder walkway up and around into the longest canyon, then proceed through a series of chambers to where the cave opens into a towering, narrow canyon. This is the 'mirror rock' that gives the outcrop its name; between 9am and 10am, depending on the time of year, the sun shines into the canyon and reflects off the walls, but it's hardly spectacular. The fee includes a guide, though navigation is not difficult.

### GUNUNG MBELING & CUNCA WULANG CASCADES

With the help of AusAID, SwissConnect and the regional government, West Flores tourism is on the rise. The goal is to get the tourism dollar into the local villages. You'll see their slick brochure upon arrival in Labuanbajo; also check out their website (www.floreskomodo.com).

Climbing up the rain-forested slopes of **Gunung Mbeling** (1239m) is the latest attraction in West Flores. The two-day trip includes eight hours of hiking, sunrise at the summit and a stop-off at the Cunca Rami Air Terjun, where you can bathe in fresh swimming holes, on the way down. The **Reo Ecotourism Association** ( ☎ 0852 3906 1205, 0813 5378 1200; www.floreskomodo .com; 750,000Rp per person) organises the treks. Reo is just an hour's drive from Labuanbajo.

If you like canyoning, you'll enjoy the **Cunca Wulang Cascades**, where local guides lead you down natural rock waterslides, off 7m rock jumps and into swimming holes beneath a series of waterfalls. Trips generally last half a day and cost 100,000Rp per person.

## Sleeping

Hotel rates include breakfast.

### CENTRAL AREA

**Gardena Hotel** ( ☎ 41258; Jl Yos Sudarso; bungalows 85,000-100,000Rp) A collection of basic bamboo huts on a rambling hillside, overlooking the gorgeous bay harbour and distant islands. The restaurant is solid, and this is easily the most popular spot in town.

**Chez Felix** ( ☎ 41032; Jl Bidaderi; r 150,000-200,000Rp) Set in a quiet location above the bay and run by a friendly family who all speak good English, this is a good option, with cute, clean tiled rooms.

**Golo Hilltop** ( ☎ 41337; www.golohilltop.com; d with fan 175,000, d with air-con 325,000-450,000Rp) Modern, superclean concrete bungalows in a hilltop garden setting with magnificent views of Teluk Labuanbajo (but not the harbour). Deluxe rooms are on the top ridge and have safety boxes. The purple and yellow colour scheme works…kind of. They arrange transport to and from town as needed.

**our pick Bayview Gardens Hotel**( ☎ 41549; www.bay view-gardens.com; Jl Ande Bole; s/d 400,000/450,000Rp; ❄ ) A new Dutch-Indo-owned hillside property. The five sweet cottages each have queen beds, private terraces (where breakfast is served), security boxes, a gorgeous garden (with over 450 plant species) and commanding harbour views. They collect rainwater for showers and use grey water to irrigate the garden. It books up, so reserve in advance.

### BY THE BEACH

This is where Labuanbjao's newest hotels are rising. At the time of writing the Jayakarta hotel chain was set to open its 100-room resort in 2010.

**Bajo Komodo Eco Lodge** ( ☎ 41362; www.ecolodges indonesia.com; s/d 660,000/720,000Rp; ❄ ) This imposing neocolonial house has six bright and spacious rooms and two detached bungalows, each with stylish pebble-floored bathrooms. It doesn't feel like an ecolodge, but it is solar-powered, collects rainwater for the showers, and grey water is recycled.

**Puri Sari Hotel** ( ☎ 42010; Jl Pantai Pede; d US$90; ❄ ) Another brand-new luxe hotel, set 2km down a rutted dirt road and on the beach. Rooms are huge, with king beds, wi-fi, wood furnishings and marble sinks. The garden needed work when we visited. Show up in low season and you may be able to get the room for the promotional rate of 500,000Rp.

**Bintang Flores** ( ☎ 42000; Jl Pantai Pede; d/ste US$120/230; 🖳 🏊 ) Relatively swish, and built like a classic tower hotel, it's set on a private beach with an attractive pool area. Rooms are large, with high ceilings, modern wood furnishings and international satellite TV. There's an internet cafe off the lobby.

### ISLAND HOTELS
It's an hour's boat ride – free for guests – to reach the following hotels from Labuanbajo. Both have a minimum two-night stay.

**Serayu Island Bungalows** (Map p529; ☎ 41258; www.serayaisland.com; s/d with fan & mosquito net 120,000/135,000Rp) Get-away-from-it-all bliss exists on Pulau Serayu. Bunk in simple bamboo bungalows with *mandis* set on a white-sand beach, with offshore snorkelling. Contact the Gardena Hotel to get here.

**Kanawa Island Bungalows** (Map p529; ☎ 0852 3917 6718; bungalows s/d 150,000/200,000Rp) A lovely beach hideaway with a strip of white sand, turquoise lagoon, endless island views and a long crooked jetty. Accommodation is basic and romantically weathered. Meals cost from 25,000Rp to 40,000Rp. Contact the Kanawa office opposite restaurant Nirvana for a lift.

## Eating & Drinking
**Porto Moro** (Jl Yos Sudarso; dishes 10,000Rp) Across from The Lounge, this funky two-storey place with warped floors and harbour views serves the cheapest food in town. It's always packed with locals, and not just because of the price.

**Matahari** ( ☎ 41083; Jl Yos Sudarso; dishes 10,000-23,000Rp) Terrific views from the deck, particularly at sunset, and a tasty menu recommended by locals that includes sandwiches, soups and hot plates.

our pick **The Lounge** ( ☎ 41962; Jl Yos Sudarso; tapas from 20,000Rp, mains 22,000-60,000Rp, espresso from 18,000Rp) Across from Porto Moro is a sleek dining room with red lounges, Balinese art and (of course) amazing views. Tapas are exceptional, as are the pizzas and homemade ravioli. But they may need to upgrade the soundtrack – c'mon, Céline Dion?

**Pesona** ( ☎ 41950; Jl Soekarno Hatta; meals 26,000Rp) Cute, ramshackle wooden restaurant perched above the harbour, specialising in fresh seafood. Try the whole snapper steamed or grilled. Meals include salad and fries or rice.

There's no real bar scene in Labuanbajo and most are content to enjoy a beer or two

with their meal. But **Paradise Bar** ( 🌙 6pm-2am Fri & Sat), set up a steep hill on the north side of town, does attract a regular weekend crowd. It satisfies all the requirements of a tropical watering hole. There's ample deck space, a natural wood bar, massive sea and island views, ice-cold beer and live music.

## Getting There & Away
### AIR
**Transnusa** ( ☎ 41800, 41955; Jl Yos Sudarso) offers daily flights departing at 11.30am from Labuanbajo's **Bandar Udara Komodo** (Komodo Airport) bound for Denpasar (700,000Rp). It also flies to Kupang (956,000Rp) on Wednesday and Friday at 10am. **IAT** (BCB Travel; Jl Kasimo) has daily noon flights to Denpasar (850,000Rp) on much newer planes. **Merpati** ( ☎ 41177) offers four flights a week to Denpasar (705,000Rp), leaving at 11am on Monday, Wednesday, Thursday and Saturday. Its office is 1.5km from town on the road to the airport.

Departure tax from Labuanbajo is 11,000Rp.

### BOAT
The ferry from Labuanbajo to Sape (60,200Rp, eight to nine hours) leaves at 8am daily. Tickets for Sape can be purchased at the harbour master's office (in front of the pier) one hour before the vessel's departure. See also p528 for Sape boat schedules.

The **Pelni agent** ( ☎ 41106) is easy to miss, tucked away in a side street in the northeast of town. The monthly Pelni ship, *Tilongkabila*, heads to Makassar and the east coast of Sulawesi; or to Bima, Lembar and Benoa.

Many travellers choose to take a boat trip between Flores and Lombok, stopping at Komodo and Sumbawa along the way for snorkelling and exploration. For more on this option, see boxed text, p540. The local Perama boat contact is **PT Diana Perama Matteru** ( ☎ 42015, 42016; www.peramatour.com; Jl Soekarno Hatta). It also books Transnusa flights.

### BUS
With no bus terminal in Labuanbajo, most people book their tickets through a hotel or agency, which makes them more expensive than they should be. If you get an advance ticket, the bus will pick you up from your hotel.

Buses to Ruteng (40,000Rp, four hours) depart every two hours from the terminal in Garantolo. One Bajawa-bound bus (100,000Rp, 10 hours) leaves at 6am daily, and buses to Ende (150,000Rp, 15 hours) run regularly via Ruteng and Bajawa, so just take the first available eastbound bus. There's also a decent minibus service. **Bajo Express** ( ☎ 42068) runs regular routes to Bajawa, Ruteng, Maumere and Ende, and they leave on time, without looping around town in search of passengers.

## Getting Around

The airfield is 1.5km from the town. Hotel reps and dive shops will meet flights and offer free lifts. A private taxi to town costs 30,000Rp. Once you're in town you can walk to most places, or hop aboard an *ojek* (3000Rp) or into a bemo (2000Rp); they do continual loops following the one-way traffic. After dark, however, the bemos cease running, *ojeks* are hard to find and you may be forced to hoof it.

Speak to transport wrangler **Jak Terming** ( ☎ 0852 3896 4782; jakflores@gmail.com) about renting a Kijang (500,000Rp to 550,000Rp a day, including driver and fuel) for trips across Flores. **Sipriano Muda** ( ☎ 0852 3924 2406) is a terrific driver, and he speaks good English. Motorbike rental is possible through most hotels.

## RUTENG

☎ 0385 / pop 37,000

Cool, refreshing and nestled among lush volcanoes and rice fields in the heart of Manggarai country, Ruteng is surrounded by beauty. But this sprawling market town is otherwise rather charmless. There are some interesting tribal villages nearby, which is why it does get its share of overnight guests in the high season. Don't miss Ruteng's lively, sprawling **pasar** (Jl Kartini), a vital lifeline to the outside world for villagers in the surrounding hills.

## Information

**BNI bank** (Jl Kartini; ☼ 8am-3.30pm Mon-Sat) Changes cash and travellers cheques and also has a Visa/Plus ATM.

**BRI bank** (Jl Yos Sudarso; ☼ 7.30am-3pm Mon-Fri, 8am-1pm Sat) MasterCard/Cirrus ATM.

**Post office** (Jl Baruk 6; ☼ 7am-2pm Mon-Sat)

**Telkom** (Jl Kartini; ☼ 24hr)

**Z-Net** ( ☎ 21347; Jl Adi Sucipto 8; per hr 10,000Rp; ☼ 9am-6pm) Ruteng's only connection.

## Sleeping

**Rima Hotel** ( ☎ 22196; Jl A Yani 14; economy s/d 75,000/100,000Rp, standard s/d 125,000/175,000Rp) One of the two best options in town. Clean standard rooms all have queen beds, wood furnishings, showers and *mandis*. Economy rooms have shared baths with *mandis*, and showers. There's also a sweet patio garden and a streetside terrace. Motorbike hire can often be arranged here.

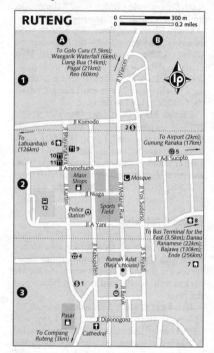

## THE FLORES 'HOBBIT'

The Manggarai have long told folk tales of *ebo gogo* – hairy little people with flat foreheads who once roamed the jungle. Nobody paid them much attention until September 2003, when archaeologists made a stunning find.

Excavating the limestone cave at Liang Bua, they unearthed a skeleton the size of a three-year-old child but with the worn-down teeth and bone structure of an adult. Six more remains appeared to confirm that the team had unearthed a new species of human, *Homo floresiensis*, which reached around 1m in height and was nicknamed the 'hobbit'.

Lab tests brought another surprise. The hominid with the nutcracker jaw and gangly, chimplike arms lived until 12,000 years ago, practically yesterday in evolutionary terms, when a cataclysmic volcanic eruption is thought to have wiped out the little people and devastated the island of Flores.

It seems that *Homo floresiensis* could represent the first ever example of human dwarfism, an evolutionary phenomenon that has been well documented in the animal world, particularly on islands. In Jersey, one of the British Channel Islands, red deer shrank to a sixth of their normal European size in just 6000 years, while California's Channel Islands were once home to the ultimate oxymoron of the animal world – a pygmy mammoth.

Flores is particularly rich in these evolutionary quirks of nature. It had minielephants called 'stegodon' as well as examples of gigantism (which tend to occur in the same locations as dwarfism), such as colossal rats and Komodo dragons (see boxed text, p530).

But not all scientists are convinced about the origins of the Flores find. The prevailing school of thought argues that the Flores hominids are descendants of *Homo erectus*, a species that fled Africa around two million years ago and spread throughout Asia – though no DNA has yet been extracted to confirm this. Until recently it was thought that the arrival of *Homo sapiens* in Asia led to the demise of *Homo erectus* around 50,000 years ago. Flores humans could indicate that the species survived in isolated places.

Anthropologists opposed to this suggest that the Flores find could represent *Homo sapiens* (who were known to be travelling between Australia and New Guinea 35,000 years ago) that suffered from microcephaly – a neurological disorder causing stunted head growth, and often dwarfism, that runs in families.

But the momentum still seems to be with the original theory, given that in 2005 a second large jawbone was found, of similar dimensions to the first discovery. And with tools very similar to those found in Liang Bua reportedly unearthed in Timor, and possibly in Sulawesi, more little people could yet emerge from the evolutionary backwoods.

For details about visiting Liang Bua, see p540.

---

**ourpick Kongregasi Santa Maria Berdukacita**
( ☎ 222 834; Jl A Yani 45; standard s/d 140,000/160,000Rp, VIP r 200,000Rp) Set on serene convent grounds, this welcome new option has gorgeous valley views and 10 large, spotless guestrooms with high ceilings, crown mouldings and plenty of natural light. The VIP room is huge, with a TV, two beds and two bathrooms, and can sleep three comfortably.

**Hotel Dahlia** ( ☎ 21377; Jl Bhayangkara; economy/ standard r 150,000/200,000Rp, VIP s/d 250,000/275,000Rp) From the outside the place looks abandoned, condemned even, but the lovely courtyard garden is surrounded by dozens of tiled rooms, and they do have up-to-date travel info. The VIP rooms are miles cleaner than the rest.

## Eating

**Rumah Makan Surya** (Jl Bhayangkara; dishes 3000Rp-10,000Rp) Heaped portions of tasty, spicy Padang food.

**Agape Cafe** ( ☎ 22561; Jl Bhayangkara 6-8; dishes 8000-30,000Rp) A darling newcomer a few years ago, its move to the large, soulless dining room was not a shrewd one. But even if the atmosphere has suffered, the coffee, roasted on the premises (check out the large roasters in the back) is still the best in town. It also has decent Indo grub, pasta dishes, Guinness and Heineken.

**Restaurant Merlin** ( ☎ 22475; Jl Bhayangkara 32B; mains 30,000Rp) This somewhat dingy dining room is the place to be for tasty Chinese food and fresh juices. Try the squid in oyster sauce or the chicken with chilli sauce.

---

**BOAT TOURS BETWEEN LOMBOK & FLORES**

Travelling by sea between Lombok and Labuanbajo is a popular way to get to Flores, as you get to see more of the region's spectacular coastline and dodge some painfully long bus journeys. Typical itineraries from Lombok take in snorkelling at Pulau Satonda off the coast of Sumbawa, and a dragon-spotting hike on Komodo. From Labuanbajo boats usually stop at Rinca and Pulau Moyo.

Be warned, this is no luxury cruise – a lot depends on the boat, the crew and your fellow travellers. Some shifty operators have reneged on 'all-inclusive' deals en route, and others operate decrepit old tugs without lifejackets or radio. And this crossing can be extremely hazardous during the rainy season, when the seas are rough.

The well-organised tours on decent boats run by Perama (see Gili Trawangan, Mataram or Senggigi sections for contact details) are safe, however. Current charges for cabin/deck are 2,600,000/2,000,000Rp for the three-day trip.

---

## Getting There & Away

### AIR

The airport is 2km southeast of town, but at research time it was still under renovation with no flights available.

### BUS

The bus terminal for eastern destinations is located 3.5km and a 2000Rp bemo ride out of town. Local buses heading west still run from the central bus/bemo terminal near the police station.

There are regular buses and bemos to Reo, which stop off at Pagal (10,000Rp, every 1½ hours). It's best to leave early from Ruteng and aim to be out of Pagal by 3pm. Gunung Mas buses going to Bajawa (60,000Rp, five hours) and Ende (120,000Rp, nine hours) depart at 7am. Buy your ticket in advance through your hotel. Buses to Labuanbajo leave at 7am, 1pm and 3pm (40,000Rp, four hours).

## Getting Around

Bemos cost 2000Rp around town. Contact Rima Hotel about motorcycle rental.

## AROUND RUTENG

**Compang Ruteng**, a 'traditional' village 3km from Ruteng has a *compang*, a traditional ancestor altar composed of a raised stone burial platform and a couple of renovated *rumah adat* (traditional houses). One is the Mbaru Gendrang, a ceremonial meeting-house that contains heirlooms, including a gold-and-silver *panggal*, a mask shaped like a buffalo horn and used in ceremonial *caci* (a martial art in which participants duel with whips and shields).

Visitors are asked to sign in and make a donation (about 20,000Rp). Ask around Ruteng for information on ceremonies held further afield.

**Golo Curu**, a hill to the north of Ruteng, offers spectacular early morning views of the rice paddies, terraced slopes and distant mountain valleys. Walk down the Reo road and, when you're about 20 minutes past Hotel Karya, turn right at the small bridge. There's a derelict shrine on the hilltop with a statue of the Virgin Mary on a pedestal. You can also drive here by *ojek* (20,000Rp). Further north, 6km from Ruteng, near Cancar, is the waterfall, **Air Terjun Waegarik**.

Manggarai sarongs are black with pretty embroidered patterns. They are sold in the main Ruteng market; or visit the weaving village of **Pagal**, 21km north of Ruteng on the main road to Reo. See left for transport information.

The 2400m **Gunung Ranaka**, an active volcano that erupted in 1987, can be reached by road from the 8km mark east of town past the airport, but views are obscured by young trees.

The limestone cave of **Liang Bua**, where the Flores 'hobbit' was found (see boxed text, p539), is about 14km north of Ruteng, down a very rough dirt track that is often not passable after periods of heavy rain. Archaeologists believe that the lip along the entrance permitted sediments to build up steadily as water flowed through the cave over millennia, sealing the remains of the humans and animals that lived and died here. There is not much to see, although some sticks mark the place where the little folk were found. Local guides, whose service is included in your 20,000Rp entry fee, will meet you at the cave's entrance and explain why Liang Bua is considered sacred. To get here take an *ojek* (10,000Rp) from Ruteng.

**Danau Ranamese**, a circular aquamarine lake 22km from Ruteng, is right next to the main Bajawa road. There are picnic spots here, and a couple of waterfalls tumble from the rear of the crater, flooding the rice paddies below. Trails loop around the lake and visitors centre, where you may be charged a 10,000Rp entrance fee. Bajawa–Ruteng buses pass the lake.

## BAJAWA
☎ 0384

Framed by forested volcanoes and blessed with a pleasant climate, Bajawa, a laid-back hill town at 1100m, is a great base from which to explore dozens of traditional villages that are home to the local Ngada people. Bajawa is the Ngada's de facto trading post, and you'll mingle with them as you stroll these quiet streets edged by blooming gardens and surrounded by cornfields. Gunung Inerie (2245m), a perfectly conical volcano looms to the south where you'll also find some hot springs. The recently emerged volcano, Wawo Muda, with its Kelimutu-esque lakes, is another favourite among the trans-Flores set.

### Information
**BNI bank** (Jl Pierre Tendean; ⏰ 8am-3pm Mon-Fri, to 12.30pm Sat) Has an ATM. Exchanges dollars and travellers cheques.
**Post office** (Jl Soekarno Hatta; ⏰ 8am-2pm Mon-Sat)
**Telkom** (Jl Soekarno Hatta; internet per hr 15,000Rp; ⏰ 24hr) The cheapest place for international calls and decent internet service.
**Tourist office** ( ☎ 21554; Jl Soekarno Hatta; ⏰ 8.30am-3pm Mon-Fri, to 1pm Sat)

### Sleeping
There once was a good choice of budget digs in Bajawa, but virtually all the cheap rooms have suffered from neglect. A good scrub and a coat of paint are needed across the board. All prices include breakfast.

**Hotel Korina** ( ☎ 21162; Jl Ahmad Yani 81; s/d 50,000/60,000Rp) The bottom of the Bajawa barrel in terms of room size, frills and cleanliness, but the staff are friendly and it will do for a night.

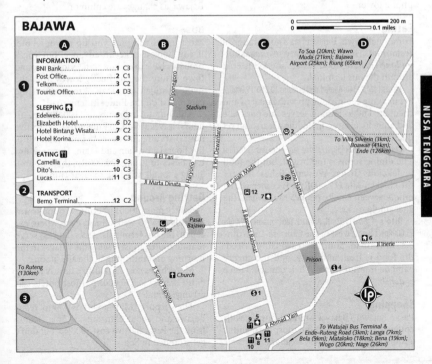

**BAJAWA**

0 — 200 m
0 — 0.1 miles

| INFORMATION | |
| --- | --- |
| BNI Bank | 1 C3 |
| Post Office | 2 C1 |
| Telkom | 3 C2 |
| Tourist Office | 4 D3 |

| SLEEPING 🛏 | |
| --- | --- |
| Edelweis | 5 C3 |
| Elizabeth Hotel | 6 D2 |
| Hotel Bintang Wisata | 7 C2 |
| Hotel Korina | 8 C3 |

| EATING 🍴 | |
| --- | --- |
| Camellia | 9 C3 |
| Dito's | 10 C3 |
| Lucas | 11 C3 |

| TRANSPORT | |
| --- | --- |
| Bemo Terminal | 12 C2 |

Stadium

Jl Diponegoro

To Soa (20km); Wawo Muda (21km); Bajawa Airport (25km); Riung (65km)

Jl El Tari

Jl KH Dewantara

To Villa Silverin (3km); Boawae (41km); Ende (126km)

Jl Hayono

Jl Gajah Mada

Jl Soekarno Hatta

Jl Marta Dinata

Pasar Bajawu

Mosque

Jl Basoeki Rahmat

Jl Inerie

Prison

To Ruteng (130km)

Jl Soryo Pranoto

Church

Jl Ahmad Yani

To Watujaji Bus Terminal & Ende–Ruteng Road (3km); Langa (7km); Bela (9km); Mataloko (18km); Bena (19km); Wogo (20km); Nage (26km)

NUSA TENGGARA

**ourpick** Villa Silverin ( ☎ 222 3865; www.villa silverinhotel.com; Jl Bajawa; economy/standard/VIP r 75,000/ 175,000/275,000Rp) Set just outside of town on the road to Ende, with beckoning verandahs and jaw-dropping valley views. VIP rooms have queen beds, hot water and are the cleanest rooms in Bajawa.

Edelweis ( ☎ 21345; Jl Ahmad Yani 76; economy/standard/ VIP r 90,000/100,000/120,000Rp; 💻 ) Even Edelweis needs a little TLC. Nevertheless, their nice gardens, great volcano views, reasonably clean VIP rooms and friendly ownership, which may boil water for a very welcome hot-water morning *mandi*, make this an appealing choice.

Elizabeth Hotel ( ☎ 21223; Jl Inerie; s/d 100,000/ 125,000Rp) Set in a quiet corner of town away from the restaurants (a car comes in handy here), rooms are cleanish, airy and very pink. Some are brighter than others. Be choosy.

Hotel Bintang Wisata ( ☎ 21744; Jl Palapa 4; standard s/d 150,000/175,000Rp, VIP r 320,000Rp) This newer place has modern rooms, from plain 'standard' class to 'VIP' rooms with TVs and shared balconies that have views of the volcano…obscured by a beautiful mobile-phone tower.

## Eating

For a small town, Bajawa has a good range of restaurants, including plenty of *makassan-Padang* (Padang-food restaurants) clustered around the bus terminal.

Lucas ( ☎ 21340; Ahmad Yani 6; mains 10,000-15,000Rp) Set in a cute cabin, done up with lanterns and chequered tablecloths, it serves fine pork sate and other local faves, including a fearsome yet quaffable *arak*.

Camellia ( ☎ 21458; Jl Ahmad Yani 74; mains 15,000Rp) The dining room is too bright, but the food is delicious. It has Western dishes, but try the chicken sate (17,000Rp). It comes with a unique sweet, smoky pepper sauce. And the guacamole rocks.

Dito's ( ☎ 21162; Jl Ahmad Yani; mains 15,000-25,000Rp) The newest of the Chinese-Indo diners on Ahmad Yani. It's reasonably priced, the food is fresh and tasty, and the cheery bamboo interior works. Their tamarillo juice is *delish*.

## Shopping

Pasar Bajawu (Bajawa Market) bustles with colourful commerce in the mornings, and is a fun scene. Local women wear and sell their ikat, and there's tons of beautiful fresh fruit to sniff and sample.

## Getting There & Away

### AIR

Merpati has resumed its Bajawa–Kupang hop. Contact its office in Kupang (see p569).

### BEMO & TRUCK

Regular bemos travel from the **terminal** (Jl Basoeki Rahmat) to Soa, Mangulewa, Mataloko, Langa and Boawae. Bemos to Bena run irregularly, two or three times a day. There is also at least one truck a day that runs to Jerebuu, passing through Bena.

### BOAT

The ASDP fairly fast ferry *Perum* runs from Aimere, on the coast near Bajawa, to Waingapu (60,000Rp) in Sumba, leaving on Monday at 4pm. It returns to Aimere overnight and then leaves for Kupang (80,000Rp) on Tuesday morning at around 9am. Take a bemo or bus from the Watujaji terminal to Aimere (15,000Rp) and buy the ticket on the ferry. Ask for the latest schedule at hotels in Bajawa, as changes are common.

### BUS

Most buses will pick you up at your hotel if you book a ticket in advance, but you'll probably have to endure endless loops around town before the bus finally leaves from the main Watujaji terminal, 3km south of the centre just off the Ende–Ruteng road.

The bus to Labuanbajo (100,000Rp, 10 hours) leaves at 6am, to Ruteng (60,000Rp, five hours) at 7am, and buses to Ende (35,000Rp, five hours) go at 7am and 11am. There are also two buses to Riung (20,000Rp, three hours), along a tough, winding road, at 1pm.

## Getting Around

Yellow bemos (2000Rp) cruise around town, but it is easy to walk almost everywhere except to the bus terminals. *Treks* (trucks) serve remote routes, most leaving the villages in the morning and returning in the afternoon.

Motorbikes cost 75,000Rp a day. A Kijang (with driver) is 550,000Rp. Most hotels can arrange rental.

The airport (Map p544) is 25km from Bajawa and about 6km outside Soa. Bemos from the Pasar Bajawu cost 5000Rp, but don't get stranded in Soa.

## AROUND BAJAWA

Bajawa's big draw is the chance to explore traditional villages in the gorgeous countryside. Their fascinating architecture features carved poles supporting a conical thatched roof. It is certainly possible to visit the area alone, but you'll learn a lot more about the culture and customs (like the caste system) with a good guide. Some organise meals in their home villages. Guides linger around hotels and can arrange day trips for 250,000Rp per person with transport, village entry fees and lunch.

The villagers are now quite used to tourists. If visiting, it is customary to sign the visitors' book and make a donation. Taking photos is usually OK, but ask first and remember that entering a village is like entering someone's home. Bena and Wogo are the most traditional and impressive villages. Bena has spectacular views.

### Langa & Bela

There are totem pole–like *ngadhu* (dedicated to male ancestors) and *bhaga* (miniature thatched-roof house, dedicated to female ancestors) in Langa, which is 7km from Bajawa, but this village is fairly modern. Bemos travel here from Bajawa's bemo terminal. Bela is more interesting and traditional and is a couple of kilometres away, off the main road.

### Bena

On the flank of the **Gunung Inerie** (2245m) volcano, 19km from Bajawa, Bena is one of the most traditional Ngada villages, and its fabulous stone monuments are the region's best.

Houses with high thatched roofs line up in two rows on a ridge, the space between them filled with fine *ngadhu*, *bhaga* (smeared with sacrificial blood) and megalithic tomblike structures. Most houses have male or female figurines on their roofs, while doorways are decorated with buffalo horns and jawbones – a sign of the family's prosperity.

A small Christian shrine sits on a mound at the top of the village and behind it a recently built lookout offers a spectacular view down a jagged valley to the sea – a two-hour walk away. Gunung Inerie can be climbed from Watumeze, between Langa and Bena, in about four hours.

Bena is the most visited village, and weavings and souvenir stalls line the front of houses. Although the village is crowded when tour groups arrive during high season and all villagers are now officially Catholic and attend a local missionary school, traditional beliefs and customs endure. Sacrifices are held three times each year, and village elders still talk about a rigidly enforced caste system that prevented 'mixed' relationships, with those defying the *adat* facing possible death.

Bena is 12km from Langa down a degraded road that's passable only in a 4WD vehicle or by motorbike. There's one daily bemo to/from Bajawa (15,000Rp); it leaves Bena at 7am and returns from Bajawa at 1pm.

### Nage

Nage is a traditional village on a plateau about 7km from Bena, with views of Gunung Inerie. A number of *ngadhu*, *bhaga* and tombs lie

---

**THE NGADA**

Over 60,000 Ngada people inhabit the upland Bajawa plateau and the slopes around Gunung Inerie. Older animistic beliefs remain strong, and most Ngada practise a fusion of animism and Christianity. They worship Gae Dewa, a god who unites Dewa Zeta (the heavens) and Nitu Sale (the earth).

The most evident symbols of continuing Ngada tradition are pairs of *ngadhu* and *bhaga*. The *ngadhu* is a parasol-like structure about 3m high, consisting of a carved wooden pole and thatched 'roof', and the *bhaga* is a miniature thatched-roof house.

The *ngadhu* is 'male' and the *bhaga* is 'female', and each pair is associated with a particular family group within a village. Some were built over 100 years ago to commemorate ancestors killed in long-past battles.

In addition to *ngadhu*, *bhaga* and the ancestor worship that goes with them, agricultural fertility rites continue (sometimes involving gory buffalo sacrifices), as well as ceremonies marking birth, marriage, death and house building. The major annual festival is the six-day Reba ceremony at Bena, 19km from Bajawa, held in late December or early January. Villagers wear specially made all-black ikat, sacrifice buffalo and sing and dance through the night.

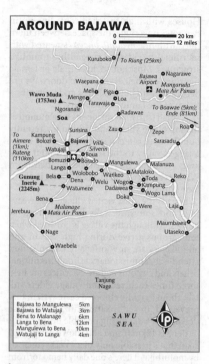

AROUND BAJAWA

| Bajawa to Mangulewa | 5km |
| Bajawa to Watujaji | 3km |
| Bena to Malanage | 6km |
| Langa to Bena | 12km |
| Mangulewa to Bena | 10km |
| Watujaji to Langa | 4km |

between two rows of high-roofed houses. About 2km before Nage are the **Malanage Mata Air Panas** (hot springs), where a fast-flowing, hot, emerald-green river mixes with a cold-water stream.

You can walk from Nage to Bena; just continue north on the sealed road through the village. Morning and afternoon bemos run from Bajawa via Bena and Mangulewa.

## Wogo

Wogo is a large village with nine sets of *ngadhu* and *bhaga,* ringed by traditional houses. This is one of the area's largest and most traditional villages, though a few mod cons have arrived, including electricity.

About 1km further on from Wogo, turn off at the Dadawea sign and follow the track to the left to Wogo Lama, where vast groups of jagged stones jut out from the ground. These megalithic **ancestor tombs** are still used in ceremonies.

Wogo is 1.5km from Mataloko, which is 18km from Bajawa on the Ende road and easily reached by bus or bemo – very regular bemos shuttle to Wogo from behind Pasar

Bajawu (2000Rp). Mataloko is famous for its huge seminary, located on the highway.

### Wawo Muda

Wawo Muda (1753m) is the latest volcano to emerge in Flores, exploding in 2001 and leaving behind a mini-Kelimutu, complete with several small lakes coloured a burnt orange inside its crater. Pine trees charred by the eruption stand in isolated patches, and there are spectacular views of Gunung Inerie.

The volcano is best visited in the wet season from November to March, if the trails are not too muddy. The lakes usually evaporate in the dry. To get there take one of the regular bemos from Bajawa (8000Rp, 50 minutes) or an *ojek* to the village of Ngoranale, near Menge, and walk an hour up an easy-to-follow trail. Some *ojek* drivers may offer to take you the whole way up, as the path is doable on a motorbike.

## BOAWAE

Charming, remote Boawae is 41km from Bajawa on the highway to Ende and is the centre for the Nage-Keo people. It sits at the base of **Gunung Ebulobo**, a steaming volcano, which can be climbed with a guide (50,000Rp). It usually involves an overnight stop on the mountain, then a two-hour ascent early the next morning. Trails are closed during the rainy season

This is also the source of the best Bajawa-area ikat, which you can see modelled by the locals when they descend here for a massive **market** every Wednesday from 8am to 2pm. Turn down the town's only 'T' intersection and you'll find it.

Ritual buffalo sacrifices also take place here, and an equally messy form of boxing called *etu* is part of the May to August harvest festivities. The boxers wear tree-bark armour painted with animal blood, and their gloves may be studded with broken glass. Talk about ultimate fighting.

Few visitors bother to stop at Boawae, but **Hotel Sao Asih Melati** ( ☎ 0813 3947 4289; s/d 60,000/80,000Rp), set off a dirt road (follow the signs) on a family plot amidst gorgeous gardens, has clean wooden rooms with flush toilets and showers. Meals are available, and they can help arrange guides to Gunung Ebulobo.

**Wisma Nusa Bunga** (r 70,000Rp) has basic concrete rooms just off the main road. It's run by a lovely family who can help you find a mountain guide.

# RIUNG

This quiet fishing village 65km from Bajawa lies opposite a scattering of offshore islands with white-sand beaches and excellent snorkelling known as the **Seventeen Islands Marine Park**. There are actually 21 islands, but government authorities decided on the number as a convenient tie-in with Indonesia's Independence Day (17 August).

Riung sprawls along a shoreline of mudflats and mangroves that is home to a Muslim Bugis stilt-house community.

## Information

The PHKA office on the main drag has information about the Riung area. Before going to the islands you must sign in and pay 15,000Rp per person (plus a 20,000Rp boat fee) at a separate booth by the dock.

There's no ATM or official currency exchange facilities in Riung. Come with ample rupiah.

## Sights & Activities

Guides will appear at your hotel offering to organise **boat trips** to the islands. **Al Itchan** ( ☎ 0813 8759 0964) is one of Riung's most experienced and dependable guides, and is highly recommended. A day trip costs 250,000Rp (for up to six), not including park admission, boat fee, snorkel gear or lunch. Three or four islands are usually included in the boat trip, including **Pulau Ontoloe**, which has a massive colony of flying foxes (these huge fruit bats blacken the sky around Riung at sunset). **Pulau Tiga** is also not to be missed. The sea is a glassy turquoise, the small reef is pristine with clouds of tropical fish, and there's a long sweep of white sand perfect for barefoot strolls.

It's also possible to **dive** the islands with **Awing Muhammad** ( ☎ 0812 3019 8727), an experienced Divemaster. Two dives cost 600,000Rp per person including gear, for two or more divers.

Hike up **Bukit Watujapi**, about 3km from Riung, for a magnificent view of the coast and the Seventeen Islands Marine Park. It's 10,000Rp to get here by *ojek*. A trek to the **Buntang Ireng** waterfall is the region's newest activity. The trail begins 8km from Riung and winds for an hour beneath cathedral trees before reaching the towering 27m cascade. Guided trips cost 275,000Rp including lunch transport to and from the trail by *ojek*. The coastline east and west of Riung is beauti-

ful and makes for some great motorbiking. Rent yours (50,000Rp to 60,000Rp per day) and drive the gorgeous 16km west to **Ruki** village, then double back and head 14km east of Riung to **Pantai Watulajar**, the best of Riung's white-sand beaches.

## Sleeping & Eating

At the time of writing, **Hotel Bintang Wisata** of Bajawa was set to open a Riung property in autumn 2009.

**Pondok SVD** ( ☎ 0813 3934 1572; standard s/d 110,000/190,000Rp, superior s/d 270,000/300,000Rp) Clean as a whistle, this missionary-run place has absolutely spotless rooms with desks, reading lights and Western toilets. The superior-class rooms have an additional living area with a sofa and a TV.

**Nirvana** ( ☎ 0813 3710 6007; bungalows 150,000-185,000Rp) Here's your Robinson Crusoe Riung outlet, with six well-constructed detached bamboo bungalows, all with open-air bathrooms. They don't serve meals.

There are only a few restaurants in Riung. The best is **Rumah Makan Murah Muriah** (mains 15,000-30,000Rp, large beer 15,000Rp), your destination for delicious, fresh grilled fish and icy Bintang.

## Getting There & Away

From Ndao terminal in Ende (40,000Rp, four hours) a bus leaves every afternoon at 1pm. The road to Ende is narrow but sealed and in mostly good condition. Two buses from Bajawa (20,000Rp, three hours) leave at 1pm. This road is a mess and is 4WD-only. The Riung–Ende bus leaves at 7am, and the bus to Bajawa departs at 6am.

# ENDE

☎ 0381 / pop 65,000

The saving grace of this muggy, dusty and crowded south-coast port and important transport hub is its spectacular setting. The eye-catching cones of Gunung Meja (661m) and Gunung Iya (637m) loom over the city and the nearby black-sand and blue-cobblestone coastline. Sukarno was exiled here in the 1930s, when he reinvented himself as a playwright…kind of.

The aristocratic families of Ende link their ancestors through mythical exploits and magical events to the Hindu Majapahit kingdom of Java. Today the population of Ende is evenly split between Christians and

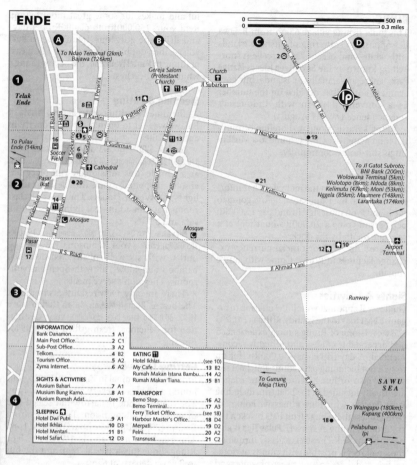

# ENDE

**INFORMATION**

| | |
|---|---|
| Bank Danamon | 1 A1 |
| Main Post Office | 2 C1 |
| Sub-Post Office | 3 A2 |
| Telkom | 4 B2 |
| Tourism Office | 5 A2 |
| Zyma Internet | 6 A2 |

**SIGHTS & ACTIVITIES**

| | |
|---|---|
| Musium Bahari | 7 A1 |
| Musium Bung Karno | 8 A1 |
| Musium Rumah Adat | (see 7) |

**SLEEPING**

| | |
|---|---|
| Hotel Dwi Putri | 9 A1 |
| Hotel Ikhlas | 10 D3 |
| Hotel Mentari | 11 B1 |
| Hotel Safari | 12 D3 |

**EATING**

| | |
|---|---|
| Hotel Ikhlas | (see 10) |
| My Cafe | 13 B2 |
| Rumah Makan Istana Bambu | 14 A2 |
| Rumah Makan Tiana | 15 B1 |

**TRANSPORT**

| | |
|---|---|
| Bemo Stop | 16 A2 |
| Bemo Terminal | 17 A3 |
| Ferry Ticket Office | (see 18) |
| Harbour Master's Office | 18 D4 |
| Merpati | 19 D2 |
| Pelni | 20 A2 |
| Transnusa | 21 C2 |

Muslims, and there are decent connections from here to other destinations in eastern Nusa Tenggara.

## Orientation

Ende is at the neck of a peninsula jutting south into the sea. The old port and most of the shops are on the western side. The main port, Pelabuhan Ipi, is on the eastern side.

## Information

### INTERNET ACCESS & TELEPHONE

**Telkom** (Jl Kelimutu; ☼ 24hr) Offers cheap international calls and internet access (10,000Rp per hour).

**Zyma Internet** (☎ 24697; Jl Yos Sudarso 3; per hr 5000Rp; ☼ 11am-10pm) Good connection in the cathedral's shadow.

### MONEY

**Bank Danamon** (Jl Soekarno; ☼ 8am-3.30pm Mon-Fri, to noon Sat) Has an ATM and offers larger credit-card withdrawals.

**BNI bank** (Jl Gatot Subroto) Situated out near the airport, this bank offers the best exchange rates and also has an ATM.

### POST

**Main post office** (Jl Gajah Mada) Out in the northeastern part of town.

**Sub-post office** (Jl Yos Sudarso) Sells stamps; opposite Hotel Dwi Putri.

### TOURIST INFORMATION

**Tourism Office** (☎ 21303; Jl Soekarno 4) Enthusiastic staff dispenses up-to-date transport information.

NUSA TENGGARA

## Sights

Meander through the aromatic **waterfront market** (Jl Pasar) with the requisite fruit pyramids and an astonishing fish section including giant tuna and sharks. The adjacent **ikat market** (cnr Jl Pabean & Jl Pasar) sells hand-woven tapestries from across Flores and Sumba.

History buffs can visit Sukarno's house of exile, now **Musium Bung Karno** (Jl Perwira; admission by donation; ☯ 7am-noon Mon-Sat). Most of the original period furnishings remain. This is where the beloved revolutionary penned the *Frankenstein* knock-off, *Doctor Satan*. Thank God for his day job.

The **Musium Bahari** (Maritime Museum; Jl Hatta; admission 10,000Rp; ☯ 7am-8pm) has a large collection of seashells but little else. Next door, the **Musium Rumah Adat** (admission 10,000Rp; ☯ 8am-2pm Mon-Sat) is a large, traditional house with a stylised village compound in front of it that has a *tubu musu* (sacrificial stone altar).

**Wolotopo**, approximately 8km east of Ende, has traditional houses built on several levels, and stunning sea views. Bemos run from Ende about twice a day. Otherwise, it's a 45-minute walk from Wolowana along the **Nanga Nesa** black-sand beach.

Northeast of Ende the road rises along a ridge opposite misty, jagged jungled peaks, overlooking a roaring river and gushing with ribbons of waterfalls in the wet season. Throw in the jade rice terraces and you have some of Flores' most jaw-dropping scenery. Yes, it's a beautiful drive to Kelimutu.

## Sleeping

Accommodation is spread all over town, but frequent bemos make it easy to get around.

**Hotel Ikhlas** ( ☎ 21695; Jl Ahmad Yani 69; economy s/d/tr 50,000/60,000/85,000Rp, standard s/d/tr 60,000/80,000/90,000Rp) This well-run place has plenty of basic but neat little rooms at good prices. Those at the rear, around a sunny courtyard, are the most desirable.

**Hotel Safari** ( ☎ 21997; Jl Ahmad Yani 65; economy s/d 100,000/125,000Rp, with air-con s/d 200,000/250,000Rp; ✷ ) Right next door to Hotel Ikhlas, this is a step-up. Rooms are large, clean and open onto a courtyard garden. Air-con rooms should be booked in advance. Breakfast is included.

**Hotel Dwi Putri** ( ☎ 21685; Jl Yos Sudarso 27-29; standard/ VIP r 150,000/250,000Rp; ✷ ) Big, white, modern and air-conditioned, this hotel feels almost classy at first, but should be cleaner. Some standard rooms have mountain views, but VIP rooms, which have air-con and hot water, are the best of the bunch.

**our pick** **Hotel Mentari** ( ☎ 21802; Jl Pahlawan 19; standard/superior/VIP r 250,000/300,000/350,000Rp; ✷ 🛜 ) Another whitewashed hotel with a brushed-up exterior. The rooms are clean, with high ceilings, and are easily the best in Ende. Some rooms have garden views and catch a bit of breeze. Be choosy. The standard class are quite sufficient unless you need a fridge and a TV. There's wireless internet access throughout.

## Eating

The waterfront market has a concentration of warungs.

**Hotel Ikhlas** ( ☎ 21695; fax 22555; Jl Ahmad Yani; dishes 3500-12,000Rp) This hotel-restaurant has bargain-priced Indonesian and Western food – the fish and chips come highly recommended.

**Rumah Makan Tiana** (Jl Pahlawan 31; dishes 6000-15,000Rp) A fun hole-in-the-wall with terrific Indonesian soul food, including a gingery *soto ayam* (chicken soup), a chilli-fired *rendang* (beef coconut curry), and *ayam sate* (chicken sate) drenched in ginger sauce.

**My Cafe** ( ☎ 22755; Jl Banteng 10; meals 12,500-17,000Rp, coffee drinks from 6000; ☯ 5pm-11pm) Ende's hipster central has a coffee bar, cold Bintang, a few standard Indo dishes (ie *nasi goreng* and *mie goreng*) and a bakery-case packed with cakes, cookies and doghnuts.

**our pick** **Rumah Makan Istana Bambu** ( ☎ 21921; Jl Kemakmuran 30A; mains 15,000-35,000Rp) Here's a classic, funkified Chinese fish house. The cast includes a sweet mouthy matriarch, her dour smirking sisterhood, and a hot, flirty waitress. But the food is the star. There's fresh fish, squid, shrimp and lobster, addictively spicy *sambal* (which they bottle and sell), and a shelf of freshly baked cakes, breads and pastries.

## Getting There & Away

### AIR

Schedules are historically fluid in eastern Nusa Tenggara, so always check flight information in advance. At the time of research, **Transnusa** ( ☎ 24333, 0852 3925 8392; Jl Kelimutu 37) offered daily flights to Denpasar. **Merpati** ( ☎ 21355; Jl Nangka) offered four flights a week to Denpasar (Monday, Wednesday, Thursday, Saturday) and Kupang (Monday, Wednesday, Thursday, Saturday).

Departure tax is 10,000Rp.

## BOAT

Ende is the major port for southern Flores and is well connected to other islands. A new ferry port was recently built 11.5km north of Ende, but the seas are too rough around this 'improved' harbour to make it useful most of the year. Ships almost always dock at Pelabuhan Ipi, which is the main port, 2.5km southeast from the town centre. Nevertheless, it's worth double-checking where your boat will arrive.

The following schedules change frequently. At research time **ASDP** ( ☎ 0813 3948 9103) ferries to Waingapu (60,000Rp, seven hours) were leaving Ende every Thursday night at midnight, before looping back again and heading to Kupang (125,000Rp) at 7pm on Friday. Buy tickets at the harbour.

Pelni's *Awu* stops in Ende every two weeks. It sails west to Waingapu, Benoa and Surabaya, then east to Kupang, Kalabahi and Larantuka. Visit the helpful **Pelni office** ( ☎ 21043; Jl Kathedral 2; ☯ 8am-noon & 2-4pm Mon-Sat).

### BUS & KIJANG

It's about 5km from town to Wolowana terminal, where you catch buses for eastern Flores. Buses to Moni (15,000Rp, two hours) operate from 6am to 2pm. Buses to Maumere (40,000Rp, five hours) leave at 7am, 9am and 4pm. Maumere buses will drop you off in Moni but charge the full fare through to Maumere. A bus to Nggela leaves between 6am and 7am, and a through bus to Larantuka leaves at 7am (nine hours).

Buses heading west leave from the Ndao terminal, 2km north of town on the beach road. Departures from Ende are to Ruteng (120,000Rp, nine hours) at 7.30am, Labuanbajo (150,000Rp, 15 hours) at 7am, Bajawa (35,000Rp, five hours) at 7am and 11am, and Riung (40,000Rp, four hours) at 1pm.

A handful of Kijang SUVs operate as shared taxis between Ende and Maumere (62,500Rp, 4½ hours).

## Getting Around

The airport is just east of the centre. Taxis to town cost around 20,000Rp.

Bemos run frequently to just about everywhere (even Pelabuhan Ipi) for a flat rate of 2000Rp. You can easily flag a bemo on the street; or find the bemo stop on Jl Hatta (near the old port).

## KELIMUTU

There aren't many better ways to wake up than to sip ginger coffee as the sun crests Kelimutu's western rim, filtering mist into the sky and revealing three deep, volcanic lakes – each one a different striking shade. That's why the tri-coloured lakes of **Kelimutu National Park** have long been considered a Nusa Tenggara must. During our research one was turquoise, the other dark brown with flecks of rust, and the third was black glass. Colours are so dense that the lakes seem the thickness of paint. It's thought that dissolving minerals (a process that can accelerate in the rainy season) account for the chameleonic colour scheme – although the turquoise lake never changes, the others fluctuate to countless shades of yellow, orange, red and brown. The summit's moonscape gives Kelimutu an ethereal atmosphere, especially when clouds billow across the craters and sunlight shafts burn luminescent pinpoints to the water's surface.

Kelimutu is sacred to local people, and legend has it that the souls of the dead go to these lakes: young people's souls go to the warmth of Tiwu Nuwa Muri Koo Fai (Turquoise Lake), old people's to the cold of Tiwu Ata Polo (Brown Lake) and those of the wicked to Tiwi Ata Mbupu (Black Lake).

Ever since locals led early Dutch settlers here, sightseers have made the sunrise trek. Today there's a sealed road up to the lakes from Moni, 13.5km away at the base of the mountain. Kelimutu's relative isolation means that surprisingly few visitors make it here outside of the July–August high season, and even then it's not too hard to find a peaceful spot to enjoy the scene. Visit in the rainy season or in the afternoon and you will probably have Kelimutu to yourself.

There's a staircase up to the highest lookout, Inspiration Point, from where all three lakes are visible. It's not at all advisable to scramble around the fringes of the craters. There once was a trail winding around them, but it crumbled years ago. Now it's just loose scree. The footing's so bad and the drop so steep, a couple of hikers perished here recently.

Pray for a sunny day – the turquoise lake reaches its full brilliance in the sunlight, and clouds may hover over the other two unless the sun is out. If the weather is not good, come back the next day – Kelimutu is really worth seeing at its best.

## Getting There & Away

Moni is the usual base for visiting Kelimutu. It's normally best to view the lakes in the early morning after the predawn mist rises, and before clouds drift in. Public bemos to Kelimutu (25,000Rp) only run from June to August. You can catch them on the main road in Moni, but you should book your seat through your hotel the day before. They leave around 4am and return to town at 7.30am. The rest of the year you'll have to charter an *ojek* (one way/return 35,000/60,000Rp), bemo (one way/return 150,000/250,000Rp, maximum four people) or car (400,000Rp return, maximum five people). Actual prices may depend on your negotiating skills. There's a PHKA post halfway up, where you'll pay the 20,000Rp admission. From the car park it's a nice 20-minute walk up through the pines to Inspiration Point.

If the skies look particularly clear and you have your own transport, it's well worth considering a trip to Kelimutu later in the day when everyone has gone, the silence of the mountain returns and the natural spectacle becomes even more moving.

Some prefer to hire transport to the top and stroll down the mountain, through the village past rice fields and along cascading streams all the way to Moni. The walk down takes about 2½ hours and isn't too taxing. A *jalan potong* (short cut) leaves the road back to Moni 1km south of the PHKA gate and goes through Manukako village, then meanders back to the main road 750m uphill from Moni.

A second short cut diverges from the trail and goes through Tomo, Mboti, Topo Mboti, Kolorongo and Koposili villages, skirts a waterfall and returns to Moni without rejoining the highway.

## MONI

Moni is a picturesque village sprinkled with upcountry rice fields and ringed by soaring volcanic peaks and distant sea views. It's a slow-paced, easy-going town that serves as a gateway to Kelimutu, and the comfortable climate invites long walks, and staying a few extra days. The turn-off to Kelimutu is 2km west of town.

Moni unfurls along the Ende–Maumere road in the heart of the Lio region, which extends

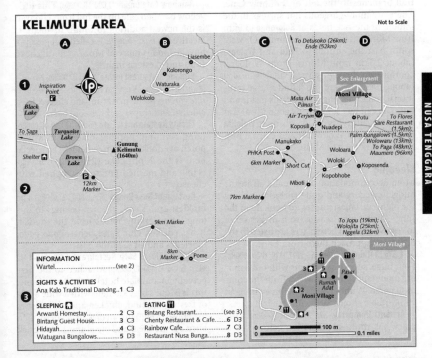

### KELIMUTU AREA

Not to Scale

To Detusoko (26km); Ende (52km)

Liasembe

Kolorongo

Inspiration Point

Black Lake

Waturaka

Wolokolo

Mata Air Panas

Moni Village

See Enlargement

Air Terjun

Koposili · Nuadepi

To Saga

Turquoise Lake

Gunung ▲ Kelimutu (1640m)

Manukako

PHKA Post

6km Marker · Short Cut

Shelter

Brown Lake

Wolojo

Potu · To Flores Sare Restaurant (1.5km); Palm Bungalows (1.5km); Wolowaru (13km); To Paga (48km); Maumere (96km)

Woloara

Wolokі · Koposenda

Kopobhobe

12km Marker

7km Marker

Mboti

To Jopu (19km); Wolojita (25km); Nggela (32km)

9km Marker

8km Marker · Pome

**INFORMATION**
Wartel....................................(see 2)

**SIGHTS & ACTIVITIES**
Ana Kalo Traditional Dancing...**1** C3

**SLEEPING**
Arwanti Homestay.......................**2** C3
Bintang Guest House..................**3** C3
Hidayah.......................................**4** C3
Watugana Bungalows.............**5** D3

**EATING**
Bintang Restaurant...............(see 3)
Chenty Restaurant & Cafe.....**6** D3
Rainbow Cafe...........................**7** C3
Restaurant Nusa Bunga..........**8** D3

Moni Village

Pasar

Rumah Adat

0          100 m
0                0.1 miles

NUSA TENGGARA

from east of Ende to beyond Wolowaru. Lio people speak a dialect of the Ende language and are renowned for their weaving; pieces are adorned with bands of blue and rusty-red. The Monday market, held on the soccer pitch, is a major local draw and a good place to snare local ikat.

## Information

There are no banks here and exchange rates are appalling. Carry cash. There's an expensive wartel at Arwanti Homestay.

## Sights & Activities

**Ana Kalo Traditional Dancing** (admission 25,000-35,000Rp) presents nightly shows in their large, thatched performance space during the peak season. Private shows (150,000-200,000Rp) can be commissioned during low season. Your guest house can help make arrangements.

Apart from the trek to/from Kelimutu, there are several other walks from Moni. About 750m along the Ende road from the centre of Moni, paths lead down to a 10m **air terjun** (waterfall), with a swimming hole and **mata air panas** (hot springs) near the falls. The trail branches to the left of Rainbow Cafe. There are more gorgeous hot springs in the middle of the rice fields at **Kolorongo** (3.5km from Moni) on the way to Kelimutu. Or walk south past the church to **Potu** and **Woloara** (about 2.5km from Moni). From Woloara, continue on through several villages to **Jopu** (about 19km), where you'll find a large traditional home with engraved beams inside and out. You can buy some really good Moni ikat here. Energetic types could walk on to **Wolojita** or loop back to Wolowaru and catch a bus, truck or *ojek* back to Moni.

## Sleeping

Moni accommodation is virtually all in the budget category and quite spread out along the highway. Guest houses do book up in the June–August high season, so it makes sense to reserve ahead. These places are listed in the order you approach them from Ende.

**our pick Hidayah** ( ☎ 0853 3901 1310; d 200,000Rp) Four huge, superclean rooms with outstanding mountain and valley views from the common porch. Without question, this is the most comfortable choice in town.

**Arwanti Homestay** (s/d 75,000/100,000Rp) This place has three spacious bungalows, each equipped with bamboo furnishings, two bedrooms, a sitting room, a bathroom with shower and a front verandah. Unfortunately, they aren't so clean, and the staff could certainly be a little more helpful.

**Bintang Guest House** ( ☎ 0852 3790 6259; s/d 60,000/75,000Rp) Just four tidy rooms with little garden patios out front and great views of the valley below. You'll be hanging around with Mr Tobias and his brood. They rent motorbikes for 75,000Rp per day.

**Watugana Bungalows** (s/d/tr 75,000/90,000/125,000Rp) Reasonably priced, older tiled rooms with a shady porch, set downhill from the main road. The management is very friendly and informative.

**Palm Bungalows** ( ☎ 0813 3914 7983; d from 75,000Rp) This is your secluded sweet spot, a ramshackle bungalow on a farm with incredible mountain views. The dusty turquoise stream that skirts the property sings a tremendous lullaby and an even better wake-up call.

## Eating

The places are listed in the order you approach them from Ende.

**Rainbow Cafe** (mains 11,000-18,000Rp) This little yellow bamboo cafe up the hill from Hidayah is the newest addition to Moni. Its menu is creative (its *nasi campur* is called 'hot gossip'), but the food is more of Moni's typical cheap Indo and Western mains.

**Bintang Restaurant** (dishes 12,000-47,000Rp) Moni's standard Indo-Western fare (*nasi goreng* and *mie goreng*, pasta, macaroni and cheese, fried chicken and chips) and ice-cold beer.

**Chenty Restaurant & Cafe** (dishes 12,000-40,000Rp) Long-running, popular place with a nice porch overlooking the rice fields. The special here is the Moni cake (25,000Rp), a vegetable and mashed potato pie topped with cheese.

**Restaurant Nusa Bunga** (dishes 8000-27,000Rp) The funkiest grub shack in town belongs to this long-time standby across from the market. It has chicken club sandwiches, *gado gado*, omelettes and all the Indo basics.

**our pick Flores Sare Restaurant** ( ☎ 0852 3902 9357; dishes 15,000-45,000Rp) Attached to the perpetually incomplete hotel of the same name, this is Moni's best kitchen, with a wide array of fresh fish, squid, chicken and pork dishes to choose from. Hire an *ojek* to get here, then burn off the meal and stroll the 1.5km back to town.

## Getting There & Away

Moni is 53km northeast of Ende and 98km west of Maumere. Buses travel to Ende (15,000Rp, two hours), starting at around 7am, and there's a bus all the way to Labuanbajo at noon.

For Maumere (35,000Rp, four hours), the first buses from Ende start coming through at around 9am or 10am and the last one passes through town at around 6pm. It's always best to travel in the morning, when buses are often half-empty. Afternoon buses are usually overcrowded. Don't book through your homestay – hail the bus as it passes through town.

Shared taxis also make the Ende–Maumere run via Moni. They travel in both directions all day until 9pm. It'll cost you 25,000Rp to Ende and 50,000Rp to Maumere.

## AROUND MONI
### Wolowaru

The village of Wolowaru, straggling along the Maumere road just 13km southeast of Moni, is a handy transport hub for the ikat-weaving villages of Wolojita and Nggela. There's a daily morning market that winds down at around 9am, except on Saturday, the main market day.

All Maumere–Ende buses stop in Wolowaru. A few morning buses originate here – check schedules at **Rumah Makan Jawa Timur** (mains 8000-16,000Rp). Most buses stop here for a meal break.

### Nggela & Wolojita

Nggela has a gorgeous hilltop position perched above the coast, but the chief attraction is the weaving, usually done by hand and still using plant-based dyes. In former times the size, colour and pattern of the ikat shawls of this region indicated the status of the wearer. Nggela ikat typically has black or rich dark-brown backgrounds, with patterns in earthy red, brown or orange. Nggela locals have earned a bad reputation for slashing tires and harassing drivers if their clients aren't buying. Bottom line: if you do come here, buy something. Or simply bypass Nggela altogether, and peruse ikat of similar quality in Wolojita, situated about 7km inland.

A road branches off the Ende–Maumere road at Wolowaru and heads to Wolojita (12km) and Nggela (19km). One bus per day leaves Ende between 6am and 7am for Nggela, passing Moni at about 9am and then Wolojita. Otherwise, it's a good half-day's walk to Nggela from Wolowaru. Your Kijang won't make it unless it's a 4WD. It's only 2km or 3km further from Moni via Woloara, so you could start from there. The volcano-studded scenery is beautiful, particularly on the downhill stretch of the road as it runs into Nggela.

From Wolojita to Nggela, either follow the road or take a short cut past the hot springs (ask for the *jalan potong ke Nggela*). It would be pushing it to do the return walk on the same day. Locals will offer you a bed for the night, but there might be a late truck going back to Wolowaru, from where you can easily find transport back to Moni.

### Detusoko

Wedged into the misty peaks above an emerald valley blanketed with rice fields is the friendly village of Detusoko. Located half-way between Ende and Moni, and just a 45-minute drive to Kelimutu, it's a great alternative to bunking in Moni. You can sleep at **Wisma Santo Fransiskus** ( ☎ 0813 2561 5488, 0813 1435 0522; d 125,000-175,000Rp), a convent with a dozen tidy guestrooms with private patios and mosquito nets. The cheaper rooms have better views, but a western-style shared bath. Breakfast is included and dinner is 50,000Rp.

### Paga

Located halfway between Moni and Maumere, is this quaint fishing village with a lovely, lonely beach and a placid bay with good snorkelling at its western edge. But you're here to lunch at the fabulous **Restaurant Larys** (0813 3941 8893; Jl Raya Maumere-Ende; meals 30,000-45,000Rp), a tumbledown fish joint on the beach. Choose your fresh catch and have it grilled or fried to perfection. And don't skimp on the fiery fresh *sambal*. Owner Agustinus Naban speaks German and English and can show you megalithic stone graves and amazing ocean views from the nearby village of **Nuabari**. If you're, um, lucky, you'll happen upon a burial ceremony and witness the ritual slaughter of pigs and buffalo. You can barely see his restaurant from the road east of town and buses won't stop here, so you'll need private transport. Drivers know it well.

# MAUMERE

☎ 0382 / pop 51,000

Blessed with a long, languid coastline backed by layered hills, Maumere should be a nice place to hang out for a while. Unfortunately the city – a sprawling, sweaty port town with a graffiti-scrawled jumble of concrete buildings, crumbling streets, a profound litter problem and relentless heat – gets in the way. Still, it is one of the main gateways to Flores, and remains well connected with Bali and Timor, so you'll probably wind up here for a night.

Thankfully, you don't have to stay in the city. There are sweet beach bungalows on the coast, along with some pleasant diversions to nearby ikat-weaving villages, the once-legendary Maumere sea gardens, and a sunken WWII wreck.

Maumere is a vortex of Sikkanese language and culture, which extends east between central Flores and Larantuka, and has been the centre of Flores' Catholic missionary activity since Portuguese Dominicans arrived 400 years ago.

## Information

### INTERNET ACCESS & TELEPHONE

**Comtel** (Jl Bandeng 1; per hr 10,000Rp; 🔀 ) The best connection in Maumere.

**Telkom** (Jl Soekarno Hatta; ⏰ 24hr) Opposite BNI.

### MONEY

**Bank Danamon** (Jl Pasar Baru Barat) Has an ATM.

**BNI bank** (Jl Soekarno Hatta) Has the best rates in town and an ATM. There's another branch opposite the market in Geliting, on the way to Waiterang.

### POST

**Post office** (Jl Pos) Next to the soccer field.

### TOURIST INFORMATION

**Tourist office** ( ☎ 21652; Jl Wairklau) Out of the way, and not particularly helpful.

### TRAVEL AGENCIES

**PT Floressa Wisata** ( ☎ 22281; Jl Sudirman; www .floressa-bali.com) This efficient company can book boat and airline tickets and offers organised tours.

## Sleeping

There's one good budget choice in Maumere, some terrific beach spots west of the city, and along the road to Larantuka in Waiara and Waiterang (see p554).

**Hotel Wini Rai** ( ☎ 21388; Jl Gajah Mada 50; s 50,000-250,000Rp, d 90,000-350,000Rp; 🔀 ) About 1km west of the centre, this sprawling courtyard hotel has five classes of rooms. The best deal here is on the spotless, air-con rooms out back. It's close to the Ende (west) bus terminal. A second branch, **Hotel Wini Rai II** ( ☎ 21362; Jl Soetomo) has near-identical room categories and prices.

**Gardena Hotel** ( ☎ 22644; Jl Patirangga 28; s/d with fan 60,000/80,000Rp, with air-con 100,000/120,000Rp; 🔀 ) A terrific budget spot on a quiet residential street east of the harbour crush. Fan rooms have newish tile, shower and *mandi*, while the air-con rooms also have TV. Rates include breakfast.

**Hotel Nara** ( ☎ 22001; Jl Moan Subu Sadipan; r with fan/air-con 90,000/130,000Rp; 🔀 ) It's a 2.5km hike from the harbour and city centre, but its clean, bright, freshly painted rooms are tremendous value. Management is warm, attentive and can arrange transport to your boat, bus or plane.

**Gading Beach Hotel** ( ☎ 0852 3900 4490; Jl Raya Don Siripe; r with fan/air-con 90,000/130,000Rp; 🔀 ) A new beach property, right on the sea, 8.5km west of town. This one is a collection of very clean bamboo bungalows with imaginative paint jobs. The barefoot bamboo restaurant has an upstairs terrace that catches the rare sea breeze, and management offers free transport to the airport and bus stations.

**Wailiti Hotel** ( ☎ 23416; Jl Raya Don Silva; s 200,000-350,000Rp, d 250,000-290,000Rp; 🔀 ) Another brand-new beach hotel with views of offshore islands, 6.5km from the city. Immaculate tiled rooms spill onto a black-sand beach. Some standard rooms are larger and nicer than the superior class, and they're closer to the sea.

## Eating

The best Maumere kitchens belong to inexpensive fish houses on the harbour.

**ourpick Rumah Makan Jakarta** ( ☎ 0812 379 5559; most dishes 6000-30,000Rp) The popular choice among sailors for a reason. And it isn't the cute, friendly staff, or its proximity to the pier. It's the fish – fresh and perfectly prepared and served almost instantly with a sensational roasted chilli *sambal* that will make you sweat. There may not be a better fish house outside of Makassar and Padang – and we do not say this lightly.

**Restaurant Bamboo** ( ☎ 0857 3755 9981; dishes 10,000-32,500Rp) Bringing a little design panache to Maumere's funky harbour is this new spot,

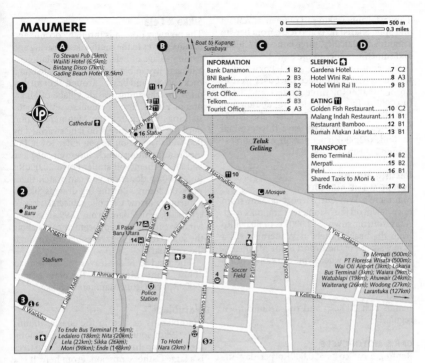

# MAUMERE

dressed tastefully in black bamboo with floor and table seating. It offers pasta, steak and Japanese dishes like beef *yakiniku*.

**Malang Indah Restaurant** ( ☎ 0813 3943 0303; mains 10,000-38,000Rp) This breezy diner grills and fries seafood at market prices. It has a nice menu of fresh juices and patio seating with harbour views.

**Golden Fish Restaurant** ( ☎ 21667; Jl Hasanuddin; large fish 35,000Rp) Hidden in town, there's another exceptional seafood choice. Walk through their open kitchen and peruse the day's live catch – including crab and lobster – on your way to the breezy second-storey dining room.

## Entertainment

There's one disco, though it's usually empty, even on Saturday. Nightlife generally revolves around karaoke and Javanese working girls.

**Stevani Pub** ( ☷ 8pm-2am) Still a funky little garden pub near the sea, 5km west of town. It can get busy late at night.

**Bintang Disco** ( ☷ 7pm-2am Fri & Sat) If you're looking for a classy night out, don't come to this beer-distribution warehouse turned

nightclub, 7km from town. It's dark, cavernous, loud and beer-soaked.

## Getting There & Away

### AIR

Maumere has good air connections. **Merpati** ( ☎ 21393; Jl Raya Don Tomas) has daily flights to/ from Kupang and Denpasar with connections to Jakarta.

Departure tax is 10,000Rp.

### BOAT

There are no longer any ASDP ferries calling in Maumere, but Pelni's *Wilis* sails fortnightly to Kupang, Larantuka, Kalimantan and Makassar. *Siguntang* sails to Lewoleba and Kupang every two weeks. **Pelni** ( ☎ 21013; Jl Suryo Pranoto) is near the entrance to the port.

### BUS & KIJANG

Maumere has two bus terminals. Departure times are rarely precise – be prepared to wait around until there are sufficient passengers.

Buses to Larantuka (32,000Rp, four hours), and buses and bemos to Geliting, Waiara, Ipir and Wodong leave from the Lokaria (or

Timur) terminal, 3km east of town, at 7.30am and 3pm. Shared taxis also leave from here to Larantuka (60,000Rp, three hours) at 7.30am, and sometimes later in the day.

The Ende (or Barat) terminal, 1.5km south-west of town, is the place for buses west to Moni (35,000Rp, three hours) and Ende (40,000Rp, five hours), leaving at 7am and 3pm. Buses to Sikka and Ledalero also depart from here. Shared taxis leave this terminal for Ende (62,500Rp per person, 4½ hours) at around 7.30am.

## Getting Around
### TO/FROM THE AIRPORT

Maumere's Wai Oti Airport is 3km from town, 800m off the Maumere–Larantuka road. A taxi to/from town is 12,000Rp, or 50,000Rp from the beach hotels in Waiterang. It's a 1km walk out of the airport to the Maumere–Larantuka road where you can hop a bemo (2000Rp) into town.

### BEMO

Bemos cost 2000Rp and run around town regularly.

### CAR & MOTORCYCLE

Renting a car costs 550,000Rp per day, in-cluding driver and fuel for trips around the Maumere region. Those organising road trips to Moni and further west should agree on an itinerary and a schedule of staggered pay-ments before departure. PT Floressa Wisata and the Gardena Hotel can organise rental cars. Gardena staff can also arrange motorbike (75,000Rp per day) rental.

## AROUND MAUMERE
### Ledalero & Nita

Many Florinese priests studied at the Roman Catholic **Seminari Tinggi St Paulus Ledalero** in Ledalero, 18km from Maumere on the Ende road. The chief attraction on these shady grounds is the **museum** (suggested donation 10,000Rp; 7am-2pm Mon-Fri, 7am-noon Sat), which houses a collection of historic stone tools, old Portuguese weaponry, and Florinese ikat, with designs and natural dyes that are either rare or no longer produced.

Nita is 2km beyond Ledalero and has a Thursday market, where you should be able to purchase some extremely good-quality Sikka-style ikat. Bemos to Ledalero and Nita leave from Maumere's Ende terminal.

### Sikka & Lela

The highway descends through coconut and banana groves to the south-coast weaving and fishing village of Lela, 22km from Maumere. Villagers live in bamboo huts sprinkled on a rocky black-sand beach. Around 4km further on is the charming seaside village of Sikka, one of Flores' first Portuguese settlements. Its kings dominated the Maumere region until the 20th century. You'll be swarmed by ikat-wallahs as soon as you enter town, but they're a charming bunch. Buy even one piece and all of them will smile. For a 20,000Rp to 50,000Rp donation you can watch them work the looms. But the big draw is Sikka's gorgeous, narrow Catholic **cathedral** (admission by donation), which dates from 1899. The open windows in the arched, beamed eaves allow the sound of crashing waves to echo through the sanctuary.

The road to Sikka leaves the Ende road 20km from Maumere. Regular bemos (5000Rp) run from Maumere to Sikka.

### Watublapi

Watublapi is nestled in the coastal moun-tains 19km southeast of Maumere. Among the swaying palms, mango and avocado trees is a large Catholic mission. From here, it is a pleasant walk to **Ohe**, set on a spiny ridge with views over both coasts of Flores. Locals will no doubt be confused, even startled by your pres-ence, but it's a very safe town. **Bola** is a large village 6km from Watublapi, and 2km further on is the traditional coastal weaving village of **Ipir**. Market day in Ipir is Monday and bemos go there from Maumere (5000Rp, 1½ hours). On other days bemos usually finish at Bola. It may be possible to stay with villagers or the *kepala desa* in Bola or Ipir.

### Waiara

Waiara is the departure point for the Maumere 'sea gardens', once regarded as one of Asia's finest dive destinations. The 1992 earthquake and tidal wave destroyed the reefs around Pulau Pemana and Pulau Besar, but they've recovered a fair bit.

Just off the Larantuka road, 9km east of Maumere, Waiara has two resorts. The past-its-prime **Flores Sao Resort** ( 21555, 0813 3906 2904; s/d 200,000/350,000Rp; ) has dated rooms with 1970s sitcom decor on a gorgeous stretch of black sand. The dive shop has shut down, and some of the rooms are pretty musty. **Sea World**

**Club** (Pondok Dunia Laut; ☎ 21570; www.sea-world-club
.com; bungalows US$25-60; ❄ ) is not just a suburban
Maumere beach resort, it's an Indo-German
Christian collaborative started to provide local
jobs and build tourism. The cabanas and bungalows are clean and comfortable, with ikat
bedspreads, hot water and air-con. And even
if they are a bit overpriced, they are on a quiet
black-sand beach with views of Pulau Besar.
The restaurant is decent, and they have a dive
shop (US$60 for two dives including gear).

To get to the hotels, catch any Talibura-
or Larantuka-bound bus from Maumere to
Waiara (3000Rp). Both hotels are signposted
from the highway; Flores Sao Resort is about
500m further along the road.

## Ahuwair, Wodong & Waiterang

The greater Maumere area does not get any
more tranquil or beautiful than the narrow,
palm-dappled beaches of Ahuwair, Wodong
and Waiterang, 26km to 29km east of the
city. There are two simple bungalow operations here and a shockingly inexpensive and
classy barefoot resort with a scuba school and
tremendous Indonesian cuisine.

There's an impressive variety of dive and
snorkelling sites here, as well, with plenty
of marine life around Pulau Babi and Pulau
Pangabaton, a sunken Japanese water-trans-
port ship from WWII, and colourful microlife in the 'muck' (shallow mudflats). All the
hotels can organise snorkelling trips to the
islands for around 95,000Rp per person, including lunch and equipment, with a minimum of three people. Local fishermen also
offer extended snorkelling trips from their
boats (350,000Rp, maximum five people).
**Happy Dive** (☎ 0812 466 9667), based at Ankermi
cottages, charges €55 for two dives, including
gear and boat transfers. In November whale-
watching trips are also offered, although you'll
probably see migrating sperm whales breach
and spout from the beach.

All of the following places are signposted
from the highway and are located down trails
10m to 500m from the road; they are listed in
the order you approach them from Maumere.
Rates include breakfast.

**Sunset Cottages** (☎ 0852 5309 9597; sunsetcottages@
yahoo.co.uk; Maumere–Larantuka Rd Km 25; s/d bungalows
with mandi 60,000/100,000Rp) Nest on a secluded
black-sand beach, with views of offshore islands, shaded by swaying coco palms. The
seven thatched, coconut-wood and bamboo
bungalows have Western toilets and *mandis*,
with decks overlooking the sea. Snorkel gear
is available for hire, and they offer overnight
camping trips to the islands' deserted beaches.
Order ahead for fresh fish.

**Lena House** (☎ 0813 3940 7733; bungalows with mandi
45,000Rp) Chill out in one of three clean bamboo
bungalows, operated by a sweet young family
and set on a spectacular stretch of beach, with
jungled mountains painted against the eastern
horizon. Owners arrange snorkelling trips, but
you may be just as happy to let your mind drift
as you watch local fishermen ply the glassy bay
in their dugouts. It's convenient to stay here
if you're diving with Happy Dive.

**our pick Ankermi** (☎ 0812 466 9667; www.ankermi
happydive.com; bungalows per person 165,000Rp, mini-
villa incl 2 meals & afternoon tea 210,000Rp) A groovy
Swiss-Javanese couple own the area's sweetest
choice. She's the dive instructor; he's the dive
guide, designer and chef. The cute, thatched
concrete and bamboo bungalows have Indo
toilets and showers, and front decks with
ocean views. Their dive shop, Happy Dive, is
the best in the Maumere area. They grow their
own organic rice and vegetables on site, and
their imaginatively prepared and presented
Javanese meals are spectacular.

Wodong, the main village in the area, is
on the Maumere–Larantuka road. Take any
Talibura, Nangahale or Larantuka bemo or
bus from the Lokaria terminal in Maumere
(3000Rp). A bemo from Wodong to Waiterang
costs another 1000Rp. A taxi or chartered
bemo from Maumere is around 50,000Rp.
Buses and shared taxis to Larantuka pass by
throughout the day.

## Around Waiterang

The five- to six-hour climb of the hulking, still
steaming **Gunung Egon** (1703m) is a popular day
trip. Charter a bemo (15,000Rp) to the village
of **Blidit**, 6km back toward Maumere, where
you can arrange a guide (75,000Rp) and walk
or drive another 7km to **Andalan**. From here it's
another 2.5km hike to the crater. Once back
in Blidit, you can soak in riverside **hot springs**
before catching a bemo back to Waiterang.
The climb can only be attempted in the dry
season, and you'll need solid walking shoes.
Start early to avoid the heat.

**Nangahale**, 10km northeast of Wodong, is
an interesting boat-building village that was
settled by survivors from Pulau Babi after
the 1992 earthquake and tsunami. It's easily

reached by bemo or bus from Waiterang. On the way to Nangahale, the road passes **Patiahu**, 33km from Maumere, which has the area's best white-sand beach.

## LARANTUKA
☎ 0383

A busy port of rusted tin roofs at the easternmost end of Flores, Larantuka rests against the base of **Gunung Ili Mandiri** (1510m), separated by a narrow strait from Pulau Solor and Pulau Adonara. It has a fun street-market vibe at dusk, when Jl Yos Sudarso and its tributaries come alive with the commerce of fresh fruit and fish, but most visitors stay just one night on their way to Kupang or the Solor and Alor Archipelagos.

Larantuka was one of Indonesia's first ports to attract European interest, as it lay on the route used by Portuguese sandalwood runners based in Timor. By 1575 more than 20 Dominican missions were built in the area. Portugal maintained a presence in Larantuka until the mid-19th century, and their descendents, called 'Topasses', still live in Larantuka.

Easter is a particularly good time to be in town, when there are huge processions of penitents and cross-bearers.

### Orientation & Information
Most hotels, the ferry pier, shipping offices and the main bus terminal are in the southern part of town. Further northeast is the Muslim quarter, as well as the **tourist office** (☉ 8am-2pm Mon-Fri), post office, **Telkom warnet** (per hour 10,000Rp; ☉ 24hr), which has solid internet access, and airport. **BNI bank** (Jl Fernandez 93) and **BRI bank** (Jl Udayana) both have branches with ATMs and change dollars and travellers cheques.

### Sights & Activities
Catholicism flourishes in Larantuka. There's a large **cathedral**, and the smaller **Kapela Tuan Maria** (Holy Mary Chapel) contains Portuguese bronze and silver known as *ornamento*. Across the street from the chapel is the **Mater Dolorosa Shrine** with a series of Passion reliefs.

### Sleeping & Eating
**our pick** **Hotel Rulies** (☎ 21198; Jl Yos Sudarso 40; s/d/tr 50,000/75,000/90,000Rp) This funky spot, near the harbour and across the street from the sea, has clean rooms with concrete floors, mostly saggy beds and shared *mandis*. Management is friendly, English-speaking and on top of current transport schedules.

**Hotel Fortuna I** (☎ 21140; Jl Basuki Rahmat 170; s/d with mandi 60,000/90,000Rp; r with air-con 175,000-200,000Rp; ✷ ) By far the best of the three Fortunas in town. It rambles along the water in the north end of town, but somehow manages to avoid ocean views at all costs. The rooms are a bit scruffy, but have queen beds and air-con.

**Hotel Tresna** (☎ 21072; Jl Yos Sudarso 8; s/d 75,000/125,000Rp, with air-con 125,000/175,000Rp; ✷ ) Has soulless rooms, but a nice little garden. If Rulies is full, it's a good alternative.

**Rumah Makan Nirwana** (Jl Yos Sudarso; dishes 5000-14,000Rp) Larantuka's first choice. The Chinese and Indonesian dishes come in filling portions, and if you buy the fresh fish at the late-afternoon sidewalk market on Jl Yos Sudarso, only steps from its front door, they'll grill it up for a modest fee.

Or stop by the **night market** (Jl Yos Sudarso; dishes 8000-27,000Rp), where you can get *mie ayam* (chicken noodles), *bakso* (meatball soup) and grilled chicken and fish opposite the Hotel Tresna.

### Getting There & Away
#### AIR
At the time of research, **Transnusa** (☎ 232 5386; 0852 3910 9100) was about to reopen links between Larantuka and Kupang (590,000Rp, 45 minutes), leaving Larantuka on Tuesday and Friday.

#### BOAT
All boats – from large Pelni cruisers to wooden ferries – depart from the main pier in the centre of town. Double-check departure times in advance, especially in the rainy season, when schedules are more like suggestions. Boats can get crowded, so arrive early to claim a seat, and bring food and water with you.

Wooden boats to Lewoleba on Lembata (30,000Rp, four hours), all via Waiwerang (Adonara, 12,000Rp) and Lamakera (Solor, 16,000Rp), depart from the pier in the centre of town at 8am and 1pm.

Three useful Pelni services call on Larantuka. *Siguntang* serves Lewoleba, Kupang and Makassar every two weeks. *Wilis* sails to Makassar, Kalimantan, Maumere and Kupang. *Sirimau* docks at Kalabahi, Kupang and Makassar, then sails west to Semarang and Jakarta. The **Pelni office** ( ☎ 21155; Jl Diponegoro) has details on all Pelni services.

## BUS

The main bus terminal is 5km west of town, but drivers may drop you off at a hotel if you ask. Buses also pick up passengers in the centre of town – speak to your hotel staff about this.

Buses to/from Maumere cost 32,000Rp and take almost five hours. You'll also find Kijangs waiting at the terminal; these speedy shared taxis cost 60,000Rp per person for an air-con three-hour ride to Maumere. Transport to Maumere is regular until around 5pm.

## Getting Around

Bemos (3000Rp) run up and down Jl Niaga and Jl Pasar, and to outlying villages. *Ojeks* also run to the pier and bus terminal for about 5000Rp.

## AROUND LARANTUKA

Six kilometres north of Larantuka, **Weri** is a popular sundown swimming spot among locals. The views from here are gorgeous and the beach has a nice mix of white and black sand, but the floating rubbish will tempt you to stay dry. You can get there by bemo from the central bemo stop in Larantuka. If you arrive by *ojek*, return to town via the narrow coastal road, which winds through banana groves and offers glimpses of front-porch family life.

# SOLOR & ALOR ARCHIPELAGOS

This is where you land if you crave the under-explored Indonesia, if you are dreaming of jade volcanic islands dropped in dimpled blue glass, if you're hoping to trek to authentic head-hunting villages, or shove off with indigenous whalers in rowboats, armed with nothing but bamboo harpoons. Adonara, Solor and Lembata form the Solor Archipelago, just east of Flores and separated by a swift, narrow strait. Lembata attracts the most attention because of the ethnic Lamalera whalers, but it receives barely a trickle of tourism. Adonara and Solor were settled by the Portuguese in the 16th century and haven't seen a major *bule* influx since. Together their people are known as the Lamaholot.

Thanks to its gorgeous anemone gardens, underwater walls draped in fluorescent sponges, migrating whales and schooling hammerheads, the Alor Archipelago gets the bulk of the region's tourism and offers almost daily flights to Kupang. But its recently expanded access masks the fact that churning cold water surrounds the islands and that it kept them remote and pristine for centuries, which explains why on the islands of Pantar and Alor you can venture deep into the countryside and visit some of the friendliest and most authentic tribal villages in Indonesia. Here you can hike red-earth trails from village to

**NUSA TENGGARA**

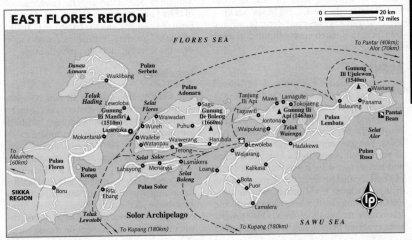

EAST FLORES REGION

village, chew betel nut, smoke home-cured tobacco, learn to handle a bow and arrow, and spend the night in traditional huts with massive sea views. Kalabahi (Alor), a burgeoning port town teeming with migrants and merchants from Java and Flores, is Alor's commercial centre.

You'll definitely need some basic Bahasa Indonesia to get by, and because foreigners are so few and far between, constantly being the centre of attention can make you feel like Britney Spears on an island of paparazzi. Still, the Lamaholot islanders mean well, so breathe deep and try not to lash out.

Food quality and general hygiene are not great away from the urban centres of Kalabahi and Lewoleba (Lembata). Rupiah won't be a problem with ATMs in both Lewoleba and Kalabahi.

## History

European contact was made as early as 1522 when the last remaining ship of Magellan's fleet sailed through Selat Alor (Lembata-Pantar Strait). By the middle of the century, the Dominican Portuguese friar Antonio Taveira had landed on Solor to spread his gospel. The Solor mission became the base for extending Christianity to mainland Flores, and a fort was built to protect the converts from Muslim raids. The Dutch eventually forced the Portuguese out of Solor in the mid-19th century.

## Getting Around

Alor and Lembata have bemos, *mikrolet* (small taxi) and a few ancient buses, but most of the islands have only one decent road, and transport to isolated areas is limited to a few trucks.

## ADONARA

Adonara, edged by a network of coastal mangroves and pearl farms, and more than a few empty beaches, remains a place to be discovered. It was known as the 'Island of Murderers' because of a feud between two clans. The feud apparently ran for hundreds of years, with people in the hills being killed and houses burned – it was very likely a case of ritual conflict between the Demon and Paji groups. Animist traditions remain influential in the hinterland, where Christianity and Islam have tenuous footholds. One traveller even reported placing her hands on a sacred

rock above one village and being unable to remove them. The chief settlements, Wailebe (on the west coast) and Waiwerang (on the south coast) are linked by a few bemos.

### Waiwerang

With the jumble of tin roofs, fishing boats, mosques, churches and coconut groves, even a few hours here offers the romance of wandering a remote tropical outpost. Waiwerang's markets on Monday and Thursday attract villagers from throughout the island and from Solor. Waiwerang has a post office, a wartel and a bank, but money cannot be changed.

There's only one decent place to stay. **Hotel Ile Boleng** (Jl Pasar Baru; s/d 75,000/120,000Rp) has English-speaking management, and meals can be arranged. Rooms at the back have sea views.

All the boats from Larantuka to Lewoleba on Lembata call at Waiwerang (12,000Rp, two hours). Passenger ferries usually dock at the main wharf in the centre of town, but at low tide may dock at the car-ferry port 1km west of town.

Small boats run between Waiwerang and the towns of northern Solor (Lamakera, Menanga and Lahayong) on Monday and Thursday. Otherwise you can charter a boat to Solor for around 250,000Rp.

## LEMBATA

With just over 300 tourists per year, Lembata, a rugged island laced with earthen roads and knitted together with cornfields, banana, papaya and coconut groves, is barely on the tourism radar. But thanks to the smoking cone of **Ili Api** (1463m), which towers over the main town of Lewoleba, and the fascinating whaling village of Lamalera, it usually manages to win over the intrepid ones who pass through.

### Lewoleba
☎ 0383
The nearby, smouldering Ili Api notwithstanding, Lewoleba, the commercial centre on Lembata, is just a sprawling, muggy, laid-back town with a couple of large government buildings and a Telkom office. Locals will notice you, so get used to the 'Hey, mister!' symphony.

Boats stop at the pier, which is a 10-minute walk west of town – take an *ojek* for 5000Rp. Extending over the water, 500m from Lile Ile guest house, is the stilted village of Bajo. Stroll over at low tide to meet local pearl divers who will probably invite you out on diving trips.

## ORIENTATION & INFORMATION

The centre of Lewoleba is the market place, which comes alive every Monday. There are **BNI** and **BRI** branches with ATMs on the main road. You can change dollars inside.

The post office is off the main street near the southern side of the market. The **Telkom office** (☯ 7am-11pm) is 500m west of town past the **Government Plaza** (per hr 12,000Rp; ☯ 8am-2pm), where you'll find the only web portal in town.

## SLEEPING & EATING

**Lile Ile** ( ☎ 41250; s/d 25,000/40,000Rp) This long-running homestay is hidden behind a concrete plant and owned by Jim, an affable Dutch-Indonesian transplant. He is a great conversationalist, an authority on local travel information, and he has a tremendous DVD collection, which is why despite the ramshackle rooms and overgrown grounds (he once had volcano views), backpackers still crash here. He did promise a renovation when we passed through.

**Hotel Lewoleba** ( ☎ 41012; Jl Awololong 15; s/d with fan 45,000/60,000Rp, s/d with air-con 90,000/110,000Rp; ✷ ) The somewhat upmarket lobby, complete with cushy sofas, sets the tone in this fairly slick place, which has the largest rooms in town. It's down the road opposite the Losmen Rejeki, past the post office. The owners speak good English and can book Merpati flights.

**Losmen Rejeki** ( ☎ 41028; Jl Trans Lembata 93; s/d 75,000/100,000Rp, with air-con 100,000/150,000Rp; ✷ ) Opposite the market, this family operation has comfortable rooms, some with very efficient air-con. Management speaks good English and can arrange Pelni reservations.

**Rumah Makan Idaman** (meals 8000-15,000Rp) On the main road, west of the commercial crush, this simple Javanese joint serves smoked and grilled fish, baked chicken wings, and spinach in a tangy peanut sauce.

**Warung Makan Berkat Lomblen** ( ☎ 41647; Jl Rayuan Kelapa; meals 10,000-18,000Rp) The best meals on the island can be found at the bamboo dining room adjacent to the mosque. Pak Tanto, the engaging, English-speaking owner cut his teeth as a food and beverage manager at the Grand Hyatt in Nusa Dua, and he serves up terrific grilled and fried fish and chicken dinners. The powdered-sugar doughnuts are addictive.

## GETTING THERE & AWAY

Merpati operates three flights a week to Kupang (596,000Rp), leaving at 7am on Tuesday, Wednesday and Thursday. Flights depart from the Lamahora airstrip, 4km west of Lewoleba.

Daily ferries to Larantuka (30,000Rp), via Pulau Adonara, depart at 8am and 1pm. At research time there was also one ferry a week to Kalabahi (59,000Rp) on Alor, leaving on Monday night at 9pm, passing through Baranusa and arriving at 2pm. But rough seas lead to frequent cancellations in the wet season. Pelni's *Siguntang* offers an almost weekly service to Kupang (economy/private cabin 120,000Rp/270,000Rp, eight hours), leaving at 11pm and arriving the next morning. You can check the schedule and buy tickets at Losmen Rejeki.

## GETTING AROUND

*Mikrolet* cost 2000Rp and run around town and to the harbour. *Ojeks* cost 3000Rp for anywhere in Lewoleba and 5000Rp to the docks.

There are no longer any ferries between Lewoleba and Lamalera; a truck convoy (30,000Rp, four hours) covers this route, leaving daily at around 1pm. The road is extremely rough, rutted and muddy. If you've missed the noon truck, consider chartering a 4WD through **Robert 'Obet' Keraf** ( ☎ 0813 3940 5412; 700,000-800,000Rp).

Buses run northeast from the Lamahora terminal, 4km west of town, to Wairiang (40,000Rp, three hours), where there's a good Thursday market and wooden ferries to Alor. *Mikrolet* run to Hadakewa (10,000Rp, 45 minutes) and direct to Balauring (25,000Rp, two hours).

Hiring a motorbike costs 75,000Rp per day; best arranged through your guest house.

# Around Lewoleba

Lembata's best ikat, recognisable by its burgundy base and detailed patterns, comes from the villages on the slopes of Ili Api, 15km to 20km from Lewoleba. On the north coast, **Atawatun** and **Mawa** are two sources of fine weaving. At **Jontona**, on the eastern side of a deep inlet on Lembata's north coast, it's possible to stay with the *kepala desa*. An hour's walk from Jontona towards Ili Api is the **Kampung Lama** (Old Village), where you'll find some traditional houses. These contain sacred and prized objects, including a huge number of elephant tusks, but are occupied by villagers only for ceremonies such as the *kacang* (bean) festival in late September or early October. It is possible to climb **Ili Api** from Lama; it takes a full day to go up and down and is easiest with a guide (best arranged in Jontona).

Regular bemos from Lewoleba head to Waipukang (30 minutes), from where you can walk to Jontona in an hour. Infrequent bemos also run to Atawatun, Mawa and Lamagute, though this region is best explored with your own wheels.

Lembata has some good **beaches**. Take an *ojek* to Pantai Lerahinga, where there's good snorkelling. Sunbathing is difficult, as crowds of kids block all sunlight.

## Lamalera
### pop 1900

Like characters from an Indonesian *Moby Dick*, the hard-scrabble men of Lamalera village on the south coast of Lembata hunt sperm and pilot whales using nothing more than bamboo harpoons (with iron warheads), wooden boats and prayer (see boxed text, opposite). Because of the small numbers of whales taken – around 15 to 25 a year – these hunters are exempt from the international ban on whaling, and their hazardous livelihood continues. The whaling season runs from May to October, when the seas aren't too rough. Locals welcome guests-gone-primal on whale hunts. It costs 100,000Rp for the goriest thrill of your life.

Lamalera itself is a tiny, fascinating little village centred on a black-sand cove lined with 22 thatched boathouses where you'll find oars, nets, harpoons and more than a little bit of whale bone. Local men will pose for pictures and allow you to watch them build and repair boats, and will deeply appreciate a pack of smokes. Homes arc around the beach and ramble up the steep hillside offering views of the deep-blue sea and migrating whales. And if there's been a recent kill, bits of drying whale meat hang from the eaves. You won't find any phones, internet or banks, and electricity exists between 6pm and 6am only. There's some decent snorkelling around the rocky outcropping at the west end of the bay, and you can charter a boat and troll for tuna if you bring a rod and reel.

On Saturday there's an interesting **barter-only market** at Wulandoni, about a 1½-hour walk along the coast from Lamalera. Another nice walk along the coast is to **Tapabali**, where you can see local weaving – the ikat has motifs of whales and mantas.

## SLEEPING & EATING

There are four small homestays in Lamalera. Rates include all meals.

**White House** (r 60,000Rp) Here's a – dare we say – Mediterranean perch overlooking the beach and rock reef. Rooms have queen or bunk beds, private baths and share a living room and deck. It was quite dirty when we visited, but nothing a little elbow grease couldn't fix. Meals are not recommended; eat at Mama's.

**Abel Beding** (r with shared/private bath 60,000/75,000Rp) Across the road from the beach is the best-appointed homestay in town. Rooms are clean, tiled, and some have sea views. Abel speaks some English and has a boat available for private charter.

**Mama Maria's Homestay** (r 75,000Rp) Nestled just behind the main square, the cramped rooms in mama's house have cracked concrete floors and curtains where doors should be – but nobody in town cooks better than she. If you want to eat but not sleep here, arrange meals (10,000Rp to 15,000Rp) in advance.

**Guru Ben's** (r 75,000Rp) Up the steep staircase west of the town square, there is no better view in town. Rooms have concrete floors, double beds, but no fans and shared baths with *mandis*. There is one breezy room off the front porch with an incredible panorama of the soaring green peaks and the undulating ocean.

## GETTING THERE & AWAY

From Lewoleba, a daily truck convoy is scheduled to leave the market at 1pm (30,000Rp, four hours) bound for Lamalera. Returning to Lewoleba, a daily truck leaves at 4.30am. It wasn't running when we visited, but we were assured that there's usually a much more comfortable group taxi service (30,000Rp, 3½ hours) running between Lewoleba and Lamalera. Shared SUVs supposedly leave Lewoleba at 11am and return at 4pm. You may also consider chartering a 4WD through **Robert 'Obet' Keraf** ( ☎ 0813 3940 5412; 700,000-800,000Rp).

## Wairiang

This small town on the eastern peninsula is a departure point for weekly wooden ferries linking Alor and Lembata, but there's no pressing reason to stay, although there is a good Thursday market here and nearby **Pantai Bean** is arguably the island's best white-sand beach.

## LAMALERA'S WHALERS

'*Baleo, Baleo!*' the shout goes when potential targets are spotted in the waters off Lamalera. This is the last village on earth where humans still regularly hunt whales by hand, using bamboo-shafted harpoons. It's a hazardous way of life that takes around 15 to 25 sperm whales from the ocean in an average year, a subsistence livelihood that conservation groups have determined does not threaten sperm whale numbers (estimated at over a million worldwide).

Be warned that if you accompany the whalers on a hunting trip it can be an extremely harrowing and bloody experience that can drag on for hours. However, your chances of seeing a whale hunt or the bloody butchering of a whale are quite small. Note that, if a whale has been speared but is not dead, the hunters will not necessarily want to head for home as night approaches so you can get your evening meal – their food supply for the next few weeks is on the other end of the line.

The wooden whaling boats (called *tena*) are around 10m long and held together with wooden dowels and lashed twine. Some engine-powered boats are now being used in Lamalera for hunting dolphins and manta rays, but all whaling vessels still carry a mast, a sail made from palm leaves and a crew who row furiously to bear down on a whale when one is spotted. As the gap between the boat and the whale narrows, the harpooner – balanced on a protruding plank – takes a bamboo harpoon and attempts to leap onto the back of the whale (using the force of his weight to drive home the harpoon). An injured whale will try to dive, dragging the boat with it, but cannot escape since it has to resurface. Often the whale will need to be speared with several harpoons before it weakens, and the ocean becomes a blood bath as the hunters prod the great mammal with knives, attempting to speed up its death.

Every part of the sperm whale is used. The dark meat is shared according to traditional dictates, with most of it reserved for the crew and portions going to virtually every family in the village. Spermacetu oil from the head (which was particularly prized by 19th-century whalers and used to burn lamps) is used for cooking. Innards are traded for fruit and vegetables in a barter-only market in the hills. Tourists buy the teeth.

The sperm whale is particularly prized, though other toothed whales (pilots and orcas) are occasionally taken. Baleen whales (plankton-eaters with sieve-like feeding mechanisms) are never touched. Mantas, dolphins, sharks (mainly hammerheads but also the odd whale shark) are hunted throughout the year – all are caught using harpoons.

Buses (40,000Rp, three hours) run from Wairiang over the sealed road to Lewoleba.

## ALOR

The final link of the island chain that stretches east of Java is wild, volcanic and drop-dead gorgeous. There are crumbling red-clay roads, jagged peaks, white-sand beaches and chilly, crystal-clear bays that have some remarkable diving – with plenty of pelagics and sheer walls draped in eye-popping sponges. The cultural diversity here is simply staggering. In this tiny archipelago alone there are over 100 tribes who, by some accounts, speak eight languages and 52 dialects. The terrain and lack of roads isolated the 185,000 inhabitants from one another and the outside world for centuries. Although the Dutch installed local rajas along the coastal regions after 1908, they had little influence over the interior, where people were still taking heads in the 1950s.

Today, Alor is around 75% Protestant and 20% Muslim, although indigenous animist traditions endure. Most islanders survive on subsistence fishing and farming, and are cultivating new cash crops, including vanilla, turmeric, candlenuts and cloves. The export of seaweed is also increasing thanks to the work of European NGO SwissConnect. But make no mistake, Alor is very poor and in some pockets children are morbidly malnourished.

Though a network of new roads now covers the island, boats are still a common form of transport. The few visitors who land here tend to linger on nearby Pulau Kepa or dive these waters from live-aboards. But if you take the time to explore the tribal interior, you will meet some of the most upbeat, charming people on earth; folks who are always psyched to share their culture – and their home-cured tobacco – with visitors. And if you want to spend the night, all you have to do is ask.

## Kalabahi
☎ 0386 / pop 59,000

Kalabahi is the chief town on Alor and is located at the end of a spectacular 15km-long, palm-fringed bay on the west coast. Not that the city planners have taken advantage of it. The town's main drag is a long, hot concrete sprawl that doesn't so much as hint at the sea, although you can grab a sea breeze – and a tasty grilled-fish dinner – at the night market on the harbour. Thanks to the punishing heat, the streets only come to life in the morning, and again an hour before sundown, when the city park is a jumble of volleyball and basketball games.

Kalabahi is very Indonesian and relatively prosperous, but extreme poverty lurks just outside town. There are some interesting villages and beautiful beaches nearby, some with spectacular snorkelling and diving.

### INFORMATION
It's best to bring plenty of cash to Alor as rates for US dollars and travellers cheques are poor, although there is a MasterCard/Cirrus ATM at **BRI bank** (Jl Sutoyo; ☼ 7.30am-2pm) and a Visa/Plus ATM at **BNI Bank** (Jl Sutomo 5). There's a **Telkom office** (Jl Soetomo; ☼ 24hr), about 2km north of town, and a **warnet** (Jl Sudirman 56; per hr 7000Rp) on the main drag.

### SIGHTS & ACTIVITIES
Kalabahi's modest **museum** (Jl Diponegoro; ☼ 8am-3.30pm Mon-Sat), just west of the market, has fine ikat, *moko* (bronze drums; see boxed text, opposite) and assorted artefacts.

**Scuba diving** in Alor can be exceptional. La Petite Kepa (see opposite) offers two dives for €60, including gear. Other scuba schools offering dives around the island include **Alor Dive** (☎ 222 2663, 0813 3964 8148; www.alor-dive.com; Jl Gatot Subroto 33) in Kalabahi, **Alor Divers** (☎ 0813 1780 4133; www.alor-divers.com) on Pulau Pantar, and **Dive Alor** (www.divealor.com), based in Kupang. Five Bali-based live-aboard dive boats cruise and plunge these waters in the high season, including **Grand Komodo Tours** (www.komodoalordive.com) and **The Seven Seas** (www.thesevenseas.net).

### SLEEPING
The most popular place to stay around Alor is La Petite Kepa homestay (opposite) on Pulau Kepa, near Alor Kecil.

**Hotel Nusa Kenari Indah** (☎ 21208; Jl Diponegoro 11; economy s/d with fan & mandi 40,000/50,000Rp, standard s/d with air-con 110,000/140,000Rp, VIP r 240,000Rp; ⊠ ) Has clean and fairly comfortable air-con rooms; the VIP rooms here are modern and smart, with tiled floors and fancy furnishings. It's near the Pelangi Indah.

**Hotel Pelangi Indah** (☎ 21251; Jl Diponegoro 100; economy s/d 50,000/100,000Rp, standard s/d with air-con & shower 90,000/150,000Rp, VIP s/d 135,000/200,000Rp; ⊠ ) Set on the main drag, the reasonably clean rooms flank a flower garden, and the VIP rooms have new spring-mattresses.

**Hotel Adi Dharma** (☎ 21280; Jl Martadinata 26; standard r with fan & bathroom 67,500-87,500Rp, VIP r with TV & air-con 97,500-112,500Rp; ⊠ ) Cheap, and just 200m from the harbour. Rooms are cleanish, and they'll do for a night if you have an early morning ferry.

**Hotel Nur Fitra** (☎ 222 2124; Pasar Kadelang; standard/VIP r 100,000/200,000Rp; ⊠ ) Rooms are large and very clean. VIP bungalows are air-conditioned, landscaped and have sun porches, and the terrace restaurant raised over the mangroves is beautiful. However, the in-room air-con units don't always work, standard-room ceiling fans rattle, and food takes forever to emerge from the kitchen. Still, it has great potential.

### EATING
Kalabahi is no culinary diamond, but the half-dozen warungs, which set up near the harbour on **Pantai Reclamasi** (☼ 7pm-11pm), turn out tasty sate, *soto ayam, nasi goreng* and tremendous fresh grilled fish. It's also the closest thing to nightlife in Kalabahi.

**Didha Cafe** (☎ 0813 1007 0227; dishes 8000-18,000Rp) Come here for simple, clean food opposite the night warungs. They have assorted noodle dishes, fresh blended juices and freshly baked roti.

### GETTING THERE & AWAY
The airport is 9km from town, and offers one of the most dramatic approaches in the country. Transport schedules are subject to frequent changes.

**Transnusa** (☎ 21039; Jl Sudirman 100) flies to and from Kupang six times a week on a newish plane. Departure tax is 13,000Rp.

Kalabahi is also linked by passenger/car ferries to Kupang (West Timor) and Larantuka (Flores) via Baranusa (Pantar), Balauring and Lewoleba (Lembata). These ferries leave from the ferry terminal 1km southwest of the town centre, a 10-minute walk or 1500Rp bemo ride.

To Kupang, ferries leave on Tuesday and Sunday (70,000Rp, around 18 hours). Ferries depart Kalabahi for Larantuka (75,000Rp, around 24 hours) on Sunday and Thursday, passing through Baranusa, Balauring and Lewoleba (59,000Rp, 14 hours). Bring plenty of food and water. Irregular wooden ferries also cross to Alor from Wairiang (50,000Rp, 6 hours) on Lembata.

**Pelni** ( ☎ 21195) ships leave from the main pier in the centre of town (the Pelni office is opposite the pier). The *Awu* sails every two weeks between Kalabahi and Kupang, Ende, Waingapu and Larantuka. Finally, the *Sirimau* connects Kalabahi with Kupang, Larantuka and Makassar.

Daily wooden boats from the central wharf head to Baranusa (25,000Rp, four hours) at 8am.

### GETTING AROUND
Transport around town is by red bemo (2000Rp). It's possible to rent a motorbike through the Hotel Adi Dharma for 50,000Rp to 60,000Rp per day. *Ojeks* are easily hired for 30,000Rp per day.

## Around Kalabahi
**Takpala** is a stunning traditional village etched into a hillside about 13km east of Kalabahi. There are several *talihutan* (traditional high-roofed houses), held together with lashings and scattered beneath mango trees, papaya and banana groves. The villagers are charming, and will be more than happy to teach you how to use a traditional bow and arrow, or roll you one of their home-cured cigarettes, which go well with a pinch of betel. And you'll probably notice the massive sea

views from every angle. To get here take a Mabu bus (3000Rp) from the terminal at Kalabahi market. Walk about 1km uphill on a sealed road from where the bus drops you off.

You can also do a fascinating village tour of Alor's bird head. From Kalabahi head to **Mombang**, up through the clove trees and coffee plots of **Kopidil** to **Julta**, and then down to the stunning sweep of white sand and coconut palms that is **Batu Putih**. It's backed by granite bluffs and cornfields, and cradles a turquoise and emerald lagoon 10km north of Mali. You'll either need to hire a motorbike (50,000Rp to 60,000Rp) or charter an *ojek* (30,000Rp per day) for this. Bring plenty of water, a boxed lunch, betel nut and a few essential food items to share with your new friends, and the best Bahasa Indonesia you've got.

Nearby, the fishing villages of **Alor Kecil** and **Alor Besar** are nice white-sand beaches with excellent snorkelling. The best is at **Sebanjar**, 3km north of Alor Kecil. The water here is wonderfully cool, with a gorgeous soft-coral garden offshore. Alor Kecil is the jumping-off point for beautiful Pulau Kepa, an offshore islet with Alor's most popular guest house, **La Petite Kepa** ( ☎ 0813 3820 0479; www.la-petite-kepa.com; bungalows incl meals per person 150,000-200,000Rp). This French-run, solar-powered property has eight beachfront bungalows, three of which are replicas of traditional Alor homes. All have sea and island views. Meals are tasty and eaten family-style. There are two beaches on Kepa, including an exquisite sliver of white sand on the west side with spectacular sunset views and good snorkelling offshore. The owners offer scuba

### MOKO
Alor's fame lies in its mysterious *moko* – bronze drums about 50cm high and 33cm across, tapered in the middle like an hourglass and with four ear-shaped handles around the circumference. Thousands of them are scattered around the island – the Alorese apparently found them buried in the ground and believed them to be gifts from the gods, though they were probably brought by traders from India, China or Makassar. There's a good collection in Kalabahi's museum.

Most *moko* have decorations similar to those on bronze utensils made in Java in the 13th- and 14th-century era, but others resemble earlier Southeast Asian designs and may be connected with the Dongson culture that developed in Vietnam and China around 700 BC and then pushed its influence into Indonesia.

*Moko* have acquired enormous value among the Alorese. In years past, wars were fought over prized *moko*, and they remain an essential part of a bride's *belis* (dowry). Export of *moko* is illegal.

diving (€$60 for two dives, including equipment), with price breaks at six dives or more. You can rent snorkelling gear for 50,000Rp per day and join the dive boat for snorkelling excursions at 90,000Rp per trip. July and August books up months in advance, so reserve ahead.

Buses and blue bemos to Alor Kecil (5000Rp, 30 minutes) and Alor Besar leave from the Kalabahi Pasar Inpres, or catch them on the harbour-front road. You can also charter a taxi from the airport (100,000Rp to 150,000Rp). If you're heading to Kepa, stop by the pier and the resort will ferry you across for free.

The traditional village of **Bumpa Lola** makes a nice excursion from Kepa. Once back on Alor, it's an easy half-day round-trip hike to where you can hang out with villagers in their peaked-roof huts and check out their *moko* drums.

### Pantar
☎ 0386

The second-largest island of the Alor group is about as far off the beaten track as Indonesia gets. Ferries between Larantuka and Alor stop at **Baranusa**, the island's sleepy main town, with a straggle of coconut palms and a couple of general stores.

**Homestay Burhan** (r 60,000Rp), Baranusa's only accommodation, is a friendly place with just three rooms; the price includes meals.

The main reason to visit Pantar is to climb **Gunung Sirung** (1372m), an impressive, smouldering volcano. From Baranusa take a truck to Kakamauta, and walk for three hours to Sirung's crater. Bring water from Baranusa and stay with the *kepala desa* in Kakamauta.

Pantar is also home to the area's newest and most upscale dive resort. **Alor Divers** ( ☎ 0813 1780 4133; www.alor-divers.com; multinight packages from €500), built and operated by a French-Slovenian couple on the island's eastern shore, caters exclusively to divers. Guests stay a minimum of three nights, in smart, thatched bungalows, and dive at least twice daily. If you land here in June or December, make your way to the west coast where you may glimpse migrating orcas, sperm and pilot whales.

Sandwiched between Pantar and Alor is **Pulau Pura**, which has a couple of fishing villages. The water is crystal-clear here and has some of Alor's best dive sites.

# WEST TIMOR

With rugged countryside, empty beaches and scores of traditional villages, West Timor is an undiscovered gem. Deep within its lontar palm–studded interior, animist traditions persist alongside tribal dialects, and ikat-clad, betel nut–chewing chiefs govern beehive-shaped hut villages; while Kupang, its coastal capital and East Nusa Tenggara's top metropolis and transport hub, buzzes to a typical Indonesian beat.

Aggravated by dry winds from northern Australia, the dry season is prolonged and often results in food shortages, which explains Kupang's sizable NGO presence. Maize is the staple crop, but coffee and rice are also important. Hit one of the many weekly markets

---

### EAST TIMOR VISA RUN

Hitting Dili in East Timor is one way to renew your Indonesian visa from Nusa Tenggara. If you decide to go, be aware that East Timor is considerably more expensive than Indonesia and the return trip normally takes more than a week by the time you've got to Dili, hung around for your visa and travelled back to West Timor.

Starting in Kupang, West Timor, book a Dili-bound minibus from Kupang (see p569), which will take you to the border at Motoain. Once over the border with your East Timor visa (available at the border for US$30) secured, you'll find your onward bus waiting for the 2½ hour trip to Dili.

The next morning, head to the Indonesian consulate for your visa (US$35), which all passport holders must have to re-enter West Timor. The consulate is near the Pertamina office on the western outskirts of Dili. Travellers have been issued with 60-day visas here upon request. Visas take five working days to issue, though some persuasive visitors have received theirs in three. Enjoy the delights of Dili and then run the route in reverse.

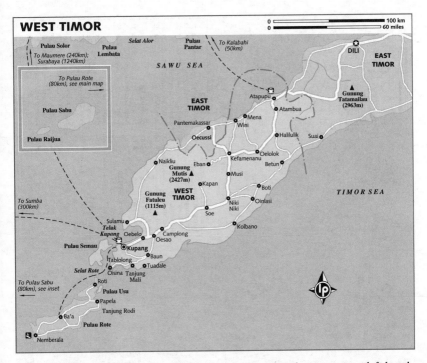

WEST TIMOR

in tribal country and you'll get a feel for rural Timor life, while eavesdropping on several of some 14 languages spoken on the island. Yes, in West Timor even Bahasa Indonesia can be a foreign tongue.

## History

The Tetum of central Timor are one of the largest ethnic groups on the island, and boast the dominant indigenous language. Before Portuguese and Dutch colonisation, they were fragmented into dozens of small states led by various chiefs. Conflict was common, and head-hunting a popular pastime.

The first Europeans in Timor were the Portuguese, who prized its endemic sandalwood. In the mid-17th century the Dutch landed in Kupang, beginning a prolonged battle for control of the sandalwood trade, which the Dutch eventually won. The two colonial powers divvied up the island in a series of treaties signed between 1859 and 1913. Portugal was awarded the eastern half plus the enclave of Oecussi, the island's first settlement.

Neither European power penetrated far into the interior until the 1920s, and the island's political structure was left largely intact. The colonisers spread Christianity and ruled through the native aristocracy, but some locals claim Europeans corrupted Timor's royal bloodlines by aligning with imported, and eventually triumphant, Rotenese kingdoms. When Indonesia won independence in 1949 the Dutch left West Timor, but the Portuguese still held East Timor, setting the stage for the tragedy that continued until the East's independence in 2002.

During August 1999, in a UN-sponsored referendum, the people of East Timor voted in favour of independence. Pro-Jakarta militias, backed by the Indonesian military, went on a murderous rampage in East Timor, destroying buildings and infrastructure before peacekeepers intervened. Back in West Timor, the militias were responsible for the lynching of three UN workers in Atambua in 2000, making West Timor an international pariah.

By 2006, relations had stabilised and transport links by road and air were thriving. Today, Kupang and the rest of West Timor are safe.

NUSA TENGGARA

# KUPANG

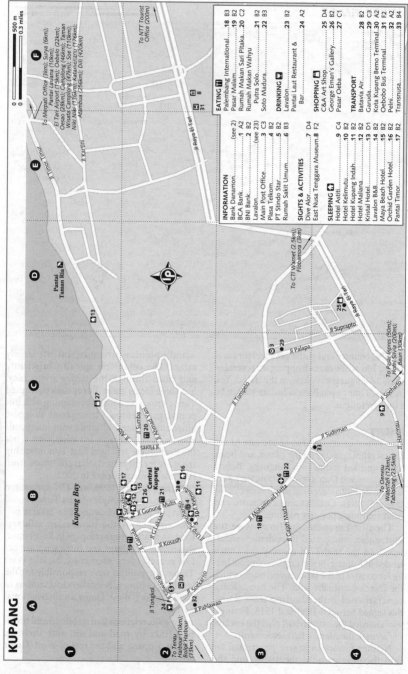

NUSA TENGGARA

500 m
0.3 miles

To NTT Tourist
Office (200m)

To Merpati Office (3km); Surya (6km);
Pantai Lasiana (10km); Oebelo (22km);
El Tari Airport (15km); Oesao (29km); Tanam
Wisata Camplong (47km); Soe (110km);
Niki Niki (136km); Katanecizaru (176km);
Atambua (256km); Dili (420km)

**INFORMATION**

| | |
|---|---|
| Bank Danamon.....................(see 2) | |
| BCA Bank................................**1** A2 | |
| BNI Bank.................................**2** B2 | |
| Lavalon................................(see 23) | |
| Main Post Office...................**3** C3 | |
| Plasa Telkom........................**4** B2 | |
| PT Stindo Star.......................**5** B2 | |
| Rumah Sakit Umum...............**6** B3 | |

**SIGHTS & ACTIVITIES**

| | |
|---|---|
| Dive Alor..............................**7** D4 | |
| East Nusa Tenggara Museum.**8** F2 | |

**SLEEPING**

| | |
|---|---|
| Hotel Astifi...........................**9** C4 | |
| Hotel Kelimutu....................**10** B2 | |
| Hotel Kupang Indah.............**11** B2 | |
| Hotel Maliana.....................**12** B2 | |
| Kristal Hotel.......................**13** D1 | |
| Lavalon B&B.......................**14** B2 | |
| Maya Beach Hotel...............**15** B2 | |
| Orchid Garden Hotel...........**16** B2 | |
| Pantai Timor.......................**17** B2 | |

**EATING**

| | |
|---|---|
| Palembang International......**18** B3 | |
| Pasar Malam.......................**19** B2 | |
| Rumah Makan Sari Pitaka....**20** C2 | |
| Rumah Makan Wahyu.........**21** B2 | |
| Putra Solo..........................**22** B3 | |
| Soto Madura......................**23** B2 | |

**DRINKING**

| | |
|---|---|
| Lavalon..............................**23** B2 | |
| Pantai Laut Restaurant & | |
| Bar..................................**24** A2 | |

**SHOPPING**

| | |
|---|---|
| C&A Art Shop.....................**25** D4 | |
| George Eman's Gallery........**26** B2 | |
| Pasar Oeba........................**27** C1 | |

**TRANSPORT**

| | |
|---|---|
| Batavia Air.........................**28** B2 | |
| Garuda..............................**29** C3 | |
| Kota Kupang Bemo Terminal.**30** A2 | |
| Oebobo Bus Terminal.........**31** F2 | |
| Pelni.................................**32** A2 | |
| Transnusa.........................**33** B4 | |

Pantai
Taman Ria

Kupang Bay

Central
Kupang

To CTI Warnet (2.5km);
Flobamora (3km)

To Pasar Inpres (50m);
Hotel Silvia (200m);
Baun (30km)

To Oenesu Waterfall (12km);
Tablolong (23.5km)

To Tenau Harbour (10km);
Bolok Harbour (13km)

# KUPANG

☎ 0380 / pop 340,000

When East Nusa Tenggara (Nusa Tenggara Timur; NTT) teens dream of attending university in the big city, they picture Kupang, its wide streets abuzz with high-speed traffic, and its funky bass-heavy bemos jammed full of hip and beautiful students from Java, Flores and beyond. Kupang is the capital of NTT, and although the city's waterfront is scruffy, its newer commercial district a sprawling gnarl of deafening traffic, and there are almost no endearing cultural or architectural elements, this is a place you can get used to. Chalk it up to Kupang's easy-to-navigate but still vaguely chaotic public transport system, the romantic, ramshackle Lavalon bar with its incredible oceanfront perch, and the fantastic pedestrian-only night market that takes over the old seaside commercial corridor and draws out Kupang's young, diverse population. Given its role as a regional transport hub, you will do some Kupang time. Just don't be surprised if you linger between trips to the interior, East Timor, Alor or Rote, and discover that you actually dig it. After all, England's Captain Bligh had the same epiphany when he spent 47 days here after that emasculating mutiny on the *Bounty* incident in 1789.

## Orientation

Kupang sprawls, and you'll need to take bemos or *ojeks* to get around. You will likely land in one of two main areas. The waterfront district, which stretches along Jl Sumba, Jl Sumatera, Jl Garuda and Jl Siliwangi, and rambles inland with Jl Ahmad Yani, has the bulk of the budget lodging options, plenty of restaurants, and hosts the fantastic night market. Jl Mohammad Hatta/Jl Sudirman to the south, is the new commercial centre with a selection of business hotels, bookstores, restaurants, hospitals and internet cafes. El Tari airport is 15km east of town; Tenau and Bolok harbours are 10km west and 13km west, respectively.

## Information

### INTERNET ACCESS & TELEPHONE
**CTI Warnet** (Jl Lalamentik 38; per hr 4500Rp; ☒ 11am-11pm)

**Plasa Telkom** (Jl Urip Sumoharjo 11; ☒ 8am-4pm Mon-Fri, 8am-noon Sat) A new building offering international calls, and a free, air-conditioned hot spot.

### MEDICAL SERVICES
**Rumah Sakit Umum** ( ☎ 832 892; Jl Mohammad Hatta 19) A large, full-service hospital with ambulances on call.

### MONEY
Kupang has scores of banks and ample ATMs in both ends of town.

**Bank Danamon** (Jl Sumatera) Equipped with an ATM and offers cash advances.

**BCA bank** (Jl Siliwangi 37) ATM and decent rates.

**BNI bank** (Jl Sumatera) Has an ATM and fair rates.

### POST
**Main post office** (Jl Palapa 1) Take bemo 5.

### TOURIST INFORMATION
**Lavalon** ( ☎ 832 256, 0812 377 0533; www.lavalon touristinfo.com; Jl Sumatera 44; ☜ ) You gotta love a town where a bar is by far the best place to find out what's what. Owner Edwin Lerrick dishes the knowledge, and his website is worth checking too. He offers free high-speed internet.

**NTT Tourist Office** ( ☎ 21540; ☒ 7am-3pm Mon-Thu) Has maps and a few brochures, but little else. It's about 4km east of the centre; take bemo 10 or 7, get off at Jl Raya El Tari at the SMP5 secondary school and walk 200m east.

### TRAVEL AGENCIES
**PT Stindo Star** ( ☎ 809 0583, 809 0584; Jl Urip Sumohardjo 2) An efficient travel agency that arranges flights to Bali, Java and throughout NTT.

## Sights & Activities

The **East Nusa Tenggara Museum** (Jl Raya El Tari; admission 2000Rp; ☒ 8am-noon, 1-4pm Mon-Sat), near the tourist office, houses a collection of skulls, seashells, stone tools, swords, gourds and antique looms from across the province. To get there, take bemo 10 from the Kota Kupang Terminal.

### EXPLORING TIMOR
Kupang is a gateway to West Timor's fascinating and welcoming traditional villages. Bahasa Indonesia – let alone English – is often not spoken, so a local guide is advisable. **Oney Meda** ( ☎ 0813 3940 4204) is a highly recommended English-speaking guide with 15 years of experience who organises anthropological tours and treks throughout West Timor and Alor. His guiding services run from 300,000Rp to 600,000Rp per day depending on the itinerary.

## DIVE TRIPS

Nearby Alor has some spectacular diving. Kupang-based **Dive Alor** ( ☎ 821 154; www.divealor .com; Jl Raya El Tari 19), run by the Australian father-son team of Graeme and Donovan Whitford, is an experienced scuba outfit that arranges trips to the island.

## Sleeping

### BUDGET

**Lavalon B&B** ( ☎ 832 236; Jl Sumatera I 8; r with shared baths 40,000Rp, with fan 55,000Rp) The best value in town with clean, ceramic tiled rooms and western-style bathrooms. Guests can use the kitchen. Run by the much-loved Oney Meda, West Timor guide extraordinaire.

**our pick** **Hotel Maliana** ( ☎ 821 879; Jl Sumatera 35; r with fan/air-con 100,000/160,000Rp; ✷ ) These basic yet comfy motel rooms are a popular budget choice. Rooms are clean and have ocean views from the front porch. Breakfast is included, and the helpful staff can arrange early morning taxis to the airport.

**Maya Beach Hotel** ( ☎ 832 169; Jl Sumatera 31; r with air-con & TV 115,000Rp, with hot water 135,000Rp; ✷ ) A decent choice, this large concrete hotel has plenty of cleanish rooms just a cut above basic. Some have sea views.

**Pantai Timor** ( ☎ 831 651; Jl Sumatera 44; standard/deluxe r 175,000/200,000Rp; ✷ ) This large hotel is both centrally located and on the water. Rooms are huge with new tile floors, high ceilings and crown mouldings, as well as TV and air-con. Bathrooms are basic, but the standard rooms are still tremendous value.

**Orchid Garden Hotel** ( ☎ 833 707; fax 831 339; Jl Gunung Fateleu 2; s/d from 175,000/200,000Rp; ✷ ) Even a fresh coat of lime paint can't hide its age, but the rooms, set around a garden and empty pool, are quite clean and spacious, with air-con and framed ikat on the walls.

Or try these:

**Hotel Kupang Indah** ( ☎ 21919; Jl Kelimutu 21; r with fan & bathroom 50,000Rp, with air-con 65,000Rp; ✷ ) Management is lovely and the air-con rooms are Kupang's cheapest.

**Hotel Kelimutu** ( ☎ 831 179; Jl Kelimutu 38; r with fan 100,000Rp, with air-con & TV 140,000Rp; ✷ ) Friendly management and decent-sized rooms.

### MIDRANGE

**Hotel Astiti** ( ☎ 832 622; Jl Sudirman 166; standard/superior/deluxe r 190,000/250,000/300,000Rp) This large business hotel, with an attached BNI bank ATM, has 60 rooms with minibar, international satellite TV, laundry and room service. Recently renovated deluxe rooms are the best in town. Location is the only drawback.

**Hotel Silvia** ( ☎ 825 191; Jl Soeharto 51-53; standard/superior/VIP r 300,000/350,000/500,000Rp; ✷ ☎ ) Less cosy than Astiti, this spot has all the business-hotel perks. They sell wireless internet vouchers to laptop luggers (11,000Rp for four hours).

**Kristal Hotel** ( ☎ 825 100; kristal@kupang.wasantara .net.id; Jl Timor Raya 59; standard/superior d 610,000/762,000Rp, ste 1,600,000Rp; ✷ ☎ ) Like a past-their-prime Hollywood star, this aging megahotel by the beach, 2km east of the centre, just had work done. There are ballrooms and a nice pool area by the sea. Rooms in the new wing have the nicest bathrooms in town and satellite TV.

## Eating

Kupang was never considered a good eating town until the wonderful, lamp-lit **pasar malam** (Jl Garuda; dishes from 6000Rp; ⏰ 6pm-10pm) was launched. With motorised traffic blocked every night, Jl Garuda has become the domain of streetside grill and wok chefs that expertly prepare inexpensive fresh fish (choose yours from the cooler), chicken and vegetable dishes.

**Rumah Makan Sari Pitaka** (Jl Sumba 4; meals 7000-12,000Rp) Enjoy cheap and tasty Balinese soul food. The *babi* (pork) comes shredded, grilled and stewed, and is served with rice and stir-fried *kangkung* (local spinach).

**Soto Madura** ( ☎ 809 9505; Jl Mohammad Hatta 21; most dishes 7,000-18,000Rp) A clean Javanese sate depot with huge simmering vats of *soto* (soup).

**Rumah Makan Wahyu Putra Solo** ( ☎ 821 552; Jl Gunung Mutis 31; meals 10,000-25,000Rp) Kupang's best pick-and-mix warung offers beef, chicken, fish, potatoes and greens deep- and stir-fried, stewed in coconut sauce, and chilli-rubbed and roasted. Even vegetarians will find something delicious here.

**Palembang International** ( ☎ 822 784; Jl Mohammad Hatta 54; dishes 17,500-50,000Rp; ⏰ 11am-10pm) A popular Chinese-Indo seafood house, with a clean dining room accented by dozens of potted plants. Try the fish in black bean sauce (30,000Rp to 50,000Rp).

## Drinking

**Lavalon** ( ☎ 832 256, 0812 377 0533; www.geocities.com/ lavalon_edwin; Jl Sumatera 44; ⬛ ☎ ) This rickety-looking, open-air, tin-roof watering hole with spectacular sea views is a must for any new traveller in town. Edwin and his local crew will give you an earful on all their favourite

NTT sweet spots. The beer is cold, and the wireless high-speed internet is free.

**Pantai Laut Restaurant & Bar** ( ☎ 0852 3910 9999; Jl Tongkol 3; 🛜 ) A new tropical bar with a huge thatched roof, no walls, beach views and the ever-present sound of rolling surf. It has free wi-fi internet, a pool table, a menu of day-glow cocktails, and the coldest beer in town.

## Shopping

Kupang's main shopping mall is the **Flobamora** (Jl Lamamentik), 3km southeast of town. Take bemo 6 from the roundabout at Jl Beringin.

The main market is the rambling **Pasar Inpres** ( 🕙 7am-4pm) off Jl Soeharto in the south of the city. To get there, take bemo 1 or 2 and follow the crowd. The smaller **Pasar Oeba** (Jl Alor) is about 1km east of town.

**C&A Art Shop** ( ☎ 802 6969; Jl Raya El Tari 27) One of several places in town that sells new production and antique ikat (with a great selection of the naturally dyed variety), masks and sculpture. The owner speaks English and prices are low.

**George Eman's Gallery** ( ☎ 0812 368 3562; Jl Taruna 2; 🕙 by appointment only) Based in the artist's home, and stacked with oil and mixed-media canvasses that blend cubism with tribal Sumba art. You'll recognise *marapu* (spiritual forces), megalithic figures and Pasola warriors.

## Getting There & Away

### AIR

Kupang is the most important hub for air travel in Nusa Tenggara. **Merpati** ( ☎ 833 833; Jl Timor Timur Km 5) flies to Denpasar (daily), Mataram (daily), Waingapu (four weekly), Waikabubak (three weekly), Maumere (daily), Ende (four weekly), Lewoleba (three weekly) and Atambua (twice weekly).

**Transnusa** ( ☎ 822 555; fax 832 573; Jl Sudirman 68) flies to Kalabahi (six weekly), Ende (twice daily), Maumere (twice daily) and Rote (twice weekly).

**Garuda Air** ( ☎ 827 333; www.garuda-indonesia.com; Jl Palapa 7) flies daily to Denpasar and on to Surabaya, Yogyakarta and Jakarta.

**Batavia Air** ( ☎ 830 555; Jl Ahmad Yani 73) flies daily to Surabaya and on to Jakarta. **Lion Air** ( ☎ 882 119; El Tari Airport) flies exactly the same route. Both operate flexi-fares, depending on how early you book.

At research time, Darwin flights had been cancelled for over a year, but were getting set to re-launch.

Departure tax is 20,000Rp for domestic flights and 70,000Rp for international flights.

### BOAT

Pelni ships depart from Tenau Harbour, 10km southwest of Kupang (4000Rp, bemo 12); ferries leave from Bolok Harbour, 13km southwest of Kupang (4000Rp, bemo 13). Expect to pay approximately 25,000Rp for a hotel drop when coming into town by bemo.

Boats are routinely late and schedules shift, particularly during the rainy season, when seas are rough.

**Pelni** ( ☎ 824 357; Jl Pahlawan 3; 🕙 8.30am-3pm Mon-Sat, 9-11am Sun) is near the waterfront. Pelni's *Dobonsolo* runs every two weeks from Bali to Kupang, and on to Kota Ambon and Papua. The fortnightly *Awu* sails from Kupang to Ende, Waingapu, Lombok and Bali, or Kalabahi, Larantuka and Sulawesi. *Sirimau* sails between Kupang, Alor and Makassar every two weeks. The fortnightly *Pangrango* sails from Kupang to Surabaya, Waingapu and Bima. The *Tatamailau* connects Kupang with Maumere, Bima and Benoa, and on the return trip heads to Saumlake and Tual. Finally, the *Siguntang* links Kupang with Lewoleba and Maumere.

From Bolok Harbour, ferries sail to Larantuka (Sunday and Thursday), and to Ende on Friday. The Ende ferry continues on to Waingapu. For Rote ferry info, see p577.

### BUS & BEMO

Long-distance buses depart from Oebobo terminal on the eastern side of town – catch bemo 10. Daily departures include Soe (45,000Rp to 60,000Rp, three hours) and Niki Niki (45,000Rp to 60,000Rp, 3½ hours) every hour from 5am to 6pm; Kefamenanu (50,000Rp to 70,000Rp, 5½ hours) and Atambua (75,000Rp, eight hours) at 7am, 9am, noon and 5pm.

Direct minibuses (175,000Rp one way, 11 hours) to Dili are operated by **Timor Travel** ( ☎ 881 543), **Paradise** ( ☎ 823 120) and **Livau** ( ☎ 821 892). Call for a hotel pick-up.

---

**OJEK WARNING**

Sadly, sexual assault against women by their *ojek* drivers has become an issue in Kupang. Don't hail an *ojek* randomly. Ask hotel staff to recommend someone.

## Getting Around

### TO/FROM THE AIRPORT

Kupang's El Tari Airport is 15km east of the town centre. Taxis from the airport to town cost a fixed 50,000Rp. For public transport, turn left out of the terminal and walk 1km to the junction with the main highway, from where bemos to town cost 3000Rp. Going to the airport, take the Penfui bemo to the junction and then walk.

### BEMO

A ride in one of Kupang's unique bass-thumping hip-hop bemos (2000Rp) is one of the city's essential experiences. Windscreens are festooned with girlie silhouettes, Jesus of Nazareth or his mom, and English premiership football stars. The low-rider paint job is of the *Fast & Furious* technicolour variety, while banks of subwoofers will have your ass involuntarily shaking to the drivers' C-list hip-hop soundtrack. They stop running by 9pm.

Kupang is too spread out to walk. The bemo hub is the Kota Kupang terminal. Useful bemo routes:

**1 & 2** Kuanino–Oepura; passing many popular hotels.

**5** Oebobo–Airnona–Bakunase; passing the main post office.

**6** Goes to the Flobamora shopping mall and the post office.

**10** Kelapa Lima–Walikota; from terminal to the tourist office, Oebobo bus terminal and East Nusa Tenggara Museum.

Several bemos use names instead of numbers. **Tenau** and **Belok Harbour** bemos run to the docks. The **Penfui** bemo links to the airport.

### CAR & MOTORCYCLE

It's possible to rent a car with a driver from 400,000Rp per day. Motorcycles cost around 60,000Rp per day. Ask at your hotel or travel agent.

## AROUND KUPANG

### Islands

**Pulau Semau** to the west of Kupang has some decent sandy beaches and snorkelling. Collective boats (10,000Rp) make the run from Tenau Harbour throughout the day, but there's no lodging here. Chartered boats cost around 500,000Rp.

**Pulau Kera** (Monkey Island), an uninhabited blob of trees and sand, surrounded by clear water, is visible from Kupang. Access is by chartered boat (750,000Rp to 1,000,000Rp) only.

### Beaches

Kupang's beaches are grubby and flotsam-strewn. **Pantai Lasiana**, about 10km east of town by bemo 17, is a wide sandy beach and a busy weekend picnic spot. There's playground equipment, football games, offshore island views, and shady snack stalls where you can enjoy fresh young coconut (3000Rp).

The road to Tablolong, 27km southwest of Kupang, rises and falls along a ridge with some spectacular ocean views. Get off the bemo at the cell tower and make the next left down a rugged 3km road, past lontar huts to **Tuadale**, where you'll find an undiscovered surf break along the offshore reef. Head southwest from here and you'll find **Air Cina**, another golden beach and turquoise bay that's the domain of fishermen and seaweed farmers. Bring plenty of food and water, and check when the last bemo goes back to Kupang from Tablolong, so you don't get stranded.

### Oenesu

Hidden in this sleepy farming village just off the Kupang–Tablolong road, is an impressive three-stage, turquoise-tinted waterfall (admission 4000Rp). There's a nice swimming hole beneath the last cascade. Locals love it, which explains the rubbish issue. The turnoff is 13km from Kupang near Tapa village, serviced by regular bemos from Tabun. From the main road it's a 2.5km walk to the falls. Take the road to Sumlili; after the Immanuel church turn and walk 800m along a rough road.

### Baun

A leafy and relatively prosperous market town 30km southeast of Kupang in the hilly Amarasi district, Baun is an ikat-weaving centre with one Dutch colonial building of note: the *rumah rajah,* now occupied by Ibu Mari, the late raja's charming widow. Inside is an enclosed porch, a blooming backyard garden and some aged black-and-white photos of old rajas in tribal dress. Market day in Baun is Saturday. From Baun to the south coast is a solid day's hike; there's a good surf beach down there.

To get to Baun, take a bemo from Kupang's bus terminal or Pasar Inpres.

## Oebelo & Oesao

Oebelo, a small salt-mining town 22km from Kupang on the Soe road, is notable for a terrific Rotenese musical-instrument workshop, **Sasandu** ( ☎ 0813 3913 7007, 0852 3948 7808), run by Pak Pah and his family. Traditional 20-stringed harps, aka *sasando* (featured on the 5000Rp note), are made and played in all sizes, along with coconut-shell drums and electrified versions of the Rotenese lontar-leaf hat, *ti'i langga*. Pak may treat you to a haunting instrumental number, or *Yellow Submarine*.

Oesao is another 6km down the road and has a war memorial dedicated to the 2/40th Australian Infantry Battalion.

## SOE

☎ 0388 / pop 30,000

The cool, leafy market town of Soe (800m) makes a decent base to explore West Timor's interior, which comes dotted with ubiquitous *ume kebubu* (beehive-shaped hut) villages that are home to local Dawan people. With no windows and only a 1m-high doorway, *ume kebubu* are cramped and smoky. Government authorities have deemed them a health hazard and are in the process of replacing them with cold concrete boxes, which the Dawan have deemed a health hazard. They build new *ume kebubu* behind the approved houses, and live there.

### Information

The **tourist information centre** ( ☎ 21149; Jl Diponegoro) has good detail on the surrounding area and is the best place to arrange guides. **Pae Nope** ( ☎ 0813 3914 1576) has royal bloodlines and is a terrific English-speaking guide who organises ethnological and bird-watching trips throughout West and East Timor. Both **BNI** (Jl Diponegoro) and **BRI** (Jl Hatta) banks have ATMs, but exchange rates for cash and travellers cheques are poor. Hotel Bahagia II has an attached internet cafe (15,000Rp per hour).

### Sleeping

**Nope's Royal Homestay** ( ☎ 21711; Jl Merpati 8; bungalows incl breakfast 100,000Rp) One aging little bungalow with *mandi* on the grounds of Pae Nope's family home. Pae speaks fluent English, is Soe's best guide, and lived in Darwin for years.

**Hotel Bahagia II** ( ☎ 21095; Jl Gajah Mada 55; d 145,000Rp, cottages 225,000-495,000Rp; 🖵 ) A decent choice with plenty of spacious rooms, queen beds (with wooden headboards), and a few cottages that make sense for families.

**Hotel Gajah Mada** ( ☎ 21197; Jl Gajah Mada; standard/VIP r 150,000/250,000Rp) Soe's newest rooms have queen beds, crown mouldings and hot water. The odd, isolated location nets some nice mountain views from the second-storey terrace.

### Eating

**Bundo Kanduang** ( ☎ 0813 3947 0896; Jl Gajah Mada; dishes 6000-18,000Rp) If you've been waiting to find a clean, fresh spot to try Padang food, this is it. There are devilled eggs with chilli, fried and curried fish, *rendang*, stewed veggies, and potato cakes. Almost everything is spicy and it all rocks. It's 1.5km west of the centre.

**Rumah Makan Favorite** ( ☎ 21031; Jl Diponegoro 38; dishes 10,000-15,000Rp) The newest, cleanest and hippest spot in Soe. You'll dig the 1970s paint job, tablecloths and silk flowers. The menu is all chicken and shrimp dishes made to order, and those fresh ginger muffins are lovely.

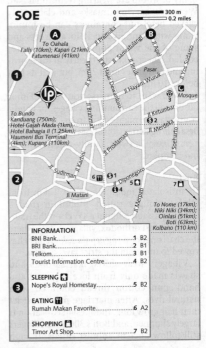

| SOE | | 0 ——— 300 m / 0 ——— 0.2 miles |
|---|---|---|
| **INFORMATION** | | |
| BNI Bank | 1 | B2 |
| BRI Bank | 2 | B1 |
| Telkom | 3 | B1 |
| Tourist Information Centre | 4 | B2 |
| **SLEEPING** 🛏 | | |
| Nope's Royal Homestay | 5 | B2 |
| **EATING** 🍴 | | |
| Rumah Makan Favorite | 6 | A2 |
| **SHOPPING** 🛍 | | |
| Timor Art Shop | 7 | B2 |

NUSA TENGGARA

## Shopping

If you're interested in antiques and handicrafts, do not miss **Timor Art Shop** ( ☎ 21419; Jl Bill Nope 17; ◷ by appointment) where you'll find Timor's best selection of masks, sculpture and carvings at unbelievable prices. There's no sign, so call owner Alfred Maku before coming over. He speaks excellent English

## Getting There & Away

The Haumeni bus terminal is 4km west of town (2000Rp by bemo). Regular buses go from Soe to Kupang (45,000Rp to 60,000Rp, three hours), Kefamenanu (25,000Rp, 2½ hours) and Oinlasi (10,000Rp to 15,000Rp, 1½ hours), while bemos cover Niki Niki (5000Rp) and Kapan (5000Rp).

# AROUND SOE
## Oinlasi

Regular buses from Soe (10,000Rp, two hours) make the 51km trip along a winding mountain road to Oinlasi. Its Tuesday market, which spreads for blocks along a ridge overlooking two valleys, attracts villagers from the surrounding hill districts, many of whom are wearing traditional ikat. Weavings, carvings, masks and elaborately carved betel-nut containers can be found, along with fruit, livestock, local sweets and some of the worst popular music ever recorded. The market starts early in the morning and continues until 2pm, but is at its best before 10am.

If you want to immerse yourself in Timor life or troll the surrounding villages for handicrafts, stay the night 1.5km from Oinlasi at the **Desa Anin Homestay** ( ☎ 0812 3641 2317; per person incl meals 50,000Rp), a sweet, family-run traditional hut complex.

## Boti

In an isolated mountain valley, 12km from Oinlasi along a rutted, mountain road – often impassable without a 4WD – is the traditional, almost orthodox, village of Boti, where the charismatic young *kepala suku* (chief) has vowed to maintain the strict laws of *adat*.

Villagers wear shirts, ikat sarongs and shawls made only from locally grown and hand-spun cotton thread coloured with natural dyes. After marriage men must let their hair grow long. Indonesian education is largely shunned, and Boti's 300 or so villagers still follow ancient animist rituals, though

another 700 neighbouring families who live in Boti's geographical sphere of influence have adopted Protestantism and attend public schools.

On arrival you will be led to the raja's house, where, keeping with tradition, you will offer betel nut to the chief as a gift. It's possible to stay with the raja in his house with all meals provided for 75,000Rp per person. Day-trippers are expected to contribute a donation (25,000Rp should work).

The Boti chief requests that you do not visit independently; bring a guide from Soe conversant with local *adat*.

### GETTING THERE & AWAY

From Niki Niki, there is a new turn-off to Boti. It's 20km on a rocky, hilly road that's passable by motorcycle or 4WD. Make sure to bring water from Soe. An *ojek* charter from Niki Niki is around 50,000Rp, or you can hire a 4WD in Soe for 750,000Rp.

## Niki Niki

Niki Niki is 34km east of Soe along the Soe–Kefamenanu road and is the site of some old royal graves and two palaces, one imposing structure belonging to Rajah Nope. The village has a busy Wednesday market, a couple of restaurants, but no accommodation. Regular buses and bemos link Niki Niki and Soe (5000Rp).

## Nome

17km east of Soe is Kefa's last head-hunting village and one of the area's best attractions. A trail begins 1km from where the bemo will drop you off on the main road. Stroll past corn and bean fields and hop over a meandering stream and you'll reach scattered *ume kebubu*, where parents still bury their baby's placenta in the centre of their hut. The village is protected by a native rock fort, which abuts a sheer cliff. At the cliff's edge you'll find a 200-year-old banyan tree and a totem pole where shamans once met with warriors before they left on head-hunting expeditions. The wise ones consulted chicken eggs and their wooden staff before predicting if the warriors would prevail. Villagers are warm and welcoming, and break out their looms at the village *lopo* (meeting place) for weaving demonstrations. It is so peaceful here that it's hard to believe they were taking heads just two generations ago.

---

**THE MIDWIFE**

Living in her dark, smoky beehive hut in the head-hunting village of Nome is a humble silver-haired woman, with *sirih*-stained lips, a generous smile and a gift. Helena Talam is a midwife, and for the past three decades she's delivered all the village children and hundreds, maybe thousands of others whose mothers come from kilometres away to see 'the one with blessed fingers'. As she tends the cook fire in the centre of her hut, the smoke snaking into the roof's storage cavity preserving bushels of rice and corn, she says 'I never studied as a nurse, what I have is a blessing from God.' She shares her wisdom with other Timorese midwives freely. 'They listen because I have never had a fatality. I just want to make mothers' lives easier and safer before, during and after delivery.' And while the government has built her a modern home that seems a good deal cleaner, she isn't moving. 'I prefer to stay here', she says.

---

## Kapan & Around

10km from Soe, on the way to Kapan, the **Oahala Falls** are tucked into a forested grotto, where the aqua water seems to paint the boulders as it threads through the forest. It's nothing spectacular but it has gravitas. During the head-hunting days, when the Molo and Amanuban kingdoms were going at it, they met here in 1911 to make peace – hence the name, Ohala (aka peaceful) Falls. Kapan buses will drop you off on the highway, from where it is a 2.5km walk to the falls, or you can hire an *ojek* (15,000Rp) or car (75,000Rp) from Soe.

Some folks call the pastureland around **Bola Plelo** 'little Scotland'. It slopes into river canyons and crawls up limestone ridges, 12km from Soe. Around 9km further on, **Kapan** rambles along a steep ridge with views of **Gunung Mutis** (2427m). There's an interesting regional market here on Thursday. From Kapan, trucks run to **Fatumenasi**, 20km away, with even more spectacular alpine scenery. Mattheus Anin runs the government **homestay** (per person incl all meals 75,000Rp). Guests nest in lontar huts and join Anin for guided walks up Gunung Mutis (100,000Rp).

## Kolbano

The village of Kolbano is on Timor's southern coast, 110km from Soe. The empty white-sand beaches see good surf between May and August. The easiest access is by bus from Noilmina on the Kupang–Soe road (about six hours).

## KEFAMENANU

☎ 0388 / pop 32,000

A former Portuguese stronghold, Kefamenanu was just another quiet hill town as recently as 2007, but with a magnesium boom in full effect, commerce has arrived along with new construction. It remains devoutly Catholic and has a couple of impressive colonial churches. There's a terrific range of accommodation in town, and it's the jumping-off point to Temkessi, one of West Timor's 'can't miss' villages. Known locally as Kefa, it lies at the heart of an important weaving region. Prepare to haggle with the ikat cartel.

### Orientation & Information

Kefa stretches in all directions from the old market, *pasar lama,* which is around 2.5km north of the bus terminal.

**BRI Bank** (Jl El Tari) Change dollars or use the MasterCard/Cirrus ATM at this gleaming new building.

**Dinas Pariwisata** ( ☎ 21520; Jl Sudirman) The tourist office, opposite the field north of the highway, can help locate a guide.

**Post office** (Jl Imam Bonjol) Opposite the market.

**Telkom** (Jl Sudirman; internet per hr 10,000Rp; ⏰ 7am-midnight) Your speedy internet connection.

### Sleeping & Eating

**Hotel Cendana** ( ☎ 31168; Jl Sonbay; r with mandi & fan 75,000Rp, with air-con 140,000-160,000Rp; ✸ ) Cendana's new rooms (160,000Rp) are terrific value, with fresh paint, crisp linens, air-con, hot-water *mandis* and flat-screen TVs. It's down a quiet side street with a small convenience store attached. Staff can help you charter bemos, find a guide, and they rent motorcycles, but they don't speak much English.

**ourpick** **Hotel Livero** ( ☎ 233 2222; Jl El Tari; standard/deluxe r 250,000/300,000Rp; ✸ ) Brand-new and sparkling in the centre of town. Rooms have wooden bed-frames, flat-screen TVs, private terraces and rain showerheads. The restaurant out back features daily live music. Outstanding value.

**Litani** (Jl El Tari; dishes 10,000-30,000Rp) If you're over Padang food, dine in these breezy bamboo environs, and munch fresh fish, prawns and squid.

**Rumah Makan Padang 2** ( ☎ 31641; Jl El Tari; meals 20,000-25,000Rp) They do all your Padang faves: curried fish and coconut greens, chilli-rubbed chicken thighs, and devilled eggs; they also pack lunch to go if you're planning a day out in the villages.

## Getting There & Away

Terminal Bus Kefa is a few kilometres south of the town centre. From here there are regular buses to Kupang (50,000Rp to 70,000Rp, 5½ hours), Soe (25,000Rp, 2½ hours) and Atambua (15,000Rp, two hours) from 6am until about 4pm.

## AROUND KEFAMENANU
### Oelolok

Oelolok, a weaving village 26km from Kefa by bus and a further 3km by bemo, is home to **Istana Rajah Taolin**, a massive beehive hut with a huge outdoor patio and carved beams dangling with corn from decades of harvests. Royals have lived here for five generations, and its current residents (the aging prince and his princess) are more than happy to share the myths and legends of their culture and kingdom. Ask about the power of the 'sword with seven lines'.

### Temkessi & Around

Accessible through a keyhole between jutting limestone cliffs, 50km northeast of Kefa, is

one of West Timor's most isolated and best-preserved villages. The raja's house overlooks the village. That's your first stop, where you'll offer gifts of betel nut, make a donation and pay your respects. After that you can shoot pictures of the low-slung beehive huts built into the bedrock and connected by red clay paths that ramble to the edge of a precipice. If you drop something, don't pick it up. Let local villagers do it, lest you bring bad vibes into your life. Oh, and about that vertical rock on the left. At least once every seven years, young warriors climb its face, *sans* rope, with a pure white goat strapped to their back. They slaughter the animal on top and can't come down until they roast and eat it in full. This Natamamausa ritual is performed to give thanks for a good harvest or to stop or start the rain. Very little Bahasa Indonesia is spoken here, so a guide is essential.

Regular buses run from Kefa to Manufui, about 8km from Temkessi. On market day in Manufui (Saturday), trucks or buses should run through to Temkessi. Otherwise, charter an *ojek* in Manufui or hike over limestone ridges with Oecussi sea views.

**Gua Santa Maria**, a sacred pilgrimage site for West Timor's Catholics 22km from Kefa on the Manufui road, is a deep limestone cave with a mother Mary statue inside, teeming with thousands of bats!

**Maubesi** is home to the Kefa regency's best textile market. You'll find it 19km from Kefa on the road to Temkessi. Market day is Thursday when goods are spread beneath riverside shade trees. Sometimes cockfights break out. **Maubesi Art Shop** ( ☎ 0852 8508 5867) has a terrific selection of local ikat, antique masks, statues, and carved beams, reliefs and doors from old Timorese homes. Prices are quite low. Look for the plain yellow-and-black 'Textile' sign. They can also organise traditional war dances (1,000,000Rp) with advance notice.

## ATAMBUA & AROUND
☎ 0389 / pop 38,000

Atambua is a scruffy border town close to East Timor. Large numbers of pro-Jakarta refugees and militias from East Timor – some with blood on their hands – settled here after East Timor's independence, and three UN workers were murdered here in 2000. Most Timor locals would rather you not pass through, and now that the Alor ferry from the nearby port of **Atapupu** has stopped running, and with a regular fleet of direct Dili–Kupang minibuses available for visa runs, there's absolutely no reason to visit.

**Betun** is a prosperous town 60km south, near the coast, which has a couple of hotels, including the recommended **Cinta Dama** (r 90,000Rp). A few intrepid travellers have visited the nearby villages of **Kletek**, **Kamanasa** and **Bolan** – you can see flying foxes and watch the sun set over the mountains at Kletek.

### Information

There's a **tourist office** ( ☎ 21483; Jl Basuki Rahmat 2) and a branch of **BNI bank** ( 🕒 8.30am-3.30pm Mon-Fri), which has an ATM and exchanges foreign currencies.

### Sleeping & Eating

**Hotel Nusantara Dua** ( ☎ 21773; Jl Kasimo; standard/VIP r 90,000/200,000Rp; 🕸 ) The best in town, with comfortable rooms. It's close to the bus terminal but a fair walk from the centre.

Tuck in at **Padang Raya** (Jl Soekarno) for a fiery point-and-eat meal.

### Getting There & Away

Merpati has two flights a week between Atambua and Kupang.

The bus terminal is 1km north of town (1000Rp by *mikrolet* 3 or 4). Destinations include Kupang (75,000Rp, eight hours) and Kefamenanu (15,000Rp, two hours). Bemos to the border cost 5000Rp (50 minutes). Buses for Dili leave from the other side when full. For more details about the trip over the border, see the boxed text on p564.

# ROTE

A slender, rain-starved limestone jewel with powdery white-sand beaches and epic surf, Rote floats just southwest of West Timor, but has an identity all its own. From a tourism perspective it's all about the surf, which is gentle enough for beginners and sick enough for experts. Stunning Pantai Nemberala is home to the world-renowned T-Land break, and there are dozens of hidden white-sand beaches, aquamarine lagoons, and seldom-surfed waves on the beaches, south and north of Nemberala. To find them you'll roll through thatched traditional villages, over natural limestone bridges and through an undulating savannah that turns from green in the November–March

---

**LONTAR PALM**

Rote is extraordinarily dependent on the drought-resistant lontar palm. The palm is extremely versatile; its tough yet flexible leaves are woven to make sacks and bags, hats and sandals, roofs and dividing walls. Lontar wood is fashioned into furniture and floorboards. But what nourishes the islanders is the milky, frothy *nirah* (sap) tapped from the *tankai* (orange-stemmed inflorescences) that grow from the crown of the lontar. Drunk straight from the tree, the *nirah* is refreshing, nutritious and energising. If left to ferment for hours, it becomes *laru* (palm wine), which is hawked around the lanes of Rote. With a further distillation, the juice is distilled into a ginlike *sopi* – the power behind many a wild Rote night.

---

'wet season' to gold in the 'dry season' which also happens to be when the offshore winds fold swells into perfect tubes. The whole experience lends a nostalgic Endless Summer feeling, even as 21st-century Rotenese voice typical Indonesian pride in their beloved Barack Obama. And don't overlook the tiny offshore islands where you can find gorgeous ikat, more silky white sand and life-affirming turquoise bays, and, of course, more surf.

Historically, the simple local economy revolved around the majestic and nutritious lontar palm (see boxed text, above). Then in the late 17th century, after a bloody campaign, Rote became the source of slaves and supplies for the Dutch. But the Rotenese also took advantage of the Dutch presence, adopted Christianity and, with Dutch support, established a school system that eventually turned them into the NTT's best-educated island. This allowed them to influence the much larger island of Timor both politically and economically.

## Ba'a

☎ 0380

Ba'a, Rote's commercial centre, is a sleepy port town that snakes south along the island's west coast among banyan trees, banana and coconut groves. The fast ferry and twice-weekly flights land here. Some houses have curious boat-shaped thatched roofs, but the town doesn't offer enough of a reason to linger, although the coast from the ferry port at Pantai Baru to Ba'a is sparsely populated and has some superb beaches. There is a **BRI bank** (Jl Pabean) with an ATM on the main drag, but it won't accept Visa. Bring plenty of rupiah from Kupang, as exchanging cash is difficult here.

If you do stick around, **Hotel Ricky** ( ☎ 871 045; Jl Gereja; r with fan 75,000Rp, s/d with air-con 150,000/200,000Rp; ✹ ) has cleanish tiled rooms that are far more welcoming than the industrial exterior would have you believe. Air-con rooms are larger and cleaner than the fan-cooled variety. They have a decent restaurant and can spot you out with transport to Nemberala. But the best place to stay is **Grace Hotel** ( ☎ 871 055; Jl Pabean; r 250,000Rp). The rooms are spotless and some overlook the harbour. They only serve breakfast, but they do offer free transport to the new **Rumah Makan Pantai Permai Prinov** ( ☎ 871 030; Jl Raya Ba'a-Papela Km 2; dishes 18,000-60,000Rp), where you can munch fresh seafood with spectacular sea views. **Rumah Makan Kelapa Satu** (Jl Pabean; meals 15,000-40,000Rp) has a decent selection of Chinese-Indonesian dishes. Meals are served on a seafront terrace.

When they can get it, shops sell the local delicacy, *susu goreng*, made from buffalo milk that's cooked until it becomes a brown powder. It's sweet and very tasty.

## Papela

This Muslim Bugis fishing village in the far east of Rote is set on a beautiful harbour, a two-hour drive north from Ba'a. Every Saturday it hosts the biggest market on the island. There is one hotel, the **Wisma Karya** (Jl Lorong Asem), but a day trip is a better bet. Buses go to Papela from Ba'a and Pantai Baru on an occasionally crumbling road.

## Nemberala

A surfers' secret for years, the word is slowly leaking out about Nemberala, a chilled-out fishing village on an exquisite white-sand beach sheltered by a reef that helps form the legendary 'left', **T-Land**. This wave gets big, especially between June and August, but it's not heavy, so the fear factor isn't ridiculous. Just north of the Nemberala fishing-boat harbour is a terrific beginners' break called **Squealers**. And if you rent a bike and drive the occasionally rutted coastal road, you'll notice that you're within reach of a half-dozen other desolate beaches and superb uncharted surf breaks. If the world is just a little too mapped out for you, you'll love Nemberala.

## SLEEPING & EATING

The surf and tourist season peaks between June and September. Accommodation range and value are solid, but there aren't a lot of rooms. Book ahead.

**Tirosa** (per person incl meals 100,000Rp) These lime-green and concrete bungalows are the cheapest beach option available. It's run by a sweet local *ibu* (older woman), and budget surfers love it. Some book rooms for the season. Turn right at the first intersection in town, and head north along the dirt road for 500m.

**Losmen Anugurah** ( ☎ 0852 3916 2645; per person incl breakfast 150,000Rp) You'll love the cute, compact, superclean lontar-palm bungalows with front patios and *mandis*, right on the beach opposite T-Land. They also have older, concrete rooms, but you don't want one of those, so reserve ahead during surf season. Their restaurant, which is decked out with ikat tablecloths, serves *ikan bakar* (grilled fish), fried squid and other basics.

**our pick** **Malole Surf House** ( ☎ 0813 3776 7412; per person incl three meals US$75-130) Built by surf legend Felipe Pomar and run by his business partner Diego Arrarte, this surf lodge blends comfort, cuisine and style better than anywhere else in Rote. The four rooms are set in a large wooden house and guest house with accent lighting, day beds, ikat bedspreads, limitless laundry and bottled water, and security boxes. Diego, the longest-tenured expat in Nemberala, will be your surf guide and get you to the right waves at the right time. Maria, the chef, carves fresh sashimi, blends spectacular soups and serves up what are among the best tapas in Indonesia. Mountain bikes, fishing trips and island excursions are also on offer. Closed during the wet season.

**Nemberala Beach Resort** ( ☎ 0813 3773 1851; www.nemberalabeachresort.com; per person US$175; ✹ ✹ ) Right on the ocean, this relaxed four-star spot has spacious slate-and-timber bungalows with ceiling fans, outdoor baths and freshwater showers. There's a swimming pool, volleyball court and pool table, and a terrific beach bar and restaurant specialising in seafood, including sashimi and lobster. A speedboat can whisk you out to other nearby surf breaks; excursions to limestone caves and tidal lagoons, and fishing trips for dog-toothed tuna and mackerel can also be arranged. Price includes all meals and transfers. It's closed during the wet season.

While all but one of the lodges and guest houses are all-inclusive, a few local warungs have popped up in recent months, so you do have a (very) few options if you've soured on *makan* homestay. **Rumah Makan Tessa Lifu** does cheap eats from her house next to the soccer pitch. **Jenet's Place** is a cute patio joint with table-cloths, silk flowers and a simple menu (think pastas, *nasi goreng* and burgers) during the high season. Cold Bintang is here year-round.

## Around Nemberala

You really must explore this lonely limestone coast by motorbike in order to absorb its majesty. If you prefer a heavier, hollow wave, your first stop should be 3km north to **Suckie Mama's**. About 8km south of Nemberala, **Bo'a** has a spectacular white-sand beach and consistent off-season surf. However, the wave is usually inconsistent when Nemberala is cranking. From Bo'a continue south over the dry rocky road, look out for monkeys, and after you traverse the natural limestone bridge, negotiate the descent and reach **Oeseli** village; then make a right on the dirt road which leads to another superb beach with some good waves, and a huge natural tidal lagoon that shelters local fishing boats and floods limestone bat caves.

The southernmost island in Indonesia, **Pulau Ndana** can be reached by local fishing boat from Nemberala. It's currently a military camp, but for years it was uninhabited. Legend has it that the entire population was murdered in a 17th-century revenge act, staining the island's small lake red with the victims' blood. Ndana has wild deer and a wide variety of birds. Its beaches are prime turtle-nesting territory, and the snorkelling here is superb.

**Boni** is about 15km from Nemberala, near the northern coast, and is one of the last villages on Rote where traditional religion is still followed. Market day is Thursday. To get here, rent a motorcycle in Nemberala.

**Pulau Do'o** is a flat spit of pale golden sand with terrific though finicky surf. You can see it from Pantai Nemberala. Further on is the stunning **Pulau Ndao**, which has more powdery white-sand beaches, limestone bluffs, and a tidy, charming ikat-weaving, lontar-tapping, fishing village that is home to nearly 600 people who speak their own indigenous dialect, Bahasa Ndao. There are some fantastic swimming beaches up the west and east coast, and good though inconsistent surf off the southern

point. Ndao is 10km west of Nemberala. To get here you'll have to charter a boat (700,000Rp to 800,000Rp, maximum five people). You could easily do both islands in one trip.

## Getting There & Away

**Transnusa** (in Kupang ☎ 0380-822 555) offers two flights a week between Rote and Kupang (250,000Rp, 20 minutes). Flights leave Kupang at 6am on Monday and return from Rote at 8am. Friday flights depart Kupang at 11am and return at noon.

The Rote–Kupang slow ferry sank in 2006 and cost many lives. But there's a new slow ferry (40,000Rp, four hours) in town. It docks at Pantai Baru, north of Ba'a, and leaves for Kupang between 9am and 10.30am daily, returning at around 3pm. The better bet is the **Baharai Express** (executive 100,000Rp, VIP 140,000Rp, two hours), a fast ferry that departs from Kupang at 8.30am daily, docks at Ba'a and returns at 11am. The service is sometimes cancelled due to rough seas.

## Getting Around

A pack of buses and bemos greet boats at Pantai Baru and run to Ba'a (1½ hours). Buses leave Ba'a for Pantai Baru around 10am to meet the slow ferry. Regular bemos run from Ba'a to Busalangga, and at least one bemo runs to Papela in the morning, while trucks service more remote locations. To get to Nemberala you'll have to charter a bemo (250,000Rp to 350,000Rp, two hours), or hire an *ojek* (100,000Rp to 200,000Rp). Price depends on your negotiation skills.

The Hotel Ricky in Ba'a and most of the Nemberala resorts can arrange a car and driver to meet you at the dock and carry you to the beach, but this will cost around 500,000Rp. Once you're in Nemberala, hire a motorbike (75,000Rp per day) through your hotel or guest house, and explore.

# SUMBA

Sumba is a dynamic mystery. With its rugged undulating savannah and low limestone hills knitted together with more maize and cassava than rice, physically it looks nothing like Indonesia's volcanic islands to the north. Sprinkled throughout the countryside are hilltop villages with thatched clan houses clustered around megalithic tombs, where

**NUSA TENGGARA**

# SUMBA

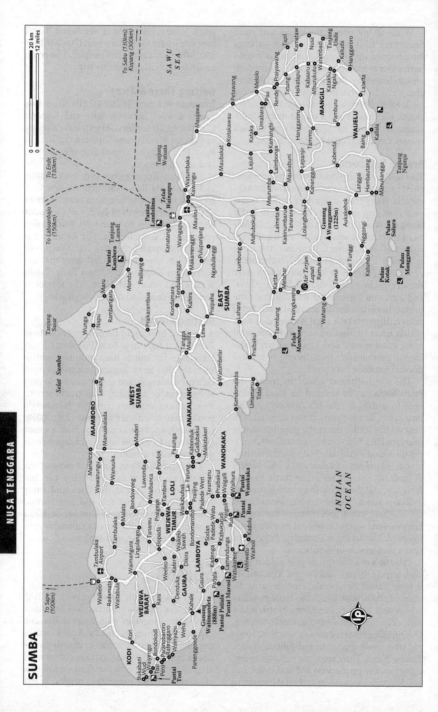

villagers claim to be Protestant but still pay homage to their indigenous *marapu* with bloody sacrificial rites. Throw in outstanding hand-spun, naturally dyed ikat, and the annual **Pasola festival** – where bareback horsemen ritualise (and stir up) old tribal conflicts as they battle one another with hand-carved spears – and it's easy to see that Sumba runs deep. It's also the poorest island in Indonesia's poorest province, and an influx of international and government aid is changing the landscape. Thatched roofs are becoming tin, tombs are now made from concrete, traditional dress is becoming increasingly rare, and remote villagers expect larger and larger donations from visitors – whether they be government officials, NGO staff or tourists.

Some traditions still persist, however. Sumba's extensive grasslands make it one of Indonesia's leading horse-breeding islands. Horses still serve as a mode of transport in more rugged regions; they remain a symbol of wealth and status and are still used to win a bride. Sumba is also one of the last Indonesian islands where water buffalo are essential to rice cultivation, particularly in the fertile and remote western half where tribal traditions are strongest.

## History

According to local legend, a great ladder once connected heaven and earth. Down it clambered the first people on earth to Sumba, and they settled at Tanjung Sasar, on the northern tip of the island.

Though 14th-century Javanese chronicles place Sumba under Majapahit control, Sumbanese history is more a saga of internal wars over land and trading rights between small kingdoms. Despite their mutual hostility, they often depended on each other economically. The inland regions produced horses, timber, betel nut, rice, fruit and dyewoods, while coastal people concentrated on ikat production and trade with other islands.

The Dutch initially paid little attention to Sumba because it lacked commercial possibilities. But in the early 20th century they finally decided to bring Sumba under their control and invaded the island.

In 1913 a civilian administration was set up, but Sumbanese nobility continued to reign as the Dutch ruled through them. When the Indonesian republic ceased to recognise the native rulers' authority, many of them became government officials. These long-time ruling clans continued to exert hegemony by monopolising local government appointments.

It all came to a head during the 1998 Waikabubak riots. Initially sparked by demonstrations against such nepotism, and Suharto-era corruption in general, the bad political blood developed into a full-scale tribal conflict perpetrated by a horseback posse of at least 3000 men. Armed with machetes, they rampaged through town and hacked at least 26 people to death (though fatalities were thought to be vastly under-reported).

## Culture

### IKAT

Sumbanese ikat is the most dramatic and arguably best executed in Indonesia. Natural dyes are still preferred by weavers who sell their wares to serious collectors in Bali and beyond. The earthy orange-red colour comes from *kombu* tree bark, indigo-blue and yellow tones are derived from *loba* leaves. Some motifs are historical: a record of tribal wars and precolonial village life. Others depict animals and mythical creatures, such as *marapu*.

Traditionally, ikat cloth was only worn ceremonially. Less than 90 years ago, only members of Sumba's highest clans and their personal attendants could make or wear it. The most impressive use of the cloth was at royal funerals, where dancers and the guards of the corpse were dressed in richly decorated costumes. The deceased was dressed in the finest textiles, bound with dozens – sometimes hundreds – more, so that the corpse resembled a huge mound before burial.

Dutch conquest broke the Sumbanese royal ikat monopoly and opened up a large external market, which increased production. In the late 19th century ikat was collected by Dutch ethnographers and museums (the Rotterdam and Basel museums have fine collections), and by the 1920s visitors were already noting the introduction of nontraditional designs, such as lions from the Dutch coat of arms.

A Sumbanese woman's ikat sarong is known as a *lau*. A *hinggi* is a large rectangular cloth used by men as a sarong or shawl.

### SUMABANESE TRADITIONS

Old beliefs fade, customs die and rituals change: the Sumbanese still make textiles but no longer hunt heads; 25 years ago the bride price may have been coloured beads and buffalo – today it might include a bicycle. Certainly, though, the bride price can still be high, and many Sumbanese men migrate just to find wives who don't expect gifts.

Some Sumbanese elders still carry their long-bladed knife in a wooden sheath tucked into their waistband. They wear scarves as turbans and wrap their brightly coloured sarongs to expose the lower two-thirds of their legs, with a long piece of cloth hanging down in front. A woman may have her legs tattooed after the birth of her first child as a mark of status; often it will be the same motifs that adorn her sarong. Another custom, teeth-filing, has all but died out, but some older people have short brown teeth from the time when jagged white teeth were considered ugly.

Churches are now a common sight, and though in some areas traditions are dying, they continue to thrive in the west.

### VILLAGES

A traditional Sumba village usually consists of two parallel rows of houses facing each other, with a square between. In the middle of the square is a stone with another flat stone on top of it, on which offerings are made to the village's protective *marapu*. These spirit stones, or *kateda*, can be found in the fields around the village and are used for offerings to the agricultural *marapu* when planting or harvesting.

The village square also contains the stone-slab tombs of important ancestors, once finely carved, but nowadays virtually always made of cement and occasionally covered in garish bathroom tile. In former times the heads of slain enemies would be hung on a dead tree in the village square while ceremonies and feasts took place. These skull trees, called *andung*, can still be seen in some villages today and are a popular motif on Sumbanese ikat.

A traditional Sumbanese dwelling is a large rectangular structure raised on stilts, and held together with lashings and dowels rather than nails; it houses an extended family. The thatched (or nowadays often corrugated tin) roof slopes gently upwards from all four sides before abruptly rising to a peak. *Marapu maluri* objects are placed in the loft (for more details, see right).

Rituals accompanying the building of a house include an offering, made at the time of planting the first pillar, to find out if the

*marapu* agree with the location. One method is to cut open a chicken and examine its liver. Many houses are decked out with buffalo horns or pigs' jaws from past sacrifices.

### RELIGION

The basis of traditional Sumbanese religion is *marapu*, a collective term for all the spiritual forces, including gods, spirits and ancestors. At death the deceased join the invisible world, from where they can influence the world of the living. *Marapu mameti* is the collective name for all dead people. The living can appeal to them for help, especially their own relatives, though the dead can be harmful if irritated. The *marapu maluri* are the original people placed on earth by god; their power is concentrated in certain places or objects, much like the Javanese idea of *semangat*.

### DEATH CEREMONIES

On the day of burial, horses or buffalo are sacrificed while ornaments and a *sirih* (betel nut) bag are buried with the body. The living must bury their dead as richly as possible to avoid being reprimanded by the *marapu mameti* and to ensure the dead can enter the invisible world – which, some say, is accessed via a ladder from Tanjung Sasar.

Funerals may be delayed for up to 10 years (the body of the deceased is sometimes stored in the loft of the family's house or given a temporary burial) until enough wealth has been accumulated for a full ceremonial funeral, and a massive stone- or concrete-slab tomb.

When the Indonesian republic was founded, the government introduced a slaughter tax in an attempt to stop the destruction of hundreds of livestock. This reduced the number of animals killed, but it didn't alter basic attitudes. The Sumbanese believe you *can*, and should, take the animal with you.

### VISITING VILLAGES

Many Sumbanese villagers are now accustomed to tourists, but still may have difficulty understanding the strange desire of Westerners to simply observe their daily life. If you're interested in their weavings or other artefacts, the villagers put you down as a potential trader. If all you want to do is chat and look around, they may be puzzled about why you've come; and if you simply turn up with a camera and start putting it in their faces, they're likely to be offended.

On Sumba, offering *sirih pinang* (betel nut) is the traditional way of greeting guests or hosts. You can buy it at most markets in Sumba. Offer your gifts to the *kepala desa* and to other village elders.

Many places also keep a visitors' book, which villagers will produce for you to sign, and you should donate a few thousand rupiah. Hiring a guide, at least to isolated villages, is a big help and offers some protection from getting into the wrong situation. No matter where you go, taking the time to chat with the villagers helps them see you more as a guest than a customer or alien.

## WAINGAPU
☎ 0387 / pop 53,000

Waingapu is a leafy, laid-back town that is plenty walkable and makes a decent base to explore the surrounding villages. It became an administrative centre after the Dutch military 'pacified' the island in 1906 and has long been Sumba's main trading post for textiles, prized Sumbanese horses, dyewoods and lumber.

The town has a groovy harbourfront dining scene, a few ikat shops and workshops.

Traders with bundles of textiles and carvings hang around hotels or walk the streets touting for rupiah.

## Orientation & Information

Waingapu stretches for 1.5km between its northern harbour and the town's main centre.

**BNI bank** (Jl Ampera) ATM accepts Visa/Plus cards. It usually has the best exchange rates.

**BRI bank** (Jl Ahmad Yani) MasterCard/Cirrus ATM.

**Post office** (Jl Hasanuddin; ⏰ 8am-4pm Mon-Fri) Close to the harbour.

**Telkom** (Jl Tjut Nya Dien; ⏰ 24hr)

**Warnet Green Corner** (Jl El Tari 4; per hr 5000Rp; ⏰ 11am-10pm)

## Sleeping

Breakfast and free airport transfer (if you call in advance) are included.

**Hotel Sandle Wood** ( ☎ 61887; Jl Panjaitan 23; s/d 2nd class 77,000/99,000Rp, 1st class 99,000/143,000Rp, VIP 187,000/209,000Rp; 🅿 ) Decent-value rooms set around a bright courtyard on a quiet street. Second-class rooms have shared baths. VIP rooms come with air-con. Management is

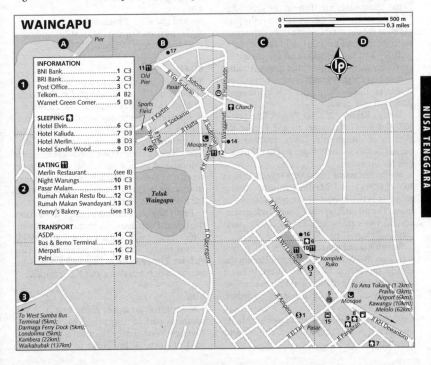

WAINGAPU

**INFORMATION**
BNI Bank..........................1 C3
BRI Bank..........................2 C3
Post Office.......................3 C1
Telkom.............................4 B2
Warnet Green Corner........5 D3

**SLEEPING**
Hotel Elvin.......................6 C3
Hotel Kaliuda...................7 D3
Hotel Merlin.....................8 D3
Hotel Sandle Wood...........9 D3

**EATING**
Merlin Restaurant..........(see 8)
Night Warungs................10 C3
Pasar Malam....................11 B1
Rumah Makan Restu Ibu..12 C2
Rumah Makan Swandayani..13 C3
Yenny's Bakery.............(see 13)

**TRANSPORT**
ASDP.............................14 C2
Bus & Bemo Terminal......15 D3
Merpati.........................16 C2
Pelni.............................17 B1

NUSA TENGGARA

top-notch and can hook you up with cars (with drivers) and motorbikes.

**Hotel Elvin** ( ☎ 61462; Jl Ahmad Yani 73; r with mandi-air-con 80,000/275,000Rp; ✿ ) This is where package tourists and business travellers converge for the new air-con rooms with queen beds and terraces. The fan rooms are aging, however, and management was pulling an air-con/fan room bait and switch at the airport when we visited.

**ourpick** **Hotel Merlin** ( ☎ 61300; Jl Panjaitan 25; r with fan 110,000Rp, with air-con & TV 200,000Rp; ✿ ) The long-standing travellers' favourite has a decent assortment of rooms on three floors, with Flores views from the rooftop restaurant. Rooms are large, with wood furnishings, fresh paint and room service, but they vary in quality. For instance, the top-floor fan rooms are a lot nicer and cleaner than the VIP rooms on the 1st floor.

**Hotel Kaliuda** ( ☎ 61264; Jl Lalamentik 3; r 125,000Rp) This reasonably clean, quiet motel has just six basic rooms with fans at a decent value. It also has a small antique collection.

## Eating

Good restaurants are thin on the ground in Waingapu. The best dinner option is the **pasar malam** at the old wharf, where three permanent warungs and half a dozen gas-lit carts set up to grill, fry and sauté seafood on the cheap. It's especially nice when the moon glows. Another collection of **night warungs** blooms across from Komplek Ruko. They offer *mie ayam, gado gado* and *soto ayam*.

**Yenny's Bakery** ( ☎ 62449; Komplek Ruko; pastries 2000-12,000Rp) Got a sweet tooth? Peruse the shelves of doughnuts, cakes, pastries and breads at this friendly bakery. They'll pack a box for the road.

**Merlin Restaurant** ( ☎ 61300; Jl Panjaitan 25; mains 7000-25,000Rp) Hotel Merlin's rooftop dining room is actually one of the best choices in town. The menu is typical Chinese Indonesian, and the views are superb. Try the chicken with mustard greens (10,000Rp).

**Rumah Makan Swandayani** ( ☎ 256 4145; Komplek Ruko; dishes 7000-25,000Rp) The biggest deal in the slowly sputtering Komplek Ruko, it has a substantial menu of Indo and Chinese cuisine featuring seafood, chicken and veggie dishes. The *soto ayam* is tasty and so is their fiery *tempeh penyet* (deep-fried tempeh). Mains are served with tangy pickled chillies and cucumbers.

The long-running **Rumah Makan Restu Ibu** ( ☎ 61218; Jl Ir Juanda 1) was in the midst of a complete reconstruction when we visited. But we were assured that Ibu's pick 'n' mix buffet would be back soon.

## Shopping

Waingapu has a few 'art shops' selling Sumbanese ikat and artefacts. Vendors also descend on hotels – some will squat patiently all day. Prices are actually very fair, and there's far more choice here than in the countryside.

**Ama Tukang** ( ☎ 62414, 0852 3747 4140; Jl Hawan Waruk 53) Do not miss this ikat workshop, even if you've overdosed on weaving. You'll see the whole process from motif design to colouring to weaving, and the collection – featuring *marapu*, village scenes, horsemen and buffalo, is simply spectacular; arguably the best in all of Indonesia. To get there, head south of the bridge on the southern side of Waingapu and turn left onto Jl Hawan Waruk. It's on the left.

## Getting There & Away
### AIR

**Merpati** ( ☎ 61323; Jl Soekarno 4) has four weekly flights to/from Kupang (742,000Rp), and three weekly flights to Denpasar (978,000Rp).

### BOAT

Waingapu is well serviced by ASDP ferries, all departing from the old pier in the centre of town. One ferry departs from Ende for Waingapu on Thursday at midnight, returning to Ende (60,000Rp, seven hours) and continuing on to Kupang at 7pm on Friday. There's also a connection to Aimere in Flores (Monday at around midnight) and a regular service to Pulau Sabu. Schedules are subject to change – check them at the **ASDP office** ( ☎ 61533; Jl Wanggameti 3).

**Pelni** ( ☎ 61665; Jl Hasanuddin) ships leave from the newer Darmaga dock to the west of town. Don't try and walk – it's further than it looks; bemos charge 5000Rp per person. The *Awu* sails for Ende and on to Larantuka, Kalabahi, Benoa in Bali, Surabaya and Kalimantan.

### BUS

The terminal for buses going east is in the southern part of town, close to the market. The new West Sumba terminal is about 5km west of town, where buses to Waikabubak

(30,000Rp, five hours) depart at around 7am, 8am, noon and 3pm.

Southeast-bound buses head to Melolo (20,000Rp, two hours), Rende (35,000Rp, two hours) and Baing (30,000Rp, four hours). Several travel through the morning and afternoon to Melolo, with a few continuing on to Rende, Ngalu (30,000Rp, four hours) and Baing. Most return to Waingapu on the same day.

There are also daily trucks southwest to Tarimbang (35,000Rp, five hours).

### Getting Around
#### TO/FROM THE AIRPORT
The airport is 6km south on the Melolo road. A taxi into town costs about 20,000Rp, but most hotels offer a free pick-up and drop-off service for guests.

#### BEMO
It's 3000Rp for a bemo ride to any destination around town, and 5000Rp to the western bus terminal.

#### CAR & MOTORCYCLE
Sumba has some of the highest car-hire rates in Nusa Tenggara. Even after bargaining, 600,000Rp is a good price per day, including driver and petrol. The Elvin, Sandle Wood and Merlin hotels can all help sort you out.

Virtually any hotel worker can arrange a motorbike (from 75,000Rp per day).

### AROUND WAINGAPU
**Londolima**, a sliver of sand about 7km northwest of town, is a favourite local swimming spot on weekends and holidays. The bay is turquoise and glassy; the beach isn't so magical. Bemos from Terminal Kota (the local name for the West Sumba bus terminal) pass by regularly. Continue along this road and you'll reach an even better beach, **Kambera**, and then come to **Maru**, about 35km from Waingapu, which has some fine traditional houses. Three daily buses (5000Rp) go to/ from Waingapu and Maru.

Three kilometres southeast of Waingapu, **Prailiu** is an ikat-weaving centre that's worth a quick look. Alongside traditional thatched houses are some concrete tombs bearing carvings of crocodiles and turtles, as well as empty graves that will be filled when the deceased's family can afford the funeral (see p580). Visitors are asked for a cash donation.

Bemos to Prailiu run from Waingapu's main bus and bemo terminal. Continuing southeast, it's a further 7km to **Kawangu**, which has two massive stone-slab tombs in the pasture, 300m off the road to Melolo.

### EAST SUMBA
Southeast of Waingapu, nestled in dry undulating savannah interspersed with cashew orchards, are several traditional villages, some with striking ancestral tombs. The area produces some of Sumba's best ikat. Most villages are quite used to tourists – you'll have to pay to visit, and be prepared for plenty of attention from ikat vendors.

### Umabara & Pau
Pau, about 4km southwest of Melolo and set along the banks of a wide, muddy river, is not the traditional village of your dreams. The large original homes are falling apart and being replaced with replicas made of new wood, tin roofs and paid for by the government. But villagers do sell terrific ikat here.

Nearby Umabara (population 150, admission by donation 10,000Rp) has 10 thatched and lashed traditional Sumbanese houses scattered beneath swaying coconut palms and set among some fantastic stone megaliths. The largest tombs are carved with images of crocodiles and turtles. Villagers form a sweet yet persistent ikat army. You will feel compelled to buy something.

The turn-off to the villages is on the main Waingapu–Melolo road, from where you head 1.5km down a side road until you come to a horse statue; here you can fork right for Umabara or left for Pau, both just a few minutes further on. Trails link the two villages.

### Praiyawang & Rende
Nestled in a shallow valley between grassy hills, Praiyawang is a traditional compound of Sumbanese houses and is the ceremonial focus of the more modern village of **Rende**, located 7km south of Melolo). It has an imposing line-up of nine big stone-slab tombs. The largest is that of a former chief. Shaped like a buffalo, it consists of four stone pillars 2m high, supporting a monstrous slab of stone about 5m long, 2.5m wide and 1m thick. Two stone tablets stand atop the main slab, carved with figures. A massive Sumbanese house with concrete pillars faces the tombs, along with a number of older *rumah adat*.

Several buses go from Waingapu to Rende (35,000Rp), starting at about 7am; otherwise, take a bus to Melolo (20,000Rp), from where bemos and trucks run throughout the day. The last bus back to Waingapu leaves at 3pm.

### Mangili

The Mangili district, centred on the villages of **Ngalu** and **Kaliuda**, is famed for its fine weaving. Kaliuda ikat is reputedly the best in Indonesia and is noted for its rich natural colours and fine lines. Much of the best stuff is made to order for traders and gets shipped off to Bali (and beyond). Kaliuda also has some fine stone-slab tombs and a gaudy modern grave painted red, yellow and blue and decorated with animal figures and crosses. Seven buses a day head here from Waingapu (30,000Rp, four hours), passing through Melolo and Ngalu. Kaliuda is a 3km walk from Ngalu towards the coast.

### Kallala

Kallala, 126km from Waingapu and 2km down a dirt road from the nearby village of **Baing**, has emerged as the surf capital of east Sumba. It's an absolutely stunning stretch of white-sand beach that arcs toward the coastal mountains, which tumble down to form East Sumba's southernmost point. Waves break 500m offshore.

If you plan on spending the night, you'll bunk at the once-renowned **Mr David's** ( ☎ 0813 3787 3589; all-inclusive bungalows 250,000Rp). Mr David (as he is referred to throughout East Sumba) has lived in Sumba for over 30 years, but the resort has seen better days. Bungalows have warped wooden floors, weathered mattresses and no furnishings. But the open dining room has some definite remote surf-camp appeal. Old boards decorate the rafters and there's a stack of boards for rent. Plus, Mrs David (the lovely Yohanna) can whip up some outstanding meals in short order. Dedicated surf rats won't mind it here at all.

Four buses a day go to Baing (30,000Rp, four hours), leaving Waingapu between 7am and 8am, and then again at around 11am and 1pm. The road is sealed all the way but is bumpy past Melolo. A dirt track with many branches runs from Baing to Kallala. Buses will drop you off at the beach if you ask the driver.

## SOUTH-CENTRAL SUMBA

This part of the island is gorgeous, but difficult to access. Although there are daily buses from Waingapu to Tarimbang and trucks to Praingkareha, getting around may require a 4WD or motorcycle and, often, some hiking.

If you're looking for uncrowded waves, check out **Tarimbang**, a life-altering crescent of white sand framed by a massive limestone bluff 88km southwest of Waingapu. The beach thumps with terrific surf, there's some nearby snorkelling, and rustic accommodation at Marthen's Homestay and the *kepala desa*'s six-room place. Both charge about 50,000Rp per person including meals. Daily trucks to Tarimbang leave Waingapu in the morning (35,000Rp, five hours).

**Praingkareha**, 26km east of Tarimbang on a terrible 4WD road, has a majestic wet-season waterfall, the 100m-high **Air Terjun Laputi**. There's a pond with eels above the falls and a beautiful pool at its base. Tradition forbids women to look into the pool, but an exception is made for foreigners. The falls are about 3km from the village. If you walk via the valley, locals will offer to guide you there (this is recommended). Otherwise, follow the main road to a fork, take the old road to the left and walk down a steep path to the falls. This is a full-day excursion that may not be possible by motorbike. Ask around before you make the trip.

## WAIKABUBAK

☎ 0387 / pop 19,000

A dusty, country market town, home to both thatched clan houses and rows of concrete stores, administrative buildings and tin-roof homes sprouting satellite dishes, Waikabubak makes Waingapu feel like a metropolis. It's a welcoming place, and at about 600m above sea level, it's a little cooler than the east and a good base for exploring the traditional villages of West Sumba.

### Information

**BNI bank** (Jl Ahmad Yani; ☼ 8am-3.30pm Mon-Fri) Has an ATM and offers fair exchange rates.

**BRI bank** (Jl Gajah Mada) Its ATM only accepts Cirrus cards.

**Post office** (Jl Sudirman; ☼ 8am-3.30pm Mon-Fri)

**Telkom** (Internet per hr 10,000Rp; ☼ 24hr) Their dial-up connection is the only internet connection you'll find in town.

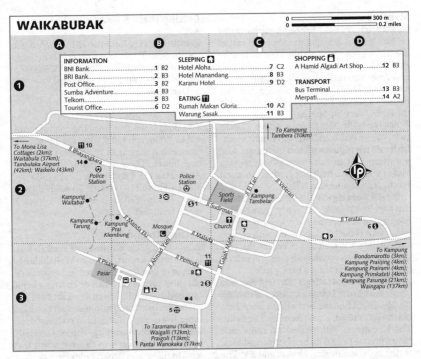

## WAIKABUBAK

| INFORMATION | | SLEEPING | | SHOPPING | |
|---|---|---|---|---|---|
| BNI Bank | 1 B2 | Hotel Aloha | 7 C2 | A Hamid Algadi Art Shop | 12 B3 |
| BRI Bank | 2 B3 | Hotel Manandang | 8 B3 | | |
| Post Office | 3 B2 | Karanu Hotel | 9 D2 | TRANSPORT | |
| Sumba Adventure | 4 B3 | | | Bus Terminal | 13 B3 |
| Telkom | 5 B3 | EATING | | Merpati | 14 A2 |
| Tourist Office | 6 D2 | Rumah Makan Gloria | 10 A2 | | |
| | | Warung Sasak | 11 B3 | | |

**Tourist office** ( ☎ 21240; Jl Teratai 1; ☺ 8am-3pm Mon-Sat) On the outskirts of town. Staff are well informed about forthcoming funerals and cultural events.

## Sights

### TOMBS & TRADITIONAL KAMPUNG

Within the town are some friendly and quite traditional *kampung* (villages) with stone-slab tombs and thatched houses. You don't need a guide here. Locals will love to show you their spacious homes lashed with old ironwood columns and beams. Charming children will mug for the camera. Old folks will offer betel nut. Bring gifts, offer a donation (5000Rp to 25,000Rp), or buy a handicraft or two and the villagers will beam with gratitude and pride.

**Kampung Tambelar**, just off Jl Sudirman, has very impressive tombs, but the most interesting *kampung* are on the western edge of town. It's only a short stroll from most hotels to **Prai Klembung** and then up the slippery slope to **Tarung** and **Waitabar**.

In November, Kampung Tarung, reached by a path off Jl Manda Elu, is the scene of an important month-long ritual, the Wula Podhu. This is an austere period when even weeping for the dead is prohibited. Rites consist mainly of offerings to the spirits (the day before the ritual ends, hundreds of chickens are sacrificed), and people sing and dance for the entire final day.

Other interesting *kampung* occupying ridge or hilltop positions outside town include **Praiijing**, with nine traditional huts set around some cool primitive stone tombs and surrounded by coconut palm and bamboo groves, and **Bondomarotto**. **Kampung Prairami** and **Kampung Primkateti** are also beautifully located on adjacent hilltops. You can take a bemo to the turn-off for Praiijing (2000Rp).

## Tours

**Sumba Adventure** ( ☎ 21727, 0813 3710 7845; sumba adventure@yahoo.com; Jl Pemuda) Experienced professional guide Philip Renggi is the best in West Sumba. He leads trips into seldom-explored villages north of Waikabubak, including his native Manukalada village and Wawarungu, where there are several sacred *marapu* houses that only shamans can enter. He charges 150,000Rp per day for guiding services or 650,000Rp per day with car and driver.

## Sleeping

**Karanu Hotel** ( ☎ 21645; Jl Sudirman 43; economy/standard r 85,000/110,000Rp) A bright garden hotel east of the downtown swirl within view of nearby rice fields. Rooms are clean, with new tiles and crisp sheets, though the mattresses are a bit tired. They don't have air-con, but they do have a fading 'Last Supper' rug framed in the lobby. Very un-Sumba.

**Hotel Aloha** ( ☎ 21245; Jl Sudirman 26; r from 100,000Rp, r with TV/air-con 150,000/225,000Rp; ✖ ) Bright, clean-ish, basic fan rooms with soft mattresses, and one overpriced air-con room, all set around a plot of grass and a fledgling garden. Cheapest rooms have Indonesian toilets.

**Hotel Manandang** ( ☎ 21197; Jl Pemuda 4; 2nd-/1st-class r 185,000/285,000Rp; ✖ ) Tidy, good-value rooms, and management works hard to keep it that way. If the 1st-class rooms with air-con and satellite TV are too pricey, try the very decent 2nd-class rooms with fans and private baths, clustered around a back garden.

**ourpick Mona Lisa Cottages** ( ☎ 21364; www.mona lisacottages-sumba.com; Jl Adhyaksa 30; s/d 300,000/350,000Rp; 🖥 ✖ ) You'll find the best night's sleep 2km northwest of town, across from the rice fields. The 10 cottages with peaked tin roofs each have a private patio with bamboo furnishings, spring beds, minifridge, air-con and TV. The deluxe master cottage (500,000Rp) has a king-sized bed, DVD player and a bathtub. Dial-up internet access is 15,000Rp per hour.

## Eating

**Warung Sasak** ( ☎ 0813 3954 5222; Jl Pemuda; dishes 8000-25,000Rp) A humble nod to Lombok, get cheap *nasi campur* here if you don't mind the roadside, bamboo-shack environs.

**ourpick Rumah Makan Gloria** ( ☎ 21389; Jl Bhayangkara 46; dishes 10,000-20,000Rp) Cute and cheerful, with chequered tablecloths, silk flowers and colourful handwritten menus, it rolls out all the Indo-Chinese hits, including a mean *ifu mie* (chinese noodles) with seafood (25,000Rp).

## Shopping

Traders gather at hotels with ikat from East Sumba, locally made bone, wood, horn and stone carvings, and jewellery.

**A Hamid Algadi Art Shop** ( ☎ 21170; Jl Ahmad Yani 99) Fantastic stone carvings in the front yard, wooden antiques and some cool old stone grinders and bronze jewellery indoors. Not to mention its all-natural ikat. Your Sumbanese treasure hunt starts here.

## Getting There & Away
### AIR

**Merpati** ( ☎ 21051; Jl Bhayangkara 20) has three flights weekly from Tambulaka airport (42km north-west of Waikabubak) to Kupang (829,000Rp) and four to Denpasar (852,000Rp).

Departure tax is 10,000Rp.

### BUS

Five daily buses run from the central termi-nal to Waingapu (30,000Rp, five hours) and throughout the day to Waitabula (12,000Rp, one hour). There are frequent bemos to Anakalang (25,000Rp), Wanokaka (5000Rp) and Lamboya (10,000Rp). To Kodi district, take a bus to Waitabula and catch a truck or bemo from there.

## Getting Around

Tambulaka, 42km northwest of Waikabubak, is the closest airport. A bus to Waitabula and a bemo or *ojek* from there is the cheapest ride, but most people get a taxi or charter a bemo (around 100,000Rp) from Waikabubak.

Bemos, trucks and minibuses service most other towns and villages in West Sumba; for details, see individual village entries. Generally, it's best to leave early in the day, when they tend to fill up and depart quickest.

Waikabubak is the place to rent a motor-bike for exploring West Sumba. Expect to pay 75,000Rp a day. For car rental (around 650,000Rp with a driver), contact Hotel Manandang or Sumba Adventure.

## WEST SUMBA
☎ 0387

If you're hungry for traditional Sumba cul-ture, you'll head west into the golden rice fields that crawl up blue mountains, carved by rivers and sprouting with bamboo and coco-nut palms. *Kampung* of high-roofed houses are still clustered on their hilltops (a place of defence in times past), surrounding the large stone tombs of their ancestors. Rituals and ceremonies for events like house-building and marriage often involve animal sacrifices and can take place at any time. Some *kampung* are unaccustomed to foreigners; gifts of betel nut help warm the waters.

Give yourself a few days around West Sumba. Once you have learned some basic manners as a guest arriving in a village – hope-fully armed with some Bahasa Indonesia – it's possible to do without a guide.

## Anakalang Villages

Set in a fertile valley carpeted in rice fields, the Anakalang district (east of Waikabubak) has some exceptional stone megaliths that are worth seeing, but traditional values have been eroded somewhat. Right beside the main road to Waingapu, 22km east of Waikabubak, **Kampung Pasunga** boasts one of Sumba's most impressive tombs. The grave of particular interest consists of an upright stone slab carved with images of a chief and his wife with their hands on their hips. This monument dates from 1926 and took six months to carve; 150 buffalo were sacrificed for the funeral ceremony. It is visible from the road. Pasunga's *kepala desa,* whose house has racks of buffalo horns, is friendly if you share some *sirih* or cigs with him. He will ask you to sign the visitors' book and leave a donation.

At **Gallubakul**, 2.5km down the road from the modernising village of **Kabonduk**, most of the tombs are crafted from concrete and cheesy tile, but it's also home to Sumba's heaviest tomb, weighing in at 70 tonnes. It is said that 6000 workers took three years to chisel the Umbu Sawola tomb out of a hillside and drag it 3km to town. The tomb is a single piece of carved stone, about 5m long, 4m wide and nearly 1m thick. At its eastern end is a separate upright slab with carvings of the raja and queen who are buried here, as well as buffalo and cockerel motifs. The raja's son lives right by the tomb with his wife and can tell its story. He'll also ask you to sign in and make a donation.

Regular minibuses run between Waikabubak and Anakalang (fewer after 1pm). Buses to Waingapu can drop you off on the highway.

## South of Waikabubak

The Wanokaka district south of Waikabubak has stunning mountain and coastal scenery and several very traditional *kampung*. It's a gorgeous drive from Waikabubak, taking a sealed but narrow road that splits at Padede Weri junction 6km from town. This is where golden, white-headed eagles soar over mountains, which tumble to the azure sea. Turn left at the junction, and the road passes through the riverside settlement of **Taramanu** 4km further on. It's 2km or so downhill to **Waigalli**, which has fine tombs and is the scene of one of the March Pasola events (see boxed text, p589). Just up a side road on the western side of the Waigalli valley, you'll find the nearly 200-year-old Watu Kajiwa tomb in the deeply traditional and isolated village of **Praigoli**. It's one of Sumba's best, with a striking symbol that resembles the fleur-de-lis.

From Praigoli it's just a short drive further on to lovely **Pantai Wanokaka**, where there's a crescent of sand, a bay bobbing with fishing boats, and a beachfront Pasola site. In the rocky coves west of the beach the water becomes clearer and rolls into decent, if inconsistent, surf. Nearby is the traditional village of **Wangli**, with views of rice fields, a river, the sea and coastal mountains, and another stone tomb with a 2.5m-tall fleur-de-lis.

**Rua**, the next in a series of luscious south Sumba beaches, is 5km southwest of the Padede Weri junction. You'll have more pale golden sand and turquoise water, and great waves when the swell hits between June and September. There's only one very basic lodging option. Heading west again, the road passes through the villages of Kabukarudi and **Kadenga**, another exceptional *kampung* with a terrific hilltop Pasola field in the coco palm–studded hills, before there's another turn-off south to the idyllic white sands of **Pantai Marosi**, 32km from Waikabubak. The sweet Sumba Nautil resort overlooks it all; they can point out the secluded, powdery white **Pantai Etreat**, the glassy **Pantai Tarikaha**, and take you to **Magic Mountain**, a coral-draped underwater volcano that is one of Sumba's best dive sites. Just before Sumba Nautil, the road forks. If you take the right fork you'll reach *kampung* **Litikaha**. From here it's just a 30-minute hike to **Tokahale**, **Kahale**, and **Malisu**, three marvellous and seldom-visited villages with spectacular panoramas. Sumba does not get more beautiful.

The world-class surf spot known as Occy's Left, featured in the film *The Green Iguana*, is on **Pantai Nihiwatu**, east of Morosi on another absolutely stunning stretch of sand buffered by a limestone headland. Unfortunately, this beach suffers from bad vibes perpetuated by Nihiwatu Resort's narrow definition of exclusivity. Only paying guests have the right to walk this beach, and surfers who try to ride its legendary waves are chased off by resort security. Thankfully, there are a few more 'lefts' and 'rights' scattered within a 30-minute boat ride from both Marosi and Nihiwatu.

NUSA TENGGARA

## SLEEPING & EATING

**Ama Homestay** (r incl all meals 100,000Rp) Give new meaning to the term 'surf camp' and crash in this thatched, wall-less pagoda mere steps from the waves.

**Sumba Nautil** ( ☎ 21806, 0868 1211 5302; www .sumbanautilresort.com; cottages US$136-156, plus 21% tax; ☒ ☒ ) West Sumba's answer to a French country resort. These brick cottages on the hill above Pantai Morosi all have ceiling fans, hot water, minibar, day beds and outrageous sea views. The menu (dishes US$3 to US$9) is French, just like the owners, who make their own pastas, breads, ice creams and chocolate. Meals are served in a marvellous open-air dining room. They have trail maps for hikers, a courtesy car to shuttle you to the beaches and surf breaks, and a dive shop. Village visits can be organised. Rates include breakfast.

**Nihiwatu Resort** (www.nihiwatu.com; bungalows & villas from US$420-1500, plus 21% tax; ☒ ☒ ) Luxury hotel in extensive grounds, perched above idyllic Pantai Nihiwatu. The American hotel owner has restricted access to the beach itself, allowing only guests, tour groups and only a few locals. Seven air-con bungalows and three villas all face the ocean and are fully equipped with modern amenities. Plenty of activities – fishing, surfing, diving, horse riding and mountain biking – are offered for additional costs. The minimum stay is five nights.

## GETTING THERE & AWAY

Two daily buses run southeast to Waigalli from Waikabubak. Lamboya district buses cover the southwest towns and run through Padede Watu to Kabukarudi, Kadenga and Walakaka. Four buses a day run between Wanokaka and Waikabubak, stopping in Praigoli village.

By far the best way to visit the area is by car or motorbike. Most roads are sealed and traffic is light. The hills south of Waikabubak are a taxing yet exhilarating ride for cyclists.

## Kodi

Kodi is the westernmost region of Sumba, and the small town of Bondokodi, about 2km from the coast, is the centre of this district. Sumba is at its most lush on this corner of the island, which is alive with teak plantations, avocado, mango and cashew groves. Local villages have incredible high-peaked houses and unusual megalithic tombs; and the long white-sand beaches come with pounding waves and offshore reefs.

The region's biggest **market** (held every Saturday) is at Kori village. A couple of buses run from Bondokodi in the morning, before 8am.

Kodi does have a reputation for lawlessness, and Sumbanese from other districts of the island are wary of Kodi people. Exploring with a guide is highly recommended.

## Pero

Pero is a friendly, modern coastal village situated on spectacular coastline just a few kilometres from Bondokodi. There are a couple of surf breaks just offshore and one directly in front of Pantai Pero. From here you won't hit land again until Africa. The long-running **Homestay Stori** (per person incl all meals 100,000Rp) is run by a hospitable family, has neat little rooms and delicious local food. To visit traditional *kampung*, go north or south along the coastline.

To reach **Ratenggaro**, take the new paved road from Bondokodi, or go off-road for about 3km along Pantai Radukapal, a sliver of white sand along a pasture, until you come to the *kampung* of Ratenggaro, framed by a low rock wall. Visitors are asked to contribute a 10,000Rp admission.

The view from Ratenggaro along the coastline is breathtaking – coconut palms fringe the shoreline, waves pound the rocks and the high roofs of **Wainyapu**, a collection of 12 *kampung* and more than 40 homes, peek out above the trees across the river. On the near side of the river mouth – where the mocha river meets the turquoise sea – unusual stone tombs occupy a small headland. To get to Wainyapu, you'll probably have to wade across the river at low tide.

On the way to Ratenggaro, look out for the thinner, high-peaked roofs of **Kampung Paranobaroro** through the trees, about 1km inland. Stone statues decorate the public space and pig jaws and numerous buffalo horns dangle on every front porch. During the day only women and children are in the village. Women are often weaving and happy to chat.

To reach **Tosi**, about 6km north and the scene of the Kodi Pasola in March, head north from Bondokodi market along the sealed road. Coming from Pero, it's a simple left at the T-junction. About 1km further on is a track on the left: follow it for 5km, past a series of tombs. Many people have reported

## PASOLA: LET THE BATTLES BEGIN

A riotous tournament between two teams of spear-wielding, ikat-clad horsemen, the Pasola has to be one of the most extravagant (and bloodiest) harvest festivals in Asia. Held annually in February and March, it takes the form of a ritual battle – not so much a quarrel between opposing forces as a need for human blood to run to keep the spirits happy and bring a good harvest. The riders gallop at each other, hurling their *holas* (spears) at rival riders (it's not permitted to use a spear as a lance). Despite the blunt spears, there will be blood, and sometimes deaths still do occur.

Pasola takes place in four areas, its exact timing determined by the arrival on nearby coasts of a certain type of sea worm called *nyale*. Two days before the main events, brutal boxing matches called *pajura* are held, the combatants' fists bound in razor-sharp local grasses.

Before the Pasola can begin, priests in full ceremonial dress must first wade into the ocean to examine the worms at dawn; they're usually found on the eighth or ninth day after a full moon. Fighting begins on the beach, and continues further inland later that same day. Opposing 'armies' are drawn from coastal and inland villages.

In February, Pasola is celebrated in the Kodi area (centred on Kampung Tosi) and the Lamboya area (Kampung Sodan); in March it's in the Wanokaka area (Kampung Waigalli) and the remote Gaura area, west of Lamboya (Kampung Ubu Olehka). Call hotels in Waingapu or Waikabubak to find out the approximate dates before travelling to Sumba, or contact a travel agent in Bali, Flores or Timor.

aggression here, so you may wish to bypass the village itself.

From Waikabubak there are direct buses to Waitabula and frequent bemos and trucks from there to Pero.

## Waitabula
☎ 0387

This sleepy market town, on the main highway between Tambulaka airport and Waikabubak, is a useful transport hub with frequent connections to Bondokodi, Pero, Waikelo and Waikabubak.

**Penginapan Melati** ( ☎ 24055; r with fan/air-con 125,000/275,000Rp; 🛑 ) Despite its ramshackle entrance, this friendly spot has excellent rooms with white tiled floors, wooden bed frames and spotless bathrooms.

The alternative, **Losmen Anggrek** (r 50,000Rp), is a basic, concrete-floor job with a fresh coat of paint.

Daily direct buses make the run all the way to Waingapu (12,000Rp). Public bemos to the airport are 5000Rp. *Ojeks* are 10,000Rp and chartered bemos are 15,000Rp.

## Waikelo
☎ 0387

This small and predominantly Muslim town north of Waitabula has a small picturesque harbour that is the main port for West Sumba. The town has a superb, powdery white-sand beach with flecks of red coral that give it a pink hue. It's a great swimming spot at high tide and ideal for beachcombing at low tide.

**Newa Sumba Resort** ( ☎ 021-522 9117; www.newa sumbaresort.com; s/d 500,000/650,000Rp) A secluded beach resort with fine timber *kampung*-style bungalows in a garden set back from the beach. The location is worth the price, but the grounds could use some maintenance. Meals are generally pretty tasty (especially if you get the lobster) and cost about 50,000Rp. Regular buses and bemos travel between Waikelo and Waitabula, and a few continue on to Waikabubak.

There is a ferry service between Waikelo and Sape (Sumbawa) twice a week. It departs from Sape for Waikelo on Monday and Friday at around 10pm and returns to Sape (50,000Rp, eight hours) at 5pm on Tuesday and Saturday.

**NUSA TENGGARA**

# Kalimantan

Shrouded in mystery, Kalimantan on the island of Borneo shelters many of Indonesia's deepest secrets and richest treasures; home to ancient forests, fantastic creatures and people living as they did centuries ago. But Kalimantan requires meticulous examination to reveal its bounties.

Occupying two-thirds of Borneo's land mass, Kalimantan offers great rewards for visitors who make the often-substantial effort to lift its veils. Home to one of the world's last great rainforests, Kalimantan's slice of Mother Earth's lungs is sanctuary to most of the planet's remaining orangutans, Dayak tribes balancing ancient traditions with modern opportunities and pioneers from across the archipelago who seek profit from Kalimantan's treasures.

While forests capture headlines, Kalimantan's best attractions flow from its waters. The mighty Sungai Mahakam and Sungai Kapuas lead to longhouse communities in pristine settings, accessible by *kapal taxi* (river ferry) and *ces* (pronounced 'chess'; motorised canoe). Jungle rivers lead to orangutans and proboscis monkeys in Tanjung Puting National Park. Off the east coast, Pulau Derawan has great diving from a village where life floats at the pace of a bygone era.

Despite an emerging consensus supporting conservation, much of Kalimantan's natural heritage remains under extreme threat. For visitors, that means get to Kalimantan fast…then take it slow.

## HIGHLIGHTS

- Plotting *ces* moves on jungle rapids in **Sungai Mahakam** (p642) or **Kapuas Hulu** (p604) in search of Dayak longhouses, drive-through earlobes, evocative tattoos and other ancient traditions
- Charting manta rays' underwater flight paths off **Pulau Derawan** (p648), fishing for dinner and docking in time for sunset volleyball
- Trading high-fives at wash time and nailing breakfast at a floating market along **Banjarmasin**'s waterways (p623)
- Reviving cinema's *African Queen* riding a *klotok* (houseboat with water-pump motor) chugging upriver to see orangutans in **Tanjung Puting National Park** (p614), lulled to sleep by cicadas, awakened by gibbons' morning whoops
- Getting into the jungle swing on bamboo bridges over river valleys in breathtaking **Pegunungan Meratus** (p631), finishing by river raft to hot springs

| POPULATION: 13.7 MILLION | LAND AREA: 558,266 SQ KM | HIGHEST PEAK: BUKIT RAYA (2278M) |

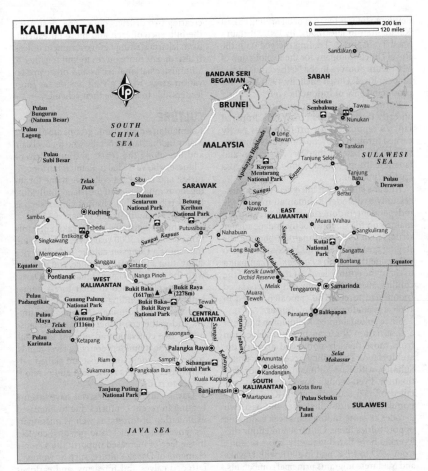

## KALIMANTAN

## HISTORY

Separated from Southeast Asia's mainland 10,000 years ago by rising seas, Kalimantan drew traders along the India–China corridor from at least 300 BC for exotic delights such as birds' nests, black pepper and precious stones. Trading contacts brought Hinduism, and by AD 500 Chinese settlers in present-day West Kalimantan. The 15th-century Melaka empire brought Islam. After Portugal conquered Melaka in 1511, ports including Kutai (now Tenggarong) and Banjarmasin became independent sultanates, safe havens for Muslim traders fleeing Portuguese control.

Following Portugal's lead, Dutch trading monopoly Vereenigde Oost-Indische Compagnie (VOC; United East India Company) began mining diamonds at Sambas in 1610, while Britain's East India Company (EIC) grabbed Kalimantan's pepper trade. The Dutch evicted the British after a failed 1701 revolt that likely received British support. The 1824 Anglo-Dutch Treaty confirmed Dutch rule over present day Kalimantan, at least in European eyes. When English adventurer James Brooke became raja of neighbouring Sarawak in 1839, Dutch officials began expanding commerce and signing treaties with sultanates to solidify their hold on Kalimantan. Banjarmasin rebelled in 1859 and resistance wasn't snuffed until 1905.

By then, the Dutch had established rubber, pepper, copra, tin, coffee and other plantations plus coal mines. But the most significant

**KALIMANTAN**

development was the start of oil drilling in East Kalimantan in late 1890s. In 1907, Britain's Shell Transport & Trading merged with the Royal Dutch Company for the Exploitation of Petroleum Sources in the Netherlands Indies to form Royal Dutch Shell. By 1930 Shell was producing 85% of Indonesia's oil.

Borneo's oil and other resources made it an early target for Japan in WWII. Imperial Japan's reputation for brutality was partly earned through its occupation of Kalimantan (see p598). Late in the war, Australian and Japanese troops fought bloody battles across East Kalimantan.

At war's end, Dutch intriguers tried unsuccessfully to dislodge Kalimantan from newly independent Indonesia, but the region remained on the sidelines of the independence struggle. In 1963, Kalimantan became the staging area for attacks on Malaysian Borneo in President Sukarno's *konfrontasi* campaign to claim the entire island. At the height of the conflict, 50,000 Commonwealth troops faced Indonesian forces. The campaign fizzled in 1966, a year after Sukarno's ouster.

Since colonial times, Kalimantan has been a destination for *transmigrasi*, relocation from more densely populated areas of the archipelago. The policy accelerated under Suharto, with East Kalimantan a major destination. Even though government has curtailed official transmigration, Kalimantan's population has doubled over the past two decades as more Indonesians seek economic opportunities there. Cultural and ethnic differences have flared violently, most recently from 1997 to 1998, and in 2001, with Dayaks and Madurese migrants principal combatants. Many Madurese have been re-relocated out of Kalimantan.

Migration is closely linked to the environmental issues that put Kalimantan in global headlines. Rising population has pushed Dayak shifting cultivators into peat lands unsuited for their traditional slash-and-burn farming techniques, contributing to annual fires and haze that blanket the island and beyond. Transmigrants also provide a labour pool for mining, logging and other environmentally degrading activities, legal or otherwise.

Local autonomy, accelerated under President Susilo Bambang Yudhoyono, is supposed to help Kalimantan meet these challenges. But greater local rule often means creating two districts out of one, decreasing the influence of each and more bureaucrats from Jakarta staffing new government offices. It also means more pieces to knit together to administer national parks and other preservation areas, while giving businesses more leaders able to approve their schemes.

## CULTURE

Kalimantan's main ethnic groups are *Melayu*, Malay Indonesians generally who follow Islam and live along the coasts and major rivers; Chinese, who've traded in Kalimantan for centuries; and Dayaks, a collective name for indigenous inhabitants of the island. Individual Dayak tribes use their distinct names, such as Kenyah, Kayan, Iban and Punan.

Anthropologists believe Dayaks' ancestors came to Borneo 3000 years ago, imbued with Indochina's Dongson culture including rice cultivation and buffalo sacrifice, and mingled with the island's original inhabitants. Dayak lifestyles, closely tied to their forest homelands, vary depending on those conditions. Groups, such as Punan, are nomadic hunters and gatherers. Other Dayaks specialise in dry rice cultivation adapted to local soil. Some are boat builders coursing river rapids, some are herders and most are skilled rattan weavers. Others mine gold and precious stones to trade.

Dayak culture and lifestyles have taken a beating in recent centuries due to increased exploitation of forests, as well as missionaries, government edicts and personal choices in the face of increased opportunities. Some elements of Dayak culture, such as women's tattooed calves and forearms, and earlobes stretched outlandishly by gold or brass rings, are difficult to find (and expensive to photograph). Men still get tattoos, but no longer earn them through headhunting. Dayak culture is now mainly expressed through birth, marriage and death rituals (see p622). Some Dayaks abandon traditional Kaharingan religion for Christianity (or Islam), others combine them.

Many Dayak tribes traditionally lived in longhouses (*rumah betang, rumah panjang, rumah adat Dayak* [fill in tribe name], *lamin* or *balai*). Details differ, but all share the basic blueprint of a carved log ladder to an elevated communal area with doors to individual family apartments. Totems in front signify buffalo sacrifices. The cemetery nearby includes spirit houses and *sandung*, above-ground coffins, often vividly painted. Longhouses remain throughout Kalimantan, some solely for rituals (or tourism), many still communal homes.

Most longhouses welcome overnight guests; ask the *ketua rumah* (elder) for permission (see p604). You've come to sample Dayak culture but you'll see only as much as is normally practised. Don't expect anyone to turn off the TV and start a traditional dance or dump their instant noodles to hunt a boar because you showed up. At a Western home, you wouldn't expect Christmas carols in July.

Visitors can commission welcome ceremonies, usually around 500,000Rp. During traditional ceremonies, expect much singing, dancing and *tuak* (homemade fermented coconut drink) drinking. You'll likely receive an invitation to sing. Go with the cross-cultural flow and let it rip. The crowd will love you, even (especially?) if you make a fool of yourself.

## WILDLIFE

Kalimantan is home to most of the world's orangutans, Asia's only great ape. Orangutans and humans share 97% of DNA, and family resemblance renders them extraordinarily endearing. This endangered species is most easily found in former rehabilitation centres at Tanjung Puting National Park, with large wild populations in Kutai, Gunung Palung and Sebangau National Parks. Like orangutans, long-nosed, potbellied proboscis monkeys (*bekantan*) unique to Borneo live along rivers and in marsh areas, along with crocodiles and macaques.

Forests also provide habitat for gibbons, clouded leopards, sun bears, giant butterflies, and stunning birdlife, including hornbills, a spiritual symbol for many Dayaks. Sungai Mahakam has a critically endangered population of freshwater dolphins. Rich fishing grounds off East Kalimantan are visited by migratory species, with Sangalaki archipelago renowned for diving, featuring sea turtles and manta rays.

## GETTING THERE & AWAY

Visa on arrival (see p839) is available at Balikpapan's Seppingan Airport, Pontianak's Supadio Airport, and West Kalimantan's Entikong land border crossing from Sarawak.

For all other entry points from outside Indonesia, obtain a visa first.

### Air

**Silk Air** (www.silkair.net) flies between Balikpapan and Singapore. **Batavia Air** (www.batavia-air.co.id) flies between Pontianak and Kuching in Sarawak, plus Batam near Singapore. Most connections to/from other parts of Indonesia pass through Jakarta or Surabaya.

### Boat

Ferries connect Tarakan and Nunukan in East Kalimantan with Tawau in Sabah daily except Sunday. Speedboats run daily between Nunukan and Tawau.

State shipping line **Pelni** (www.pelni.co.id) and other carriers link most coastal cities to Java and Sulawesi. Cargo ships offer rides in many ports.

### Bus

Air-con buses connect downtown Pontianak with Kuching. Economy buses to the Entikong border crossing leave from Batu Layang outside Pontianak, and from Singkawang and Sintang. At the time of research, immigration officials allowed foreigners to exit at Entikong, immediately obtain a new visa, and re-enter Indonesia.

## GETTING AROUND

Vast distances, dense jungle, and mountain ranges make travel difficult, especially by land. Where possible, boats are often more direct and comfortable, but pricier. For long distances, flights can spare days on the road, particularly during rainy season, at reasonable prices.

### Air

Kalimantan's air schedules and carriers constantly change due to rapid growth and, following major accidents in 2007, heightened safety concerns. At the time of research, at least eight airlines had flights to Kalimantan destinations including otherwise isolated interior communities. Main air hubs are Pontianak, Balikpapan and Banjarmasin. Bookings often require cash payment for confirmation. Usually, travel agents provide the best information, service, and prices for flights. **KalStar** ( ☎ 021-5315 3456) gets high marks for variety of destinations and reliability.

KALIMANTAN

## KALIMANTAN'S TOP JUNGLE ADVENTURES

Kalimantan has spectacular jungle journeys for intrepid travellers. Treks require resilience, respect, Bahasa Indonesia and a keen sense of adventure.

### Putussibau to Long Apari (p606)

The meek need not apply for this trip, crossing dense jungle with all the primal trimmings. It involves two days of river travel and six or seven of trekking, crossing from West to East Kalimantan.

### Loksado & Around (p631)

This combo tour is easy to organise from Banjarmasin, but simple enough to do independently with some Bahasa Indonesia ability. Bus from Banjarmasin to Loksado, take a few days to trek around Tanuhi and then return by bamboo raft – the best fun ever on floating foliage.

### The Apokayan Highlands (p650)

Ride the rapids on Sungai Pujungan, then take a five-day trek past ancient burial grounds and towering waterfalls, climbing into the Apokayan via the Apo Napu high pass to Data Dian, the last Dayak Kayan village in the highlands.

### Krayan Hulu & Kayan Mentarang National Park (p650)

From Kalimantan's remote north along Sungai Krayan, travel by foot and motorised canoe into the 'Heart of Borneo', exploring some of the last pristine rainforest on this spectacular island. Forays into Kayan Mentarang National Park reveal stunning flora and perhaps clouded leopards.

### What to Bring?

Jungles are steamy and wet. A waterproof jacket is essential and layers of clothing are recommended. For camping shelter, use strong, waterproof material. Tough footwear is mandatory, not just for the terrain, but to thwart leeches and fire ants. Basic medicines and iodine for drinking water are wise. Most importantly, keep the load light, since you'll probably carry your own gear.

### Anything Else I Should Know?

These itineraries require trekking experience, and most require a guide. Guide fees vary depending on the length and remoteness of the trek, but bank on paying 200,000Rp to 500,000Rp per day. You'll also need to pay for food (around 50,000Rp per person per day) and transport costs.

---

Flight cancellations are frequent, so always check before going to the airport. It's also often worthwhile going to the airport even if a flight is supposedly full. Be polite, but firm, and you may get aboard. For some small planes, passengers are weighed along with their luggage and pay by the kilo.

### Boat

Boat travel is disappearing as more roads are built. That's unfortunate, since river ferries (*kapal biasa* or *kapal taxi*) or *long bots* (narrow wooden boats with covered passenger cabins) are pleasant alternatives to buses and best for exploring the jungle. The journey up Sungai Mahakam to Dayak communities remains a Kalimantan highlight, and there's no other way to the headwaters of Sungai Kapuas. There are few coastal boat routes within Kalimantan. Scheduled and chartered speedboats and *ces* reach small towns and tributaries.

### Bus

Roads now connect most major towns, and where roads run, buses follow. Travel conditions vary dramatically by location and season; rainy season shifts durations from hours to days. Air-con, smoke-free buses remain rarities. Kijangs (a popular SUV brand) run scheduled routes between some cities and can be chartered everywhere, independently or through hotels and travel agencies. A car and driver cost 450,000Rp to 800,000Rp per day, depending on location, circumstances and bargaining prowess. Where necessary and available, 4WD vehicles are far more expensive.

# WEST KALIMANTAN

From Kalimantan's oldest longhouses to its most cosmopolitan city, West Kalimantan (Kalimantan Barat or KalBar) offers Indonesian Borneo's widest menu of attractions, spiced by a sizeable Chinese minority. Traditional villages, wild orangutans, antique palaces, virgin forests and idyllic beaches beckon. Many are defended by formidable natural barriers, including Sungai Kapuas,

Kalimantan's longest river at 1143km, coupled with underdeveloped tourist infrastructure that will test the most intrepid travellers' mettle. Successes are amply rewarded, and, unlike many parts of Kalimantan, can be toasted with widely available alcohol.

## PONTIANAK
☎ 0561 / pop 520,000
Bang on the equator, Pontianak is a gateway to Dayak settlements in wild Kapuas Hulu (Upper Kapuas River) and South China Sea beaches. But KalBar's capital is also Kalimantan's most ardently urban destination with a vibrant, compact centre. Pontianak buzzes with commerce driven by produce from the interior, displayed at fruit

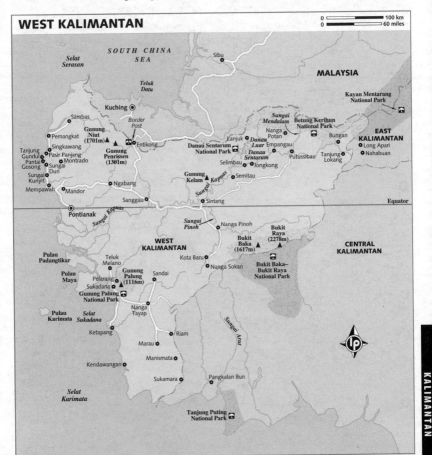

WEST KALIMANTAN

KALIMANTAN

# PONTIANAK

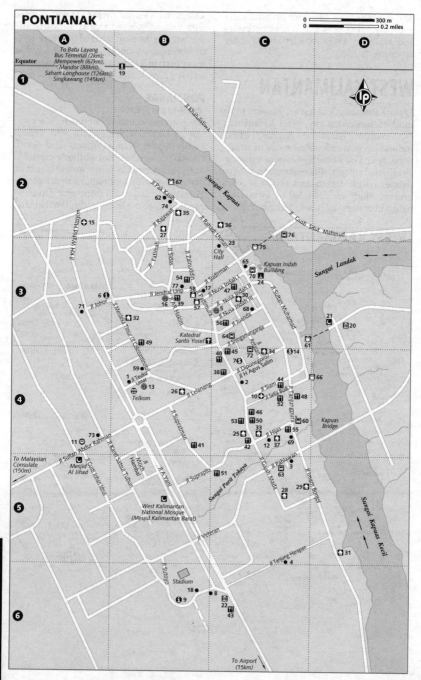

0 — 300 m
0 — 0.2 miles

KALIMANTAN

| INFORMATION | | |
|---|---|---|
| Antya Tour................................**1** B4 | Central Hotel.........................**26** B4 | Somay Bandung.....................**54** B3 |
| Aria Tour.................................**2** C4 | Grand Mahkota Hotel.............**27** B2 | Warung Dim Sum....................**55** C4 |
| Berjaya Tour & Travel...............**3** C5 | Hosanna Inn..........................(see 3) | Warung Lamongan Pak |
| Borneo Access Adventure.........**4** C5 | Hotel Kapuas.........................**28** C5 | Ari....................................**56** C3 |
| Centrine Online ......................**5** C3 | Hotel Kapuas Dharma.............**29** C5 | |
| City Tourist Office....................**6** A3 | Hotel Kini..............................**30** C3 | SHOPPING 🛍 |
| Haji Tunrung Star.....................**7** C4 | Hotel Merpati.........................**31** D5 | Crafts Shops..........................**57** B3 |
| Immigration Office...................**8** C6 | Hotel Patrisia.........................**32** B3 | Matahari Mall.........................**58** B3 |
| Kalimantan Barat Tourist Office..**9** B6 | Hotel Queen...........................**33** C4 | |
| Karisma................................(see 58) | Hotel Santika.........................**34** C4 | TRANSPORT |
| Klinik Kharitas Bhakti..............**10** C4 | Hotel Surya............................**35** B2 | Batavia.................................**59** B4 |
| Main Post Office.....................**11** A4 | Kartika Hotel..........................**36** C2 | Bintang Jaya.........................**60** C4 |
| Mentari Tour ..........................**12** C4 | Mess Hijas.............................**37** C4 | Canoe Ferry to Istana |
| Mitra Tour & Travel.................**13** B4 | | Kadriyah...........................**61** C3 |
| PT Safari...............................**14** C4 | EATING 🍴 | Dharma Kencana....................**62** B2 |
| RS Santo Antonius..................**15** A2 | Apollo..................................**38** C4 | Executive Buses to Kuching....**63** C5 |
| Spectra Gaming & Internet.......**16** B3 | Bakso PSP.............................**39** B3 | Executive Buses to Kuching....**64** C4 |
| Toko Buku Populer..................**17** B3 | Borneo Coffee Club...............**40** C4 | Garuda.................................**65** C3 |
| | Bubur Ikan Sudirman.............**41** B4 | Hak Senghee Harbour............**66** D4 |
| SIGHTS & ACTIVITIES | Capcai.................................**42** C4 | Harbour Terminal for |
| Dayak Longhouse....................**18** B6 | Hypermarket..........................**43** C6 | Java..................................**67** B2 |
| Equator Monument..................**19** B1 | Kabar Gembria.......................**44** C4 | IAT......................................**68** C3 |
| Istana Kadriyah......................**20** D3 | Kaisar..................................**45** C4 | KalStar.................................**69** C4 |
| Mesjid Abdurrahman...............**21** D3 | Ligo Mitra.............................**46** C4 | Kapuas Indah Opelet & Bus |
| Museum Provinsi Kalimantan | Oukie...................................**47** C3 | Terminal............................**70** C3 |
| Barat................................**22** C6 | Oukie II................................**48** C4 | Mandala Air..........................**71** A3 |
| Taman Alun Kapuas.................**23** C3 | Putera Borneo.......................**49** B3 | Opelet Terminal Antasari........**72** C4 |
| Vihara Bodhisatva Karaniya | Restoran Gaja Mada...............**50** C4 | Pelni...................................**73** A4 |
| Metta................................**24** C3 | Restoran Hawaii.....................**51** C5 | Prima Vista...........................**74** B2 |
| | Rumah Makan Borneo............**52** C4 | River Ferry to Siantan.............**75** C3 |
| SLEEPING 🛏 | Rumah Makan Rumah | Siantan Bus & Ferry |
| Ateng House..........................**25** C4 | Betang...........................(see 18) | Terminal............................**76** C2 |
| | Sam Hak Heng.......................**53** C4 | Sriwijaya..............................**77** B3 |

stalls peddling whatever's come downriver this morning, and fabulous food in warungs and street stalls, mixing Dayak, Malay and Chinese cooking, washed down with coffee and conversation at kerbside tables.

## Orientation

Pontianak's centre remains between Jl Tanjungpura, just west of the traditional Sungai Kapuas harbour area, and Jl Pattimura, which becomes Jl Gajah Mada south of Jl Diponegoro/H Agus Salim (Diponegoro on the north side, H Agus Salim on the south).

## Information

### BOOKSTORES

Plentiful newsstands and bookstores stock city and regional maps.

**Karisma** (2nd fl, Matahari Mall, cnr Jl Jendral Urip & Jl Pattimura) Features children's books, ideal for longhouse gifts (see p604).

**Toko Buku Populer** (Jl Pattimura B3&4) Carries the English-language *Jakarta Post* newspaper.

### IMMIGRATION OFFICES

**Immigration office** ( ☎ 765 576; Jl Sutoyo)

**Malaysian Consulate** ( ☎ 732 986, 736 061; www.imi .gov.my; Jl Sultan Syahrir 21; ⏱ visa applications 9-11am)

### INTERNET ACCESS

Smoking is not permitted in the following internet centres.

**Centrine Online** (off Jl Nusa Indah III; per hr 3500Rp; ⏱ 7.30am-10pm) Signposted in a short alley.

**Mitra Tour & Travel** ( ☎ 733 544; Komplek Pontianak Mall, Jl Teuku Umar; per hr 4000Rp; ⏱ 9.30am-10pm) Shares space with an excellent travel agency.

**Spectra Gaming & Internet** (Jl Jendral Urip; per hr 3000; ⏱ 24 hr)

### MEDICAL SERVICES

**Klinik Kharitas Bhakti** ( ☎ 734 373; Jl Siam 153; ⏱ 7.30am-9pm)

**RS Santo Antonius** ( ☎ 732 101; Jl KH Wahid Hasyim 249) Hospital.

### MONEY

ATMs abound, with major banks on and around the north half of Jl Tanjungpura. Moneychanging options:

**Haji Tunrung Star** (Jl Diponegoro 155)

**PT Safari** (Jl Tanjungpura 12)

### POST

**Main Post Office** (Jl Sultan Abdur Rahman 49; ⏱ 7.30am-9.30pm Mon-Sat, 8am-2pm Sun) Poste restante.

## KALIMANTAN'S KILLING FIELDS

Mandor is a lush, sleepy settlement on the main road into West Kalimantan's interior. Diminutive in size, it's a place of overgrown jungle and rice fields. But its serenity is tainted by a tragic past; Mandor is burial ground for 21,037 victims murdered by Japanese troops during their three-year occupation, making Mandor Kalimantan's killing fields.

When the Japanese navy arrived in West Kalimantan in 1942, Indonesia was readying for independence. Dutch authorities had returned home, leaving a leadership vacuum. Japan quickly established troops from Sambas to Ketapang. Treatment of the local population was shocking. Despite ethnic and cultural differences, the desire to resist occupation prompted a secret summit of regional sultans, Dayak, Chinese and Malay leaders in Pontianak. With accurate information from an informant, the Japanese targeted leaders and brought them one by one to Mandor for execution. At first, victims were sultans and their families, intellectuals and ethnic leaders, but the Japanese soon targeted any potential threat, including most men above age 17 and influential women.

The massacre spanned three years and went unrecognised until 1971, when Mandor resident Pak Sambad, presented West Kalimantan's governor with a report appealing for commemoration. His efforts succeeded, prompting a road to the killing site and monument honouring victims.

Today Pak Sambad lives outside the gates of the memorial site and is happy to talk about the area's history (in Bahasa Indonesia). The site contains 10 mass graves, including a shrine to the family of Sultan Abdul Hamid II. A carved-stone storyboard depicts tragedies from Japan's invasion to withdrawal. It is an exquisitely peaceful and reverent place, the flourish of green and wildflowers a fitting tribute to victims. There's no admission fee but Pak Sambad maintains the site and donations are welcomed.

Buses to Mandor (18,000Rp, two hours) run daily from Pontianak's Batu Layang terminal. Buses to Ngabang will also stop at Mandor on request. The journey is beautiful, passing kilometres of rice fields, with forested hills and low-slung cloud hovering above.

## TOURIST INFORMATION

**City tourist office** ( ☎ 732340; Jl Johar 1) Mixed bag of publications and information.

**Kalimantan Barat tourist office** ( ☎ 736172; fax 743104; Jl Sutoyo 17) English-speaking staff member Pak Iwan presses pamphlets and ambitious itineraries.

## TOUR & TRAVEL AGENCIES

**Antya Tour** ( ☎ 733 688; Jl Teuku Umar 62) Kijang and car-rental specialist.

**Aria Tour** ( ☎ 577 868; fax 741 963; Jl Gaja Mada 3) Local jetsetters' pick for flights.

**Berjaya Tour & Travel** ( ☎ 737 325; www.berjayatour .com; Jl Pahlawan 224/2) All travel services (including rooms; see opposite).

**Borneo Access** ( ☎ 081 257 680 66; www.borneoac cessadventurer.com; Jl Tanjung Harapan Gang HD Usman 46) West Borneo Tour Guide Association chairman Alex Afdhal gets mixed reviews for his journeys into KalBar's wilds.

**Mentari Tour** ( ☎ 767196; mentari_tour_ptk@yahoo .com.sg; Jl Hijas 108) Responds to English emails.

**Times Tours & Travel** ( ☎ /fax 770 259; www .timestravelpnk.com) Delivers air tickets, organises tours to Kapuas Hulu and beyond.

## Sights

### TAMAN ALUN KAPUAS

This riverside **park** (Jl Rahadi Usman) includes the ferry crossing to Siantan and vistas of Kapuas activity. At night, it swells with families, kiddie rides, hawkers and food stalls.

### ISTANA KADRIYAH & MESJID ABDURRAHMAN

On the east bank of Sungai Kapuas, **Istana Kadriyah** (admission by donation; ☷ 8.30am-4pm) was completed in 1771 for Pontianak's first sultan, Abdurrahman Habib Hussein Al Kadrie. The ironwood palace is now a museum of royal relics.

Just north of the dock, the sultan's mosque, **Mesjid Abdurrahman** (also known as Mesjid Jami'), with its Sumatran-style square-tiered roof, holds a commanding spot on the Kapuas. Cross wobbly planks to village houses on stilts over the water, busiest at early- or late-day washing times.

Get there by canoe taxi (2000Rp) from the foot of Jl Mahakam or charter (10,000Rp) from nearby piers.

## VIHARA BODHISATVA KARANIYA METTA
KalBar's oldest and biggest **Chinese temple** (Jl Sultan Muhammad) dates to 1679. Amid the sensory festival, note huge urns bookending the entrance and cement rock gardens.

## MUSEUM PROVINSI KALIMANTAN BARAT & DAYAK LONGHOUSE
The **West Kalimantan Provincial Museum** (Jl A Yani; ☯ 8am-2pm Tue-Thu, 8-11am Fri, 8am-1pm Sat-Sun, closed Mon) features artefacts of the province's Dayak, Malay and Chinese inhabitants plus *tempayan*: Asian ceramics dating to the 16th century. Its garden has replicas of traditional houses, factories and Perahu Lancang Kuning, the sultan's golden yacht.

Around the corner, a replica *rumah betang* or **Dayak longhouse** (Jl Sutoyo) sports genuine totems and carved log steps. **Rumah Makan Rumah Betang** ( ☎ 792 9975; mains 8000-25,000Rp) serves Indonesian and Kenayant Dayak favourites, including *ular* (snake) and *asu* (dog), some cooked in bamboo tubes, and sells handicrafts.

Take a red or pink *opelet* (intracity minibus) south along Jl A Yani.

## EQUATOR MONUMENT
Grown from a simple marker in 1928 into a collage of circles and arrows with a huge replica outside marking *its* spot, **Patung Khatulistiwa** (Equator Monument; Jl Khatulistiwa) makes much – too much – of Pontianak's geography. It draws crowds every equinox to experience shadowless sunlight.

Take a *bis kota* (intercity bus; 2500Rp) going south along Jl Tanjungpura across the bridge to the monument or the ferry to Siantan and an *opelet* heading northwest. Patung Khatulistiwa is alongside the highway. Believe us, you can't miss it.

## SAHAM LONGHOUSE
Located in Pahauman, this **longhouse** is one of KalBar's oldest (more than 200 years) and longest (180m).

Visit by bus from Batu Layang to Ngabang (35,000Rp, 3½ hours, 114km) or take any downtown executive bus east. Get dropped at the Pahauman turn, then catch a local taxi or *ojek* (motorcycle taxi; 12km). Chartered Kijangs from Pontianak cost up to 500,000Rp.

## Festivals & Events
Pontianak's geography inspires the **Equatorial Culture Festival** around the March and September equinoxes with Dayak, Chinese and Malay traditional dancing, singing, and competitions.

**Robok-Robok** celebrates neighbouring Mempawah's kingdom with a royal yacht procession, dragon boat races and terrestrial events in Mempawah (15,000Rp, 1½ hours, 67km). Dates follow the Islamic calendar; falling mid-January in 2011, moving approximately two weeks earlier annually.

**Gawai Dayak** harvest festival in May centres on Pontianak's **longhouse** (Jl Sutoyo).

## Sleeping
### BUDGET
**Hotel Patrisia** ( ☎ 736 063; Jl Cokroaminoto 497; r 50,000-85,000Rp; ✺ ) Clean, sparse rooms, all with private (some Western) bathrooms and two beds. Higher rate buys air-con and TV.

**Mess Hijas** ( ☎ /fax 744 068; 081 256 960 03; Jl Hijas 106; s 75,000Rp, d 110,000-135,000Rp; ✺ ) Every room at this business-traveller favourite includes air-con, TV and Western bathroom, many with hot water, plus a friendly, efficient vibe throughout.

**Hotel Merpati** ( ☎ 745 481; fax 762 662; Jl Imam Bonjol 111; r 84,000-156,000 plus 10% tax, ste 270,000Rp plus 10% tax; ✺ 🛜 ) Budget rooms include air-con and private *mandi*. Good value are the main-building rooms from 126,000Rp with minibar, hot/cold shower and free wi-fi in the lobby.

**Hotel Queen** ( ☎ 767 232, 081 522 036 89; Jl Gajah Mada 141-143, entrance on Jl Hijas; r 90,000-150,000Rp; ✺ ) Simple rooms here all have air-con and TV. The cheapest rooms share spotless bathrooms with Western toilets.

**Ateng House** ( ☎ 732 683; attenghouse@yahoo.com; Jl Gajah Mada 201; s/d incl breakfast 110,000/125,000Rp plus 15% tax; ✺ ) Bright rooms include air-con, TV, private bathroom and homely frills like bedspread, water dispenser and curtains.

More budget options:

**Hosanna Inn** ( ☎ 735 052; www.hosannainn.com; Jl Pahlawan 224/2; s 80,000-98,000Rp, d 118,000-195,000Rp, all incl breakfast; ✺ 🛜 ) Above Berjaya Tour, most rooms have shared bath and no windows. Smoking is restricted to the terrace.

**Hotel Surya** ( ☎ 734 337; fax 760 334; Jl Sidas 11A; r 120,000Rp; ✺ ) Reliable rooms with air-con, TV and private bathroom with shower.

### MIDRANGE & TOP END
Many hotels offer substantial discounts at airport kiosks.

**our pick** **Central Hotel** ( ☎ 737 444; fax 734 993; Jl Cokroaminoto 232; r incl breakfast 160,000-250,000Rp; ☒ ) Ignore that ground-floor barber shop: Central's no clip joint. Weathered standard rooms include hot-water shower, air-con and extraordinarily helpful staff. Pricier renovated rooms add style.

**Hotel Kapuas Dharma** ( ☎ 766 669; fax 735 399; Jl Imam Bonjol 89; r incl breakfast 172,500-340,400Rp; ☒ ) Midrange sibling of Hotel Kapuas offers comforts including hot-water shower, minibar and elevator at value rates.

**Kartika Hotel** ( ☎ 734 401; fax 738 457; Jl Rahadi Usman 2; r incl breakfast 200,000-320,000Rp plus 20% tax; ☒ ⓢ ) Riverside terrace, bright yellow decor, modern furnishings, tennis court: advantage Kartika.

**Hotel Kapuas** ( ☎ 736122; www.hotelkapuas.com; Jl Gajah Mada 889; r incl breakfast 315,000-624,000Rp; ste 720,000-1,632,000Rp; ☒ ▯ ▨ ⓢ ) Posh rooms in a resort setting with fitness centre, vast pool and bar.

**Hotel Kini** ( ☎ 732 223; fax 742 882; Jl Nusa Indah III; r incl breakfast 481,800-650,000Rp, ste 880,000-1,880,000Rp; ☒ ⓢ ) A new wing opened in 2009 adding more large, comfortable rooms, often discounted by 25%. Suites shine.

**Hotel Santika** ( ☎ 733 777; pontianak@santika.com; Jl Diponegoro 46; r incl breakfast 601,000-640,500Rp; ste 677,700-1,322,000Rp plus 21% tax; ☒ ▯ ⓢ ) Angle for 30% discounts at this branch of a national chain offering relaxed elegance in swanky rooms. The 3rd-floor features a lounge with live music. Nonsmoking rooms available.

**Grand Mahkota Hotel** ( ☎ 736 022; fax 736 200; Jl Sidas 8; r incl breakfast 605,000-726,000Rp, ste 1,442,000-4,235,000Rp; ☒ ▯ ⓢ ) This contender for Pontianak's best puts luxury furnishings and original art in each room and offers steep weekend discounts. Swimming pool under construction during our visit. Nonsmoking rooms are available.

## Eating

Fresh ingredients, Chinese influence, and street culture make Pontianak Kalimantan's best destination to travel your tastebuds. Warungs and stalls abound along major streets and surrounds, with Jl Diponegoro/H Agus Salim, Jl Pattimura, Jl Hijas and Jl Setia Budi (Pontianak's computer district) especially notable. At night, new stalls sprout, particularly along Jl Gajah Mada. Despite Pontianak's late-night soul, some restaurants close at 9pm. Most top hotel restaurants serve Western, Chinese and Indonesian food at reasonable prices.

**Somay Bandung** (Jl Zainuddin 15; mains 7000-14,000Rp) Mobbed at lunch for the national version of

*siomay*: steamed dough, potatoes, tofu, and cabbage drowned in rich peanut sauce.

**Warung Dim Sum** ( ☎ 706 4584; Jl Hijas 8; dishes 8000-12,000Rp; ⓢ 6am-3pm) Sunday brunch Chinese style, all day, every day.

**Kabar Gembira** (Jl Siam 206; mains 10,000-14,0000Rp; ⓢ 7am-8pm) This is the most popular of many Chinese vegetarian options and has the latest closing time.

**our pick** **Oukie** (Jl Nusah Indah I; mains 10,000-16,000Rp; ⓢ 6am-5pm, closed Monday) Third-generation local institution serving noodles at the intersection of Indonesian and Chinese cooking. There is also a branch on Jl Tanjungpura.

**Warung Lamongan Pak Ari** (Jl Juanda; mains 10,000-18,000Rp; ⓢ 4pm-midnight) Crowded nightly for deep-fried fish and chicken *lalapan* style, served with sambal and fragrant raw *kemangi* leaves, a taste like very strong basil.

**Bakso PSP** (Jl AR Hakim; mains 12,000Rp) Ationg and Yuli – he's Chinese, she's Bugis – blend Pontianak's best beef ball soup.

**Restoran Hawaii** ( ☎ 742 277; Jl Suprapto 16; per person 40,000-60,000Rp; ⓢ 9.30am-9.30pm) Local Chinese-cuisine legend, recently relocated. Some contend newcomer **Restoran Gaja Mada** ( ☎ 766 580; Jl Gajah Mada 202; per person 60,000-70,000Rp; ⓢ 10am-10pm) now dishes Pontianak's best Chinese chow.

### LOCAL FARE

Get a Chinese street feed and cooking demonstration at **Sam Hak Heng** (cnr Jl Gajah Mada & Jl Darwis; mains 12,000-22,000Rp; ⓢ 5-10.30pm), or **Capcai** (cnr Jl Gajah Mada & Jl Suprapto; mains 17,000-25,000Rp; ⓢ 10am-9.30pm).

Discover *sotong pangkong* (roasted dried squid; per squid 25,000Rp to 40,000Rp) smashed by hammer, best with beer, in an alley off Jl Nusa Indah I late afternoons to the wee hours. Try *tauswan* (sweet greenbean soup; 5000Rp) and *kaloci* (or *moci*; glutinous rice coated with peanuts and sugar; 5000Rp) on Jl H Agus Salim, 25m east of Jl Gajah Mada, from mid-morning to night.

Other Pontianak specialties:

**Apollo** (Jl Pattimura; mains 13,000Rp) Founded in 1968, dishes up *mie tiau daging sapi* (fried noodles with beef aka beef *kway teow*).

**Bubur Ikan Sudirman** (Jl Supratman 40; bowl 12,000Rp; ⓢ 6.30-10.30am, 5-9.30pm) Front-yard warung serving Teochew-style fish porridge.

**Rumah Makan Borneo** (Jl Setia Budi; mains 8000-14,000Rp) Specialises in *fuyung hai* (deep-fried seafood omelette).

## COFFEE SHOPS

Pontianak brims with coffee shops and stalls, open day and night, mainly patronised by men. Many *warung kopi* add simple food, a full drinks menu and TV sports to the brew. **Borneo Coffee Club** (Jl Pattimura 71E; mains 11,000-16,000Rp; ☻ 10am-10pm; ☎ ) and **Putera Borneo** (Jl Cokroaminoto 475; mains 10,000-15,000Rp; ☎ ), a gender-neutral juice joint, get the blend right, including free wi-fi.

### SELF CATERING

Top supermarkets:

**Hypermarket** (A Yani MegaMall, Jl A Yani)

**Kaisar** (Jl Pattimura) Also KalBar's biggest bakery chain.

**Ligo Mitra** (Jl Gajah Mada 77)

## Shopping

Specialty items at **crafts shops** along Jl Pattimura include *songket* (handwoven cloth with gold or silver threads), Dayak *mandau* (daggers), beadwork and carvings, honey and other secondary forest products.

## Getting There & Away

### AIR

**Batavia** ( ☎ 734 488; fax 736 604; Jl Cokroaminoto 278A), **Garuda** ( ☎ 734 986; Jl Tanjungpura), **Sriwijaya** ( ☎ 768 777; Jl Jendral Urip 19), **Lion** ( ☎ 706 6111) and **Mandala Air** ( ☎ 766 447; Jl KH Ahmad Dahlan 6) all fly to Jakarta. Batavia also flies to Kuching and to Surabaya via Yogyakarta. **KalStar** ( ☎ 739 090; Jl Tanjungpura 429) and **IAT** (Indonesia Air Transport; ☎ 762 247; Jl Juanda 40) fly to Ketapang and Pangkalan Bun. KalStar also serves Banjarmasin. IAT flies to Putussibau and Semarang in Central Java.

### BOAT

Boats to Java leave from the **main harbour** on Jl Pak Kasih, north of the Kartika Hotel. **Prima Vista** ( ☎ 761 145; Jl Pak Kasih 90B), **Dharma Kencana** ( ☎ 765 021; Jl Pak Kasih 42F) and **Pelni** ( ☎ 748 124; fax 748 131; www.pelni.co.id; Jl Sultan Abdur Rahman 12) serve Jakarta (250,000Rp, 36 hours), Semarang (225,000Rp, 34 hours) and Surabaya (270,000Rp, 40 hours). Travel agents sell tickets and know schedule details.

Scheduled passenger boats to Putussibau are extinct, but try finding passage by *bandung*, a combination freighter and general store that can take a month for the 800km journey.

Daily **jet boats** head south to Ketapang (140,000Rp to 180,000Rp, eight hours) from **Hak Senghee Harbour** on Jl Barito; air-con class is worth the extra fare. Longboats to Sukadana (160,000Rp, six hours) leave from behind the Kapuas Indah Building.

### BUS

Batu Layang terminal, northwest of town, has buses to Singkawang (25,000Rp, three hours), Sambas (40,000Rp, five hours), Sanggau (48,000Rp, six hours) and the Entikong border crossing (55,000Rp, nine hours), plus minibuses to Mempewah (15,000Rp, 1½ hours). To reach Batu Layang, take a cross-Kapuas ferry to Siantan and catch a white *opelet* north, or, direct but longer, take the orange-and-white *bis kota* (2500Rp) running south along Jl Tanjungpura.

Door-to-door service by shared Kijang is a popular option to Singkawang (70,000Rp, three hours). Book through hotels or travel agents.

Along Jl Sisingamangaraja, several companies run air-con **express buses to Kuching** (economy/executive 165,000/230,000Rp, 11 hours) through Entikong. **SJS** ( ☎ 734 626; Jl Sisingamangaraja 155) has the most choices. Bus clusters on Jl Pahlawan, and Jl Tanjungpura serve Kuching and other destinations, including Sintang (100,000Rp, 10 hours), Nanga Pinoh (115,000Rp, 11 hours), even Brunei (550,000Rp, 27 hours). **Damri** ( ☎ 744 859; Jl Pahlawan 226/3) has the broadest menu. **Bintang Jaya** ( ☎ 659 7402; Jl Tanjungpura 310A) has the newest Kuching fleet.

Buses to Putussibau (175,000Rp to 270,000Rp, 16 to 18 hours) via Sintang leave from the Kapuas Indah Building. **Perintis** ( ☎ 767 886; Komplek Kapuas Indah 1-2) has the most frequent service.

### CAR & MOTORCYCLE

Travel agencies or hotels arrange cars (without/with driver per day 250,000/450,000Rp) for exploring KalBar at your pace. Shop around as terms can vary substantially. For experienced riders, motorcycles rent for 150,000Rp per day.

## Getting Around

Airport taxis cost 70,000Rp to town (15km).

*Opelet* (2500Rp) routes converge around Jl Sisingamangaraja. Becaks are widely available. Taxis are unmetered and scarce. Some hotels have Kijangs standing by; fares for these 'hotel taxis' start at Rp20,000.

KALIMANTAN

Cross-river ferries (1000Rp) to Siantan terminal leave from Taman Alun Kapuas. Canoe ferries to Istana Kadriyah (2000Rp) leave from the pier at end of Jl Mahakam. Motorised canoes for hire (cross-river 10,000Rp; per hour 100,000Rp) are plentiful along the riverfront.

## SUNGAI KAPUAS

Indonesia's longest river, Sungai Kupuas remains a highway for goods from the interior to Pontianak. In its upper reaches, the 1143km river and its tributaries provide access to Dayak communities and fabulous forests, and begin cross-Borneo journeys.

Buses have replaced boats for long-distance travel along the lower Kapuas. Along Kapuas Hulu (upper Kapuas) tributaries and beyond Putussibau, travel is still primarily by boat. Where public boats run, they usually won't leave until full. Chartering is an expensive alternative.

### Sintang
☎ 0565 / pop 40,000

Against the grey backdrop of Gunung Kelam, Sintang marks the start of Kapuas Hulu and its confluence with Sungai Melawi. The town branches out from the river banks.

International ATMs are scattered around town. For medical emergencies, consult **Rumah Sakit Ade Mohammad Djoen** ( ☎ 22805/07/09; Jl Pattimura).

Across the river, the sultan's palace is now **Dara Janti Museum**. The keeper will open it for a donation. Boats to cross (10,000Rp) congregate around riverfront warungs. Founded by missionaries to preserve local craft traditions, Kobus Centre (Jl Mohammad Saad; ☻9am-2pm), features renowned local ikat. Kobus and local government support ikat production at **Ensaid Panjang** (one hour), one of several *rumah betang* outside town. In the dry season, these longhouses can be reached by minibus, but require private transport in wet months.

**Taman Baning** (2km) is a 215-hectare tropical forest for watching birds and wild orchids. Take an *opelet* (3000Rp) or *ojek* (10,000Rp).

**Gunung Kelam** (18km) features butterflies, a waterfall *(air terjun)*, panoramic views and a testing climb up its 900m peak with steel ladders on its toughest rock faces. Take an *opelet* to Pasar Impres (3000Rp) and then a Kelam *opelet* (7000Rp) to the gaudy park entrance.

**Bukit Baka–Bukit Raya National Park** (see right) is about eight hours south by road and river.

It's four hours by very rough road or seven hours by boat to **Danau Sentarum National Park** (see p605), but most visitors reach the park via Putussibau.

### SLEEPING & EATING
**Sakura Hotel** ( ☎ 23418; Jl MT Haryono 58A; r 78,000-248,000Rp; 🛂 ) Beyond the rustic lobby, rooms feature modern comforts including refrigerator, air-con and Western bathroom with hot water. Economy rooms have *mandi* and fan.

**Hotel Setia** ( ☎ 23433; Jl Mahapahit 1-4; r 100,000-105,000Rp; 🛂 ) In central Sintang, Setia's identical rooms include private *mandi*, TV and air-con.

**Sintang Permai Hotel** ( ☎ 22725; Jl MT Haryono 117; r 155,000-185,000Rp; 🛂 ) Sintang's newest hotel, on a hill about 600m from Sintang's centre, has bright rooms with refrigerator, TV and hot-water shower. Friendly staff will arrange chartered cars, and a 24-hour canteen dishes Indonesian basics (mains 6000Rp to 14,000Rp).

Riverfront warungs on stilts offer cheap eats. Fruit vendors, more food stalls and restaurants line Jl Sugioso, one block inland. **Intar** (Jl Sugioso) sells groceries and other essentials.

### GETTING THERE & AWAY
At the time of research there were no flights to Sintang; check in Pontianak for updates.

Buses to Putussibau (125,000Rp, seven hours), Semitau (60,000Rp, four hours), and Pontianak (100,000Rp, 10 hours) leave from Pasar Durian terminal on Jl Wisapati. Roads to Putussibau are good, roads to Pontianak dreadful.

For buses south to Nanga Pinoh (10,000Rp, one hour), take an *opelet* (10,000Rp) to Sungai Ukoi bus terminal, 10km southwest.

### Bukit Baka–Bukit Raya National Park

Named for two of Kalimantan's highest peaks, **Bukit Baka–Bukit Raya National Park** offers extraordinary montane forest vistas, breathtaking waterfalls, meandering rivers, giant rafflesia blooming every March and barely any tourist facilities. The park is a southern option for cross-Borneo treks. Before visiting, contact the **park office** ( ☎ /fax 0565-23521; Jl Dr Wahidin Sudirohusodo) in Sintang.

Reach the sprawling 181,000-hectare Schwaner Range reserve, about eight hours south of Sintang, by boat and 4WD via Nanga Pinoh and Nanga Popai. From Palangka Raya in Central Kalimantan, the route combines road, river and trekking via Tumbang Jatuh, Tumbang Manggu and Tumbang Gagu.

## Putussibau

☎ 0567 / pop 17,000

Last stop for airlines and long distance buses, Putussibau is launch point for excursions to Kapuas Hulu's traditional communities, national parks and untouched forests.

To develop sustainable ecotourism, local government, national park authorities, WWF and villagers created **Kompakh** ( ☎ 085 650 021 01; http://www.kompakh.org; Jl Pasar Impres, Gang D Salam 1). Kompakh offers touring options including Danau Sentarum National Park, longhouse visits, river cruising, whitewater adventures, mild to extreme jungle treks and even trans-Borneo journeys by foot and boat. Tours can be customised, and prices depend on group size and precise itinerary. Independent guide **Usman** ( ☎ 081 649 959 61; usman_tour@hotmail.com) also gets good recommendations.

Sandwiched between Sungai Kapuas and Sungai Sibau, Putussibau's main street is Jl Yos Sudarso. There's *angkot* (minibus; 3000Rp) service along this street that, north past the traffic light, becomes Jl Panjaitan – home to Putussibau's lone international ATM – and leads to **internet access** (Jl Gaja Mada; per hour 3500Rp; ☺ 8am-4pm). The name changes to Jl A Yani heading south, toward the bus and boat terminals, morning market and bridge across Sungai Kapuas to the airport. **Rumah Sakit Dr Achmad Diponegoro** ( ☎ 21129; Jl Yos Sudarso 42) offers medical services.

### SLEEPING

**Aman Sentosa Hotel** ( ☎ 21691; fax 21357; Jl Diponegoro 14; r 50,000-120,000Rp; ❄ ) Once Putussibau's best hotel, Aman Sentosa's rooms are battered but clean. The cheapest digs have fans and shared *mandi*. Pricier rooms add TV, air-con, refrigerator and private *mandi*, plus a verandah overlooking its parking lot turned scrap yard.

**Permata Bunda Inn** ( ☎ 22249; Jl Yos Sudarso 87; r 50,000-150,000Rp; ❄ ) Highest grade rooms here boast hot and cold water – for drinking, not bathing. All have private *mandi*.

**Sanjaya Hotel** ( ☎ 21653; fax 22366; Jl Yos Sudarso 129; r with breakfast 75,000-375,000Rp; ❄ ) Highest priced rooms include Putussibau's only hot/cold showers, but the real find are shared *mandi*, economy rooms with two beds in this clean, modern hotel.

**Mess Pemda** ( ☎ 21010; Jl Merdeka 11; r 125,000-150,000Rp; ❄ ) 'Wisma Uncuk Kapuas Terhitang' by its sign outside, this government hostel's spotless rooms, all with air-con, TV, Western toilet and *mandi*, offer great value. From Jl A Yani, turn left on Jl Dahar and make two rights to Jl Merdeka.

### EATING

There are warungs and coffee joints aplenty along Jl Yos Sudarso, and more near the bridge serving noodles, juices and desserts. Try local specialty *krupuk basah*, ground fish steamed in banana leaf, sprinkled with shrimp crackers and spicy peanut sauce.

**our pick** **Depot Cak Nur** (Jl Yos Sudarso; mains 4000-12,000Rp) Serve yourself fresh East Java specialties, including lots of vegetable choices. Busy at breakfast.

**Pondok Fajar** (Jl Yos Sudarso; mains 10,000-18,000Rp; ☺ 6am-1am) This Padang place packs 'em in for its buffet.

**Pondok Meranti** ( ☎ 21454; Jl Yos Sudarso; mains 12,000-15,000Rp) Serves up fried or barbecued chicken, soups and noodles on its sprawling veranda or hangar-like interior.

**Pondok Flamboyan** (Jl Yos Sudarso; mains 12,000-29,000Rp) Delicious, ambitious Chinese fish and seafood by the portion, plus crab and *udang galah* (giant river prawns) by the ounce.

**Famili** ( ☎ 21378; Jl KS Tubun; mains 15,000-20,000Rp; ☺ 10am-8pm) Putussibau's Chinese standby, 50m from the traffic light.

For self-catering, **Diamond** (Jl Amin) has the best grocery selection.

### GETTING THERE & AWAY

**IAT** (Indonesia Air Transport; ☎ 22663; Jl Danau Sentarum 21A) flies to/from Pontianak (800,000Rp) three times weekly. Taxis from the airport (10km) cost 35,000Rp, if you can find one; *ojeks* cost 20,000Rp.

Several companies operate economy buses to Pontianak (175,000Rp, 16 hours) and Sintang (100,000Rp, 10 hours). **Perinitis** ( ☎ 21237, Jl Yos Sudarso 71) runs three trips daily, including two 'executive' buses (non air-con/ air-con 210,000/270,000Rp). Pontianak service passes through Sintang for connections to the border at Entikong. The local bus, *angkot* and *ojek* **terminal** is on Jl Diponegoro, near the market.

River boats use the pier on Sungai Kapuas east of the bridge. From Jl Merdeka, take any street south to the waterfront.

## Around Putussibau

Many of Kalimantan's most intriguing long-houses survive in **Kapuas Hulu**. Most accept overnight guests and welcome participation in community activities (see below).

**Baligundi longhouse** was purpose-built for tourism in a Taman Dayak farming community 12km north of Putussibau (*opelet* 8000Rp). You can stay overnight at basic homestays (per person 30,000Rp; meals per day 55,000Rp). Residents also can stage welcome ceremonies (500,000Rp).

On Sungai Mendalam, **Semangkok I** and much older **Semangkok II** are accessible by *ojek* (100,000Rp return, 30 minutes) or longboat (300,000Rp return, 30 minutes).

North on Sungai Sibau two hours by long-boat (300,000Rp), **Nanga Potan** has Dayak Bukat, Kantuk and Taman inhabitants and a lodge (per person 25,000Rp; meals per day 50,000Rp). The community's ecotourism group organises dawn and dusk **wildlife cruises** (per boat 150,000Rp). Village activities include **slingshot fishing** using a primitive form of wire-guided missile. Ambitious travellers can track wild orangutans inside Betung Kerihun National Park (see opposite).

**Sungkok Apalin** (admission 10,000Rp) is the oldest longhouse in Borneo, according to experts. At nearly 8m off the ground, it's indisputably one of the highest. This Tamambaloh Dayak community welcomes overnight visitors (per person 25,000Rp; meals per day 40,000Rp). Reach the village by *opelet* from Putussibau (13,000Rp, one hour, 38km), running at 9am and 12 noon; visitors may want to stay overnight or take an *ojek* (75,000Rp)

back. Or continue by bus (40,000Rp) through Iban longhouses with their characteristic terraces toward Danau Sentarum National Park (see opposite).

### ALONG SUNGAI KAPUAS

Upstream from Putussibau on Sungai Kapuas, there's a string of Taman longhouses, starting with Sauwe (or Saui), 3km east of the airport. Take a ferry across the river (10,000Rp) to **Melapi I**, a renovated longhouse that retains its original flavour, and **Melapi II**, in original condition, with five other new longhouses nearby. These areas have a twice-daily *opelet* service (15,000) with the option of return by *ojek* (50,000Rp).

Continuing east, **Unsah** (also called Lunsah) has two longhouses. Unsah I is among the region's oldest. In dry season, it's accessible by *ojek* (50,000Rp, one hour), but the water route by chartered longboat (350,000Rp return, 1½ hour) or speedboat (500,000Rp return, one hour) includes river vistas and views of other longhouses. For overnight stays, add 100,000Rp to transport charges.

Beyond Unsah, Riam Delapan (Eight Rapids) on Sungai Kapuas make travel more challenging and expensive. Kompakh organises whitewater longboating: it has safety equipment for challenging the rapids, but no rafts.

**Bungan** (3,500,000Rp to 4,000,000Rp return, eight hours) and **Tanjung Lokang** (6,000,000Rp return, 10½ to 14 hours) are traditional villages on the fringes of Betung Kerihun National Park accessible only by longboat. Don't expect longhouses; residents are Punan

---

### LONGHOUSE GIFT TIPS

It's traditional to give gifts when you visit a longhouse. Some say the tradition began with guided tours. Standard suggestions for gifts – cigarettes and candy – appal many visitors. So we asked guides and Kalimantan Dayaks for alternatives.

First, ask your host (if you've been invited) or your tour guide what the longhouse needs. Practical items such as fishing line are hard to find in the jungle. Fruits or spices common in the city may be longhouse luxuries.

Communal gifts are presented to the longhouse leader, who then parcels them out as he (invariably, it's a man) sees fit. Individually packaged, pre-portioned items work best. A couple dozen envelopes of powered milk may be welcome in some areas. Toothbrushes and/or toothpaste can help combat rampant tooth decay. Books for sharing or notebooks and pencils for school children seem ideal, but beware that logging for paper production is an issue in some Dayak communities.

If you've been invited by a family, give them an individual gift and benefit the community by hiring a guide or taking a canoe trip.

Dayaks, ancestral cave dwellers. In Bungan (also called Nanga Bungan), inhabitants remain principally hunters and gatherers, so everyone's usually in the forest except for old people and children. Villagers practice traditional rattan crafts and prospect in the river, with the modern twist of a compressor for underwater breathing. Bungan's **lodge** (per person 25,000Rp) has no facilities. Village homestays (per person 50,000Rp) are more comfortable for travellers without full gear.

In Tanjung Lokang, there's a more complete **community-run lodge** ( ☎ 086 812 114 807; per person 25,000Rp), though visitors must bring their food. The village is a starting point for trans-Borneo treks and base for exploring Betung Kerihun National Park. Local activities include gold mining, incense making, farming, and boat building.

Going west on Sugnai Kapuas, **Danau Empangau** is a protected lake habitat of prized fish species such as *arowana* and giant snakehead, seen in the lake (bring a torch) or village fish farms. The village runs a **lodge** ( ☎ 085 654 587 797; per person 25,000Rp), and **lake tours** (boat with guide per day 200,000Rp). From nearby Teluk Aur, take **orangutan cruises** ( ☎ 085 650 848 556) into the mangroves. Public boats to Empangau leave daily from Putussibau (150,000Rp, 2½ hours).

## DANAU SENTARUM NATIONAL PARK

A seasonal lake that regulates water levels throughout Sungai Kapuas, **Danau Sentarum National Park** (admission per day 15,000Rp; camera 30,000Rp) is a 132,000-hectare wetland area with a variety of inhabitants.

The lake is famous for super red *arowana* (*Scleropages formosus*), a trophy aquarium fish frequently spotted leaping. During rainy season, lake depths reach 8m and flood surrounding forests. During dry season, fish huddle in isolated pools.

Wildlife in peat swamps and lowland rainforest include orangutans, proboscis monkeys, crocodiles, stork and great argus pheasant. At least four Dayak groups – Iban, Sebaruk, Sontas and Punan – with several longhouses live in and around the park.

Most visitors enter through the ranger post at **Lanjuk**. Bring copies of your passport and Indonesian visa for registration. Bukit Lanjuk offers a panoramic view of the park. From Lanjuk travel by speedboat, longboat, or houseboat (*klotok* or *bandung*) that may offer accommodation. Guides cost 50,000Rp to 250,000Rp per day. Prices for speedboats are fixed (quoted below); *klotok* prices are negotiable from 500,000Rp per day.

**Pulau Tekenang** (650,000Rp, one hour) has a Malay fishing village with floating houses and a basic research facility open to visitors; negotiate terms with villagers. Bukit Tekenang is a good vista point. **Pulau Melayu** (250,000Rp, 15 minutes) has a lodge with no facilities (bring food and bedding) and good views. **Sungai Pelaik** (750,000Rp, one hour) has an Iban longhouse. At the lake's south end, **Meliau** (950,000Rp, two hours) has access to marsh areas with orangutan, crocodiles, proboscis monkeys and abundant birdlife. Most times of year, motor canoe (per hour 100,000Rp; guide per day 50,000Rp) is the best way to spot wildlife.

Reach Danau Sentarum from Sintang by longboat (2,000,000Rp, five to seven hours) or bus (80,000Rp, four hours) to Semitau, then speedboat (1,500,000Rp, two hours). From Putussibau, take a minibus to Lanjuk (100,000Rp, 3½ hours) or a longboat to Empangau (150,000Rp, 2½ hours), then charter a speedboat (1,500,000Rp, 2½ hours).

For more information, contact the **park office** ( ☎ 0567-22242; Jl Oesiang Oeray 43), **WWF** ( ☎ 0567-22258; fax 0567-22787; Jl Yos Sudarso 97), or Kompakh (see p603), all in Putussibau.

## BETUNG KERIHUN NATIONAL PARK

Tracing the border with Sarawak in Malaysia, mountainous **Betung Kerihun National Park** (admission per day 15,000Rp; camera 30,000Rp) shelters the headwaters of Sungai Kapuas amid diverse ecosystems. WWF's Heart of Borneo initiative aims to link Betung Kerihun with Malaysia's Lantjak Entimau Wildlife Reserve.

The 800,000-hectare park, named for two Muller Range peaks, has eight types of forest, from lowland to montane, and varied wildlife, including orangutan, gibbon, tarsier, leaf monkeys, sun bear, clouded leopard and 300-plus bird species. Spot wildlife at salt springs dotting the park.

A main attraction is Kahnung Cave (Liang Kaung in Dayak language) and Kuburan Tahapan, a cemetery, a three- to four-hour trek from Tanjung Lokang. Get permission to enter from the villagers. Other caves have swiftlets producing the key ingredient of bird's nest soup.

To track wild orangutans, enter the park from Nanga Potan on Sungai Sibau via longboat (500,000Rp, three hours), then trek 12km into their habitat. Guides (per day 150,000Rp to 250,000Rp) from the park or Kompakh are required, and it's rough camping in the jungle. A typical trip lasts two nights and can end with building a raft from *purang*, a fast growing hardwood, and riding it six hours back to Nanga Potan.

For details, contact the **park office** ( ☎ 0567-21773; fax 0567-21935; Jl Tendean 49), **WWF** ( ☎ 0567-22258; fax 0567-22787; Jl Yos Sudarso 97), or Kompakh (p603), all in Putussibau.

### TRANSBORNEO: PUTUSSIBAU TO LONG APARI

Trekking across the world's third-largest island is a challenge steeped in romance. For a reality check, meet George Muller. In 1825, Muller became the first European to cross from East to West Kalimantan over the mountain range that now carries his name. After his historic journey, Muller was beheaded. Reasonably fit and motivated travellers will likely have better results.

From Putussibau, trans-Kalimantan travel begins by boat to Tanjung Lokang. Then it's five to seven days walking across the Muller Range and pristine forests to the headwaters of Sungai Mahakam at Long Apari. From there, progressively larger boats bring travellers to Samarinda in three or four days.

Aside from drive and legs, the trip requires substantial dosh. Figure 4,000,000Rp for transport to Tanjung Lokang. A guide (per day 250,000Rp to 350,000Rp) is essential beyond there. Porters (per day 150,000Rp to 250,000Rp) are strongly recommended; negotiate in advance whether you'll pay for their return travel. Budget at least 3,000,000Rp for East Kalimantan travel. Food costs around 50,000Rp per person daily for all, including guides and porters.

Few guides in Tanjung Lokang speak English. Chances are somewhat better in Putussibau and much better in Pontianak (see p598). Kompakh (p603) can also provide information and arrange tours. Packages start from 25,000,000Rp per person for two.

Cross-Kalimantan treks can also begin in Samarinda (see p638) or Balikpapan (see p633).

Aside from where and how (and why), consider when to trek. In rainy season, cooler temperatures somewhat compensate for the wet. July and August are dry but very hot, and annual forest fires follow. May and June seem ideal: honeybees agree, often plaguing trekkers during those months.

## SINGKAWANG
☎ 0562 / pop110,000

Chinese-majority Singkawang attracts men from Taiwan seeking brides. Nearby beaches attract travellers and Pontianak weekenders seeking sun and surf.

Jl Diponegoro is Singkawang's north–south spine, with ATMs, banks and moneychanger **Tricoin** (Jl Diponegoro 39). Particularly to the east, classic shophouses abound: listen hard to hear a scratchy recording of a 1930s Shanghai chanteuse. The main Chinese temple is at the intersection of Jl Niaga and Jl K Mahmud. Check your email at **Cyber X** (Jl Diponegoro 126; per hr 3000Rp; ☉ 9am-11pm). For medical issues, consult **RS Santo Vincentius** (Jl Diponegoro 9).

The yearly **Cap Go Meh** festival, climaxing on the fifteenth day of the Chinese New Year, attracts visitors from across the region. Contact the **tourism office** ( ☎ 631 423) for schedules.

### SLEEPING

**Hotel Kalbar** ( ☎ 631 460; Jl K Mahmud 1; r 70,000-210,000Rp; ❄ ) From basic fan-cooling to hot/cold water VIP, every room has a private bathroom with Western toilet. Location is dead centre downtown.

**Hotel Putera Kalbar III** ( ☎ 631 551; Jl Diponegoro 7; r 85,000-100,000Rp; ❄ ) Freshly painted rooms all include air-con, TV, shower and free drinking water.

**Hotel Restu** ( ☎ 636 904; fax 633 706; Jl Stasium 77; r 145,000-398,000Rp; ❄ ) Facing the bus station, Restu's extras include international TV stations and Combo Café ( ☉ 7pm to midnight) on the roof.

**Hotel Prapatan** ( ☎ 636 888; Jl Sejahtera 1; r incl breakfast 165,000-350,000Rp; ❄ ) Business-class rooms, losmen-class service. Bargain for discounts.

**Hotel Mahkota** ( ☎ 631 244; fax 631 491; Jl Diponegoro 1; r incl breakfast 450,000-650,000Rp; ste 750,000-1,250,000Rp; ❄ ⌨ ☏ ) This graceful, venerable four-star hotel has welcoming rooms – angle for discounts up to 40% – classy furniture, tennis court and swimming pool (admission 5000Rp for nonguests). Free wi-fi in outdoor Café Teras and the 24-hour Restoran Saleras Putri (mains 11,000Rp to 45,000Rp plus 21% tax;) serving Western and Indonesian mains, pizza, burgers and sashimi.

With Cap Go Meh crowds thick and choices thin, try:

**Century Hotel** ( ☎ 632 047; Jl Diponegoro 59; r 60,000-250,000Rp; ❄ )

**Hotel Khatulistiwa 2** ( ☎ 632 854; Jl Diponegoro 25; r 120,000-450,000Rp; ❄ )

**Hotel Paseban** ( ☎ 631 449; Jl Ismail Tahir 41; r incl breakfast 124,000-176,000Rp; ❄ )

**Hotel Sankubana** ( ☎ 631 990; Jl Gn Kerinci 9; r 120,000Rp; ❄ )

**Hotel Sinar Khatulistiwa I** ( ☎ 631 697; Jl Selamat Karman 17; r 60,000-145,000Rp; ❄ )

## EATING

Warungs abound on Jl Niaga, called Jl Stasiun near the bus terminal.

**Rumah Makan Vegetarian Maitreya** (Jl Tsjafioedin 7; meals 10,000-15,000Rp; ☯ 6am-7.30pm) Popular Chinese vegetarian buffet.

our pick **Warung Hangku** (Jl Sejahtera 76; mains 12,000-18,000Rp) The no-smoking, air-con section sets apart this Chinese warung specialising in fish and seafood.

**Villa Bukit Mas** (Jl Bukit Mas; mains 13,000-18,000Rp) South of downtown, this hilltop restaurant has Indonesian standards plus *shabu-shabu* (57,000Rp), panoramic views and a swimming pool (admission 10,000Rp).

**Restoran 889** ( ☎ 631 411; Jl Tsjafioedin 29; per person 40,000-60,000Rp; ☯ 10am-9pm) Singkawang's top Chinese for group feeds.

Singkawang's after-dark place to be, **Pasar Hong Kong** (Hong Kong Market) runs from 5pm until dawn along Jl Setia Budi, concurrent with produce markets on Jl Hasan Said. Snack and coffee stalls (whose owners are happy to pour beers over ice) dominate, though some offer full meals.

## Getting There & Away

Buses to Pontianak's Batu Layang (25,000Rp, 3½ hours) and Sambas (20,000Rp, three hours) leave frequently until late afternoon from the terminal on Jl Stasiun. Companies nearby run buses to Sintang (77,000Rp, 10 hours), Pontianak's centre (air-con 40,000Rp, four hours), and the Entikong border crossing (65,000Rp, eight hours). **Antya** ( ☎ 733 688; Jl Stasiun 8) and **Amanah Taxi** ( ☎ 330 5848) run Kijangs to Pontianak (70,000Rp, 3 hours) and charters to other destinations.

*Opelet* service from the terminal runs around town (3000Rp) and to nearby Gunung Poteng (5000Rp), Pasir Panjang (3000Rp) and Tanjung Gundul (7000Rp). See right.

## AROUND SINGKAWANG

See the world's largest flower at **Gunung Poteng**, (5000Rp), 12km east of Singkawang – ask to get dropped at the foot of the hill. Each rafflesia plant only blooms once a year, but there are flowerings year-round. The 3km hike to the top requires two hours.

**Ceramics factories** 5km south of town produce huge, colourful Chinese urns. The Semanggat Baru factory, 100m from the main road, has an ancient kiln and ships purchases. Prices start from 250,000Rp. Sinar Terang, 400m further, is another cool kiln.

## Beaches

Coastal forests around Singkawang shelter some of KalBar's best beaches.

Mobbed on weekends and holidays, **Taman Pasir Panjang** (Long Beach Park; admission 3000Rp), located 14km south of Singkawang, has a public pool, warungs and other facilities. **Palapa Beach Hotel** ( ☎ 633 402; fax 633 400; r 279,000-479,000Rp, cottages 449,000Rp; ❄ ) features clean, casual rooms and odd cottages with carports. There is a 25% discount on weekdays. Its **Palapa Discotheque** (admission 50,000Rp; ☯ Thu & Sat nights) crosses Cinderella's castle with a Chinese temple. The hotel runs boats (per person 150,000Rp, 40 minutes) to **Pulau Randayan** for snorkelling and pristine beaches. There is also a two-bedroom villa (rooms 350,000Rp). Take an *opelet* (3000Rp, 20 minutes) or *ojek* (15,000Rp) to the park gate and walk 500m to the beach.

**Tanjung Gundul** (20km) is more isolated and relaxed. **Kura Kura Resort** ( ☎ 085 822 181 173; Charlie@ kurakurabeach.com; r incl meals per person 150,000Rp, villa incl breakfast 600,000Rp) owners Charlie Robertson and wife Siska strive to preserve this patch of white sand sheltered by unspoiled hills and an unpaved road 3km from Tanjung Gundul village. Comfortable, all wood accommodation includes homestay rooms and a villa sleeping up to seven. Snorkelling, trekking, sailing and fishing can be arranged, although a lie-about on the beach to drink in the vista and perhaps a cold beer (guests bringing beer and ice for Charlie are especially welcome) is the right agenda for most visitors. From Singkawang, take an *opelet* (7000Rp to village, 15,000Rp to resort).

The beach at Batu Payung (22km south) has been revived by **Batu Payung Village** ( ☎ 464 2888/2999; Pontianak office ☎ 0561-738 278, fax 0561-737 131; r US$20-100; ❄ ) opened in mid-2009.

Well hidden **Pantai Gosang** (44km) overlooks offshore islands including Pulau Pelaplis for day trips or camping. For transport, see Bapak Dendy, head of the local fisherman's association.

North of Singkawang, **Pemangkat Beach**, (25km) is another popular weekend destination. Stay at beachfront **Hotel Fortuna** (☎ 380 123; Jl Trikora; r 60,000-165,000Rp; ❀) or in-town **Grand Hotel** (☎ 242 558; fax 242553; Jl Nusantara 69; r 120,000-220,000Rp; ❀). Sambas-bound buses pass Pemangkat (15,000Rp; two hours); specify if you want to be dropped at the beach or in town.

## Sambas

☎ 0562 / pop 56,000

Flashing diamonds and gold, Sambas had contact with 6th-century India and Sumatra's Sriwijaya kingdom. The Dutch VOC came in 1610 and 18th-century gold strikes brought Chinese settlers. Sambas is now best known for *songket*, but prices may be cheaper in Pontianak.

**Keraton Sambas** (4km from town), the former palace turned museum, has charming architecture and views along Sungai Sambas. Hire a canoe for 10,000Rp and paddle over. Or charter a motorised canoe to tour riverside **stilt homes**. It's similar to canal tours in Banjarmasin (see p626), but since Sambas receives fewer visitors, receptions are grander.

Sambas is usually a day-trip destination from Singkawang. For accommodation, try clean, comfortable **Hotel Pantura** (☎ 392 438; Jl Tabrani 62A; r 76,000-278,000Rp; ❀).

Beyond Sambas, long stretches of isolated beach, including Tanjung Datok (two hours) at Kalimantan's northwest tip, offer Robinson Crusoe–type holidays.

## KETAPANG

☎ 0534 / pop 69,000

Isolated from most of KalBar, Ketapang connects with nature. The town is the gateway to **Gunung Palung National Park** (see p610) and KalBar's southwest coast. Government officials are trying to develop further ecotourism activities. But the first new attraction is **Rumah Melayu** (Jl Basuki Rachmad; ❀ 8-11am, 2-6.30pm), a traditional Indonesian-Malay house on steroids with giant furniture. It balances a ceremonial **longhouse** (Jl R Suprapto) north of town. The other local houses of note

are *rumah walet,* windowless dwellings for swiftlets producing the key ingredient for bird's nest soup.

**Kendawangan** (80km south) has unspoiled, largely undeveloped beaches with quaint fishing settlements and simple losmen. Reach it by bus (35,000Rp, three hours) or charter.

### ORIENTATION & INFORMATION

Ketapang spreads along the east bank of Sungai Pawan. Travel around town by *opelet* (Rp3000). Silver shops, supplied by area mines and supported by local artisans, cluster around the Jl Suprapto circle. Many businesses close around 4pm and reopen from 7pm to 9pm.

**Hypernet** (Jl A Yani; per hr 5000Rp; ❀ 8am-1am) Pass the game room for air-con internet. No smoking.

**Karya Tours** (☎ /fax 303 6633; Jl A Yani 49) Flights and Gunung Palung National Park arrangements.

**Mulia Tour** (☎ 770 0907, 081 2562 0680; mulia.keta pang@yahoo.com; Jl MT Haryono 142) Formerly Berjaya Tour, still Ketapang's top information source, wife and husband team Mulia Lie and Rudy Salim advise on flights, ferries and local attractions.

**Tourism office** (☎ 32072; Jl Jend Sudirman 61) Contact local tourism head Yudo Sudarto (☎ 081 2562 0342; yudo_sudarto@yahoo.co.uk) for new ecotourism initiatives.

### SLEEPING

**Hotel Bersaudara** (☎ 32874; Jl Diponegoro 5; r 30,000-60,000Rp; ❀) Clean but tiring rooms in a pink house featuring a 2nd-floor balcony shaded by a huge tree. Economy class has shared *mandi* and ceiling fan; a little more money buys a lot more comfort.

**Losmen Patra** (☎ 32742; Jl Diponegoro 63; r 40,000-120,000Rp; ❀) On a quiet block, Losmen Patra has exceptionally bright rooms and friendly vibe to match.

**Hotel Anda** (☎ 32575; Jl R Suprapto; r 50,000-100,000Rp plus 10% tax; ❀) Simple, scrubbed rooms with very helpful staff.

**Putra Tanjung Hotel** (☎ 32574; Jl Pak Nibung I 12A; r 88,000-143,000Rp, ste 176,000Rp; ❀) Small, tidy rooms in the original wing, with an extension under construction when we visited.

**ourpick Hotel Perdana** (☎ 33333; fax 32740; Jl Merdeka 112; r 110,000-320,000Rp plus 10% tax; ❀ ▯) Once indisputably Ketapang's best hotel, Perdana is responding to competition with free wired internet in each rustic but comfortable room, 24-hour warnet (per hour

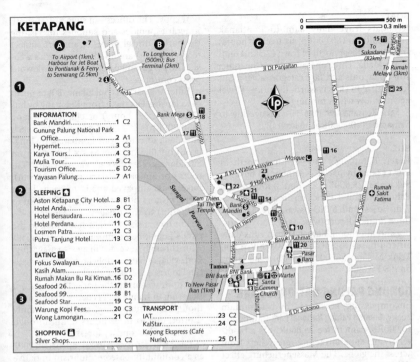

## KETAPANG

**INFORMATION**
| | |
|---|---|
| Bank Mandiri | 1 C2 |
| Gunung Palung National Park Office | 2 A1 |
| Hypernet | 3 C3 |
| Karya Tours | 4 C3 |
| Mulia Tour | 5 C2 |
| Tourism Office | 6 D2 |
| Yayasan Palung | 7 A1 |

**SLEEPING**
| | |
|---|---|
| Aston Ketapang City Hotel | 8 B1 |
| Hotel Anda | 9 C2 |
| Hotel Bersaudara | 10 C2 |
| Hotel Perdana | 11 C3 |
| Losmen Patra | 12 C3 |
| Putra Tanjung Hotel | 13 C3 |

**EATING**
| | |
|---|---|
| Fokus Swalayan | 14 C2 |
| Kasih Alam | 15 D1 |
| Rumah Makan Bu Ra Kiman | 16 D2 |
| Seafood 26 | 17 B1 |
| Seafood 99 | 18 B1 |
| Seafood Star | 19 C2 |
| Warung Kopi Fees | 20 C3 |
| Wong Lamongan | 21 C2 |

**SHOPPING**
| | |
|---|---|
| Silver Shops | 22 C2 |

**TRANSPORT**
| | |
|---|---|
| IAT | 23 C2 |
| KalStar | 24 C2 |
| Kayong Ekspress (Café Nuria) | 25 D1 |

10,000Rp) in the lobby, and a daily 10,000Rp coupon for its restaurant (mains 15,000Rp to 22,000Rp) serving Indonesian food and cold beer.

**Aston Ketapang City Hotel** ( ☎ 303 777; www.astonketapang.com; Jl R Suprapto 68A; r incl breakfast 298,000-378,000Rp, ste 698,000-798,000Rp; ✖ ▢ ☎ ) This Southeast Asian chain's new three-star branch seems misplaced. Its minimalist rooms feature wraparound chairs straight out of *Austin Powers* and showers with floor-to-neck voyeur windows.

### EATING & DRINKING

Find warungs, street stalls and fruit stands along Jl Diponegoro and Jl A Yani, and at Pasar Baru.

**Warung Kopi Fees** ( ☎ 34575; Jl Basuki Rahmat; drinks & snacks 3000-25,000Rp; ☎ ) Friendly indoor-outdoor cafe with free wi-fi from late afternoon.

**Rumah Makan Bu Ra Kiman** ( ☎ 34575; Jl Haji Agus Salim 139; mains 6000-8000Rp; ⏱ 6-11am) Try *nasi kuning* (saffron rice) or *ketupat cholet* (stewed beef with steamed coconut rice) at this breakfast spot.

**Wong Lamongan** (Jl R Suprapto 22; mains 10,000-22,000Rp) Want fresh? Pick from fish swimming in the *mandi*. Open until at least 11pm.

**Kasih Alam** (Jl Brigjen Katamso; meals 10,000-15,000Rp) Visit early for the widest selection at this popular vegetarian buffet.

**Seafood Star** (Jl MT Haryono 89; mains 12,000-23,000Rp; ⏱ 4pm-midnight) Quality and taste far exceed prices at this Chinese warung.

**Seafood 99** ( ☎ 34222; Jl R Suprapto 162; mains 14,000-60,000Rp; ⏱ 10am-10pm) Locally renowned Chinese seafood in air-con comfort. Budget per person 50,000Rp for a group feed. Nearby Seafood 26 ( ☎ 34575; Jl R Suprapto 139; mains 14,000Rp to 60,000Rp) is its open-air counterpart.

Self-caterers should head to **Fokus Swalayan** (Jl R Suprapto).

### Getting There & Away
#### AIR

**IAT** ( ☎ 303 6971; Jl K Haji Mansur) and **KalStar** ( ☎ 35588; fax 35599; Jl R Suprapto 44) fly to Pontianak several times daily. Both fly daily to Pangkalan Bun, KalStar continuing to Banjarmasin, IAT to Semarang. Taxis to/from Rahadi Osman Airport (6km) cost 50,000Rp, 25,000Rp by *ojek*.

**BOAT**

Jet boats leave daily 8am to Pontianak (140,000Rp to 180,000Rp, six to eight hours) from the **harbour** north of town (2.5km) on Jl Gajah Mada. Three operators share the route; seating layouts and fare categories vary, but for all air-con class is worth the price. Travel agents know who's running when.

**Satia Kencana** ( ☎ 303 6736) sails weekly to Semarang (205,000Rp, 30 hours).

**BUS**

Reach Ketapang's bus terminal north of town (2km) by *opelet*. Northbound buses to Sukadana (25,000Rp, 2½ hours) for Gunung Palung National Park run frequently from 7am. Buses south to Kendawangan (35,000Rp, three hours) depart twice daily, early morning and afternoon. **Kayong Ekspres** runs daily air-con buses to Sukadana (30,000Rp) and Teluk Melano (40,000Rp) from Café Nuria on Jl S Parman.

# GUNUNG PALUNG NATIONAL PARK

Encompassing seashores and mountain peaks, **Gunung Palung National Park** (admission 10,000Rp, camera fee 25,000Rp) is a biodiversity treasure, attracting researchers from across the globe. The Massenerheburg effect compresses vegetation zones, creating several forest types within this compact 90,000-hectare park. The richness extends to wildlife, with an estimated 10% of the world's wild orangutans living here among three dozen species of mammals and nearly 200 types of birds, representing every avian family, if not every species, in Kalimantan. Gunung Palung has also been a top choice for illegal logging and poaching, but park management has taken effective countermeasures, including patrols by microlight aircraft, and encouraged tourism.

**Yayasan Palung** (Map p609; ☎ /fax 0534-303 6367; www.savegporangutans.org; yayasanpalung@gmail .com; Jl Gajah Mada 97, Ketapang) supports tourism development in the park as part of its conservation and education mission

## Orientation & Information

Obtain permits for Gunung Palung at the **park office** (Balai Taman Nasional Gunung Palung; Map p609; ☎ 0534-32720; btngp@yahoo.com; Jl Gajah Mada; ☒ 8am-3pm Mon-Fri) in Ketapang or at its **Sukadana office** (Jl Tangjungpura 41; ☒ 8am-3pm Mon-Fri) with BTNGP painted on the wall. Bring a passport copy. The offices can suggest transport, itineraries, guides and supplies for visiting the park. Official prices (transport subject to negotiation) are listed on the park's website (http://gunungpalungnationalpark.word press.com/prices/).

Enter the park via Sukadana, 80km north of Ketapang. Get there from Ketapang by bus (25,000Rp, 2½ hours) or charter a Kijang (350,000Rp). It's also possible to reach Sukadana directly from Pontianak by longboat (160,000Rp, four to six hours). From Sukadana, access the park via Air Pauh (3km south) or Simpang Pelarang (17km north); buses pass unpaved roads to each. From there, visitors often take *ojeks* (20,000Rp to 30,000Rp) to the villages. To Air Pauh it's 3.5km then a six- to eight-hour walk to the park's Lubuk Baji camp. From Pelarang, it's 9km through several villages to Begasing. Both villages have simple homestays for cultural tourism. Begasing also has guides, necessary for travel inside the park. The trail from Begasing to Lubuk Baji is better maintained, though less interesting, and it's certainly shorter, one to three hours uphill through primary and secondary forest.

**Lubuk Baji** (per person 25,000Rp), opened in 2007 as a community-based ecotourism initiative by Yayasan Palung, has simple sleeping and cooking facilities (bring food and bedding), views of **Gunung Palung** (1116m) and **Gunung Panti** (1050m) plus the distinctive temples of Balinese *transmigrasi* villages below. Around the camp, find *keladi* leaves up to 2m tall, waterfalls including a 30m beauty just below camp, plus swimming holes, all with clear, potable mountain water year round. For orangutans, trek 30 minutes to an hour; about one in five treks encounter apes.

**Batu Barat** in lowland swamp forest has orangutans, proboscis monkeys, sun bears and freshwater crocodiles. Black orchids bloom February to April. Accommodation is rough camping or very basic homestays (per person 25,000Rp). For Batu Barat, continue north past Sukadana to Teluk Melano (32km), then take a speedboat (per person 250,000Rp) or along Sungai Matan.

Many Gunung Palung visits end with a splash in the sea at Sukadana's Pulau Datok beach.

Park officials plan to add facilities, but Cabang Panti research camp no longer welcomes tourists.

# CENTRAL KALIMANTAN

Visitors to Central Kalimantan (Kalimantan Tengah, or KalTeng) overwhelmingly focus on Tanjung Puting National Park, renowned for close encounters with orangutans. Otherwise, Indonesia's third-largest province at 153,564 sq km, barely gets a look. That's partly because KalTeng is mainly flat, poorly drained and heavily logged. But it is Kalimantan's lone Dayak majority province, separated from South Kalimantan in 1957. Travellers willing to get beyond KalTeng's well-beaten path will find surviving swathes of forest and traditional life, including longhouses over a century old, and one of the world's largest wild orangutan populations.

## PANGKALAN BUN

☎ 0532 / pop 40,000

Flight schedules may allow Tanjung Puting travellers to head directly from the airport to the park. But there's no reason to avoid Pangkalan Bun, a pleasant town along Sungai Arut. Riverside boardwalks present photo opportunities including stilt houses and diving schoolboys. Main street Jl P Antasari runs parallel to the river. Tour operators for Tanjung Puting often offer help getting around town.

Local law prohibits sale of alcohol, so bring your own along.

Self-described 'orangutan group that works with people, not orangutans' **Yayorin** (Yayasan Orangutan Indonesia; ☎ 29057; www.yayorin .org; Jl Bhayangkara Km1) runs **Kampung Konservasi** (Conservation Village; ☼ 7am-5pm, closed Mon) a model farm educating local people on how to 'become protectors, not destroyers, of their own environment' (see p615). Ask to stop there on the way to/from Tanjung Puting. From Pangkalan Bun, take a taxi or *ojek*; tell the driver, 'Yayorin, near Perumahan Pinang Merah'.

**Istana Kuning** (Yellow Palace; ☼ 8am-2pm Mon-Thu, 8am-1pm Fri, 8-11am Sat, closed Sun), the sultan's hilltop fortress above the police station on Jl P Antasari, preserves royal relics.

**Pantai Kubu** is a white-sand beach 28km southeast of town; buses run via Kumai.

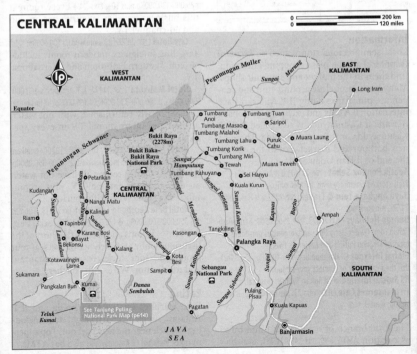

**CENTRAL KALIMANTAN**

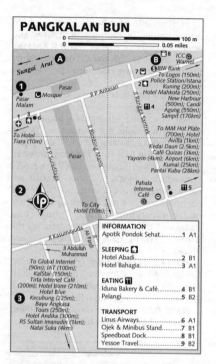

## PANGKALAN BUN

| INFORMATION | |
| --- | --- |
| Apotik Pondok Sehat............1 A1 | |

| SLEEPING | |
| --- | --- |
| Hotel Abadi...........................2 B1 | |
| Hotel Bahagia.......................3 A1 | |

| EATING | |
| --- | --- |
| Iduna Bakery & Café..............4 B1 | |
| Pelangi.................................5 B2 | |

| TRANSPORT | |
| --- | --- |
| Linus Airways........................6 A1 | |
| Ojek & Minibus Stand...........7 B1 | |
| Speedboat Dock...................8 B1 | |
| Yessoe Travel.......................9 B2 | |

## Information

Local semiprecious stones such as *kecubun* (sapphire) are the main shopping attraction; find them in the market and souvenir shops. Many businesses close around 4pm and reopen at 7pm. Banks along Jl P Antasari have international ATMs and exchange US dollars. Beware: Jl Kasumayuda is also called Jl PRA Kasumayuda or Jl Prakasumayuda. There's a new harbour and market area to the east, at the end of Jl Haji Udan Said.

**Apotik Pondok Sehat** ( ☎ 21167; Jl P Antasari 86) Well-stocked pharmacy with doctors' offices.

**Bayu Angkasa Tour & Travel** ( ☎ 22374; Jl Hasanudin 11/75) Air bookings.

**Borneo Holidays** ( ☎ 29673, 081 2500 0508; harnovia@yahoo.com) Owner Harry Purwanto organises personalised tours of Tanjung Puting and KalTeng's rivers.

**Global Internet** (Jl Hasanudin; per hr 4000Rp; ⏲ 24hr) Use their computer or connect your laptop.

**RS Sultan Imanudin** (Jl Sultan Syahrir) Hospital.

**Tirta Internet Café** (Jl Domba 23; per hr 4000Rp) BYO laptop; wartel, too.

The local branch of national tour and travel association **ASITA** ( ☎ 081 349 021 411; asitakobar@gmail.com) provides info on tour operators for Tanjung Puting and beyond. The province's **guide association** (Himpunan Pramuwisata; ☎ 085 252 745 600; hpikobar07@gmail.com) lists qualified guides.

## Sleeping

**Hotel Bone** ( ☎ 21213; Jl Domba 21; room r 40,000-100,000Rp; ✿ ) Pronounced Bo-nay, the hotel is on a quaint side street serviced by *opelet*. Fan-cooled economy rooms are bare 'Bone'; VIP rooms have air-con, TV and private *mandi*.

**Hotel Andika** ( ☎ 21218; Jl Hasanudin 20A; s incl breakfast 50,000Rp, d incl breakfast 70,000-85,000Rp; ✿ ) Simple rooms with charming porches. Hotel arranges cars, and its restaurant (mains 8,000Rp to 15,000Rp) dishes Indonesian favourites.

**Hotel Tiara** ( ☎ 22717; fax 25151; Jl P Antasari 150; r 55,000-135,000Rp plus 10% tax; ✿ ) Reliable, meticulously maintained place with private *mandi* and TV in every room. Some rooms have three beds.

**Hotel Bahagia** ( ☎ 21226; fax 24085; Jl P Antasari 100; r 60,000-220,000Rp; ✿ ) Clean rooms and central location are two reasons they named it 'Hotel Happiness'.

**Hotel Abadi** ( ☎ 21021; fax 22800; Jl P Antasari 150; r 85,000-130,000Rp plus 10% tax; ✿ ) Every room at this business-traveller favourite has air-con and 40-channel TV.

**City Hotel** ( ☎ 28569; Jl Kasumayuda; r 100,000Rp; ✿ ) Targeting foreigners, modern rooms include air-con, Western bathroom and international TV.

**Hotel Mahkota** ( ☎ 21172; Jl P Antasari; s 160,000-290,000Rp, d 200,000-330,000Rp, f 360,000Rp, all incl breakfast; ✿ ) Newly refurnished, with hot water, air-con and international TV in every spacious room.

**Hotel Avilla** ( ☎ 27710; avila2182004@telkom.net; Jl Diponegoro 81; r incl breakfast 250,000-350,000Rp; ✿ 🖳 🛜 ) Cushy rooms all have hot water, air-con and international TV, plus accommodating staff. Wi-fi with voucher.

**Hotel Blue Kecubung** ( ☎ 21211; fax 21513; Jl Domba 1; s 350,000-500,000Rp, d 420,000-570,000Rp, all incl breakfast; ✿ 🛜 ) Rooms and service fall short of the luxurious lobby at this choice of overseas tour groups with four stories, basement restaurant and no elevator. Wi-fi with voucher.

## Eating

Find warungs on Jl Kasumayuda and Jl P Antasari, supplemented by night stalls, including a clutch near the new harbour. Top supermarket **Pelangi** (Jl Kasumayuda) also has ATMs.

**Kedai Daun** ( ☎ 29953; Jl Malijo; mains 10,000-25,000Rp; ⏰ 5pm-1am; 🛜 ) By day, the office of Friends of the National Parks (see p616), by night, a restaurant and coffee house with Indonesian and Western food plus free wi-fi where anyone's liable to pull out a guitar and start a sing-along.

**Café Quizas** (Jl Iskandar 63; mains 20,000-50,0000Rp) Discover karaoke can be fun even when sober at this restaurant serving Indonesian favourites plus steaks.

**Iduna Bakery & Café** ( ☎ 24007; Jl Rangga Santrek 5; mains 15,000-32,000Rp; ⏰ 9am-9pm) Get your burger fix at this cosmopolitan joint with hip coffees, juices and ice cream in smoke-free air-con. Adjacent bakery opens 7am to 4.30pm.

**MM Hot Plate** ( ☎ 25088; Jl Diponegoro 43; mains 17,500-35,000Rp) Rangy menu includes Indonesian, Japanese, Chinese and Western dishes, all good and fresh.

### Getting There & Away
#### AIR
**KalStar** ( ☎ 21266; fax 27509; Jl Hasnuddin 39) and **IAT** ( ☎ 21224, 6708222; Jl Hasnuddin 20) fly daily to Pontianak via Ketapang. KalStar also flies to Banjarmasin. **Linus Airways** ( ☎ 22923; www .linusairways.com; Jl P Antasari 1) flies daily to Jakarta and Semarang, but frequently cancels flights or shuffles its schedule. IAT also flies to Semarang. At the time of research, service to Java was so erratic that we suggest flying via Pontianak, Ketapang or Banjarmasin, if feasible.

#### BOAT
Public speedboats leave behind the minibus terminal for Kotawaringin Lama (60,000Rp, two hours) and Nanga Bulik (70,0000Rp, 2½ hours) on Sungai Lamandau.

**Pelni** ( ☎ 244305; Jl Diponegoro 71) and other boats to Java leave from Kumai. See p614.

#### BUS
Buses to Palangka Raya (economy/air-con 80,000/120,000Rp, 12 to 14 hours) are run by **Logos** ( ☎ 27275; Jl P Antasari), **Candi Agung** ( ☎ 27475; Jl Hahi Udan Said), and **Yessoe Travel** ( ☎ 21212; Jl Rangga Santrek), all connecting or continuing to Banjarmasin (125,000Rp, 17 to 19 hours). Ask about pick-up and drop options at both ends of the trip. For example, Yessoe's inbound Pangkalan Bun service ends at its remote terminal where *ojek* is

the only transport available. Other inbound buses drop passengers in town and yet others at the long distance bus station Natai Suka (4km), where there's *opelet* service into town, plus buses to Kotawaringin Lama and Tapinbini.

### Getting Around
Taxis to/from Isklandar Airport (6km) cost 50,000Rp. *Opelet* rides around town cost 3000Rp. Minibuses to Kumai (10,000Rp) leave from the terminal near the market on Jl P Antasari.

## SUNGAI LAMANDAU & SUNGAI BALANTIKAN
Visiting Sungai Lamandau and its tributaries that sustain Dayak villages with longhouses and traditional lifestyles requires patience with irregular, expensive transport. A guide is also recommended.

Located two hours from Pangkalan Bun by public speedboat (60,000Rp), **Kotawaringin Lama** has a longhouse and frail wooden sultan's palace. From there, travel by road to Sukamara (60,000Rp) for speedboats to **Manismata** and **Riam** in West Kalimantan. Hearty travellers can continue from Riam to Ketapang.

Continuing north from Kotawaringin Lama, villages pepper the river to **Bekonsu** with longhouses, traditional mausoleums, and homestays. Get there from Pangkalan Bun by irregular public speedboat (80,000Rp) or charter from Kotawaringin Lama (1,000,000Rp, three hours) or Nanga Bulik (600,000Rp, 1½ hours). From Bekonsu it's about an hour by speedboat (500,000Rp) to **Tapinbini**, where a handful of longhouses defy centuries of weathering and fire. There's daily minibus service between Tapinbini and Pangkalan Bun (125,000Rp, eight hours), a less expensive, less comfortable substitute to river travel.

Alternatively, veer off Sungai Lamandau onto more remote **Sungai Balantikan**, where villagers may invite visitors to share *tuak* – traditional rice wine, more potent than palm sugar *tuak* elsewhere in Indonesia. Hire a speedboat from Pangkalan Bun to **Bayat** (3,000,000Rp, five hours) and stay overnight with a family. From Bayat, rapids require travel by motorised canoe. A feisty rapid at **Nanga Matu** often requires hauling vessels on land for a kilometre or two. From Bayat, in two days, it's possible to explore north by motorised canoe (2,000,000Rp) to **Petarikan**, staying in **Kalingai** or other villages along the way.

Though well beyond the beaten path, even by KalTeng standards, tour companies, including **Borneo Holidays** ( ☎ 0532-29673, 081 2500 0508; harnovia@yahoo.com), organise itineraries along both rivers.

## KUMAI
☎ 0532 / pop 23,000

A lively harbour town, Kumai is homeport for the *klotok* (houseboat) fleet to Tanjung Puting National Park as well as passenger ships to Java, freighters, Bugis *pinisi* and Maduran schooners.

Main street Jl HM Idris follows Sungai Kumai. Hotels are within walking distance, either here or up Jl Gerliya. There are no money-changers or ATMs, and non-nautical travel is best arranged in Pangkalan Bun.

### Sleeping & Eating

**Losmen Aloha** ( ☎ 61210; Jl HM Idris 465; s/d 35,000/45,000Rp) Above a travel agency and commendable warung of the same name, Aloha's basic rooms have fans and shared *mandis*.

**Losmen Permata Hijau** ( ☎ 61325; Jl HM Idris; r 60,000-100,000Rp; 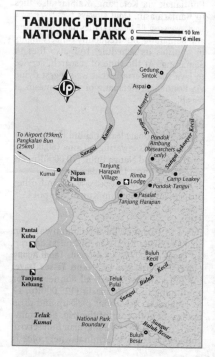 ) Staff constantly wield a broom or mop at this immaculate guest house. Even shared *mandis* for fan-cooled budget rooms sparkle.

**Hotel Mentari** ( ☎ 61558; Jl Gerliya 98; r incl breakfast 100,000Rp; ) Mentari is fresh and very clean. Rooms are bright and well furnished.

At warungs and food stalls along Jl HM Idris near the market, try fresh fish, caught a fly cast away.

### Getting There & Away

Reach Kumai by minibus from Pangkalan Bun (10,000Rp, 35 minutes). Taxis from Pangkalan Bun airport to Kumai cost 150,000Rp, including all stops for visiting Tanjung Punting National Park (p616).

Pelni boats connect Kumai with Semarang (145,000Rp, 24 hours) and Surabaya (153,000Rp; 26 hours) three times weekly. The **Pelni office** (Jl HM Idris) is opposite the market. **Dharma Lautan Utama** ( ☎ 61205, 61250; Jl Bahari 561) runs more frequent boats to Semarang (160,000Rp, 19 to 22 hours), including a fast ferry (265,000Rp, 18 hours), and Surabaya (165,000Rp, 23 to 26 hours).

## TANJUNG PUTING NATIONAL PARK

Our pick as the world's best place to see orangutans in their natural habitat, **Tanjung Puting National Park** may also be the world's easiest adventure travel. Unlike other jungle wildlife destinations, there's little physical exertion required, so anyone aged two to 92 can handle the trip. (Our almost-two-year-old daughter had the time of her life.) Purists may assail the merits of Tanjung Puting as a wildlife destination, but there's no disputing that seeing orangutans up close in the jungle is a thrilling experience.

Like other orangutan rehabilitation sites, Tanjung Puting guarantees plenty of these irresistible auburn primates. What sets Tanjung Puting apart is the journey straight out of *The Heart of Darkness* via *klotok*, your floating luxury losmen, put-putting up Sungai Sekonyer.

Cruising gently between walls of pandanus fringing the river like spiky-haired stick figures, sharp-eyed captains or guides may spot orangutans perched on riverside branches or macaques scurrying through the forest canopy shared among 200-plus bird species. Tanjung Puting is also home to sun bears, wild

**TANJUNG PUTING NATIONAL PARK**

0 — 10 km
0 — 6 miles

Gedung Sintok
Aspai
Sungai Sekonyer
Sungai Kumai
Pondok Ambung (Researchers only)
Sungai Sekonyer Kecil
To Airport (19km); Pangkalan Bun (25km)
Kumai
Nipas Palms
Tanjung Harapan Village
Rimba Lodge
Camp Leakey
Pondok Tangui
Pasalat Tanjung Harapan
Pantai Kubu
Buluh Kecil
Tanjung Keluang
Teluk Pulai
Sungai Buluh Kecil
Teluk Kumai
National Park Boundary
Sungai Buluh Besar
Buluh Besar

---

### AXING ILLEGAL LOGGING

Yayasan Orangutan Indonesia (Yayorin; Indonesia Orangutan Foundation; www.yayorin.org) aims to make the world safe for orangutans by teaching humans to preserve the species and its environment. Its projects include community education and sustainable farming projects that others can replicate. Arsyad is a 30-year-old who never got past elementary school, trying to support his wife and seven-year-old in Central Kalimantan. He was an illegal logger for more than a decade until Yayorin showed him an alternative. Arsyad talked to Lonely Planet about his transformation.

**What have you learnt from Yayorin?** There are many things that I have learnt from Yayorin, including the consequences human beings must pay for destroying nature. The most important thing that I learn from Yayorin is how sustainable agriculture can actually sustain my family's economic needs.

**Why did you decide to become a farmer?** I was looking for a more peaceful life compared to the time when I was a logger. Life as a logger was dangerous for me, my family and others. Moreover, the income I was making from it was not worth the amount of destruction I created, as well as the risk that I had to take.

**What has changed in your life since you became a farmer?** My family life has become much more comfortable, safer and free of fears. I no longer have to move from one place to another; I am happier and feel proud now that I own a rubber plantation and vegetable gardens, as well as a house on my own land.

**Do you make more money now as a farmer?** I have been making around 2,000,000 to 2,500,000 rupiah per month as a farmer. It is almost the same as I made before as a logger, but without the danger and high risk.

**What message would you give to others who are illegal loggers?** Stop being an illegal logger because it is very dangerous for yourself, destroying the environment and disadvantageous for others. Moreover, illegal logging is not a job that can sustain your life for a long time into the future.

---

boars, clouded leopards, spotted cats, pythons, gibbons, porcupines and Sambar deer, none likely to turn up along the riverbank.

Absolutely count on seeing proboscis monkeys (*bekantan*). Found only in Borneo, these odd creatures with their potbellies, awkward movements (by monkey standards), and white faces highlighted by a tubular nose (when colonists showed up, natives rechristened the proboscis *monyet belanda*, Dutch monkey) anxiously await *klotok* arrivals. A troop of 30 light-brown monkeys may plunge from branches 10m or higher into the dark river and cross directly in front of the boat, acting out Kalimantan's version of 'Why did the chicken cross the road?' Answer: because boat engines and propellers scare crocodiles, which find *bekantan* delicious.

Orangutans (see boxed text, p379), the only great apes outside Africa, face a very real extinction threat this century as their rainforest habitat is converted to palm-oil plantations and furniture from often-illegally cut timber. Canadian researcher Dr Biruté Galdikas began research here in 1971. Least famous of three female ape experts mentored by legendary anthropologist Dr Louis Leakey, Dr Galdikas' discoveries include the orangutan's eight-year birth cycle, making the species highly vulnerable to extinction. Valuable studies continue at Tanjung Puting, mainly at Pondok Ambung, a research station closed to the public.

The 415,040-hectare park was Indonesia's first site for the now-controversial practice of orangutan rehabilitation: training orphaned or former captive orangutans to live in the wild (sometimes known as referalisation). But after prolonged, close contact with human rehabilitators, orangutans never lose their taste for it. Orangutans can also pick up human diseases and spread them to wild populations. Current practice specifies reintroduction into areas without native orangutan populations. Tanjung Puting's rehabilitation work is being phased out.

Part of the rehabilitation process that survives is daily feedings to released orangutans at jungle platforms. That's where visitors go to see orangutans. Feedings take place at three camps: **Tanjung Harapan** at 3pm, **Pondok Tangui** at 9am, and **Camp Leakey** at 2pm (check for schedule changes). Reaching camp feeding stations requires a short walk through jungle from the dock. Trails can be slippery when wet and teem with leeches. Wear boots or closed shoes, bring sun/rain protection and vats of insect repellent. Camp Leakey and Tanjung Harapan have information centres. Tanjung Harapan also has a garden displaying dozens of native medicinal plants.

**Pasalat** is a reforestation camp where saplings of sandalwood, ironwood and other native trees are being reintroduced to combat logging, mining and fires. On Paslat's bulletin board:

> Hutan...
> Bukan hanya milik kita
> Hutan...
> Warisan bagi anak cucu kita
> Lestarikan Hutan

> (The Forest...
> Not only ours
> The Forest...
> Our grandchildren's inheritance
> Preserve the Forest)

## Orientation & Information

Visiting Tanjung Puting begins with registration at Pangkalan Bun's police station. Bring photocopies of your passport and visa. (Airport taxi drivers know the steps.)

Next stop, the **PHKA office** (national parks office; ☎ 61500; Jl HM Idris, Kumai; ❍ 7am-2pm Mon-Thu, 7am-11am Fri). Park registration costs per day 65,000Rp per person, 35,000Rp for cameras, and 5000Rp per day for a *klotok* (15,000Rp for a speedboat). Call ahead for weekend arrivals. Provide a copy of your police letter from Pangkalan Bun and another photocopy of your passport. Then head to Kumai's docks to begin chugging upriver. When the park office is closed, it may be possible to register at the park's boundary checkpoint. Ask your boat captain or guide.

For additional information about Tanjung Puting's orangutans, conservation efforts and volunteer opportunities, contact **Friends of the National Parks Foundation** ( ☎ 29953; www .fnpf.org; Jl Malijo). Headquartered in Bali, FNPF runs Tanjung Harapan, Pasalat, plus community education and ecofriendly enterprise initiatives (see opposite). US-based **Orangutan**

**Foundation International** (OFI; ☎ 1-323-938 6046; www .orangutan.org) runs Camp Leakey and publishes *A Guidebook to Tanjung Puting National Park* by Dr Biruté Galdikas and Gary Shapiro.

Dry season falls from May to September. Reduced rainfall makes journeys more enjoyable and may increase the number of orangutans seeking feeding, since fewer jungle trees are fruiting. But higher water during the wet season expands boat access. Tanjung Puting's 200 varieties of wild orchids bloom mainly from January to March.

## Guides

Guides are not required in the park, but are helpful for touring camps and essential for travel beyond them. *Klotok* captains are usually excellent wildlife spotters, but few speak much English. Camp rangers often don't speak English and focus on orangutans, not tourists.

Guide fees range from 150,000Rp to 250,000Rp per day. In Kumai, freelance guides abound and boat operators can provide suggestions. Tour operators may or may not include a guide in their packages; if not they'll have recommendations. PHKA staff can work as guides; some speak English and know the park. Camp rangers or residents of Tanjung Harapan village, across the river from that camp, are another option. The province's **guide association** (Himpunan Pramuwisata; ☎ 085 252 745 600; hpikobar07@gmail.com) lists qualified guides. For more on hiring guides, see p823.

## Rules & Conduct

Follow park regulations to ensure the health of ecosystems and their inhabitants; don't disregard them for the sake of a photo. Never travel park trails without a ranger or guide. Many orangutans are ex-captives and unafraid of humans. No matter what boat crew or rangers do, don't feed orangutans or initiate contact with them. Young ones especially are very hard to resist, but they are highly susceptible to human diseases, so you can inflict great harm. Orangutans are also very strong and may grab your camera, bag or anything else they can reach. In a tug-of-war, they'll win.

Resist the temptation to swim in rivers. Crocodiles lurk; several years ago a British volunteer was killed swimming just off a dock. Water may also be polluted due to mining activities upstream. Wash safely at the river pool at Camp Leakey dock. Elsewhere, get advice before drawing river water.

## Klotok Hire

*Klotok* travel is a windfall pleasure of visiting Tanjung Puting. These eight-to-10m houseboats serve as transportation, accommodation and restaurant, generally for up to four adults. At night, crews moor well away from settlements, so passengers can enjoy sunsets and wildlife peacefully. Sleep on deck on mattresses under mosquito nets, wake to the haunting cries of gibbons and lilting songs of sunbirds: 'It's like those tapes of the rainforest,' one visitor said.

Three days is a reasonable length of stay, though it's possible to see all three camps with just an overnight stay. Some travellers spend a week or more. Three days allows time to survey the rivers unhurriedly and explore around and beyond the camps. Plan river travel for dawn or dusk, when primates come to the banks.

Book a *klotok* through tour operators in Pangakalan Bun (see p612) or tour agencies across Kalimantan and Indonesia; Tanjung Puting is a premier tourist destination. Boat demand peaks in July and August and around local school holidays, but outside these times hiring a *klotok* independently in Kumai is a simple matter – operators will generally find you. Basic boat designs are similar, but there are differences in size, standard, deck configuration and furnishings, so shop around. The **Association of Tourist Boat (Klotok) Kumai** ( ☎ 081 2508 6105, 532-61319; kumaitouristboat@gmail.com), can provide a list of Kumai's *klotok* fleet. It numbered 26 at the time of research, with at least a dozen more boats under construction.

Daily rates run 400,000Rp to 450,000Rp for a boat and captain, including fuel. Cooks cost 75,000Rp daily. Food is generally per person 50,000Rp per day. It's optional to provide the crew's food (and poor form to decline).

Travellers have given particularly good reviews of trips on *Kingfisher*, the Majid family's *Satria* group and *Cahaya Purnama* with Captain Emeng. But there are few bad trips on any *klotok*.

## Tanjung Harapan Village

Across the river from the orangutan camp of the same name, **Tanjung Harapan village** offers several community-based ecotourism activities through the Sungai Sekonyer villagers' association **Tegari Lestari** ( ☎ 081 251 647 27; tegari_lestari@yahoo.co.id). Tegari Lestari, named for a type of jungle orchid and supported by FNPF, doesn't just talk the conservation talk.

Tanjung Harapan residents participate in reforestation projects, including Beguru, a 120-hectare predominantly ironwood area 3km from Tanjung Harapan hit hard by fires in 2006. Carvings from burnt trees are among local handicrafts featured at the **cooperative shop** at the village dock. Ask your captain to stop for a look.

Visitors can join villagers and walk the conservation walk on one- and two-night **jungle treks** (one/two nights per person 600,000Rp/ 1,000,000Rp) through areas Tegari Lestari protects from encroaching plantations and loggers. Covering about 10km per day, the treks fit well with other Tanjung Puting activities.

**Batimu**, a traditional steam bath and massage (200,000Rp) using local spices, is the perfect end to a trek, or just thinking about one.

Tanjung Harapan's **homestays** (d with meals 200,000Rp) are best enjoyed with participation in village activities.

Tegari Lestari also organises Sunday trips to Tanjung Puting. Intended to help school children and their parents appreciate their natural heritage at the bargain price of 7500Rp, anyone can tag along on a space-available basis for 75,000Rp. Bring food or buy simple meals on board. From Kumai, the *klotok* visits Tanjung Harapan, and the feeding at Camp Leakey. Get details from Tegari Lestari or FNPF.

## Sleeping

*Klotok* camping is as much a part of the Tanjung Puting experience as primates. Only visitors that absolutely must sleep on terra firma should miss it. Some visitors alternate nights on *klotok* and land.

**Rimba Lodge** ( ☎ 0532-671 0589; www.rimbalodge.com; s US$55-125, d US$60-130, all incl breakfast; ❄ ) Rimba registers charmless and drab, even by ecolodge standards. Plus it's pricey at US$95 or US$100 for hot water and air-con, the main reasons to move here from a *klotok*. There's internet access via radio. Nonsmoking rooms are available. The restaurant (mains 25,000Rp to 55,000Rp, plus 21% tax) serves Chinese and Indonesian food.

**Sekonyer Ecolodge**, near Tanjung Harapan village, was closed and for sale at the time of research.

## Getting There & Around

Access to Tanjung Puting is by boat only. From Kumai, it's 1½ hours by *klotok* to Tanjung Harapan, 2½ hours to Pondok Tanggui and 3½ hours to Camp Leakey.

Wooden canoes, a quiet alternative for exploring Sungai Sekonyer's shallow tributaries, rent at camps for 30,000Rp per day. Bring an umbrella or hat and lots of drinking water.

Speedboats from Kumai cost about 400,000Rp, but they're a last resort. It takes less than two hours to reach Camp Leakey but the trip is uncomfortable, motor noise chases away wildlife, and propellers wreak havoc on river dwellers.

## PALANGKA RAYA

☎ 0536 / pop 207,000

Once a dusty village called Pahandut, Palangka Raya means 'great and holy place'. This capital city of KalTeng was mooted as a potential capital for all Kalimantan. It has a network of appropriately grand boulevards and handsome government buildings, plus cantilevered Kahayan Bridge, a striking sight, day or night. Stilt houses and plank walks near Rambang Pier on Sungai Kahayan recall the area's roots.

Action for inhabitants and much of the town's wealth reside in the suburbs. Activity nodes around the core include the market off Jl Ahmad Yani, and **Bundaran Besar** (Big Traffic Circle) with night stalls for eating, drinking, seeing and being seen along Jl Yos Sudarso. Also on the circle, **Palma** (Palangka Raya Mall) has the best supermarket in town, a bakery with Western-style bread, food court with wi-fi (voucher required), and Books City with maps and a good selection of children's books for longhouse gifts (see p604).

### Information

Several banks along eastern Jl Ahmad Yani exchange dollars and have ATMs accepting international cards. Beer isn't widely available; ask where to find it. Newsagent **Fathir** (Jl Ahmad Yani 12) sells the English language *Jakarta Post*.

**Apotik Sehat Bahagia** (Jl Ahmad Yani 20) Well-stocked pharmacy with doctors' practices and lab on site.

**Dinas Pariwisata** (Regional Tourism Office, Jl Tjilik Riwut Km 5; ☉ 7am-2pm Mon-Thu, 7-10.30am Fri) Maps and tips for travel into interior. Some staff speak English. Look for 'Disparsenibud Propinsini Kalimantan Tenggah' between Mitsubishi and Toyota signs on taxi route A.

**Kalimantan Tour Destinations** (☎ /fax 322 2099; www.wowborneo.com; kalimantantours@gmail.com; Jl Milono Km 1) Unique itineraries to Dayak communities and wilderness along Sungai Kahayan and Sungai Rungan, including cruises aboard floating ecohotels *Raha'i Pangun* and *Spirit of Borneo*.

**Kevin Maulana Tours** (☎ 323 4735; newkevin _maulana@telkom.net; Jl Milono Km 1) Full service, full price tours. Also flights, Kijangs and charter cars.

**Mulio Angkasa Raya Tour & Travel** (☎ 322 1031; fax 322 3723; Jl Ahmad Yani 55) Best bet for all flights, plus tours, car rental and Kijangs.

**Palangka Raya Guide Association** (☎ 081 349 062 797; Dandang Tingang Hotel, Jl Yos Sudarso 13) Chairman Yusuf Kawaru provides information on guides for trips into the interior.

**Warnet Patrick** (Jl Batam 29; per hour 3500Rp; ☉ 8am-midnight) Best internet hub in town can connect your laptop, print and fax.

Central Kalimantan is renowned for rattan and bamboo crafts. **Souvenir shops** along Jl Batam sell 'export quality' Japanese-style mats, some with *kanji* labels.

**Kalaweit Care Centre** (☎ /fax 322 6388; www.kalaweit.org) accepts volunteers (not visitors) for rehabilitating ex-captive gibbons (see p840) and broadcasts 'Good morning, Kalimantan' ecoradio 99.1FM.

### Sights & Activities

Longhouse-style **Mandala Wisata** (Jl Panjaitan) is an arts centre and venue for traditional performances. Check posted schedule for times.

**Museum Balanga** (Jl Tjilik Riwut Km 2.5; admission by donation; ☉ 8am-1.30pm Mon-Thu, 8-10.30am Fri, 8am-12.30pm Sat, 10am-1.30pm Sun), on taxi route A, has enlightening exhibits on Ngaju Dayak culture. Agau leads a staff of excellent guides whose limited English can't mask their enthusiasm.

Ask hotels or tour agents about **river cruises** on Sungai Kahayan to admire Kahayan Bridge and see stilt houses. Or try your luck around Rambang Pier.

### Sleeping

#### BUDGET

**Hotel Melati Serasi** (☎ 322 3682; Jl Dr Murjani 54; s 27,500-38,500Rp, d 38,500-110,000Rp, t 49,500-66,000Rp; ❄ ) Friendly, clean, quiet place with rooms ranging from shared *mandi* and fan to air-con and international TV off a charming courtyard.

**Hotel Mahkota** (☎ 322 1672; Jl Nias 5; r 44,000-250,000Rp; ❄ ) Breakfast is included for all except the fan-cooled economy rooms. Accessed via an ugly car park, rooms here are large with

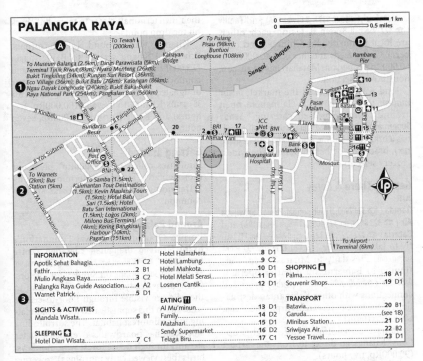

# PALANGKA RAYA

refrigerator and TV. Staff pushes foreigners into huge, high-priced digs.

**Losmen Cantik** ( ☎ 322 2399; Jl Halmahera 22; s 75,000Rp, d 95,000-110,000Rp; ✹ ) At this new entry, rooms, all with TV and shared bathrooms, are spotless. Shared air-con units mean arctic temperatures without neighbourly cooperation.

**Hotel Dian Wisata** ( ☎ 322 1241; Jl Ahmad Yani 32; r incl breakfast 100,000-170,000Rp; ✹ ) Watch your head descending to economy rooms with shared *mandi* via the central atrium. Standard and 'VIP' rooms have air-con and private *mandi*; all are clean.

**Hotel Halamahera** ( ☎ 322 1222; fax 322 1993; Jl Halmaherea 24; r incl breakfast 160,000-250,000Rp; ✹ 🛜 ) Great value with international TV, hot/cold shower and unlimited coffee, tea and water. Room quality varies, so pick a good one.

## MIDRANGE

**Hotel Lampang** ( ☎ 322 0003; Jl Irian 2; s incl breakfast from 228,000Rp; d incl breakfast 276,000-360,000Rp; ✹ 🛜 ) Stylishly refurbished with Western bathrooms and free wi-fi.

**Hotel Batu Sari** ( ☎ 322 6535; fax 323 8269; Jl Raden Saleh 1; r incl breakfast 240,000-384,000Rp, ste 600,000Rp; ✹ ) Located near Hotel Batu Sari International, the precursor to Hotel Batu Sari International (see below) has a stronger longhouse motif and gives 25% discounts for one, 15% for two. Located off Jl Milono on taxi route E.

**Hotel Batu Sari International** ( ☎ 324 4765; fax 322 8549; Jl Raden Saleh 4; r incl breakfast 288,000-366,000Rp, ste 576,000Rp; ✹ ) Plush rooms have refrigerator, international TV, hot-water shower and wired internet.

**Rungan Sari Resort** ( ☎ 333 3878; Jl Tjilik Riwut Km 36; www.kmc-rs.com; s & d incl breakfast 580,800-701,800Rp; ✹ 🚲 🖳 ) This a luxurious conference retreat north of town, near Bukit Tangkiling (see p620). It shares facilities with adjacent **Eco Village** ( ☎ 331 7777; Jl Tjilik Riwut Km 36.3; r incl breakfast 200,000-350,000Rp; ✹ 🚲 🖳 ).

## Eating

**Samba** ( ☎ 322 4322; Jl Milono 15; mains 12,000-18,000Rp; ⏰ 7am-3pm, closed Sun) Dayak warung featuring fried fish, savoury soups and unique sambal.

**Al Mu'minun** ( ☎ 322 4322; Jl Darmosugondo 5; mains 14,000-20,000Rp) Popular, friendly place for barbecued fish.

**Matahari** ( ☎ 322 5333; Jl Bawean 3A) and **Family** ( ☎ 322 9560; Jl Bawean 8), facing each other, are local favourites for Chinese food (and beer). Group feeds at either cost 40,000Rp to 60,000Rp per person. Matahari has an air-con, nonsmoking section.

Find warungs around the market; *pasar malam* food stalls on Jl Halmahera open around 4pm. For self-catering, **Sendy Supermarket** (cnr Jl Ahmad Yani & Jl Dr Murjani) which has a branch at Palma, and **Telaga Biru** (Jl Ahmad Yani), bracketed by bakeries, have the widest grocery selections.

## Getting There & Away

### AIR

**Garuda** ( ☎ 323 2900; Jl Kinibalu front, Palma), **Sriwijaya Air** ( ☎ 323 8124; fax 323 4095; Jl Imam Bonjol 19A) and **Batavia** ( ☎ 322 6777; fax 322 1275; Jl Ahmad Yani 11E) all fly to Jakarta. **Susi Air** ( ☎ 081 1211 3080/90; info@ susiair.com) flies daily to Muara Teweh, continuing to Banjarmasin. Charter operator **Aviastar** ( ☎ 320 4009; www.aviastar.biz) proposed connections with other Kalimantan destinations at the time of research. Airport taxis cost 60,000Rp (6km).

Banjarmasin offers more flight options. Kijangs go direct to/from the airport (90,000Rp, five hours).

### BOAT

Boats south to Sebangau and Pagatan leave mornings from Kering Bangkirai, the terminus of taxi route E. Service is by speedboat and *klotok* on different days, so travel times vary. Call **Haji Polo** ( ☎ 085 249 541 999) for details.

### BUS & KIJANG

Buses for Banjarmasin (50,000Rp, five hours), Buntok (90,000Rp to 125,000Rp, 12 hours), Muara Teweh (150,000Rp, 16 hours) and other points east leave from **Milono bus terminal** (Bundaran Burung, Jl Milono Km 4.5) on taxi route E.

Day and night buses to Pangkalan Bun (economy/air-con 80,000/120,000Rp, 14 hours) and Lamandau (150,000Rp to 200,000Rp, eight hours), as well as service to Sampit (60,000, four hours), leave from **Tjilik Riwut Km 8** on taxi route A. Minibuses to west to Kasongan and beyond also depart from here.

**Yessoe Travel** ( ☎ 322 1436; Jl Banda 7) and **Logos** ( ☎ 338 6090; Jl Milono Km 2) run buses to Pangkalan Bun and other destinations from

their own terminals closer to town, but check on the drop points.

Kijangs wait around bus terminals. Scheduled Kijang service to Banjarmasin (75,000Rp, five hours) is well organised and comfortable, with pickup and drop at your designated location. **Gian Travel** ( ☎ 081 251 638 38) runs Kijangs to Tewah (100,000Rp, five hours) and Kuala Kurun (120,000Rp, seven hours).

## Getting Around

Minibuses, called 'taxis' (3000Rp), ply major thoroughfares. The eastern terminus is along Jl Darmosugondo. *Ojek* and becaks are also common.

## Around Palangka Raya

Borneo Orangutan Survival Foundation's **Nyaru Menteng Orangutan Education Centre** ( ☎ 330 8414; Jl Tjilik Riwut Km 29; admission by donation; 9am-3pm Sun) opens on Sunday for visitors. Orangutans readying for reintroduction to the wild are visible through floor-to-ceiling windows in this sophisticated facility simulating their rainforest habitat. The surrounding **arboretum** has boardwalks over black water streams through dense forest with monkeys, birds (best viewed early mornings), towering trees, butterflies and mosquitoes, leading to a lake with pedal boats.

**Bukit Tangkiling**, a series of hills, begins at Tjilik Riwut Km 34, where the turnoff leads to a **convent**. Ask for permission to climb the hill here that has the Christian Stations of the Cross depicted at the top amid spectacular views of the extraordinarily flat KalTeng countryside. A branch of the road continues to **Taman Alam**, a zoo and botanical garden. Further north along Jl Tjilik Riwut, Tangkiling town has a wharf and busy weekend market. Opposite the turnoff, Bukit Banama is named for the boat that, in Dayak belief, carries spirits to the next world. Use taxi route A to Tjilik Riwut Km 8 terminal and take a minibus.

After Tangkiling, the road bends west. National hero and KalTeng's first governor Tjilik Riwut frequently meditated at **Bukit Batu** (Jl Tjilik Riwut Km 76) in a stone seat overlooking the plain and slept between balanced rocks. **Kasongan**, 10km further west on Sungai Mendawai, is a centre for rattan processing and crafts. Many visitors pay respects at the *sandung* of Tjilik Riwut's mother behind the market.

For **Buntuoi longhouse**, take taxi E to Milono terminal for a minibus to Pulang Pisau (20,000Rp, 2½ hours, 98km), or take a Kijang (40,000Rp), then a taxi to Mintin (10km) for a *klotok* to the riverside longhouse. Either return to Palangka Raya or continue east to Banjarmasin.

Sungai Sebangau's black waters lead to **Pagatan**, a picturesque port accessible only by water. Charter a *klotok* (300,000Rp) for a sunset cruise into the mangroves to see proboscis monkeys. The wharf showcases Indonesian cargo vessels, particularly the elegant Bugis *pinisi*. From Palangka Raya, take taxi E south to Kering Bangkirai for public boat service ( ☎ 085 249 541 999; *klotok*/speedboat 82,000/252,000Rp) with different boats sailing different days. Pagatan's clean losmen (r 70,000Rp) near the pier has private *mandi* and a balcony overlooking the river.

Reach **Bukit Baka–Bukit Raya National Park** by road, river and trekking from Palangka Raya via Tumbang Samba, Tumbang Manggu and Tumbang Gagu. In Tumbang Manggu, arrange welcoming ceremonies and treks into the national park through the village's new longhouse and **Ngau Dayak cultural centre** ( ☎ 081 335 296 5670, 0536-323 6621). Climbing Bukit Raya (2278m), the home of a spirit army, according to Dayak legend, requires three days, including ceremonies before and after the climb.

## SEBANGAU NATIONAL PARK

A peat swamp forest between Sungai Katingan and Sungai Sebangau south of Palangka Raya, **Sebangau National Park** (admission 15,000Rp) is home to 9000 orangutans, among the world's largest wild populations. Sebangau's biodiversity includes more than 100 bird species, 35 mammal species and several forest types within its 568,700 hectares.

**WWF Indonesia** (www.wwf.or.id) campaigned to establish the park, gazetted in 2004, and remains at the forefront of involving nearby residents in low-impact logging, home industry, reforestation and ecotourism. The park area was home to 13 logging concessions, all expired by 1990. Yet in 2001 there were still 147 sawmills operating in the area, according to WWF. The area also experienced severe fire damage in 1997–98. Canals dug to transport illegally cut timber dried the underlying peat lands, making them more susceptible to burning. WWF works with villages neighbouring the park to fill in canals and replant trees.

Ecotourism is still in its infancy but WWF has established two camps for visitors, both with equally slim chances to spot orangutans. Stays include participation in local community activities along with jungle walks. On Sungai Sebangau, visitors can stay at the **SSI Canal field station**, named for a notorious logging concession. This area is a key reforestation site, and views from the station's 5m observation tower illustrate the contrast between burned and replanted areas. The camp has four basic rooms with mattresses and mosquito nets, shared *mandi* and cooking facilities – and no fixed price. Bring your own food, though fresh caught fish is available (per kilo 50,000Rp). Guides for treks to search for orangutans cost 85,000Rp per day. Get here by public boat from Kering Bangkirai in Palangka Raya or charter, from 200,000Rp, depending on boat size. By speedboat, the trip takes one hour.

**Keruing village** on Sungai Katingan is more remote, and accommodation at the field station on Lake Panggualas is less developed. Visitors need to bring bedding and, if they want a cook, recruit one from the village. Local guide Surakhmansyah ( ☎ 085 252 801 658) can assist. **Losmen Cikia** ( ☎ 085 248 510 195; r 50,000-80,000Rp), about two hours away by *klotok*, may be more comfortable. Guides cost 85,000Rp per day, and canoe (per day 100,000Rp) is the best way to seek orangutans. From Palangka Raya, travel to Kasongan, then take a public *klotok*, last departure 10am, to Kuruing (150,000Rp, five hours). Alternatively, charter a *klotok* (1,500,000Rp to 2,000,000Rp) or speedboat (4,000,000Rp, two hours).

For more information about visiting the park, contact the **park office** ( ☎ 0536-332 7093; Jl Mahir Mahan Km 1.2) or **WWF office** ( ☎ 0536-323 6997; fax 0536-322 0993; Jl Pangrango 59), both in Palangka Raya.

## SUNGAI KAHAYAN

Every route is an adventure following Sungai Kahayan to traditional Dayak communities and primary forests deep in KalTeng's interior. Isolation has limited modernisation in the Kahayan's headwaters. Independent travel here is often improvised, expensive and challenging, with Bahasa Indonesia essential. Prices may fluctuate wildly from quotes below.

From Palangka Raya, start by Kijang to **Tewah** (100,000Rp, five hours) for its exquisitely carved longhouse. Then take a *klotok*

**DAYAK RITES OF CENTRAL KALIMANTAN**

**Tiwah, Ijambe & Wara Ceremonies**

KalTeng is famous for *tiwah*: colourful ceremonies in which dozens of Ngaju Dayak families retrieve the remains of their dead from temporary graves and send them on their way to the next life, according to the traditions of Kaharingan (a religion practiced by many Dayaks). Groups of villages participate, dispatching up to 150 or more long-dead 'spirits' in a month of feasting and ceremonies. The peak of activity is when bones are taken from the graves and washed and purified to cleanse the spirit of sins. Water buffalo, pigs, chickens and everything else needed for the journey to the next life are tethered to a totem then slaughtered. After more feasting, dancing and ceremonies, the purified human remains are transferred to the family *sandung* (brightly painted coffin on stilts).

Most *tiwah* ceremonies occur along Sungai Kahayan once or twice a year, with a major one every four or five years. Everyone is welcome, even foreigners. Introduce yourself to the chief of the organising committee, explain why you are there, ask permission to take photos, then enjoy the hospitality. Nothing happens in a hurry, so don't be too surprised if organisers are a bit vague about the program.

The *ijambe* is a Ma'anyan and Lawangan Dayak variation on *tiwah*. In sending their dead relatives on the journey to the next life, the bones are cremated and the ashes are stored in small jars in family apartments.

*Wara* is the funeral ritual practiced by the Tewoyan, Bayan, Dusun and Bentian Dayak people of northern Sungai Barito. They are far less concerned about the physical remains; instead, they use a medium to tell spirits of the dead the way to Gunung Lumut, nirvana for this branch of Kaharingan.

**Potong Pantan Ceremony**

Potong Pantan is a welcoming ceremony. Important guests are met by the head of the village, offered a machete and invited to cut through *pantan* (lengths of wood placed at the village's entrance) to purge themselves of bad spirits. As they cut, guests introduce themselves and explain the purpose of their visit. *Tapung tawar* is an extension of Potong Pantan, in which guests have their faces dusted with rice flour and their heads sprinkled with water to protect them from bad spirits and illness.

up Sungai Hamputung to **Tumbang Miri** (200,000Rp, six hours; charter 3,000,000Rp one way, 5,000,000Rp return) via river rapids. Stay at **Losmen Berkat Karunia** (s/d 44,000/55,000Rp) or try the longhouse settlement at **Tumbang Korik**.

Next day, trek to the Dayak village of **Tumbang Malahoi** with its fabulous 150-year-old ironwood longhouse. From here, charter a *klotok* to the historic village of **Tumbang Anoi** (500,000Rp, three hours; speedboat 1,000,000Rp, two hours) with a traditional longhouse still in use. Spend the night with a family, and return to Tumbang Miri by *klotok*. Figure at least five days for this route.

A three-day option from Tumbang Miri heads southwest to **Tumbang Rahuyan** or the gold-mining area near **Sungai Antai** (three hours). Continue downriver to **Tumbang Baringei** (three hours), by road via Tumbang Malahoi to **Tumbang Jutuh**, then by *klotok* or

speedboat south to **Tangkiling** or by road to Tewah (2½ hours) and on to Palangka Raya. Boats from Tumbang Jutuh leave mornings only and don't run during dry season.

For a four- to five-day trip, take a Kijang from Palangka Raya to **Kuala Kurun** (120,000Rp, seven hours), the site of **Batu Suli**, a rock Dayaks consider sacred, and by *ojek* north to **Sei Hayu**. Take a *klotok* on Sungai Kapuas to **Sungai Mendaun** and on to **Jarak Masuparia**. Hike to **Masuparia**, a gold field in the jungle. Continue by *ojek* to **Tumbang Masao** then by *klotok* downstream to **Puruk Cahu** and **Muara Teweh**. Or continue from Tumbang Masao to Sungai Barito's headwaters, past several rapids north of **Tumbang Tuan**, then take a boat downstream.

Given the difficulty, expense and need to negotiate each step, even confirmed independent travellers may want professional help for this journey; see p618.

## MUARA TEWEH

☎ 0519 / pop 37,500

In the heart of Sungai Barito logging country, Muara Teweh is the last riverboat stop unless the water is high enough to reach **Puruk Cahu**. From Puruk Cahu you can go further north by boat and hire Dayak guides to trek into the northeastern mountains and forest featuring waterfalls, stone carvings and orchids. Climbing **Gunung Bondang**, a holy peak to some Dayaks, takes a day. Near Gunung Pacungapung, on the border between Central and East Kalimantan, a cement pillar marks the geographic **centre of Borneo**.

You can also trek overland to **Long Iram** in East Kalimantan for boats down Sungai Mahakam to Samarinda. Different routes are possible, via jungle or logging roads to try hitching rides with passing vehicles, for this journey of up to two weeks.

Muara Teweh's main settlement is on the north bank of Sungai Barito. Jl Panglima Batur, parallel to the river, is the main drag. Rooms at very comfortable **Wisma Pacifik** ( ☎ 21231; Jl Panglima Batur 87; s incl breakfast 157,000-194,000Rp, d incl breakfast 194,000-218,000Rp; ✖ ) have TV, refrigerator and air-con, with hot water in larger 'VIP' rooms. **Permata Barito** ( ☎ 22882; Jl A Yani 176; s/d 77,000/143,000Rp; ✖ ) and **Barito Hotel** ( ☎ 21080; Jl Panglima Batur 43; s/d 50,000/65,000Rp) are decent alternatives.

Find warungs along Jl Panglima Batur west of Barito Hotel, up the hill on Jl Surapati, and near the market.

In Puruk Cahu there are a couple of **losmen** (r around 35,000Rp), or try the longhouse at Konut (10km).

**Muksin Hussein** ( ☎ 22342), an English teacher in Muara Teweh, assists tourists. In Puruk Cahu, ask for Mahrani, a Siang Dayak who speaks English.

### Getting There & Away

Daily (and nightly) buses travel equally long and uncomfortable routes to Palangka Raya (150,000Rp, 16 hours) and Banjarmasin (125,000Rp, 12 hours) from the terminal across the bridge (3km). Minibuses to Puruk Cahu (50,000Rp, three hours) use the terminal on Jl Surapati.

Cargo ships plying Sungai Barito may take riders.

The airport is 5km north of town. **Susi Air** ( ☎ 081 1211 3080/90; info@susiair.com) flies daily to/from Banjarmasin (600,000Rp) and Palangka Raya (450,000Rp). At the time of research, **Aviastar** (www.aviastar.biz) had proposed service to/from Palangka Raya.

# SOUTH KALIMANTAN

In just 37,660 sq km, South Kalimantan (Kalimantan Selatan, or KalSel) combines the region's largest and most beguiling city, scenic Pegunungan Meratus (Meratus Mountains), 10,000 sq km of wetlands and three million people. This seat of Banjar kings that once ruled much of Kalimantan is now Borneo's smallest province, so visitors can easily combine the urban and natural jungles.

## BANJARMASIN

☎ 0511 / pop 607,000

Beyond its space-age mosque, office towers and extensive air links, Banjarmasin's back streets still teem with old-time charm. The city is known as the Venice of Asia for its network of canals featuring stilt houses teetering over the water. Banjar tall roof architecture is on display at **City Hall** (Jl Martadinata) and the **Provincial Legislature** (DPRD; Jl Lambung Mangkurat).

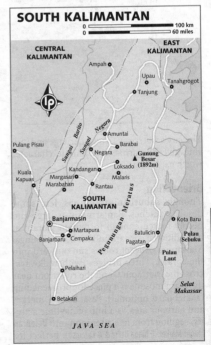

SOUTH KALIMANTAN

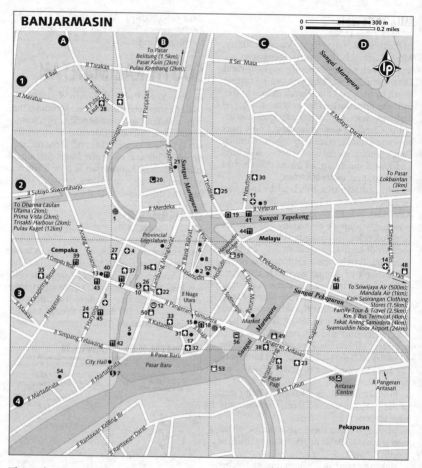

The city's waterways, royal heritage and cuisine give Banjarmasin a unique character worth exploring.

## Orientation

Though suburbanisation has left some desolate patches, Banjarmasin is large and deeply rooted enough to remain vibrant at its traditional core around the bend of Sungai Martapura. *Angkot* routes run outward into the sprawl. Three bridges (with walkways) cross the Martapura, and the riverfront near the main mosque is a place for promenading (skateboard optional). **Pasar Baru**, a market and harbour area, is a hub of daytime activity, seguing from late afternoon into **Belauran** (Night Market; Jl Niaga Utara & Jl Katamso), perfect for

sampling local food and culture. The harbour for boats to Java is west of town on Sungai Barito.

## MAPS

**Gramedia** (Jl Veteran 55-61 & Duta Mall)
**Usaha Jaya** (Jl Niaga Utara 1)

## Information
### INTERNET ACCESS

**1899 Exclusive** (Jl R Suprapto 18; per hr 4000Rp; 10am-midnight) Remove your shoes before going to computers upstairs. Smoking is not permitted.
**Warnet Kyagi** (Jl Pangeran Samudera 94-96; per hr 3000Rp; 8am-midnight Sun-Fri, 8am-2am Sat)

At **Pos Indo Plaza** (cnr Jl Pangeran Samudera & Jl Lambung Mangkurat) shopping centre, **Starbright** (drinks & snacks 3000-18,000Rp; 8am-3am) and **Bright Café** (mains 20,000-30,000Rp; 10am-1am) have free wi-fi.

## MEDICAL SERVICES

**Apotek Piala** ( ☎ 436 7500; Jl Haryono 3A) Top druggist.

**Rumah Sakit Ulin** ( ☎ 325 2180; www.rsudulin.com; Jl A Yani Km 2 No 43; 24hr) Hospital.

Pharmacies **Kimia Farma** ( ☎ 325 0682; Jl Veteran 61; 24 hr) and **Apotek Sari Mulia** ( ☎ 335 4650; Jl Haryono 15) have multiple doctors' practices.

## MONEY

Banks exchanging money abound along Jl Lambung Mangkurat. Major streets and malls have ATMs, with a cluster at **Hotel Istana Barito** (Jl Haryono 16-20). For non-US currency exchange, see **Haji La Tunrung Star Group** (Jl Pangeran Samudera 17C).

## TOURIST INFORMATION

**City Information Kiosk** (Jl Martadinata; 9am-3pm Mon-Fri)

## TRAVEL AGENCIES

See p626 for more guided tours.

**Adi Angkasa Travel** ( ☎ 436 6100; fax 436 6200; Jl Hasanudin 27) Flight bookings and contact for independent guide Tailah.

**Arjuna Tours & Travel** ( ☎ 335 8150; arjuna_travel@ telkom.net; ground fl, Arjuna Plaza, Jl Lambung Mangkurat) Books domestic flights and regional tours. Operates Amandit River Lodge in Loksado (p630).

**Family Tour & Travel** ( ☎ 326 8923; www.bestbor neotour.com; Komp Aspol Bina Brata 1E, Km 4.5 Jl A Yani) Flights and tours throughout Kalimantan, plus car rental and hotel bookings. Helpful owner Syamsuddinnor speaks English.

**NES Tour & Travel** ( ☎ 336 1923; nes_travel@telkom .net; Jl Pangeran Samudera 25) Air and boat bookings with 24-hour phone service.

**Tekat Aneng Samudera** ( ☎ 327 2330; Jl Pramuka 21) At the Km 6 bus terminal, Ibu Yuni and her team sort air, sea and ground transport.

## Sights & Activities

### MESJID RAYA SABILAL MUHTADIN

In a park-like setting, this massive **mosque** (Jl Sudirman) resembles a landed spaceship. Wear long pants and, for women, long sleeves, to see its interior. During Ramadan, enjoy renowned **Pasar Wadai** cake market along the adjacent riverfront.

### CHINESE TEMPLES

Central Banjarmasin has a pair of monumental Chinese temples, the older one at the corner of Jl Niaga and Jl Niaga Utara, and the newer one across Sungai Martapura at the start of Jl Veteran.

### CANAL TRIPS

Cruising in filthy brown water through people's bathrooms during wash time hardly sounds appealing. But as water-villagers wash, scrub clothes on wooden-plank porches, paddle or swim alongside your boat, or just

**KALIMANTAN**

lounge in the late afternoon breeze, their smiles light up these waterways where life dates back at least 350 years. Children star but everyone joins in, trading waves, splashes and high fives.

Enjoy the spectacle with a tour operator and guide or charter a boat (150,000Rp to 200,000Rp) from beneath Hasanudin Bridge.

### FLOATING MARKETS

Brave the 5.30am boarding call to shop at the *pasar tarapung* (floating market) amid canoes laden with vivid produce manoeuvring intricately in tight quarters. For breakfast, supplement fruit purchases at the floating cafe, using a bamboo pole with a nail pushed through the end to spike cakes.

**Pasar Kuin** (30 minutes) is the best known floating market. **Pasar Lokbaintan** (45 minutes) is often busier.

### PULAU KEMBANG

Pulau Kembang is home to long-tailed macaques that greet visitors noisily at the dock. Charter a boat (100,000Rp return) or elect the optional stop on Pasar Kuin tours. Caution: macaques can be aggressive.

### PULAU KAGET

This set of islands in Sungai Barito has troupes of proboscis monkeys, a primate found only in Borneo. Charter a boat (200,000Rp return, four to five hours) from Triskati Harbour or take a tour. Monkeys are scarce enough and shorelines long enough that a guide really helps.

## Tours

Many travel agencies and hotels offer city and Pegunungan Meratus touring with English-speaking guides. **South Kalimantan Tour Guide Association** (www.hpikalsel.com) lists registered guides. Agencies and guides can also assist with visiting Tanjung Puting National Park (see p614) and Sungai Mahakam (see p642). Shop around because prices vary drastically.

**Tailah** ( ☎ 327 1685; 085 821 035 791), based at **Diamond Homestay** ( ☎ 436 6100; Jl Hasanudin 58; s/d 30,000/40,000Rp), is our favourite independent guide; see opposite. Friendly, fluent in English and utterly genuine, he's adept at all itineraries and well connected. He lives his motto: 'Enjoy your trip as a family trip'.

Other guides with good reputations include **Mulyadi Yasin** ( ☎ 081 351 936 200; yadi_yasin@yahoo

.co.id), affiliated with **Borneo Homestay** ( ☎ 436 6545; borneo@banjarmasin.wasantara.net.id; Jl Hasanudin 33; s/d 45,000/50,000Rp) and independent guide **Sarkani Gambi** (Kani Dayak; ☎ 081 351 877 858; kani286@ yahoo.com).

Rates per person run from 100,000Rp for floating markets and 75,000Rp for canal tours for groups of two or more, including guide and transport. Guide fees for forest trekking start from 250,000Rp per day, plus food, accommodation and transport. See p823 for more on choosing guides.

## Sleeping
### BUDGET

Cheap sleeps are clustered around Belaruan Niaga or Pasar Pagi off Jl Pangeran Antasari.

**Hotel Perdana** ( ☎ 335 2376; perdanahotel@plasa .com; Jl Katamso 8; s incl breakfast 70,000Rp, d incl breakfast 80,000-325,000Rp; 🗙 ) Best of the *belaruan* budget bunch, spotless Perdana is a sweet deal with free afternoon cake, TV and private bathroom for all; economy rooms have fan only. Listed prices include breakfast. Many will appreciate management's zero tolerance for prostitutes.

**Hotel Asia Baru** ( ☎ 325 3260; asiabaru_hotel@yahoo .co.id; Jl Sugiono 48; r 85,000-155,000Rp; 🗙 ) Sleek new place near Pasar Pagi has a Western bathroom and 42 TV channels in every room. Choose economy with fan or air-con comfort.

**Samudera Guest House** ( ☎ 336 2250; fax 436 8817; Jl Pangeran Samudera 29; r incl breakfast 100,000-255,000Rp; 🗙 ) In a *gang* (alley) 50m north of Jl Pangeran Samudera, every well-furnished room at this new entry has air-con and TV. There's an attractive 2nd-floor sitting area.

**Hotel SAS** ( ☎ 335 3054; fax 336 5967; Jl Kacapiring Besar 2; r incl breakfast 125,000-250,000Rp, ste/f 242,500/293,500Rp; 🗙 ) This teakwood classic bridges budget to midrange with generous rooms and helpful staff. But, especially at midrange prices, many hotels now offer better value.

Other budget options:
**Hotel Biuti** ( ☎ /fax 335 4493; Jl Haryono 2; r 75,000-225,000Rp; 🗙 ) Nicely renovated.
**Hotel Niaga** ( ☎ 335 2595; Jl Niaga 14; s 35,000-40,000Rp, d 60,000Rp, t 75,000Rp) Clean and basic.
**Hotel Niagara** ( ☎ 335 6355; Jl Katamso 1; s 35,000-60,000Rp, d 60,000-80,000Rp; 🗙 ) This upmarket cousin of Hotel Niaga has some air-con rooms.

### MIDRANGE & TOP END

There's a range of new and old choices along Jl Lambung Mangkurat from 250,000Rp to

---

**TOWN & COUNTRY TOURING**

'When I began, there were hardly any guides', M (for Muhammad) Tailah recalls. 'At first, I just did it as a hobby because I like making friends and practising my English. Back then, not many people in Banjarmasin could speak English.'

A fixture on South Kalimantan tour scene and in central Banjarmasin, independent guide Tailah (who goes by that one name) was born in Barabai, about 165km north of South Kalimantan's capital. He moved to the big city when he was 10 and began working as a guide at Borneo Homestay when it pioneered tourism for foreigners in the 1990s. Tailah's favourite tours reflect the two sides of his background.

'In Banjarmasin as a youngster, I used to swim in the rivers or play in a *jukung* (canoe). I like to show people the waterways around Banjarmasin, so they understand the city's connection with the water.' Those trips include canal tours of neighbourhoods on liquid backstreets and 5.30am visits to the floating markets. 'When people see these places, they can understand the culture.'

Tailah also enjoys showing visitors his Pengungungan Meratus roots, including visits to *balai*, the region's unique, rectangular longhouses. But most of all he's about trekking through the mountain forests and trains for it by running every morning.

'I love showing guests the natural richness of Meratus with its beautiful scenes of mountains, jungle trees, flowers and surprises like *kayu manis* (cinnamon)', Tailah says, noting that even here, there are connections to the water: 'clear mountain springs, waterfalls and bamboo rafting' at the end of many treks.

'I hope that when people see these natural and cultural treasures, they'll want to help preserve them.'

---

350,000Rp. At its airport kiosk, **Kaha Tours** ( ☎ 747 3102; fax 470 6161) deeply discounts many upmarket hotels. Also ask there about hotels near the airport in Banjarbaru if you have an early departure.

**Hotel Midoo** ( ☎ 325 8918; fax 325 0626; Jl Nasution 8; r 155,000-175,000Rp; ✗ 🖭 ) Cross the bridge into Banjarmasin's Chinatown for large, boxy rooms with air-con, hot-water shower, international TV channels and lobby wi-fi (per hour 10,000Rp).

**Hotel Cahaya** ( ☎ 325 3508; fax 326 6748; Jl Tendean 22/64; r incl breakfast 160,000-230,000Rp; ✗ ) Just across Hasanudin bridge, newish Cahaya has the cheapest rooms in town with hot/cold shower and breakfast.

**Hotel Mira** ( ☎ 336 3955; fax 335 2465; Jl Haryono 49; r incl breakfast 175,000-200,000Rp; ste 275,000Rp; ✗ ) Centrally located modern, spotless rooms with hot-water showers, some without windows.

**Hotel Roditha** ( ☎ 336 2345; rodithahotel@yahoo.com; Jl Antasari Pasar Pagi 41; r incl breakfast 250,000-375,000Rp, ste 400,000-495,000Rp plus 21% tax; ✗ 🖭 🖭 ) Newest and swishest near Pasar Pagi, business-friendly Roditha has free wi-fi in its bright rooms.

**Hotel Grand Mentari** ( ☎ 436 8944; hotelgrandmentari_bjm@yahoo.com; Jl Lambung Mangkurat 32; r incl breakfast 273,000-544,000Rp; ✗ 🖭 ) Overshadowed by its 'Grand' addition, Mentari's original wing rooms are exceptional value.

**Hotel Arum Kalimantan** ( ☎ 436 6818; banjarmasin@arumhotel-banjarmasin.com; Jl Lambung Mangkurat; s 509,000-649,000Rp, d 536,000-676,000Rp, ste from 1,929,000Rp, all incl breakfast; ✗ 🖭 🖭 🖭 ) Four-star 'Hotel Kalimantan' has classy, cushy rooms behind its cold facade and a full line-up of facilities.

Kartikas and company:

**Hotel Kartika** ( ☎ /fax 335 5518; Jl Pulau Laut 1; r 150,000-180,000Rp; ✗ ) Modern, all Western bathrooms with hot water.

**Hotel Kartika Dua** ( ☎ 436 5801; Jl Taman Sari 8; r incl breakfast 175,000Rp; ✗ ) Homely feel, hot-water shower and 40-channel TV.

**Kartika Antasari** ( ☎ 336 3119; Jl Lambung Mangkurat 26; r incl breakfast 209,500-248,500Rp; ✗ ) Small hotel, huge rooms.

**Hotel Istana Barito** ( ☎ 335 2240; fax 436 7300; Jl Haryono 16-20; r incl breakfast from 450,000Rp; ✗ 🖭 ) As aging Barito teeters, try slipping into a still-comfortable room for 250,000Rp or less.

**Swiss-Belhotel Borneo** ( ☎ 327 1111; www.swiss-belhotel.com; Jl Pangeran Antasari 86A; s/d incl breakfast 890,000/940,000Rp; ✗ 🖭 🖭 ) Also known as 'Hotel Borneo', luxuries include frequent 25% discounts. Windows optional.

## Eating

Banjar cooking is renowned; try it at Belauran Niaga stalls. For alcoholic drinks, try Chinese restaurants and hotels. For ice cream, try **Yasuka** ( ☎ 335 8827; Jl Pangeran Samudera 21) which has homemade ice cream by the scoop (5000Rp) or half-litre (25,000Rp) featuring fruit flavours in season.

**Depot Kalimantan** ( ☎ 325 8286; Jl Veteran 19; mains 8000-15,000Rp) Bright, air-con, no-smoking refuge for Banjar and Chinese dishes plus fruit juices. Popular with families and couples.

**Rumah Makan Abdullah** (Jl A Yani Km 1; mains 13,000-18,000Rp) *Nasi kuning* (saffron rice with coconut milk), a breakfast food found elsewhere in Indonesia, is served all hours with fish, meat or vegetable toppings.

**ourpick** **Soto Banjar Haji Anang** (Jl Pekapuran; mains 15,000-20,000Rp; ☯ 6am-5.30pm Sat-Thu, closed Fri) Riverside warung renowned for *soto banjar* with a full chicken part, not a few shavings. Broth here is savoury, *lontong* (rice steamed in banana leaf) lush, homemade sambal scorching.

**Rumah Makan Jayakarta** ( ☎ 336 4301; Jl Haryono 7; mains 20,000-40,000Rp; ☯ 11am-2.30pm, 5-11pm) Javanese name, Chinese cooking dished with air-con and beer.

**Cendrawasih** (Jl Pangeran Samudera; mains 15,000-30,000Rp) Delve deeper into Banjar cuisine at this renowned spot. Pick fish, seafood or chicken for grilling, served with an array of Banjar sauces. Or just have a selection of dishes brought to your table and pay for ones you eat. Neighbouring **Kaganangan** ( ☎ 436 4203; Jl Pangeran Samudera 8; mains 9000-25,000Rp) has similar options, with smaller, cheaper portions and an occasional bad attitude toward foreigners.

### BUBUR AYAM
Banjarmasin breakfasts on *bubur ayam* (chicken rice porridge).

**Depot Soraya** (Jl Simpang Telawang 51; bubur 8000Rp, mains 8000-17,000Rp; ☯ 6.30am-10pm) Serves *bubur* till noon and other Banjar specialities until 10pm.

**Bubur Ayam Cempaka** (Jl Cempaka Besar 4; bubur 20,000Rp; ☯ 6.30am-10pm) This place gets mobbed on Sunday.

### SELF CATERING
**Hero Supermarket** (Mitra Plaza, Jl Pangeran Antasari)
**Hypermarket** (Duta Mall, Jl A Yani Km 2)

## Shopping
Shops along Jl Pangeran Antasari sell Dayak and other traditional souvenirs, including Banjar specialty *kain sasirangan*, tie-dyed

batik. Stores at Jl A Yani Km 3.7 sell *kain sasirangan* clothing, but large sizes are hard to find.

Banjarmasin residents are fussy about *belauran* (night markets). Huge groups of night stalls around Antasari Centre and along Jl Anang Andenansi aren't *belauran*. On the north side of town, **Pasar Belitung** (Jl Belitung) is a 2km *belauran* also known as Pasar Tunging, Banjar for squat toilet, once its top-selling item. Visit during early evening to sample modernised, urbanised traditional life.

## Getting There & Away
### AIR
**Garuda** ( ☎ 335 9065; Jl Hasanudin 13), **Sriwijaya Air** ( ☎ 327 2377; Jl A Yani Km 2.5), **Lion Air** ( ☎ 470 5277) and **Batavia Air** ( ☎ 335 8996) fly to Jakarta. Lion and affiliate **Wings Air** ( ☎ 470 5277), Sriwijaya, **Citilink** ( ☎ 080 4108 0808; www.citilink.co.id), Batavia and **Mandala Air** ( ☎ 326 6737; Jl A Yani Km 3) serve Surabaya. **KalStar** ( ☎/fax 436 4465) flies to Pangkalan Bun, Ketapang and Pontianak. Batavia flies to Balikpapan, as does **Trigana Air** ( ☎ 757 6249), which also serves Kota Baru. Mandala flies to Yogyakarta. **Susi Air** ( ☎ 081 1211 3080/90; info@susiair.com) flies daily to Muara Teweh, continuing to Palangka Raya.

Taxis to/from Syamsuddin Noor Airport (26km) cost 75,000Rp. Alternatively, take a Jl A Yani *angkot* to Km 6 terminal, then catch a Martapura-bound Colt (minibus; 10,000Rp). Get off at the airport approach road, and walk 1.5km to the terminal. From the airport, walk to the highway for a Colt to Km 6.

### BOAT
**Pelni** ( ☎ 335 3077; Jl Martadinata 10) sails weekly to Semarang (333,000Rp, 24 hours) from **Trisakti Harbour** (3km) on Sungai Barito. **Dharma Lautan Utama** ( ☎ 442 0547; Jl Yos Sudarso 8) and **Prima Vista** ( ☎ 335 9487; Jl Sutoyo 1) ferries depart for Surabaya (235,000Rp, 18 hours) on alternate days.

Longboats from **Sudi Mampir wharf** leave to Marabahan (15,000Rp, six hours) Monday and Tuesday at 9am, and from **Pasar Lima** wharf to Negara (20,000Rp, 18 hours) Tuesday and Saturday at 1pm.

### BUS
The main bus terminal is at Jl A Yani Km 6, southeast of downtown. Colts depart frequently for Banjarbaru (16,000Rp, 25 minutes), Martapura (16,000Rp, 35 minutes), Kandangan (30,000Rp, four hours), Negara

(35,000Rp, five hours) and other Pegunungan Meratus destinations.

Several companies run day and night buses to Balikpapan (economy/air-con 110,000/165,000Rp, 10 hours), Samarinda (economy/air-con 135,000/180,000Rp, 13 hours), Muara Teweh (economy/air-con 125,000/150,000Rp, 12 hours), Palangka Raya (economy/air-con 60,000/75,000Rp, five hours) and Pangkalan Bun (economy/air-con 125,000/165,000Rp, 17 hours).

One bus leaves daily from Km 6 to Marabahan, but it's easier to go to Kayu Tani Ujung by *angkot* (3000Rp) in northern Banjarmasin for a Colt (25,000Rp, three hours). There's a 1000Rp charge for the short ferry crossing.

### Getting Around

*Angkot* routes (3000Rp) fan out from terminals in the city core at Jl Pangeran Samudera circle and Jl Hasanudin and from Antasari Centre to the east. Becak and *ojek* gather around market areas. Unmetered taxis wait on Jl Bank Rakyat Indonesia.

Charter boats near Jl Hasanudin bridge for canal cruising. Rates are by destination, not duration.

## AROUND BANJARMASIN

Three towns southeast of Banjarmasin make interesting day trips, separately or combined.

### Banjarbaru

Amid ancient banyan and lontar trees, **Museum Lambung Mangkurat** (Jl Ahmad Yani 36; admission 5000Rp; 9.30am-2.30pm Tue-Thu, Sat & Sun, 9.30-11am Fri, closed Mon) exhibits relics from pre-Islamic Hindu temples, Dayak artefacts and *halat*, Banjar carved-wood walls and doors. The museum is on the Banjarmasin–Martapura Colt route.

### Martapura

Precious stones are the most notable regional produce at the colourful **market** in Martapura, just east of Banjarbaru. Purchasing uncut gems (many from local mines) silver jewellery and trading beads here requires hard bargaining – your knowledge and the seller's reputation are the only indicators of authenticity.

Area mines close Friday, so the market swells with workers and families. To avoid crowds, visit another day.

### Cempaka

See the dirty business of pursuing prized pebbles at Cempaka's **diamond fields** ( closed Fri). Prospectors work up to their necks in water, hoisting silt to be washed in makeshift contraptions and sifted for gold specks, diamonds or agate.

Since 1846, multicarat diamonds have been found here – largest of all, the 167.5-carat Tri Sakti (Thrice Sacred) in August 1965. Most diamonds are tiny, but hope for a huge find keeps miners focused.

To reach Cempaka, take a Banjarmasin–Martapura Colt to the huge roundabout just past Banjarbaru. Switch to a green *angkot* to Alur (2000Rp) and walk 1km from the main road. Touts eagerly show the way in hopes of collecting the customary 2000Rp tip.

## MARABAHAN & MARGASARI

To observe river life, cruise 65km up Sungai Barito from Banjarmasin to Marabahan, a small town with some traditional Banjar-style 'tall roof' wooden houses. Losmen on the river, such as **Hotel Bahtera** (r 30,000Rp), have adequate accommodation with shared *mandis*.

From Marabahan, charter a boat to Margasari, known for rattan and bamboo handicrafts. Colts run daily between Marabahan and Banjarmasin (25,000Rp, three hours). Boats run twice weekly from Banjarmasin's Sudi Mampir (15,000Rp, six hours).

## KANDANGAN
☎ 0517

With its crumbling colonial-era market and minibus terminal as hubs, Kandangan is the place to stock supplies and begin Pegunungan Meratus explorations.

**Losmen Loksado** ( ☎ 21352; Jl Suprapto 8; r 50,000-150,000Rp; ), around the corner from the minibus terminal, has comfortable, fan-cooled rooms. Harder to find, **Wisma Duta** ( ☎ 21073; Jl Permuda 9; r incl breakfast 150,000-200,000Rp; ) in a converted family house, offers homely accommodation on a quiet street.

Kandangan's specialty food is *ketupat*, sticky rice triangles enjoyed across Indonesia, served with broiled *harawan*, a river fish, coconut sauce and a squeeze of lime. Try it at **Warung Ketupat Kandangan**, 1km northwest of the minibus terminal on the road to Barabai.

The government **tourism office** ( ☎ 21363; Jl Jend Sudirman 26), on the main road, 2km south of the town centre, has information on trekking and renting holiday cottages at Muara Tanuhi, see right.

Colts run frequently to/from Banjarmasin's Km 6 terminal (30,000Rp, four hours) until mid-afternoon. Night buses stop en route from Banjarmasin to Balikpapan at around 7pm at a terminal 2km east of town. Catch a Negara-bound minibus (5000Rp) there, or take an *ojek* (15,000Rp).

## NEGARA

Home to some of the world's most spectacular swimmers, Negara, northwest of Kandangan, is a wetland during the rainy season and surrounded by water year-round. Negara's buildings are on stilts and the only land above water is the road, and even that can disappear – in floods of mosquitoes if not rain.

Negara's incredible aquatists are water-buffalo. Farmers rear buffalo on wooden platforms, releasing them daily for grazing and drinking. Buffalo swim up to 5km until 'canoe cowboys' herd them home.

Tour Negara by boat – it may cost 150,000Rp, depending on your bargaining skill. The wetlands are remarkable for prolific fish and bird life. The town is also known for forging swords, *mandau* and kris.

Surprisingly, Negara has no hotel. You might find a homestay, but Kandangan is a better bet.

Colts from Banjarmasin to Negara (35,000Rp, five hours) leave from Km 6 terminal. From Kandangan to Negara choose among public minibus (10,000Rp, one hour), shared sedan with four people (per person 20,000Rp, charter 80,000Rp), or *ojek* (40,000Rp). Twice-weekly boats leave from Pasar Lima in Banjarmasin (20,000Rp, 18 hours).

## UPAU

One of the smallest Dayak groups, Deah Dayaks live at the remote northern edge of Pegunungan Meratus, isolated by centuries of aristocratic intrigue and refusal to embrace Islam. In Upau (meaning 'jackfruit', abundant locally) Deah traditional rites are still performed, including the *balian* (shaman) ceremony to drive evil spirits from the sick, and *aru* preparing warriors for head-hunting (although they now skip the head-hunting).

English is rare, and there's no formal accommodation, but some families accept guests. Bring food from Tanjung or Upau's Friday market, and offer a modest sum of money.

There's prime trekking in hills 2km away. Villagers Aman and Dudang know the mountains and act as guides. Take a moderate one-day trek into the foothills. For two- or three-day adventures over rough terrain, only experienced trekkers need apply.

To reach Upau, catch a minibus from Negara (45,000Rp, two hours) or Colt from Banjarmasin's Km 6 (70,000Rp, six hours) to Tanjung, then a red and yellow *angkot* to Upau (7,000Rp, 1½ hours).

## LOKSADO

Largest of about 20 villages spread around Pegunungan Meratus, Loksado is at the end of the road 40km east of Kandangan. Road access makes Loksado an important market village and base for trekking in this 2500 sq km mountain range roughly bounded by Kandangan and Amuntai to the west and coastline to the east.

**Amat** ( ☎ 081 348 766 573), a personable Dayak who speaks good English, is Loksado's tourism coordinator. A visitor information kiosk lists standard prices for services.

After years of false rumours, comfortable **Hotel Wisma Loksado** ( ☎ 085 251 544 398; r 150,000Rp) finally opened across from a bamboo bridge from the village centre.

**Amandit River Lodge** (r 200,000Rp), 3km west of Loksado, has simple, charming rooms, and staff can organise meals. Amandit opens by appointment; give two days' notice to **Arjuna Tours & Travel** (p625) in Banjarmasin.

Muara Tanuhi's **hot springs** (admission adult/child 3000/2000Rp), 2km west of Loksado, have **holiday cottages** ( ☎ 21363; cottage 275,000Rp) with kitchens and sleeping for four. Grounds include two pools, tennis court and suburban aesthetic targeting Banjarmasin weekenders.

### Getting There & Away

Pick-up trucks leave Kandangan terminal for Loksado (15,000Rp, 1½ hours) afternoons, and leave Loksado for Kandangan early mornings.

After treks, many travellers charter bamboo rafts down Sungai Amandit. The usual drop-off point is Muara Tanuhi, two hours downstream (125,000Rp for up to three passengers). Continuing downstream to Muara

## LOKSADO AREA

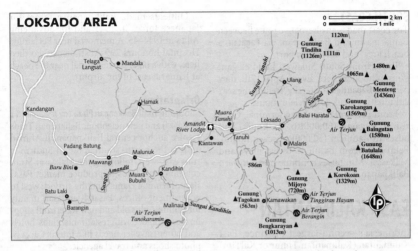

Bubuhi crosses some exciting rapids when the river is high, takes another three hours and costs at least double. From the nearby road at Muara Bubuhi, take a minibus or *ojek* to Kandangan. Rafting Loksado to Kandangan takes a full day.

## AROUND LOKSADO

From Loksado hundreds paths lead through the hills, many crossing streams via suspension bridges of rope and bamboo. Residents negotiate the bridges easily, but visitors often set them rocking, amusing onlookers.

### Malaris

A 30-minute walk (1.5km) or 10-minute *ojek* ride through bamboo forest southeast of Loksado leads to Malaris. Its aged *balai* (longhouse) once housed 32 families; modernisation means separate houses for families. Ask the *kepala balai* (village head) about **homestays** (30,000Rp).

### Treks

Combining limestone mountainsides, dense tropical forests, rolling hills and river valleys, Pegunungan Meratus presents breathtaking vistas and opportunities to visit *balai*, rectangular longhouses built around a central temple. Treks vary from moderate to extreme. Guides are usually necessary to find the right paths and best vistas. Enlist one in Loksado, though if you require an English speaker, hire in Banjarmasin. Pegunungan Meratus treks are a specialty of **Tailah**: see p626. Guide rates

run from 250,000Rp per day, plus transport costs and other expenses.

To sample the hills, follow the path from Loksado upstream along Sungai Amandit for three hours (8km) to a series of **air terjun** (waterfalls) past Balai Haratai. Finding the first waterfall is easy, but the middle and top falls and a nearby cavern require assistance. Ask for help at Haratai.

Longer treks begin from Loksado or 2km west in **Tanuhi**. The combination of mountains and rivers means plenty of waterfalls and suspension bridges. The primary forest is a tranquil yet awe-inspiring spectacle. Accommodation is at *balai* along the way, including Haruyan, about four hours from Tanuhi; Kepayang, one to two days; Niwak, two days; and Pangong, three days. Return downstream by bamboo raft.

**Barabai**, renowned for its scenic views, is another terminus for treks. **Fusfa Hotel** ( ☎ 0517-41136; Jl Hasan 144; s/d/tr incl breakfast from 150,000/200,000/250,000Rp; ✷ ) has pleasant rooms and a restaurant. From Barabai, minibuses go to Kandangan (8000Rp, one hour) and Banjarmasin (35,000Rp, five hours)

It's also possible to trek from Loksado to the coast. Reaching **Kota Baru** on Pulau Laut via Gunung Besar (1892m), KalSel's highest peak, takes three or four days by foot, minibus and boat. Kota Baru has traditional boat building and fishing. Return to Banjarmasin by bus (85,000Rp, nine hours including ferry) or take the coast road north to Balikpapan.

**KALIMANTAN**

## SOUTH COAST

The coast road is an alternative route between Banjarmasin and Balikpapan, via **Pagatan**, a beach area, and **Batulicin**, a port.

Bugis from South Sulawesi build elegant *pinisi* schooners here. Every April 17th, they perform **Mapan Retasi**, literally 'feeding the sea', culminating week-long celebrations.

From Banjarmasin's Km 6 terminal, Colts run to Pagatan (50,000Rp, six hours) and buses to Batulicin (50,000Rp, seven hours). Pelni sails from Batulicin to Surabaya and Makassar. Minibuses continue north toward Balikpapan.

# EAST KALIMANTAN

Indonesia's second-largest province, East Kalimantan (Kalimantan Timur or KalTim) has Borneo's richest and most diverse natural and human resources. Previously famed for timber and oil, now coal is king. KalTim's environment, wildlife and traditional cultures have suffered from these extractive industries. But at 202,000 sq km, KalTim has room enough for effective preservation, including vast areas where distance and natural obstacles fend off chainsaws, bulldozers, and other 21st-century intruders. With enough time, patience and money, travellers can leap these barriers to see traditions surviving in longhouse villages amid ancient forests. Some of KalTim's best destinations are actually easy to reach, including the province's signature journey into Sungai Mahakam's Dayak communities. Plus there's direct access from abroad with visa on arrival at Balikpapan's Seppingan Airport and ferry service from Sabah in Malaysia.

## BALIKPAPAN

☎ 0542 / pop 460,000

This gateway to Kalimantan usually gets the short shrift from travellers other than corporate executives. But oil and coal aren't the only energy flowing in Balikpapan. It's Indonesia's urban frontier, attracting ambitious people from across the archipelago seeking their fortunes. They add to the welcoming, cosmopolitan flavour, appropriate for Kalimantan's leading airline hub. Sungai Mahakam journeys can originate here via Loajanan, and many find Balikpapan more pleasant than Samarinda.

Oilfields made Balikpapan a target for Japanese forces in 1941 and for advancing Allies in 1944–45. A memorial near Pertamina Hospital honours 229 Australians who died here, with a Japanese memorial near the beach at Lamaru, east of the airport.

### Orientation

Shopping mall **Balikpapan Plaza** (cnr Jl Sudirman & Jl Ahmad Yani) and new neighbour Balikpapan Trade Centre anchor central Balikpapan. Jl Ahmad Yani is the north–south spine. Jl Sudirman runs east–west, following the Makassar Strait coastline: east leads to produce market Pasar Baru, Terminal Damai and the airport; west to government offices, Pasar Klandasan mainly for clothing, plus old and new waterfront shophouses sprinkled with restaurants, clubs, hotels and other traveller needs like internet access, photo shops and travel agencies.

### MAPS
**Gramedia** (2nd fl, Balikpapan Plaza)

### Information
#### IMMIGRATION
**Immigration Office** (☎ 421 175; Jl Sudirman 23)

#### INTERNET ACCESS
Cruise Jl Sudirman for abundant connections open until at least 10pm.
**Global Net** (RT2 No 35 Klandasan; per hr 6000Rp; ◷ 9am-11pm; ⚟)
**Java Net** (Jl Pranoto; per hr 5000Rp; ◷ 24 hr)
**Vagabond Cybernet** (Jl KH Agus Salim 71; per hr 4000Rp; ◷ 9am-7am)

#### MONEY
Most banks along Jl Sudirman exchange currency and have ATMs accepting international cards.
**Bank Mandiri** (Jl Ahmad Yani 15) Extended hours, foreign-exchange counter.
**Haji La Tunrung Star Group** (Jl Ahmad Yani 51) Money changer.

#### MEDICAL SERVICES
**Pertamina Hospital** (☎ 734 020; www.rspb.co.id; Jl Sudirman 1)

#### TRAVEL AGENCIES
**Agung Sedayu** (☎ 420 601; agung_sedayu_trv@ yahoo.com.sg; Jl Sudirman 28; ◷ 7am-9pm) Tops for Pelni info and all boat bookings. Also handles domestic flights.

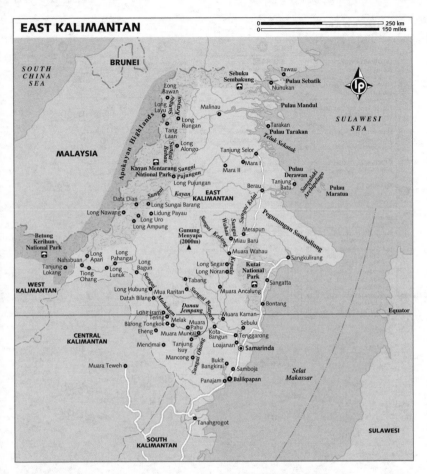

## EAST KALIMANTAN

0 ————— 250 km
0 ————— 150 miles

SOUTH CHINA SEA

BRUNEI

Tawau

Sebuku
Sembakung

Pulau Sebatik
Nunukan

Long Bawan

Pulau Mandul

Long Layu
Sungai Kayan
Malinau

Long Rungan
Tang Laan

Tarakan
Pulau Tarakan
Teluk Sekatak

SULAWESI SEA

MALAYSIA

Apokayan Highlands

Long Alongo

Tanjung Selor

Mara I

Kayan Mentarang National Park

Sungai Pujungan

Mara II

Pulau Derawan
Tanjung Batu
Sungai Kelai
Sungai Segah Archipelago

Long Pujungan

Berau

Pulau Maratua

Data Dian

Sungai Kayan
EAST KALIMANTAN

Long Sungai Barang
Long Nawang

Lidung Payau

Sungai Kelai

Long Uro
Long Ampung

Pegunungan Sambaliung

Betung Kerihun National Park

Gunung Menyapa (2000m) ▲

Sungai Kelong
Sungai Wahau

Merapun

Miau Baru

Muara Wahau

Long Apari
Long Pahangai
Long Bagun

Sungai Kapuas

Long Segar
Long Norang

Sangkulirang

Nahabuan

Tanjung Lokang
Tiong Ohang
Long Lunuk

Kutai National Park

Sangatta

WEST KALIMANTAN

Long Hubung
Datah Bilang

Sungai Mahakam

Tabang

Muara Ancalung

Sangatta

Long Iram

Mua Raritan

Sungai Belayan

Muara Kaman

Bontang

Equator

Danau Jempang

Tering
Melak

Muara Pahu

Sebulu

CENTRAL KALIMANTAN

Barong Tongkok
Eheng

Muara Muntai

Kota Bangun

Tenggarong

Mencimai
Tanjung Isuy

Sungai Ohong

Loajanan

Samarinda

Mancong

Bukit Bangkirai

Samboja

Selat Makassar

Muara Teweh

Panajam
Balikpapan

SULAWESI

Tanahgrogot

SOUTH KALIMANTAN

**Gelora Equatorial Travel** (GET; ☎ 423 251; getbpp@yahoo.com; Jl ARS Muhammad 7) Foreigner-friendly travel and tour agency. Fluent English, Dutch and more.

**TX Travel** ( ☎ 444 099; tgs_lestari@hotmail.com; Jl Ahmad Yani 24) Aggressive newcomer offering all flights, hotel vouchers and free ticket delivery.

## Tours
**East Kalimantan Guide Association** ( ☎ 8000 9549; guide_borneo@hotmail.com) Chaired by the owner of River Tours (below).
**Puri Tours & Travel** ( ☎ 749 540; puri_bpn@indo.net .id; Jl Sutoyo 88) Sungai Mahakam specialist.
**River Tours** ( ☎ 081 253 312 333; fax 422 211; www .borneokalimantan.com) Ecotourism pro with 1st-class itineraries throughout KalTim and beyond.

**Transborneo Adventure** ( ☎ 762 671; tborneo@indo .net.id; Jl Sudirman 21) Established agency with broad menu.

## Sleeping
Most hotels are clustered north and west of Balikpapan Plaza with a clutch of budget places in Gunung Kawi, 2km up Jl Ahmad Yani on *angkot* routes 3 or 5.

### BUDGET
**Hotel Murni** ( ☎ 738 692; Jl P Antasari 2; s 60,000Rp, d 90,000-135,000Rp; ⊠ ) Popular family-run losmen has immaculate rooms on three floors, all with private *mandi*, some with Western toilet. Enjoy free flow water, coffee, tea and conversation on the lobby's enormous red leather sofa.

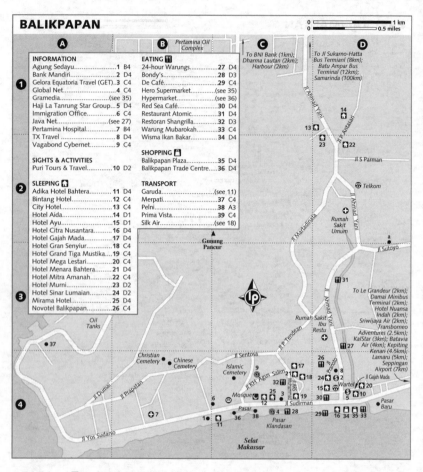

# BALIKPAPAN

| INFORMATION | | EATING 🍴 | |
|---|---|---|---|
| Agung Sedayu...................1 | B4 | 24-hour Warungs..............27 | D4 |
| Bank Mandiri....................2 | D4 | Bondy's.........................28 | D3 |
| Gelora Equatoria Travel (GET)..3 | C4 | De Café.........................29 | C4 |
| Global Net......................4 | C4 | Hero Supermarket........(see 35) | |
| Gramedia...................(see 35) | | Hypermarket...............(see 36) | |
| Haji La Tanrung Star Group....5 | D4 | Red Sea Café...................30 | D4 |
| Immigration Office..............6 | C4 | Restaurant Atomic..............31 | D4 |
| Java Net.....................(see 27) | | Restoran Shangrilla.............32 | D3 |
| Pertamina Hospital.............7 | B4 | Warung Mubarokah.............33 | C4 |
| TX Travel.......................8 | D4 | Wisma Ikan Bakar..............34 | D4 |
| Vagabond Cybernet.............9 | C4 | | |
| | | SHOPPING 🛍 | |
| SIGHTS & ACTIVITIES | | Balikpapan Plaza................35 | D4 |
| Puri Tours & Travel.............10 | D2 | Balikpapan Trade Centre.....36 | D4 |
| | | | |
| SLEEPING 🛏 | | TRANSPORT | |
| Adika Hotel Bahtera........11 | D4 | Garuda......................(see 11) | |
| Bintang Hotel.................12 | C4 | Merpati.........................37 | C4 |
| City Hotel......................13 | C4 | Pelni...........................38 | A3 |
| Hotel Aida....................14 | D1 | Prima Vista.....................39 | C4 |
| Hotel Ayu.....................15 | D1 | Silk Air.....................(see 18) | |
| Hotel Citra Nusantara......16 | D4 | | |
| Hotel Gajah Mada..........17 | D4 | | |
| Hotel Gran Senyiur..........18 | C4 | | |
| Hotel Grand Tiga Mustika...19 | C4 | | |
| Hotel Mega Lestari..........20 | C4 | | |
| Hotel Menara Bahtera.......21 | D4 | | |
| Hotel Mitra Amanah.........22 | C4 | | |
| Hotel Murni..................23 | D2 | | |
| Hotel Sinar Lumaian.........24 | D2 | | |
| Mirama Hotel................25 | D4 | | |
| Novotel Balikpapan.........26 | C4 | | |

---

**Hotel Ayu** ( ☎ 425 290; Jl P Antasari 18; r 120,000-180,000Rp; 🗗 ) Cosy hidden gem with a variety of homely layouts, including triples.

**Hotel Citra Nusantara** ( ☎ 425 366; fax 410 311; Jl Gajah Mada 76; r incl breakfast 125,000-235,000Rp; 🗗 ) Rule against unmarried couples sharing keeps this guest house extra clean. Higher priced options include hot water.

**our pick** **Hotel Gajah Mada** ( ☎ 734 634; fax 734 636; Jl Sudirman 328; s 125,000-275,000Rp, d 165,000-325,000Rp, all plus 10% tax; 🗗 ) Comfortable, spotless rooms off breezy corridors leading to waterfront terraces, and prime location make Gajah Mada a favourite with Indonesian travellers. Reservations a must.

**Hotel Mitra Amanah** ( ☎ 422 857; mitraamanah@ yahoo.com; Jl ARS Muhammad 31; s 150,000-345,000Rp, d

215,000-399,000Rp, all incl breakfast; 🗗 🛜 ) Friendly place with free extras including lobby wi-fi and airport shuttle.

More choices:

**Hotel Aida** ( ☎ 421 006; fax 733 940; Jl Ahmad Yani 1/12; d 105,000-245,000Rp, tr 135,000-275,000Rp, all incl breakfast; 🗗 ) Long red staircase leads to basic digs popular with students.

**Hotel Sinar Lumaian** ( ☎ 736 092; Jl Ahmad Yani 5/49; r 75,000-230,000Rp; 🗗 ) Range of well-kept, mainly fan-cooled rooms.

## MIDRANGE & TOP END

**City Hotel** ( ☎ 427 500; fax 419 789; Jl Sudirman 45; r incl breakfast 200,000-250,000Rp; ste 300,000Rp; 🗗 ) Still a deal – but not at prices on some websites – with hot-water shower and TV. Huge family suites include kitchen table, refrigerator and bathtub.

**Bintang Hotel** ( ☎ 735 908; bintangh@indosat.net .id; Komplek Pantai Mas Permai, Jl Sudirman; r incl breakfast 245,000-300,000Rp, f/ste 395,000-565,000Rp; ✗ ☐ ☎ ) Reliable waterfront rooms with friendly staff, in-room wi-fi with voucher, and travel agent on site.

**Hotel Nuansa Indah** ( ☎ 418 555; fax 412 138; Jl Sudirman 1; r incl breakfast 312,200-445,300Rp, ste 481,600-530,000Rp plus 21% tax; ✗ ☐ ☎ ☎ ) Opposite Damai Terminal, Nuansa Indah's new wing features a huge pool, fitness centre, plus free wi-fi in its swish lobby and 24-hour coffee shop. Simple to stylish rooms are good value and just a short walk to the beach. Nonsmoking rooms are available.

**Hotel Grand Tiga Mustika** ( ☎ 733 788; www.grandti gamustika.com; Jl ARS Muhammad 51; r incl breakfast 430,000-620,000Rp, ste 680,000-1,880,000Rp plus 21% tax; ✗ ☎ ) Rooms at this self-proclaimed 'three-star plus with four-star facilities' hotel include wired internet access, minibar, kettle, international TV and Chinese furnishings bordering on kitsch. For nonguests, pool packages (per person 30,000Rp weekdays, 40,000Rp weekends) include choice of meal or snack.

**Adika Hotel Bahtera** ( ☎ 738 000; www.bahteraho tel.com; Jl Sudirman 2; r incl breakfast 445,000-495,000Rp; ✗ ☐ ☎ ). This three-star predecessor of Hotel Menara Bahtera (below) features wi-fi in public areas and free cabled internet among in-room comforts. Shared facilities include swimming pool and business centre.

**Hotel Menara Bahtera** ( ☎ 758 7333; bahtera.bpn@ bahterahotel.com; Jl Gajah Mada 2; r incl breakfast weekends 450,000-500,000Rp, weekdays 550,000-700,000Rp; ✗ ☎ ☎ ) This sophisticated new four-star tower just behind Adika Hotel Bahtera (above) has wi-fi in the lobby and free cabled internet in the rooms.

**Hotel Mega Lestari** ( ☎ 411 811; www.hotelmeg atlestari.com; Jl ARS Muhammad 31; r incl breakfast 487,000-600,000Rp, ste 734,000-1,400,000Rp; ✗ ☐ ☎ ☎ ) Plush newbie has must-see staircase murals from Michelangelo to *Les Miserables*. Its richly furnished rooms, 20m pool, glass elevator with seaview, free wi-fi in the lobby and 24-hour coffee shop, frequently come with 20% discounts. Nonsmoking rooms are available.

**Le Grandeur** ( ☎ 420 155; bppres@legrandeurhotels .com; Jl Sudirman; r incl breakfast 740,000-890,000Rp; ste 750,000-1,250,000Rp; ✗ ☐ ☎ ☎ ) Luxury facilities at beachfront Le Grandeur (formerly The Dusit) include swimming pool, fitness centre, tennis courts and lounge bar. Special rates on indulgent rooms add extras like in-room wi-fi and executive lounge access.

**Hotel Gran Senyiur** ( ☎ 820 211; gran@senyiurhotels .com; Jl ARS Muhammad 7; r incl breakfast US\$120-140, ste US\$180-1100; ✗ ☐ ☎ ☎ ) Balikpapan's classiest choice mixes Kalimantan style – wood floors, Dayak *doyo* (bark beaten into cloth) on walls – with five-star luxury. Nonsmoking rooms are available.

More choices:

**Mirama Hotel** ( ☎ 412 442; www.hotel-mirama.com; Jl Pranoto 16; r incl breakfast 285,000-455,000Rp; ✗ ☐ ) Crisply renovated business-class rooms with 5% weekend discounts.

**Novotel Balikpapan** ( ☎ 820 820, 080 717 777 77; www.novotel.com/asia; Jl Brigjen Ery Suparjan 2; r 765,000-895,000Rp; ste 1,300,000Rp; ✗ ☎ ) Chic international sterility.

## Eating & Drinking

Find cheap eats along the waterfront particularly around Pasar Klandasan plus a pair of all-night warungs on Jl Pranoto. Most large hotels have international-class restaurants serving Western and tame Indonesian cuisine, plus pubs with some mix of live music, karaoke, and dancing. There's a fluid cast of clubs and karaoke among waterfront shophouses.

**our pick Warung Mubarokah** (Jl ARS Muhammad; mains 10,000-15,000Rp) Versatile, friendly warung on a breezy ridge with precooked *nasi campur* (rice with a choice of side dishes), fresh grilled fish and chicken, and beef soup bubbling on the cooker.

**Red Sea Café** ( ☎ 720 3379; F03, Ruko Bandar, Jl Sudirman; mains 20,000-30,000Rp; ☾ 5pm-midnight) Looking for a hookah? This eclectic spot in the burgeoning waterfront area worth exploring feeds the local fad for *shisha* (44,000Rp), Middle Eastern water pipes with sweet tobacco blends.

**Wisma Ikan Bakar** (Jl Sudirman 16; mains 20,000-45,000Rp; ☾ 11am-9.30pm) At 'Grilled Fish Inn' pick fish or seafood from the cooler and enjoy it *lalapan* style with hot sambal and fragrant *kemangi* leaves.

**Restoran Shangrilla** ( ☎ 423 124; Jl Ahmad Yani 250; mains 25,000-50,000Rp; ☾ 11am-3pm, 6-10.30pm) Specialities at this popular, family-run Chinese restaurant include *ikan delapan rasa* (eight-flavour fish) and steamboat.

**Restaurant Atomik** ( ☎ 422 868; Jl Pranoto 10; mains 20,000-50,000Rp; ✹ 10am-2pm, 6-10pm) Extensive Chinese menu features vegetarian options and 110,000Rp group packages.

**De Café** ( ☎ 739 267; Ruko Bandar Balikpapan, Jl Sudirman; mains 30,000-50,000Rp; ✹ 11am-2pm, 6-11pm; 📶 ) Expat-oriented spot to indulge cravings for Western (Chinese, Japanese or Indonesian) food, pizza, fancy coffees or treats from the bakery (open from 8am to 11pm), featuring free wi-fi and no-smoking section.

**Bondy's** ( ☎ 424285; Jl Ahmad Yani; mains 30,000-50,000Rp; ✹ 10am-10pm) Bondy's built its reputation as a beery garden oasis featuring fish on ice, imported steaks (80,000Rp to 110,000Rp), and Indonesian favourites. It's also a great place to enjoy bread, coffee and desserts from its bakery (open from 8am to 10pm) featuring homemade ice cream, and has an air-con, smokeless section.

**Kepiting Kenari** ( ☎ 764 018; Jl Marsuma R Iswahyudi; crabs 110,000Rp; ✹ 11am-10pm) Black-pepper crabs here are so good that seafood joints all over Kalimantan claim to be Kenari's partners. Each portion, in five varieties, serves three to four people. There's also chicken, fish and prawns on the menu, but why bother? On *angkot* route 7 toward the airport.

### SELF CATERING
These self-catering options have adjacent food courts:

**Hero Supermarket** (Balikpapan Plaza)
**Hypermarket** (Balikpapan Trade Centre)

## Getting There & Away
Visa on arrival is available at Seppingan Airport, Kalimantan's main air hub.

### AIR
**Silk Air** ( ☎ 730 800; Hotel Gran Senyiur, Jl ARS Muhammad 7) flies daily to Singapore. Fly to Jakarta with **Garuda** ( ☎ 422 301; Adika Hotel Bahtera, Jl Sudirman 2), **Batavia Air** ( ☎ 760 655, 887 0808; Jl Haryono), **Lion Air** ( ☎ 707 3761), **Mandala Air** ( ☎ 410 708; Blk H1/04, Jl Sudirman), **Sriwijaya Air** ( ☎ 749 777; H2/4 Komplek Balikpapan Permai), or **Air Asia** ( ☎ 021-5050 5088). Batavia, **Citilink** ( ☎ 080 410 808 08), Lion, Mandala and Sriwijaya fly to Surabaya. **Merpati** ( ☎ 424 452; B3-2, Komplek Pantai Mas Permai, Jl Sudirman), Garuda and Sriwijaya fly to Makassar, Sriwijaya via Palu. Batavia serves Yogyakartra and Manado.

Within Kalimantan, Batavia and **Trigana Air** ( ☎ 762 298) fly to Banjarmasin, Trigana

via Kota Baru. **KalStar** ( ☎ 737 473; Jl Sudirman 86), Batavia, Mandala and Swijiaya fly to Tarakan. Batavia, KalStar and Trigana fly to Berau. KalStar also flies to Samarinda and Nunukan. **Bintang Sendawar** ( ☎ 765 594) and **Susi Air** ( ☎ /fax 764 416, 081 1211 3086; Jl Pupuk Raya 33) fly to Samarinda and Melak. Susi continues to Data Dawai twice weekly.

### BOAT
**Agung Sedayu** ( ☎ 420 601) is the best source for all nautical transport information and tickets. See opposite.

**Dharma Lautan** ( ☎ 423 292; Ruko Tanah Citra Rapat, Jl Sukarno-Hatta) runs ferries twice weekly to Surabaya (275,000Rp, 36 hours) and weekly to Makassar (175,000Rp, 24 hours). **Prima Vista** ( ☎ 732 607; Jl Sudirman 138) serves Pare Pare (190,000Rp), Makassar and Surabaya. **Pelni** ( ☎ 424 171; Jl Yos Sudarso 76) sails to Makassar, Pare Pare (14 hours), Tarakan (195,000Rp, 24 hours), Pantoloan (115,000, 12 hours), Surabaya and beyond.

### BUS
Buses to Samarinda (economy/air-con 22,000/27,000Rp, 2½ hours) leave from Batu Ampar bus terminal at the north end of town. Buses to Banjarmasin (economy/air-con 130,000/150,000Rp, 12 hours) leave from a terminal on Jl Sukarno-Hatta. Use *angkot* route 3 for both.

## Getting Around
Taxis to/from Seppingan Airport cost 45,000Rp. Alternatively, route 7 *angkot* wait on the highway just outside the airport gate, bound for Damai Terminal. Transfer to route 1 or 3 for central Balikpapan.

Balikpapan Plaza is a focal point for *angkot* (3000Rp) routes in town, with *ojek* drivers along the fringes there and at other strategic spots.

## AROUND BALIKPAPAN
### KWPLH Sun Bear Centre
Sheltering five rescued *beruang madu*, **KWPLH Sun Bear Centre** (Kawasan Wisata Pendidikan Lingkungan Hidup, Environmental Education & Recreation Centre; ☎ 0542-710 8304; www.beruangmadu.org; Jl Balikpapan–Samarinda Km 23; ✹ 9am-5pm) showcases Asia's only bear species in its natural habitat. The bears' 1.3-hectare enclosure includes their favourite fruit trees. Visitors can observe the bears and feedings at 9am and 3pm from an elevated

boardwalk. There are also educational exhibits, flower gardens and a playground, plus children's activities on weekends. Take minibus number 8 (10,000Rp, 30 minutes) from Batu Ampar.

## Bukit Bangkirai

A 1500-hectare reserve noted for *bangkirai* trees, a hardwood favoured for roofing and shipbuilding, **Bukit Bangkirai** ( ☎ 0542-736 066; admission 15,000Rp; ☽ 8am-4pm) is best known for its rope **canopy bridge** (admission 50,000Rp), 30m above the jungle floor. From that perch, spot red monkeys, hornbills, macaques and gibbons. There's no public transport; charter a Kijang from Balikpapan (200,000Rp return, one hour, 50km) or Samarinda (300,000Rp return, two hours, 100km). The road can be impassable during rainy season.

## Mangrove Cruising

Sungai Wain's inlet to Balikpapan Bay features extensive mangrove forest to observe proboscis monkeys and bird life. For a boat tour, contact **Pak Rudeng** ( ☎ 0542-722 4099; per day 500,000Rp) or ask a tour agency.

## Samboja Lestari

This 1850-hectare reserve houses **Borneo Orangutan Survival Foundation** (BOS; www.orangutan.or.id) projects including orangutan reintroduction, sun bear protection, reforestation and research. Samboja Lestari is open to visitors on Saturday morning by appointment – other times by special arrangement – for **day visits** ( ☎ 0542-707 0485; fax 0542-413 069; www.sambojalodge.com; Jl Balikpapan-Handil Km 44; admission donation US$50 Saturday, US$70 other times). Charter a Kijang from Balikpapan (200,000Rp return, 45 minutes). BOS also operates **Samboja Lodge** ( ☎ 0542-711 1484; www.sambojalodge.com; s/d with meals US$110/160, ste US$130-320; ☒ ▯ ) for overnight stays. All rooms are nonsmoking. Guests can participate in projects by observing animal behaviour, cleaning enclosures or planting trees. Samboja Lestari also accepts volunteers; see p840

## SAMARINDA

☎ 0541 / pop 356,000

Usual launch point for journeys up spectacular Sungai Mahakam, Samarinda's reputation as a travellers' oasis is overdone. Suburban sprawl puts much of East Kalimantan's capital city beyond visitors' reach. Don't sweat what you may be missing in this urban jungle and head straight upriver to the forest.

## Orientation

Samarinda spreads from **Pasar Pagi** (Morning Market; Jl Sudirman) and **Mesra Indah Mall** (Jl Khalid) just opposite. *Angkot* (3000Rp) congregate here. Hotels cluster here, running north toward Tumendung Airport. The town centre extends east though **Citra Niaga** market, featuring souvenir and food vendors, to **Ramayana Mall** (or 'Samarinda Centre Plaza'; Jl Mulawarman) and west to Jl Awang Long. The striking central mosque, **Mesjid Raya Darussalam** (Jl Niaga Selatan), with its missile-like minarets, is between the markets. Riverboats leave from docks 3km west. En route, note the ornate **Islamic Centre**, opened in 2008, reputed to be the largest mosque in Southeast Asia. Long distance bus terminals are scattered around town.

### MAPS
**Karisma** (2nd fl, Ramayana Mall)

## Information
### INTERNET ACCESS
**Borneo Warnet** (Jl Abul Hassan; per hr 5000Rp; ☽ 9am-midnight)
**Sumangkat Internet** (Jl Haji Agus Salim 35; per hr 6000Rp; ☽ 8am-midnight) As well as intenet, it offers a postal service and wartel.

### MEDICAL SERVICES
**RS Bhakti Nguraha** ( ☎ 741 363; Jl Basuki Rahmat 150) Clinic.
**RS Haji Darjad** ( ☎ 732 698; Jl Dahlia) Large, modern hospital.

### MONEY
Banks along Jl Sudirman, including several just west of Pasar Pagi, exchange currency.

### TOURIST INFORMATION
**East Kalimantan Tourism office** ( ☎ 736 850; cnr Jl Sudirman & Jl Awang Long)

### TRAVEL AGENCIES
Many Samarinda travel agencies offer Mahakam tours. For air tickets:
**Angkasa Express** ( ☎ 200 281; aexsri@telkom.net; Plaza Lembuswana, Jl S Parman)
**Cendana Travel** ( ☎ 739 791; Jl Cendana 7) Delivers tickets.
**Prima Tour & Travel** ( ☎ 737 777; www.travelprima.com; Hotel MJ, Jl Khalid 1)

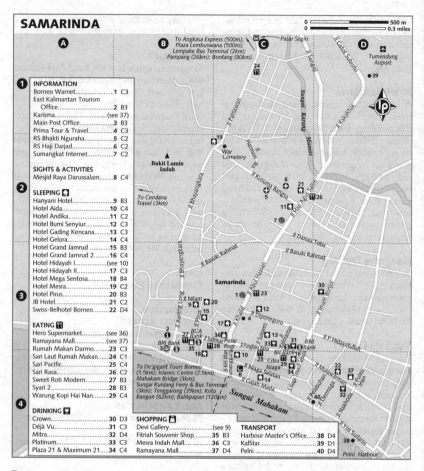

**SAMARINDA**

## Tours

Abundant independent guides help make Samarinda the preferred starting point for touring the mighty Mahakam and beyond. Guides with good reputations include **Junaid Nawawi** ( 081 253 630 0057; junaid.nawawi56@yahoo.com; Hotel Pirus; 2-5pm), **Rustam** ( 735 641, 081 258 549 15; rustam_kalimantan@yahoo.co.id) and **Suryadi** ( 081 645 982 63; Hotel Hadiyah I). **Jailani** ( 081 346 338 343; jailani.borneo_tours@yahoo.com; Hotel MJ) is a veteran guide recently returned to the trade.

**De'gigant Tours Borneo** ( 081 258 465 78; fax 777 6848; www.borneotourgigant; Jl Martadinata Rauda 1 No 21) is the new agency run by touring expert Lucas Zwaal. De'gigant is a Dayak word for clever.

For more information on Sungai Mahakam travel, see p642.

## Sights

Samarinda-style sarongs and *songket* are woven in **Samarinda Seberang** on the south side of Sungai Mahakam. Take a yellow *angkot* from Pasar Pagi or the nearby cross-river ferry then an *angkot* to Jl Nuri or Jl Aminah Syukur.

**Pampang** (26km west) has Kenyah Dayak ceremonies at its longhouse Sunday at 2pm. These are not made-for-tourist performances, and rituals are relatively unadulterated. Offer a small donation for snapping photographs. Public minibuses to Pampang (15,000Rp, one hour) leave from Segiri terminal. Chartering a taxi or Kijang with other travellers for around 150,000Rp is an alternative.

## Sleeping

### BUDGET

**Hotel Gelora** ( ☎ 742 024; gelora@smd.mega.net.id; Jl Niaga Selatan 62; r incl breakfast 100,000-225,000Rp; ste 300,000Rp; ✖ ) Samarinda's best budget choice, Gelora overlooks Citra Niaga market and is routinely overlooked by foreigners. Immaculate rooms include private *mandi*, with air-con from 150,000Rp. There's a canteen, travel agent and photocopy shop on premises.

**Hotel Gading Kencana** ( ☎ 731 512; fax 731 954; Jl Sulawesi 4; r incl breakfast 135,000-235,000Rp; ✖ ) Even fan-cooled economy rooms are spacious and have private *mandi* or Western bathroom. The 2nd-floor restaurant has a bright, breezy terrace.

**Hotel Aida** ( ☎ 742 572; Jl KH Mas Tumenggung 12; r incl breakfast 135,000-260,000Rp; ✖ ) Popular with domestic travellers, Aida's rooms all have private *mandi*, TV and telephone.

**Hotel Andika** ( ☎ 742 358; fax 747 389; Jl Haji Agus Salim 7; r incl breakfast 160,000-400,000Rp; ✖ 🛜 ) Bridging budget and midrange, Andika rooms all include air-con, TV and telephone. Economy rooms have shared bathrooms, and older rooms have better furniture than renovated ones. Wi-fi with voucher.

More choices:

**Hanyani Hotel** ( ☎ 742 653; Jl Pirus 31; r 100,000-170,000Rp; ✖ ) Large but neglected rooms merit discounts.

**Hotel Hidayah I** ( ☎ 731 210, 731 261; Jl KH Mas Temenggung; r incl breakfast 125,000-225,000Rp; ✖ ) Has seen better days.

**Hotel Hidayah II** ( ☎ 741 712; Jl Khalid 25; s 100,000Rp, d 175,000-200,000Rp, t 275,000Rp; ✖ ) Clean but worn.

### MIDRANGE

**Hotel Pirus** ( ☎ 741 873; fax 735 890; Jl Pirus 30; r from 195,000-350,000Rp; ✖ ) Renovated up from budget class, Pirus rooms have homely furnishings.

**JB Hotel** ( ☎ 737 688; management@jbhotel.net; Jl Haji Agus Salim 16; r 196,000-299,000Rp; ✖ 🖥 🛜 ) JB takes care of business travellers with big, bright rooms, and free wi-fi. Optional buffet breakfast costs 35,000Rp for two.

**Hotel Mega Sentosa** ( ☎ 749 218; fax 787 489; Jl Veteran 88; r incl breakfast 200,000-312,000Rp, ste 375,000Rp; ✖ ) Comfortable rooms (though most with tiny windows) and accommodating staff on a side street near Pasar Pagi. Extras include buffet breakfast, Western bathroom with hot/cold water, free-flow drinking water and 24-hour room service.

**Hotel Grand Jamrud** ( ☎ 743 828; fax 743 837; Jl Jamrud 34; r incl breakfast 200,000-385,000Rp; ✖ ) Grand Jamrud has sparkling, cosy rooms in a quiet spot. Very popular for business and government meetings.

**Hotel Grand Jamrud 2** ( ☎ 731 233; fax 736 096; Jl Panglima Batur 45; r incl breakfast 270,000-450,000Rp; ✖ ) Squeaky clean rooms with classy touches, such as wood floors, and has friendly staff. Is situated in the nightclub district.

### TOP END

**Hotel Mesra** ( ☎ 732 772; www.hotelmesra.com; Jl Pahlawan 1; r incl breakfast 400,000-750,000Rp, cottage 1,000,000Rp, ste 1,600,000Rp; ✖ 🖥 🛜 ) Mesra's sleek new, nosmoking, free wi-fi 'International' addition doesn't mesh with the rustic hilltop original. But its oversized cottages with Kalimantan decor still flawlessly combine extravagance and charm. Outsiders can use its two pools for 30,000Rp.

**Hotel Bumi Senyiur** ( ☎ 741 443; www.senyiurho tels.com; Jl Diponegoro 17-19; r incl breakfast 720,000-980,000Rp, ste 1,700,000-2,700,000Rp; ✖ 🖥 🛜 🛜 ) Absolutely 1st-class luxury. Tastefully indulgent rooms feature hardwood floors and rattan or wooden furniture. Nonsmoking rooms are available.

**Swiss-Belhotel Borneo** ( ☎ 200 888; www.swiss-belho tel.com; Jl Mulawarman 6; r incl breakfast 1,000,000-1,490,000Rp, ste 1,490,000Rp; ✖ 🖥 🛜 🛜 ) International-style hotel with bright, attractive rooms – half with river views – and a full range of facilities. Ask for discounts and deals for free wi-fi and spa. Nonsmoking rooms are available.

## Eating

For cheap Indonesian food and local specialties such as *udang galah*, try Jl Nilam, Jl Khalid or Citra Niaga. Mesra Indah Mall has a 4th-floor **food court** (mains 10,000-15,000Rp; 🕙 9am-9pm; 🛜 ) for Indonesia mainstays and free wi-fi, but music there is ridiculously loud.

**Syari 2** (Jl Sudirman; mains 10,000-15,000Rp) Busy, bright, family-run warung dishing homecooked, Banjar-style grilled fish and chicken, vegetarian choices, *nasi campur* and soups. Breakfast menu features *nasi kuning*.

**our pick Rumah Makan Darmo** ( ☎ 737 287; Jl Abul Hassan 38; mains 15,000-30,000Rp; 🕙 11am-2.30pm, 6-10pm) Rare Chinese restaurant attuned to individual diners and couples specialises in fresh seafood, with smoke-free air-con upstairs.

**Sari Laut Rumah Makan** ( ☎ 735 848; Jl Pahlawan; mains 25,000-40,000Rp; ⏰ 6-10pm) Local legend for *udang galah*, served fragrant, spicy or Padang style.

Outside major hotels and clubs (see below), it's tough finding restaurants that serve alcohol. For air-con dining with cold beer, try **Sari Rasa** ( ☎ 742 771; Jl Haji Agus Salim 26; mains 20,000-50,000Rp; ⏰ 10.30am-10.30pm) specialising in Chinese food and imported steaks (90,000Rp to 95,000Rp). Affiliate **Sari Pacific** ( ☎ 743 289; Jl Pagima Batu A5-7; mains 30,000-50,000Rp; ⏰ 11am-9.30pm) features Japanese food and steaks. Both also have Indonesian dishes, Western items and, for better or worse, karaoke.

Self-catering and snacks:

**Warung Kopi Hai Nan** (Jl Niaga Utara 50) A clean, well-lighted Chinese-Indonesian-Western bakery and coffee shop.

**Hero supermarket** (Mesra Indah Mall)

**Sweet Roti Modern** (Jl Sudirman 8) Bakery.

## Drinking

Samarinda's club scene has grown lately. Although karaoke and prostitution remain prominent, there's also live music, a friendly vibe and often interesting dining. Clubs open as early as 7pm, but nothing happens before 10.30pm. Closing times run 1am to 3am, cover charges 30,000Rp to 70,000Rp.

**Crown** (Jl Imam Bonjol 9) Focussed on music and booze.

**Deja Vu** (Jl Panglima Batur) Stylish club with sleek contemporary restaurant (mains 35,000Rp to 150,000Rp).

**Mitra** ( ☎ 741 335; Jl Mulawarman 17) Before live music, hostesses and karaoke in back, there's a relaxed cafe (mains 35,000Rp to 70,000Rp) serving eclectic international fare, plus free wi-fi.

**Platinum** (Jl Panglima Batur 61A) Hostess in high school uniform greets visitors.

**Plaza 21 & Maximum 21** (Jl Niaga Timur 21) Old school discos.

## Shopping

Citra Niaga shops sell Dayak rattan, *doyo*, carvings and other souvenirs. **Fitriah Souvenir Shop** (Jl Sudirman 10) offers high-quality items priced that way.

Get souvenirs of Bali, without visiting at **Devi Gallery** ( ☎ 081 346 533 888; Jl Nilam), a bright yellow shed with sarongs, bags, sandals, and other things Bali.

**Mesra Indah Mall** (Jl Khalid) has a mix of local and chain stores. **Ramayana Mall** (or 'Samarinda Centre Plaza'; Jl Mulawarman) is more upmarket, with more national and international chains, plus a four-screen cinema.

## Getting There & Away

### AIR

**KalStar** ( ☎ 742 110; Jl Gatot Subroto 80) and **Trigana** ( ☎ 746 721) fly to Berau, Tarakan and Nunukan. Trigana also flies to Balikpapan. **Bintang Sendawar** ( ☎ 707 0045) flies to Balikpapan and Melak.

**Susi Air** ( ☎ 791 3282/3) flies to Balikpapan, Long Ampung four times weekly and Data Dawai three times weekly. Balikpapan has a bigger airport and better connections.

### BOAT

Mahakam river boats (called *kapal biasa* or *kapal taxi*) leave by 7am (sometimes 6.30am) from Sungai Kunjang terminal (3km via *angkot* C) for Tenggarong (25,000Rp, two hours), Melak (124,000Rp, 16 hours), Long Iram (155,000Rp, 21 hours) and, sometimes, Long Bagun (250,000Rp, 36 hours).

Cross-Mahakam ferries to Samarinda Seberang (4000Rp) leave from the end of Jl KH Mas Tumenggung.

**Pelni** ( ☎ 741402; Jl Yos Sudarso 76) serves Pare Pare (170,000Rp, 24 hours), Surabaya (383,000Rp, three days) and Batu Licin (287,000Rp, two days) in South Kalimantan from the main harbour on Jl Yos Sudarso.

After an early 2009 sinking, private ferry service to/from Pare Pare was suspended. Ask the **harbour master** ( ☎ 741 046; Jl Yos Sudarso 2) for updates and for ships in port that may accept passengers.

### BUS

Samarinda has multiple bus terminals. Sungai Kunjang terminal serves Tenggarong (12,000, one hour), Kota Bangun (23,000Rp, three hours), Melak (125,000Rp, eight hours) and Balikpapan (economy/air-con 25,000/27,000Rp, 2½ hours). Use Lempake terminal on *angkot* route B at the north end of town for Bontang (25,000Rp, three hours), Sangatta (30,000Rp, four hours) and Berau (135,000Rp, 20 hours, but days during rainy season). Buses leave as filled from 6am until early afternoon. Minibuses for Sunday afternoon Dayak rituals at Pampang (15,000Rp, one hour) leave from Segiri terminal at the north end of Jl Pahlawan.

## Getting Around

Minibuses or taxis (3000Rp, be careful here you're not overcharged), converge at Pasar Pagi.

KALIMANTAN

Taxis from **Tumendung Airport** (3km) cost 50,000Rp. *Angkot* B passes the airport and drops passengers at the terminal for 10,000Rp. For an *angkot* from the airport, walk 100m to Jl Gatot Subroto and turn left.

## KUTAI NATIONAL PARK

Favourite of wild orangutan buffs, **Kutai National Park** (admission 15,000Rp, camera 30,000Rp, video 125,000Rp) encompasses 200,000 hectares of diverse ecosystems, from mangrove swamps to highland hardwoods, including Indonesia's largest, relatively untouched ironwood (*ulin*) forest. Still recovering from fires in 1997–98 it faces new threats from illegal loggers and wildcat miners for its coal, oil and gas. Park authorities have enlisted legitimate timber and energy companies working nearby in preservation efforts.

Orangutans are concentrated in Kutai's coastal areas, along with other primate species, including slow loris, proboscis and leaf monkeys. Sun bear, deer, flat-headed cat and other mammals are found throughout the park. Bird species includes sea eagle, stork and myna. Treks feature encounters with golf ball–sized, tiger-striped beetles straight out of Alice's Wonderland, as well as jungle orchids. Cruising the park's numerous waterways is another option for spotting wildlife.

Visitors must register with the park's **Bontang headquarters** (PHKA; ☎ 0548-27218; Jl Mulawarman 236; ☺ 7.30am-4pm Mon-Thu, 8am-noon Fri) or **Sangatta office** (PHKA; ☎ 0549-24651; Jl Suromo; ☺ 7.30am-4pm Mon-Thu, 8am-noon Fri); call ahead for weekend arrivals. Park personnel can help with transport and guides (per day 200,000Rp). Buses run from Samarinda's Lempake terminal to Bontang (25,000Rp, three hours) and Sangatta (30,000Rp, four hours).

Overnight accommodation is at basic **guest houses** (per person 100,000Rp) at Sangkimah near Bontang and Camp Kakap near Sangatta. Facilities are rudimentary; bring your own food and bedding, plus mosquito repellent. Visitors give higher marks to Camp Kakap, particularly if there's room at the University of Kyoto research facility with mattresses and a better equipped kitchen. Contact **Pak Willis** ( ☎ 081 347 423 297) for availability and details. The 30-minute boat ride from Sangatta costs 400,000Rp (return) for up to four people.

Orangutans are best seen early mornings and late afternoons. Wild orangutans can be hard to find, though sightings are reported most often around Camp Kakap.

Many guides and tour agencies in Balikpapan (p633) and Samarinda (p638) offer Kutai itineraries.

## TENGGARONG

☎ 0541 / pop 78,000

Once capital of the mighty Kutai sultanate, Tenggarong is now visited for its Dayak festival and museum recalling those glory days, usually as a day trip from Samarinda or stop on Sungai Mahakam journeys.

In the former palace of sultans who ruled for 19 generations, **Mulawarman Museum** (Jl Diponegoro; admission 2500Rp, camera 5000Rp, video 10,000Rp; ☺ 9am-4pm, closed Mon & Fri) displays royal relics, ceramics and an (unintentionally) hilarious collection of traditional headwear from every Indonesian province. Behind the museum, the current **Kedaton Kertanegara** (Sultan's Palace) has elaborate wooden balconies and stained-glass windows.

Dayaks from throughout Kalimantan attend the annual **Erau Festival**. Though touristy, it's a chance to see traditional dances and rituals amid a vast intertribal party. The festival is usually held in late September for one to two weeks. Get upcoming dates from Tenggarong's **tourism office** ( ☎ 661 042; fax 661 093; Jl Ahmad Yani 12) or the Bahasa Indonesia website http://erau.kutaikartanegara.com.

For overnight stays, **Hotel Anda Dua** ( ☎ 661 817; Jl Sudirman 52; r incl breakfast 120,000-160,000Rp; ✷ ) and **Hotel Karya Tapin** ( ☎ 661 258; Jl Maduningrat 29; r incl breakfast 175,000-200,000Rp; ✷ ) are good budget options. **Hotel Lesong Batu** ( ☎ 663 499; www.kutaikartanegara.com/lesongbatu; Jl Panji 1; r incl breakfast 531,000-601,000Rp, ste 2,108,000Rp; ✷ ) is fit for a sultan.

**Rumah Makan Tepian Pandan** (Jl Diponegoro 23; mains 15,000-25,000Rp) has tasty Indonesian meals on the river opposite the museum. Cheerful **Rumah Makan Banjar** ( ☎ 661 782; Jl Sudirman 62; meals 18,000Rp-30,000Rp; ☺ 9am-9pm) features grilled fish and chicken.

Find buses to/from Samarinda (12,000Rp, one hour) and Kota Bangun (25,000Rp, two hours) at **Petugas terminal** on Tenggarong's southern riverfront. Get to town by *angkot* (3000Rp) or *ojek* (10,000Rp).

From Samarinda, you can take a morning bus or *kapal biasa* (25,000Rp, two hours), visit the museum and then continue upriver from Kota Bangun by *kapal biasa* that afternoon.

**KALIMANTAN**

## SUNGAI MAHAKAM

Combining cultural and natural wonders, 920km-long Sungai Mahakam is rightly renowned and richly rewarding. The river provides easy access – by Kalimantan standards – to traditional communities and stunning scenery. Along the river, there are signs of industrialisation, especially massive coal barges; on tributaries and small lakes, they're overwhelmed by jungle and communities that accept modernisation on their terms.

Double-deck passenger ferries (*kapal biasa* or *kapal taxi*) leave Samarinda daily by 7am. On the open lower deck, passengers use sarongs or newspapers to mark personal space. A canteen serves instant noodle variations. On the upper level, simple mattresses are laid across the floor for sleeping. If you are travelling overnight, head upstairs to claim one for 20,000Rp. Bedding is clean (usually), and the atmosphere is relaxed and friendly. Better boat engines have worked to slash travel times.

Alternatively, combine bus or ferry travel with chartering your own *ces*. Rates start from 100,000Rp per hour and 500,000Rp per day. Most tour operators offer houseboats, some with air-con cabins, but expect to pay plenty for the luxury.

Much of the year, *kapal biasa* terminate at Long Iram (155,000Rp, 18 hours), 409km from Samarinda. When the river is right, boats continue to rapids at Long Bagun (250,000Rp, 36 hours, 523km).

To explore further, charter a *ces*. It's an 18-hour trip from Long Bagun to **Long Pahangai** through some of the Mahakam's most explosive waters. Only attempt this stretch with seasoned local boaters. Running with the current back to Long Bagun takes six or seven hours.

Boats continue upriver to Long Apari, focal point for cross-Borneo trips. From there it's a trek of at least three days to Sungai Kapuas' headwaters in West Kalimantan.

On the lower Mahakam, it's easy to travel independently. In its upper reaches, Bahasa Indonesia and/or guides are essential. Some travellers hire guides along the river, others begin the trip with them (see p633 and p638 for Mahakam guides and tour operators). Guide rates start at 150,000Rp per day (plus food, transport and accommodation). Even without a guide, Mahakam travel gets expensive beyond *kapal biasa*, with charter

---

> ### MOWING DOWN THE MAHAKAM
>
> The most common form of transport beyond Sungai Mahakam's beaten waterways is the *ces*, a motorised canoe with a long propeller shaft. This innovation was launched in 1990 when an enterprising boater attached a 2½HP engine to the back of his canoe. The name – pronounced chess – comes from the sound of the engine starting, and it stuck. Coursing the river with the power of a lawnmower must have been rough; most engines these days are 20HP or more.

---

rates from 100,000Rp per hour for a *ces* and 1,000,000Rp per hour for speedboats.

Along the river, ask about Dayak festivals and celebrations. As modernisation steams ahead, such events are the best opportunities to observe genuine traditional culture. Sometimes modernisation helps: West Kutai's provincial tourism website, www.wisata-kutaibarat.com, has information on festivals and other useful tips, albeit in Bahasa Indonesia.

### Kota Bangun

A shipbuilding town and transport interchange, Kota Bangun is the gateway to Mahakam lake country. From Samarinda, travellers can take a bus here (23,000Rp, three hours, 105km) instead of eight hours via *kapal biasa*. From Kota Bangun, bargain for a *ces* along Mahakam 'backroads' via Muara Muntai (150,000Rp; 1½ hours), Tanjung Isuy (350,000Rp; three hours), and Mancong (500,000Rp; six hours). Boat operators set official prices for *ces* routes, but you'll need luck (or a good guide) to get those rates.

For an English-speaking guide, contact local schoolteacher **Maskur** ( ☎ 085 250 529 777). His wife runs **Warung Anneesha** ( ☎ 081 2553 2287; Jl Ahmad Yani; mains 10,000-15,000Rp), serving fresh grilled fish with mild, tomato-rich *sambal*, 10m from the bus station.

To try spotting the critically endangered Irrawaddy dolphin (*pesut* in Bahasa Indonesia; see opposite) take a *ces* – never a speedboat for dolphins – to Muara Muntai via Danau Semayang and Sungai Pela. But there's better dolphin watching at Muara Pahu (p644).

Alternatively, charter a *ces* to Muara Kaman, 1½ hours north, site of Kalimantan's first Hindu kingdom, with renowned fishing.

It's about 30 minutes further through Kedang Kepala to Danau Siran for abundant birdlife, monkeys and spectacular sunsets. Beware: the losmen in Muara Kaman is dismal.

In Kota Bangun, **Losmen Mukjizat** (Jl Mesjid Raya 46; r 50,000Rp), opposite the main mosque, has clean, basic rooms with shared *mandis*.

## Muara Muntai

In the heart of Mahakam lake country, Muara Muntai's handsome ironwood buildings are connected by sturdy boardwalks over mud flats. At prayer times, this Banjar village may resemble a ghost town. It's a good spot for chartering *ces* to Tanjung Isuy (250,000, 1½ hours) or Mancong (350,000Rp, 3½ hours) through scenic Sungai Ohong.

The three losmen in town all offer shared bathrooms, fans and free-flowing coffee, tea and water. Left of the dock, **Penginapan Srimuntai** (per person 50,000Rp) is newest, with spotless rooms and a TV on its terrace overlooking the central boardwalk. Further along, behind a photocopy shop, **Penginapan Adi Guna** (☎ 0541-205 871, 081 545 146 578; per person 50,000Rp) has Western bathrooms and its own TV terrace. Around the bend, right of the dock, friendly **Penginapan Tiara** (☎ 081 347 376 794; s/d 30,000/50,000Rp) features a breezy balcony with views of the river and will whip up meals with advance notice. Otherwise, try the handful of warungs along the boardwalk.

Reach Muara Muntai from Samarinda by *kapal biasa* (100,000Rp, 10 hours) or bus to Kota Bangun (50,000Rp, three hours) then *ces* (150,000Rp, 1½ hours).

## Tanjung Isuy

A favourite with tour groups, Tanjung Isuy on the southwest shore of Danau Jempang is the Mahakam's first longhouse village, with Banuaq Dayak (and Banjar) residents. Don't expect traditional dress and tattoos, but mobile phones and motorcycles. Modernity remains largely skin deep, though. Village life is still about rising with the roosters, watching the river flow and chatting on the front porch while catching the evening breeze.

Welcome ceremonies greet tour groups at **Louu Taman Jamrout**, a longhouse vacated in the 1970s, refurbished by provincial authorities as a craft centre and losmen. Performances in Louu Taman Jamrout are certainly commercial, but they're also lively, rhythmic and fun for all. Social anthropologists may find the combination of Kenyah, Kayan and Banuaq dance disconcerting, but it's a real crowd

---

### RASI TO SAVE DOLPHINS

The Irrawaddy dolphin (*Ocaella brevirostris*; *pesut* in Bahasa Indonesia) is a provincial symbol of KalTim, and into the 1980s, *pesut* were common all along Sungai Mahakam to Samarinda. A completely protected species since 1990, *pesut* suffer high mortality rates due to gillnet entanglement and, to a lesser extent, boat collisions. More subtly, their habitat is threatened by pollution from speedboats and coal barges, chemical waste from mining, depletion of prey through unsustainable fishing techniques and sedimentation in lakes.

**Yayasan Konservasi RASI** (Conservation Foundation for Rare Aquatic Species of Indonesia; www.geocities.com/yayasan_konservasi_rasi) fights to save the *pesut*. It runs education, sustainable fisheries and reforestation programs to fight habitat destruction. These efforts have helped *pesut* population increase from 65 in 2003 to 91 in 2009. The foundation also works to move coal traffic off the river to create a 70km conservation area along the Mahakam and tributaries, centred at Muara Pahu, where YK-RASI has opened a **Mahakam Information Centre** with a riverside verandah for dolphin-watching.

The foundation has trained boatmen on the best techniques to spot dolphins. From Muara Pahu, **dolphin spotting trips** (☎ 081 253 729 933) run one hour to all day (150,000Rp to 500,000Rp) starting with Sungai Bolowan to Kedang Pahu, or to Jintan, a black-water river leading into peat swamp. For long trips, bring lunch and plenty of water. **De'gigant Tours Borneo** (☎ 081 258 465 78; fax 777 6848; www.borneotourgigant) arranges trips here direct from Balikpapan or Samarinda, donating a portion of the proceeds to YK-RASI.

Combine dolphin watching with *ces* transport to Maura Muntai or Tanjung Isuy (450,000Rp; via Mancong 600,000Rp) through Sungai Baroh, rich with birds and monkeys; to Melak (600,000Rp); or south to Dayak villages Damai or Lambing (750,000Rp).

pleaser. If there's no ceremony scheduled during your visit, arrange one for 500,000Rp.

Tanjung Isuy's two best losmen are next to each other, about 500m from the jetty. **Losmen Wisata** (Jl Indonesia Australia; per person 50,000Rp) has one- and two-bed rooms off a central dining area. The airy common space has wall-to-wall windows for superior views, and long, conversation-inducing tables. Neighbouring **Louu Taman Jamrout** ( ☎ 081 347 183 352; Jl Indonesia Australia; per person 50,000Rp), the dance venue, has a more rustic feel and one large bed per room. Both losmen have shared *mandis*, mosquito nets and fans, plus generators to cope with frequent power outages.

*Doyo*, weavings and *mandau* (machetes) with carved handles (as well as a lot of junk) are available at reasonable prices at Louu Taman Jamrout's shop. Some villagers also sell crafts.

### GETTING THERE & AWAY
Tanjung Isuy is not on the *kapal biasa* route. Chartering a *ces* from Muara Muntai (250,000Rp, 1½ hours) or Melak (650,000Rp, four hours) is the easiest way there. A public *ces* to Muara Muntai leaves daily in the early evening (from 60,000Rp, depending on the number of passengers). You can charter a *ces* direct to Kota Bangun (350,000Rp, three hours), then catch a bus and be in Samarinda or Balikpapan that night. In dry season, Tanjung Isuy is 30 minutes by Kijang (250,000Rp) or ojek (100,000Rp) from Mancong.

### Muara Pahu
Critically endangered Irrawaddy dolphins (*pesut*; see box p643) are the reason to linger at Muara Pahu, Sungai Mahakam's confluence with Sungai Kedang Pahu. Less than 100 *pesut*, lacking the bottle nose of their saltwater cousins, remain, mainly in the small section of wetland from Danau Semayang through various tributaries to Muara Pahu.

*Kapal biasa* to/from Samarinda (100,000Rp, 12 hours) reach Muara Pahu in the early evening. **Pengingapan Anna** (per person 60,000Rp), left of the dock, has spotless rooms in a family home. Find warungs along the boardwalk.

### Mancong
Cruising to Mancong along Sungai Ohong, its banks teeming with wildlife and flowering trees reaching into and across the waterway, is one of Kalimantan's scenic highlights. Majestic hornbills soar above, dazzling kingfishers skim the water and proboscis monkeys paddle across while macaques skitter along branches above.

Mancong recalls life on the Mahakam before logging, oil and coal dominated. Forest still surrounds the village almost entirely. A two-storey **longhouse** (*lamin*) is the grandest structure with a dozen totems in front, rebuilt with government assistance in 1987 on the ruins of the 1930s original. The village's 32 families have separate houses, so the *lamin* is reserved for folk dances and ceremonies. Just one family lives in the longhouse, so it must be the cleanest, most orderly in Borneo. Overnight guests are welcome (per person 60,000Rp; no bedding, food or electricity). Ask for permission to stay from the family or at the crafts shop in front of the longhouse. Ceremonies can be arranged here; ask a guide or tour agency in Samarinda or Balikpapan for help.

To visit Mancong, charter a *ces* from Tanjung Isuy (250,000Rp return) early in the morning. Ask the boater to go slowly to enjoy the scenery, lengthening the trip to as much as three hours each way. Or visit en route to/from Melak (700,000Rp, four hours). In dry season, it's possible to go to/from Tanjung Isuy in 30 minutes by *ojek* (100,000Rp) or Kijang (250,000Rp) but travelling by land misses the riverside scenery.

## UPPER MAHAKAM
### Melak & Around
Founded as a depot serving rubber plantations, Melak is now a coal centre, a far cry from local fishing villages. Busloads of miners in safety vests and rubber boots hit town at every shift change. For tourists, the quarry is Dayak communities and other attractions on the Barong Tongkok peninsula west of town, reaching as far as Tering by road. Amid modern trappings, traditional beliefs remain particularly strong in these areas, making ceremonies real treats. You can also find genuine crafts at the *Pasar Seni* (Art Market) to the left of the dock on Jl A Yani. To finance shopping, BRI bank's ATM on Jl Tendean accepts international cards.

The famed black orchids of Kersik Luway **orchid reserve** (16km southwest) bloom mainly in December and January, but there are flowers galore year round. Fires in 1997–98 and since have cut orchid species from 72 to 53, still plenty to please aficionados and amateurs alike. Bring water for the trails. Motorcycles handle the execrable road here better than cars.

The area also has several waterfalls, including 3m-high **Ambau Asa** (15km southwest), and across the Mahakam at **Gemuruh** (7km northeast), accessible by *ojek* or *ces* through riverside rice fields.

**Mencimai** (24km southwest) has an excellent **museum** ( ☎ 081 347 146 063; admission by donation; ☽ 8am-2pm Mon-Fri) with explanations in English and Bahasa Indonesia of Banuaq methods of shifting cultivation, collecting wild honey, trapping pigs (and monkeys) and producing *doyo* (bark beaten into cloth). It also displays antique *mandau*, rattan and other relics. Outside regular hours, call for a private opening.

Tiny **Eheng** (27km southwest) has a patched longhouse built in 1960 housing 30 Benuaq families, although they spend most of their time away, farming rice or collecting rattan, rubber and other forest products. Many return Monday night to gossip and gamble ahead of Tuesday's weekly market. Residents welcome visitors to join the fun, even stay overnight, but it helps to speak Bahasa Indonesia. You'll need to pay to stay – rates vary – provide your own bedding and food (there's a warung across the road), plus gifts (see p604). Crafts, mainly woven-rattan items, are specialities. There's another small modern Benuaq longhouse at **Pasek** (17km southwest).

The Benauq longhouse at **Benung** (20km southwest) is older, larger and more tourist-friendly. It has seven families and an excellent group of totems outside. *Sandung*, the final resting place for Dayak bones, are richly decorated with carvings and lively colours. The longhouse has mattresses for guests and lets them cook up whatever they buy at the nearby warung.

Some guides offer treks between Eheng and Benung (two hours), continuing south to **Damai** and **Lambing** (one day) featuring rattan longhouses. It's possible to continue from there to Tanjung Isuy, sleeping in the jungle, with the option of joining a village hunting trip.

## Sleeping & Eating

In Melak, look for accommodation along the two main streets, riverfront Jl A Yani and Jl Tendean, which runs west, becoming Jl Dr Sutomo.

**Penginapan Rahmat Abadi** ( ☎ 0545-41007; Jl Tendean; s 30,000Rp; d 55,000-65,000Rp) Clean guest house above a shop with fans, shared *mandi*, TV lounge and long tables to enjoy free-flow coffee, tea and water. Its lone room with private bathroom has enough electric outlets to recharge your phone, camera and MP3 player.

**Hotel Flamboyant** ( ☎ 081 253 231 994; Jl A Yani; r 80,000-130,000Rp; ✖ ) Friendly place with big rooms featuring choice of private or shared bathroom (all with *mandi* and Western toilet), fan or air-con and TV. Along the riverfront, 40m to the right of the dock, beware of flooding during rainy season.

**Hotel Monita** ( ☎ 0545-41798; Jl Dr Sutomo 76; r incl breakfast 110,000-300,000Rp plus 21% tax; ✖ ) About 2km uphill from the dock, thoroughly modern Monita has immaculate rooms, all with private bathrooms. Options include hot water shower and air-con.

**Warung Ketapang** (Jl A Yani; mains 10,000-15,000Rp) Serves barbecued river fish with a home-cooked veggie buffet. Find food stalls around the bus station, adjacent to *Pasar Seni*.

## Getting Around & Away

The best way to visit sights around Melak is by *ojek* (per half-day/day 100,000-125,000/150,000Rp). You can rent a motorcycle without a driver for the same price, but you're inviting hassles. Kijangs cost 550,000Rp to 650,000Rp per day, depending on destinations. Ask your accommodation about transport or contact **Pak Aripin** ( ☎ 081 347 385 842), self-appointed local tourism coordinator.

*Kapal taxi* from Samarinda to Long Iram (35,000Rp, five hours) arrive between 9pm and 11pm and leave 30 minutes after docking. Boats to Samarinda (124,000Rp, 16 hours, 325km) depart between 11am and 2pm. To/from Tanjung Isuy, charter a *ces* (700,000Rp, four hours).

Buses to Samarinda (125,000Rp, eight hours) over good roads leave several times daily beginning at 7am from the terminal left of the dock. Buses pass Muara Lawa (22,000Rp, two hours) near Damai and Lambing. Both villages have losmen. Paved roads now run northeast to Tering but the only land transport is by chartered car (150,000Rp, 1½ hours).

**Bintang Sendawar** ( ☎ 0545-41969) flies to Samarinda (680,000Rp) and Balikpapan (815,000Rp); at the time of research, Data Dawai service was suspended pending runway reconstruction there.

## Tering & Long Iram

Often the last stop for *kapal taxi*, **Long Iram** (155,000Rp, 21 hours from Samarinda) is a pleasant village on a bend in Sungai Mahakam with a handful of colonial buildings. Beyond here rapids make the river impassable when water gets too high or too low.

From the village centre it's a stroll through market gardens or a short *ces* (60,000Rp, 40 minutes) to **Tering**, three settlements straddling the Mahakam. Walk north along Jl Soewondo, turn right at the path to the police station and cross scenic bridges to **Danau Gap** (3km). Some residents of **Tering Lama**, a Bahau Dayak village on the northern bank, still sport traditional tattoos and elongated earlobes. The village also has four wooden totems and a magnificent church at its eastern end. Ceremonies can be arranged here for 1,500,000Rp. **Losmen Susanti** (r per person 75,000Rp) has simple, decent accommodation.

To stay overnight in Long Iram, get dropped at the floating cafe on the east bank, climb to the main road, turn right and look for the tiny sign (opposite the two-storey shops) for **Penginapan Wahyu** (Jl Soewondo 57; r per person incl breakfast 40,000Rp).

Down the road, **Warung Lestari** (Jl Soewondo; mains 12,000-20,000Rp) still has the best food on the Mahakam. Order whatever's on the stove.

## Datah Bilang

Site of several longhouses, Datah Bilang is a Protestant community of Kenyah and Bahau Dayaks, relocated from the Apokayan Highlands in the 1970s. Some older women have traditional elongated earlobes and charge from 25,000Rp for photographs. **Long Hubung** is another Bahau Dayak village with a basic **losmen** (r 50,000Rp).

Travellers with a thirst for back roads and good knowledge of Bahasa Indonesia can tackle Sungai Merah northeast into the highlands then cross to Tabang, a rare route that takes around four to five days, with a two day option to Maura Wahau before reaching Sungai Belayan. Or continue directly to Kota Bangun via Sungai Belayan (see opposite). Trekking experience, equipment, food and a Kenyah or Punan guide are essential; ask around in Datah Bilang and expect to pay at least 250,000Rp per day.

## Long Bagun to Long Apari

Under favourable conditions, *kapal biasa* from Samarinda reach **Long Bagun** (250,000Rp, 36 hours), a small settlement with an abandoned longhouse, a decent shop for supplies, and basic accommodation at **Penginapan Artomorow** (r 50,000Rp) and **Losmen Polewali** (☎ 081 350 538 997; r 50,000Rp). Rapids and shallows that restrict access for large vessels also protect forests to the east and dampen the impact of modernisation.

From Long Bagun, travellers can charter boats or trek through primary and secondary forests. Losmen Polewali organises treks to **Batu Ayu**. A two-night trip costs about 1,000,000Rp for two; contact the losmen or **Ibu Sari** (☎ 081 253 117 493) in Samarinda. It's an exciting trip through treacherous rapids – sometimes too rough for boats – to the next major settlement, **Long Pahangai**, (650,000Rp, four hours), then another day to Long Apari. **Long Lunuk**, between Long Pahangai and Long Apari, is a base for visiting Kenyah villages, featuring tall houses rather than longhouses. Alternatively, stay at **Tiong Ohang**, a strongly traditional community two hours upstream from Long Lunuk (250,000Rp). **Long Apari**, the uppermost longhouse village on the Mahakam is spectacularly scenic. A boat from Long Lunuk takes five to six hours (1,000,000Rp). From here, cross-Borneo trekkers veer toward West Kalimantan. Or turn north toward the Apokayan Highlands; see p650 for more information.

It's possible to see Sungai Mahakam from the top by flying to Data Dawai, an airstrip near Long Lunuk. However, at the time of research, the airstrip was closed for reconstruction.

## SUNGAI KEDANG KEPALA

Sungai Kedang Kepala branches north from the Mahakam near **Muara Kaman** and has regular boat service. The trip from Samarinda to **Muara Wahau** takes three days and two nights, via Kenyah and Bahau villages: **Tanjung Manis**, **Long Noran** and **Long Segar**. The main attraction is seeing what few tourists see. Villages are isolated and many inhabitants have moved to more convenient locations. Nearby caves held 5th-century Sanskrit finds, now in Tenggarong's museum. To explore independently, charter a motorised canoe for 250,000Rp daily or a speedboat for 1,500,000Rp.

An alternative route from Samarinda to Berau goes north by boat from Muara Wahau to **Miau Baru**. Then try finding a boat on Sungai Kelai, or continue by land, hitching rides or hiring a Kijang to Berau.

## SUNGAI BELAYAN

An adventurous yet cultural route follows Sungai Belayan, branching northwest from the Mahakam at Kota Bangun, to **Tabang**. Chartered longboats from Samarinda to Tabang (650,000Rp) take three days and two nights. A chartered *ces* from Kota Bangun to Tabang only takes a day, but the convenience costs more than 2,500,000Rp.

Tabang can also be reached from the upper Mahakam (see opposite). Find a guide at either end to trek through traditional rainforests of nomadic Punan Dayaks.

## BERAU

☎ 0554 / pop 60,000

At the confluence of Sungai Kelai and Sungai Segah (forming Sungai Berau), Berau is also known as Tanjung Redep. Tourists visit primarily en route to Pulau Derawan.

Technically, Tanjung Redep is the spit of land between the rivers that's Berau's centre. Before dark, there aren't many surprises. At night, Jl A Yani comes alive with coffee and snack stalls lining the riverfront (and wi-fi with voucher until 10pm). Turning the corner onto Jl Antasari, fruit vendors and food stalls feature more substantial fare, leading to the night market on Jl Soetomo.

### Information

Find ATMs and banks for currency exchange along Jl P Antasari/Jl Maulana.

**HG Computer** (Jl Mangga II; per hr 6000Rp; ⊙ 24hr) HG has chairs or floor booths, plus air-con. Tell the *angkot* driver 'Jl Mangaa Dua'.

**MicroNet** (Jl Anggur 379; per hr 6000Rp; ⊙ 9am-midnight) Well-hidden internet for grown-ups take Jl Pemuda to the (asphalt) soccer field, turn left on Jl Mangga I, left again on Jl Anggur.

**Rumah Sakit Abdul Rifai** (Jl Pulau Panjang) Hospital.

**Speedy** (Jl Mangga II; per hr 6000Rp; ⊙ 24hr) About 100m from HG Computer with comfy floor pillows and air-con.

**THM Travel** (☎ 21238; Jl Niaga II) Friendly agency for local advice and flight bookings.

**Tourism office** (☎ 21159; Jl Permai 35) Enthusiastically dispenses limited information.

### Sights & Activities

Across Sungai Segah, **Museum Batiwakkal** (admission by donation; ⊙ 8am-1pm Mon-Thu & Sat, 8-11am Fri) recounts the local sultanate's complex history with rival Sambaliung, across Sungai Kelai.

Across the bridge from the market, there's a big **Balinese Temple** built by islanders employed in the region.

### Sleeping & Eating

At the time of research, budget favourite **Hotel Central Graha** (☎ 22580; Jl A Yani) was closed for renovation.

**Penginapan Family** (☎ 24334; Jl Panglima Batur 384; r 50,000-60,000Rp) Welcoming, clean, worn place to crash if you blew your budget diving.

**Hotel Nirwana** (☎ /fax 21893; Jl Aminuddin 715; r incl breakfast 77,000-209,000Rp; ✷ ) Choose between fan and shared *mandi* upstairs, and fan or air-con with private *mandi* downstairs, at what management calls 'the hotel with the Muslim atmosphere', despite its Buddhist name.

**Sanggam Hotel** (☎ 21353; Jl Sudirman; r incl breakfast 110,000-230,000Rp; ✷ ) New hotel in an old building, Sanggam's renovation preserves many enchanting details. Rooms range from fan-cooled with one bed to air-con with two queen-size beds, all including private Western bathroom and attentive staff.

**Hotel Rahayu** (☎ 21142; cnr Jl Panglima Batur & Jl Gajah Mada; r 120,000-160,000Rp; ✷ ) Blindingly efficient and absolutely spotless Rahayu's cosy rooms all feature private *mandi* or Western bathroom. Great value in a central spot.

**Hotel Sederhana** (☎ 21353; Jl P Antasari; r incl breakfast 235,000-325,000Rp; ✷ ⊚ ) Sederhana has big, fully featured rooms, free evening wi-fi in the coffee shop, and a tasty breakfast buffet. But it needs a good scrubbing.

**Hotel Derawan Indah** (☎ 24255; fax 24252; Jl Panglima Batur 396; r incl breakfast 250,000-350,000Rp, ste 700,000Rp; ✷ ⊚ ) Immaculate, generous rooms, swimming pool and lighted tennis court on the roof are a hit with families.

**Bumi Segah** (☎ 24041; fax 21534; Jl Pulau Sampit 747; r incl breakfast 300,000-375,000Rp; ✷ ⊚ ) Favoured by travellers for Berau Coal and the Nature Conservancy, Bumi Segah's pampering rooms set a new milestone in carbon offsetting.

**Sari Ponti Restaurant** (☎ 23616; Jl AK Sanipa I; mains 15,000-25,000Rp; ⊙ 11am-2.30pm, 5-9.30pm) This family-run place aims to please with Chinese seafood, chicken, pigeon, beef and vegetarian choices. Look for young coconuts outside.

Warungs along Jl A Yani and Jl Niaga serve Indonesian standards from early morning until late night. For a fish dinner, find a crowded food stall along Jl Antasari.

Self-caterers can use **Solo SWA** (Jl Sudirman) or **Kharisma** (Jl A Yani).

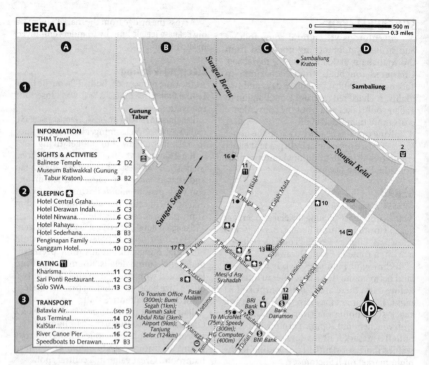

**BERAU**

INFORMATION
THM Travel....................1 C2

SIGHTS & ACTIVITIES
Balinese Temple...................2 D2
Museum Batiwakkal (Gunung
    Tabur Kraton)..................3 B2

SLEEPING
Hotel Central Graha.............4 C2
Hotel Derawan Indah...........5 C3
Hotel Nirwana.....................6 C3
Hotel Rahayu......................7 C3
Hotel Sederhana.................8 B3
Penginapan Family...............9 C3
Sanggam Hotel..................10 D2

EATING
Kharisma.............................11 C2
Sari Ponti Restaurant...........12 C3
Solo SWA............................13 C3

TRANSPORT
Batavia Air.......................(see 5)
Bus Terminal......................14 D2
KalStar.............................15 C3
River Canoe Pier................16 C2
Speedboats to Derawan......17 B3

## Getting There & Away

### AIR
**KalStar** ( ☎ 21007; fax 20279; Jl Maulana 45) **Trigana Air** ( ☎ 202 7885) and **Batavia Air** ( ☎ 26777; Hotel Derawan Indah, Jl Panglima Batur 396) fly to Balikpapan. KalStar also flies daily (except Sunday) to Tarakan, Tanjung Selor and Samarinda. Trigana also serves Samarinda.

### BOAT
Speedboats (*sepit*) to Pulau Derawan (three hours) wait off Jl A Yani. Negotiations start at 2,000,000Rp one way; anything under 1,000,000Rp is a bargain. Cheaper Derawan transport goes by Kijang to Tanjung Batu; see opposite for more information.

Canoe ferries cross Sungai Segah (3000Rp) to Museum Batiwakkal, or can be chartered for river cruises (per hour 50,000Rp to 100,000Rp).

### BUS
The convenient **bus terminal** (Jl Haji Isa) is south of the market on *angkot* routes. Buses over good roads to Tanjung Selor (50,000Rp, 2½ hours) and Malinau (175,000Rp, six hours) are sched-

uled hourly from 8.30am to 11.30am but won't roll with fewer than 15 passengers. Buses to Samarinda (150,000Rp, 18 hours), via Sangatta and Bontang for Kutai National Park (see p641), are scheduled until 1pm. This route, over atrocious roads, can take days during rainy season. Kijangs for Tanjung Selor (50,000Rp, two hours) and Samarinda (200,000Rp, 15 hours) gather across from the terminal and demand a minimum of four passengers; buy multiple seats to leave faster. Kijangs for Tanjung Batu wait on Jl A Yani from 9am.

## Getting Around
Taxis to the airport (9km) cost 40,000Rp. Berau a*ngkot* (3000Rp) drivers are Kalimantan's most common compliant, breaking routes to reach your destination. River crossings by fan-tail canoe cost 3000Rp; charters for river cruising cost 50,000Rp per hour.

## PULAU DERAWAN & SANGALAKI ARCHIPELAGO
World renowned diving in the Sangalaki Archipelago is not the best reason to visit **Pulau Derawan**. Even if you never put on a mask

and fins, you'll plunge into village life of a bygone era.

This island is a 45-hectare teardrop-shaped oasis that can be circled on foot in an hour, with electricity supplied only from dusk to dawn. (Generators violate the island's spirit, as do motorcycles; both are blissfully rare.) News travels from front porch to front porch, scattered warungs sell traditional Bajau palm sugar sweets (and maybe beer out the backdoor), time is marked by the arrival of the daily vegetables from the 'mainland', and all are welcome to late afternoon volleyball matches, women first. There's always fresh fish on the menu, turtles and sea horses swimming between the pilings of the docks, and just beyond the village, stretches of white sand beach to call your own. In short, Derawan is the tropical island you came to Southeast Asia dreaming about.

Diving in this Sulawesi Sea chain of 30-odd island deserves its acclaim. Derawan has rich coral reefs, turtles and schooling fish. Off **Pulau Sangalaki**, majestic mantas wing through the water. The island is also home to green turtles, a **Turtle Foundation** (www.turtle-foundation .org) monitoring outpost, and, sporadically, a dive resort. **Kakaban** has an ecologically intriguing lake where jellyfish have lost their sting. **Nabucco** and **Maratua** also have accommodation, but staying there misses Derawan village life.

## Activities

On Pulau Derawan, diving is organised at Derawan Dive Resort, Losmen Danakan, and, sometimes, Peningapan Lestari. The losmen charge 250,000Rp for dives, including tank and equipment hire. Snorkelling gear costs 50,000Rp per day. Village boats to other islands cost around 500,000Rp, including fishing for dinner on the trip back. At the resort, a la carte dives cost about US$40, including tank and weight belt only.

## Sleeping & Eating

At the time of writing, **Sangalaki Dive Resort** (www .sangalaki.net) on Pulau Sangalaki was closed.

**Losmen Ilham** (Pulau Derawan; r 40,000-45,000Rp) This small guest house has clean rooms with fans (when the electricity is on) and shared *mandi*. The attached warung serves Indonesian food (meals 8000Rp to 16,000Rp).

**our pick Losmen Danakan** ( ☎ 081 350 982 799, 081 347 733 701; Pulau Derawan; r per person incl meals 100,000-125,000Rp; ✷ ) If Ernest Hemingway came back as a sensitive new age guy, he'd check in to fish, write and revel in the sunsets. This immaculate homestay on stilts over the water features comfortable all-wood rooms (choose fan or air-con), and shared *mandi*, some with Western toilets. Meals are simply lovely.

**Derawan Dive Resort** ( ☎ 0542-707 2615; www .divederawan.com; Pulau Derawan; r US$45-120, 5-night package per person from US$970; ✷ ) Timber cottages have rustic charm and air-con, and the generator is well hidden. Packages include transfer from Berau, meals, and three boat dives daily, plus unlimited shore diving. Walk-ins may bargain for a room at 350,000Rp.

More accommodation options:

**Penginapan Derawan Lestari** (Pulau Derawan; r 75,000Rp) Haji Ismail's simple losmen on a pier resembles Danakan but lacks its soul.

**Penginapan Derawan Lestari II** ( ☎ 081 347 615 894; Pulau Derawan; r 50,000-100,000Rp; ✷ ) Clean, family-home option with air-con nightly.

**Maratua Paradise Resort** (www.borneo.org; Pulau Maratua; 6-night package per person US$1305-1395; ✷ ) Packages include beach chalet or stilt cottage accommodation, meals, scheduled island transfers and four dives daily.

**Nabucco Island Resort** ( ☎ /fax 0542-593635; www .nabuccoislandresort.com; Pulau Nabucco; s/d/t incl meals per person €102/74/67; ✷ ) The rate covers cottages over the surf (add €5 for air-con, deduct €10 for breakfast and dinner only) without dives (10- 20-dive package €345/652) or transfers (scheduled per person/charter per boat €110/625) to this isolated, indulgent resort. Management professes a soft spot for backpackers, so request discounts.

A handful of warungs on Pulau Derawan offer simple meals and snacks. Bring fruit for variety, and alcoholic beverages. We don't recommend Derawan Beach Cafe & Cottage. When we visited, there was a noisy, smelly generator, and we experienced less than courteous treatment.

Tanjung Batu, a fishing village, has a couple of warungs and **Losmen Famili** (r 30,000Rp) for rooms with shared *mandi* (no fan), in case you're stuck waiting for a boat.

## Getting There & Away

A direct speedboat from Berau to Derawan costs up to 2,000,000Rp (three hours). Save with a Kijang (50,000Rp, two hours) to Tanjung Batu and boat from there. Kijangs wait along the riverfront from 9am, but won't leave with fewer than five passengers, which often means departing mid-afternoon. At Tanjung Batu, hire a speedboat (200,000Rp, one hour) to Pulau Derawan or try to negotiate a ride with a fishing boat. Stay close to Indonesians arriving with you and you may get lucky; at the very least, you can share boat costs.

From Derawan, losmen can arrange a local boat to Tanjung Batu (150,000Rp, 2½ hours). Leave early: Kijangs for Berau depart 8am sharp.

## SUNGAI KAYAN & APOKAYAN HIGHLANDS

Elevation and rough water has kept away loggers, miners and most outsiders from the northwest quadrant of KalTim, preserving traditional lifestyles and pristine forests. **Kayan Mentarang National Park** follows the province's border with Malaysia from Sungai Kayan's headwaters northward. This 1.36-million-hectare park, the largest forest area in Southeast Asia, is a storehouse of global biodiversity – new plant and even animal species are discovered regularly – and centrepiece of WWF's Heart of Borneo initiative to protect contiguous forests in Indonesia, Malaysia and Brunei.

Around the park, an estimated 20,000 to 25,000 Dayaks from the Kenyah, Punan, Lun Daye, Lun Bawang and other groups have lived for centuries by maintaining natural balances in the environment. In recent years, with help from WWF, villagers along Sungai Kayan to Apokayan and Sungai Pujungan have begun to welcome tourists.

Trading boats from **Tanjung Selor** at the mouth of Sungai Kayan travel to Long Bia or follow Sungai Pujungan branching west (as Sungai Kayan branches south) to **Long Pujungan** (400,000Rp, one to 1½ days). The boat ride through rapids is part of the adventure. From Long Pujungan, the local ecotourism committee can arrange boats upriver to Long Ketaman (one or two people 250,000Rp), Long Pua (one or two people 350,000Rp) and Long Jelet (one or two people 350,000Rp), and **village homestays** (per person incl meals 90,000Rp).

The ecotourism committee organises activities, including treks. In Long Ketaman, a village of about 100, visitors can observe production of rattan crafts and tools, plus traditional farming, hunting and gathering in the forest. There's a good trail from Long Jelat with lots of wildlife and birds along way, though hunting makes the animals wary of humans. Guides cost 90,000Rp per day and porters 70,000Rp. Destinations include day trips to Batu Ului and U'ung Melu'ung waterfall, a moderate two-day trek to 70m Sungai Bum waterfall and ancient burial caves, and a rugged five-day climb into

Apokayan through the Apo Napu high pass to Data Dian, the last Kayan village in Apokayan, returning via Sungai Kat.

To begin trekking from the other end, **Susi Air** ( ☎ 081 1211 3080/90; info@susiair.com) flies to Long Ampung from Tarakan (1,200,000Rp) via Nunukan (800,000Rp). Destinations include a leisurely 2½-hour walk to the longhouse of **Long Uro**, or about an hour farther to **Lidung Payau** with boats back to Long Ampung. Hardy travellers may include treks north and west to longhouses and dry rice farms in Long Nawang and Data Dian via Sungai Anei and Long Metun or difficult five-hour jungle walk east from Lidung Payau to **Long Sungai Barang**.

Forking north, Sungai Bahau has more ecotourism areas. There's longboat transport from Long Pujungan to Long Alongo (one or two people 1,100,000Rp) with homestays (per person including meals 80,000Rp) and a lodge (per person including meals 100,000Rp). WWF's research station in the traditional protected forest area at Lalut Birai has deepened global understanding of tropical ecosystems since opening in 1991. Further upstream into Bahau Hulu, find a burial site in Long Pulung, cultural performances and traditional crafts in Long Berini and Apau Ping. The grasslands beyond Apau Ping offer good opportunities for seeing wildlife. It's also possible to trek from here into Krayan Hulu (see below).

For details on visiting, check www.borneo-ecotourism.com or contact the **WWF office** ( ☎ 0553-21523; km@indo.net.id) in Malinau. Reach Tanjung Selor from Berau by bus (50,000Rp, 2½ hours) or Tarakan by speedboat (80,000Rp, 1½ hours) or 20-minute **Trigana** ( ☎ 0551-31800; fax 0551-31890; 135,000Rp) flights. **KalStar** ( ☎ 0552-22205) flies to Tanjung Selor daily except Sunday from Balikpapan (924,000Rp) via Berau (197,000Rp). Contact **Missionary Air Fellowship** (MAF; ☎ 0551-34348) about its flights into Apokayan from Tarakan.

## KRAYAN HULU

The highlands of upper Sungai Krayan (Krayan Hulu) in KalTim's northwest corner are more easily reached from Sarawak in Malaysia Kalimantan. Isolation helps safeguard the landscape and customs of several Dayak groups, including Sa'ban, Lengilu, Lun Dayeh and Punan. About 1000m above sea level, the climate is refreshingly cool.

The **Krayan Hulu Ecotourism Committee** (Tana Tam Krayan Hulu; tana_tam@yahoo.com; Tarakan office

(☎ 551-34010; Jl Diponegoro 17) organises activities around Long Rungan (also called Tanjung Pasir), Long Layu, Tang Laan (also Pa' Upan), Binuang, Long Padi and Ba' Liku at the south end of Sungai Krayan. Tan Tam also manages the Kayan Mentarang National Park watershed between Krayan Hulu and Bahau Hulu, supported by WWF.

Ecotourism activities include **homestays** (per person incl meals 90,000Rp) featuring participation in village activities including wet and dry rice farming, buffalo raising, rattan weaving and tool production. **Treks** (packages per person 700,000-1,800,000Rp) cover heath forest with edible plants, fruits and flowers, including black orchids. Nearby destinations include springs around Long Layu where villagers produce mountain salt, ancient burial grounds with human images carved in stone, Batu Sichen (Honey Rock) where bees live under a scenic peak, and river rapids between Long Rungan and Tang Laan. Treks of up to five days cross into Sarawak's Kelabit or Bario Highlands or south to Apau Ping in Bahau Hulu through ancient forest, grassland with lots of wildlife, and abandoned village sites. Guides cost 90,000Rp per day and porters 70,000Rp.

The only practical way into Krayan Hulu is by air. **Missionary Air Fellowship** (MAF; ☎ 0551-34348) flies from Tarakan to/from Long Rungan; book as far in advance as possible. **Susi Air** (☎ 081 121 130 80/90; info@susiair.com) flies Tarakan to/from Long Bawan direct (165,000Rp) four times weekly and twice weekly via Nunukan (500,000Rp). MAF also flies between Long Rungan and Long Bawan; check schedules and book as far ahead as possible. During dry season, you can get from Long Bawan to Long Layu by motorcycle, 4WD or a day's trek. In Long Bawan, **Penginapan Agung Raya** (☎ 081 350 170 517; r 50,000-60,000Rp) is a small, clean losmen.

## SEBUKU SEMBAKUNG

Kalimantan's only elephant habitat, Sebuku Sembakung is a 400,000-hectare mix of protected and production forest plus oil-palm plantations along KalTim's north border with Sabah, included in WWF's Heart of Borneo initiative. Sebuku Sembakung has six forest types, from tidal swamp to green hills with limestone outcrops. Elephants inhabit Sebuku Sembakung's central lowland forest plains, but they are extremely difficult to find. Elephants are more easily sought (and more often seen) across the border along Sabah's Sungai Kinabatangan.

**Borneo Ecotourism** (www.borneo-ecotourism.com) or the **WWF office in Malinau** (☎ 0553-21523; km@indo.net.id) can help arrange visits. Access is via Sungai Sembuku from Nunukan by *ces* (4,000,000Rp, one day). Speedboats run regularly between Nunukan and Tarakan (170,000Rp, 2½ hours). **KalStar** (☎ 0551-25840 in Tarakan, 0556-23013 in Nunukan), **Trigana** (☎ 0551-31800; fax 0551-31890) and **Susi Air** (☎ 081 121 130 80/90; info@susiair.com) fly Tarakan to/from Nunukan (300,000Rp; 25 minutes).

## TARAKAN

☎ 0551 / pop 103,000

Tarakan's leaders liken their city to Singapore. Both are clean island towns near Malaysia, but obvious similarities end there. This Celebes Sea port linked to Tawau in East Sabah by ferry is a pleasant way to greet Indonesia – though visa on arrival would help – or bid farewell.

**THM Plaza**, a mix of local shops, national chains and hawkers at the corner of Jl Yos Sudarso and Jl Sudirman, marks Tarakan's centre, flanked by newer **Grand Tarakan Mall**. Down Jl Gajah Mada, **Gusher Plaza** (pronounced 'guesser') has Tarakan's only department store amid more shops and a traditional market. Harbours are to the south, Tingkayu into KalTim's interior and Malundung for Tawau and Pelni service.

### Information

Banks changing dollars are along Jl Yos Sudarso with more ATMs along Jl Sudirman and at Gusher Plaza. **Karisma** at THM Plaza and **Granmedia** at Grand Tarakan Mall sell maps of Tarakan and beyond. Many businesses close Sunday.

**Angkasa Express** (☎ 30288; aex_trk@yahoo.com; Hotel Tarakan Plaza, Jl Yos Sudarso) Air and Pelni tickets with free delivery.

**Haji La Tunrung Star Group** (☎ 21405; Jl Yos Sudarso 32) Moneychanger.

**HappyCom** (3rd fl; Grand Tarakan Mall; per hr 6000Rp; ⏰ 10am-9.30pm) Internet.

**Immigration office** (☎ 21242; Jl Sumatra) Information on visas and crossings to/from Malaysia.

**Melati Ekspres** (☎ 25622, 081 357 514 971; Jl Sudirman 23) Striving travel agent offering 24-hour SMS service and free delivery.

**Perta Medika Hospital** (☎ 31403; Jl Mulawarman)

**Post office** (Jl Sudirman)

**StarCorp Internet** (THM Plaza; per hour 6000Rp; ⏰ 10am-10pm)

**Tanjung Harapan Mulia** (☎ 21572; tjharapanmulia@gmail.com; Jl Yos Sudarso 38) Travel agency for all domestic flights and Tawindo boat to Tawau.

**Tourism office** (☎ 32100; Jl Sudirman 76, 4th fl) Good maps.

**Warnet Kopegtel** (☎ 35000; kopegteltravel@yahoo .com; Jl Sudirman 19; per hr 4000Rp; ⏰ 8am-10.30pm; 🛜) Internet access with wi-fi, attached to a travel agency.

## Sights

The **mangrove forest** (Jl Gajah Mada; ⏰ 8am-5pm) holds two Borneo exclusives, proboscis monkeys and *ikan tempankul*, a fish that walks out of the water. Spread over nine hectares with shaded boardwalks and benches, just 300m from the town centre, the mangroves also shelter macaques and many bird species.

Japanese and Australian forces clashed bloodily over Tarakan late in WWII. There's an **Australian memorial** (*kuburan Australia*; Jl Sumatra) at the Indonesian military barracks. A **Japanese gravesite** (*kuburan Jepang*) is in nearby hills, amid old bunkers.

**Pantai Amal** (11km) is a swimming beach that can be reached by minibus (3000Rp) or taxi (50,000Rp).

## Sleeping

**Hotel Bunga Muda** (☎ 21349; Jl Yos Sudarso 7; r 66,000-150,000Rp; ❄) Clean, friendly, basic accommodation between the harbours. Economy rooms have shared bathrooms. Only VIP rooms have air-con and sleep up to four.

**Hotel Bahagia** (☎ 37141; fax 24778; Jl Gajah Mada; r incl breakfast 80,000-200,000Rp; ❄) Big, bright economy digs at 'Hotel Happiness' opposite Gusher Plaza have shared Asian and Western bathrooms. Higher-priced rooms include private Western bathrooms and air-con, but some lack windows.

**Hotel Gemilang** (☎ 21521; fax 35588; Jl Diponegoro 4; r 90,000-160,000Rp; ❄) Miles ahead of typical budget haunts, all rooms are meticulously kept and boast fabulous wood furniture.

**Hotel Makmur** (☎ 31988, 085 246 570 888; fax 23565; Jl Sudirman 18; s 160,000Rp, d 200,000-250,000Rp, all incl breakfast; ❄) Snug, ultramodern standard rooms have hot-water shower, air-con, refrigerator, kettle, cable TV, but no window. Deluxe accommodations add windows and cushiony chairs.

**Hotel Harmonis Classic** (☎ 21783; fax 24503; Jl Diponegoro 5; r incl breakfast 215,000-320,000Rp; ❄ 🛜) Sleek, luxurious rooms with all the trimmings, plus free wi-fi in the lobby and restaurant.

**Hotel Tarakan Plaza** (☎ 21870; fax 21029; Jl Yos Sudarso 1; r incl breakfast 433,000-540,000Rp; ste 620,000-1,034,000Rp; ❄ 🛜) Reconstruction has catapulted this landmark straight over the top.

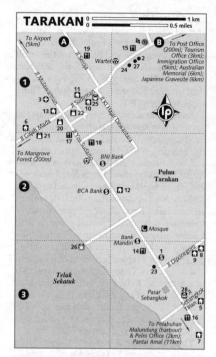

Rooms no longer represent value for money; even wi-fi costs extra.

**Swiss-Belhotel Tarakan** (☎ 21133; fax 36633; Jl Mualwarman 15; s 599,00-799,000Rp, d 699,000-859,000Rp, ste 1,379,000-2,299,000Rp plus 10% tax, all incl breakfast; ❄ 🖥 🛗 🛜) The former Garden City Hotel has received an elegant makeover. Ask for discounts and deals, especially on weekends. Nonsmoking rooms are available.

Other options:

**Hotel Asia** (☎ 36706; Jl Sebangkok Tirian 5; r incl breakfast 88,000-165,000Rp; ❄) Decent rooms, cement jungle in the lobby, harbour views from upper floor terraces.

**Hotel Sakura** (☎ 22730; Jl Sudirman 20; r 120,000-160,000Rp; ❄) Save money across from Hotel Makmur at its budget cousin.

## Eating

In 2009, a new local administration took the Singapore fantasy too far, banning food stalls from most streets, without following the Lion City's model of building hawker centres for the displaced vendors. The move eliminated opportunities to sample fabulous local fish street cheap. **Turi Ikan Bakar** (☎ 21153; Jl Yos Sudarso 32; per person 50,000-70,000Rp; ⏰ 10am-3pm,

| INFORMATION | | EATING 🍴 | |
|---|---|---|---|
| Angkasa Express | (see 12) | Bagi Alam I | 14 B3 |
| Granmedia | (see 20) | Cahaya | 15 B1 |
| Haji La Tunrung Star Group | 1 B3 | Makmur Supermarket | (see 10) |
| Happy Com | (see 20) | Nasi Lalap Niaga | 16 B3 |
| Karisma | (see 22) | Toko Setia Budi | 17 A2 |
| Melati Ekspres | 2 B1 | Turi Ikan Bakar | 18 A2 |
| Perta Medika Hospital | 3 A1 | Warung Jember | 19 A1 |
| StarCorp Internet | (see 22) | | |
| Tanjung Harapan Mulia | (see 1) | SHOPPING 🛍 | |
| Warnet Kopegtel | 4 B1 | Grand Tarakan Mall | 20 A1 |
| | | Gusher Plaza | 21 A2 |
| SLEEPING 🛏 | | THM Plaza | 22 A1 |
| Hotel Asia | 5 B3 | | |
| Hotel Bahagia | 6 A1 | TRANSPORT | |
| Hotel Bunga Muda | 7 B3 | Batavia Air | 23 B3 |
| Hotel Gemilang | 8 B3 | KalStar | 24 B1 |
| Hotel Harmonis Classic | 9 B3 | Mandala Airlines | (see 23) |
| Hotel Makmur | 10 A1 | Ojek Stand | 25 A1 |
| Hotel Sakura | 11 A1 | Pelabuhan Tengkayu, boats to Tanjung Selor | 26 A3 |
| Hotel Tarakan Plaza | 12 B2 | Sriwijaya Air | 27 B1 |
| Swiss-Belhotel Tarakan | 13 A1 | Taxi & Minibus Terminal | 28 B3 |
| | | Trigana Air | (see 12) |

6-10pm) and **Bagi Alam I** ( ☎ 22371; Jl Yos Sudarso 17; per person 40,000-60,000Rp; ⏰ 10am-10pm) offer restaurant fish feasts. For economical eats, the best bets are THM and Jl Seroja off Jl Sudirman. Large hotels' restaurants serve local favourites, Western and/or Chinese food.

**Warung Jember** (Jl Seroja; mains 6,000-12,000Rp) Home-cooked, East Java *nasi campur*.

**Nasi Lalap Niaga** ( ☎ 36954; Jl Yos Sudarso 32; mains 9,000-12,000Rp; ⏰ 9.30am-9.30pm) Busy hole-in-the-wall dishing the richest *capcay* in KalTim. Laden with chicken giblets, one portion serves two. Vegetarians request, '*Sayur saja*' ('Just vegetables').

**Cahaya** ( ☎ 21917; Jl Sudirman 105; mains 20,000-45,000Rp; ⏰ 7am-1.30pm, 5-10pm) Popular Chinese restaurant featuring seafood and cold beer.

For self-catering, try **Makmur Supermarket** (Jl Sudirman 20), next to the Hotel Makmur entrance, or popular **Toko Setia Budi** (Jl Yos Sudarso 5).

## Getting There & Away
### AIR
**Batavia Air** ( ☎ 32262; Jl Yos Sudarso 11), **KalStar** ( ☎ 25840; Jl Sudirman 9), **Lion Air** ( ☎ 202 6009), **Mandala Airlines** ( ☎ 22929; fax 32656; Jl Yos Sudarso 10) and **Sriwijaya Air** ( ☎ 33777; Jl Sudirman 21) fly to Balikpapan, connecting to Jakarta, Surabaya and beyond. KalStar and **Trigana Air** ( ☎ 31800; fax 31890; Hotel Tarakan Plaza, Jl Yos Sudarso) serve Berau, and Samarinda. **Susi Air** ( ☎ 081 121 130 80/90; info@su siair.com) flies to Malinau, Long Bawan and Long Apung. Trigana flies to Tanjung Selor, and along with KalStar to Nunukan. Check with **Mission Aviation Fellowship** (MAF; ☎ 34348) for scheduled and charter flights into the interior.

### BOAT
**Pelni** ( ☎ 51169; Jl Yos Sudarso) ships steam weekly to Pantaloan (261,000Rp), Pare Pare (377,000Rp), Makassar (379,000Rp), Surabaya (561,000Rp), and bi-weekly to Nunukan (75,000Rp), Maumere (409,000Rp), Kupang (587,000Rp), Jakarta (687,000Rp) and Kijang (841,000Rp), all from Pelabuhan Malundung, the main harbour at the south end of Jl Yos Sudarso. Travel agents are generally more helpful than Pelni's office.

Morning ferries to Tawau in Sabah (300,000Rp, 3½ hours) depart daily except Sunday from Pelabuhan Malundung. *Indomaya* and *Tawindo Express* run on alternate days and are very similar; choose the day, not the boat. Immigration formalities are at the ferry terminal. Officials take your passport and return it, stamped for Malaysian entry, upon arrival in Tawau.

Eight boats run daily to Tanjung Selor (80,000Rp, 1½ hours) from Pelabuhan Tengkayu, closer to Tarakan's centre off Jl Yos Sudarso. Speedboats from Tengkayu also serve Malinau (180,000Rp, three hours) and Nunukan (170,000Rp, 2½ hours), where boats to Tawau (90,000Rp, 1¼ hours) run daily.

## Getting Around
Taxis to/from Juwata Airport (6km) cost 50,000Rp. Alternatively, walk 200m to the street for an *angkot* (3000Rp). *Angkot* routes follow Jl Yos Sudarso, Jl Sudirman and Jl Gajah Mada. *Ojek* drivers gather on Jl Sudirman above THM Plaza and across from Gusher.

KALIMANTAN

# Sulawesi

If you think Sulawesi looks crazy on the map, just wait until you see it for real. The massive island's multilimbed coastline is drawn with sandy beaches, fringing coral reefs and a mind-boggling variety of fish. Meanwhile, the interior is shaded by impenetrable mountains and jungles thick with wildlife such as the rare nocturnal tarsiers and flamboyantly colourful maleo birds. Cultures have been able to independently evolve here, cut off from the rest of the world by the dramatic topography. Meet the Tana Toraja with their elaborate funeral ceremonies in which buffaloes are sacrificed and *balok* (palm wine) flows freely; nearby in Mamasa life revolves around the Christian church, and in the far north the Minahasans offer you spicy dishes of everything from stewed forest rat to grilled fish; the coastal regions are mainly inhabited by the Bugis, Indonesia's most famous seafarers.

Most people take the route from Makassar to Tana Toraja, then continue to the Togean Islands and farther north to Pulau Bunaken, but to do this on a one-month visa you'll need to move fast. The north is the best choice for those on a time budget, since distances are short and you can dive the world's top coral reefs one day, then see jungle critters and rare birds at the Tangkoko Nature Reserve the next. To get way off the beaten track, head to Southeast Sulawesi and its fabulous Wakatobi Marine National Park, to the ancient megaliths and forests of Lore Lindu National Park in Central Sulawesi or to the pristine Sangir-Talaud Islands in the north.

## HIGHLIGHTS

- Snorkelling or diving along unbelievably rich coral drop-offs – some of Asia's best – around chilled-out **Pulau Bunaken** (p710)
- Wondering if you didn't just wander into a cultural documentary when attending an elaborate funeral ceremony in **Tana Toraja** (p672)
- Island-hopping from one outrageous beach to the next in the laid-back **Togean Islands** (p696), an island paradise
- Feeling the cool air off glistening Danau Poso at the quiet lakeside towns of **Pendolo** (p686) and **Tentena** (p687)
- Spotting sprightly tarsiers and discovering ancient megaliths at **Lore Lindu National Park** (p690)

★ Pulau Bunaken

★ Togean Islands

Lore Lindu National Park ★

★ Tentena and Pendolo

Tana Toraja ★

■ POPULATION: 16 MILLION  ■ LAND AREA: 202,000 SQ KM  ■ HIGHEST PEAK: GUNUNG RANTEMARIO (3440M)

# SULAWESI

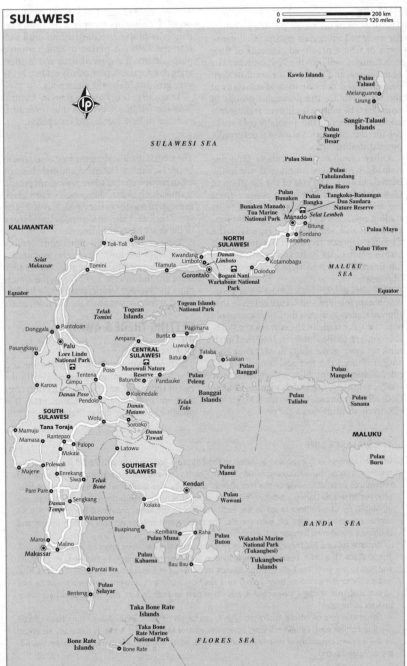

200 km
120 miles

Kawio Islands

Pulau
Talaud

Melanguane
Lirung

Tahuna

Sangir-Talaud
Islands

SULAWESI SEA

Pulau
Sangir
Besar

Pulau Siau

Pulau
Tahulandang

Pulau Biaro

Pulau
Bunaken

Tangkoko-Batuangas
Dua Saudara
Nature Reserve

Pulau
Bangka

KALIMANTAN

Bunaken Manado
Tua Marine
National Park

Selat Lembeh

Manado

Pulau Mayu

Bitung

Tondano

Buol

Tomohon

NORTH
SULAWESI

Toli-Toli

Pulau Tifore

Kwandang

Danau
Limboto

Selat
Makassar

Tomini

Tilamuta

Limboto

Kotamobagu

MALUKU
SEA

Gorontalo

Doloduo

Equator

Bogani Nani
Wartabone National
Park

Equator

Teluk
Tomini

Togean
Islands

Togean Islands
National Park

Donggala

Pantoloan

Ampana

Bunta

Pagimana

Luwuk

Pasangkayu

Palu

Batui

Tataba

Salakan

Lore Lindu
National Park

Poso

Central
Sulawesi

Pulau
Banggai

Pulau
Mangole

Tentena

Morowali Nature
Reserve

Karosa

Gimpu

Baturube

Pandauke

Pulau
Peleng

Pulau
Taliabu

Pulau
Sanana

Danau Poso

Kolonedale

Pendolo

Banggai
Islands

SOUTH
SULAWESI

Danau
Matano

Teluk
Tolo

MALUKU

Mamuju

Tana Toraja

Wotu

Soroako

Mamasa

Rantepao

Danau
Towuti

Palopo

Pulau
Buru

Makale

Latowu

Polewali

Majene

Enrekang

SOUTHEAST
SULAWESI

Pulau
Manui

Siwa

Teluk
Bone

Pare Pare

Kendari

Danau
Tempe

Sengkang

Pulau
Wowoni

Watampone

Kolaka

BANDA SEA

Buapinang

Kembara

Raha

Maros

Malino

Pulau Muna

Pulau
Buton

Wakatobi Marine
National Park
(Tukangbesi)

Makassar

Pulau
Kabaena

Bau Bau

Tukangbesi
Islands

Pantai Bira

Pulau
Selayar

Benteng

Taka Bone Rate
Islands

Taka Bone
Rate Marine
National Park

Bone Rate
Islands

FLORES SEA

Bone Rate

## HISTORY

The interior of the island provided a refuge for some of Indonesia's earliest inhabitants, some of whom preserved elements of their rich cultures well into the 20th century. The Makassarese and Bugis of the southwestern peninsula and the Christian Minahasans of the far north are the dominant groups of Sulawesi. The unique traditions, architecture and ceremonies of the Toraja people make the interior of South Sulawesi a deservedly popular destination.

Other minorities, particularly Bajo Sea nomads, have played an integral role in the island's history. The rise of the kingdom of Gowa – Sulawesi's first major power – from the mid-16th century was partly due to its trading alliance with the Bajo. The Bajo supplied valuable sea produce, especially the Chinese delicacy trepang (sea cucumber), tortoiseshell, birds' nests and pearls, attracting international traders to Gowa's capital, Makassar.

Makassar quickly became known as a cosmopolitan, tolerant and secure entrepôt that allowed traders to bypass the Dutch monopoly over the spice trade in the east – a considerable concern to the Dutch. In 1660 the Dutch sunk six Portuguese ships in Makassar harbour, captured the fort and forced Gowa's ruler, Sultan Hasanuddin, into an alliance in 1667. Eventually, the Dutch managed to exclude all other foreign traders from Makassar, effectively shutting down the port.

Even after Indonesia won its independence, ongoing civil strife hampered Sulawesi's attempts at postwar reconstruction until well into the 1960s. A period of uninterrupted peace delivered unprecedented and accelerating development, particularly evident in the ever-growing Makassar metropolis.

Tragically, the Poso region in Central Sulawesi fell into a cycle of intercommunal violence in 1998 (see boxed text, p688).

## CLIMATE

The wettest months along the west coast tend to be late November, December and early January, when northwesterly and westerly winds prevail. Southeasterly winds dump heavy rains along the eastern regions in late April, May and early June. The Palu Valley in Central Sulawesi is one of the driest areas in Indonesia.

Temperatures drop quite considerably going from the lowlands to the mountains. Average temperatures along the coast range from around 26ºC to 30ºC, but in the mountains the average temperature drops by 5ºC. See also the climate chart for Manado, p827.

## GETTING THERE & AWAY
### Air
#### DOMESTIC

The three transport hubs are Makassar and Manado, which are well connected with the rest of Indonesia, and Palu, which offers connections to Balikpapan in Kalimantan. It is possible to arrange direct flights to Java, Bali,

---

### THE WALLACE LINE

Detailed surveys of Borneo and Sulawesi in the 1850s by English naturalist Alfred Russel Wallace resulted in some inspired correspondence with Charles Darwin. Wallace was struck by the marked differences in wildlife, despite the two islands' proximity and similarities in climate and geography. His letters to Darwin, detailing evidence of his theory that the Indonesian archipelago was inhabited by one distinct fauna in the east and one in the west, prompted Darwin to publish similar observations from his own travels. The subsequent debate on species distribution and evolution transformed modern thought.

Wallace refined his theory in 1859, drawing a boundary between the two regions of fauna. The Wallace Line, as it became known, divided Sulawesi and Lombok to the east, and Borneo and Bali to the west. He believed that islands to the west of the line had once been part of Asia, and those to the east had been linked to a Pacific-Australian continent. Sulawesi's wildlife was so unusual that Wallace suspected it was once part of both, a fact that geologists have since proven to be true.

Other analyses of where Australian-type fauna begin to outnumber Asian fauna have placed the line further east. Lydekker's Line, which lies east of Maluku and Timor, is generally accepted as the western boundary of strictly Australian fauna, while Wallace Line marks the eastern boundary of Asian fauna.

Kalimantan, Maluku and Papua, but you'll need transit for connections to Sumatra or Nusa Tenggara. Merpati Nusantara Airlines and Lion Air are the main carriers, but Batavia Air, Garuda Indonesia, Sriwijaya Air and Wings Air also service Sulawesi. See the individual Getting There & Away sections for details about all domestic flights.

### INTERNATIONAL

Silk Air flies between Manado and Singapore four times a week (Monday, Wednesday, Friday and Saturday) for US$335 (one way). Wings Air flies between Manado and Davao in the southern Philippines once a week for US$150 one way. This is useful for a visa run, but it is important to note that you need an onward ticket before you can enter the Philippines.

Tickets for all international flights from Makassar and Manado are often cheaper through travel agencies.

### Sea

Sulawesi is well connected, with more than half the Pelni's fleet calling at Makassar, Bitung (the seaport for Manado), Pare Pare and/or Toli-Toli, as well as a few other minor towns.

Some of the more important boats that stop at Makassar and/or Bitung (Manado) include the following:

**Bukit Siguntang** To East Kalimantan and Nusa Tenggara.
**Ciremai** To Maluku, Papua and Java.
**Ganda Dewata** To Jakarta.
**Kelimutu** To Java, Bali, Nusa Tenggara and Maluku.
**Kerinci** To East Kalimantan.
**Labobar** To Java and Papua.
**Lambelu** To Java, Maluku and Northern Maluku.
**Sirimau** To Nusa Tenggara, Java and East Kalimantan.
**Tilongkabila** To Nusa Tenggara.

## GETTING AROUND
### Air

Merpati and Lion Air are the main carriers within Sulawesi, but Batavia Air and Sriwijaya also operate selected routes. See the individual Getting There & Away sections for details of flights around Sulawesi.

### Boat

The few Pelni ships that link towns within Sulawesi are a comfortable alternative to long and rough bus trips. Every two weeks the following boats sail from Makassar: the *Kerinci* and *Bukit Siguntang* go to Balikpapan; at least

six ships go to Bau Bau and onto various destinations including Ambon and Bitung (for Manado). The *Lambelu* and *Labobar* go to Surabaya; the *Labobar* goes to Sorong and the *Sirimau* goes to Larantuka.

The most useful service is the *Tilongkabila*, which sails every two weeks from Makassar to Bau Bau, Raha and Kendari; up to Kolonedale, Luwuk, Gorontalo and Bitung; across to Tahuna and Lirung in the Sangir-Talaud Islands; and returns the same way to Makassar.

Elsewhere along the coast, and to remote islands such as the Togean and Banggai, creaky old passenger ships, or *kapal kayu* (wooden boats), are the normal mode of transport, although speedboats are also occasionally available for charter. Around the southeastern peninsula, the *kapal cepat* (fast boat) or 'super-jet' are the ways to go.

### Bus, Bemo & Kijang

Regions around Makassar and the southwestern peninsula, and around Manado and the northeastern peninsula, have good roads and frequent, comfortable buses (and less comfortable bemos or minibuses, known in Sulawesi as *mikrolet* or *pete-pete*). Elsewhere, roads are often rough, distances are long, and public transport can be crowded and uncomfortable. Allow plenty of time to travel overland in Central Sulawesi, especially in the wet season. On the southeastern and southwestern peninsulas, sharing a Kijang (a type of 4WD taxi) is a quick, but not necessarily more comfortable, way of getting around.

# SOUTH SULAWESI

South Sulawesi (Sulawesi Selatan; often shortened to Sul-sel) is immense, and in Sulawesi big equals diverse. Makassar in the far south is the capital of the island and is fittingly tumultuous and surprisingly cosmopolitan. Stop here a day or two to get your last chance for nightlife plus feast on some of the best seafood on the island. From here you could head farther south to Bira, which has the sleepy feel of a Greek isle with its dry climate and goats aplenty, or do what most people do and go directly to Tana Toraja to experience a dizzying blend of mountains carved with rice paddies, outlandish funeral ceremonies involving animal sacrifices and some of the

SULAWESI

# SOUTH SULAWESI

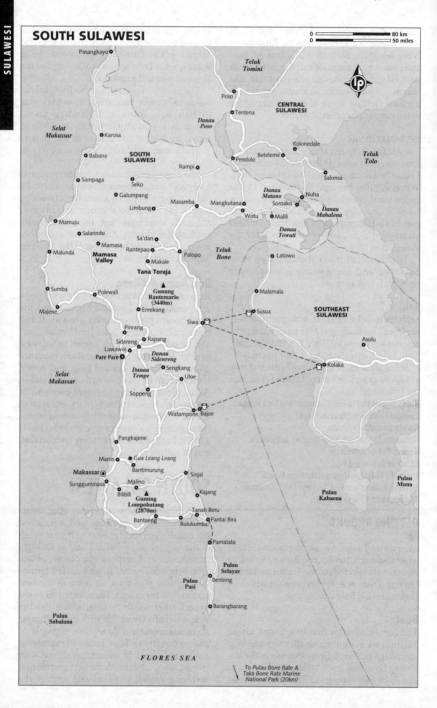

0          80 km
0          50 miles

Pasangkayu

*Teluk Tomini*

Poso

*CENTRAL SULAWESI*

Tentena

*Danau Poso*

*Selat Makassar*

Karosa

Kolonedale

Beteleme

*Teluk Tolo*

Babana

**SOUTH SULAWESI**

Pendolo

Sampaga

Rampi

Salonsa

Seko

Galumpang

Masamba

Mangkutana

*Danau Matano*

Nuha

Limbung

Soroako

*Danau Mahalona*

Mamuju

Wotu

Malili

Salarindu

*Danau Towuti*

Mamasa

Sa'dan

**Mamasa Valley**

Rantepao

Palopo

*Teluk Bone*

Latowu

Malunda

Makale

**Tana Toraja**

Sumba

Polewali

▲ **Gunung Rantemario (3440m)**

Malamala

Majene

Enrekang

Susua

Siwa

**SOUTHEAST SULAWESI**

Pinrang

Sidereng

Rapang

Asolu

Lawawoi

*Danau Sidenreng*

**Pare Pare**

Sengkang

Kolaka

*Danau Tempe*

Uloe

*Selat Makassar*

Soppeng

Watampone Bajoe

Pangkajene

Maros

*Gua Leang Leang*

Bantimurung

Sinjai

*Pulau Muna*

**Makassar**

Malino

Sungguminasa

Kajang

*Pulau Kabaena*

Bilibili

▲ **Gunung Lompobatang (2870m)**

Tanah Beru

Bantaeng

Bulukumba

Pantai Bira

Pamatata

**Pulau Selayar**

*Pulau Pasi*

Benteng

*Pulau Sabalana*

Barangbarang

*FLORES SEA*

↓ To Pulau Bone Rate &
Taka Bone Rate Marine
National Park (20km)

craziest local-style architecture in Asia. In between these places there are plenty of buzzing towns and ports not used to seeing visitors, where you could stop awhile and soak in the culture. On the long bus rides in between you'll pass coastal salt farms and coffee, cotton and sugarcane plantations inland.

The estimated nine million–plus inhabitants include the Bugis (who make up two-thirds of the population), the Makassarese (a quarter) and the Toraja. The Makassarese are concentrated in the southern tip, mainly around Makassar. The Bugis (centred around Watampone) and Makassarese have similar cultures; both are seafaring people who for centuries were active in trade, sailing to Flores, Timor and Sumba, and even as far afield as the northern coast of Australia. Islam is the dominant religion, but both people retain vestiges of traditional beliefs.

### History

The leading powers of the south were long the Makassarese kingdom of Gowa (around the port of Makassar) and the Bugis kingdom of Bone. By the mid-16th century, Gowa had established itself at the head of a major trading bloc in eastern Indonesia. The king of Gowa adopted Islam in 1605 and Bone was soon subdued, spreading Islam to the whole Bugis-Makassarese area.

The Dutch United East India Company found Gowa a considerable hindrance to its plans to monopolise the spice trade. It found an anti-Gowa ally in the exiled Bugis prince Arung Palakka. The Dutch sponsored Palakka's return to Bone in 1666, prompting Bone to rise against the Makassarese. A year of fighting ensued and Sultan Hasanuddin of Gowa was forced to sign the Treaty of Bungaya in 1667, which severely reduced Gowa's power. Bone, under Palakka, then became the supreme state of South Sulawesi.

Rivalry between Bone and the other Bugis states continually reshaped the political landscape. After their brief absence during the Napoleonic Wars, the Dutch returned to a Bugis revolt led by the queen of Bone. This was suppressed, but rebellions continued until Makassarese and Bugis resistance was finally broken in the early years of the 20th century. Unrest lingered on until the early 1930s.

The Makassarese and Bugis are staunchly Islamic and independent-minded – revolts against the central Indonesian government again occurred in the 1950s. Makassar and Pare Pare are still the first to protest when the political or economic situation is uncertain.

## MAKASSAR

☎ 0411 / pop 1.6 million

The metropolis of Makassar is thick with honking horns, strong smells and general pandemonium, but it maintains a nearly backwater charm thanks to its friendly people and delicious, down-home seafood warungs (food stalls). The city's seething mass is expanding in every direction, with new suburbs everywhere. Tanjung Bunga looms to the southwest of the city and may become the centre one day, while Panukkukang to the east is chock-a-block with mighty, modern shopping malls. Not surprisingly, Makassar has the liveliest night scene this side of Surabaya.

As the gateway to eastern Indonesia for centuries, it was from Makassar that the Dutch controlled much of the shipping that passed between the west and the east. Today it's still a thriving port and important transport hub. Fort Rotterdam, once an ancient Gowanese fort, is Makassar's main tourist attraction and stands as a reminder of the Dutch occupation.

In the area surrounding Makassar are the palace of the Gowanese kings, waterfalls where the naturalist Alfred Wallace collected butterflies and cave paintings left by the first inhabitants of Sulawesi.

### Orientation

Makassar is *huge*, but you'll only need to venture into the eastern suburbs to catch a bus or go to the airport. The port is conveniently located in the northwest part of the city; Fort Rotterdam is in the centre of the older commercial hub.

---

**WHAT'S IN A NAME?**

From the early 1970s until 1999 the official name of Makassar was Ujung Pandang. During his final days as president, BJ Habibie made the popular decision to change the name back to Makassar. In reality both names are still used, as they have been for centuries, and neither title is politically charged.

SULAWESI

# MAKASSAR

0 ——— 1 km
0 ——— 0.5 miles

Ⓐ　　　　　Ⓑ　　　　　Ⓒ　　　　　Ⓓ

**INFORMATION**
Bank Bali................................1 B4
Bank Mandiri..........................2 B4
BII Bank.................................3 B4
BNI Bank................................4 B4
BNI Bank................................5 A5
Caraka Travelindo...............(see 28)
Expresso Cafe Net...................6 A4
Immigration Office...................7 B2
Internet Centre....................(see 8)
Lippo Bank..........................(see 1)
Main Post Office......................8 A4
Police Station.........................9 A4
Port Entrance........................10 A2
Post Office...........................11 C4
PT Haji Moneychanger...........12 A4
Rumah Sakit Pelamonia.........13 B5
Sulawesi Tourism Information
　Centre..............................14 B6
Telkom...............................(see 8)

Wartel.................................15 A5
Wartel.................................16 B4

**SIGHTS & ACTIVITIES**
Fort Rotterdam.....................17 A4
Makam Pangeran Diponegoro..18 C3
Monumen Mandala................19 B5
Museum Negeri La Galigo.....(see 17)
Paddle Boats.......................20 A6
Taman Anggrek Clara Bundt...21 B5

**SLEEPING**
Asoka Homestay....................22 A6
Hotel Dinasti.......................23 B3
Hotel Grand Wisata...............24 B5
Hotel Lestari.........................25 B4
Hotel Losari Beach.................26 A5
Hotel Maracaya.....................27 C6
Hotel Pantai Gapura...............28 A4
Hotel Yasmin........................29 A4
Imperial Aryaduta Hotel.........30 B4
Kenari Tower Hotel................31 B6
Losmen Semeru.....................32 A4
New Legends Hostel...............33 A4
Pondok Suada Indah...............34 A5
Quality Hotel........................35 A5
Santika Hotel........................36 B5

**EATING**
Club Velvet........................(see 30)
Fish Warung..........................37 A4
Galeal Supermarket................38 A5
Kantin Baik dan Murah.........(see 38)
Kios Semarang.....................(see 47)
Lae Lae...............................39 B5
Mie Titi...............................40 B6
Night Warung........................41 A6
Pizza Ria.............................42 B4
Rumah Makan Kayangan........43 A5
Rumah Makan Malabar...........44 B3
Sentosa...............................45 A5
Shogun...............................46 A5
Swensen's.........................(see 38)

**DRINKING**
Ballairate Sunset Bar............(see 28)
Kafe Kareba..........................47 A5

**ENTERTAINMENT**
Botol Cafe..........................(see 35)
Colors.................................48 A4
Makassar Theatre...................49 B4

**SHOPPING**
Makassar Mall.......................50 B3

**TRANSPORT**
Batavia Air............................51 B4
Boats to Pulau Kayangan & Pulau
　Samalona............................52 A4
Central Pete-Pete Terminal.......53 B4
Garuda................................54 A4
Lion Air...............................55 B4
Merpati...............................56 D4
Pelabuhan Makassar (Pelni Port)..57 A3
Pelni..................................58 B5

To Pelabuhan
Paotere (3km)
7

10

LP

57

Jl Butung
Jl Tentara Pelajar
Jl Sangir
Jl Hatta
Jl Lembeh
Jl Martadinata
Jl Nusantara
Jl Sulawesi
Jl Lombok
Jl Bali
Jl Sumba
Jl Serui Sama
Jl Ahmad Yani
Jl Slamet Riyadi
Jl Balaikota
Jl Pasar Ikan
Jl Irian
Jl Supratman
Jl Pattimura
Jl Thamrin
Jl Sumba
Jl Opu
Jl Daeng Tompo
Jl Baumassepe
Jl Ranggong
Jl Penghibur
Jl Alimalaka
Jl Mochtar Lutfi
Jl Datu Musseng
Jl Yosep Latumahina
Jl Kenari
Jl Sultan Hasanuddin
Jl Bonto Lempangan
Jl Khairitan War
Jl Sawengading
Jl Aritake
Jl Sam Ratulang
Jl Mero Tanjung Bunga

Jl Buru
Jl Akademis
Jl Mohammadyah
Jl Hasyim
Jl Irian
Jl Cokroaminoto
Jl Ramli
Jl Bulusaraung
Jl Sungai Cerekang
Jl Gunung Lompobattang
Jl R A Kartini
Jl Amannagappa
Jl Ince Nurdin
Jl Jendral Sudirman
Jl Sultong

Jl Bandang
Jl Andalas
Jl Diponegoro
Jl Mesjid Raya
Jl Bawakaraeng
Jl Sungai Poso
Jl Sungai Paremang
Jl Gunung Merapi
Jl Gunung Kelabat
Jl Gunung Nona
Jl Sungai Saddang
Jl Sarif Alqadri
Jl Monginsidi
Jl Sungai Limboto
Jl Gunung Salahutu
Jl Veteran Utara
Jl Kerung Kerung
Jl Abubakar Lambogo
Jl Latimojong
Jl Lamadukelleng

Masjid Al
Markas al Islami

Lapangan
Karebosi

Marannu
Hotel

Selat
Makassar

Governor's
Residence

Taman
Hiburan
Makasar

Canal

Panampu

To Panukkukang Mall (6km);
M Club (7km); Hasanuddin Airport;
Terminal Regional Daya (22km);
Pare Pare (160km);
Rantepao (328km)

To G Mall
(4km)

To Kampung
Expeditions
(1.5km)

To Ratu Indah Mall (200m);
Losari Holidays Tours & Travel (1km);
Terminal Mallengkeri (5km);
Old Gowa (7km); Terminal
Sungguminasa (12km); Malino (75km)

## Information

### EMERGENCY
**Police station** ( ☎ 110; Jl Ahmad Yani)

### IMMIGRATION
**Immigration office** (Jl Tentara Pelajar) Has a reputation of being difficult with visa extensions.

### INTERNET ACCESS & POST
Internet centres are springing up across the city, most charging 7000Rp per hour.

**Expresso Cafe Net** (cnr Jl Pasar Ikan & Jl Ahmad Yani; ⏲ 8am-12am) Clean private booths and fast connections.

**Main post office** (Jl Slamet Riyadi; ⏲ 8am-9pm) Has a poste restante service, a Telkom office and an internet centre.

### MEDICAL SERVICES
**Rumah Sakit Pelamonia** ( ☎ 324 710; Jl Jendral Sudirman) The most convenient and well-equipped hospital.

### MONEY
The streets surrounding Lapangan Karebosi are loaded with banks and ATMs that accept all major credit cards. Most are on Jl Ahmad Yani and can also change cash and travellers cheques. At the airport several moneychangers offer slightly lower rates than in the city, and some of the ATMs there accept credit cards.

### TELEPHONE
Wartel (private telephone offices) are everywhere, so it is easy enough to make calls from almost anywhere in town. There are international telephones at the airport.

### TOURIST INFORMATION
**Sulawesi Tourism Information Centre** ( ☎ 872 336; cnr Jl Sam Ratulangi & Jl Sungai Saddang; ⏲ 8am-4pm) There is little on offer here, but the staff are helpful and friendly. Take any pete-pete travelling south along Jl Jendral Sudirman to get here.

### TRAVEL AGENCIES
There are travel agencies through which you can book flights and Pelni ship voyages all around Makassar and at many hotels.

Just about everyone in Makassar wants to take you on a tour of Tana Toraja. Recommended tour agencies to destinations all over Sulawesi include the following:

**Caraka Travelindo** ( ☎ 318 877; www.sulawesi-in donesia.com; Hotel Pantai Gapura) Dutch-run and one of the biggest.

**Kampung Expeditions** ( ☎ 582 639; www.kampungx .com; Jl Palapa VI 129) Has Japanese and Australian partners and runs tours all over South Sulawesi.

**Losari Holidays Tours & Travel** ( ☎ 506 3884; Jl Mappanyukki 1) The agent for Operation Wallacea projects in Sulawesi (see p723).

**Nell Tours** ( ☎ 852 445; www.nelltours.com; Jl Cendrawasih 103)

## Sights

### FORT ROTTERDAM
One of the best-preserved examples of Dutch architecture in Indonesia, **Fort Rotterdam** (Jl Pasar Ikan; entry by donation, suggested 10,000Rp; ⏲ 7.30am-6pm) continues to guard the harbour of Makassar. A Gowanese fort dating back to 1545 once stood here, but failed to keep out the Dutch. The original fort was rebuilt in Dutch style after the Treaty of Bungaya in 1667. Parts of the crumbling wall have been left untouched and provide a comparison with the restored buildings, but really the fort isn't anything spectacular.

Inside the fort are two **museums** (admission 1700Rp; ⏲ Tue-Sun) which have an assortment of exhibits, including rice bowls from Tana Toraja, kitchen tools, musical instruments and various costumes. It's hardly riveting, but at this price who can complain? The museums seem to keep the same hours as the fort.

Guides approach you at the fort's entrance and charge 50,000Rp for worthwhile though lengthy (count on two hours) historic tours of the grounds and museums. Avoid visiting on Sunday when schoolchildren and English students swarm the place.

### MAKAM PANGERAN DIPONEGORO
Prince Pangeran Diponegoro of Yogyakarta led the Java War (1825–30), but his career as a rebel leader came to a sudden halt when he was tricked into going to the Dutch headquarters to negotiate peace, was taken prisoner and then exiled to Sulawesi. He spent the last 26 years of his life imprisoned in Fort Rotterdam. His tomb and monument can be seen in a small **cemetery** (Jl Diponegoro; entry by donation).

### OLD GOWA
Remnants of the former kingdom of Gowa, 7km from town on the southeastern outskirts of Makassar, include **Makam Sultan Hasanuddin** (Jl Pallantiang, off Jl Sultan Hasanuddin), which memorialises the ruler of Gowa from the mid-17th

century. Outside the tomb compound is the **Pelantikan Stone**, on which the kings of Gowa were crowned.

**Benteng Sungguminasa** (Jl Kh Wahid Hasyim; admission free; ☺ 8am-4pm), a fort that was once the seat of the sultan of Gowa, is 5km further south at Sungguminasa. The former royal residence, now known as **Museum Balla Lompoa**, houses a collection of artefacts, including gifts from Australian Aborigines of Elcho Island, who have a history of trade with the Bugis. Although the royal regalia can be seen only on request, the wooden Bugis-style palace itself is the real attraction.

To go to Old Gowa and Sungguminasa, take a *pete-pete* marked 'S Minasa' from Makassar Mall to the turn-off for the 1km walk to the tomb. A becak (bicycle-rickshaw) from there to the fort should cost around 9000Rp. Another becak will take you to Mallengkeri Terminal, from where *pete-pete* return to central Makassar; the *pete-pete* should cost about 4000Rp.

### OTHER SIGHTS
**Pelabuhan Paotere** (Paotere Harbour; admission 500Rp), a 15-minute becak ride north of the city centre, is where the Bugis sailing ships berth and is arguably the most atmospheric part of the city. There is usually lots of activity on the dock and in the busy **fish market** a few streets south.

**Taman Anggrek Clara Bundt** (Clara Bundt Orchid Garden; Jl Mochtar Lufti 15; entry by donation) is a sanctuary hidden behind the Bundt family home. It contains exotic hybrids (some up to 5m high). There's also a verdant fruit orchard and an extensive shell collection.

The towering **Monumen Mandala** (Jl Jendral Sudirman; admission 5000Rp; ☺ 8am-4pm) is a smaller version of Jakarta's Monas (National Monument), and celebrates the 'liberation' of Irian Jaya (now known as Papua).

## Activities
Top-end hotels such as Hotel Pantai Gapura and Imperial Aryaduta Hotel have **swimming pools** which the public can use for 20,000Rp, although they get crowded on Sunday. Comedic fish-shaped **paddle boats** (15,000Rp per hr; ☺ 11am-9pm) are available for hire near the night warungs (food stalls) for a sunset paddle.

Makassar isn't known for diving, but Kapoposang and islands off the coast do offer abundant marine life and some of the largest wrecks off the Sulawesi coast. In mid-2009 there was no dive centre in Makassar, but you can charter a speedboat from Pelabuhan Paotere (about 500,000Rp; two hours) to go on your own, or contact the **Makassar Dive Club** (☎ 411326056), which is not a dive centre but a small organisation of local divers, for information about any upcoming chartered dive trips.

## Sleeping
The most pleasant area to stay is along the waterfront south of the port (which also has the best nightlife), while choices a few blocks away from the sea or around Jl Ahmad Yani are central and a short walk to the action. Unless noted otherwise, all of the following prices include breakfast. All places listed here have Western-style bathrooms.

### BUDGET
**New Legends Hostel** (☎ 313 777; Jl Jampea 5G; dm 65,000Rp, r 90,000-125,000Rp; ⌨ ) Catering to backpackers, this clean and very helpful place has an upstairs cafe where you can meet other travellers over breakfast or movies at night. The rooms and dorms, however, are small, windowless and box-like. Cheaper rooms are fan-only and have shared bathrooms.

**Losmen Semeru** (☎ 318 113; Jl Jampea 28; r 70,000Rp; ⌨ ) This long-running budget stalwart still offers some of the best basic crash pads in town. Rooms are minuscule but have TVs, attached *mandis* and air-con. The atmosphere isn't exactly glamorous but service is friendly. No meals are served.

**Hotel Grand Wisata** (☎ 324 344; grandwisht@yahoo.co.id; Jl Sultan Hasanuddin 36-38; r 100,000-265,000Rp; ⌨ ) This is a sprawling place with options ranging from fan-cooled cheapies with shared bathrooms to larger though worn-looking rooms with all the mod cons. A skinny courtyard with palms and some potted plants adds some light and a feeling of space.

**Hotel Lestari** (☎ 327 337; Jl Savu 16; r 145,000-200,000Rp; ⌨ ) Freshly painted rooms, all with satellite TV, minibar, hot water and air-con, are among the best deals in Makassar. There's not much character but for friendly service, a clean comfy bed and a good night's sleep it's hard to do better than this.

**Pondok Suada Indah** (☎ 317 179; fax 312 856; Jl Sultan Hasanuddin 12; r from 175,000Rp; ⌨ ) One of Makassar's more interesting options, this place is set in a spacious, old colonial-era house that feels far from the city's hubbub just out the front door. Rooms are huge and are decorated with a tatty mix of heavy antiques and cheap modern furniture; some have age-worn bathtubs and all have little TVs with local channels.

## MIDRANGE

**our pick** **Asoka Homestay** ( ☎ 873 476; Jl Yosep Latumahina; r 200,000-300,000Rp) An oasis just steps from the waterfront, this charming family-run place has five rooms surrounding an immaculate flowery courtyard. Everything from the little breakfast tables draped in pink lace to the large and airy rooms is tended with love. The one 'super' room has a small terrace and kitchen and is a good option for families.

**Hotel Maracaya** ( ☎ 876 787; JC0808@yahoo.co.id; Jl Kijang 2; r 200,000-330,000Rp; ✖ ) You'll have to pay the high end of the price range to get a window, but all the rooms at this newish hotel are sparkling clean, with uncommonly big beds draped in crisp sheets. Enjoy your HBO after a hot shower.

**Hotel Dinasti** ( ☎ 325 657; hotel_dinasti@yahoo.com; Jl Lombok 30; r from 330,000Rp; ✖ &#x267f; ) The Dinasti takes its Chinese theme seriously, from bell-boys in silk caps with a fake braid hanging down the back, to the rather elegant rooms all decorated with traditional Chinese furniture. The welcome is very friendly and all rooms include satellite TV and fridge. There is also a whirlpool hot tub available for guests.

**Hotel Yasmin** ( ☎ 328 329; yasminmakassar@yahoo .co.id; Jl Jampea 5; r from 336,000Rp; ✖ 🖳 ) Victorian patterned wallpaper and upholstered chairs add a little decadence to this bustling business hotel. Rooms are small but in good shape and the staff are formally professional. There's a cafe-restaurant and karaoke-dance bar on site.

**Hotel Losari Beach** ( ☎ 326 062; los-htl@indosat.net .id; Jl Penghibur 10; r from 400,000Rp; ✖ 🖳 ) Boasting a great location overlooking the seafront, the bland rooms are a bit disappointing for the price. Prices rise rapidly for a premium sea view.

**Kenari Tower Hotel** ( ☎ 874 250; hotelkenari@yahoo .co.id; Jl Yosep Latumahina 30; r from 500,000Rp; ✖ 🖳 ) Muted lighting, a beige-and-mauve colour scheme and minimalist Bali-style decor make this brand-new hotel the most stylish place in town. A stone's throw from the seafront, even some standard rooms have sea views, and the

rooftop terrace restaurant is a prime location for sunset cocktails. Chill out afterwards in the jacuzzi or the on-site spa.

**Santika Hotel** ( ☎ 332 233; www.santika.com; Jl Sultan Hasanuddin 40; r from 525,000Rp; ✖ 🖳 ) The second most chic hotel in Makassar, after Kenari Tower, the Santika isn't as well located for views, but the rooms are luxurious and have a calming beige-and-white decor.

**Quality Hotel** ( ☎ 333 111; www.qualityhotelmakassar .com; Jl Somba Opu 235; r from 525,000Rp; ✖ 🖳 ) The liveliest hotel in Makassar. Staff here are young and fun and there's a happening nightspot in the basement (see p665). Rooms (request a sea view) are modern, very comfy and excellent value. There's a lovely jacuzzi with ocean panoramas, plus a sauna and steam room.

## TOP END

Both these places offer frequent promotions, with discounts between 10% and 25%.

**Hotel Pantai Gapura** ( ☎ 325 791; www.pantaigapura .com; Jl Pasar Ikan 10; r 600,000Rp, cottages from 1,000,000Rp; ✖ ✖ ) The closest thing you'll find to a resort in the city centre, Hotel Pantai Gapura is a bit kitsch but the ocean views, swimming pool, palm trees and water gardens do feel like a holiday. Rooms are poor value but the giant Bugis-style over-the-water cottages are truly special. There is also a sunset bar-restaurant in a funny old cargo boat.

**Imperial Aryaduta Hotel** ( ☎ 870 555; www.aryaduta .com; Jl Somba Opu 297; r from 1,200,000Rp; ✖ 🖳 ✖ ) This is *the* place to see and be seen with the ritzy Asian business elite. Huge rooms with amazing sea views would be better if the carpets weren't stained, but you could easily forget about this at the spa, the seaside pool or by holding your nose at any of the several smoky bars.

## Eating

For many, it's the food that makes Makassar a great destination. There's an abundance of seafood, Chinese dishes, local specialities such as *coto Makassar* (soup made from buffalo innards), and a few international surprises.

Hundreds of night warungs just off Jl Metro Tanjung Bunga serve up fresh and cheap Indonesian and Chinese meals for around 15,000Rp, and you can (just about) see Makassar's famous sunset.

Just as good are the string of makeshift fish warungs set up every night on the foreshore opposite Fort Rotterdam that serve some of the tastiest, cheapest seafood in town (about 15,000Rp per fish, baked, grilled or fried). Roaming buskers provide tableside entertainment.

Jl Timor, in the heart of the Chinese quarter, is where you'll find restaurants serving delicious *mie pangsit* (wonton soup).

**Sentosa** ( ☎ 326 062; Jl Penghibur 26; soup 6000Rp) Locals flock to this basic cafe with sea views (across the street) and delicious wonton soup.

**Mie Titi** (Jl Datu Museng; small/large noodles 15,000/16,000Rp; ☺ 10am-2am) Makassar institution for its *mie kering* (dry noodles) – deep fried thin noodles that stay crunchy under a rich sauce of greens, dough, *bakso* and precisely one shrimp per portion. Ask for extra garlic and try the pickled chillis.

**Kios Semarang** (Jl Penghibur; mains 15,000-35,000Rp; ☺ lunch & dinner) At the closest thing to a Makassar institution, climb the stairs to the 3rd floor where you will be rewarded with a rowdy crowd, good seafood and cheap beer. Start with a sunset and a Bintang or two before trying the fresh squid or shrimp.

**our pick Lae Lae** ( ☎ 334 326; Jl Datu Museng 8; fish from 20,000Rp; ☺ lunch & dinner) A very basic dining hall jam-packed with food-frenzied locals, this place is as social as the seafood is good. Servers lead you to the ice box where you choose your fish (or squid, crab or just about any other sort of sea critter) that gets grilled while you make friends at your table. Wash up, roll up your sleeves and dive into the flaky fish, sambal (chilli sauce) and sauces hands-first.

**Rumah Makan Kayangan** ( ☎ 325 273; Jl Datu Museng 20; fish from 20,000Rp; ☺ lunch & dinner) Kayangan is a slightly more upmarket affair than Lae Lae, with tablecloths and air-con. The fish is fresh, the service swift and the Bintangs are ice-cold.

**Rumah Makan Malabar** ( ☎ 319 776; Jl Sulawesi 264; curry 20,000Rp; ☺ lunch & dinner) Run by a second-generation Keralan, Malabar is a little slice of the Indian subcontinent, serving up flaky naan and tender *kare kambing* (goat curry).

**Pizza Ria** (cnr Jl Kajaolalido & Jl Ahmad Yani; pizza from 20,000Rp; ☺ lunch & dinner) The atmosphere here is a little cheesy, but the pizzas are surprisingly good and a few have a spicy Indonesian twist.

**Shogun** ( ☎ 324 102; Jl Penghibur 2; sushi & sashimi platters from 95,000Rp; ☺ lunch & dinner) The only authentic Japanese restaurant in town is right next door to Hotel Losari Beach. The sushi is excellent, but portions are small in comparison to the hefty price tag. There are also teppanyaki sets (from 128,000Rp), yakitori, sate and steaks.

**Club Velvet** (Imperial Aryaduta Hotel; Jl Somba Opu 297) A smoky evening jazz lounge that offers sumptuous platters for two with all sorts of flamboyant flavours.

If the hot weather is just too much, duck into Swensen's for an ice cream. Upstairs in the same food court, above the well-stocked **Galeal Supermarket** (Jl Sultan Hasanuddin), is Kantin Baik dan Murah turning out good, cheap Indonesian food at affordable prices.

## Drinking

A lot of the bars around the port area are little more than brothels disguised as karaoke bars and are best avoided by all but the proverbial drunken sailor. You really want to know how bad it is? Locals call it Vagina St.

Further south on Jl Penghibur, there are several lively places. The aforementioned Kios Semarang is definitely *the* watering hole in town.

**Kafe Kareba** (Jl Penghibur) On the corner opposite the Hotel Losari Beach, this outdoor beer garden features live bands and the drinks flow. It also has a pretty extensive menu of food for those wanting entertainment while they eat.

**Ballairate Sunset Bar** (Hotel Pantai Gapura; Jl Pasar Ikan 10) Built on stilts over the sea, this is the best-located bar in town. Walk right through the hotel to discover draft Bintang by the pitcher and a perfect view of the sunset. Sundays are a bad idea as the Makassar jet-ski crowd strut their stuff on the water here.

## Entertainment

### CINEMAS

There are several modern multiscreen cinemas showing current Western films in their original language (with Indonesian subtitles):

**Makassar Theatre** (Jl Bali) Hidden away in the back streets near many of the budget hotels.

**Studio 21** (Jl Sam Ratulangi) On the top floor of the Ratu Indah Mall complex.

### NIGHTCLUBS

Drinking at nightclubs can be prohibitively expensive, as this is how they rake in the cash. It is best to warm up at a bar before delving into the dance zone. Most of the clubs rumble on until about 3am.

Many of the top-end hotels house night-clubs with pricey drinks and bands playing MTV hits. Entry costs 30,000Rp to 50,000Rp, which usually includes a soft drink or beer.

**Colors** (Jl Pasar Ikan; admission varies) Housed in the old Benteng Theatre, this is the 'in' club in town. DJs and bands from Jakarta, ladies' night on Wednesday and expensive drinks all round, this is where the hipsters hang out.

**M Club** (admission incl 1st drink from 25,000Rp) On the eastern edge of town, this warehouse club is one of the biggest in Sulawesi. The music is tech-no prisoners and the lighting strobe-heavy, but if you want the Makassar experience, this is an essential stop. Foreigners often get in free. All taxi drivers know the place – a ride should cost about 30,000Rp.

**Botol Cafe** (Quality Hotel; Jl Somba Opu 235) By far the most popular of the hotel nightclubs, this one is tucked away rather uninvitingly in the basement car park.

## Shopping

Jl Somba Opu has plenty of shops with great collections of jewellery, 'antiques' and souvenirs, including crafts from all over Indonesia, such as Kendari filigree silver jewellery, Torajan handicrafts, Chinese pottery, Makassarese brasswork, and silk cloth from Sengkang. Shopping centres are the place to be for most Makassarese:

**G Mall** The massive centrepiece of the new Tanjung Bunga development.

**Makassar Mall** A sprawling mess and more like a market than a mall – go here to experience Makassar at its craziest.

**Panukkukang Mall** Bigger than an Indonesian village, this is a popular mall in the affluent eastern suburbs.

**Ratu Indah Mall** (Jl Sam Ratulangi) The best of the more central malls, this one could be anywhere in the world.

## Getting There & Away

### AIR

Makassar is well connected to the rest of Indonesia, as many flights between Java and the easternmost islands call here en route. Shop around and check for the current prices with airlines and agents.

**Batavia Air** (☎ 365 5255; Jl Ahmad Yani 35) of-fers flights three to four days a week to and from Gorontalo, Luwuk, Manokwari and Jayapura (via Manokwari) and daily flights to Kendari.

**Garuda** (Garuda Indonesia; ☎ 365 4747; Jl Slamet Riyadi 6) flies directly to and from Manado, Denpasar, Jakarta, Jayapura and Biak every day of the week.

**Lion Air** (☎ 327 038; Jl Ahmad Yani 22) flies daily to and from Manado, Kendari, Gorontalo, Palu, Jakarta, Surabaya and Denpasar.

**Merpati** (☎ 442 892; Jl Bawakaraeng) connects Makassar to Jakarta, Balikpapan, Kendari, Surabaya, Luwuk and Palu. There is also a handy daily Yogyakarta service.

**Sriwijaya Air** (☎ 424 800; Jl Boulevard Raya 23) flies to Surabaya, Palu, Gorontalo, Kendari and Ambon.

### BOAT

More than half the Pelni fleet stops in Makassar, mostly on the way to Surabaya and Jakarta, East Kalimantan, Ambon and Papua.

Useful services include the *Kerinci* and *Tidar* to Balikpapan (economy/1st class 146,000/407,000Rp), the *Sirimau* to Larantuka in Flores (309,000/886,000Rp), and the *Tilongkabila* to Bau Bau and then up along the east coast to Kendari (181,000/465,000Rp), Kolonedale, Luwuk, Gorontalo and Manado.

The **Pelni office** (☎ 331 401; Jl Sam Ratulangi; ⊙ 8am-2pm Mon-Sat) is efficient and computer-ised. Tickets are also available at any Pelni agency around town. The chaotic Pelabuhan Makassar port, which is used by Pelni boats, is only a short becak ride from most hotels.

### BUS & KIJANG

Makassar has numerous terminals but three are most useful. Terminal Daya is in the eastern suburbs on the road to the airport, where there are buses and Kijangs to all points north, including Pare Pare (24,300Rp, three hours), Sengkang (38,000Rp, four hours) and Rantepao (51,600Rp, eight hours). Kijangs often take shorter routes than the buses and are worth the slightly more expensive tick-ets. VIP **Bintang Prima** (☎ 47728) buses are the most comfortable choice for Rantepao, although **Litha Bus** (☎ 324 847) is a close sec-ond. Both cost 80,000Rp and offer better leg room than business class on an aeroplane – no kidding. To get to Terminal Daya, catch any *pete-pete* (3000Rp, 30 minutes) marked 'Daya' from Makassar Mall or from along Jl Bulusaraung.

Terminal Mallengkeri is about 10km southeast of the city centre. From here, buses and Kijangs go to places southeast of Makassar, including Bulukumba (32,000Rp, three hours) and Pantai Bira (55,000Rp, four hours). For Pantai Bira, you may have to change in Bulukumba.

Terminal Sungguminasa has regular *pete-pete* services to Malino (14,000Rp, 1½ hours). To get to Mallengkeri or Sungguminasa, take a *pete-pete* marked 'S Minasa' from Makassar Mall or from along Jl Jendral Sudirman. Ask to be dropped at Mallengkeri, or continue on to Terminal Sungguminasa.

Buses run all day but are most frequent in the morning, so it's good to get to the terminals no later than 8am.

If you're arriving by plane, buses to Pare Pare, Toraja and all points north can be flagged down on the Makassar–Maros road, 300m from the terminal (there's a free shuttle), saving a trip into town. However, you may need to wait a while for an empty seat.

## Getting Around
### TO/FROM THE AIRPORT

Hasanuddin Airport is 22km from the centre of Makassar. Prepaid taxis are easy to arrange at the arrivals area. There are three fares from 75,000Rp to 95,000Rp, depending on the destination, but most hotels are in the centre, which costs 85,000Rp. To the airport, a metered taxi is about 80,000Rp.

For public transport from the airport to central Makassar, free shuttles run from the basement level of the airport to the main road (about 500m from the terminal) about every 15 minutes; that's where you can flag down a *pete-pete* into town (although you'll probably have to change to another *pete-pete* at Terminal Daya). From central Makassar to the airport, catch a *pete-pete* from Makassar Mall to Maros (8500Rp) and tell the driver to let you out at the airport. If you're lucky, the shuttle will be there and take you to the terminal, or you'll have to walk the 500m.

It's also possible to get an *ojek* (motorcycle taxi) to the airport for around 60,000Rp.

### PUBLIC TRANSPORT

Makassar is hot, so using a becak, *pete-pete* or taxi can be a relief. The friendly old crooks that are the becak drivers like to kerb-crawl, hoping you'll succumb to their badgering

and/or the heat. The going rate is 5000Rp around town, but you inevitably have to bargain for this. The main *pete-pete* terminal is at the Makassar Mall, and the standard fare around town is 3000Rp. Air-conditioned taxis have meters and are worth using; it works out at about 4500Rp a kilometre.

## AROUND MAKASSAR
### Pulau Samalona

A tiny speck just off Makassar, Pulau Samalona is popular for fishing and snorkelling, particularly on Sunday. Otherwise, there's nothing much to do – it takes a full two minutes to walk around the island. If you ask around, you can buy cold drinks and fresh fish meals. Snorkelling gear is also available. Compared to Makassar harbour, the water's pretty clear!

To get here you will have to charter a boat for about 250,000Rp one way or return from the special jetty in Makassar and prearrange to be picked up later. On Sunday you can probably share a boat with some day-trippers.

### Pulau Kayangan

This tiny island is cluttered with strange tourist attractions and is not great for swimming (although plenty of locals do it). It's very busy on Sunday, but almost completely empty for the rest of the week. Some of the restaurants around the island are positioned over the water, and many are perfect for sunsets. If you feel like staying here, **Wisata Bahari Pulau Kayangan** ( ☎ 0411-315 752; r 180,000-450,000Rp) has somewhat overpriced rooms, although the deluxe options are huge and include satellite TV and air-con.

Boats travel from the special jetty in Makassar every 15 minutes (per person return 20,000Rp, on Sunday 30,000Rp) until 10pm – perfect for a sunset cruise followed by a meal on the island.

### Bantimurung

**Air Terjun Bantimurung** (admission 10,000Rp), 42km from Makassar, are waterfalls set amid lushly vegetated limestone cliffs. Looking up, it's straight out of Jurassic Park, but then you scan the ground level and it's a classic *objek wisata* (tourist object). That translates as crowded with day-trippers on weekends, and peppered with litter and creative concrete, but it remains a wonderful and picturesque retreat from the heat of Makassar. Upstream from the main waterfall there's another smaller waterfall and a pretty, but treacherous, pool. However, you will need a torch to make it through the cave en route. Bantimurung is also famous for its beautiful **butterflies**. The naturalist Alfred Wallace collected specimens here in the mid-1800s. However, numbers are plummeting as locals trap them to sell to visitors, so try not to encourage the trade.

Catch a Damri bus or *pete-pete* (8500Rp, one hour) to Maros from Makassar Mall in Makassar, and a *pete-pete* to Bantimurung (5000Rp, 30 minutes).

### Gua Leang Leang

A few kilometres before Bantimurung is the road to these caves, noted for their ancient paintings. The age of the paintings is unknown, but relics from nearby caves have provided glimpses of life from 8000 to 30,000 years ago. There are 60 or so known caves in the Maros district, as the limestone karsts here have more holes than a Swiss cheese.

Catch a *pete-pete* from Maros to the 'Taman Purbakala Leang-Leang' turn-off on the road to Bantimurung, and then walk the last couple of kilometres. Alternatively, charter a *pete-pete* from Maros and combine it with a trip to Bantimurung.

### Malino
☎ 0417

Malino is a hill resort, once famous as the meeting place of Kalimantan and East Indonesian leaders who endorsed the Netherlands' ill-fated plans for a federation. More recently, peace agreements have been struck for Maluku and Poso in the Resort Celebes. There are many scenic walks, and **Air Terjun Takapala** is a spectacular waterfall set amid rice fields 4km east of town. Look for the 'Wisata Alam Lombasang Malino' sign as you come into town for the waterfall turn-off.

**Hotel Pinang Mas** ( ☎ 21173; Jl Karaeng Pado; r from 170,000Rp) is the place for huge views, but the prices are equally huge given the standard of the rooms. It's on the main road, about 150m above the muddy market.

**Resort Celebes** ( ☎ 21300; Jl Hasanuddin 1; r from 280,000Rp) is a must for those with a sense of history, as many an important political agreement has been hammered out here. All rooms include satellite TV and hot water. It's a very peaceful place.

Both hotels have popular restaurants; otherwise you can eat at hole-in-the-wall warungs.

Terminal Sungguminasa has regular *pete-pete* services to Malino (14,000Rp, 1½ hours). Make sure you leave early before Malino's infamous rain sets in.

## PANTAI BIRA
☎ 0413

Goats outnumber vehicles in the charmingly lethargic beach village of Bira, and it's a particularly inexpensive spot for backpackers to take off their packs and chill out. The powdery white-sand beach gets spacious at low tide and there's great snorkelling a short swim from the shore. There are several more remote beaches, hiking and a few caves with freshwater pools to explore in the surrounding area. The diving here is very good, with more fish than you'll find at Bunaken or in the Togeans, but strong currents make it suitable only for experienced divers.

### Orientation & Information

Almost everything is located along a small section of the road into Pantai Bira, Jl Kapongkolang. Foreign tourists must pay 5000Rp per person at the toll booth when they first enter 'town'. The Bira Beach Hotel has a wartel, which also acts as a postal agency, Pelni agency and moneychanger. At the time of research there was no internet and no bank in Bira.

### Sights

Boat builders use age-old techniques to craft **traditional ships** at Marumasa near Bira village and at Tanah Beru on the road to Bulukumba. Boats of various sizes can be seen at different stages of construction.

Weavers gather under raised houses to work and gossip. You can hear the click-clack of their looms as you walk along the streets in Bira village. There is a small **market** (Pasar Bira) held in the village every two days.

A short hike from the road near Pantai Timur takes you to the top of **Pua Janggo**, a small hill with great views. Staff of all the hotles and guest houses can tell you how to get to caves and some deserted beaches nearby by public transport.

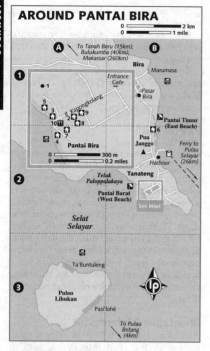

# AROUND PANTAI BIRA

## Activities

### DIVING & SNORKELLING

The waters off Bira are particularly popular with sharks, rays and huge groupers, plus there is superb coral at several drop-offs. May to June is whale shark season although you'd be lucky to see one. The best spots are around Pulau Selayar, Marumasa, northern Pulau Lihukan, and southern and eastern Pulau Betang.

The only dive centre in Bira is **South Sulawesi Diver** ( ☎ 82125; www.south-sulawesi-diver.com), based at Anda Bungalows. It's run by a German instructor who has been exploring the waters for a few years. Fun dives are available, but the price depends on numbers and the centre is only open six months a year.

Snorkelling is also impressive off Bira and it's worth chartering a boat to get to the best spots. A trip around Pulau Lihukan and Pulau Betang will cost about 250,000Rp per day. The beach in front of Bira View Inn is good, but don't venture too far because the currents can be surprisingly strong and people have drowned. Equipment can be rented for about 50,000Rp per day from several hotels, including Riswan Guest House, Bira View Inn and Bira Beach Hotel.

### SWIMMING

The tides can be severe, but **Pantai Barat** (West Beach) is a perfect stretch of beach, about 100m northwest of Bira Beach Hotel. You can hire huge inflatable rubber tyres, and enjoy the serenity – except on Sunday, when the place is usually crawling with day-trippers from Makassar. **Pantai Timur** (East Beach) is more your serene, coconut-fringed affair. Bear in mind that the locals are fairly conservative around here, so topless bathing for women is a major no-no.

## Sleeping

Places are close together so you can shop around before deciding where to stay – a good idea since most are not very well kept.

**Salassa Guest House** ( ☎ 081 2426 5672; r 60,000Rp) A family-run place, Salassa has basic rooms with an Indonesian-style shared bathroom in a wooden house on stilts. The owners are very helpful, speak English and can direct you to some great off-the-beaten-track locations around Bira. You can join the family meals on request.

**Riswan Guest House** ( ☎ 82127; r 75,000Rp) Rooms here are simple but very clean and have attached bathrooms. Host Riswan is friendly and knowledgeable and the family atmosphere is simply charming. You can also get a room including all meals (which are served with the family) for 150,000Rp; rooms with breakfast only are 100,000Rp.

**our pick Nini's Place** ( ☎ 0813 5541 5379; nini bone@hotmail.com; r with breakfast 90,000Rp) Perched up on a hill with ocean views, American-Indonesian-run Nini's has a fresh coat of paint, a wonderful communal terrace with sea breezes, a convivial atmosphere and is easily the best-tended place in Bira. Comfy rooms in a big wooden house have spotless shared bathrooms.

**Bira View Inn** ( ☎ 82043; fax 81515; cottages 100,000-200,000Rp; ⊠ ) Barbed wire, a few semidestroyed bungalows and graffiti makes this place look abandoned, but there's still a snoozing receptionist in the main office and a few of the big bungalows with terraces are in surprisingly good shape on the inside. It's a heartbreaker because the seafront location here is fantastic.

**Kaluku Kafe** (www.kalukukafe.com; d in bungalow/cottage 120,000/280,000Rp) The only choice on Pantai Timur, Kaluku Kafe has a pristine setting amid palm trees. There is one bungalow, and the owner has recently added a cottage that can take up to six people. There is also a beachfront restaurant and craft shop, making it easy to lose days here.

**Bira Beach Hotel** ( ☎ /fax 83522; bungalows 150,000-250,000Rp; ⊠ ) This is hands-down the busiest place in town, although all the rooms are pretty rickety. Only the high-end 'sea-view' rooms are worth staying in, but this is because of the happy yellow decor, not because of the minuscule view. The restaurant here is one of the best in Bira. Prices go up 20% in July and August.

**Hotel Sapolohe** ( ☎ /fax 82128; r 245,000-510,000Rp; ⊠ ) While this hotel has a good location on the beach, the rooms are worn, musty and overpriced. The most expensive rooms have OK sea views and all have hot water. Rates go through the roof during holidays.

**Anda Bungalows** ( ☎ 82125; fax 85033; bungalows 250,000-350,000Rp; ⊠ ) All the bungalows here have air-con and are set around a lovely landscaped garden away from the sea; the new cement bungalows are by far the most comfortable in Bira. Cheaper wooden bungalows aren't as posh but are still OK value and the big restaurant here has lots of choices.

## Eating

Most guest houses serve family-style meals while the hotels have more expensive restaurants. The Bira Beach Hotel is by far the best place for a sunset Bintang followed by a meal; expect to pay around 20,000Rp for a main course.

There is also a couple of local Indonesian restaurants along the main drag for cheap eats.

Opposite the Bira Beach Hotel there is a cluster of food and drink stalls and a couple of nameless warungs serving cheap Indonesian fare and freshly grilled fish.

## Getting There & Away

### BOAT

The harbour at Pantai Timur has daily services to Pulau Selayar (two hours, 60,000Rp). Every Sunday night, there is a direct boat to Labuanbajo (150,000Rp) in Flores, but it's a slow ride, taking almost two days.

---

### SULAWESI SEAFARERS

The Bugis are Indonesia's best-known sailors, trading and carrying goods on their magnificent wooden schooners throughout Indonesia.

The Bugis' influence expanded rapidly after the fall of Makassar, resulting in a diaspora from South Sulawesi in the 17th and 18th centuries. They established strategic trading posts at Kutai (Kalimantan), Johor (north of Singapore) and Selangor (near Kuala Lumpur), and traded freely throughout the region. Bugis and Makassarese *pinisi* (schooners) are still built along the south coasts of Sulawesi and Kalimantan, using centuries-old designs and techniques. You can see boats being built at Marumasa and Tanah Beru, both near Bira.

The Bajau, Bugis, Butonese and Makassarese seafarers of Sulawesi have a 500-year history of trading and cultural links with the Australian Aborigines, and their ships are featured in pre-European Aboriginal cave art in northern Australia. British explorer Matthew Flinders encountered 60 Indonesian schooners at Melville Bay in 1803; today many more still make the risky (and illegal) journey to fish reefs in the cyclone belt off the northern coast of Australia.

Many Minahasans of North Sulawesi, relative newcomers to sailing folklore, work on international shipping lines across the world. Like with their Filipino neighbours, the Minahasans' outward-looking culture, plus their language and sailing skills, make them the first choice of many captains.

### BUS, BEMO & KIJANG

From Makassar (Terminal Mallengkeri), a few Kijangs go directly to Pantai Bira for 55,000Rp. Alternatively, catch a Kijang or bemo to Bulukumba, and another to Pantai Bira (transport from Bulukumba to Pantai Bira stops at around 3pm).

Direct Kijangs from Pantai Bira to Makassar (55,000Rp) can sometimes be booked through your hotel the day before; otherwise get a *pete-pete* from Pantai Bira to Bulukumba and take a Kijang to Makassar from there; the price also works out to 55,000Rp.

## PULAU LIHUKAN & PULAU BETANG

Weavers at **Ta'Buntuleng** make heavy, colourful cloth on hand looms under their houses. On the pretty beach west of the village there is an interesting old **graveyard**, and off the beach there are acres of sea grass and coral, but mind the currents and sea snakes. To see the best coral, which is further out, you'll need a boat. In fact, you'll need to charter a boat to visit Lihukan and the nearby, uninhabited Pulau Betang, also known as Pulau Kambing.

## PULAU SELAYAR
☎ 0414

This long, narrow island lies off the southwestern peninsula of Sulawesi and is inhabited by the Bugis, the Makassarese and the Konjo. Most reside along the infertile west coast and in **Benteng**, the main town. Like at Pantai Bira, Selayar's long coastline is a repository of flotsam from nearby shipping lines, perhaps accounting for the presence of a 2000-year-old Vietnamese Dongson drum, kept in an annexe near the former **Benteng Bontobangun** (Bontobangun Fort), a few kilometres south of Benteng.

Selayar's main attractions are its sandy **beaches** and picturesque scenery. The snorkelling near small **Pulau Pasi**, opposite Benteng, is good, but you will have to charter a boat.

Stay at **Selayar Island Resort** ( ☎ 21750; www.selayarislandresort.com; cottages per person €40-70; 🗙 🛜 ), a relatively new place perched on a rocky outcrop next to its own beach. There's a range of comfortable rooms as well as a dive centre that leads dives to some extraordinary, little-visited sites.

There are daily ferries (two hours, 60,000Rp) from Pantai Timur harbour near Pantai Bira to/from Pamatata on Selayar. The hotel should know the current schedule or can arrange private transport. Buses leave Terminal Mallengkeri in Makassar each morning to link with the ferry from Pantai Bira.

## TAKA BONE RATE

Southeast of Pulau Selayar and north of Pulau Bone Rate, is the 2220-sq-km Taka Bone Rate, the world's third-largest coral atoll. The largest, Kwajalein in the Marshall Islands, is just 20% bigger. Some of the islands and extensive reefs in the region are now part of **Taka Bone Rate Marine National Park** (Taman Laut Taka Bone Rate), a marine reserve with a rich variety of marine and bird life.

There is no official accommodation on the islands, but if you manage to get here you can stay with villagers if you ask the *kepala desa* (village head) at Bone Rate on Pulau Bone Rate. Boats leave irregularly from Selayar. Most visitors are divers on liveaboard trips.

## WATAMPONE
☎ 0481 / pop 84,000

Known more simply as Bone (bone-eh) by locals, Watampone is a small town with a good range of hotels. The only reason most foreigners come here is to go to/from Kolaka in Southeast Sulawesi from the nearby port of Bajoe.

While in town, visit **Museum Lapawawoi** (Jl Thamrin; admission free; 🕑 7am-4pm), a former palace housing one of Indonesia's most interesting regional collections, including an odd array of court memorabilia and dozens of photographs of state occasions.

If you do end up staying overnight, try **Wisma Bole Ridie** ( ☎ 21412; Jl Merdeka 6; r 45,000Rp, s/d 60,000/80,000Rp), a former royal residence, built in the Dutch colonial style. The cheaper rooms are rather small and located out the back, while in the main building there are huge, charming, yet dusty rooms. **Hotel Wisata Watampone** ( ☎ 21362; fax 22367; Jl Jendral Sudirman 14; r from 150,000Rp; 🗙 🖭 ) is the best hotel in town, and the big rooms have satellite TV, hot water and air-con.

There is a cluster of simple *rumah makan* (local restaurants) in the market area, and night warungs and Padang-style *rumah makan* along the main shopping street, Jl Ponggawae.

The BNI bank on Jl Sukawati has one of the only ATMs in town, and you can try to find internet connections at the Telkom office on Jl Monginsidi.

## Getting There & Away

### BOAT
Bajoe is the major regional port, 8km from Watampone, for connections to Kolaka.

Three ferries (eight hours) leave every evening at 5pm, 8pm and 11pm from Bajoe for Kolaka, the gateway to the southeastern peninsula. Tickets are 55,000/70,000Rp for deck/business class.

From Watampone, bemos go to Bajoe every few minutes from a special stop behind the market. From the bus terminal at the end of the incredibly long causeway in Bajoe, buses head off to most places, including Makassar and Rantepao, just after the ferry arrives. Get off the ferry and jump on an *ojek,* bus or bemo to Watampone.

### BUS & BEMO
Several Kijangs and buses travel to Bulukumba (45,000Rp, three hours) for connections to Bira and Makassar (55,000Rp, five hours). Buses also run to Palopo and Pare Pare. The terminal is 2km west of town, so take an *ojek* or bemo from Jl Sulawesi. Kijangs to Sengkang (25,000Rp, two hours) leave from Jl Mangga in the centre of Watampone.

If you're heading to Rantepao (55,000Rp), get a connection in Palopo. Several bus agencies along Jl Besse Kajuara, on either side of the bus terminal, sell tickets for the through trip to Kendari (120,000Rp).

## SENGKANG
☎ 0485

Sengkang is a small yet traffic-clogged town with a nearby scenic lake and a traditional hand-woven silk industry. **BNI bank** (Bank Negara Indonesia; Jl Ahmad Yani) has an ATM and can change money. For telephone calls, there is a Telkom office on Jl Pahlawan.

## Sights & Activities

### DANAU TEMPE
Danau Tempe is a large, shallow lake fringed by wetlands, with floating houses and magnificent birdlife. Geologists believe the lake was once a gulf between southern Toraja and the rest of South Sulawesi. As they merged, the gulf disappeared and geologists believe the lake will eventually disappear too…silt from deforestation is speeding up the process.

There are no organised boat tours, but the guest houses can help you arrange a charter boat for about 80,000Rp for two hours (100,000Rp with a guide), in which time you can speed along **Sungai Walanae**, visit **Salotangah village** in the middle of the lake, go across to **Batu Batu village** on the other side, and come back. A boat trip is particularly charming at dusk.

You could try to haggle for a cheaper rate on your own at the longboat terminal opposite the sports field on Jl Sudirman.

### SILK WEAVING
Sengkang's other attraction is its *sutera* (silk) weaving industry. **Silk-weaving workshops** are found around 5km out of town, while the nearest **silkworm farms** are about 15km from Sengkang. Ask the staff at your hotel to recommend some workshops, and charter a *pete-pete* from the terminal. Alternatively, just walk around the **market** in Sengkang, where silk scarves and sarongs are on sale.

## Sleeping
All room prices include breakfast.

**Hotel Al Salam II** ( ☎ 21278; fax 21893; Jl Emmi Saelan 8; r 50,000-170,000Rp) This is the busiest hotel in town, with friendly, helpful service and a range of large rooms with attached bathrooms. Unfortunately, mattresses are musty and there is plenty of dust in the room corners. There's also a little restaurant and bar on the premises.

**Hotel Apada** ( ☎ /fax 21053; Jl Nangka 9; r 100,000-150,000Rp; ✗ ) Formerly owned by a princess, this large, rambling hotel has smart rooms that include attached bathrooms. The hotel can also organise traditional Bugis dinners and will lend you fancy sarongs to dress for the occasion.

**Pondok Eka** ( ☎ /fax 21296; Jl Maluku 12; r 165,000-220,000Rp; ✗ ⌨ ) If you want clean, head here, although the ambiance isn't as lively as at the Al Salam II. Rooms, surrounding a sparkling courtyard with a murky pool, are huge and all have air-con and HBO. It's family-run and helpful.

## Getting There & Away
Sengkang is readily accessible from Pare Pare (25,000Rp, two hours) by bus or Kijang. If you're travelling to/from Rantepao (six hours), take a bemo to Lawawoi (20,000Rp) and catch a bus from there (40,000Rp); alternatively you can go through Palopo. There are plenty of buses and Kijangs along the road to Watampone (25,000Rp, two hours) and Bajoe. There are regular buses to/from Terminal Daya in Makassar (38,000Rp, six hours), but Kijangs and bemos (55,000Rp, four hours) take a shorter route.

Bemos to local destinations leave from the bus terminal behind the market on Jl Kartini. Agencies for long-distance buses, Kijangs and Pelni boats are a few metres south of the terminal.

## PARE PARE
☎ 0421 / pop 114,000
Pare Pare is a smaller, greener version of Makassar, and a quiet stopover between Tana Toraja or Mamasa and Makassar. It's also the second-largest port in the region, with many Pelni services and boats to Kalimantan.

### Orientation & Information
The town is stretched out along the waterfront. At night, the esplanade turns into a lively pedestrian mall with warungs. Most of what you might need is on the streets running parallel to the harbour. The major banks change money and internet can be found at the main post office on Jl Karaeng Burane.

### Sleeping & Eating
**Hotel Gandaria I** ( ☎ 21093; Jl Bau Massepe 395; s/d with fan 40,000/70,000Rp) A friendly, family-run spot which has good-value rooms. There's a second location, with the same prices, on Jl Samporaja.

**Hotel Kenari Bukit Indah** ( ☎ 21886; Jl Jendral Sudirman 65; s/d from 163,000/200,000Rp; 🗙 ) This hotel is a little way out of town, but for those with transport it is worth it for the superb sea views and a well-regarded restaurant. The rooms are some of the most comfortable in Pare Pare, with air-con, TV and hot water.

There are several small *rumah makan* along Jl Baso Daeng Patompo, in the vicinity of Hotel Siswa. At night, warungs line the esplanade, each with exactly the same choice of rice and noodle dishes.

### Getting There & Away
**BOAT**
The main reason to come to Pare Pare is to catch a ship to East Kalimantan. Every two weeks, **Pelni** ( ☎ 21017; Jl Andicammi) runs the *Tidar* to Nunukan in Kalimantan and the *Dobonsolo* to Balikpapan.

Every one or two days, several passenger boats travel between Pare Pare and Samarinda and Balikpapan (both 125,000Rp, 22 hours) and Nunukan (266,000Rp, two nights), but these boats are far less safe than the Pelni ships (in January 2009 one of these passenger boats sank, killing 180 people). Details and bookings are available from agencies near the port and just north of Restaurant Asia.

**BUS**
Plenty of buses and Kijangs go to Makassar (24,300Rp, three hours) and Rantepao (35,000Rp, five hours). Most buses travel through Terminal Induk several kilometres south of the city, but it's often easier to hail a bus as it flies through town. Kijangs to Polewali (21,000Rp, two hours) leave from Terminal Soreang, 3km northeast of town.

## PALOPO
☎ 0471 / pop 93,000
This Islamic port on the east coast of the peninsula is the administrative capital of the Luwu district. Before the Dutch, it was the centre of the old and powerful Luwu kingdom. The former palace is now the tiny **Museum Batara Guru** (Jl Andi Jemma), which is opposite the police station, and contains relics of the royal era. On the waterfront is a **Bugis village**, and a long pier where you can get a closer look at the fishing boats.

Palopo is a sprawling town with an inordinate number of becak. There is no reason to come here except to catch public transport. Vehicles regularly leave from just outside Terminal Bolu in Rantepao for the *very* winding trip to Palopo (24,000Rp, two hours). Plenty of buses and minibuses go from Palopo's organised terminal to Rantepao, Pare Pare, Makassar and Watampone.

# TANA TORAJA

A trip to Tana Toraja is like a cultural documentary brought to life. Sweeping and elaborately painted houses with boat-shaped roofs dot terraced rice paddies where farmers work the fields alongside their doe-eyed buffalo. It's an island hemmed in by mountains on all sides and rich with traditional culture. Life for the Toraja revolves around death, and their days are spent earning the money to send away their dead properly. Funeral ceremonies bring together families who may have dispersed as far as Papua or even Australia. Buffalo and pigs are sacrificed, there is a slew of traditional dances and enough food and drink for everyone who can make it to the party. High-class Toraja are entombed in cave graves or hanging graves in the steep cliffs, which are guarded over by *tau tau* (life-sized

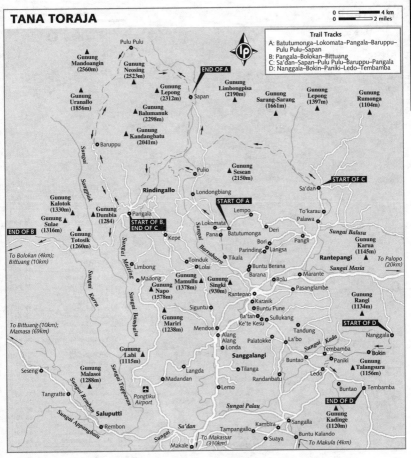

TANA TORAJA

0 — 4 km
0 — 2 miles

**Trail Tracks**
A: Batutumonga–Lokomata–Pangala–Baruppu–
   Pulu Pulu–Sapan
B: Pangala–Bolokan–Bittuang
C: Sa'dan–Sapan–Pulu Pulu–Baruppu–Pangala
D: Nanggala–Bokin–Paniki–Ledo–Tembamba

wooden effigies) carved in their image – you'll
find these eerie yet beautiful cliff cemeteries
scattered throughout the region.

The biggest funerals (see boxed text, p676)
are usually held in the dry-season months of
July and August, but there are funerals (even
big ones) year-round. During July and August
the tourist numbers swell to uncomfortable
proportions and prices soar. Outside these
months, you'll share this cool countryside
with the locals and only a handful of foreign
travellers. While most people consider attending a funeral a highlight, Tana Toraja also
offers some great do-it-yourself trekking opportunities where you can explore the fresh
and clean outdoors and meet some of the most
hospitable people you'll ever encounter.

## RANTEPAO

☎ 0423 / pop 45,000

Rantepao is an easy-to-manage place that's in
striking distance of most of the major sites and
has a good range of accommodation and restaurants. It's the largest town and commercial
centre of Tana Toraja, but traffic isn't too heavy
and the wide streets are fringed by greenery. It's
the obvious place to base a trip to the region.
Nights can be cool and there is rain throughout
the year – even in the dry season.

## Information
### INTERNET ACCESS & POST

There are internet cafes all over town and the
cheaper ones charge 5000Rp per hour.

**Post office** (Jl Ahmad Yani; ☼ 8am-4pm Mon-Sat)

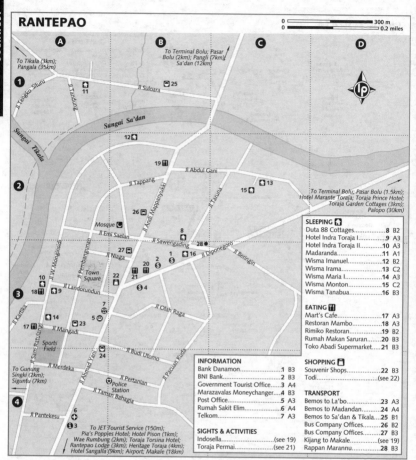

# RANTEPAO

## MAPS

If you're doing some serious hiking, pick up a copy of the detailed *Tana Toraja* (1:85,000) map, published by Periplus.

## MEDICAL SERVICES

**Rumah Sakit Elim** ( ☎ 21258; Jl Ahmad Yani) The main hospital in town. If anything serious should befall you in Toraja, make for Makassar, as facilities here are basic.

## MONEY

The best exchange rates are available from moneychangers.

**Bank Danamon** (Jl Diponegoro) Has an ATM; also offers heftier cash advances.

**BNI bank** (Bank Negara Indonesia; Jl Diponegoro) Another popular ATM.

**Marazavalas** (Jl Diponegoro) Moneychanger with reasonable rates.

## TOURIST INFORMATION

**Government tourist office** ( ☎ 21277; Jl Ahmad Yani 62A) The friendly staff here can provide accurate, independent information about local ceremonies, festivals and other activities as well as arrange guides. It's just south of the hospital.

## TELEPHONE

There are several wartel in town, and many hotels offer international calls from rooms.
**Telkom** (Jl Ahmad Yani; ⏰ 24hr) Next door to the post office.

## Sights

Rantepao's main **market**, Pasar Bolu, is held every six days (but operates in a reduced capacity daily). The main market is a very big, social occasion that draws crowds from all over Tana Toraja. Ask around Rantepao for the exact day, or seek out other markets in the area. There is a 10,000Rp charge to enter the livestock market, where the leading lights from the buffalo community are on parade. Many cost more than a small car. Pasar Bolu is 2km northeast of town and easily accessible by bemo.

## Activities
Most of the activities lie in the hills beyond (see p679). However, most of the hotels that have **swimming pools** allow nonguests to swim for a fee of about 10,000Rp.

## Tours
See p679 for information on independent guides to the countryside around Rantepao.

There are also several reliable, long-running agencies in Rantepao, which can arrange more luxurious tours (including trekking and cultural tours), vehicles and guides:

**Indosella** ( ☎ 25210; www.sellatours.com; Jl Andi Mappanyukki 111)

**JET Tourist Service** ( ☎ 21145; fax 23227; Jl Pontingku 31)

**Toraja Permai** ( ☎ 21785; fax 21236; Jl Andi Mappanyukki 10)

## Sleeping
Prices in Rantepao usually rise in the tourist season (June–August), when some private homes also accept guests. Most budget and midrange places include breakfast in their prices, but they don't offer air-conditioning or a fan, as the nights are cool.

Location and views are often the selling points for midrange places, which are mostly located along the roads from Rantepao to Makale or Palopo. They cater almost exclusively for tour groups with their own transport, but individuals are welcome, and rates are pretty negotiable during the long, quiet low season.

### BUDGET
**Wisma Maria I** ( ☎ 21165; adespasakal@yahoo.com; Jl Sam Ratulangi 23; s/d 50,000/80,000Rp, with hot water 120,000/150,000Rp) At our favourite rock-bottom cheapie in the town centre, welcoming mama bakes fresh bread for breakfast while her grown-up kids rent out scooters (60,000Rp per day) and bicycles (30,000Rp per day) and suggest itineraries. Rooms are plain but good-sized, bright and very clean. It's all set around a large garden.

**Wisma Irama** ( ☎ 21371; Jl Abdul Gani 16; r from 60,000Rp) On a quiet road, the ageing rooms here surround a grassy courtyard with a traditional rice barn in the centre. It's not as friendly as some of the other places in town but rooms are a good deal.

**Wisma Tanabua** ( ☎ 21072; Jl Diponegoro 43; r without/with attached bathroom 60,000/80,000Rp) A friendly, family-run central spot that has basic rooms and doubles as a beauty salon. You can get a one-hour massage for 100,000Rp.

**our pick** **Pia's Poppies Hotel** ( ☎ 21121; s/d 66,000/88,000Rp) Pia's is the type of place where you can settle in, relax and be pampered after some long days on the road. Rooms have some quirky details like stone bathrooms and each terrace overlooks a languorous garden. Sheets are changed daily, everything is spotless, there's hot water and you're even served a welcome fruit juice on arrival. The service here is better than at most of Sulawesi's business hotels. Plus the charming cafe serves the best food in the region – don't miss the Torajan specialties ordered a few hours in advance. Breakfast is not included in the price and it's about a five- to 10-minute walk (or short becak ride) to the town centre.

**Wisma Imanuel** ( ☎ 21416; Jl W Monginsidi 16; r 80,000-100,000Rp) Set in a large house backed by the river (but there's no access), the rooms here are a generous size and the more expensive include hot-water showers. Big balconies out front offer views over the garden and street action beyond.

**Wisma Monton** ( ☎ 21675; Jl Abdul Gani 14A; r 80,000-125,000Rp) Hidden away down a side lane, this three-storey establishment has clean and comfortable rooms with hot water. Almost deserted when we visited, the building is speckled with Toraja decoration and there's a rooftop restaurant with fine views.

**Hotel Pison** ( ☎ 21344; s/d 85,000/100,000Rp) Literally opposite Pia's, the bland but good-value Pison has 32 rooms, each with a clean bathroom and minibalcony with mountain views. All rooms come with hot water.

**Toraja Garden Cottages** ( ☎ 23336; fax 25397; cottages incl breakfast 100,000Rp) This place was closed for the low season when we passed, but the big cottages are in a very pretty hillside-forest setting on the road towards Palopo. The thoughtful design includes a verandah with countryside views, and both TV and hot water are available.

## THE TORAJA

Inhabiting the vast, rugged landscape of the South Sulawesi highlands are the Toraja, a name derived from the Bugis word *toriaja* that had negative connotations similar to 'hillbilly' or 'bumpkin'.

For centuries Torajan life and culture had survived the constant threat from the Bugis from the southwest, but in 1905 the Dutch began a bloody campaign to bring Central Sulawesi under their control. The missionaries moved in on the heels of the troops, and by WWII many of the great Torajan ceremonies (with the exception of funeral celebrations) were rapidly disappearing from their culture.

### Beliefs

Prior to the arrival of Christianity, the Toraja believed in many gods but worshipped Puang Matua as the special god of their family, clan or tribe. Christianity undermined some traditional Torajan beliefs, but the ceremonies are still a vital part of life.

Torajan mythology suggests that their ancestors came by boat from the south, sailed up Sungai Sa'dan (Sa'dan River) and dwelled in the Enrekang region before being pushed into the mountains by the arrival of other groups.

Buffalo are a status symbol for the Toraja and are of paramount importance in various religious ceremonies. The buffalo has traditionally been a symbol of wealth and power – even land could be bought with buffalo. Sought-after albino buffalo can change hands for more than US$8000.

Despite the strength of traditional beliefs, Christianity in Toraja is a very active force. One of the first questions asked of you will be your religion, and Protestants are given immediate approval.

### Traditional Houses

One of the most noticeable aspects about Tana Toraja is the size and grandeur of the *tongkonan* (traditional house). It is the place for family gatherings and may not be bought or sold.

The towering roof, rearing up at either end, is the most striking aspect of a *tongkonan*. Some believe the roof represents the horns of a buffalo; others suggest it represents the bow and stern of a boat. The more buffalo horns visible, the higher the household's status.

**Duta 88 Cottages** ( ☎ 23477; Jl Sawerigading 12; r 120,000Rp) A slight step up in rupiah from the rest of the budget choices gets you a lovely *tongkonan*-style (traditional Torajan) cottage, set around a verdant little garden. It's a friendly oasis that feels far from the action though it's right in the centre of things. The immaculate cottages with terraces are large, have attached bathrooms and even little dressing areas. All come with hot water and satellite TV. Rates include breakfast.

**Hotel Indra Toraja** ( ☎ 21163; fax 21547; Jl Landorundun 63; standard/deluxe r 180,000/216,000Rp; ✹ ) Right in the centre of Rantepao, the Indra has two annexes opposite each other. The riverside option was undergoing major remodelling at the beginning of 2009 and was already looking quite flashy. Rooms at the streetside location are still in good shape and have terraces overlooking a common courtyard area. All are clean, have hot water and HBO and the service is stellar.

### MIDRANGE

Many of the midrange places are strewn throughout the buffalo-infested valleys, which is great for those with transport, but not so straightforward for those without it. To get to these places, either hop in a bemo or take a becak.

**Rantepao Lodge** ( ☎ 23717; fax 21248; r 200,000-300,000Rp; ✹ ) At this sprawling compound near the Toraja Torsina Hotel, the deluxe rooms are the draw. They have private balconies with a view over the rice fields, TV, fridge and hot water. The standard rooms are pretty basic for the money. There is also a swimming pool here.

**Madaranda** ( ☎ 23777; Jl Sadan 21; d 250,000Rp) The huge, modern and clean rooms inside Torajan-style houses are great value for the money. In low season you can easily bargain for better rates – this place was empty when we passed. Staff is friendly and the grounds are pleasant, central to town and shady.

## Funerals

Of all Torajan ceremonies, the most important is the *tomate* (funeral; literally 'deceased'). Without proper funeral rites the soul of the deceased will cause misfortune to its family.

The Toraja generally have two funeral ceremonies, one immediately after death and an elaborate second funeral after preparations have been made. The bigger ones are usually scheduled during the dry months of July and August, but there are funerals year-round.

Before the second funeral, the deceased remains in the family house. An invitation to visit the deceased is an honour. If you accept, remember to thank the deceased and ask permission of the deceased when you wish to leave – as you would of a living host.

The second funeral can be spread over several days and involve hundreds of guests. The Toraja believe that the souls of animals should follow their masters to the next life, hence the importance of animal sacrifices.

Visitors attending a funeral should wear black or dark-coloured clothing and bring gifts of sugar or cigarettes for the family of the deceased.

## Graves & Tau Tau

The Toraja believe that you can take possessions with you in the afterlife, and the dead generally go well equipped to their graves. Since this led to grave plundering, the Toraja started to hide their dead in caves.

These caves are hollowed out by specialist cave builders. Coffins go deep inside the caves, and sitting on balconies in the rock face in front of the caves are *tau tau* – wooden effigies of the dead.

You can see *tau tau* carvers at work at Londa. There are many *tau tau* at Lemo and a few elsewhere, but it's becoming increasingly difficult to see them in Tana Toraja. So many have been stolen that the Toraja now keep them in their homes.

## Books

In the souvenir shops and supermarkets in Rantepao there are a few decent locally produced guides: *A Guide to Toraja* by AT Marampa is available in English, German and French, and lists dances, ceremonies and some local walks. *Toraja – An Introduction to a Unique Culture* by LT Tangdilintin and M Syafei is written in an equally unique style. *Life and Death of the Toraja People* by Stanislaus Sandarupa is readable and informative.

**Hotel Sangalla** ( ☎ /fax 24485; r 250,000Rp) Located on the road to Makale, the rooms here are all set in *tongkonan*-style houses. Bamboo and wood furnishings predominate and the bathrooms are spotlessly clean. Check the rates before you commit.

**Toraja Prince Hotel** ( ☎ 21430; www.torajaprince hotel.com; r 300,000-350,000Rp; 🛇 🛋 ) A few kilometres from town on the road to Palopo, the Prince was nearly deserted when we passed but the colonial-style rooms are in good shape. There's an old 1970s-style swimming pool and lots of lush garden space, so this isn't a bad choice for families with transportation. The staff we met spoke no English.

**Toraja Torsina Hotel** ( ☎ 21293; s/d from US$30/40; 🛋 ) Set in the rice fields near the turn-off to Ke'te Kesu, the rooms here are clean and comfortable and worth the rupiah considering the swimming pool.

### TOP END

**Hotel Marante Toraja** ( ☎ 21616; www.marantetoraja .com; deluxe r US$60, cottages US$78; 🛋 ) Cement cottages with Torajan-style roofs look great from the outside but are far more bland on the inside. Rooms have the same interiors as the cottages and could use a coat of paint. Fortunately, the staff is exuberant and helpful.

**Heritage Toraja** ( ☎ 21192; www.torajaheritage.com; r US$90-135; 🛇 🛋 ) The Heritage is by far the swankiest place in town, with many of the elegant rooms set in huge *tongkonan*-style houses. Standards are high (with some odd details like a fresh flower in the toilet bowls) and there are lush gardens and a lagoon-like pool. Rooms in the more ordinary block are just as nice as the ones inside the Torajan-style houses but are less expensive. Ask for a top-floor room with a view. It's about 3km from town towards Ke'te Kesu.

## Eating

Going to ceremonies or local restaurants offers a great opportunity to sample Torajan food. The best-known dish is *pa'piong* (meat stuffed into bamboo tubes along with vegetables and coconut). If you want to try it in a restaurant, order several hours in advance because it takes time to cook. The following places are all open for breakfast, lunch and dinner.

**Rumah Makan Saruran** (Jl Diponegoro 19; mains around 15,000Rp) Indonesian-style Chinese food is served at this hopping restaurant that's popular with young travelling Indonesians. The atmosphere is basic but the food is good and cheap.

**Mart's Cafe** (Jl Sam Ratulangi 44; dishes 15,000-45,000Rp) The best tourist trap in town, Mart's gets lively in the evenings when the resident guides start crooning and strumming their guitars. The food is bland but OK and includes Western fare, Indonesian staples and Torajan specialties (order in advance). The Bintang flows and it's almost like a real night out.

**Rimiko Restoran** (Jl Andi Mappanyukki; dishes from 20,000Rp) This place serves the best food of the tourist-oriented restaurants and has a few Torajan specialties on the menu that don't require ordering in advance. It's two doors down from the Indosella office.

**Restoran Mambo** (Jl Sam Ratulangi; dishes from 20,000Rp) Geared towards tourists, this place has a long menu including everything from an interesting interpretation of a burrito (40,000Rp) to buffalo meat (40,000Rp).

**Toko Abadi** (Jl Andi Mappanyukki) For trekkers and self-caterers, this is the best-stocked supermarket in town, although for fruit and veg, make for the market.

---

### NEVER MIND THE BALOKS

Rantepao and Makale markets have whole sections devoted to the sale of the alcoholic *balok* (palm wine, also known as *tuak* and toddy). *Balok* is sold in huge jugs around town and comes in a variety of strengths, colours (from clear to dark red, achieved by adding bark) and flavours (sweet to bitter).

Coffee is Toraja's other famous brew, an excellent antidote to a night of *balok*-tasting.

---

## Shopping

Woodcarving, weaving and basketry are the main crafts of Tana Toraja – some villages are noted for particular specialities, such as Mamasan boxes (used to store magic, salt, betel nuts), huge horn necklaces and wooden figurines. Woodcarvings include trays, panels and clocks, carved like the decorations on traditional houses. The carvers at Ke'te Kesu and Londa are renowned for the quality of their work.

Artefacts sold in souvenir shops, especially around the market building in town, include small replicas of Torajan houses with exaggerated overhanging roofs; Torajan weaving (especially good in Sa'dan); and the longer cloths of the Mamasa Valley. Necklaces made of seeds, chunky silver, and amber or wooden beads festoon the gift shops, but the orange-bead necklaces are the authentic Torajan wear. Black-and-red velvet drawstring bags are popular with tourists, much to the amusement of locals who use them for carrying betel nut to funerals.

**Todi** (Jl Andi Mappanyukki 25) The leading ikat (cloth in which the pattern is produced by dyeing the individual threads before weaving) gallery in Tana Toraja has a stunning showroom upstairs, and there are some fine pieces available. Prices are high and an optimistic sign says 'no bargaining'.

## Getting There & Away

### AIR

Rantepao has an airstrip, but in mid-2009 no airlines were servicing the town.

### BUS & BEMO

Most long-distance buses leave from the bus company offices along, or just off, Jl Andi Mappanyukki. There's also a small shop for **Rappan Marannu** ( ☎ 23537; 6 Jl Sawerigading) that sells bus tickets to Poso, Palu and points between. The most comfortable buses (with slightly higher prices to match) are Bintang Prima and Litha. Try to book the ticket a day or so in advance.

There are plenty of buses heading north to Pendolo (80,000Rp, eight hours), Tentena (110,000Rp, 10 hours), Poso (120,000Rp, 12 hours) and Palu (150,000Rp, 20 hours). Even more buses head south to Pare Pare (35,000Rp, five hours). To Terminal Daya in Makassar (52,000 to 80,000Rp, eight hours), buses often run at night, and prices vary according to speed and the level of comfort and space. Various companies also have services to Mamuju via Polewali, from where there are connections to Mamasa. The only direct bus between Tana Toraja and Mamasa leaves from Makale (see p684).

From Terminal Bolu, 2km north of Rantepao, there are regular vehicles to Palopo. From outside Rimiko Restoran, Kijangs leave every minute to Makale (5000Rp, 20 minutes). See right for more details about transport between Rantepao and other places in Tana Toraja. Plenty of bemos travel between Rantepao and Terminal Bolu.

## Getting Around

Rantepao is small and easy to walk around. A becak should cost around 5000Rp in town.

## MAKALE
☎ 0423

Makale is the administrative capital of Tana Toraja, but has very few of the amenities of Rantepao. It's a small town built around an artificial lake and set amid cloud-shrouded hills. The town also boasts whitewashed churches sitting atop each hill and a busy market. Makale is well connected to most of Tana Toraja by bemo.

Makale's **market** (Jl Pasar Baru) is a blur of noise and colour. On the main market day, held every six days, you'll see pigs strapped down with bamboo strips for buyers' close inspection, buckets of live eels, piles of fresh and dried fish, and a corner of the market is reserved just for *balok* sales.

## Sleeping & Eating

In all honesty, it is far more sensible to stay in Rantepao, which has a good selection of hotels to suit every budget.

**Rumah Makan Idaman** (Jl Merdeka; meals 5000-25,000Rp; ⏱ breakfast, lunch & dinner) The only real restaurant in town is a small, friendly place that serves the usual Indonesian fare, as well as tasty baked fish. It is next door to Makale's *mesjid* (mosque).

When the market's pumping, you'll find local dishes for sale at warungs, such as *pa'piong*, seasonal fruit and *kueh* (cakes).

## Getting There & Away

From dawn to dusk, Kijangs race between Rantepao and Makale (5000Rp, 20 minutes) – just flag one down. Most of the bus companies

based in Rantepao also have offices near the corner of Jl Merdeka and Jl Ihwan Rombe in Makale. Buses will pick up prebooked passengers in Makale for any destination from Rantepao (see opposite). The only direct bus connection between Tana Toraja and Mamasa is with Disco Indah several times a week (98,000Rp, 10 hours).

See below for regional public transport details from Makale.

## AROUND TANA TORAJA

To really experience all that Tana Toraja has to offer, you'll need to spend a few days – or, even better, a few nights – in this tantalising countryside. Stunning scenery, cascading rice fields, precipitous cliff graves, other-worldly *tau tau*, hanging graves, soaring *tongkonan* and colourful ceremonies – this is the wild world of Tana Toraja and it lies just a short walk or ride away from Rantepao.

Most of the places in this section can be reached on day trips from Rantepao, but longer trips are possible, staying overnight in villages or camping out. Public transport, organised tours, motorbike or mountain-bike rental, vehicle rental with a driver-cum-guide or, best of all, walking – anything is possible. The roads to major towns, such as Makale, Palopo, Sa'dan, Batutumonga, Madandan and Bittuang, are paved, but many other roads around Tana Toraja are constructed out of compacted boulders – vehicles don't get stuck, but your joints get rattled loose. Walking is often the only way to reach the remote villages.

A few areas such as Londa, Lemo, Tampangallo, Ke'te Kesu and, to a lesser extent, Palawa have become a bit like tourist traps with lots of stalls selling trinkets and a jaded welcome, but it happened because these places are exceptionally beautiful. There are still plenty of less-visited gems to get to, especially if you take off on foot far from the tour-bus circuit.

### GUIDES

Guides will approach you everywhere and charge 200,000Rp for an all-day circuit by motorbike, including a funeral if there's one on. You can also hire a guide with a car (for up to four people) for 275,000Rp per day, but much of the Toraja region is only accessible on foot or by motorbike so this is a limiting option. All-inclusive two-day treks cost around 1,000,000Rp for two people.

**CHOOSING A GUIDE**

In this region, many guides hold a government-approved licence, obtained by undertaking a course in culture, language and etiquette, and being fluent in the local language. Nevertheless, there are competent guides with no certificate (and incompetent licensed guides). The best way to choose a guide is to sit down and talk through a trip before committing. There is often a lively discussion about Toraja's better guides on the Thorn Tree forum at www.lonelyplanet.com. For more on hiring guides, see boxed text, p823.

Hiring a guide can be useful to help you get your bearings, learn about the culture and cover a lot of ground quickly, but if you have a sense of direction, a decent map (see p674 for map recommendations), know a few relevant phrases of Bahasa Indonesia and are not going too far off the beaten track, you won't go too wrong travelling without one. Many people hire a guide for one day, then set out on their own the next. For a list of agencies in Rantepao offering organised tours of the region, see p675.

## ACTIVITIES
### Trekking
This is the best way to reach isolated areas and to really get a feel for the countryside and the people. Always take good footwear; a water bottle and food; a strong torch (flashlight) in case you walk at night, stay in villages without electricity or want to explore caves; and an umbrella or raincoat – even in the dry season, it's more likely than not to rain. If you're taking advantage of Torajan hospitality, bring gifts (1kg sacks of sugar and cigarettes are favourites) or pay your way.

If you prefer a professional trekking company, contact **Indosella** ( ☎ 0423-25210; www.sellatours.com; Jl Andi Mappanyukki 111, Rantepao). Shorter hikes are mentioned in the individual sections later in this chapter, but a few of the popular longer treks include the following routes:

**Batutumonga–Lokomata–Pangala–Baruppu–Pulu Pulu–Sapan** Three days of superb scenery. Batutumonga to Pangala is on a motorbike-accessible road, while the rest is more serious uphill-trail hiking.

**Bittuang–Mamasa** Three days; see p685.

**Pangala–Bolokan–Bittuang** Two days on a well-marked trail through pristine villages.

**Sa'dan–Sapan–Pulu Pulu–Baruppu–Pangala** Three days; tough and mountainous – a real mountain trek.

For an overview of these trekking routes, check out the Tana Toraja map (Map p673).

### Rafting
**Indosella** ( ☎ 0423-25210; www.sellatours.com; Jl Andi Mappanyukki 111, Rantepao) is the most professional and reliable outfit offering rafting trips on Sungai Sa'dan's 20 rapids, including a few that are Class IV (read: pretty wild). Rafting trips, including transport to/from your hotel (anywhere in Tana Toraja), equipment, guide, insurance and food, cost €50 for one day on Class II to III rapids, or €155 for two days on Class III to IV rapids, with an overnight stay in local rest huts.

A cheaper and more minimalist approach is to hire an independent guide (they usually do not have insurance or good equipment – ask first) for around 120,000Rp per day per person without an overnight stay.

### ENTRANCE FEES
Most of the tourist sites around Tana Toraja have an entry fee of 10,000Rp. There is usually a ticket booth at each place, complete with the odd souvenir stall…or 10 or more in the case of Lemo and Londa.

### GETTING AROUND
Motorbikes and mountain bikes are available through hotels and some agencies. Remember that roads out of Rantepao and Makale are good but often windy, steep and narrow, so they are more suitable for experienced bikers. Bikes can be used along some walking trails, but the trails are often too rocky.

Local public transport leaves from central Rantepao and Makale, as well as from the scruffy and muddy Terminal Bolu north of Rantepao; there are regular bemos and Kijangs to all main villages, but the vehicles are poorly signed so you may have to ask around the terminal. See the Rantepao map (Map p674) for where to catch bemos in central Rantepao heading to La'bo, Madandan, Sa'dan and Tikala.

Some of the more useful services head to the following destinations from Rantepao and Makale:

**Bittuang** For treks to Mamasa, only leaves from Makale.
**La'bo** Via Ke'te Kesu.
**Lempo** Useful for hiking up to Batutumonga.
**Pangala** Via Batutumonga.
**Sa'dan** Usually via Tikala.
**Sangalla** Only leaves from Makale.

## Batutumonga

One of the easiest places to stay overnight and also one of the most beautiful, Batutumonga occupies a dramatic ridge on the slopes of Gunung Sesean, with panoramic views of Rantepao and the Sa'dan Valley, and stunning sunrises. Located about 20km north of Rantepao to Deri, you could also day-trip here for some hiking and a local lunch.

### SLEEPING & EATING

The last two sleeping options are right on the roadside before Batutumonga.

**Mama Siska's Homestay** ( ☎ 0813 4253 2534; r incl all meals per person 75000Rp) This place is as homey and friendly as you can find, but the two rooms (which can sleep four people) in a bamboo hut with basic shared *mandis* are very rustic. It's between Lempo and Batutumonga and is signposted; it's about a 500m walk from the main road.

**Mama Rina's Homestay** ( ☎ 0852 5592 5540; r incl breakfast & dinner per person 75,000Rp) Another very rustic family affair, this place has rooms in a *tongkonan* with saggy mattresses and grotty bamboo walls, but it's a warm, friendly ambience and the views are stunning.

**Mentirotiku** ( ☎ 081 142 2260; bed per person 75,000Rp, r with views 220,000Rp) With commanding views across the valley below, this place has very authentic traditional *tongkonan* crash pads – as in, there are three mattresses squashed together in a space about the size of a small elevator. There are also large modern rooms with bathroom. The rather classy restaurant serves basics from 15,000Rp and traditional Toraja dishes for around 27,000Rp. It's all clean and the grounds are charming.

**Coffee Shop Tinimbayo** (tea 5000Rp) Located a few kilometres east of Batutumonga, this little cafe has a killer location, perched on a hairpin bend with infinite views over the cascading rice fields. Basic meals are possible, but most people stop for tea or a cold drink.

### GETTING THERE & AWAY

Simply take a bemo (10,000Rp) to Batutumonga from Terminal Bolu in Rantepao. Sometimes the bemo only goes as far as Lempo (2km downhill), but the walk from Lempo to Batutumonga is pleasant.

## North of Rantepao

Trekking in the north is the most scenic Tana Toraja option, with dramatic bowls of cascading rice terraces. From Batutumonga, a beautiful walk west takes you to **Lokomata**, a village with cave graves hewn into a rocky outcrop, and outstanding scenery. Backtrack and take the well-marked trail down the slopes to **Pana**, with its ancient hanging graves, and some baby graves in nearby trees. You can see tiny villages with towering *tongkonan*, women pounding rice, men scrubbing their buffalo and children splashing in pools. The path ends at **Tikala** and, from there, regular bemos return to Rantepao.

Alternatively, backtrack through Lempo to **Deri**, the site of rock graves, walk down to the Rantepao–Sa'dan road and catch a bemo back to Rantepao. This is a very pleasant downhill walk (five hours) through some of the finest scenery in Tana Toraja.

At 2150m above sea level, **Gunung Sesean** is not the highest peak on Sulawesi, but it's one of the most popular for trekking. The summit is accessible via a trail from Batutumonga. The return trip to the summit takes five hours. A guide is a good idea if you're inexperienced or speak no Bahasa Indonesia.

Beyond Gunung Sesean is **Pangala** (35km from Rantepao; 20,000Rp by bemo), one of the biggest villages in the region – it has a few streets and a little *ayam goreng* (fried chicken) stall – that's famous for being the hometown of Pongtiku, a fearless warrior who fought against the Dutch. Pongtiku's tomb and a cement statue of the warrior can be seen just at the edge of the village. From here it's a lovely 10km trek to **Baruppu**, a village noted for its dancers.

**Losmen Sando** (r per person 80,000Rp), Pangala's accommodation, looks abandoned from the outside but has surprisingly comfortable rooms, and a spacious restaurant overlooking a coffee plantation. Aptly named Merry (the owner) offers good advice about local trekking.

The traditional village of **Palawa**, east of Batutumonga, is similarly attractive but less popular than Ke'te Kesu, and has *tongkonan* houses and rice barns. In the dry season you can walk southwest, fording a river and walking through rice fields to **Pangli**, with its *tau tau* and house graves, and then to **Bori**, the site of an impressive *rante* (ceremonial ground) and some towering megaliths. About 1km south of Bori, **Parinding** has *tongkonan* houses and rice barns. From here you can walk back to Rantepao or on to Tikala.

Further north is the weaving centre of **Sa'dan** (12km north of Rantepao; take a bemo from Terminal Bolu for 6000Rp), where local women set up a market to sell their woven cloth. It's all handmade on simple looms, but not all is produced in the village.

### West of Rantepao

About 2km west across the river from Rantepao, **Gunung Singki** (930m) is a steep hill. There's a slippery, overgrown hiking trail to the summit, which has panoramic views across Rantepao and the surrounding countryside. Return to the road to **Siguntu** (7km from Rantepao), which offers more superb views of the valleys and Rantepao.

The 3km walk from Siguntu to the Rantepao–Makale road at Alang Alang is also pleasant. Stop on the way at the traditional village of **Mendoe**. From Alang Alang, where a covered bridge crosses the river, head to Londa, back to Rantepao, or remain on the western side of the river and continue walking south to the villages of **Langda** and **Madandan**.

### South of Rantepao

Many popular cultural sights are in this region and most are accessible by car, so it's not a great region for walking – but it is for a motorbike day tour. Tour buses love this area for the easy access but also because the sights are simply stunning.

On the outskirts of Rantepao, just off the road to Makale, is **Karasik**, with traditional-style houses arranged around a cluster of megaliths. The houses may have been erected some years ago for a single funeral ceremony, but some are now inhabited.

Just off the road to Ke'te Kesu is **Buntu Pune**, where there are two *tongkonan* houses and six rice barns. According to local legend, one of the two houses was built by a nobleman named Pong Marambaq at the beginning of the 20th century. During Dutch rule he was appointed head of the local district, but planned to rebel and was subsequently exiled to Ambon (Maluku), where he died. His body was returned to Tana Toraja and buried at the hill to the north of Buntu Pune.

About 1km further along from Buntu Pune is **Ke'te Kesu** (5km from Rantepao), renowned for its woodcarving and traditional *tongkonan* and rice barns. On the cliff face behind the village are some cave graves and very old hanging graves. The rotting coffins are suspended on wooden beams under an overhang. Others, full of bones and skulls, lie rotting in strategic piles.

From Ke'te Kesu you can walk to **Sullukang**, which has a *rante* marked by a number of large, rough-hewn megaliths, and on to **Palatokke**. In this beautiful area of lush rice paddies and traditional houses, there is an enormous cliff face containing several cave graves and hanging graves. Access to the caves is difficult, but the scenery makes it worthwhile. From Palatokke there are trails to **La'bo** and **Randanbatu**, where there are more graves, and on to Sangalla, Suaya and Makale.

**Londa** (6km south of Rantepao) is a very extensive burial cave at the base of a massive cliff face. The entrance to the cave is guarded by a balcony of *tau tau*. Inside the cave is a collection of coffins, many of them rotted away, with the bones either scattered or heaped in piles. A local myth says that the people buried in the Londa caves are the descendants of Tangdilinoq, chief of the Toraja when they were pushed out of the Enrekang region and forced to move into the highlands.

It's mandatory to take a guide (who will be a family member of the deceased) to take you through the cave with an oil lamp (20,000Rp). The guides speak excellent English (and a few other languages) and are happy to answer all your questions. If you're thin, and don't suffer from claustrophobia, squeeze through the tunnel connecting the two main caves, past some interesting stalactites and stalagmites. A bemo between Rantepao and Makale will drop you off at the turn-off, about 2km from the cave. Visit in the morning for the best photos.

Further south, 2km (east) off the Rantepao–Makale road, is **Tilanga** (10km from Rantepao), a lovely, natural cool-water swimming pool. You can swim in the pool, but don't be surprised if some friendly eels come to say hello.

**Lemo** (10km south of Rantepao) is the best-known burial area in Tana Toraja. The sheer rock face has a whole series of balconies for *tau tau*. According to local legend, these graves are for descendants of a Toraja chief who reigned over the surrounding district hundreds of years ago and built his house on top of the cliff into which the graves are now cut. Because the mountain was part of his property, only his descendants could use it. The chief himself was buried elsewhere because the art of cutting grave caves had not yet been developed. The biggest balcony has a dozen figures with white eyes and black pupils, and outstretched arms like spectators at a sports event. It's a good idea to go before 9am for the best photos. A Rantepao–Makale bemo will drop you off at the turn-off to the burial site, from where it's a 15-minute walk to the *tau tau*.

### East of Rantepao

**Marante** is a fine traditional village, just north of the road to Palopo. Near Marante there are stone and hanging graves with several *tau tau*, skulls on the coffins and a cave with scattered bones. From Marante you can cross the river on the suspension bridge and walk to pretty villages set in rice fields.

About 7km off the Palopo road to the south is the traditional village of **Nanggala** (16km from Rantepao); take a bemo from Terminal Bolu for 4000Rp, but you may have to walk from the Palopo road. The village has a particularly grandiose traditional house and an impressive fleet of 14 rice barns. The rice barns have a bizarre array of motifs carved into them, including soldiers with guns, Western women and cars. Keep an eye out for a colony of huge black bats hanging from trees at the end of the village.

From Nanggala you can walk south to **Paniki**, a tough hike (five hours) along a dirt track up and down the hills. The trail starts next to the rice barns, and along the way are coffee-plantation machines grinding away. From Paniki walk (two hours) to Ledo and **Buntao** (15km from Rantepao), which has some house graves and *tau tau*. Alternatively, catch a bemo from Paniki to Rantepao. About 2km from Buntao is **Tembamba**, which has more graves and is noted for its fine scenery.

### East of Makale

South of Sangalla are the Kambira baby graves, and even farther south are the hot springs at **Makula**, well signposted from the Rantepao–Makale road. At Makula, you can stay at the upmarket **Hotel Sangalla** (☎ 0423 24112; r from 150,000Rp; 🏊). The public can use the hot-springs swimming pool for 10,000Rp.

One of the most stunning sights in Tana Toraja is the *tau tau* at **Tampangallo**, between Sangalla and Suaya. The graves belong to the chiefs of Sangalla, descendants of the mythical divine being Tamborolangiq, who is believed to have introduced the caste system, death rituals and agricultural techniques into Torajan society. The former royal families of Makale, Sangalla and Menkendek all claimed descent from Tamborolangiq, who is said to have descended from heaven on a stone staircase. Take a Kijang from Makale to Sangalla, get off about 1km after the turn-off to Suaya, and walk a short distance (less than a kilometre) through the rice fields to Tampangallo.

# MAMASA VALLEY

Another area of outstanding natural beauty in Sulawesi, the Mamasa Valley is often referred to as West Tana Toraja, but this overplays the connection between Mamasa and Tana Toraja. Mamasan *tongkonan* have heavy wooden roofs, which are quite different from the exaggerated boat-shaped bamboo roofs to the east. Torajan ceremonies and funerals survive in the Mamasa Valley, but on the whole these are far less ostentatious affairs than those around Tana Toraja.

Mamasans have embraced Christianity with unfettered enthusiasm: choir groups regularly meet up and down the valley, flexing their vocal cords in praise of God. *Sambu* weaving is a craft that still thrives in the hills around Mamasa village. These long strips of heavy woven material are stitched together to make blankets, which are ideal insulation for the cold mountain nights.

Like in Tana Toraja, the best way to explore the valley is on foot. The paths tend to follow the ridges, giving hikers stunning views of the mountainous countryside. There are few roads, and many paths to choose from, so you'll need to constantly ask directions or hire a guide. The other source of confusion is that village districts, such as Balla, cover broad areas and there are few villages within them. Even centres within the village area, such as Rante Balla, Balla Kalua and Buntu Balla, are very spread out.

SULAWESI

## MAMASA

Mamasa is the only large village in the valley. The air is cool and clean, and the folk are hospitable. The rhythm of life has a surreal, fairytale quality for those used to the hustle of Indonesia's big cities. The highlight of the week is the market every Monday, where hill people trade their produce. Look for locally made woven blankets, a must for those cold mountain nights. While walking through hill villages, trekkers will also be offered plenty of fine-looking blankets direct from weavers, so take money or goods, such as condensed milk, chocolate, sugar or *kretek* (Indonesian clove cigarette), to barter with.

### Sleeping & Eating

**Mantana Lodge** (Jl Emmy Saelan 1; s from 50,000Rp, d 95,000-140,000Rp) The most sophisticated digs in town, the rooms are bright, with attached bathroom. The restaurant here is arguably the best in town and has cold beer. You might catch a spirited church service downstairs.

**Losmen Mini** (Jl Ahmad Yani; s/d 60,000/75,000Rp) A sort of creaky old mountain lodge in the heart of town. The rooms upstairs are a lot brighter than the dark offerings down below.

**Mamasa Cottages** (s/d US$40/46) Built over hot springs at Kole, 3km north of Mamasa. It offers lovely rooms for a negotiable price. Hot-spring water flows to every bathroom.

Other options:

**Guest House Gereja Toraja** (Jl Demmatande 182; r 75,000Rp) Reasonable rooms in an old house.

**Mamasa Guest House** (off Jl Buntu Budi; r 75,000Rp) Tucked away down a side street but offers good views.

There aren't any real restaurants in Mamasa and most visitors end up chowing down in their guest house. Basic supplies are available in local shops, and there's a good selection of fresh produce in the market.

### Getting There & Away

On a map, Mamasa looks tantalisingly close to Rantepao, but there's no direct transport because the road is so bad. You can travel from Makale to Bittuang by Kijang or bemo, but from Bittuang you'll have to walk (see opposite). A new road is under construction, but due to the tough terrain it may take several years to complete. At the time of writing, jeeps were running from Mamasa to Ponding for 80,000Rp every day, where you can hook up with a horse on to Bittuang for about 150,000Rp.

The only direct connection between Tana Toraja and Mamasa is the bus (98,000Rp, 10 hours), three times a week from Disco Indah Bus in Makale. Otherwise, from Tana Toraja (or anywhere else), catch a bus towards Majene or Mamuju and get off at Polewali. From here lots of creaky minibuses go to Mamasa (45,000Rp, three hours) along a rough road, often prone to mudslides. Start early as services dry up in the afternoon.

## AROUND MAMASA

The countryside surrounding Mamasa is strikingly beautiful. You can hire motorbikes around town for a negotiable 100,000Rp per day. You can charter a bemo or Kijang along the valley's couple of main roads, but footpaths and very slender suspension bridges are the only access to most villages.

The following places (with distances from Mamasa given in kilometres in brackets) are easy to reach from Mamasa, but take warm clothes and gifts for your hosts if you plan to stay overnight. As most people grow their own coffee here, in return for any hospitality bring condensed milk, chocolate, sugar, *kretek* and other goods from town.

### North of Mamasa

**Rante Buda** (4km) has an impressive 25m-long *tongkonan* building known as Banua Layuk (High House), an old chief's place with colourful motifs. This *tongkonan* is one of the oldest and best preserved in the valley, built about 300 years ago for one of five local leaders, the chief of Rambusaratu. A donation (about 5000Rp) is expected.

**Kole** (3km) has hot springs, tapped for the guests at Mamasa Cottages. **Loko** (4km) is a traditional village with old houses, set in the jungle. The only way there is to hike via Kole or Tondok Bakaru. Hardy hikers can continue from Loko up the steep hill to **Mambulilin Sarambu** (Mambulilin Waterfall), and on to the peak of **Gunung Mambulilin** (9km). **Taupe** (5km) is a traditional village with jungle walks and panoramic views.

### South of Mamasa

**Rante Sopang** (12km) is a busy centre for weaving and retailing crafts. The path up the hill from the roadside craft shop leads to a few workshops, where women weave long strips of heavy cloth for Mamasa's distinctive, colourful blankets.

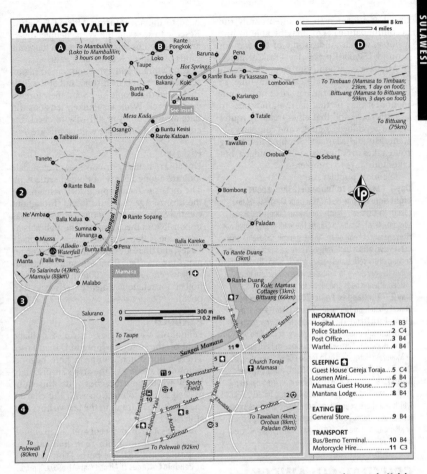

## MAMASA VALLEY

**INFORMATION**
Hospital........................**1** B3
Police Station..................**2** C4
Post Office.....................**3** B4
Wartel..........................**4** B4

**SLEEPING** 🏠
Guest House Gereja Toraja....**5** C4
Losmen Mini.....................**6** B4
Mamasa Guest House..........**7** C3
Mantana Lodge..................**8** B4

**EATING** 🍴
General Store...................**9** B4

**TRANSPORT**
Bus/Bemo Terminal.............**10** B4
Motorcycle Hire................**11** C3

**Osango** (3km) is the site of *tedong-tedong* (burial houses), which are supposedly up to 200 years old. There are lots of paths and the village is *very* spread out, so you may find that you'll need to ask for directions along the way. **Mesa Kada** (2km) are hot springs that are suitable for a swim.

**Tanete** (8km) has mountain graves under a cave. Tanete and nearby **Taibassi** are also centres for traditional weaving and carving. **Rante Balla** (12km) has big, beautiful *tongkonan* and woven blankets and baskets.

**Buntu Balla** (15km) has beautiful views, traditional weaving and *tedong-tedong* burial sites. Close to Buntu Balla there's a waterfall at **Allodio**, a traditional village at **Balla Peu**, megalithic remains at **Manta** and views along the whole valley from **Mussa**. Further south, **Malabo** (18km) has *tedong-tedong* burial sites.

Southeast of Mamasa, **Orobua** (9km) has a fine old *tongkonan*, one of the best in the area. There are more sweeping views from **Paladan** further south.

## Mamasa to Bittuang

This route is the only direct way between the Mamasa Valley and Tana Toraja. The 59km hike takes three days, but with an early start and legs of steel you can make it to Ponding in one and to Bittuang the next day. The track is easy to follow, and there are plenty of villages along the way for food and accommodation. Bring appropriate gifts – or pay your way – in return for any hospitality if you don't stay or eat at a losmen (basic, often family-run accommodation). You may be able to hire a horse, with a guide, some of the way for around 150,000Rp per day – ask at hotels in Mamasa or around Bittuang. The area is chilly at night and rain can hit anytime, so come prepared. As the new road nears completion, it may be that more traffic starts to use this route and that other trekking routes will be developed by guides and companies in Rantepao and Mamasa. An up-and-coming route takes in Salurea and Bulo Sandana, but takes four days to complete.

The most popular route:

**Day 1 – Mamasa to Timbaan (23km, about eight hours)** Rante Buda (4km from Mamasa)–Mama (3km)–Pa'kassasan (2km)–Lombonan (3km)–Tadokalua summit (4km)–Timbaan (7km). The walk is easy uphill but rises sharply at Lombonan. At the summit Tadokalua offers great views across both valleys. There's a simple stall here serving gritty coffee and packet noodle soup. The trail then winds its way down to Timbaan, where there are three losmen offering beds and meals for around 60,000Rp.

**Day 2 – Timbaan to Paku (20km, about six hours)** Mawai (4km from Timbaan)–Tabang (4km)–Ponding (5km)–Paku (7km). The path undulates its way past rice fields, through villages and over rivers. At Ponding you can stay at Homestay Papasado; or continue to Paku and stay at Mountain Homestay, both for 60,000Rp (with meals).

**Day 3 – Paku to Bittuang (16km, about three hours)** It's easier to walk, but there is an irregular jeep service from Ponding and Paku to Bittuang for 30,000Rp, which will shake your fillings loose. There are three simple losmen at Bittuang, but you're better off catching a bemo or Kijang to Makale (25,000Rp, two hours), from where there are Kijangs to Rantepao.

# CENTRAL SULAWESI

Nearly abandoned by tourism during and after a period of religious violence spanning over eight years (see boxed text, p688), Central Sulawesi is finally back on the itinerary for travellers who are moving up or down between the Togean Islands and Tana Toraja. The refreshing towns on the vast Danau Poso are an ideal place to stop awhile or break up a long bus ride, but there's much, much more to this province and it's simply begging to be explored. Tranquil Tentena is the easiest place to arrange treks into the Lore Lindu National Park, which is filled with mysterious megaliths and has a wildlife-rich jungle; those with lots of time and a nose for anthropology should head to the adventurous Morowali Nature Reserve to seek out the Wana people; divers and beach bums can laze around on the white sands of Tanjung Karang near Palu.

It's a vibrant and extremely varied region scarred by its recent history and still a little shaky, but the people here want their foreign visitors back. While it's unlikely tensions will flare again soon, it is still wise to check the current situation before visiting this area.

## History

Undated remains from a cave near Kolonedale indicate a long history of human settlement. The most spectacular prehistoric remains are the Bronze Age megaliths found throughout Central Sulawesi, but no one knows who was responsible for their creation. The highest concentration is along Sungai Lariang in the Bada Valley, and there are others throughout the region, down to Tana Toraja in South Sulawesi.

Between 1998 and 2006 this area was a hotbed for religious violence (see boxed text, p688).

## PENDOLO

Pendolo is a dusty, sparse strip of a village right on the southern shore of Danau Poso. There's not much going on here beyond swimming at some of the area's surprisingly lovely white-sand beaches – it's this calm as well as the connection with the charming locals what draws in the few visitors that stop here.

There's a strip of decent and cheap *rumah makan* along the main road that cater to stopping long-distance buses. You can stay at **Pendolo Cottages** (Jl Ahmad Yani 441; r 60,000Rp, bungalow s/d 55,000/80,000Rp), right next to the boat landing, about 1km east of the village centre, which is a rustic place that gets good traveller reviews on service and ambience. More upmarket is **Mulia Poso Lake Hotel** (Jl Pelabuhan Wisata 1; r from 100,000Rp, cottages from 150,000Rp), the smartest place in Pendolo which also has an elegant restaurant.

## Getting There & Away

Pendolo is on the main Palopo–Poso highway, but there is no bus terminal. To go north, the best option is to catch a bemo to Tentena (45,000Rp), then transfer there. If you're going south, see if your hotel can help you reserve a seat on one of the many long-distance buses that blaze through town. You could also try

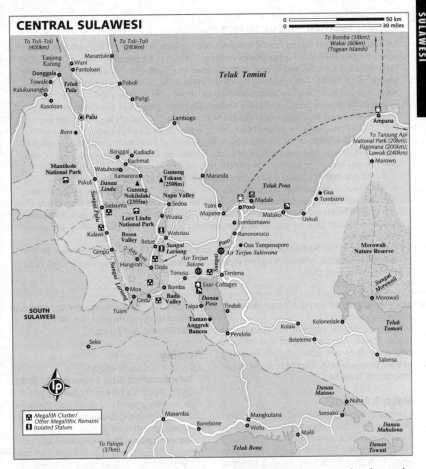

## CENTRAL SULAWESI

your luck flagging one down from the main road (heading to destinations such as Poso, Palu and Rantepao) – but many are full.

In mid-2009 there was no public boat between Pendolo and Tentena, but with some determination you could charter one for around 350,000Rp for the three-hour trip.

## TENTENA
☎ 0458

Tentena is a town of white picket fences and churches, cool breezes from the lake and lots of wonderfully strange things to eat. Surrounded by clove-covered hills, it's a peaceful and very easy-to-manage town with several good places to stay, an interesting market and some natural treasures to

explore nearby. There are no beaches in the town itself, but it's easy to hire a motorbike or an *ojek* to get to some.

Tentena is the host of the annual **Festival Danau Poso**, the undisputed highlight of Central Sulawesi's social calendar, in late August. Villagers from far afield gather for a colourful celebration of culture, with dancing, songs and traditional sports.

## Information

There are only a handful of guides in Tentena but they all organise treks to Lore Lindu National Park and Morowali Nature Reserve. All guides speak English and know the area well. As soon as you arrive in town, they'll find you and offer their services – they are helpful

---

**CENTRAL SULAWESI'S TROUBLED PAST**

It's been pretty quiet around Central Sulawesi since late 2006, but for eight years prior the region was torn apart by Christian versus Muslim violence. The big trouble began in 1998 when a drunken brawl between Christian and Muslim youths sparked clan fighting in Poso. By 2000 paramilitary groups called the Red Force (backing the Christians) and the Laskar Jihad (backing the Muslims) were engaged in full warfare against each other, armed with machetes and bows and arrows as well as homemade bombs and heavy artillery. Christians grouped in predominantly Christian Tentena, while Muslims stood their ground in Poso and Palu. The Indonesian government stepped in in 2001 by organising the Malino Peace Treaty, signed in 2002 by both sides, which produced a decline in the violence but did not stop it. By the end of 2006, more than 1000 people had been killed, houses had been burned, markets bombed and children beheaded. Tourists were never targets but the region was, for obvious reasons, best avoided.

It's still debated what caused these communities to start fighting each other after generations of living peacefully together. Some analysts believe this was just another arm in the fighting that had been going on between Muslim and Christian communities in the Maluku Islands (see p726). The more common belief is that the influx of Muslim immigrants from Java under President Suharto's transmigration program abruptly shifted the Christian majority and power in the region.

Today locals chat easily about this dark time and about how happy they are it's over. As one Poso Muslim told us, 'Nowadays I go on vacation to Tentena but before I was afraid I'd get killed if I even went near there.'

---

and pleasant even if you don't plan on taking a trip with them.

There's a tourist office at the market, but it was closed when we visited and by local reports it does not offer English-speaking service or much help. There are no banks or internet in Tentena.

## Sights & Activities

Most of the things to do and see are around Tentena. The best way to spend a day is to either rent a motorbike (full/half-day 70,000/60,000Rp – ask at your hotel) or hire an *ojek*. With wheels you can visit **Air Terjun Salopa** (entrance fee 10,000Rp), a waterfall about 15km from Tentena from where you can hike through the forest and up alongside the falls for a few kilometres. The forest is clean and shady and the falls are a spectacular place for a swim. From here drive another 5km to Siuri Cottages (right), where you can swim in the lake at the white-sand **beach** and have lunch. An *ojek* to get to these two spots for a half-day should cost about 80,000Rp.

In town, Tentena's pretty, covered 210m bridge marks where the lake ends and Sungai Poso begins its journey to the coast. V-shaped **eel traps** north of the bridge snare the 2m monsters for which Tentena is famous. Live specimens are available for inspection and sale at warungs in the centre of town.

Chartering a boat to explore the lake can be surprisingly difficult – the asking rate is 100,000Rp for two hours.

## Sleeping

All prices include breakfast.

**Hotel Victori** ( ☎ 21392; Jl Diponegoro 18; r 65,000-150,000Rp; ❄ ) It's a bit scruffy but the price is right, service is good and the rooms are clean. Only the higher-end rooms have air-con. This is a good spot to meet guides.

**Losmen Tropicana** ( ☎ 21224; r 80,000Rp) The small rooms here have real spring mattresses and the semioutdoor cafe in front has some flair from the bright paintings on the walls. It's almost directly across the street from the bridge and the market.

**Hotel Pamona Indah Permai** (Jl Yos Sudarso 25; r from 110,000Rp) This place doesn't take any advantage of its lakeside location, but the rooms are bright and tidy and the restaurant here is the best in town.

**Hotel Intim Danau Poso** ( ☎ 21345; fax 21488; Jl Yos Sudarso 22; r 175,000Rp) The rooms are dark and the staff speak little English, but this is the only place in town that's posh enough to have hot-water showers. The rooms on the 2nd floor have OK lake views.

**Siuri Cottages** ( ☎ 0813 4116 7345; s/d 215,000/225,000Rp) Twenty kilometres from Tentena on the road to Pendolo, these big, well-kept but simple cottages are lined up along a sparkling white, lakeside beach with views that take in all the size and splendour of Danau Poso. The owner speaks English and there's a basic restaurant for meals, but note that this place is completely isolated. To get here from Tentena, you can catch an afternoon bemo for 15,000Rp; from Pendelo a bemo should cost 30,000Rp. The owner can help you rent a canoe to explore the lake, but you'll have to haggle for the price.

### Eating

The local speciality is *sugili* (eel) and *ikan mas* (goldfish). For these specialties as well as spicy bat dishes, pull up a chair at one of the riverside *rumah makan* at the market near the bridge – the best is **Rumah Makan Kawana** (meals around 1000Rp). After dinner don't miss trying the tasty *pisang molen* (banana fried in a sweet pastry) at stalls in front of the eastern part of the bridge.

The only real restaurant in town is at the **Hotel Pamona Indah Permai** (meals from 15,000Rp), which has an extensive menu offering everything from nasi goreng to both *sugili* (45,000Rp) and *ikan mas* (30,000Rp) in a variety of sauces.

### Getting There & Away

#### BOAT

Public local boats travel to nearby villages, but in early 2009 there were no public boats to Pendelo. Chartering a boat to Pendelo (three hours) can be difficult to arrange but should cost around 350,000Rp.

#### BUS & BEMO

You'll need to catch an *ojek* (6000Rp) to/from Tentena's bus and bemo terminal, 3km from

---

**DANAU POSO**

Indonesia's third-largest lake, Danau Poso, covers an area of 32,300 hectares and reaches an average depth of 450m. The lake is 600m above sea level – so the evenings are pleasantly cool without being too cold. With mountains on all sides and mist hovering over the calm waters in the early morning, it's a breathtaking spot.

The lake is famous for its wild orchids, especially in **Taman Anggrek Bancea** (Bancea Orchid Garden). It is accessible on foot (about 11km), by chartered vehicle, or by irregular bemos to Taipa from Pendolo.

---

town centre. There are plenty of buses and bemos that make the run to Poso (20,000Rp, 1½ hours) and on to Palu. For longer distances, such as the trip to Rantepao, you can book tickets at the bus offices around Tentena; ask at your hotel. Bemos to Pendolo run in the afternoon and cost 45,000Rp.

#### JEEP

The availability and price of jeeps to Gintu in Lore Lindu National Park depends on the condition of the road. The price should be around 100,000Rp per person by public jeep, and up to 800,000Rp to charter one.

## POSO

☎ 0452 / pop 47,000

Poso is the main town, port and terminal for road transport on the northern coast of Central Sulawesi. It's a spread-out, noisy place and there's little reason to stay other than to use an ATM, check your email or change buses.

The northern part of Poso, around Jl Haji Agus Salim, is more like a small village but it has limited shops and restaurants. Most facilities are along or near busy Jl Sumatera.

Poso is the last chance for Togean- and Tentena-bound travellers to change money; the best option is BNI bank, with an ATM, near the port about 2km from town centre – take an *ojek*. Internet access is at the **Telkom office** (Jl Yos Sudarso; per hr 7000Rp), which is 1km or an easy *ojek* ride (2000Rp) from town centre.

If you're just changing buses, stay at **Losmen Alugoro** ( ☎ 21336; Jl Sumatera 20; s/d 40,000/55,000Rp, d with air-con 110,000-175,000Rp; ❄ ), a reliably decent but characterless place that's central for the bus offices and restaurants on Jl Sumatera. For something more interesting, try **Rumah Makan & Losmen Lalang Jaya** ( ☎ 22326; Jl Yos Sudarso; r 75,000Rp), right next to the port and the BNI bank. This rickety place perched over the sea looks like somewhere Popeye would have lived had he been Indonesian. There's also a basic seafood restaurant here.

### Getting There & Away

From the bus terminal, about 5km out of town, there are buses to Kolonedale (eight hours, 90,000Rp), Rantepao (13 hours, 120,000Rp), and Manado (30 hours), as well as regular minibuses to Tentena (1½ hours, 25,000Rp).

From the terminal it's a 3000Rp bemo ride into central Poso.

For Palu (six hours, 65,000Rp) and Ampana (five hours, 60,000Rp), it's best to catch comfortable minibuses that leave from offices along Jl Sumatera – sometimes these minibuses fish for customers at the bus terminal as well. Bemos to nearby villages and beaches leave from a terminal next to the market.

## AROUND POSO

There are plenty of good places for swimming and snorkelling around Poso. **Pantai Madale** is a snorkelling spot 5km east of Poso; **Pantai Matako** is a white-sand beach about 20km further east; and **Pantai Toini**, 7km west, has a few *rumah makan* with great seafood. All three can be reached by bemo from the terminal near the market in Poso.

**Lembomawo**, 4km south of Poso, is renowned for its ebony carving. Take a bemo from the terminal at the Poso market.

## LORE LINDU NATIONAL PARK

As if the lush jungle filled with butterflies larger than a human hand, impressive hornbills and shy tarsiers weren't enough, Lore Lindu is also home to several indigenous tribes and is famous for its megalithic remains – giant freestanding stones. Covering an area of 250,000 hectares, this remote national park (a Unesco Biosphere Reserve) has been barely touched by tourism. It's a wonderful area for trekking and the perfect place to seek out an of-the-beaten-path adventure.

### Information

The main national park office, rangers station and visitor centre are about a 1km walk from Kamarora village. You can buy permits here (20,000Rp), as well as at the small field offices (which have no accommodation) at Kulawi and Wuasa, and at the **Balai Taman Nasional Lore Lindu office** ( ☎ 0451-457 623; Jl Prof Mohammad Yamin SH).

### Sights

Attractions in the park include ancient megalithic relics, mostly in the **Bada**, **Besoa** and **Napu Valleys**; remote peaks, some more than 2500m high; birdwatching, including hornbills, around **Kamarora**; and the 3150-hectare lake, **Danau Lindu**.

### Activities

For **trekking**, the rangers at Kamarora can show you the start of several short trails, which don't require a guide – such as the 10m-high **waterfall** about 2km from Kamarora, and the hot springs at **Kadidia** (3km), where you can bathe. To reach the summit of the 2355m **Gunung Nokilalaki** (6km), you'll need a guide.

Other longer hikes (with a guide) include Rachmat to Danau Lindu (six hours one way) and Sadaunta to Danau Lindu (four hours one way). An exciting alternative is to go on horseback; horses and handlers are available from 100,000Rp per day at Watutau and Gimpu.

The roads around Lore Lindu have improved in recent years and now many of the old trekking routes are used by buzzing motorbikes. The best place to get into the jungle, free of motor noise but rich in wildlife, is the trail between Doda and Gimpu (a two-day walk), but there aren't any megaliths on this route. Megalithic remains are found mostly along the motorbike road between Tonusu and Gimpu, via Tuare and Moa, or Doda and Hangirah. There are also megaliths to see along the road between Doda and Wuasa that is accessible by car. For trekking, take a public (or chartered) bemo to Tonusu, Doda or Gimpu, and then tackle the trail like this:

**Tonusu–Bomba** From Tonusu, walk for two days, sleeping under covered bridges. You'll need to carry food and water-purification tablets. You could also charter a motorbike the whole way, stopping to look for the Bomba, Bada and Sepe megaliths. At Bomba, stay at the friendly Ningsi Homestay.

**Bomba–Doda** It's 10km to Gintu, from where you begin the trek towards Doda. Along this trail you'll be rewarded with views over the two valleys, but it's a tough hike that is better tackled in two days and there's no official losmen along the way – there is a losmen in Doda. This road is accessible by motorbike, so that is another option.

**Doda–Gimpu** From here you are really in the jungle, so take all the necessary precautions. This is a two-day walk and there is a sleeping hut halfway through, although you might need a guide to find it. From Gimpu you can hike into the Besoa Valley, or travel back by public (or chartered) transport to Palu.

### GUIDES

For long-distance trekking a guide is compulsory, and also necessary if you're intent on finding the megaliths. An organised trek from Tentena will cost around 3,700,000Rp for two people for five days, including food, transport and accommodation. The guides from Tentena speak English.

If travelling independently, arrange a guide at the visitor centre (Kamarora), the two field offices (Kulawi or Wuasa), or the tourist office or national park office in Palu. Guides start at 200,000Rp per day but rarely speak English.

Food is readily available in the villages, but it's wise to bring other necessities, such as mosquito repellent and sunblock lotion, plus gifts to repay any hospitality. If trekking, you may have to sleep under roofs of covered bridges, which can get cold. Conversely, during the day it can get very hot, so the wildlife will be resting in the forest and is often difficult to spot. See boxed text, p822 for more information on safe and responsible trekking.

## Getting There & Away

There are three main approaches to the park, one from Tentena and two from Palu. From Palu buses run all the way to Gimpu and Doda twice a day from Terminal Petobu. From Tentena you'll need to take a jeep; they run according to demand and road conditions to Bomba or Gintu.

From Gimpu, Doda and Bomba you should be able to hire *ojeks* that can tackle the tracks between Gintu and Gimpu via Moa and from Gintu to Doda. You can also hike this scenic route, but you will have motorbikes buzzing by you. The track between Doda and Gimpu can only be done on foot.

## PALU

**☎ 0451 / pop 282,000**

Palu, the capital of Central Sulawesi, is characterless but loaded with banks and ATMs, cheap internet, travel agencies, supermarkets and, oddly, pharmacies (all along Jl Emmi Saelan). It's a good place to do errands when arriving from or heading out by ship to Kalimantan or treks to Lore Lindu National Park. Nearby is the rarely visited yet wonderfully quaint village of Dongalla and beach area of Tanjung Karang (see p693). Situated in a rain shadow for most of the year, Palu is one of the driest places in Indonesia.

There's not much in the way of sights apart from the large **Museum Negeri Propinsi Sulawesi Tengah** (☎ 422 290; Jl Sapri 23), which features interesting traditional art and other geological and archaeological items but is inconveniently located. The best part of town to wander around is the busy Jl Hasanuddin II area.

## Information

### EMERGENCY
**Police station** (☎ 421 015; Jl Sam Ratulangi)

### INTERNET ACCESS, POST & TELEPHONE
Warnet (internet stalls) are everywhere in Palu and generally charge 4000Rp per hour.
**Main post office** (Jl Prof Mohammad Yamin SH 161) Inconveniently located.
**Telkom** (Jl Ahmad Yani)

### MEDICAL SERVICES
**Rumah Sakit Umum Propinsi Undata** (☎ 421 270; Jl Suharso) Large and reasonably well-equipped hospital.

### MONEY
Palu has banks and ATMs at every corner. The BNI banks are the best and most convenient for changing money.

### TOURIST INFORMATION
**Balai Taman Nasional Lore Lindu office** (☎ 457 623; Jl Prof Mohammad Yamin SH) No English is spoken but they do their best to help and can set you up with Indonesian-speaking guides.
**Tourist office** (☎ 455 260; Jl Dewi Sartika 91) Inconveniently located and hard to find; has some information about Lore Lindu National Park.

## Sleeping & Eating

All rates include breakfast.

**Purnama Raya Hotel** (☎ 423 646; Jl Wahidin 4; s/d 40,000/50,000Rp) This is a family-run place that has a village feel even though it's in the heart of Palu. Rooms with attached Indonesian-style bathrooms are clean but can be a little noisy from the traffic outside. Some English is spoken (which is a big deal for Palu) and the family is helpful with arranging guides to Lore Lindu and other onward travel.

**Hotel Sentral** (☎ 422 789; Jl Kartini 6; r 150,000-650,000Rp; 🟦 🖳) Even the cheapest rooms here have satellite TV and air-con, and it's a smiling, friendly place. There's a travel agent and warnet here as well.

**Rama Garden Hotel** (☎ 429 500; Jl Monginsidi 81; r 165,000-440,000Rp; 🟦 🟦 🛜) It looks like nothing from the outside, but this place is a garden of tranquillity inside, with winding paths, lots of plants and mini-lawn areas, plus a pool and a terrace dining area. Take a swim, order room service and watch a movie on HBO.

There are plenty of night warungs along the breezy seafront esplanade, Jl Raja Moili. **Mall Tatura Palu** (Jl Emmi Saelan) has a good food court

SULAWESI

# PALU

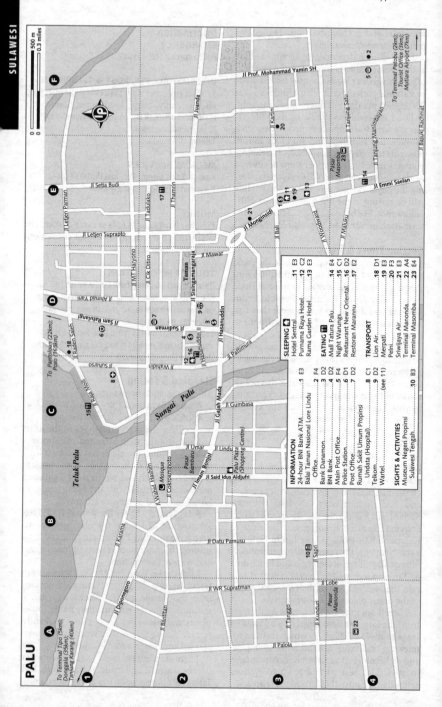

To Terminal Tipo (5km);
Dongaala (35km);
Tanjung Karang (40km)

To Pantoloan (22km);
Poso (165km)

To Terminal Petobu (2km);
Tourist Office (3km);
Mutiara Airport (7km)

Teluk Palu

Sungai Palu

Jl Prof. Mohammad Yamin SH

Jl Juanda

Jl Kartini

Jl Tanjung Satu

Jl Tanjung Manimbaya

Pasar
Masomba

Jl Emmi Saelan

Jl Basuki Rachmat

Jl Setia Budi

Jl Tadulako

Jl Thamrin

Jl Monginsidi

Jl Bali

Jl Maluku

Woodward

Jl Letjen Parman

Jl Letjen Suprapto

Jl MT Hayono

Jl Cik Ditiro

Jl Mawar

Jl Ahmad Yani

Jl Sam Ratulangi

Taman

Jl Sisingamangaraja

Jl Hasanuddin

Jl Raden Saleh

Jl Sudirman

Jl Imam Bonjol II

Jl Patimura

Jl Suharso

Jl Wahidin

Jl Imam Bonjol

Jl Wolter
Monginsidi

Jl Gajah Mada

Jl Gumbasa

Jl Umar

Jl Lindu

Jl Said Idus Aldjufri

Palu Plaza
(Shopping centre)

Pasar
Bambaru

Jl Wahid Hashim

Jl Cokroaminoto

Mosque

Jl Karama

Jl Datu Pamusu

Jl Diponegoro

Jl Banttan

Jl WR Supratman

Jl Sapri

Jl Lobe

Jl Tanggo

Jl Kunduri

Pasar
Manonda

Jl Palola

## INFORMATION

| | |
|---|---|
| 24-hour BNI Bank ATM....................1 | E3 |
| Balai Taman Nasional Lore Lindu | |
| Office............................................2 | F4 |
| Bank Danamon..............................3 | D2 |
| BNI Bank.......................................4 | F4 |
| Main Post Office............................5 | D1 |
| Police Station................................6 | D2 |
| Post Office....................................7 | D2 |
| Rumah Sakit Umum Propinsi | |
| Undata (Hospital).........................8 | C1 |
| Telkom.........................................9 | D2 |
| Wartel.......................................(see 11) | |

## SIGHTS & ACTIVITIES

| | |
|---|---|
| Museum Negeri Propinsi | |
| Sulawesi Tengah.........................10 | B3 |

## SLEEPING ⌂

| | |
|---|---|
| Hotel Sentral...............................11 | E3 |
| Purnama Raya Hotel.....................12 | C2 |
| Rama Garden Hotel......................13 | E3 |

## EATING 🍴

| | |
|---|---|
| Mall Tatura Palu...........................14 | E4 |
| Night Warungs.............................15 | C1 |
| Restaurant New Oriental..............16 | D2 |
| Restoran Marannu........................17 | E2 |

## TRANSPORT

| | |
|---|---|
| Lion Air........................................18 | D1 |
| Merpati........................................19 | E3 |
| Pelni............................................20 | F3 |
| Sriwijaya Air.................................21 | E3 |
| Terminal Manonda.......................22 | A4 |
| Terminal Masomba.......................23 | E4 |

0                    500 m
0                    0.3 miles

on the top level, as well as a few more upmarket restaurants and cafes and a supermarket.

**Restoran Marannu** (Jl Setia Budi; mains 20,000-40,000Rp; ⊙ breakfast, lunch & dinner) At one of the smarter spots in town, the menu includes tasty seafood and Chinese cuisine.

## Getting There & Away

### AIR
There are flights to Makassar with **Merpati** ( ☎ 423 341; Jl Monginsidi), **Sriwijaya Air** ( ☎ 428 777; 37 Jl Monginsidi) and **Lion Air** ( ☎ 428 777; Jl Raden Saleh 1). Merpati also flies from Palu to Kendari, Sriwijaya has services to Balikpapan, while Lion Air flies to Manado.

### BOAT
Travelling by boat is one way to avoid long and uncomfortable bus rides through Central Sulawesi. Palu is also well connected to East Kalimantan.

Every two weeks, the Pelni liner *Tidar* sails to Balikpapan, the *Dobonsolo* sails to Makassar, the *Tidar* also goes to Pare Pare, and the *Dorolonda* goes to Bitung. These boats dock at Pantoloan, 22km north of Palu, which is accessible by shared taxi from Terminal Manonda in Palu, or by metered taxi (about 40,000Rp). The **Pelni office** ( ☎ 421 696; Jl Kartini) in Palu is efficient; there's another one at Pantoloan.

### BUS & SHARED TAXI
Buses and minibuses to Poso (75,000Rp, six hours), Ampana (125,000Rp, 11 hours), Rantepao (150,000Rp, 19 hours) and Manado (24 hours) all leave from bus-company offices inconveniently dotted around the suburbs of Palu.

Kijangs to Donggala (for Tanjung Karang) leave from Terminal Tipo, about 5km northwest of Palu, but it's easier to take an *ojek* – see p694. There are buses to Gimpu and Doda (for Lore Lindu National Park) that leave twice a day from Terminal Petobu, about 2km east of Palu.

## Getting Around
Mutiara Airport is 7km east of town. Public transport is difficult to find, so take a metered taxi for about 45,000Rp from the city centre.

Transport around Palu is by bemo. Routes are not signed and are flexible, so flag down one that looks like it's going your way. Taxis are cheap and air-conditioned and drivers generally use the meters.

## DONGGALA & TANJUNG KARANG
☎ 0457

Donggala is an old-fashioned country town that's full of colourful houses, small flower gardens, a few dirt roads and lots of interesting local characters. From here it's a short *ojek* ride to Tanjung Karang's slice of white sand studded with rickety beach bungalows, buffalo roaming around and a decent dive centre.

Although it's hard to believe, Donggala was once the administrative centre under the Dutch and was briefly the most important town and port in Central Sulawesi. When the harbour silted up, ships used the harbours on the other side of the bay, and Palu became the regional capital.

## Activities
The main attractions are sun, sand and water at Tanjung Karang (Coral Peninsula), about 5km north of Donggala. The reef off Prince John Dive Resort is good for **snorkelling** and beginner-level **diving**. Individual dives cost around €35 and PADI courses are also run here. Diving and snorkelling equipment is available.

## Sleeping & Eating
There's nowhere to eat at Tanjung Karang, so you'll be relying on what's served at your homestay or resort.

**Kaluku Cottages** (cottages per person incl meals 75,000Rp) You'll have to ask around to see if you can find the owner and get him to open this place up, but it's worth it to get a bungalow here on Tanjung Tuluku, a few kilometres north of Tanjung Karang, and its better beach. There is great coral off the coast and free coconuts are on offer throughout the day. Ask an *ojek* driver to take you from Donggala.

**Harmoni Cottages** ( ☎ 71573; cottages incl meals per person 175,000Rp) This place is absurdly overpriced for how rustic it is (a small shack with a terrace, mattress on the floor and a mosquito net), but the beach location, friendly welcome and the delicious food might make you want to pay the price anyway. The helpful owner speaks English and can help arrange tours to Lore Lindu National Park.

**Prince John Dive Resort** ( ☎ 71104; www.prince-john-diveresort.de; bungalows for 2 people incl meals from 380,000Rp) For almost the same price as Harmoni, you can stay at this resort in a comfortable varnished-wood bungalow with a large bathroom and a sea view. The only dive resort in the Palu area, it has bungalows spread out on a well-planted hillside and there's a small beach with a few umbrellas for rent for nonguests, as well as a restaurant.

### Getting There & Away

Kijangs to Donggala (15,000Rp) leave when full from Terminal Tipo, about 5km outside Palu – you'll have to flag down a bemo from anywhere in Palu to take you to the terminal (3500Rp). From Donggala you can catch an *ojek* to Tanjung Karang (5000Rp). It works out to be almost the same price (and takes half the time) to take an *ojek* directly from Palu to Tanjung Karang (30,000Rp).

## KOLONEDALE

☎ 0465

Kolonedale is a small tangle of long, dusty streets set on the stunning Teluk Tomori, and is the gateway to Morowali Nature Reserve. Rainfall in the bay area is heavy and constant, and the best time to visit is from September to November.

There is a small post office behind the main mosque, and a **Telkom office** ( 🕑 24hr) up the hill from the Pelni office.

### Sleeping & Eating

Most accommodation, shops and the market are adjacent to the main dock.

**Penginapan Sederhana** ( ☎ 21124; Jl Yos Sudarso 64; r 20,000-115,000Rp) Formerly just another basic budget crash pad, this little guest house has added several smarter rooms in the past few years, making it the best all-rounder in town. It is managed by the local environmental group, Sahabat Morowali (Friends of Morowali), so has top information on Morowali Nature Reserve.

**Losmen Jungpandang** ( ☎ 21091; Jl Yos Sudarso; r from 25,000Rp) Handy for the dock, the rooms are very basic with shared *mandis*. The attached restaurant offers simple Indonesian fare.

There are basic warungs around the bus terminal and the market.

### Getting There & Away

The intersection in front of the market serves as the bus and bemo terminal. Several buses a day travel between Kolonedale and Poso (eight hours) via Tentena. From the south, cross Danau Matano by boat from Soroako to Nuha, rent a motorbike or jeep to Beteleme, then wait for a bus to Kolonedale.

The Pelni liner *Tilongkabila* stops at Kolonedale about once a week on its way to Gorontalo (economy/1st class 52,000/189,000Rp, eight hours) or Kendari. *Perahu* (traditional outrigger boats) leave the main dock most days at about 11pm for the overnight trip east to Baturube and Pandauke, from where there are buses to Luwuk (five hours).

## TELUK TOMORI

Most visitors to Kolonedale head straight to Morowali, so they miss much of the stunning beauty of the islands and inlets around Teluk Tomori, where limestone cliffs plunge into emerald waters, and unbroken forests cover islands and surrounding hills. To properly explore the bay, rent a boat from Kolonedale: for around 100,000Rp per day, you can charter a small 'Johnson' (dugout canoe with an outboard motor), or for about 300,000Rp a larger boat holding up to 10 people.

Sights include a **limestone cliff** across the water from Kolonedale with faint painted outlines of prehistoric handprints and fossils embedded in the rock; the oddly shaped **mushroom rock**; tiny **fishing villages**; and some fine **beaches** on uninhabited islands at the mouth of the bay. There are also **coral reefs** with plenty of marine life, but the visibility can be poor.

## MOROWALI NATURE RESERVE

This 225,000-hectare nature reserve was established in 1980 on the northern shore of Teluk Tomori after Operation Drake, a British-sponsored survey of the endangered species in the area. The reserve includes islands in the bay, accessible lowland plains and densely vegetated peaks up to 2421m high.

Morowali is home to about 5000 Wana people, who live mostly by hunting and gathering and from shifting agriculture. The park is rich in wildlife, such as *anoa* (pygmy buffalo), maleo birds, *babi rusa* (wild deer-like pig) and the world's tiniest bat, but dense jungle is often all you'll see.

### Trekking

You will need at least four days to properly visit the park, plus a few extra to get there and back, and the going is tough. Treks can be organised with guides in Tentena (see p687) for about 3,700,000Rp for two people, including transport, food and accommodation, for a five- to six-day trek.

However, you can also wait to find a guide (which is necessary to see the wildlife) until you reach Kolonedale. In Kolonedale guides may approach you in the street, you can organise one through your hotel, or you can visit the KSDA (National Parks) office – where you must register and buy a permit (20,000Rp per day). A good source of independent advice and a good place to organise guides is **Friends of Morowali** (Sahabat Morowali; ☎ 0465-21124; Penginapan Sederhana, Jl Yos Sudarso 64), a local environmental group based in Kolonedale.

From Kolonedale it's a two-hour boat trip across Teluk Tomori and up Sungai Morowali to drop-off points for hikes to **Kayu Poli**, a small Wana settlement. You can stay in a local home there or at another village, and spend some time with the Wana people. West of Kayu Poli (three hours) is the eerily silent **Danau Rahu**, which takes about five hours to cross by canoe. You can leave the park via Sungai Rahu and return to Kolonedale by boat.

## LUWUK

☎ 0461 / pop 48,000

Luwuk is the biggest town on Sulawesi's isolated eastern peninsula, and the stepping-off point for the remote Banggai Islands. Nearby attractions include **Air Terjun Hengahenga**, the 75m-high waterfall 3km west of Luwuk; and the **Bangkiriang Nature Reserve**, which is 80km southwest of Luwuk and home to Central Sulawesi's largest maleo-bird population.

**Ramayana Hotel** (☎ 21502; Jl Danau Lindu; s/d from 75,000/90,000Rp) is the best of the town's few hotels. The rooms are clean and the seaside restaurant attracts a breeze. VIP rooms run to 325,000Rp if you are feeling very important.

**Maleo Cottages** (☎ /fax 324 068; www.maleo -cottages.com; Jl Lompobattang; s/d incl breakfast 100,000/120,000Rp) is by far the best place to stay in the Luwuk area, about 16km from town. There are rooms in the main house and three atmospheric cottages. Meals are available at 35,000Rp. This is the base for **Wallacea Dive Cruise** (www.wallacea-divecruise.com), so it's a good place to arrange diving in the Banggai Islands or liveaboards to the Togean Islands. The hotel also offers treks to some remote forest regions nearby.

**Merpati** (☎ 21523; Jl Sam Ratulangi 50) has daily flights to/from Manado, and **Batavia Air** has three or four flights a week to Makassar.

Every week the Pelni liner *Tilongkabila* links Luwuk with Kolonedale (economy/1st class 57,000/189,000Rp, eight hours) and Gorontalo (65,000/204,000Rp, 11 hours); it is an excellent way to travel to this remote part of Sulawesi. There's a **Pelni office** (☎ 21888; Jl Sungai Musi 3) in town.

There are also buses to Pagimana, Poso and Bunta for connections to Ampana.

## BANGGAI ISLANDS

With a *lot* of time and patience you can visit the wild and remote Banggai Islands. It's a superb area for **swimming**, **diving** and viewing **marine life** such as whales and dugongs. Alfred Wallace called the area 'the mother of all living coral reefs'. Boats can be chartered from most villages, but it is easiest to arrange diving and snorkelling trips through Maleo Cottages near Luwuk (see left).

The largest and most populous island is **Pulau Peleng**, with the main settlements at Tataba and Salakan. There is still no accommodation on the islands, but you can stay at a local home in any village if you check with the *kepala desa* first.

There is a daily ferry between Luwuk and Tataba. Once every two weeks the Pelni ship *Sinabung* visits Banggai from Makassar, then travels onward to Ternate.

## TANJUNG API NATIONAL PARK

The 4246-hectare Tanjung Api (Cape Fire National Park) is home to *anoa, babi rusa,* crocodiles, snakes and maleo birds, but most people come to see the burning coral cliff fuelled by a leak of natural gas. To get here you need to charter a boat around the rocky peninsula from Ampana (from there it's 24km east). It's more interesting at dusk.

## AMPANA

☎ 0464

The main reason for travellers to come to Ampana is to catch a boat to/from the Togean Islands, but it's a laid-back, pleasant town with a vibrant market and a good stopover while you recover from, or prepare for, an assault on the Togeans.

Note that the sole ATM in town only takes MasterCard and maximum withdrawals are 500,000Rp per day. **Friends Internet** across from Losmen Irama is often not open, so try **Frenzy Net** (Jl P Talataka 15; per hr 7000Rp; 🕑 9-12am) about 300m inland.

## Orientation

The main Poso–Luwuk road goes through Ampana and is called Jl Hatta. Many hotels are along Jl Kartini, which heads towards the sea from Jl Hatta. The main dock, market and bus terminal are all close to Jl Kartini.

## Sleeping & Eating

**Losmen Irama** ( ☎ 21055; Jl Kartini; r 60,000Rp, with air-con 110,000Rp; ✷ ) Catering mostly to locals, this basic place has clean rooms with Indonesian-style bathrooms.

**Oasis Hotel** ( ☎ 21058; Jl Kartini; dm 60,000Rp, r from 90,000Rp; ✷ ) Run in conjunction with the Kadidiri Paradise Resort in the Togeans, this place has clean rooms and dorms, but don't expect to sleep till the karaoke shuts down at 11pm. The most expensive rooms include air-con and hot water.

**Marina Cottages** ( ☎ 21280; cottages 90,000Rp) Perched on a very rocky beach, the cottages boast a seafront setting and friendly service, and are in a perfect location for boats to Bomba. They are in Labuhan village, a 10-minute *bendi* (horse-drawn cart) ride from Ampana. The restaurant is worth visiting for the sunsets alone.

**Rumah Makan Ikan Bakar** (Jl Kartini; mains 15,000Rp) A good place for some cold beer and baked fish.

## Getting There & Away

Several minibuses travel each day to Luwuk (100,000Rp, six hours), Poso (60,000Rp, five hours) and Palu (125,000Rp, 11 hours).

A chartered car to Pagimana (four to five hours) for the ferry to Gorontalo costs about 600,000Rp.

Boats to Poso, Wakai in the Togean Islands and beyond leave from the main boat terminal at the end of Jl Yos Sudarso, in the middle of Ampana. Boats to Bomba in the Togeans leave from a jetty in Labuhan village, next to Marina Cottages. See opposite for more details.

# TOGEAN ISLANDS

Yes, it does take some determination to get to the Togean Islands, but believe us, it takes much more determination to leave. Island-hop from one forested golden-beach beauty to the next, where hammocks are plentiful, the fish is fresh and the welcome is homey. Most islands, such as Pulau Tomken, Bolilangga, Malenge and Togean have only one or two family-run guest houses that can accommodate just a few people, while popular Kadidiri has a small but lively beach scene with night-time bonfires and cold beers all around. The surrounding sea of Teluk Tomini is still recovering from its past brushes with cyanide and dynamite fishing, but the corals are coming back and most divers and snorkellers are thrilled with the rich diversity of marine life they find.

When you decide to pull yourself out of the water, there's a surprising variety of wildlife to look for in the undisturbed and wild jungles, as well as other remote beaches to find and even an active volcano to climb on Una Una

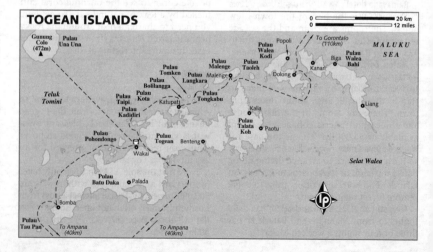

**TOGEAN ISLANDS**

0 ————— 20 km
0 ————— 12 miles

Gunung Colo (472m) ▲
Pulau Una Una
Popoli
To Gorontalo (110km)
MALUKU SEA
Pulau Walea Kodi
Pulau Walea Bahi
Biga
Kanari
Pulau Tomken
Pulau Malenge
Pulau Taoleh
Dolong
Pulau Bolilangga
Pulau Langkara
Malenge
Teluk Tomini
Pulau Taipi
Pulau Kota
Katupati
Pulau Tongkabu
Liang
Pulau Kadidiri
Kalia
Pulau Talata Koh
Paotu
Pulau Pohondongo
Pulau Togean
Benteng
Wakai
Selat Walea
Pulau Batu Daka
Palada
Bomba
Pulau Tau Pan
To Ampana (40km)
To Ampana (40km)

---

### DIVING & SNORKELLING AROUND THE TOGEANS

The Togeans are the only place in Indonesia where you can find all three major reef environments – atoll, barrier and fringing reefs – in one location. Two atolls and their deep lagoons lie to the northwest of Pulau Batu Daka. Barrier reefs surround many islands at the 200m-depth contour (5km to 15km offshore), and fringing reefs surround all of the coasts, merging with sea grass and mangroves. There is also a sunken WWII B-24 bomber plane, which is a 30-minute trip by speedboat (or one hour by regular boat) from Kadidiri.

The mix of coral and marine life is spectacular and unusually diverse, although many reefs were badly damaged by dynamite and cyanide fishing (see boxed text, p698). The more conspicuous residents include brightly marked coral lobsters, a colony of dugong, schools of a hundred or more dolphins, the occasional whale, commercially important species of trepang (sea cucumber), and natural pearls.

**Snorkelling** gear is available at most homestays for about 25,000Rp, but it's always better to bring your own. **Diving** can be arranged at a number of places, including **Black Marlin** (p699) and **Kadidiri Paradise** (p699) on Pulau Kadidiri, **Island Retreat** (p699) near Bomba and the upmarket **Walea Dive Resort** (p701) on Pulau Walea Kodi. Prices start from €24 per dive and PADI courses are also available.

---

(by day trip). Seven or so ethnic groups share this region, but all are happy see visitors and are exceptionally hospitable.

While there are no five-star resorts in the Togeans, there are some very comfortable options as well as your standard basic beach huts. Most of the rooms are in wooden cottages and right on the beach. Most have a mosquito net but no fan because the sea breezes keep everything cool. Bathroom facilities range from communal and rustic to private and porcelain. All prices quoted in this section are per person and all rates include local meals. It is a good idea to bring along some snacks and treats. Beer, soft drinks and mineral water are available from shops and homestays. Bring plenty of cash as there are no banks in the islands.

## Getting There & Away

Representatives from resorts and hotels will usually meet the ferries at each stop and shuttle you to their accommodation free of charge, or for a small fee if you don't end up staying with them.

The quickest way to get to the Togeans is to fly from Manado to Luwuk and travel by road from there to Ampana (six hours) – you'll have to stay overnight, then catch the ferry the next morning. Alternatively, you could fly to Palu and take a minibus from there to Ampana (11 hours). Otherwise, if you can get the boat schedule right, you can fly to Gorontalo from Manado, then catch the overnight ferry to the Togeans. Overland travellers often make their way up from Tana Toraja to Ampana, while plenty of people also take the bus from Manado to the port in Gorontalo.

### AMPANA

The bulk of transport to the Togeans leaves from Ampana. Every Monday morning the *Puspita* ferry makes the 15-hour journey from Ampana to Gorontalo via Wakai (40,000Rp, three hours), Katupat (one hour from Wakai), Malenge (45 minutes), Dolong (one hour), then on through to Gorontalo (110,000Rp, nine hours from Dolong). The ferry schedule tends to chop and change, so don't plan flight connections around it.

More reliable are the three local Ampana ferries that depart at 10am every day except for Thursday and Sunday to Wakai (40,000Rp, three hours), then to Katupat, Malenge and Kalia on Pulau Talata Koh before returning to Ampana. You can usually pay the captain an extra 40,000Rp to stop at Bomba, but don't count on it. To go direct to Bomba it's better to take small local boats that leave from a jetty in Labuhan village, next to Marina Cottages, at 9.30am on Sunday, Tuesday and Thursday and cost about 25,000Rp.

### GORONTALO

Every Wednesday evening the *Puspita* ferry makes the return 15-hour trip (110,000Rp) to Ampana via Dolong, Malenge, Katupat and Wakai. On Friday the larger, steel *Tuna Tomini* travels direct to Wakai, then on to Ampana (110,000Rp), making the return trip on Saturday morning.

---

**CONSERVATION OF THE TOGEANS**

Home to over 500 types of coral, 600 reef fish species and an estimated 500 mollusc, Teluk Tomini around the Togean Islands is one of the richest reef areas in all of Indonesia. In 2004 the Indonesian Ministry of Forestry signed a bill that turned 362,000 hectares of this fragile area into a national park – great news to conservation groups – but some local NGOs claim national-park status restricts local livelihoods and leaves the region open to other types of exploitation. It will take time to find out the real impacts.

The Togeans' shaky ecological record really started when cyanide and dynamite fishing was introduced to the islands in the early 1990s. While this boosted the local catch, it also caused untold damage to fragile reef ecosystems. By the early 2000s locals (often with help from local NGOs and the dive centres) began to understand the destructiveness of these practices and many went back to traditional fishing techniques. Some villages even began creating their own protected areas, and a guardhouse was completed in 2006 to patrol certain regions against illegal fishing practices. Today, islanders are hailing larger fishing yields closer to home and healthy coral beds – proof that reef protection works.

But the Togeans are relatively poor islands and the fishing ain't what it used to be. The fishing of valuable Napoleon fish (for foreign Chinese restaurants) has all but wiped this fish out of these waters and resulted in a catastrophic increase in the number of crown-of-thorns starfish, which destroy coral at an alarming rate.

Luckily, as the water quality has improved, some families are starting seaweed farms. Seaweed farming's potential twice-yearly harvest and a stable market price offer another lucrative option.

---

The only other option is the overnight, non-stop *Baronang* ferry to Pagimana (140,000/85,000Rp A/B class, 10 hours, once a week), which is a five-hour drive east of Ampana, from where you can catch regular ferries (see p697).

### MARISA

Anyone who is loaded with rupiah (about 2,000,000Rp) can charter a speedboat between Marisa (about 150km west of Gorontalo) and Wakai or Kadidiri. Both Black Marlin Dive (opposite) and Kadidiri Paradise (opposite) can arrange boat charters.

### BUNTA

Few people go this way, but it's one of the fastest routes to the Togeans. Take a morning flight from Manado to Luwuk, charter a car to Bunta (800,000Rp, four hours) and then charter a boat to Kadidiri (1,000,000Rp). It quickly adds up, but is not a bad option for a small group.

## Getting Around

Allow plenty of time to get around, because transport within the Togeans is infrequent. Schedules for public boats bend and break, but you can usually fall back on chartering something.

Charters are not hard to arrange in Wakai, Bomba and Kadidiri, but are far more difficult to arrange in smaller settlements be-

cause there are simply not many boats around. You'll often have to accept anything that's available. The rates should be negotiable but are often fairly standard among the cartel of local operators (250,000Rp from Wakai or Kadidiri to Bomba on a speedboat).

Ask your homestay or anyone around the village about the current timetables for boats to other islands, or further on to Ampana and Gorontalo. The locals rely heavily on these boats, so they always know what is going where and when.

## PULAU BATU DAKA

The largest and most accessible island is Pulau Batu Daka, which is home to the two main villages, Bomba and Wakai.

## Bomba

Bomba is a tiny outpost at the southwestern end of the island, which most travellers sail past on the way to and from Wakai (for Pulau Kadidiri). Bomba is an appealing alternative to Kadidiri, as the coral is in much better shape here and it sees fewer visitors.

It's a pleasant walk to the **bat caves** in the hills behind Bomba, but you'll need a guide and a torch (flashlight).

**Poya Lisa Cottages** (cottages 125,000Rp) is located on a pretty beach on its own little island. The friendly owners drop you there then bring you meals four times per day. The same family runs **Losmen Poya Lisa** (r 90,000Rp) in the village, where guests stay their first night if they arrive late in the day on the boat.

**Island Retreat** (www.togian-island-retreat.com; r per person US$15-28) is run by an expat Californian woman and her band of friendly dogs. Set on the beautiful beach at Pasir Putih, the 20 cottages are very well cared for and the cheapest ones have shared bathrooms. Some guests rave about the professionalism and relative luxury of this place, while others complain it lacks the family-style ambience available elsewhere in the Togeans – everyone, however, loves the internationally inspired food. There's a dive centre here, plus snorkelling gear. Boat charters can be arranged from Ampana and Marisa.

To leave Bomba to get to the other islands, you can sometimes flag down one of the ferries coming from Ampana or you can hire an *ojek* for the bumpy ride to Wakai (100,000Rp, three hours). For transport to Ampana, see p697.

## Wakai

The largest settlement in the Togeans, Wakai is mainly used as the departure point for boats to Pulau Kadidiri, but there are several well-stocked general stores and a lively market. A small **waterfall**, a few kilometres inland from Wakai, is a pleasant hike – ask directions in the village.

## PULAU KADIDIRI

This is definitely the island to go to if you're feeling social, but during the low season you could still potentially wind up on your own here. Just a short boat trip from Wakai, the three lodging options here (all right next to each other) are on a perfect strip of sand with OK snorkelling and swimming only metres from the door and superb diving beyond.

---

**COCONUT CRABS**

Coconut crabs, the world's largest terrestrial arthropods, once lived on islands throughout the western Pacific and eastern Indian Oceans, but unsustainable human exploitation has reduced stocks to a handful of isolated islands, including the Togeans. Mature crabs weigh up to 5kg and their large-clawed legs can span 90cm.

---

A short walk west of the beach brings you to a series of craggy coral cliffs, home to coconut crabs the size of small footballs. Put your hand into any hole in the sand and you may never see it again!

## Activities

A range of activities are on offer on Kadidiri. Apart from diving, snorkelling gear can be rented for about 25,000Rp per day and you can hike around the island on a series of complicated trails (bring something along to mark your path as some visitors got *very* lost). There are treks around volcanic Pulau Una Una (500,000Rp for up to eight people), and visits to other nearby islands for snorkelling (from around 150,000Rp). All the accommodation places have a small book exchange, which is great because you'll do a lot of reading.

## Sleeping

**Pondok Lestari** (cottages 75,000Rp) Stay with a charming Bajo family who take their guests on free daily snorkelling trips and fishing excursions where you can catch your own dinner. The older bamboo bungalows are very rustic, but a few newer wooden ones were under construction when we stayed here. All share a *mandi* bathroom.

**Black Marlin Cottages** ( ☎ 0435-831 869; www.blackmarlindive.com; cottages from 145,000Rp) This is arguably the liveliest place on Kadidiri and is home to British-run Black Marlin Dive. Cottages are large, wooden, well decorated and have particularly good bathrooms, but water is in short supply during certain hours of the day. Travellers from the three hotels tend to amass on the pontoon here for sunsets, and if Ali is around be prepared for a night of drinking *arak*, the local fermented beverage. Visa and MasterCard are accepted but sometimes the machine doesn't work – bring cash anyway.

**Kadidiri Paradise Resort** ( ☎ 0464-21058; www.visitkadidiriparadise.com; r per person €16-27) On the same stretch of beach as Black Marlin (although the two places don't get along), this resort on stunning planted grounds nearly surrounded by water is Kadidiri's poshest option. Rooms are huge and all have generous decks and big stone bathrooms. The dive centre here is particularly well run – don't miss the sea horses right off the dive centre's dock. Credit cards are accepted here too, but again, the machine doesn't always work. You can always pay in Ampana.

---

**THE BAJO**

Nomadic Bajo 'sea gypsies' still dive for trepang, pearls and other commercially important marine produce, as they have done for hundreds, perhaps thousands, of years. The Bajo are hunter-gatherers who spend much of their lives on boats, travelling as families wherever they go.

There are several permanent Bajo settlements around the Togean Islands, and even some stilt villages on offshore reefs, but the itinerant character of Bajo culture still survives. Newlyweds are put in a canoe and pushed out to sea to make their place in the world. When they have children, the fathers dive with their three-day-old babies to introduce them to life on the sea.

The rare intrusions from the outside world can sometimes result in tragedy. When Bugis and Chinese traders introduced air compressors to enable the Bajo to dive longer and deeper for trepang, the lethal nature of caisson disease (the bends) was rarely explained properly. Around 40 men were killed, and many more crippled, in one area alone. These days the Bajo divers' only concessions to modernity are goggles fashioned from wood and glass, and handmade spear guns. Land-loving Indonesians tend to look down on the Bajo, in much the same way gypsies are discriminated against in Europe.

---

## Getting There & Away

The public boats don't stop on Kadidiri, so you must go to Wakai first (see p699). Hotel representatives will usually meet the ferry and take you to Kadidiri for free. Once or twice a day a boat delivers fresh water and supplies to Kadidiri from Wakai; ask your homestay in Kadidiri or Wakai about the schedules. You can also charter a boat between Wakai and Kadidiri for about 50,000Rp one way.

## PULAU UNA UNA

The Togeans are part of an active volcanic belt. Pulau Una Una, which consists mostly of **Gunung Colo** (472m), was torn apart in 1983 when the volcano exploded for the first time in almost 100 years. Ash covered 90% of the island, destroying all houses, animals and most of the crops. Thankfully, Una Una's population had been safely evacuated. These days you can trek to the top of the volcano (three hours) and admire the awesome lava landscapes all around the island.

A public boat leaves Wakai about twice a week, but there is nowhere to stay on Una Una. The bigger homestays and resorts on Kadidiri and at Bomba can organise guided treks up the volcano, plus snorkelling stops along the way.

## PULAU TOGEAN

The main settlement on this island is the very relaxed Katupat village, which has a small market and a couple of shops. Around the island there are magical **beaches** and some decent **hikes** for anyone sick of swimming, snorkelling and diving.

**Losmen Melati** (r 90,000Rp), near the boat jetty in Katupat, offers the traveller simple accommodation.

## PULAU TOMKEN & PULAU BOLILANGGA

These two islands are a five-minute boat ride from Katupat. **Fadhila Cottages** (cottages from 125,000Rp) on Pulau Pangempa has so-so food, but it's clean and has superb snorkelling (lots of lionfish). **Bolilangga Cottages** (cottages from 80,000Rp) on Pulau Bolilangga only opens up on demand but is perfect if you're looking for a secluded hideaway.

## PULAU MALENGE

Malenge is remote and secluded, with wonderful **snorkelling** just offshore from the village. Some locals, with the aid of NGOs, have established excellent **walking trails** around the mangroves and jungles to help spot the particularly diverse fauna, including macaques, tarsiers, hornbills, cuscuses and salamanders.

The best place to stay is **Lestari Cottages** (r 80,000Rp, cottages 100,000Rp) run by friendly Rudy who offers rooms at the boat jetty in Malenge village and cottages on a secluded beach about 1km away by boat. Also near the jetty, **Malenge Indah** (cottages 80,000Rp) is attractively situated over the water.

## PULAU WALEA KODI

Dolong is a busy fishing village, and the only settlement on the island. Facilities are basic, transport is limited, and the island doesn't offer the picturesque beaches and snorkelling found elsewhere.

On an island just off Walea Kodi is the stunning Italian-run **Walea Dive Resort** (www .walea.com). Package deals, including cottage, three meals (including Italian cuisine), transport and three dives a day, start from €173 per person per day.

# NORTH SULAWESI

Northern Sulawesi has lots to offer in a relatively condensed space. You can dive over some of the world's best coral reefs at Bunaken one day, climb a volcano near Tomohon the next and visit the lowland Tangkoko-Batuangas Dua Saudara Nature Reserve and its wildlife the next. With cheap flights linking Manado to major destinations of Southeast Asia with quick connections to Europe, and easy transport between attractions, it's no wonder Indonesia is pushing this region as a major tourist destination. Economic prosperity from tourism and agriculture (mostly cloves and coconuts) means that North Sulawesi is the most developed province on Sulawesi and prices are higher here than elsewhere on the island.

The two largest distinct groups in the region are the Minahasans and the Sangirese, but there are many more subgroups and dialects. The kingdoms of Bolaang Mongondow, sandwiched between Minahasa and Gorontalo, were also important political players. The Dutch have had a more enduring influence on this peninsula than anywhere else in the archipelago: Dutch is still spoken among the older generation, and well-to-do families often send their children to study in the Netherlands.

The Sangir-Taulaud island group forms a bridge to the Philippines, providing a causeway for the movement of peoples and cultures. As a result, the language and physical features of Filipino peoples can be found among the local Minahasans.

## History

A group of independent states was established at a meeting of the linguistically diverse Minahasan peoples around AD 670 at a stone now known as Watu Pinabetengan (near Kawangkoan).

At the time of the first contact with Europeans in the 16th century, North Sulawesi

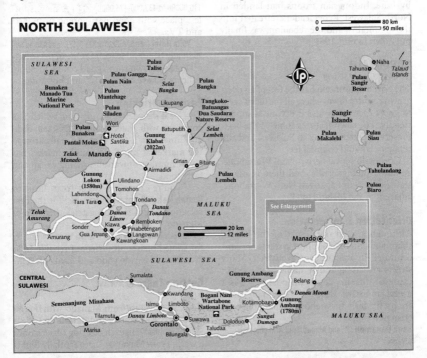

had strong links with the sultanate of Ternate (North Maluku) and Bugis traders from South Sulawesi. In 1677 the Dutch occupied Pulau Sangir and, two years later, a treaty with the Minahasan chiefs saw the start of Dutch domination for the next 300 years.

Although relations with the Dutch were often less than cordial, and the region did not actually come under direct Dutch rule until 1870, the Dutch and Minahasans eventually became so close that the north was often referred to as the '12th province of the Netherlands'.

Christianity became a force in the early 1820s, and the wholesale conversion of the Minahasans was almost complete by 1860. Because the school curriculum was taught in Dutch, the Minahasans had an early advantage in the competition for government jobs and positions in the colonial army.

The Minahasan sense of identity became an issue for the Indonesian government after independence. The Minahasan leaders declared their own autonomous state of North Sulawesi in June 1957. The Indonesian government then bombed Manado in February 1958 and, by June, Indonesian troops had landed in North Sulawesi. Rebel leaders retreated into the mountains, and the rebellion was finally put down in mid-1961.

## GORONTALO
☎ 0435 / pop 150,000
The port of Gorontalo has the feel of an overgrown country town, where all the locals seem to know each other and everyone is superfriendly. The town features some of the best-preserved Dutch houses in Sulawesi and still retains a languid colonial feel.

Gorontalo's local hero is Nani Wartabone, an anti-Dutch guerrilla, and there is a large statue of him in Lapangan Nani Wartabone, adjacent to the Melati Hotel.

### Orientation & Information
Although spread out, most of the hotels, shops and other life-support systems are concentrated in a small central district. Many streets are ambiguously named, which can cause confusion. The main post office is a useful landmark. Note that Gorontalo banks are particularly fussy about exchanging only crisp new bills.

**Bank Danamon** (Jl Jend Ahmad Yani) ATM plus cash advances.

**Black Marlin** ( ☎ 831 869; Jl Kasuari 9A) The office for Black Marlin on Pulau Kadidiri in the Togean Islands.
**BNI bank** (Bank Negara Indonesia; Jl Jend Ahmad Yani) ATM and currency exchange.
**Telkom** (Jl Parman; ☒ 24hr) Efficient.
**W@rsinet** (Jl Jend Ahmad Yani 14A) Internet access available.

### Activities
Diving is available in Gorontalo area with **Miguel's Diving** (www.miguelsdiving.com; Jl Agus Salim 29) at the Gorontalo Oasis Hotel next door to the Yulia Hotel, but it is only seasonal, from November to April.

### Sleeping
**Melati Hotel** ( ☎ 822 934; avelberg@hotmail.com; Jl Gajah Mada 33; r 80,000-175,000Rp; ☒ ☐ ) The friendly Melati is the long-time backpacker favorite. It's based around a lovely home, built in the early 1900s for the then harbour master (current owner Pak Alex's grandfather). The rooms in the original house are basic but atmospheric; the newer rooms are set around a pretty garden and are well furnished.

**Hotel Karina** ( ☎ 828 411; Jl Jend Ahmad Yani 28; s 110,000Rp, d 132,000-176,000Rp; ☒ ) A new, spotless place with good nasi-goreng breakfasts and TVs.

**Yulia Hotel** ( ☎ 828 395; fax 823 065; Jl Jend Ahmad Yani 26; s/d from 181,500/203,500Rp; ☒ ) One of the smartest hotels in town with a good central location. All rooms have satellite TV and hot water.

### Eating & Drinking
The local delicacy is *milu siram,* which is a corn soup with grated coconut, fish, salt, chilli and lime. You'll find it at the stalls around the market at night. The night market has a vast number of warungs selling cheap and tasty food.

If you're craving a sweet treat, head to **Rumah Makan Brantas** (Jl Hasanuddin) for the best selection of cakes and pastries this side of Manado.

**Rumah Makan Viva** (off Jl Gajah Mada) is handy for some hotels, and turns out reliable Indo favourites like gado gado and fried chicken.

### Getting There & Away
#### AIR
You can travel to/from Manado with **Lion Air** ( ☎ 830 035; Jl Rachmat 15) and **Batavia Air** ( ☎ 823 388; Jl DI Panjaitan 233), each offering service once a week. From Makassar there are daily flights

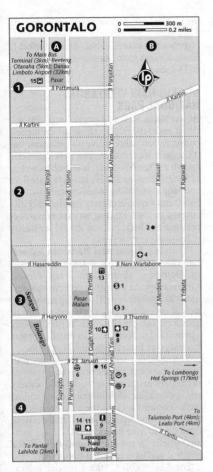

**GORONTALO**

Once a week the stable *Baronang* crosses the gulf from Gorontalo to Pagimana (A/B class 140,000/85,000Rp, 10 hours) and returns the next day. It leaves both places at about 9pm, and arrives at about 6am.

Direct boats also connect Gorontalo to the Togeans; see p697 for more details. You can book tickets at the office for **Black Marlin** ( ☎ 831 869; Jl Kasuari 9A).

**BUS**

The main bus terminal is 3km north of town and accessible by bemo, *bendi* or *ojek*. There are direct buses to Palu (110,000Rp, 17 hours) and Manado (regular/air-con 65,000/80,000Rp, 10 hours), departing every hour. Most people make the Manado trip by minibus or in 4WD Toyotas. Seats are priced by how close they are to the front: 100,000Rp to 150,000Rp.

From the terminal next to the market, *mikrolet* go in all directions to regional villages.

## Getting Around

The airport is 32km north of Gorontalo. For 50,000Rp a share-car can be booked at the taxi desk inside the terminal, and you'll be taken to your requested address. To get to the airport, book the same service through the airline, travel agency or your hotel.

## AROUND GORONTALO

On the outskirts of Gorontalo, on a hill at Lekobalo overlooking Danau Limboto, is **Benteng Otanaha**. The fort was probably built

divided between the carriers **Lion Air**, **Sriwijaya** ( ☎ 827 878; Jl Agus Salim18) and **Batavia Air**. All airlines have offices at the airport, or tickets can be bought at agencies around town.

## BOAT

Gorontalo has two ports, both about 4km from the town centre: Talumolo port for the Togeans and Leato port for Pagimana and Pelni ferries. Both are easily accessible by *mikrolet* (small taxi) along Jl Tantu. Tell the driver your boat's destination and he'll drop you off at the right place.

Every two weeks the Pelni liner *Tilongkabila* links Gorontalo with Bitung (for Manado). The **Pelni office** ( ☎ 821 089; cnr Jl 23 Januari & Jl Gajah Mada) is efficient and convenient.

by the Portuguese and supposedly used by Gorontalo kings as a bastion against the Dutch when relations soured. Today there are the remains of just three towers. Take a *bendi* or *mikrolet* from the *mikrolet* terminal to a path at the foot of the hill.

**Pantai Lahilote** is a white-sand beach 2km south of Gorontalo, and accessible by *bendi* or *mikrolet*. **Lombongo hot springs**, 17km east of Gorontalo, at the western edge of Bogani Nani Wartabone National Park, have a swimming pool filled with hotspring water. A nicer spot is the **swimming hole** at the foot of a 30m waterfall, which is a 3km walk past the springs. To get to the springs, take the *mikrolet* marked 'Suwawa' from in front of the hospital in Gorontalo.

## KOTAMOBAGU
☎ 0434

Kotamobagu (or 'Kota') was once the seat of power for the precolonial Bolaang Mongondow kingdoms, but is now a prosperous market town in a fertile valley of towering coconut plantations. There's little to do here, but it's a useful stopover between Manado and Gorontalo, and the gateway to the Bogani Nani Wartabone National Park.

### Orientation & Information
The main road from the Bonawang bus terminal is Jl Adampe Dolot. This turns into Jl Ahmad Yani through the centre of town, and has several well-stocked supermarkets and a BNI bank branch (which changes money).
**Bogani Nani Wartabone National Park office**
( ☎ 22548; Jl AKD) Along the road to Doloduo, about 5km from central Kotamobagu. Permits, maps and helpful trekking tips.
**Tourist office** (Jl Ahmad Yani 188) Not much in the way of spoken English or handouts.

### Sleeping & Eating
**Hotel Ramayana** ( ☎ 21188; Jl Adampe Dolot 50; s/d 50,000/85,000Rp) This hotel has clean, quiet accommodation, and is the best all-rounder in town.

There aren't all that many contenders, but Rumah Makan La Rose is probably the nicest restaurant in town.

### Getting There & Away
The main Bonawang bus terminal is a few kilometres from Kotamobagu, in the village of Monglonai, and accessible by *mikrolet*. There

are regular buses to Manado (three hours) and Gorontalo (eight hours).

From the central Serasi **bemo terminal** (Jl Borian), Kijangs go to Manado and bemos head to Dolotuo.

## BOGANI NANI WARTABONE NATIONAL PARK
About 50km west of Kotamobagu, this national park (193,600 hectares) has the highest conservation value in North Sulawesi, but it's mostly inaccessible. The park (formerly known as Dumoga-Bone) is at the headwaters of Sungai Dumoga and is a haven for rare flora and fauna, including black-crested macaque (*yaki*) and a species of giant fruit bat only discovered in 1992. Finding rare fauna requires patience and luck, but you should see plenty of hornbills and tarsiers.

Visit the **Bogani Nani Wartabone National Park office** ( ☎ 0434-22548; Jl AKD), on the road to Doloduo, about 5km from central Kotamobagu. At this office you can buy permits (20,000Rp per visit), pick up useful tips, look at decent trekking maps and ask lots of questions. You can also enter the park and buy a permit at Limboto, near Gorontalo, but this is a long way from the main hiking trails.

You could day-trip from Kotamobagu with private transport, but it's best to base yourself in the park in order to appreciate the scenery and spot wildlife while hiking at dawn and/or dusk. The area around the park entrance at Kosinggolan village has several trails, lasting from one to nine hours, and there are various options for overnight jaunts through the jungle if you have camping equipment.

For Kosinggolan, take a regular *mikrolet* to Doloduo from the Serasi terminal in Kotamobagu. Then walk about 2km west (or ask the *mikrolet* driver to continue) to the ranger station at Kosinggolan, just inside the park, where you must register and pick up a compulsory guide for 60,000Rp per short hike (more for longer trips).

## MANADO
☎ 0431 / pop 500,000
With an overabundance of bland shopping malls and cavernous holes in the sidewalk exposing the city's litter problem, Manado doesn't usually register as one of North Sulawesi's highlights. It's a well-serviced and friendly place, however, with more than its share of comfortable hotels and some good

places to eat. Around the city are nearby adventures at Bunaken, Tomohon, the Lembeh Strait and Tangkoko-Batuangas Dua Saudara Nature Reserve, and to get to these places most travellers will have to spend one night or more in Manado.

## History

In 1844 Manado was levelled by earthquakes, so the Dutch redesigned it from scratch. Fourteen years later the famous naturalist Alfred Wallace visited and described the city as 'one of the prettiest in the East'. That was 150 years ago and time hasn't been kind to the place.

Rice surpluses from Minahasa's volcanic hinterland made Manado a strategic port for European traders sailing to and from the 'Spice Islands' (Maluku). The Dutch helped unite the diverse Minahasan confederacy. By the mid-1800s, compulsory cultivation schemes were producing huge crops of cheap coffee for a Dutch-run monopoly. Minahasans suffered from this 'progress', yet economic, religious and social ties with the colonists continued to intensify. Elsewhere, Minahasan mercenaries put down anti-Dutch rebellions in Java and beyond, earning them the name *anjing Belanda* (Dutch dogs).

The Japanese occupation of 1942–45 was a period of deprivation, and the Allies bombed Manado heavily in 1945. During the war of independence that followed, there was bitter division between the nationalists and those favouring Dutch-sponsored federalism, and the city was bombed by Indonesian military in 1958.

Today, the development of Bitung's deep-sea port, and direct air links with the Philippines, Malaysia and Singapore, have helped to promote Manado's trade and tourism.

## Orientation

Along Jl Sam Ratulangi, the main road running north–south, there are upmarket restaurants, hotels and supermarkets. The 'boulevard', Jl Piere Tendean, is a monstrous thoroughfare with hotels and shopping malls; it has limited coastal access.

## Information

### EMERGENCY

**Main police station** ( ☎ inquiries 852 162, emergencies 110; Jl 17 Agustus)

### IMMIGRATION

**Immigration office** ( ☎ 841 688; Jl 17 Agustus)

### INTERNET ACCESS & POST

The best internet places in town can be found at the IT Center mall across from the Mega Mall.
**Main post office** (Jl Sam Ratulangi 23; ☼ 8am-7.30pm Mon-Fri, 8am-6pm Sat & Sun)

### MEDICAL SERVICES

**Rumah Sakit Umum** ( ☎ 853 191; Jl Monginsidi; Malalayang) The general hospital is about 4.5km from town and includes a decompression chamber.

### MONEY

Manado is overflowing with banks, and it's the best place in the region to exchange money. ATMs can be found at the banks along Jl Sam Ratulangi, plus out at the airport.
**BCA bank** (Bank Central Asia; Jl Sam Ratulangi) Has good rates and provides cash advances of up to 3,000,000Rp on Visa and MasterCard.
**BII bank** (Bank Internasional Indonesia; Jl Sam Ratulangi)
**BNI bank** (Bank Negara Indonesia) ATM and cash advances available at the airport.

### TELEPHONE

Numerous wartel around town offer competitive long-distance rates.
**Telkom** (Jl Sam Ratulangi; ☼ 24hr)

### TOURIST INFORMATION

**North Sulawesi Tourism Office** ( ☎ /fax 852 723; Jl Diponegoro 111; ☼ 8am-2pm Mon-Sat) You can get a map and sign the guest book, but that's about it.
**Tourist information** ( ☎ 0812 4403 7100) At the airport and only open for international arrivals, this glass booth has very helpful service. If you arrive on a domestic flight you can call the number above for any questions you might have.

## Sights

Most of the main sights lie beyond the city; however, the **Public Museum of North Sulawesi** (Museum Negeri Propinsi Sulawesi Utara; ☎ 870 308; Jl Supratman 72; admission 1000Rp; ☼ 8am-4pm Mon-Thu, 8-11.30am Fri, 9am-2pm Sat) is a possible diversion. It features a large display of traditional costumes and housing implements, with captions in English.

The 19th-century **Kienteng Ban Hian Kong** (Jl Panjaitan) is the oldest Buddhist temple in eastern Indonesia and has been beautifully restored. The temple hosts a spectacular festival in February (dates vary according to the lunar calendar).

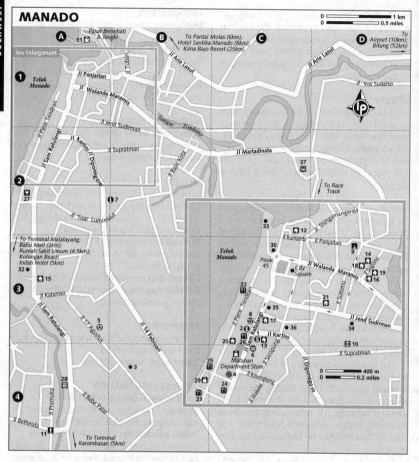

MANADO

0 — 1 km
0 — 0.5 miles

Pasar Bersehati & Jengki

To Pantai Molas (6km);
Hotel Santika:Manado (8km);
Kima Bajo Resort (25km)

To Airport (10km); Bitung (52km)

Jl Arie Lasut

Jl Yos Sudarso

Teluk Manado

Jl Panjaitan

Jl Walanda Maramis

Jl Piere Tendean

Jl Jend Sudirman

Sungai Tondano

Jl Martadinata

Jl Sam Ratulangi

Jl Kartini/Jl Diponegoro

Jl Supratman

Jl Balai Kota

To Race Track

Jl Toar Lumimuut

To Terminal Malalayang;
Bahu Mall (2km);
Rumah Sakit Umum (4.5km);
Kolongan Beach
Indah Hotel (5km)

Jl Katamso

Jl Sam Ratulangi

Jl 17 Agustus

Jl 14 Februari

Jl Pramuka

Jl Babe Palar

Jl Bethesda

To Terminal
Karombasan (5km)

Teluk Manado

Sisingamangaraja

Jl Rumambi

Jl Panjaitan

Pasar 45

City Square

Jl Walanda Maramis

Jl Sutomo

Jl Sugiono

Jl Piere Tendean

Jl Sam Ratulangi

Jl Kartini

Jl Jend Sudirman

Jl Sarapung

Matahari
Department Store

Jl Walanga

Jl Korengkeng

Jl Diponegoro

Jl Supratman

0 — 400 m
0 — 0.2 miles

## Activities

For relief from the incessant heat or an escape from the buzz of *mikrolet*, nonguests can use the **swimming pool** at Hotel Sahid Kawanua for 10,000Rp. At the Mega Mall there's a **Superbowl** on the top floor if you're craving some bowling, and **Tikala Shiatsu** ( ☎ 340 525; 1hr massage 90,000Rp; 9am-12am) to work out the kinks afterwards.

## Festivals & Events

Minahasans love an excuse to party. Watch out for these main festivals:

**Tai Pei Kong festival** Held at Kienteng Ban Hian Kong in February.

**Pengucapan Syukur** A harvest festival that can take place any time from June to August.

**Traditional horse races** Second week of August.

## Sleeping

Hotels near and on Jl Sam Ratulangi are an easy walk to food and shopping but can be noisy from the traffic. Places a little farther from the city centre are more peaceful and you can easily hop on one of the ubiquitous *mikrolet* to get wherever you need to go.

### BUDGET

The better budget places fill quickly with Indonesian business people, so reserve in advance.

**Rex Hotel** ( ☎ 851 136; fax 867 706; Jl Sugiono 3; s 35,000-50,000Rp; d 75,000-90,000Rp; ) These are the best budget rooms in town: all are clean and have windows letting in natural light. Shared-bathroom economy rooms are microscopic, but standards with private bathrooms are quite comfortable.

**New Angkasa Hotel** ( ☎ 864 062; Jl Sugiono 10; r with fan/air-con from 60,000/85,000Rp; 🖳 ) This place is always full because of its good-value though basic rooms.

**Hotel Anggrek** ( ☎ 851 970; Jl Kartini 5; r 90,000-150,000Rp; 🖳 ) There are plans to turn this place, recently purchased by an Italian-Indonesian couple, into a bona fide backpackers' pad. When we passed it had the most character of the town's cheapies (fish tank in the lobby, plenty of people milling about etc) but the matchbox-sized dark rooms were pretty scruffy.

**Hotel Angkasa Raya Inda** ( ☎ 862 039; Jl Sugiono 12A; r from 100,000Rp) Lives off the overflow from its better-value neighbours, but not half-bad if you're in a bind.

**Hotel Wisata** ( ☎ 860 908; wisatahotel_mdo@yahoo .com; Jl Sam Ratulangi 7; r 180,000-300,000Rp; 🖳 )Rooms here are priced according to size, but all have new double beds and are bright and comfortable. The sweeping spiral staircase in the lobby adds a little pizzazz, and the staff are helpful and speak decent English. It's the best deal in the city centre.

**Hotel Regina** ( ☎ 855 0091; Jl Sugiono 1; r from 190,000; 🖳 ) Bland but big rooms here are spotless and very plush for the price. The hearty Indonesian breakfasts are another perk.

**our pick Hotel Minahasa** ( ☎ 862 559; minahasa hotel@hotmail.com; Jl Sam Ratulangi 199; r with fan/air-con from 195,000/320,000Rp; 🖳 🖳 ) Manado's answer to a boutique hotel has flower-filled grounds stretching up the hill to a luxurious pool and fitness centre with city views. Fan rooms are basic and OK value if you consider the facilities, though you'll be tempted to upgrade to

a much more elegant, superior room with a terrace and a view. The staff are uncommonly helpful, breakfasts are copious and there are lots of little touches like umbrellas on lend and welcome fruit juice.

### MIDRANGE
Hot water and included breakfasts are standard at all the midrange places.

**Celebes Hotel** ( ☎ 870 425; hotelcelebesmdo@yahoo .com; Jl Rumambi 8A; r 210,000-400,000Rp; 🖳 ) As this place towers over the port area, ask for a room on either the 4th or 5th floors for big vistas over the water. All rooms are spotlessly clean and include air-con and hot water. The rooftop restaurant has great views over the action below and is a fine spot for a sundowner.

**Kolongan Beach Indah Hotel** ( ☎ 853 001; Jl Walter Monginsidi; r 260,000Rp; 🖳 ) Out in Malalayang, this is a quiet, attractive alternative to Manado, and is very handy for the Malalayang bus terminal, about 100m away. The smart rooms have air-con, hot water and satellite TV, and the restaurant is a good spot to wait for a bus.

**Ritzy Hotel** ( ☎ 855 555; www.ritzymanado.com; Jl Piere Tendean; s/d from 560,000/1,665,000Rp; 🖳 🖳 ) Spacious rooms have giant windows that make the best of the city or sea views. There's a near-constant 'special rate' here of 550,000Rp for a double.

**Hotel Santika Manado** ( ☎ 858 222; www.santika -manado.com; r from 650,000Rp; 🖳 🖳 ) This place feels like a world away from Manado, with a large swimming pool and walkway access through mangroves to the sea. While the dive centre gets rave reviews, the rooms are definitely past their prime.

## TOP END

At the time of research, seven upmarket hotels were under construction to accommodate visitors at the five-day World Ocean Conference 2009.

**Sintesa Peninsula Hotel** ( ☎ 855 008; www.sintesapeninsulahotel.com; Jl Jend Sudirman; r from US$110; ❄ 💻 ⌨ ) A gleaming new, white fortress on a hill in the middle of town, the Sintesa has all bases covered from the marble-clad lobby to its fitness centre, free internet and a big swimming pool. Great service and security. Promotional rates as low as 450,000Rp can sometimes be found on their website.

**Kima Bajo Resort** ( ☎ 860 999; www.kimabajo.com; r from US$180; ❄ ⌨ ) The leading boutique resort in the Manado area (it's about a 30-minute drive to the city), Kima Bajo offers indulgent rooms in a choice of bungalows and villas, plus there's a good dive centre here. The Mayana Spa is the place to unwind after a week of diving.

## Eating

Adventurous Minahasan cuisine can be found around Manado, especially at the stalls that open up at night on Jl Piere Tendean. Get a taste for *rica-rica*, a spicy stir-fry made with *ayam* (chicken), *babi* (pork) or even *r.w.* (pronounced 'air weh' – dog!). *Bubur tinotuan* (corn porridge) and fresh seafood are local specialities worth looking out for.

Most of the malls have extensive food courts on their upper floors. The best ones are those at Mega Mall and Bahu Mall, but even the smaller shopping centres have cheap eats. Choose from Indonesian, Chinese, Italian and more.

Hidden behind the massive Mega Mall on Jl Piere Tendean is an excellent stretch of surprisingly chic seafood warungs open every night. The price, variety and sunsets are unbeatable. **Blue Terrace** (sheesha pipe 35,000Rp) is the hippest and doubles as a candlelit sheesha bar, while **Piglet** (mains from 15,000Rp) is the best stop for Minahasan food.

There is another stretch of warungs behind the Bahu Mall, on Jl Walter Monginsidi, 2km south of the town centre. Live bands sometimes play on a stage here.

**Singapura Bakery** (Jl Sam Ratulangi 22; pastries from 5000Rp) Has a mind-boggling array of baked goods, fresh juices and shakes, plus a popular cheap cafe next door serving yummy Javanese fare.

**Raja Sate** (Jl Pierre Tendean 39; sate from 10,000RP) Just south of the Mega Mall. Chose from a tasty array of sate, curries and even New Zealand steaks.

**Rumah Makan Green Garden** (Jl Sam Ratulangi; lunch 19,000Rp) Looks a bit funky but the food here is really good. Try the tofu dishes and fresh juices.

**Famili Cafe** (Jl Pierre Tendean; mains 20,000-50,000Rp; ☽ lunch & dinner) Excellent grilled-fish lunch specials that include rice, greens and sambal.

## Drinking

The drinks of choice are *saguer*, a very quaffable fermented sago wine, and Cap Tikus (literally, Rat Brand), the generic name for distilled *saguer*. Cap Tikus is sold as No 1, No 2 or No 3, referring to its strength (No 1 is the strongest!). It is best diluted and served over ice.

The best option for a sunset drink is to head to one of the seaside warungs behind the Mega Mall. Stick around and sink some drinks here, as the price rises rapidly in the clubs.

**Gacho** (Jl Piere Tendean) One of the best of the pool bars, just south of Mega Mall.

**Styx** (Bahu Mall) Even more sophisticated, and straight out of New York or London.

**Corner** (Bahu Mall) A couple of floors above Styx, this is a huge sports bar, but it is pretty quiet during the week, only picking up late on Saturday. Bands from Jakarta sometimes play here and attract a cover charge of 25,000Rp or more.

Be very wary of places promoting karaoke. These are usually dark dens of iniquity, with overpriced drinks and working girls.

## Entertainment

Music is a way of life for the Minahasans. They love jazz, and there are always small concerts and backroom gigs happening, so ask around.

### CINEMAS

**Studio 21 Cinema** (Jl Sam Ratulangi; entry 17,500Rp) The most sophisticated cinema in Manado, it features recent Western releases with Indonesian subtitles.

### NIGHTCLUBS

**Ha Ha Cafe** (entry incl 1 drink 50,000Rp) The leading club in town, this place is on the top floor of the Mega Mall. It is so vast that it looks like an aircraft hangar and only really fills up on Wednesday (ladies' night), Friday and Saturday. Once the smuggled flasks of Cap Tikus are drained, the crowds loosen up and mob the dance floor.

## Getting There & Away
### AIR
Manado is well-connected by air internationally and with other parts of Indonesia.

**Merpati** ( ☎ 842 000; Jl Jend Sudirman 111) has daily flights to Jakarta and three flights a week to/from Makassar.

**Garuda** ( ☎ 877 737; Jl Sam Ratulangi) flies daily to/from Makassar, Balikpapan and Denpasar, with connections to Jakarta.

**Lion Air** ( ☎ 847 000; Mega Mall) flies daily to/from Makassar, Jakarta, Denpasar, Ternate, Sorong and Singapore, five days a week to Kuala Lumpur and once a week to/from Gorontalo.

**Wings Air** ( ☎ 847 000; Airport) has flights to/from Davao, Philippines once a week.

**Silk Air** ( ☎ 863 744; Jl Sarapung) offers services to/from Singapore six days a week.

**Air Asia** ( ☎ 2150-505 088; Airport) has flights to Kuala Lumpur three days a week that link up with European flights.

**Batavia Air** ( ☎ 386 4338; Mega Mall) offers flights to/from Balikpapan, Gorontalo, Surabaya and Jakarta.

Tickets for domestic flights often cost slightly less at travel agencies, and agencies often sell international tickets at substantial discounts.

See p657 for more details about international flights to/from Manado. The international departure tax is 150,000Rp.

### BOAT
All Pelni boats use the deep-water port of Bitung, 55km from Manado. Several of the Pelni liners call by once or twice every week: the *Sangiang* goes to Ternate (economy/1st class 436,000/1,473,000Rp), the *Lambelu* goes to Namlea (111,000/317,000Rp) and Ambon (233,000/617,000Rp), the *Dorolonda* to Sorong (228,000/695,000Rp) and Fak Fak, and the *Tilongkabila* to Luwuk (168,000/442,000Rp) and other ports along the southeastern coast.

There's no Pelni office in Manado – the nearest one is in Bitung – but **PT Virgo Ekspres** ( ☎ 858 610; Jl Sam Ratulangi 5) is a reliable Pelni agent for checking information and purchasing tickets.

Every Monday, Wednesday and Friday afternoon the **Ratu Maria** ( ☎ 855 851) makes the overnight trip to Pulau Siau (75,000Rp) and Tahuna (115,000Rp) in the Sangir-Talaud Islands.

Small, slow and uncomfortable boats leave Manado every day or two for Tahuna and Lirung, also in the Sangir-Talaud Islands; and to Mangole, Sanana, Tobelo and Ambon in Maluku. Tickets are available from the stalls outside the port. From Bitung, four overnight ferries a week also travel to Ternate in North Maluku.

### BUS
There are three reasonably orderly terminals for long-distance buses and the local *mikrolet*.

From Terminal Karombasan, 5km south of the city, buses go to Tomohon (6000Rp), Tondano (7000Rp) and other places south of Manado. From the far-southern Terminal Malalayang, very regular buses go to Kotamobagu (20,000Rp) and Gorontalo (70,000Rp, eight hours).

From Terminal Paal 2, at the eastern end of Jl Martadinata, varied public transport runs to Bitung (7000Rp) and the airport (3500Rp).

## Getting Around
### TO/FROM THE AIRPORT
*Mikrolet* from Sam Ratulangi International Airport go to Terminal Paal 2 (3500Rp), where you can change to a *mikrolet* heading to Pasar 45 or elsewhere in the city, for a flat fee of 2300Rp. Fixed-price taxis cost 85,000Rp from the airport to the city (13km).

### PUBLIC TRANSPORT
Manado's *mikrolet*, literally clog up Manado's streets so that finding one with a spare seat is a matter of waiting a second or two. *Mikrolet* heading south on Jl Sam Ratulangi with 'Wanea' on the window sign will go to Terminal Karombasan. Most *mikrolet* heading north go through Pasar 45 and past the Pasar Jengki fish market, but some go directly to Terminal Paal 2 along Jl Jend Sudirman. *Mikrolet* heading to Terminal Malalayang go down Jl Piere Tendean. The fare for any destination around town is 2300Rp.

Private taxis circle the city but very few drivers are willing to use the meter, so negotiate before setting off.

**SULAWESI**

# PULAU BUNAKEN

☎ 0431

This tiny, coral-fringed isle is North Sulawesi's top tourist destination but (so far) it's managed to avoid becoming resort-land and maintains a rootsy island soul. Tourist accommodation is spread out along two beaches – other than that, the island belongs to the islanders; these friendly folk have a seemingly endless reserve of authentically warm smiles. There are no hassles here, just laid-back beachy bliss.

However, most people come to Bunaken for the diving. The marine biodiversity is extraordinary, with more than 300 types of coral and 3000 species of fish, so when you first get your head in the water and see the abundant corals, sponges and phenomenally colourful life all around you, it's a life-shaking experience. The 808-hectare island is part of the 75,265-hectare **Bunaken Manado Tua Marine National Park** (Taman Laut Bunaken Manado Tua), which includes: Manado Tua (Old Manado), the dormant volcano that can be seen from Manado and climbed in about four hours; Nain and Mantehage islands; and Pulau Siladen, which has some more accommodation options.

With the developing and expanding city of Manado right next door, Bunaken is becoming more and more accessible. Within two hours of arriving to Manado from Singapore, Kuala Lumpur or most parts of Indonesia, you can be in a bamboo beach shack on Bunaken watching the sunset. Unfortunately, this proximity also means that the huge amounts of garbage generated by the city can sweep onto Pantai Liang, turning the picturesque tropical beach into a refuse heap. The scarcity of fresh water has limited the island's development, and villagers must import their drinking water from Manado. Washing water is drawn from small, brackish wells.

Many tourists who come to Bunaken are on short vacations from Europe and elsewhere, so prices from accomodation to a Bintang are much higher than in mainland Sulawesi. It also means some of the resorts actively discriminate against nondivers, either by charging higher accommodation prices or turning them away.

## Orientation

There is a concrete and dirt path connecting Pangalisang and Liang, about a 30-minute walk. Pangalisang is connected to Bunaken

village by a new paved road used by scooters, while Liang has a complicated network of forest footpaths towards the main village (hint: stay on the overgrown paved part and keep going straight). A third village, Alung Banua at the northwest of the island, is rarely visited by tourists.

## Information

In an attempt to finance conservation activities, rubbish disposal, mangrove rehabilitation, local education program and the policing of any illegal fishing practices, the Bunaken Manado Tua Marine National Park charges an entry fee of 50,000Rp (for a day pass) to 150,000Rp (if you stay any longer; good for one year). Pay at your hotel or dive centre. If no one asks you to pay, go to the national park headquarters on Pantai Liang to pay yourself since the money truly goes to a good cause. The plastic-tag permit should be worn while within the park boundaries.

There's an informative diorama-style museum about the flora and fauna of Bunaken at the national park headquarters with helpful information.

## Activities

Most people go to Bunaken to dive or snorkel, but it's a lovely island to walk around, with very friendly villages and beautiful scenery.

If you're on the island during the second to third week of September, you'll be able to catch the **Bunaken Festival** which features arts and cultural performances by all the ethnic groups around North Sulawesi.

For those with less time and more money, some of the dive operators and hotels can organise day trips to Bunaken from Manado.

## Sleeping & Eating

There are plenty of budget and midrange resorts on Bunaken, but no luxurious hideaways, so if you want serious comfort, stick with the mainland resorts or go to Pulau Siladen. Most rooms include at least a fan and a mosquito net and most places throw in transfers to and from the jetty in Bunaken village, in some cases to the mainland. Consider bringing some snacks and treats from the mainland, as there is not much available on the island beyond the set meals. All prices quoted below are per person and include three meals per day.

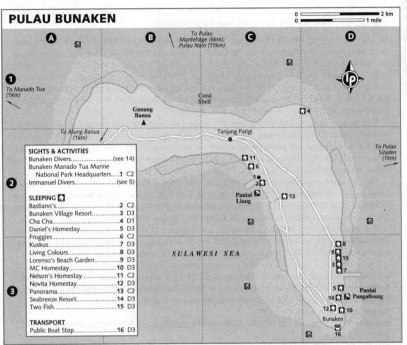

**PULAU BUNAKEN**

## PANTAI PANGALISANG

Pantai Pangalisang is a stretch of white sand tucked behind the mangroves with some outrageous snorkelling just beyond. The beach all but disappears at high tide.

### Budget

**Novita Homestay** (r 125,000) Right in Bunaken village (at the northern end), these spotless rooms with shared bathrooms in a charming family home are the place to stay for an authentic local experience.

**Lorenso's Beach Garden** ( ☎ 0852 5697 3345; www .lorenso-bunaken.com; r 125,000Rp, bungalows 175,000-250,000Rp) Lorenso's has no-frills bamboo huts plus two cheaper rooms with a shared *mandi*-style bathroom and a social atmosphere. Meals invariably involve lots of fresh fish, and some of the island's best snorkelling is just through the mangroves.

**Daniel's Homestay** ( ☎ 813 143; daniels@indostat.net .id; bungalows from 150,000Rp) There has to be at least 20 friendly workers and their family milling around at this flower-filled outfit. Wood cottages are very basic but spacious. Pay a little more for a seafront cottage.

**Two Fish** ( ☎ 081 143 2805; www.twofishdivers.com; r €12-25; 🖳 ) This is a big, impersonal place with a handful of small cheapies with shared bathroom and some larger but still plain 'superior' rooms with attached bathrooms. All options are on the shabby side, making only the budget rooms worth the money.

**Seabreeze Resort** ( ☎ 081 143 9558; www.bunakendiv ers.com; cottages €13-25) A large, sprawling resort, it has quite a few different types of bungalows, so shop around before committing. Attractions include a verdant garden, good beach access and very cold beers thanks to the Aussie owner.

**Kuskus** ( ☎ 081 3400 37657; www.bunakenkuskusre sort.com; bungalows €15) Excellent-value, big wood bungalows are nestled in a particularly lush garden. Cross the small road to the restaurant on the beach. The ambience and the food here get fantastic reviews from travellers.

### Midrange

**MC Homestay** (www.mcdivebunaken.com; bungalows €20) Located on the northern edge of Bunaken village, this homestay is just above the best beach on Bunaken and has solid, cement bungalows.

## DIVING & SNORKELLING AROUND PULAU BUNAKEN

Bunaken's unique situation of being surrounded by deep water with strong, nutrient-laden currents, plus having a mangrove ecosystem that protects much of the beaches and subsequently the corals from erosion, makes it one of the best diving and snorkelling spots in the world. Beyond drop-offs you'll find caves and valleys full of brightly coloured sponges, thriving corals and fish – it is also common to see turtles, rays, dolphins and sharks. The most accessible site is the flat coral off Pantai Liang, which takes a dramatic 90-degree turn less than 100m offshore, plummeting from 1m to 2m depths into dark oblivion.

The best snorkelling and diving sites are marked on maps in most homestays on Bunaken. Well-worn snorkelling equipment can be rented from most homestays for about 50,000Rp per day, but it is often worth paying a little more to rent some quality equipment from one of the dive centres. The best option is to put in near Lorenso's Beach Garden and exit at Two Fish. The closer you get to Bunaken Village, the less thriving the reef becomes.

Trips around Bunaken and nearby islands will cost from €45 for two dives (there's nearly always a two-dive per trip minimum – for one dive you'll have to wait out the second dive on the boat) and around €375 for PADI courses. Equipment rental is extra and costs around €15 per day for scuba gear, fins, mask and snorkel. Snorkellers can go along with the dive boats for around €5 per person.

It is worth checking whether companies are members of the **North Sulawesi Watersports Association** (NSWA; www.divenorthsulawesi.com), which promotes conservation activities and local community initiatives. This organisation has almost 20 members and keeps on growing.

The places that charge more per dive usually do so because they invest in better equipment. Check out the state of what's on offer and ask about the centre's safety procedures before you commit.

**Bastiano's** ( ☎ 0431-853 566; www.bastianos.com; Bastiano's) Caters mainly to European dive tourists on packages.

**Bunaken Divers** ( ☎ 0431-330 6034; www.bunakendivers.com; Seabreeze Resort) Friendly Australian-run outfit that has been around a while.

**Bunaken Village Resort** ( ☎ 081 3407 57268; www.bunakenvillage.com; Bunaken Village Resort) Small and competitively priced.

**Cha Cha Divers** ( ☎ 081 2430 1356; www.bunakenchacha.com; Cha Cha) Small operator with the emphasis on a personal touch.

**Froggies Dive Centre** ( ☎ 0431-850 210; www.divefroggies.com; Froggies) Pioneers of the famed lazy dive where the current does the work.

**Immanuel Divers** ( ☎ 0431-813 143; www.divedaniels.com; Daniel's Homestay) Intimate and cheap.

**Living Colours** ( ☎ 081 2430 6063; www.livingcoloursdiving.com; Living Colours) Has some of the best equipment on the island and is very professionally run.

**Two Fish Divers** ( ☎ 081 143 2805; www.twofishdivers.com; Two Fish) Popular English-run operation that does small groups with no time limits.

There are also several operators based at resorts on the mainland and other islands that offer fully inclusive dive packages for five days or more:

**Barracuda** ( ☎ 0413-854 279; www.barracuda-diving.com) Based at their own bungalow resort on Pantai Molas, northeast of Manado.

**Eco Divers** ( ☎ 0431-824 445; www.eco-divers.com) Based at the charming Tasik Ria Resort, about 20km south of Manado.

**Gangga Island Resort & Spa** ( ☎ 0413-889 4009; www.ganggaisland.com; r per person incl meals US$165-225; 🗶 💻 🖳 ) Live on remote Pulau Gangga that has access to the dive sites at Bunaken and the Lembeh Strait. Service and room quality are excellent as is the safety and equipment of the dive center. This posh place even has satellite TV and a spa.

**Lumba Lumba Diving** ( ☎ 0431-826 151; www.lumbalumbadiving.com) Promoting personal service, this homely dive centre and resort has a loyal following. It's about 20km south of Manado.

**Murex** ( ☎ 0431-826 091; www.murexdive.com) One of the longest-running dive operators in the area, with a resort to the south of Manado and liveaboards roving further afield.

**Nusantara Diving Centre** ( ☎ 0413-863 988; www.ndcmanado.com) The daddy of dive operators around Bunaken, with its own impressive resort on Pantai Molas, northeast of Manado.

**Odyssea Divers** ( ☎ 0431-860 999; www.odysseadivers.com) Based at the luxurious Kima Bajo Resort on the mainland.

For more on diving the Lembeh Strait, see p715.

Service can be iffy though, and standards are dependent on whether or not the owners are there.

**Bunaken Village Resort** ( ☎ 081 3407 57268; www .bunakenvillage.com; cottages from €30; 🏊 ) With a chic dipping pool, a fabulously friendly welcome and a refreshing Javanese-Balinese style, this is one of Bunaken's most comfortable options and is a good choice for families.

**our pick** **Living Colours** ( ☎ 081 2430 6063; www .livingcoloursdiving.com; cottages from €35; 🖥 ) By far the most upmarket choice on this main strip of beach, this Finnish-run place has wooden bungalows with enormous terraces, stylish furniture clad in drapy white fabrics and spacious hot-water bathrooms. It's perched up on a little hill and both the food and service get excellent traveller reviews.

**Cha Cha** ( ☎ 081 3560 03736; www.bunakenchacha.com; cottages from US$60; 🎲 ) In splendid isolation on the northeastern tip of the island, 'The Last Resort' as it is sometimes nicknamed, has an intimate atmosphere thanks to just seven bungalows. The menu is more varied than most, with Italian and Japanese to complement the local meals. Everyone who stays here raves about it.

### PANTAI LIANG

The beach at Pantai Liang has suffered from considerable erosion (it was destroyed by a storm in early 2009) and rising sea levels, and has thus become a svelte though pleasant strip of white sand. Bungalows are closer together and there's more beachside action here (such as seaside food and trinket vendors), as well as a higher likelihood of impromptu beach parties. However, it's a sorry sight when the rubbish washes in from Manado.

The beach just south of Pantai Liang is a protected turtle nesting ground, so keep off of it even though it looks inviting.

### Budget

**Panorama** ( ☎ 01340830872; ester_kasehung@hotmail .com; cottages from 125,000Rp) Tucked in corner up on a hillside, the basic wood bungalows with terraces and commanding views are the best budget deal on the island. It's a friendly, family-style place; some more upmarket bungalows (under Dutch management) were under construction when we visited.

**Nelson's Homestay** ( ☎ 0431856288; cottages 175,000Rp) These basic huts are built on the cliffs and have bay views and an OK stretch of beach below.

### Midrange

**Bastiano's** ( ☎ 853 566; www.bastianos.com; r €18-25) The cheaper rooms at this sprawling hotel are basic for the price, but the more expensive ones have skylights and some pretty terracotta *mandi* bathing jugs in the bathrooms. It's on a long stretch of beach and the service is great. Food is not as good as you might hope for at an Italian-run place.

**Froggies** ( ☎ 081 2430 1356; www.divefroggies.com; cottages €25-35) Very professionally run, this was one of the first dive centres on the island and it's still going strong. It has a good beachfront location, rooms are well decorated and spotless, and the interesting restaurant area feels a bit like the bat cave. Nondivers are not welcome.

### PULAU SILADEN

**Siladen Resort & Spa** (www.siladen.com; r from €250) A beautiful resort on Siladen, with 15 cottages that are sumptuously furnished and have a great reputation. Facilities include a lagoon pool, an indulgent spa and dive centre.

**Tanta Moon** (r 130,000Rp) Basic, friendly and clean, this place gets points for its good, fresh food.

## Getting There & Away

Every day (except Sunday) at about 3pm, a public boat (50,000Rp, one hour) leaves the harbour, near Pasar Jengki fish market in Manado, for Bunaken village and Pulau Siladen. You'll have to walk from the boat landing in Bunaken village to your homestay. The boat leaves Bunaken between 7am and 8am daily (except Sunday), so it's not possible to day-trip from Manado using the public boat.

The more upmarket options on Bunaken offer on-demand boat shuttles to/from Manado for their clients for around €5 each way per person – you can also usually hop on these services if you've been diving with the place. Otherwise, most guest houses can help you charter a boat (often small and rickety) for around 200,000Rp each way for the whole boat. When conditions are rough the public boat stops running, but private boats will usually make the shorter, half-hour crossing between Bunaken and either the **Hotel Santika** (see p707; about one hour from Manado) or the town of Wori (two hours from Manado). Bear in mind that conditions are sometimes too choppy for any boats to make the crossing.

At the beginning of 2009 a second, larger pier was under construction at Bunaken village, with goals of welcoming a regular tourist-calibre ferry to/from Manado that might also connect Bunaken to Gangga and Bangka islands.

## TOMOHON

☎ 0431 / pop 30,000

Tomohon is a pleasant, cool respite from Manado, with a stunning setting below Gunung Lokon volcano. It's popular with city folk on weekends; for travellers, it's a possible (though spread-out) alternative to Manado, and an ideal base from which to explore the many nearby attractions.

### Sleeping

If you plan on climbing Gunung Lokon stay at Volcano Resort which is right at the base. To get here, get out at 'Gereja Pniel', about 3km before Tomohon from Manado. From here you'll have to walk or catch an *ojek* the remaining 500m towards the mountain.

To get to Onong's Palace or Highland Resort, get off the *mikrolet* from Manado at 'Kinilow', about 5km before Tomohon, and walk the 300m signposted from the main road.

All of the following places have restaurants, and breakfast is included in the price.

**Volcano Resort** ( ☎ 352 988; cottages 100,000-150,000Rp) Spread out around a grassy garden, these clean, wooden bungalows are a great deal, plus the staff are helpful and speak English. There are also some budget rooms with shared bathroom at 80,000Rp.

**Onong's Palace** ( ☎ 315 7090; www.tomohon-onong.com; r 250,000Rp) The chic bungalows here are perched along an exceptionally lush and shady hillside. All have big decks, massive windows, artistic bamboo Bali-style details and hot water. There's a reasonably good on-site restaurant.

**Highland Resort** ( ☎ 353 333; www.highlandresort.info; r €30-80) A tidy place with all the staff in matching red T-shirts, Highland Resort has a huge collection of plain but clean wooden rooms of varying sizes. Lots of tours and tour information are on offer, and there are nice views over the jungle. There's also a full spa.

**Gardenia Country Inn** ( ☎ 353 333; www.gardeniacountryinn.com; r/chalets from US$60/80) An oasis in beautifully manicured gardens. The chalets here are like a Balinese hideaway. Discounts available.

> ### TOMOHON'S MACABRE MARKET
>
> It's said that the Minahasan people will eat anything on four legs, apart from the table and chairs, and nowhere is this more evident than at Tomohon's daily market. Visiting the market (which is right next to the *mikrolet* terminal) is a slaughterhouse-like experience, with dead and alive dogs, pigs, rats and bats all on display. The most radical moments are when yelping dogs are pulled out of their cages and killed by a bludgeon on the back of the head. The market is at its 'best' on Saturday morning when the snake butchers come to town.

### Eating

Minahasan adventurous cuisine is served in a string of restaurants on a cliff overlooking Manado, just a few kilometres before Tomohon. The food at **Pemandangan** (meals 15,000-45,000Rp) is as impressive as the spectacular views, with great seafood plus Indonesian staples. The bus from Manado to Tomohon will drop you off at any restaurant, but buses back to Manado are often full.

### Getting There & Around

*Mikrolet* regularly travel to Tomohon (6000Rp, 40 minutes) from Terminal Karombasan in Manado. From the terminal in Tomohon, *mikrolet* go to Manado, and *mikrolet* and buses go to Tondano and various other towns.

There are a few *bendi* around town, but a good way to see local sights in little time is to charter a *mikrolet* or a more comfortable, but expensive, taxi. The taxis line up opposite the *mikrolet* terminal.

## AROUND TOMOHON

**Gunung Lokon** (1580m) contains a simmering crater lake of varying hues, which takes about three hours to reach (and another hour to the peak) from Tomohon. Before climbing any volcano in the area, report to the **vulcanology centre** (Kantor Dinas Gunung Berapi; ☎ 351 076; Jl Kakashashen Tiga). The centre can provide advice about the hike. Happy Flower Homestay and Volcano Resort in Tomohon can help arrange this and other hikes in the area, for guests.

You can drive almost all the way to the top of **Gunung Mahawu**, where you'll be rewarded with views over the whole region and into a

180m-wide, 140m-deep sulphuric crater lake. There's no public transport but lots of tours go here. This place gets swarmed by locals on the weekends.

There are numerous other places to explore from Tomohon, and all are accessible by *mikrolet*. **Danau Linow**, a small, highly sulphurous lake that changes colours with the light, is home to extensive birdlife. Take a *mikrolet* to **Sonder**, get off at **Lahendong** and walk 1.5km to the lake. From Danau Linow you can hike 8km to Danau Tondano, but you'll need to ask directions.

## DANAU TONDANO

This lake, 30km south of Manado, is 600m above sea level. It's a beautiful area for **hiking**, and is popular with Manado's upper class especially on weekends. Just before Remboken village, along the road around the lake, **Objek Wisata Remboken** has a swimming pool, a mediocre restaurant overlooking the lake and some gardens to wander around. There are also several decent seafood restaurants along the road around the lake.

*Mikrolet* regularly leave for Tondano village (7000Rp) from Terminal Karombasan in Manado, or you can get there by *mikrolet* from Tomohon (2500Rp). From Tondano, catch another *mikrolet* to Remboken, and get off anywhere you like along the road around the lake.

## AIRMADIDI

Airmadidi (Boiling Water) is the site of mineral springs, but the real attraction are the odd little **pre-Christian tombs** known as *waruga*. Corpses were placed in these carved stone boxes, in a foetal position, with household articles, gold and porcelain, but most have been plundered. There's a group of these tombs at Airmadidi Bawah, a 15-minute walk from the Airmadidi *mikrolet* terminal.

*Mikrolet* to Airmadidi leave from Terminal Paal 2 in Manado (4000Rp), and there are connections between Airmadidi and Tondano and Bitung.

### Gunung Klabat

Gunung Klabat (2022m) is the highest peak on the peninsula. The obvious path to the crater at the top starts behind the police station at Airmadidi, where you must register and take a guide. The climb (about four hours to the top, two for the descent) goes through

rainforest where you can see superb flora and fauna, but it's a tough hike.

It's best to camp overnight near the top and be there for the sunrise and the stupendous views across the whole peninsula. Your guide should be able to provide a tent. Try to avoid Sunday, when the mountain can be crowded with local hikers.

## BITUNG

☎ 0438 / pop 137,000

Bitung is the chief regional port and home to many factories. Despite its spectacular setting, the town is unattractive, so most travellers make for Manado or beyond as soon as possible.

Regardless of what time you arrive by boat in Bitung, there will be buses going to Manado, but if you need to leave Bitung by boat early in the morning, it may be prudent to stay overnight. Be vigilant around the docks, as plenty of pickpockets turn up to greet the Pelni liners.

**Hotel Nalendra** ( ☎ 32072; Jl Samuel Languyu 5A; r from 150,000Rp) has been recommended by readers who have been stranded in Bitung over the years. The clean rooms include hot water, TV and air-con.

There are plenty of basic *rumah makan* in the town centre and near the port.

### Getting There & Away

All sorts of vehicles leave regularly from Terminal Paal 2 in Manado (7000Rp, one hour). The driver stops at Terminal Mapalus, just outside Bitung, from where you have to catch another *mikrolet* (10 minutes) to town or the port.

See p709 for details about boats to Bitung. The port is in the middle of Bitung, and the **Pelni office** ( ☎ 35818) is in the port complex.

## PULAU LEMBEH & THE LEMBEH STRAIT

Lembeh is known almost exclusively for its diving and has emerged as the critter capital of Indonesia. For the uninitiated, welcome to an alien world on our very own planet. Critters are the weird and wonderful creatures that inhabit the murky depths and are much admired by underwater photographers. However, this is muck diving and not for beginners thanks to strong currents. If it's coral you are after, you're better off around Bunaken.

## Sleeping & Eating

As Lembeh's fame grows, so does the number of dive resorts, and most have a sister operation on either Bunaken or around Manado. All are set in their own secluded bays, but without transport it is near-impossible to travel between them. Packages that include diving are usually available, but the following prices are for room and board only per person.

**Bastiano's** ( ☎ 0431-332 5678; www.bastianoslembeh.com; r € 18-23, cottages €26-38; ✂ 💻 🍴 ) One of the newer resorts, Bastiano's has good-value rooms, but the cottages are much nicer.

**Divers Lodge** ( ☎ 081 2443 3754; www.diving-on-sulawesi.com; cottages €30) One of the more popular options in the Lembeh area has good food and even better service.

**Kungkungan Bay Resort** (www.divekbr.com; cottages US$115-180; ✂ 💻 🍴 ) This small, elegant resort is intimate and very well run.

**Lembeh Resort** ( ☎ 0438-30667; www.lembehresort.com; cottages US$125-175; ✂ 💻 🍴 ) This is a lovely Balinese-style resort that gets many returning customers.

## TANGKOKO-BATUANGAS DUA SAUDARA NATURE RESERVE

With 8800 hectares of forest bordered by a sandy coastline and offshore coral gardens, Tangkoko is one of the most impressive and accessible nature reserves in Indonesia. The park is home to black macaques, cuscuses and tarsiers, maleo birds and endemic red-knobbed hornbills, among other fauna, and rare types of rainforest flora. Tangkoko is also home to a plethora of midges, called *gonones*, which bite and leave victims furiously scratching for days afterwards. Always wear long trousers, tucked into thick socks, and take covered shoes and plenty of insect repellent.

Sadly, parts of the park are falling victim to encroachment by local communities, but money generated from visitors might help stave that off.

Bring plenty of cash as the nearest ATM, in Girian, often runs dry.

## Sights & Activities

Most people arrive at the park entrance at Batuputih in the afternoon, take a guided night walk into the park to see the tarsiers (when sightings are nearly guaranteed), and then another guided walk the next morning to see lively troupes of black macaques. Guided walks cost 85,000Rp per person. It's worth staying longer to enjoy the gorgeous beach setting and friendly folk at Batuputih and to take a variety of other tours including **dolphin-spotting boat tours** (full day up to 4 people 300,000Rp), that also include a visit to nearby hot springs, and **birdwatching** or **fishing tours** (half-day up to 4 people 200,000Rp). All tours and walks can be arranged at your guest house, which will invariably be swarming with guides.

## Sleeping & Eating

There are several basic losmen in Batuputih village which all include three meals in their prices.

**Tarsius Homestay** ( ☎ 0813 5622 5545; r 150,000-200,000Rp) One of a few cheaper but less lively places down the road towards the beach from Mama Roos, this place has clean rooms with attached bathrooms in a big house.

**Mama Roos** ( ☎ 0813 4042 1454; mamaroos@eudoramail.com; r 250,000-300,000Rp) This is the most popular option and it's bright and friendly.

**Pulisan Jungle Beach Resort** ( ☎ 0431-838 185; www.pulisanresort-sulawesi.com; bungalows per person incl meals from €22-40) Located just to the north of

---

**TARSIERS**

If you're visiting Sulawesi's Tangkoko-Batuangas Dua Saudara Nature Reserve or Lore Lindu National Park, keep your eyes peeled for something looking back at you: a tiny nocturnal primate known as a tarsier. These creatures are recognisable by their eyes, which are literally larger than their stomachs, so big in fact that they cannot rotate them within their sockets. Luckily, their heads can be rotated nearly 360 degrees, so their range of vision isn't compromised. Tarsiers also have huge, sensitive ears, which can be retracted and unfurled, and disproportionately long legs, which they use to jump distances 10 times their body length. They use their anatomical anomalies and impressive speed to catch small insects. Tarsiers live in groups of up to eight, and communicate with what sounds like high-pitched singing. They are found only in some rainforests of Indonesia and the Philippines.

the nature reserve. Dive into pristine waters, go birdwatching, hike or just take it easy. Boat trips to the national park are available and there is a beautiful stretch of sand here.

### Getting There & Away

To get to Batuputih from Manado, take a bus to Bitung, get off at Girian and catch a *mikrolet* or pick-up truck to Batuputih. Some of the dive centres and hotels in and around Manado also run day trips to the park, but you'll miss most of the animal action if you go on these.

## SANGIR-TALAUD ISLANDS

☎ 0432

Strewn across the sea between Indonesia and the southern Philippines are the volcanic island groups of Sangir and Talaud. There are 77 islands, of which 56 are inhabited. The main islands in the Sangir group are Sangir Besar and Siau; the main islands in the Talaud group are Karakelong, Salibabu and Kaburuang. The capital of the group is Tahuna on Sangir Besar; the other major settlement is Lirung on Pulau Salibabu.

The islands offer dozens of unspoilt sandy beaches, a few crumbling **Portuguese forts**, several **volcanoes** to climb, many caves and waterfalls to explore, and some superb **diving** and **snorkelling** (bring your own gear). But like most wonderfully pristine places, the islands are not easy to reach.

There's a **tourist office** (☎ 22219; Jl Tona) in Tahuna.

### Sleeping & Eating

**Penginapan Chindy** (s/d 30,000/45,500Rp) and **Penginapan Sederhana** (s/d 30,000/45,500Rp) are both in Lirung, but don't expect too much luxury or privacy.

**Hotel Nasional** (☎ 21185; Jl Makaampo 58, Tahuna; s/d with fan 50,000/75,000Rp, with air-con from 90,000/120,000Rp; ❄ ) Head here for a range of decent rooms, plus it has the best restaurant in Tahuna.

**Rainbow Losmen** (r 55,000Rp) Located further south along the coast from Tahuna in nearby Tamoko, this is a simple, friendly establishment in a pretty village.

**Hotel Victory Veronica** (☎ 21494; Jl Raramenusa 16, Tahuna; r with fan/air-con 60,000/90,000Rp; ❄ ) The smartest place anywhere on the islands. It also has the decent Deniest Coffee Shop.

### Getting There & Away

#### AIR

Once a week, Merpati flies from Manado to Naha, which is about 20km from Tahuna, and on to Melanguane, which is near Lirung in the Talaud group. There's a **Merpati office** (☎ 21037; Jl Makaampo) in Tahuna.

#### BOAT

Travelling by boat will give you a look at the stunning set of volcanic islands along the way. From Bitung, the Pelni liner *Sangiang* stops at Tahuna and Lirung once every two weeks. Pelni boats are far more comfortable than the other options, such as the *Pulo Teratai* and the *Agape Star*, which sail between Manado and Lirung (15 hours), often stopping in Tahuna (11 hours), every one or two days. Book at the boat offices near the port in Manado.

Every Monday, Wednesday and Friday afternoon the **Ratu Maria** (☎ 0431-855 851) makes the overnight trip from Manado to Siau (75,000Rp) and Tahuna (115,000Rp).

Also from Manado, small, slow and uncomfortable boats leave every day or two for Tahuna and Lirung. Tickets are available from the stalls outside the port.

The seas can get quite rough during the high wind from October to April.

# SOUTHEAST SULAWESI

Few visitors make it to Southeast Sulawesi, but the handful of travellers that are prepared to venture a little off the beaten track will find themselves rewarded with some striking scenery and hospitable cultures, and surprisingly good transport links. The top attraction here is Wakatobi Marine National Park, located in the remote Tukangbesi Islands off the southern tip, offering some of Indonesia's best snorkelling and diving.

## History

Some of the earliest records of life in Southeast Sulawesi are depicted in prehistoric paintings on the walls of caves near Raha. The red ochre paintings include hunting scenes, boats and warriors on horseback.

The region's most powerful pre-colonial kingdom was Buton, based at Wolio, near Bau Bau. Its control and influence over other regional states was supported by the Dutch

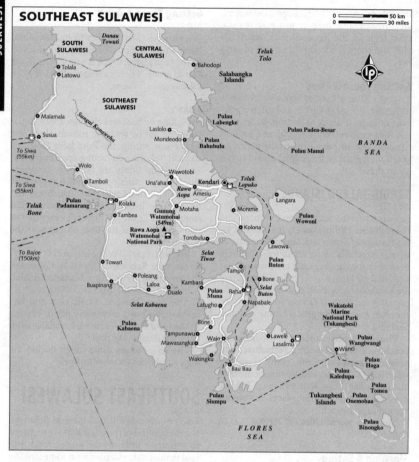

**SOUTHEAST SULAWESI**

colonialists. Buton came under direct Dutch rule after the fall of Makassar in 1669, and was granted limited autonomy in 1906.

Other local trading centres maintained a low profile, probably for reasons of self-preservation. Kendari was one of the busiest, but the island of Bungkutoko at the mouth of Kendari harbour hid the town so well it was not really 'discovered' by the Dutch until 1830.

The civil strife of the 1950s and 1960s was a time of extreme hardship for the people of the province. Farms and villages were plundered by rebel and government forces alike, decimating the region's agricultural sector. Today Southeast Sulawesi is supported by mining, agriculture and timber plantations

and is a centre for transmigration (see p57), which has boosted its population to almost two million.

## KOLAKA
☎ 0405

Kolaka is readily accessible by boat from Bajoe, and is the major gateway to Southeast Sulawesi province. The centre of town is the bus terminal, about 500m north of the ferry terminal. You can change money at **BNI bank** (Bank Negara Indonesia; Jl Repelita), not far from Hotel Family.

There are not many facilities in town, so try to carry on to Kendari or Bajoe.

**Hotel Family** ( ☎ 21350; Jl Cakalang 6; r 30,000-40,000Rp), a quiet spot 150m southwest of the bus terminal, is the best place to stay. It has airy, clean rooms and the more expensive ones include an attached bathroom.

## Getting There & Away

All day and night, plenty of buses, bemos and Kijangs travel between Kolaka and Kendari (65,000Rp, six hours). While you are on the ferry you may be able to find a spare seat on a bus going directly to Kendari or Makassar – just check with the bus drivers.

Three ferries travel overnight from Kolaka to Bajoe (60,000/75,000Rp deck/business class, eight hours), the main port on the eastern coast of the southwest peninsula. The ferries leave at 5pm, 8pm and 11pm, and are all timed to connect with services for a convenient arrival in Makassar.

## KENDARI
☎ 0401 / pop 235,000

The capital of Southeast Sulawesi province has long been the key port for trade between the inland Tolaki people and seafaring Bugis and Bajo traders. The town's isolation continues to cushion it from dramatic developments elsewhere. Kendari is a bustling town with little to recommend it except the range of decent accommodation that makes it a good place to break the long haul from Makassar to Wakatobi.

## Orientation

Kendari begins in a tangle of lanes in the old *kota* (city) precinct adjacent to the original port in the east, and becomes progressively more modern as each era has added another suburb to the west. The one very, *very* long main road has most of the facilities, except the bus terminals. The main road's many names are confusing, especially at the *kota* end where Jl Sudirman and Jl Soekarno are used interchangeably.

## Information

**Bank Danamon** (Jl Diponegoro) The best place to change money.

**BNI bank** (Bank Negara Indonesia; Jl Sudirman)

**Hospital** (☎ 321 773; Jl Sam Ratulangi) A reliable public hospital, 6km west of town.

**Main post office** (Jl Sam Ratulangi) Also has an internet centre.

**Telkom office** (Jl Ahmad Yani; ⊘ 24hr)

**Tourist office** (☎ 326 634) Inconveniently located and of limited use.

## Festivals & Events

**Festival Teluk Kendari** (Kendari Bay Festival) is held each April and is the highlight of the social calendar, with dragon-boat races, traditional music and plenty of partying.

## Sleeping & Eating

**Hotel Cendrawasih** (☎ 321 932; Jl Diponegoro 42; r with fan/air-con 66,000/110,000Rp; ✂) A long-running place, just off the main road, with friendly staff and good service. The fan rooms are ageing these days, but have balconies. The air-con rooms are in better shape.

**Kendari Beach Hotel** (☎ /fax 321 988; Jl Hasanuddin 44; r 100,000-150,000Rp; ✂) This is located on a small hill; take advantage of the private balcony to enjoy the views and breezes. All rooms come with satellite TV, while the more expensive options come with hot water and better views. There is also a restaurant overlooking the bay with an extensive menu at affordable prices.

**Hotel Kartika Kendari** (☎ /fax 321 484; Jl Parman 84; r from 160,000Rp; ✂) This large hotel has smart rooms with satellite TV and hot water. You may have to pester staff to get the hot water working. Discounts available.

**Rumah Makan Marannu** (Jl A Silondae; mains 25,000-40,000Rp; ⊘ breakfast, lunch & dinner) Some of the best Chinese food in town, but watch the weight on the seafood, as it adds up quickly.

The night warungs lining the esplanade along Jl Bung Tomo are a popular hang-out in the evening.

## Getting There & Away

### AIR

**Merpati** (☎ 322 242; Jl Sudirman) and **Lion Air** (☎ 329 911; Jl Parman 84) connect Kendari and Makassar, and Merpati also flies to Palu. Don't forget to ask the staff about transport to the remote airport.

### BOAT

Adjacent to a church on top of a hill, the **Pelni** (☎ 321 915) office is just up from a roundabout, and not far from the Pelni dock.

Kendari is not well serviced by Pelni, but is relatively close to the major port of Bau Bau. Every two weeks the slow boat *Tilongkabila* heads up the coast to Kolonedale (economy/ 1st class 85,000/258,000Rp, 12 hours), and then goes on to Luwuk, Gorontalo and Bitung for Manado; and to Raha, Bau Bau and Makassar (131,000/405,000Rp, 22 hours).

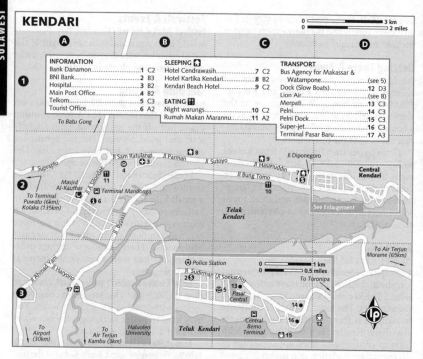

**KENDARI**

| INFORMATION | | SLEEPING | | TRANSPORT | |
|---|---|---|---|---|---|
| Bank Danamon | 1 C2 | Hotel Cendrawasih | 7 C2 | Bus Agency for Makassar & | |
| BNI Bank | 2 B3 | Hotel Kartika Kendari | 8 B2 | Watampone | (see 5) |
| Hospital | 3 B2 | Kendari Beach Hotel | 9 C2 | Dock (Slow Boats) | 12 D3 |
| Main Post Office | 4 B2 | | | Lion Air | (see 8) |
| Telkom | 5 C3 | EATING | | Merpati | 13 C3 |
| Tourist Office | 6 A2 | Night warungs | 10 C2 | Pelni | 14 C3 |
| | | Rumah Makan Marannu | 11 A2 | Pelni Dock | 15 C3 |
| | | | | Super-jet | 16 C3 |
| | | | | Terminal Pasar Baru | 17 A3 |

The Super-jet *kapal cepat* (fast boat) leaves the Pelni dock at Kendari at about 7.30am and 1pm daily for Raha (75,000Rp, 3½ hours) and Bau Bau (100,000Rp, five hours). You can buy your ticket directly from the **Super-jet** ( ☎ 329 257; Jl Sukowati 8) office near the Pelni dock.

### BUS, BEMO & KIJANG

The main terminal is at Puwatu, about 10km west of town. From there, plenty of buses, Kijangs and bemos go to Kolaka (45,000Rp, six hours). It's more convenient to book a ticket (and board the bus) at one of the agencies in town. Most buses leave Kendari at about 1pm to link with the 8pm ferry (which means arriving in Bajoe at about 4am). The fare to Watampone/Makassar is 95,000/120,000Rp, and includes the ferry trip in deck class, but you can upgrade to business class.

### Getting Around

Contact the airline office about transport to the airport, which is 30km southwest of Kendari – both airlines usually run a bus with certain pick-up points in town. From

the airport, you can jump in a shared vehicle or if you don't mind the extra cost, charter one.

Kendari is *very* spread out. For short distances, take a becak; for anything along the main road, take a *pete-pete*; to anywhere else, catch an air-conditioned taxi.

## AROUND KENDARI
### Air Terjun Kambu

The closest attraction to Kendari is this **waterfall** at the foot of Gunung Kambu, 3km upstream from Haluoleo University. Walk from the university, or charter a *pete-pete*.

### Air Terjun Morame

This impressive waterfall is 100m of tumbling water set amid ebony, teak and banyan trees on Sungai Kali Osena, situated 65km south of Kendari. There is a deep pool at the base of the falls, which is excellent for **swimming**.

Take a bus from Terminal Pasar Baru (one hour), or charter a boat (about two hours) from near the Pelni dock in Kendari. If you have a boat, arrange a slight detour to **Teluk Lapuko**, a great spot for **swimming** and **snorkelling**, with white-sand beaches and clear water.

## Pulau Hari
This tiny island, 18km off the Kendari coast, is a **nature reserve** with white-sand beaches and opportunities for **snorkelling** and **walking**. Get a group together, and charter a boat from near the Pelni dock in Kendari. It should cost about 200,000Rp for the day, but bring your own snorkelling gear.

## RAHA
☎ 0403
Raha, the main settlement on Pulau Muna, is a quiet backwater about halfway between Kendari and Bau Bau. Raha is famous for its horse fighting, cave paintings and lagoons. You can change money at **Bank Danamon** (Jl Sutomo) and **BNI bank** (Bank Negara Indonesia; Jl Sukawati), but don't (ahem) count on it.

### Sleeping & Eating
**Hotel Alia** ( ☎ 21218; Jl Sudirman 5; r from 65,000Rp) Convenient for its proximity to the causeway, this quiet hotel has basic but clean rooms or you can become a VIP for just 125,000Rp. There is also a small restaurant that is open to all comers.

**Hotel Permata Sari** ( ☎ 21164; Jl A Yani 67; s/d 65,000/75,000Rp) Conveniently located opposite the bus/bemo terminal, and still reasonably quiet. It has large, clean rooms.

**Hotel Ilham** ( ☎ 21070; Jl Jati 16; r with fan 66,000Rp, with air-con 175,000Rp; 🌀 ) One of the few places in town to offer an air-con escape during the hot season, this is a friendly operation.

**Rumah Makan Cahaya Pangkep** (Jl Sudirman; meals 10,000-25,000Rp; 🕒 breakfast, lunch & dinner) The best option in Raha, with excellent baked fish, but bear in mind this is not the culinary capital of Indonesia.

### Getting There & Away
Raha is the only stop between Kendari and Bau Bau on the fast Super-jet. Purchase tickets the day before departure from the **Super-jet** ( ☎ 22018; Jl Dewantara) office in Kendari. These boats are scheduled to leave for Kendari (75,000Rp, 3½ hours) at 8.30am and 1.30pm; and for Bau Bau (50,000Rp, 1½ hours) at about 10am and 3.30pm. Be ready for the onboard scramble to claim a seat.

Every two weeks the Pelni liner *Tilongkabila* stops at Raha on its way up (via Kendari)

and down (via Bau Bau) the east coast of Sulawesi. The **Pelni** office is at the end of the causeway.

## AROUND RAHA
### Napabale
Raha's main attraction is Napabale, a pretty lagoon at the foot of a hill. The lagoon is linked to the sea via a natural tunnel, so you can paddle through when the tide is low. It is a great area for **hiking** and **swimming**, and you can hire boats to explore the lake. Napabale is a scenic ride (15km) from Raha. You can reach it by *ojek*, or by regular *pete-pete* to Lohia village, from where the lagoon is another 1.5km walk, at the end of the road. There is usually a couple of food stalls, and often a few more on Sunday, when it's generally crowded.

### Pantai Melerua
Not far from Napabale, Melerua beach has superb scenery and unusual rock formations. Although you can swim and snorkel (bring your own gear), there isn't a sandy beach as such. Take the regular *pete-pete* towards Lohia and ask the driver to drop you off at the unmarked turn-off. From here, walk (or take an *ojek*) about 7km until the very rough path finishes.

### Gua Mabolu
The solid 10km walk from Mabolu village to Gua Mabolu (Mabolu Caves), through plantations and pretty walled gardens, is probably more interesting than the caves themselves. The caretakers can take you to a selection of the best caves, starting with **Liang Metanduno**, which has paintings of a horse with two riders, headless warriors and some boats.

It is 12km from Raha to Mabolu village, so catch (or charter) a *pete-pete* to Mabolu and ask the driver to drop you off at the path to the caves. The paths are not clear, so you'll need someone from Mabolu to show you the way to the caves, and to the caretakers who live nearby.

### Latugho
**Festival Danau Napabale** is held each June at the village of Latugho, 30km inland from Raha. The festival features horse combat, as well as the more gentle spectacle of kite flying. Horse fighting is a Muna tradition with a robust following – it's not for the tender-hearted.

SULAWESI

# BAU BAU
☎ 0402 / pop 83,000

With comfortable accommodation, great views from the well-preserved citadel walls and some decent beaches within easy *ojek* range, Pulau Buton's prosperous main town of Bau Bau is a great place to await a boat connection to Maluku, North Sulawesi, or the diving paradise of Tukangbesi.

## Orientation & Information
The terminal, main mosque and market are about 500m west of the main Pelni port, along Jl Kartini, which diverges from the seafront esplanade, Jl Yos Sudarso. Jl Kartini crosses a bridge then curves south past the post office towards the *kraton* (walled city palace).

The best internet cafe is a block inland from the main mosque. Around 1.5km east of the main port is a second harbour, with the offices for the **tourist department** ( ☎ 23588), Telkom and Pelni. The **BNI bank** (Bank Negara Indonesia; Jl Kartini) has an ATM that shouldn't be relied upon, as well as exchange.

## Sights & Activities
Banking steeply behind the town centre is the **kraton**, the Wolio royal citadel with impressively long and well-preserved 16th-century walls that offer great views over the town and its north-facing bay. Amid trees and flowers within the walls are timeless semi-traditional homes and the old royal mosque. Some 500m beyond the citadel's south gate is **Pusat Kebudayaan Wolio**, a cultural centre and museum in a restored old mansion-palace, which is the focal point of Bau Bau's **Festival Kraton** each September. Eleven kilometres southwest of Bau Bau, the nearest white-sand beach is the attractively palm-lined **Pantai Nirwana**, though there is a certain amount of rubbish. Locals prefer **Pantai Batauga**, 10km beyond, for swimming.

## Sleeping & Eating
**Wolio Homestay** ( ☎ 040 226 999; 16 Jl Mayjen Sutoyo; r 35,000Rp) About 200m from the harbour. The owner here speaks English and the price includes breakfast.

**our pick** **Hillhouse Resort** ( ☎ 21189; r with breakfast 100,000Rp) This little place has one of the most spectacular settings anywhere in Sulawesi. It's about half a click above Pusat Kebudayaan Wolio, set amid a hilltop flower garden with outstanding panoramic views of the bay and beyond. The rooms are simple, with mosquito nets and shared bathroom. Be sure to call ahead to alert staff of your arrival and to order any meals (35,000Rp) in advance; there are no shops or eateries nearby.

**Hotel Ratu Rajawali** ( ☎ 22162; Jl Sultan Hasanuddin 69; r from 195,000Rp; ❄ 🖥 ) Right opposite the Pelni office, 2km east of the port, this hotel is a real gem. The well-appointed rooms include air-con and TV, plus small balconies that overlook the gardens and swimming pool towards the sea beyond. This is the preferred hotel of the Operation Wallacea teams (see opposite) when transferring to and from Pulau Hoga in Wakatobi.

You'll find restaurants and warungs (many set up at night) along the esplanade, a few hundred metres west of the port.

## Getting There & Away
The fast Super-jet boat takes 1½ hours to Raha (55,000Rp) and five hours to Kendari (100,000Rp), and leaves at 7am and 12.30pm daily. Demand can often be greater than supply, so book ahead (from 5pm the day before) at the **Super-jet** ( ☎ 22497) office, which is opposite Warung Pangkep, about 500m west of the port.

Every two weeks the Pelni liners *Umsini, Ciremai, Lambelu, Sinabung, Tilongkabila* and *Kelimutu* link Bau Bau with Makassar (economy/1st class 112,000/365,000Rp), and most also go to Ambon, southern Maluku and/or Papua. Every two weeks the *Tilongkabila* goes up and down the east coast of Sulawesi, stopping off at Kendari and Bitung (for Manado), among other places.

# TUKANGBESI ISLANDS
According to Jacques Cousteau, the Tukangbesi Islands offered 'possibly the finest diving in the world' when he surveyed the area in the 1980s. Most of the islands are now part of **Wakatobi Marine National Park** (Taman Laut Wakatobi). Positioned remotely off the far southeast coast, the islands are difficult to reach, but they do offer superb snorkelling and diving, a blaze of corals and marine life, isolated beaches and stunning landscapes. For good information online check out www.wakatobi.org.

## Sleeping
All accommodation except Wakatobi Dive Resort are on Pulau Hoga. It is also possible to arrange informal homestays on this island for

about 50,000Rp including meals. Some basic snorkelling equipment is available, but bring your own if you want to be sure.

**Hoga Island Resort** (diving@sulawesi-indonesia.com; bungalow per person from 50,000Rp) A Dutch-run place on the beach catering to backpackers.

**Island Garden** ( ☎ 0815 819 4119; http://home.arcor.de/islandgarden; bungalow per person 100,000Rp) Has a good reputation and comfortable bungalows.

**Operation Wallacea** (www.opwall.com) This British-based NGO organises pre-booked 'volunteer' programs in marine conservation. The organisation has a study centre on Pulau Hoga and may be able hook people up with a homestay during busy periods.

**Wakatobi Dive Resort** (www.wakatobi.com; one-week packages from US$3125) On Pulau Onemobaa, this ultra-exclusive hideaway offers beautiful

bungalow accommodation and one of the most celebrated house reefs in Indonesia. Packages include diving, full board and charter flights from Bali. It is also the base for the elegant liveaboard **Pelagian** (www.pelagian.wakatobi.com).

## Getting There & Away

Getting to Hoga is the big headache. From Bau Bau, take the daily boat to Wanci on Pulau Wangiwangi (about 100,000Rp; eight hours), which usually leaves in the evening and arrives very early the next day. Wait around for another boat, or more likely charter one, to Hoga (count on 100,000Rp). Once every four weeks the Pelni liner *Kelimutu* travels from Makassar to Bau Bau then on to Ambon via Wanci.

# Maluku

Welcome to the original 'spice islands'. Back in the 16th century when nutmeg, cloves and mace were global commodities that grew nowhere else, Maluku was a place where money really did 'grow on trees'. Incredibly, it was the search for Maluku's valuable spices that kick-started the whole process of European colonisation in Asia. Today spices have minimal economic clout and Maluku (formerly 'the Moluccas') has dropped out of global consciousness.

The region is protected from mass tourism by distance, unpredictable transport and memories of a brief yet tragically destructive period of intercommunal conflict (1999–2002). But peace has long since returned to this scattering of idyllic islands where the complex web of effusively welcoming cultures envelops visitors with an almost Polynesian charm. While transport can prove infuriatingly inconvenient, with flexibility and patience you can snorkel the brilliant Bandas, explore the beach-strewn Kei Islands, survey North Maluku's mesmerising volcano islands and explore ruined Dutch fortresses, all well within the limits of a two-month visa.

With picture-perfect desert-island beaches at backpacker prices and world-class snorkelling right in front of your guest house, this is the ideal place for travellers prepared to wind down many gears, learn Bahasa Indonesia and revel in a tropical discovery that seems almost too good to be true.

---

## HIGHLIGHTS

- Snorkelling some of the world's finest accessible coral gardens in the historically fascinating **Banda Islands** (p756)

- Unwinding at **Ohoidertawun** (p767) or **Pasir Panjang** (p767), two stunning yet virtually undiscovered sweeps of the purest white sand

- Dining at Floridas on **Pulau Ternate** (p733) as the sunset burnishes golden highlights onto the jungle-furred volcanic cone of neighbouring **Pulau Tidore** (p735)

- Staying at one of the offbeat getaways on **Pulau Saparua** (p751) before mainstream tourism discovers the island's white-sand beaches, friendly villages and extensive diving potential

- Discovering idyllic empty beaches and WWII remnants on the desert islands scattered around **Morotai** (p740)

★ Morotai

Pulau Ternate ★
Pulau Tidore ★

**PAPUA**

Pulau Saparua ★

★ Banda Islands

Ohoidertawun
Pasir Panjang ★★

---

| ◾ POPULATION: 2.1 MILLION | ◾ LAND AREA: 85,728 SQ KM | ◾ HIGHEST PEAK: GUNUNG BINAYA (3027M) |

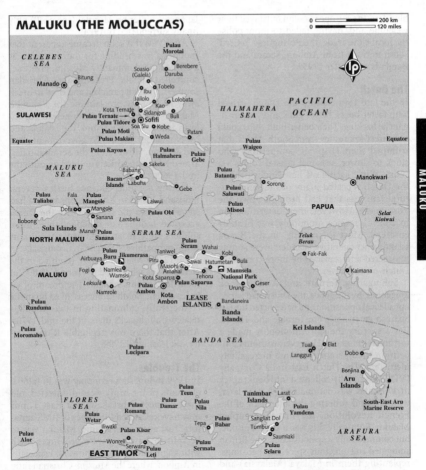

**MALUKU (THE MOLUCCAS)**

MALUKU

## HISTORY
### Precolonial Times

The name Maluku probably originated as *Jazirat-al-Muluk* (Land of Many Kings). The 'kings' in question ruled Ternate, Tidore, Bacan and other Maluku 'spice islands'. Their majestic fleets of *kora-kora* war canoes policed empires that sometimes extended as far afield as Sulawesi and Papua. Their fabulous wealth came from a global monopoly of clove and other spice production. Spices preserved food in a world without refrigerators. And they complemented leeches to offer the best available medical hope against an array of medieval ailments. By the 1st century AD, Maluku spices were reaching Europe via tortuous and risky caravan routes through India

and the Persian Gulf. This made them vastly expensive. Eventually, Europeans figured out that they could save money by seeking the source of the spices for themselves.

### The Portuguese

The Portuguese showed up in 1510. Their intercontinental expedition incurred awful losses of lives and ships but still managed to prove financially profitable. The Portuguese cheekily tried to reduce their costs by demanding a trade monopoly. Without any intention to respect such terms, Ternate's sultan agreed to a Portuguese clove monopoly in return for help against arch-enemy Tidore. Tidore responded by enlisting Spanish military assistance. Consistently committing cultural blunders, the Europeans soon outstayed their welcome and, having failed to monopolise the local clove trade, the Portuguese 'retired' south to trade from Ambon, Seram and the Banda Islands after 1795.

## The Dutch

In the late 16th century the Dutch arrived with faster boats, better guns and greater financial backing. Their better-built ships could use direct sea routes from South Africa that trumped their Hispanic competitors who stuck to slower, seasonal coastal routes via India. While seeing off new English rivals, the Dutch repeated many of the same cultural faux pas that had brought down the Portuguese. However, their determination to control a spice monopoly was brutally enforced. Most infamously, in the Banda Islands uncooperative islanders were simply massacred and replaced by more compliant Dutch-owned slaves.

Subjugating Ternate and Ambon took longer but, by the 1660s, the Dutch had wiped out all local opposition and had evicted the last Spanish garrisons from Ternate and Tidore. For a century the spice monopoly made a fortune for Holland. However, without competition the operation became increasingly inefficient. The Dutch East India Company (VOC) eventually collapsed into bankruptcy in 1795 and was nationalised. A year later, with Holland suffering the aftermath of the French Revolution, the British occupied Maluku. Politically this was a short episode, but commercially it spelt disaster. The British smuggled out precious spice-tree seedlings, replanting them in Malaya (Malaysia) and Ceylon (Sri Lanka). Thus within a few short decades Maluku's once unique spices were being produced more cheaply elsewhere. As the spice trade declined, many Christian Ambonese and Kei Islanders found themselves new employment in the Royal Netherlands Indies Army (KNIL), where they became respected as loyal fighters.

## WWII & Independence

Maluku's remoteness meant it was used as an open prison for independence activists Hatta and Syahrir who remained on Bandaneira until 23 February 1942, just minutes before Japanese bombardments began. Japan controlled the archipelago until General MacArthur's allied counterattacks of 1944, though the last Japanese soldier on Morotai (see p740) only finally surrendered in 1973!

After WWII it soon became apparent that Indonesia was heading for independence as a unified, predominantly Muslim, Javanese-controlled republic. Predominantly Christian southern Maluku panicked and tried to break away in 1950 by proclaiming the Republik Maluku Selatan (RMS). Indonesian republican troops steadily retook the islands and by November the RMS 'government' had fled Ambon. However, in the Seram jungles, armed RMS opposition rumbled on until the mid-1960s.

During the independence tussles, several thousand Malukan KNIL troops in Java had stayed loyal to the Dutch. Once the Dutch accepted Indonesian independence, these soldiers were in an awkward position: as RMS sympathisers they feared reprisals, so some 12,000 Malukans were resettled in the Netherlands where today around 40,000 of their descendants remain. The dream of an independent 'South Moluccas' lived on in the Netherlands, culminating in two Maluku-related train hijacks there in the mid-1970s. After that there was negligible RMS activity...at least until 1999.

## The Troubles

In 1999 Indonesia's economy was in tatters, elements of the army were disaffected and the unexpected breakaway of East Timor may have rekindled the hopes of RMS agitators. Just at this tense time, Maluku was to be split into two separate provinces, each with augmented regional powers. Especially in Ambon, where the Muslim-Christian ratio was finely balanced, each religious community could see the political benefits of frightening away members of the other. Although Malukan society had long been a model of peaceful Christian-Muslim coexistence, intercommunal squabbles turned to riots and full-blown massacres. To avenge an infamous mass killing of Muslims in Tobelo, a fundamentalist Islamic group called Laskar Jihad shipped around 3000 jihadis from Java in April 2000, racking up tensions even higher. Churches, mosques and whole villages were torched with thousands displaced or left homeless. Tempers began to cool with the February 2002 Malino II Accord and especially in October when Laskar Jihad suddenly disbanded and left Ambon, probably thanks to American pressure on Indonesia following the New York terrorist attacks of 11 September 2001.

## Maluku Today

Apart from a few 2004 riots in Kota Ambon, recovery was remarkably swift. With the dust settled, locals wonder how they had ever been duped into the destructive spiral, most blaming outside *agents provocateurs* for stirring up the bloodbath. Today all is peaceful while many local economies are receiving significant boosts from the upgrading of *kecamatan* (subdistricts) to *kabupaten* (regencies). Such seemingly minor semantic differences result in a cascade of new building projects, infrastructure improvements and bureaucratic jobs.

## CULTURE

Maluku's people have very mixed blood. To Malay and Melanesian precursors have been added Indian, Arab, Chinese and Portuguese genes, with more recent additions of Bugis (from Sulawesi seafarers) and Javanese (from transmigrants). Melanesian features are strongest on the Kei and Aru Islands. Although there are still traditional communities of Nua-ulu (Seram) and Togutil (Halmahera), don't expect Papua-style tribal garb: Malukans, especially in Ambon, see themselves as one of the most Westernised groups in Indonesia. But a great diversity remains. Incredibly, the region has over 130 distinct traditional languages, many now used in blended pidgin forms with additions from Bahasa Indonesia. Muslims are more numerous in most of North Maluku. Christians form majorities in several central and southern areas.

## GETTING THERE & AWAY
### Air

Ambon and Ternate are the region's air hubs. Both have several daily connections to Jakarta, mostly via Makassar or Manado (Sulawesi). There are several connections from Ambon to Papua but only one weekly flight to Nusa Tenggara, Merpati's heavily booked Ambon–Kisar–Kupang run.

### Sea

Four Pelni liners visit Ambon on bi-weekly cycles from Bau Bau (southeast Sulawesi, 12 hours), Makassar (31 to 36 hours), Surabaya (60 to 68 hours) and/or Jakarta (Tanjung

---

**TOP BUDGET CHILLOUTS**

Watch the waves and unwind at these delightful yet very inexpensive little Maluku retreats:

- Savana Cottages, Ohoidertawun, Kei Islands (p767)
- Vita Guest House, Bandaneira, Banda Islands (p760)
- Penginapan Lisar Bahari, Sawai, Seram (p756)
- Penginapan Benteng Duurstede, Kota Saparua, Lease Islands (p751)
- Hotel Harapan Indah, Saumlaki, Tanimbar Islands (p769)
- Molana Bungalows, Pulau Molana, Lease Islands (p752)

---

Priok; four days). Newest and fastest is *Dempo*, which bypasses Bau Bau. *Ciremai* handily continues east via the Banda and Kei Islands. Along with the *Nggapulu*, these three ships continue on to various ports in Papua. The *Lambelu* instead swings north via Buru and Ternate to terminate in Bitung (northern Sulawesi). *Sinabung* and *Dorolonda* both stop in Ternate between Bitung and Sorong. The *Pangrango* links Kupang to Ambon using a thrillingly offbeat loop via Saumlaki, Tepa, Leti and Kisar. Slower *Kelimutu* makes only monthly loops, is infamously variable and often claustrophobically crowded.

Non-Pelni vehicular ferries and/or slow *kapal motor* (wooden boats) from Sulawesi (mostly Bitung or Manado) run to Ternate, Tobelo (Halmahera) and the Sula Islands.

## GETTING AROUND
### Air

Merpati and Trigana Air operate numerous regional flights. However, with only four aging little prop-planes between them, engine trouble, bad weather or one-off charters can and will throw out the schedules for days. Annoyingly, Merpati only sells one-way tickets booked from the departure point, making return trips hit and miss. Smaller planes have 10kg baggage limits. Pelita (Ternate–Sanana–Ambon), Express Air (Ambon–Saumlaki–Langgur) and Wings (Ambon–Langgur) all advertise intra-Maluku flights but as yet only the Wings flight actually operates.

## MALUKU FERRIES

many areas have only mud tracks or no roads at all. On most islands shorter routes are operated by bemo (minibus), known locally as *mobil*. On Halmahera and Seram, pricey shared Kijangs (fancy seven-seater Toyotas) are more common than long-distance buses. Renting an *ojek* (motorbike taxi) is a pleasant, inexpensive way to travel if the rain holds off.

# NORTH MALUKU

Although dwarfed by crazy K-shaped Pulau Halmahera, North Maluku's historically and politically most significant islands are the string of pyramidal volcanic cones off Halmahera's western coast. Ternate, Tidore and Bacan are ancient Islamic sultanates that were once the world's only sources of cloves. Nowadays cloves may seem trivial additions to mulled wine or *kretek* cigarettes. But in the Middle Ages they were enormously valuable as food preservatives and were considered cures for everything from toothache to halitosis to sexual disinterest. Funded by the spice trade, Ternate's and Tidore's sultans became the most powerful rulers in the medieval Indies but wasted much of their wealth fighting each other.

In 1511 the first Portuguese settlers arrived in Ternate. Tidore quickly responded by inviting in the Spaniards. Both islands found their hospitality rapidly exhausted as the Europeans tried to corner the spice market and preach Christianity. Ternate's Muslim population, already offended by the Europeans' imported pigs and heavy-handed 'justice', were driven to rebel in 1570 when Ternate's Sultan Hairun (Khairun) was executed and his head exhibited on a pike. The besieged Portuguese held out in their castle until 1575 when the new Ternatean sultan took it over as his palace. Five years later he entertained the English pirate-adventurer Francis Drake. After an amicable meeting, Drake astounded his host by his almost total disinterest in buying cloves. In fact, Drake's ship *Golden Hind* was already so full of stolen Spanish-American gold that he simply couldn't carry anything more.

The Spaniards and later the Dutch made themselves equally unpopular. In a history that's as fascinating as it is complicated and Machiavellian, they played Ternate off against Tidore and also confronted one another for control of an elusive clove monopoly. The Dutch prevailed eventually, though the sul-

## Boat

Pelni services *within* Maluku are patchy and notoriously changeable. Some medium-range hops are served by uncomfortable ASDP ferries or by wooden boats known as *kapal motor*. The latter have limited wooden-board 'bed' spaces, but you may need to arrive several hours before departure to grab one. Perintis cargo boats are bigger but not at all designed with passengers in mind. Bring waterproofs.

Speedboats link nearby islands and roadless villages. Locals use very specific terms for boat types: if there isn't a *spid* (covered multiengine speedboat) to your destination, there might still be a *Johnson* (outboard-powered longboat) or a *ketingting/lape-lape* (smaller, short-hop motorised outrigger canoe). Regular speedboats often depart very early in the morning when seas are calmest. If chartering, smaller or diesel-powered speedboats will be slower but significantly cheaper than multi-engined petrol ones.

## Road Transport

In mountainous Maluku, the few asphalted roads are often potholed and narrow while

tanates continued almost uninterrupted for most of the period and remain well-respected institutions to this day.

Today Ternate remains the main hub of North Maluku (Malut), though in 2007 Sofifi on Halmahera was named the province's official capital. The full move is still incomplete while construction of new offices continues in Sofifi.

Few islands in North Maluku have any real history of tourism, so visits beyond Ternate will often prove to be something of an adventure.

## PULAU TERNATE
☎ 0921

The dramatic volcanic cone of 1721m Gunung Api Gamalama *is* Pulau Ternate. Settlements are sprinkled around its lower coastal slopes with villages on the east coast coalescing into North Maluku's biggest town, Kota Ternate. The city makes a useful transport gateway for the region and neighbouring volcanic islands look particularly photogenic viewed from the few remnant stilt-house neighbourhoods, harbours full of colourful boats or hillside restaurant terraces.

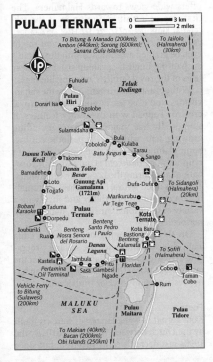

**PULAU TERNATE**

To Bitung & Manado (200km);
Ambon (440km); Sorong (600km);
Sanana (Sulu Islands)

To Jailolo
(Halmahera)
(30km)

Fuhudu

Teluk
Dodinga

Pulau
Hiri

Dorari Isa

Togolobe

Sulamadaha

Bula

Tobololo

Kulaba

*Danau Tolire
Kecil*

Batu Angus

Tarau

Takome

Sango

*Danau Tolire
Besar*

Bamadehe

Loto

Gunung Api
Gamalama
(1721m)

Dufa-Dufa

To Sidangoli
(Halmahera)
(20km)

Togafo

Marikurubu

Air Tege Tege

Bobani
Karaoke

Taduma

Pulau
Ternate

Kota
Ternate

Dorpedu

Benteng
Santo Pedro
i Paulo

Kota Baru

Jouburiki

Benteng
Nosra Seniora
del Rosario

Benteng
Bastiong

Rua

*Danau
Laguna*

Benteng
Kalamata

To Sofifi
(Halmahera)

Kastela

Jambula

Pitu

Floridas

Pertamina
Oil Terminal

Sasa Gambesi

Ngade

Cobo

Taman
Cobo

Vehicle Ferry
to Bitung
(Sulawesi)
(200km)

Rum

*MALUKU
SEA*

Pulau
Maitara

Pulau
Tidore

To Makian (40km);
Bacan (200km);
Obi Islands (250km)

0 ........... 3 km
0 ........... 2 miles

## Kota Ternate
**pop 106,000**

Stretching around 10km from the airport to beyond Bastiong port, Kota Ternate's main north–south through-road has multiple names: Jl Sultan Khairun, Jl Merdeka, Jl Mononutu, Jl Hasan Esa and eventually Jl Raya Bastiong. The main commercial centres are Jl Pattimura and Jl Pahlawan Revolusi culminating at the Swering waterfront promenade. Jatiland is a middle-class suburb where virtually every road is called Jl Jati but confusingly the Jati Mall (under construction) and Jatiland BS (a long-terraced 'Bisnes Senter' of new shops) are on a central waterfront land-reclamation area. Jl Nuri was recently renamed Jl Alfred Wallace.

### INFORMATION
#### Internet Access

**D@gimoi** (Map p732; Jl Sultan Khairun; internet/wi-fi per hr 8000/13,000Rp; ⏰ 8am-midnight) Passable connection indoors, attractive outdoor garden-cafe for wi-fi use.

**Muara C@feNet** (Map p732; Jl Pahlawan Revolusi; per hr 7000Rp; ⏰ 9am-midnight) OK connection, but sweaty; above the Muara Hotel lobby.

**One-Net** (Map p732; Jl Pattimura; per hr 7000Rp; ⏰ 10am-midnight; 🖳 ) Connection variable to poor; air-con could be stronger.

#### Money

Several banks on Jl Pahlawan Revolusi have ATMs but only **BNI** (Bank Negara Indonesia; Map p732; ⏰ 8am-3pm Mon-Thu, 8am-noon Fri) changes money, and then only US dollars in new, unfolded $100 bills!

#### Telephone

**Plasa Telkom** (Map p732; Jl Pattimura & Jl Pahlawan Revolusi; ⏰ 8am-6pm)

#### Tourist Information

**Aketajawe-Lolobata National Park Office** (Map p730; ☎ 0852 4003 7036; aketajawe@gmail.com; Airport Rd; ⏰ 8am-4pm Mon-Fri) Good source of information if planning forest trips or bird-watching on Halmahera. Dani and O-on speak English.

**North Maluku Tourist Office** (Map p732; ☎ 312 7396; www.malukuutaraprov.go.id; Jl Kamboja 14; ⏰ 8am-4pm Mon-Fri) Helpful English-speaking staff can answer questions, organise guides and even have a compressor and some full-set diving equipment for rent to scuba fans (450,000Rp per person per dive).

**Ternate City Tourist Office** (Map p732; ☎ 311 1211; Benteng Oranye; ⏰ 8am-2.30pm Mon-Fri) Friendly staff, some speaking English but information is limited.

## SIGHTS
### Keraton (Istana Kesultan)

Built in 1834 and restored in semi-colonial style, the Sultan's Palace is still a family home. However, there is a **museum section** (donation appropriate) containing a small but interesting collection of historic weaponry plus memorabilia from the reigns of past sultans whose lineage dates back to 1257. The airy veranda offers wide views towards Halmahera. The first step of a visit is signing in at the **sekretariat kiosk** (Map p732; ☎ 312 1166; ⏰ 8am-5pm, closed 10am-2pm Fri). If you're lucky, you might even be granted an audience with the sultan's enchanting English-speaking sister and hear tales of the royal family's amazing life sagas.

Without a special invitation from the sultan, visitors won't see the famous **mahkota** (royal crown). Topped with cassowary feathers, it supposedly has magical powers including growing 'hair' which needs periodic cutting. Some claim it can even stop Gamalama from erupting. The *mahkota* is only worn at coronations and during the Legu Gam ceremonies, Ternate's main **festival** (⏰ 6-13 April), culminating on the sultan's birthday and involving a variety of traditional musicians, dancers and performers.

On the 27th evening of Ramadan, Laila Tulqadr celebrations see the sultan's procession arrive to a mass of flaming torches at the **royal mosque** (Map p732; Jl Sultan Babullah), which has impressive heavy interior timberwork.

### Forts

Kota Ternate's three fortresses were (re)built by the Dutch between 1606 and 1610. By the 1990s just decrepit ruins survived, but since then the empty, remnant shells have been heavy-handedly over-renovated.

The biggest, most central but least complete is the 1606 **Benteng Oranye** (Map p732; originally Fort Malayo), once headquarters of the Dutch VOC operation and later the residence of Ternate's Dutch governors. Today you can wander some sections of cannon-topped bastion accessed through a hefty, restored gateway arch.

Dinky little **Benteng Tolukko** (Map p730; 10,000Rp donation appropriate), the first Portuguese stronghold on Ternate (1512), has beautifully manicured floral gardens and attractive sea views. The family living beside the entrance keeps the key.

The 1540 **Benteng Kalamata** has an unusual waterside location 1km southwest of Bastiong, waves lapping right up to its angled walls. There are great views across to Tidore. Take Rua, Sasa or Jambula bemos.

### Religious Buildings

With an eye-catching dome covered in stylised Arabic calligraphy (the repeating name of Allah), the new **Masjid Al Munawwah** (Map p732) is so vast that it overshoots its new land-reclamation site with outer minarets rising directly out of the sea. Dozens more mosques attractively pimple the skyline, several churches have been rebuilt and there's a colourful 2007 **Chinese temple** (Map p732) replete with gaudy rearing dragons.

### SLEEPING

You'll probably value a powerful new air conditioner given Ternate's oppressive heat and sauna-like humidity.

### Budget

Accommodation under 150,000Rp is plentiful around Ahmad Yani Port but conditions are often abysmal. Although there are a few exceptions, even the nicest cheapies often have

---

**HELLO MISTER**

Few places in Indonesia have so many ultra-keen English-language students desperate to help tourists in return for conversation practice. They pop up everywhere. This can result in delightful friendships or infuriating feelings of being pestered, depending on your outlook and good fortune.

---

damp patches, a slimy *mandi* (a large water tank from which water is ladled over the body) and a hint of dysfunction.

**Penginapan Purnama** (Map p732; ☎ 312 4649; Mohajarin Falajawa; s/d/tr 50,000/100,000/150,000Rp) In a modest family home full of old Chinese porcelain, four bare guestrooms without fan share concrete outside *mandis*.

**Hotel Pantai Indah** (Sulamadaha; d 50,000Rp) A 20-minute drive from town, this homestay-style place lies behind a motorbike repair shop, 50m from the beach at Sulamadaha (p734). The five simple fan rooms have private *mandi* attached. Bring mosquito repellent.

**Penginapan Kembar Emas** (Map p730; ☎ 311 0750; Jl Feri, Bastiong; r without/with bathroom 60,000/70,000Rp) Rooms are a little grubby but very handy if you're leaving on an early boat from Bastiong. Oddly, access required crossing a wall.

**Hotel Indah** (Map p732; ☎ 312 1334; Jl Bosoiri 3; s/tw with fan 66,000/77,000Rp, with air-con 93,500/110,000Rp, with hot water 137,500/154,000Rp; ✹ ) Modest old-style *penginapan* (simple lodging house) with a little garden area and quaintly dated sitting room.

**Saqavia Guest House** (Map p732; ☎ 311 1147; Mohajarin Falajawa; s/d 110,000/165,000Rp; ✹ ) Not exotic, new air-con rooms are fair value if the custard-yellow paintwork doesn't turn your tummy.

**Taman Ria** ( ☎ 322 2124; d with fan/air-con 125,000/165,000Rp) Set back behind an under-construction waterfront menagerie-zoo, 700m beyond Benteng Kalamata, most rooms are new and well appointed but fan rooms overheat and a handful of older cheapies (double 75,000Rp) are very sad.

### Midrange

Several hotels including the Corner Palace, Nirwana and Zhavitry look great from the outside but are disappointing within, often lacking windows in all but the priciest rooms. The great-value Tiara doesn't take foreigners.

**Losmen Gamalama** (Map p732; ☎ 312 5943; Jl Merdeka; s/d 200,000/250,000Rp; ✹ ) Eight fresh new rooms around an interior courtyard, one floor above an attractive Japanese-styled water feature and prayer area.

**Losmen Kita** (Map p732; ☎ 312 1950; Jl Stadion; tw with cold/hot showers 200,000/250,000Rp; ✹ ) Rambling low-rise bed factory with nearly 50 clean but bland rooms around a tree-shaded car park.

MALUKU

MALUKU

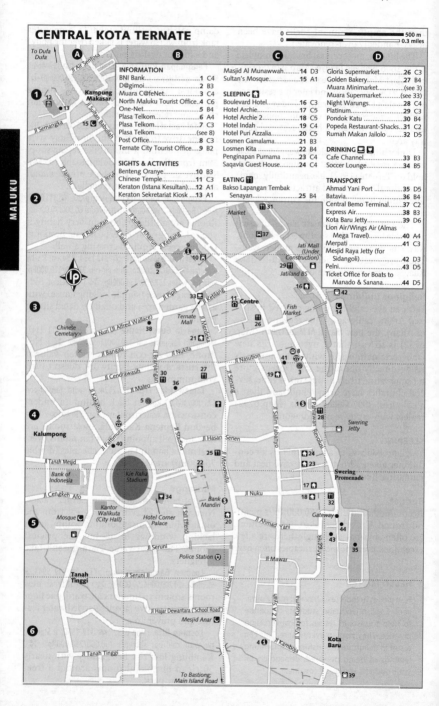

# CENTRAL KOTA TERNATE

0       500 m
0       0.3 miles

### INFORMATION
| | |
|---|---|
| BNI Bank | **1** C4 |
| D@gimoi | **2** B3 |
| Muara C@feNet | **3** C4 |
| North Maluku Tourist Office | **4** C6 |
| One-Net | **5** B4 |
| Plasa Telkom | **6** A4 |
| Plasa Telkom | **7** C3 |
| Plasa Telkom | (see **8**) |
| Post Office | **8** C3 |
| Ternate City Tourist Office | **9** B2 |

### SIGHTS & ACTIVITIES
| | |
|---|---|
| Benteng Oranye | **10** B3 |
| Chinese Temple | **11** C3 |
| Keraton (Istana Kesultan) | **12** A1 |
| Keraton Sekretariat Kiosk | **13** A1 |

| | |
|---|---|
| Masjid Al Munawwah | **14** D3 |
| Sultan's Mosque | **15** A1 |

### SLEEPING
| | |
|---|---|
| Boulevard Hotel | **16** C3 |
| Hotel Archie | **17** C5 |
| Hotel Archie 2 | **18** C5 |
| Hotel Indah | **19** C4 |
| Hotel Puri Azzalia | **20** C5 |
| Losmen Gamalama | **21** B3 |
| Losmen Kita | **22** B4 |
| Penginapan Purnama | **23** C4 |
| Saqavia Guest House | **24** C4 |

### EATING
| | |
|---|---|
| Bakso Lapangan Tembak | |
| Senayan | **25** B4 |

| | |
|---|---|
| Gloria Supermarket | **26** C3 |
| Golden Bakery | **27** B4 |
| Muara Minimarket | (see **3**) |
| Muara Supermarket | (see **33**) |
| Night Warungs | **28** C4 |
| Platinum | **29** C3 |
| Pondok Katu | **30** B4 |
| Popeda Restaurant-Shacks | **31** C2 |
| Rumah Makan Jailolo | **32** D5 |

### DRINKING
| | |
|---|---|
| Cafe Channel | **33** B3 |
| Soccer Lounge | **34** B5 |

### TRANSPORT
| | |
|---|---|
| Ahmad Yani Port | **35** D5 |
| Batavia | **36** B4 |
| Central Bemo Terminal | **37** C2 |
| Express Air | **38** B3 |
| Kota Baru Jetty | **39** D6 |
| Lion Air/Wings Air (Almas | |
|   Mega Travel) | **40** A4 |
| Merpati | **41** C3 |
| Mesjid Raya Jetty (for | |
|   Sidangoli) | **42** D3 |
| Pelni | **43** D5 |
| Ticket Office for Boats to | |
|   Manado & Sanana | **44** D5 |

**Bukit Pelangi Hotel** (Map p730; ☎ 312 2180; Jl Jati Selatan 338; d 210,000-299,000Rp, ste 325,000Rp; ✺ ) The old building rises amid palms like a colonial palace, though rooms here are variable: look at a few and avoid the cheap back ones (145,000Rp). The appealing new building has a stylish, Escheresque feel and upstairs is wonderfully airy with fine balcony spaces overlooking Tidore. Suites are especially recommended.

**Boulevard Hotel** (Map p732; ☎ 311 0777; Jatiland BS; standard/business/deluxe/view 256,450/302,450/325,450/350,450Rp; ✺ ) After the inviting exterior and Klimt-dominated lobby, most rooms are disappointingly windowless and generic. 'View' rooms (3rd floor, no lift) are altogether more appealing.

**Hotel Archie** (Map p732; ☎ 311 0555; Jl Nuku 6; d/ste 286,000/357,500Rp; ✺ ) Vastly better than most equivalently priced competitors, Archie has English-speaking staff, immaculately kept rooms with hot water, fancy ceiling mouldings, multichannel TV, toilet paper, minibar and several 'secret' sitting spaces. Rooms in swish Archie 2 across the road are brand new with curious theatrical columns in front of the bathtubs.

**our pick** **Hotel Puri Azzalia** (Map p732; ☎ 312 1959; puri.azzalia@yahoo.com; Jl Mononutu 275; d/ste 308,000/396,000Rp; ✺ ) Behind a stylish 50s-retro facade, this charming little boutique hotel is tastefully appointed with local artefacts, hung fabrics and fresh orchids.

### Top End

**Amara Hotel** (Map p730; ☎ 312 1800; www.belainternationalhotel.com, www.amarahotels.com; Jl Jati Raya; d rack/walk-in rates from 1,000,000/550,000Rp; ✺ 🅿 🛜 ) Far and away Ternate's most luxurious option, the Amara has 195 immaculate, gently fashionable rooms in coffee-and-cream colours, all with balconies and views. Even the cheapest one is spacious and equipped to international standards. 'Executive' rooms (1,250,000/687,500Rp) add bathtub and free wi-fi. 'Cabana' rooms (1,300,000/715,000Rp) have direct access to the vast central swimming pool in which lie 'islands' of palm trees.

### EATING

*Rumah makan* (eating houses) offer cheap eats around the markets with several shacks north of the bemo terminal serving local specialities *ikan gohu* (raw-fish morsels in a tangy peanut-edged marinade) and *popeda*

(Malukan sago) as part of 20,000Rp all-you-can-eat spreads including fish, cassava and a dozen other side dishes.

Numerous warungs (food stalls) appear at night on the Swering promenade (Jl Pahlawan Revolusi). A couple of unmarked eateries in Bastiong Harbour sporadically produce superb roast fish (from 12,000Rp with rice) that's arguably better than anything at the city's far more expensive seafood restaurants.

**Rumah Makan Jailolo** (Map p732; Jl Pahlawan Revolusi 7; meals from 13,000Rp; ⏱ 7am-9.30pm) Bright, reliable place for inexpensive point-and-pick meals.

**Bakso Lapangan Tembak Senayan** (Map p732; Jl Mononutu; meals 19,250-41,000Rp, juices 14,500Rp; ⏱ 10am-10pm) The new-meets-old architecture keeps you cool without air-con and attracts an unpretentious middle-class crowd for snacks, meals and drinks.

**Pondok Katu** (Map p732; ☎ 312 7332; Jl Branjangan 28; mains 25,000-37,000Rp; ⏱ 10am-10pm; ✺ ) This long-lasting family favourite serves seafood lunches and good Chinese food in a gently attractive columned dining hall.

**our pick** **Floridas** ( ☎ 321 4430; meals 20,000-45,000Rp, crab meals 250,000Rp, drinks 6000-20,000Rp; ⏱ 10am-11pm) A 10,000Rp *ojek* ride southwest of town, Floridas sits high above a steep slope of banana trees that twinkle at night with fireflies. Behind the main dining hall, ledge tables provide splendid bay views across to the superimposed volcanic cones of Tidore and Maitara. Try the delicious *ikan woku kenari*, fish steak (not boneless!) marinated in a mildly spicy sauce of kenari almonds, sweet chilli and lemongrass, then roasted in a banana leaf.

**Platinum** (Map p732; ☎ 312 2820; Jatiland BS; mains 38,000-155,000Rp, juices 16,500Rp, rice 6000Rp; ⏱ 11am-midnight; ✺ ) Maluku's hippest Western-style cafe-restaurant has a trendy retro interior from which you can watch chefs at work through a giant glass window. A very wide-ranging multilingual menu includes pastas (49,000Rp), steaks (111,000Rp to 155,000Rp) and numerous Indonesian favourites.

Supermarkets include **Gloria** (Map p732; Jl Bosoiri) and **Muara** (Map p732; Jl Pahlawan Revolusi & Ternate Mall). **Golden Bakery** (Map p732; Jl Pattimura; ⏱ 9am-10pm) bakes a fine selection of fresh bread and pastries.

### DRINKING

In Ternate alcohol isn't sold in restaurants and is fiercely expensive in karaoke bars (beer from 60,000/160,000Rp per bottle/pitcher).

**The Soccer Lounge** (Map p732; Corner Palace Hotel; Jl Stadion; beer 60,000Rp) This bar's once fine decor is looking seriously worn, but its large windows overlook the Kie Raha Stadium, so when Ternate's major-league football team Persiter is playing at home, you could watch beer-in-hand from here without risking heatstroke in the overcrowded, unshaded stands.

**Cafe Channel** (Map p732; Ternate Mall, Jl Merdeka; coffees & juices 11,000-14,300Rp; ☺ 8am-10pm; ✷ ) Good if pre-sweetened coffee is misnamed 'espresso' at this attractive cafe with ball lamps, black and tangerine furniture and an open roadside terrace section.

## GETTING THERE & AWAY
### Air
**Lion Air/Wings Air** (Map p732; Almas Mega Travel; ☎ 311 1555; Jl Pattimura; ☺ 8am-8pm) flies three times daily to Manado with connections to Makassar, Jakarta and Surabaya. For Jakarta via Makassar, **Batavia** (Map p732; ☎ 312 2799; Jl Pattimura; ☺ 8am-6pm & 8pm-10pm) flies daily, and **Express Air** (Map p732; ☎ 312 2846; Jl Nuri/Jl Alfred Wallace; ☺ 9am-6pm) four times weekly. **Merpati** (Map p732; ☎ 312 1651; Jl Bosoiri; ☺ 8am-4pm Mon-Sat, 10am-noon Sun) flies daily to Makassar, twice weekly to Galela and Gebe, and weekly to Morotai (Friday), Fala (Wednesday) and Sanana (Tuesday via Labuha, Bacan).

**Trigana Air** (Map p730; Archie Travel; ☎ 312 8484; Jl Raya Bastiong; ☺ 8am-5pm Mon-Sat) flies three times weekly Ternate–Sanana–Ambon–Tual, Ternate–Manado and Ternate–Buli.

### Boat
Ahmad Yani port is the passenger harbour for **Pelni** (Map p732; ☎ 312 1434; ☺ 8am-4pm Mon-Sat) liners. *Sangiang* loops around Halmahera. Eastbound *Dorolonda* and *Sinabung* head to Sorong (183,000Rp, 14 to 16 hours) and other Papuan ports. Westbound ones both go to Bitung (northern Sulawesi; 135,000Rp, seven hours), *Sinabung* continuing to Bau Bau via Banggai (24 hours), *Dorolonda* proceeding to Balikpapan (47 hours) via Pantoloan near Palu, Sulawesi. *Lambelu* links Ternate with Ambon (155,000Rp, 19 hours) via Namlea (Buru; 137,500Rp).

Non-Pelni boats *RM Theodora/Intim Teratai* both sail from here to Manado (165,000Rp, 21 hours) on Friday/Sunday and to Sanana (Sula Islands, 260,000Rp, 16 hours) at 2pm on Tuesday/Thursday.

Other jetties:

**Bastiong ferry port** (Map p730) Vehicle ferries daily to Rum (Tidore; 5000Rp, 7am, 1pm, 4pm), Sidangoli (9am), three times weekly to Sofifi and overnight to Bitung (Sulawesi; 75,000Rp, 11pm Saturday).

**Bastiong 'first' port** (Map p730) Speedboats to Rum (Tidore; 8000Rp), Gurapin (Kayoa; 80,000Rp, 5am three times weekly) and Makian (50,000Rp, 5am daily). Boats to Babang (Bacan; 100,000Rp, 7pm), Lelei (8am, three times weekly), Obi and western Halmahera.

**Dufa-Dufa jetty** (Map p730) To Jailolo (Halmahera) by speedboat (38,000Rp, one hour) or 2pm *kapal motor* (27,000Rp, 1½ hours, returns 8am).

**Kota Baru jetty** (Map p732) Speedboats to Sofifi (Halmahera, 30,000Rp to 50,000Rp).

**Mesjid Raya jetty** (Map p732) Speedboats to Sidangoli (Halmahera, 28,000Rp).

## GETTING AROUND
For the 6km from Babullah Airport to central Ternate taxis want an outrageous 50,000Rp, but if you walk 10 minutes south, bemos from outside Hairun University cost only 3000Rp to the central market. From there bemos run in all directions (3000Rp) but *ojeks* (4000Rp per hop) are generally more convenient.

## Gunung Api Gamalama
Ternate's central volcano erupted in 1840, destroying almost every house on the island. Although it has blown its fiery nose as recently as 2003, it is not considered imminently dangerous. A vulcanology unit keeps careful watch from Marikurubu village, where traditionally anyone planning the five-hour climb to Gamalama's summit (steep, hazardous and foolish without a guide) should seek the blessing of the *kepala adat*. There are pleasant, shorter clove-grove hikes from Air Tege Tege village (near the transmitter tower), but even here the going rapidly gets very steep. The tourist offices can help you find guides.

## Outside Kota Ternate
This section works anticlockwise, leaving Kota Ternate via **Batu Angus**. That's a spiky 300-year-old lava flow, not a type of steak. At the top of the island, **Sulamadaha** has a popular if somewhat litter-strewn black-sand beach with heavy swells. From a cove some 800m east, public longboats (5000Rp per person) cross to the offshore volcanic cone of **Pulau Hiri** around 8am, 1pm and 5pm each way. Hiri was the last step of the sultan's family's *Sound of Music*–style escape from Ternate during WWII. Northern Hiri has relatively good snorkelling by Ternate standards.

Beyond the village of **Takome**, the main road returns to the coast beside the small, muddy Danau Tolire Kecil. Less than a kilometre further, a paved side lane (2000Rp fee) climbs to the rim of **Danau Tolire Besar**. Startlingly sheer cliffs plummet down to the lugubriously green, crocodile-infested waters of this deep crater lake. Local children offer guide services should you want to descend yourself (1½ hours return on foot).

A footpath from the southern edge of Dorpedu leads down to **Jouburiki**, the beach where Ternate's very first sultan was supposedly crowned in 1257. More picturesque black-sand beaches are found at **Rua** and **Kastela**. The latter village is named for the 1522 Portuguese fort of **Benteng Nosra Senora del Rosario**, whose ruins have been partially renovated. Topped with a giant clove, a concrete monument here graphically reminds you that the Portuguese murdered Sultan Hairun in 1570, then got their comeuppance five years later.

**Danau Laguna** is a pleasant, spring-fed bowl-lake with a lushly forested perimeter. Across the straits lie the conical islands of Tidore and Maitara as featured on Indonesia's 1000Rp notes. Those volcanoes align perfectly when viewed from the Floridas restaurant (p733) just beyond Ngade. Across the road are only the stubby roadside remnants of **Benteng Santo Pedro i Paulo**, once Ternate's main line of defence against a 1606 Spanish attack.

### GETTING AROUND

From Kota Ternate's central terminal, bemos run frequently to Sulamadaha (5000Rp, anti-clockwise) and Kastela (4000Rp, clockwise). No single bemo goes right around the island but some north-route vehicles drive as far as Togafo (6000Rp). From there it's a pleasantly windy 2km walk to Taduma, where the longest south-route bemos start. Consider chartering an *ojek* to loop around the island with photo stops (around 30,000Rp per hour).

## PULAU TIDORE

☎ 0921

Gently, charming Tidore makes a refreshing day-trip escape from the bustle of Ternate, its neighbour and implacable historical enemy. An independent Islamic sultanate from 1109, Tidore's sultanate was abolished in the Sukarno era but the 36th sultan was reinstated in 1999. The island's proud volcanic profile looks especially magnificent

when viewed from Bastiong on Ternate. In Tidorean language *sukur dofu* means 'thank you', *saki* means 'delicious' and *sterek* (*lau*) means '(very) good'.

### Soasio

Above the southernmost edge of Tidore's capital, Soasio, lie the sparse, overgrown remnants of **Benteng Tohula**, Tidore's 17th-century Spanish fort. Around 200m north the **Sonyine Malige Sultan's Memorial Museum** displays the sultan's sedan chair and giant spittoons, plus the royal crown topped with cassowary feathers. The crown is considered as magical as Ternate's *mahkota* (see p730). Getting in, you'll have to find the curator, Umar Muhammad, who works at the DIKNAS office in the Dinas Pendidikan dan Kebudayan building, 2km north. Outside office hours try his home in Gamatufgange. Umar has been known to demand rather hefty entry fees of up to 100,000Rp.

A block inland from the museum, sturdy whitewashed base bastions are all that remains of the original **kraton** royal citadel (Istana Sultan) which now contains an unfinished contemporary palace-villa with a garish blue roof.

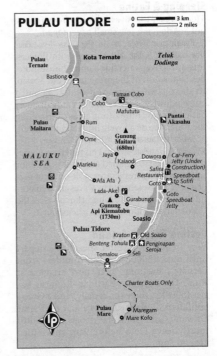

### Lada-Ake

High up a disconcertingly steep road, Lada-Ake village retains a few traditional homes made of split bamboo set on mossy dry-stone bases. Curious *guwige* basket poles offer nests to chickens. Many women still use traditional *saloi* (conical back baskets) when foraging in the surrounding lush forest. Glimpses of Ternate are an inspiring view from the approach road from Gurabunga. *Ojeks* cost 50,000Rp for a return trip from Goto. Rare bemos charge 12,000Rp each way.

### Around Tidore

Most other Tidorean villages are simply strips of homes on either side of the round-island coast road. None of these are outstanding, though several have small ribbons of beach. **Pantai Akasahu** is typically underwhelming but popular for its grubby little hot-spring pool. From here the quiet road to **Rum** is attractive, with fine views over Ternate. A three-minute speedboat hop from Rum, **Pulau Maitara** has clear blue waters for better snorkelling and swimming. **Pulau Mare** is famed for its attractive, no-frills pottery.

### Sleeping & Eating

Tidore's easy to visit as a day trip from Ternate but Soasio has a few small *penginapan*.

**Penginapan Seroja** ( ☎ 316 1456; Jl Sultan Hassanuddin; s/tw 75,000/150,000Rp; ✲ ) Decked with flowers, this attractive waterside family house-hotel lies 50m south of the museum in old Soasio. Its air-con twin rooms are decently appointed but windowless. Singles with fan are extremely basic but enjoy little sitting areas overlooking the water across a lovely little orchid garden.

**Safira Restaurant** ( ☎ 0813 4017 9499; mains 12,000-30,000Rp; ☉ 7am-9pm Mon-Sat) This waterside house-restaurant serves limited food but is ideal for sipping 9000Rp fresh juices at sit-on-floor garden pavilions serenaded by waves amid colourful bougainvillea. It's around 1km north of the Goto market, Tidore's most extensive.

### Getting There & Around

Very frequent 12-seater speedboats depart until dusk (8000Rp, seven minutes) from Ternate's Bastiong 'first' port arriving at Rum. There are also Bastiong–Rum car ferries (5000Rp, three times daily) and a Goto-Sofifi ferry is planned from a new dock near Dowora. Goto–Sofifi speedboats (30,000Rp) mostly leave Goto before 9am and return around 2pm.

Frequent bemos run Rum–Soasio–Goto (9000Rp, 30 minutes) using the south-coast road. No bemos use the quiet Rum–Mafututu route but that pretty road is now asphalted. Rum–Goto *ojeks* cost 40,000Rp.

## SOUTH OF TIDORE
### Makian

Spiky-topped **Pulau Makian** is an impressive, 1357m volcano with a photogenically huge gash in the cone's northern flank. Its rare eruptions killed over 2000 people in 1760 and caused a full-scale temporary evacuation in 1988.

### Lelei

West of low-slung **Pulau Kayoa**, the **Guraici** group is a sprinkling of small, low, palm islands. Here the idyllically peaceful little two-village island **Pulau Lelei** is touted somewhat misleadingly as a dive resort. There's certainly a remarkable wealth of colourful reef fish just off Lelei's northern village, and a 100,000Rp boat ride away Pulau Rajawali offers a good chance of getting personal with large rays (especially on full- and new-moon days). However, the islands' gently sloped coral gardens have received a pretty severe battering. **Diving** (dives incl boat & equipment 450,000Rp) using good new scuba gear is available only when the helpful organiser, **Mr Tamrin** ( ☎ 0852 4064 2284; Desun Satu), is in residence, but there's no real dive master. Lelei's 12 beautifully designed, three-room Minahasan-style **beach villas** (d 150,000Rp) have large sitting rooms and great balconies, but cleaning is haphazard, there's no restaurant and there's little hope of electricity when you're the only guest. Arachnophobes, beware. Mr Tamrin's family keep the villa keys, provide **meals** (breakfast/dinner 10,000/30,000Rp), free snorkel rental and alternative homestay rooms (50,000Rp).

Cramped slow boats *KM Rahmat Ilahi* or *SS Bajoi* depart Bastiong at 8am on Tuesday, Wednesday and Friday, stopping at a string of remote islands including Lelei (65,000Rp, seven hours). On return they pick up from Lelei around 10am two days later. Alternatively, charter Mr Tamrin's speedboat (350,000Rp) to Gurapin (Pulau Kayoa), where there's a *penginapan*, a Wednesday morning boat to Bacan (returns Thursday) and a 5am speedboat to Ternate (Monday, Wednesday and Saturday).

## Pulau Bacan
☎ 0927

Bacan is the fourth of North Maluku's traditional Kie Raha ('four mountain') sultanates (along with Ternate, Tidore and Jailolo). Its main island, Pulau Bacan, is pleasant enough but its 'sights' are fairly pitiful. **Air Panas** is a patch of ferric-orange pebbles discoloured by volcanic bubbling in pretty sea shallows off **Kupal** village. 'Waterfall' **Air Belanda** (Dutch Water) is about as exciting as watching your *mandi* overflow. And the small, exaggeratedly fortified Portuguese-Dutch fort **Benteng Barnevald** is the one minor attraction of Bacan's languid little capital, **Labuha**. Nonetheless, Labuha has several modestly appealing guest houses, and beach cottages are under construction on little **Pulau Nusara**. Contact **Pak Ameruddin** ( ☎ 0812 4416 3254) for a progress report.

**Merpati** ( ☎ 21603) flies Ternate–Labuha–Sanana and back on Monday. Overnight boats (100,000Rp, eight hours) run daily at 7pm from Bastiong (Ternate) to Babang, 16km east of Labuha, arriving around 4am. Bemos await. There's no regular Ambon–Bacan boat service.

## PULAU HALMAHERA

Maluku's biggest island is eccentrically shaped, with four mountainous peninsulas, several volcanic cones and dozens of offshore islands. As it's sparsely populated and hard to get around, the island's potential for diving, bird-watching and beach tourism remains almost entirely untapped. In the riverine interior the nomadic, seminaked Togutil people still hunt deer with wooden spears, but change is coming with gold mining at Buli and the Weda Bay nickel-mining concession near Kobe. The creation of new regional capitals at Sofifi (North Maluku province), Weda (central Halmahera) and Jailolo (western Halmahera) is also stimulating local building booms. The movement of big bureaucracies out of Ternate and Tidore finally seeks to reverse a history throughout which Halmahera has been largely dominated by those tiny islands. Although occasionally breaking away as the independent Jailolo sultanate, Halmahera was ruled (at least nominally) by a deposed or renegade branch of the Ternate (or sometimes Tidore) royal family, or by loyalists regrouping to resist European incursions on Ternate. Halmahera is predominantly Muslim, with Christian villages in several areas of the more developed northern peninsula.

### GETTING THERE & AWAY

Merpati has air links to Morotai, Bacan, Gebe and Galela. Trigana flies Ternate–Buli. Pelni's *Sangiang* loops around Halmahera once or twice a month from Ternate and/or Bitung (Sulawesi). There's also a weekly Tobelo–Manado boat. But by far the most popular access is by speedboat from Ternate (see p734). For the northwestern coast head for Jailolo. For Tobelo, Galela and the east cross initially to Sofifi.

## Jailolo
☎ 0922

Famed for its fragrant durians, attractive little Jailolo port steams gently amid the mangroves at the base of a lush volcanic cone. Before being incorporated by Ternate, Jailolo was an independent sultanate, though be aware that medieval historians used the term Jailolo (Gilolo) to refer to the whole island of Halmahera. Today, not even a stone remains of Jailolo's former *kraton* (palace), abandoned in the 1730s. However, the sultan was reinstated in 2003 and now lives in a modest beachfront villa in Marimbati.

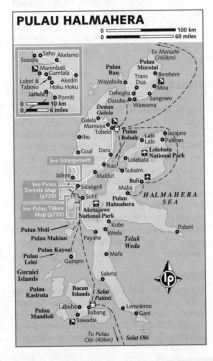

**PULAU HALMAHERA**

MALUKU

---

**RUMAH ADAT & BAILEU**

Known as *baileu* in Ambon and the Lease Islands (which also have fine examples), *rumah adat* are airy open-sided thatched structures doubling as village meeting places and general hang-outs. Some even have a communal TV. Many were burnt during the 1999–2002 troubles and others have been tastelessly modernised. However, those in several Christian villages north of Jailolo remain original, some dating from the villages' foundation (eg 1910 at Lolori). Several Jailolo-area *rumah adat* display a pair of *sasadu*, hairy balls hung from palm pennants at the end of an elongated apex beam. Rather than crude innuendo, their intended symbolism is as the 'feet' (representing stability) of the community. Tucked away into the palm-woven beams you may spot a *sie-sie* (bamboo pipe-cup) used for quaffing distilled palm wine on special occasions.

---

Facing the market, five minutes' walk from Jailolo's main jetty, is the simple but homely **Penginapan Jailolo** ( ☎ 222 1022; s/d 75,000/150,000Rp). Very close by, **Penginapan Camar** ( ☎ 222 1100; Jl Gufasa; r 75,000-200,000Rp; ✷ ) has fully refurbished, mostly air-con rooms sharing a lovely rear sitting area that surveys the bay, mangroves and jetty. Newer and out-wardly plusher, the boxy **Hotel d'Hoek** ( ☎ 222 1200; Jl Hatebicara; d 300,000-650,000Rp; ✷ ) has less charm and is inconveniently located 3km out of centre near the Marimbati junction.

Hole-in-the-wall eateries in the market serve superb *nasi ikan* (fish with rice) at 11,000Rp. Large speedboats to Dufa Dufa (Ternate; 38,000Rp, one hour) typically take an hour or so to fill up. The last departure is around 5pm.

### Around Jailolo

A very pleasant 12km *ojek* excursion takes you to **Marimbati**, set on a long black-sand beach (beware of currents if swimming). En route the floral villages of **Hoku Hoku**, **Taboso**, **Lolori** and **Gamtala** each maintain their own traditionally thatched *rumah adat* meeting hall (see boxed text, above). Those speaking OK Bahasa Indonesia (or Dutch) might gain an audience with the present sultan who lives 1.6km north of Marimbati village. Reached by entirely different road via Akelamo, **Susupu** is a picturesque volcano-backed village at the far-northern end of Marimbati beach.

### Sofifi

For most travellers this small market village is just a connection point on the Tobelo–Ternate journey. However, Sofifi is now officially the capital of North Maluku (Malut) province and numerous government departments will even-tually be relocated here from Ternate. The huge new governor's office is almost complete on a hilltop 5km east of Sofifi port and has sweeping views. A Sofifi visitors' centre for the remote **Aketajawe & Lolobata National Parks** ( ☎ 0852 4003 7036; aketajawe-lolobata@gmail.com; Jl 40) was due to open in 2010 at the time of writing. Ornithologists seeking the exceedingly rare Wallace's stand-ard-wing bird of paradise *(burung bidadari)* should ask park staff (some English-speaking) for help locating the local bird-guide Demianus ('Anung') whose hard-to-find house is accessed by hiking from Tanah Putih, itself around 30 minutes by *ojek* fsrom Sidangoli.

Sofifi–Bastiong speedboats (40 minutes) cost 50,000Rp for fast-filling 12-seaters, and 30,000Rp for bigger versions that might take an hour to fill up. Kijangs bound for Tobelo (80,000Rp, 3½ hours) and Weda (120,000Rp) wait by the Sofifi dock till early afternoon, but guessing which vehicle will be the first to leave can prove hit and miss.

### Tobelo
☎ 0924

Modest Tobelo is northern Halmahera's only real 'town'. The main Kao–Galela road (Jl Kemakmuran/Jl H Simange) is bisected just north of the market by Jl Pelabuhan leading 300m to the main port. In contrast to most of North Maluku, Tobelo is predominantly Christian, so beers are sold and you can even get lunch during Ramadan. Its bay is fronted by a pretty jigsaw of islands, many ringed with golden sandy beaches. The most accessible is **Pulau Kumo**, just a 10-minute ride away by shared outrigger. It's crowded on Sunday.

#### INFORMATION
**BNI** (Bank Negara Indonesia; Jl Kemakmuran) 24-hour ATM. No money exchange.

**Star Computer** (Jl Elim; internet/wi-fi per hr 10,000/5000Rp; ☼ 8am-10pm Mon-Sat) Connection is somewhat temperamental but there's a pleasant Wild West–styled wi-fi hot-spot cafe (juices 8000Rp).

**Tourist Office** (Dinas Parawisata; ☎ 262 1001; www .halmaherautara.com; Jl Puskesmas; ☼ 8am-4pm Mon-Fri) One block inland from Jl Kemakmuran, this attractively appointed new tourist office is working on a map of the region's scuba and snorkelling sites. It plans a dive centre on Pulau Kakara in the bay off Tebelo. English is spoken.

### SLEEPING & EATING

There are a dozen perfectly survivable options but most are rather lacklustre.

**Penginapan Asean Jaya** ( ☎ 262 1051; Jl Pelabuhan; s/tw 40,000/65,000Rp) Typical bed-in-a-box budget rooms share small *mandis*. Anis, the delightful owner, speaks English.

**Penginapan Meraksi Flower** ( ☎ 262 1129; Jl Bhavangkara; tw 110,000-165,000Rp; ☒ ) Pleasant rooms are pretty standard but fair value and reasonably well kept. It's 50m inland from the Hotel President.

**Wisma Slasabila** ( ☎ 262 2389; Jl Kemakmuran; standard/ spring bed 165,000-220,000Rp; ☒ ) Lemon-and-lime rooms around a narrow central strip of water garden are cleaner, fresher and more spacious than most in Tobelo. It's easy to miss, two doors north of the better-known Penginapan Regina.

**Hotel President** ( ☎ 262 1312; Jl Kemakmuran; d 185,000-250,000Rp; ☒ ) Decor and wood-veneer ceilings look a little dated but most rooms are comfortable and the 2nd-floor lounge has sea views.

**Elizabeth Inn** ( ☎ 262 1885; Jl Kemakmuran; d 200,000-250,000Rp; ☒ ) Rooms are brand new so relatively clean and comfortable, but they lack style and windows are minimal.

**Kusu-Kusu** ( ☎ 262 1870; Wosio; d 250,000Rp; ☒ ) Primarily a 'spa' offering 100,000Rp massages in thatched, octagonal pavilion booths, Kusu-Kusu has three new guest rooms that are well equipped though less stylish than the signs might imply. It's 3km south of Tobelo, 200m beyond the new bemo terminal.

**Kakara Cafe** ( ☎ 262 1908; Jl Kemakmuran; meals 17,000-40,000Rp, juice 12,500Rp, beer 30,000Rp; ☼ 9am-midnight Mon-Sat, 6pm-11pm Sun) This seafood restaurant, 500m south of Galaxy Mart supermarket, is marginally more polished than most of Tobelo's simple eateries.

### GETTING THERE & AWAY

The nearest airports are in Kao (temporarily inactive at the time of research) and Galela

from which **Merpati** ( ☎ 0813 4089 0899) flies twice weekly to Ternate. The *KM Elisabet II* sails to Manado (295,000Rp, 21 hours) on Thursday at 2pm, returning Monday. Pelni's *Sangiang* loops around Halmahera from Bitung (Sulawesi) on a Ternate–Babang (Bacan)–Gebe–Buli–Tobelo–Bitung route, monthly in either direction.

Speedboats for Morotai (50,000Rp, two hours) leave at 9am and there's a *kapal motor* at 1pm (45,000Rp, four hours).

Most Kijangs to Sofifi (80,000Rp, 3½ hours) leave around 4am. Book ahead and they'll pick you up at your hotel. Others leave later in the morning if and when full (90,000Rp) from in front of the harbour office, but waits can be lengthy. Chartering is possible from 300,000Rp. Bemos run regularly to Galela (15,000Rp, one hour) from the main market. Bemos to Kao (25,000Rp) via Daru (20,000Rp) start from a new terminal 3km south, 2000Rp away by shuttle bemo. Within town, *ojeks* cost 4000Rp, and *bentor* (motorbike-rickshaws) cost 5000Rp.

## South of Tobelo

**Pantai Karlen** is a beach of strikingly pure black sand 1km east of Pitu, 5km south of Tobelo. Around 10km further south, then 2km off the main road, **Kupa Kupa** has a white-sand swimming beach heavily shaded with mature trees. It's very photogenic when looking north, less so looking south thanks to the Pertamina Oil Terminal next door. Three simple but pleasantly furnished thatched **beach cottages** ( ☎ 0815 2785 6971; d 100,000Rp) have mosquito nets, bucket *mandis* and bamboo walls. They're tucked behind a charming little **cafe** (fish & cassava 25,000Rp, beer 30,000Rp) that caters mostly to Sunday picnickers and Saturday-night karaoke. Other days the site is peacefully calm except for the generator.

**Danau Paca** is a photogenic little lake backed by steep, lushly forested mountains. The scene is surveyed by an idyllic little weekend cafe built on stilt walkways above the waters at Talaga Paca. A tiny palm island floats around according to the wind's whim. Talaga Paca village is 2km west of the main road, 23km south of Tobelo: turn just south of the tall communication mast.

There's reputedly good snorkelling off the sandy southern tip of **Pulau Bobale**, accessed by 5000Rp shared boat from **Daru**. Daru is also the departure point for speedboats to eastern

Halmahera. A shipwrecked Japanese freighter lies just off Pantai Sosol at **Malifut**, where it was scuttled at the end of WWII.

## North of Tobelo

The road north is well surfaced with several very attractive woodland sections, glimpses of coast and a fine brief view (8km) of the active volcano Dukono smoking on the horizon. At **Luari** (13km) there's a Sunday **beach** with creamy coloured sand shaded by *ketapang* trees in a pretty horseshoe bay. Turning 1.5km inland at **Galela** (aka Soasio, 25km) you come to **Danau Galela** (Danau Duma), a sizeable lake lined with villages that suffered particularly in the 1999 troubles. Several burnt-out church ruins remain. Bullock carts are common on the lake's 16km 'ring' road. On the south bank in Soakonora, **Penginapan Talaga Maloha** ( ☎ 0852 5683 2276; d 100,000Rp, full-board per person extra 50,000Rp) is a comfortable family homestay whose rear terrace and best rooms (4 and 5) survey the lake, where local fishermen still punt around on bamboo rafts.

Galela has its own language, in which *daloha* means 'good', *sukur dala dala* means 'thank you' and *to-tagi tagi* rather than *jalan jalan* is the ideal answer to the eternal question, 'Where are you going?'.

## Eastern Halmahera

Way off the tourism radar, eastern Halmahera appeals to travellers who fancy being an area's first foreigner in a generation. One place with potential is Jarajara, whose fine sandy beach is ringed by a protective coral reef with diving possibilities. Deep in the riverine hinterland, at least a two-day trek from Subaim, Jarajara or Patlean, live the nomadic Togutil people, often dressed in nothing but a loin cloth. Keen if relatively inexperienced **Ilham Hiabdullah** ( ☎ 0852 9836 0813; http://ilhamtravelguide.blogspot.com; soplo_1984@yahoo.com) is an English-speaking Ternate-based guide who organises tailor-made adventures starting from his family's Jarajara home.

Boats from Tobelo run to Patlean (Sunday), Jarajara (some Tuesdays) and Maba (four weekly). Preorganised longboat transfers allow hop-offs at intermediate villages en route. From Pelabuhan Penyebangan, 6km north of Tobelo, car ferry *Inerie* crosses to Subaim (six hours) on Thursday and Saturday nights. Trigana Air flies three times weekly between Ternate and mine-ravaged Buli.

## PULAU MOROTAI
☎ 0923

A minor Japanese base during WWII, Morotai leapt to prominence when it was captured by the Allies and used to bomb Manila to bits. That was the sadly destructive fulfilment of General MacArthur's 'I will return' pledge to retake the Philippines. Among the Japanese defenders who retreated to Morotai's crumpled mountain hinterland was the famous Private Nakamura: only in 1973 did he discover that the war was over. A WWII US amphibious tank still lies rusting in a hidden palm grove, a five minutes' *ojek*-ride behind Morotai's village capital **Daruba**. There are attractive palm-backed fishing beaches along the narrow Nefelves Peninsula that stretches south from Daruba. But for better beaches explore the array of offshore islands in Morotai's sparkling turquoise waters. With a decent longboat (300,000Rp to 500,000Rp) you can make a great day trip combining Zum Zum, Kolorai, Dodola and the pearl-farming island of Ngelengele.

Around an hour's longboat ride from Daruba, idyllic **Pulau Dodola** is actually a pair of uninhabited islands linked by a low-tide sandbar. The utterly perfect white sand is so soft that it feels like you're walking on warm snow. The western lagoon offers sheltered swimming but the island's reputation for good snorkelling is exaggerated by Maluku standards. The clumps of surviving coral are marginally better around tiny **Pulau Kolorai**, a one-village island famous for its lobsters (from 150,000Rp per kilogram).

On **Pulau Zum Zum (Sum Sum)**, 25 minutes' ride from Daruba, there's a comically unrecognisable bust of General MacArthur who had his temporary WWII command base here. The island is mostly ringed by mangroves, but on its small, spongy white-sand beach you'll still find the rusty foundations of a wartime pier which deposits metal 'pebbles' amid all the discarded giant clam shells. Locals still 'fish' for WWII machine guns, shell casings and other valuable scrap.

## Sleeping & Eating

Daruba has four homestay-style *penginapan*. Passengers arriving at the port or airport race each other into town to nab a room at the unmarked **Penginapan Muslim** ( ☎ 0812 4480 2587; d 120,000Rp; ▨ ), which is rightly considered the best on offer. **Penginapan Tonga** ( ☎ 222 1204; r with fan/air-con 85,000/130,000Rp) is slightly less homely. In an unmarked two-storey house, **Simpang 4** ( ☎ 0813 5667 3548; s 50,000Rp) has shared *mandis* but is more attractive than Muslim Dua. There are half a dozen *rumah makan*. Morotai's 2009 'promotion' to regency means that Daruba's facilities are likely to improve very considerably in coming years.

### Getting There & Away

**Merpati** ( ☎ 222 1063) operates Ternate–Daruba flights on Friday. Daily to Tobelo there's a 9am speedboat (50,000Rp, two hours) and the 10am *KM Galang* (45,000Rp, four hours). A twice-weekly car ferry service should restart when the new ferry dock is finished at Juanga, 5km south of Daruba. The *KM Kie Raha* and Pelni's *Sangiang* sail to Ternate twice monthly.

# SULA & BURU

For the very rare travellers passing this way, Buru and Sanana (Sula Islands) are most likely to be visited as stepping stones when taking local boats between Ternate and Ambon. Neither have money exchange nor international ATMs. In Sula language *berahi* means 'good', *mina* is 'sweet' and *sukur* (*eb-eb*) means 'thank you (very much)'.

### Getting There & Away

**Merpati** ( ☎ Namlea 0813 4313 5533, Sanana 0929-222 1078) flies Ambon–Namlea–Namrole (Saturday), Ambon–Namlea–Sanana (Monday), Sanana–Bacan–Ternate (Tuesday) and Ternate–Fala (Wednesday). **Trigana Air** ( ☎ 0929-222 1505) flies Ambon–Sanana–Ternate three times weekly.

On alternate days the *Bahari Express* jet-boat (205,000Rp, four hours) departs Namlea at 8am for Ambon. An overnight car ferry runs the same days to Galala (Pulau Ambon, 70,000Rp, 13 hours). Namlea–Sanana car ferries (120,000Rp, 14 hours) run every three to five days, and there's a *kapal motor* (150,000Rp, 14 hours) roughly twice weekly. Pelni's *Lambelu* calls at Namlea between Ternate (14 hours) and Ambon (four hours) but can't actually dock resulting in a photogenically chaotic melee as perilously overcrowded lighters ferry hoards of passengers to shore. Pelni's monthly *Sangiang* runs Ambon–Namlea–Sanana–Ternate–Bitung.

*KM Intim Teratai* sails overnight Thursday from Ternate to Sanana (dorm/air-con berth 260,000/350,000Rp, 15 hours), proceeds to Dofa/Fala (five/seven hours), then returns directly to Ternate. *Theodora* sails Ternate–Sanana on Tuesday night, shuttles to Dofa and Fala on Wednesday then returns to Sanana (Thursday) before overnighting back to Ternate. Once the *Theodora* has arrived (Wednesday evening), *KM Funka* departs Fala for Jorjoga (access point for Pantai Anjing) and Bobong (Pulau Taliabu's main village), continuing on to Pulau Banggai and Bau Bau (Sulawesi).

## SULA ISLANDS
### Pulau Sunana
☎ 0929

Although you're quite likely to be the Sulas' only foreign visitor all year, the astoundingly underutilised **tourist information office** ( ☎ 21227; 9am-5pm Mon-Fri) in **Sanana** has friendly English-speaking staff waiting to assist. It's hidden within the modest whitewashed shell of the 1652 Dutch fort **Benteng De Verlachting**. Around 8km north, **Bajo** is Pulau Sanana's most photogenic village, with fishermen's stilt cottages linked together by wooden plank pathways above the tidal waters.

Sanana's best accommodation choice is **Hotel Green Sula** ( ☎ 0812 4441 4277; Jl Telkom; s/d 150,000/200,000Rp; 🐾 ), an airy house with ample communal seating guarded by a concrete chicken. Half a dozen basic cheapies include four-room **Penginapan Budi** ( ☎ 21292; Jl Merpati; r 50,000Rp).

### Pulau Mangole
☎ 0929

Although speedboats run from Sanana to Mangole town, there's no road between there and Dofa or Fala, Pulau Mangole's main settlements, so you'll need to wait for the twice-weekly Sanana–Dofa–Fala ferry.

The Sulas' most famous attraction is a quadruple set of tidal whirlpools (*palung* or *sempeh*) in the narrow strait between Taliabu and Mangole islands (Selat Capalulu). The whirlpools appear as the tide changes on full- and new-moon days. A viewpoint from which to observe the phenomenon (becoming progressively less impressive as years go by) is **Tanjung Batu Gosok**, accessed by an 8km path from Dofa. The nearest accommodation is at Fala, 18km from Dofa by *ojek*. Part way along you'll pass through Lekokadai village, from which it's a short *ketinting* (outrigger) ride to the uninhabited island **Pas Leko**, where you'll find the most accessible of the Sulas' white-sand beaches.

## PULAU BURU

☎ 0913

Famed for its medicinal eucalyptus oil *(minyak kayu putih)*, Buru (http://burukab.go.id) became Indonesia's 'anti-Siberia' in the 1960s, when communist suspects were exiled here in significant numbers. Short of quaffing *sopi* (distilled palm wine) with dumbstruck fishermen, there's not a great deal for tourists to do here, but capital **Namlea** has a gentle charm, with grassy hills giving its surroundings a very un-Malukan appearance. Over a dozen small, simple *penginapan* include friendly **Maya** ( ☎ 21645; Jl Mesjid Jami; r 60,000Rp). It's beside a noisy mosque and the typical box rooms share *mandis*, but bay views are very pleasant from the communal balcony. Much more luxurious, **Hotel Grand Sarah** ( ☎ 213 021; Jl A Yani; standard/bungalow/VIP r 250,000/350,000/400,000Rp) is unexpectedly one of Maluku's best hotels. Perched on a garden view ridge directly above town, a grand sweep of stairway leads up from its inviting lobby to immaculate bedrooms with pseudo-antique furniture and acres of sash curtain.

A four-room *penginapan* is under construction 17km northwest of Namlea at **Jikumerasa**, a stunning bay of turquoise water and dazzling white sand backed by sparse palms and Sunday picnic shacks. Bemos (5000Rp, 25 minutes) run roughly hourly till 3pm.

Buru's spiritual heart is the mystical mountain lake, **Danau Rana**, but despite tales of giant eels and 'flowers of longevity', its boggy banks are visually disappointing after the two days' sweaty trek to reach it.

# PULAU AMBON

Maluku's most prominent island is lush and gently mountainous, indented with two great hoops of bay. Around capital Kota Ambon, villages merge into a long, if still green, suburban ribbon. But further out light sparkles brilliantly through alluring flower gardens and swaying tropical foliage, with a particularly inspiring string of timeless coastal villages west of the airport. Disregard misleadingly out-of-date websites that claim

there's any sort of danger to visiting this delightful place. Ambon is well and truly back in business, a pleasant transport hub for reaching the lovely Lease and Banda Islands, but also a charming retreat and dive base in its own right.

## History

Until 1512 Ambon was ruled by Ternate. The sultans brought the civilising force of Islam to the island's north coast and developed Hitu Lama as a major spice-trading entrepôt. When the Portuguese displaced the Ternateans, they found Ambon's less developed, non-Islamicised south more receptive to Christianity, and built the fortress around which Kota Ambon would eventually evolve. In 1599 the Dutch renamed this fort Victoria and made Kota Ambon their spice-trading base.

During WWII Kota Ambon became a Japanese military headquarters, resulting in extensive Allied bombing that destroyed most of its once-attractive colonial architecture. In 1950 Ambon was briefly the centre of the southern Malukan independence movement. This was extinguished within a few months by Indonesian military force, with a last stand at Passo village.

From 1999 until mid-2002, Ambon was ripped apart by Christian-Muslim intercommunal violence, leaving Kota Ambon looking like 1980s Beirut. However, there have been no disturbances since 2004, and strong economic resurgence has wiped away almost every visible scar of that tragic era. It's as though everyone suddenly awoke from a bad dream to find themselves back in their busy little South-Sea paradise.

## KOTA AMBON

☎ 0911 / pop 368,000

By the region's dreamy tropical standards, Maluku's capital, commercial centre and transport hub is a busy, throbbing metropolis. Sights are minimal and architecture wins no prizes, but compared to cities elsewhere, Kota Ambon retains a languid charm emphasised by a perfect arc of bay and its lushly tree-dappled mountainous backdrop.

### Orientation

Almost all public road transportation emanates from the traffic-clogged Mardika market area. Jl Dr Sam Ratulangi, Jl Said Perintah and

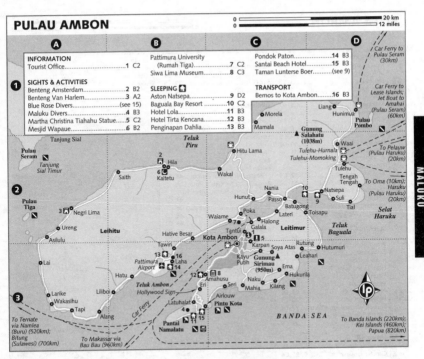

**PULAU AMBON**

| INFORMATION | | |
|---|---|---|
| Tourist Office | 1 | C2 |

**SIGHTS & ACTIVITIES**
| Benteng Amsterdam | 2 | B2 |
| Benteng Van Harlem | 3 | A2 |
| Blue Rose Divers | (see 15) | |
| Maluku Divers | 4 | B3 |
| Martha Christina Tiahahu Statue | 5 | C2 |
| Mesjid Wapaue | 6 | B2 |

| Pattimura University | | |
| (Rumah Tiga) | 7 | C2 |
| Siwa Lima Museum | 8 | C3 |

**SLEEPING**
| Aston Natsepa | 9 | D2 |
| Baguala Bay Resort | 10 | B3 |
| Hotel Lola | 11 | B3 |
| Hotel Tirta Kencana | 12 | B3 |
| Penginapan Dahlia | 13 | B3 |

| Pondok Paton | 14 | B3 |
| Santai Beach Hotel | 15 | B3 |
| Taman Lunterse Boer | (see 9) | |

**TRANSPORT**
| Bemos to Kota Ambon | 16 | B3 |

*0 — 20 km*
*0 — 12 miles*

**MALUKU**

Jl AY Patty are the major commercial streets. Busy Jl Sultan Babullah comes cacophonously to life at dusk.

## Information
Maluku's phone numbers currently have 5-, 6- and 7-digit varieties. Expect rationalisation.

### INTERNET ACCESS
Several places are grindingly slow. The following are faster:

**K@tongNet** (Jl Sam Ratulangi 91; per hr 5000Rp; 8am-2am) Rather sweaty.
**Target** (Jl Sultan Hairun; per hr 7500Rp; 10am-11pm) Central though cramped.
**Warnet Tifa** (Jl Rijali; per hr 5000Rp; 9am-1am) Good air-conditioning.
**Wartel Aladin** (Jl Sultan Babullah; per hr 6000Rp; 24hr if custom dictates) Reasonably spacious with good air-con.

With your own laptop, there's free wi-fi at gently trendy **Cafe Beta** (Jl Pantai Mardika; juice 12,000Rp, coffee 7000-10,000Rp; 6pm-11pm) and in the lobby cafe of **Hotel Amans** (p746; great connection).

### MONEY
Change or withdraw enough money in Ambon for trips to outlying islands where there are no exchange facilities whatever.

**Bank Mandiri** (Jl Pantai Mardika; 9am-3pm Mon-Fri) Best available rates for new US$100 bills, albeit still relatively low.
**BCA** (Bank Central Asia; Jl Sultan Hairun 24; 9am-3pm Mon-Fri) Exchanges euros, Aussie and US dollars, but you can expect a long wait. ATMs allow 2,500,000Rp withdrawals.
**BNI** (Bank Negara Indonesia; Jl Said Perintah 12; 9am-3pm Mon-Fri) Poor exchange rates but relatively swift service (counter 08).
**PT Indova** (☎ 352 590; Jl Kopra) Abysmal rates but dollar exchange is possible at virtually any time. Call to have the door opened.

### TOURIST INFORMATION
**Laszlo Wagner** (www.east-indonesia.info) This very experienced Hungarian-born Maluku fanatic has contributed numerous informative Maluku webpages to www.virtual tourist.com and now leads tailor-made tours into remote areas of Maluku and Papua.
**Tourist Info Desk** (Pattimura Airport; 10am-3pm Mon-Sat) Unmarked but useful desk straight ahead on leaving baggage claim.

**MALUKU**

# KOTA AMBON

0 | 500 m
0 | 0.3 miles

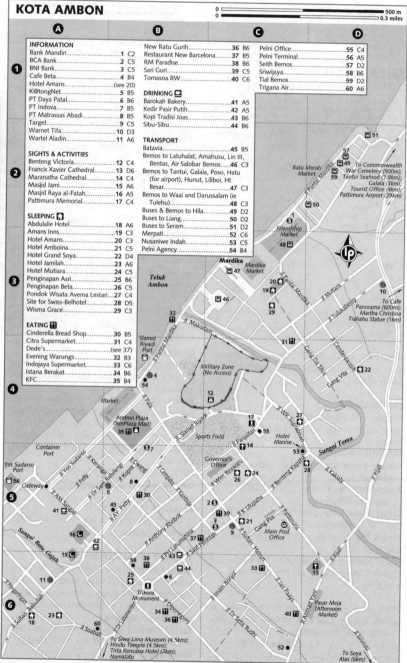

### INFORMATION
Bank Mandiri....................................1 C2
BCA Bank.........................................2 C5
BNI Bank..........................................3 C5
Cafe Beta.........................................4 B4
Hotel Amans.............................(see 20)
K@tongNet.......................................5 B5
PT Daya Patal...................................6 B6
PT Indova.........................................7 B5
PT Matrassas Abadi..........................8 B5
Target...............................................9 C5
Warnet Tifa....................................10 D3
Wartel Aladin..................................11 A6

### SIGHTS & ACTIVITIES
Benteng Victoria.............................12 C4
Francis Xavier Cathedral..................13 D6
Maranatha Cathedral.......................14 C4
Masjid Jami.....................................15 A6
Masjid Raya al-Fatah.......................16 A5
Pattimura Memorial.........................17 C4

### SLEEPING
Abdulalie Hotel...............................18 A6
Amans Inns.....................................19 C3
Hotel Amans...................................20 C3
Hotel Amboina................................21 C5
Hotel Grand Soya............................22 D4
Hotel Jamilah..................................23 A6
Hotel Mutiara..................................24 C5
Penginapan Asri..............................25 B6
Penginapan Beta.............................26 C5
Pondok Wisata Avema Lestari..........27 C3
Site for Swiss-Belhotel.....................28 D5
Wisma Grace...................................29 C3

### EATING
Cinderella Bread Shop.....................30 B5
Citra Supermarket...........................31 C4
Dede's.....................................(see 37)
Evening Warungs............................32 B3
Indojaya Supermarket......................33 C6
Istana Berakat.................................34 B6
KFC................................................35 B4

New Ratu Gurih...............................36 B6
Restaurant New Barcelona...............37 B5
RM Paradise....................................38 B6
Sari Guri..........................................39 C5
Tomasoa RW...................................40 C6

### DRINKING
Barokah Bakery...............................41 A5
Kedir Pasir Putih..............................42 A5
Kopi Tradisi Joas.............................43 B6
Sibu-Sibu........................................44 B6

### TRANSPORT
Batavia...........................................45 B5
Bemos to Latuhalat, Amahusu, Lin III,
   Bentas, Air Salobar Bemos......46 C3
Bemos to Tantui, Galala, Poso, Hatu
   (for airport), Hunut, Liliboi, Ht
   Besar...........................................47 C3
Bemos to Waai and Darussalam (ie
   Tulehu)........................................48 C3
Buses & Bemos to Hila....................49 D2
Buses to Liang.................................50 D2
Buses to Seram................................51 D2
Merpati...........................................52 C6
Nusaniwe Indah...............................53 D2
Pelni Agency...................................54 B4

Pelni Office.....................................55 C4
Pelni Terminal.................................56 A5
Seith Bemos....................................57 D2
Sriwijaya.........................................58 B6
Tial Bemos......................................59 D2
Trigana Air......................................60 A6

To Commonwealth
War Cemetery (900m);
Tantui Seafood (1.8km);
Galala (3km);
Tourist Office (4km);
Pattimura Airport (29km)

Batu Merah
Market

Jl Pantai Mardika

Friendship
Market

Mardika
Mardika
Market

Teluk
Ambon

Jl Mutiara

To Cafe
Panorama (600m);
Martha Christina
Tiahahu Statue (1km)

Jl Tulukabessy

Jl Makodam

Slamet
Riyadi Port

Jl Pantai Mardika

Gang Da Silva

Jl Cenderawasih

Gang Vila

Military Zone
(No Access)

Jl WR Supratman

Market

Jl Pala

Jl Yos Sudarso

Yos Sudarso
Port

Container
Port

Ambon Plaza
(AmPlaza Mall)

Jl Slamet Riyadi

Sports Field

Jl Panjaitan

Hotel
Manise

Sungai Tomu

Jl Keranjang

Jl Dr Sam Ratulangi

Jl Kopra

Jl Cengkeh

Jl Cempaka

Jl Kambulu

Governor's
Office

Jl Wim Reawaru

Jl Benteng Kapaha

Jl Kakialy

Jl Rijali

Gateway

Jl AM Sangaji

Jl Felly

Jl AY Patty

Jl Anthony Rhebok

Jl Pti Latumahina

Jl Silet Perintah

Jl JK Ulupaha

Jl Sultan Hairun

Gang Pos

Main Post
Office

Pattioura

Sungai Batu Gajah

Jl Sultan Babullah

Jl Pengerang

Trikora
Monument

Jl Diponegoro

Imam Bonjol

Jl Jan Paays

Jl Dr Setia Budhi

Pasar Meja
(Afternoon
Market)

Jl Ahmad Yani

Jl Rijali

Jl Soabali

To Siwa Lima Museum (4.5km);
Hindu Temple (4.5km);
Tirta Kencana Hotel (7km);
Namalatu

To Soya
Atas (6km)

Jl Sirimall

**Tourist Office** (Map p743; Dinas Parawisata; ☎ 312 300; Jl Jenderal Sudirman, Tantui; ◷ 8am-4pm Mon-Fri) Offers fistfuls of colourful free brochures. Tantui bemos pass by, a 4km loop outbound from Mardika but less than 1km returning.

### TRAVEL AGENCIES

**PT Daya Patal** ( ☎ 353 344; spicetr@gmail.com; Jl Said Perintah; ◷ 8am-6pm) Ever-obliging agency with several knowledgeable English-speaking staff. Sells airline and Pelni tickets and is creating a dive lodge on Pulau Saparua.
**PT Matrassas Abadi** ( ☎ 311 111; mattras_amq@ hotmail.com; Jl AY Patty 52; ◷ 8am-9pm) Well-organised English-speaking travel agency for domestic air tickets.

## Sights

The town's biggest mosque, **Masjid Raya al-Fatah** (Jl Sultan Babullah) is a modern concrete affair. The fanciful green **Masjid Jami** next door is much more photogenic. **Maranatha Cathedral** (Jl Pattimura) has a staid if iconic tower. **Francis Xavier Cathedral** (Jl Pattimura) has a facade crusted with saint statues and silver-strut steeples which glimmer mysteriously. Undramatic **Benteng Victoria** (out of bounds, army use) is the Dutch-era fortress. It's fronted by a gilded statue of Slamet Riyadi, an Indonesian commander who died retaking the place from RMS rebels in 1950. A bellicose **Pattimura Memorial** brandishes his *parang* (machete) and *salawaka* (spindly Malukan shield) in the park behind. A hilltop **Martha Christina Tiahahu statue** (Map p743) commemorates Pattimura's contemporary (see boxed text, p752) and enjoys wonderful views.

Allied servicemen who died in WWII are remembered in a beautifully manicured **Commonwealth War Cemetery** (Tantui), shaded beneath towering trees fuzzed with epiphytes.

In the southern suburbs, the **Siwa Lima Museum** (Map p743; ☎ 341 652; admission 3000Rp; ◷ 8am-4pm Mon-Fri) has two main buildings separated by 500m of road snaking beautifully up through steep, lovingly tended gardens. The upper ethnographic building displays regional costumes, building styles, totems, *doti-doti* (voodoo-style curse-boats), local fabrics, weapons and *kepala desa* 'power sticks'. Diorama windows demonstrate *sopi* distillation and sago production and there's a walk-through recreation of a neolithic cave dwelling. The lower maritime museum lacks English captioning but the crustacea, model boats and gigantic whale skeletons are self-explanatory. Air Salobar *mobils* (2000Rp)

from Ambon turn around at the gardens' eastern gateway. An *ojek* to the door saves the sweaty climb.

## Festivals & Events

The annual **Darwin–Ambon Yacht Race** (www.darwin ambonrace.com.au; ◷ July), once Ambon's main international sporting event, restarted modestly in 2007. The **Darwin–Saumlaki Rally** (www .sailindonesia.net) also sails to Ambon.

## Sleeping

There are alternatives around the airport (see p750) and on beaches at Latuhalat (p749) and Natsepa (p749).

### BUDGET

If you're unfussy, there's plenty of choice, but only a few budget places make even the most cursory attempt to hide their cockroaches and damp stains.

**Penginapan Asri** ( ☎ 311 217; tw with fan & shared bathroom 65,000-80,000Rp; r with air-con 110,000-160,000Rp; ✷ ) Many rooms lack natural light, but the Asri is very central and much better kept than most other hotels in this price range.

**Penginapan Beta** ( ☎ 353 463; Jl Wim Reawaru; tw with fan/air-con 80,000/120,000Rp; ✷ ) The 'pink prison' looks like a mouldering dump from outside, but while the compact rooms lack privacy they're fairly well kept and reasonably priced with ensuite bathrooms.

**Abdulalie Hotel** ( ☎ 352 057; Jl Sultan Babullah; tw with fan/air-con from 82,500/176,000Rp; ✷ ) Well run and eternally popular with local petty salesmen. The cheap rooms attract plentiful mosquitoes, but the 'executive' rooms are tastefully decorated off an almost colonial-feel hallway. Air-con is often trumped by power cuts.

**Hotel Jamilah** ( ☎ 353 626; Jl Soabali; d 125,000Rp; ✷ ) Behind a grotto of fake golden rocks, this 15-room family hotel has a peaceful, homely charm and ample areas of communal lounge space. Rooms are freshly painted though the lurid pink attached *mandis* are a slight let-down.

**Pondok Wisata 'Avema' Lestari** ( ☎ 355 596, 0813 4303 3842; Jl WR Supratman 18; s/d/tr 150,000/165,000/ 220,000Rp; ✷ ) This welcoming family homestay has neat, clean air-conditioned rooms and airy communal spaces. Helpful owner Jan speaks fluent Dutch and English, but finding him to check in or out can sometimes take a while: there's no reception. Doors lock at 11pm.

MALUKU

**Wisma Grace** ( ☎ 234 1717; tw without/with hot water 170,000/220,000Rp; ✖ ) Comparatively new, Grace has good, clean, beige-brown tiled floors, and better rooms have minibars, but some walls already need repainting.

**our pick Hotel Tirta Kencana** (Map p743; ☎ 345 840; tirta.kencana@yahoo.co.id; Jl Raya, Amahusu; d cottage/stand-ard/deluxe/ste 181,000/212,000/272,000/333,000Rp; ✖ ) This immaculately maintained waterside hotel has particularly appealing deluxe rooms with balconies facing the limpid blue bay through a line of palms. There's a lovely open-air water-front cafe-restaurant and a small massage-spa. It's 7km southwest from central Ambon, 2km beyond Siwa Lima Museum. Take Amahusu or Latuhalat bemos.

### MIDRANGE

Ambon's better hotels are all air-conditioned, bathrooms have hot showers and at least some staff speak basic English. Several offer sig-nificantly cheaper 'discount rates' without even asking.

**Hotel Grand Soya** ( ☎ 312 019; Jl Cenderawasih 20; discount-/full-price tw from 234,000/390,000Rp; ✖ 🖳 ) With attractive, dark wood furniture and useful extras like in-room safes, this is one of Ambon's most popular, central addresses. Wi-fi (11,000Rp per hour) is available in the slightly chintzy lobby.

**Hotel Amboina** ( ☎ 355 514; Jl K Ulupaha; s 375,000Rp, d standard/executive/ste from 300,000/450,000/500,000Rp; ✖ ) Reception is stylishly minimalist and a sooth-ing cream-colour scheme prevails. However, while rooms have been recently redecorated, most are windowless and those that aren't suffer from oppressive road noise.

**Hotel Amans** (Ambon Manise; ☎ 353 888; www .amans-hotel.com; Jl Pantai Mardika 53A; discounted/annex d from 320,000/190,000Rp; ✖ 🖳 🖳 ) Neither luxu-rious nor dowdy, the Amans has over 150 unremarkable but fairly priced midrange rooms whose rack rates are regularly slashed without ado for walk-in guests. English-speaking staff abound and there's free wi-fi in the pleasantly refurbished rear-lobby area. If you don't mind a higher proportion of carpet burns and minor furniture damage, try the tattier Amans Inns annex (190,000Rp to 240,000Rp) which is located directly be-hind. Look first, as a few rooms are cruddy but most of the spacious, upper-floor 'gold' rooms are a great deal and you still get soap, top sheet, hot water, air-con and multichan-nel TV.

**Hotel Mutiara** ( ☎ 353 873; hotel_mutiara_ambon@ yahoo.com, www.hotelmutiaraambon.com; Jl Pattimura; s/d deluxe 407,000/484,000Rp, VIP 495,000/550,000Rp; ✖ ) Behind a dainty curtain of tropical foliage, this cosy, tastefully executed 26-room hotel has a welcoming European atmosphere and small but mostly well-appointed rooms sport-ing superclean bathrooms and framed local fabrics. Four cheaper rooms (single/double 264,000/3300,000Rp) are a significant step down in quality. The hotel's bouncy carpets are just starting to age.

At the time of research, a 10-storey **Swiss-Belhotel** (Jl Benteng Kapaha) was under construc-tion opposite the overpriced Hotel Manise.

## Eating

Cheap *rumah makan* abound, especially around Mardika market, the ports, the Pelni office and Jl Sultan Babullah. Evening warungs appear on Jl Sultan Babullah and Jl Pantai Mardika. An intriguing variety of restaurants and coffee shops lie within two blocks of the Trikora monument, especially down Jl Said Perintah.

**RM Paradise** (Jl PH Latumahina; dishes 5000Rp, fish mar-ket price; ✖ lunch Mon-Sat) Outwardly a typical, cheap dining barn, the Paradise is considered *the* place for hard-to-find genuine Ambonese food including *papeda* (see the boxed text, opposite).

**Tomasoa RW** (Jl Jan Paays; dog with cassava 10,000Rp; ✖ 4.30-11pm Mon-Sat) Cooked in spicy ginger chunks, dog meat is eaten in tiny shack dives like this one, washed down with half-bottles of *sopi* (13,000Rp).

**KFC** (Ambon Plaza Mall, 2nd fl; chicken per piece 11,000Rp; ✖ 9am-9pm) Ambon's contemporary fast-food palace has luxuriant air-conditioning.

**Restaurant New Barcelona** ( ☎ 347 728; Jl Said Perintah; mains 15,000-40,000Rp, beer 20,000Rp; ✖ 10am-10pm Mon-Sat, 6-10pm Sun) Inexpensive if unspec-tacular Chinese dishes bolster a free-wheeling menu including seafood-, tofu-, pigeon- and even frog-based dishes.

**Cafe Panorama** ( ☎ 351 884; Jl CM Tiahahu; mains 23,000-65,000Rp, juices 10,000-20,000Rp, beer 25,000Rp; ✖ 11am-11pm) Pseudo-colonial and ethnic de-sign elements add to the strikingly wide city view from this agreeable hillside resto-cafe. Partly English menus include local favourites, sizzler-plate steaks, calamari rings and valiant attempts at chicken cordon bleu in thick gar-lic-cream sauce. Karpan bemos drive past, but so does the endless deafening traffic.

---

### MALUKAN FOOD

Despite what you'll see in most restaurants, Maluku's traditional staple isn't rice but *kasbi* (boiled cassava) or *papeda* (sago), called *popeda* in Ternate. That's served as an amorphous, colourless goo that you ladle into plates of *kuah-ikan* (fish soup), then suck down as though trying to swallow a live jellyfish. Odd, but surprisingly good when accompanied with *sayur garu* (papaya flower), *kohu-kohu* (green-bean/coconut/fish mix), *papari* (a unique mixed vegetable), *keladi*-root and cassava-leaf spinach. For protein, fish and seafood are king, typically served with a lightly spiced citrus dip called *dabu dabu* or *colo colo*. But some locals also eat pigeon, frog and even dog – known as RW ('eyre-weh'), as in Manado.

Originally unique to the Banda Islands, the spice-yielding kernel of nutmeg (*pala*) grows within a fruit that itself makes deliciously tart jams and distinctive sweet 'wine' (available at Ambon's Sibu Sibu; see below). Nutmeg grows best in the shade of magnificent *kenari* trees which themselves yield an almond-like nut locally used in confectionery and sauces. *Kenari* nut chunks float atop *air goraka*, a distinctive ginger-coffee hot beverage.

*Sageru* (palm wine) is distilled into powerfully alcoholic *sopi* even in Muslim areas, but even though they're commonly supped by off-duty fishermen and used for some *adat* (traditional law) ceremonies, neither are openly sold in normal shops.

---

**Tantui Seafood** ( ☎ 0852 3223 7888; Tantui; mains from 25,000Rp, juice 15,000Rp; ☷ 11am-11pm; ☷ ) Sit inside or out on faintly silly, bow-wrapped chairs or out on the waterside terrace for generous portions of shrimp-rich nasi goreng seafood with perfectly grilled fish or spicy squid (*cumi bakar*).

**Istana Berakat** (Jl Diponegoro; mains 35,000-55,000Rp; ☷ 10am-10pm) Decor is entirely lacklustre but the seafood and vegetarian *sapo tohu* (tofu sizzler, 42,500Rp) are excellent. Across the street its sister restaurant Berakat Ambonia is renowned for pork dishes.

Other reliable places for fresh fish include bright if bland **New Ratu Gurih** (Jl Diponegoro; meals 30,000-50,000Rp), **Sari Guri** (Jl Dana Kopra; mains 25,000-50,000Rp, beer 25,000Rp; ☷ 9am-11pm) and more attractive but less busy **Dede's** (Jl Said Perintah; fish meals 25,000-40,000Rp, beer 23,000Rp; ☷ 9am-10pm).

### SELF-CATERING

Mardika is the biggest market. Useful stores include:

**Cinderella Bread Shop** (Jl AY Patty; ☷ 8am-8pm) Try the brilliantly named *Shaggy Twist*, a soft croissant-shaped roll topped with cheese (5000Rp).

**Citra Supermarket** (Jl Tulukabessy; ☷ 8am-9pm)

**Indojaya Supermarket** (Jl Jan Paays; ☷ 8.30am-8.30pm Mon-Sat, 11am-8pm Sun)

## Drinking

**Barokah Bakery** (Jl AM Sangaji; ☷ 6.30am-7pm) Reduce plastic waste by refilling water bottles for 500Rp at this little bakery-cafe. Handy for the port.

**Kopi Tradisi Joas** (Jl Said Perintah; coffee 5000-11,000Rp; ☷ 6.30am-7.30pm Mon-Sat) Local bigwigs talk politics for hours over Joas' rich mocha-style 'secret-recipe' coffees and slices of deep-fried breadfruit (*sukun goreng*, 1000Rp) in this simple but attractive cafe with wood-panelled walls and a central avocado tree.

**Kedir Pasir Putih** (Jl Sultan Babullah; tea/juices/snacks from 4000/12,000/15,000Rp; ☷ 7am-2am) South-Sea island-themed juice-bar which comes to life after dark when the lanterns and fairy lights twinkle through the faux foliage.

**our pick** **Sibu-Sibu** ( ☎ 312 525; Jl Said Perintah; juices 8000-14,000Rp, beer 24,000Rp, coffee 5000-7000Rp, fish'n'chips 20,000Rp; ☷ 8am-10pm Mon-Sat, 1.30-8pm Sun) Ambon-born star portraits deck the walls of this sweet little coffee shop which plays Malukan music and serves local snacks like *koyabu* (cassava cake, 3000Rp), *lopis pulut* (sticky rice with palm jaggery) and *kenari* nut brownies. Owner June speaks English.

Comparatively stylish places for a beer include the convivial lobby bars of Hotels Mutiara (beer 38,500Rp), Amans (27,500Rp) and Amboina (27,500Rp). The last one suffers from live 'music'.

## Getting There & Away

### AIR

#### Beyond Maluku

Between them, **Batavia** ( ☎ 346 380; www.batavia-air.co.id; Jl AY Patty 31; ☷ 8am-5pm Mon-Sat, 8am-2pm Sun), **Lion/Wings Air** ( ☎ 351 532; Pattimura Airport) and **Sriwijaya** ( ☎ 354 498; www.sriwijayaair-online.com; Jl AM Sangaji 79; ☷ 9am-6pm) operate five daily

Jakarta–Ambon flights, typically costing around 800,000Rp. Both Wings and **Express Air** (☎ 323 807; Pattimura Airport) fly three times weekly to Sorong, with connections to Jayapura and Manokwari. Express's advertised Ambon–Manado flight (999,000Rp) is oddly routed via Sorong too. Alternatively, for Manado take Lion/Wings via Makassar (daily). Merpati's Ambon–Kisar–Kupang flight currently departs on Monday, returning on Thursday.

### Within Maluku

**Merpati** (☎ 352 481; Jl Ahmad Yani; ☽ 9am-4.30pm Mon-Fri, 9am-3pm Sat-Sun) connects several smaller airports. Flights can only be booked one way.

**Trigana Air** (☎ 343 393; Jl Soabali; ☽ 8am-8pm) offers handy Langgur–Ambon–Sanana–Ternate flights, returning next day. Beware that both Merpati and Trigana schedules are notorious for last-minute changes and cancellations.

### BOAT

Pelni services include *Ciremai* heading to Papua via Bandaneira (Banda Islands; seven hours) and Tual (Kei Islands; 21 hours), typically departing Ambon at 5pm on alternate Saturdays. The new *Dempo* sails non-stop to Sorong, continuing to Jayapura via Biak. Westbound *Ciremai*, *Lambelu*, *Nggapulu* and *Dempo* run to Makassar (34 hours) via Bau Bau (24 hours, except for *Dempo*). All but *Nggapulu* continue to Tanjung Priok (Jakarta, four days).

For Ternate the most comfortable option is *Lambelu*, currently departing at 2pm on alternate Tuesdays. It takes 20 hours via Namlea (Buru, four hours) and continues on to Bitung (northern Sulawesi), arriving at 9pm

Wednesday. Slower, less predictable *Sangiang* runs direct to Ternate (27 hours) one Tuesday per month, and via Namlea and Sanana on a different Monday (38 hours).

*Pangrango* runs to Kupang (four days) via Saumlaki (33 hours) and remote southwestern Maluku (p771). *Kelimutu* heads monthly to Tual (57 hours) via Banda (12 hours) and Saumlaki (36 hours).

Timetables are infamously changeable, so copy the monthly schedule at the glass-faced **Pelni** (☎ 348 219; ☽ 9am-3pm Mon-Fri, 9am-noon Sat) office. To buy tickets head down, around the back, then upstairs again, or purchase from any Pelni agency.

For non-Pelni boats see the boxed text, below. For Lease Islands car ferry timetables see p751.

Two yacht races also stop in Ambon, but to participate you must start in Darwin, Australia; see p745 for details.

### BUS & BEMO

Road transport (including buses to Seram via the Hunimua car ferry) starts from various points along Jl Pantai Mardika. For Natsepa (4000Rp), Tulehu-Momoking (5000Rp) and Tulehu-Hurnala (7000Rp) take Waai or Darussalam bemos. Latuhalat (3000Rp) and Amahusu bemos also pick up passengers beside the Trikora monument on Jl Dr Latumenten.

## Getting Around
### TO/FROM THE AIRPORT

Pattimura Airport is 30km round the bay from central Kota Ambon. Hatu- and Liliboi-bound bemos pass the airport gates (6000Rp,

---

**WHICH PORT?**

| Port | Destination | Notes |
|---|---|---|
| Galala | Namlea (Buru) | car ferry; alternate days |
| Hunimua | Waipirit (Seram) | main car ferry; six daily |
| Slamet Riyadi | Wahai, Kobi, Bula (Seram) | *kapal motor* |
| | Leksula (Buru) | *kapal motor* |
| Tulehu–Hurnala | Amahai (Seram) | jet boat; 8.30am & 3.30pm Mon-Sat |
| | Lease Islands, Seram | car ferry |
| | Haria (Pulau Saparua) | *kapal motor*; 1pm Mon-Sat |
| Tulehu market | Haruku, Oma, Rohomoni | speedboats; daily when full |
| | Kailolo (Pulau Haruku) | speedboats; daily when full |
| Tulehu–Momoking | Haria (Pulau Saparua) | speedboats; daily when full |
| | Pelauw (Pulau Haruku) | speedboats; daily when full |
| | Nusa Laut | speedboats; 7am Tue & Sat |
| Yos Sudarso | various | Pelni ships |
| | Namlea (Buru) | Bahari Express; alternate days |

70 minutes from Mardika). **Nusaniwe Indah** ( ☎ 353 714; Jl WR Supratman) runs a 5am airport minibus (50,000Rp, 50 minutes, prebooking essential) from outside Hotel Manise. Taxis charge 150,000Rp (sometimes negotiable).

### BEMO

For any bemo ride consider getting on/off at least 200m away from Mardika market (the terminus), where vehicles typically jostle interminably through chaotic traffic jams.

Ultrafrequent Lin III bemos *(mobils)* head southwest down Jl Pantai Mardika and either Jl Dr Sam Ratulangi or Jl AY Patty, swinging around the Trikora monument onto Jl Dr Latumenten. After 2km they loop back via Jl Sultan Babullah and Jl Yos Sudarso.

Tantui bemos run northeast from Mardika, passing the Commonwealth War Cemetery and Tantui Seafood, then looping back past the tourist office.

## AROUND PULAU AMBON

### Soya Atas

High above Ambon on the cool slopes of **Gunung Sirimau** (950m) is **Soya Atas** village, whose convincingly rebuilt **church** has risen from the ashes after being torched during the intercommunal strife of 2002. Across the road, a tacky **St Francis Xavier statue** recalls the original Jesuit's 1546 Christianising mission here. Steep footpaths lead down to Ema and other villages beyond.

### Southern Leitimur

**Latuhalat** straddles a low pass culminating in a pair of popular, well-shaded 'Sunday beaches' (admission 2000Rp), **Santai** and **Namalatu**. Neither offers great swimming but both have a hotel and dive operation (see boxed text, p750). Walk between the two in 15 minutes or take one of the famous **musical becak** (bicycle-rickshaws), which hit customers with maximum-decibel Indonesian pop.

Further east are two attractive **Pintu Kota** 'recreation parks', perched atop attractive meadows which end in cliffs plunging towards the crashing waves below. The coast road deadends at the forgotten little fishing village of **Seri**, where outriggers and drying cloves lie quietly beneath the giant *ketapang* trees.

### SLEEPING & EATING

There's an inexpensive village homestay tucked behind the Maluku Divers office.

**Santai Beach Hotel** ( ☎ 323 109; Pantai Santai, Latuhalat; r with fan/air-con 110,000/225,000Rp; ✖ ) Eight sea-facing air-con rooms come with terraces and curtained parking. Fan rooms are good value but set back with no view. The large restaurant is popular with Ambon weekenders.

**Hotel Lola** ( ☎ 323 882; www.divingmaluku.com; Namalatu, Latuhalat; per person full-board US$70; ✖ Oct-May) Operated by Maluku Divers but not restricted to their clients, this attractive if somewhat incomplete little resort has stylish garden bungalows with wicker furniture and framed dive photos. There's a laid-back waterfront beach bar but no beach.

### GETTING THERE & AWAY

Green 'Lt Halat' bemos from Kota Ambon (3000Rp, 40 minutes) run to Namalatu along a pretty waterside road through Eri, where an amusing **Hollywood sign** is painted in giant letters on the sea defences.

### Eastern Leihitu

A handful of bayside retreats offer a striking contrast to the bustle of Ambon 20km away. Family-friendly **Baguala Bay Resort** ( ☎ 362 717; Jl Raya; deluxe/cottage/ste 300,000/350,000/450,000 Rp; ✖ ➚ ) is set around a pair of well-kept swimming pools in a lovely waterfront palm garden that looks especially enchanting at night. Rooms attractively counterpoint white walls with dark wooden floors and oddments of local decor. The good-value seafront cafe serves Western and local food.

Around 3km further east, **Aston Natsepa** ( ☎ 362 257; www.astonambon.com; promotional/rack rate d from 726,000Rp/US$108; ✖ ➚ ) is Ambon's first full-blown four-star resort, complete with infinity pool, professional, ever-bowing English-speaking staff and a soaring Zen-modernist atrium. Fashionably mellow-toned new rooms come with fine white linen, minibar, safe and sea-facing balconies. Construction and landscaping remained incomplete when we visited. Minimal beach.

Right next door, the much simpler **Taman Lunterse Boer** ( ☎ 361 366; www.picturetrail.com/nat sepa; info@natsepa.org; d with fan/air-con 250,000/300,000Rp; ✖ ) has its own idyllic little beach (admission 2000Rp for nonguests) and six decent ensuite rooms with clean tiled floors and faintly old-fashioned little terraces with sea views.

Beyond, a 300m strip of very simple waterside snack-shack cafes leads to busier **Natsepa Main Beach** (admission 2000Rp), where three attractive

MALUKU

---

**DIVING AMBON**

Although there are alternatives on Saparua (p752) and Lelei (p736), Ambon is Maluku's main **scuba diving** centre. High-visibility highlights include coral-crusted volcanic pinnacles off Mahia and Hukurila, an underwater arch at Pintu Kota, a 1960s shipwreck at Waiame and red-toothed trigger-fish off Pulau Tiga's vertical wall. But Ambon is most celebrated for muck diving. Numerous bizarre critter species include the unique *Histiophryne psychedelica*, a weird, jet-propelled form of frogfish first spotted in October 2008 in an unaesthetic rubbish-strewn twilight zone off Laha port.

Professionally run **Maluku Divers** ( ☎ 323 882; www.divingmaluku.com; Namalatu, Latuhalat; 1/2/3 dives per day US$45/85/130, plus equipment rental US$35; ☼ Sep-late May) has local and expat dive masters who know the spots intimately.

Also recommended, **Blue Rose Divers** ( ☎ 323 883; www.bluerosedivers.com; Santai Beach Hotel, Latuhalat; 1/2/3 dives per day 750,000/1,000,000/1,100,000Rp, plus equipment rental 350,000Rp negotiable) are less fluent in spoken English but have similarly new equipment and a powerful dive boat. In the off-season ( ☼ May-Aug) their dives start from Hitu and visit the Tanjung Setan area.

Aston Natsepa (p749) also plans a dive centre.

---

new cottages are being built onto the wooded cliff behind.

**Waai** is famous for its 'lucky' *bulut* (Moray eels). For 10,000Rp, a gentleman named Bapak Minggus tempts the eels out of the dark recesses in a concrete-sided carp pond (Jl Air Waysilaka) by feeding them raw eggs. To find the pond (which doubles oddly as the village washing pool), get off Waai bemos one block before the thatched *baileu* (see boxed text, p738) and walk two blocks inland.

Kota Ambon–Natsepa–Waai bemos run remarkably frequently till around 8pm.

## Northern & Western Leihitu

Western Leihitu is home to some of Ambon's most picturesque and archetypal coastal villages. In **Alang**, a traditional thatched *baileu* rebuilt in 2004 sports a carved crocodile. In photogenic **Wakasihu** village elders while the day away at seaside platforms with views of an offshore, tree-topped mini-island. A sharper rock shard appears at the roadside beyond **Larike**. In north **Asilulu** there are multiple boat racks and fine views across to Seram's Tanjung Sial. Offshore lies Pulau Tiga, a trio of islands around which lie several diving and snorkelling spots.

**Negri Lima** hides the dumpy two-storey ruin of **Benteng Van Harlem**, a roofless Dutch-era tower. In **Hila** the decidedly more impressive 1649 **Benteng Amsterdam** (10,000Rp donation expected) retains hefty ramparts and a three-storey keep that's recently been reroofed though it's empty except for the swooping swallows. Seek out a key-holder to enter. That Hila should now be renowned for a Dutch fort is somewhat ironic considering it

was originally the power base of anticolonial Ambon. Five minutes' walk inland, then across a school football field, is Kaitetu's pretty little thatch-roofed **Mesjid Wapaue**. Originally built in 1414 on nearby Gunung Wawane, the mosque was supposedly transferred to the present site in 1664 by 'supernatural powers'.

### SLEEPING & EATING

Several simple options cater for travellers taking early flights from Pattimura Airport. Michael ( ☎ 0813 4302 8872) at the airport's tourist desk arranges simple 75,000Rp family homestays. Almost directly opposite the terminal, **Penginapan Dahlia** ( ☎ 0812 4722 8528; r with fan/air-con 120,000/160,000Rp; ✱ ) is a lime-green bungalow with simple new box rooms, private *mandi* and 'double' beds so narrow they'll challenge even the most intimate sleeping partners. Hidden in Laha village 2km away, **Pondok Paton** ( ☎ 0813 4323 0559; s/d 125,000/150,000Rp, with air-con 200,000/225,000Rp; ✱ ) has a pleasant little rear sitting area on stilts overlooking a boat-and-mangrove filled creek.

No other Western Leihitu villages have accommodation or restaurants, but roadside stalls in Lai and Wakal sell fruit and barbequed fish in the afternoon.

### GETTING THERE & AWAY

Bemos (5000Rp) leave semiregularly from Hunut to Hila and from Kota Ambon to Liliboi. To close the loop, charter an *ojek* from near the airport. The road is mostly new asphalt, but one short, rough section between the two halves of Asilulu village may prove too steep for cars.

# LEASE & SERAM

## LEASE ISLANDS

☎ 0931

Pronounced 'leh-*a*-say', these conveniently accessible yet delightfully laid-back islands have a scattering of old-world villages, lovely bays, great diving possibilities and a couple of great-value budget beach retreats. Foreign tourists remain very rare and little English is spoken, but Saparua is just starting to get 'rediscovered'.

Access is by boat, mostly from one of three ports at Tulehu (Pulau Ambon). Morning speedboats run to Tulehu-Momoking from Haria, Pelauw, Itawaka (5am only) and Nusa Laut (6.45am Monday and Friday, returning 7am next day). Heading from Haria (Saparua) a 7am *kapal motor* runs to Tulehu-Hurnala (two hours) returning at 1pm (not Sundays).

There are two car ferries, both starting from Tulehu-Hurnala. On Monday and Thursday *Mujair* departs at 9am and runs to Wailey (Pulau Seram, four hours) and back stopping en route both ways at Ume Putih (Pulau Saparua, 11.30am and 3pm). On Tuesdays *Samandar* departs at 9am and runs one way to Masohi (8½ hours) via Ume Putih (11.30am) and Nalahia (Nusa Laut, 2.15pm). It returns the same way Wednesday leaving Masohi at 8am and stopping in Nalahia about 11am and Ume Putih at 2pm. Timings can vary somewhat.

### Pulau Saparua

A sprinkling of offbeat accommodation choices lies amid Saparua's shaggy forests, friendly part-thatched villages and crystal-clear fish-filled waters. Dugongs reportedly appear in Saparua Bay and you might spot dolphins en route to uninhabited Pulau Molana, where you don't need Hollywood riches to have a desert island all for yourself.

#### KOTA SAPARUA

The low-walled 1676 **Benteng Duurstede** (admission free), famously besieged by Pattimura in 1817 (see boxed text, p752), has been refaced with mouldering grey concrete, but the gateway is original and the cannon-studded ramparts survey a gorgeous sweep of turquoise bay. Opposite, a large but sparse **museum** displays sweetly naive, glassed-in scenes where doll figures recreate scenes from Pattimura's anticolonial exploits. Bring a torch (there's no light inside) and get the key from Robert Mual. Robert runs the unsigned **Penginapan Benteng Duurstede** ( ☎ 21099; d 50,000Rp) directly behind. Its seven clean, simple rooms are superb value with little terrace areas facing a delightful sandy beach that's idyllic at dawn when you'll have it almost to yourself but gets noisy with local kids on afternoons and weekends. Cold beers and excellent home-cooked food are available to savour on your terrace if you preorder.

Two minutes' walk from the fort on one of Kota Saparua's two parallel main streets is the

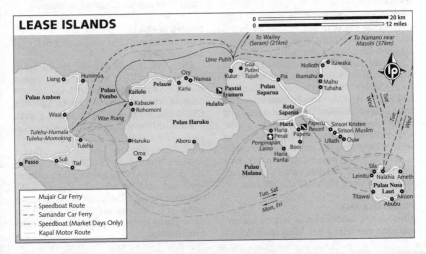

**LEASE ISLANDS**

0    20 km
0    12 miles

To Wailey (Seram) (21km)

To Namano near Masohi (37km)

Ume Putih

Liang   Hunimua

Pulau Ambon

Waai

Tulehu-Hurnala
Tulehu-Momoking

Passo   Suli   Tial
Tulehu

Ory
Pelauw   Namaa
Kailolo   Kariu
Kabauw
Rohomoni

Wae Riang

Haruku   Aboru

Oma

Pulau Pombo

Pulau Haruku

Goa Puteri
Kulur   Tujuh   Pia
Pantai
Iyanaen

Hulaliu

Nolloth   Itawaka
Ihamahu   Mahu
Tuhaha

Pulau Saparua

Kota Saparua

Haria   Paperu   Sirisori Kristen
Hania   Paperu   Sirisori Muslim
Perak   Ullath   Ouw
Penginapan   Booi
Laino
Hania
Pantai

Pulau Molana

Tue, Sat

Mon, Fri

Sila
Leinitu   Nalahia   Ameth
Pulau Nusa Laut
Titawai   Akoon
Abubu

Tue   Wed

Resort

— Mujair Car Ferry
⋯ Speedboat Route
– – Samandar Car Ferry
– · Speedboat (Market Days Only)
— Kapal Motor Route

## PATTIMURA & TIAHAHU

In 1817 the Dutch faced a small but emotionally charged uprising led by Thomas Matulessy, who briefly managed to gain control of Saparua's Benteng Duurstede. He killed all the fortress defenders but spared a six-year-old Dutch boy. For this minor 'mercy' Matulessy was popularly dubbed Pattimura ('big-hearted'). The rebels were rapidly defeated and dispatched to the gallows but have since been immortalised as symbols of anticolonial resistance. Today their statues dot the whole of Maluku, and Pattimura even features on Indonesia's 1000Rp banknotes. A much-romanticised heroine of the same saga is Martha Christine Tiahahu, whose father supported Pattimura. After his execution on Nusa Laut, Martha was put on a ship to Java but, grief-stricken, she starved herself to death. Her remains were thrown into the sea but her memory lingers on.

**Penginapan Lease Indah** (☎ 21040; Jl Muka Pasar; tw 70,000-80,000Rp; 🔀 ). Also great value, its well-maintained rooms are set around a pleasant palm garden culminating in a pair of bay-view pavilion seats decked in bougainvillea. It's hidden behind the co-owned **Penginapan Perdana** (☎ 21040; Jl Muka Pasar; d without/with TV 150,000/175,000Rp), whose flashy faux-marble reception desk covers both hotels, though its rooms aren't noticeably better.

Further along Jl Muka Pasar are a few *rumah makan,* the **market** (🕙 Wed & Sat) and a Telkom building, directly behind which is the **bemo terminal** (Jl Belakang). Facing the Zeba'ot Church, the innocently ill-named **SS Restaurant** (Jl Belakang; meals 15,000-35,000; 🕙 8am-8pm) is the most comfortable eatery in town.

From Kota Saparua *ojek* fares include Haria (5000Rp), Itawaka (15,000Rp), Ouw (10,000Rp) and Kulur (25,000Rp). Rare bemos cost about 40% less.

### HARIA

Saparua's main port is **Haria**, with two boxy churches, a big thatched *baileu* (see boxed text, p738) and a giant white cross above the sapphire-blue bay. A five-minute *ketinting* ride across that bay (or a convoluted 7km *ojek* trip by road and unpaved track) is **Haria Perak**, from which an 800m trail crosses a scrubby headland to the four-room **Penginapan Laino** (per person full board 100,000Rp). Utterly unsigned and astonishingly isolated, this do-nothing getaway commands a long, picturesque sweep of white, if none too soft, sand. Rooms are simple boxes with bucket *mandis*, basic vinyl flooring and no fans, but each has a sea-facing terrace with lovely views towards Pulau Molana.

### PULAU MOLANA

Uninhabited, roadless Pulau Molana has several great snorkelling and diving spots. A beak

of soft, dazzlingly white sand at the island's northernmost tip may be rather prone to snag driftwood, but there's great swimming here as the sand slopes down towards the east while directly west a coral wall offers excellent snorkelling. Best of all, you can stay directly behind the beach at the brand-new **Molana Bungalows** (http://molanaisland.com; tw full board 200,000-350,000Rp), a superb Robinson Crusoe hideaway that would be ideal for a small group of friends. Their bigger, thatched wooden bungalow called 'Marlatu' is spacious, with private bathroom and balcony. There's also a smaller bungalow ('Pieter'), plus two rather cramped rooms within the sturdy timber restaurant (shared bathrooms). The site is only staffed when guests are expected, so forewarn the owner **Pak Agus Kaya** (☎ 0813 4307 7423; umel_molanaislands@yahoo.co.id; Jl Sikar, Kampong Baru, Haria) or his English-speaking daughter Evie (☎ 0812 4716 4455) well ahead of your planned arrival. Meals (25,000Rp) are somewhat basic. A *ketinting*/speedboat from Haria costs around 120,000/250,000Rp.

### DIVING RESORTS

Saparua's crystal-clear waters offer richly rewarding diving.

On a wonderfully peaceful private headland 3km from Kota Saparua, Swiss-owned dive base **Cape Paperu Resort & Spa** (☎ 0811 470 0183; www.capepaperu.com; Paperu; s/d/tr from €76/130/165) limits dives to resident guests. Their sturdy thatched bungalows are spacious, airy and lightly decorated with stylish Balinese furniture and carvings. Bigger cottages (from €107/184/234) have partial sea views. Nondiving guests aren't encouraged and walk-ins are not accepted without reservation. The resort is 800m down unpaved Jl Tamasya off the Booi road but most guests arrive by private-boat transfer from Ambon.

The 15-room **Mahu Lodge** (Mahu village; per person half-board 150,000Rp) will be a much less exclusive dive operation when reconstruction is complete in 2010. Contact Tony at **Daya Patal** ( ☎ 0811 470 608; spicetr@gmail.com).

### NORTHEAST SAPARUA

**Nolloth** has Saparua's finest traditional *baileu*, a thatched if barn-like **church** (Gereja Darurat) and a selection of colourfully gaudy Christian statuettes. From adjoining **Itawaka** a 50,000Rp boat transfer takes you to Dutch-owned five-room **Penginapan Tolau Indah** (siahayav@xs4all.nl; r €25-50) nearing completion in blissful roadless isolation on a sea-facing cape with snorkelling possibilities. The best room (number 1) has a fabulous balcony overlooking Seram. Decor is tasteful and the shared bathrooms well built.

### SOUTHEAST SAPARUA

At **Ullath** is a traditional-style *baileu*, over-shadowed by the pointy-hatted tower of the Protestant church. The road dead-ends at **Ouw**, famous for its elegantly simple **pottery** *(sempe)*. None is obviously on show but any local can lead you to a workshop, where 5000Rp is a reasonable donation to watch craftsmen build up a typical bowl on an unpowered spindle device. Misleading advertisements suggest that there's a *penginapan* on a minuscule 'beach' called Nukuwoni around a roadless cape from Ouw. In fact this place has been closed and derelict for years.

### NORTHWEST SAPARUA

If you're heading to Kulur/Ume Putih for the ferry, you could make a short detour to the **Goa Puteri Tujuh** (Cave of Seven Princesses) containing a seven-section pool whose waters are so crystal-clear they're almost invisible. The access path heads inland 1.1km east of Ume Putih. After four minutes' walk, descend a short stairway beside a rusty pavilion.

### GETTING THERE & AWAY

Predawn speedboats run from Itawaka (55,000Rp) to Tulehu-Momoking (Ambon) and from Ihamahu (45,000Rp, one hour) to Namano near Masohi (Seram). Arrive by 4.30am, get your name on the passenger list, then pay for the ticket later when your name is called. From Haria to Ambon there's a 7am *kapal motor* (35,000Rp, two hours, not Sundays) and several speedboats (mostly early morning, 45,000Rp, leave when full).

## Pulau Nusa Laut

Nusa Laut's 'capital' **Ameth** strictly protects its very fine offshore **coral gardens** by *sasi* (see boxed text, p768), so before snorkelling here, pay a 25,000Rp per person *sasi*-removal fee to the village raja (chief). The village has a kitschy 'clock-carrying' **statue** and an unusual octagonal **Beth-Eden church**. Unmarked **Penginapan Pari Nussa** (Jl Pendidikan; per person 50,000Rp) is a relatively new house facing the football pitch at Ameth's easternmost end. Rooms have fans, en-suite bucket *mandis* and clean squat toilets.

In **Sila** the attractive 1719 **Ebenhaezer church** is Maluku's oldest, but fake tiling on the roof is garishly new. Nearby the cube-shaped 1654 Dutch fort, **Benteng Beverwyk**, has been completely rebuilt with thatched roof and cement wall rendering that needs time to age. Crawling through the window slits you can access a wooden stairway to the roof terrace for bay views. Between fort and church, friendly local English teacher **Robert Abraham** ( ☎ 0852 4355 5106) offers a single twin-bed **homestay room** (per person 50,000Rp; ⏲ from 3pm) in his typical cottage home.

The island's most picturesque villages are **Nalahia** with its steep stairways and **Akoon** with a small thatched *baileu* and shuttered church. **Titawai**'s setting backed by steep forests is relatively dramatic. **Abubu** features a statue of Martha Christina Tiahahu and the large 1895 Irene Church.

More daring *ojek* drivers are prepared to do a full loop of the island for around 100,000Rp (two hours including short stops), but beware that the Titawai–Leinitu section is a narrow, overgrown footpath, not a road.

### GETTING THERE & AWAY

For the weekly car-ferry timetable see p751. Speedboats leave Ameth and Sila for Tulehu-Momoking on Monday and Fridays(60,000Rp, 6.45am), returning the next day. Wednesday and Saturday dawn speedboats from each Nusa Laut village shuttle to Kota Saparua market (25,000Rp each way), returning by lunchtime. Chartering a *Johnson* longboat *from* Nusa Laut is easy enough and cheapest if you head for Ouw (from 150,000Rp departing Sila, 250,000Rp from Ameth). Chartering *to* Nusa Laut is tougher and relatively expensive as no appropriate boats moor in Ouw.

MALUKU

MALUKU

## Pulau Haruku

Pulau Haruku has no formal accommodation, so visits are easiest as day trips from Ambon or in linking Ambon with Pulau Saparua. The quietly quaint Christian village of **Haruku** is famous for its November **Sasi Lompa festival**, marking the end of the annual prohibition (see boxed text, p768) on catching *lompa* flying fish. **Rohomoni** sports Maluku's most impressive **thatch-roofed mosque**. There are some attractive beaches located east of **Kailolo**.

**Pelauw**, Pulau Haruku's main village, has a pitiful fortress ruin and a tacky **Cakalele monument** celebrating the island's other major festival. At the western end of **Hulaliu** village, **Pantai Iyanaen** is a narrow, sandy beach with some lovely sweeps of view towards Saparua and Seram.

### GETTING THERE & AWAY

Speedboats leave when full (fairly regularly till afternoon) from behind Tulehu market (Ambon) to Haruku, Oma, Rohomoni and Kailolo villages (15,000Rp, 15 minutes). From beside a prominent orange building at Tulehu-Momoking, speedboats depart when full to Pelauw (25,000Rp, 25 minutes), mostly from 10am to 4pm. From Hulaliu a chartered speedboat to Haria (Saparua) costs around 150,000Rp.

### GETTING AROUND

Rare bemos run between Pelauw and Kailolo. Sample *ojek* fares include Kailolo–Rohomoni (5000Rp), Kailolo–Haruku (40,000Rp) and Pelauw–Hulaliu (20,000Rp).

## PULAU SERAM
☎ 0914

Some Malukans call Seram 'Nusa Ina' (Mother Island), believing that all life sprang from 'Nunusaku', a mythical peak ambiguously located somewhere in the island's western mountains. The best known of Seram's indigenous minority tribes, the Nua-ulu ('upper-river') or Alifuro people, sport red bandana headgear and were head-hunters as recently as the 1940s. They live in Seram's wild, mountainous interior whose thick forests are alive with cockatoos and colourful parrots, but seeing them usually requires a punishingly masochistic trek into the remote Manusela National Park for which you'll need guides and extra permits. Bula

on the northeast coast is an oil town (www .citicresources.com/eng/business/oil.htm) serving the inland Oseil field. Seram's greatest tourist attraction is dramatic Teluk Sawai on the northern coast.

### GETTING THERE & AWAY

**Merpati** ( ☎ 0813 4339 5512, 0813 3043 1092; Jl MC Tiahahu) flies Amahai–Banda–Ambon both ways on Sunday, with Amahai–Banda tickets often easier to procure than Ambon–Banda runs. Ambon–Wahai–Ambon flights operate on Thursday.

Cramped, direct buses perfumed with durian and sweat operate from Mardika in Kota Ambon to various Seram towns including Masohi, Tehoru and Piru (they typically leave Ambon at 3am and 7am), using the Hunimua–Waipirit car ferry (12,000Rp extra). Overnight departures leave Ambon on alternate days, including the 7.30pm **Gumilang** ( ☎ 0812 4717 9632) bus to Sawai (120,000Rp, 11 hours).

It's more comfortable to start with the twice-daily Amahai jet boat (75,000Rp, 2½ hours) departing Tulehu-Hurnala at 8.30am and 3.30pm, returning at 8am and 1.30pm (no Sunday service). Daily speedboats from Namano cross to Ihamahu (Pulau Saparua) at around 7am (45,000Rp, one hour).

## Masohi, Namano & Amahai

Neat if slightly dull, Masohi is the spacious purpose-built capital of central Maluku. It's only really useful to travellers as a transport interchange, though technically you're still supposed to sign in with the **Masohi Police** (Jl Dr Siwabessy; ⏰ 9am-2.30pm Mon-Fri) before proceeding elsewhere in Seram. Main street Jl Soulissa heads southwest from the terminal, market and Masohi Plaza shopping mall becoming Jl Martha Tiahahu in the Christian suburbs and continuing 6km through Namano to Amahai. Here, just before Amahai's main port, the larger road turns 90 degrees heading 1km to the airport, passing the minuscule statuette-fronted **Sangar Budaya Seram Museum** ( ☎ 22102; Soahuku; suggested donation 10,000Rp; ⏰ by request) opposite Amahai's Ebenhaezer church. It's not really a museum at all; you'll see a few very gaudy mock-Alifuro *salawaka* (thin shields), tacky head-dresses (for sale) and *tipa* (drums) on which neighbours might accompany curator Nus Tamaela as he plays

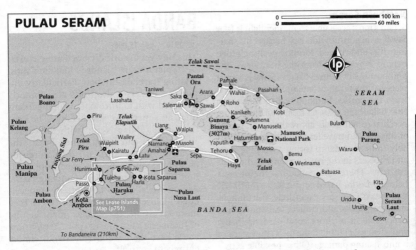

PULAU SERAM

SERAM SEA

BANDA SEA

the *totobuan* (12-bell gamelan, or traditional Javanese/Balinese orchestra) or tells stories in easy Bahasa Indonesia about traditional Nua-ulu/Alifuro ceremonies. Most involve severed heads.

Masohi has a warnet (internet centre) and several ATMs. Friendly if far from informative, the **Central Maluku Tourist Office** (Dinas Kebudayan & Parawisata; ☎ 21462; Jl Imam Bonjol; ☷ 8am-2pm Mon-Sat) is where you'd start the three-stage application process for Manusela National Park permits.

When time allows, friendly English teacher **Max Dopeng** ( ☎ 0812 4705 6459) doubles as freelance guide, tourist helper and 'super-*ojek*'.

### SLEEPING

There's plenty of accommodation if you're stuck here though much of it (especially in central Masohi) is a little unkempt. Ultrafrequent Masohi–Amahai bemos pass by or near all of the following.

**Penginapan Irene** ( ☎ 21238; Jl MC Tiahahu, Masohi; s/d/tw with fan from 70,000/85,000/120,000Rp, with air-con from 160,000/185,000/180,000Rp; ❄ ) The Irene (pronounced 'ee-reh-neh') is friendly, professionally run and suffers less road noise than most. Best choices are in the 200,000Rp range, around an attractive floral shrubbery. Many cheaper rooms are windowless.

**Hotel-Restaurant Isabella** ( ☎ 22637; Jl Manusela 17; s with fan 75,000-95,000Rp, d with air-con from 185,000Rp; ❄ ❄ ) A colourful lobby leads to mostly cramped and/or windowless rooms, but 'executive' rooms (265,000Rp) are comfortable,

with windows, hot showers and settee seating. Oddly plonked in the car park is a sizeable swimming pool open to nonguests for 10,000Rp. From the New Lelemuku head one block south, then two blocks inland.

**Hotel New Lelemuku** ( ☎ 21581; Jl MC Tiahahu, Masohi; tw with fan/air-con 90,000/185,000Rp) Decent new rooms around an ill-conceived indoor water feature.

**Lounusa Beach Hotel** ( ☎ 21379; Jl MC Tiahahu, Namano; d 100,000-150,000Rp; ❄ ) Rooms are clean if not extraordinary, but the attraction here are the free cups of tea taken on delightful little rough-wood pavilion-platforms that extend on stilts into the bay behind the hotel's patch of mangrove bank (despite the name, there's no beach). Owners speak Dutch and limited English.

### EATING

Numerous cheap eateries and evening warung tents are dotted along Masohi's main drag, especially within a block or two of Masohi Plaza.

**Cak Eko** (Jl Soulissa; meals 9000-20,000Rp, bakso 10,000Rp; ☷ 8am-11pm) Naturally cooled by traditional design, this bright, thatched barn is part of the Bakso Malang Kota chain.

**Afsal** (Jl Binaya; meals 13,000Rp; ☷ 7.30am-10.30pm) Attached to the otherwise disappointing Afsal Hotel, this restaurant has Masohi's most appealing interior with solid black furniture, mirrored wall panels and checkerboard floors. Food is a good if typical preprepared selection.

MALUKU

## Northern Seram

Seram's most accessible scenic highlight is **Teluk Sawai**, a beautiful wide bay backed by soaring cliffs and rugged, forested peaks. Hidden behind a headland from the best views, the photogenic stilt-house village of **Sawai** is a great place to unwind and contemplate moonlit seas from the creaky, bamboo-walled **Penginapan Lisar Bahari** (per person full board 200,000Rp). Being perched romantically above the water, rooms at this age-old traveller favourite are predictably somewhat damp (bring a sleeping mat) and showers in the basic en-suite bathrooms are salty. There's no phone but the owner's helpful Masohi-based cousin **Wati** ( ☎ 0852 3050 5806) speaks English. Cost includes fish dinners, assorted snacks and endless tea. Snorkelling is possible in offshore coral gardens (bring your own gear) though the reefs show signs of bomb-fishing damage. Other possible activities include boat rides to Pulau Raja or to the bay's most spectacular western side, where dramatic cliffs rise up above the picturesque village of **Saleman**. It's famed for flocks of bat-like **Lusiala birds**, which emerge at dusk supposedly bearing the souls of human ancestors. En route, tempting little **Ora** is a handkerchief of marvellously spongy, white-sand beach on which the six rooms and pavilion restaurant of **Ora Beach Hotel** (per person full board 400,000Rp) were finally nearing completion at the time of writing. Check opening details through Ambon's Baguala Bay Resort (p749).

Well east of Sawai, lethargic little **Wahai** once housed Seram's main Dutch garrison, but a small, cannon-topped mound of stones is all that remains of the fort. There's inexpensive accommodation but little incentive to visit.

### GETTING THERE & AWAY

Bus-ferry-bus combinations (120,000Rp) run Ambon–Sawai on alternate days. Masohi–Sawai Kijangs run according to customer numbers (per person/vehicle 125,000/600,000Rp, 3½ hours). Rare Masohi–Wahai buses can drop you off at a deserted junction 6km above Sawai to make the sweaty descent on foot. If the rain holds off, Masohi–Sawai is much more appealing by ojek (around 150,000Rp), with some attractive areas of mountain forest en route. By prior arrangement the Lisar Bahari can arrange a longboat-Kijang connection via Saka, a beautiful boat ride from Sawai.

# BANDA ISLANDS

☎ 0910 / pop 15,000

This tiny yet historically fascinating cluster of 10 picturesque islands is Maluku's most inviting travel destination. Particularly impressive undersea drop-offs are vibrantly plastered with multicoloured coral gardens offering superlative snorkelling. The central islands Pulau Neira (with the capital Bandaneira) and Pulau Banda Besar (the great nutmeg island) curl in picturesque crescents around a pocket-sized tropical Mt Fuji (Gunung Api; 666m). Outlying Hatta, Ai and Neilaka each have utterly undeveloped picture-postcard beaches. Were they more accessible, the Bandas might be one of Indonesia's top tourist spots. Yet for now you'll have these wonderful islands almost entirely to yourself.

## History

Nutmeg, once produced almost exclusively in the Banda Islands, was reputed to ward off bubonic plague, making it one of the medieval world's most expensive commodities. Growing nutmeg takes knowledge but minimal effort, so the drudgery of manual labour was virtually unknown in the Bandas. Food, cloth and all necessities of life could be easily traded for spices with eager Arab, Chinese, Javanese and Bugis merchants who queued up to do business. Things started to go wrong when the Europeans arrived, the Portuguese in 1512, then the Dutch from 1599. These strange barbarians had no foodstuffs to trade, just knives, impractical woollens and useless trinkets of mere novelty value. So when they started demanding a trade monopoly, the notion was laughable nonsense. However, since the Dutch were dangerously armed, some orang kaya (elders) signed a 'contract' to keep them quiet. Nobody took it at all seriously. The Dutch sailed away and were promptly forgotten. But a few years later they were back, furious to find the English merrily trading nutmeg on Pulau Run and Pulau Ai. Entrenching themselves by force, the dominant Dutch played cat and mouse with the deliberately provocative English, while trying unsuccessfully to enforce their mythical monopoly on the locals. In 1621 Jan Pieterszoon Coen, the new governor general of the VOC (Dutch East India Company), ordered the virtual genocide of the Bandanese. Just a few hundred survivors escaped to the Kei Islands.

# BANDA ISLANDS

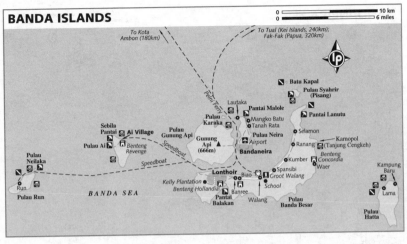

MALUKU

Coen's VOC thereupon provided slaves and land grants to oddball Dutch applicants in return for a promise that they'd settle permanently in the Bandas and produce fixed-priced spices exclusively for the company. These folk, known as *perkeniers* (from the Dutch word *perk,* meaning 'ground' or 'garden'), established nearly 70 plantations mostly on Banda Besar and Ai.

This system survived for almost 200 years but corruption and mismanagement meant that the monopoly was never as profitable as it might have been. By the 1930s, the Bandas were a place of genteel exile for better-behaved anti-Dutch dissidents including Mohammed Hatta (future Indonesian vice president) and Sultan Syahrir (later prime minister). The small school they organised while in Bandaneira inspired a whole generation of anticolonial youth.

In the 1999 troubles, churches were burnt and at least five people were killed at Walang including the 'last *perkenier*', Wim de Broeke. Most of the Christian minority fled to Seram, but the islands rapidly returned to their delightfully torpid calm.

## Activities
### SNORKELLING
Crystal-clear seas, shallow-water drop-offs and coral gardens teeming with multicoloured reef life offer magnificently pristine snorkelling off **Pulau Hatta**, eastern **Banda Besar** and **Pulau Ai**. Some Bandaneira homestays rent fins and snorkels to guests.

### DIVING
Bandaneira's Hotel Maulana (p760) has the Bandas' only diving operation. Rental of their new *Scubapro* BCDs, regulators, wetsuit sets costs US$38.50 in addition to dive prices (single/double/triple dive US$49.50/93.50/132) and various fuel surcharges. That's especially expensive considering that there's no resident dive master. If groups book well ahead, Maluku Divers (www.divingmaluku.com; see boxed text, p750) can send an experienced dive leader across from Ambon.

## BANDANEIRA
pop 6000

Little Bandaneira has always been the Bandas' main port and administrative centre. In the Dutch era the townsfolk virtually bankrupted themselves maintaining a European lifestyle in spacious mansions that needed rebuilding whenever Gunung Api's volcanic huffs burnt them down again. Today Bandaneira's sleepy, flower-filled streets are so quiet that two becak count as a traffic jam. It's a charmingly friendly place, ideal to wander aimlessly admiring late-colonial houses, pondering mouldering ruins, watching glorious cloudscapes over Gunung Api and stumbling across the odd historic cannon lying randomly in the grass.

## Information
There's no tourist office, but several guest houses have helpful English-speaking owners. Delfika (p760) gives its guests a free, basic island map and produces souvenir DVDs

MALUKU

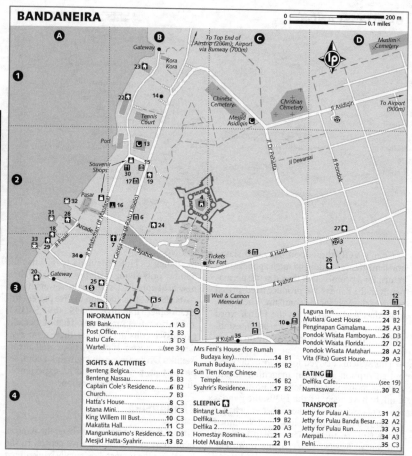

## BANDANEIRA

0 ————— 200 m
0 ————— 0.1 miles

To Top End of
Airstrip (200m); Airport
via Runway (700m)

Gateway
Kora
Kora

Muslim ×
Cemetery

To Airport
(900m)

Chinese
Cemetery

Christian
Cemetery

Mesjid
Asidiqin

Jl Asidiqin

Tennis
Court

Port

Jl Dr Palatta

Jl Dewanai

Jl Pondok

Souvenir
Shops

Pasar

Arcade

Jl Pasar

Jl Pelabuhan (Jl Ratu Untuelo)

Jl Gereja (Jl Ratu Untuelo)

Jl Syahrir

Tickets
for Fort

Jl Hatta

Jl Syahrir

Gateway

Well & Cannon
Memorial

Jl Kujali

**INFORMATION**
BRI Bank.................................1 A3
Post Office..............................2 B3
Ratu Cafe...............................3 D3
Wartel................................(see 34)

**SIGHTS & ACTIVITIES**
Benteng Belgica.....................4 B2
Benteng Nassau.....................5 B3
Captain Cole's Residence.......6 B2
Church...................................7 B3
Hatta's House........................8 C3
Istana Mini............................9 C3
King Willem III Bust.............10 C3
Makatita Hall.......................11 C3
Mangunkusumo's Residence..12 D3
Mesjid Hatta-Syahrir............13 B2

Mrs Feni's House (for Rumah
  Budaya key)......................14 B1
Rumah Budaya.....................15 B2
Sun Tien Kong Chinese
  Temple..............................16 B2
Syahrir's Residence..............17 B2

**SLEEPING**
Bintang Laut.........................18 A3
Delfika..................................19 C3
Delfika 2...............................20 A3
Homestay Rosmina...............21 A3
Hotel Maulana......................22 B1

Laguna Inn...........................23 B1
Mutiara Guest House ..........24 B2
Penginapan Gamalama.........25 A3
Pondok Wisata Flamboyan...26 D3
Pondok Wisata Florida.........27 D2
Pondok Wisata Matahari......28 A2
Vita (Fita) Guest House.........29 A3

**EATING**
Delfika Cafe.......................(see 19)
Namasawar..........................30 B2

**TRANSPORT**
Jetty for Pulau Ai................31 A2
Jetty for Pulau Banda Besar..32 A3
Jetty for Pulau Run..............33 A3
Merpati.................................34 A3
Pelni....................................35 C3

(50,000Rp). For great historical background, read *Indonesian Banda* by Willard A Hanna, available from some souvenir shops and (more expensive) from the Rumah Budaya museum.

Very slow web access is available at guest houses Mutiara and Delfika (25,000Rp per hour).

Bring ample rupiah from Ambon. **BRI bank** (Bank Rakyat Indonesia; Jl Kujali) has no exchange facilities and no ATM (yet). In extremis, Abba at Mutiara Guest House (p760) can change US dollars and euros when he's in town.

A tiny area around **Ratu Cafe** (Jl Hatta) is nicknamed 'SMS corner' as it's the only place in the Bandas to receive a mobile phone signal.

## Sights

### FORTRESSES

In 1608, Dutch Admiral Verhoeven ordered the building of **Benteng Nassau** on foundations abandoned by the Portuguese in 1529. This was against the most express wishes of local island leaders, who ambushed and executed some 40 Dutch 'negotiators' including Verhoeven himself. The Dutch retaliated in 1621 with the infamous beheading and quartering of 44 *orang kaya* within the fortress, followed by the virtual genocide of the entire Bandanese population.

Three years later the more commanding **Benteng Belgica** (admission 20,000Rp; ☾ sporadic) was added on the hill above. It's a classic Vauban-style star fort named Belgica for Governor

General Pieter Both's native Flanders. The five massive sharp-pointed bastions were expensively crafted to deflect the cannon-fire of a potential English naval bombardment. So in 1796 it caused quite a scandal in Holland when the Brits managed to seize it (albeit briefly) without firing a shot.

From the 1860s both fortresses lapsed into ruin. Benteng Nassau remains largely overgrown, but Benteng Belgica was extensively restored in the 1990s. To reach the upper ramparts (with great views), take the second arch on the left from the central courtyard.

### MUSEUM

Bandaneira's main museum, **Rumah Budaya** (Jl Gereja Tua; admission 20,000Rp), houses scatterings of amphorae, Dutch coins, *genever* flagons, a working wind-up gramophone and enough minicannons to marry off a whole village of Kei Islanders. Several lurid paintings, maps and fading photos have English captions. When closed, the museum's key is available from caretaker Mrs Feni, who lives about 200m further north.

### HISTORIC HOUSES

Several historically significant Dutch-era buildings have been restored. If you manage to gain access at all (knock and hope!), much of the fun of a visit is hearing the fascinating life stories of the septuagenarian caretakers, assuming your Bahasa Indonesia is up to the task. Donations (around 10,000Rp per person) are appropriate.

Of three early-20th-century 'exile houses', **Hatta's House** (Jl Hatta) is the most appealing. It's partly furnished and Hatta's distinctive spectacles and neatly folded suit are visible in a display cupboard. Behind is the little schoolhouse that he ran in the late 1930s. **Mangunkusumo's Residence** ( ☎ 21215; Jl Kujali) has a grander portico but only one very sparse 'museum room'. **Syahrir's Residence** (Jl Gereja Tua) has just a few mementos of specialist interest.

**Captain Cole's Residence** (Jl Gereja Tua) is the supposed lodgings of the British Marine commander who recaptured Benteng Belgica in 1810. This was just after they'd handed it back to the Dutch, having grabbed it in 1796. The roof is collapsing and it's closed to the public.

The grand but eerily empty 1820s **Istana Mini** (Jl Kujali) was a later residence for the Bandas' Dutch governors, and a haughty, medal-spangled bust of Dutch King Willem III rusts quietly in the side garden. **Makatita Hall** (Jl Kujali) occupies the site of the former Harmonie Club (aka 'the Soc') that once boasted seven snooker tables and was the focus of colonial-era social events.

### RELIGIOUS BUILDINGS

Behind the main port is the eye-catching **Mesjid Hatta-Syahrir**. Some locals claim this was converted into a mosque from the mansion that first accommodated Hatta and Syahrir on their arrival in 1936.

The 300-year-old **Sun Tien Kong Chinese Temple** (Jl Pelabuhan) looks intriguing glimpsed through the exterior wall at night.

The restored 1852 **church** (Jl Gereja Tua) has a portico of four chubby columns, a decorative bell-clock and an antique tombstoned floor.

Separate Chinese, Christian and Muslim cemeteries are ranged around Mesjid Asidiqin in the Merdeka area.

## Activities

Though not Banda's best place for **snorkelling**, Bandaneira has pleasant coral gardens at the southern end of **Tanah Rata** village, off the eastern end of the airstrip and to the northeast off **Pantai Malole**. A notable marine attraction is spotting populations of **mandarin fish** that emerge at dusk from rubble piles within Neira harbour. Though tiny, these fish are dazzlingly colourful, their whirring fins and lurid blue-orange markings seemly designed by artistic six-year olds on acid. Snorkellers can find them in the shallows between the Vita and Bintang Laut guest houses. Divers can find deeper water populations just off the Hotel Maulana. Bring underwater torches.

## Sleeping

### BUDGET

Over a dozen family guest houses and homestays offer simple but clean rooms, almost all with en-suite *mandi*. Vita, Mutiara and Delfika are best set up for foreign travellers, with spoken English, great free breakfasts, snorkel rentals (15,000Rp per day) and help with boat hire always at hand. Vita and Delfika 2, along with Bintang Laut and the otherwise lacklustre Matahari, offer the major plus of a waterfront location. Where air-con is available, choosing not to have it turned on means you'll pay only the fan rate.

MALUKU

**Delfika** (☎ 21027; delfika1@yahoo.com; r with fan 60,000-125,000Rp, with air-con 125,000-150,000Rp; ✶ ) There are two locations. For great bay views, upstairs rooms at the brand-new Delfika 2 annex are hard to beat. Meanwhile, the original Delfika has an old-world charm with appealing sitting room, atmospheric garden courtyard and a range of rooms mostly well renovated. The Delfika Cafe is one of Banda's most convivial.

**Bintang Laut** (☎ 21183; Jl Pasar; tw with fan/air-con 75,000/95,000Rp) The big plus here is a communal view jetty, but little English is spoken and clean rooms are rather dark, facing each other across a covered hallway.

**Penginapan Gamalama** (☎ 21053; Jl Gereja Tua; tw with fan/air-con 75,000/100,000Rp; ✶ ) Functional, relatively large rooms beyond some gratuitous tree-effect concrete pillars. There's plenty of communal seating.

**Homestay Rosmina** (☎ 21145; Jl Kujali; s/tw 75,000/85,000Rp) Small, lacklustre homestay where manager 'Bob' speaks rather frenetic English.

**OUR PICK Vita Guest House** (Fita; ☎ 21332; al landarman@gmail.com; Jl Pasar; d with fan/air-con from 80,000/100,000Rp; ✶ ) Seven comfortable rooms form a colonnaded L around a waterfront palm garden whose wonderful wooden jetty area is an ideal perch from which to gaze at Gunung Api while sipping a cold beer. Allan and family are endlessly helpful and quietly entertaining. There's a useful communal kitchen and fridge.

**Mutiara Guest House** (☎ 21344, 0813 3034 3377; banda_mutiara@yahoo.com; s/d/air-con r 80,000/90,000/125,000Rp; ✶ 🖳 ) The Mutiara has superb-value new rooms and sturdy, classically styled furniture. Some elements suggest nouveau-riche suburban America, but the curious melange includes parrots, an artificial waterfall, a spice garden and a veritable museum of local collectables. Ever-energetic owner 'Abba' is tirelessly helpful when he's not globetrotting for his pearl business. Most guests meet up for the generous, convivial dinner (50,000Rp).

**Pondok Wisata Matahari** (☎ 21050; Jl Pasar; tw 80,000-100,000Rp) Three of the rather tired rooms look out towards Gunung Api.

**Pondok Wisata Flamboyan** (☎ 21233; Jl Syahrir; s/tw full-board 100,000/150,000Rp) Quiet if fairly ordinary rooms with hard beds and no mosquito screens around a lawn with a *jambu* tree. Renowned for great home cooking.

**Pondok Wisata Florida** (☎ 21086; Jl Hatta; r 100,000Rp) Although this aging family home has some curious oddments of old furniture including antique bedsteads and lamps, rooms are rather basic and underlit.

### MIDRANGE

**Hotel Maulana** (☎ 21022; lawere@cbn.net.id; standard/ deluxe/ste US$60/78/84; ✶ ) This pseudocolonial-style palace hotel has a lovely verandah overlooking the waterfront between palms and shaggy *ketapang* trees, with the best views from top-floor suites (no elevators). However, room decor lacks personality, and cleaning and service seem a little haphazard given the prices (negotiable). Save $10 for single occupancy. Save another $10 for rooms at the Laguna Inn annex, which has similar pros and cons.

## Eating

Frequent cups of tea and a light breakfast are generally included in room prices, and almost every place will serve lunch or dinner (35,000Rp to 50,000Rp per person) on advance request. Mutiara, Vita and Gamalama serve cold beer (30,000Rp) to their guests. Delicious local favourites worth requesting include fish in nutmeg-fruit sauce and eggplant with *kenari*-almond sauce. These are available along with seasonal fruit juices (9500Rp) and delicious nutmeg-jam pancakes at **Delfika Cafe** (mains 15,000-30,000Rp; no alcohol).

Half a dozen non–guest house eateries lie a bone's throw of Bandaneira's port, offering *nasi ikan* from 6000Rp. **Namasawar** (☎ 21136; Jl Pelabuhan; mains 10,000-30,000Rp) has the nicest decor with split-level bamboo seating and gingham tablecloths. Several places will cook fresh seafood to order: you can accompany the owner to the market to choose your fish.

Street vendors sell presmoked fish on a stick, sticky rice, dried nutmeg-fruit slices, and pricey but delicious *halua-kenari* almond brittle. In December try *anggur*, fruits which look like black olives but taste like mildly astringent grapes.

## Shopping

Several souvenir shops on Jl Pelabuhan sell a small variety of souvenirs, postcards, 'antiques', pearls, contrived artefacts and genuine local snacks.

## Getting There & Away

As you tear your hair over minimalist, ever-changeable transport connections, bear in mind that were it not so infuriatingly awkward to reach, Banda would not be the blissfully unspoilt delight that it is today.

### AIR

**Merpati** ( ☎ 21060; Jl Pelabuhan) flies both ways Ambon–Bandaneira–Amahai on Sunday. Consider phoning your guest house and asking them to prebook your return flight before you even arrive. Beware that last-minute itinerary changes and cancellations are all too common.

### BOAT

**Pelni's** ( ☎ 21196; Jl Kujali; ☼ 8.30am-1pm & 4-6pm Mon-Sat) *Ciremai* arrives at Bandaneira every second Saturday night just before midnight from Makassar (47 hours) via Bau Bau (Sulawesi) and Ambon (seven hours). After circling through Tual (Kei Islands; 11 hours) and two Papuan ports, the ship returns the other way departing Banda at 7pm on Tuesday…assuming it's on time. That means you'll have less than three days on Banda if making a return to/from Ambon. Once a month there's an extra Ambon–Banda run on the smaller, overcrowded *Kelimutu* (12 hours) continuing to Saumlaki. Beware of pickpockets at any Pelni embarkation. Irregular cargo boats run without schedule (roughly weekly) to Tehoru or Masohi in southern Seram. Chartering a longboat to Tehoru is pricey (diesel/petrol 2,000,000/3,000,000Rp, 10/six hours).

## Getting Around

The island is walkably small but *ojeks* save sweat at 3000Rp per hop, 10,000Rp to the airport or 15,000Rp to Pantai Malole. Mutiara and Vita guest houses rent mountain bikes (40,000Rp per day). Several guest houses offer free airport pick-ups. Typical boat-charter rates for full-day trips including snorkelling stops include Ai (350,000Rp), Hatta (450,000Rp), Karnopol and Pisang (300,000Rp), and Run, Neilaka and Ai (500,000Rp). Diesel boats are cheaper but considerably slower.

## PULAU GUNUNG API

This devilish little 666m volcano has always been a threat to Bandaneira, Lonthoir and anyone attempting to farm its fertile slopes. Its most recent eruption in 1988 killed three people, destroyed over 300 houses and filled the sky with ash for days. Historically, Gunung Api's eruptions have often proved to be spookily accurate omens of approaching intruders.

The volcano can be climbed for awesome sunrise views in around three hours up and back, but the unrelenting slope is arduous and the loose scree is scary especially when descending. Take ample drinking water. Guides (from 50,000Rp) are prepared to accompany hikers but the path up is obvious.

The waters around Gunung Api hide several attractive coral gardens, home to lurid purple-and-orange sea squirts, remarkably fast-growing table corals and concentrations of (mostly harmless) sea snakes. Especially good for snorkelling are the submerged north-coast lava flows ('New Lava') and areas off little Pulau Karaka's handkerchief of beach reached by chartered *ketinting* from Bandaneira (half-day around 100,000Rp).

## PULAU BANDA BESAR
### pop 6000

The largest island of the group, hilly Banda Besar makes a great day trip and offers some interesting woodland walks. Boats shuttle regularly from Bandaneira to several Banda Besar jetties, most frequently to **Walang** (per person/boat 4000/30,000Rp, 15 minutes). *Ojeks* (5000Rp) run via **Biao** village (home of a scraggy pet cassowary) to **Banree** where the asphalt ends. If you walk 10 minutes west along the narrow concrete sea-defence wall, you'll emerge at the new but photogenic **Masjid Al Taqwa** mosque in **Lonthoir** (pronounced 'lontor'). This is Banda Besar's sleepy, steeply layered 'capital' village whose main 'street' is actually a long stairway. That starts beside **Homestay Leiden** (Jl Warataka; per person 50,000Rp), which offers two neat guest rooms (thin mattresses, shared *mandi*) in the attractive house of earnest, English-speaking Usman Abubakar. At the top of the stairway turn right to find the **Kelly Plantation** where centuries-old, buttressed *kenari* trees tower protectively over a nutmeg grove. Or turn left to find **Benteng Hollandia**. Built in 1624, this was once one of the biggest Dutch fortresses in the Indies until shattered by a devastating 1743 earthquake. The chunky overgrown ruins are easy to miss but the site, high above the village, offers perfect palm-framed views of Gunung Api with a magical foreground of sapphire-blue shallows.

Between the steps and the fort, look for a colonnade-wrapped mosque called Masolah Asalihim and take a hidden path behind to descend southwards to **Pantai Balakan** (aka Laerkoey Beach). That's a pleasant sandy bay dotted with fishing boats, though one female reader has reported harassment here.

An alternative path with broken steps descends to Biao from near the fortress.

Bandaneira's Vita Guest House occasionally organises guided forest walks across Banda Besar combined with boat pick-up and snorkelling stops during the return ride.

### Eastern Banda Besar

East-coast Banda Besar is roadless and generally accessed by boat charter from Bandaneira. **Waer** village is fronted by unreconstructed **Benteng Concordia**, a small star fortress retaining three of its four corner bastions. **Karnopol** (aka Tanjung Cengkeh) offers snorkellers very rich sea life including reef sharks, though visibility is somewhat poorer than at Hatta or Ai. **Pantai Lanutu** is a pleasant, family-friendly beach stop with a gently sloping stretch of safe sand beneath your feet.

On **Pulau Pisang (Syarhir)**, sunset views from semidormant **Guest House Mailena** (per person full-board 130,000Rp) are better than the snorkelling. Four simple rooms share two bathrooms, but the place is usually unmanned and nominal manager Ahmad Kadiri (Jl Pondok Pantai, Bandaneira) lacks a decent boat, adding to the logistical difficulties.

### PULAU HATTA
pop 800

Formerly called Rozengain, isolated Hatta had no nutmeg. Thus its only historical relevance was a comical episode where eccentric English Captain Courthope raised a flag merely to enrage the Dutch. The island's two tiny settlements have no facilities, but right in front of Lama village is a lovely white-sand beach off which are Banda's clearest waters and richest reefs. Around 300m west of Lama, a natural underwater 'bridge' creates a beautiful blue hole over part of Hatta's stunning vertical drop-off. Pristine coral, clouds of reef fish and superb visibility make this Banda's top snorkelling spot. Some dive trips continue 20 minutes south to an underwater atoll known as Skaru, but most of the shallow-water coral here is depressingly bombed-out.

From Bandaneira count on around 450,000Rp to charter a suitably powerful boat including stops on Hatta, eastern Banda Besar and Pulau Pisang.

### PULAU AI
pop 1000

Seventeenth-century English agents had built a fortress and trained Ai citizen-fighters so well that they managed to resist a 1615 Dutch attack. Indeed, the islanders then stunned the astonished Dutch with an unexpected counterattack, inflicting some 200 casualties. A year later the humiliated Dutch were preparing to make a revenge attack when a small British fleet appeared, apparently in the nick of time to defend their Ai comrades. But after a few volleys of cannon fire the English commander ceased hostilities and invited his Dutch opponent for a cup of tea. After a little chat the Dutch offered the Brits nominal trading rights and sovereignty in Pulau Run. Suitably bribed, the duplicitous Brits sloped off to Seram. When they returned, almost the entire Ai population had been massacred or had fled. The Dutch repopulated the island with slaves and prisoners. Ai's four-pointed star fortress, now an overgrown ruin, has been known poignantly ever since as **Benteng Revenge**.

Ai village has a gentle charm, and beach views back towards Bandaneira from the jetty are magnificent. But the island's greatest attraction is snorkelling the remarkably accessible, brilliantly pristine coral drop-offs just

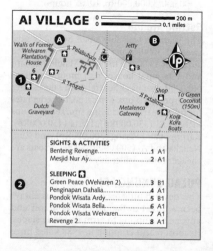

| SIGHTS & ACTIVITIES | |
|---|---|
| Benteng Revenge | 1 A1 |
| Mesjid Nur Ay | 2 A1 |

| SLEEPING 🏠 | |
|---|---|
| Green Peace (Welvaren 2) | 3 B1 |
| Penginapan Dahalia | 4 A1 |
| Pondok Wisata Ardy | 5 B1 |
| Pondok Wisata Bella | 6 A1 |
| Pondok Wisata Welvaren | 7 A1 |
| Revenge 2 | 8 A1 |

MALUKU

---

**GO ON, TAKE NEW YORK!**

After the 1616 Dutch ravaging of Ai, English forces retreated to their trading post on Run and built an 'impregnable' fort (now entirely disappeared) on the tiny, waterless islet of Neilaka. Increasingly besieged, the same eccentric Captain Courthope who had taunted the Dutch on Hatta (formerly Rozengain), put honour above survival in a preposterously futile last stand, refusing even the most reasonable offers to leave. Somehow British sovereignty was maintained even after the 1621 Dutch atrocities during which all of Run's nutmeg trees were systematically destroyed. That left the English with an economically worthless scrap of land. Eventually in 1667 Britain agreed to a 'swap', giving Holland Run for a (then equally useless) North American island. That island was Manhattan. Not a bad deal, as it turned out.

---

a flipper flap away. There's masses to see directly in front of the village, and sea life is even more impressive off **Sebila Pantai**, 15 minutes' walk west where a wrasse 'cleaning station' attracts sharks, batfish and turtles.

### Sleeping & Eating

Virtually none of the homestays have signs. Use the map and ask! Be extra careful not to waste water: Ai has no springs and all needs are provided by collecting rainwater or by laboriously transporting purchased water from Bandaneira when supplies run out. There are no restaurants, but accommodation prices (per person) include three meals.

**Revenge 2** (per person 75,000Rp) Two rooms with shared bathroom offered by an enthusiastic English-speaking young owner. Has great food.

**Green Coconut** (Jl Patalima; per person 100,000Rp) Although food is comparatively basic, the Green Coconut has the best seafront location with wonderful sea views from its common balcony and dining room (plus room 4).

**Penginapan Dahalia** (per person 100,000Rp) This family house has two en-suite guest rooms and regularly recommended food.

**GreenPeace/Welvaren 2** (mg_oderadjaidi@yahoo .co.id; per person 100,000Rp) Purpose-built new guest house where rooms 1 and 2 overlook the jetty and have private *mandis*. Free wake-up calls from the nearby mosque.

Three Pondok Wisatas, **Welvaren** (per person 75,000Rp), **Ardy** (per person 100,000Rp) and **Bella** (per person 75,000Rp), have a mixed bag of rooms.

### Getting There & Away

Two or three passenger boats (20,000Rp, one hour) leave Ai for Bandaneira when full around dawn, returning between 10.30am and 1pm. To make day trips *from* Bandaneira you'll have to charter.

## PULAU RUN (RHUN)

pop 1000

Run village is an appealing little network of steps and floral concrete paths backed by vine-draped limestone cliffs with attractive views between the tamarind trees from the top end of Jl Eldorado. Run's main attraction is diving the deeper-water drop-off that lies 70m to 150m off the island's northwestern coast (access by boat). Visibility is magnificent but the coral has suffered some damage of late. Alternatively, beach yourself briefly on the picture-perfect white sands of **Pulau Neilaka**, an isle so small you can saunter around it in 10 minutes. There are dazzlingly photogenic views towards Gunung Api from the eastern sand spit.

A morning boat (30,000Rp, two hours) leaves Run for Bandaneira, returning around noon. Chartering (350,000Rp to 450,000Rp return from Bandaneira) makes more sense as Run has no formal accommodation and you'll need a boat anyway to reach Neilaka and the offshore drop-offs.

# SOUTHERN MALUKU

## KEI ISLANDS

☎ 0916

The Kei Islands' trump cards are kilometres of stunning yet almost entirely empty white-sand beaches. Landscapes are unspectacular except on Kei Besar, but comparative accessibility and the deeply hospitable population add considerably to the islands' appeal. Beneath the mostly Christian facade, Kei culture is fascinatingly distinctive with three castes, holy trees, bride prices paid in *lela* (antique mini-cannons!) and strong belief in *sasi* (see boxed text, p768). In Kei language *bokbok* means 'good', *hanarun (li)* means '(very) beautiful' and *enbal* (cassava) is a local food staple.

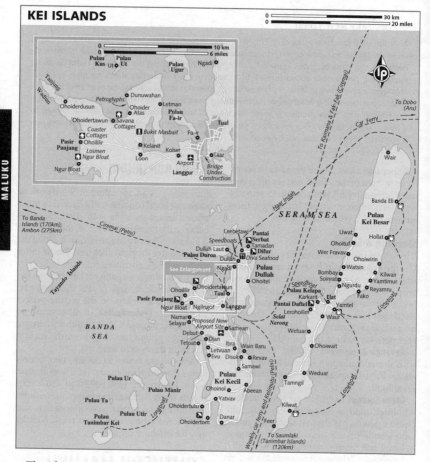

# KEI ISLANDS

The driest season is September to December, with *Belang* war-canoe races held in November. The Darwin–Saumlaki yacht rally (www.sailindonesia.net) visits Debut harbour in late July, welcomed by a cycle of traditional cultural events.

## Tual & Langgur
### pop 65,000

Bridging the two central islands, these twin towns together form the Kei Islands' main commercial centre and transport gateway. Sights are minimal though neotraditional **Mesjid Muharjirin** (Jl Soekarno-Hatta) is stylish, **Gereja Anugerah** (Jl Soekarno-Hatta) has a space-ship-shaped bell-tower, and a **graveyard** behind Tual's stilted Kyombawa quarter

makes an attractive sunset-watching spot. Jl Jenderal Sudirman and Jl Pattimura (one-way southbound) are the main commercial streets.

**BNI bank** (Bank Negara Indonesia; Jl Dr Laimena; 8am-3pm Mon-Fri) has the only official currency exchange (terrible rates) and the best ATM (1,200,000Rp maximum). **LiveCom** (per hr 10,000Rp; 3-10pm Mon-Sat) has more reliable internet than **Ronevan Computer** (Jl Kartini; per hr 10,000Rp; 9am-6pm Mon-Sat).

The **tourist office** (Dinas Parawisata; ☎ 24063; Jl Jenderal Sudirman; 8am-2.30pm Mon-Sat, 8am-noon Fri) answers questions and dispenses maps and brochures. Friendly, well-informed Viki ( ☎ 0813 4331 2704; budhitoffi@yahoo.com) speaks English.

## SLEEPING

Tual and Langgur have ample accommodation though many travellers make straight for the beachside options (see p767).

**Losmen Amelia** ( ☎ 21387; Jl Fidnang Armau, Tual; s 25,000-40,000Rp) Box rooms with shared *mandi* are as miserable as you'd expect for the price, but the losmen's owner, Umbra, speaks some English.

**Losmen Bahtera** ( ☎ 21973; Jl Kayu Hitam, Langgur; r 60,000Rp) Basic little en-suite rooms in an unmarked three-storey mansion with lemon-yellow trim overlooking the mangroves.

**Penginapan Asnolia** ( ☎ 22106; Jl Mayor Abdullah, Tual; d 140,000-195,000Rp; 🕸 ) Attractively upgraded new rooms are freshly painted and solidly furnished off pleasantly airy, common sitting rooms. All but two (80,000Rp, with fan) have decent air-con but bathrooms could be better.

**Hotel Vilia** ( ☎ 21878; Jl Telaver, Langgur; d 150,000-250,000Rp; 🕸 ) Clean and airy but somewhat soulless with mangrove views from the shared 3rd-floor balcony.

**Hotel Dragon** ( ☎ 21812; Jl Jenderal Sudirman, Langgur; s/tw from 175,000/200,000Rp; 🕸 ) Reliable, friendly and well equipped if slightly dated, the Dragon's upper-floor rooms are good value but suffer from road noise and minor plumbing niggles.

**ourpick Aurelia Hotel** ( ☎ 23748; Jl Jenderal Sudirman, Langgur; d 250,000-350,000Rp; 🕸 ) Brand-new Western-standard rooms line a kitschy ribbon of manicured garden with gilded Corinthian columns hidden away at the side of the Kimson Center fitness-and-games complex. English is spoken in the small reception booth.

**Hotel Suita** ( ☎ 24007; hotelsuitatual@telkom.net; Jl Jenderal Sudirman, Langgur; d/deluxe/ste 325,000/600,000/ 850,000Rp; 🕸 ) Bilingual service is obliging but rucked carpets and distressingly widespread damp patches thoroughly spoil the once-stylish decor. Overpriced.

## EATING

Several cheap but unremarkable eateries are strung along Langgur's Jl Jenderal Sudirman with more huddling near Tual's Pasar Masrun.

**Risa Cafe** (Jl Jenderal Sudirman; cakes 2000-4000Rp, coffee 5000Rp, rice dishes 12,000Rp; 🕔 8am-midnight) The Kei Islands' only Western-style cafe, Risa is spacious, pleasantly lit at night and serves a mean *kopi jahe* (ginger coffee, 5000Rp).

**Ayah/Family Restaurant** (beside Watdek Bridge; meals 8000-25,000Rp; 🕔 9am-2am) It's not especially polished but you get to sit on a pierlike area overlooking the bridge and mangroves. The preprepared food is no more expensive than at the numerous warungs that spring up outside each evening.

**Diva Seafood** ( ☎ 21337; mains 20,000-40,000Rp, juice 15,000Rp; 🕔 9am-midnight) It's well worth trekking 10km north of Tual to sit beside an iridescent blue bay at this unusually well-appointed restaurant with indoor, outdoor and pavilion seating. Sip a fresh *sirsak* (soursop) juice or tuck into a variety of fresh fish dishes including some pseudo-Thai variants.

## GETTING THERE & AWAY
### Air

**Wings Air** ( ☎ 22186; Jl Jenderal Sudirman; 🕔 9am-5pm Mon-Sat, 9am-2pm Sun) and/or **Trigana Air** ( ☎ 23743; Jl Pattimura; 🕔 8am-4pm Mon-Sat) have flights to/ from Ambon (1,050,000Rp, 1½ hours) almost daily, providing gorgeous views of Tayando and Bandas en route (south windows). Some Trigana flights continue on to Sanana and Ternate. Baggage limit is 10kg.

**Merpati** ( ☎ 21376; Rahmat Jayamatra, Jl Fidnang Armau) flights to Dobo (Friday and Saturday) are generally full, with passengers originating in Ambon.

### Bemo (Mobil) & Ojek

*Mobil* for Debut (3000Rp), Disuk (5000Rp) and southern Kei Kecil operate from a station beside Pasar Langgur. Those for Dullah (3000Rp, fairly frequent) and Difur Beach (Sunday only) leave from Tual's Pasar Masrun. From Langgur's Pasar Ohoijang roughly one *mobil* per hour leaves to Ngur Bloat (for southern Pasir Panjang) or Ohoililir (for Coaster Cottages). Or you can take an *ojek* (15,000Rp, 25 minutes).

### Boat

**Pelni** ( ☎ 22520; Jl Pattimura; 🕔 8am-2pm) liner *Ciremai* links Tual to Ambon (18 hours) via Bandaneira (10 hours). Eastbound, it loops through Kaimana and Fak-Fak in Papua, returning 36 hours later. Ferries depart from behind Pasar Masrun on Friday at 5pm to Dobo and Benjina (Aru) and on Monday to Saumlaki and Larat (Tanimbar). For Perintis cargo-ship timetables ask at the **port office** (Kantor Pelabuhan; ☎ 22475), up an unlikely back stairway.

MALUKU

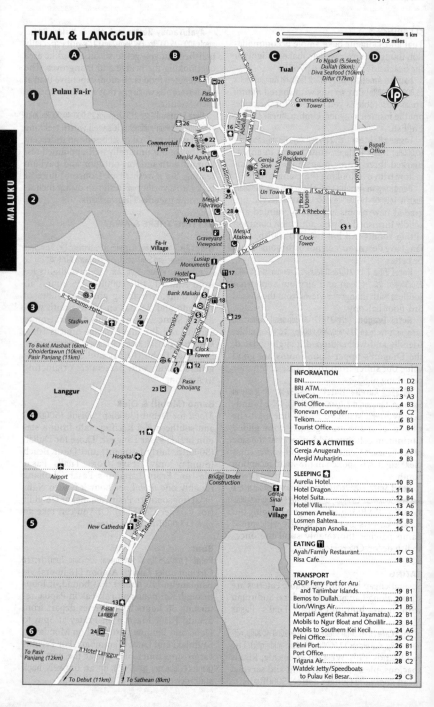

# TUAL & LANGGUR

**MALUKU**

## GETTING AROUND
Bemos (2000Rp per hop) are so common they form a virtual conveyer belt along Langgur's Jl Jenderal Sudirman, mostly continuing to Tual's big Pasar Masrun market via BNI bank and/or the Un (not UN!) Tower. Southbound from Tual, 'Langgur' bemos pass Hotel Vilia and terminate at Pasar Langgur. 'Perumnas' bemos divert to the area around the Anugerah church. Ojeks cost 5000Rp per hop.

## Kei Kecil
### BUKIT MASBAIT
With great views over Langgur, the island's highest point is an important Easter pilgrimage site for Catholics. An open-armed Christ statue stands atop a globe and tower surrounded by various scenes from the crucifixion. Notice the strikingly Asian features of the Roman centurion. Access takes 10 minutes up an unmarked track (then steps) from the low pass on the Letman road just beyond Kelanit village.

### OHOIDERTAWUN
The charming village of **Ohoidertawun** surveys a lovely bay that becomes a vast, white sand flat at low tide. Craftsmen sit in the palm shade carving out canoes with adzes. An elfin Elim church and pyramidal mosque coexist harmoniously. A 'holy tree' on the waterfront beside Savana Cottages is believed to enforce peace or bind relationships. And it seems to work an intangible magic on visitors who are frequently mesmerised by this wonderfully peaceful little place. A footpath and stairway leads north to Ohoider Atas village. At low tide you can splash across the sand flats past small caves cut in the limestone cliffs (some contain human bones). After around 25 minutes notice red-and-orange **petroglyphs** painted on the cliff faces. Although some designs look new, many are antique and their origin baffles archaeologists.

### Sleeping
**OUR PICK** **Savana Cottages** ( ☎ SMS only 0813 4308 3856; d 110,000Rp) For pure narcotic serenity, few budget guest houses in Indonesia can beat Savana Cottages. Watch the changing moods of nature, the swooping curlews and the tide retreating in the moonlight, while sipping an ice-cold beer or swinging from the hammock between sighing casuarinas. Four simple, double-bed cottage-style rooms come with rat-

tan balcony chairs and towels for the shared *mandis*. Mosquito nets are available and hearty breakfasts included. There's a sweet little cafe (dinner 50,000Rp) decorated with gongs, carvings and tinkling wind chimes. When not away in Holland, English-speaking owner Gerson offers a variety of interesting excursions and explanations on some of the bizarre intricacies of Kei social life.

### PASIR PANJANG
The Kei Islands' most famous tourist draw is **Pasir Panjang**, 3km of white sand so powdery it feels like flour. Obliging coconut palms curve across it for your photographic delectation. And despite the brochure-cover beauty, the beach is almost entirely deserted except at weekends when a couple of karaoke outfits crank up the volume near the beach's access points: Ngur Bloat (south) and Ohoililir (north).

At the beach's reputedly haunted north end, 700m beyond Ohoililir village, **Coaster Cottages** (http://keikecil.tk) comprises three very different beach houses, each with excellent sunset-facing balcony-terraces. Although each one has different owners, bookings for all three are organised through English-speaking Ogbert ('Bob') Asyz ( ☎ 0813 4347 2978; bob.azyz@yahoo.co.id). The **Grand Villa** (house €60) is a fully equipped holiday home that's brilliantly airy, stylishly designed and lovingly maintained. The two bedrooms come elegantly draped with two vast mosquito nets. It's one of Maluku's best-quality beachside options, so consider booking way ahead. The **Middle House** (tw 150,000Rp) is contrastingly simple, with two unadorned, fanless rooms whose overly soft double mattresses come with musty pillows. Some readers consider the price excessive, but you're paying

---

### WOMA
The spiritual centre of every Kei village is marked by an open-air shrine known as a *woma*, into whose offering dish superstitious people drop coins for good luck. Many modern *woma* are tackily painted concrete monstrosities. But in Waur you can find a rare original one in the form of an unembellished five-legged stone altar. Sitting beside it, a VOC (Dutch East India Company) mini-cannon points at the vast, recently rebuilt church. A message?

MALUKU

---

**SASI SAVVY**

Call it 'magic' or 'earth knowledge', Maluku experiences many hidden undercurrents of almost voodoo-esque beliefs, beautifully described in Lyall Watson's book *Gifts of Unexpected Things*. One such belief still widely prevalent is *sasi*, a kind of 'prohibition spell' used to protect property and prevent trespass. Physically the only barrier is a *janur* palm frond. But few would dare to break a *sasi* for fear of unknown 'effects'. For countless generations *sasi* have prevented the theft of coconuts and ensured that fish aren't caught during the breeding season. However, in 2003 some cunning Kei Islanders put a *sasi* on the Tual–Langgur bridge. All bemo traffic stopped. Nobody dared to walk across. The result was, not unintentionally, a prolonged bonanza for boatmen until the authorities finally stumped up the cash for a *sasi*-removal ceremony. Other jokers made a *sasi* across the access route to Tual's government offices so employees couldn't get to work. The 21st-century *sasi* seems to have become a unique version of the protection racket.

---

for a unique location. The **Doctor's House** (house 200,000Rp; 🛏) is spacious and equipped with kitchenette, fridge and air-con. However, it's somewhat aging and much less hip than the Grand Villa. For 75,000Rp per person, guests at any of the houses can enjoy two well-cooked meals and a cursory breakfast.

Near the beach's southern end, a handful of Sunday snack kiosks lie amid palms around 400m north of Ngur Bloat (aka Pasir Panjang village). Here **Losmen Ngur Bloat** (d incl breakfast 100,000Rp, dinner 35,000Rp, beer 30,000Rp) has four rooms with mosquito nets, AC Milan bed sheets, step-down *mandi* and private (if broken-seated) toilet. You can hear but not quite see the waves from the rickety communal terrace. When unmanned, get the keys from Evlyn Dresubun in Ngur Bloat village.

Nearby **Rahan Vatar** (r 75,000Rp, beer 30,000Rp) has a trio of narrow queen-bed rooms in a reasonably well-built, timber stilt hut – but be warned that it's primarily a karaoke shack, so expect nocturnal nuisances.

**SOUTHERN KEI KECIL**

From **Debut** outrigger ferries cross to Tetoat, from which a rough road continues to **Ohoidertutu Beach**. Also from Debut, daily longboats cross to **Pulau Tanimbar Kei**, the most traditional of all the Kei Islands. There's no way back till next morning (unless you charter at around 2,000,000Rp), but the tourist office is planning to have bungalow accommodation operational by 2011.

About 4km south of Debut an unmarked track to the right leads down steps to **Gua Lian Hawan**, a pair of cave pools with ice-blue water and lots of butterflies. The good new asphalt ends at picturesque **Letvuan**, where locals dry a special type of medicinal seaweed.

A rougher road continues to **Evu**, source of Kei Kecil's fresh water. Evu's artificial splashing pool behind a *lela* (minicannon) monument is popular with weekenders, and Evu's upper village is gently photogenic.

## Pulau Dullah

A series of **outlying islands** with lovely beaches and turquoise waters face **Ngadi** village, where English-speaking Ebi Renwarin can help you organise island homestays.

**Dullah** is famous for its *kora-kora* (canoe) rowing team, and two open-sided **boat sheds** are visible beside the main road 2km before the brilliant Diva Seafood restaurant (p765).

With blinding white sand, **Difur** is idyllic on weekdays but predictably busy on Sunday.

## Pulau Kei Besar

Scenic Kei Besar is a long ridge of lush, steep hills edged with picturesque villages and several picture-perfect beaches (better for taking photos than for swimming). Expect intense curiosity from locals and take your best *kamus* (dictionary) as nobody speaks English.

### ELAT & AROUND

Attractively set on a bay featuring three temptingly sand-ringed islets, Elat is Kei Besar's main village. A short walk from the port in an unmarked peach-coloured house, **Penginapan Sanohi** ( ☎ 23013; Jl Pelabuhan; d 75,000) is the island's only formal accommodation, with pleasant new rooms off a family living area sharing two rudimentary *mandis*. The rooftop quads (100,000Rp) are older and more basic.

Elat has a market and three rice-and-fish *rumah makan*. All close by dusk, so eat early or snack on biscuits from the few tiny evening shops.

Southwest of Elat, a lane through palm fronds and bougainvillea leads 6km to **Pantai Daftel**, a superb, if shallow-water, white-sand beach that stretches 1.8km to **Lerohoilim**, where there's a scattering of ancient graves atop a rocky outcrop called Batu Watlus. Coastal views are delightful.

Other easy *ojek*-excursions from Elat include picturesque **Yamtel** village (20 minutes east), **Waur** (15 minutes south) with its celebrated little *woma* (see boxed text, p767), or the charming west-coast villages of **Ngurdu** (3km), **Soinrat** (4km), **Bombay** (7km) and **Watsin** (8km), all with bay views, stone stairways and rocky terraces.

### EAST COAST

The eastern coastline has attractive, tidal rock pools but no beaches. Villages are comparatively isolated, steeped in superstitious traditions and locals tend to speak the local Kei language rather than Bahasa Indonesia. The only current access is by boat from Yamtel, since the coast road was washed away between Fako and **Reyamru**, whose high forests hide a mysterious **batu kapal** (stone boat). Straight-faced locals will assure you this was once a Portuguese shipwreck that somehow became petrified and ran up the mountain! Some 10 minutes' walk along the beach north of **Kilwair**, Anderius Uwaubun is happy to show off his private turtle pool. Walk five minutes further to find a triple-arched rock promontory, **Watngasoar**, site of local fairy tales in which a woman turned into a *kuel* fish.

Several hours north by longboat, **Banda Eli** is home to many Bandanese who fled here from the Dutch-led massacres of 1621 (see p756). The Bandanese language, now extinct in the Banda Islands, is still spoken here and the people are renowned for metalwork. Contact Tual-Langgur's tourist office to find out whether the planned visitor cottages have yet been built.

### GETTING THERE & AWAY

Torpedo-shaped 50-seater speedboats shuttle between Watdek (Langgur) and Elat (25,000Rp, 65 to 80 minutes), leaving when full. That's roughly hourly between around 8.30am and 4pm. En route notice the *bagang* (fishing platforms) sitting above the waters like giant wooden spiders. Occasional *kapal motor* sail from Watdek to southern Kei Besar. The *Haar Indah* from Tual's main port sails to Banda Eli (60,000Rp, three hours) at 8am Monday, Wednesday and Saturday, returning next day.

### GETTING AROUND

*Mobil* are very rare. By *ojek* prebook a return ride if you don't want to be stranded in traffic-less outer villages. East-coast settlements are served from Yamtel by multistop *Johnson* longboats. These depart at dawn from both Kilwat and Banda Eli, returning from Yamtel around noon (70,000Rp, around four hours). Take sunscreen, rain protection and sandals for wading through rock pools to the uncovered boats.

## TANIMBAR ISLANDS
☎ 0918

The nominally Christian Tanimbar Islands are known for wild orchids, endemic parrots, woodcarvings and mysterious 'stone boats'. Although declared a conservation area in 1971, continuing logging on the group's biggest island, Pulau Yamdena, has caused international concern (see www.earthaction.org/end-yamdena-logging.html).

### Saumlaki
pop 15,000

In WWII Saumlaki was the site of a suicidally heroic WWII battle, when Julius Tahija's 13 KNIL (Royal Netherlands Indies Army) troops temporarily repelled a whole Japanese invasion force. Today the unexciting little town is undergoing a sudden economic boom as the capital of the new Tanimbar 'regency'. However, there's still no money exchange, the **BRI Bank** (Jl Bhineka) ATM is unreliable and the only internet cafe had closed down when we visited. The **tourist office** (Dinas Parawisata; Jl Sukarno; ☽ 8am-2pm Mon-Fri) can provide free, vaguely misleading city maps once somebody finds the relevant cupboard keys. It's 500m inland from the smart new **Hotel Galaxy** (☎ 22222; Jl Urayana; d/ste 270,000/390,000Rp).

Saumlaki's greatest attraction is unwinding on the lovely boardwalk terrace of the appealing bayfront **Hotel Harapan Indah** (☎ 21019; Jl Bhineka; s with fan 176,000Rp, s/tw/tr with air-con 275,000/286,000/396,000; ✹ ). It's an ideal spot for watching spectacular sunsets while washing down fresh seafood with a cold Bintang or three. The hotel terrace also displays woodcarvings in Tanimbar's distinctive Picasso-meets-Indiana-Jones style. Such carvings make attractive souvenirs, but don't believe claims that they're 'antiques'. The 'tradition' was revived in the late 20th century as a job-creation scheme for villagers in **Tumbur** (18km north), now the island's main craft centre.

**TANIMBAR ISLANDS**

Obliging English-speaking *ojek*-driver Nus (a trained dive guide) will likely find you and be keen to help out with your transport arrangements.

## Around Saumlaki

### WELUAN

An easy 5km *ojek* ride leads to **Pantai Weluan**, where a convex sweep of palm-backed grey-white sand is revealed at low tide, facing some funky offshore rock islands. It's overwhelmed with picnickers on Sunday (and with their rubbish on Monday). Better beaches on offshore islands are accessible by private boat.

Reached by a parallel road, **Kristus Raja** is a vaguely manic Jesus Christ statue thrusting forth his out-of-scale arms towards an invisible multitude in an isolated area of overgrown secondary scrub.

### SANGLIAT DOL

Centuries ago, the Tanimbars' first settler families commemorated their seaborne arrivals by building remarkable **stone boats** which formed the spiritual heart of their original villages. The most intact example lies in scenic **Sangliat Dol** village, 42km north of Saumlaki. Overlooked by a tall church tower, the 15m 'boat' has a mast stone and megalithic 'altar', but the stone prow's finely carved top piece was stolen in 2005. Before snapping photos, you're expected to present cash (around 25,000Rp per group) and a bottle of *sopi* (available in situ) to both the *kepala desa* (whose house is across the volleyball court) and the *tuan tanah* (traditional 'boatman'). The latter then beseeches spirit ancestors not to be annoyed by your camera-toting antics. Being a 'Christian' village, these fascinating *adat* (traditional laws) prayers start and end incongruously with a Catholic body-crossing!

There's a second, smaller stone boat on the village beach: descend the steep ceremonial stone stairway and turn left.

Up to four Arui-bound buses lurch past Sangliat Dol daily (15,000Rp, 1½ hours), the last returning around 3.30pm. The *kepala desa* can organise homestays and (with sufficient notice) local dancing for a suitable fee.

In the sea's calm season (December–April) it's fun to arrive in Sangliat Dol by boat. That costs around 200,000Rp for a return trip from attractive **Lorolun** village, which retains one of the Tanimbars' last traditional twin-level timber houses with stylised bull-horn eaves. Lorolun's uncommercialised beach sweeps northeast towards a headland with possible surfing potential (May–August). Bemos to Lorolun leave Saumlaki every couple of hours till 4pm (12,000Rp).

## Getting There & Away

A new 'Saumlaki International' airport is under construction 4km from Lorolun, but for now only tiny prop-planes can land on the ultrashort runway of Olilit Airport, 1km east of central Saumlaki. On Sunday **Merpati** ( ☎ 21027; Hotel Harapan Indah) flies Ambon–Saumlaki–Larat–Langgur and back. Three times weekly **Trigana Air** ( ☎ 270 5355; Jl Nusantara; ⌚ 8am-6pm) flies Ambon–Saumlaki–Langgur–Ambon, but to fly Saumlaki–Langgur you'll generally be charged the full Saumlaki–Ambon fare unless you risk going 'stand-by'.

The Ambon–Saumlaki trip takes 36 hours on Pelni's monthly *Kelimutu* (via Banda, 22 hours), or 33 hours direct on the *Pangrango*, which continues on a three-day odyssey to Kupang, West Timor. The uncomfortable *Koromolin* ferry (see boxed text, opposite) from

MALUKU

---

**CACOPHONOUS KOROMOLIN: THE ASDP FERRY EXPERIENCE**

Is this a ferry or a bazaar? At Tual, the ro-ro gantry opens but no cars drive on. Instead, the vehicle deck of the aging ferry is quickly covered with vinyl matting from which a noisy trade in meals, drinks and more mats takes place. Extraordinary numbers of people come and go, but as the ferry prepares to leave the rusty car deck remains full, traders becoming almost organically replaced by groups of travellers. While there are in fact seats and around 80 *Kelas 1* bunks upstairs, these are stuffy, enclosed and much more prone to seasickness-inducing roll once at sea. Thus many passengers stay downstairs hoping that rain squalls don't shower them too badly through the big open-sided boat frame. Arriving at Dobo, you understand why no vehicles were brought aboard. There's no way to get them off again! Instead, as the ferry docks, an extraordinary tsunami of porters and meeter-greeters surge over the boat's sides in an endless wave. Welcome to Aru!

---

Tual travels overnight on Monday via Larat, returning Wednesday at 5pm (150,000Rp).

Sail Saumlaki Rally (www.sailindonesia.net, www.manta.org.au/saumlaki/DSCLogJuly2006.pdf) is an annual yacht expedition from Darwin, Australia.

## SOUTHWESTERN MALUKU

A comparatively arid arc of islands swings west towards Timor. The region's capital is Wonreli on **Kisar**, which anecdotally got its current name from a 1665 mix-up. A lost Dutch VOC official arrived on one of its white-sand beaches and asked the bemused locals where he was standing. Reasonably enough, he was told 'kiasar!' (on the sand!). The name stuck. A weekly Merpati flight connects Kisar with both Ambon and Kupang in Nusa Tenggara. Apart from Perintis cargo boats, the only other public transport is on Pelni's *Pangrango* running each way from Saumlaki to **Tepa** (11 hours), **Leti** (25 hours), Kisar (33 hours), **Iliwaki** (Wetar, 38 hours) and eventually Kupang (59 hours). Once a year (November or December), Bali-based diving outfit **Seatrek** ( ☎ 0361-283 358; http://seatreksailingadventures.blogspot.com, www.anasia-cruise.com) offers live-aboard cruises in a refitted nine-berth Bugis schooner between the Kei Islands and Timor, stopping in the Tanimbars, Dai (Pulau Babar), Damar, Romang and Wetar.

## ARU

☎ 0917 / pop 40,000

This steamy, low-lying island group was once part of the land bridge between New Guinea and Australia to which its flora and marsupial fauna are biologically similar. Alfred Wallace's classic *The Malay Archipelago* records his five-month stay here in 1857. Most visitors come to retrace Wallace's footsteps in search of Aru's famous birds of paradise (*cendrawasih*),

but the only one you're likely to see in Aru's busy little capital **Dobo** is a garish concrete version surveying the town's main road junction. For the real thing you'll need the time, money and linguistic skills to organise expeditions to prime spots like Pulau Baun or Pulau Maekor, both at least five hours by powerful longboat from Dobo. Don't forget mosquito repellent: malaria is prevalent.

If you're stranded in Dobo, **Pantai Durjela**, 9km west, would be idyllic but for the numerous trucks which are busily removing its gorgeous white sand.

There's lots more sand and better high-tide swimming off **Kota Lama**, a minuscule fishing village on Pulau Wokam (150,000Rp, 40 minutes by longboat from Dobo), where the very scanty ruins of a 1659 Dutch fort lie overgrown beyond the graveyard.

Dobo's most congenial accommodation is the professionally run **Penginapan Suasana Baru** ( ☎ 21940; Jl Ali Murtopo; d with fan/air-con from 137,500/165,000Rp; ✕ ), where rear rooms are built on platform which extends on stilts above the shallow bay, making for great views. It's hidden behind a comically naive statue of 1965 naval hero **Yos Sudarso** standing on a chunk of warship. Hotels Grand Aru and Sinar Harapan are also good choices, while **Penginapan Cendrawasih** ( ☎ 21095; Jl Yos Sudarso; tw from 88,000Rp; ✕ ) is marginally the best port-area cheapy.

**Merpati** ( ☎ 21260; Jl Kapitan Malongo; ✕ 9am-3pm Mon-Sat) flights from Ambon via Langgur (Friday and Saturday) are typically booked solid over a week ahead. The uncomfortable ASDP *Koromolin* ferry (see boxed text, above) departs Tual at 5pm Friday, arriving at Dobo (59,000Rp) at 5am Saturday, then continuing to the pearl-farming settlement of Benjina. At 5pm Saturday it departs Dobo for the return to Tual.

# Papua

Even a country as full of adventure as Indonesia has to have its final frontier, and here it is – Papua, half of the world's second-biggest island, New Guinea. Here the modern world is still clawing at the edges of a very traditional one, where some people buy food in supermarkets but others hunt it with bows and arrows, where one woman dons the *jilbab* and another just a grass skirt. In this youngest part of Indonesia no roads connect the dozen or so towns, and to travel any distance you must take to the air or the water. In many ways, Papua seems a different country – which is what most Papuans, who are ethnically distinct from other Indonesians, would like it to be.

Some tribes were still hunting heads and fighting village wars just a couple of decades ago. Under the influence of missionaries and Dutch and Indonesian governments, such pastimes are now history. Travelling in Papua's interior today will awe you only with the charm of its peoples, the resilience of their cultures and the splendour of their landscapes.

Nor is awesome any exaggeration for the islands and beaches around Papua's coasts or the marine life on their coral reefs. The diversity of life around the Raja Ampat islands, in particular, has biologists and scuba divers reaching for ever more original superlatives.

Travel in Papua is undoubtedly a challenge, and not one that comes cheap. But everything you do here is an adventure, and those who take on Papua's challenge are guaranteed that combination of trepidation and exhilaration of which only the very best travels are made.

## HIGHLIGHTS

- Trekking among the thatched-hut villages, unique culture and mountain grandeur of the **Baliem Valley** (p801)

- Diving and snorkelling in the real-life tropical aquarium of the **Raja Ampat islands** (p782)

- Discovering the pristine beaches and waters and friendly folk of **Pulau Biak** (p796)

- Exploring the surprisingly traditional villages around beautiful **Danau Sentani** (p794) by longboat

- Searching out the indigenous lowland culture and Australia-like flora and fauna of **Wasur National Park** (p814)

Pulau Biak ★
★ Raja Ampat Islands
Danau Sentani ★
Baliem Valley ★
Wasur National Park ★

▪ POPULATION: 2.8 MILLION  ▪ LAND AREA: 422,000 SQ KM  ▪ HIGHEST PEAK: CARSTENSZ (PUNCAK JAYA; 5030M)

# PAPUA

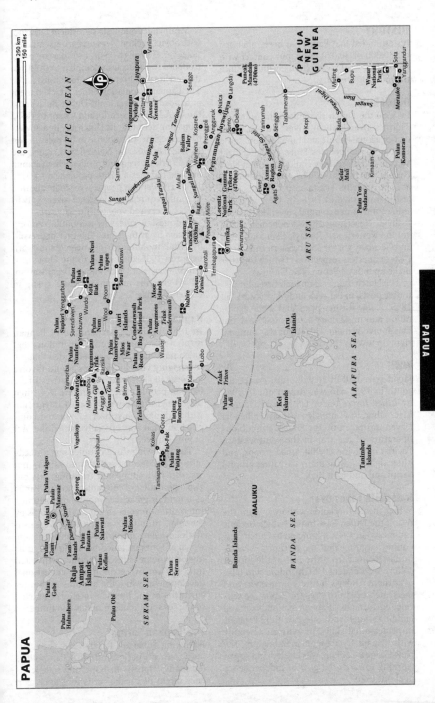

PAPUA

# HISTORY

It's estimated that Papua has been inhabited for 30,000 or 40,000 years, but contact with the outside world was extremely limited until the mid-20th century.

## Dutch Rule

In 1660 the Dutch recognised the Sultan of Tidore's sovereignty over New Guinea, based on occasional tribute and homage from some Papuan coastal peoples. Since the Dutch held sway over Tidore, they could argue that New Guinea was theirs too. Their first settlement, at Lobo on Teluk Triton, near Kaimana, only lasted from 1828 to 1838. By the end of the 19th century three colonial powers had agreed to divide New Guinea between them: Holland got the western half (today's Papua); Britain and Germany got the southeastern and north-eastern quarters respectively (which together make up today's Papua New Guinea).

The Dutch didn't set up their first administrative posts, in Fak-Fak and Manokwari, till 1898. A few further posts and some exploration and missionary activity followed, but Dutch involvement with Papua was minimal right up to WWII.

## WWII

Japan seized all of New Guinea except the south in 1942 and was driven out in 1944 by Allied forces under US general Douglas MacArthur, in a campaign that saw Hollandia (Jayapura) taken by the largest amphibious operation of the war in the southwestern Pacific, involving 80,000 Allied troops, and bitter fighting, with many casualties around Sarmi and on Pulau Biak.

## Indonesia Takes Over

When the Netherlands withdrew from the rest of the Dutch East Indies (which became Indonesia) in 1949, it hung on to Dutch New Guinea, arguing that the territory was culturally distinct from the rest of the former colony. Subsequent Dutch-Indonesian talks over the territory's future got nowhere and the Dutch began to prepare Papua for self-rule, encouraging Papuan nationalism and building schools and colleges to train Papuans in professional skills. In 1961 an assembly with a majority Papuan membership, the New Guinea Council, was elected and began working towards the goal of independence in about 1970.

Meanwhile Indonesia's President Sukarno, with Soviet backing, was preparing a military takeover. Through 1962 Indonesian paratroopers and marines attempted to infiltrate the territory in preparation for an invasion. The Papuan population either attacked them or handed them over to the Dutch. But by now the USA had decided it didn't want to risk a damaging defeat for its Dutch ally by a Soviet-backed regime. In response to US pressure, on 15 August 1962 the Netherlands signed the New York Agreement, under which Papua became Indonesia's 26th province on 1 May 1963. The Papuan people were to be allowed to confirm or reject Indonesian sovereignty in a UN-supervised vote within six years.

Indonesian rule was unpopular among Papuans from the start. The first big revolt, by Arfak mountain tribes near Manokwari, began in 1965, giving rise to the Organisasi Papua Merdeka (Free Papua Organisation; OPM) guerrilla movement, which is still in existence today.

## Papua under Suharto

In 1969, against a background of Papuan revolt and military counter-operations that killed thousands, Indonesia decided that the sovereignty vote by Papuans would involve just over 1000 selected 'representatives' of the Papuan people. The chosen few were then threatened if they voted against integration with Indonesia. Just over a thousand complied, in what was officially named the 'Act of Free Choice'.

The following three decades saw a steady influx of Indonesian settlers into Papua – not just officially sponsored transmigrants but also 'spontaneous' migrants who saw Papua as a land of greater economic opportunity. Intermittent revolts and sporadic actions by the small, primitively armed OPM were usually followed by drastic Indonesian retaliation, which at times included bombing and strafing of Papuan villages. Indonesia invested little in Papuans' economic or educational development, while the administration, security forces and business interests extracted resources such as oil, minerals and timber.

## The 'Papuan Spring'

Following Suharto's fall in 1998, the *reformasi* (reform) period in Indonesian politics led many Papuans to hope that independence might be on the cards for Papua as it

**A LOT IN A NAME**

When the Portuguese first encountered New Guinea and its surrounding islands in the early 16th century, they called them Ilhas dos Papuas (Islands of the Fuzzy-Hairs), from the Malay word *papuwah*. In 1545, Spanish sailors named the island Nueva Guinea (New Guinea). The Dutch later named the western half of the island Dutch New Guinea. As this territory prepared for independence in the 1950s and 1960s, local leaders chose West Papua as the name for their future nation. When Indonesia took over in 1962, Sukarno named the territory Irian Barat (West Irian), using a Biak name for New Guinea that means 'Hot land rising from the sea'. In 1973 Irian Barat was changed to Irian Jaya (Victorious Irian).

To most native Papuans, the name Irian symbolises unwanted Indonesian rule. Papuan nationalists still refer to their land as West Papua. In a nod to their feelings, the reformist Indonesian President Abdurrahman Wahid renamed it Papua in 2000. His successor Megawati Sukarnoputri seemed to forget all about this in 2003 when she announced her plan to divide the province of Papua into three, to be named Irian Jaya Barat (West Irian Jaya), Irian Jaya Tengah (Central Irian Jaya) and Irian Jaya (the eastern part). After violent protests, only the western province was hived off, and it was renamed Papua Barat (West Papua) in 2007. So today Papua comprises one small province, Papua Barat, and one large one, still called Papua – and the name West Papua means one thing to administrators and another, much bigger thing to Papuan independence activists.

was for East Timor. In June 2000 the Papua People's Congress (over 2500 Papuan delegates meeting in Jayapura) declared that Papua no longer recognised Indonesian rule and delegated a smaller body called the Papua Council Presidium to seek a UN-sponsored referendum on Papuan independence.

But what some commentators have called the Papuan Spring was short-lived. The second half of 2000 saw a big security-force buildup in Papua, and attacks on pro-independence demonstrators. And in November 2001 the Papua Council Presidium's leader Theys Eluay was murdered by members of the Indonesian army (see the boxed text, p793).

### 'Autonomy' & Human Rights

November 2001 also saw the passing of a Special Autonomy charter for Papua – Jakarta's response to Papuan grievances, whose major provision was to give Papua a bigger share (70% to 80%) of the tax take from its own resources and more money to develop education and health. Many Papuans rejected the very concept of Special Autonomy – they wanted full independence – and its implementation has received much criticism, chiefly that little benefit is seen at grassroots level because too much of the money disappears into the hands of a fast-expanding bureaucracy.

Sporadic OPM actions have continued and pro-independence protests are on the rise. The increased concern for human rights seen elsewhere in Indonesia is less evident in Papua, where torture, rape, murder and disappearances continue to be documented by organisations such as the United Nations, the US State Department, Amnesty International and Human Rights Watch. Papuans regularly receive jail sentences of 10 years or more for simply raising the Morning Star flag, symbol of Papuan independence.

Living standards in Papua's cities have risen in the past few years, but the poverty rate in Papua as a whole is double the national average. The villages and countryside, where most ethnic Papuans live, remain among Indonesia's poorest. The AIDS rate in Papua is the highest in Indonesia, and rising. Most Papuans want to be free of Indonesian rule, but their chances of that seem as slim as ever now that Papua is home to over a million non-Papuans.

### CLIMATE

In general, the drier season is from May to November, but all parts of Papua get some rain year-round. December to April sees roughly twice as much rain per month in most areas – which can be inconvenient and uncomfortable but doesn't make travel impossible. Sorong and the Raja Ampat islands at the tip of the Vogelkop are exceptions to the general pattern, getting their heaviest rain between April and September. The far south is the only area with a proper dry season: Merauke normally receives less than 50mm of rain per month from June to October.

Temperatures and humidity are high all year in the lowlands, but it's cooler in the highlands, and highland nights can be positively cold.

## WILDLIFE

Thanks to its former existence as part of the Australian continent – New Guinea was still joined to Australia as recently as 10,000 years ago – Papua's terrestrial wildlife has big differences from that of the rest of Indonesia. Here dwell marsupials such as tree kangaroos, wallabies, bandicoots, cuscuses and possums, as well as echidnas, which are among the planet's few egg-laying mammals.

Papua is still about 75% covered in forest and its habitats range from savannas, coastal mangroves and river floodplains, to lowland rainforest, higher-altitude montane forest and the glaciers around 5030m Carstensz Pyramid (Puncak Jaya), the highest peak in Oceania. These diverse ecosystems harbour more than half the species found in Indonesia, including over 190 mammals, 550 breeding birds, 2650 fish species and more than 2000 types of orchid. Papua shares many plants with Indonesia as well as Australia.

The megastars of the feathered tribe are the birds of paradise, whose fantastically coloured males perform weird and wonderful mating dances. Papua and neighbouring Papua New Guinea (PNG) are home to nearly all the world's 40-plus species of birds of paradise. Also here are large, ground-dwelling cassowaries, colourful parrots and lorikeets, unique types of kookaburra, crowned pigeons, cockatoos, and the curious bowerbirds, whose males decorate large ground-level dens

in their efforts to find mates. See the boxed text, p788, for more on birds of paradise and birdwatching in Papua.

Marine life is even more fantastic and varied, especially around the Vogelkop, which sits at the heart of the 'Coral Triangle' stretching from the Philippines to Indonesia's Nusa Tenggara and east beyond PNG. Most stunning of all are the still-being-explored seas around the Raja Ampat islands (p782), which are now a fast-developing mecca for divers.

New species continue to be found on land too. A 2005 Conservation International expedition in the almost untouched Foja Mountains, on the edge of the vast Mamberamo basin, found types of bird of paradise and bowerbird that had been thought extinct, four new species of butterfly, 20 new frogs, and the golden-mantled tree kangaroo, which was previously known only on one mountain in PNG.

Modern economic developments and some older human activities threaten Papua's wildlife. Forests are under assault from logging (much of it illegal, with the timber smuggled out to Asia), road construction, mining, transmigration settlements and new oil-palm plantations. This means a loss of habitat for many birds and forest animals such as the tree kangaroo. Commerce in brightly coloured birds or their feathers has been a fact of life here for centuries. Birds of paradise continue to be smuggled out of Papua even though trade in their feathers has been illegal in Indonesia since 1990.

The classic, if weighty, text on Papuan wildlife is Marshall and Beehler's two-volume *The Ecology of Papua*.

---

### TOP FIVE READS

■ *Throwim' Way Leg* by Tim Flannery (2000) – a mammalogist's travelogue of sorts, detailing his research years in Papua and PNG – full of lovely, funny observations and wonderful insights into the people and environment.

■ *Under the Mountain Wall* by Peter Matthiessen (1987) – a beautifully written book chronicling his daily life among the Kurulu people of the Baliem Valley way back in 1961.

■ *The Lost World of Irian Jaya* by Robert Mitton (1983) – compiled from his letters, diaries, maps and photographs after his death in 1976; criticises the reckless way that Papuans were forced into the modern world.

■ *Poisoned Arrows* by George Monbiot (1989) – details a remarkable journey to the wilds of Papua with the objective of uncovering the truth about *transmigrasi* and anti-Indonesian resistance.

■ *The Open Cage* by Daniel Start (1997) – first-hand experience of a hostage taken by the OPM; he creates a commendably thorough backdrop of the Papuan context leading to his situation.

**PAPUA TRAVEL WARNING**

Outbreaks of civil unrest and violence do happen in Papua, but they shouldn't deter you from visiting the region unless some generalised outbreak occurs. Political demonstrations in Abepura, Jayapura and elsewhere sometimes turn violent, and the 2009 local election period was marked by several OPM attacks in the western highlands as well as the stabbing to death of four *ojek* (passenger motorcycle) drivers in Wamena and an assault on the Abepura police station by attackers armed with bombs, spears and bows and arrows. In 2002, one Indonesian and two American teachers from the international school near Timika were shot dead in an ambush, and in 2001 two Belgians were kidnapped by the OPM near Ilaga (and later freed). But mainstream tourists have not been targeted and are welcomed by the great majority of people here. Unrest tends to be localised, so you should stay abreast of current events and ask the police if you have concerns about particular places.

# CULTURE

Papua is a land of hundreds of cultures – those of the 200-plus indigenous peoples and those of all the immigrants from other parts of Indonesia, who dominate in the cities and now make up over 40% of Papua's population. Relations between native Papuans and immigrants are often good on a person-to-person level but poor when it comes to group dynamics. Papuans tend to resent the increasing numbers and dominance of non-Papuans as well as the conduct of the Indonesian security forces. Non-Papuans may consider Papuans 'primitive', uneducated and uncultured. The immigrants are predominantly Muslim, while Papuans are mostly Christian with an undercoat of traditional animism, but violent clashes between Papuan and non-Papuan civilians are mercifully rare.

Indigenous Papuan culture is much more apparent in the villages than the towns. It has altered a lot in the past few decades, under the influence of Christian missionaries and Dutch and Indonesian governments. Tribal warfare, headhunting and cannibalism, practised by some tribes well into the second half of the 20th century, have all but disappeared. But reverence for ancestors and pride in cultural traditions such as dances, dress and wood-carving persist. Papuan woodcarving is prized throughout Indonesia and beyond: the Asmat, Kamoro, Sentani, Biak and Yapen peoples produce the most striking work.

Tribal culture varies from area to area, starting with languages, of which Papua has approximately 280. Traditional housing shows marked differences according to environment: while waterside people often live in stilt houses, the Dani of the Baliem Valley inhabit snug, round, wood-and-thatch huts known as *honai*, and the Korowai and Kombai tribes of the southern interior build their homes high in trees as a refuge against animals, enemies and floods. Gender roles remain traditional among the tribal peoples: polygamy is still practised by some men, and women do most of the carrying as well as domestic tasks.

# GETTING THERE & AWAY
## Air

You must first get to Jakarta, Makassar, Denpasar, Manado or Ambon, then take an onward domestic flight. Visitors heading straight for the Baliem Valley must fly first to Jayapura, which is served by five airlines from Jakarta and Makassar, and by Garuda from Denpasar. For the Raja Ampat islands, fly to Sorong from Jakarta, Makassar, Ambon or Manado. You can also fly to Manokwari, Biak or Timika from Makassar or Jakarta, and to Fak-Fak from Ambon. Most flights to Papua from Jakarta are overnight, with a small-hours stop in Makassar. The cheapest Jakarta–Jayapura fares at research time, from around 1,500,000Rp one way, were with Batavia Air and Lion Air.

Book as far ahead as possible with all airlines, as low fares or even seats may not be available in the last few days before departure. Following are the airlines linking Papua with other parts of Indonesia.

**Airfast** (www.airfastindonesia.com)
**Batavia Air** (www.batavia-air.co.id)
**Expressair** (www.expressair.biz)
**Garuda** (www.garuda-indonesia.com)
**Lion Air** (www.lionair.co.id)
**Merpati** (www.merpati.co.id)
**Wings Air** (www.lionair.co.id)

**PAPUA**

**TRAVEL PERMIT**

Foreigners are required to obtain a travel permit known as a *surat keterangan jalan* (commonly called a *surat jalan*) before they can visit many places in Papua.

Rules and procedures for this change from time to time, and enforcement varies from place to place. At the time of writing, you could visit Jayapura, Sentani, Pulau Biak and Sorong without a *surat jalan*. Elsewhere, it is safest to assume you need one, even for day trips out of the above places, though sometimes you won't need to show it.

A *surat jalan* is usually easily and quickly obtained from the police in regency capitals (of which Papua has about 30). See city sections in this chapter for details of specific police stations issuing the *surat jalan*. The relevant departments are typically open from 9am to 3pm Monday to Friday, although some may be able to attend you outside those hours. Take your passport, two passport photos, and one photocopy each of the passport pages showing your personal details and your Indonesian visa. The procedure normally takes about an hour with no payment requested.

Some police stations will only issue a *surat jalan* for their own regencies or limited other destinations. The best place to go to obtain a wide-ranging *surat jalan* is Polresta in Jayapura (p790), where you can present a list of every place that you intend to visit and then get them all listed on one *surat jalan*. Don't omit any obscure, off-the-beaten-track places that you plan to visit. Having them already covered by your *surat jalan* when you arrive can save hassles and wasted time.

Once you have your *surat jalan*, make several photocopies of it. Each time you arrive in a new town, your hotel should report your arrival to the police and they will need photocopies of your passport and/or *surat jalan* to do so. In a few places you may need to report to the police yourself. Carry your *surat jalan* whenever you take out-of-town trips.

Some parts of Papua are sometimes off-limits to tourists, usually because of OPM activity. This was the case at research time with the Ilaga area in the highlands. Police to whom you apply for a *surat jalan* will tell you if anywhere on your itinerary is off-limits.

The permit lasts from one week to one month, depending on how long you request and the expiry date of your visa.

## Boat

Several Pelni liners link Papuan ports with Maluku, Sulawesi and Java every two or four weeks. Almost all pass through Sorong, which has six inbound and six outbound sailings every two weeks. Jayapura has five arrivals and departures every two weeks. See p848 for general information about sailing on Pelni ships.

A few Perintis boats regularly link the north coast of Papua with Sulawesi and northern Maluku, and connect the south coast with southeast Maluku.

## GETTING AROUND

Inter-city roads are an unknown concept in Papua's undeveloped terrain. Boats are an option for travel between coastal towns if you have enough time, or along rivers if you have enough money. Aircraft go almost everywhere, and are generally the most convenient, and sometimes the only, option for getting around Papua.

## Air

The hubs for flights within Papua are Jayapura and Sorong. Some direct flights between other towns exist, but you will probably have to return to Jayapura or Sorong for some connections. Most flights within Papua cost around 1,000,000Rp, give or take a hundred thousand or two.

Delays and schedule changes are common, and the routes operated by different airlines change frequently. It also has to be said that, even by Indonesian standards, Papua seems to suffer more than its fair share of aviation incidents and crashes. The number of small aircraft negotiating tricky highland landing strips obviously has something to do with this.

In addition to flights between the bigger towns by commercial airlines, missionary airlines such as the Roman Catholic **Associated Mission Aviation** (AMA; www.ama-papua.com) and Protestant Mission Aviation Fellowship (MAF) do a lot of flying between small, remote airstrips. Tourists are not a priority for them, but they will often carry them if there are spare seats.

For destinations not served by scheduled flights, chartering a small plane for seven to 10 people is another option, typically costing around 7,000,000Rp for a short hop under 100km, or 20,000,000Rp to 35,000,000Rp for a longer flight such as Wamena to Ewer (Agats). **Trigana Air** (www.trigana-air.com), **Aviastar** (www.avia star.biz) and Merpati are among charter carriers, and AMA mission planes are sometimes available for charter.

## Boat

Five big Pelni liners – the *Dorolonda*, *Gunung Dempo*, *Labobar*, *Nggapulu* and *Sinabung* – sail from Sorong to Jayapura and back every two weeks, stopping at various combinations of the main ports en route (Manokwari, Wasior, Nabire, Serui and Biak). The *Nggapulu* also sails between Sorong and Fak-Fak, while the *Tatamailau* links Fak-Fak to Timika, Agats and Merauke along Papua's southern coast (once every two weeks in each direction), and the *Kelimutu* sails between Timika, Agats and Merauke every four weeks.

The next best option is a Perintis boat along either coast, but these are much slower and less comfortable, with bare boards for sleeping. The basic Perintis routes around Papua are Sorong to Jayapura, Sorong to Merauke, and Manokwari–Sorong–Ternate. Perintis boats stop at more, and smaller, ports than Pelni liners, and some go up rivers such as the Mamberamo or Digul to inland villages or towns.

On routes without any public service, or just to get there quicker, you can charter a boat. This will usually be a longboat (motorised outrigger canoe). Costs are highly negotiable and depend on the distance, price of fuel (about 10,000Rp per litre at research time) and size of boat.

## Tours

Given the logistical difficulties of Papua travel, it can make sense to take an organised tour, and particular sense for more challenging destinations such as the Asmat, Korowai or Kombai areas or the little-explored Mamberamo basin in the north. It's well nigh essential (given the bureaucracy involved) for mountaineers

---

### TRAVELLING BETWEEN PAPUA & PNG

There are no flights between Papua and PNG, and the only route across the border that is open to foreigners is between Jayapura (northeast Papua) and Vanimo (northwest PNG, about 65km from Jayapura).

You can charter a *taksi* (small minibus) from the market at Abepura (called Pasar Abepura or Pasar Yotefa), 13km south of downtown Jayapura, to the border at Wutung (1½ hours) for 200,000Rp to 400,000Rp. Cross the border itself on foot, then hire a car to Vanimo for about 10 kina (US$3.50). Air Niugini links Vanimo with Port Moresby three times weekly.

Another option, more expensive but possibly useful if the land border is suffering one of its occasional closures, is to charter a boat to Vanimo. You can ask around the ports at Argapura or Hamadi near Jayapura, or check with PT Kuwera Jaya (p790) in Jayapura.

Most visitors to PNG need a visa; the standard 60-day tourist visa (225,000Rp) can be obtained at the **Consulate of Papua New Guinea** ( ☎ 0967-531 250; congenpng_id@yahoo.com; Blok 6 & 7, Ruko Matoa, Jl Kelapa Dua, Entrop; ☻ 9am-noon & 1-2pm Mon-Fri) 4km south of downtown Jayapura. To get there catch an Entrop-bound *taksi* (2500Rp) from Jl Percetakan Negara or Terminal Mesran in Jayapura. The consulate is in the same street as the Entrop *taksi* terminal.

Details of the visa procedure change often, but you can expect it take two to five working days and to be asked for two photos, a copy of an onward ticket out of PNG or Indonesia, and a typed letter requesting a 60-day tourist visa. Travellers from Eastern European, Asian or African countries should make advance enquiries at a PNG consulate, as PNG has different regulations for some of these nationalities.

Travellers *entering* Indonesia from Vanimo cannot get an Indonesian visa at the border; you must obtain one beforehand. Indonesian 30-day tourist visas are available in Vanimo or Port Moresby for US$25. The Vanimo consulate usually issues them within one working day. If you're travelling to/from Jayapura by boat, visit Jayapura's **immigration office** (Map p790; ☎ 0967-533 647; Jl Percetakan 15; ☻ 9am-2pm Mon-Fri) to make sure you have the correct entry/exit stamp in your passport.

---

**EXCHANGING MONEY IN PAPUA**

Only a handful of banks in Papua will exchange any kind of foreign money, and those that do (chiefly in Jayapura and Kota Biak) will only accept cash US dollars, usually in US$100 bills only – and they like clean ones! There are fairly reliable ATMs in all towns, however, with Visa, Visa Electron, MasterCard, Maestro, Cirrus and Plus cards all widely accepted.

---

wanting to climb Papua's high peaks such as Carstensz Pyramid (Puncak Jaya) or Gunung Trikora. The following local and specialist operators can all be recommended.

**Baliem Valley Resort** (www.baliem-valley-resort.de) The most upmarket hotel in the Baliem Valley (p805) offers challenging trips to destinations like Carstensz and the Korowai and Kombai regions, and also general Baliem Valley tours.

**Benneti Expeditions** ( ☎ 0967-573 310; www.ben netiexpeditions.com; Kompleks Ruko Denzipur 9, Jl Raya Sentani, Waena) An experienced outfit based in Waena, near Jayapura, with a speciality in the Asmat, Korowai and Kombai.

**Biak Paradise Tours** ( ☎ 0981-23196; www.discover papua.com; Hotel Arumbai, Jl Selat Makassar 3, Kota Biak, Biak) An established, efficient, Biak-based operator that offers a wide range of tours in many parts of Papua.

**Grand Irian Tours & Travel** ( ☎ 0967-536 459; www .grandiriantours.com; Jl Batu Putih 49, Jayapura) Efficient Sumatran-run agency offering a range of adventurous trips.

**Papua Adventure Tours & Travel** ( ☎ 0967-572 622; www.papuaadventure.com; Jl Raya Sentani 20, Waena) Based between Sentani and Jayapura, this agency offers tours in the Baliem Valley, Asmat, Korowai, Kombai and other areas. You're looking in the region of US$2000 for a 10-day Baliem Valley trip.

**Papua Expeditions** (www.papuaexpeditions.com) This ecotourism-minded, Sorong-based company specialises in birdwatching trips in all the best Papuan destinations.

**Papua/Irian Jaya Adventure** ( ☎ 0852-4413 1512; justinus_daby@yahoo.com; Jl Gatot Subroto 15, Wamena) Run by a Baliem Valley native who offers trips in the Baliem Valley, Asmat and Korowai and Kombai regions.

**Papua Trekking** (www.papuatrekking.com) Czech-based company specialising in the most challenging destinations such as Carstensz, Mamberamo, Asmat and Korowai and Kombai. Also covers the Baliem Valley area.

For more information on hiring guides, see the boxed text, p823.

# WEST PAPUA

The controversially hived-off province of West Papua chiefly comprises two large peninsulas – the Vogelkop (Bird's Head/Kepala Burung/Semdoberai) and the more southerly Bomberai Peninsula – and several hundred offshore islands. The attractions here are primarily natural, especially the world-class diving and gorgeous island scenery of the Raja Ampat islands, and the birdlife of Pegunungan Arfak. Sorong and Manokwari are well-provided urban bases from which to launch your explorations.

## SORONG
☎ 0951 / pop 140,000

Papua's second biggest city, Sorong sits at the northwestern tip of the Vogelkop. It's a busy port and base for oil and logging operations in the region, which has many transmigration settlements. Few travellers stay longer than it takes to get on a boat to the Raja Ampat islands, but Sorong is quite fun to stay in for a day or two.

### Orientation & Information

Sorong stretches 6km following the coast from the airport at the eastern end of town to Pantai Lido and the Kampung Baru area at the western end, then another couple of kilometres north. One main street runs the whole way, called Jl Basuki Rahmat outside the airport, then Jl Yani and Jl Yos Sudarso after it turns north along Pantai Lido. You'll find most of what you need along this street. Three ATMs cluster outside the biggest supermarket, **Saga** ( ☎ 322 794; Jl Yani; ☯ 9am-10pm Mon-Sat, 10am-10pm Sun).

**Aloysius Computer College** (Jl Kesehatan, Kampung Baru; internet access per hr 6000Rp; ☯ 9am-7pm) Has an air-conditioned public internet room. It's 300m off Jl Yos Sudarso, along the street next to the hospital.

**Kennko Tours** ( ☎ 0813 4437 3398, 0812 4864 8838; rudie-rajaampat.blogspot.com; airport) This small, welcoming, English-speaking operation provides travel agency services, help with obtaining a *surat jalan*, luggage storage (per hr 5000Rp) and snorkel-gear rental (per day 200,000Rp). It's based at Kennko Café (follow 'Raja Ampat Tourism Center' signs outside the arrivals hall).

**Polresta Sorong** ( ☎ 0812 4876 4928; Jl Basuki Rahmat; ☯ 8am-3pm Sun-Fri) Head to this police station, 1km west of the airport, for a *surat jalan*.

**Raja Ampat Tourism Office** ( ☎ /fax 326 576; JE Meridien Hotel, Jl Basuki Rahmat km 7; www.gorajaam pat.com, www.diverajaampat.org; ☯ 9am-4pm Mon-Fri)

This incredibly helpful office will tell you all you need to know about the Raja Ampat islands. It even has maps and printed information sheets in English. It also runs a booth in the airport arrivals hall, open when flights arrive. You must pay your 500,000Rp fee to visit the islands at one of these places.

## Sights & Activities

**Pantai Kasuari** (Cassowary Beach), 5km north of grubby Pantai Lido, is a long, sandy strand with some coral, ideal for swimming and snorkelling (bring your own gear). You can get there by public *taksi* to Tanjung (Cape) Kasuari from Boswesen market in town (5000Rp). For a taste of Sorong city life, wander through **Pasar Remu** (Jl Selat Sagawin; ☼ from 6am), the large main market, on a side street off Jl Basuki Rahmat about 500m from the airport gate.

## Sleeping

Breakfast is included at all these places.

**Hotel Tanjung** ( ☎ 323 782; Jl Yos Sudarso; s 126,000-225,000Rp, d 136,000-255,000Rp; ✷ ) Situated on the Pantai Lido waterfront, popular Hotel Tanjung has a range of acceptable rooms, though the cheapest ones share bathrooms and lack air-con.

**Hotel Waigo** ( ☎ 333 500; Jl Yos Sudarso; s 250,000-378,000Rp, d 300,000-476,000Rp; ✷ ) Playfully decked out in pink paint, psychedelic tiles and stylised murals, Hotel Waigo is a good deal. Standard rooms are good-sized; the oceanview 'suites' are massive. All rooms come with air-con, hot showers and drinking-water dispensers, and you can order meals in your room.

**JE Meridien Hotel** ( ☎ 327 999; hoteljemeridiensorong .blogspot.com; Jl Basuki Rahmat km 7; r 350,000-650,000Rp, ste 750,000-850,000Rp; ✷ ☐ ☜ ) Handily placed opposite the airport, Sorong's newest hotel offers solid, modern comfort in cool, white, good-sized rooms with a touch of kitschy art. The quoted prices include the normal 20% discount from official rates.

Also recommended:

**Cenderawasih Hotel** ( ☎ 322 367; Jl Sam Ratulangi 54, Kampung Baru; s/d 191,000/221,000Rp; ✷ )

**Hotel Mariat** ( ☎ 323 535; mariathotel@gmail.com; Jl Yani 1; r 350,000-682,000Rp, ste 825,000-1,500,000Rp; ✷ ✿ ☜ )

## Eating

Most of the best eateries cluster on and just off Jl Yos Sudarso near Hotel Tanjung. Restaurants in Sorong are generally better stocked with alcohol (beer, at least) than those elsewhere in Papua. For cheaper eats, seafood warungs set up in the evenings at the southern end of the Yos Sudarso waterfront.

**our pick** **Rumah Makan Ratu Sayang** ( ☎ 321 184; Jl Yos Sudarso; mains from 20,000Rp; ☼ noon-3pm & 6-10pm) Pick up the scent of fish on the grill and head inside this popular spot, 200m from Hotel Tanjung, for delicious *ikan bakar* (grilled fish). With rice, spinach and three sauces, this will set you back 60,000Rp.

**Sunrise** ( ☎ 322 709; Jl Yos Sudarso; mains 25,000-100,000Rp; ☼ noon-midnight) Sunrise overlooks Pantai Lido and faces west for spectacular sunsets. It's nice for a beer as well as good rice, noodle, seafood, meat, tofu and vegetable dishes.

## Shopping

**Irian Jaya Art & Souvenirs** ( ☎ 321 713; Jl Yani; ☼ 10am-9pm) This shop 1km east of Hotel Mariat has some of the most original wares in Papua, including antique Chinese, Dutch and Indonesian ceramics.

## Getting There & Away

### AIR

You can book at the airlines' airport counters or at their offices or travel agents. **Merpati** ( ☎ 327 000; Jl Sam Ratulangi 50, Kampung Baru), **Expressair** ( ☎ 328 200; JE Meridien Hotel, Jl Basuki Rahmat km 7) and **Lion Air** ( ☎ 321 444; Jl Basuki Rahmat km 7) all fly daily to Makassar and Jakarta. Expressair also goes daily to Jayapura, and three times weekly to Manokwari, Fak-Fak, Ambon and Manado. Merpati heads to Manokwari and Fak-Fak three times weekly, and Lion goes three times a week to Ambon and Manado.

### BOAT

**Pelni** ( ☎ 321 716; Jl Yani 13), near the western end of Jl Yani, has five ships sailing every two weeks east to Jayapura (via various combinations of intermediate ports including Manokwari, Biak and Serui) and west to ports in Maluku, Sulawesi and Java. The *Tatamailau* heads round to Fak-Fak, Timika, Agats and Merauke on Papua's southern coast. Sample fares (1st class/economy) are 820,000/263,000Rp to Biak, 937,000/299,000Rp to Jayapura, 1,383,000/437,000Rp to Merauke and 602,000/171,000Rp to Ambon.

## Getting Around

Official airport taxis charge 70,000Rp to hotels in town; out on the street you can charter a public *taksi* for half that. Using the yellow public *taksi* (2500Rp), first get one going west outside the airport, then change to another at a local terminal after 600m. Hordes of *taksi* run along Jl Basuki Rahmat/Yani/Yos Sudarso.

Short *ojek* rides of 2km to 3km are 5000Rp; to/from the airport is 10,000Rp to 20,000Rp.

## RAJA AMPAT ISLANDS

### pop 40,000

This group of 610 mostly uninhabited islands off Sorong offers some of the best – if not *the* best – diving in Indonesia. Raja Ampat's sheer number and variety of fish, and its huge reef systems, with hundreds of hard and soft corals, have divers in raptures. It's like swimming in a tropical aquarium! Little known until the last few years, Raja Ampat now sees a steady traffic of liveaboard dive boats, and the current handful of land-based dive resorts is growing. The sparsely populated islands – though not geared to travellers on tight budgets – are also great for snorkelling, birdwatching and just exploring amid sublime scenery of steep, jungle-covered islands, pristine white-sand beaches, hidden lagoons and pellucid waters.

The four biggest islands are Waigeo in the north, with the fast-growing new regional capital, Waisai; Salawati, just southwest of Sorong; Batanta, off northern Salawati; and Misool to the southwest. The Dampier Strait between Waigeo and Batanta has many of the best dive sites, so most accommodation options are on Waigeo, Batanta or two smaller islands between them, Mansuar and Kri.

Useful websites on Raja Ampat include those of **Raja Ampat Culture & Tourism Affairs** (www .gorajaampat.com, www.diverajaampat.org), **Papua Diving** (www.papua-diving.com) and **Misool Eco Resort** (www .misoolec oresort.com).

## Activities

### DIVING

You can get up close with huge manta rays and giant clams, gape at schools of barracuda, fusiliers or parrotfish, peer at tiny pygmy seahorses or multicoloured nudibranchs ('sea slugs'), and with luck encounter a wobbegong or an epaulette shark, which uses its fins to 'walk' on the sea bottom. The reefs have hundreds of brilliantly coloured soft and hard corals, and the marine topography varies from vertical walls and pinnacles to reef flats and underwater ridges.

Most dives are drift dives due to the currents washing over the reefs. You can dive year-round, although the usually smooth seas can be rougher in July, August and September. The dive resorts offer packages of seven days or more but also provide diving services to people visiting independently, normally for €30 to €40 per dive, with equipment rental at around €30 per day.

Here's a selection of the best dive sites, in approximate north-to-south order:

**Wayag Islands** These small, uninhabited islands with white-sand beaches 30km northwest of Waigeo feature varied coral gardens and sloping walls with schools of anthias (small fish that can change sex), sea fans and soft corals. Grey reef sharks hang out in a cave off Pulau Uranie.

**Teluk Kabui** Between Waigeo and the smaller Pulau Gam, Kabui is packed with picturesque jungle-topped limestone islets. Visibility isn't fantastic, but Nudibranch Rock, with an amazingly varied population of brightly coloured nudibranchs, is a Raja Ampat highlight.

**The Passage** This 20m-wide channel between Waigeo and Gam is effectively a saltwater river. It's heaven for macro photographers with its shrimp gobies, nudibranchs, sponges and tunicates ('sea squirts'). Sharks, archerfish, turtles, barracuda, rays and schools of bumphead parrotfish are seen here too.

**Fam Islands** At the western end of the Dampier Strait, this island cluster has very calm waters, stunning coral and masses of fish, notably at the Melissa's Garden site.

**Manta Point** Near Pulau Arborek between the Gam and Mansuar islands, this famous site is a manta cleaning station, where huge manta rays, some with wing spans over 5m, wait above large coral heads to be cleaned by small wrasses. You can get very close to 15 or more mantas.

**Cape Kri** The number and variety of fish at the northeastern point of Pulau Kri, just off the eastern end of Pulau Mansuar, have to be seen to be believed. Schools of barracuda, jacks, batfish and snapper coexist with small reef fish, rays, sharks, turtles and a few giant Queensland groupers. There's beautiful coral too.

**Sardine Reef** About 3km northeast of Pulau Kri, this offshore reef, sloping down to 33m, has so many fish that it can get quite dark at times. The fish-and-coral combination is great for photographers.

**Pulau Wai** The reefs around this small island off the north coast of Batanta are home to masses of unusual sea life including the recently discovered Raja epaulette shark, wobbegong shark, crocodile fish and double-ended pipefish (a seahorse relative). There are also manta rays, and a WWII US fighter-plane wreck. The night diving is spectacular.

**PROTECTING THE MARINE EPICENTRE**

Marine biologists consider eastern Indonesia to be the world's epicentre of marine life, and Raja Ampat harbours probably the greatest diversity of all – including at last count 1223 species of coral reef fish, 565 hard corals (over 75% of the world total) and some 700 molluscs. Ocean currents carry coral larvae from here to the Indian and Pacific Oceans to replenish other reefs.

Seven Marine Protected Areas (MPAs) were declared in Raja Ampat in 2007 to protect the reefs from threats such as cyanide and dynamite fishing, large-scale commercial fishing, and the effects of mining, logging and road building. The MPAs cover over 9000 sq km and sustainable marine tourism plays a big part in the conservation effort. As part of this, foreign visitors must pay a 500,000Rp entrance fee to visit the islands (Indonesians pay 250,000Rp). You can do this at Sorong airport or the Raja Ampat Tourism Office (p780) in Sorong. The money goes to local conservation and community development and the Raja Ampat Tourism Department.

**Pulau Misool** This remote southern island – especially the small islands off its southeastern corner – has stunningly beautiful coral life. The pristine reefs attract pygmy seahorses, epaulette sharks, manta rays and a vast range of other fish.

**SNORKELLING**

There are strong currents in some areas, but the Fam Islands, northwestern Misool, Pulau Wai and Mios Kon (10km east of Kri) are all fine, and you can see plenty of coral and sea creatures close to the shore in many places. If you don't have your own gear, some accommodation places can rent or lend it, and you can rent it at Kennko Tours (p780) in Sorong.

**BIRDWATCHING**

Two fantastically coloured birds of paradise, the red and the Wilson's, are endemic to just a few areas of the Raja Ampat islands. The red male has a spectacular courtship dance in which he spreads his wings and shakes like a big butterfly. The best base for seeing both species is Wailebet (or Wai Lebed) village on the southern coast of Batanta, although this area is less attractive than it was because of illegal logging. Ask for guides Kris Sauyai or Yehuda Dei. Basic accommodation is available in the village.

Village guides in Yenwaupnor and Sawingrai on Pulau Gam will also take you to nearby spots where you may see the red bird of paradise. They charge 50,000Rp for about three hours.

Birds of paradise – like many other birds – usually do their stuff soon after dawn, which usually means a very early start to walk to viewing spots. Lorikeets, parrots, kingfishers, eagles and hornbills are fairly abundant around the islands.

Sorong-based **Papua Expeditions** (www.papuaexpeditions.com) offers specialised birding trips to Raja Ampat.

## Sleeping & Eating
### ON LAND

A few villages have constructed basic tourist accommodation where you sleep on mats for around 150,000Rp per person (take a mosquito net and some food; the villagers will usually cook for you). Options:

**Wailebet** Southern coast of Batanta.

**Yenbuba** Eastern end of Pulau Mansuar; contact English-speaking Pak Dedy ( ☎ 0812 4855 7279).

**Yensawai** Northern coast of Batanta; the 'homestay' is on Pulau Dayan, a few kilometres away. Contact Pak Leo ( ☎ 0813 4475 4379).

If you just turn up at a village you can usually sleep in someone's house. You can pay anything from 10,000/20,000Rp for a mat/bed, and another 10,000Rp if they provide a meal.

**Kobe Oser Resort** ( ☎ 0813 4437 3398; fax 0951-335 692; mariarumbiak@yahoo.com; Yenwaupnor, Pulau Gam; full-board per person 350,000Rp) Kobe Oser, also known as Ibu Maria's, has two rustic stilt bungalows set over the water at Yenwaupnor on the southern coast of Pulau Gam. Meals are basic, but it's a welcoming, relaxed place and they can provide snorkel gear and will run you round in their boat for a reasonable charge (around 300,000Rp for a typical day excursion).

**Raja Ampat Dive Resort** ( ☎ 0812 4844 2284; www.rajaampatdiveresort.com; Waiwo, Waigeo; r/cottages full-board per person from 250,000/300,000Rp, 7-night dive package US$900–1035) This place a few kilometres west of Waisai is further from the best dive sites than the other island resorts are, but it can be convenient if you just want to come for a few days. Packages include an average two dives a day, meals and transfers from/to Waisai. Cottages and rooms all hold two people, but the cottages are newer and nicer, with private bathrooms. Guests have free use of snorkelling gear.

**our pick** **Kri Eco Resort** ( ☎ 0951-328 038; www .papua-diving.com; Pulau Kri; 7-night dive package per person €998-1295) Kri Eco, operating since 1994, is the original Raja Ampat dive lodge, and belongs to Papua Diving, whose Dutch founder, Max Ammer, pioneered scuba in Raja Ampat. It has a gorgeous setting on little Pulau Kri, off the eastern tip of Mansuar, and six of the spacious, airy, wooden guest bungalows are built over crystal-clear waters along the jetty. Bathrooms are shared. Packages run Sunday to Sunday and include at least 12 dives a week, meals and Sorong transfers.

**Misool Eco Resort** (www.misooleco resort.com; Pulau Batbitim; 11-night dive package per person €1810-3535; closed Jul-Sep; 🌣 ) Set on a beautiful small island off southwestern Misool, this comfortable, well-equipped dive resort has a strong conservation and community ethos, and plenty of great dive sites within a few minutes' boat ride. Dive packages include excellent meals, excursions and Sorong transfers (four to six hours each way). Most of the cottages have air-con and a verandah over the water; all have private bathroom.

**Sorido Bay Resort** ( ☎ 0951-328 038; www.papua-div ing.com; Pulau Kri; 7-night dive package per person €1791-2247; 🌣 🖳 🛜 ) Papua Diving's newer, more luxurious option offers Western-style comforts, with air-con and hot showers in spacious waterside bungalows, internet access and special facilities for underwater photographers. As at Kri Eco, packages run Sunday to Sunday and include meals and Sorong transfers.

At least two more dive lodges were due to open by the end of 2009:

**Papua Paradise** (www.papuaparadise.com) On Pulau Birie, off Batanta.

**Raja Ampat Dive Lodge** (www.dive-paradise-indone sia.com) On the north coast of Pulau Mansuar.

### LIVEABOARDS

The ultimate Raja Ampat experience could be cruising around on a twin-masted Bugis-style schooner specially kitted out for divers. A couple of dozen Indonesian- and foreign-owned liveaboards now do regular 10- to 12-day dive cruises around the islands, usually starting

and ending in Sorong. There are also itineraries combining Raja Ampat with Maluku or Triton Bay (Teluk Triton) south of Kaimana. Most boats carry 12 to 16 passengers and some are luxurious, with air-conditioned cabins and en suite bathrooms. The majority of cruises run between November and April, when Raja Ampat seas are calmest. Some can rent diving gear, but generally it's better if you can bring your own.

Total costs typically range between US$3000 and US$5000 per person per cruise. **Dive Paradise Indonesia** (www.dive-paradise-indonesia .com), a long-running Indonesian operation with five liveaboards, operates year-round and is among the least expensive. The **Seven Seas** (www.thesevenseas.net) is probably the last word in Raja Ampat liveaboard luxury. Other established boats include the **Cheng Ho** (www .kararu.com), **Ondina** (www.thebestdivingintheworld.com), **Pindito** (www.pindito.com) and **Seahorse** (www.indo cruises.com).

### Getting There & Around

Mega Express operates fast passenger boats with airline-style seating (economy/VIP 105,000/125,000Rp, two hours) to Waisai from Sorong's Usaha Mina harbour at 9am Monday to Saturday, and noon Sunday, starting back from Waisai at 2pm. The harbour is on Jl Yani, 1km east of Sorong's Pelni port. The slower but breezier *Gracelia* sails at 2pm Wednesday, Friday and Sunday (per person 100,000Rp, four hours) from Sorong's Pelabuhan Rakyat, off Jl Baru, and starts back from Waisai at 2pm Monday, Thursday and Saturday. The *Raja Ampat I*, *Raja Ampat II* and *Raja Ampat III* sail various routes around the islands from Sorong: ask at Usaha Mina or Pelabuhan Rakyat for details of their itineraries.

The main dive resorts include boat transfers from and back to Sorong in their dive packages. Smaller accommodation places will usually collect you at Waisai if you contact them ahead. If you have to charter a boat yourself from Waisai, it's all very negotiable. Ask around the pier where the ferries arrive, or take an *ojek* to the motorboat jetty (*pelahu-ban speedboat*) or the river behind the town-centre market. You might pay 200,000Rp to 300,000Rp to Yenbuba or Yenwaupnor.

It's possible to hire a small longboat in island villages for several days with captain and shipmate and follow your own itinerary round the islands, sleeping under the stars or in village homes. A fair price is around 300,000Rp per day plus fuel and food.

# FAK-FAK
☎ 0956

This port and regency capital rambles up and down green hills on the Bomberai Peninsula. Along with Manokwari, Fak-Fak was one of the first successful Dutch settlements in Papua, established in 1898. It merits a special trip if you have an interest in ancient rock paintings. Beware: outbound flights are often heavily booked.

## Orientation & Information

Fak-Fak's shoreline stretches between two inlets – one with the main port, and the other, 1.5km west, with the tidy Tambaruni market and Tambaruni *taksi* terminal. Jl Izak Telussa, the main street, and its westward continuation Jl Tambaruni, connect the two.

**Bank Mandiri** (Jl Izak Telussa 26) Doesn't exchange any form of foreign money but has a very busy Visa, Visa Electron and Plus ATM.

**Police** ( ☎ 22200; Jl Tambaruni) For a *surat jalan*, report to this police station halfway between the port and Terminal Tambaruni.

**Toko Alfa** ( ☎ 22224; Jl Cenderawasih 9; internet access per hr 10,000Rp; ☉ 9am-1pm & 6-10pm Mon-Sat, 6-10pm Sun) The young, English-speaking owner, Alex Ferdinand, is very willing to dispense helpful information. Alfa is in the Puncak district, 2.5km uphill from Jl Izak Telussa – take a *taksi* or *ojek*.

## Sights & Activities

If you have time for a spell on the beach, take a *taksi* from Terminal Tambaruni west to Pasar Seberang (3000Rp), then another to Pasir Putih (5000Rp) – a total trip of about half an hour to reach the three beaches of **Pasir Putih**, all with white sands, azure waters and no crowds on weekdays.

## Sleeping & Eating

**Hotel Tembagapura** ( ☎ 22136; Jl Izak Telussa 16; r 125,000-150,000Rp; ☒ ) It's central and the rooms are clean and reasonable, all with air-con and private *mandi* (Indonesian-style bath).

    **Fak-Fak Hotel** ( ☎ 23196; fax 24281; Jl Suprapto 9; s 120,000-200,000Rp, d 130,000-220,000Rp; ☒ ) A couple of winding streets up the hill from Jl Izak Telussa, the top-price rooms here have hot water, minibars and balconies with bay views. Cheaper rooms are dilapidated and most lack

hot water, but staff are amiable. Snack breakfast is included, and you can order other meals in your room.

    **Hotel Grand Papua** ( ☎ 24695; grandpapua_hotel@ yahoo.com; Jl Panjaitan 1A; r incl breakfast 424,000-635,000Rp; ☒ ) Half a kilometre uphill from the Fak-Fak Hotel, the Grand Papua has clean, spacious, comfy rooms, a bland atmosphere and a reasonable restaurant (mains 35,000Rp to 50,000Rp).

    **Warungs** (Jl Baru; dishes 15,000-50,000Rp; ☉ evening) For ocean breezes and excellent *ikan bakar* or *udang asam manis* (sweet-and-sour prawns), head for the line of warungs out along the reclaimed road in front of Pasar Tamburani.

## Getting There & Away

**Merpati** ( ☎ 22130; Jl Izak Telussa 57; ☉ 8am-12.30pm Mon-Sat) flies three days a week to Sorong, and once to Kaimana and Manokwari. **Wings Air** ( ☎ 25555; Hotel Grand Papua, Jl Panjaitan 1A; ☉ 8am-5pm Mon-Sat) heads to Ambon twice a week. **Expressair** ( ☎ 25377; Jl Izak Telussa; ☉ 8am-5pm Mon-Sat) flies to Jayapura daily except Sunday, alternately via Sorong–Manokwari and Kaimana–Nabire.

    **Pelni** ( ☎ 23371; Jl Panjaitan) has five sailings every fortnight, including two each to Sorong (1st class/economy 329,500/108,500Rp) and Ambon (446,000/144,500Rp), and one each to Timika, Agats, Merauke, Tual and Banda. The office is about 1km uphill from the town centre.

## Getting Around

Little Torea airport is on a hillside 7km west of town. A chartered *taksi* should cost 50,000Rp to or from the town. Hundreds of red, yellow, green and white public *taksi* (2500Rp) follow incomprehensible routes around Fak-Fak's hilly, circuitous streets. An *ojek* in town costs 4000Rp.

# AROUND FAK-FAK

A trip out to **Kokas**, on the north coast of the peninsula 42km by mostly paved road from Fak-Fak, is the most interesting thing to do in the area. In Kokas **Freddy Bola** (bollafreddy@yahoo .com; Toko Jaya, Jl Rumagesar), by the main jetty, can organise a motorboat trip along the coast to see several sites of striking **rock paintings** (of marine life, crocodiles, human handprints and other motifs), as well as groups of **human skulls** on cliff ledges – all of uncertain age and origin. There is also a muddy WWII **'Japanese cave'** (actually a set of tunnels) in the village,

PAPUA

and an unusual European-style 19th-century **mosque** at Patimburak, a 10-minute boat ride away. Bolla charges around 600,000Rp for a two- to three-hour boat trip to the main sites, and can provide accommodation should you need it.

Public *taksi* to Kokas (20,000Rp, 1½ hours) leave when full from Fak-Fak's Terminal Kokas, reached by local *taksi* (2500Rp) from Terminal Tambaruni. If you miss the last *taksi* back from Kokas, an *ojek* is 200,000Rp.

# MANOKWARI

☎ 0986 / pop 59,000

Capital of West Papua (Papua Barat) province since it was created in 2003, Manokwari sits on Teluk Cenderawasih near the northeastern corner of the Vogelkop. It's a mellow enough place but only merits a special trip for out-of-town attractions, especially hiking and birding in Pegunungan Arfak.

## Orientation & Information

Most travellers' facilities are in the area known as Kota, on the eastern side of the Teluk Sawaisu inlet. Local transport terminals and the airport (7km) are to the west and southwest.

**Arfak Paradigalla Tours** ( ☎ 0813 4475 1664; yoris_tours@yahoo.com) This effusive, one-man, English-speaking outfit offers city tours, as well as birdwatching trips and treks around Pegunungan Arfak and the Anggi lakes, for a guide fee of 250,000Rp per day (500,000Rp overnight outside town), not counting transport, accommodation or food.

**ATMs** (Jl Yos Sudarso) You'll find several cash machines across the street from the Swiss-belhotel.

**BNI bank** (Bank Negara Indonesia; Jl Merdeka 44) ATM good for most international cards.

**Flashlink.net** (Jl Merdeka 46; internet access per hr 9000Rp; ☺ 9am-9pm Mon-Sat) Slow connections tempered by soothing air-con.

**Police station** ( ☎ 211 359; Jl Bhayangkhara) A *surat jalan* for surrounding areas is easy to obtain here, 1km southeast of the port.

**Tourist office** ( ☎ 211 689; Jl Percetakan Negara; ☺ 9am-3pm Mon-Fri) Worth visiting, especially if you plan to visit Pegunungan Arfak or Cenderawasih Bay National Park.

## Sights & Activities

A reasonably level 2.5km path crosses picturesque **Taman Gunung Meja** (Table Mountain Park), a protected forest with plenty of birdlife and butterflies. The trail is well marked, but

the start is unsigned: if you take a public *taksi* towards Amban you can ask the driver to let you off at the right place. The **Tugu Jepang** (Japanese Monument), 1km before the end of the trail, offers great views.

Two German missionaries settled on **Pulau Mansinam** off Manokwari in 1855 and became the first in Papua to spread 'The Word'. The picturesque island is home to a small village, a **ruined church**, a **memorial** to the missionaries, and a pleasant **beach**. It's best to report to the *kepala desa* (village head) before wandering around too far. A passenger boat (3000Rp one way) sails between Kwawi, 2.5km southeast of central Manokwari, and Mansinam whenever it fills up with passengers.

Teluk Doreri in front of Manokwari is peppered with the wrecks of WWII ships and planes lying in shallow, clear water, as well as abundant coral and marine life. There is no local dive operator, but Papua Diving (p784) or Dive Paradise Indonesia (p784) can bring you here.

About 5km southeast of the centre, **Pantai Pasir Putih** is a curved bay of white sand and clear water, good for **swimming** and **snorkelling** if you have gear. It's a little unkempt in parts, but quiet – except on Sunday when half Manokwari invades the beach. The other half visits black-sand **Pantai Amban**, 7km north of Manokwari and perfect for **surfing**. Regular public *taksi* to both Pantai Pasir Putih and Amban village (4km before the beach) start from Terminal Sanggeng and run through town en route.

## Sleeping

All these hotels include breakfast in their rates, and some throw in afternoon tea.

**Losmen Apose** ( ☎ 211 369; Jl Kota Baru 4; s/d 120,000/250,000Rp) This is a friendly place opposite the Merpati office. Most rooms have private *mandi*, but they vary in quality, so view a few before deciding.

**Hotel Mokwam** ( ☎ 211 403; Jl Merdeka 49; r 180,000-204,000Rp; ✷ ) This hotel has been around a while, but it's still clean and quite comfy, with good-sized rooms (all upstairs), airy walkways and amiable staff.

**Billy Jaya Hotel** ( ☎ 215 787; fax 215 827; Jl Merdeka 51; s 181,500Rp, d 224,000-333,000Rp; ✷ ) The clean, cosy, lower-end rooms at this efficient, friendly hotel are a terrific deal. Rattan ceilings, TVs and minibars add to the atmosphere and comfort. The Billy company is also building a grander new hotel next door.

Also recommended:
**Hotel Maluku** ( ☎ 211 948; Jl Sudirman 52; r 125,000–180,000Rp; ❄ ) Fairly quiet, but rather airless and with only squat toilets.
**Swiss-belhotel** ( ☎ 212 999; fax 212 777; www.swiss-belhotel.com; Jl Yos Sudarso 8; r 900,000–2,130,000Rp; ❄ 🖴 🛜 ) Way above anywhere else for service and style. Check the website for discounts.

## Eating
**Hawai Billy Bakery & Coffee Shop** ( ☎ 212 189; Jl Sudirman 100; cakes & pastries 6000–9000Rp; ⏲ 6am-1am) An arm of the Billy empire, this relaxed spot serves espresso, pizza and Indonesian soups, and features a wall of house-baked pastries including chocolate muffins.

**Abressio Café** (Jl Merdeka 87; mains 20,000–60,000Rp) A large and spacious restaurant, with a quiet air-con section and plenty of well prepared dishes. Try the excellent *ikan rica-rica* (fish in a spicy sauce made with ginger, shallots and lime).

**Billy Café** ( ☎ 211 036; Jl Merdeka 51; mains 25,000–60,000Rp) The menu details a few Western selections like hamburgers, but you're better off with the Indonesian or Chinese food, which comes in generous portions. The main dining room blasts moderately effective air-con and live music in the evenings.

## Getting There & Away
**Merpati** ( ☎ 211 153; Jl Kota Baru 39) flies three times a week to Jayapura, Sorong, Makassar and Jakarta and theoretically twice to Biak. **Batavia Air** ( ☎ 215 666; Jl Sudirman 30) heads to Jayapura, Makassar and Jakarta four times weekly. There are also flights by Expressair: three weekly to Jayapura, Sorong, Makassar, Jakarta and Fak-Fak.

Every two weeks **Pelni** ( ☎ 215 167; Jl Siliwangi 24) has four sailings each to Jayapura (1st class/economy 685,000/230,000Rp) and Sorong (364,000/124,000Rp), three each to Serui and ports in Sulawesi, two each to Ternate and Jakarta, and one each to Biak, Fak-Fak and Ambon. ASDP Indonesia Ferry's *Teluk Cenderawasih II* sails to Biak (88,000Rp, about 26 hours) via Pulau Numfor every Thursday at 6pm.

## Getting Around
You can get a taxi to town on the road outside the airport for 30,000Rp or 40,000Rp. Some public *taksi* (3000Rp) come past here too, bound for Terminal Wosi, halfway to the centre. From Wosi get another to Terminal Sanggeng on the western side of Teluk Sawaisu, then another (or walk) to Kota. *Ojeks* cost 4000Rp within town, and 10,000Rp to or from the airport.

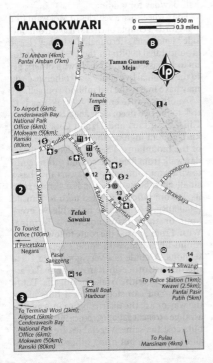

| INFORMATION | |
|---|---|
| ATMs................................................ | **1** A2 |
| BNI Bank........................................ | **2** B2 |
| Flashlink.net.................................. | **3** B2 |

| SIGHTS & ACTIVITIES | |
|---|---|
| Tugu Jepang.................................. | **4** B1 |

| SLEEPING 🛏 | |
|---|---|
| Billy Jaya Hotel............................. | **5** B2 |
| Hotel Maluku................................. | **6** A2 |
| Hotel Mokwam............................... | **7** B2 |
| Losmen Apose................................ | **8** B2 |
| Swiss-belhotel............................... | **9** A2 |

| EATING 🍴 | |
|---|---|
| Abressio Café................................. | **10** A2 |
| Billy Café........................................ | (see 5) |
| Hawai Billy Bakery & Coffee Shop....... | **11** A2 |

| TRANSPORT | |
|---|---|
| Batavia Air..................................... | **12** A2 |
| Merpati.......................................... | **13** B2 |
| Pelni.............................................. | **14** B3 |
| Port............................................... | **15** B3 |
| Terminal Sanggeng......................... | **16** A3 |

**PAPUA**

**FEATHERED PARADISE**

Papua is a spectacular destination for bird lovers, and of all the many exotic and rare birds found here, the undoubted stars are the 30 birds of paradise (cenderawasih), which include astrapias, sicklebills, riflebirds and manucodes as well as those actually named 'bird of paradise'. Papua and neighbouring PNG are the chief homes of these fantastically colourful birds, whose males perform spectacular mating 'dances'.

Papuans have long used bird-of-paradise feathers in traditional dress, and the feathers have also been exported for many centuries. Because traders often removed the birds' legs and wings to highlight their beautiful plumage, Europeans once believed the birds had no feet and spent their entire lives in flight. The plumes became so popular and valuable as European women's fashion accessories that by the late 19th century more than 50,000 skins were being exported from Papua every year, bringing the birds close to extinction. After WWI conservationist pressure and changes in fashion put an end to the trade.

Birds of paradise are elusive and tend to live in remote areas, but with patience, time and a knowledgeable guide, it's quite possible to spot some in the wild. The easier sites include the Raja Ampat islands (p783), Pegunungan Arfak (below), Pulau Yapen (p800) and Danau Habbema (p811). The same areas are generally excellent for many other birds too.

Most good Papuan tour companies (see p779) can arrange specialised birding trips with expert local guides. UK-based **Birdquest** (www.birdquest.co.uk) is one overseas operator that regularly brings groups to Papua.

Terminal Sanggeng is the starting point for very frequent public *taksi* running through Kota and out to Kwawi and Pantai Pasir Putih, or Amban, as well as west to Terminal Wosi.

## PEGUNUNGAN ARFAK

The thickly forested Arfak mountains, rising to more than 2800m south of Manokwari, are a region of beautiful tropical mountain scenery, exotic wildlife (especially birds) and a mostly indigenous Papuan population (the Hatam and other peoples). You can spend a few days trekking here or select one base and focus on the wildlife. The Arfak region was the scene of the first and one of the biggest Papuan revolts against Indonesian rule, in 1965–68.

The best **birdwatching** base is **Mokwam** village, about a 50km drive from Manokwari. Ask for Zeth Wonggor in the part of Mokwam known as Syobri. Zeth is a highly experienced bird guide who has worked here with, among others, Sir David Attenborough. He has forest hides for viewing birds such as the magnificent bird of paradise, western parotia (another bird of paradise) and Vogelkop bower bird. There are many other rare and exotic birds to be spotted – along with spectacular, iridescent birdwing butterflies with wingspans of up to 25cm. You might also see marsupials such as the tree kangaroo. Zeth has tourist **accommodation** (per person 30,000Rp) in a well-built wooden

house. Bring a sleeping bag, and any food you want beyond rice and a vegetable or two. Zeth charges about 150,000/300,000Rp per half-day/day for guiding.

Four-wheel-drive vehicles to Mokwam (the road fords a couple of rivers) leave from outside Manokwari's Terminal Wosi. They charge around 1,000,000Rp for the 1½-hour trip for up to 12 passengers. To share with others, get to the terminal by about 7am – otherwise you may have to pay the full million yourself.

Another way to enjoy the Arfak area is to trek to the two deep, clear **Anggi Lakes**, Danau Giji (29 sq km) and Danau Gita (24.5 sq km), 2030m high on the southwestern side of the mountains. They're a two- or three-day walk from **Ransiki**, a coastal *transmigrasi* town 80km south of Manokwari that has a small **guest house** (per person 50,000Rp) next to its Telkom office. Crowded *taksi* to Ransiki (50,000Rp, two to three hours) leave every hour or so from Manokwari's Terminal Wosi. From Ransiki the route follows Sungai Momi upstream, with some steep, muddy sections. A guide is a very good idea – ask the district office in Ransiki or make arrangements with Arfak Paradigalla Tours (p786). You can sleep in local huts along the way or ask the district office in Anggi to arrange **accommodation** (per person 50,000Rp) – the huts cost the same. Vegetables are available along the way, but bring other food. From the lakes it's possible to continue round to Mokwam in about three days via Dimaisi and Minyambou villages.

## CENDERAWASIH BAY NATIONAL PARK

This reserve (Taman Nasional Teluk Cenderawasih), with about 20 islands and 500km of coastline, is easily the biggest protected area in what conservationists call the Bird's Head Seascape – the waters around the Vogelkop, which harbour a vast diversity of marine life. The potential for diving, snorkelling, hiking and birding is obvious, but there is very little regular transport and no dedicated tourist accommodation. Before visiting, consult the **Cenderawasih Bay National Park office** (Map p787; ☎ 0986-212 303; btntc@telcom.net; Jl Drs Esau Sesa, Sowi, Manokwari), on a hillside above Manokwari airport, or Manokwari tourist office (p786). Arfak Paradigalla Tours (p786) can help set up a trip.

The larger inhabited islands are Rumberpon, Mios Waar, Roon and Angrameos. You can explore the coastline or islands by boat from Ransiki for about 800,000Rp per day, or base yourself on **Pulau Rumberpon**, which offers **snorkelling** among superb coral and marine life, outstanding **hiking** and the possibility of boat trips to smaller islands. Public speedboats (about two hours) leave Ransiki for Rumberpon most days, or you can charter one for 250,000Rp. On Rumberpon, you should be able to camp on the beach (bring everything with you) or stay in a village hut.

# THE NORTH

Papua province's capital, Jayapura, and its airport town of Sentani, in the northeastern corner of Papua, are the hubs of Papuan travel, and there's a variety of appealing things to see and do in and around these towns. Further west the islands of Biak and Yapen in Teluk Cenderawasih are fine places for a spot of beach relaxation, with good snorkelling and diving, wildlife to search for and WWII sites to investigate.

## JAYAPURA
☎ 0967 / pop 150,000

Central Jayapura's streets are fairly grungy, but they have a beautiful setting between steep, forested hills opening on to Teluk Imbi. If you just want to get up to Wamena as soon as

possible, you can often make all arrangements in Sentani without coming into Jayapura. But if you want to see Papua's biggest and most important city, this is it.

A small settlement named Hollandia, established by the Dutch in 1910, was the target of the large-scale American amphibious attacks of April 1944. After WWII Hollandia became the capital of Dutch New Guinea. Following the Indonesian takeover in 1963, it was renamed Kota Baru, then Sukarnapura, then Jayapura ('Victory City') in 1968. With nearby towns and villages that it has now engulfed, and Kotaraja, Abepura and Waena a bit further south, the Jayapura conurbation now counts perhaps 300,000 people. Cenderawasih University at Abepura is a particular focus of Papuan nationalism.

## Orientation

Most of what you'll need is on the parallel main streets, Jl Yani and Jl Percetakan, and the waterfront streets Jl Sam Ratulangi and Jl Koti. From the centre Jayapura stretches about 6km northeast along the coast, and is joined to a string of formerly separate towns and villages to the south: Argapura (2km), Hamadi (3km) and Entrop (4km).

## Information
### INTERNET ACCESS
**Warnet Andhika** (Jl Yani 16; per hr 8000Rp; ☽ 9am-1am) Slow but open late.
**Warnet Media Papua** (Jl Percetakan; per hr 7000Rp; ☽ 9am-10pm) As slow as everywhere else, but bigger and with better prices.

### MEDICAL SERVICES
**Rumah Sakit Umum Daerah** ( ☎ 533 616; Jl Kesehatan 1, Dok II) Jayapura's large public hospital is in the northern foothills, 1km from downtown.

### MONEY
**Bank Mandiri** (Jl Yani 35; ☽ 8am-3pm Mon-Fri) You can exchange cash US dollars here, and there's a Visa ATM.
**BII bank** (Bank Internasional Indonesia; Jl Percetakan 22; ☽ 8am-3pm Mon-Fri) Will change cash US dollars and has an ATM for most international cards.
**BNI ATM** (Jl Yani 14) Accepts Visa, Visa Electron, MasterCard, Cirrus, Plus and Maestro cards.

### POST & TELEPHONE
**Main post office** (Jl Koti 3; ☽ 7.30am-6.30pm Mon-Sat)
**Plasa Telkom** (Jl Koti; ☽ 8am-midnight) You can phone from here.

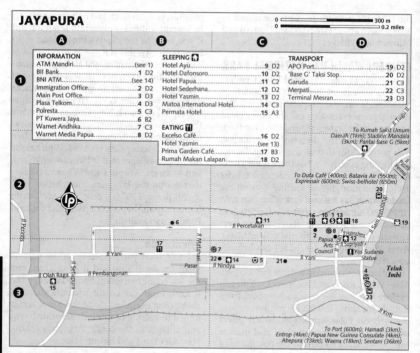

**JAYAPURA**

| INFORMATION | |
|---|---|
| ATM Mandiri | (see 1) |
| BII Bank | 1 D2 |
| BNI ATM | (see 14) |
| Immigration Office | 2 D2 |
| Main Post Office | 3 D3 |
| Plasa Telkom | 4 D3 |
| Polresta | 5 C3 |
| PT Kuwera Jaya | 6 B2 |
| Warnet Andhika | 7 C3 |
| Warnet Media Papua | 8 D2 |

| SLEEPING | |
|---|---|
| Hotel Ayu | 9 D2 |
| Hotel Dafonsoro | 10 D2 |
| Hotel Papua | 11 C2 |
| Hotel Sederhana | 12 D2 |
| Hotel Yasmin | 13 D2 |
| Matoa International Hotel | 14 C3 |
| Permata Hotel | 15 A3 |

| EATING | |
|---|---|
| Excelso Café | 16 D2 |
| Hotel Yasmin | (see 13) |
| Prima Garden Café | 17 B3 |
| Rumah Makan Lalapan | 18 D2 |

| TRANSPORT | |
|---|---|
| APO Port | 19 D2 |
| 'Base G' Taksi Stop | 20 D2 |
| Garuda | 21 C3 |
| Merpati | 22 C3 |
| Terminal Mesran | 23 D3 |

## TRAVEL AGENCIES

**PT Kuwera Jaya** ( ☎ 533 333; Jl Percetakan 96; ⏰ 8am-9pm Mon-Sat, 10am-9pm Sun) This efficient company sells tickets for flights and Pelni boats from Jayapura and also for some flights from other Papuan cities.

## TRAVEL PERMIT

**Polresta** ( ☎ 531 027; Jl Yani 11; ⏰ officially 7am-3pm Mon-Fri) Police elsewhere in Papua will usually only issue a *surat jalan* for their own regencies, but here you can get one for everywhere you want to go in Papua (that's not off-limits). It normally takes one to two hours. See p778 for more on the *surat jalan*.

## Sleeping

Rates include breakfast at all these hotels.

### BUDGET

**Hotel Ayu** ( ☎ 532 174; Jl Tugu Il 1; s 82,500-198,000, d 110,000-198,000Rp, tr 297,000Rp; ❄ ) Being the best cheap choice in Jayapura, this place is often full, and no wonder – it's snug and bright, with a pleasant common hall. Fan-only rooms have shared *mandis*, while air-con rooms have private ones.

**Hotel Sederhana** ( ☎ 531 561; Jl Halmahera 2; r 110,000 or 220,000Rp; ❄ ) It's drab, but central and quite clean. The cheaper rooms (often full) have fans and shared *mandis*; the others have air-con with private *mandis*.

### MIDRANGE & TOP END

**Hotel Dafonsoro** ( ☎ /fax 531 695, 534 055; Jl Percetakan 20; r 198,000-330,000; ❄ ) The Dafonsoro is friendly, quiet and clean, with hot showers, though the rooms are characterless and only the most expensive have windows (they have small terraces over the street too). Breakfast is fairly minimal.

**ourpick Permata Hotel** ( ☎ 531 333; hotelpermata@ yahoo.co.id; Jl Olah Raga 3; s 195,000-355,000Rp, d 270,000-430,000Rp; ❄ ) This new hotel on the edge of the market zone provides good, modern rooms with hot showers, shiny tile floors and kettles. Staff are welcoming and the restaurant is open 24 hours – it's good value.

**Hotel Papua** ( ☎ 535 800; fax 533-700; Jl Percetakan 78; r 400,000-550,000; ❄ ) Along with bonuses like hot water, satellite TV and bathtubs in the most expensive rooms, this place goes the extra decorating mile with colourful, quite tasteful

PAPUA

murals and photos. It's a bit overpriced, and staff can be sleepy, but there's a reasonable restaurant (with beer).

**Swiss-belhotel** ( ☎ 551 888; www.swiss-belhotel .com; Jl Pasifik Permai; r 672,000-1,340,000Rp; ☒ ☒ ☒ ) Opened in 2007, the Swiss-bel provides high-quality, European-style comfort right by the sea on the northern side of the centre. There's nothing very Papuan about it, but with a lovely open-air pool, a business centre and a good restaurant (mains 50,000Rp to 170,000Rp, lunch buffet for 79,000Rp from 11.30am to 2.30pm Monday to Friday), you can't beat it for comforts.

Also recommended:

**Matoa International Hotel** ( ☎ 531 633; Jl Yani 14; s/d 365,000/475,000Rp; ☒ ) Rooms are good and comfy, and there's interesting Papuan art in the lobby.

**Hotel Yasmin** ( ☎ 533 222; Jl Percetakan 8; s 381,000-610,000Rp, d 457,000-686,000Rp; ☒ ) A quite classy place with well-equipped but small rooms.

## Eating & Drinking

Jayapura is 'dry' except for the restaurants of the better hotels.

**Prima Garden Café** ( ☎ 532 038; Jl Yani 28; cakes & pastries 3000-4500Rp, drinks 7000-14,000Rp; ☒ closed Sun) Join locals relaxing over coffee, tea, juice and *wajik* (sweet black rice cake) at this old-fashioned, fan-cooled upstairs joint.

**Duta Café** ( ☎ 0852-4450 6672; Jl Pasifik Permai; rice & noodle dishes 15,000-30,000Rp, fish mains 30,000-55,000Rp; ☒ evening) Long lines of warungs open in the evening along Jl Pasifik Permai, cooking up all sorts of Indonesian goodies including seafood galore. You won't go wrong at the large, clean Duta Café. An excellent *ikan bakar* comes with five *sambals* (chilli sauces) lined up on your table, and the juice drinks go down very nicely too.

**Rumah Makan Lalapan** ( ☎ 531 949; Jl Percetakan 8; mains 20,000-50,000Rp) The best of a poor lot downtown (hotels excepted), with fish, chicken and *nasi goreng* choices, and oddly successful decor of dangling plastic leaves.

**Excelso Café** ( ☎ 534 450; Jl Percetakan 38; coffee, cakes & snacks 22,000-55,000Rp; ☒ ☒ ) Recline in large easy chairs and choose from a range of Indonesian and international coffees (hot or iced), sandwiches, ice cream and serious Black Forest gateau!

**Hotel Yasmin** ( ☎ 533 222; Jl Percetakan 8; mains 30,000-130,000Rp; ☒ 24hr; ☒ ) The lobby restaurant here has about the best prepared and presented food downtown, from good *nasi* *goreng istimewa* (special fried rice) to steaks, fish and American breakfasts. It'll serve you a cold beer too – and it never closes.

## Entertainment

Jayapura's soccer team, Persipura (nicknamed Mutiara Hitam – the Black Pearls), were champions of the Indonesia Super League in 2005 and 2009 – a big source of Papuan pride! Stadion Mandala is 3km northeast of the centre, reachable by 'Base G' *taksi* from Jl Sam Ratulangi. Check www.bli-online.com for fixtures.

## Getting There & Away

### AIR

**Jayapura airport** ( ☎ 591 809), actually at Sentani, 36km west, is the hub of Papuan aviation and many people's first point of arrival in Papua. If you do much travelling around Papua you'll probably pass through here a few times. Tickets are available in the airport departures hall and at travel agencies and the airlines' offices. The airport desks require cash payment and usually close when their flights are finished for the day.

**Aviastar** Flies to Wamena four times daily (tickets sold at check-in counter).

**Batavia Air** airport ( ☎ 591 745); Jayapura ( ☎ 550 666; Blok B 3A, Jl Pasifik Permai) Flies to Manokwari, Makassar and Jakarta four times weekly.

**Expressair** Jayapura ( ☎ 550 444; Blok G 10/2, Jl Pasifik Permai) Flies to Manokwari, Sorong, Makassar and Jakarta daily; connections in Sorong for Manado, Ambon and Ternate.

**Garuda** airport ( ☎ 594 111); Jayapura ( ☎ 522 221/2; Jl Yani 5-7; ☒ 9am-5.30pm Mon-Fri, 10am-3pm Sat & Sun) Flies to Biak, Timika, Denpasar, Makassar and Jakarta daily.

**Lion Air** ( ☎ 594 042/3, 594 576/7) At the airport. Flies to Makassar and Jakarta daily.

**Merpati** airport ( ☎ 591 288); Jayapura ( ☎ 533 111; Jl Yani 15; ☒ 8am-5pm Mon-Fri, 9am-3pm Sat & Sun) Flies to Biak, Timika, Merauke, Makassar and Jakarta daily, and to Manokwari and Manado three times weekly.

**Trigana Air** airport ( ☎ 594 592); Sentani (Map p792; ☎ 594 383/4; Komplek Ruko Multijaya No 266, Jl Raya Kemiri) Flies to Wamena four or more times daily.

### BOAT

Five Pelni liners leave here every two weeks bound for Sorong (1st/economy class 950,000/315,000Rp, two days) via selections of the intermediate ports – including Biak (495,000/174,000Rp), Serui and Manokwari (685,000/230,000Rp) – and then on to Maluku and/or Sulawesi. The **port** (Jl Koti) is accessible by any *taksi* heading to Hamadi or Entrop. Tickets for all major boats are available there or at agencies including PT Kuwera Jaya (p790).

Perintis boats also head along the coast, putting in at smaller ports too and even heading to villages up rivers such as the Mamberamo. They normally leave from the **APO port** (Jl Sam Ratulangi) and typically take about a week to reach Sorong, with fares of around 75,000Rp to Biak, 100,000Rp to Manokwari and 110,000Rp to Sorong.

### Getting Around

Official airport taxis from Sentani airport to central Jayapura cost a hefty 200,000Rp. Outside the airport gate you can charter one for 100,000Rp to 120,000Rp with bargaining. Going by public *taksi* from Sentani to Jayapura involves three changes and takes about 1½ hours. It's less bad than it sounds, as each change is just a hop into another vehicle waiting at the same stop. First get one from Sentani (outside the airport gate or heading to the right along the main road 400m straight ahead) to Waena (4000Rp, 20

to 30 minutes). The other stages are Waena to Abepura (3000Rp, 10 minutes), Abepura to Entrop (3500Rp, 20 minutes) and Entrop to Jayapura (2500Rp, 20 to 30 minutes).

Heading back south from Jayapura, go through the same routine in reverse. You can pick up Entrop-bound *taksi* on Jl Percetakan or at **Terminal Mesran** (Jl Koti).

## SENTANI
☎ 0967

Sentani, the growing airport town 36km west of Jayapura, is a place you'll almost certainly pass through on your Papuan travels and also an interesting spot to base yourself for a couple of days. Set between the forested Pegunungan Cyclop and beautiful Danau Sentani, it's quieter, cooler and more convenient than Jayapura and has most of the facilities you'll need.

### Orientation & Information

The older area, near the airport, has wide, tree-lined streets. West along very busy Jl Raya Kemiri is the much busier part of town where most of the inhabitants and local com-

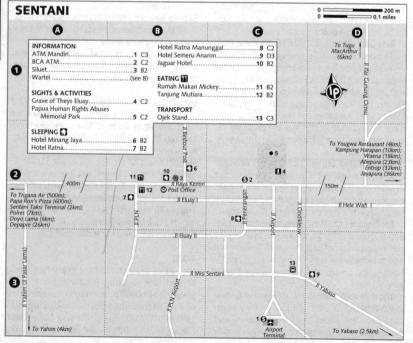

**SENTANI**

| INFORMATION | |
| --- | --- |
| ATM Mandiri | 1 C3 |
| BCA ATM | 2 C2 |
| Siluet | 3 B2 |
| Wartel | (see 8) |

| SIGHTS & ACTIVITIES | |
| --- | --- |
| Grave of Theys Eluay | 4 C2 |
| Papua Human Rights Abuses Memorial Park | 5 C2 |

| SLEEPING | |
| --- | --- |
| Hotel Minang Jaya | 6 B2 |
| Hotel Ratna | 7 B2 |

| | |
| --- | --- |
| Hotel Ratna Manunggal | 8 C2 |
| Hotel Semeru Anaron | 9 D3 |
| Jaguar Hotel | 10 B2 |

| EATING | |
| --- | --- |
| Rumah Makan Mickey | 11 B2 |
| Tanjung Mutiara | 12 B2 |

| TRANSPORT | |
| --- | --- |
| Ojek Stand | 13 C3 |

To Tugu MacArthur (6km)

To Yougwa Restaurant (4km);
Kampung Harapan (10km);
Waena (18km);
Abepura (23km);
Entrop (32km);
Jayapura (36km)

To Trigana Air (500m);
Papa Ron's Pizza (600m);
Sentani Taksi Terminal (2km);
Polres (7km);
Doyo Lama (6km);
Depapre (26km)

Jl Raya Kemiri
Post Office
Jl Eluay I
Jl Eluay II
Jl Misi Sentani
Jl Hele Wafi I
Jl Yabaso

To Yahim (4km)

To Yabaso (2.5km)

Airport Terminal

Jl Yahim Di Pasar Lama
Jl PLN
Jl PLN Airport
Jl Bestour Post
Jl Penerangan
Jl Airport
Jl Ondikleuw
Jl Itki Gunung Ormu

PAPUA

---

**THEYS ELUAY**

Right by the junction of Jl Airport and the main road in Sentani, where no arriving visitor can miss it, a former football field is now the **Papua Human Rights Abuses Memorial Park** (Jl Raya Kemiri). This contains nothing but the grave and memorial of the Papuan independence leader Theys Eluay, a Danau Sentani tribal chief, who was murdered in November 2001 by members of the Indonesian army's Kopassus special forces. Eluay was chairman of the Papua Council Presidium, which had been delegated by the Papua People's Congress of mid-2000 to seek a UN-sponsored referendum on Papuan independence. He was strangled while travelling in a car with Kopassus soldiers, who later received light sentences for the crime (3½ years' jail for their leader). The death triggered riots in Sentani, and thousands attended Eluay's funeral here.

---

merce are found. If you need to change cash dollars, you must go to Jayapura.

**ATM Mandiri** (airport) Outside the arrivals hall, this dispenses convenient cash to Visa and Plus cards.

**BCA ATM** (Bank Central Asia; Jl Raya Kemiri) Good for Visa, Plus, MasterCard and Cirrus.

**Polres** ( ☎ 591 110; Jl Yowanibi, Doyo Baru; ☺ officially 8am-3pm Mon-Fri) This police station 5km west of Sentani takes about an hour to issue a *surat jalan* for the Baliem Valley area. An *ojek* from Sentani costs around 10,000Rp.

**Siluet** (Jl Raya Kemiri 60; internet access per hr 8000Rp; ☺ 8am-10pm) Has four computers.

**Wartel** (Hotel Ratna Manunggal, Jl Penerangan; ☺ 7am-1am) Convenient spot to make phone calls.

## Festivals

The **Lake Sentani Cultural & Art Festival**, for a few days around 20 June, was only inaugurated in 2008 but promises to be well worth attending. Music, dance, art and crafts of the lake peoples and nearby coastal communities are featured.

## Sleeping

**Hotel Minang Jaya** ( ☎ 591 919; Jl Bestour Post 2; r 120,000-140,000Rp; ☒ ) Rooms are rather dark and far past their prime, but the hotel is kept reasonably clean. The cheapest rooms share *mandis*; the most expensive have air-con. A small breakfast is included.

**Hotel Semeru Anaron** ( ☎ 591 447; Jl Yabaso 10; r 150,000-250,000Rp; ☒ ) The best-value cheapie, and very convenient to the airport. Rooms are slightly worn, but clean and comfortable. Breakfast is do-and-brew yourself.

**Hotel Ratna Manunggal** ( ☎ 592 277; fax 582 340; Jl Penerangan 2; s/d incl breakfast from 225,000/275,000Rp; ☒ ) A decently kept and run, if rather soulless hotel, this has big, blue, clean, air-con rooms, with *mandis* and sit-down toilets.

**ourpick** **Hotel Ratna** (Hotel Ratna Keyko; ☎ 591 119; fax 594 449; Jl PLN 1; s/d incl breakfast 250,000/280,000Rp;

☒ ) The Ratna's rooms are very clean and comfortable, and mostly good-sized, with cable TV and homey touches. Most of the efficient, friendly staff speak English, and the standard is the best in Sentani for the price, though the showers aren't heated. Dinners (20,000Rp to 35,000Rp) are available and airport drop-offs are free.

**Jaguar Hotel** ( ☎ 510 0201; Jl Raya Kemiri; r 250,000-350,000Rp; ☒ ) A friendly new place with just six freshly painted rooms, all equipped with air-con, hot showers and TV. Cake-and-tea breakfast included.

**Yougwa Restaurant** (Map p795; ☎ 571 570; Jl Raya Kemiri; r incl breakfast 262,000-523,000Rp; ☒ ) This excellent lakeside restaurant (below) has four sparkling guest rooms, with their own bathrooms and balconies over the lake.

## Eating

**Tanjung Mutiara** (Jl Raya Kemiri; mains 10,000-25,000Rp; ☺ 7am-7pm) Tasty Padang *nasi campur* in clean premises under cooling fans. You can easily fill up for 25,000Rp.

**Rumah Makan Mickey** ( ☎ 591 339; Jl Raya Kemiri 49; mains 12,000-40,000Rp; ☺ 9am-2.30pm & 5-9.30pm) Brightly painted, diner-style Mickey remains the most popular place for travellers and expats. The big range of Indonesian, Chinese and Western-style dishes is good on quantity but ordinary on flavour.

**ourpick** **Yougwa Restaurant** (Map p795; ☎ 571570; Jl Raya Kemiri; mains 30,000-45,000Rp; ☺ 9am-8pm Mon-Sat, 11am-5pm Sun & holidays) Sentani's most charming dining is on the Yougwa's breezy wooden terraces over the lakeside 4km east of town. Try the *ikan gabus* (snakehead), a lake fish that doesn't fill your mouth with little bones. While here you can take a trip in the Yougwa's sturdy motorboat (holding half a dozen passengers) with a knowledgeable driver-cum-guide, for a reasonable 200,000Rp per hour.

**PAPUA**

**Papa Ron's Pizza** ( ☎ 591 944; Sentani City Square Mall, Jl Raya Kemiri 286; medium pizzas 45,000-70,000Rp; ⏱ 10am-10pm) Wouldn't mind a familiar feed after trekking in the mountains? You might just have to head to this unashamedly Western-style joint inside Papua's glitziest mall. No pig products among the toppings, but there are plenty of tempting options – and a decent salad bar (23,000Rp).

## Getting There & Around

See p791 for information on flights from Sentani and p792 for transport between Sentani, Jayapura and intermediate points.

A taxi from the airport to most Sentani hotels costs 20,000Rp, but you can easily walk or hop an *ojek* (5000Rp).

Public *taksi* (3000 Rp) marked 'Trm Sentani-Hawai' shuttle up and down Jl Raya Kemiri between their terminal at the western end of town and the Hawai area out east.

## AROUND JAYAPURA & SENTANI
☎ 0967

Several interesting places around Jayapura and Sentani can be easily visited on day trips from either town. For details on transport along the Sentani–Jayapura road, see p792.

## Pantai Base G

Base G Beach (also known as Pantai Tanjung Ria) is nearly 3km long and desolate – except on Sunday, when locals come in droves for a picnic and walk. It's the best beach easily accessible from Jayapura. Here was established the administrative HQ of the American forces in 1944. Frequent 'Base G' *taksi* start from Jl Sam Ratulangi in Jayapura for the 5km trip to Tanjung Ria; the beach is a 10-minute walk down the hill.

## Hamadi

Hamadi, 3km south of central Jayapura, has several specialist **Papuan craft shops** ( ⏱ daily) along its main street, Jl Pasar Hamadi. The drums, statues, shields, stone axes, arrows, bark paintings and penis gourds – some mass-produced for a tourist market – are from many parts of Papua and even PNG. Hamadi's daily **fish market** is down a side street 300m further south.

**Pantai Hamadi**, site of one of the US amphibious landings on 22 April 1944, is another 2km south. The beach is long, sweeping and picturesque, but it's far from secluded and

fairly dirty. The remains of two landing craft and one tank sit on pedestals at its near end. It's 500m off the Hamadi–Entrop road, along a side road starting beside a large navy barracks (where you may have to show a copy of your *surat jalan*).

*Taksi* head to Hamadi (2500Rp) from Jl Koti in Jayapura every few seconds; you can also catch one from the terminal at Entrop. From Hamadi to the barracks, take an Entrop-bound *taksi* or an *ojek*.

## Temples

Halfway along the road between Entrop and Abepura, it's worth stopping for a look around two huge temples – if mainly for the magnificent views of Teluk Yotefa. The Balinese Hindu **Pura Agung Surya Bhuvana** (admission free; ⏱ daylight hours), on the inland side of the road, is architecturally nothing special, but the vistas are more than enough reason to visit. About 300m further down the road towards Abepura, the Buddhist **Vihara Arya Dharma** is signposted to the left at a sharp right turn. Again, it wasn't built in any special style, but the setting and views are worth the steep 400m walk up from the road.

## Museum Loka Budaya

Cenderawasih University's **Cultural Museum** ( ☎ 581 227; Jl Abepura, Abepura; admission 5000Rp; ⏱ 8am-3pm Sun-Fri) contains a fascinating range of Papuan artefacts between 80 and 300 years old, including the best collection of Asmat carvings and 'devil-dance' costumes outside Agats, plus fine crafts from several other areas, historical photos and musical instruments. With luck you'll be guided round by an English-speaking staff member and learn a lot about Papuan culture. The museum is 250m west of the main-road *taksi* stop in Abepura.

## Danau Sentani

You get a bird's-eye view of 96.5 sq km Danau Sentani, snaking its way between picturesque green hills, if you fly in or out of Sentani. Down at water level, this beautiful lake, with its 19 islands and numerous Papuan fishing villages of wooden stilt houses, is well worth a day or two of your time. A visit to any of the islands or villages is quite a change of pace – in fact, it's a bit like travelling back in time.

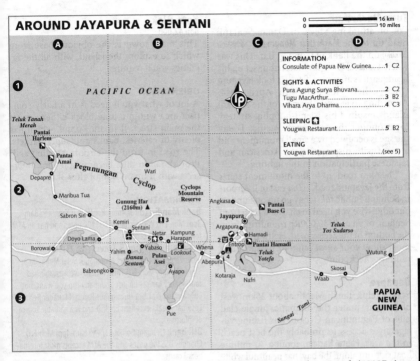

## AROUND JAYAPURA & SENTANI

| INFORMATION | |
|---|---|
| Consulate of Papua New Guinea | **1** C2 |

| SIGHTS & ACTIVITIES | |
|---|---|
| Pura Agung Surya Bhuvana | **2** C2 |
| Tugu MacArthur | **3** B2 |
| Vihara Arya Dharma | **4** C3 |

| SLEEPING | |
|---|---|
| Yougwa Restaurant | **5** B2 |

| EATING | |
|---|---|
| Yougwa Restaurant | (see **5**) |

### PULAU ASEI

Asei Island is the main centre for Sentani bark paintings. Originally done only on bark clothing for women of chiefs' families, bark paintings are now a Sentani art form. To reach Asei, take a *taksi* to Kampung Harapan, then an *ojek* 2km south to the lake, where you can get a boat to the island – 20,000Rp per person if there's one going anyway, or 150,000Rp for a round-trip charter.

### YABASO

An inexpensive way to explore the lake is to stroll 3km southeast along Jl Yabaso from the airport gate in Sentani. The road (then path) goes through Yabaso village and continues around the lake past several villages.

### BABRONGKO

Babrongko village's woodcarvers produce beautifully worked knives, dishes, masks and drums. At the western end of the village you'll find the **Sanggar Kegiatan** (Craft Workshop) where locals learn the carving art and sell some work: you can pick up a nice piece for 100,000Rp to 200,000Rp.

From Sentani, take an *ojek* (5000Rp) or bemo (4000Rp) south along Jl Yahim to Yahim (4km), where boatmen will take you across to Babrongko for around 250,000Rp round-trip (about 30 minutes each way plus waiting time).

### DOYO LAMA

This village sits on its own bay 6km west of Sentani. On the right as you enter Doyo Lama you'll see the entrance to **Situs Megalitik Tutari** (Tutari Megalithic Site; admission free). This mysterious hillside site comprises various arrangements of rocks and stones and dozens of rock paintings of fish, turtles, crocodiles and lizards, all of uncertain age but still considered sacred by the villagers. The stones and paintings are in six different fenced areas, all reached by a good 1km concrete path. Try to recruit a local to show you everything and explain some of its significance.

Public *taksi* to Doyo Lama (5000Rp) go infrequently from the terminal in Sentani. *Ojek* riders charge 6000Rp to 8000Rp one way.

## Tugu MacArthur

For breathtaking views of Danau Sentani, head up to the **MacArthur Monument** (admission 5000Rp) on the flank of Gunung Ifar. This was where General Douglas MacArthur set up his headquarters after his US forces took Jayapura (then called Hollandia) in April 1944. According to legend, the view of the Sentani islands inspired his island-hopping strategy to reconquer the southwest Pacific. Today the site is occupied by a small monument and a room with displays on the American and Japanese participation in the fighting.

The 6km road up to the monument starts from the Jayapura road, 700m east of Jl Airport in Sentani. Public *taksi* may go up on Sunday, but otherwise you need to charter a *taksi* from Sentani, or an *ojek* (30,000Rp roundtrip) from the bottom of the access road. Halfway up, you must show your *surat jalan* or passport at a military checkpoint.

## Depapre

Set on Teluk Tanah Merah about 26km west of Sentani, under the dramatic, jungle-clad hills of Pegunungan Cyclop, this fishing village gives access to probably the best beach in the area. **Pantai Harlem**, about a 30-minute boat ride out along the bay, has beautiful white sands backed by jungle, and a coral reef good for snorkelling. It gets a few visitors at weekends but is never anything like crowded. Boats from Depapre's pier will carry you there for around 250,000Rp return. **Pantai Amai**, nearer to Depapre, is cheaper to reach but less appealing, with grey sand and a concrete boardwalk.

Public *taksi* to Depapre (5000Rp, 45 minutes) leave when full from the *taksi* terminal in western Sentani. It's a pretty ride.

## PULAU BIAK
☎ 0981

Sitting in the north of the broad Teluk Cenderawasih, Biak (1898 sq km) is one of Papua's biggest offshore islands. It's a relaxed place to chill out for a few days with, even by Papuan standards, exceptionally friendly people, and has good beaches and snorkelling spots. The coral reefs and beautiful beaches of the offshore Padaido Islands provide diving and further snorkelling opportunities.

Biak was the scene of fierce fighting in WWII, with over 6000 Japanese and nearly 500 Americans killed in the month-long Battle of Biak in 1944.

## Kota Biak
pop 42,000

This main town is the obvious base from which to explore the island, with all the facilities you'll require.

### ORIENTATION

A lot of what you'll need is in a fairly compact area within a long block either side of the main street, Jl Imam Bonjol, which has plenty of eateries, banks and supermarkets. The road in from the airport, starting as Jl Prof M Yamin then becoming Jl Yani, intersects with Jl Imam Bonjol after 3km.

### INFORMATION

**Bank Mandiri** (cnr Jl Imam Bonjol & Jl Yani; ◷ 8am-3pm Mon-Fri) Will exchange US$100 notes and has an ATM for Visa and Plus cards.

**Biak Paradise Tours & Travel** ( ☎ 23196; www.discoverpapua.com; Hotel Arumbai, Jl Selat Makassar 3; ◷ 8am-4pm Mon-Fri) This efficient, well-established tour agency can set up just about any trip you want, not only around Biak but throughout Papua. Manager Benny Lesomar speaks excellent English and is a valuable source of information.

**BNI bank** (Jl Imam Bonjol 23; ◷ 8am-4pm Mon-Fri) Changes US$100 notes and the ATM accepts most international cards.

**DiBiak.com** (Jl Sudirman 4; internet access per hr 9000Rp; ◷ 8am-9pm Mon-Sat, 4-9pm Sun) Popular internet centre with quite speedy connections in heavenly air-con comfort.

**Janggi Prima Tours & Travel** ( ☎ 22973; cme_pino@yahoo.co.id; Jl Pramuka 5) This experienced one-man show can take you on a range of trips around Biak and Yapen islands, including snorkelling and birdwatching.

**Police station** ( ☎ 21294; Jl Diponegoro 3; ◷ 8am-4pm Mon-Sat) *Surat jalan* are issued in an hour or so here. For Biak you only need one if you stay on an offshore island or go to neighbouring Pulau Supiori.

**Tourist office** ( ☎ 21663; Jl Prof M Yamin 56; ◷ 7.30am-2pm Mon-Fri) Two kilometres from the centre along the airport road. It has a brochure and staff do their best to answer queries.

### ACTIVITIES

Though Biak has been overshadowed by the Raja Ampat islands as a scuba destination, there is still some good **diving** and **snorkelling** to be done here. In general you'll see the biggest numbers of fish in May, June and July. Some fishermen don't help by continuing to practise dynamite and cyanide fishing.

# PULAU BIAK

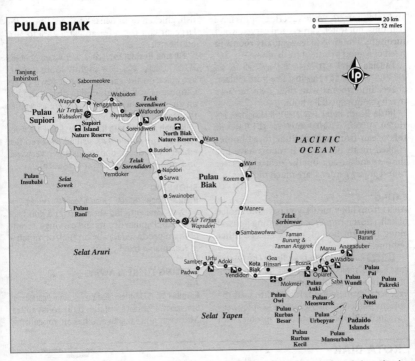

There are some worthwhile spots along the coast east of Kota Biak, with wall dives at Marau, Saba and Wadibu, which are also good snorkelling spots, as is Anggaduber a few kilometres further east. But the best diving, and some excellent snorkelling, is around the Padaido Islands (p800).

Local PADI dive master **Erick Farwas** ( ☎ 0813 4436 6385; laurenslexy@yahoo.co.id) offers two-dive outings to all the best spots. For two people, he asks 1,600,000Rp to 1,800,000Rp on the mainland, or 2,300,000Rp to 2,700,000Rp for the Padaido Islands (negotiable). Equipment rental is 250,000Rp per full set. Farwas also takes all-day snorkelling and sightseeing tours to the islands (1,700,000Rp to 3,200,000Rp for two people). Night dives and overnight island stays are further options.

## SLEEPING

All places listed here offer rooms with private bathroom or *mandi*, and breakfast included.

### Budget

**Hotel Maju** ( ☎ 21841; Jl Imam Bonjol 45; s/d 85,000/115,000Rp; ☒ ) Biak's best budget option:

the rooms are nothing special, but they're clean and reasonably sized. Those at the back are far quieter.

**Hotel Irian Biak** ( ☎ 21939; fax 21458; Jl Prof M Yamin 4; r 160,000-285,000Rp; ☒ ) Almost opposite the airport terminal, this rambling, colonial-era hotel, with large, grassy gardens overlooking the sea, is at last getting a renovation to realise its charm potential. Meantime, the cheaper rooms are reasonable value, with wood floors, cold showers, air-con and balconies, while the more expensive ones are bigger, better and more private, sitting close to the ocean.

### Midrange

**our pick** **Hotel Nirmala** ( ☎ 22005; Jl Selat Madura 13; s/d 225,000/290,000Rp; ☒ ) Terrific value, with amiable staff and three meals included in room rates. The rooms are immaculate and recently renovated, with good air-con, comfy beds, spacious bathrooms with hot showers, and little sitting areas along a tidy courtyard that catches cool breezes.

**Hotel Arumbai** ( ☎ 21835; fax 22501; Jl Selat Makassar 3; s 236,000-363,000Rp, d 315,000-448,000Rp; ☒ ☒ ) Standard rooms come with cool marble floors and cold showers, while superior rooms have bathtubs, hot water, carpets and carved wood furniture. The air-con leaves many rooms in need of a good breath of fresh air.

**Padaido Hotel** ( ☎ 22144; Jl Monginsidi 16; s/d 250,000/270,000Rp; ✹ ) Has just five immaculate, cheery little rooms with their own terraces overlooking a small harbour.

**Intsia Beach Hotel** ( ☎ 21891; Jl Monginsidi 7; s 250,000-300,000Rp, d 350,000-400,000Rp; ✹ ) Rates at this ocean-front spot include three home-cooked meals per day. All rooms have hot showers and air-con, but the 'deluxe' ones, set round grassy gardens, are much nicer.

### EATING

Apart from hotel meals, you have the choice of half a dozen *rumah makan* (eating houses) along Jl Imam Bonjol, plus scattered other options.

**our pick Rumah Makan Jawa Timur** ( ☎ 22544; Jl Imam Bonjol 37; mains 12,000-30,000Rp; ✹ ) The pick of the Imam Bonjol joints, this place serves excellent Javanese food. It's hard to beat the options that combine rice, *pecel* (a spicy peanut sauce with spinach and bean sprouts) with

fish, chicken or prawns. You can dine in the large air-con room for an extra 25% to 30% on the prices.

**Furama Restaurant** ( ☎ 22022; Jl Yani 22; mains 25,000-70,000Rp; ✹ ) This slightly more upmarket place on the eastern side of town offers Chinese as well as Indonesian dishes and has an air-con room and outdoor cafe as well as the regular dining room.

**Rumah Makan Cinta Rasa Baru** (Jl Yani; fish dishes 40,000Rp) The *ikan bakar*, grilled over red-hot embers outside the door, goes down very well and comes with rice and spicy sauces.

### SHOPPING

**Iriani Art Shop** ( ☎ 21457; Jl Imam Bonjol 40; ✹ 8am-2pm & 5-9pm) This enticing shop carries a good selection of Papuan drums and carvings – some of them produced locally on Biak or Yapen – at reasonable fixed prices.

### GETTING THERE & AWAY
#### Air

**Garuda** ( ☎ 25737; Jl Sudirman 3; ✹ 7.30am-9pm Mon-Fri, 8am-noon & 5-9pm Sat & Sun) flies daily to Jayapura, Makassar and Jakarta and has an appealingly

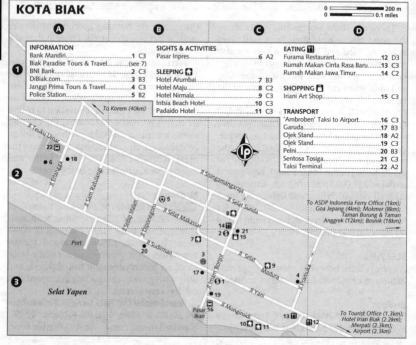

**KOTA BIAK**

0 —— 200 m
0 —— 0.1 miles

| INFORMATION | |
| --- | --- |
| Bank Mandiri | 1 C3 |
| Biak Paradise Tours & Travel | (see 7) |
| BNI Bank | 2 C3 |
| DiBiak.com | 3 B3 |
| Janggi Prima Tours & Travel | 4 C3 |
| Police Station | 5 B2 |

| SIGHTS & ACTIVITIES | |
| --- | --- |
| Pasar Inpres | 6 A2 |

| SLEEPING | |
| --- | --- |
| Hotel Arumbai | 7 B3 |
| Hotel Maju | 8 C2 |
| Hotel Nirmala | 9 C3 |
| Intsia Beach Hotel | 10 C3 |
| Padaido Hotel | 11 C3 |

| EATING | |
| --- | --- |
| Furama Restaurant | 12 D3 |
| Rumah Makan Cinta Rasa Baru | 13 C3 |
| Rumah Makan Jawa Timur | 14 C2 |

| SHOPPING | |
| --- | --- |
| Iriani Art Shop | 15 C3 |

| TRANSPORT | |
| --- | --- |
| 'Ambroben' Taksi to Airport | 16 C3 |
| Garuda | 17 B3 |
| Ojek Stand | 18 A2 |
| Ojek Stand | 19 C3 |
| Pelni | 20 B3 |
| Sentosa Tosiga | 21 C3 |
| Taksi Terminal | 22 A2 |

To Korem (40km)

Jl Teuku Umar

Jl Eridanga

Jl Sam Ratulangi

Jl Sedap Malam

Jl Dipoonegoro

Port

Jl Sisingamangaraja

Jl Selat Sunda

Jl Selat Makassar

Jl Sudirman

Jl Imam Bonjol

Jl Selat Madura

Jl Yani

Jl Monginsidi

Pasar Ikan

Selat Yapen

To ASDP Indonesia Ferry Office (1km);
Goa Jepang (4km); Mokmer (8km);
Taman Burung & Taman
Anggrek (12km); Bosnik (18km)

Jl Iriamuka

To Tourist Office (1.3km);
Hotel Irian Biak (2.2km);
Merpati (2.3km);
Airport (2.3km)

PAPUA

air-conditioned, computerised downtown office. **Merpati** ( ☎ 24900; Jl Prof M Yamin; ☺ 8am-4pm Mon-Fri, 10-2pm Sat & Sun) flies daily to Jayapura and Makassar, four times a week to Jakarta and twice weekly to Manokwari. Its office is opposite the airport, so you may find it easier to use one of the town-centre ticket agencies. Susi Air flies every morning to Serui (900,000Rp): buy tickets at **Sentosa Tosiga** ( ☎ 21398; Jl Imam Bonjol 42; ☺ 8am-8pm Mon-Sat, 8am-noon & 5-8pm Sun).

### Boat

**Pelni** ( ☎ 23255/6; Jl Sudirman 37; ☺ 9am-noon & 2-5pm Mon-Fri, 9am-1pm Sat, 10am-5pm Sun) has three liners serving Biak. The *Sinabung* (every two weeks) and *Gunung Dempo* (every four weeks) head to Jayapura (1st/economy class 495,000/174,000Rp), via Serui in the *Sinabung's* case. Westbound, both ships, as well as the *Nggapulu* (every two weeks), go to Sorong (820,000/263,000Rp) – *Gunung Dempo* direct, *Sinabung* via Manokwari (300,000/110,000Rp), and *Nggapulu* via Serui, Nabire and Manokwari – and then on to Maluku.

Two ships of **ASDP Indonesia Ferry** ( ☎ 22577; Jl Bosnik Raya 38; ☺ 8am-5pm Mon-Fri) make weekly trips from Biak to ports around Teluk Cenderawasih. The *Gutila* sails to Serui (economy/business class 58,000/82,000Rp) and beyond, usually departing on Friday afternoon. The *Teluk Cenderawasih II* leaves on Tuesday afternoon for Pulau Numfor and Manokwari (88,000Rp). The office is on the eastern edge of Kota Biak, but the boats leave from Mokmer, about 8km east.

### Taksi

Public *taksi* to places around the island leave from the terminal on Jl Erlangga, next to Pasar Inpres. On most routes service winds down in the afternoon. Blue *taksi* to Bosnik (5000Rp, 30 to 40 minutes), passing Mokmer and Taman Burung, normally go every few minutes. *Taksi* to Anggaduber (9000Rp, one hour) normally go at least hourly. There are also *taksi* up Biak's east coast to Warsa (10,000Rp, two hours) via Korem.

### GETTING AROUND

Yellow public *taksi* (2500Rp) going to the right (west) outside the airport terminal head to the town centre. Returning, take one marked 'Ambroben' from the corner of Jl Imam Bonjol and Jl Monginsidi or heading east along Jl Yani. *Ojek* drivers charge 5000Rp for rides in town.

## Around Pulau Biak & Nearby Islands

Many interesting places are dotted around Pulau Biak, and roads circle the island. Public *taksi* and buses (left) reach most places, but you can make things easier by chartering a car or *ojek*, or taking a trip with Janggi Prima (p796) or Biak Paradise (p796). A three-person outing to the main sites east of Kota Biak as far as Anggaduber with Janggi Prima will cost approximately 600,000Rp to 750,000Rp.

Remember that villages on the island may look biggish on a map, but most are little more than a handful of huts, with no accommodation or food for travellers.

### GOA JEPANG

The **Japanese Cave** ( ☎ 26641; Jl Goa Jepang 47; admission incl museum 20,000Rp; ☺ 7am-5pm), 4km northeast of Kota Biak, was used a base and hideout in WWII by thousands of Japanese soldiers. A tunnel from the cave is said to lead 3km to the coast at Parai, another Japanese base. In 1944, an estimated 3000 Japanese died when US forces located the cave, dropped petrol drums into it and then bombarded it from above.

From the end of a concrete walkway, steps lead down into the biggest cave, with a small tunnel off one chamber that led to the officers' quarters below. In and around the ticket office, and in a small museum over the road, is a remarkable collection of Japanese and US weapons, equipment and photos.

An *ojek* from town costs 10,000Rp. Sumberker-bound public *taksi* from the Inpres terminal (2500Rp) can drop you at the cave, or you can take a more frequent Bosnik *taksi* and ask to be dropped at the unsigned road that leads 700m up to the cave. At the top of a steepish uphill bit after 300m, you pass a Japanese gun emplacement overlooking the airport, which was the focus of all the fighting.

### TAMAN BURUNG & TAMAN ANGGREK

At Ibdi, 12km east of downtown Kota Biak, the **Bird & Orchid Garden** (Jl Raya Bosnik km 12; admission 10,000Rp; ☺ 7am-6pm) contains a sizeable collection of (caged) Papuan birds, including strikingly coloured lories, hornbills, cockatoos and birds of paradise, as well as dozens of types of orchid. Several semi-tame cassowaries roam freely, so keep your eyes peeled.

### BOSNIK

Bosnik, 18km from Kota Biak, is a laid-back village strung along the coast for 2km, where you could happily base yourself for a relaxing few days. The site of the US landing in 1944, today Bosnik holds a busy little morning **market** every Tuesday, Thursday and Saturday. The best section of the beach is **Pantai Segara Indah** at the eastern end, with good sand, shelters (30,000Rp per day) and some coloured coral offshore. It's virtually empty weekdays.

**Guest House Beach Bosnik** ( ☎ 81078; Jl Bosnik Raya; s 100,000Rp, d 150,000-250,000Rp; 🔀 ), about 500m east of the market, has half a dozen spotless upstairs rooms, four of them air-conditioned and two with private bathroom, in a sturdy brick-and-ironwood house facing the sea. Owner Agustina speaks English, rates include breakfast and other meals are available.

About 100m further east, little **Warung Pareke** (mains 10,000-30,000Rp) will do you good noodle or rice dishes or *ikan bakar*, and has homemade doughnuts for breakfast.

### EAST OF BOSNIK

The road turns inland just before Opiaref, 3km east of Bosnik, but you can continue on foot 6km along the coast through Opiaref to Marau, Saba and Wadibu, where a road heads about 500m inland to rejoin the Anggaduber road. **Pantai Marau** is overlooked by the shell of a large luxury hotel built by 'Tommy' Suharto in the early 1990s. The hotel closed when Garuda's Los Angeles–Biak–Jakarta flights ceased in 1997. It continues to disintegrate by the day as villagers strip it of all usable materials. The coral and fish in front of the beach make for good snorkelling and diving, as do the rocky islets in front of and beyond the next village east, **Saba**.

Bosnik-route *taksi* from Kota Biak usually go as far as the Opiaref turning. Or you could take an Anggaduber *taksi* and walk 1km down to Marau or Saba from the main road.

**Anggaduber**, 3km beyond Wadibu, is an attractive village with grass-lawned houses and a good, palm-lined, sandy beach. The snorkelling is good along the first, western, part from where the road hits the coast.

### PADAIDO ISLANDS

This lovely cluster of 36 reefs and islands (only 13 of them inhabited) makes for a great day trip from Kota Biak or Bosnik, and you can stay over on some islands. Virtually all the islands have jungle-backed, white-sand beaches with crystal-clear waters, coral reefs and plenty of marine life. The best **snorkelling** spots include Pulau Wundi, which has particularly good coral and many fish near the surface; the eastern side of unpopulated Pulau Rurbas Kecil; Pulau Meoswarek; and Pulau Nusi. Top **diving** sites include the western end of Pulau Owi, with good coral and big fish; Pulau Rurbas Besar for coral, sharks, turtles, sea fans and more big fish; Pulau Wundi, with a cave, a long wall and good coral; and Barracuda Point, south of Pulau Meoswarek.

You can charter a boat from Bosnik for around 300,000Rp to 400,000Rp round-trip to Owi (just 2km from Bosnik), or 500,000Rp to Auki (5km), the two nearest and most populated islands. You can also find boats in Kota Biak, but they take longer and cost about twice as much.

Erick Farwas (p797) offers diving trips and also sightseeing-and-snorkelling trips, which are an attractive way for nondivers to explore the islands. In addition, Farwas has a basic three-room **guest house** (r incl meals 150,000Rp) on Pulau Wundi.

If you plan to stay on the islands, the cheapest way to get there is from Bosnik on Tuesday, Thursday or Saturday, when islanders are returning from Bosnik market about 3pm or 4pm and you should be able to get a place in a boat for the local price of 30,000Rp to 50,000Rp. You can normally find accommodation in a village house or by asking the local churchkeeper – bring food and expect to pay 20,000Rp to 50,000Rp per night.

### KOREM

On the east coast of Pulau Biak, Korem was mostly destroyed by an earthquake and tsunami in 1996. The village has been rebuilt inland of the main road, but the **beach** is still delightful, though most locals refuse to visit it because of the number of people who died there in 1996. Ask the *taksi* driver to drop you at the beach turn-off, and wait for a lift or walk (about 30 minutes).

## PULAU YAPEN
☎ 0983

This elongated, mountainous, rainforest-covered island, south of Pulau Biak, offers the chance to see **birds of paradise** and superb snorkelling in several spots. The only town of any size is the regency capital, Serui (population 25,000). A *surat jalan* for Yapen can be easily obtained in Kota Biak.

The lesser bird of paradise dwells near **Aikakoba** village, a 45-minute boat ride from Poom near the western end of the north coast. A trip by boat from Serui with a local guide and an overnight village stay should cost 1,000,000Rp to 1,500,000Rp for a small group. Alternatively, go by boat from Biak through one of Kota Biak's two travel agencies (p796). Another site for the lesser bird of paradise is **Barawai** in eastern Yapen. Around both places you should see a good number of other interesting birds such as hornbills, cockatoos and lorikeets.

Less than one hour south of Serui (you'll have to charter a boat), **Pulau Ambai** offers wonderful **snorkelling** (bring your own gear) among coral reefs and dolphins, and is home to thousands of cockatoos and hornbills.

Yapen's only hotels are in Serui:

**Bersaudara Hotel** ( ☎ 31123; Jl Sudirman 56; r 150,000Rp) Offers basic but clean rooms, without air-con.

**Hotel Merpati** ( ☎ 31154; Jl Yos Sudarso 8; r incl breakfast 180,000-300,000Rp; 🔀 ) Serui's best: staff are cluey about transport arrangements, all rooms are air-conditioned, and lunch and dinner are available.

Susi Air flies daily between Biak and Serui, and ASDP Indonesia Ferry's *Gutila* sails weekly from Biak to Serui and back (see p799 for further information). Pelni's *Sinabung* sails from Sorong to Jayapura via Manokwari, Biak and Serui, and vice versa, every two weeks. The *Dorolonda* and *Nggapulu* also call at Serui.

# THE BALIEM VALLEY

The Baliem Valley (Lembah Baliem in Bahasa Indonesia) is the most popular destination in Papua and the most accessible place in the interior. The Dani people who live here were still dependent on tools of stone, bone and wood when the first white men (a natural-history expedition led by American Richard Archbold) chanced upon the valley in 1938. The Dani have since adopted various modern ways and new beliefs, but the valley remains one of the world's last truly fascinating, traditional areas.

The valley is about 60km long and 16km wide and bounded by high mountains on all sides. Wamena sits at its centre at an altitude of 1550m. The powerful Sungai Baliem running through the valley escapes through a narrow gorge at the southern end, then drops about 1500m in less than 50km on its way to Papua's southern coast. Amid this spectacular scenery, the majority of the Dani still live close to nature, tending their vegetable plots and pigs, around villages composed of circular thatched huts called *honai*.

The first Christian missionaries arrived in 1954 (missionary activity is still a big feature of highland life today), and a Dutch government post was established in Wamena in 1956. These days, Indonesia has added its own brand of colonialism, bringing schools, police, soldiers, shops, motor vehicles and becaks to the valley, though the local culture has in many ways proved resilient. Tensions between Papuans and non-Papuans sometimes erupt into violence – notably during a large-scale highland uprising in 1977 and again in 2000 when clashes led to a temporary exodus of non-Papuans.

## Climate & When To Go

In the drier months from May to November, most days are fine and warm and the evenings cool. From December to April you can still trek, but more mud and rain can make it harder work. At all times of year, you should be prepared for rain, and always take cold-weather gear for higher areas, such as Danau Habbema. During the busiest tourism season, July and August, the Baliem Valley can be quite busy with groups of tourists and trekkers. ·

## Travel Permit

You must have a *surat jalan* (p778) for Wamena and the Baliem Valley. If you're going beyond the main Baliem Valley (for example to Danau Habbema or the Yali or Lani country) make sure your *surat jalan* covers this. You can obtain your *surat jalan* at Sentani (p793) or Jayapura (p790). The Wamena police (p803) will also issue one if you haven't already got it. If you already have a *surat jalan* when you arrive in Wamena you must report to the police there within 24 hours.

In the countryside, you should show your *surat jalan* to police stations or village authorities if you *stay* (ie not visit on a day trip) anywhere outside Wamena.

PAPUA

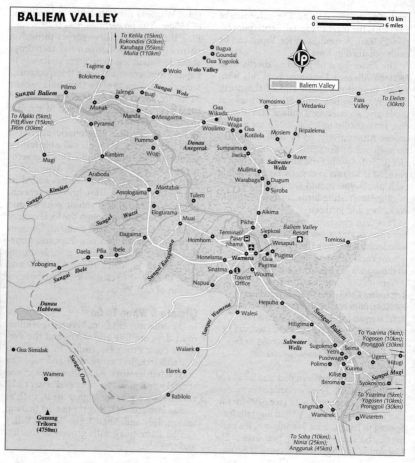

## BALIEM VALLEY

Some more remote areas in the region may be off limits to foreigners; the Wamena police can tell you about the current situation.

## Getting There & Around

Flying into Wamena (p805) is the only way to reach the Baliem Valley. Once you're here, trekking is the best way to explore the landscape and local life. But it is also possible to get around the main valley – and see traditional people and villages, as well as mummies, markets and hanging bridges – by car, bemo or *ojek* (p805). Three main roads head out from Wamena:

- North up the eastern side of the valley to Pikhe, Aikima, Jiwika and Wosilimo, then west to Manda, Munak, Bolokme

(the asphalt ends here), Tagime, Kelila, Bokondini, Karubaga and Mulia
- Northwest up the western side of the valley to Kimbim, Pyramid (end of asphalt), Makki, Pitt River and Tiom
- South to Hitigima and Sugokmo (nearly all asphalt)

The only vehicle bridge over Sungai Baliem in the main valley is at Pikhe, 3km north of Wamena.

## WAMENA

☎ 0969 / pop 8500

The main town in the Baliem Valley, Wamena is dusty and sprawling, but it's the obligatory starting point for any travels around the valley. The population is a mix of Papuans and non-Papuans and there's little that's traditional about it. Penis gourds are no longer banned here, as they were during Indonesia's 'Operasi Koteka' in the 1970s, but rarely will you see one being worn.

Wamena is expensive by Indonesian standards, since almost everything has been flown in from Sentani, and much of it has been shipped to Jayapura first.

## Information
No banks exchange foreign cash or travellers cheques, but two ATMs accept international cards. Wartel are dotted along Jl Trikora.

**Bank Mandiri** (Jl Trikora 92) ATM for Visa, Visa Electron and Plus.

**BRI bank** (Bank Rakyat Indonesia; cnr Jl Yos Sudarso & Jl Trikora) The ATM accepts MasterCard, Maestro and Cirrus.

**Papua.com** (☎/fax 34488; fuj0627@yahoo.co.jp; Jl Ahmad Yani 49; internet access per hr 15,000Rp; ☺ 9am-8.30pm Mon-Sat, 1-8.30pm Sun) Busy, efficient internet cafe that also functions as an informal tourist-information centre. Owner Kazutaka 'Fuji' Fujiwara is a highly experienced Papua traveller and a willing mine of information.

**Police station** (☎ 31972; Jl Safri Darwin; ☺ 9am-3pm Mon-Sat, 3-5pm Sun) For reporting on arrival or issuing a surat jalan, they can often attend you outside regular hours.

**Rumah Sakit Umum** (☎ 31152; Jl Trikora 9) If you need a hospital you'll get a minimum of care here.

**Tourist office** (☎ 31365; Jl Yos Sudarso 73; ☺ 8am-3pm Mon-Fri) About 2.5km from central Wamena; staff have little on-the-ground knowledge of the area.

### THE DANI

Several groups in the Baliem Valley come under the umbrella name 'Dani', a partly pejorative term given by neighbouring tribes. The Dani are friendly but can be shy. Long handshakes allowing time to really feel the other's hand are common.

Most Dani speak Bahasa Indonesia but appreciate a greeting in their own language. Around Wamena, the general greeting is la'uk to one person, and la'uk nyak to more than one – except that men say nayak to one other man and nayak lak to more than one man.

Many Dani men still wear a penis sheath (horim in Dani, koteka in Bahasa Indonesia), made from a cultivated gourd and held upright by a thread looped around the waist or chest. These guys generally wear little else apart from a few neck, head or arm adornments made from feathers, shells or bones. Other Dani men now prefer T-shirts and trousers or shorts. Very few women now go bare-breasted, though some still sport the traditional skirts of grass for unmarried women or fibre coils for married women. Women often carry string bags around their heads, often heavily laden with vegetables, babies or even pigs. Some Dani wear pig fat in their hair and cover their bodies in pig fat and soot for warmth. Most men, and some women, are enthusiastic smokers.

Many Dani now consider themselves Christian and one traditional pastime that has gone out of the window is village warfare. Dani villages used to go to war with each other over land disputes, wife stealing and even pig stealing, with combat taking place in brief, semi-ritualised clashes (with deaths and woundings nevertheless). Today such quarrels are settled by other, usually legal means. (The last village conflict took place in 1988–89 over a land dispute between Wouma and Walesi.)

Villages are still mostly composed of extended-family compounds each containing a few honai (circular thatched-roof huts). The men sleep apart from the women and children in a dedicated men's hut, visiting the women's huts only for sex. After a birth, sex is taboo for the mother for two to five years, apparently to give the child exclusive use of her milk. Perhaps because of this, many Dani are still polygamous – a man may have as many wives as he can afford the standard bride price of four or five pigs for, and his social status is measured partly by the number of wives and pigs he has. Dani life expectancy is around 60 years, relatively high among traditional people.

One of the more unusual (and now prohibited) Dani customs is to amputate one or two joints of a woman's finger when a close relative dies – you'll see many older women with fingers missing up to their second joint.

One thing that hasn't changed and probably never will is the Dani's love for the sweet potato, grown on extensive plots and terraces all over the valley.

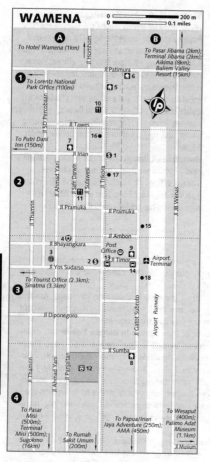

## BUDGET

**Hotel Syahrial Makmur** ( ☎ 31306; Jl Gatot Subroto 51; r 150,000Rp) Each room is different at this cheapest place in town, but most are simple, with squat toilets and no hot water. The management are quite simpatico and speak some English.

**Hotel Srikandi** ( ☎ 31367; Jl Irian 16; r 200,000Rp) The rooms are small and dark, with squat toilets, and it can get noisy. At least the price is low for Wamena.

**Nayak Hotel** ( ☎ 31067; Jl Gatot Subroto 63; r 200,000-300,000Rp) Directly opposite the airport, this has seen much better days. Rooms are sizeable but tired, and staff not very interested. A decent breakfast is available for 25,000Rp.

## MIDRANGE & TOP END

Breakfast is included at all these places.

**Hotel Mas Budi** ( ☎ 31214; Jl Patimura 32; s 240,000-360,000Rp; d 290,000-410,000Rp) A very well-run place with 12 clean, good-sized rooms. All except the cheapest have hot showers in ample bathrooms, and the hotel's restaurant is one of the better ones in town.

**our pick Putri Dani Inn** ( ☎ 31685; Jl Irian 40; s 280,000Rp, d 300,000-350,000Rp) About 600m west of Jl Trikora, this little family-run place offers spotless, comfortable rooms with hot showers. The friendly owners provide endless tea and coffee. It's often full, so try to book ahead.

## Dangers & Annoyances

Local guides contrive to latch on to almost every tourist stepping off a plane at Wamena airport. Guides can be useful for many tasks from trekking to arranging pig feasts, but you might not want to choose the one who's trying to choose you. Shaking them off can be hard – it's usually a matter of firmness, patience and if necessary some blunt language or low cunning. See the boxed text, p808, for further information on Baliem Valley guides.

## Sleeping

Hotels without water heaters can usually provide a bucket of heated water for guests who don't fancy a frigid bath!

**Hotel Wamena** (☎ 31292; fax 32715; Jl Homhom 61; r incl breakfast 300,000-350,000Rp) Worth considering for some seclusion, 1km north of Jl Patimura. The rooms around the little central garden are clean and decent, though their bathrooms need some work.

**Baliem Pilamo Hotel** (☎ 31043; fax 31798; Jl Trikora 114; r incl breakfast 350,000-460,000Rp) The efficiently run Pilamo makes an effort towards charm with a couple of pretty garden-courtyards. The more expensive rooms have surprising garden-style bathrooms too! The cheaper, TV-less rooms are still a reasonable deal, with hot showers. The restaurant (mains 25,000Rp to 95,000Rp) is one of the best in Wamena, and the included breakfast is an excellent buffet-style affair.

**Baliem Valley Resort** (www.baliem-valley-resort.de; s/d €100/110) This surprising hotel occupies a gorgeous position in the eastern hills, about a 15km drive from Wamena, with 14 large, rustic-style but very comfortable guest cottages in picturesque grounds. A superb collection of Papuan (especially Asmat) art adorns the semi-open-air dining hall. The German owner has a wealth of Papua expertise, and a variety of excursions and expeditions are on offer. Meals are €8 to €10.

## Eating

The local delicacies are goldfish (*ikan mas* in Bahasa Indonesia) – far larger than the variety found in your goldfish bowl – and prawns (*udang*), which are more like crayfish. Both are expensive and sometimes in short supply, however.

**Restaurant Mas Budi** (☎ 31214; Jl Patimura 32; mains 20,000-80,000Rp) The food and service are commendable, and the place is deservedly popular, though the menu is fairly standard, ranging from rice and noodle dishes to chicken and fish.

**Rumah Makan Remuja** (☎ 34400; Jl Safri Darwin; mains 25,000-35,000Rp) One of the best cheaper places, with duck on offer as well as chicken, fish and *nasi goreng*.

**Restoran Blambangan** (☎ 32444; Jl Trikora 99; mains 25,000-150,000Rp) Has a pleasant ambience and a typical Indonesian-Chinese menu of reasonably well-done dishes, from inexpensive fried rice to expensive fish or prawns. It serves beer.

## Entertainment

Unbelievably, little, remote Wamena's Persiwa soccer team regularly occupies high placings in the Indonesia Super League. They are almost unbeatable in their home games at **Stadion Pendidikan** (Jl Panjaitan) – partly thanks to Wamena's altitude!

## Shopping

Though they aren't woodcarvers, the Dani are still fine craftspeople, especially in the arts of body adornment. Generally, it's cheaper to buy in the villages, but it's also worth checking out prices at Pasar Jibama (Pasar Baru) or the handful of craft shops on Jl Trikora north of Jl Ambon. Traders also hang around the doorways of hotels and restaurants. Bargaining is expected.

The cost of stone axe blades (*kapak* in the Dani language) can vary from 45,000Rp to 500,000Rp or more, depending on the size and the labour involved; bluestone is considered the finest material and is more expensive. *Noken*, costing from about 25,000Rp to 100,000Rp, are string bags made from the inner bark of certain trees and shrubs, which is dried, shredded and then rolled into thread. The bags are coloured with vegetable dyes, resulting in a strong smell.

Other handicrafts include necklaces, pectorals and armbands (*mikak*) of cowrie shells, carved stone, feathers, bone or pig tusks; grass skirts (*jogal* and *thali*); carved spears and arrows; and assorted head decorations (*suale*), which may be made of cassowary feathers and topped off with the tusks of a wild pig. Asmat and PNG artefacts are also available in the souvenir shops.

Of course, the most popular souvenir is the penis gourd. These cost from 5000Rp to 60,000Rp depending on size, materials and negotiation!

## Getting There & Away
### AIR
Flights are often heavily booked, especially in August. Always allow a couple of days' leeway for possible flight delays due to poor weather or other causes.

The main carriers between Jayapura (Sentani) and Wamena are **Trigana Air** (☎ 31611; airport) and **Aviastar** (☎ 34872; airport). Both normally fly four or more times daily each way, charging 825,000Rp from Jayapura to Wamena but less than half that going 'downhill', when they carry much less cargo.

Aviastar also makes four or five daily scheduled flights to Dekai (1,200,000Rp), on Sungai Brazza about 100km southeast of Wamena.

**Merpati** ( ☎ 33707; Jl Trikora 104) flies once a week to Karubaga, Tiom and Mulia, northwest of Wamena; you need to book about a week ahead for these flights. **Susi Air** ( ☎ 32226; Jl Gatot Subroto) goes daily to Dekai (1,300,000Rp) and some days to Mulia.

Airlines frequently change schedules and add or cancel destinations – Merpati has at times flown between Wamena and Merauke, for example – so it's always worth checking the latest possibilities.

The mission airlines **AMA** ( ☎ 32400; Jl Gatot Subroto) and **MAF** (Jl Gatot Subroto) fly small planes to many small highland airstrips. Tourists are not their priority but they may carry tourists if seats are available. Contact them as soon as you reach Wamena if you're interested. There is generally more chance of seats flying back to Wamena from villages than for outbound flights. As a rule MAF doesn't carry tourists outbound at all. AMA's one-way fare to Angguruk, for example, is around 2,000,000Rp. But fares from Angguruk to Wamena can be as low as 450,000Rp.

Charter flights are another possibility. Aviastar does charters to places such as Merauke, Bokondini, Mulia and Karubaga. AMA and Merpati also sometimes do charters. You pay around 12,000,000Rp from Wamena to Angguruk or Kosarek for six or seven passengers.

### PUBLIC BEMO

Overcrowded bemos head out along the main roads from several starting points around Wamena. Most don't have schedules; they just leave when they are full. They get scarce after 3pm and are less plentiful on Sunday. Few villages or attractions are signposted, so ask your driver (or guide) to let you know where to get off.

Most bemos are coded with numbers and/ or letters:

**Baliem Valley – northeast** These bemos leave from Terminal Jibama (right): 'MM' to Aikima (5000Rp, 15 minutes), 'KL' to Jiwika (7000Rp, 30 minutes), 'WL' to Wosilimo (13,000Rp, 40 minutes), 'TM' to Meagaima (20,000Rp, one hour), Manda (20,000Rp, one hour) and Wolo (25,000Rp, 1½ hours), and 'BT' to Bolokme (25,000Rp, 1½ hours) and Tagime (25,000Rp, 1¾ hours) at around 9am and 2pm. Bemos to Pass Valley (150,000Rp), Kelila (80,000Rp), Bokondini (130,000Rp) and Karubaga (250,000Rp) go some days from outside Bank Mandiri in the early morning (around 5am) – ask at least one day ahead about what is going and when.

**Baliem Valley – northwest** Bemos marked 'KMP' go to Kimbim (15,000Rp, 50 minutes) and Pyramid (20,000Rp, one hour) from Terminal Jibama. From the street opposite the market in Sinatma, bemos depart for Makki and Tiom as early as 3am (rarely later than 5am), and for Ibele (10,000Rp, one hour) until about noon.

**Baliem Valley – south** 'SG' bemos go to Sugokmo (15,000Rp, 30 minutes) from Terminal Misi (Jl Yani).

### CHARTERED BEMO

It is well worth considering chartering a bemo for about 100,000/600,000Rp per hour/day (probably more for remote and rougher roads) in order to avoid the public sardine-cans-on-wheels or to reach more remote places.

### OJEK

Typical one-way *ojek* prices for out-of-town destinations include 50,000Rp to Jiwika, 60,000Rp to Ibele, 80,000Rp to Wosilimo, 150,000Rp to Kimbim or Manda, and 250,000Rp to Bolokme.

## Getting Around

For longer trips around town, you can ride an *ojek* (10,000Rp) or a becak (3000Rp to 5000Rp). Becak don't run at night (or when it rains!) and they're not allowed along Jl Yos Sudarso at any time.

Bemos marked 'A2' (4000Rp) go along Jl Irian and up Jl Trikora to Terminal Jibama, 2km north of town beside Pasar Jibama (Pasar Baru) market. This is the main departure point for bemos up the eastern side of the Baliem Valley (see left).

## AROUND WAMENA
### Wesaput

This pleasant little village is just across the airport runway from Wamena. Bemos marked 'A3' (4000Rp) run from Jl Timor in Wamena.

At the end of Jl Musium, 1.2km from the airport fence, is the **Palimo Adat Museum**. It's dusty and decrepit and has no regular opening hours, but if you arrive by about noon, Monday to Saturday, someone should be able to open it, show you round and make it very interesting. The collection covers the Dani, Lani and Yali peoples and ranges from skulls of tribal-war victims to penis gourds, stone axes, musical instruments, rattan armour and specialised arrows for hunting different types of prey. Give a donation.

At the back of the museum is the nearest **hanging bridge** to Wamena. Strung across Sungai Baliem, it's 90m long.

## Pugima

The mostly flat trail beyond the Wesaput bridge leads in one hour, past Dani farms and villages, to Pugima, which has a few Dani compounds (past the huge church). The scenery is magnificent and halfway along, behind a small lake, **Gua Pugima** is an eerie cave.

## Sinatma

At the end of Jl Yos Sudarso, about 3.5km west of central Wamena, Sinatma village has a busy daily **market**. Bemos marked 'A1' run to Sinatma (3000Rp) from Jl Timor in Wamena.

Facing back to Wamena from the crossroads by the market, take the street to the right and easy **walking trails** lead to the raging Sungai Wamena, some pretty Dani compounds and dense woodlands. A **hanging bridge** crosses the river near the small hydroelectric station further up the hill.

## BALIEM VALLEY – SOUTH

South of Wamena, the valley narrows and Sungai Baliem becomes a ferociously raging torrent known as the Baliem Falls. The dramatic scenery and traditional lifestyle of many villages down here make this the best trekking area, for anything up to a week's walking. Walking times in what follows are based on an average 'tourist pace', including a few stops.

The paved road ends at **Sugokmo**, a sizeable village 16km from Wamena with some traditional *honai*. It's a 20-minute walk from Sugokmo down to a hanging bridge over

the raging Baliem, beside which is a small **memorial** to a Japanese tourist and his Dani guide who drowned when a previous, less solid bridge collapsed. From the bridge a path leads along the east bank to the neat village of **Seima** (about two hours from Sugokmo), then climbs gradually to **Ugem** (two hours from Seima). Here the path turns east along the flank of the beautiful Mugi valley to **Hitugi**, about three hours from Ugem. You will meet groups of Yali heading to or from Wamena along this path.

Below Seima you can return to the west bank by another hanging bridge at **Kurima**, a pleasant, largish village with a police station, and accommodation in houses at the southern end of the village. There's a guest house at **Polimo**, a mission base on the hill just above Kurima.

Several trails fan out from Kurima. One follows the Baliem downstream to a hanging bridge, across which the trail veers into the Mugi valley and crosses Sungai Mugi on a fabulous hanging bridge constructed entirely of wood and natural twine. From this bridge you can continue to little **Syokosimo** (three to four hours from Kurima), which has two guest houses. Another route from Kurima (four to five hours) leads southwest over forested hills and down to **Tangma** in a deep side-valley, where you can stay in a church house (ask for Tinus Hesegem) or mission building. Or you can head one hour uphill south from Kurima to **Kilise**, a *honai* village with glorious views.

**our pick** **Alberth Elopore's guest house** in Kilise is one of the best in the area, with cosy *honai*-style huts and a wonderful grotto-like *kamar mandi*. Alberth is Kilise's *kepala desa*.

From Kilise it's half an hour south to Ibiroma, where you can descend to the Baliem bridge downstream of Kurima and continue to Syokosimo, or continue south to **Wamerek** in the lower Tangma valley (with accommodation), or cross over to Tangma itself. All these are about half a day's walk from Kilise.

A hanging bridge over Sungai Baliem below Wamarek leads to **Wesagalep**, high on the east bank, from which you can head north on an up-and-down trail to **Wuserem**. Both these stages are half-day to one-day walks and there is school or teacher-house accommodation in both villages. From Wuserem it's two to three hours round to Syokosimo, or five hours back to Kurima.

---

### HIGHLAND MARKETS

Highland markets can be good places to mingle with locals in a relaxed, quotidian setting. You can find souvenirs like the colourful *noken* (bark-string bags) that women sling over their foreheads, or pick up bundles of veggies for your trek.

There are daily markets at Sinatma and Pasar Jibama, both just outside Wamena. Markets in villages happen as and when people have stuff to sell and buy. Those in Jiwika and Kimbim usually happen every day, with bigger gatherings on Sunday and Saturday respectively.

**PAPUA**

**PAPUA**

## HIKING & TREKKING IN THE BALIEM VALLEY

You can see some sights without straying far from the main roads, but getting out along the paths brings you closer to the traditional Dani lifestyle. You'll find most of the people extraordinarily friendly. In a day you can climb narrow rainforest trails, stroll well-graded paths past sweet-potato terraces, wend through villages of thatched-roof *honai*, traverse hillsides where the only sounds are birds, wind and water far below, and cross rivers on hanging footbridges held together by natural twine.

The classic trekking area is in the south of the valley (p807), from Sugokmo down, with the branch valleys to the east and west. Beyond the reach of roads, Dani life here is still pretty traditional, the scenery gorgeous and the walking varied, and there's a good scattering of villages. This is also the jumping-off point for more demanding treks into the Yali country (p812). Another lightly trekked area is the Wedanku valley (p810). The Wolo Valley (p811) has beautiful scenery and pretty villages, though its culture is no longer very traditional. It's a similar case with the northwestern area around Bokondini and Karubaga, and the Lani country (p811) further west, though these are still good walking areas. The hike to or from Danau Habbema (p811) is another wonderful route.

A handful of maps is sometimes available in Wamena, but none is very detailed or more than partly accurate. Don't use them as substitutes for a knowledgeable guide.

### What to Bring

You'll need a sleeping bag and torch (flashlight); a mosquito net can be useful. Bring warm clothes, and something waterproof for when it rains. Cooking equipment will be provided by most guides. Villages can normally supply firewood for 10,000Rp. If you'll be camping, bring your own tent.

You have to carry at least some food with you from Wamena, where you can stock up at Pasar Misi or Pasar Jibama. Larger villages have kiosks selling basics like biscuits, noodles and rice (the final reliable supplies are at Manda and Kimbim in the north and Kurima in the south). You can obtain some other foods, such as sweet potatoes, other vegetables, fruit and eggs, locally. Start with a couple of bottles of drinking water before you get down to boiling the local stuff.

### Accommodation

Accommodation is available in just about every village. Some have dedicated guest houses, which could be in a mission building, or Dani-style huts erected by a local family. In other villages you can often stay in the teacher's house, the school or other houses. If necessary, ask the village police or the *kepala desa* where you can stay. You'll usually be asked between 50,000Rp and 80,000Rp per person. Blankets and a mat to go under your sleeping bag will probably be provided, and your hosts can boil water for drinking. Sleeping on the floor of a Dani *honai* can be cheaper but is a last resort, as they are insect havens. Make sure you've been invited before entering a compound or hut. If you have to overnight *between* villages, there are a few basic shelters on some routes, but you'll be cold without a tent.

### Guides & Porters

For hiking off the main roads or paths, a guide is essential. Guides can help you decide where to go, facilitate communication with locals, find places to stay, and explain the local customs and ecology – and you'll get to know a local person.

Finding a reliable guide may be the biggest challenge of trekking in the Baliem Valley. Guides will often latch on to you as soon as you step off the plane in Wamena and it can be hard to shake them off. Most are clever bargainers: there's no such thing as a standard price in the Baliem trekking world.

Tricks played by unscrupulous guides include pocketing some of the money you've given them to get supplies (to avoid this, go with them or get the supplies yourself); sending a junior replacement guide at the last minute; using public bemos to the trek starting point when you have paid for a charter; asking for more money along the way and refusing to finish the trek unless they get it; or disappearing partway into the trek and leaving you in the hands of an unpaid porter.

Fortunately, there are ways to find a reliable guide. Ask advice from other travellers or anyone else you trust. A good source of recommendations in Wamena is Papua.com (p803), and hotels can put you in touch with guides. You can also ask to see a guide's badge *(tanda pramuwisata)*. Authorised senior guides have undergone six weeks' training in Jayapura and have a badge stamped by the provincial governor; authorised junior guides have done four weeks at Jayapura and have a badge stamped by the local *bupati*. We can recommend **Papua/Irian Jaya Adventure** ( ☎ 0852-4413 1512; justinus_daby@yahoo.com; Jl Gatot Subroto 15), which is run using authorised guides by Justinus Daby, an English-speaking Dani who has been guiding since the year dot and heads the local branch of the Indonesian Tourist Guide Association. His house/office is identifiable by the bamboo tree in front of it.

For more on hiring guides, see the boxed text, p823.

Allow a few days in Wamena to arrange things, and bargain hard. Perhaps try out a guide on a day trip before committing to anything longer. For an experienced, English-speaking guide who knows the area, expect to pay around 250,000Rp to 400,000Rp per day.

In addition to a guide, porters are a good idea and cost 50,000Rp to 100,000Rp per day, depending partly on the toughness of the trek. On longer treks you may need two porters per trekker: one for a backpack and another for camping and cooking gear and food. A cook costs another 75,000Rp to 150,000Rp per day – porters and guides can double as cooks if you're looking to cut costs. You'll have to provide enough food for the whole team (this might amount to 30,000Rp to 40,000Rp each per day), and probably cigarettes for them and for your village hosts. A 10% tip at the end of a trek is also expected for each member of staff. If you're willing to chance it, in the more frequented trekking areas you can head off alone and ask the way as you go, or pick up a local porter-cum-guide for 50,000Rp to 100,000Rp a day.

For transport to/from the start and end points of the trek, chartering a vehicle is more comfortable than squeezing into a public bemo. You can charter a bemo to Sugokmo, for instance, for 200,000Rp one way.

### Day Hikes Without a Guide
Following paths and/or roads, you can easily enjoy these short hikes without a guide.

- Aikima–Suroba–Dugum–Mulima (three hours) – follow the foothills from Aikima to Dugum, then head back to the main road
- Elagaima–Ibele (three hours) – follow the main road, and take a bemo one way
- Kimbim–Pummo (three hours) – mostly flat countryside, but only possible in the dry season when Sungai Baliem isn't too high

### Short Hikes With a Guide
For these hikes, a guide can help you find the best paths. Only some of the many possibilities are listed. Some require an overnight stop.

- Bolokme–Tagime–Kelila (seven hours) – consider staying in Kelila
- Kurima–Hitugi (five hours) – down the Baliem Valley then up the Mugi valley
- Kurima–Tangma (five hours) – up one valley and down into another
- Meagaima–Manda–Bugi–Wolo (four hours)
- Meagaima–Manda–Munak–Pyramid (four hours) – can be combined with Pyramid–Pummo–Meagaima (3½ hours)
- Sugokmo–Seima–Kurima–Kilise (four hours) – follow Sungai Baliem, crossing it twice on hanging bridges, then climb to picturesque Kilise
- Wolo–Ilugua (three hours) – two-thirds of the way, a track leads around a sinkhole and down to Gua Yogolok and Goundal, a village on the floor of a canyon

### Tour Agencies
Depending on the number of trekkers in your group and the company you deal with, using an agency may not cost much more than setting up a trek yourself. Budget trekking companies in Wamena have trouble staying afloat, but the operators listed on p779 can set up treks for you. Some also offer non-trekking Baliem tours, visiting the main sights and arranging special events like pig feasts.

# BALIEM VALLEY – NORTHEAST

Daily public transport along the paved road up the eastern side of the valley reaches as far as Tagime. Several interesting places along here are within day-trip reach from Wamena, and some side-valleys offer good hiking. Several villages have *honai*-style guest huts.

## Aikima

Just east of the Jiwika road about 8km from Wamena, nondescript Aikima is famous for its 270-year-old **Werapak Elosak mummy** (admission 30,000Rp; ☼ daylight hours), though the mummy at Sumpaima (below) is in better condition.

## Suroba & Dugum

Just off the main road, the pretty villages of Suroba and Dugum are worth exploring. Ask the bemo driver to let you off at the nearest spot to Suroba along the main road. Then walk 1km along the path through pretty scenery, crossing a flimsy wooden hanging bridge over a small river. At a clearing near the bridge, traditional **pig feasts** and **warrior dances** (based on traditional Dani warfare) are sometimes staged for around 1,000,000Rp each, mainly for tour groups. Both villages have basic tourist accommodation in *honai*-style huts.

## Jiwika

Jiwika (pronounced Yiwika) is a local administrative centre and an inexpensive base for exploring the northeastern Baliem Valley. This is another place where prearranged **warrior dances** and **pig feasts** (around 1,000,000Rp each) can be staged for tourists. If you are staying you should report to the Kurulu district police station by the roadside just south of the village.

At Iluwe, about 1½ hours up a steep path from Jiwika (with some scrambling at the top), are some **saltwater wells** (admission 5000Rp; ☼ daylight hours). To extract the salt, banana stems are beaten dry and put in a pool to soak up the brine. The stem is then dried and burned, and the ashes are used as salt. Ask a local boy in Jiwika to show you the way and to find out if anyone is working at the wells. Start the hike from Jiwika before 10am.

**Sumpaima**, just north of Jiwika (look for the blue 'Mumi' sign), is home to the **Wimontok Mabel mummy** (admission 30,000Rp; ☼ daylight hours). Wimontok Mabel was a powerful chief here in the 18th century and his blackened corpse is the best and most accessible of its kind near Wamena.

## SLEEPING

**Lauk Inn** (r 80,000Rp) Opposite the turn-off to Iluwe is this pleasant spot with basic but clean rooms (as opposed to Dani-style huts). Basic dinners (15,000Rp) are available, but it's still best to bring some of your own food.

**Wiyok Huts** (per person 80,000Rp) This *honai*-style place is about 200m south of the police station – you can contact Justinus Daby (see the boxed text, p808) in Wamena to make arrangements.

## Gua Kotilola

The road between Jiwika and Wosilimo is flanked by rocky hills in which some of the valley's 50 listed **caves** are located. **Gua Kotilola** (admission 10,000Rp; ☼ 8am-4pm) is a sizeable cavern up a short, pretty path behind a Dani compound near Waga Waga, about 5km north of Sumpaima. It contains the bones of past tribal-war victims – though they don't show these to outsiders.

## Wosilimo

Wosilimo (or 'Wosi') is a relatively major village with a couple of shops. Here, **Gua Wikuda** (admission incl tour 10,000Rp; ☼ 8am-4pm) is said to be several kilometres long, with an underground river that reaches Danau Anegerak, but disappointingly only the first 100m or so of the cave may be open for visits.

One hour southwest from Wosi on foot, along a small path behind a church and over a hanging bridge, is **Danau Anegerak**. During the wet season the path may be impassable, but otherwise this is a delightful area for **hiking**, and locals rent out basic fishing gear. There's accommodation in a Dani-style **hut**.

## Pass Valley

A rough road heads up over the hills from Wosilimo to Pass Valley, then descends to Elelim, about 60km from Wosi (one day, this road is planned to reach Jayapura). The small **Wedanku valley** between Wosilimo and Pass Valley still retains a strong, traditional Dani culture. Wedanku village's Catholic mission can provide accommodation, and from there you can hike one day up through the forest to **Ikipalekma**, then on the next day to Jiwika via the Iluwe wells (left). From **Dombomi**, between Pass Valley and Landikma, you can hike to **Sumpuleh**, with a waterfall and good birding (the yellow bird of paradise is one to look

---

**BALIEM VALLEY FESTIVAL**

To coincide with the busiest time for tourism, a festival is held in the Baliem Valley between about 7 and 12 August each year. The highlight is mock 'tribal fighting', where village men dress up in full traditional regalia and enact an old-fashioned tribal battle and accompanying rituals. The festival also features plenty of traditional dancing, and Dani music on instruments such as the *pikon*, a kind of mouth harp. Pig races are fun, too – if not for the pigs, which usually end up roasted on a spit. Other goings-on include spear-throwing contests and archery exhibitions.

In recent years the main events have taken place at Wosilimo and at Muliama between Kimbim and Araboda. Although the festival is set up for tourists, it's still a magical (and very photogenic) time to visit.

---

for). All the mentioned villages can provide accommodation in local houses. At Dombomi ask for Yakob Endama.

## Manda

This enticing village has a shop and market, as well as friendly people and wonderful landscapes to hike around. Ask if the **honai-style huts**, behind the market, are open. There's also *honai*-style accommodation in Meagaima, a few kilometres before Manda (ask for Isaak Aut).

## Wolo Valley

This is one of the most spectacular Baliem side-valleys. Inspired by a resolute strain of Evangelical Protestantism, **Wolo** is a nonsmoking village with lovely flower gardens. There is plenty of great **hiking** in the area.

## BALIEM VALLEY – NORTHWEST

The western side of the valley is less scenic or interesting. **Kimbim** is a pleasant administrative centre with a few shops and a busy **market**. About one hour away on foot (ask directions), **Araboda** is home to the 250-year-old **Alongga Huby mummy** (admission 10,000-20,000Rp; ☺ erratic hours). About 7km past Kimbim is **Pyramid**, a graceful mission village with a theological college and sloping airstrip.

## DANAU HABBEMA

This beautiful lake, 30km west of Wamena as the crow flies, sits amid alpine grasslands at about 3400m above sea level, with dramatic, snow-capped mountains in view (4700m Gunung Trikora rises to the south). The fauna and flora are a big draw for nature-lovers. Visitors need a permit from the Wamena office of **Lorentz National Park** (Taman Nasional Lorentz; Map p804; ☎ /fax 0969-34098; Jl Patimura 47): just show them your *surat jalan* with its Wamena stamp and pay a fee of about 20,000Rp.

It's possible to visit the lake in a day trip from Wamena – the drive is around two hours each way. You can rent a car and driver in Wamena for around 2,500,000/3,000,000Rp one way/return, or go by motorbike for about 800,000/1,000,000Rp. The road is paved as far as Napua, 7km from Wamena, where the military post may charge you 200,000Rp or so to proceed.

The ideal way to visit Habbema is to drive there and trek back (three to four days), for which you will need to hire a guide. Much of the route is through rainforest. The usual route starting from the lake is via Yobogima (a forest clearing) and then through a spectacular gorge to Daela village and on to Pilia and Ibele. En route you stand a fairly good chance of seeing cuscus, three birds of paradise (MacGregor's, King of Saxony and superb) and, if you're lucky, tree kangaroos. Ibele is connected to Wamena by public transport.

An alternative, more southerly route back on foot (four days) goes via Babilolo, Walaek and Walesi. It's also possible to walk back down the motor road in one very long day.

## LANI COUNTRY

Up the Baliem Valley west from Pyramid is the home of the Western Dani, or Lani. Though the nearer areas are no longer particularly traditional, the Lani are by and large friendly folk and the walking here is easier than in the Yali country to the east. Makki, Pitt River and Tiom, 25km to 50km west of Pyramid, mark the beginning of Lani country and are accessible by public transport from Wamena. It's possible to fly to Tiom or to Mulia or Ilaga, further west beyond the Baliem watershed. The OPM is active in the western Lani area, and Ilaga in particular is often off-limits for foreigners.

PAPUA

**FREEPORT INDONESIA**

No business in Papua, and few if any in Indonesia, matches the Freeport mine for size, profitability or controversy. At an elevation of 4000m, a few kilometres from 5030m Carstensz Pyramid (Puncak Jaya), **PT Freeport Indonesia** (www.ptfi.co.id), a local affiliate of US-based **Freeport McMoRan Copper & Gold Inc** (www.fcx.com), is mining the world's largest gold reserve and largest recoverable copper reserve.

Freeport signed its original contract for the site with the Suharto government back in 1967, and the initial Ertsberg site, where mining started in 1972, was mined out by the mid-1980s. Only then were even greater gold deposits discovered at the nearby Grasberg site, which is still being mined today. The large lowland town of Timika, about 80km southwest of the mine, was founded in the early 1970s as Freeport's logistics base. Visiting the mine or the mine town of Tembagapura ('Copper City' in Bahasa Indonesia) requires a permit from the company, but if you fly over you might spot Grasberg, a gigantic hole in the ground.

Freeport employs some 20,000 people directly and in contracting and service companies, the great majority of them Indonesian but only about a quarter of them Papuan. Its output accounts for 40% of Papua province's GDP and over 1.3% of Indonesia's. The company is one of Indonesia's biggest taxpayers, contributing more than 2% of the national budget (it paid a total of over US$8 billion in taxes, dividends and royalties to the Indonesian government from 1992 to 2008).

While people who work for Freeport generally love the company, Papuans critical of Indonesian rule see it as a symbol of Jakarta's exploitation of Papua's people, resources and environment. The company itself stresses its value to the local economy and support for local communities.

Opponents' grievance No 1 is over land rights and local communities, principally the highland Amungme and lowland Kamoro peoples, whose traditional lands the mine operations use. After locals rioted against Freeport in 1996, the company pledged to commit 1% of its gross revenue

# YALI COUNTRY & BEYOND

Over the eastern walls of the Baliem Valley, amid scenery that is often as stunning, lies the home of the Yali people. They have a shorter history of contact with outsiders than the Dani, and are one of the more traditional highland peoples, although traditional dress is now seen a lot less than it was 10 years ago. The men may wear 'skirts' of rattan hoops, with penis gourds protruding from underneath. Missionaries provide much of the infrastructure here, such as schools and transport.

Yali country is a great destination for more adventurous trekkers who have enough time. The most direct route from the Baliem Valley runs from Sugokmo to Ugem, then up the lovely Mugi valley to Hitugi, Yuarima, Yogosen, Kiroma and Wonggol (a forest shelter), over 3000m-plus Gunung Elit, and down to Piliam and Pronggoli in Yali country. Nights are typically spent at Hitugi, Yogosen or Kiroma, Wonggol, and Piliam if you don't make it as far as Pronggoli on day four. The section over Gunung Elit involves several hours of steep ascent. From Pronggoli to Angguruk, the biggest Yali village, with a large market twice a week, takes another day.

An easier but longer option – about six days from Sugokmo to Angguruk and still with plenty of up and down – is the southern loop via Kurima, Wesagalep, Soba and Ninia.

Once in Yali country, accommodation and local guides can be cheaper than in the Baliem proper. You might be able to get a mission flight back to Wamena (see p805), but you can't count on it unless it's organised in advance. Villages with airstrips include Angguruk, Pronggoli and Kosarek in Yali country; Nipsan, Endoman, Nalca and Eipomek in Mek country (east of the Yali); and Langda in Una country (south of the Mek).

An onward route of four to six days from Angguruk, with mountainous and rainforest sections, goes northeast to Helariki, Membahan, Telambela, Pimohon, Serkasi and Kosarek. The mission village of Kosarek is near the border of the next tribal people, the Mek – similarly small in stature to the Yali. From Kosarek you can trek several days southeast to Nipsan, Endoman and Eipomek. You can also reach Eipomek from Angguruk, via the chief Mek settlement, Nalca. If you're still hankering for more, from Nalca or Eipomek it's possible to cross Papua's north-south watershed, probably camping out at least one night,

to health, education and economic development of local indigenous communities through the Amungme & Kamoro Community Development Organisation. By 2008 the company had paid nearly US$329 million to this fund. In total the company says it has invested over US$600 million in social infrastructure of direct benefit to local people (such as schools, hospitals and business development) since 1992. Grievance No 2 is 'Where does all the Freeport money go?' Even though the 2001 Special Autonomy law for Papua stipulated that 80% of government revenues from mining in the province were to be returned to Papua, Papuans claim they have still to see much evidence of the money being spent on the ground.

Grievance No 3 is that the mine uses the Indonesian military as part of its security force, despite the military's notoriously heavy-handed treatment of indigenous Papuans. For 2007, Freeport Indonesia reported that it contributed US$9.4 million towards the costs of the 2100 personnel of 'government-provided security'. Some Papuans argue that the army provokes violent incidents to bolster its claims that the mine needs its protection.

Grievance No 4 is the mine's environmental record. In 2008 this led the government of Norway to sell all its shares in the mining company Rio Tinto, which is a partner in Freeport Indonesia. The principal concern is over the large amounts of mine tailings (finely ground rock residue) that are dumped into Sungai Aikwa, which flows through Timika to the Arafura Sea. The company argues that local conditions make this the best available option for tailings disposal.

Freeport is the subject of many protests locally and in Jayapura, and has been the object of OPM attacks – most infamously in 1977 when the mine's slurry line was bombed, leading to Indonesian military reprisals against the Amungme, reportedly including aerial attacks on villages.

But such is Freeport's importance to Indonesia, some analysts believe, that it alone makes Papuan independence unthinkable.

to Langda, main village of the Una people (considered pygmies!), where there's a mission guest house.

# THE SOUTH

Relatively few travellers make it to the low-lying, river-strewn south, but Wasur National Park near Merauke is one of the best wildlife destinations in Papua (albeit for only a few months a year), while the hard-to-reach Asmat region is famed for its headhunting past and marvellous woodcarving artisanry.

## MERAUKE
☎ 0971 / pop 55,000
Merauke is a reasonably prosperous and orderly town of wide, straight streets, renowned as the most southeasterly settlement in Indonesia. The Merauke area and its hinterland, as far north as Tanahmerah, have one of the most extensive collections of transmigration settlements in Papua, and a heavy military presence. The best reason to visit is nearby Wasur National Park (p814), which is like a small slice of Australian bush in Indonesia, wallabies and all.

## Information
It's 6km from the airport at the southeastern end of town to the port on Sungai Maro at the northwestern end. The main street, running almost the whole way, is Jl Raya Mandala.
**BNI bank** (Jl Raya Mandala 173) Close to the Megaria and Nakoro hotels, with an ATM for Visa, Visa Electron, MasterCard, Cirrus, Maestro and Plus.
**Police station** (☎ 371 716; Jl Brawijaya 27) Opposite the main market; come here if you need a *surat jalan*.
**Tourist office** (☎ 324 738; Jl Yos Sudarso 14; 8.10am-2.30pm Mon-Thu, to 11am Fri, to 1pm Sat) About 100m from the port gate; staff are willing but have limited material to hand out.

## Sights
Merauke's beach, **Pantai Lampu Satu**, is named after its lighthouse. Motorbike or horse races are held here some afternoons. The beach is 3km along Jl Nowari, off the northwestern end of Jl Raya Mandala.

Several buildings from Merauke's Dutch days survive in the older part of town near the port, notably the Hotel Asmat and a quaint 1920 **post office** (Jl Sabang).

Wildlife enthusiasts may find Merauke's main market, **Pasar Baru** (Jl Pembangunan), 2.5km north of the airport, grimly instructive.

Venison, wallaby meat and wild pork from Wasur National Park are all sold here – recognise the wallaby meat (around 30,000Rp a chunk) by their little heads sitting in a row beside it. About 7am bat, bandicoot, snake and lizard meat (if that's what you call it) are sold by the road at the market's southeastern end.

## Sleeping & Eating

**Hotel Nakoro** ( ☎ 322 287; Jl Ermasu 96; r 200,000-250,000Rp; ) You'll feel at home in the friendly, relaxed atmosphere in this sweet spot on a quiet street, roughly halfway between airport and port. All rooms have good air-conditioning and private *mandi*, and the slightly cheaper, smaller ones upstairs get more breeze. Prices include snack breakfast.

**Hotel Megaria** ( ☎ 321 932; Jl Raya Mandala 166; r 248,000-325,000; ) Along a short lane from about the halfway point of Jl Raya Mandala, the Megaria was under renovation at research time but has a good selection of large, well-furnished rooms with bathrooms. The most expensive have hot water. Breakfast snack included.

**Hotel Asmat** ( ☎ 321 065; Jl Trikora 3; s 363,000-451,000Rp; d 418,000-506,000Rp; ) Hotel Asmat offers comfortable, quiet rooms, all with their own little front patios, breakfast and amenities like satellite TV, as well as excellent service. It's just off the northwestern end of Jl Raya Mandala.

**Rumah Makan Serumpun Indah** ( ☎ 325 364; Jl TMP Trikora; meals from 25,000Rp; 5am-10pm) Though a bit out of the way on the inland edge of town, this big, clean, busy eating hall is well worth a ride. Check the offerings at the counter and they'll bring your meal to your table. A brilliant *nasi campur* with prawns, egg, *sambal* and coconut sauce will cost you 32,000Rp.

## Shopping

If you can't get to the Asmat region, visit Merauke's own Asmat woodcarver. **Andreas Puer** ( ☎ 0813 8082 6281; Jl Gudang Arang) has been here since 1970 and carves some original pieces, which he sells at reasonable prices. His house is on the northern edge of town.

## Getting There & Away

**Merpati** ( ☎ 321 242; Jl Raya Mandala 257; 8am-4.30pm Mon-Sat, 10am-noon Sun) flies daily to and from Jayapura, Makassar and Jakarta. You need to reconfirm your outbound flight *and* check in

good and early. Merpati also flies to several southern Papua airports including Ewer (for Agats).

Every two weeks Pelni's *Tatamailau* sails from Merauke to Agats (1st/economy class 182,000/566,000Rp), Timika, Fak-Fak and Sorong (392,000/1,240,000Rp). The *Kelimutu* links Merauke with Agats, Timika and Maluku every four weeks. Smaller boats run up and down the coast to Kimam (Pulau Yos Sudarso), Bade, Agats and as far inland as Tanahmerah.

**PT Bima Suci Irja** port area ( ☎ 325 726; Jl Sabang) midtown ( ☎ 321 948; Jl Raya Mandala) sells tickets for both Pelni and Merpati. The midtown office is next to BNI bank.

## Getting Around

An airport taxi costs 50,000Rp into town. An *ojek* is 5000Rp or so. Walk 300m to Jl Raya Mandala and you can climb into one of the public *taksi* (3000Rp) that bustle up and down it every nanosecond.

# WASUR NATIONAL PARK

The 4130-sq-km Taman Nasional Wasur, stretching between Merauke and the PNG border, will fascinate anyone with an interest in wildlife, especially birds and marsupials. But come in the later part of the dry season (August to November), otherwise most of Wasur's tracks will be impassable and the only wallabies you'll see will be the concrete ones that welcome you at Merauke port and airport.

To naturalists, Wasur is part of the region known as the Trans-Fly, which straddles the Indonesia-PNG border (the name comes from PNG's Fly River). It's a flat, low-lying area of savannas, swamps, forests and slow-moving rivers that inundate much of the land during the wet season. Wasur's wildlife includes at least three species of wallaby (locals call them all *kangguru*) and nocturnal cuscuses, sugar gliders and bandicoots. Deer and wild pigs have been introduced. Among the 400 birds are cassowaries, kookaburras, palm cockatoos, brolgas, magpie geese, gorgeously coloured rainbow lorikeets and two types of bird of paradise. Wasur's wetlands attract migratory birds from Australia (July to October) and even Siberia (October to March).

The southern part of the park is the best for wildlife spotting as it has more open grasslands and coastal areas. In the dry season you can see a reasonable amount of the park (and probably reach the observation tower on the plains at Ukra) in a long day trip, but better is to spend a night or two camping, or staying in a village for around 100,000Rp per person (take food). A good route around the park is to head south from Merauke via the small villages of Ndalir, Kuler, Onggaya, Tomer and Tomerau, then head northeast to Ukra and the indigenous villages of Rawa Biru and/or Yanggandur. From either of these you can return to Merauke via the paved 'Trans-Irian Hwy' – a total trip of around 150km for which you need a 4WD vehicle or at least a motorbike.

The park office, **Balai Taman Nasional Wasur** (☎ 0971-324 532; Jl Garuda Leproseri 3; ☒ 8.10am-2pm Mon-Thu & Sat, to noon Fri), 4km southeast of Merauke airport on the road towards the park's Wasur village entrance, may be able to help you set up a trip. Alternatively, contact Lea Kanisia Mekiuw of the local NGO **Yapsel** (☎ 0971-323 204, 0971-321 688; lkanisia@yahoo .co.id; Jl Missi, Merauke), who can arrange an airport pickup and put you in touch with a good, English-speaking, Papuan guide. Or call the guide, **Bony Kondahon** (☎ 0813 4458 3646), direct. You'll probably pay 700,000Rp per day for vehicle, guide and driver, plus food, drinks and any accommodation costs.

It's also possible to charter a *taksi* or even an *ojek* from Merauke to park villages. Carry your passport, *surat jalan* and photocopies to show to military posts in the villages.

# THE ASMAT REGION

The Asmat region is a massive, remote, low-lying area of hundreds of muddy, snaking rivers, mangrove forests and tidal swamps. The Asmat people, formerly feared for their headhunting and cannibalism, are now most celebrated for their woodcarvings – the most spectacular of Papuan art.

To appreciate what the Asmat region has to offer requires a *lot* of time, money and patience. Most visitors who make it here come on organised tours or with experienced guides from elsewhere, and spend time boating to carving villages, and maybe seeing a traditional dance performance or demo of the uses of the sago palm. Sizeable areas have been deforested: many Asmat were subjected to forced logging labour in their own forests in the 1970s.

The one time when more than a handful of visitors appears here is during the annual **Asmat Art & Culture Festival**, or 'Asmat Show', an early-October festival of traditional dance and dress, canoe races and woodcarving, with Agats as the main venue. Most of the agencies listed on p779 offer trips to the Asmat region; expect to pay about US$200 per person per day, plus airfares.

## Agats
☎ 0902 / pop 1400
The capital of the region is the small town of Agats, on the Aswetsj estuary. Agats has two hotels, limited electricity and limited fresh water. Due to the extraordinary tides and

**PAPUA**

---

### THE ASMAT PEOPLE

The Asmat traditionally believe that no person, except the very young and very old, dies from any cause other than tribal fighting or magic. So every family member's death must be 'avenged' so that the dead can rest in the spiritual world known as *safan*. Not long ago, 'avenging' took the form of headhunting raids. Today, though more ceremonial, 'avenging' is still taken seriously.

The centre of Asmat traditional belief is the figure of Fumeripitisj, who 'created' the first Asmat people by carving them from wood. The Asmat remain in contact with their ancestors through their carvings. Each village appoints a *wow ipits* (woodcarver) based on his skills. Carvings were originally made only for ritual use, but today there is also strong tourist and collector demand, which has encouraged some new forms and designs in Asmat carving.

The famous phallic *bis* poles of interlocked human and animal figures are carved from mangrove trees and can be 6m or more tall. Traditionally they were carved as objects where the spirits of slain warriors could reside until they were liberated by the killing and eating of enemies. Decorated shields used in funeral ceremonies also represent and avenge dead relatives. Other ceremonial items include rattan 'devil' costumes used in dances to drive out evil spirits, lizard-skin drums, paddles and horns that were once used to herald the return of headhunting raids.

Asmat people revere their dead ancestors and may still keep their skulls as sources of spiritual strength.

location, it is traversed on raised (and often broken) wooden walkways – watch your step! Report to the police station (er, hut) with your *surat jalan* when you arrive.

The **Museum Kebudayaan & Kemajuan** (Museum of Culture & Progress; admission by donation; ☉ about 8am-1pm Mon-Sat), one 'block' behind (south of) the mosque, has a very worthwhile collection of traditional and modern Asmat art and artefacts, from *bis* poles and skulls to full-body dance outfits. Try to recruit an English-speaking guide as there is little interpretative information.

The **Pusat Asmat & Pusat Pendidikan Asmat** (Asmat Education Centre & Asmat Centre; Jl Yos Sudarso; admission free; ☉ erratic hours), 400m northeast of the mosque, is an impressive group of traditional architecture.

### SLEEPING & EATING
**Losmen Pada Elo** ( ☎ 31038; Jl Kompas Agats; r 150,000-200,000Rp) Near the dock where boats from the airstrip arrive, this guest house offers acceptable rooms and friendly, helpful service. Rooms share *mandis*. You can order meals for around 30,000Rp.

There are a couple of *rumah makan* near the waterfront and reportedly a second, recently opened hotel.

### GETTING THERE & AWAY
Agats' airfield is a grass strip at Ewer, a 20-minute boat ride north. Merpati normally flies several times weekly from both Timika and Merauke, but flights can be cancelled in the wet season if the airstrip is waterlogged. It's also possible to charter a small plane from Timika, Wamena or Merauke, for 20,000,000Rp to 35,000,000Rp one way (maybe less from Timika) for seven to 10 passengers.

Pelni's *Tatamailau* leaves Agats every two weeks for Merauke (1st class/economy 566,000/182,000Rp) southbound, and Timika, Fak-Fak and Sorong northbound. The *Kelimutu* comes every four weeks, to Merauke southbound and Timika and Maluku northbound. It's possible to charter a boat for the two- to three-day river trip from Dekai (served by scheduled flights from Wamena) for 6,000,000Rp or 7,000,000Rp per day for up to six to seven passengers.

Longboats are the only form of transport to the surrounding area. A sturdy boat from Agats with a reputable driver costs about 6,000,000Rp per day. You might get cheaper rates in Sjuru village, a 10-minute walk southwest of Agats.

### Around the Asmat Region
If you're not on an organised tour, in addition to the expensive boat hire, you'll need a guide (250,000Rp or more per day) and probably a porter or cook (100,000Rp or more). And take all your own supplies (shops in Agats sell basic items). Don't forget the mosquito repellent and be ready for a lot of mud!

A few villages such as Atsy and Senggo have basic guest houses with rooms for 100,000Rp to 200,000Rp. Elsewhere you can usually sleep at missions, teachers' houses or schools (around 50,000Rp to 70,000Rp per person).

Villages you might visit for their carving include **Owus**, **Biwar Laut** and **Atsy**, respectively about 35km, 60km and 80km by boat south of Agats. Biwar Laut, Atsy, and **Omandesep**, a couple of hours further south, are places where traditional Asmat performances can be laid on (2,500,000Rp or more). From Atsy it's about 50km southward to **Ocenep**, reputed to hold the skull of Michael Rockefeller, ethnologist and son to a former US vice-president, who disappeared nearby in 1961 when headhunting was still a living tradition among the Asmat.

## KOROWAI & KOMBAI REGIONS
Inland from the Asmat in the region of the Dairam rivers is the territory of the Korowai and Kombai tribes, seminomadic dwellers in tree houses perched 10m to 30m high as refuges against animals, enemies, floods and mosquitoes. The Korowai and Kombai were not contacted by missionaries until the 1970s and many still live their traditional way of life most of the time, wearing few clothes and employing stone and bone tools. It's thought headhunting and cannibalism might persist in some remoter parts of the area.

Several of the agencies listed on p779 offer challenging and expensive tours to the Kombai and Korowai areas, which normally start by flying to the mission settlement of Yaniruma, boating upriver from Agats to Yaniruma or Basman (beyond Senggo), or boating down Sungai Brazza from Dekai. This last can be the least expensive as you may reach the northern edge of Korowai territory in one day (6,000,000Rp to 7,000,000Rp). From these starting points you typically spend several days walking into the Korowai and/or Kombai zones, often along muddy trails through hot, swampy forests, sleeping in tents, huts or tree houses, and witnessing tribal life. It's best to avoid the wettest season, January to March.

# Directory

## ACCOMMODATION

Accommodation in Indonesia ranges from a basic box with a mattress to the finest five-star luxury resorts. Costs vary considerably across the archipelago, but in general Indonesia is one of the better bargains in Southeast Asia.

Travellers' centres have plenty of reasonably priced food and accommodation; Bali has the highest standards and whether you want to spend US$5, US$50 or US$500 per night you will get excellent value. Accommodation prices don't necessarily increase in outer and more remote provinces, but less competition often means lower standards.

Some hotels have fixed prices and display them, but prices are often flexible, especially in quiet periods. This applies particularly to midrange and top-end hotels, where discounts of 10% to 50% are readily available both in person and online.

Accommodation reviews in this book are chosen at the authors' discretion and based solely on merit. Reviews are listed in order of price, starting with budget and winding up with the most expensive option, unless otherwise stated. Quoted rates are high season (May to September and Christmas/New Year) and may drop by 20% or more during low season.

The range of prices used in this book is based on the average price per night in high-season rooms at a property (except in Bali):

**Budget** Less than 200,000Rp.
**Midrange** Between 200,000Rp and 700,000Rp.
**Top End** More than 700,000Rp (more than US$70).

On Bali and the nearby Gili Islands off Lombok the prices, which are often quoted in US dollars, are as follows:
**Budget** Less than 280,000Rp (less than US$30).
**Midrange** Between 280,000Rp (around US$30) and 1,100,000Rp (around US$120).
**Top End** More than 1,100,000Rp (more than US$120).

'Budget' often consists of a fan-cooled room in a losmen (simple, family-run hotel) or basic hotel, with a bed and shared *mandi* (Indonesian-type bath), although in the main cities like Jakarta and Yogyakarta rooms often come with a private *mandi*. Midrange accommodation is usually in a hotel and you can expect a private *mandi* or Western bathroom,

---

**BOOK YOUR STAY ONLINE**

For more accommodation reviews and recommendations by Lonely Planet authors, check out the online booking service at www.lonelyplanet.com/hotels. You'll find the true, insider low-down on the best places to stay. Reviews are thorough and independent. Best of all, you can book online.

more comfortable beds with a modicum of furniture, air-con and TV. Of course standards vary greatly depending on where you are. Top end is generally a more comfortable version of midrange, with newer interiors and satellite TV. Luxury resorts in Bali rival those anywhere in the world. Hotel and resort rooms reviewed in this book have a bathroom unless otherwise stated.

All hotels charge a 10% government tax, although many cheap hotels either ignore the tax or absorb it into their room rates. Midrange and top-end hotels have a 21% tax-and-service charge (called 'plus plus'), but not all include it in their advertised tariffs, so ask when checking in to avoid a headache on your way out. Prices in this book include tax unless otherwise stated.

For hotels, especially midrange and top-end places, you can often find the best deal by shopping around online. Some hotels offer internet deals on their websites; many more work with agents and brokers to sell their rooms at discounts off the published rates.

Besides the main internet travel bookers such as Expedia, Orbitz and Travelocity, the following sites often have good rates on rooms in Java, Bali and other well-touristed areas.

- www.asiarooms.com
- www.balidiscovery.com
- www.directrooms.com
- www.hotelclub.net
- www.otel.com
- www.zuji.com

## Camping

Camping in national parks is popular among Indonesian youth, though formal camping grounds with power and other facilities are rare. Outside of the parks, camping is unknown, and villagers will regard campers as a source of entertainment.

A sleeping sleeve or just a sarong will be sufficient for the lowlands, but you must be properly equipped to camp at higher elevations. Late-afternoon or night rain is common in mountain areas all year round, which can pose a danger of exposure to the inexperienced or unprepared. You'll also want a mosquito net, to guard against insects and other things that crawl and slither in the night.

## Hostels

Indonesia doesn't have many hostels, mainly because there are so many inexpensive hotels. One exception is Jakarta, where there are places offering dormitory accommodation. There are a handful of hostels in a few other places, but it's easy to travel through Indonesia on a tight budget without ever staying in one.

The main thing to be cautious about in hostels is security. Few places provide lockers, and it's not just local thieves you must worry about – foreigners have been known to rip off other people's valuables.

If you want to avoid nocturnal visits by rats, don't store food in your room, or at least have it sealed in jars or containers.

## Staying in Villages

In many places in Indonesia you'll often be welcome to stay in the villages. If the town has no hotel, ask for the *kepala desa* (village head), who is generally very hospitable and friendly, offering you not only a roof over your head in a homestay, but also meals. You may not get a room of your own, just a bed.

Payment is usually expected: about the same price as a cheap losmen (50,000Rp in Java) as a rule of thumb. The *kepala desa* may suggest an amount, but often it is *terserah* ('up to you'), and you should always offer to pay. While the village head's house sometimes acts as an unofficial hotel, you are a guest and often an honoured one. Elaborate meals may be prepared just for you. It's also a good idea to have a gift or two to offer – cigarettes, photographs or small souvenirs from your country are popular. Homestays and village stays are a great way to socialise with families and neighbours, contribute to the local economy and experience life at a much closer level.

In towns where no accommodation is available, ask at the local police station or any vaguely official-looking office. Oil-palm plantations generally have accommodation for visiting employees. Act friendly and don't mention rainforest conservation. For more information on cultural considerations when staying at villages, see the boxed text, p55.

## Villas & Long-Term Accommodation

Luxury villas are popular accommodation on Bali, although they are not without their environmental costs in terms of water usage and placement amidst once pristine rice fields. Many villas are literally straight out of the pages of *Architectural Digest* and other design magazines, and come with pools, views, beaches and more. Often the houses are staffed and you have the services of a cook, driver etc.

Rates typically range anywhere from US$500 per week for a modest villa to US$4000 per week and beyond for your own tropical estate. There are often deals, especially in the low season. For longer stays, you can find deals easily for US$800 a month. Look in the *Bali Advertiser* (www.baliadvertiser.biz). If your tastes are simple, you can find basic bungalows among the rice fields in Ubud for US$200 a month.

The following agencies are among the many in Bali.

**Bali Tropical Villas** ( ☎ 0361-732 083; www.bali-tropical-villas.com)
**Bali Ultimate Villas** ( ☎ 0361-857 1658; www.baliultimatevillas.com)
**Bali Villas** ( ☎ 0361-703060; www.balivillas.com)
**House of Bali** ( ☎ 0361-739541; www.houseofbali.com)

## ACTIVITIES

Indonesia's volcanic, archipelagic geography creates a wide range of adventure opportunities. The many seas hold superb diving, snorkelling, swimming and surfing venues. Inland, the rugged peaks, dense jungles and rushing rivers are an adventurer's delight.

### Cycling

Cycling in Indonesia is generally a means of transport, now booming in popularity as petrol prices skyrocket. Lowland towns such as Yogyakarta and Solo in Java teem with bikes, and bicycles are gaining popularity in Bali. Lombok has good roads for bikes.

---

**SAFETY GUIDELINES FOR DIVING**

Before embarking on a scuba-diving, skin-diving or snorkelling trip, carefully consider the following points to ensure a safe and enjoyable experience:

- Possess a current diving certification card from a recognised scuba-diving instructional agency.
- Be sure you are healthy and feel comfortable diving.
- Obtain reliable information about physical and environmental conditions at the dive site.
- Dive only at sites within your realm of experience and engage the services of a certified dive instructor.
- Check your equipment thoroughly beforehand.
- Be aware that underwater conditions vary significantly from one region, or even site, to another. Seasonal changes can also significantly alter any site and its dive conditions.

You can enjoy bike tours in Ubud (p313). In most tourist centres you can rent city bikes for around 15,000Rp per day, and organised tours on midrange mountain bikes are available in Bali and Java.

You can purchase a good-quality, locally manufactured mountain or road bike in most major cities. Be sure to buy a model with quick-release wheels to make it easier to squeeze the bike onto public transport if required. See p848 for more information.

## Diving & Snorkelling

With so many islands and so much coral, Indonesia presents wonderful possibilities for diving. In some areas, frequent storms reduce visibility during the wet season (October to April).

If diving is beyond your depths, try snorkelling. Many of the dive sites described can also be explored with a snorkel, and there are beautiful coral reefs on almost every coastline in Indonesia. While you can usually buy or rent the gear, it's best to take your own.

Some of Indonesia's best dive sites:

**Bali** Padangbai (p331), Nusa Lembongan (p301), Candidasa (p335), the Amed area (p339) and Tulamben (p341). See also the boxed text, p303.
**Java** Pulau Seribu (p118), Pulau Kotok (p119), Carita (p122) Ujung Kulon National Park (p133) and Cimaja (near Pelabuhan Ratu, p139).

**Kalimantan** Pulau Derawan and Pulau Sangalaki (p649).
**Maluku** Banda Islands (p756) as well as Saparua (p751) and Ambon (p742).
**Nusa Tenggara** Flores (p532), Alor (p561), Komodo and Labuanbajo (see the boxed text, p531), Gili Islands (see the boxed text, p497) and Senggigi (p488).
**Papua** Raja Ampat Islands (p782).
**Sulawesi** Pantai Bira (p667), Togean Islands (see the boxed text, p697), Tukangbesi Islands (p722), Pulau Bunaken (see the boxed text, p712) and Tanjung Karang (p693).
**Sumatra** Pulau Weh (p409).

## Hiking & Trekking

Hiking, at least in areas near large towns, is a popular activity among Indonesian youth, but infrastructure is minimal at best. The national parks often have good hiking opportunities.

Some highlights:

**Bali** Bali's central volcanic spine (p348), Bali Barat National Park (p347) and around Munduk (p354).
**Java** Gunung Halimun National Park (p139) and Ujung Kulon National Park (p133).
**Kalimantan** Pegunungan Meratus (p631) and the Apokayan Highlands (p650).
**Nusa Tenggara** Gunung Rinjani (p506) and Gunung Tambora (p523).
**Papua** Baliem Valley (p801)
**Sulawesi** Tana Toraja (p679)
**Sumatra** Gunung Leuser (p417) and Mentawai Islands (p425).

---

### RESPONSIBLE DIVING

The popularity of diving puts immense pressure on many sites. Consider the following tips when diving and help preserve the ecology and beauty of reefs:

■ Do not use anchors on the reef, and take care not to ground boats on coral.

■ Avoid touching living marine organisms with your body or dragging equipment across the reef. Never stand on corals, even if they look solid and robust.

■ Be conscious of your fins. The surge from heavy fin strokes near the reef can damage delicate organisms. When treading water in shallow reef areas, take care not to kick up clouds of sand. Settling sand can easily smother delicate reef organisms.

■ Practise and maintain proper buoyancy control. Major damage can be done by divers descending too fast and colliding with the reef. Make sure you are correctly weighted and that your weight belt is positioned so that you stay horizontal.

■ Resist the temptation to collect corals or shells. The same goes for marine archaeological sites (mainly shipwrecks).

■ Ensure that you collect all your rubbish and any litter you find as well. Plastics in particular are a serious threat to marine life. Turtles can mistake plastic for jellyfish and eat it.

■ Resist the temptation to feed fish.

■ Minimise your disturbance of marine animals. In particular, do not ride on the backs of turtles as this causes them great anxiety.

## RESPONSIBLE TREKKING

To help preserve the ecology and beauty of Indonesia, consider the following tips when trekking.

### Rubbish

- Carry out *all* your rubbish. Don't overlook easily forgotten items, such as cigarette butts, and make an effort to carry out rubbish left by others.
- Never bury your rubbish: it can take years to decompose and digging encourages erosion. Buried rubbish will likely be dug up by animals, which may be injured or poisoned by it.
- Minimise waste by taking minimal packaging and no more food than you will need. Take reusable containers or stuff sacks.
- Sanitary napkins, tampons, condoms and toilet paper should be carried out despite the inconvenience. They burn and decompose poorly.

### Human Waste Disposal

- Contamination of water sources by human faeces can lead to the transmission of all sorts of nasties. Where there is a toilet, please use it. Where there is none, dig a small hole 15cm (6in) deep and at least 100m (320ft) from any watercourse. Cover the waste with soil and a rock.

### Washing

- Don't use detergents or toothpaste in or near watercourses, even if they are biodegradable.
- For personal washing, use biodegradable soap and a water container (or even a lightweight, portable basin) at least 50m (160ft) away from any watercourse.
- Wash cooking utensils 50m (160ft) from watercourses using a scourer instead of detergent.

### Erosion

- Stick to existing tracks.
- If a track passes through a mud patch, walk through the patch so as not to increase its size.
- Avoid removing the plant life that keeps topsoils in place.

### Fires & Low-Impact Cooking

- Don't depend on open fires for cooking. The cutting of wood for fires in popular trekking areas can cause rapid deforestation. Cook on a lightweight kerosene, alcohol or Shellite (white gas) stove and avoid those powered by disposable butane gas canisters.
- Fires may be acceptable below the tree line in areas that get very few visitors. If you light a fire, use an existing fireplace. Use only minimal, dead, fallen wood.
- Ensure that you fully extinguish a fire after use.

### Wildlife Conservation

- Do not engage in or encourage hunting. Indonesia is full of endangered critters, which need all the help they can get to survive.
- Don't buy items made from endangered species.
- Discourage the presence of wildlife by not leaving food scraps behind you.
- Do not feed the wildlife; it can make them dependent on handouts or seriously ill.

Sudden rainstorms are common at high altitudes, and Indonesia is no longer tropical once you get above the 3000m mark. Death from exposure is a real possibility, so a good rain poncho is essential. Other necessities include warm clothing in layers, proper footwear, and sunscreen. With mobile network coverage extending even into wilderness areas, you should take a GPS-equipped cell phone along with your map and a compass. It should go without saying that you must bring sufficient food and water. Don't underestimate your need for water – figure on at least 2L per day, more in extreme heat. It's worth bringing a lightweight kerosene stove (other fuels are less readily available in Indonesia).

### Guides

Hikers, both local and tourist, frequently run into serious problems in the Indonesian wilderness. It is strongly recommended to hire a competent guide even for short treks near population centres. However, you must be prepared to haggle over the price. A private guide will typically cost around 100,000Rp to 200,000Rp per day, and more through a travel agency. Take some time to talk to your guide to make sure he (Indonesian guides are always male) really understands the route and won't simply help you get lost.

In areas that see a lot of hiker traffic, a system of licensing guides may be in place. If your guide claims to be licensed, ask to see the licence and copy down his name and number.

That way, if you encounter some really big problems (eg the guide abandons you on a mountainside), you can report him.

For more on selecting a guide, see opposite.

### Watching Wildlife

For the best places in Indonesia to see its vast and diverse range of wildlife, see p125

### White-Water Rafting

Sulawesi's Sungai Sa'dan (p680) lures adventure junkies to tackle its 20-odd rapids (some up to Class IV). Rafting agents in Rantepao organise trips down its canyon.

Several Bali-based adventure-tourism operators run trips down the Ayung and the Teleagawaja Rivers. Both are suitable for rafting novices and families (see p313).

In Sumatra dinghies are swapped for tubes on Sungai Bohorok (p382), where navigating the rapids in a truck tyre is all the rage. Guides in Bukit Lawang also organise trekking and rafting tours in the area (see p382).

In Java, white-water rafting is well established on Sungai Citarak (p139), which churns out Class II to IV rapids.

It may not raise the hairs on your neck, but bamboo rafting down South Kalimantan's Sungai Amandit (p630) is a highlight of touring the area. It's easy enough to organise on your own, but several companies in Banjarmasin can do the work for you.

There are also a number of unrafted rivers in Papua, but tackling these will require expedition-style preparations – roads are

---

**SAFETY GUIDELINES FOR TREKKING**

Before embarking on a trekking trip, consider the following points to ensure a safe and enjoyable experience:

- Pay any fees and obtain any permits required by local authorities.
- Be sure you are healthy and feel comfortable walking for a sustained period.
- Obtain reliable information about physical and environmental conditions along your intended route.
- Be aware of local laws, regulations and etiquette about wildlife and the environment.
- Walk only in regions and on trails/tracks within your realm of experience.
- Be aware that weather conditions and terrain vary significantly from one region, or even from one trail/track, to another. Seasonal changes can significantly alter any trail/track. These differences influence what to wear and what equipment to carry.
- Ask before you set out about the environmental characteristics that can affect your walk and how local, experienced walkers deal with these considerations.
- Strongly consider hiring a guide. There are often good ones available in Indonesia who have invaluable local knowledge.

**A CONSUMER GUIDE TO GUIDES**

A guide can make or break a trip. Here are some tips for choosing one. Some travellers report disappointing trips with cheap guides, but high fees alone don't guarantee satisfaction.

First, quiz the guide about the itinerary. That can begin by email or telephone, also providing a sample of their ability in your language. (Be aware that guides using email may have a helper, often their child, handling that correspondence.) The guide should be able to offer a range of destination and transport options, and tell you which options are best for you and why. Listen to their ideas, and see if they listen to yours.

The guide should also inform you of local festivals and other events worth a detour or longer stay, and weather or travel conditions that may impact your plans. Also ask where the guide is from and about their relatives in the area you'll visit. Family ties can mean a chance to get an inside look at how people really live.

Regarding fees, guides usually offer package prices and should be able to roughly itemise trip costs. Make sure you're clear on what's included in the package, particularly regarding transport and food. Fixed expenses such as transport and the guide's lodging and food mean you'll get a better price per person travelling in a group of two or more.

Some guides offer the option of charging you only their fee (250,000Rp to 500,000Rp per day) while you pay other expenses directly; good guides will get you the local price, or close to it, for those items. Under this arrangement, guides may raise their fee for additional travellers multiplying chances of mishaps.

Most importantly, meet the guide before finalising any trip. (If you're dealing with a tour agency, insist on meeting the guide you'll travel with, not the head of the agency.) Get a feel for their language ability and their style. Discuss the trip and expectations with the guide – and see if they're someone you'd like at your side under frequently fantastic, often challenging conditions.

nonexistent, crocodiles will probably find Western cuisine delightful and there may be unexpected surprises like waterfalls.

## BUSINESS HOURS

Government office hours are roughly 8am to 3pm Monday to Thursday and 8am to noon on Friday, but they are not completely standardised. Post offices are open from about 8am to 2pm Monday to Friday; in tourist centres, the main post offices are often open longer and/or on weekends. Banking hours are generally 8am to 2pm Monday to Thursday, 8am to noon Friday and 8am to about 11am Saturday. The banks enjoy many public holidays.

In this book it's assumed that restaurants and cafes are usually open from about 8am to 10pm or 11pm daily in touristed areas. Elsewhere, things close by 9pm. Shops and services catering to tourists are open from 9am to about 8pm (as early as 5pm other places). Where the hours vary from these, they are noted in the text.

## CHILDREN

Travelling anywhere with children requires energy and organisation. Most Indonesians adore children, especially cute Western kids;

however, children may find the constant attention overwhelming.

Health standards are low in Indonesia compared to the developed world, but with proper precautions, children can travel safely. As with adults, contaminated food and water present the most risks, and children are more at risk from sunstroke and dehydration. It depends where and how you travel. Indonesians may have to take their toddlers on gruelling eight-hour journeys in hot, stuffy buses, but you'd be well advised to take an air-con bus or rent a car. And many adults can comfortably sample warung food, but parents with kids will want to be more careful.

If you're travelling only to the main cities and tourist areas, like the resorts of southern Bali, the malaria risk is minuscule, but it's probably not worth the risk to travel to known malarial areas like Papua or Pulau Nias in Sumatra.

## Practicalities

Kid-friendly facilities such as high chairs in restaurants and cots in hotels are generally limited to Bali, which caters well to holidaying families. Bali has a ready supply of babysitters (often called 'babysisters') and plenty for kids

# SURF'S UP *Andrew Tudor & Justine Vaisutis*

Indonesia lures surfers from around the globe, many with visions of empty palm-lined beaches, bamboo bungalows and perfect barrels peeling around a coral reef. The good news is that mostly the dreams come true, but just like anywhere else, Indonesia is subject to flat spells, onshore winds and crowding (particularly in Bali). A little research and preparation go a long way.

## WHEN TO GO

The dry season (May to September) is more likely to produce solid ground swell, initiated in the Indian Ocean. Trade winds blow from the east or southeast, which means winds are offshore in Bali, from Kuta to Ulu Watu. During the wet season (October to April), trade winds are west or northwest, and are offshore on the other side of Bali (Sanur to Nusa Dua).

Traditionally June to August provides the most consistent and largest swells – and the largest crowds. Outside the high season, it's still possible to find good waves without drop-ins and jostling.

## WHAT TO BRING

On arrival at Denpasar, it pays to carry some Indonesian rupiah as officials sometimes charge a 'surfboard tax' (import duty) for bringing two or more boards into the country – try to refuse to pay.

Indonesia's waves mostly break over shallow reefs and therefore break more sharply. Given this, you'll need to have a few more inches underneath you to avoid getting pitched on the takeoff. Taking a quiver is a good idea. Seven-foot to 7½ft boards are commonly used, but shorter boards are handy for Bali, and you'll need an 8ft board if you're planning on tackling the big swells.

Surfboards can be hired relatively easily in Bali; expect to pay between 30,000Rp and 50,000Rp per day.

## INFORMATION & TOURS

Camps and charter cruises catering specifically to surfers lace Indonesia's coastlines and many advertise their wares on the internet. See the regional chapters for details.

Useful websites:

**www.globalsurfers.com** Global online forum for surfers.
**www.indosurf.com.au** Web links and general info.
**www.island-aid.org** Surfer-run aid organisation.
**www.surfaidinternational.org** Surfer-run aid organisation.
**www.surftravel.com.au** Australian outfit with camps, yacht charters, destination information, surfer reviews and more.
**www.surftravelonline.com** Information on remote Indonesian locations.
**www.wannasurf.com** Surf reports, current conditions and a message board.

## WHERE TO GO

### Bali

Bali is touted as a surfing mecca. Though getting to the breaks can be an adventure in itself, the rewards at the end of the road can be well worth it.

Ulu Watu on the west coast (p291) is a true surfers' paradise. The wave has three left-handers. The Peak is a high-tide wave that handles small and big swells, and is in front of the cave. Racetracks, further down the reef, is a hollow wave that starts to work on the mid-tide and gets better as it runs out. It handles up to about 1.8m and is very shallow. On a big swell and a low tide, try Outside Corner for a long ride on a huge face.

Nearby Bingin is one of several excellent and currently very hot surf spots here.

Kuta and Legian Beaches (p269) are two places where beginners can learn how to surf, although waves can get big and sometimes currents are strong, so take care.

Medewi (p345) in west Bali has a long left-hander over a rock-and-sand bottom. Though a long ride, it's not hollow. Like Canggu (p284), the trade winds are onshore, so early morning on a mid- to high tide is the best time for a surf.

Shipwreck at Nusa Lembongan (p301) is so named because of the rusted hull that pokes out of the reef. It's known for its back-door tubes and fast walling sections.

See boxed text, p273, for hot tips.

## Nusa Tenggara

On Sumbawa's west coast, Scar Reef (p517) is a left-hander that breaks over sharp coral and is usually best on the high tide. If it's small at low tide, don't despair; the wave often jacks 0.6m to 0.9m on the incoming tide.

Aptly named Supersuck (p518) turns inside out and is a tube-rider's dream. The steep take-off funnels into a long sucking bowl over a shallow reef. Unfortunately, Supersuck requires a big swell to turn on, but in its favour the dry-season winds are mostly offshore.

Yo Yo's (p518), a right-hand reef break, is reasonably deep compared with Supersuck, but the end section gets shallow on a mid- to low tide. Early-morning surfs are best.

It's possible to surf year-round at Lakey Peak (p523) on the southeastern coast. It's a classic A-frame peak with a left and a right. It's usually better for holding big swells and providing hollow tube sections. Watch out for surfers trying to backdoor the peak.

Sumba and Timor are gaining popularity. Around southwestern Sumba, Rua (p587) is a good place to head. It's a left-hand reef break and the dry-season trade winds are cross-shore to offshore. Tarimbang (p584) on Sumba's central southern coast also has good waves, and Baing (p584) has emerged as east Sumba's surf capital.Lombok

Tanjung Desert (Desert Point; p487) on Lombok's southwest peninsula was recently voted the best wave in the world by one surf-mag poll. A left hollow break of reef and coral, this wave reaches 1.5m to 3m on a good day. It's one for experienced surfers.

Kuta (Lombok; p512) has world-class waves and turquoise water. There are excellent lefts and rights right in front of Kuta's bay as well as the reefs east of Tanjung Aan.

## Java

Grajagan (G-Land) at Alas Purwo National Park (p254) on Java's southeastern tip is home to what has become a world-famous and world-class surfing break. G-Land is a freight train left-hander that has several take-off sections, monster barrels and speeding walls. From the camp at Pantai Plengkung, the reef stretches east up around the headland as far as the eye can see and, when a ground swell hits and big tubing left-handers line up all the way round, it's truly a sight to behold.

In West Java, the beaches near Pelabuhan Ratu (see p139) offer some excellent reef breaks and beachies (waves that break over a sand bank). Batu Karas (p160), near Pandangaran, has one of the coast's best surf beaches and is a good spot to learn.

For hollow waves head to Pulau Panaitan (p134) in Ujung Kulon National Park. The waves here break over super-shallow coral reef and get faster and more hollow towards the end section. This place is for experienced surfers only.

## Sumatra

Northern Sumatra's Pulau Nias (p395) is the most-visited surfing destination in the province. The right-hander at Teluk Lagundri is a relatively short wave, but at size is a high and tight tube from take-off to finish. The outside reef only starts to work on a solid ground swell of about 1.2m to 1.8m, but holds huge swells and the tubes are perfect. Nearby, Sorake's world-famous right consistently unrolls between June and October (see the boxed text, p400).

An increasing number of surf charters are establishing camps on the Mentawai Islands (p428), which enjoy swells year-round, although they're biggest in the dry season.

DIRECTORY

to do. Java doesn't have Bali's mega-tourism industry, so it caters less to children, but it's well developed with a range of amenities, transport, hotel and food options. Travel outside cities requires patience, hardiness and experience – for both parents and kids.

Nappy-changing facilities usually consist of the nearest discreet, flat surface. Baby wipes, disposable nappies and baby formula are all readily available in cities and big towns but seldom elsewhere.

Breastfeeding in public is acceptable in areas such as Papua and Sumatra but virtually unseen in Maluku, Sulawesi and Kalimantan. In parts of Java it's simply inappropriate. The rule of thumb of course is always to take your cue from local mothers with infants.

### Sights & Activities

Travelling in some areas of Indonesia is probably too hard for most people to tackle with small children. Transport and facilities are best in Bali and there are plenty of safe beaches suitable for kids. South Bali has most of the island's family-friendly resorts and there are specific activities to keep little tackers occupied – see p274 for suggestions.

In Java the islands of Karimunjawa (p218) are isolated and some can be difficult to get to, but the calm seas and pace make for tranquil family holidays.

The once-heady tourism influx of Sumatra's Danau Toba (p388) has left a legacy of decent infrastructure, and families with young kids will find it easy to cope here. It's actually a popular spot for weekend-away expats from Medan and Aceh.

### CLIMATE CHARTS

Sitting atop the equator, Indonesia tends to have a relatively even climate year-round. Rather than four seasons, Indonesia has two – wetter (roughly April to September) and drier (roughly October to March) – and there are no extremes of winter and summer. See p20 for more information.

### COURSES

Many cultural and language courses are available, particularly in the main tourist areas. Once again Bali takes the lead, offering a little something to just about everyone. Ubud is Bali's culinary capital and there are courses to teach the inquisitive gastronome a thing or two; see p85 for details. Look for advertise-

ments at your hotel, enquire at local restaurants and bars, ask fellow travellers and hotel staff, and check out the tourist newspapers and magazines.

Culture vultures and art addicts are also looked after, with a plethora of courses in Ubud teaching painting, woodcarving, batik, textile and more (see p313 for more information). Short batik courses are popular in Yogyakarta (see p182) and in Solo (p201).

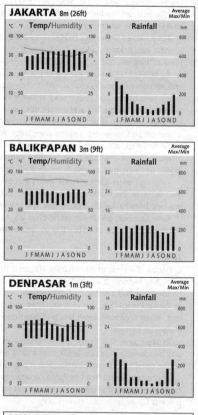

Also in Java, dance and art classes are held at the Mangun Dhama Art Centre in Candi Jago (p238).

Many students come to Indonesia to study Bahasa Indonesia. The better private courses can charge US$15 or more per hour, though many offer individual tuition. Some of the embassies arrange courses or have information about teachers and language institutes. Courses are offered in Yogyakarta (p182) in Java.

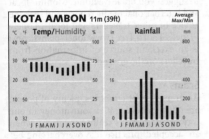

KOTA AMBON 11m (39ft)

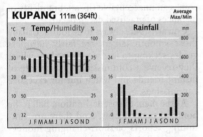

KUPANG 111m (364ft)

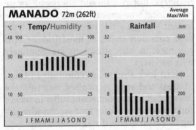

MANADO 72m (262ft)

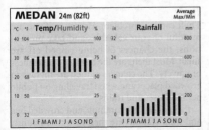

MEDAN 24m (82ft)

## CUSTOMS REGULATIONS

Indonesia has the usual list of prohibited imports, including drugs, weapons, fresh fruit and anything remotely pornographic.

Each adult can bring in 200 cigarettes (or 50 cigars or 100g of tobacco), a 'reasonable amount' of perfume and 1L of alcohol.

Surfers with more than two or three boards may be charged a 'fee', and this could apply to other items if the officials suspect that you aim to sell them in Indonesia. If you have nothing to declare, customs clearance is usually quick.

There is no restriction on foreign currency, but the import or export of rupiah is limited to 5,000,000Rp. Amounts greater than that must be declared.

Indonesia is a signatory to the Convention on International Trade in Endangered Species (CITES), and as such bans the import and export of products made from endangered species. In particular, it is forbidden to export any product made from green sea turtles or turtle shells.

## DANGERS & ANNOYANCES

It's important to note that, compared with many places in the world, Indonesia is fairly safe. There are some hassles from the avaricious, but most visitors face many more dangers at home. Petty theft occurs, but it is not prevalent.

It's best to avoid buying arak, the locally produced fermented booze made from rice or palm. Several people died in Bali after a producer tried to stretch a batch with what turned out to be a deadly chemical.

### Drugs

Indonesia has demonstrated its zero-tolerance policy towards drugs with a spate of high-profile arrests and convictions. Australian Schapelle Corby captured news headlines around the world when she received a 20-year prison sentence for smuggling marijuana. In the same year five Australians were caught with several kilograms of heroin strapped to their bodies at Denpasar Airport. Along with their accomplices they became known (sensationally) as the 'Bali Nine'. Seven received life sentences (later reduced to 20 years) and two were sentenced to death by firing squad.

Indonesia is now a major supplier of ecstasy, both for export and to fuel the local rave scenes in Bali, Jakarta and other big cities.

Random raids of nightclubs in Jakarta and Bali and mandatory urine tests for anyone found with drugs occur regularly. Private parties on Bali have also been raided, and hotel owners are required by law to report offenders. The law does not provide for differentiation of substance types or amounts. Whether found with a full bag of heroin or a few specks of marijuana dust in your pocket, you will be in very serious trouble.

In areas where nightclubs are concentrated, such as Bali, freelance entrapment of tourists is a lucrative vocation.

## Personal Space

You tend to get stared at when in places few foreigners visit, but overall Indonesians stand back and look rather than gather around you. Those who do come right up to you are usually kids. The other habit that is altogether ordinary to Indonesians is touching between those of the same gender. The Indonesians are an extraordinarily physical people: they'll hold onto your knee for balance as they get into a bemo, reach out and touch your arm while making a point in conversation, or simply touch you every time they mean to speak to you. All this is considered friendly, as is the highly personal questions you will be asked by everyone. Interrogating a total stranger about their origin, age, and marital status is considered polite, and a refusal to answer is regarded as discourtesy.

## Safety

Security in touristed areas increased after the 2002 and 2005 Bali bombings but has since tended to fade. The odds you will be caught up in such a tragedy are low. Large luxury hotels that are part of international chains tend to have the best security, though they also make the most tempting targets, as shown in Jakarta in 2003 and 2009.

Security issues in Indonesia are often exaggerated by the foreign media, who portray rambunctious protest rallies and minor incidents of civil unrest as nationwide pandemonium. Foreign governments add to the hype with heavy-handed, blanket travel warnings. While it's true that small sections of Indonesia experience flashes of conflict, overall the archipelago is quite safe.

On the other hand, regional and separatist conflicts remain an ongoing problem in Papua. Western mining companies are targeted by frustrated indigenous people here and also in Nusa Tenggara. But most people know the difference between a multinational and a tourist and conflicts rarely affect travellers.

Of course the best ways to ensure your safety are to keep abreast of the news, plan accordingly and apply common sense. Check official travel advisories (see the boxed text, opposite), keeping in mind they often seem to suggest you not leave home. Monitor local and international media reports and seek the advice of other travellers and locals. Lonely Planet's Thorn Tree (www.lonelyplanet.com) is an excellent source of information from travellers on the ground.

## Scams

As in most poor countries, plenty of people are out to relieve you of your money in one way or another. It's really hard to say when an 'accepted' practice like overcharging becomes an unacceptable rip-off, but plenty of instances of practised deceit occur.

Con artists are always to be found. Usually those smooth talkers are fairly harmless guides seeking to lead you to a shop where they receive a commission. Just beware of instant friends and watch out for excessive commissions.

As the main tourist destination, Bali is the home of many scams. And there are continuing reports of short-changing moneychangers. But you should always be aware of any local who appears out of nowhere the instant you get a flat tyre. As always, trust your common sense, as most Indonesians you meet in such situations are genuinely trying to help.

Hard-luck stories are common in tourist areas and are a recognised way to make money. But most Indonesians suffer in silence and would never ask for money; consider giving to aid programs if you want to help.

## Theft

Theft can be a problem. However, if you are mindful of your valuables and take precautions, the chances of being ripped off are small. Most thefts are the result of carelessness or naivety. The chances of theft are highest in crowded places and when travelling on public bemos, buses and trains.

Pickpockets are common, and crowded bus and train stations are their favourite haunts, as are major tourist areas. Compared to most Indonesians, tourists are rich and this attracts thieves. The Bahasa Indonesia word for thief is *pencuri*.

Most precautions are simple common sense and should be practised worldwide: do not leave your valuables unattended, and in crowded places hold your handbag or day pack closely. A money belt worn under your clothes is the safest way to carry your passport, cash and travellers cheques.

Keep an eye on your luggage if it's stored on the roof of a bus; bag slashing and theft from bags next to you inside the bus are also hazards. Locks on your bags are mandatory – travelling without them is like waving a 'come and get it' banner.

Always lock your hotel-room door and windows at night and whenever you go out, even if momentarily. Don't leave valuables, cash or travellers cheques lying around in open view inside your room. It is wise to keep valuables hidden and locked inside your luggage; better hotels have safe storage facilities.

Report any theft to the police, but without witnesses don't expect action. Bus companies and hotels will automatically deny any responsibility. Reported theft is usually termed *kehilangan*, or 'loss' – you lost it and it is your responsibility to prove theft. Police will provide a report, which is necessary for replacement passports and travellers cheques, and for insurance claims.

Be wary and know where your valuables are at all times – but at the same time remember that the overwhelming majority of Indonesians are honest and will go out of their way to look after a visitor. Out in the villages, far removed from the big cities and tourist areas, theft is a foreign concept.

## DISCOUNT CARDS

The International Student Identity Card (ISIC) is useful for discounts on some domestic flights, although maximum age limits (usually 26) often apply. A few attractions offer student discounts. Check out www.istc. org for information and details on the application process.

## EMBASSIES & CONSULATES

It's important to realise what your own embassy can and can't do to help you if you get into trouble. Generally speaking, it won't be much help if whatever trouble you're in is remotely your own fault. Remember that you are bound by the laws of the country you are in. In genuine emergencies you might get some assistance, but only if other channels have been exhausted. If you have all your money and documents stolen, your embassy might assist with getting a new passport, but that's about it.

Foreign embassies are located in Jakarta; Bali and Medan have many consulates. There are also some in towns close to foreign borders; see regional chapters for details.

### Bali

All telephone numbers take the area code ☎ 0361:

**Australia** (Map pp298-9; ☎ 241 118; www.dfat.gov.au/bali; Jl Tantular 32, Denpasar; ☺ 8am-noon, 12.30-4pm Mon-Fri) The Australian consulate has a consular sharing agreement with Canada, and may also be able to help citizens of New Zealand, Ireland and Papua New Guinea.

**France** (Map p286; ☎ 285 485; consul@dps.centrin.net.id; Jl Mertasari, Gang II 8, Sanur)

**Germany** (Map p286; ☎ 288 535; germanconsul@bali-ntb.com; Jl Pantai Karang 17, Batujimbar, Sanur)

**Japan** (Map pp298-9; ☎ 227 628; konjpdps@indo.net.id; Jl Raya Puputan 170, Renon, Denpasar)

**Netherlands** (Map p272; ☎ 752 777; Jl Raya Kuta 127, Kuta)

**Switzerland** (Map p272; ☎ 751 735; swisscon@telkom.net; Kuta Galleria, Blok Valet 2, 12, Kuta)

**UK** (Map p286; ☎ 270 601; bcbali@dps.centrin.net.id; Jl Tirtanadi 20, Sanur)

**USA** (Map pp298-9; ☎ 233 605; amcobali@indosat.net.id; Jl Hayam Wuruk 188, Renon, Denpasar; ☺ 8am-4.30pm) A consular agent.

---

**OFFICIAL ADVICE**

It is always worthwhile to check with official government sources before visiting Indonesia in order to check current travel conditions and the overall safety situation. But bear in mind that government sources generally take a conservative and over-cautious view. It's also worth following news sources in order to get a realistic picture.

Government travel advisories:

**Australia** (www.smarttraveller.gov.au)

**Canada** (www.voyage.gc.ca)

**New Zealand** (www.mfat.govt.nz)

**UK** (www.fco.gov.uk/travel)

**US** (www.travel.state.gov)

## Jakarta

All phone numbers take area code ☎ 021:

**Australia** (Map p98; ☎ 2550 5555; www.indonesia
.embassy.gov.au; Jl HR Rasuna Said Kav 15-16)

**Brunei** (Map p104; ☎ 3190 6080; Jalan Teuku Umar 9,
Menteng)

**Canada** (Map p98; ☎ 2550 7800; www.geo.intern
-ational.gc.ca/asia/jakarta/; World Trade Centre, 6th fl, Jl
Jenderal Sudirman Kav 29-31)

**France** (Map p104; ☎ 2355 7600; www.ambafrance
-id.org/; Jl Thamrin 20)

**Germany** (Map p104; ☎ 3985 5000; www.jakarta.diplo
.de; Jl Thamrin 1)

**Japan** (Map p104; ☎ 3192 4308; www.id.emb-japan
.go.jp/; Jl Thamrin 24)

**Malaysia** (Map p98; ☎ 522 4947; www.kln.gov
.my/perwakilan/Jakarta; Jl HR Rasuna Said Kav X/6 No 1)

**Netherlands** (Map p98; ☎ 524 8200; www.indonesia
.nlembassy.org; Jl HR Rasuna Said Kav S-3)

**New Zealand** (Map p98; ☎ 2995 5800; www.nzem
bassy.com; 10th fl, Sentral Senayan 2, Jl Asia Afrika No 8)

**Papua New Guinea** (Map p98; ☎ 725 1218; 6th fl,
Panin Bank Centre, Jl Jenderal Sudirman 1)

**Singapore** (Map p98; ☎ 2995 0400; www.mfa.gov
.sg/jkt/; Jl HR Rasuna Said, Block X/4 Kav 2)

**Thailand** (Map p104; ☎ 390 4052; www.thaiembassy
.org/Jakarta/; Jl Imam Bonjol 74)

**UK** (Map p104; ☎ 2356 5226; www.ukinindonesia.fco
.gov.uk; Jl Thamrin 75)

**USA** (Map p104; ☎ 3435 9000; www.usembassyjakarta
.org; Jl Merdeka Selatan 4-5)

## Medan

All phone numbers take area code ☎ 061:

**Australia** (Map p372; ☎ 415 7810; Australia Centre, Jl
RA Kartini 32)

**India** (Map p372; ☎ 4531308; Jl Uskup Agung)

**Japan** (Map p372; ☎ 457 5193; Wisma BII 5, Jl Diponegoro 18)

**Malaysia** (Map p372; ☎ 453 1342; Jl Diponegoro 43)

**Netherlands** (Map p372; ☎ 456 9853; Jl Monginsidi 45T)

**USA** (Map p372; ☎ 451 9000; Jl MT Haryono A-1, Uni Plaza)

## FESTIVALS & EVENTS

With such a diversity of people in Indonesia,
there are many local holidays, festivals and
cultural events.

Regional tourist offices are the best source
of information for all national holidays, regional festivals, and many of the music, dance
and theatre performances held throughout
the year.

Unless otherwise stated, the dates for the
following festivals vary from year to year.

## January

**Tabut** (p422) An Islamic festival held in January or February in Pariaman, West Sumatra. Painted effigies, dancing,
singing and music.

**Gerebeg** (p183) Java's three most colourful festivals
are held annually at the end of January and April and the
beginning of November.

**Cap Go Mei** (p606) Chinese New Year celebration in
Chinese-majority Singkawang.

## February

**Tai Pei Kong festival** (p706) In Manado, Kienteng Ban
Hian Kong, Eastern Indonesia's oldest Buddhist temple,
plays host to this magnificent festival every February.

**Pasola** (see the boxed text, p589) Nusa Tenggara's biggest
festival: vividly dressed teams of horsemen engage in
mock, though sometimes bloody, battles. Often coincides
with Nyale.

**Nyale** (see the boxed text, p513) Huge fishing festival
celebrated by the Sasaks of Lombok. Usually February or
March.

## March

**Kirab Pusaka** (p201) This festival has been celebrated
in Solo on the first day of the Javanese month of Suro (any
time from March to May) since 1633.

**Equatorial Culture Festival** (p599) Around the March
(and September) equinoxes, with traditional dancing,
singing, and competitions.

## April

**Festival Teluk Kendari** (p719) The Kendari Bay festival
turns the capital of Southeast Sulawesi into a frenzy of
celebrations, with dragon-boat races, traditional music
and partying.

**Galungan-Kuningan** (p263) Ten-day festivals held in
Balinese temples during full-moon periods in April to May
and September to November.

**Gerebeg** See above.

**Legu Gam** (p730) In Ternate, a weeklong annual celebration leading up to the sultan's birthday on April 13th.

## May

**Waisak** (p174) Borobudur flourishes with thousands
of pilgrims and the saffron hue of Buddhist monks to
celebrate the Buddha's birth, enlightenment and reaching
of nirvana.

**Sekaten** (p201) The birth of the Prophet Muhammad is
celebrated in the Islamic month of Maurud (from May to
July) in Solo, Java. The closing ceremony includes a fair and
a huge rice mountain.

## June

**Yogya Arts festival** (p183) Annual festival from 7 June
to 7 July, with a wide range of shows and exhibitions.

**Bali Arts Festival** (p296) Month-long festival starting in mid-June, showcasing traditional Balinese dance, music and crafts.

**Danau Toba Festival** (p392) Week-long festival held in mid-June with cultural performances and colourful canoe races.

**Festival Danau Napabale** (p721) Horse combat and kite flying in Latugho, Southeast Sulawesi.

**Jakarta Anniversary** (p107) Fireworks and the Jakarta Fair kick off Jakarta's birthday, celebrated on 22 June but continuing all the way into mid-July.

**Festival of Borobudur** (p174) This Borobudur festival features Ramayana-style dance, folk-dancing competitions, handicrafts, white-water rafting and a whole lot more.

**Lake Sentani Cultural & Art Festival** (p793) A few days around 20 June.

## July

**Tana Toraja funeral festival** (see the boxed text, p676) A Sulawesi highlight. Held during July and August, Toraja working throughout the country return home for celebrations and funeral rituals.

## August

**Bidar race** (p465) Spectacular canoe races held on South Sumatra's Sungai Musi every 17 August (Independence Day) and 16 June (the city's birthday).

**Independence Day** (p107) Jakarta becomes a spectacle of parades and celebrations every 17 August to mark the country's independence.

**Baliem Festival** (see the boxed text, p811) A celebration of indigenous culture in Papua's Baliem Valley, with mock 'tribal fighting', full traditional regalia, dance and music. Usually 7 August to 12 August.

### RAMADAN

One of the most important months of the Muslim calendar is the fasting month of Ramadan. As a profession of faith and spiritual discipline, Muslims abstain from food, drink, cigarettes and other worldly desires (including sex) from sunrise to sunset. Exemptions from fasting are granted to pregnant women, the ill or infirm, young children and those undertaking extreme physical labour.

Ramadan is often preceded by a cleansing ceremony, Padusan, to prepare for the coming fast (*puasa*). Traditionally, during Ramadan people get up at 3am or 4am to eat (this meal is called *sahur*) and then fast until sunset. Many Muslims visit family graves and royal cemeteries, recite extracts from the Koran, and sprinkle the graves with holy water and flower offerings. Special prayers are said at mosques and at home.

The first day of the 10th month of the Muslim calendar is the end of Ramadan, called Idul Fitri or Lebaran. Mass prayers are held in the early morning, followed by two days of feasting. Extracts from the Koran are read and religious processions take place. During this time of mutual forgiveness, gifts are exchanged and pardon is asked for past wrongdoing. This is the big holiday of the year, a time for rejoicing, and the whole country is on the move as everyone goes home to be with their families.

During Ramadan, many restaurants and warungs are closed in Muslim regions of Indonesia. Those owned by non-Muslims will be open, but in deference to those fasting, they may have covered overhangs or will otherwise appear shut. Ask around for open restaurants. In the big cities, many businesses are open and fasting is less strictly observed. For night owls, the cities come alive for the night meal.

Though not all Muslims can keep to the privations of fasting, the overwhelming majority do and you should respect their values. Do not eat, drink or smoke in public or in someone's house. If you must, excuse yourself and go outside.

Ramadan is an interesting time to travel but it can be difficult. Apart from having to hunt down restaurants and abstain from imbibing in public, the first few weeks are not too restrictive, but travel is a real hassle towards the end of Ramadan.

Around a week before and a week after Idul Fitri, transport is chaotic and packed to the gunwales. Don't even consider travelling during this time. You will be better off in non-Muslim areas – eg Bali, east Nusa Tenggara, Maluku or Papua – but even these areas have significant Muslim populations and Idul Fitri is a big national holiday of two days' duration for everyone. Plan well, find yourself an idyllic spot and stay put.

Ramadan and Idul Fitri move back 10 days or so every year, according to the Muslim calendar.

## October

**Ubud Writers & Readers Festival** (p314) A global festival celebrating the art of writing.

**Asmat Art & Culture Festival** (p815) Held in the Asmat Region of eastern Papua, this festival showcases renowned woodcarving and traditional dancing. Usually in the first week of October.

## November

**Gerebeg** See p830.

## December

**JiFFest** (Jakarta International Film Festival; p107) Indonesia's premier film festival takes place in early December.

## FOOD

Eating reviews in this book are listed in order of budget, from cheapest to most expensive. Prices vary from region to region of course, but in most of Indonesia you can tuck into a simple meal at a warung for around 10,000Rp, spend another 15,000Rp or so for a meal at a restaurant and splurge on dinner and a Bintang beer for 30,000Rp and upwards. You can spend much more in major cities and Bali and – especially in the latter – enjoy cuisine that is simply excellent.

Indonesia's vast array of culinary delights and regional specialities are explained in detail in the Food & Drink chapter, p79.

## GAY & LESBIAN TRAVELLERS

Gay travellers in Indonesia will experience few problems. Physical contact between same-sex couples is quite acceptable, even though a boy and a girl holding hands may be seen as improper. Homosexual behaviour is not illegal, and the age of consent for sexual activity is 16 years. However, in Bali and Jakarta, police and social organisations are cracking down on suspected paedophiles, and several foreigners have been extradited or have received lengthy jail terms. Gay men in Indonesia are referred to as *homo* or *gay*; lesbians are *lesbi*.

Indonesia's community of transvestite/transsexual *waria* – from the words *wanita* (woman) and *pria* (man) – has always had a very public profile. Also known by the less polite term *banci*, they are often extroverted performers as stage entertainers and street-walkers. Islamic groups proscribe homosexuality, but such views are not dominant and there is no queer-bashing or campaigns against gays. It pays to be less overt in some orthodox areas, though.

Indonesia has a number of gay and lesbian organisations. The coordinating body is **GAYa Nusantara** (www.gayanusantara.or.id), which publishes the monthly magazine *GAYa Nusantara*. In Kuta, **Hanafi** ( ☎ 0361-756454; www.hanafi.net) is a gay-friendly tour operator. **Utopia Asia** (www.utopia-asia.com) also has an extensive list of gay and lesbian venues throughout Indonesia and the rest of Asia.

## HOLIDAYS
### Public Holidays

Following are the national public holidays in Indonesia. Unless stated, they vary from year to year.

### JANUARY/FEBRUARY

**New Year's Day** Celebrated on 1 January.
**Muharram (Islamic New Year)** Usually late January.
**Imlek (Chinese New Year)** National holiday in late January to early February.

### MARCH/APRIL

**Good Friday** Late March or early April.
**Paskah (Easter)** Late March or early April.
**Nyepi (Balinese New Year)** The island of Bali closes down for one day, usually in March, sometimes in April; it's a cultural marvel, albeit a quiet one.

### APRIL/MAY

**Maulud Nabi Muhammed** The birthday of the Prophet Muhammed. Celebrated on one day between late March and early May.
**Waisak Day** Marks the Buddha's birth, enlightenment and death. Falls in May.
**Ascension of Christ** May.

### AUGUST

**Hari Proklamasi Kemerdekaan (Independence Day)** 17 August. Independence Day is a national public holiday.

### SEPTEMBER

**Isra Miraj Nabi Muhammed** Celebration of the ascension of the Prophet Muhammed. Held on one day between late August and mid-September.

### OCTOBER/NOVEMBER

**Idul Fitri** Also known as Lebaran, this two-day national public holiday marks the end of Ramadan. Held sometime between mid-October and mid-November.

### DECEMBER

**Idul Adha** Muslim festival held between December and January.
**Hari Natal (Christmas Day)** Celebrated on 25 December.

## School Holidays

Indonesian school holidays vary slightly from province to province, but the following should give you a good idea of when they fall. 'Winter holiday' usually falls in the first week of March, 'spring holiday' spans two weeks, usually from late April to early May, 'summer holiday' runs from the very end of June to the first week in September. Then there's a mid-term holiday during the last two weeks of October, and the Christmas holiday runs from around December 21 to the first week in January.

## INSURANCE

A travel-insurance policy to cover theft, loss and medical problems is essential. There is a wide variety of policies, most sold online; if you're planning to travel to remote areas it's wise to take a policy that will facilitate a speedy evacuation in the event of a medical emergency.

Theft is a potential problem in Indonesia (see p828), so make sure that your policy covers expensive items adequately. Many policies have restrictions on laptops and expensive camera gear, and refunds are often for depreciated value, not replacement value.

Worldwide travel insurance is available at www.lonelyplanet.com/travel_services. You can buy, extend and claim online anytime – even if you're already on the road.

For information on health insurance see p856, and for details on car insurance see p852.

## INTERNET ACCESS

Indonesia is somewhat wired, but speed varies from blindingly fast to painfully slow. All sizeable population centres have at least one warnet (public internet facility) where you can update your blog for 3000Rp to 5000Rp an hour. Wi-fi is increasingly available in hotels and cafes in larger towns and tourist centres. At these places you can download your digital camera, burn CDs or chat on Skype. You can also network your laptop.

Elsewhere in Indonesia, speed varies but is often painfully slow. Expect to pay 300Rp to 500Rp per minute; centres are common anywhere there are tourists. Several national telecommunications operators have set up 3G networks, and Blackberry and iPhone services are available in most towns and tourist areas.

Many hotels have internet centres for their guests. In tourist areas, in-room wi-fi access is moving down the price chart in availability, but watch out for places with high charges pegged to time or data use (we tried one where two emails exhausted the 80,000Rp connection allowance). Most are free or cheap. In South Bali, Ubud, Jakarta and Yogya, wi-fi access in cafes is increasingly common and is often free.

## LEGAL MATTERS

Drugs, gambling and pornography are illegal, and it is an offence to engage in paid work without a formal working permit. Visa length of stay is strictly enforced, and many a careless tourist has seen the inside of an immigration

---

### STOPPING CHILD-SEX TOURISM IN INDONESIA

Unfortunately, Indonesia has become a destination for foreigners seeking to sexually exploit local children. A range of socio-economic factors render many children and young people vulnerable to such abuse and some individuals prey upon this vulnerability. The sexual abuse and exploitation of children has serious, life-long and even life-threatening consequences for the victims. Strong laws exist in Indonesia to prosecute offenders and many countries also have extraterritorial legislation which allows nationals to be prosecuted in their own country for these intolerable crimes.

Travellers can help stop child-sex tourism by reporting suspicious behaviour. In Bali, call the **Women and Children Care Unit** (☎ 0361-226 783 ext 127) of the Bali police. Elsewhere in Indonesia, reports can be made to the **Anti-Human Trafficking Unit** (☎ 021 721 8309) of the Indonesian police. If you know the nationality of the individual, you can contact their embassy directly.

For more information, contact the following organisations:

**ECPAT** (End Child Prostitution and Trafficking; www.ecpat.org) A global network working on these issues, with over 70 affiliate organisations around the world. Child Wise (www.childwise.net) is the Australian member of ECPAT.

**PKPA** (Center for Study and Child Protection; ☎ 061 663 7821 in Medan, Sumatra) An organisation committed to the protection of Indonesia's children and the prevention of child-sex tourism.

**DIRECTORY**

detention facility. Being caught with drugs will result in jail and quite probably a harsh prison sentence (see p827). Generally, you are otherwise unlikely to have any encounters with the police unless you commit a traffic infringement.

Despite claims of reform, corruption remains a fact of life, as police salaries and operational budgets are woefully inadequate. Most police officers are actually embarrassed about having to solicit bribes to buy petrol for their patrol vehicle, so if you are pulled over for a dubious traffic infringement, be polite and respectful as the officer lectures you and then suggests an alternative to a trip to the police station and a courthouse date. Generally, 50,000Rp is usually plenty, but the Balinese police seldom settle for less than 100,000Rp.

On the other hand, the police will leap to protect a foreigner in genuine difficulty. In the case of an accident involving serious injury or death, the best advice is to drive straight to the nearest police station, unless you are in an isolated area and can offer assistance. The police may detain you, but they will sort it out and you will be safe from possible reprisal.

Tourists are unlikely to come across any other problems with officialdom or requests to pay bribes. If you need to report a crime, head to a police station in respectable dress with an Indonesian friend or interpreter in tow. If you find yourself in real trouble with the law contact your embassy or consulate immediately. They will not be able to arrange bail but will be able to provide you with an interpreter and may be able to suggest legal counsel.

## MAPS

Locally produced maps are often inaccurate. Periplus produces excellent maps of most of the archipelago and includes maps of the major cities. The Nelles Verlag map series covers Indonesia in a number of separate sheets, and they're usually reliable although they can be dated for places such as Bali. Both series are available in Indonesia and overseas.

Free tourist maps of major Javanese, Sumatran and Balinese cities can be found in hotels but are of highly variable quality and usefulness.

Hikers will have little chance of finding accurate maps of remote areas. It's far more useful (and wise) to employ the services of a local guide, who will be able to navigate seemingly uncharted territory.

## MONEY

The unit of currency used in Indonesia is the rupiah (Rp). Denominations of 50Rp, 100Rp, 200Rp and 500Rp are in circulation in both the old bronze-coloured coins and the much more common, newer aluminium models. A 1000Rp coin is also minted but rarely seen. Notes come in 500Rp, 1000Rp, 5000Rp, 10,000Rp, 20,000Rp, 50,000Rp and 100,000Rp denominations. For change in amounts below 50Rp, expect to receive a few sweets.

See this book's inside front cover for exchange rates and p20 for more information about general costs in Indonesia.

There are plenty of options for exchanging money in Indonesia, and it's wise to use all of them: carry some plastic, an ATM card and cash.

### ATMs

ATMs are common in larger towns and cities on the main islands of Indonesia; most now accept Visa, Mastercard, Maestro, Plus and Cirrus. Confirm with your bank at home to ensure you can use ATM facilities in Indonesia, and also ask what charges or service fees apply.

ATMs in Indonesia have a maximum limit for withdrawals; sometimes it is 2,000,000Rp, but it can be as low as 400,000Rp, which is not much in foreign-currency terms, especially if you want to get large amounts to limit service charges.

Many ATMs have a sticker that specifies whether the machine dispenses 50,000Rp or 100,000Rp notes. When possible go with the former as the latter are always hard to break.

There have been several instances of ATM fraud in tourist or business areas, so try to select a machine in a bank branch or heavily guarded area.

### Cash & Travellers Cheques

The US dollar and, to a lesser degree, the euro, are the most widely accepted foreign currencies in Indonesia. Australian, British and Japanese currencies are exchangeable in the most touristed areas of Bali and Java. Few people carry any travellers cheques these days and many banks won't exchange them. When heading for really remote places, carry stacks of rupiah, as foreign exchange may be limited to US dollars or simply impossible.

Emergency cash in the money belt is a wise stash for Maluku and Papua, where credit cards are rarely accepted anywhere and ATMs are uncommon. Have a mix of notes – breaking even a 20,000Rp note in a warung can be a major hassle out in the villages.

## Credit Cards

If you are travelling on a low budget, credit cards are of limited use for day-to-day travel expenses, as it is only non–bare bones hotels, restaurants and shops that accept them (and they're virtually useless in places like Papua and Maluku). In touristed areas and Jakarta you'll find plenty of opportunities to use plastic. Credit cards are useful for major purchases like airline tickets (though smaller offices in the backblocks may not accept them) or carefree stays in better hotels.

MasterCard and Visa are the most widely accepted credit cards. Amex is a distant third. Cash advances are possible at many ATMs or banks. If you'll be off the main track, check with your card issuer to find out where you can get cash. Remember, however, that in more remote areas you're asking for trouble if all you have is a credit card.

## Moneychangers

Moneychangers and banks can be very particular about the condition of cash: torn or marked notes are often refused, as are notes more than five years old. Outside the main cities in Java and Bali, exchanging currencies other than US dollars will require more legwork – first to find a bank that will accept them and second to find one that gives a good rate, but also be aware that in places like Papua and Maluku there may be no place to exchange money.

Rates vary, so it pays to shop around. The best rates of exchange are found in Jakarta and Bali. Touristy places have lots of money changers as well as banks. When changing cash, bigger notes are better – a US$100 note may attract a better exchange rate than a US$20 note.

Moneychangers in Bali offer some of the best rates in Indonesia *if* you don't fall for any of many schemes. Signboard rates are often a fabrication, and after signing your travellers cheque or forking over your notes you may find that a 10% (or higher) commission applies. Be sure to double-check the conversion rate and be aware that some dubious operators

rig their calculators; short-changing is rampant at non-bank exchanges and bars are filled with travellers moaning about being fleeced by a moneychanger (often they thought they could outwit the pro, ha!).

Always count your rupiah first before you hand over your money. Only when you are satisfied that you have received the correct amount, hand over your currency or travellers cheques. If there are any problems during the transaction, leave with your cash travellers cheques and try another moneychanger.

Moneychangers outside touristed areas are more likely to be honest, although it is best to sacrifice a bit of the exchange rate and use a bank, which are usually completely honest. Better yet, use an ATM, knowing that the rate is closer to the real exchange rate and doesn't come with hidden 'costs'.

To check bank exchange rates, go to the website of BNI (www.bni.co.id), a large Indonesian bank.

## PHOTOGRAPHY & VIDEO

Digital cameras are easily accommodated in the main tourist areas. Photo shops are ubiquitous, and all now stock memory cards and batteries, and will download your images and burn them onto a CD or make prints. Warnet also offer download and burn services. More esoteric regions, however, may offer little support. Your best bet is to carry some extra memory so you'll never be caught short of pixels.

Indonesia and Indonesians can be very photogenic, but whatever you do, photograph with discretion and manners. It's always polite to ask first, and if the person says no, don't take the photo. A gesture, a smile and a nod are all that is usually necessary. Few subjects expect payment, but all will appreciate a copy of the photo or at least a glimpse of its digital form.

Blank video cassettes are only found in major tourist centres. Be sure that any charger for your video camera will work with the local electricity.

## POST

Sending postcards and normal-sized letters (ie under 20g) by airmail is cheap but not really fast. A postcard/letter to the USA costs 5000/10,000Rp (allow 13 days); to Australia costs 7500/15,000Rp (15 days); and to the UK costs 8000/18,000Rp (21 days).

For anything over 20g, the charge is based on weight. You can send parcels up to 20kg and you can get them properly wrapped and sealed at any post office.

Every substantial town has a *kantor pos* (post office). In tourist centres, there are also postal agencies. They are often open long hours and provide postal services. Many will also wrap and pack parcels.

Have poste restante mail sent to you at major post offices. It should be addressed to you with your surname underlined and in capital letters, then 'Kantor Pos', the name of the town, and then the name of the island and 'Indonesia'. You can also have mail sent to a hotel.

Express companies such as FedEx and UPS can be found in Bali and Jakarta and offer reliable, fast and expensive service.

## SHOPPING

Indonesia is a great place to buy arts and crafts. The range is amazing and the prices cheap.

Souvenir vendors positively swarm around heavily touristed places. Off the beaten track, shopping is more relaxed. If you're an art collector, you'll find plenty of chances to stock up on unusual items. Woodcarvings are on sale everywhere. Batik and ikat (a form of dyed woven cloth; see p68) attract a steady stream of foreign art enthusiasts. Good pottery is available, mostly in Lombok and Java. See p70 for an overview.

Bali is a shoppers' paradise, with crafts from all over Indonesia. Jl Legian in Kuta (p283) has kilometres of shops selling crafts, antiques, clothes and shoes. Sanur, Ubud and other tourist centres are also worthwhile. Yogyakarta (p188) is the best place to shop in Java, where you can purchase handcrafted batik, silver, puppets and leatherwork. In Sulawesi shopping is not great, but you might find some woodcarvings or betel-nut bags you like.

*Songket*, which is silk cloth woven with gold or silver thread (see p69), is painstakingly made into ceremonial sarongs in parts of Sumatra, and exquisite examples are up for grabs in Palembang (p466).

Kalimantan is also good for *songket* and excellent for sought-after Dayak rattan backpacks. In Nusa Tenggara, West Timor, Alor and Sumba have some spectacular naturally dyed ikat for sale.

Elsewhere in Indonesia you tend to see only locally produced crafts, but of course the price for those items will be much cheaper than in the tourist shops of Bali or Jakarta.

You can take some tasty packaged wares home; supermarket chains such as Hero and smaller general stores are well stocked. Look for things that will remind you of your trip such as *sambal* (chilli sauce), *kecap manis* (sweet soy sauce; ABC is a popular brand), sachets of *jamu* (herbal medicine), ready-to-fry *kerupuk* (crackers) and strange-flavoured lollies (candy) such as durian or *asam* (tamarind). A popular treat from the Banda Islands in Maluku is dried nutmeg fruit. If you can lift it, a *cobek* and *ulek-ulek* (mortar and pestle) is needed for making your own *sambal*.

Many foreigners get addicted to Indonesian coffee, which is superb. Both ground coffee and beans can be bought in supermarkets, but the best coffee is bought fresh in markets. In coffee-growing areas such as Bali, highland markets adjacent to plantations offer the best-quality beans. Indonesian tea – black, jasmine or green, loose leaf or in bags – is another popular product. And perhaps you'll want to pick up some tea lids to keep your brew warm.

### Bargaining

Many everyday purchases in Indonesia require bargaining. This applies particularly to handicrafts, artwork and any tourist items, but it can also apply to almost anything you buy. As a general rule, if prices are displayed, prices are fixed; if not, bargaining may be possible. The exception is tourist shops, especially those selling artwork, where price tags are often absurdly inflated for the unwary – hard bargaining is always required.

When bargaining, it's usually best to ask the seller their price rather than make an initial offer. As a rule of thumb, your starting price could be anything from a third to two-thirds of the asking price – assuming that the asking price is not completely crazy, which it can be in tourist areas. Then with offer and counter-offer you move closer to an acceptable price.

A few rules apply to good bargaining. First of all, it's not a question of life or death, where every rupiah you chisel away makes a difference. Don't pass up something that you really want that's expensive or unobtainable at home because the seller won't come down a few hundred rupiah. Second, when your offer is accepted you have to buy it – don't then change your mind and decide you don't want it after all. Third, while bargaining may seem to have a competitive element to it, try to apply it mostly to shopping. It's a mean victory knocking a poor becak (bicycle-rickshaw) driver down from 4000Rp to 3500Rp for a ride.

Don't get hassled by bargaining and don't go around feeling that you're being ripped off all the time – too many travellers do. It is very easy to become obsessed with getting the 'local' price. Even locals don't always get the local price. In Indonesia, if you are rich it is expected that you pay more, and *all* Westerners are rich when compared to the grinding poverty of most Indonesians.

## SOLO TRAVELLERS

Solo travellers will receive little attention in Bali and the more heavily populated areas of Java. Outside these places, however, people are simply curious and a single traveller sporting a backpack will always attract wide eyes and various forms of 'hello'. The more remote the area the greater the focus. Maluku, Papua, Sumatra and Kalimantan encompass vast areas that are virtually untouristed. Be prepared for celebrity status; be prepared for lots of photos. It's generally harmless and a warm smile will surpass the language barrier and elicit the same in return.

Women travelling on their own in these areas may feel less like a celebrity and more like an enigma. For most rural people, the concept of a woman travelling unaccompanied for no reason other than to travel is somewhat unfathomable. Even if you explain that your husband (real or imagined) is at home/in the next town/on the bus in the next street, it still doesn't explain why you aren't at home rearing children. In Sumatra in particular men are bold and the attention can become more than unwelcome. The best thing to do is simply ignore it and employ common sense. If you've attracted undue attention in daylight, don't head out for a beer at night. Be aware of your own personal security. Remote beaches in Papua and Maluku aren't the best places to unwind unless you have a companion in tow. If you're planning a trek into seldom visited territory, take the time to research a genuine and reliable guide. See p841 for more information.

## TELEPHONE

To call any country direct from Indonesia dial ☎ 001 plus the country code followed by the number, or make a call via the international operator (☎ 101). The country code for Indonesia is ☎ 62. Area codes are listed at the start of each city and town in this book. Phone numbers beginning with ☎ 08 are mobile (cell) phones.

The telecommunications service within Indonesia is provided by Telkom, a government monopoly. Local directory-assistance operators (☎ 108) are helpful and some of them speak English. If you call directory assistance and have to spell out a name, try to use the 'Alpha, Bravo, Charlie' system of saying the letters.

Calling internationally can easily cost from US$0.25 to US$1 or more a minute no matter which of the methods you choose to opt for as outlined below.

Some foreign telephone companies issue cards that enable you to make calls from Indonesian phones and have the cost billed to your home phone account. However, the catch is that most public telephones, wartel and hotels won't allow you to call the toll-free ☎ 008 or ☎ 001 access numbers needed to use these phonecards or other home-billing schemes, and the few hotels and wartel that do permit it charge a fee for doing so.

### Internet Calling

Internet connections fast enough to support Voice Over Internet (VOI) services like Skype are now common in the most popular parts of Bali, Jakarta and other modern areas. Some internet centres are hip to this and some allow it, while others add a surcharge for the call to your connection time (perhaps 3000Rp per minute). If you're staying at a place with fast wi-fi in the room, you're really set.

### Mobile Phones

There are several local cell/mobile phone service providers, including Telkomsel and Pro XL. If your phone company offers international roaming in Indonesia, you can use your own mobile telephone in Indonesia – but check rates (often outrageous) with the company.

Alternatively, a mobile phone (called a handphone in Indonesia) using the GSM system (but not the North American GSM system) can be used cheaply if you purchase a prepaid SIM card in Indonesia. This will cost about 50,000Rp and will give you your own local telephone number. However, make certain the phone you bring is both unlocked and able to take SIM cards. Basic phones bought locally start at US$20.

Usually the person selling you your SIM card will install it and make certain things are working. There is also a requirement that you show some ID so your number can be registered with the government, but often busy clerks will suggest you return 'some other time', thus saving you this formality.

Long-distance and international calls from a mobile can be less expensive than through the regular phone system. When you buy your SIM card and usage credit, ask about special access codes that can result in international calls for as low as US$0.25 per minute.

### Phonecards

The vast majority of public phones use phonecards. Some use the regular *kartu telepo* (phonecards) with a magnetic strip. Others use a *kartu chip*, which has an electronic chip embedded in it. You can buy phonecards in denominations of 5000Rp, 10,000Rp, 25,000Rp, 50,000Rp and 100,000Rp at wartel, moneychangers, post offices and many shops. An international call from a card phone costs about the same per minute as a call from a wartel.

### Telephone Offices

A *kantor telekomunikasi* (telecommunications office) is a main telephone office operated by Telkom, usually found in bigger towns. Wartel are sometimes run by Telkom, but the vast majority are private, and there are a lot of them. You can make local, *inter-lokal* (long-distance) and international calls from any wartel.

The official Telkom price of a one-minute call is about the equivalent of US$1 to most parts of the world. Many wartel, however, will charge higher per-minute rates.

You can sometimes make reverse-charge (collect) calls from a Telkom wartel, though most private ones don't allow it and those that do will charge a set fee.

### TIME

There are three time zones in Indonesia. Java, Sumatra, and West and Central Kalimantan are on Western Indonesian Time, which is seven hours ahead of GMT/UTC. Bali, Nusa Tenggara, South and East Kalimantan, and Sulawesi are on Central Indonesian Time, which is eight hours ahead of GMT/UTC. Papua and Maluku are on Eastern Indonesian Time, nine hours ahead of GMT/UTC. In a country straddling the equator, there is of course no daylight-saving time.

Allowing for variations due to summer or daylight-saving time, when it is noon in Jakarta it is 9pm the previous day in San Francisco, midnight in New York, 5am in London, 1pm in Singapore and Makassar, 2pm in Jayapura and 3pm in Melbourne and Sydney.

Strung out along the equator, Indonesia has days and nights that are approximately equal in length, and sunrises and sunsets occur very rapidly with almost no twilight. Sunrise is around 5.30am to 6am and sunset is around 5.30pm to 6pm, varying slightly depending on distance from the equator.

### TOILETS

One thing you'll have to learn to deal with is the Indonesian bathroom, which features a large water tank and a plastic scooper. *Kamar mandi* means bathroom and *mandi* means to bathe or wash.

Climbing into the tank is very bad form indeed – it's your water supply and it's also the supply for every other guest that comes after you, so the idea is to keep the water clean. What you're supposed to do is scoop water out of the tank and pour it over yourself.

Most of the tourist hotels have showers, and the more expensive ones have hot water, especially in Bali and Jakarta.

Indonesian toilets are basically holes in the ground with footrests on either side, although Western-style toilets are common in tourist areas. To flush the toilet, reach for that plastic scooper, take water from the tank and flush it away.

As for toilet paper, it is seldom supplied in public places, though you can easily buy your own. Indonesians rarely use the stuff and the method is to use the left hand and copious quantities of water – again, keep that scooper handy. Some Westerners easily adapt to this method, but many do not. If you need to use toilet paper, see if there is a wastebasket next to the toilet (that's where the paper should go, not down the toilet). If you plug up a hotel's plumbing with toilet paper, the management is going to get pissed.

*Kamar kecil* is Bahasa Indonesia for toilet, but people usually understand 'way-say' (WC). *Wanita* means women and *pria* means men.

## TOURIST INFORMATION

Indonesia's national tourist organisation, the **Ministry of Culture and Tourism** ( ☎ 021-383 8167; www.budpar.go.id; Jl Merdeka Barat 17, Jakarta), maintains a head office in Jakarta as well as offices in each province. Its website is a good source of links; otherwise, you won't find it overly useful.

Most tourist offices in Indonesia offer little of value, although they at times make up for the dearth of material with a surfeit of enthusiasm. One notable exception is the tourist office in Ubud, Bali (p307), which is an excellent resource. Another is the excellent office in Yogyakarta (p178).

## TRAVELLERS WITH DISABILITIES

Indonesia has very little supportive legislation or special programs for disabled people, and it's a difficult destination for those with limited mobility.

At Indonesian airports, arriving and departing passengers usually have to walk across the tarmac to their planes. Check with airlines to see what arrangements can be made and if they can provide skychairs. Airports at Bali and Jakarta have direct access and lifts, but not all flights use these facilities. International airlines are usually helpful, but domestic flights are much more problematic.

Building regulations in Indonesia do not specify disabled access, and even international chain hotels often don't have facilities.

Pavements are a minefield of potholes, loose manholes, parked motorcycles and all sorts of street life, and are very rarely level for long until the next set of steps. Even the able bodied walk on roads rather than negotiate the hassle of the pavement (sidewalk).

Public transport is also difficult, but cars with driver can be hired readily at cheap rates and are much more common than self-drive rentals. Minibuses are easily hired, but none has wheelchair access. Guides are found readily in the tourist areas and, though not usual, they could be hired as helpers if needed.

Bali, with its wide range of tourist services and facilities, is the most favourable destination for travellers with disabilities.

For unsighted travellers or those with only limited vision, Indonesia would definitely be a rewarding destination. Music is heard everywhere, Indonesians are always ready to chat, and the exotic smells of incense and tropical fruit linger in the air. With a sighted companion, many places should be reasonably accessible.

There are no Indonesia-specific resources for disabled travellers; however, **Disability World** (www.disabilityworld.org) is a useful website for global trends and progress.

## VISAS

Visas are the biggest headache many travellers face in their Indonesian trip. They are not hard to obtain, but the most common – 30 days – is awfully short for such a big place. Many travellers find even the 60-day visa restricting.

The following information was correct at the time of writing, but Indonesian visa requirements are prone to fluctuations so you need to contact the Indonesian embassy in your home country before you plan your trip.

The Department of Foreign Affairs website (www.deplu.go.id) has links to Indonesian embassies and consulates worldwide where you can find the latest up-to-date visa information.

### Study & Work Visas

You can arrange visas for study, short-term research, visiting family and similar purposes if you have a sponsor, such as an educational institution. These social/cultural (*sosial/budaya*) visas must be applied for at an Indonesian embassy or consulate overseas. Normally valid for three months on arrival, they can be extended every month after that for up to six months without leaving the country. Fees apply.

People wishing to study and work in Indonesia must apply directly to the Central Immigration Office in Jakarta (p100) for a Limited-Stay Visa (Kartu Izin Tinggal Terbatas, or Kitas). If you're planning to work in Indonesia your employer will need to organise your visa – it's a long and complicated process. In the first instance, though, call your nearest embassy for the most direct avenue. Those granted limited stay are issued a Kitas card, often referred to as the KIMS card.

## Tourist Visas

Depending on your nationality you may be able to obtain a visa on arrival (VOA) at recognised entry points in Indonesia, which comprise 15 airports and 21 sea ports. These include ports for ferries to/from Sumatra: Penang–Medan, Penang–Belawan, Melaka–Dumai and Singapore–Batam/Bintan. See the boxed text, p369, for more information. VOAs are not available at land border crossings, including the one from East Timor. There are two types of VOA; a seven day (US$10) and a 30 day (US$25). Both visas are non-extendable. To get a 60-day visa you have to apply through an embassy or consulate before your departure.

At the time of writing, citizens of 63 countries were eligible for a VOA, including those from Australia, Canada, France, Germany, Ireland, Japan, the Netherlands, New Zealand, the UK and the USA.

If you are not eligible for a VOA, or if you are arriving at a non-approved port or crossing overland, you need to apply for a visa in advance. These can be 30 day or 60 day and the costs vary from country to country (because they are charged in local currency), so again you need to seek accurate information from your nearest embassy. The main crossings that require a visa to be issued in advance include the road crossing at Entikong between Kalimantan and Sarawak (eastern Malaysia), between Tarakan (Kalimantan) and Tawau (Sabah, Malaysia), and between Jayapura (Papua) and Vanimo (Papua New Guinea). See the boxed text, p779, for more information.

You may be able to skip all the above if your nationality falls under the visa-free category. For visits of up to 30 days, visas are not required for citizens of Singapore and a smattering of other countries.

Officially, you must have a ticket out of the country when you arrive. The best answer to the ticket-out requirement is to buy a return ticket to Indonesia or to include Indonesia as a leg on a through ticket. Medan–Penang and Singapore–Jakarta tickets are cheap, popular options for satisfying this requirement. Although immigration officials usually won't ask to see an onward ticket, if you don't have one you may be forced to buy one on the spot.

In addition to (sometimes in lieu of) an onward ticket, you may be asked to show evidence of sufficient funds. The magic number is US$1000. Credit cards and travellers cheques can usually substitute for cash.

Citizens of Israel and several other countries will need special visas that are difficult to obtain. However, it's an urban myth that a stamp from Israel in your passport will cause problems.

### Travel Permits

Technically, if you're heading to Papua or parts of Maluku, you should obtain a special permit from the Indonesian Immigration Office. It rarely translates to necessity, though, but checking with your nearest Indonesian embassy before you go is wise.

### Visa Extensions

Tourist 30-day visas on arrival are not extendible and it is illegal to remain in the country if your visa has expired. Do not simply show up at the airport with an expired visa and expect to be able to board your flight. You may be sent back to the local immigration office to clear up the matter and you could be in deep trouble. However, if you genuinely cannot leave before your visa expires because of illness or a flight reservation problem, you can get a short extension if you report to immigration *before* your last legal day.

If you're already in Indonesia and you want to extend your stay you will probably need to leave the country and apply for another visa. The Indonesian embassy in Singapore is popular. See also the boxed text, p564, for more info.

However, another route to visa renewal has emerged: travellers have reported being able to extend a 60-day tourist visa if they can find an Indonesian willing to act as their sponsor. This can be done 30 days at a time for up to six months. However, there's a fair amount of paperwork involved, so first check with an immigration office to find out the latest details.

## VOLUNTEERING

There are excellent opportunities for aspiring volunteers in Indonesia. Third World poverty and the tragedy of the 2004 tsunami have created need across the archipelago.

See the boxed text, pp406-7 for details on ways you can help the ongoing recovery in Banda Aceh, Sumatra.

Bali is a hub for many charitable groups and NGOs, including the following.

**Friends of the National Parks Foundation**
( ☎ 0361-977 978; www.fnpf.org; Jl Bisma 3, Ubud)
Main office in Bali. Has volunteer programs in and around Tanjung Puting National Park in central Kalimantan.

**JED** (Village Ecotourism Network; ☎ 0361-737447; www.jed.or.id) Organises highly regarded tours (see the boxed text, p330) of small villages. Often needs volunteers to improve its services and work with the villagers.

**ProFauna** ( ☎ 0361-424731; www.profauna.or.id) A large nonprofit animal-protection organisation operating across Indonesia; the Bali office has been aggressive in protecting sea turtles. Volunteers needed to help with hatchery releases and editing publications.

**SOS** (Sumatran Orangutan Society; www.orangutans-sos .org) An Ubud-based group that works to save endangered species throughout Indonesia.

**Yakkum Bali** (Yayasan Rama Sesana; ☎ 0361-247363; www.yrsbali.org; Denpasar) Dedicated to improving reproductive health for women across Bali.

**YKIP** (Humanitarian Foundation of Mother Earth; ☎ 0361-759544; www.ykip.org) Established after the 2002 bombings, it organises health and education projects for Bali's children.

Papua has **Peace Brigades International** (www.peace brigades.org) for people committed to working for human rights and 'positive peace building'. It is also active in Jakarta.

On Sulawesi, the following are always looking for support.

**Borneo Orangutan Survival Foundation** (BOS; www.orangutan.or.id) Accepts volunteers for its orangutan and sun bear rehabilitation and reforestation programs at Samboja Lestari between Balikpapan and Samarinda.

**Kalaweit Care Centre** ( ☎ /fax 0536-322 6388; www .kalaweit.org) Accepts volunteers (not visitors) for rehabilitating ex-captive gibbons.

Kalimantan also has volunteering possibilities with the **Borneo Orangutan Survival Foundation** (BOS; volunteers@sambojalodge.com), a project that promotes reforestation and rehabilitation at Samboja Lestari.

### International Organisations

Another possible source for long-term paid or volunteer work in Bali or Lombok are the following agencies.

**Australian Volunteers International** (www .australianvolunteers.com) Organises professional contracts for Australians.

**Global Volunteers** (www.globalvolunteers.org) Arranges professional and paid volunteer work for US citizens.

**Global Vision International** (www.gviusa.com, www .gvi.co.uk) Organises short-term volunteer opportunities doing things like primate research in Sumatra (you pay costs); offices in Australia, the UK and the US.

**Voluntary Service Overseas** (www.vso.org.uk) British overseas volunteer program accepts qualified volunteers from other countries. Branches in Canada (www.vso canada.org) and the Netherlands (www.vso.nl).

**Volunteer Service Abroad** (www.vsa.org.nz) Organises professional contracts for New Zealanders.

## WOMEN TRAVELLERS

Plenty of Western women travel in Indonesia either solo or in pairs, and most seem to travel through the country without major problems. However, women travelling solo will receive extra attention, and some of it will be unwanted. To avoid this, some women invent a boyfriend or, even better, a husband, whom they are 'meeting soon'. A wedding ring can also be a good idea, while a photo of you and your 'partner' also works well. Sunglasses and a hat are a good way to avoid eye contact and to stop you feeling so exposed.

While Indonesian men are generally very courteous, there is a macho element that indulges in puerile behaviour – horn honking, lewd comments etc. Ignore them totally, as Indonesian women do; they are unsavoury but generally harmless. There are some things you can do to minimise harassment – the most important is dressing appropriately. Dressing modestly won't stop the attention, but it will lessen its severity. In fundamentalist regions such as Aceh in northern Sumatra, it is essential that women cover up as much as possible (including the arms, although a loose-fitting T-shirt which covers the tops of your arms will do). Walk around in shorts and a singlet and you'll be touched, grabbed and leered at by men in the street; cover up and they'll just call out as you walk past.

Women travelling alone in Bali are common, especially in Ubud.

## WORK

A work permit is required to work in Indonesia (see p839). These are very difficult to procure and need to be arranged by your employer. Apart from expatriates employed by foreign companies, most foreigners working in Indonesia are involved in the export business.

# Transport

**TRANSPORT** (side tab)

# GETTING THERE & AWAY

## ENTERING THE COUNTRY

Entering Indonesia by air is relatively simple and straightforward, particularly if you're eligible for a VOA (visa on arrival); see p839 for important information regarding all visas. Numerous sea ports are similarly easy; if you're arriving by land you'll have no problems as long as you have a valid visa.

## Passport

Your passport *must* be valid for six months after your date of arrival in Indonesia. Before passing through immigration you will fill out a disembarkation card, half of which you must keep to give to immigration when you leave the country. See p839 for information on visas.

## AIR

Indonesia is well connected to the rest of the world by numerous airlines. Flights from neighbouring countries also stop in several Indonesian cities. Singapore has some of the cheapest flights to Indonesia so it may be cheaper to fly there and then enter Indonesia by air or ship. From Penang in Malaysia, you can take a short flight or ferry to Medan in Sumatra.

## Airports & Airlines

The principal gateways for entry to Indonesia are Jakarta's Soekarno-Hatta International Airport (p115) and Bali's Ngurah Rai International Airport (p266), which is 15km south of Denpasar.

### AIRLINES FLYING TO & FROM INDONESIA

Airlines serving Indonesia include:

**AirAsia** (airline code AK; www.airasia.com) Serves a wide range of Indonesian destinations from Kuala Lumpur plus Bali and Jakarta from Bangkok and Singapore.

**Cathay Pacific Airways** (airline code CX; www.cathay pacific.com) Serves Bali and Jakarta from Hong Kong.

**China Airlines** (airline code CI; www.china-airlines.com) Serves Bali and Jakarta from Taipei.

**Emirates** (airline code: EK; www.emirates.com) Serves Jakarta from Dubai.

**Eva Air** (airline code BR; www.evaair.com) Serves Bali and Jakarta from Taipei.

**Firefly** (airline code: FY; www.fireflyz.com.my) Serves major cities on Sumatra from Kuala Lumpur and Penang in Malaysia.

**Garuda Indonesia** (airline code GA; www.garuda -indonesia.com) Indonesia's national airline serves Bali and Jakarta from Australia and points across Asia.

**Japan Airlines** (airline code JL; www.jal.co.jp) Serves Bali and Jakarta from Tokyo.

**Jetstar/Qantas Airways** (airline code QF; www.qantas .com.au) Serves Bali and Jakarta from Australia.

---

### THINGS CHANGE...

The information in this chapter is particularly vulnerable to change. Check directly with the airline or a travel agent to make sure you understand how a fare (and ticket you may buy) works and be aware of the security requirements for international travel. Shop carefully. The details given in this chapter should be regarded as pointers only and are not a substitute for your own careful, up-to-date research.

**KLM** (airline code KL; www.klm.com) Serves Jakarta from Amsterdam.

**Korean Air** (airline code KE; www.koreanair.com) Serves Bali and Jakarta from Seoul.

**Lion Air** (airline code JT; www.lionair.co.id) Fast-growing Indonesian budget airline serves airports across the country from major Asian cities.

**Lufthansa** (airline code LH; www.lufthansa.com) Serves Jakarta from Frankfurt.

**Malaysia Airlines** (airline code MH; www.mas.com.my) Serves Bali and Jakarta from Kuala Lumpur.

**Merpati Airlines** (airline code MZ; www.merpati.co.id) Serves Dili in East Timor from Bali.

**Pacific Blue** (airline code DJ; www.flypacificblue.com) Offshoot of Australia's Virgin Blue, serves Bali from several Australian cities.

**Philippine Airlines** (airline code PR; www.philippineair lines.com) Serves Jakarta from Manila.

**Qatar Airways** (airline code QR; www.qatarairways.com) Serves Bali from Doha.

**Royal Brunei** (airline code BI; www.bruneiair.com) Serves Bali and Jakarta from Bandar Seri Begawan.

**Silk Air** (airline code: MI; www.silkair.com) Serves numerous Indonesian destinations from Singapore including Balikpapan and Lombok.

**Singapore Airlines** (airline code SQ; www.singaporeair .com) Numerous flights to Bali & Jakarta daily.

**Thai Airways International** (airline code TG; www .thaiair.com) Serves Bali and Jakarta from Bangkok.

**Tiger Airways** (airline code TR; www.tigerairways.com) Singapore-based budget carrier serving Jakarta, Padang et al.

## Tickets

Check websites to get an idea of airfares to Indonesia. Don't just limit yourself to major sites either, search for 'Indonesian airfares' and you may well find sites belonging to small travel agents who specialise in Indonesian travel.

It can also be worth checking with travel agents for comparison's sake. However if you have plans that include flying to places beyond the busy hubs of Bali and Jakarta then a travel agent may well find ways to produce an itinerary that's cheaper than online. Airline websites are also worth checking as they may have specials not sold elsewhere.

Online sites to consider:

**Booking Wiz** (www.bookingwiz.com) Offers up searches of all other major airfare sites.

**Ebookers** (www.ebookers.com) Europe and UK-based sites.

**Expedia** (www.expedia.com) Good for flights from the US, Canada, the UK or Europe.

**Hotwire** (www.hotwire.com) Good site for US and Canadian departures.

**Kayak** (www.kayak.com) Good price comparison site.

**Opodo** (www.opodo.com) Reliable company specialising in fares from Europe.

**Orbitz** (www.orbitz.com) A full-service site for people in North America.

**SideStep** (www.sidestep.com) Compares a huge range of fares.

**STA** (www.statravel.com) Prominent in international student travel, but you don't have to be a student; site linked to worldwide STA sites.

**Travelocity** (www.travelocity.com) US site that allows you to search fares to/from anywhere.

**Zuji** (www.zuji.com) Excellent site for departures from Australasia and the Pacific.

### ROUND-THE-WORLD TICKETS

Round-the-world (RTW) tickets that include Indonesia are offered by airline alliances such as **Star Alliance** (www.staralliance.com) and **One World** (www.oneworld.com). These tickets come in many flavours, but most let you visit several continents over a period of time that can be as long as a year. It's also worth investigating Circle Pacific–type tickets, which are similar to RTW tickets but limit you to the Pacific region.

Searching for 'round-the-world' tickets will yield vast numbers of online agencies who combine legs from a variety of airlines. These tickets can be great deals. Prices for RTW tickets are often under US$2000 – not much different from what you'll pay for the flight to Bali alone from North America or Europe.

## Asia

Indonesia is closely linked to most of Asia. A plethora of airlines serves Bali and Jakarta. But newer budget carriers like AirAsia and Lion Air serve a huge range of Indonesian cities from major Asian cities.

## Australia

Australia is well served with numerous direct flights from Bali and Jakarta to all major cities on multiple carriers, including Garuda Indonesia, Jetstar/Qantas and Pacific Blue.

---

**CLIMATE CHANGE & TRAVEL**

Climate change is a serious threat to the ecosystems that humans rely upon, and air travel is the fastest-growing contributor to the problem. Lonely Planet regards travel, overall, as a global benefit, but believes we all have a responsibility to limit our personal impact on global warming.

**Flying & Climate Change**

Pretty much every form of motor travel generates $CO_2$ (the main cause of human-induced climate change) but planes are far and away the worst offenders, not just because of the sheer distances they allow us to travel, but because they release greenhouse gases high into the atmosphere. The statistics are frightening: two people taking a return flight between Europe and the US will contribute as much to climate change as an average household's gas and electricity consumption over a whole year.

**Carbon Offset Schemes**

Climatecare.org and other websites use 'carbon calculators' that allow jetsetters to offset the greenhouse gases they are responsible for with contributions to energy-saving projects and other climate-friendly initiatives in the developing world – including projects in India, Honduras, Kazakhstan and Uganda.

Lonely Planet, together with Rough Guides and other concerned partners in the travel industry, supports the carbon offset scheme run by climatecare.org. Lonely Planet offsets all of its staff and author travel.

For more information check out our website: lonelyplanet.com.

---

## Canada

From Canada, you'll change planes at an Asian hub for Bali and Jakarta.

## Continental Europe

KLM and Lufthansa link Amsterdam and Frankfurt respectively with one-stop, same-plane service to Jakarta. But a huge number of airlines, from Emirates to all the major Asian carriers, offer connections between major European cities and Jakarta, and often Bali as well.

## New Zealand

From New Zealand you will have to connect through Australia or an Asian hub.

## UK

Options to fly to Jakarta and Bali from London (or Manchester) involve connecting through a major hub *somewhere* in Asia. The range of choices is myriad. The budget carrier AirAsia now offers cheap flights from London to Kuala Lumpur that connect to flights to Indonesia.

## USA

The best connections are through any of the major Asian hubs with nonstop service to Bali and Jakarta, although residents of the East Coast may find shorter routings via Europe or the Middle East. No US airline serves Indonesia.

## LAND
## Border Crossings

There are three possible land crossings into Indonesia. In all instances you must have obtained a visa before you get to the border; see p839 for visa information.

Regular buses between Pontianak (Kalimantan) and Kuching (Sarawak, eastern Malaysia) pass through the border post at Entikong. They take around 10 hours and if travelling from Pontianak, buses stop at the border in the wee hours until it opens at 9am. You need to get off the bus and clear immigration on either side. See p601 for specifics.

The border crossing between West and East Timor at Motoain was open at the time of research; a visa is required when travelling from East to West Timor. See the boxed text on p564 for details.

The road from Jayapura or Sentani in Indonesia to Vanimo in Papua New Guinea can be crossed, depending on the current political situation. A visa is required if travelling into Indonesia; see the boxed text, p779.

# SEA

There is currently no sea travel between the Philippines and Indonesia.

## East Timor

There is a regular ferry service between Dili in East Timor and Oecussi which borders West Timor. If crossing into Indonesia from here you will have to have organised your visa already in Dili.

## Malaysia

Regular and comfortable high-speed ferries run the two-hour journey between Melaka (Malaysia) and Dumai (Sumatra); see p451 for more information. Similar ferries travel between Penang (Malaysia) and Belawan (Sumatra), taking about five hours. See p377 for specifics.

There are also boats from Pekanbaru (Sumatra) to Melaka, which take around eight hours. See p450 for more information.

From Johor Bahru in southern Malaysia, daily ferries run to Pulau Bintan (see p458) in Sumatra's Riau Islands.

Ferries connect Tarakan and Nunukan in East Kalimantan with Tawau in Sabah daily except Sunday, see p653 for details. Speedboats run daily between Nunukan and Tawau.

## Papua New Guinea

There are no longer any regular boats.

## Singapore

From Batam, speedboats travel through to Pekanbaru on the Sumatran mainland. Otherwise, Pelni ships pass through Batam to and from Belawan (the port for Medan) and Jakarta.

Boats also travel between Pulau Bintan and Singapore. Service includes **Bintan Resort**

**Ferries** (www.brf.com.sg), which handles transport between Lagoi and Singapore (p459).

## Yachts

It's possible to hop on yachts around Southeast Asia, but luck is a major factor. Yacht owners frequently need crew members – you'll usually be required to contribute for food too. As for where to look – well, yacht clubs, and anywhere that yachts pass through.

# TOURS

Most tours tend to be of the standard packaged variety, but some focus on adventure and trekking in places such as Papua, Kalimantan and areas of Java. There are so many tours that it's impossible to list them here.

Prices vary according to the standard of the accommodation. Some try so hard to maximise luxury and minimise hassles that participants are hermetically isolated from the country. Small groups that provide some independence generally also provide a more worthwhile experience. Tours will not run while there are security risks.

Again, your best bet is to search the internet using the names of places in Indonesia you wish to visit plus words describing your interest and the ever-vital 'tour'. Many of the volunteer agencies listed in the Directory (p840) offer tours that for a fee combine travel with doing good.

A few recommended tour companies include the following:

**Earthwatch Institute** (www.earthwatch.org) US-based company offering eco-sustainable tours, activities and volunteer programs.

**Footprint Adventures** (www.footventure.co.uk) UK-based company specialising in small group trekking tours to Sumatra, Kalimantan, Papua and other Indonesian destinations.

---

**INDONESIAN AIRLINE SAFETY**

There's no way around it: Indonesia's airlines do not have a good safety record. Flying conditions are often challenging (monsoons, volcanic eruptions etc), safety standards can be lax and the airlines themselves run in a less-than-professional manner. Although the major carriers have made improvements, at the time of writing all notable Indonesian airlines were on a 'black list' of airlines banned by the EU (www.ec.europa.eu/transport/air-ban/list_en.htm) from its airspace because of safety concerns.

Should you be worried? The odds of a fatal flight in Indonesia are very small, even if they are higher than First World carriers. When possible, pick a major airline over a smaller one and in really remote locations, feel free to do your own inspection of the plane and crew before you fly.

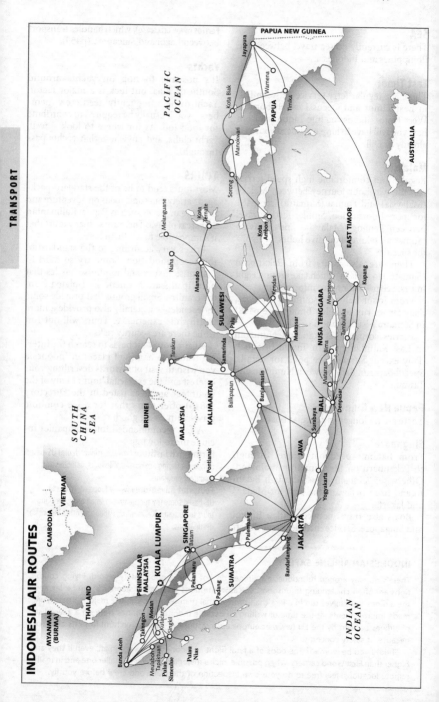

TRANSPORT

**DOMESTIC DEPARTURE TAX**

Indonesian airports typically charge a departure tax to passengers flying out. This charge varies by airport (averaging 50,000Rp but check in advance) but is payable in cash.

**Imaginative Traveller** ( ☎ 800-316 2717; www .imaginative-traveller.com) UK-based company emphasising sustainable, low-impact tourism.

**Intrepid Travel** ( ☎ 1300 360 887, 03-9473 2626; www.intrepidtravel.com.au) Australian-based company with similar ecotravel focus.

**Sustainable Travel International** (www.sustain abletravelinternational.org) Umbrella organisation lists numerous companies offering ecologically focused and volunteer-type tours and travel.

# GETTING AROUND

## AIR
### Airlines in Indonesia

The domestic flight network in Indonesia continues to grow extensively; schedules and rates are in a constant state of flux. Local carriers servicing small routes tend to operate cramped and dated aircraft, whereas flights to Jakarta, Bali and other major destinations are usually on larger, newer craft.

The larger Indonesian-based carriers have websites listing fares, however it may be hard, if not impossible, to purchase tickets over the internet from outside Indonesia because of restrictive laws that limit sales to local credit cards. You may have to call the airline in Indonesia – or better, if the option exists, an office outside of Indonesia. Note that you may not reach anyone on the phone who speaks English.

Another option is to enlist the services of one of many travel agents listed in major cities in this book. Sometimes the best way to get a ticket for travel within Indonesia is to simply go to the airport and compare prices at the various airline offices. Many airlines are strictly cash-based, and offer last-minute deals if there are empty seats.

Even if you book on the day of departure, there's a good chance you'll get a seat – except on major holidays and school vacation periods (see p20). During these times, flights may be booked on the more popular out-of-the-way routes serviced by small aircraft.

It is *essential* to reconfirm. Overbooking is a problem and if you don't reconfirm at least a few days before departure, you may well get bumped. Expect problems in the outer islands, where flights are limited, communications poor and booking procedures haphazard – you should reconfirm and reconfirm again.

Depending on the size of the airlines and where they fly, timetables will vary from accurate, national schedules to hand-adjusted printouts of localised areas or provinces on specific islands. Website information is useful for the bigger carriers but nonexistent for the smaller ones. The best option is to check with local airline offices and travel agents (see regional chapters for contact details) to see what's available.

Major airlines flying domestically include the following (many more local ones are listed in relevant sections of the destination chapters):

**Air Asia** (airline code AK; www.airasia.com) Fast-growing Malaysian-based budget carrier with a web of Indonesian domestic flights.

**Batavia Air** (airline code 7P; www.batavia-air.co.id) Serves numerous destinations; has the enigmatic slogan: 'Trust us to fly'.

**Garuda Indonesia** (airline code GA; www.garuda -indonesia.com) The national carrier serves numerous cities, it is often the connecting airline shown on travel websites.

**Lion Air** (airline code JT; www.lionair.co.id) Fast-expanding budget carrier that has a web of service across the archipelago. It carried the most passengers in 2008.

**Mandala Airlines** (airline code RI; www.mandalaair .com) Serves major routes.

**Merpati Airlines** (airline code MZ; www.merpati.co.id) Serves many smaller Indonesian cities, in addition to the main ones.

**Sriwijaya Air** (airline code: SJ; www.sriwijayaair-online .com) Serves Java, Kalimantan, Sumatra and Sulawesi.

**TransNusa** (airline code: TGN; www.transnusa.co.id) Good for flights within Nusa Tenggara and for flights from Denpasar to places like Labuanbajo.

There are some other intriguing possibilities for flying in Indonesia. The mission air services, which operate in places such as Kalimantan and Papua fly to some really remote regions of the interior of these islands. They will take paying passengers, but only if seats are available at time of takeoff. See the respective chapters' Getting There & Around sections for details.

**TRANSPORT**

## BICYCLE

If reasonably fit, and with a bit of preparation and a ton of common sense, a cyclist will enjoy an incomparable travel experience almost anywhere in the archipelago. The well-maintained roads of Bali, Lombok, East Java and South Sulawesi are suitable for cyclists of all ability levels, while the pros can head for the hills along the length of Sumatra or Nusa Tenggara.

The two primary difficulties are the heat and traffic. Resting during the hottest hours of the day remedies the first, and you can avoid most traffic problems by keeping to back roads or even jumping on a truck or bus to cover really dangerous sections. The third annoyance, being a constant focus of attention, you just have to get used to.

You can rent bikes fairly easily on Bali and other tourist centres such as Yogyakarta, just ask at your accommodation. Rates range from 15,000Rp to 50,000Rp per day. However in places like Papua, bikes for hire are as common as snowballs.

Bicycling is gaining popularity among the Indonesian middle class, and bicycle clubs will be delighted to aid a foreign guest. **Bike to Work** (www.b2w-indonesia.or.id) has an extensive national network. Many tourist areas, particularly Bali, Lombok and Yogyakarta offer organised, vehicle-supported bicycle tours; one good resource is www.ridingtheringoffire.com. At all the main sights in Java there are bicycle parking areas (usually about 1000Rp), where an attendant keeps an eye on your bicycle. See p819 for more information about cycling in Indonesia.

## BOAT

Sumatra, Java, Bali, Nusa Tenggara and Sulawesi are all connected by regular ferries, and you can use them to island-hop all the way from Sumatra to Timor. These ferries run either daily or several times a week, so there's no need to spend days in sleepy little port towns. Check with shipping companies, the harbour office or travel agents for current schedules and fares.

Going to and between Kalimantan, Maluku and Papua, the main connections are provided by Pelni (right), the government-run passenger line. The increase in competitive airline prices has had a significant impact on many of Pelni's routes and it's difficult to obtain any accurate or solid information about schedules more than a month in advance. Furthermore, Pelni ships generally only operate every two or four weeks, so regular ferries are much more convenient.

## Pelni Ships

Pelni is still the biggest shipping line, with services almost everywhere. It has modern, air-con passenger ships that operate set routes around the islands, either on a fortnightly or monthly schedule. The ships – most rather modern – usually stop for four hours in each port, so there's time for a quick look around.

Routes and schedules change every year and the best place to find accurate information is from a Pelni office, but they may only have schedules for the ships that call at their port. At the time of writing the **Pelni website** (www.pelni.com) was three years out of date, but it's useful for details regarding ports and Pelni offices. It's important to note that Pelni only serves some routes once a month, so confirm all details more than once when planning your trip.

Pelni has four cabin classes, followed by economy class, which is the modern version of deck class. It is sometimes possible to book a sleeping place in economy; otherwise, you'll have to find your own empty space. Mattresses can be rented and many boats have a 'tourist deck' upstairs. Even economy class is air-conditioned and it can get pretty cool at night, so bring warm clothes. There are no locker facilities, so you have to keep an eye on your gear.

First class is comfortable, with only two beds per cabin. Second class is a notch down in style, with four to a cabin, but still very comfortable. Third class has six beds to a cabin and 4th class has eight. Each of these classes has a restaurant with decent food, while in economy you queue up to collect an unappetising meal and then sit down wherever you can to eat it. It pays to bring some other food with you.

Economy class is OK for short trips. Fourth class is the best value for longer hauls, although fares are such that 1st is still relatively cheap; some ships only offer 1st- and 2nd- or 3rd-class in addition to economy. As a rough approximation, 4th class is 50% more than economy, 3rd class is 100% more, 2nd class is 200% more and 1st class is 400% more.

It's best to book at least a few days in advance, although you can book tickets up to a week ahead. Pelni is not a tourist operation, so don't expect any special service, although there is usually somebody hidden away in the ticket offices who can help foreigners.

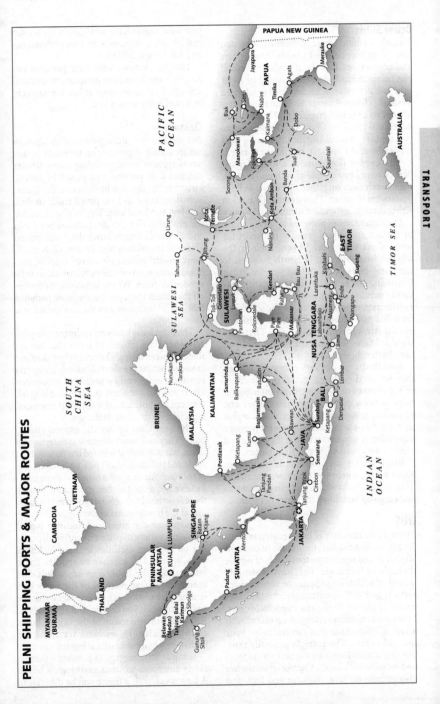

PELNI SHIPPING PORTS & MAJOR ROUTES

TRANSPORT

## Other Ships

There's a whole range of floating tubs you can use to hop between islands, down rivers and across lakes. Just about any sort of vessel can be rented in Indonesia. Fishing boats or other small boats can be chartered to take you to small offshore islands. Some of these boats are *not* reliable and engine trouble can be an occasional problem. Check out the boat before you rent it – it would be nice if it had a two-way radio and a lifeboat, but these are rare.

The *longbot* (longboat) is a long, narrow boat powered by a couple of outboard motors, with bench seats on either side of the hull for passengers to sit on. They are mainly used in Kalimantan as a standard means of transport.

Outrigger canoes powered by an outboard motor are a standard form of transport for some short inter-island hops, such as the trip out from Manado in North Sulawesi to the coral reefs surrounding nearby Pulau Bunaken. On Lombok these elegant, brilliantly painted fishing boats, which look like exotic dragonflies, are used for the short hop from Bangsal harbour to the offshore islands of Gili Air and Gili Trawangan. There are standard fares for standard routes, and you can charter these boats.

Speedboats are not very common, though they are used on some routes on the rivers of Kalimantan or for some short inter-island hops in some parts of Indonesia. They are, of course, considerably faster than *longbot* or river ferries, but are considerably more expensive. A smaller version is the motorised canoe – also used widely in Kalimantan.

River ferries are commonly found on Kalimantan, where the rivers *are* the roads. They're large, bulky vessels that carry passengers and cargo up and down the water network.

## BUS

Buses are the mainstay of Indonesian transport. At any time of the day, thousands of buses in all shapes and sizes move thousands of people throughout Indonesia. The 'leave-when-full' school of scheduling applies to almost every service, and 'full' sometimes means the aisles are occupied too. In the vast majority of cases, buses are hot, bumpy, banged-up affairs with a lack of suspension that can rearrange your internal organs. The going is generally slow. But they are undoubtedly the best way to meet and socialise with locals. Comfortable coaches also operate on Java, Sumatra and Bali, and

relatively comfortable services do the border run between Pontianak in East Kalimantan and Kuching in Malaysia.

Take precautions with your personal belongings and keep your passport, money and any other valuables close at hand, preferably in a concealed money belt.

## Classes

Bus services vary throughout the archipelago but are usually dependent on the roads: eg Java has all types of buses, including luxury air-con coaches that ply the well-paved highways. Luxury buses can also be found on the Trans-Sumatran Hwy and on paved roads in Bali, Lombok and Sumbawa. The 'Wallace Line' for the evolution of buses lies between Sumbawa and Flores, as luxury buses don't operate on Flores or the islands further east. Only small, overcrowded rattlers ply Flores' narrow, pot-holed roads, as an expensive bus would soon be wrecked on them. Within Indonesia, the further off the beaten track you go, the more potholed that 'track' becomes and the less choice you have in buses.

The most basic buses are ordinary, everyday economy-class *(ekonomi)* buses that run set routes between towns. They can be hot, slow and crowded, but they're also ridiculously cheap and provide a never-ending parade of Indonesian life. If you can get a seat and the road is good, they can be quite tolerable for short distances, especially on the main highways.

The next class up are the express *(patas)* buses. They look much the same as the economy buses, but stop only at selected bus terminals en route and (officially) don't pick up from the side of the road. Air-con *patas* buses are more comfortable and seating is often guaranteed. Usually there is no need to book and you can just catch one at the bus terminal in any big city.

Luxury air-con buses (or 'executive' buses) come in a variety of price categories, depending on whether facilities include reclining seats, toilets, TV, karaoke or snacks. These buses should be booked in advance; ticket agents often have pictures of the buses and seating plans, so check to see what you are paying for when you choose your seat. In Java, Bali and Sumatra many of the luxury buses are night buses *(bis malam)*, travelling the highways when the traffic is lighter.

Bring as little luggage as possible – there is rarely any room to store anything on buses. A large pack with a frame will be difficult to find space for (and often ends up on your lap). Many out-of-the-way places can only be reached by public bus; for real exploration it pays to leave your luggage in storage and travel with a day pack for a few days.

## Costs

Economy-class bus prices vary from region to region and with the condition of the road. The daytime buses that depart early in the morning – carrying chickens, pigs and goats – are usually the cheapest. An eight-hour journey will cost 50,000Rp to 100,000Rp. By way of comparison, an eight-hour journey on a luxurious, overnight bus will cost 150,000Rp to 200,000Rp.

## Reservations

Vehicles usually depart throughout the day for shorter routes over good roads; for longer routes, you'll have to get down to the bus terminal early in the morning in order to get a vehicle. On bad roads, there'll be fewer vehicles, so buying a ticket beforehand can be a good idea. Luxury buses should be booked in advance. In many towns and villages, the bus companies have a ticket/reservations office, or there are shops which act as agents (or own the buses). Often, hotels will act as agents or buy a ticket for you and will arrange for the bus to pick you up at the hotel – they sometimes charge a few hundred rupiah for this service but it's easily worth it.

# CAR & MOTORCYCLE
## Driving Licence

To drive in Indonesia, you officially need an International Driving Permit (IDP) from your local automobile association. This permit is rarely required as identification when hiring/driving a car in Indonesia, but police may ask to see it. Bring your home licence as well – it's supposed to be carried in conjunction with the IDP. If you also have a motorcycle licence at home, get your IDP endorsed for motorcycles too.

**TRANSPORT**

---

### GUIDEBOOK ADVENTURES

The authors of this book had some real adventures while researching.

#### Maluku *Mark Elliot*
Getting so drenched on a 50km *ojek* ride in Tanimbar that I stopped halfway to ring out my underwear in the driver's home village.

Getting so swamped by waves trying to reach Molana that I had to turn back and charter a bigger boat.

#### Papua *John Noble*
Returning from Papua's Arfak mountains to Manokwari, there was no traffic on the mountain road. I started walking – 26km to the main road, maybe I could do it before dark. Then along came a clapped-out 4WD with people hanging off the back. I was given a privileged place in the front, half of one buttock on a seat. We broke down seven times in the 50km to Manokwari. Eventually the driver extracted the fan belt, cut a piece out of it, and fixed it back together with wire. We rumbled into Manokwari at dusk. Better than walking? I wasn't sure.

#### Nusa Tenggara *Adam Skolnick*
I was suspicious of our knock-off VW van almost immediately. The paint job made it look shiny and new, yet it struggled to make it up to 60km/hr. Nevertheless, we set out from Soe for remote Temkessi village, and three hours later we were stuck in the mud. We hopped *ojeks* to continue up the steep, crumbling ridge. Soon villagers appeared waving and smiling, and when we finally walked the last 500m through a keyhole in the rocks we arrived in the most breathtaking village I've ever seen.

#### Java *Iain Stewart*
Jakarta is a sweaty, polluted metropolis not geared to walking – pavements are either nonexistent or have canyonesque cracks, and are usually blocked by *kaki lima* (mobile food carts) and street hawkers. I really didn't want to walk the kilometre or so from Kota up to Sunda Kelapa in the midday sun, so when a cyclist with an extra back seat strapped to his Dutch-era bike offered me a ride I quickly agreed. His first price? 3000Rp. He got a tip.

## Fuel & Spare Parts

After decades of subsides, fuel prices are now adjusted to reflect international oil prices. At the time of writing premium petrol cost 5500Rp per litre (still cheap by Western standards). The opening of the domestic fuel market to foreign operators has spurred national oil company Pertamina to build full-service outlets (*pompa bensin*) throughout the archipelago. Where no formal stations exist, roadside shops fill the gap by selling litres of petrol with a slight markup; look for signs that read *press ban,* or for crates of bottles with a *bensin* sign. Some vendors step on their product with the zeal of a drug dealer, so they should only be used as a last resort.

## Hire

### CAR HIRE

The price of car rental will vary according to both location and vehicle. Indonesia has car-rental agencies in the large cities such as Jakarta, where a rental costs around US$100 per day. It's generally cheaper to hire a car and driver for 350,000Rp to 500,000Rp per day. Bali is one of the cheapest places to rent a car; a Suzuki 4WD costs around 80,000Rp to 120,000Rp a day, including insurance and unlimited kilometres. In most cases, the price includes unlimited mileage, but you supply the petrol.

If you are travelling in a group, renting a minibus can be a particularly good deal. The minibuses are sturdy, comfortable, go-almost-anywhere vehicles, and can take up to six people plus luggage in comfort. Minibus rental, including driver but excluding petrol, costs 350,000Rp to 700,000Rp or more per day depending on distance to be travelled. Bargaining is usually required. It is harder to find a driver for trips lasting longer than a few days. Negotiate a deal covering food and accommodation for your driver; either you provide a hotel room each night and pay a food allowance or negotiate an allowance that covers both (figure on about 60,000Rp per day). It pays to see what your driver is like on a day trip before heading off on a lengthy expedition.

Major car-rental agencies, including **Hertz** ( ☎ 021 390 7282; www.hertz.com) and **Avis** ( ☎ 021 314 2900; www.avis.com) have offices in the main cities, such as Jakarta, Bandung, Yogyakarta, Medan, Surabaya and Denpasar, but they are more expensive than arranging a vehicle through your hotel or a tourist office.

Travel agencies in the travellers' centres are good places to try for minibus rental. Go to the cheap tour operators – agents in the big hotels will charge big prices.

### MOTORCYCLE HIRE

You'll find that motorcycles are readily available for hire throughout Indonesia. In the tourist centres they can be rented from around 30,000Rp per day, but in most places the locals rent out their own motorcycles to earn a few extra rupiah. Rental charges vary with the type of bike and the length of hire. The longer the hire period, the lower the rate; the bigger or newer the bike, the higher the rate.

Motorcycles are almost all between 90cc and 125cc, with 100cc the average size. You really don't need anything bigger; the distances are short and the roads are rarely suitable for fast speeds.

Indonesia is not the place to learn how to ride. The main highways are hectic, especially in Java and Bali. Combined with all the normal hazards of motorcycle riding there are narrow roads, unexpected potholes, crazy drivers, buses and trucks that claim road ownership, children who dart onto the road, lumbering bullocks, dogs and chickens that run around in circles and unlit traffic at night. Take it slowly and cautiously around curves to avoid hitting oncoming traffic. Keep to the back roads as much as possible, where riding can be pleasurable.

You need to have a licence, especially to satisfy travel insurance in case of an accident, though you'll rarely need to show it.

Some insurance policies do not cover you if you are involved in an accident while on a motorcycle. Check the small print.

## Insurance

Rental agencies and owners usually insist that the vehicle itself is insured, and minimal insurance should be included in the basic rental deal – often with an excess of as much as US$100 for a motorcycle and US$500 for a car (ie the customer pays the first US$100/500 of any claim). The more formal motorcycle- and car-rental agencies may offer additional insurance to reduce the level of the excess, and cover damage to other people or their property, ie 'third-party' or 'liability' cover. Your travel insurance may provide some additional protection, although liability for motor accidents is specifically excluded from many policies.

A private owner renting out a motorcycle may not offer any insurance at all. Ensure that your personal travel insurance covers injuries incurred while motorcycling.

### Road Conditions

The relentless traffic congesting every Indonesian city makes driving an exhausting activity. On the open road, expect delays due to potholes and congestion. Finding your way around the main tourist sites on any island can be a challenge, as roads are only sometimes signposted and maps are often out of date.

### Road Hazards

Aside from the above, avoid driving on rural roads after dusk, when spotting human and other living traffic becomes more difficult.

### Road Rules

Indonesians drive on the left side of the road (sometimes the right, sometimes the pavement), as in Australia, Japan, the UK and most of Southeast Asia. Indonesia has its fair share of maniacal drivers, including most bus drivers, but there are relatively few accidents. The key is defensive driving. The roads are not just for cars, but also pedestrians, animals, food carts etc.

Considering the relatively small cost of a driver in relation to the total rental, it makes little sense to take the wheel yourself. Driving requires enormous amounts of concentration and the legal implications of accidents can be a nightmare, as a foreigner – it's *your* fault (see Legal Matters, p833).

## HITCHING

Hitching is not part of the culture but if you put out your thumb, someone may give you a lift. On the back roads where no public transport exists, hitching may be the only alternative to walking, and passing motorists or trucks are often willing to help. If you snag a ride in a late-model sedan or SUV expect to be treated to a meal, otherwise you should at least offer to pitch in for petrol.

Bear in mind, however, that hitching is never entirely safe in any country, and we do not recommend it. Travellers who decide to hitch should understand that they are taking a small but potentially serious risk. People who do choose to hitch will be safer if they travel in pairs and let someone know where they are planning to go.

## LOCAL TRANSPORT
### Bajaj

These machines are noisy, smoke-belching three-wheeled vehicles with a driver who sits at the front, a small motorcycle engine below and seats for two passengers behind. They're a common form of local transport in Jakarta, but you don't see them very often elsewhere.

### Becak

These are three-wheeled bicycle-rickshaws. Unlike the version found in India where the driver sits in front of you, or the Filipino version with the driver at the side, in Indonesia the driver sits at the rear, with you riding point.

Many drivers rent their vehicles, but those who own them add personal touches: brightly painted pictures, bells or whirring metal discs strung across the undercarriage.

The becak is now banned from the main streets of some large cities, but you'll still see them swarming the back streets, moving anyone and anything.

Negotiate your fare *before* you get in; and if there are two passengers, make sure that it covers both people, otherwise you'll be in for an argument when you get to your destination. Becak drivers are hard bargainers – they need to be to survive – but they will usually settle on a reasonable fare, around 2000Rp to 4000Rp per kilometre. Fares vary from city to city and increase with more passengers, luggage, hills and night journeys. Hiring a becak for a period of time or for a round trip often makes good sense if you're planning to cover a lot of ground in one day, particularly in large places like Yogyakarta or Solo.

### Bus

Large buses aren't used much as a means of city transport except on Java. There's an extensive system of buses in Jakarta and these are universally cheap, but beware of pickpockets. They usually work in gangs and can empty your pockets faster than you can say 'gado gado'.

### Dokar

A *dokar* is the jingling, horse-drawn cart found throughout the archipelago. The two-wheeled carts are brightly coloured with decorative motifs and bells, and the small horses or ponies often have long tassels attached to their bridle. A typical *dokar* has bench seating on either side, which can comfortably fit three or four people. However, their owners try to pack in three or four families plus bags of rice etc. It's a picturesque way of getting around if you don't get upset by the ill-treatment of animals, but generally the ponies are well looked after. The carts often operate on set runs and payment is per person (1500Rp to 2000Rp). Foreigners may have to charter; 10,000Rp to 15,000Rp should get you just about anywhere around town.

In Java you'll also see the *andong* or *dilman*, which is a larger horse-drawn wagon designed to carry six people. In some parts of Indonesia, such as Gorontalo and Manado in North Sulawesi, you also see the *bendi*, which is a small *dokar* that carries two passengers.

## Ojek

*Ojeks* (or *ojegs*) are motorcycle riders who take pillion passengers for a bargainable price. They are found at bus terminals and markets, or just hanging around at crossroads. They will take you around town and go where no other public transport exists, or along roads that are impassable in any other vehicle. They are the preferred method for navigating Jakarta traffic. They can also be rented by the hour for sightseeing (starting at around 20,000Rp to 30,000Rp).

## Taxi

Metered taxis are readily available in major cities, especially in Java and Bali. If a taxi has a meter *(argo)*, make sure it is used. Most drivers will use them without fuss but like anywhere there are a few sharks. Elsewhere, meters don't exist and you will have to bargain for the fare in advance. Non-licensed taxis abound and are sometimes the only option; otherwise, opt for the licensed taxis.

At airports, taxis usually operate on a coupon system, payable at the relevant booth before you board the taxi.

## MINIBUS (BEMO)

Public minibuses are used for local transport around cities and towns, short intercity runs and the furthest reaches of the transport network.

The great minibus ancestor is the bemo, a small three-wheeled pick-up truck with a row of seats down each side, but regular minibuses are more common these days. The word 'bemo' (a contraction of 'becak' – three-wheeled bicycle-rickshaw – and 'motor') is still applied in some cities and is universally understood, but you'll encounter a mind-boggling array of names, such as *opelet, mikrolet, angkot, angkudes* and *pete-pete*. Just to make things confusing, they are called taxi in many parts of Papua, Kalimantan and East Java. Often they will be called simply by their brand name, such as Suzuki, Daihatsu or Toyota, but the most popular make by far is the Mitsubishi Colt, therefore 'Colt' is widely used.

Most minibuses operate a standard route, picking up and dropping off people and goods anywhere along the way. This is particularly the case in cities, where one fare applies, regardless of the distance. On longer routes between cities you may have to bargain a bit. Minibus drivers often try to overcharge foreigners and will have no qualms about asking you for triple the amount they just accepted from a local. It's best to ask somebody, such as your hotel staff, about the *harga biasa* (normal price) before you get on; otherwise, see what the other passengers are paying and offer the correct fare.

Beware of getting on an empty minibus – you may end up chartering it! On the other hand, sometimes chartering a bemo is worth considering: if there's a group of you, it can work out cheaper than hiring a motorcycle by the day and much cheaper than hiring a car. Regular bemos carry around 12 people, so multiplying the usual fare by 12 should give you a rough idea of what to pay.

As with all the public transport in Indonesia, the drivers wait until their vehicles are crammed to capacity before they contemplate moving, or they may go *keliling* – driving endlessly around town looking for a full complement of passengers. Often there are people, produce, chickens, baskets and even bicycles hanging out the windows and doors – at times it seems you're in danger of being crushed to death or at least asphyxiated (there's no air-con on any of these vehicles).

Luxurious, express minibuses operate between the main tourist centres in Bali, Lombok and Sumatra.

## TOURS

A wide range of tours can be booked from travel agents within Indonesia. Most operate in tourist hot spots. Some of the best tours are with local guides, such as the eco-trips to Halimun National Park in Java with Alwi (p137) or treks in the forests of South Kalimantan with Tailah (p626).

You can be certain that taking a tour will work out to be more expensive than if travelling independently, but the benefit of local dialects, in-depth local knowledge and experience is worth it. You will find local tour companies listed throughout this book and their offers will be readily apparent in tourist centres.

A few to consider contacting in advance:

**Baliem Valley Resort** (www.baliem-valley-resort.de) Offers challenging trips to destinations like Carstensz and the Korowai/Kombai region, and also general Baliem Valley tours in Papua.

**Biak Paradise Tours** ( ☎ 0981-23196; www.discover papua.com; Hotel Arumbai, Jl Selat Makassar 3, Kota Biak, Biak) A Biak-based operator that offers a wide range of tours in many parts of Papua.

**Expedition Jungle** (0813 7060 7035; www.expedi tionjungle.com) North Sumatra travel, tours and jungle treks.

**Jaker** ( ☎ 0293 788 845; jackpriyana@yahoo.com.sg) A group of guides and local activists based in the small settlement of Borobudur.

**Laszlo Wagner** (www.eastindonesia.info) An experienced Hungarian-born writer offers tailor made trips around Maluku and Papua.

**Papua Trekking** (www.papuatrekking.com) Czech-based company specialising in the most challenging destinations such as Carstensz, Mamberamo, Asmat and Korowai/Kombai in Papua.

You can also travel around Indonesia – especially between Bali, Lombok and Flores – by charter sailing boats. The website **Indonesia Traveling** (www.indonesiatraveling.com) has a good page of links to dozens of boats for hire.

## TRAIN

Train travel in Indonesia is restricted to Java and Sumatra. In Java, trains are one of the most comfortable and easiest ways to travel. In the east, the railway service connects with the ferry to Bali, and in the west with the ferry to Sumatra. Sumatra's limited rail network runs in the south from Bandarlampung to Lubuklinggau, and in the north from Medan to Tanjung Balai and Rantauparapat.

The railway's **Train Information Service** ( ☎ 0361 227 131; www.kereta-api.com) has more information; on the site, both '*Jadwal*' (schedule) and 'Info KA' can point you to schedules. For complete details of trains on Java, see p95.

# Health <small>Dr Trish Batchelor</small>

## CONTENTS

Health issues and the quality of medical facilities vary enormously depending on where and how you travel in Indonesia. Many of the major cities are well developed, although travel to rural areas can expose you to a variety of health risks and inadequate medical care.

Many visitors tend to worry about contracting infectious diseases when in the tropics, but infections are a rare cause of serious illness or death in travellers. Pre-existing medical conditions such as heart disease, and accidental injury (especially traffic accidents), account for most life-threatening problems. Becoming ill in some way, however, is relatively common when travelling in Indonesia. Fortunately most common illnesses can either be prevented with some common-sense behaviour or be treated easily with a well-stocked traveller's medical kit.

The following advice is a general guide only and does not replace the advice of a doctor trained in travel medicine.

# BEFORE YOU GO

Pack medicines in their original, clearly labelled containers. A signed and dated letter from your physician describing your medical conditions and medications, including generic names, is also a good idea. If you have a heart condition bring a copy of your ECG taken just prior to travelling.

If you take regular medication bring double your needs in case of loss or theft. You can buy many medications over the counter without a doctor's prescription, but it can be difficult to find some of the newer drugs, particularly the latest antidepressant drugs, blood-pressure medications and contraceptive pills.

## INSURANCE

Even if you are fit and healthy, don't travel without health insurance – accidents do happen. Declare any existing medical conditions you have – the insurance company *will* check if your problem is pre-existing and will not cover you if it is undeclared. If you're uninsured, emergency evacuation is expensive; bills of over US$100,000 are not uncommon.

Find out in advance if your insurance plan will make payments directly to providers or reimburse you later for overseas health expenditures. (In many countries doctors expect payment in cash.) Some policies ask you to call back (reverse charges) to a centre in your home country where an immediate assessment of your problem is made.

## VACCINATIONS

Specialised travel-medicine clinics are your best source of information. The doctors will take into account factors such as past vaccination history, the length of your trip, activities you may be undertaking and underlying medical conditions, such as pregnancy.

Most vaccines don't provide immunity until at least two weeks after they're given, so visit a doctor four to eight weeks before departure. Ask your doctor for an International Certificate of Vaccination (otherwise known as the yellow booklet), which will list all the vaccinations you've received.

### Recommended Vaccinations

The World Health Organization (WHO) recommends the following vaccinations for travellers to Southeast Asia:

**Adult diphtheria and tetanus:** Single booster recommended if none in the previous 10 years. Side effects include sore arm and fever.

## MEDICAL CHECKLIST

Consider including the following in your medical kit:

- Antibiotics – consider including these if you're travelling well off the beaten track; see your doctor, as they must be prescribed, and carry the prescription with you
- Antifungal cream or powder – for fungal skin infections and thrush
- Antihistamine – for allergies, eg hay fever; to ease the itch from insect bites or stings; and to prevent motion sickness
- Antiseptic (such as povidone-iodine or Betadine) – for cuts and grazes
- Antispasmodic – for stomach cramps, eg Buscopan
- Aspirin or paracetamol (acetaminophen in the USA) – for pain or fever
- Bandages, Band-Aids (plasters) and other wound dressings
- Calamine lotion, sting relief spray or aloe vera – to ease irritation from sunburn and insect bites or stings
- Cold and flu tablets, throat lozenges and nasal decongestant
- Contraceptives
- DEET-based insect repellent
- Ibuprofen or other anti-inflammatory
- Iodine or other water purification tablets
- Loperamide or diphenoxylate – 'blockers' for diarrhoea
- Multivitamins – consider for long trips, when dietary vitamin intake may be inadequate
- Permethrin – to impregnate clothing and mosquito nets
- Prochlorperazine or metoclopramide – for nausea and vomiting
- Rehydration mixture – to prevent dehydration, which may occur, for example, during bouts of diarrhoea; particularly important when travelling with children
- Scissors, tweezers and a thermometer – note that mercury thermometers are prohibited by airlines
- Sterile kit – in case you need injections in a country with medical hygiene problems; discuss with your doctor
- Sunscreen, lip balm and eye drops

**Hepatitis A:** Provides almost 100% protection for up to a year, a booster after 12 months provides at least another 20 years' protection. Mild side effects such as headache and sore arm occur in 5% to 10% of people.

**Hepatitis B:** Now considered routine for most travellers. Given as three shots over six months. Lifetime protection occurs in 95% of people.

**Measles, mumps and rubella (MMR):** Two doses of MMR required unless you have had the diseases. Many young adults require a booster.

**Polio:** Only one booster required as an adult for lifetime protection. Inactivated polio vaccine is safe during pregnancy.

**Typhoid:** Recommended unless your trip is less than a week and only to developed cities. The vaccine offers around 70% protection, lasts for two to three years and comes as a single shot.

**Varicella:** If you haven't had chickenpox, discuss this vaccination with your doctor.

These immunisations are recommended for long-term travellers (more than one month) or those at special risk:

**Japanese B Encephalitis:** Three injections in all. Booster recommended after two years. Sore arm and headache are the most common side effects.

**Meningitis:** Single injection. Recommended for long-term backpackers aged under 25.

**Rabies:** Three injections in all. A booster after one year will then provide 10 years' protection. Side effects are rare – occasionally headache and sore arm.

**Tuberculosis (TB):** Adult long-term travellers are usually recommended to have a TB skin test before and after travel, rather than vaccination. Only one vaccine given in a lifetime.

### Required Vaccinations

The only vaccine that is required by international regulations is yellow fever. Proof of vaccination will only be required if you have visited a country in the yellow-fever zone within the six days prior to entering Indonesia. If you are travelling to Indonesia from either Africa or South America you should check to see if you require proof of vaccination.

## INTERNET RESOURCES

There is a wealth of travel health advice on the internet. The **World Health Organization** (WHO; www.who.int/ith/) publishes a superb book called *International Travel & Health*, which is revised annually and is available online at no cost. Another website of general interest is **MD Travel Health** (www.mdtravelhealth.com), which provides travel health recommendations for every country. The **Centers for Disease Control & Prevention** (CDC; www.cdc.gov) website also has good general information. For further information, **LonelyPlanet.com** (www.lonelyplanet.com) is a good place to start. You can also check the websites of various foreign embassies in Indonesia (see boxed text, below and p829).

## FURTHER READING

Lonely Planet's *Healthy Travel – Asia & India* is a handy pocketsized book that is packed with useful travel information including pre-trip planning, emergency first-aid advice, immunisation and disease information, and what to do if you get sick on the road. Some other recommended references include *Traveller's Health* by Dr Richard Dawood and *Travelling Well* by Dr Deborah Mills – which also has a website (www.travellingwell.com.au).

---

#### HEALTH ADVISORIES

It's usually a good idea to consult your government's travel-health website before departure, if one is available:

**Australia** (www.smartraveller.gov.au)
**Canada** (www.phac-aspc.gc.ca/tmp-pmv/pub_e.html)
**New Zealand** (www.safetravel.govt.nz)
**UK** (www.dh.gov.uk/PolicyAndGuidance/HealthAdviceForTravellers/fs/en)
**US** (www.cdc.gov/travel/)

---

# IN INDONESIA

## AVAILABILITY OF HEALTH CARE

It is difficult to find reliable medical care in rural areas, but most capital cities now have clinics catering specifically to travellers and expats. These clinics are usually more expensive than local medical facilities, but are worth utilising, as they will offer a superior standard of care. Additionally, they understand the local system and are aware of the safest local hospitals and best specialists. They can also liaise with insurance companies should you require evacuation.

If you think you may have a serious disease, especially malaria, do not waste time – travel immediately to the nearest quality facility to receive attention.

Buying medication over the counter is not recommended, as fake medications and poorly stored or out-of-date drugs are common.

Local medical care in general is not yet up to international standards. Foreign doctors are not allowed to work in Indonesia, but some clinics catering to foreigners have 'international advisors'. Almost all Indonesian doctors work at government hospitals during the day and in private practices at night. This means that private hospitals often don't have their best staff available during the day. Serious cases are evacuated to Australia or Singapore.

## INFECTIOUS DISEASES
### Dengue Fever

As there is no vaccine available for this mosquito-borne disease, it can only be prevented by avoiding bites. The mosquito that carries dengue is active day and night, so use insect-avoidance measures at all times. Symptoms include high fever, severe headache and body ache (dengue was previously known as 'breakbone fever'). Some people develop a rash and experience diarrhoea. There is no specific treatment, just rest and take paracetamol – not aspirin as it increases the likelihood of haemorrhaging. See a doctor to be diagnosed and monitored.

### Filariasis

A mosquito-borne disease that is very common in the local population, yet very rare in travellers. Mosquito-avoidance measures are the best way to prevent this disease.

**EATING HEALTHY**

Ironically, roadside warung can be the best option for travellers worried about gastric distress. Soups on the boil for hours and overcooked vegetables have about as much bacteria as vitamins. Midrange hotel coffee shops and mass-market tourist restaurants tend to be the worst offenders. Tips for the gastronomically paranoid include:

- Drink only hot tea or coffee and bottled water, which is available anywhere.
- Try to eat lightly cooked food such as gado gado early in the day, before it has had a chance to sit in the sun.
- In a restaurant, do not feel shy about checking out the kitchen. Fortunately, many warung and restaurant kitchens are open to the dining room.
- Stay away from Western food, particularly salads, in areas with few foreigners. Most Indonesian food is bought, cooked and served on the day, while Western ingredients may sit around for a week or more.
- Look for food served on banana leaves and other disposable wrappings, and is eaten with your fingers. Food is only as clean as the plate and utensils.

## Hepatitis A

A problem throughout the region, hepatitis A is a food- and water-borne virus that infects the liver, causing jaundice (yellow skin and eyes), nausea and lethargy. There is no specific treatment for hepatitis A; you just need to allow time for the liver to heal. All travellers to Indonesia should be vaccinated against hepatitis A.

## Hepatitis B

The only sexually transmitted disease that can be prevented by vaccination, hepatitis B is spread by body fluids, including sexual contact. In some parts of Indonesia up to 15% of the population are carriers of hepatitis B, and usually are unaware of this. The long-term consequences can include liver cancer and cirrhosis.

## Hepatitis E

Hepatitis E is transmitted through contaminated food and water and has similar symptoms to hepatitis A, but is far less common. It is a severe problem in pregnant women and can result in the death of both mother and baby. There is currently no vaccine, and prevention is by following safe eating and drinking guidelines.

## HIV

Typically, Indonesia has been considered a relatively safe country with respect to HIV/AIDS, with only a few thousand reported infections per year. However, religious and cultural taboos have likely resulted in a systematic underreporting of the problem throughout the country. According to WHO estimates, anywhere from 50,000 to 200,000 are living with HIV in Indonesia. While this is nowhere near as severe a pandemic as in other parts of Southeast Asia, it is high enough for travellers to exercise caution and vigilance.

## Japanese B Encephalitis

While this is a rare disease in travellers, many locals are infected each year. This viral disease is transmitted by mosquitoes. Most cases occur in rural areas and vaccination is recommended for travellers spending more than one month outside of cities. There is no treatment, and a third of infected people will die while another third will suffer permanent brain damage.

## Malaria

For such a serious and potentially deadly disease, there is an enormous amount of misinformation concerning malaria. Some parts of Indonesia, particularly city and resort areas, have minimal to no risk of malaria, and the risk of side effects from the tablets may outweigh the risk of getting the disease. For most rural areas, however, the risk of contracting the disease far outweighs the risk of any anti-malarial tablet side effects. Remember that malaria can be fatal. Before you travel, seek medical advice on the right medication and dosage for you.

Malaria is caused by a parasite transmitted by the bite of an infected mosquito. The most important symptom of malaria is fever, but general symptoms such as headache, diarrhoea, cough or chills may also occur. Diagnosis can only be made by taking a blood sample.

Two strategies should be combined to prevent malaria: mosquito avoidance and antimalarial medications. Most people who catch malaria are taking inadequate or no antimalarial medication.

Travellers are advised to prevent mosquito bites by taking these steps:

- Use a DEET-containing insect repellent on exposed skin. Wash this off at night, as long as you are sleeping under a mosquito net. Natural repellents such as citronella can be effective, but must be applied more frequently than products containing DEET.
- Sleep under a mosquito net impregnated with Permethrin.
- Impregnate clothing with Permethrin in high-risk areas.
- Wear long sleeves and trousers in light colours.
- Use mosquito coils.
- Spray your room with insect repellent before going out for your evening meal.

There are a variety of medications available:

**Artesunate:** Derivatives of Artesunate are not suitable as a preventive medication. They are useful treatments under medical supervision.

**Chloroquine and Paludrine:** The effectiveness of this combination is now limited in most of Southeast Asia, including Indonesia. Common side effects include nausea (40% of people) and mouth ulcers. Generally not recommended.

**Doxycycline:** This daily tablet is a broad-spectrum antibiotic that has the added benefit of helping to prevent a variety of tropical diseases, including leptospirosis, tick-borne disease, typhus and meliodosis. The potential side effects include photosensitivity (a tendency to sunburn), thrush in women, indigestion, heartburn, nausea and interference with the contraceptive pill. More serious side effects include ulceration of the oesophagus – you can help prevent this by taking your tablet with a meal and a large glass of water, and never lying down within half an hour of taking it.

**Lariam (Mefloquine):** Lariam has received much bad press, some of it justified, some not. This weekly tablet suits many people. Serious side effects are rare but include depression, anxiety, psychosis and having fits. Anyone with a history of depression, anxiety, other psychological disorders, or epilepsy should not take Lariam. It is considered safe in the second and third trimesters of pregnancy. It is around 90% effective in most parts of Southeast Asia, including Indonesia.

**Malarone:** This drug is a combination of Atovaquone and Proguanil. Side effects are uncommon and mild, most commonly nausea and headaches. It is the best tablet for scuba divers and for those on short trips to high-risk areas.

A final option is to take no preventive medication but to have a supply of emergency medication should you develop the symptoms of malaria. This is less than ideal, and you'll need to get to a good medical facility within 24 hours of developing a fever. If you choose this option the most effective and safest treatment is Malarone (four tablets once daily for three days).

## Measles

This highly contagious bacterial infection is spread via coughing and sneezing. Most people born before 1966 are immune as they had the disease in childhood. Measles starts with a high fever and rash and can be complicated by pneumonia and brain disease. There is no specific treatment.

## Rabies

This potentially fatal disease is spread by the bite or lick of an infected animal – most commonly a dog or monkey. You should seek medical advice immediately after any animal bite and commence postexposure treatment. Having pretravel vaccination means the postbite treatment is greatly simplified. If an animal bites you, gently wash the wound with soap and water, and apply iodine-based antiseptic. If you are not prevaccinated you will need to receive rabies immunoglobulin as a matter of urgency. Rabies is now present in Bali's stray dog population, yet another reason to be wary of these often ill-tempered critters.

## Schistosomiasis

Schistosomiasis is a tiny parasite that enters your skin after you've been swimming in contaminated water – travellers usually only get a light infection and hence have no symptoms. If you are concerned, you can be tested three months after exposure. On rare occasions, travellers may develop 'Katayama fever'. This occurs some weeks after exposure, as the parasite passes through the lungs and causes an allergic reaction; symptoms are coughing and fever. Schistosomiasis is easily treated with medications.

**DRINKING WATER**

- Never drink tap water.
- Bottled water is generally safe – check the seal is intact at purchase.
- Avoid ice (although on Bali ice comes from bottled water plants and is safe).
- Avoid fresh juices – they may have been watered down.
- Boiling water is the most efficient method of purifying drinking water.
- The best chemical purifier is iodine. It should not be used by pregnant women or those who suffer from thyroid problems.
- Water filters should also filter out viruses. Ensure your filter has a chemical barrier such as iodine and a small pore size, eg less than four microns.

## STDs

Common sexually transmitted diseases include herpes, warts, syphilis, gonorrhoea and chlamydia. People carrying these diseases often have no signs of infection. Condoms will prevent gonorrhoea and chlamydia but not warts or herpes. If after a sexual encounter you develop any rash, lumps, discharge or pain when passing urine seek immediate medical attention. If you have been sexually active during your travels have an STD check on your return home.

## Tuberculosis (TB)

While rare in travellers, medical and aid workers, and long-term travellers who have significant contact with the local population should take precautions. Vaccination is usually only given to children under the age of five, but adults at risk are recommended pre- and post-travel TB testing. The main symptoms are fever, cough, weight loss, night sweats and tiredness.

## Typhoid

This serious bacterial infection is also spread via food and water. It gives a high and slowly progressive fever, headache and may be accompanied by a dry cough and stomach pain. It is diagnosed by blood tests and treated with antibiotics. Vaccination is recommended for all travellers spending more than a week in Indonesia, or travelling outside of the major cities. Be aware that vaccination is not 100% effective, so you must still be careful with what you eat and drink.

## Typhus

Murine typhus is spread by the bite of a flea, whereas scrub typhus is spread via a mite. These diseases are rare in travellers. Symptoms include fever, muscle pains and a rash. You can avoid these diseases by following general insect-avoidance measures. Doxycycline will also prevent them.

## TRAVELLER'S DIARRHOEA

Traveller's diarrhoea is by far the most common problem affecting travellers – between 30% and 50% of people will suffer from it within two weeks of starting their trip. In over 80% of cases, traveller's diarrhoea is caused by a bacteria (there are numerous potential culprits), and therefore responds promptly to treatment with antibiotics. Treatment with antibiotics will depend on your situation – how sick you are, how quickly you need to get better, where you are etc.

Traveller's diarrhoea is defined as the passage of more than three watery bowel-actions within 24 hours, plus at least one other symptom such as fever, cramps, nausea, vomiting or feeling generally unwell.

Treatment consists of staying well hydrated; rehydration solutions like Gastrolyte are the best for this. Antibiotics such as Norfloxacin, Ciprofloxacin or Azithromycin will kill the bacteria quickly.

Loperamide is just a 'stopper' and doesn't get to the cause of the problem. It can be helpful, for example if you have to go on a long bus ride. Don't take Loperamide if you have a fever, or blood in your stools. Seek medical attention quickly if you do not respond to an appropriate antibiotic.

### Amoebic Dysentery

Amoebic dysentery is very rare in travellers but is often misdiagnosed by local poor quality labs. Symptoms are similar to bacterial diarrhoea, ie fever, bloody diarrhoea and generally feeling unwell. You should always seek reliable medical care if you have blood in your diarrhoea. Treatment involves two drugs; Tinidazole or Metroniadzole to kill the parasite in your gut and then a second drug to kill the cysts. If left untreated, complications such as liver or gut abscesses can occur.

HEALTH

## Giardiasis

*Giardia lamblia* is a parasite that is relatively common in travellers. Symptoms include nausea, bloating, excess gas, fatigue and intermittent diarrhoea. 'Eggy' burps are often attributed solely to giardiasis. The parasite will eventually go away if left untreated but this can take months. The treatment of choice is Tinidazole, with Metronidazole being a second-line option.

# ENVIRONMENTAL HAZARDS

## Air Pollution

Air pollution, particularly vehicle pollution, is an increasing problem in major cities. If you have severe respiratory problems speak with your doctor before travelling to any heavily polluted urban centres. This pollution also causes minor respiratory problems such as sinusitis, dry throat and irritated eyes. If troubled by the pollution, leave the city for a few days and get some fresh air.

## Diving

Divers and surfers should seek specialised advice before they travel to ensure their medical kit contains treatment for coral cuts and tropical ear infections, as well as the standard problems. Divers should ensure their insurance covers them for decompression illness, and should get specialised dive insurance through an organisation such as **Divers Alert Network** (DAN; www.danseap.org). Have a dive medical before you leave your home country – there are certain medical conditions that are incompatible with diving and economic considerations may override health considerations for some dive operators.

## Food

Eating in restaurants is the biggest risk factor for contracting traveller's diarrhoea. Ways to avoid it include eating only freshly cooked food, and avoiding shellfish or food that has been sitting around in buffets. Peel all fruit, cook vegetables and soak salads in iodine water for at least 20 minutes. Eat in busy restaurants with a high turnover of customers.

## Heat

Many parts of Indonesia are hot and humid throughout the year. For most people it takes at least two weeks to adapt to the hot climate. Swelling of the feet and ankles is common, as are muscle cramps caused by excessive sweat-ing. Prevent these by avoiding dehydration and excessive activity in the heat. Take it easy when you first arrive. Don't eat salt tablets (they aggravate the gut) but drinking rehydration-solution or eating salty food helps. Treat cramps by resting, rehydrating with double-strength rehydration solution and gently stretching.

Dehydration is the main contributor to heat exhaustion. Symptoms include feeling weak, headache, irritability, nausea or vomiting, sweaty skin, a fast or weak pulse, and a normal or slightly elevated body temperature. Treatment involves getting out of the heat and/or sun, fanning the victim and applying cool wet cloths to the skin, laying the victim flat with their legs raised and rehydrating with water containing a quarter teaspoon of salt per litre. Recovery is usually rapid and it is common to feel weak for some days afterwards.

Heatstroke is a serious medical emergency. Symptoms come on suddenly and include weakness, nausea, a hot dry body with a body temperature of over 41°C, dizziness, confusion, loss of coordination, fits and eventually collapse and loss of consciousness. Seek medical help and commence cooling by getting the person out of the heat, removing their clothes, fanning them and applying cool wet cloths or ice to their body, especially to the groin and armpits.

Prickly heat is a common skin rash in the tropics, caused by sweat being trapped under the skin. The result is an itchy rash of tiny lumps. Treat by moving out of the heat and into an air-conditioned area for a few hours, and by having cool showers. Creams and ointments clog the skin so they should be avoided. Locally bought prickly-heat powder can be helpful.

Tropical fatigue is common in long-term expats based in the tropics. It's rarely due to disease and is caused by the climate, inadequate mental rest, excessive alcohol intake and the demands of daily work in a different culture.

## Insect Bites & Stings

Bedbugs don't carry disease but their bites are very itchy. You can treat the itch with an antihistamine. Lice inhabit various parts of your body but most commonly your head and pubic area. Transmission is via close contact with an infected person. They can be difficult to treat

## MARINE LIFE TO WATCH OUT FOR

Most venomous fish, including stingrays, stonefish and scorpion fish, are found in salt water. If you do come into contact with these species, it will usually be through stepping on them by accident.

### Sea Snakes

These beautiful creatures are found throughout coastal Indonesia. They're often inquisitive, although not aggressive. However, their venom is extremely toxic, so give them a wide berth. Symptoms of poisoning may not appear for several hours, and include anxiety and restlessness, dry throat, nausea and, eventually, paralysis.

### Sea Urchins & Other Stingers

Avoid stepping on sea urchins, as their spines can break off and are very difficult to remove. Some species can cause a severe reaction that may result in paralysis and breathing difficulties. Sometimes this results in an itchy skin rash (sea urchin dermatitis) that can last for several months.

### Stingrays

These creatures like to lie half-submerged in mud or sand in the shallows. You'll know if you step on one because they whip their tails up in defence. This can cause a nasty ragged wound, but they also have venomous spines which can sometimes be fatal. Shuffle along in the shallows to give stingrays plenty of warning of your approach.

### Stonefish & Scorpion Fish

With sharp dorsal fins through which they inject a venom, these species are the most dangerous of all venomous fish. They are found throughout Indonesia.

Stonefish are generally reef dwellers, and as their name suggests, they are masters of disguise and lie half-submerged in sand, mud or coral debris. Their stings are extremely painful and may lead to collapse and coma. There is a stonefish antivenine which should be given as soon as possible after the sting. Scorpion fish are very distinctive and much easier to avoid – the chances of being stung by one are remote. There's no antivenine available.

### Treatment

Hot (nonscalding) water can help break down the toxins in fish venom and can be surprisingly effective at relieving pain from stings. The procedure is as follows:

- If any spines are poking out, try to remove them gently (be sure to protect your hands).
- Wash any surface venom off with water.
- Bathe the wound in hot (nonscalding) water for up to 90 minutes or until the pain has gone, or apply hot packs.
- Wash the wound thoroughly. Once the pain is under control, apply a clean dressing.
- Rest with the limb raised.
- Seek medical help for antivenin if necessary, eg for a stonefish sting.

**HEALTH**

and you may need numerous applications of an antilice shampoo such as Permethrin. Pubic lice are usually contracted from sexual contact.

Ticks are contracted after walking in rural areas. Ticks are commonly found behind the ears, on the belly and in armpits. If you have had a tick bite and experience symptoms such as a rash at the site of the bite or elsewhere, as well as fever or muscle aches you should see a doctor. Doxycycline prevents tick-borne diseases.

Leeches are found in humid rainforest areas. They do not transmit any disease but their bites are often intensely itchy for weeks afterwards and can easily become infected. Apply an iodine-based antiseptic to any leech bite to help prevent infection.

Bee and wasp stings mainly cause problems for people who are allergic to them. Anyone with a serious bee or wasp allergy should carry an injection of adrenaline (eg an Epipen) for emergency treatment. For others, pain is the main problem – apply ice to the sting and take painkillers.

Most jellyfish in Indonesian waters are not dangerous, just irritating. First-aid for jellyfish stings involves pouring vinegar on to the affected area to neutralise the poison. Do not rub sand or water onto the stings. Take painkillers, and anyone who feels ill in any way after being stung should seek medical advice. Take local advice on whether there are dangerous jellyfish around and, if so, keep out of the water.

### Parasites

Numerous parasites are common in local Indonesian populations; however, most of these are rare in travellers. The two rules to follow if you wish to avoid parasitic infections are to wear shoes and to avoid eating raw food, especially fish, pork and vegetables.

### Snakes

Always wear boots and long pants if walking in an area that may have snakes. First-aid in the event of a snakebite involves pressure immobilisation via an elastic bandage firmly wrapped around the affected limb, starting at the bite site and working up towards the chest. The bandage should not be so tight that the circulation is cut off, and the fingers or toes should be kept free so the circulation can be checked. Immobilise the limb with a splint and carry the victim to medical attention. Do not use tourniquets or try to suck the venom out. Antivenine is available for most species.

### Sunburn

Even on a cloudy day sunburn can occur rapidly. Always use a strong sunscreen (at least factor 30), making sure to reapply after a swim, and always wear a wide-brimmed hat and sunglasses outdoors. Avoid lying in the sun during the hottest part of the day (10am to 2pm). If you become sunburnt stay out of the sun until you have recovered, apply cool compresses and take painkillers for the discomfort. One percent hydrocortisone cream applied twice daily is also helpful.

## WOMEN'S HEALTH

Pregnant women should receive specialised advice before travelling. The ideal time to travel is in the second trimester (between 16 and 28 weeks), when the risk of pregnancy-related problems are at their lowest and pregnant women generally feel at their best. During the first trimester there is a risk of miscarriage and in the third trimester complications such as premature labour and high blood-pressure are possible. It's wise to travel with a companion. Always carry a list of quality medical facilities available at your destination and ensure you continue your standard antenatal care at these facilities. Avoid rural travel in areas with poor transport and medical facilities. Most of all, ensure travel insurance covers all pregnancy-related possibilities, including premature labour.

Malaria is a high-risk disease in pregnancy. WHO recommends that pregnant women do *not* travel to areas with Chloroquine-resistant malaria. None of the more effective antimalarial drugs are completely safe in pregnancy.

Traveller's diarrhoea can quickly lead to dehydration and result in inadequate blood flow to the placenta. Many of the drugs used to treat various diarrhoea bugs are not recommended in pregnancy. Azithromycin is considered safe.

Urinary tract infections can be precipitated by dehydration or long bus journeys without toilet stops; bring suitable antibiotics.

## TRADITIONAL MEDICINE

Throughout Southeast Asia, traditional medical systems are widely practised. There is a big difference between these traditional healing systems and 'folk' medicine, which is dubious and should be avoided.

All traditional Asian medical systems identify a vital life force, and see blockage or imbalance as causing disease. Techniques such as herbal medicines, massage and acupuncture are utilised to bring this vital force back into balance, or to maintain balance. These therapies are best used for treating chronic disease such as chronic fatigue, arthritis, irritable bowel syndrome and some chronic skin conditions. Traditional medicines should be avoided for treating serious acute infections such as malaria.

Be aware that 'natural' doesn't always mean 'safe', and that there can be drug interactions between herbal medicines and Western medicines. If you are utilising both treatment systems ensure that you inform both practitioners what the other has prescribed.

# Language

## CONTENTS

Most of the 700-plus languages spoken around Indonesia belong to the Malayo-Polynesian group. Within this group are many different regional languages and dialects. Indonesia's national language is Bahasa Indonesia, which is very similar to Malay, and most Indonesians speak it just as well as their first language (for more on local languages, see boxed text, p870).

Like many languages, Bahasa Indonesia has a simplified colloquial form and a more developed literary form. It's considered one of the easiest spoken languages to learn – there are no tenses, plurals or genders and, even better, it's easy to pronounce.

Apart from ease of learning, there's another very good reason for trying to pick up at least a handful of Bahasa Indonesia phrases: few people are as delighted with visitors learning their language as Indonesians – they'll make you feel like you're an expert even if you only know a dozen or so words. Bargaining also seems a whole lot easier and more natural when you do it in the local language.

Written Bahasa Indonesia is equally easy for English speakers to master. Note, however, that there are sometimes inconsistent spellings of place names. Compound names are written as one word or two, eg Airsanih or Air Sanih, Padangbai or Padang Bai. Words starting with 'Ker' sometimes lose the 'e', as in Kerobokan/Krobokan. Some Dutch-influenced spellings also remain in common use, with *tj* instead of the modern *c* (as in Tjampuhan/Campuan), and *oe* instead of the *u* (as in Soekarno/Sukarno).

For lots of useful culinary terms and phrases on eating out, check out p85.

## PRONUNCIATION

Most letters are pronounced more or less the same as their English counterparts. Nearly all syllables in a word carry equal emphasis, but a general rule is to stress the second-last syllable. The main exception to the rule is the unstressed **e** in words such as *besar* (big), pronounced 'be-sarr'.

### Vowels

| | |
|---|---|
| a | as in 'father' |
| ai | as in 'Thai' |
| au | as the 'ow' in 'cow' |
| e | as in 'bet' when unstressed (and sometimes hardly pronounced at all, as in the greeting *selamat,* which sounds like 'sla-mat' if said quickly); like the 'a' in 'may' when stressed, as in *becak* (rickshaw), pronounced 'bay-cha' |
| i | as in 'unique' |
| o | as in 'hot' |
| u | as in 'put' |
| ua | as 'w' when at the start of a word, eg *uang* (money), pronounced 'wong' |

### Consonants

| | |
|---|---|
| c | always as the 'ch' in 'chair' |
| g | as in 'get' |
| h | a little stronger than the 'h' in 'her'; almost silent at the end of a word |
| j | as in 'jet' |
| k | like English 'k', except at the end of a word when it's like a closing of the throat with no sound released, eg *tidak* (no/not), pronounced 'tee-da' |
| ng | as the 'ng' in 'sing' |
| ngg | as the 'ng' in 'anger' |
| ny | as the 'ny' in 'canyon' |
| r | slightly rolled |

## MAKING A RESERVATION
(for written and phone inquiries)

| I'd like to book ... | Saya mau pesan ... |
| in the name of ... | atas nama ... |
| date | tanggal |
| from ... (date) | dari ... |
| to ... (date) | sampai ... |
| | |
| credit card | kartu kredit |
| number | nomor |
| expiry date | masa berlakunya sampai |
| | |
| Please confirm | Tolong dikonfirmasi |
| availability and | mengenai ketersediaan |
| price. | kamar dan harga. |

## ACCOMMODATION

| I'm looking for a ... | Saya mencari ... |
| camp site | tempat kemah |
| guest house | rumah yang disewakan |
| hotel | hotel |
| youth hostel | losmen pemuda |

**Where is a cheap hotel?**
Hotel yang murah di mana?
**What is the address?**
Alamatnya di mana?
**Can you write it down, please?**
Anda bisa tolong tuliskan?
**Do you have any rooms available?**
Ada kamar kosong?
**How much is it (per day/person)?**
Berapa harganya (sehari/seorang)?
**Is breakfast included?**
Apakah harganya termasuk makan pagi?

| one night | satu malam |
| one person | satu orang |
| bathroom | kamar mandi |
| room | kamar |

| I'd like a ... | Saya cari ... |
| bed | tempat tidur |
| room with a bathroom | kamar dengan kamar mandi |
| room with a double bed | tempat tidur besar satu kamar |
| room with two beds | kamar dengan dua tempat tidur |
| single room | kamar untuk seorang |

| I'd like to share a dorm. | Saya mau satu tempat tidur di asrama. |

| May I see it? | Boleh saya lihat? |
| Where is the toilet? | Kamar kecil di mana? |
| Where is the bathroom? | Kamar mandi di mana? |
| I'm/We're leaving today. | Saya/Kami berangkat hari ini. |

## CONVERSATION & ESSENTIALS

Pronouns, particularly 'you', are rarely used in Bahasa Indonesia. When speaking to an older man (or anyone old enough to be a father), it's common to call them *bapak* (father) or simply *pak*. Similarly, an older woman is *ibu* (mother) or simply *bu*. *Tuan* is a respectful term for a man, like 'sir'. *Nyonya* is the equivalent for a married woman, and *nona* for an unmarried woman. *Anda* is the egalitarian form designed to overcome the plethora of words for the second person (you).

To indicate negation, *tidak* is used with verbs, adjectives and adverbs; *bukan* with nouns and pronouns.

| Welcome. | Selamat datang. |
| Good morning. | Selamat pagi. (before 11am) |
| Good day. | Selamat siang. (noon to 2pm) |
| | Selamat sore. (3pm to 6pm) |
| Good evening. | Selamat malam. (after dark) |
| Good night. | Selamat tidur. |
| Goodbye. | Selamat tinggal. (to one staying) |
| | Selamat jalan. (to one leaving) |
| Yes. | Ya. |
| No. (not) | Tidak. |
| No. (negative) | Bukan. |
| Maybe. | Mungkin. |
| Please. | Tolong. (asking for help) |
| | Silahkan. (giving permission) |
| Thank you (very much). | Terima kasih (banyak). |
| You're welcome. | Kembali. |
| Sorry. | Maaf. |
| Excuse me. | Permisi. |
| Just a minute. | Tunggu sebentar. |
| How are you? | Apa kabar? |
| I'm fine. | Kabar baik. |
| What's your name? | Siapa nama Anda? |
| My name is ... | Nama saya ... |
| Where are you from? | Anda dari mana? |
| I'm from ... | Saya dari ... |
| How old are you? | Berapa umur Anda? |
| I'm ... years old. | Umur saya ... tahun. |
| I (don't) like ... | Saya (tidak) suka ... |
| Good. | Bagus. |
| Good/Fine/OK. | Baik. |

## DIRECTIONS

| | |
|---|---|
| Where is ...? | Di mana ...? |
| Which way? | Ke mana? |
| Go straight ahead. | Jalan terus. |
| Turn left/right. | Belok kiri/kanan. |
| Stop! | Berhenti! |
| at the corner | di sudut |
| at the traffic lights | di lampu lalu-lintas |
| here/there/over there | di sini/situ/sana |
| behind | di belakang |
| in front of | di depan |
| opposite | di seberang |
| far (from) | jauh (dari) |
| near (to) | dekat (dengan) |
| north | utara |
| south | selatan |
| east | timur |
| west | barat |

| SIGNS | |
|---|---|
| **Masuk** | Entrance |
| **Keluar** | Exit |
| **Buka** | Open |
| **Tutup** | Closed |
| **Informasi** | Information |
| **Dilarang** | Prohibited |
| **Ada Kamar Kosong** | Rooms Available |
| **Polisi** | Police |
| **Kamar Kecil/Toilet** | Toilets/WC |
| **Pria** | Men |
| **Wanita** | Women |

| | |
|---|---|
| beach | pantai |
| island | pulau |
| lake | danau |
| main square | alun-alun |
| market | pasar |
| sea | laut |

## HEALTH

| | |
|---|---|
| I'm ill. | Saya sakit. |
| It hurts here. | Sakitnya di sini. |
| | |
| I'm ... | Saya sakit ... |
| asthmatic | asma |
| diabetic | kencing manis |
| epileptic | epilepsi |
| | |
| I'm allergic to ... | Saya alergi ... |
| antibiotics | antibiotik |
| aspirin | aspirin |
| bees | tawon |
| nuts | kacang |
| penicillin | penisilin |

## EMERGENCIES

| | |
|---|---|
| Help! | Tolong saya! |
| There's been an accident! | Ada kecelakaan! |
| I'm lost. | Saya tersesat. |
| Leave me alone! | Jangan ganggu saya! |
| | |
| Call ...! | Panggil ...! |
| a doctor | dokter |
| the police | polisi |

| | |
|---|---|
| antiseptic | penangkal infeksi/antiseptik |
| condoms | kondom |
| contraceptive | kontrasepsi |
| diarrhoea | mencret/diare |
| medicine | obat |
| nausea | mual |
| sunblock cream | tabir surya |
| tampons | tampon |

## LANGUAGE DIFFICULTIES

**I (don't) understand.**
*Saya (tidak) mengerti.*
**Do you speak English?**
*Bisa berbicara Bahasa Inggris?*
**Does anyone here speak English?**
*Ada yang bisa berbicara Bahasa Inggris di sini?*
**How do you say ... in Bahasa Indonesia?**
*Bagaimana mengatakan ... dalam Bahasa Indonesia?*
**What does ... mean?**
*Apa artinya ...?*
**I can only speak a little (Bahasa Indonesia).**
*Saya hanya bisa berbicara (Bahasa Indonesia) sedikit.*
**Please write that word down.**
*Tolong tuliskan kata itu.*
**Can you show me (on the map)?**
*Anda bisa tolong tunjukkan pada saya (di peta)?*

## NUMBERS

| | |
|---|---|
| 1 | satu |
| 2 | dua |
| 3 | tiga |
| 4 | empat |
| 5 | lima |
| 6 | enam |
| 7 | tujuh |
| 8 | delapan |
| 9 | sembilan |
| 10 | sepuluh |

A half is *setengah,* pronounced 'steng-er', eg *setengah kilo* (half a kilo). 'Approximately' is *kira-kira.* After the numbers one to 10, the 'teens' are *belas*, the 'tens' *puluh*, the 'hundreds' *ratus*, the 'thousands' *ribu* and the 'millions' *juta*, but as a prefix *satu* (one) becomes *se-*, eg *seratus* (one hundred).

| 11 | sebelas |
| 12 | duabelas |
| 13 | tigabelas |
| 20 | duapuluh |
| 21 | duapuluh satu |
| 25 | duapuluh lima |
| 30 | tigapuluh |
| 99 | sembilanpuluh sembilan |
| 100 | seratus |
| 150 | seratus limapuluh |
| 200 | dua ratus |
| 888 | delapan ratus delapanpuluh delapan |
| 1000 | seribu |

## PAPERWORK

| name | nama |
| nationality | kebangsaan |
| date of birth | tanggal kelahiran |
| place of birth | tempat kelahiran |
| sex/gender | jenis kelamin |
| passport | paspor |
| visa | visa |

## QUESTION WORDS

| Who? | Siapa? |
| What is it? | Apa itu? |
| When? | Kapan? |
| Where? | Di mana? |
| Which? | Yang mana? |
| Why? | Kenapa? |
| How? | Bagaimana? |

## SHOPPING & SERVICES

| What is this? | Apa ini? |
| How much is it? | Berapa harganya? |
| I'd like to buy ... | Saya mau beli ... |
| I don't like it. | Saya tidak suka. |
| May I look at it? | Boleh saya lihat? |
| I'm just looking. | Saya lihat-lihat saja. |
| I'll take it. | Saya beli. |

| this | ini |
| that | itu |
| big(ger) | (lebih) besar |
| small(er) | (lebih) kecil |
| more | lebih |
| less | kurang |
| expensive | mahal |
| another/one more | satu lagi |

| Do you accept ...? | Bisa bayar pakai ...? |
| credit cards | kartu kredit |
| travellers cheques | cek perjalanan |

| What time does it open/close? | Jam berapa buka/tutup? |
| May I take photos? | Boleh saya potret? |
| Can you take a photo of me? | Bisa saya minta tolong dipotretkan? |

| I'm looking for a/the ... | Saya cari ... |
| bank | bank |
| church | gereja |
| city centre | pusat kota |
| ... embassy | kedutaan ... |
| food stall | warung |
| hospital | rumah sakit |
| market | pasar |
| museum | museum |
| police | kantor polisi |
| post office | kantor pos |
| public phone | telepon umum |
| public toilet | WC ('way say') umum |
| restaurant | rumah makan |
| telephone centre | wartel |
| tourist office | kantor pariwisata |

## TIME & DATES

| What time is it? | Jam berapa sekarang? |
| It's (seven) o'clock. | Jam (tujuh). |
| At what time? | Jam berapa? |
| At (seven). | Pada jam (tujuh). |
| How many hours? | Berapa jam? |
| five hours | lima jam |
| What date is it today? | Tanggal apa hari ini? |
| It's (18 October). | Tanggal (delapanbelas Oktober). |

| in the morning | pagi |
| in the afternoon | siang |
| in the evening | malam |
| today | hari ini |
| tomorrow | besok |
| yesterday | kemarin |
| day | hari |
| week | minggu |
| month | bulan |
| year | tahun |

| Monday | hari Senin |
| Tuesday | hari Selasa |
| Wednesday | hari Rabu |
| Thursday | hari Kamis |
| Friday | hari Jumat |
| Saturday | hari Sabtu |
| Sunday | hari Minggu |

LANGUAGE

| | |
|---|---|
| **January** | *Januari* |
| **February** | *Februari* |
| **March** | *Maret* |
| **April** | *April* |
| **May** | *Mei* |
| **June** | *Juni* |
| **July** | *Juli* |
| **August** | *Agustus* |
| **September** | *September* |
| **October** | *Oktober* |
| **November** | *Nopember* |
| **December** | *Desember* |

## TRANSPORT
### Public Transport

| | |
|---|---|
| **What time does the … leave/arrive?** | *Jam berapa … berangkat/ datang?* |
| **boat/ship** | *kapal* |
| **bus** | *bis* |
| **plane** | *kapal terbang* |
| | |
| **I'd like a … ticket.** | *Saya mau tiket …* |
| **1st class** | *kelas satu* |
| **2nd class** | *kelas dua* |
| **one-way** | *sekali jalan* |
| **return** | *pulang pergi* |
| | |
| **I want to go to …** | *Saya mau ke …* |
| **The train has been delayed/cancelled.** | *Kereta terlambat/dibatalkan.* |
| | |
| **first** | *pertama* |
| **last** | *terakhir* |
| **ticket** | *karcis* |
| **ticket office** | *loket* |
| **timetable** | *jadwal* |

### Private Transport

| | |
|---|---|
| **Where can I hire a …?** | *Di mana saya bisa sewa …?* |
| **I'd like to hire a …** | *Saya mau sewa …* |
| **4WD** | *gardan ganda* |
| **bicycle** | *sepeda* |
| **car** | *mobil* |
| **motorbike** | *sepeda motor* |
| | |
| **Is this the road to …?** | *Apakah jalan ini ke …?* |
| **Where's a service station?** | *Di mana pompa bensin?* |
| **Please fill it up.** | *Tolong isi sampai penuh.* |
| **I'd like … litres.** | *Minta … liter bensin.* |
| | |
| **diesel** | *disel* |
| **leaded petrol** | *bensin bertimbal* |
| **unleaded petrol** | *bensin tanpa timbal* |

| ROAD SIGNS | |
|---|---|
| **Bahaya** | Danger |
| **Beri Jalan** | Give Way |
| **Dilarang Masuk** | No Entry |
| **Dilarang Mendahului** | No Overtaking |
| **Dilarang Parkir** | No Parking |
| **Hati Hati** | Careful |
| **Jalan Memutar** | Detour |
| **Keluar** | Exit |
| **Kosongkan** | Keep Clear |
| **Kurangi Kecepatan** | Slow Down |
| **Masuk** | Entry |
| **Satu Arah** | One Way |

| | |
|---|---|
| **I need a mechanic.** | *Saya perlu montir.* |
| **The car has broken down at …** | *Mobil mogok di …* |
| **The motorbike won't start.** | *Motor tidak bisa jalan.* |
| **I have a flat tyre.** | *Ban saya kempes.* |
| **I've run out of petrol.** | *Saya kehabisan bensin.* |
| **I had an accident.** | *Saya mengalami kecelakaan.* |
| **Can I park here?** | *Saya boleh parkir di sini?* |
| **How long can I park here?** | *Berapa lama saya boleh parkir di sini?* |
| **Where do I pay?** | *Saya membayar di mana?* |

## TRAVEL WITH CHILDREN

| | |
|---|---|
| **Is there a/an …?** | *Ada …?* |
| **I need a …** | *Saya perlu …* |
| **baby car seat** | *kursi anak untuk di mobil* |
| **baby change room** | *tempat ganti popok kamar* |
| **babysitter (who speaks English)** | *suster (yang bisa berbicara Bahasa Inggris)* |
| **child-minding service** | *tempat penitipan anak* |
| **children's menu** | *menu untuk anak-anak* |
| **discount for children** | *diskon khusus anak* |
| **formula** | *susu kaleng* |
| **highchair** | *kursi anak* |
| **potty** | *pispot* |
| **stroller** | *kereta anak* |

**Do you have disposable nappies/diapers?**
*Anda jual popok sekali pakai?*
**Do you have painkillers for infants?**
*Anda jual obat penawar sakit untuk bayi?*
**Are children allowed?**
*Boleh bawa anak-anak?*
**Are there any good places to take children here?**
*Ada tempat yang cocok untuk anak-anak di sekitar sini?*

**LANGUAGE**

## LOCAL LANGUAGES

As you travel throughout the archipelago, don't forget that Bahasa Indonesia is a second language for 90% of Indonesians. More than 700 *bahasa daerah* (local languages) rank Indonesia second only to Papua New Guinea in linguistic diversity. As a visitor, you'll never be expected to speak any local languages, but there's no doubt that locals will appreciate your extra effort.

Here are some useful basic phrases in Balinese (which has around four million speakers in Bali) and Javanese (spoken by about 80 million people in Java). Note that these languages don't have phrases for greetings like 'hello' or 'goodbye'. Another interesting feature of both languages is that they have three distinct language 'levels' – the differences are related to the social status of the speaker. In the following phrases we've used the 'middle level' understood by all Balinese/Javanese speakers.

For a more extensive selection that also includes Benuaq, Bugis, Galelarese, Jani, Minang, Sasak, Sundanese, Toba Batak and Toraja, plus a handy language map of Indonesia, get a copy of Lonely Planet's *Indonesian Phrasebook*.

### Balinese

**How are you?**
  *Kenken kabare?*
**Thank you.**
  *Matur suksma.*
**What's your name?**
  *Sire wastene?*
**My name is …**
  *Adan tiange …*
**I don't understand.**
  *Tiang sing ngerti.*

**Do you speak Balinese?**
  *Bisa ngomong Bali sing?*
**I speak a little Balinese.**
  *Tiang bisa akidik.*
**What do you call this in Balinese?**
  *Ne ape adane di Bali?*
**How much is this?**
  *Ji kude niki?*
**Which is the way to (Ubud)?**
  *Kije jalan lakar kel (Ubud)?*

### Javanese

**How are you?**
  *Piye kabare?*
**Thank you.**
  *Matur nuwun.*
**What's your name?**
  *Nami panjenengan sinten?*
**My name is …**
  *Nami kula …*
**I don't understand.**
  *Kula mboten mangertos.*

**Do you speak Javanese?**
  *Sapeyan saged basa Jawi?*
**I speak a little Javanese.**
  *Kula namung saged basa Jawi sakedhik.*
**What do you call this in Javanese?**
  *Napa namine ing basa Jawi?*
**How much is this?**
  *Pinten regine?*
**Which is the way to (Kaliurang)?**
  *Menawi bade dateng (Kaliurang) langkung pundi, nggih?*

Also available from Lonely Planet:
*Indonesian Phrasebook*

# Glossary

See p86 for food and drink terms.

**ABRI** - Angkatan Bersenjata Republik Indonesia; the armed forces; now TNI
**adat** - traditional laws and regulations
**air** - water
**air panas** - hot springs
**air terjun** - waterfall
**AMA** - Associated Mission Aviation; Catholic missionary air service operating in remote regions of Papua
**anak** - child
**andong** - horse-drawn passenger cart
**angklung** - musical instrument made from different lengths and thicknesses of bamboo suspended in a frame
**angkot** - or *angkota;* short for *angkutan kota* (city transport); small minibuses covering city routes, like a *bemo*
**angkudes** - short for *angkutan pedesaan;* minibuses running to nearby villages from cities, or between villages
**anjing** - dog
**arja** - refined operatic form of Balinese theatre
**Arjuna** - hero of the *Mahabharata* epic and a popular temple gate guardian image

**babi rusa** - wild deer-like pig
**bahasa** - language; Bahasa Indonesia is the national language
**bajaj** - motorised three-wheeler taxi found in Jakarta
**bale** - open-sided Balinese pavilion, house or shelter with steeply pitched roof; meeting place
**bandar** - harbour, port
**bandar udara** - often shortened to *bandara;* airport
**banjar** - local division a Balinese village consisting of married adult males
**bapak** - often shortened to *pak;* father; also a polite form of address to any older man
**barat** - west
**Barong** - mythical lion-dog creature
**batik** - cloth made by coating part of the fabric with wax, then dyeing it and melting the wax out
**batik cap** - stamped batik
**batik tulis** - hand-painted or literally 'written' batik
**becak** - bicycle-rickshaw
**bemo** - minibus
**bendi** - two-person horse-drawn cart; used in Sulawesi, Sumatra and Maluku
**bensin** - petrol

**benteng** - fort
**bentor** - motorised *becak*
**Betawi** - original name of Batavia (now Jakarta); ethnic group indigenous to Jakarta
**bis** - bus
**bouraq** - winged horselike creature with the head of a woman
**Brahma** - the creator; with Shiva and Vishnu part of the trinity of chief Hindu gods
**bu** - shortened form of *ibu*
**bukit** - hill
**bule** - common term for foreigner
**bupati** - government official in charge of a *kabupaten*

**caci** - a ceremonial martial art in which participants duel with whips and shields
**camat** - government official in charge of a *kecamatan* (district)
**candi** - shrine or temple; usually Hindu or Buddhist of ancient Javanese design
**cenderawasih** - bird of paradise
**colt** - minibus

**dalang** - puppeteer and storyteller of *wayang kulit*
**danau** - lake
**dangdut** - popular Indonesian music that is characterised by wailing vocals and a strong beat
**Departemen Kehutanan** - Forest Department
**desa** - village
**dinas pariwisata** - tourist office
**dokar** - two-person, horse-drawn cart
**dukun** - faith healer and herbal doctor; mystic

**Gajah Mada** - famous Majapahit prime minister
**gamelan** - traditional Javanese and Balinese orchestra
**gang** - alley or footpath
**Garuda** - mythical man-bird, the vehicle of Vishnu and the modern symbol of Indonesia
**gereja** - church
**gili** - islet, atoll
**Golkar** - Golongan Karya (Functional Groupings) political party
**gua** - or *goa;* cave
**gunung** - mountain
**gunung api** - volcano; literally 'fire mountain'

**harga touris** - tourist price
**hutan** - forest, jungle

**ibu** - often shortened to *bu;* mother; also polite form of address to an older woman
**ikat** - cloth in which the pattern is produced by dyeing the individual threads before weaving

**jadwal** - timetable
**jalan** - abbreviated to Jl; street or road
**jalan jalan** - to go for a stroll
**jalan potong** - short cut
**jam karet** - 'rubber time'; time is flexible
**jamu** - herbal medicine
**jembatan** - bridge
**jilbab** - Muslim head covering worn by women

**kabupaten** - regency
**kain** - cloth
**kaki lima** - mobile food carts; literally 'five feet' (the three feet of the cart and the two of the vendor)
**kala** - demonic face often seen over temple gateways
**kamar kecil** - toilet; literally 'small room'; also known as WC (pronounced way-say)
**kampung** - village, neighbourhood
**kantor** - office
**Kantor Bupati** - Governor's Office
**karang** - coral, coral reef, atoll
**kav** - lot, parcel of land
**kebaya** - women's long-sleeved blouse
**kepala balai** - Dayak village head (Sumatra)
**kepala desa** - village head
**kepulauan** - archipelago
**ketoprak** - popular Javanese folk theatre
**Ketuktilu** - traditional Sundanese (Java) dance in which professional female dancers perform for male spectators
**kijang** - a type of deer; also a popular Toyota 4WD vehicle, often used for public transport (Kijang)
**KKN** - Korupsi, Kolusi, Nepotisme; Corruption, Collusion, Nepotism; buzz word of the post-Suharto reform era
**kora-kora** - canoe (Papua)
**kramat** - shrine
**kraton** - or *keraton;* walled city palace
**kretek** - Indonesian clove cigarette
**kris** - wavy-bladed traditional dagger, often held to have spiritual or magical powers
**krisis moneter** - or *krismon;* monetary crisis
**kulit** - leather

**ladang** - nonirrigated field for dry-land crops; often farmed using slash-and-burn agriculture
**lapangan** - field, square
**laut** - sea, ocean
**Legong** - classic Balinese dance performed by young girls; Legong dancer
**lontar** - type of palm tree; traditional books were written on the dried leaves of the lontar palm

**losmen** - basic accommodation, usually cheaper than hotels and often family-run

**MAF** - Mission Aviation Fellowship; Protestant missionary air service that operates in remote regions
**Mahabharata** - venerated Hindu holy book, telling of the battle between the Pandavas and the Kauravas
**Majapahit** - last great Javanese Hindu dynasty, pushed out of Java into Bali by the rise of Islamic power
**makam** - grave
**mandau** - machete (Kalimantan)
**mandi** - common Indonesian form of bath, consisting of a large water tank from which water is ladled over the body
**marapu** - term for all spiritual forces, including gods, spirits and ancestors
**mata air panas** - hot springs
**menara** - minaret, tower
**meru** - multiroofed shrines in Balinese temples; the same roof style also can be seen in ancient Javanese mosques
**mesjid** - *masjid* in Papua; mosque
**mikrolet** - small taxi; tiny *opelet*
**moko** - bronze drum from Alor island (Nusa Tenggara)
**muezzin** - mosque official who calls the faithful to prayer five times a day

**ngadhu** - parasol-like thatched roof; ancestor totem of the Ngada people of Flores
**nusa** - island

**Odalan** - temple festival held every 210 days (duration of the Balinese year)
**ojek** - or *ojeg;* motorcycle taxi
**oleh-oleh** - souvenirs
**opelet** - small minibus, like a bemo
**OPM** - Organisasi Papua Merdeka; Free Papua Movement; main group that opposes Indonesian rule of Papua
**ora** - Komodo dragon
**orang putih** - white person, foreigner; *bule* is more commonly used

**pak** - shortened form of *bapak*
**PAN** - Partai Amanat Nasional; National Mandate Party
**pantai** - beach
**parkir** - parking attendant
**pasar** - market
**pasar malam** - night market
**pasar terapung** - floating market
**pasir** - beach, sand
**patas** - express, express bus
**patola** - ikat motif of a hexagon framing a type of four-pronged star
**PDI** - Partai Demokrasi Indonesia; Indonesian Democratic Party

**PDI-P** - Partai Demokrasi Indonesia-Perjuangan; Indonesian Democratic Party for Struggle
**peci** - Muslim black felt cap
**pegunungan** - mountain range
**pelabuhan** - harbour, port, dock
**pelan pelan** - slowly
**pelawangan** - gateway
**Pelni** - Pelayaran Nasional Indonesia; national shipping line with a fleet of passenger ships operating throughout the archipelago
**pemangku** - temple priest
**pencak silat** - form of martial arts originally from Sumatra, but now popular throughout Indonesia
**pendopo** - large, open-sided pavilion that serves as an audience hall; located in front of a Javanese palace
**penginapan** - simple lodging house
**perahu** - or *prahu;* boat
**perahu lading** - longboat
**perahu tambing** - ferry boat
**pesanggrahan** - or *pasanggrahan;* lodge for government officials where travellers can usually stay
**pete-pete** - a type of *mikrolet* or *bemo* found in Sulawesi
**PHKA** - Perlindungan Hutan & Konservasi Alam; the Directorate General of Forest Protection & Nature Conservation; manages Indonesia's national parks; formerly PHPA
**pinang** - betel nut
**pinisi** - Makassar or Bugis schooner
**PKB** - Partai Kebangkitan Bangsa; National Awakening Party
**pondok** - or *pondok wisata;* guesthouse or lodge; hut
**PPP** - Partai Persatuan Pembangunan; Development Union Party
**prasada** - shrine or temple; usually Hindu or Buddhist of ancient Javanese design
**pulau** - island
**puputan** - warrior's fight to the death; honourable, but suicidal, option when faced with an unbeatable enemy
**pura** - Balinese temple, shrine
**pura dalem** - Balinese temple of the dead
**pura puseh** - Balinese temple of origin
**puri** - palace
**pusaka** - sacred heirlooms of a royal family
**puskesmas** - short for *pusat kesehatan masyarakat;* community health centre

**rafflesia** - gigantic flower found in Sumatra and Kalimantan, with blooms spreading up to a metre
**Ramadan** - Muslim month of fasting, when devout Muslims refrain from eating, drinking and smoking during daylight hours
**Ramayana** - one of the great Hindu holy books; many Balinese and Javanese dances and tales are based on stories from the Ramayana

**rangda** - witch; evil black-magic spirit of Balinese tales and dances
**rawa** - swamp, marsh, wetlands
**rebab** - two-stringed bowed lute
**reformasi** - reform; refers to political reform after the repression of the Suharto years
**RMS** - Republik Maluku Selatan; South Maluku Republic; main group that opposed Indonesian rule of southern Maluku
**rumah adat** - traditional house
**rumah makan** - restaurant or *warung*
**rumah sakit** - hospital, literally 'sick house'

**saron** - xylophone-like gamelan instrument, with bronze bars that are struck with a wooden mallet
**sarong** - or *sarung;* all-purpose cloth, often sewn into a tube, and worn by women, men and children
**Sasak** - native of Lombok
**sawah** - individual rice field; wet-rice method of cultivation
**selat** - strait
**selatan** - south
**selimut** - blanket
**sembako** - Indonesia's nine essential culinary ingredients: rice, sugar, eggs, meat, flour, corn, fuel, cooking oil and salt
**semenanjung** - peninsula
**sirih** - betel nut, chewed as a mild narcotic
**songket** - silver- or gold-threaded cloth, hand woven using floating-weft technique
**suling** - bamboo flute
**sungai** - river
**surat jalan** - travel permit

**taksi** - common term for a public minibus; taxi
**taman** - ornamental garden, park, reserve
**taman laut** - marine park, marine reserve
**taman nasional** - national park
**tanjung** - peninsula, cape
**tarling** - musical style of the Cirebon (Java) area, featuring guitar, *suling* and voice
**taxi** - besides the Western definition which often applies, in some places this can be a small minibus like a *bemo*
**taxi sungai** - cargo-carrying river ferry with bunks on the upper level
**telaga** - lake
**telepon kartu** - telephone card
**teluk** - bay
**timur** - east
**tirta** - water (Bali)
**TNI** - Tentara Nasional Indonesia; Indonesian armed forces; formerly ABRI
**toko (e)mas** - gold shop
**tomate** - Torajan funeral ceremony

**tongkonan** - traditional Torajan house with towering roof (Sulawesi)

**topeng** - wooden mask used in dance-dramas and funerary dances

**tuak** – homemade fermented coconut drink

**uang** - money

**ular** - snake

**utara** - north

**wali songo** - nine saints of Islam, who spread the religion throughout Java

**Wallace Line** - hypothetical line dividing Bali and Kalimantan from Lombok and Sulawesi; marks the end of Asian and the beginning of Australasian flora and fauna zones

**waringin** - banyan tree; large, shady tree with drooping branches that root and can produce new trees

**warnet** - short for *wartel internet;* internet stall or centre

**warpostel** - or *warpapostel;* wartel that also handles postal services

**wartel** - short for *warung telekomunikasi;* private telephone office

**warung** - simple eatery

**wayang kulit** - shadow-puppet play

**wayang orang** - or *wayang wong;* people theatre

**wayang topeng** - masked dance-drama

**Wektu Telu** - religion peculiar to Lombok that originated in Bayan and combines many tenets of Islam and aspects of other faiths

**wisma** - guesthouse or lodge

# The Authors

### RYAN VER BERKMOES
Coordinating Author, Bali

Ryan Ver Berkmoes first visited Bali in 1993. On his visits since he has explored almost every corner of the island – along with side trips to Lombok, and Nusas Lembongan and Penida. Just when he thinks Bali holds no more surprises, he, for example, ducks behind Pura Batukau. Better yet, he simply never tires of the place. Four visits in two years shows that; sometimes his Bali social calendar is busier than anywhere. Off-island, Ryan lives in Portland, Oregon, and writes about Bali and more at ryanverberkmoes.com.

### CELESTE BRASH
Sulawesi

Celeste first visited Indonesia in 1995 to find out if it lived up to everything she'd learned in her Southeast Asian studies courses at the University of California. It did and more, knocking her off her feet with earthquakes, volcanoes and long, bad bus rides. All this action made her other travels pale in comparison and she's since spent many months exploring the country from North Sumatra to Bali and up through Sulawesi. When in Indonesia nowadays she has to carry a map to explain the location of her home, French Polynesia, to all those questioning locals.

### MUHAMMAD COHEN
Kalimantan

Native New Yorker Muhammad Cohen first visited Indonesia in 1994 to meet an ex-neighbour from his days as a diplomat in Africa. Cohen's first mouthful of nasi goreng (fried rice) told him he wanted to explore further. From his base in Hong Kong, he's been frequenting Indonesia for more than a dozen years, picking up the language and a taste for *ikan bakar lalapan* (grilled fish served with sambal and aromatic leaves). Beyond his Lonely Planet credits, Cohen is the author of *Hong Kong on Air* (www.hongkongonair.com), a novel about the 1997 handover, television news, love, betrayal, global economic crisis and cheap lingerie.

---

**LONELY PLANET AUTHORS**

Why is our travel information the best in the world? It's simple: our authors are passionate, dedicated travellers. They don't take freebies in exchange for positive coverage so you can be sure the advice you're given is impartial. They travel widely to all the popular spots, and off the beaten track. They don't research using just the internet or phone. They discover new places not included in any other guidebook. They personally visit thousands of hotels, restaurants, palaces, trails, galleries, temples and more. They speak with dozens of locals every day to make sure you get the kind of insider knowledge only a local could tell you. They take pride in getting all the details right, and in telling it how it is. Think you can do it? Find out how at **lonelyplanet.com**.

## MARK ELLIOTT
Maluku

Since his first trip in 1987, Mark has visited virtually every corner of Indonesia, with trips ranging from relaxing holidays in blissful Bali to leech-infested upriver treks with Kalimantan Dayaks. He's jammed the harmonica in end-of-Ramadan festivities aboard a Pelni liner, survived an appallingly storm-battered sea crossing in a Bugis fishing boat and escaped from a Solo hotel hours before it was burnt down by anti-Suharto rioters. Mark remains fascinated by Indonesia's smorgasbord of cultures and considers the Maluku Spice Islands to be among the greatest undiscovered travel gems in Asia.

## TRENT HOLDEN
Sumatra

Trent's first visit to Indonesia was as a wide-eyed teenager in the 1990s. It was his first independent trip overseas, and marked the beginning of an obsession with travelling in Asia. While he's in awe of the volcanoes, exotic jungles and ridiculously beautiful beaches, it's the friendly locals and their great sense of humour that really clinches it as one of his favourite destinations. Trent was born and bred in Melbourne, where he also works as an editor for Lonely Planet. He loves listening to the Ramones and reading Charles Bukowski. Trent also cowrote *Nepal 8*.

## GUYAN MITRA
Sumatra

As a keen young history student who read all about a colonial-era land of 'untamed natural wealth, beauty and savages', Guyan made Sumatra a definite stop on his postgraduate travels. He has since returned to Indonesia many times in different guises: surfer, diver, beach bum, volunteer and, over more recent years, travel writer. When not larking about in the jungles of Asia, Guyan can be found in west London, where he maintains a career writing travel features for the *Sunday Times, Esquire* and many inflight magazines.

## JOHN NOBLE
Papua

John has rated Indonesia his favourite country to travel in ever since his first visit in the middle of the Suharto dictatorship, when he wrote surveys of the country's coal industry for the *Financial Times International Coal Report* and the *Jakarta Post*. Since then he has spent nearly a year in Indonesia, visiting all the main regions except (so far) Kalimantan. He loves Indonesia's ever-charming people, its languages, its gamelan, its Balinese dance, its Asmat carving, its dragons and birds of paradise, its spectacular landscapes and translucent seas, its unbelievable variety of cultures, boats and land transport, and above all the fact that every different island is a whole different world.

### ADAM SKOLNICK
Nusa Tenggara

Adam Skolnick became travel obsessed while working as an environmental activist in the mid-1990s. A freelance journalist, he writes about travel, culture, health, sports and the environment for Lonely Planet, *Men's Health*, *Outside*, *Travel & Leisure* and *Spa*. He has coauthored six previous Lonely Planet guidebooks: *Southeast Asia on a Shoestring* 14, *East Timor* 2, *Mexico* 11, *The Carolinas, Georgia & the South Trips* 1, *Bali & Lombok* 12 and *Nicaragua* 2. He's also the author of *Phuket Encounter* 1. To get around Nusa Tenggara he took eight buses, 18 boats and ferries, 11 planes, and hired or hitched 19 cars and 15 motorbikes. You can read more of his work at www.adamskolnick.com.

### IAIN STEWART
Java

Iain Stewart first travelled through Java in 1992 during a two-year, not-so-grand tour between India and Honduras. He's returned to Indonesia many times since, and has explored most parts of the archipelago: scuba diving in Sulawesi, hiking through rainforest in Sumatra and encountering wildlife in the clubs of Bali and Jakarta (in the interests of research, of course). Iain's written several dozen guidebooks over the years to destinations as diverse as Ibiza and Vietnam, but Java's combination of spectacular scenery, fiery food, refinement and informality means that it's never too soon for a return trip.

### STEVE WATERS
Sumatra

*Crocodile Vampires* was the movie screening on the boat from Batam to Dumai back in 1996, when Steve was investigating the Sumatran back door. His love of trekking took him across Sumatra Barat until his camera finally succumbed to the Mentawai mud. Thirteen years later he's still in mud as he climbed Gunung Kerinci, reprising his original journey. Drawn to wild lonely places, he'd rather be waiting for a lift on the Mongolian steppe, climbing a volcano in Kamchatka or bushwalking in southwest Tasmania than sitting at his desk in Melbourne keeping Lonely Planet's databases online. Steve's a regular contributor to *Wild* magazine.

## CONTRIBUTING AUTHOR

**Dr Trish Batchelor** wrote the health chapter. Trish is a general practitioner and travel-medicine specialist who works at the CIWEC Clinic in Kathmandu, Nepal, as well as being a medical advisor to the Travel Doctor New Zealand clinics. Trish teaches travel medicine through the University of Otago, and is interested in underwater and high-altitude medicine, and in the impact of tourism on host countries. She has travelled extensively through Southeast and East Asia and particularly loves high-altitude trekking in the Himalayas.

# Behind the Scenes

## THIS BOOK

The 1st edition of *Indonesia*, way back in 1986, was the collective work of Alan Samalgaski, Ginny Bruce and Mary Covernton. And cramming this immense, sprawling jewel of an archipelago into one action-packed volume has kept us busy ever since... In subsequent editions we've had 23 different authors travelling the country in search of adventure, enlightenment and ferry timetables.

The previous 8th edition was the work of co-ordinating author Justine Vaisutis along with a team of authors: Patrick Witton, Neal Bedford, Ryan Ver Berkmoes, China Williams, Iain Stewart, Nick Ray, Mark Elliott and Wendy Yanagihara. Indonesia expert journalist and author John Martinkus wrote the Indonesia's Separatist Conflicts box in the History chapter. Dr Trish Batchelor wrote the Health chapter.

For this 9th edition Ryan Ver Berkmoes took the helm as coordinating author. His crack team of authors included Celeste Brash, Muhammad Cohen, Mark Elliott, Trent Holden, Guyan Mitra, John Noble, Adam Skolnick, Iain Stewart and Steve Waters.

This guidebook was commissioned in Lonely Planet's Melbourne office, and produced by the following:

**Commissioning Editors** Judith Bamber, Tashi Wheeler
**Coordinating Editors** Laura Gibb, Trent Holden, Kate Whitfield
**Coordinating Cartographer** Andras Bogdanovits
**Coordinating Layout Designer** Frank Deim
**Managing Editors** Sasha Baskett, Katie Lynch, Laura Stansfeld
**Managing Cartographer** David Connolly
**Managing Layout Designer** Laura Jane
**Assisting Editors** Sarah Bailey, Kate Daly, Penelope Goodes, Shawn Low, Rowan McKinnon, Katie O'Connell, Alison Ridgway, Branislava Vladisavljevic
**Assisting Cartographers** James Bird, Alex Leung, Peter Shields
**Assisting Layout Designer** Aomi Hongo
**Cover** Naomi Parker, image research provided by lonelyplanetimages.com
**Language Content** Branislava Vladisavljevic
**Project Manager** Chris Love
**Thanks to** Lucy Birchley, Daniel Corbett, Sally Darmody, Indra Kilfoyle, Yvonne Kirk, Ali Lemer, Suyin Ng, Trent Paton, Sarah Sloane, Louisa Syme, Saralinda Turner

## THANKS
### RYAN VER BERKMOES

Many thanks to friends on Bali like the wise Jeremy Allan, Eliot Cohen (a coauthor and Sanur tennis champ), Jamie James, taste-masters Kerry and

---

### THE LONELY PLANET STORY

Fresh from an epic journey across Europe, Asia and Australia in 1972, Tony and Maureen Wheeler sat at their kitchen table stapling together notes. The first Lonely Planet guidebook, *Across Asia on the Cheap*, was born.

Travellers snapped up the guides. Inspired by their success, the Wheelers began publishing books to Southeast Asia, India and beyond. Demand was prodigious, and the Wheelers expanded the business rapidly to keep up. Over the years, Lonely Planet extended its coverage to every country and into the virtual world via lonelyplanet.com and the Thorn Tree message board.

As Lonely Planet became a globally loved brand, Tony and Maureen received several offers for the company. But it wasn't until 2007 that they found a partner whom they trusted to remain true to the company's principles of travelling widely, treading lightly and giving sustainably. In October of that year, BBC Worldwide acquired a 75% share in the company, pledging to uphold Lonely Planet's commitment to independent travel, trustworthy advice and editorial independence.

Today, Lonely Planet has offices in Melbourne, London and Oakland, with over 500 staff members and 300 authors. Tony and Maureen are still actively involved with Lonely Planet. They're travelling more often than ever, and they're devoting their spare time to charitable projects. And the company is still driven by the philosophy of *Across Asia on the Cheap*: 'All you've got to do is decide to go and the hardest part is over. So go!'

Milton Turner, Nicoline Dolman, Jack Daniels, Oka Wati and many more.

At Lonely Planet, thanks to the entire publishing and production teams for guidance, understanding and the ability to fix a lot of bad syntax. And huge thanks to an amazingly talented and dedicated team of coauthors: Adam, Celeste, Guyan, Iain, John and Mark are simply the best.

Finally, there's Annah, who always gives me a welcome 'merp' and Erin Corrigan, who discovered Bali for herself and proved that paradise begins at home.

## CELESTE BRASH
I had a small army of travellers and locals who helped me on this trip. Particular thanks to Pter and Hannah Vercevsky, Shiela and Glen Ord, John on Kadidiri, Annika Hartell, Tomaken, Gibson Dangnga, Blake Hodges, Maggie Behrend, the guides in Tentena and Dake in Manado. Thanks also to fellow LPers Nick Ray, Eliot Cohen, Ryan Ver Berkmoes, Judith Bamber and all the behind-the-scenes folk. My husband Josh joined me for 10 days of this trip while Diana Hammer watched my kids back in Tahiti – thanks for arranging your lives around me as usual!

## MUHAMMAD COHEN
My heartfelt appreciation goes to all who made visiting Kalimantan such a pleasure, and to those working so diligently to conserve, preserve and protect this unique and precious place. Special thanks to Kartono Tarjono for helping me eat my way across Pontianak, and to fellow traveller David Matson. Repeated acknowledgment to all who helped me get my feet wet in Kalimantan on Lonely Planet's Borneo guide, particularly Borneo Bob Kendall in Bali. Most all, kudos to my wife and our daughter, sufficiently emboldened by my experience to join in for their first visits to Kalimantan.

## MARK ELLIOTT
Terima kasih Tony and family in Ambon, Anthonius Savsavubun in Langgur, Alo in Dobo, Ilham in Ternate, Arif and Governor Thaib Armaiyn, Mr Tamrin and crew in Lelei, Viki in Kei, Nus in Saumlaki, Maxi in Masohi, Bram in Saparua, Robert and Ida on Nusalaut, Sofia and Ivan in Sanana, His Highness the Sultan of Jailolo, Mattis Persson, Bim in Daruba, chickens Glenn and Shiela, Dirk, Ivan and 'plastic fantastic' Ges. Most of all eternal thanks to my fabulous parents and wife Dani, without whose love and support the great adventure of life would be so much less fulfilling.

## TRENT HOLDEN
A big thanks to Danny, Hadi Faisal and Muhammad from Banda Aceh, Nasir and Mona Lisa, Mahmud Bangkaru, Siegfried Klein, Maxwell Sibhensana and Scott McIntyre. At Lonely Planet, biggest thanks goes to Tashi Wheeler for all her assistance, as well as Katie Lynch, Martin Heng and Darren O'Connell for their invaluable support. Thanks to Laura Gibb and Kate Whitfeld who so competently took over the coordinating of Indonesia 9. Finally I'd like to thank my family and my girlfriend Melissa Adams.

## JOHN NOBLE
Thanks to all who helped me try to piece together the Papua jigsaw, especially Rudie Yarangga, Justinus Daby, Pino Moch, 'Fuji' Fujiwara, Yoris Wanggai, Yetni from Wamena, Alex Ferdinand, Zeth Wonggor, Lea Kanisia Mekiuw, Bony Kondahon, Ignatius in Merauke, and Ibu Maria and Manches in Yenwaupnor.

## ADAM SKOLNICK
Thanks to the entire Blue Marlin team, Marcus and the Manta family, Harriet, Chris and Miriam, Astrid, Grace and their staff at Karma Kayak, Kevin Brooke on Moyo, Condo in Komodo, Sipri in Labuanbajo, Brian in Moni, Jim and Pak Tanto in Lewoleba, Odet in Lamalera, Edwin, Willy and Oney in Kupang, Pae Nope in Soe, Diego and Maria in Rote, Ann, Kirbi and the basketball mafia in Alor and Augus in Sumba. Thanks as always to Brett, Yoni and Made in Bali, Judith and Tashi in Melbourne, Ryan and my coauthors, and to sweet and lovely Georgiana Johnson.

## IAIN STEWART
This was a great, great trip, despite the efforts of the rain gods. Many Javanese people helped make it so wonderful, finding time to help out a nosy, time-pressed writer get his research done, thank you all. A few folk deserve a special mention: in Jakarta Mei and her crew were wonderful company, it was great to catch up with Yudi and my Cianjur mates again and meet Jack and the Jaker gang in Borobudur for the first time. In Yogya Wildan and Atik were wonderful hosts, guides and friends (miss you), while I owe so much to Eno I don't know where to start. I'd also like to thank Judith Bamber for signing me up, Tashi Wheeler for ensuring a smooth transition and all my fellow Indonesian authors.

## STEVE WATERS
Many thanks to all the people who made my job easier, including Subandi Keluarga in Kerinci, Kemun for the volcano, Yuli and Scuzz for boats

880

and breaks, Roni for guiding updates, Andi for recovering my diary and Ulrich for beers, borgwards, databases and 'Sway'. To Batty and Mega for sharing the lake, and your shower in KL was a lifesaver. Thanks also to Roz, Megan and Ryan for your dining-room table and to Sian for putting up with everything. Finally, big thanks go to Tashi for giving me the chance, and to Ed and Nigel for erecting the force field.

## OUR READERS

**Many thanks to the travellers who used the last edition and wrote to us with helpful hints, useful advice and interesting anecdotes:**

**A** Barry Acott, Michel Adine, John Ahern, Laura Ambrey, Justin Andrews, Graham Ashford **B** Ralph Balmer, Julie Barber, Chris Barnes, Ruth Bath, Kees Berkelaar, Bibiana Brauchle, Bas En Christel Breuker - Van Hout, Iman Brinkman, Menno Brons, Steve Buss, David Byrne **C** Agi Cakradirana, Hugo Adrian Camacho, Candice Carr Kelman, Perry Cas, James Chen, Jess Choy, Claudia Christl, Andrew Cooper, Oliver Craven, Andrej Curda **D** Patrick Daan, Pieter De Hart, Niels De Pous, David De Rango, Cathy Degaytan, Mark Degaytan, Merel Dekker, Kenny Dick, James Dimond, John Donoghue, Sally Drinkhouse, Anderson Duane, Yvonne Duijst **E** Paul Eaton, Anita En Gede, Martin Engeset, Ville Etelapaa, Pete Evans **F** Stan Ford, Marianne Fortuin **G** Jonathan Gamble, Claire Garabedian, Winke Goede, Leika Gooneratne, Brendan Griffin, Yuri Gupta **H** Ben Haberfield, Sari Handayani, Roy Hans, Jochem & Bianca Havermans, Theresa Heller, Oliver Henrich, Mirjam Hermans, Aldi Heyl, Kirsten Hietkamp, Bettie Holaday, Tom Holzinger, Raoul Hoovers, Michael Huffman, Hannes Hutzelmeyer, John Huxley **J** Harriet Jackson, Xana Jones, Mirari Judio **K** Hanne Kabel, Karsiyah Karsiyah, Karsiyah Karsiyah, Ancelikh Kaspinen, Darcy Killeen, Thomas Klueter, Suzan Kohlik, Alex Korns, Janneke Kraan,

Jane Kubke **L** Richard Lam, Hans Langendoen, Hans Langendoen, Nick Langston-Able, Bregje Laumans, Zach Leigh, Yvonne Lensink, John Lett, Raymond Liljeros **M** Matt Mackay, Sebastien Mai, Xuan Mai, Joseph Mansell, Brian Markussen, Miriam Martens, Adrian Martin, Hannah Massarella, Eliane Mattes, Reynold Mawikere, James McFadden, Mar Mercadal, Niels Meves, Kelapa Muda, Louise Murray, Juhani Mykkänen **N** Aretha N, Dario Nardi, Claire Neden, Richard Netherwood, Chris Neugebauer, Jane Nicol, Lilli Nicolson, Kathy Nitsan **O** Louise O'Flynn, Bernard Onsoe, Calvin Ow **P** John Pascoe, Barry Peacock, Sam Pearse, Nathan Petrelle, Lucie Prazak, Liz Price **Q** Bart-Anton Quispel **R** Shifra Raz, Maria Regazzoni, Mark Reniers, Gill Richards, Anselm Richter, Romy Riedel, Warner Riksen, Robin Robertson, Evan Rogers, John Rothman, Tobias Rutz **S** Jorge Saez-Guinea, Sandra Sandra, Christine Sbick, Martin Schmidt, Heiko Schmitz, Daniel Schwenk, Stephen Scott, Scott Secker, Aric Sigman, Wendy Simons, Firman Sitepu, Kristi Smith, Taressa Snelling, Jan O Staal, Mijke Steenhuisen, Made Supartika, Ernest Syrjänen **T** Sarah Tavner, Pascal Ternisien, Gareth Thomas, Sarah Tibbatts, Felix Timischl, Marianne Toll, James Travers, Victor Tumaang **U** Marc-Oliver Urban **V** Erwin Van Kemenade, Frank Van Der Heyden, Kirsten Van Der Heyden, Casper Van Der Vaart, Ton Van Dijk, Marcel Van Hak, Leon Van Kouwen, Koen Van Laar, Peter Van Luijk, Arianne Van Reedt Dortland, Hugo Van Veen, Erik Jan Van Zwieten, Adrian Vannisse, Thomas Viger, Jakko Vinken **W** Sonya Syafitri Wallenta, Jessa Wegman, Katrin Wernli, Tom Williams, Alan Wilson, Cindy Wockner, Matius Wong, Pearl Wright **Y** Michael Young **Z** Eric Zimmerman, Joost Zondervan, Agnes Zundert

## ACKNOWLEDGMENTS
**Many thanks to the following for the use of their content:**
Globe on title page ©Mountain High Maps 1993 Digital Wisdom, Inc.

# Index

INDEX

INDEX

INDEX

INDEX

INDEX

**INDEX**

# GreenDex

The following attractions, tours and accommodation choices have all been selected by Lonely Planet authors because they meet our criteria for sustainable tourism. We've selected places that are run locally or by a community group with profits remaining in the community.

We've also included businesses such as hotels and tour companies that operate to green principles. Note that in Indonesia – especially in tourist areas – many claim a green label but few actually fulfil the promise. The places we list are actually making a difference.

We want to keep developing our sustainable-travel content. If you think we've omitted someone who should be listed here, or if you disagree with our choices, contact us at www.lonelyplanet .com/contact and set us straight for next time. For more information about sustainable tourism and Lonely Planet, see www.lonelyplanet.com/responsibletravel.

## MAP LEGEND

### ROUTES

| | |
|---|---|
| Tollway | One-Way Street |
| Freeway | Street Mall/Steps |
| Primary Road | Tunnel |
| Secondary Road | Walking Tour |
| Tertiary Road | Walking Tour Detour |
| Lane | Walking Trail |
| Under Construction | Walking Path |
| Track | Pedestrian Overpass |
| Unsealed Road | |

### TRANSPORT

| | |
|---|---|
| Ferry | Rail |
| Bus Route | Rail (Underground) |

### HYDROGRAPHY

| | |
|---|---|
| River, Creek | Canal |
| Intermittent River | Water |
| Mangrove | Lake (Dry) |
| Reef | Mudflats |

### BOUNDARIES

| | |
|---|---|
| International | Regional, Suburb |
| State, Provincial | Ancient Wall |
| Disputed | Cliff |
| Marine Park | |

### AREA FEATURES

| | |
|---|---|
| Airport | Land |
| Area of Interest | Mall |
| Beach, Desert | Market |
| Building | Park |
| Campus | Reservation |
| Cemetery, Christian | Rocks |
| Cemetery, Other | Sports |
| Forest | Urban |

### POPULATION

| | |
|---|---|
| CAPITAL (NATIONAL) | CAPITAL (STATE) |
| Large City | Medium City |
| Small City | Town, Village |

### SYMBOLS

**Sights/Activities**
- Beach
- Buddhist
- Castle, Fortress
- Christian
- Diving, Snorkelling
- Hindu
- Islamic
- Monument
- Museum, Gallery
- Point of Interest
- Pool
- Ruin
- Snorkelling
- Surfing, Surf Beach

**Eating**
- Eating
- Zoo, Bird Sanctuary

**Drinking**
- Drinking
- Café

**Entertainment**
- Entertainment

**Shopping**
- Shopping

**Sleeping**
- Sleeping
- Camping

**Transport**
- Airport, Airfield
- Border Crossing
- Bus Station
- General Transport
- Parking Area
- Petrol Station
- Taxi Rank

**Information**
- Bank, ATM
- Embassy/Consulate
- Hospital, Medical
- Information
- Internet Facilities
- Police Station
- Post Office, GPO
- Telephone
- Toilets

**Geographic**
- Lighthouse
- Lookout
- Mountain, Volcano
- National Park
- River Flow
- Shelter, Hut
- Waterfall

## LONELY PLANET OFFICES

**Australia** (Head Office)
Locked Bag 1, Footscray, Victoria 3011
☎ 03 8379 8000, fax 03 8379 8111
talk2us@lonelyplanet.com.au

**USA**
150 Linden St, Oakland, CA 94607
☎ 510 250 6400, toll free 800 275 8555
fax 510 893 8572
info@lonelyplanet.com

**UK**
2nd fl, 186 City Rd,
London EC1V 2NT
☎ 020 7106 2100, fax 020 7106 2101
go@lonelyplanet.co.uk

**Published by Lonely Planet Publications Pty Ltd**
ABN 36 005 607 983

© Lonely Planet 2009

© photographers as indicated 2009

Cover photograph: Hindu female dancers in full costume, Bali, Paul Kennedy/Lonely Planet Images. Many of the images in this guide are available for licensing from Lonely Planet Images: lonelyplanetimages.com.

Printed by Toppan Security Printing Pte. Ltd.
Printed in Singapore.

Mixed Sources
Product group from well-managed forests and other controlled sources
www.fsc.org  Cert no. SGS-COC-005002
© 1996 Forest Stewardship Council